PSYCHOLOGY

PSYCHOLOGY
THE FRONTIERS

RONALD E. SMITH
IRWIN G. SARASON
BARBARA R. SARASON

THIRD EDITION

OF BEHAVIOR

1817

HARPER & ROW, PUBLISHERS, New York
Cambridge, Philadelphia, San Francisco,
London, Mexico City, São Paulo, Singapore, Sydney

Photograph and Illustration Acknowledgments can be found at the back of the text, following the Bibliography.

Sponsoring Editor: **Susan Mackey**

Development Editors: **Lauren S. Bahr and Sandra Poore**

Editorial Production Manager: **Nora Helfgott**

Project Editors: **Ellen Meek Tweedy and Dorothy Cappel**

Text Design: **Betty Binns Graphics/Martin Lubin and Karen Kowles**

Cover Design: **Betty Binns Graphics/Martin Lubin**

Cover Illustration: **Betty Binns Graphics/Martin Lubin, David Skolkin, and Ahmad Mallah**

Text Art: **Vantage Art, Inc.**

Photo Research: **Mira Schachne**

Production Manager: **Jeanie Berke**

Compositor: **York Graphic Services, Inc.**

Printer and Binder: **R. R. Donnelley & Sons Company**

Psychology: The Frontiers of Behavior, Third Edition

Library of Congress Cataloging in Publication Data

Smith, Ronald Edward, 1940–
    Psychology: the frontiers of behavior.
    Bibliography: p.
    Includes indexes.
    1. Psychology.   I. Sarason, Irwin G.   II. Sarason, Barbara R.   III. Title.
BF121.S58   1986   150   85-27071
ISBN 0-06-045728-7

86 87 88 89 9 8 7 6 5 4 3 2 1

BRIEF CONTENTS

DETAILED CONTENTS vi

TO THE INSTRUCTOR xv

TO THE STUDENT xviii

SECTION ONE **PSYCHOLOGY: ITS PERSPECTIVES AND METHODS** 1

CHAPTER ONE **PSYCHOLOGY IN PERSPECTIVE** 3
CHAPTER TWO **SCIENTIFIC PRINCIPLES AND METHODS IN PSYCHOLOGY** 32

SECTION TWO **BRAIN, CONSCIOUSNESS, AND PERCEPTION** 65

CHAPTER THREE **BIOLOGICAL FOUNDATIONS OF BEHAVIOR** 67
CHAPTER FOUR **STATES OF CONSCIOUSNESS** 109
CHAPTER FIVE **SENSATION AND PERCEPTION** 145

SECTION THREE **LEARNING, COGNITIVE PROCESSES, AND INTELLIGENCE** 193

CHAPTER SIX **LEARNING: PRINCIPLES AND APPLICATIONS** 195
CHAPTER SEVEN **INFORMATION PROCESSING AND MEMORY** 239
CHAPTER EIGHT **LANGUAGE, PROBLEM SOLVING, AND INTELLIGENCE** 267

SECTION FOUR **AROUSAL AND BEHAVIOR** 305

CHAPTER NINE **EMOTION AND MOTIVATION** 307
CHAPTER TEN **HUMAN SEXUALITY** 348

SECTION FIVE **DEVELOPMENTAL PROCESSES** 385

CHAPTER ELEVEN **LIFE SPAN DEVELOPMENT: THEORIES AND RESEARCH** 387
CHAPTER TWELVE **BIOLOGICAL, COGNITIVE, AND SOCIAL CHANGES IN DEVELOPMENT** 418

SECTION SIX **PERSONALITY, ADAPTATION, AND HEALTH** 449

CHAPTER THIRTEEN **PERSONALITY: PERSONS AND SITUATIONS** 451
CHAPTER FOURTEEN **ADJUSTING TO LIFE: STRESS, COPING, AND HEALTH** 483

SECTION SEVEN **BEHAVIOR DISORDERS AND TREATMENT** 509

CHAPTER FIFTEEN **BEHAVIOR DISORDERS** 511
CHAPTER SIXTEEN **THERAPEUTIC BEHAVIOR CHANGE** 550

SECTION EIGHT **SOCIAL BEHAVIOR** 581

CHAPTER SEVENTEEN **SOCIAL BEHAVIOR AND THE INDIVIDUAL** 583
CHAPTER EIGHTEEN **THE SOCIAL ENVIRONMENT** 619
APPENDIX **STATISTICAL CONCEPTS AND METHODS** 656

GLOSSARY G-1   BIBLIOGRAPHY B-1   ACKNOWLEDGMENTS A-1   NAME INDEX   SUBJECT INDEX

DETAILED CONTENTS

TO THE INSTRUCTOR xv

TO THE STUDENT xviii

SECTION ONE PSYCHOLOGY: ITS PERSPECTIVES AND METHODS 1

CHAPTER ONE
PSYCHOLOGY IN PERSPECTIVE 3

THE SCOPE OF PSYCHOLOGY 4
Four basic goals of psychology (and you) 9

FIVE PERSPECTIVES ON HUMAN BEHAVIOR 9
The importance of perspectives 10 **The biological
perspective: Body, mind, and behavior** 11
Historical development of the biological perspective 11
**The psychodynamic perspective: The forces
within** 14 Historical development of the psychodynamic
perspective 14 **The cognitive perspective: The
thinking human** 16 Historical development of the
cognitive perspective 16 **The behavioral perspective:
Humans as reactors** 18 Historical development of the
behavioral perspective 18 **The humanistic-existential
perspective: Choice, responsibility, and
self-actualization** 20 Historical development of the
humanistic-existential perspective 20

**APPLYING THE PERSPECTIVES:
UNDERSTANDING HUMAN AGGRESSION** 21
Biological factors in aggression 22 Evolutionary and
genetic viewpoints 22 The brain and aggression 23
Hormones, temperament, and physical appearance 23
Psychodynamic factors in aggression 24 **Cognitive
processes in aggression** 26 **The behavioral
perspective on aggression** 27 Stimulus control and
response consequences 27 Observation of aggressive
models 28 **The humanistic-existential perspective
on aggression** 29

FRONTIER 1.1 EMERGING SPECIALTY AREAS: HEALTH,
FORENSIC, AND SPORT PSYCHOLOGY 7

Study outline 29 Key terms and concepts 31
Suggested readings 31

CHAPTER TWO
SCIENTIFIC PRINCIPLES AND METHODS IN PSYCHOLOGY 32

SCIENTIFIC PRINCIPLES IN PSYCHOLOGY 35
Approaches to understanding behavior 36
After-the-fact understanding 36 Understanding through
prediction and control 37 **Constructs and
operational definitions** 37

**SCIENTIFIC METHODS: GATHERING
INFORMATION ABOUT BEHAVIOR** 39
Case studies 40 **The observational approach** 40
Uncontrolled observation: Sanity in insane places 40
Controlled observation: Blind obedience to authority 42

The correlational approach: Finding relationships 44
Boxing matches and homicides 44 Correlation and
prediction 45 **The experimental approach: Control
and manipulation of variables** 46 Independent and
dependent variables 46 Experimental and control
groups 46 Manipulating one independent variable:
Obedience revisited 47 Manipulating two independent
variables: The think-drink effect 49 Single-subject
experiments: Attention and asthma 50 Threats to the
validity of experiments 52

ETHICS IN HUMAN AND ANIMAL RESEARCH 54
STATISTICS: ANALYZING AND INTERPRETING
DATA 55

**Descriptive statistics: Organizing and summarizing
results 56   The correlation coefficient 57
Inferential statistics: Drawing conclusions about
data 58**

FRONTIER 2.1 PSYCHOLOGY AND THE COMPUTER
REVOLUTION 60

Study outline 62   Key terms and concepts 63
Suggested readings 63

SECTION TWO **BRAIN, CONSCIOUSNESS, AND PERCEPTION** 65

CHAPTER THREE
BIOLOGICAL FOUNDATIONS OF BEHAVIOR 67

GENETIC INFLUENCES ON BEHAVIOR 68
Human heredity 69   Sex determination **70**
Dominant and recessive genes **70**   Chromosome
variations and mutations **71**   **Behavior genetics 73**
Reaction ranges and heritability **73**   Research methods in
behavior genetics **75**

THE NEURAL BASES OF BEHAVIOR 77
**The neuron 77   Nerve impulses 78   Synaptic
transmission 80   Neurotransmitters 81   The
language of neural communication 82**

THE CENTRAL NERVOUS SYSTEM 83
**The spinal cord 84   The brain: Seat of
consciousness and behavior 84   The hindbrain 85**
The medulla and pons: Seat of vital functions **85**   The
reticular formation: Sentry of the brain **86**   The
cerebellum: Motor coordination center **87   The
midbrain 87   The forebrain 87**   The thalamus: The
brain's switchboard **87**   The hypothalamus: Motivation and
emotion **88**   The limbic system: Learning and organization
of behavior **88**   The cerebral hemispheres: Crown of the
brain **88**   The motor cortex **89**   The sensory
cortex **90**   Association cortex **91**   The frontal lobes:
The human difference **91**   Hemispheric localization: The
left and right brains **92   Brain damage and recovery
of function 96**   Types of injury **96**   Neural
plasticity **97**

THE AUTONOMIC AND ENDOCRINE SYSTEMS 98
The autonomic nervous system 98   Sympathetic
nervous system **103**   Parasympathetic nervous
system **103   The endocrine system 104**

FRONTIER 3.1 GENETIC ENGINEERING: THE EDGE OF
CREATION 72
FRONTIER 3.2 UNLOCKING THE SECRETS OF THE
BRAIN 100
Study outline 105   Key terms and concepts 107
Suggested readings 108

CHAPTER FOUR
STATES OF CONSCIOUSNESS 109

SLEEPING AND DREAMING 112
**Our biological clocks 113   Stages of sleep 114
The nature and functions of dreams 115**   Freud's
theory **116**   Dreams and memory consolidation **117**
Dreaming as homeostasis **117**

MEDITATION 120
Meditation and stress 120

HYPNOSIS 121
**Animal magnetism, mesmerism, and hypnosis 121
The scientific study of hypnosis 122   Hypnotic
behaviors and experiences 123**   Perceptual
distortions **124**   Physiological effects **125**   Increased pain
tolerance **125   Theories of hypnosis 126**   Role
playing **127**   Imagination **127**   Cerebral hemisphere
shifts **128**   Dissociation **128**

DRUGS AND CONSCIOUSNESS 130

Mechanisms of drug action 130   **Depressants** 131
Alcohol 131   Barbiturates and tranquilizers 132
Stimulants 133   Amphetamines 133   Cocaine 134
Narcotics 134   **Hallucinogens** 135   LSD 136
PCP 137   **Cannabis** 137

FRONTIER 4.1   SLEEP DISORDERS 118
FRONTIER 4.2   LIMITS OF CONSCIOUSNESS 140

Study outline 141   Key terms and concepts 143
Suggested readings 144

CHAPTER FIVE

SENSATION AND PERCEPTION 145

THE SENSORY SYSTEMS 147

Vision 147   The human eye 147   The rods and
cones 148   Brightness vision 150   Dark adaptation 150
Color vision 151   Visual defects: Limits on sensation 154
Audition 156   The human ear 158   Coding of
auditory information 159   **The chemical senses** 159
The skin and body senses 162   The skin senses 162
The body senses 162   **Psychophysics: The study of
sensory capabilities** 163   Stimulus detection: The
absolute threshold 163   Subliminal stimuli 164   The
difference threshold 165

PERCEPTUAL PROCESSES 165

Attention: Selecting which information gets in 166
Attentional shifts 167   Motivational and psychodynamic
factors 167   **Patterning and organization in
perception** 167   Cortical columns and blobs 168

Gestalt principles of perceptual organization 170
Perceptual hypotheses and expectancies 171   Illusions:
False perceptual hypotheses 172   **Depth and distance
perception** 176   Monocular cues 176   Binocular cues:
Stereopsis 178   **Auditory localization** 179

PERCEPTUAL DEVELOPMENT 179

**The role of experience in perceptual
development** 180   Visual deprivation studies 180
Manipulating the visual environment 182   Clinical studies
of restored vision 183

FRONTIER 5.1   ODORS AND SEXUALITY IN HUMANS 161
FRONTIER 5.2   PAIN PERCEPTION AND CONTROL 183

Study outline 189   Key terms and concepts 191
Suggested readings 191

SECTION THREE   **LEARNING, COGNITIVE PROCESSES, AND
INTELLIGENCE** 193

CHAPTER SIX

LEARNING: PRINCIPLES AND APPLICATIONS 195

WHAT IS LEARNING? 197
**CLASSICAL CONDITIONING: LEARNING
THROUGH ASSOCIATION** 197

**Acquisition, extinction, and spontaneous
recovery** 198   **Generalization and
discrimination** 200   **Some applications of classical
conditioning principles** 202   Classical conditioning and
physical disorders 202   Classical conditioning and attitude
formation 202

**OPERANT CONDITIONING: LEARNING THROUGH
CONSEQUENCES** 203

The study of operant conditioning 204   **The ABCs
of operant conditioning** 205   Antecedents: Stimulus
control of behavior 205   Differences between operant
and classical conditioning 206   **Response consequences
and behavior** 206   Positive reinforcement 206
Shaping 207   Operant extinction 208   **Schedules of
reinforcement** 209   Fixed-ratio schedule 210
Variable-ratio schedule 210   Fixed-interval schedule 211
Variable-interval schedule 212   Effects of reinforcement
schedules on learning and extinction 212   **Negative
reinforcement: Escape and avoidance
conditioning** 213   A two-factor theory of avoidance

learning 214   **Punishment** 215   Applying aversive stimuli 216   Therapeutic use of aversive punishment 216   Response cost: Punishment through removal of reinforcers 217   **Timing of behavioral consequences** 218

THE COGNITIVE PERSPECTIVE ON LEARNING 219

Cognition in classical conditioning 224
Cognition and operant conditioning 225   **The power of expectancies: Learned helplessness and learned mastery** 227   **Internal self-evaluations as rewards and punishment** 228   **Observational learning (modeling)** 229

THE BIOLOGICAL PERSPECTIVE ON LEARNING 231

Biological constraints on learning 231   The misbehavior of animals 231   Peculiarities in avoidance learning 231   Conditioned aversions 232   The concept of preparedness 232

FRONTIER 6.1   BEHAVIORAL SELF-CONTROL: OPERANT PRINCIPLES IN THE SERVICE OF SELF 220
FRONTIER 6.2   THE SEARCH FOR THE BIOLOGICAL BASIS OF LEARNING 234

Study outline 235   Key terms and concepts 237
Suggested readings 238

CHAPTER SEVEN

INFORMATION PROCESSING AND MEMORY 239

INFORMATION PROCESSING 240

Input 241   Visual input 241   Auditory input 242
Processing, coding, and storage 242   Rehearsal 242
Selective processing 243   Coding and organization 244
General organizing principles 249

RETRIEVAL FROM MEMORY 251

Context and memory 253   **Memory for complex stimuli** 254   **Reconstructive memory** 255
Episodic and semantic memory 256   **Retrieval failure or forgetting** 257   Interference 258
Biological state 258   Mood as a retrieval cue 258   **Are memories ever permanently lost?** 259

Contributions from surgery 259   Psychodynamic observations 259   The tip of the tongue phenomenon 260   Displacement of memories 260

CURRENT THEORETICAL VIEWS OF MEMORY PROCESSES 260

The duplex theory 261   **Levels of processing and elaboration** 263

FRONTIER 7.1   METACOGNITION 252

Study outline 264   Key terms and concepts 266
Suggested readings 266

CHAPTER EIGHT

LANGUAGE, PROBLEM SOLVING, AND INTELLIGENCE 267

LANGUAGE 268

The structure of language 268   **Understanding language** 269   **Language development** 270
Perspectives on language development 270   The sequence of development 272   **Biological basis of language** 273   Critical periods, sensitive periods, and language development 278   **Language and cognition** 279   Linguistic relativism 279   Language and perception 279   Language and memory 280

PROBLEM SOLVING 281

Understanding problem-solving techniques 281

Algorithms versus heuristics 281   **Common difficulties in problem solving** 283

INTELLIGENCE 285

Sources of intelligence 285   The biological perspective 285   The behavioral perspective 287   **The structure of intelligence** 287   The factor analytic approach 287   The cognitive stages approach 288
Intelligence as specific brain functioning 288   **The processes of intelligent behavior** 288   **Intelligence tests** 290   Test reliability 290   Test validity 290
Standardization 290   Individually administered tests 291

Group tests of intelligence **293**   The IQ concept **294**
Social issues and testing 296   Tests for slow
learners **296**   Aptitude tests for college admission **297**

FRONTIER 8.1   DO ANIMALS USE LANGUAGE? **275**

FRONTIER 8.2   **A NEW GENERATION OF INTELLIGENCE
TESTS?   298**

Study outline **301**   Key terms and concepts **303**
Suggested readings **303**

SECTION FOUR   **AROUSAL AND BEHAVIOR** 305

CHAPTER NINE
EMOTION AND MOTIVATION 307

EMOTION 308

**Eliciting stimuli 309   The cognitive
component 310   The physiological component 310**
The brain and emotion **311**   Autonomic and hormonal
processes **312**   **The behavioral component** 314
Expressive behaviors **315**   Instrumental behaviors **318**
Interactions among components 320   Theories of
emotion **320**   Manipulating appraisal to influence
arousal **321**   Manipulating arousal to influence
appraisal **322**   Associative networks involving
emotion **323**

MOTIVATION: THE "WHY" OF BEHAVIOR 324

Perspectives on motivation 324   The biological
perspective: Drives and their regulation **326**   The
behavioral perspective: Learning and motivation **326**   The

cognitive perspective: Expectancy and value **326**   The
psychodynamic perspective: The motivational
underworld **327**   The humanistic-existential perspective:
Deficiency and growth needs **328**   **Homeostatic needs:
To thirst and hunger 329**   Thirst **330**   Hunger **330**
Sensory needs 332   Individual differences in sensation
seeking **336**   **Social motivation 338**   The
achievement motive **338**   The need for power **340**
Motivational conflict 341

FRONTIER 9.1   EATING DISORDERS **333**
FRONTIER 9.2   MOTIVES GONE AWRY: NEW THEORIES OF
ADDICTION **343**

Study outline **344**   Key terms and concepts **346**
Suggested readings **347**

CHAPTER TEN
HUMAN SEXUALITY 348

**THREE APPROACHES TO THE STUDY OF
SEXUALITY 350**

The survey approach 351   Problems of sex survey
research **352**   Patterns and changes in sexual
behavior **353**   **The observational approach 354**
The experimental approach 356   Stimulus factors in
sexuality **356**   Effects of pornography on behavior **357**

SEX, CULTURE, AND RELATIONSHIPS 360

**Cultural influences on sexuality 360   Sex, love,
and intimacy 360**

SEXUALITY THROUGH THE LIFE SPAN 361

**Childhood sexuality 361   Development of gender
identity 365**   Transsexualism: Reversed gender
identity **366**   **Sex and aging 368**   Changes in male

sexuality **369**   Changes in female sexuality **370**
SEXUAL DYSFUNCTION 370
Psychological factors in sexual dysfunction 371
Treatment of sexual dysfunction 373
ALTERNATIVE MODES OF SEXUALITY 374
Homosexuality 374   Homosexual life styles **374**
Atypical sexual behaviors 377
SEXUAL VICTIMIZATION 378
Rape 378   Rapists **380**   **Child molestation 380**

FRONTIER 10.1   PASSIONATE LOVE **362**

Study outline **381**   Key terms and concepts **383**
Suggested readings **383**

SECTION FIVE DEVELOPMENTAL PROCESSES 385

CHAPTER ELEVEN
LIFE SPAN DEVELOPMENT: THEORIES AND RESEARCH 387

THE LIFE SPAN APPROACH 388

Factors in life span development 389   **Basic developmental concepts** 390   Maturation 390   Stages of development 390   **Research techniques for the study of development** 392

LONGITUDINAL STUDIES OF DEVELOPMENT 396

The Terman Study 397   **The New York Longitudinal Study** 399   **The Grant Study** 400

PSYCHOLOGICAL PERSPECTIVES ON DEVELOPMENT 402

Freud's theory of psychosexual development 402   Psychosexual stages 402   Evaluation 404   **Erikson's**

psychosocial theory of personality development 404   Psychosocial stages 405   Evaluation 406   **Piaget's theory of cognitive development** 407   Stages of cognitive development 408   Evaluation 411   **Kohlberg's theory of moral development** 411   Stages of moral reasoning 412   Evaluation 412   **Kübler-Ross's theory of death and dying** 414   Stages of dying 414   Evaluation 415

FRONTIER 11.1 PRACTICAL APPLICATIONS OF LIFE SPAN DEVELOPMENTAL THEORY 391

Study outline 415   Key terms and concepts 417   Suggested readings 417

CHAPTER TWELVE
BIOLOGICAL, COGNITIVE, AND SOCIAL CHANGES IN DEVELOPMENT 418

BIOLOGICAL DEVELOPMENT 420

Periods of physical change 420   Infant growth 420   Physical development in adolescence 421   Body changes in aging 422   **Motor performance** 423   **Emotional development** 424   **Sensory skills** 426   Sensory measurement techniques for infants 426   Depth perception 427

LEARNING AND COGNITIVE DEVELOPMENT 429

Learning in infancy 429   **Measuring cognitive development in infants** 431   **Cognitive changes over the life span** 432   **Age changes in learning techniques** 432

SOCIAL AND PERSONALITY DEVELOPMENT 434

Attachment 434   Attachment theories and research 434   Laboratory studies of attachment 436   Father attachment 437   **Socialization** 437   Sex role development 437   Perspectives on sex role development 438   **Plasticity of development** 440   Experimental work on critical periods 441   Invulnerability 441   High-risk children grow up 442

FRONTIER 12.1 THE EFFECTS OF DIVORCE ON CHILDREN'S DEVELOPMENT 443

Study outline 446   Key terms and concepts 447   Suggested readings 447

SECTION SIX PERSONALITY, ADAPTATION, AND HEALTH 449

CHAPTER THIRTEEN
PERSONALITY: PERSONS AND SITUATIONS 451

WHAT IS PERSONALITY? 452
PERSONALITY THEORIES 454

Freud's psychoanalytic theory 454   Psychic energy and mental events 454   The structure of personality 456

The role of defense mechanisms **457**   Contributions and evaluation **459**   **Other analytic theories 459** Adler's individual psychology **460**   Jung's analytical psychology **460**   Contributions and evaluation **461 Humanistic and existential theories** 46 I   Rogers's self theory **462**   Contributions and evaluation **463 Cognitive-behavioral theories 464**   Behavioral approaches **464**   Cognitive approaches **464**   Theories integrating cognitive and behavioral principles **465** Contributions and evaluation **467**   **Biological approaches to personality 467**   Sheldon: Body type and personality **467**   Eysenck's biological psychology **469** Contributions and evaluation **470**   **Trait theories** 47 I Contributions and evaluation **471**   **An appraisal of personality theories 472   Situations, persons, and their interactions 472**   Situations **472**   Persons **473**

Person × situation interactions **473**

PERSONALITY ASSESSMENT 475

The interview 476   **Paper and pencil questionnaires 476**   The Minnesota Multiphasic Personality Inventory **476**   **Projective techniques 477** Rorschach inkblots **477**   Thematic Apperception Test **478 Behavioral assessment 478   Cognitive assessment 480   Bodily assessment 480 Personality tests and the privacy and validity issues** 48 I

FRONTIER 13.1   EXPERIMENTAL STUDY OF PSYCHOANALYTIC CONCEPTS: A PERSON × SITUATION PERSPECTIVE **473**

Study outline **481**   Key terms and concepts **482** Suggested readings **482**

CHAPTER FOURTEEN
ADJUSTING TO LIFE: STRESS, COPING, AND HEALTH 483

STRESS 484

Factors involved in stress 484   Situational factors **484** Personal factors **485**   Biological factors **485**   **Stress arousal 486   Vulnerability to stress 488**

COPING WITH STRESS 488

Self-control 490   Social support 491

BREAKDOWNS UNDER STRESS 493

Posttraumatic stress reactions 494   Burnout 495 Quantifying life stress 495

HEALTH PSYCHOLOGY AND BEHAVIORAL MEDICINE 496

Physical disorders related to stress 497 Psychophysiological disorders **497**   Coronary heart disease **498**   **Speeding recovery from illness** 50 I Information and expectations **501**   Predictability and perceived control **502**   Social support and clinical progress **502**   **Achieving health 503**   Exercise and health **503**   Stamina and health **504**

FRONTIER 14.1   IMPROVING THE PREDICTION OF HEART ATTACK **500**

Study outline **505**   Key terms and concepts **506** Suggested readings **507**

SECTION SEVEN   **BEHAVIOR DISORDERS AND TREATMENT** 509

CHAPTER FIFTEEN
BEHAVIOR DISORDERS 511

WHAT IS ABNORMAL BEHAVIOR? 512

Abnormal behavior from various perspectives 512 How is abnormal behavior defined? 514

CLASSIFICATION OF ABNORMAL BEHAVIOR 515

The problems of constructing a classification system 515   DSM III 515

PERSONALITY DISORDERS 517

Odd or eccentric behavior **518   Dramatic or erratic behavior 518   Fearful or anxious behavior** 520

ANXIETY DISORDERS 520

Generalized anxiety disorder 521   Panic disorder 521   Phobia 521   Obsessive-compulsive disorder 523   Perspectives on anxiety

disorders 524   The psychodynamic perspective 524
The behavioral perspective **524**   The cognitive
perspective **525**   The biological perspective **526**   The
humanistic-existential perspective **526**

AFFECTIVE DISORDERS 526

Depression 526   The problem of suicide **528**
Perspectives on depression 529   Biological
theories **529**   Behavioral theories **530**   The cognitive
perspective **531**   Psychodynamic theories **533**
Humanistic-existential theories **534**   **Mania and bipolar
disorders** 534

SCHIZOPHRENIC DISORDERS 536

Characteristics of schizophrenia 536
Hallucinations and delusions 537   **Outcome
prospects** 538   **Perspectives on schizophrenia** 540
The biological perspective **540**   The cognitive
perspective **545**   The psychodynamic perspective **545**
The behavioral perspective **546**   The humanistic-existential
perspective **546**   The interaction of stress and
vulnerability **546**

FRONTIER 15.1   NEW TECHNIQUES COMPLEMENT EARLIER
RECORDS 542

Study outline 547   Key terms and concepts 549
Suggested readings 549

CHAPTER SIXTEEN
THERAPEUTIC BEHAVIOR CHANGE 550

PSYCHODYNAMIC THERAPIES 552

Psychoanalysis 553   **Other psychodynamic
therapies** 554

HUMANISTIC-EXISTENTIAL THERAPIES 555

Client-centered therapy 555   **Existential
therapy** 556

BEHAVIOR THERAPIES 556

Therapies based on operant conditioning 557
Therapies based on classical conditioning 559
Systematic desensitization **559**   Flooding **559**
Therapies based on social learning theory 559

COGNITIVE THERAPIES 561

Rational-emotive therapy 561   **Cognitive therapy
for depression** 562   **Self-instructional training** 562

GROUP THERAPY 563

Specialized group approaches 563   Transactional
analysis **563**   Gestalt therapy **563**   Experiential

groups **564**   **Family and couples therapy** 565

BIOLOGICAL THERAPIES 566

Drug therapies 566   Antianxiety drugs **568**
Antipsychotic drugs **568**   Antidepressant drugs **569**
Antimanic drugs **569**   **Electroconvulsive therapy** 569

EVALUATION OF THERAPIES 570

Meta-analysis 571   **Comparative outcome
research** 574

**DISORDERED BEHAVIOR AND PUBLIC
POLICY** 575

Criminal responsibility 575
Institutionalization 576   **Prevention** 577

FRONTIER 16.1   CAN PSYCHOTHERAPY REDUCE TOTAL
HEALTH CARE COSTS? 571

Study outline **578**   Key terms and concepts **579**
Suggested readings **579**

SECTION EIGHT **SOCIAL BEHAVIOR** 581

CHAPTER SEVENTEEN
SOCIAL BEHAVIOR AND THE INDIVIDUAL 583

**RESEARCH METHODS IN SOCIAL
PSYCHOLOGY** 584
SOCIAL PERCEPTION 585

Attribution 585   Rules of attribution **587**   The effects
of attribution **587**   **Motivation and attribution** 588

SOCIAL COGNITION 588

Schemata 589

ATTRACTION, LIKING, AND LOVE 590

What characteristics cause attraction? 590
Similarity 590   Complementarity 590   Familiarity 592
Attractiveness 593   **The development of a
relationship** 594   Reciprocity 594   Self-disclosure 595
Love 596   **Theories of interpersonal attraction** 596
The ending of a relationship 597

ATTITUDES AND BEHAVIOR 598

What are attitudes? 598   **Cognitive complexity
and evaluative simplicity** 599   **Stereotyped
attitudes and prejudice** 600   Group competition and
conflict 601   The outgroup-ingroup categorization 601
Cognitive mechanisms in the development of prejudice 602
Sexism 603   **How attitudes translate into**

behavior 604   The theory of reasoned action 604
Cognitive dissonance 605   Self-perception theory 606
Persuasion and attitude change 607   Characteristics
of the communicator 607   One-sided versus two-sided
arguments 608   Persuading through fear 608

ALTRUISM AND PROSOCIAL BEHAVIOR 609

The biological perspective 609   **The
psychodynamic perspective** 609   **The learning
perspective** 610   **The cognitive perspective** 610
The person × situation interaction in helping 611
The situation 611   The person 613

FRONTIER 17.1 WHO DONATES BLOOD AND WHY? A
STUDY OF PROSOCIAL BEHAVIOR 614

Study outline 616   Key terms and concepts 617
Suggested readings 618

CHAPTER EIGHTEEN
THE SOCIAL ENVIRONMENT 619

SOCIAL NORMS AND ROLES 621

Development of norms 622   **Conformity** 624
Extreme conformity: Brainwashing and cults 626
Deindividuation 628

GROUP DYNAMICS 629

Group influences on task performance 630   Social
facilitation 631   Social loafing: Many hands make light the
work 632   When are groups more productive than
individuals? 634   **Group decision making** 635
Group polarization 635   Groupthink 636   **Social
power and leadership** 637   Trait approaches: Born to
lead? 637   Leadership styles: The contingency model 639
Intergroup conflict and conflict resolution 640

Applying the lesson of Robbers Cave: Cooperative
learning 640

**SOCIAL IMPACT OF THE PHYSICAL
ENVIRONMENT** 646

Crowding 646   Calhoun's behavioral sink 647   Effects
on humans: Density versus crowding 647   **Noise** 649

FRONTIER 18.1 GROUP DYNAMICS IN SPORTS 642
FRONTIER 18.2 PSYCHOLOGY AND THE
ENVIRONMENT 650

Study outline 653   Key terms and concepts 654
Suggested readings 655

APPENDIX
STATISTICAL CONCEPTS AND METHODS 656

DESCRIPTIVE STATISTICS 657

Measures of central tendency 658   **Types of
distributions** 659   **Measures of variability** 660
Standard scores 662

THE NORMAL CURVE 662
**STATISTICAL METHODS FOR DATA
ANALYSIS** 664

A key concept: Variance accounted for 664
Correlational methods 665   The correlation
coefficient 665   Correlation and prediction 667   Factor
analysis 667   **Inferential statistics and hypothesis
testing** 669

Study outline 671   Key terms and concepts 672
Suggested readings 672

GLOSSARY G-1   BIBLIOGRAPHY B-1   ACKNOWLEDGMENTS A-1   NAME INDEX   SUBJECT INDEX

TO THE INSTRUCTOR

Writing this third edition gave us the opportunity to think again about the scope of the field of psychology and the introductory textbook. Although the field has changed a great deal in a short period of time, our theory of the beginning book remains basically the same as it was when the first edition was published.

There is no such thing as a standardized beginning course in psychology. Each institution and each instructor has a special set of needs and goals. Nevertheless, one issue seems to predominate whenever course instructors get together: how to make "Introduction to Psychology" come alive. *Coming alive* means getting students to *want* to learn about why people (and animals) behave as they do.

Given our inability to predict which topics will capture the imagination of particular students, the challenge of the beginning book is to do justice to the entire field of psychology and to do so in as highly interesting and clear a manner as possible. An important factor is an organizational structure that facilitates the integration of the diverse topics within psychology. We have attempted to provide this structure by organizing the whole book in terms of five basic theoretical perspectives—biological, psychodynamic, cognitive, behavioral, and humanistic-existential–that are introduced in the first chapter and frequently referred to throughout the book.

While working on this edition, we thought about undergraduate books that had influenced our own educations. We agreed that the really good texts were especially effective at getting us immersed in the subject matter. Applied to psychology, this means getting students to begin thinking as psychologists do. At every opportunity, we emphasize how psychologists get interested in topics and develop an understanding of them. All chapters have a frontier box (a few chapters have two) that provides an in-depth, challenging review of a study, controversy, or method. Among the topics included in these frontier features are computers in psychology, sleep disorders, pain mechanisms and pain control strategies, and the biological bases of learning.

We repeatedly direct the student's attention to the relationship between scientific strategies, activities, and theoretical perspectives, on the one hand, and discoveries, on the other. Implementing this device, Chapter 2 is devoted to an explanation—with numerous illustrations—of the scientific principles and methods used in the field of psychology. Together, the first two chapters give the student a working psychological vocabulary, an introduction to the logic of research, and a knowledge of the procedures that characterize psychological research. As in the second edition, we have also included an appendix on statistical techniques and research design for use in courses for which more extensive exploration of these topics is desired.

NEW TO THIS EDITION

Growth and change in the field of psychology have led us to make a variety of changes in this edition to involve students more in the frontiers of the discipline.

Material has been added on brain-behavior relationships, including recent findings concerning the functions of the frontal lobe, controversies surrounding the left and right hemispheres, and new methods of measuring brain functions.

Treatment of cognitive psychology and of memory has been expanded to reflect new evidence about metacognition, episodic memory, the influence of biological states and mood on information retrieval, and language development, among other topics. The expansion of material on cognitive processes in Chapters 7 and 8 reflects the growing awareness of the interrelationship among cognition, intelligence, problem solving, and language.

Research from the rapidly expanding areas of health psychology and behavioral medicine is covered at appropriate places throughout the book rather than in a separate chapter so that students may better understand how this material relates to other topics (for example, the chapter on psychotherapy relates evidence of the effects of psychological interventions on health and illness).

A chapter has been added on the social environment, dealing with both group dynamics and environmental psychology, to reflect the excitement that characterizes current social psychological research in these areas. A second social psychology chapter contains new and greatly expanded sections on social cognition, interpersonal attraction, and altruism.

The two chapters on developmental psychology take a life span approach to personal change. They contain critical comparisons of research designs employed in longitudinal studies and also identify important practical implications of theories of life span development. Expanded treatment is given to research on attachment, the long-term effects of divorce on children, and emotional development as well as to the findings of studies that have followed their subjects from childhood to late middle age.

The comprehensive presentation of human sexuality uses the theoretical perspectives reviewed in Chapter 1 to show the links between bodily and psychological processes. We provide an update on research relating odors to sexual behavior, as well as a discussion of attributional and opponent-process theories of love and sexual behavior.

The chapters on behavioral disorders and their treatment provide the latest on research findings concerning *DSM III*, a new section on teenage suicide, comparisons between Type I and Type II schizophrenia, expanded coverage of depression (with new case study material), and a description of meta-analytic procedures applicable to the evaluation of therapies.

In this edition we have incorporated several pedagogical aids suggested to us by people who use the text. Important terms throughout each chapter are boldfaced. All boldfaced terms, together with other terms a student may wish to clarify, are defined in the glossary.

Each chapter begins with a chapter outline and ends with both a summary in outline form that highlights important material and gives page references for coverage of major topics, and a list of key terms and concepts to make review easier. These aids are designed to facilitate the student's comprehension and organization of the material. We believe that these changes, together with the high interest value and completeness of the text, have produced a book that gives students both the incentive and the help they need to become well grounded in the basics of psychological knowledge.

The ancillary materials have been produced with care to assist both the instructor and the student.

ANCILLARY PACKAGE

Instructor's Manual, written by Ed Scholwinski (Southwest Texas State University), has been expanded to include the following: lecture outlines and lecture supplements, key terms and concepts, discussion questions, student activities and projects, and lists of mixed media materials and supplemental readings. In addition, the manual offers information on planning the course, class assignments, examinations and evaluations, and grading procedures.

Test Item File, prepared by William C. Owen (Virginia Western Community College), Barbara Jane Feinberg, and Leanne Wilson (University of Washington), consists of 2000 multiple-choice questions. One third of these are *factual questions* taken directly from the text. One third of the questions are *interpretive* and involve matching a concept to a behavior, or a research finding to a general or specific context. The remaining third are *applied* questions. These are practical applications or interpretations, usually of research findings. The questions vary in level of difficulty, allowing the instructor to satisfy specific class needs, and each question is keyed to the text for easy reference.

MICROTEST. This microcomputer test-generation package consists of the questions from the test bank on disks and the software necessary to turn them into instructor-customized tests. The 2000 multiple-choice questions are accompanied by a comprehensive set of descriptors including chapter number, item number, item type, level of difficulty (easy, moderate, difficult), cognitive type (factual, interpretive, applied), page numbers in the text on which the correct answer can be found, and the learning objective to which the question applies. MICRO-TEST is compatible with Apple, IBM-PC and most compatibles, and IBM-PC XT.

Study Guide, written by Henry J. Oles (Southwest Texas State University) and Jack B. McMahan, retains the following effective features for each chapter: a capsule summary, study objectives, key terms and concepts, a guided comprehensive review, thought stimulators, and suggested mini-projects for individual or classroom use. In addition, all the questions in the *Study Guide* are keyed to both the study objectives and to the text pages for easy referencing.

Study-Aid. This computer software version of the study guide is keyed directly to the text. *Study-Aid* helps students review chapters through various types of exercises and self-tests. Automatic scoring allows students to evaluate their progress as they learn. *Study-Aid* is compatible with Apple, Macintosh, IBM-PC, and most compatibles.

Media Policy. The most flexible media policy available for introductory psychology texts. Ask your local Harper & Row representative for more information.

Transparencies. A set of 50 transparencies, many of them full color, is available free to adopters. The transparencies, presenting material taken directly from the text, usually support class discussion.

Slides. A set of 188 slides, suitable for use with any introductory psychology text, is available free to adopters. The slides were developed to engage students in the study of important psychological concepts through an experiential approach.

In writing this edition we have benefitted from feedback received from students, adopters, reviewers, and consultants. We value the compliments we have received (particularly concerning our integrative use of the theoretical perspectives and the concept of psychological frontiers), as well as the criticisms and numerous suggestions regarding pedagogy and emphasis.

We are indebted to the following people at Harper & Row for their help with this book: Judith L. Rothman, Executive Editor; Lauren S. Bahr, Director of Development; Susan Mackey, Psychology Editor; Nora Helfgott, Editorial Production Manager; and Mira Schachne, Photo Researcher. Sandra Poore's work in revising the manuscript with an eye to style and readability has been especially helpful, and Dorothy Cappel and Ellen Meek Tweedy, Project Editors, have provided assistance throughout the various stages of production.

We are indebted to the following individuals at the University of Washington who helped us in various ways: Betty Johnson, Kathleen Springer, Katherine Kerr, Shirin Madani, Sheri Nylund, and Leslie Poppe.

We are especially indebted to Gregory Pierce for helping with text permissions, proofreading, and generally providing both knowledgeable and tangible assistance and psychological support.

We wish to express our gratitude and to specifically acknowledge the contributions made by the following people:

Robert Bolles, University of Washington
Steven Buck, University of Washington
Maurice Caldwalder, San Jacinto Community College
Ken L. Dercole, Kwantlen College
Michael Dougher, University of New Mexico
Phil Finney, Southeast Missouri State University
Cynthia A. Ford, Jackson State University
Donald G. Forgays, University of Vermont
Bruce Goldstein, University of Pittsburgh
Larry Gregory, New Mexico State University
Joy Hammersla, Seattle Pacific University
Elaine Hauff, Minneapolis Community College
Louis R. Hellwig, University of Northern Iowa
Melvyn B. King, State University of New York at Cortland
Paul J. Kulkosky, University of Southern Colorado
Robert C. Mathews, Louisiana State University
Valerie R. Padgett, Mississippi State University
Michael G. Rom, Pasco Hernando Community College
Ed Scholwinski, Southwest Texas State University
Douglas Smith, University of Wisconsin—River Falls
Michael V. Vitiello, University of Washington

RONALD E. SMITH
IRWIN G. SARASON
BARBARA R. SARASON

TO THE STUDENT

We hope that this book will serve as an informative introduction to the study of psychology. The study of behavior is one of the most fascinating of all activities. If some of our enthusiasm for the field of psychology rubs off on you as a result of reading our book, we will have achieved one of our goals in writing it.

Psychology is a vital and dynamic field. As a science, it is now exploring many frontiers of behavior. As faculty members in a large and active psychology department at the University of Washington, we are constantly struck by the fascinating diversity of topics—all interesting—being studied by our colleagues. In other settings around the world, important new discoveries and applications of knowledge are being discovered in all areas of psychology. Our emphasis on these frontiers is found throughout the book. Some of the most important and provocative of them are highlighted in special frontier sections in each chapter.

New discoveries and theoretical advances do not occur in a vacuum. They are prompted by the ways in which psychologists think about behavior and its causes. For psychologists in their work, as for all of us in our personal lives, viewpoints or perspectives serve as lenses through which the world of behavior is viewed and determine what is noticed, studied, and learned. The many topics and theories of psychology will be more understandable to you if you are aware of the lenses through which psychologists view the world. Therefore, in Chapter 1, we present in some detail the five major perspectives—biological, psychodynamic, cognitive, behavioral, and humanistic-existential—that guide the activities of most psychologists. While these perspectives may at times seem to be competitive and contradictory, they in fact often complement one another. Taken together, they provide us with a unified conception of human nature. Throughout the book, we show how these five perspectives influence important areas of psychological study, including biological foundations of behavior, ways in which we learn and think, personality and individual differences, social and emotional development, and ways in which we try to solve personal and social problems. Because of the wide range of psychological phenomena and principles covered in the introductory course, the emphasis on how the perspectives help psychologists think about behavior provides a unifying framework to pull things together.

Psychology is an inquiring science, and we think that it is essential for you to gain an appreciation for and an understanding of the methods that psychologists use to unravel the mysteries of behavior. We are bombarded daily with reports of new scientific and medical discoveries by the mass media. To be an intelligent consumer of such reports, you need to know something about research methods. No matter what your future occupation, an understanding of the scientific method will help you evaluate evidence and make decisions about important issues. A knowledge of research methods will also make you a more effective problem solver and enable you to think more logically and clearly, to be aware of potential biases, and to evaluate evidence critically. For these reasons, after introducing you to the theoretical perspectives in Chapter 1, we devote Chapter 2 to a discussion of scientific methods and issues in psychology. Throughout the book, we present not only the facts that have emerged from psychological research but also a description of how those facts were discovered and a discussion of their meaning.

Any textbook, regardless of its specific emphases and format, is, first and foremost, a medium for communicating facts and ideas. We have tried to make *Psychology: The Frontiers of Behavior* a book that will both interest and challenge you, as well as assist you in understanding and mastering the material.

Each chapter begins with an outline to help you organize its major topics and subtopics. At the end of the chapter, you will find a detailed study outline that recaps key points made in the chapter. You may find it helpful to read the study outline *before* beginning the chapter to get a preview of the material. Following the study outline is a list of key terms and concepts that you can use to test your knowledge of the material discussed in the chapter. Most of these terms are also defined in the glossary at the back of the text. Because some of these terms may be new to you, the glossary also contains a pronunciation guide for many of them.

There are two other important mastery aids available to you. One is the comprehensive *Study Guide* prepared by Henry Oles of Southwest Texas State University and Jack McMahan. The *Study Guide* is available from your campus bookstore. For those of you who have access to an Apple, Macintosh, or IBM microcomputer, Harper & Row offers *Study-Aid*, a new computerized version of the *Study Guide*. More information about *Study-Aid* is available at the back of the book.

It is our hope that this book's features and themes will enhance the value and enjoyment of your psychology course and will inspire you to pursue the challenge of exploring new psychological frontiers.

SECTION ONE
PSYCHOLOGY: ITS PERSPECTIVES AND METHODS

CHAPTER ONE: **PSYCHOLOGY IN PERSPECTIVE**

CHAPTER TWO: **SCIENTIFIC PRINCIPLES AND METHODS IN PSYCHOLOGY**

CHAPTER ONE
PSYCHOLOGY IN PERSPECTIVE

THE SCOPE OF PSYCHOLOGY

FRONTIER I.I EMERGING SPECIALTY AREAS: HEALTH, FORENSIC, AND SPORT PSYCHOLOGY

Four basic goals of psychology (and you)

FIVE PERSPECTIVES ON HUMAN BEHAVIOR

The importance of perspectives

The biological perspective: Body, mind, and behavior

The psychodynamic perspective: The forces within

The cognitive perspective: The thinking human

The behavioral perspective: Humans as reactors

The humanistic-existential perspective: Choice, responsibility, and self-actualization

APPLYING THE PERSPECTIVES: UNDERSTANDING HUMAN AGGRESSION

Biological factors in aggression

Psychodynamic factors in aggression

Cognitive processes in aggression

The behavioral perspective on aggression

The humanistic-existential perspective on aggression

STUDY OUTLINE

KEY TERMS AND CONCEPTS

SUGGESTED READINGS

We have had religious revolutions, we have had political, economic and nationalistic revolutions. All of them, as our descendants will discover, are but ripples in an ocean of conservatism—trivial by comparison with the psychological revolution toward which we are so rapidly moving. (Aldous Huxley)

We are now in the midst of the psychological revolution that Huxley predicted. On many fronts, important advances are being made in unraveling the mysteries of human behavior, in understanding how we behave, and why. In this book, we hope to communicate the excitement that exists on these frontiers of our attempts to know, to understand, and to change ourselves and the world of the 1980s. Like the world in which we live, the face of modern-day psychology is constantly changing as discoveries open up new fields of research and application.

THE SCOPE OF PSYCHOLOGY

Psychology is defined as *the scientific study of behavior and its causes.* In this definition, the term **behavior** is used in its broadest sense to include anything that a human or animal can do. We are thus concerned with both **overt** behaviors—the things we can actually see being done—and **covert** behaviors, such as thoughts, images, and biological processes that we cannot observe directly.

As a scientific discipline, psychology employs a range of specific procedures for doing research and for building and testing theories about behavior and its causes. The knowledge gained through these procedures can often be applied to important problems in today's world. A distinction is sometimes made between **basic science,** the quest for knowledge purely for its own sake, and **applied science,** research designed to solve specific practical problems. In the real world, however, the two often go hand in hand. Knowledge gained through basic research can provide solutions to

real-life problems, and the findings of applied science can fuel basic research. As we survey the major areas of psychology, we shall on many occasions see the intimate link between basic and applied science.

Although humans have always been interested in understanding the workings of their minds and the causes of their behavior, psychology as a scientific discipline is little more than a century old. The birth date of psychology is generally agreed to be 1879, the year that Wilhelm Wundt established a laboratory at the University of Leipzig, Germany, to study scientifically the structure of the mind. The new science soon spread to the United States, where 31 charter members founded the American Psychological Association (APA) in 1892. Today, the APA has nearly 60,000 members, and thousands of psychologists work in nearly every other nation in the world.

Modern-day psychology is a sprawling intellectual domain that stretches from the borders of medicine and the biological sciences to those of the social sciences, and on into the realm of philosophy. No psychologist can be an expert on all aspects of behavior, just as no physician can be an expert in all areas of medicine. Thus, in psychology, as in other professions, areas of specialization have emerged over the years. These specialty areas are described in Table 1.1. We shall not attempt to describe these areas in depth at this point, but you will encounter all of the aspects of behavior that they focus on as you proceed through this book and your introductory psychology course.

Preparation for a career in many of the subfields described in Table 1.1 requires a doctoral degree based on four to six years of training in a university graduate program. Graduate training in psychology includes broad exposure to the theories and body of knowledge in the field, special focus on one or more of the subfields, and extensive training in research methods. In some areas, an additional year of supervised practical experience in a hospital, clinic, or school may be required.

As Table 1.1 shows, the largest of the specialty areas are clinical and counseling psychology. Because both areas are oriented toward helping people resolve personal problems, clinical and counseling psychologists sometimes work closely with psychiatrists—medical doctors with several years of specialized training in the diagnosis and treatment of mental disorders. As physicians, psychiatrists can prescribe drugs and use other medical procedures that psychologists cannot. Psychologists, on the other hand, are more broadly trained in psychological testing and research methods.

Besides the fascinating nature of its subject matter, one aspect of a career in psychology that attracts many people is the rich array of career options and work settings that await the well-trained professional. Figure 1.1 shows some of the major settings in which psychologists work. Many psychologists have rich and varied professional lives in which they teach, do research, or apply psychological principles and techniques to help solve personal or social problems.

As we noted earlier, psychology is an evolving profession in which new discoveries and opportunities for applying psychological principles for human betterment are constantly occurring. Frontier 1.1 describes three emerging areas of research and application that are attracting the attention of many psychologists.

TABLE 1.1 MAJOR SPECIALTY AREAS OF PSYCHOLOGY

SPECIALTY	PERCENT	MAJOR FOCUS
Clinical	45	Diagnosis and treatment of emotional disorders; research on personality and abnormal behavior.
Counseling	12	Work with clients concerning personal adjustment and vocational and career plans; interest and aptitude testing.
Educational	10	Psychological aspects of the educational process; curriculum and instructional research; teacher training.
Experimental	8	Research on basic psychological processes such as learning, memory, perception, and motivation.
Industrial	6	Examination of behavior in work settings; study of factors related to morale and productivity; design of training programs; preparation of machines and tasks to fit human capabilities.
Developmental	4	Physical, mental, emotional, and social development across the entire life span, from birth to old age.
Social	4	All aspects of social behavior and the conditions that affect it.
Personality	3	Individual differences in personality and their effects on behavior; factors involved in personality development and change.
Physiological	2	Biological foundations of behavior; brain-behavior relationships, genetic processes, and the functioning of sensory and motor systems.
Quantitative	2	Measurement and data analysis; development of mathematical models of behavior; computer science.
Others	4	
Total	100	

Source: Courtesy, American Psychological Association.

FIGURE 1.1 *Psychologists engage in a wide variety of professional activities, including research, clinical work (here, testing attentional processes in an infant), and consultation.*

SETTING	PERCENT
Colleges and medical schools	**43.1**
Private practice	**14.7**
Clinics, counseling centers	**14.3**
Industry and government	**13.0**
Hospitals	**9.6**
School districts	**4.6**
Others	**0.7**
Total	**100.0**

EMERGING SPECIALTY AREAS: HEALTH, FORENSIC, AND SPORT PSYCHOLOGY

There is little question that the promotion of health and physical well-being is one of today's top priorities. In recent years, the contributions that psychology can make to illness prevention and recovery have become so evident that a new area of specialization known as *health psychology,* or *behavioral medicine,* has emerged.

For many years, scientists have known that stress and other emotional conditions play a major role in physical illness. Indeed, some experts believe that such factors may be involved in the development and progress of most physical diseases, and in many accidents as well. If this is so, then psychologists can make major contributions to modern health care and illness prevention. They can identify psychological conditions that make individuals susceptible to certain diseases so that preventive measures can be taken. They can isolate the mental and biological mechanisms that underlie the potentially devastating effects of life stress on the body and can develop programs to help people learn specific life skills to cope more effectively with stress. Psychologists can identify the most effective strategies for coping with serious illness and disability once they occur, for psychological factors are clearly involved in recovery from illness.

Many people engage in behaviors that increase the risk of illness and death. They smoke, they overeat, they become addicted to harmful drugs, they ignore early warning signs of serious illness, or they fail to comply with medical treatment once a disease has been diagnosed. All of these are behavioral problems that fall within the province of the psychologist. For this reason, the National Institutes of Health have designated health psychology as a priority training area and are funding the development of specialty training programs within numerous psychology departments in the United States. In Chapter 14, we shall discuss recent contributions of health psychology in greater detail.

Another growing field is *forensic psychology,* the application of psychological principles to law enforce-ment and the legal system. The province of law covers a vast terrain, extending all the way from crime prevention to punishment and rehabilitation of the offender, and psychologists have become increasingly involved with the legal system at all levels. They have developed methods for selecting police officers who are likely to be successful, and some have become skilled in counseling police officers and their families when personal problems arise. They can create personality profiles of people being sought for serious crimes, and they have trained police officers in crowd control and the handling of potentially explosive domestic disturbances. Some forensic psychologists work in correctional institutions, where they treat offenders and assist in their rehabilitation.

The court system often seeks the skills and knowledge of psychologists, who can help assess the mental competency of a defendant to stand trial and can testify in custody cases and in other instances in which psychological factors are important. Psychologists sometimes assist in jury selection, do research on factors that influence jury decisions, and help to devise new methods to reduce the possibility of injustice. An example of a procedure inspired by psychological research is the videotaping of an actual trial in the absence of the jury. The jury views the tape and makes its decision after all inadmissible evidence has been edited out.

To an increasing extent, the legal system has been relying on the results of psychological research as a basis for important decisions. In a recent U.S. Supreme Court ruling on the minimum allowable jury size, no fewer than 14 of the 32 paragraphs in the opinion cited psychological studies of jury size and decision making. Psychologists have offered testimony based on research in such areas as eyewitness identification, the effects of busing and racial desegregation, and bilingual education. The relationship between psychology and the legal system promises to grow even stronger in the coming years (see Figure 1.2).

Sport has long been an important part of our cul-

EMERGING SPECIALTY AREAS: HEALTH, FORENSIC, AND SPORT PSYCHOLOGY

ture, and it touches the lives of most of us. It is also attracting the attention of an increasing number of psychologists.

At one time, only a few psychologists referred to themselves as sport psychologists. These pioneers were usually clinical psychologists who treated athletes having psychological problems that interfered with their performance. But as awareness grew of the importance of psychological factors in sport, psychologists were increasingly attracted to the application of psychological principles in athletics. Presently, a number of psychologists serve as consultants to college, professional, and Olympic teams. In addition to helping athletes who have personal problems, they develop training programs in such vital areas as stress management, the use of mental imagery, and concentration skills.

In Europe, sport psychologists are highly involved in the training of elite athletes. Soviet and East German national teams all have at least one full-time sport psychologist, as well as others who act as consultants. Many of these psychologists are trying to identify the psychological and physiological traits that are related to success in various sports. Such information could be used to build a model of the "ideal" athlete for each sport for selection and training purposes (Schneidman, 1979). The increasingly political nature of international sporting events has led many nations to look to psychological training and preparation for the competitive edge.

Psychological researchers also see sport as an unusually rich natural laboratory for studying factors like motivation, learning, leadership and group functioning, stress, personality development, and so on. In the past decade, several new scientific journals devoted entirely to sport-related research have appeared.

Some psychologists have become involved in sports as researchers and consultants to youth athletic programs, which have frequently been criticized for an overemphasis on winning and competition. Psychologists can help adults create a more positive and less stressful environment that will contribute to the personal growth of young athletes. Some of the recent

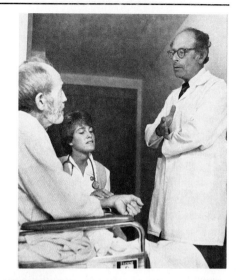

FIGURE 1.2 *Increasing numbers of psychologists are studying and applying psychological principles in the areas of health and behavior, the legal system, and sports.*

psychological research on social factors in sports will be described in Chapter 18.

Because of the relevance of behavioral research and application to many areas of our society, new opportunities for psychology to contribute to the quality of life occur continuously. Throughout the book, we will focus on these important frontiers.

Four basic goals of psychology (and you)

People's attempts to understand themselves are as old as the human race. Over the years, people have developed "theories" based on their everyday observations, have examined their own thoughts, motives, and behavior, and have sought understanding through the use of philosophical reasoning and even through divine inspiration. Psychology uses yet another approach, one based on scientific methods. These methods have four related goals: (1) to *describe*, (2) to *understand* (explain), (3) to *predict*, and (4) to *influence* behavior.

These same goals guide our behavior on a day-to-day basis. We all ask questions like "What's happening?" "What am I (or they) doing?" (description); "Why did that happen?" (understanding); "What will happen if I do that?" (prediction); and "What can I do to make sure things turn out well?" (influence). We can see, then, that description, understanding, prediction, and influence are goals shared by psychologists and lay people alike, although the specific methods used to attain these objectives may be quite different.

All of us realize that different people can achieve different "understandings" out of the same basic experiences. Our ideas and beliefs guide our perceptions of ourselves, of other people, and of events in our lives. What we perceive and how we interpret it is but one possibility among many. No one has expressed this more vividly than the early American psychologist and philosopher William James:

The mind is at every stage a theater of simultaneous possibilities. . . . The mind, in short, works on the data it receives very much as the sculptor works on his block of stone. In a sense the statue stood there from eternity, but there were a thousand different forms beside it, and the sculptor alone is to thank for having extricated one from the rest. (1890, p. 288)

Just as our basic goals are shared with scientific psychology, psychology shares with us different ways of looking at and trying to understand the complex realm of behavior. This diversity in viewpoints—or, as we shall call them, **perspectives**—guides and enriches our attempts to understand behavior and its causes. We turn now to the five major perspectives on behavior that characterize and guide modern-day psychology.

FIVE PERSPECTIVES ON HUMAN BEHAVIOR

On a hot summer evening in Austin, a University of Texas student wrote the following letter:

I don't really understand myself these days. I am supposed to be an average, reasonable, and intelligent young man. However, lately (I can't recall when it started) I have been the victim of many unusual and irrational thoughts. These thoughts constantly recur, and it requires a tremendous mental effort to concentrate on useful and progressive tasks. In March when my parents made a physical break I noticed a great deal of stress. I consulted a Dr. Cochrum at the University Health Center and asked him to recommend someone that I could consult with about some psychiatric disorders I felt I had. I talked with a doctor once for about two hours and tried to convey to him my fears that I felt overcome by overwhelming violent impulses. After one session I never saw the doctor again, and since then I have been fighting my mental turmoil alone, and seemingly to no avail. After my death I wish that an autopsy would be performed on me to see if there is any visible physical disorder. I have had some tremendous headaches in the past and have consumed two large bottles of Excedrin in the past three months. (UPI)

Later that night, Charles Whitman killed his wife and mother. The next morning he went to a tower on the University of Texas campus and began shooting the people below with a high-powered hunting rifle (see Figure 1.3). In 90 horrifying minutes he killed 14 people, wounded another 24, and even managed to hit an airplane before police stormed the tower and shot him to death.

There were many attempts to explain Whitman's murderous rampage. The letter he wrote provided a number of clues. Following up his reference to intense headaches, a postmortem examination revealed a highly malignant tumor in an area of the brain known to be involved in aggressive behavior. Some experts therefore suggested that Whitman's behavior was

FIGURE 1.3 *A terrified University of Texas student hides behind the base of a flagpole to avoid the gunfire of Charles Whitman. One of his victims is visible in the background.*

caused by his damaged brain. Others focused on the "unusual and irrational thoughts" to which he referred. Still others sought the answer in Whitman's previous learning experiences, and a study of his past revealed a long history of rewarding experiences with guns. There was also speculation that Whitman's "overwhelming violent impulses" had been bottled up inside for many years and had finally exploded into action because of the recent life stresses that he described in his letter.

We cannot be certain which of these potential causes was most important. Perhaps all of them contributed in varying degrees. But the Whitman case dramatically illustrates the many vantage points from which a given act can be viewed and explained.

The importance of perspectives

Although opposing viewpoints may sometimes be personally uncomfortable for us, they are the lifeblood of social, technical, and scientific advances. If everyone perceived the world in exactly the same way, originality and creativity would be impossible. Partly because psychology has its roots in such varied disciplines as philosophy, medicine, and the biological and physical sciences, five different perspectives for viewing people and their behavior have emerged over the years. Each perspective focuses on a different aspect of our functioning and on different causes of our behavior. Taken together, they provide us with a unifying framework for understanding who we are and why we behave as we do. The five perspectives are the *biological* perspective, the *psychodynamic* perspective, the *cognitive* perspective, the *behavioral* perspective, and the *humanistic-existential* perspective (see Figure 1.4).

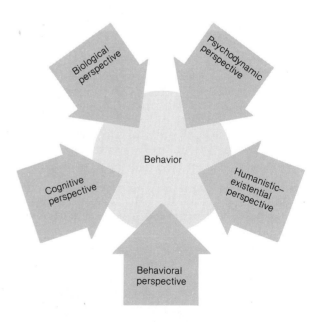

FIGURE 1.4 *Five major perspectives—biological, psychodynamic, cognitive, behavioral, and humanistic-existential— guide modern-day psychology's attempts to understand human behavior.*

These differing perspectives on behavior thread their way through the history of psychology, and they are just as important today as they were a century ago. Like our own personal viewpoints, they serve as lenses through which the world of behavior is viewed, and they reflect and shape our very conception of human nature. They also determine which aspects of behavior we see as important and worthy of study, which questions we ask, and which methods of study we employ. In a very real sense, perspectives on behavior influence the directions in which psychology develops, what it learns about our behavior, and the kinds of contributions it makes to human betterment.

The biological perspective: Body, mind, and behavior

Each of the thousands of studies being carried out in physiological psychology laboratories has the same general goal: to understand thought, emotion, and behavior in terms of physical processes taking place within the body. Most of this work would have been considered impossible by scientists as recently as 50 years ago.

HISTORICAL DEVELOPMENT OF THE BIOLOGICAL PERSPECTIVE

The **biological perspective** has its roots in philosophy as well as in the physical and biological sciences. At its core is a philosophical question that has tested and bested the greatest minds down through the ages: the body-mind problem.

The body-mind problem For thousands of years, people have tried to understand the relationship between the nonphysical mind and the physical body. Early Greek philosophers like Aristotle and Plato believed that the physical body and the spiritual mind are separate entities. Aristotle thought that the mind was localized in the heart, while Plato believed that the mind or soul interacted with the body through the brain. The Greeks and the influential seventeenth-century philosopher René Descartes ("I think, therefore I am.") also maintained that the mind, being spiritual, is not subject to physical laws. The implication of this view, known as **dualism,** is that no amount of research on the body could hope to unravel the mysteries of the mind.

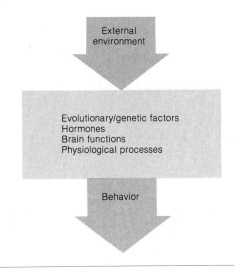

FIGURE 1.5 *The biological perspective focuses on evolutionary, genetic, and physiological foundations of behavior.*

The alternative to dualism is **monism,** derived from the Greek work *monos,* meaning "one." If mind and body are one, rather than separate entities, mental events result from physical events, and questions about mental functions can therefore be studied scientifically. Many modern scientists hold a monistic view of mind-body relationships, as typified in the statement by two prominent physiological psychologists that "answers to the great questions of psychology will ultimately be found in 'physiology.' Higher organisms, after all, are simply brains with a few minor appendages. All behavior, all experience, all feeling, indeed all the subject matter of psychology, are nothing more than the outcomes of the activity of the nervous system" (Thompson and Robinson, 1979, p. 449).

The biological perspective thus emphasizes our evolutionary history, our highly developed brain, and a process of individual development that is partly programmed by genetic factors (see Figure 1.5).

Scientific advances Because it focuses on processes that are largely invisible to the naked eye, the biological perspective has been especially dependent on scientific and technological developments. In the sixteenth century, a number of scientific advances occurred in the fields of anatomy, physiology, and biology. Physicians began to dissect dead humans to study their anatomy. Experiments were conducted on the circulatory system. The microscope was invented and cells were discovered.

One of the most important of these advances concerned the electrical nature of nerve conduction. In the seventeenth century, Luigi Galvani discovered that the severed leg of a frog would move if an electrical current was applied to it. Galvani's reports were ridiculed by dualists, who believed that all bodily movements were caused by spiritual forces from the soul, but further experiments confirmed his findings. Soon many experiments on electrical nerve conduction were under way, borne on a wave of excitement about the discovery of "nervous energy." By 1870, researchers at the University of Berlin were applying electrical stimulation directly to the exposed brains of experimental animals. They discovered that stimulation of what we now know as the *motor cortex* resulted in body movements. During this same period, many clinical reports appeared linking damage to specific brain areas with behavioral impairments.

As psychology entered the twentieth century, the study of brain-behavior relationships was in its infancy. Karl Lashley, the most important figure in the early development of physiological psychology in America, was interested in brain mechanisms in learning. His approach was to create lesions (damage) in specific brain areas and to study their effects on the maze learning of experimental animals. Lashley's research stimulated many other attempts to study brain-behavior relationships experimentally.

In the 1920s, two important technical advances occurred. First, the development of the cathode ray oscilloscope made it possible to view and measure the nerve impulse. In 1929, the invention of the electroencephalogram (EEG) allowed researchers to measure the electrical activity of large areas of the brain through electrodes attached to the scalp. Scientists could now relate brain wave patterns to behavior and states of consciousness. In the 1940s, the development of tiny microelectrodes permitted scientists to monitor the electrical activity of single nerve cells.

Many of the important discoveries about the brain and behavior have occurred since 1950, again as a result of technical advances (see Figure 1.6). The electron microscope has made it possible to study formerly invisible brain structures. New biochemical and computer-based techniques have created ways of looking into the living brain to witness the electrochemical activities that are the basis for thought, emotion, and behavior. The electrical activity of the brain is now known to be mediated by chemical substances released by nerve cells; the role of these substances in both normal and abnormal behavior is one of the most important areas of current research. We have also learned that the two hemispheres of the brain—the "right brain" and the "left brain"—have different functions and are capable under certain conditions of functioning independently of one another as if there were two minds in one body. We are on the threshold of many other revolutionary discoveries of brain-behavior relationships.

Evolution and genetics   The appearance of Charles Darwin's book *On the Origin of Species* in 1859 generated shock waves that are still felt today. Darwin pro-

---

FIGURE 1.6 *Relationships between brain functions and behavior have long been a focus of the biological perspective. Here a physiological psychologist performs brain surgery on a laboratory animal. The effects on behavior will then be studied.*

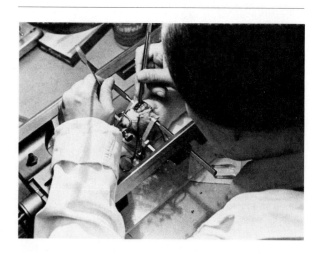

posed that new species evolve over time in response to environmental conditions through a process called **natural selection,** or "survival of the fittest." Natural selection means that any inheritable characteristic that increases the likelihood of survival will be maintained in the species because those individuals who have the trait will be more likely to survive and reproduce. On the other hand, characteristics that reduce chances for survival will be eliminated from the species over time because those creatures having them will not survive to pass on their genes. Darwin assumed that the principle of natural selection could be applied to all living things, including human beings. (Contrary to popular misconceptions, Darwin did not say that we are the direct descendants of modern apes. Rather, he believed that both human beings and apes had a common ancestor in the distant past but that at some point, the various species became different branches of the family tree.)

Evolution has relevance to more than just physical development. An organism's biology determines how it is capable of behaving, and its behavior determines whether or not it will survive. Psychologists with an evolutionary perspective stress that what evolved in the history of the human species was successful behavior as well as a changing body. One theory is that when dwindling vegetation in some parts of the world forced ape-like animals from the trees and required that they hunt

for meat, chances for survival were greater for those who were capable of **bipedal locomotion** (walking on two legs) (Pilbeam, 1984). By freeing the hands, bipedalism in turn fostered the development of improved tools and weapons, and hunting in groups encouraged social organization. Tool use and bipedal locomotion put new selective pressures on many parts of the body, including the teeth, the hands, and the pelvis. But the greatest pressure was placed on the brain structures involved in the abilities most critical to the emerging way of life: attention, memory, language, and thought. Between an early humanlike creature such as *Australopithecus* of 2 million years ago and the *Neanderthal man* of 75,000 years ago, the brain tripled in size, with the most dramatic increase in brain tissue occurring in the cerebrum, the seat of the higher mental processes (see Figure 1.7). Thus, changes in behavior contrib-

FIGURE 1.7 *The human brain evolved over a period of several million years. The greatest growth occurred in those areas concerned with the higher mental processes.*

The Brain Gets Bigger

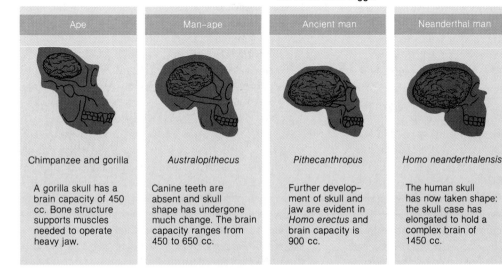

Ape	Man–ape	Ancient man	Neanderthal man	Modern human
Chimpanzee and gorilla	*Australopithecus*	*Pithecanthropus*	*Homo neanderthalensis*	*Homo sapiens*
A gorilla skull has a brain capacity of 450 cc. Bone structure supports muscles needed to operate heavy jaw.	Canine teeth are absent and skull shape has undergone much change. The brain capacity ranges from 450 to 650 cc.	Further develop– ment of skull and jaw are evident in *Homo erectus* and brain capacity is 900 cc.	The human skull has now taken shape: the skull case has elongated to hold a complex brain of 1450 cc.	The deeply convoluted brain reflects growth in areas concerned with higher mental processes.

uted to the development of the brain, just as the growth of the brain contributed to the development of human behavior.

Psychologists have had a long-standing interest in **behavior genetics,** the study of how behavioral tendencies are influenced by genetic factors. Animals can be selectively bred for specific traits like aggression or intelligence, by allowing assertive or bright animals to mate with similar partners (Snowdon, 1983). There seems to be little doubt that human behavior, too, can be influenced by genetic factors. Research with humans indicates that identical twins, who are exactly the same genetically, are much more alike in their behavior than are genetically different fraternal twins, even when the identical twins have been separated at birth and reared in different homes (Wilson, 1983).

The most recent and ambitious attempt to explain complex human behavior in genetic terms is **sociobiology.** Sociobiologists assert that all manner of human behavior, including dominance, love, and aggression, can be understood as attempts to ensure that our genes will be passed on either through ourselves or our relatives. In other words, our own survival as individuals is not as important as the survival of our genetic code (Barash, 1982). According to sociobiologists, this is why parents love and care for their children and why many parents will sacrifice their own lives so that their offspring may survive. While sociobiology is controversial, long on speculation, and short on research support (Hailman, 1982; Snowdon, 1983), the theory has stimulated new research that may shed more light on evolutionary factors underlying human behavior.

The psychodynamic perspective: The forces within

At times during your life you have probably felt as if there were some kind of a struggle going on within you. According to our second approach to understanding behavior, the **psychodynamic perspective,** the mind is a battleground where conflicting psychic forces struggle for supremacy, and our behavior often represents a compromise between these forces (see Figure 1.8). There are a number of different psychodynamic theories of behavior, but the first and most influential of them was Sigmund Freud's theory of psychoanalysis.

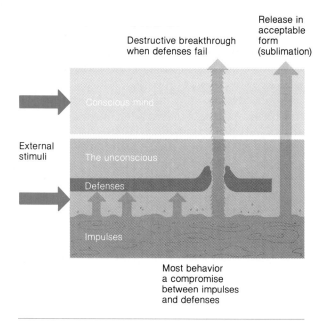

FIGURE 1.8 *In the psychodynamic perspective, there is a never-ending internal struggle between impulses and defenses.*

HISTORICAL DEVELOPMENT OF THE PSYCHODYNAMIC PERSPECTIVE

Although the shadowy underworld of hidden motives has tempted explorers throughout history, humans have traditionally viewed themselves as creatures ruled by reason and conscious thought. But late in the nineteenth century, as the aftershocks produced by Darwin's evolutionary theory were still being felt throughout the intellectual world, Sigmund Freud mounted a second and equally profound assault on the prevailing conception of human beings as rational, civilized creatures.

As a young Viennese medical student in the early 1880s, Freud became interested in the treatment of hysteria, a disorder in which physical symptoms such as blindness, pain, or paralysis develop without any apparent organic or physical cause. Freud treated hysterical patients, first by hypnosis and later by a technique he developed called *free association*. In free association, the patient was to say whatever came to mind and to let one association lead freely to another, even if the order did not seem logical or rational. To Freud's surprise, his patients (most of whom were women) consistently reported and relived extremely painful long-"forgotten" childhood sexual experiences and desires. After the patients had relived these experiences, their symptoms often showed a marked improvement. Freud concluded, however, that many of these childhood sexual "experiences" had never actually occurred. (This conclusion is a topic of current controversy within psychoanalytic circles, especially because of what we now know about the high incidence of sexual abuse in children.) Freud was faced with the problem of accounting for how "reliving" events that never happened reduced the symptoms of hysteria. Freud became convinced that his patients were driven to create these fantasies because of the existence of a compelling and unsatisfied sexual drive.

Freud also found that sexual material often emerged in dreams and slips of the tongue. These observations, plus an intensive period of self-analysis, led him to propose that much of human behavior is influenced by inner forces of which we are unaware. He claimed that we have an inborn sexual drive, or instinct, and that our adult personality is strongly shaped by the ways we cope with these forces as we grow up. Freud speculated that because early sexual desires and needs are punished, they are **repressed**, or pushed

down into the unconscious depths of the mind. There they remain as sources of energy, continually striving for release. To keep the forbidden instincts under control, the personality constructs elaborate psychological defenses. All behavior, whether it is normal or abnormal, is a reflection of the never-ending internal struggle between the instincts and the defenses. Pathological, or unhealthy, symptoms appear when the defenses either fail to control the instincts or when the need to strengthen the defenses forces the person to behave in some abnormal way.

One of the great thinkers of the twentieth century, Freud wrote numerous works of both psychological and literary interest (see Figure 1.9). Freud's theory gave rise to other psychodynamic theories, some of which differed from his in attaching less importance to sexual instincts and fantasies and more significance to conscious and reality factors. But regardless of their specifics, all psychodynamic theories emphasize the role of inner forces in explaining behavior.

FIGURE 1.9 *For more than 50 years, Sigmund Freud probed the hidden recesses of the human mind.*

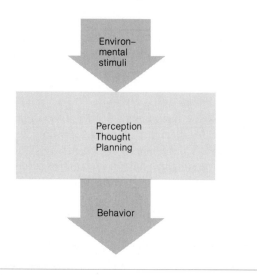

FIGURE 1.10 *The thinking human is the focus of the cognitive perspective.*

The cognitive perspective: The thinking human

The term *cognitive* comes from the Latin word *cogitare*, which means "to think." The **cognitive perspective** emphasizes the ways in which people mentally process incoming information, evaluate it, and decide how to respond to it. While psychodynamic theories focus primarily on the role of unconscious and irrational mental forces, the cognitive perspective views humans as active and rational problem solvers, as information-processing systems whose actions are governed by conscious thought and planning (see Figure 1.10).

HISTORICAL DEVELOPMENT OF THE COGNITIVE PERSPECTIVE

Psychology has been concerned with cognitive processes from its very beginning. An important assumption of present-day cognitive psychology can be traced back to the philosopher J. F. Herbart (1776–1841), who stated that the way we receive information from the world is strongly influenced by the existing contents of the mind. In later years several important "schools" of psychology developed, each of which had its own way of studying mental processes.

Structuralism and functionalism   Wilhelm Wundt, who founded the first laboratory of experimental psychology at Leipzig, Germany, believed that the structure of the mind could be studied by breaking it down into its basic components, as a chemist might study the components of chemical compounds. His approach was known as **structuralism.**

Wundt, who believed that sensations are the basic units of consciousness, set out to study them through the method called **introspection** (looking within). Subjects were exposed to all sorts of sensory stimuli—lights, sounds, tastes—and asked to report on their inner experiencing of the sensations. While structuralism as a school of psychology never really caught on, particularly in the United States, Wundt's work established a scientific tradition in the study of cognition (see Figure 1.11).

In the United States, structuralism gave way to a

FIGURE 1.11 *Wilhelm Wundt established the first laboratory of experimental psychology to study the nature of consciousness.*

new approach called **functionalism.** The chief architects of this school of psychology were William James and John Dewey. As its name suggests, functionalism was more interested in how the mind functions than in how it is structured. In part, functionalism was influenced by evolutionary theory, which stressed the importance of adaptive behavior in survival, and much of the early research on the nature of learning and problem solving in humans and animals was done by functionalists. Although it no longer exists as a formal school of psychology, the tradition of functionalism endures in modern-day cognitive psychology as an emphasis on how our minds process information and govern our behavior.

Gestalt psychology In the 1920s, a German school of thought known as **Gestalt psychology** became influential in the United States. The word *gestalt* may be translated as "whole" or "organization." Instead of trying to break consciousness down into its basic elements, as the structuralists did, the Gestalt psychologists argued that our perceptions and other mental processes are organized so that the whole is not only greater than, but also quite different from, the sum of its parts. For example, most people see Figure 1.12 as three groups of vertical lines rather than nine vertical lines. The Gestalt psychologists believed that such grouping tendencies reflect principles of perceptual organization that are built into our nervous systems.

Wolfgang Köhler, one of the leaders of Gestalt psychology, conducted research with apes and other animals while he was stranded at a research station in the

FIGURE 1.13 *A modern-day Sultan demonstrates insight learning as he uses a series of shorter sticks to pull in a stick that is long enough to reach the delicacy.*

Canary Islands during World War I. Köhler concluded that the ability to perceive relationships is the essence of what we call intelligence, and he called the sudden perception of a useful relationship **insight.**

Several examples of insight were demonstrated by Sultan, one of Köhler's apes. One day, Köhler hung a banana from the top of Sultan's cage, out of his reach. Sultan scratched his head a few times, looked about his cage, noticed a box in one corner, and placed the box beneath the dangling banana so that he could reach it. Another time, Sultan attached two sticks together to reach a banana that had been placed on the ground outside his cage, a feat that has gone down in history as an act of simian genius (see Figure 1.13). Gestalt psychology's demonstrations of insight learning in both animals and humans stimulated new interest in human cognitive processes.

Piaget and the development of thought A final figure in our brief excursion through the history of cognitive psychology is a scientist who reshaped our conceptions

FIGURE 1.12 *Through the processes of perceptual organization, most people "see" this as three groups of three lines rather than as nine lines. The Gestalt psychologists emphasized our tendency to organize our perceptions so that the whole is greater than and different from the sum of its parts.*

FIGURE 1.14 *Jean Piaget was a master of observation. Many of his conclusions about stages of cognitive development came from watching children solve problems and inferring how they must have thought about them.*

of how thought develops in children. A zoologist by training, Jean Piaget spent more than 50 years studying how children think, reason, and solve problems. His primary techniques were careful observation and **empathic inference,** the technique of watching how children approach specific problems and then imagining how they must have experienced the situation in order to respond as they did (see Figure 1.14). Piaget concluded that new and specific stages of cognitive growth that cannot be explained by the accumulation of past experiences emerge naturally in the course of development.

The cognitive perspective gives us a far more active role in shaping our own behavior than the biological and psychodynamic perspectives do. In the cognitive view, people are less what their experience makes them than what they make of their experience. Far from being passive reactors to our environment, we partly create the reality to which we respond. Indeed, as may already have occurred to you, our emphasis on the five perspectives is based on this assumption from the cognitive perspective.

The behavioral perspective: Humans as reactors

The biological, psychodynamic, and cognitive perspectives see processes within the individual—biological factors, needs, conflicts, perception, and thought—as the important determinants of behavior. The **behavioral perspective** concentrates instead on the role of the external environment in shaping and governing our actions. Although behaviorists acknowledge biological factors, they deny that people freely choose the ways in which they respond. The factors that control human behavior, they say, reside in the external environment rather than within the individual. People's behavior is jointly determined by their previous life experiences and by their immediate surroundings.

HISTORICAL DEVELOPMENT OF THE BEHAVIORAL PERSPECTIVE

The behavioral perspective is rooted in a seventeenth-century school of philosophy known as **British empiricism.** The empiricists believed that all ideas and knowledge are gained *empirically*—that is, through the senses. According to John Locke, one of the early empiricists, the human mind is initially a *tabula rasa*, a "blank slate," on which our experiences make imprints. Human beings thus behave according to the dictates of their environment. Empiricism also maintained that observation is a more valid approach to knowledge than is reason, an idea that has been enormously influential in shaping the development of science.

Radical behaviorism   Behaviorism emerged early in this century as an outspoken alternative to the cognitive schools of psychology. A leader in the new movement was John B. Watson, who argued that the proper subject matter of psychology was observable, or overt, be-

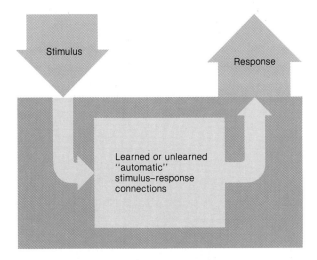

Stimulus

Response

Learned or unlearned "automatic" stimulus–response connections

FIGURE 1.15 *Radical behaviorism views our actions as the result of past conditioning and current stimuli. References to mental events are avoided.*

havior, not unobservable inner consciousness. Human beings, he said, are products of their learning histories, and their behavior can be controlled completely by manipulating their environment. Watson likened animals and humans to machines that react automatically to certain stimuli (cues). In a sense, Watson put a lid on the box of internal processes that is the human being and declared that it was, for scientific purposes, empty (see Figure 1.15). Behaviorists devoted their efforts to discovering the laws that govern learning and performance. They believed that the same basic principles of learning held true for all organisms, and their research with both humans and animals led to many applications of these concepts. Many behaviorists would argue that the discovery of the laws of learning was the greatest contribution of American psychology.

The leading contemporary figure in what has come to be called radical behaviorism is B. F. Skinner of Harvard University (see Figure 1.16). Although Skinner does not deny that mental events, images, and feelings occur within us, he maintains that these are themselves behaviors rather than causes. The erroneous belief that human behavior is caused by inner factors, Skinner says, diverts attention from the real causes of behavior, which reside in the outer world. If human beings are to be changed, indeed saved, Skinner main-

FIGURE 1.16 *B. F. Skinner is a major contemporary figure in behaviorism.*

tains, we must manipulate the environment that determines behavior through its pattern of rewards and punishments. Skinner believes that large-scale control over human behavior is possible today but that the chief barrier to social engineering is an outmoded conception of people as free agents.

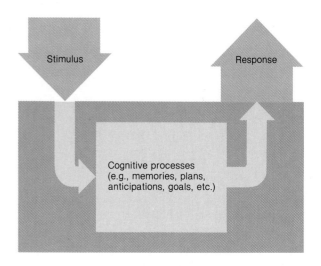

Cognitive behaviorism Another behavioral approach that has become highly influential in recent years is known as **cognitive behaviorism.** Cognitive behaviorism is an attempt to combine the behavioral and cognitive perspectives into a more comprehensive theory. Cognitive behaviorists believe that the environment exerts strong effects on behavior, but that it does so through the influence of thought (see Figure 1.17). That is, our behavior is influenced not only by our immediate environment but also by our memories of the past and our anticipations of the future. In this view, our learning experiences do not automatically stamp in responses, but rather give us the information we need to behave effectively (Bandura, 1981; Staats, 1975). Moreover, we can learn new behaviors by observing the actions of others and storing this information in our memories. In combining the cognitive and behavioral perspectives, cognitive behaviorists believe that a more comprehensive and useful conception of human behavior and its causes will emerge.

The humanistic-existential perspective: Choice, responsibility, and self-actualization

Our final perspective presents a completely different conception of human nature from those we have seen so far. As different as the psychodynamic and behavioral perspectives might seem, they do share a belief that human behavior is predictably controlled (either by internal or environmental factors) and that human freedom is an illusion. But not all psychologists are willing to subscribe to such a conception of human nature. Some prefer to view humans as free, creative, and inherently good beings who are striving to become all that they can be. The **humanistic-existential perspective** thus presents a sharp contrast to the psychodynamic and behavioral perspectives that have dominated psychology in the United States (see Figure

1.18). Abraham Maslow, an important humanistic theorist, called humanism the "third force" in contemporary psychology.

HISTORICAL DEVELOPMENT OF THE HUMANISTIC-EXISTENTIAL PERSPECTIVE

The historical roots of the humanistic-existential perspective are found in philosophical and religious systems that have stressed the dignity, inherent goodness, and freedom of human nature. The growth of this perspective within psychology was partly a product of this tradition and partly a reaction to the less flattering conceptions of human nature presented by psychoanalysis and radical behaviorism.

Among the most influential of the humanistic theories are those of Carl Rogers (1951, 1981) and Abraham Maslow (1970, 1971). Both theorists assume that in every human there is an active force toward growth and **self-actualization.** When the human personality unfolds in a benign environment that allows these creative forces free rein, the positive inner nature of humans emerges. Human misery and pathology, on the other hand, are fostered by environments that frustrate these innate tendencies toward self-actualization.

Closely related to the humanistic movement is the existential perspective, which became popular in Europe as psychologists and philosophers like Jean-Paul Sartre (1956) sought to understand how the horrors of World War II could have occurred and how certain people were able to rise above them and find meaning

Behavior

Free will and innate
motives toward self–
actualization and the
discovery of the meaning
of our existence

FIGURE 1.18 *The humanistic-existential perspective emphasizes the freedom and self-determination of beings striving for self-actualization.*

in life. Whereas the humanistic theories focus on the process of self-actualization, existential theorists like Rollo May (1961) and R. D. Laing (1967) emphasize rising above environmental forces through *self-determination*, choice, and responsibility. "We are our choices," the existentialists maintain. Our existence and its meaning are squarely in our own hands, for we alone can decide what our attitudes and behaviors will be.

Humanistic-existential theorists believe that scientific psychology is missing the mark if it dwells only on observable behavior and neglects the inner life of a person. They believe that inner experience and our search for the meaning of our existence are the core of our being-in-the-world and should be a primary focus of psychology. To them, introspection is not simply a valid source of psychological information—it is an indispensable one (Tageson, 1982).

The humanistic-existential perspective is more a philosophical position than a formal scientific theory. Nevertheless, this perspective is an important and vital force within psychology because it addresses crucial aspects of human existence. It has particularly enriched our understanding of motivation, personality, and disordered behavior.

APPLYING THE PERSPECTIVES: UNDERSTANDING HUMAN AGGRESSION

Psychology stands at the scientific crossroads of the five perspectives. The causes of behavior are many and varied, and each perspective focuses on different pieces of the jigsaw puzzle of causality. Let us now examine how these five perspectives can be applied to the understanding of a behavior of major social importance—violence and aggression.

The Charles Whitman incident in Texas is only one example of the violence and aggression that is an all-too-familiar aspect of human behavior. We are the most destructive creature ever to inhabit the earth, and aggression is perhaps the greatest threat to our survival. Here are just a few stark reminders of our legacy of violence (cf., Archer and Gartner, 1984):

Over 800,000 violent crimes are committed against Americans every year.

Every 23 minutes someone is murdered in the United States; every 6 minutes a woman is raped; every 48 seconds a man, woman, or child is assaulted.

If you are between the ages of 17 and 24, your chances of being a homicide victim are twice as great today as they would have been in 1961.

The total destructive force unleashed by all the armies during World War II was about 3 megatons (3 million tons of TNT). Today, hostile nations stand poised for confrontation with an estimated 15 *thousand* megatons of destructive power at their fingertips. If the arsenal were unleashed, Hiroshima-size nuclear weapons could rain down on us at a rate of one every three seconds for 40 days and 40 nights.

If human aggression had a single cause, perhaps we would be more successful in controlling it. But like most human behavior, aggression is very complex, and so are its causes. As we shall see, each of the perspectives can provide us with important clues to understanding the factors that underlie violence and aggression.

Biological factors in aggression

The biological perspective looks for causes of aggression in our evolutionary history, in genetic factors, and in the workings of the brain and the physiology of our bodies.

EVOLUTIONARY AND GENETIC VIEWPOINTS

Ethologists are scientists who study animal behavior in its natural environment. Much of their work is concerned with innate or instinctual patterns of behavior that occur in response to specific environmental stimuli called **releasers.** Ethologist Konrad Lorenz (1966) has argued that aggression is instinctive to human beings as well as to other animals. The difference, however, is that most lower animals have developed internal, genetically based controls against killing members of their own species, usually by displaying ritualized behaviors through which members can signal submission and thereby escape unharmed (see Figure 1.19).

FIGURE 1.19 *Rattlesnakes could quickly kill one another with their deadly fangs, but they limit their combat to attempts to force each other's heads to the ground. The loser thereafter submits to the victor. Konrad Lorenz believes that because humans are physically harmless by comparison with many other animals, they never developed internal inhibitions against killing their own kind.*

But people often fail to respond to such signs of submission from their fellows. Lorenz believes that because human beings are physically rather harmless creatures in comparison with many predatory animals, they did not develop genetically based internal inhibitions and controls against killing their own kind. Once they began to use their brains to construct weapons, there was nothing to curb their acquired deadliness except the thin veneer of societal prohibitions.

From an evolutionary standpoint, aggressiveness has been important to the emergence and survival of the human species. Prehistoric humans survived by becoming hunters, and ethologists have suggested that our cruelty can be traced to this prehistoric adaptation. Obviously, aggressiveness was also important in competing successfully for resources and in defending territory. It is ironic that a form of behavior that may have figured so prominently in humankind's past survival has now become the problem that most endangers our future survival. As biologist Loren Eiseley has written, "The need is now for a gentler, a more tolerant people than those who won for us against the ice, the tiger, and the bear" (1946, p. 140).

Although there is no compelling scientific evidence that human beings have an innate aggressive instinct that programs us to respond violently to specific releasers, genetic factors do appear to play a more general role in aggressive behavior. In lower animals, the linkages are quite clear. Animal breeders have for many years raised animals for specific traits through **selective breeding,** which involves mating animals with selected characteristics. Strains of pedigreed dogs, thoroughbred race horses, fighting cocks, and the "brave bulls" have been developed in this way. In Thailand, gambling on contests between fighting fish has for centuries been a national pastime, and the selective breeding of winners has resulted in the emergence of the vicious Siamese fighting fish, which will instantly attack other fish or even its own image in a mirror.

There is evidence that genetic factors may also contribute to aggressiveness in humans. Identical twins, who are genetic carbon copies of each other, are more similar in their aggressive and dominant behavior patterns than are fraternal twins, who differ genetically from one another (Gottesman, 1963; Loehlin and Nichols, 1976). This is the case even if the identical twins are raised in different homes with presumably different social environments (Bouchard, in press).

THE BRAIN AND AGGRESSION

Many attempts have been made to locate and study areas of the brain involved in aggressive behavior. One approach is to damage or electrically stimulate certain areas of the brain in animals and to study the subsequent effects on aggressive behavior. Such studies have shown that several structures deep within the brain are involved in triggering and inhibiting aggressive behavior. Surgical destruction of these areas can produce either extremely tame or very aggressive animals, and electrical stimulation of specific regions can cause an animal to make vicious attacks and kill other animals (Flynn, 1975).

Although certain areas of the brain may have coordinating functions in aggression, we also know that these regions are closely regulated by other areas of the brain that process information coming in from the environment. The manner in which neural (nerve) and environmental factors are jointly involved in aggression is illustrated in a famous experiment conducted by José Delgado (1967).

Delgado implanted electrodes in the brains of several members of a gibbon colony and observed the social behavior of the animals both under normal circumstances and when a so-called aggression area was electrically stimulated in selected animals through radio transmission. Because the animals had been living together for some time, a **dominance hierarchy** (or "pecking order") had been established. Delgado found

that an animal's position in the dominance hierarchy had a strong influence on the way it behaved when its brain was stimulated. When a dominant male was stimulated, he would attack subordinate male members, but not females (see Figure 1.20). But stimulation of the same area in a subordinate male elicited cowering and submissive behavior.

Certain kinds of brain damage or disorders can produce violent and unpredictable behavior in humans, too. During one 8-month period, a total of 45 people appeared at Massachusetts General Hospital complaining of violent impulses. About a quarter of these patients had symptoms of neurological disorders, and 11 of them either owned or carried deadly weapons (Lion and others, 1969).

HORMONES, TEMPERAMENT, AND PHYSICAL APPEARANCE

Three other biological factors that have been studied in relation to aggression are hormones, temperament, and physical appearance. In males, levels of the male sex hormone **testosterone** are related to self-reports of

FIGURE 1.20 *Depending on the animal's relative position in the dominance hierarchy, electrical stimulation of the identical brain site can result in either submission in the presence of a dominant animal (left) or an attack on an animal lower in the pecking order (right).*

physical and verbal aggression, particularly in response to provocation and threat (Olweus and others, 1980; Mazur, 1983). Men with high testosterone levels tend to be impatient and irritable, and their moods may increase the likelihood that they will respond aggressively to frustration or threat. Links between hormones and aggression have not been established in women (Parke and Slaby, 1983).

Anyone who has observed babies knows that temperamental differences are present from birth. Some babies can be charitably described as "difficult," and this infant characteristic is related to later aggressive behavior in both childhood and adolescence (Bates, 1982; Olweus, 1980). Here again, however, there is probably an interaction between a biologically based trait and the environment. It is hard for parents to react to crabby and obnoxious children with warmth and approval. Disapproval and, at times, outright dislike expressed by parents may help to encourage the development of a hostile child (Bates, 1982).

There is hardly a more obvious biological trait than physical appearance, and homeliness seems to be a definite handicap. As early as age 3 to 5, unattractive children are liked less by both adults and other children, and negative traits like "meanness" are attributed to them even by those who do not know them (Lerner and Lerner, 1977). By age 5, unattractive children, perhaps in response to the negative reactions of others, are more likely to be aggressive, to hit playmates, and to play in a loud and boisterous manner (Langlois and Stephan, 1981).

Although biological factors can contribute to aggression, we must keep in mind that learning experiences and features of the environment combine with physical factors in critically important ways. The other perspectives focus on some of these other influences.

Psychodynamic factors in aggression

According to the psychodynamic perspective, human aggression is an outgrowth of the continuous conflict between strong and often unconscious impulses and the defenses that the individual develops to keep them in check. Freud believed that behavior is largely directed toward satisfying inborn biological drives, one of which is aggression. But how does one go about releas-

FIGURE 1.21 *According to the psychodynamic perspective, aggressive impulses can be expressed in a variety of indirect ways.*

ing aggressive impulses in a world in which people are made to feel guilty and fearful about their violent desires? Freud's answer was that the defense mechanisms help to control our unacceptable impulses and to create acceptable ways of releasing them. He noted that there are many disguised forms in which hostile impulses may be released, such as in competitive sports, law enforcement, debate, and hunting (see Figure 1.21).

But what if people's defenses become so rigid that they cannot express their aggressive impulses even in indirect or disguised forms? Will the unreleased pressures build up to an explosion point? In some cases the answer appears to be yes.

Aggressive acts are often committed by individuals who have a history of such behavior, but some of the most brutal crimes are committed by those who are described by psychologist Edwin Megargee (1966) as people with **overcontrolled hostility.** Instead of showing immediate reaction to provocations, they repress or bottle up their anger, and over time the pressure to aggress builds up. At a critical point their rigid defenses shatter, and then they erupt into violence that is often extreme and brutal. Often, the provocation that triggers their destructive outburst is a trivial straw that breaks the camel's back. For example, one overcontrolled 10-year-old boy with no previous history of aggression stabbed his sister more than 80 times with an ice pick after she changed the channel during his favorite television show. After the aggressive outburst, such people revert to their former passive state, appearing again as unassertive individuals quite incapable of violence (Quinsey and others, 1983).

Psychodynamic theorists have also sought to understand the person for whom aggression has become a life style. Such individuals, far from being overcontrolled, use aggression as their primary means of achieving their goals and dealing with interpersonal problems (see Figure 1.22). According to Hans Toch (1969), violence-prone people fall into a number of fairly distinct personality patterns. **Self-defenders** behave aggressively out of intense fear of others. They consistently view others as wanting to harm them, and they regard their aggression as a legitimate way of protecting themselves. **Self-indulgers,** on the other hand, have an infantile view of the world and seem to think that others exist solely to satisfy their every need. When others fail to cater to their whims, they feel betrayed and strike out in blind fury. A third violence-prone group, **bullies and sadists,** simply like to harm others. They seek out vic-

tims who are relatively defenseless, and signs of submission from their victims cause them to engage in even more cruelty. (In the Freudian view, these people exemplify the unchecked instinct to aggress. For Lorenz, they serve as examples of a lack of internal inhibitions against aggression in the presence of submissive signals.) Finally, **self-image compensators** aggress as the result of feelings of insecurity and low self-esteem. Successful aggression shores up their poor self-image and demonstrates their power to others. Such people are extremely sensitive to signs that they are being laughed at or belittled by others and often respond to such perceptions with unprovoked attacks.

Megargee's and Toch's findings illustrate different ways in which psychodynamic factors can result in aggressive behavior. They also show that similar behaviors can have completely different underlying causes.

FIGURE 1.22 *Some people use aggression as their primary means of solving problems or of getting what they want. Hans Toch's research on violent men indicated several different personality patterns.*

Cognitive processes in aggression

How we perceive and interpret situations and the actions of others helps to determine how we behave. Aggression is just one possible response to the psychological world that people mentally construct for themselves. Through our thought processes, we can create enemies and justify aggression toward them.

By blaming a person or group for real or imagined wrongs, people can promote an image of a hated enemy fully deserving of whatever aggression is directed at it. Before and during wars, participants on both sides come to view themselves and their adversaries in black-and-white terms and develop a "diabolical enemy image" and a "moral self-image" (White, 1968). The adversaries become the incarnation of evil, and one's own side is regarded as the defender of all that is right and good (see Figure 1.23). These extreme images help to justify aggression and to foster the idea that the victims brought the suffering on themselves.

A variety of other cognitive self-deceptions may be used to reduce guilt reactions and thereby weaken inhibitions against aggressive behavior. For example, people sometimes minimize their own aggression by comparing it with even more repulsive deeds. Each side in the seemingly endless struggle between Arabs and Jews in the Middle East has justified its escalating brutality by pointing to "acts of terrorism" committed by its adversary.

The belief that the end justifies the means also helps to minimize guilt and self-condemnation. The pages of history are filled with accounts of brutal acts performed in "holy wars" and "moral crusades." Here is Adolf Hitler's justification for a policy that was to result in the murder of more than six million Jews:

By warding off the Jews, I am fighting for the Lord's work. . . . What we have to fight for is the security of the existence and the increase of our race and our people, the nourishment of its children, and the preservation of the purity of the blood, the freedom and independence in the fatherland in order to enable our people to mature for the fulfillment of the mission which the Creator of the universe has allotted also to them.

After Germany's defeat in World War II, many of Hitler's followers found themselves using another technique for minimizing guilt over aggression: **displacement of responsibility** for one's deeds onto another person. Nazi war criminals disclaimed personal accountability for their acts by displacing it onto those in command: "I was only following orders."

A related method of minimizing guilt is **diffusion of responsibility.** If a decision is made by a group, no single individual needs to feel totally responsible for the consequences. Sometimes the diffusion of responsibility can enable a group (for example, a lynch mob) to commit an act of violence no individual within the group would commit alone.

FIGURE 1.23 *During confrontations with the United States, Iran's Ayatollah Khomeini painted an image of his adversary as evil incarnate, "the Great Satan."*

Another self-justifying cognitive mechanism is **dehumanization.** If the victims are stripped of all human qualities, the aggressor can treat them as objects rather than as individuals with hopes, sensitivities, and feelings. Often the process involves attaching demeaning labels, such as "gooks," "pigs," or "niggers," to the victims so that they can be viewed as members of a despised group rather than as individual human beings.

In the cognitive view, human beings are thinking and reasoning problem solvers. But the tragedy of our existence is that our higher mental processes frequently result in our choosing violent solutions to our problems.

The behavioral perspective on aggression

The behavioral approach rejects the instinct theories of aggression. Rather, it views aggression as a learned response (Stuart, 1981). The behavioral approach to the study of aggression involves an analysis of the following elements:

Present stimulus conditions and previous learning → Aggressive behavior → Consequences of aggression → Probable future behavior

STIMULUS CONTROL AND RESPONSE CONSEQUENCES

Aggression is a social behavior and thus occurs at least partly in response to stimuli in the environment. Even animal aggression directly elicited by electrical stimulation of the brain is affected by environmental factors such as the presence of dominant or submissive individuals (Delgado, 1967). Aggression may be said to be under **stimulus control** as a result of previous learning when certain stimuli acquire the ability to trigger aggression. Specific individuals, circumstances, or objects such as weapons may thus set off aggressive behavior (Berkowitz, 1984).

The cornerstone of the behavioral perspective is the influence of past consequences on present behavior. Behaviors that have led to positive outcomes in the past are more likely to recur in the future, while those that have had negative consequences are less likely to be repeated. Following this assumption, it seems obvious

FIGURE 1.24 *Research has shown that the more success children have in attaining their goals through aggressive behavior, the more aggressive they become over time.*

that people who are rewarded for aggressive behaviors are more likely to behave aggressively.

Research with both animals and humans supports this prediction. A number of studies have shown that formerly nonaggressive animals can be trained to become vicious aggressors if conditions are arranged so that they are consistently victorious in fights with weaker animals. Conversely, if conditions are arranged so that an animal is defeated in its early battles, it becomes extremely submissive. Moreover, the younger an animal is when it first suffers repeated defeats, the more submissively it will react to attacks by other animals (Zillmann, 1979).

The rewarding of aggression affects people in much the same way. In one study of 4-year-old nursery school children, the investigators recorded a total of 2583 aggressive acts and their consequences. Children whose aggressive behavior produced positive outcomes for them (such as forcing another child to give up a desired toy) became increasingly more aggressive (see Figure 1.24). Those whose aggressive behavior was unsuccessful or who experienced unpleasant consequences were less likely to be aggressive in the future (Patterson and others, 1967). A particularly ominous finding was that about 80 percent of the aggressive behaviors paid off for the aggressor.

In some social groups aggressive behavior receives a great deal of social support and provides aggressors with important rewards. Consider the following statement made by a youth involved in a gang killing: "If I would of got the knife, I would have stabbed him. That would have gave me more of a build up. People would have respected me for what I've done and things like that. They would say, 'There goes a cold killer'" (Yablonsky, 1962, p. 8).

OBSERVATION OF AGGRESSIVE MODELS

There is a great deal of evidence that aggressive behavior can be *learned* simply by observing others' behavior (Parke and Slaby, 1983). Whether or not the observer later *performs* the behavior depends on the consequences he or she has observed. If a child sees another child deliver an exotic karate chop to a victim, the child is more likely to *imitate* the aggression if he or she sees the model being rewarded. But regardless of what

happens to the model, the child will probably have learned the aggressive behavior, and if you offer him or her a reward for reproducing the karate chop, chances are the child will be able to do it. Many studies have shown that aggressive and delinquent children tend to have parents who frequently display hostile behavior (Bandura, 1973; Baron, 1977). Many parents who abuse their children have been abused themselves as children, which also suggests the possibility of modeling effects (Straus and others, 1980).

Modeling can be accomplished through description as well as through direct demonstration. News accounts of criminal activities often provide detailed information about how antisocial behaviors are performed and what consequences they are likely to produce. News of a sensational crime, such as a political kidnapping or terrorist bombing, is often followed by a sharp rise in acts of a similar nature. It has also been found that suicides show an abrupt increase immediately after highly publicized suicides, suggesting that media presentations can provide models for this form of destructive behavior (Phillips, in press).

A good deal of public attention and debate have focused on the possible role of televised violence in the

FIGURE 1.25 *There is much scientific evidence that viewing violent television programs and movies can increase the tendency to behave aggressively.*

learning of aggressive behavior, and this issue has been the subject of scientific investigation for over a decade. There is now substantial evidence that exposure to television and movie violence can increase the tendency of both children and adults to behave aggressively (Parke and Slaby, 1983; *Television and Behavior*, 1982). It appears that television and the movies can indeed function as schools of violence (see Figure 1.25).

The humanistic-existential perspective on aggression

Freud, Lorenz, and others have maintained that violence and aggression are natural expressions of human nature. In contrast, humanists distinguish between natural or positive aggression directed toward self-defense or against prejudice, injustice, and other social ills, and the pathological violence that results when our inner nature is twisted, denied, or frustrated (Maslow, 1968). But regardless of the reasons why we aggress, existential theorists will not allow us to deny that we ultimately choose to do so and are personally responsible for our actions.

Irving Yalom (1980), a leading existential theorist, suggests that people use aggression to deny and rise above their lack of control over death. He suggests that our sense of mortality can be lessened somewhat by enlarging our sphere of control over others through domination and aggression. Yalom believes that much human aggression, especially that which appears to be performed for its own sake, has this purpose. But dominance over other creatures cannot buy us dominance over the final fate that we share with all other creatures. Future death is a fact of present life.

Frustrations are a part of everyone's life, so all of us are certain to feel resentful at times. Humanistic and existential theorists stress that when we can accept rather than deny such feelings, we can channel them more easily into positive attempts to solve our problems and improve society (Jourard and Landsman, 1980). When we can accept our own feelings of frustration and hostility, we can be more understanding and tolerant of others as well. Consequently, personal relationships can improve and social conflict can decrease (Rogers, 1951). The hypothesis that self-acceptance is

associated with acceptance of others is generally supported by research evidence (Wylie, 1978).

Each of the five perspectives discussed in this chapter focuses on different factors that are important in understanding human behavior. In a general sense, the perspectives emphasize the role of either personal or environmental factors. The biological, psychodynamic, cognitive, and humanistic-existential perspectives stress the personal factors—the role of biological functions, mental processes, or personality. In contrast, the behavioral perspective focuses on environmental determinants. As we have seen in our discussion of the perspectives in relation to aggression, however, all of these factors must be taken into account if we are to have a truly comprehensive understanding of behavior. We need to understand how internal processes, the person's behavior, and the environment relate to and influence one another. Throughout this book, we shall attempt to tie these diverse causal elements together.

STUDY OUTLINE

THE SCOPE OF PSYCHOLOGY (p. 4)

1. Psychology is the scientific study of behavior and its causes. Most psychologists use the term behavior in its broadest sense to include anything a human or animal can do, including both overt and covert acts.

2. Psychologists specialize in a number of subfields and work in a variety of settings. Their professional activities include teaching, research, clinical work, and the application of psychological principles in numerous social settings.

3. Three emerging areas of research and application that are attracting many psychologists are behavioral medicine, or health psychology, forensic psychology (psychology and the law), and sport psychology.

FOUR BASIC GOALS OF PSYCHOLOGY (AND YOU) (p. 9)

The basic goals of scientific psychology are to describe, understand (explain), predict, and influence behavior.

FIVE PERSPECTIVES ON HUMAN BEHAVIOR (p. 9)

A number of important perspectives on human behavior have shaped the development of psychology. These perspectives serve as lenses through which the world of behavior is viewed, and they help to determine which aspects of behavior are studied, and how. Each perspective provides us with a different conception of human nature.

THE BIOLOGICAL PERSPECTIVE: BODY, MIND, AND BEHAVIOR (p. 11)

1. Positions on the body-mind problem have ranged from dualism (the body is physical and the mind is spiritual) to monism (the workings of the mind are physical in nature).

2. The biological perspective views humans as complex animals and focuses on genetic and physiological influences on behavior. The approach of sociobiology regards many social behaviors as innately determined attempts to ensure that our genes will be passed on to our descendants.

THE PSYCHODYNAMIC PERSPECTIVE: THE FORCES WITHIN (p. 14)

The psychodynamic perspective emphasizes the role of internal conflicts and unconscious motivation on behavior. The mind is a battleground with conflicting psychic forces and counterforces striving for superiority, and behavior often represents a compromise between these forces. Freud's psychoanalytic theory is perhaps the most influential of the psychodynamic theories.

THE COGNITIVE PERSPECTIVE: THE THINKING HUMAN (p. 16)

The cognitive perspective views humans as rational information processors and problem solvers whose higher mental processes allow them to think, judge, imagine, and plan. The roots of the cognitive perspective lie in structuralism, functionalism, Gestalt psychology, and the work of Jean Piaget.

THE BEHAVIORAL PERSPECTIVE: HUMANS AS REACTORS (p. 18)

1. The behavioral perspective has its roots in the philosophical tradition of empiricism. Behaviorists emphasize the role of the external environment and learning in behavior. They deny that we freely choose how to behave.

2. Radical behaviorists like Watson and Skinner believe that psychology should restrict itself to the study of observable stimuli and responses, whereas cognitive behaviorists try to combine the behavioral and cognitive perspectives into a more comprehensive theory of behavior.

THE HUMANISTIC-EXISTENTIAL PERSPECTIVE: CHOICE, RESPONSIBILITY, AND SELF-ACTUALIZATION (p. 20)

The humanistic-existential perspective presents a conception of free and responsible humans with an innate drive toward self-actualization. Unless thwarted by the environment, this drive will help them to fulfill themselves. This perspective rejects the deterministic assumptions of psychoanalysis and behaviorism.

APPLYING THE PERSPECTIVES: UNDERSTANDING HUMAN AGGRESSION (p. 21)

1. The biological perspective stresses the role of evolutionary forces, genetic processes, brain mechanisms, and other biological factors in explaining aggression. Konrad Lorenz suggested that, unlike other animals, humans have not developed internal inhibitions against killing their own kind. Animals can be selectively bred for aggression, and studies of twins suggest that genetic factors might influence human aggression as well. Brain functions have also been implicated in aggressive behavior.

2. Psychodynamic factors can be important determinants of aggression. Studies of overcontrolled individuals who erupt into violent behavior and of people who show little control of aggression point to a variety of psychodynamic processes that can contribute to violent behavior.

3. The role of perceptual and mental processes in aggression is emphasized by the cognitive perspective. Guilt about aggressing can be reduced through self-justification, displacement and diffusion of responsibility, and dehumanization.

4. The behavioral perspective stresses present stimulus conditions and previous learning, particularly the rewarding and punishing consequences of previous aggressive acts. The importance of modeling in the learning of aggression has been emphasized by cognitive behaviorists. There is substantial evidence that viewing televised aggression can increase the tendency to behave aggressively.

5. Humanistic-existential theorists suggest that aggression can be a way of dealing with our own limitations and mortality by demonstrating power and increasing our sphere of influence.

KEY TERMS AND CONCEPTS

At the end of each chapter, the major concepts will be listed in the order in which they appear in the chapter. In the text itself, these terms almost always appear in *boldface*. You should be able to define each concept as well as recall the major points that the text makes about it. Being able to do so will help you to gauge your mastery of the material in the chapter. Most of these terms are defined in the glossary at the end of the book as well as in the chapter.

psychology
overt behavior
covert behavior
basic and applied science
health psychology
forensic psychology
biological perspective
dualism
monism
natural selection
bipedalism
behavior genetics
sociobiology

psychodynamic perspective
repression
cognitive perspective
structuralism
functionalism
Gestalt psychology
insight (Gestalt)
empathic inference
behavioral perspective
(British) empiricism
radical behaviorism
cognitive behaviorism

humanistic-existential perspective
self-actualization
ethologist
releasers
selective breeding
dominance hierarchy
testosterone
overcontrolled hostility
self-defenders

self-indulgers
bullies/sadists
self-image compensators
displacement of responsibility
diffusion of responsibility
dehumanization
stimulus control
modeling

SUGGESTED READINGS

AMERICAN PSYCHOLOGICAL ASSOCIATION (1983). *Careers in psychology.* Washington, D.C.: American Psychological Association. A useful booklet describing career opportunities and educational requirements in various areas of specialization. A copy can be obtained by writing the American Psychological Association, 1200 Seventeenth Street N.W., Washington, D.C. 20036.

GEEN, R. G., and DONNERSTEIN, E. I. (Eds.) (1983). *Aggression: Theoretical and empirical reviews.* New York: Academic Press. A comprehensive overview of current theories and research on aggression.

WANDERSMAN, A., POPPEN, P., and RICKS, D. (Eds.) (1976). *Humanism and behaviorism: Dialogue and growth.* Elmsford, N.Y.: Pergamon Press. A book that grew out of a conference at which leading behaviorists and humanists discussed whether these perspectives might be integrated.

WERTHEIMER, M. A. (1979). *A brief history of psychology.* New York: Holt, Rinehart and Winston. A historical overview of the various schools and perspectives of psychology.

CHAPTER TWO

SCIENTIFIC PRINCIPLES AND METHODS IN PSYCHOLOGY

SCIENTIFIC PRINCIPLES IN PSYCHOLOGY
Approaches to understanding behavior
Constructs and operational definitions

SCIENTIFIC METHODS: GATHERING INFORMATION ABOUT BEHAVIOR
Case studies
The observational approach
The correlational approach: Finding relationships
The experimental approach: Control and manipulation of variables

ETHICS IN HUMAN AND ANIMAL RESEARCH

STATISTICS: ANALYZING AND INTERPRETING DATA
Descriptive statistics: Organizing and summarizing results
The correlation coefficient
Inferential statistics: Drawing conclusions about data

FRONTIER 2.1   PSYCHOLOGY AND THE COMPUTER REVOLUTION

STUDY OUTLINE

KEY TERMS AND CONCEPTS

SUGGESTED READINGS

CHAPTER TWO

SCIENTIFIC PRINCIPLES

AND METHODS IN PSYCHOLOGY

What do you think of when you hear the word *executive*? Perhaps your images include a big office, a fancy car and an expensive home, and an important person handling big problems every day. In our psychology-conscious world, the term may also evoke the image of driven, distressed people whose insides are being eaten away by the never-ending pressures of making decisions that affect their careers, the lives of others, and the survival of their businesses. This image reflects our awareness that stress, pressure, and too much responsibility can have devastating effects on our bodies. A steady stream of discoveries by medical and psychological researchers has taught us a great deal about stress, coping, and health.

This is the story of one such discovery. It can teach us a lot about the process of research and discovery and about the pitfalls that await the unwary.

In the late 1950s, at the Walter Reed Army Institute of Research, Joseph Brady and his colleagues were studying the physiological responses of monkeys as they learned to cope with stress. The experimental task that Brady and his co-workers created was rather simple. A monkey was placed in a restraining chair to minimize its movement and to allow its emotional responses to be measured. Electrodes through which electric shock could be delivered were attached to the monkey. In front of the monkey was a control box with a lever. The animal could learn to avoid the shock by pressing the lever at least once every 20 seconds. Monkeys are pretty bright animals, and Brady's subjects were soon merrily pushing the lever while the researchers measured their physiological responses.

The essence of good experimental research is control over any extraneous factors that might influence results. Brady knew, for example, that merely being restrained is stressful for animals as active as monkeys. How could Brady be sure that the stress he observed and measured was related to the electric shock and not simply to being restrained for hours in the experimental chair? The researchers came up with an ingenious solution. They put a second monkey into an identical restraining chair next to the monkey who was learning to avoid the shock (see Figure 2.1). Electrodes were also attached to the second monkey so that whenever the first monkey failed to push the lever in time, the second monkey would be shocked, too. The second monkey even had an identical control box and lever that it could push, but the box wasn't connected to anything and the lever had no effect on the shock. This arrangement was a painstaking attempt to control all

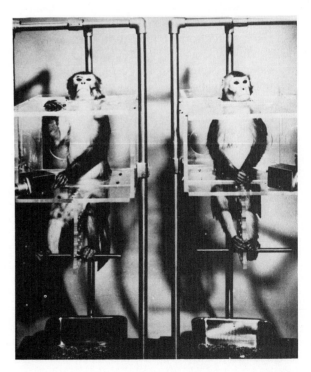

FIGURE 2.1 *The experimental apparatus used by Brady in his "executive monkey" studies. The two chambers are identical except that the control box on the right does not allow that animal to avoid the shock. Only the monkey on the left can avoid the shock for both animals.*

aspects of the situation except the crucial factor: whether or not the animal could learn to control the shock.

The experiment began uneventfully. The monkey responsible for avoiding the shock for himself and his helpless partner quickly learned the task. He averaged more than 15 lever presses per minute and never slowed down. Then, on the twenty-third day, he died! A postmortem examination revealed a massive perforated stomach ulcer. The second monkey was still in good health.

This was totally unexpected, but it occurred to the researchers that, quite by accident, they might have stumbled onto something important. Could it be that the responsibility for the welfare of both animals shouldered by what they termed the "executive monkey" resulted in a unique form of stress that led to the development of ulcers?

Brady quickly changed the direction of the research project. Another set of two monkeys—an executive and a control animal—was run in the identical situation. Again, the executive monkey died, this time after 25 days. A third executive lasted but 9 days, and a fourth for 48 days. In each case, the cause of death was massive ulceration. None of the control monkeys showed these ill effects.

These results seemed to confirm the widely held belief that high levels of responsibility place executives at risk for ulcers and possibly other physical disorders. Although Brady urged caution in extending the results to humans, his research created headlines in the popular media and attracted a great deal of attention from other researchers. Brady's "executive monkey" study became a classic that was cited in virtually every psychology textbook. (Nevertheless, the nation's business colleges survived.)

But the story doesn't end here. The study seemed so well controlled that no one noticed a possibly fatal flaw in Brady's research design until years later. But there was one. Recall that Brady was originally interested in studying monkeys' physiological responses while the animals learned to cope with stress. To save time and to minimize the amount of pain they would have to inflict, the researchers had selected monkeys who were known to learn shock avoidance quickly. After the first monkey died, these "fast learners" were consistently assigned to the executive role, and other, less bright monkeys served as their partners. Unfortunately, later research showed that the fastest learners in shock-avoidance situations are those who are the most highly emotional to begin with. Moreover, such animals have the lowest stress tolerance and are most likely to develop ulcers under stressful circumstances.

Thus, there was an alternative explanation for Brady's finding. Perhaps it was not the degree of "responsibility" that caused their ulcers. Maybe these high-strung animals were primed to break down under stress regardless of whether they were executives or controls. In fact, it was possible that having no control over being shocked—as was the case with the partner monkey—would actually have been even more stressful for them.

The only way to answer the question, of course, was to eliminate the flaw that existed in Brady's study. To minimize differences in emotionality, the animals should have been assigned to the executive and control conditions on a random basis. When researcher Jay Weiss at Rockefeller University did so with rats, it was the helpless controls, not the executives, who fared more poorly. They lost more weight and developed more severe ulcers than did the executives who controlled their fate (Weiss, 1971). Subsequent research with both animals and humans has shown that while responsibility may be a source of stress, having no control in the face of a stressor has even more damaging physical and psychological effects (Miller, 1983; Seligman, 1975). Studies with human executives have also shown that those exercising considerable control and responsibility have fewer stress-related disorders than middle-level executives who have considerable responsibility but relatively less control (Eyer and Sterling, 1973; Metropolitan Life Statistical Bulletin, 1975).

Science frequently has all the mystery and drama of a detective story. The mysteries that challenge the psychologist relate to behavior and its causes. But nature does not give up her secrets easily. False leads, blind alleys, and apparent contradictions are all part of the scientific enterprise. The case of the executive monkeys is an example of how easy it is for even highly competent and experienced researchers to draw false conclusions.

Like the master detective, the good scientist is an incurable skeptic. Even when it looks like the evidence is in and the mystery solved, he or she asks: How reliable is the evidence? Was the research designed and carried out carefully enough to control for other possible influences? Are there other possible explanations for the results? If so, what additional information is needed to rule them out? It is our hope that by the end of this course, you will share this same healthy skepticism. Becoming more aware of scientific standards for making observations and drawing conclusions can help you to become a more acute observer and conclusion drawer in your own life.

SCIENTIFIC PRINCIPLES IN PSYCHOLOGY

Scientific study involves a continuous interplay between observations and attempts to explain and understand what was observed. Typically, the path of scientific understanding involves these steps:

1. Informal observation and formulation of a question

2. Tentative initial attempts to answer the question

3. Formal hypotheses to test our understanding

4. Performing the observations needed to test the hypotheses

5. Theory building

The scientific process always begins with some kind of noteworthy observation. Researchers often stumble onto important discoveries quite by accident. When this happens, a good researcher heeds B. F. Skinner's advice: "When you run into something interesting, drop everything and study it" (Skinner, 1959, p. 363). Brady recognized immediately that the death of the first executive monkey might herald the discovery of something more important than what he was originally studying, and he adapted his research to focus on that new possibility.

At the second stage of the scientific process, Brady and his colleagues tried to figure out what could have been responsible for the fatal ulcers. Behaving just as you would, they used reason, logic, and perhaps a little guesswork to arrive at an initial and tentative explanation. It seemed perfectly logical to conclude that since the amount of control over the shock was the obvious difference between the dead monkey and the still-healthy control, it was the critical factor. (With the power of 20/20 hindsight, we might surmise that the

responsibility factor was so obvious that it blinded the researchers to the unintentional bias in assigning the monkeys to the two conditions—the factor that turned out in the end to be the critical one.)

Where casual observers might be satisfied at this point that they understood why the fatal ulcers had occurred, the scientific method takes us a crucial step further. We recognize that the explanation is still only tentative, and we go on to *test* our understanding by means of additional observations. First, though, we formulate a **hypothesis.** A hypothesis is an "if . . ., then . . ." statement that can be tested with new observations. Brady and his colleagues used new pairs of monkeys to test the hypothesis: "*If* a monkey has control of the shock, *then* it is more likely to develop ulcers than one whose lever exerts no influence on the shock." When subsequent observations at the fourth stage of hypothesis testing were consistent with this prediction, the investigators considered the hypothesis confirmed.

Years later, when Jay Weiss realized that a crucial factor had not been controlled, he had the observations necessary to test an altered hypothesis: "*If* animals are assigned on some random basis to the executive and control conditions to rule out preexisting differences in stress proneness, *then* the executives will develop more severe ulcers." Of course, the results came out exactly the opposite, indicating that when the subject groups are similar in emotionality, helplessness is more likely to produce ulcers than is control and responsibility.

The goal of the first four steps of the scientific process is the development of theories. A psychological **theory** is a system of generalizations that specify lawful relationships between specific behaviors and their causes. A good theory has three important characteristics:

1. It is able to incorporate many existing facts, observations, and known relationships within a single broad framework.

2. It gives rise to additional hypotheses that can be tested by means of new observations. In this way, a

theory leads to the development of new knowledge. Even if the new observations do not support the theory, as in the case of the executive monkeys, the theory will still serve a valuable function by leading to an even better and more inclusive theory. Sometimes it is just as important to know what is *not* true as what is true.

3. It must be testable and capable of being refuted. It should be able to tell us which kind of relationships are *not* possible as well as which ones are. Theories that seem capable of accounting for everything, even seemingly contradictory facts, are not good theories.

Compared with those of other sciences, psychological theories are still rather primitive, largely because of the bewildering complexity of behavior. Saying that it is difficult to pin down all the causes of a complex behavior is a little like saying that Hitler had his faults. The trend now in psychology is away from the grand theory that explains everything and toward small-scale theories that relate to a limited area of behavior and generate precise and testable hypotheses.

Approaches to understanding behavior

The basic goal of science is understanding—the ability to answer the questions "Why?" and "How?" Applied to behavior, understanding means being able to specify the *causes* of behavior—the conditions responsible for its occurrence. There are two basic approaches to understanding, and they serve to illustrate the difference between nonscientific and scientific understanding.

AFTER-THE-FACT UNDERSTANDING

One sometimes hears the statement that psychology is nothing more than common sense. In fact, exactly this criticism was leveled by a *New York Times* book reviewer some years ago. The report he was reviewing, *The American Soldier* (Stouffer and others, 1949), summarized the results of a large-scale study of the goals, attitudes, and behavior of American soldiers during World War II. The reviewer blasted the government for spending a considerable amount of money to "tell us nothing we don't already know."

How would you account for each of the following findings?

1. The motivation to become officers was higher among white soldiers than among blacks.

2. During basic training, soldiers from rural backgrounds had higher morale and adapted better than did soldiers from large cities.

3. During combat, soldiers with high intelligence were more fearful and more likely to develop psychosomatic disorders (emotionally caused physical illnesses) than were soldiers of low intelligence.

4. Soldiers serving in Europe were more highly motivated to return home while the fighting was going on than they were after the war ended.

If you're anything like our students, you should have no difficulty arriving at perfectly reasonable psychological explanations for these results. A typical line of reasoning might be: (1) Because of widespread prejudice, black soldiers knew that their chances of becoming officers were remote. Why strive for something you can't have? (2) It makes sense that the rigors of basic training would be more tolerable for people from farm settings who were accustomed to working hard and getting up at the crack of dawn. (3) The brighter soldiers were smart enough to realize what might happen to them in combat; hence, they experienced more anxiety. (4) Who in his right mind would *not* want to go home while the bullets were flying? The explanation here is easy: survival!

Do these explanations resemble yours? If so, place your hand on a rock and declare yourself a lay psychologist. There *is* one catch, however. The results you've just explained are the exact opposite of the actual findings. Black soldiers were actually more highly motivated to become officers; city boys had higher morale during basic training; soldiers of low intelligence were more anxious and more likely to develop psychosomatic problems; and soldiers were actually more eager to return home *after* the war ended than they were during the fighting.

We often use this demonstration in our own psychology classes to illustrate how easy it is to arrive at a completely reasonable **after-the-fact understanding** of almost any result. Indeed, after-the-fact explanations—the process by which we try to explain a behavior by taking into account the conditions that existed at the time—are probably our most common method of trying to understand our own and others' behavior. After the good-natured volley of apple cores and umbrellas, our students are quickly able to find equally plausible explanations for the real findings. (They also learn that they must pay closer attention when being taught by sneaky professors!)

As we've seen, then, the major problem with after-the-fact understanding is that it is possible to explain past events in many ways, and there is no sure way to determine which, if any, of the alternative explanations is correct. We are not saying that after-the-fact understanding is never useful or valid. Since we can't always reconstruct past events, there is often no alternative. Because this approach can give us valuable leads and insights, it is usually the foundation upon which further scientific inquiry is built.

UNDERSTANDING THROUGH PREDICTION AND CONTROL

Scientists favor an approach to understanding that allows them to test their theories about causes directly. For them, real understanding is the ability to make accurate predictions. If we understand the causes of a given behavior, then we should be able to specify the conditions under which that behavior will occur in the future. Furthermore, if those conditions can be controlled or manipulated, then it should be possible to control the occurrence of the behavior. This is precisely what we are doing when we test a scientific hypothesis. Understanding through prediction and control is thus the scientific alternative to after-the-fact understanding.

Even when a hypothesis is supported by successful prediction and control, it is never regarded as an absolute truth because it is always possible that some new observation will contradict it. When this happens, however, scientists don't necessarily wring their hands in despair, because the disproving of accepted and established hypotheses frequently opens up new frontiers for investigation. The displacement of old beliefs and "truths" is the lifeblood of science.

FIGURE 2.2 *Unless psychologists can operationally define the constructs they use in their theories, they cannot communicate their ideas.*

Constructs and operational definitions

The vocabulary of psychology is filled with terms like *aggression, personality, learning,* and *motivation.* All of these are simply words or concepts—scientists prefer the term **constructs**—that refer to classes of behaviors and situations. Because these words represent nonmaterial ideas and not real things, they may have different meanings for different people. The term *dependency,* for example, refers to a particular class of behaviors, but the specific types of behavior that are labeled *dependent* may vary from one person to another. "What do you mean by that?" is a question to which psychologists must give a precise answer if they are to study the behavior in question. Unless two people have a common understanding of what each one means by *dependent,* they can't be sure they're communicating effectively when they talk about *dependent people* (see Figure 2.2).

"I can't put it into layman's language for you. I don't know any layman's language."

(DRAWING BY DANA FRADON; © 1975 THE NEW YORKER MAGAZINE, INC.)

Operational definitions help solve the communication problem by translating an abstract term into something that is observable and measurable. That observable event may be a stimulus, something that is *done to* a subject (for instance, the term *hunger* may be operationally defined as "the number of hours that a subject is deprived of food"), or it may be a response, something that the subject *does* (such as a subject's rating of how hungry he or she feels). A construct, then, may be operationally defined either in terms of conditions imposed on the subject (that is, in terms of a *stimulus*) or in terms of subject *responses*. Figure 2.3 shows some of the stimulus and response operational definitions for the construct *stress* that have been used in psychological research.

Unless a construct can be tied down to something observable, it cannot be studied scientifically. For example, the construct *free will* is an important concept in the history of Western thought, but it cannot be studied by scientists because no one can agree on how to operationally define or measure it. On the other hand, it is possible for psychologists to study the causes and effects of a *belief* in free will, because we can measure people's beliefs by interviewing them or giving them questionnaires about their beliefs.

Operational definitions don't solve every problem, however. Different scientists may not agree on a particular definition, just as you and a friend may not agree about whether an acquaintance is *really* dependent. Likewise, different operational definitions of the same construct may not always agree with one another. For example, subjects' ratings of their level of stress do not

---

FIGURE 2.3 *Some operational definitions of the construct* stress. *It may be operationally defined either in terms of stimulus conditions to which subjects are exposed or in terms of various kinds of responses made by subjects.*

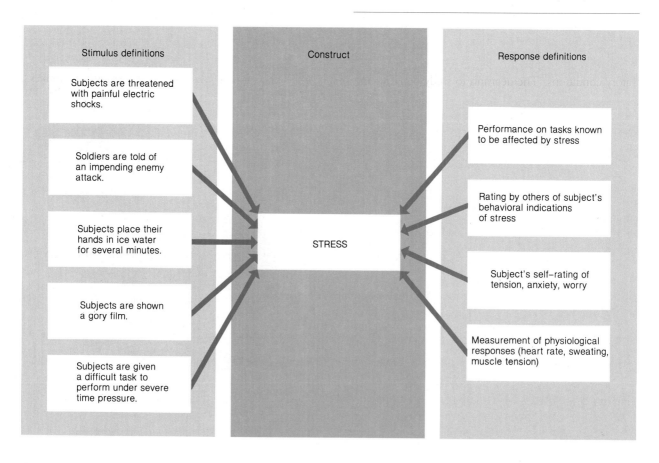

always correspond with measures of their actual physiological responses, since different aspects of the total stress response are being measured (Katkin and Hastrup, 1982). Thus, researchers must state their operational definitions in very precise terms. Otherwise, they might well find that they are still talking about apples and oranges.

SCIENTIFIC METHODS: GATHERING INFORMATION ABOUT BEHAVIOR

Having considered some of the principles underlying the scientific study of behavior, we now examine the specific ways in which observations, or *data*, are collected by psychologists. The methods chosen by a researcher depend on the nature of the particular problem being studied, the objectives of the study, and the researcher's personal preferences.

Some types of behavior can be studied only in their natural setting, where little or no control is possible; others can be examined under highly controlled laboratory conditions. The decision to study behavior in a natural setting as opposed to a laboratory involves some important trade-offs. Identifying the true causes of behavior observed in a natural setting poses problems because there is no way to rule out other possible causes by controlling them. On the other hand, the subjects are being observed in their native habitat, and the researcher can have more confidence that the results may be applied to other, similar real-life settings.

The highly controlled conditions possible in laboratory research allow the researcher to be more confident that the causes of behavior have been identified. But there is a trade-off here as well. Can the results be generalized beyond the laboratory setting in which they occurred? To what extent do the results mirror what happens out in the real world? The answers to these questions depend on how well the researcher has captured the important elements of the real-world situation to which the results are to be applied. Throughout the book, you will see many examples of the ingenuity that is required to achieve this goal.

Before describing the research methods themselves, we should say a word or two about *sampling*, since it

relates in important ways to the interpretation of research results. There are few if any situations in which a researcher can study every member of the larger group to which the results are expected to apply, which may be as inclusive as "people in general." We are almost always restricted to a segment, or **sample,** of that larger group, which is called the **population.** If valid conclusions are to be drawn, the sample must reflect the important characteristics of the larger population. Public opinion pollsters use samples that possess the important traits (age, gender, political party, geographical location, and so on) in the same proportion as in the population. The responses of such a **representative sample** are therefore likely to mirror those of the larger population. Election forecasts derived from representative samples are often strikingly accurate, even if the sample constitutes less than 1 percent of the population.

As we saw in the case of the executive monkeys, biased samples can have crucial effects on results. The most common way to avoid this is to have sufficiently large samples so that a few unusual subjects cannot greatly distort the overall results and then, by **random assignment,** to place the subjects in the various conditions that are being studied. If this had been done in Brady's studies, the results might have been quite different.

Always consider the nature of the sample when you interpret research results. Just as the results of laboratory studies may not always generalize to real-life settings, research results derived from samples of college students or white rats (probably the two most-studied populations) may not apply to other populations, such as children or middle-aged males. Indeed, one of the most interesting topics of research in psychology is the way different populations behave differently within similar situations.

We now consider the major methods used to help us to understand the causes of behavior. To show you how these are used, we will describe an actual study done with each method.

Case studies

Case studies—detailed observations of a single person's behavior—are often used by clinical and personality psychologists. The goal of most case studies is to identify or illustrate certain principles of individual behavior that are assumed to apply in a general sense. Case studies can also be performed on groups or even whole organizations. Many theories of personality, group behavior, and organizational functioning were derived originally from intensive case studies.

Rare or spectacular examples of situations or behavior are often the subject of case studies. The following case study illustrates the profound effects that faith in a medicine can have on a physical illness.

The patient was suffering from the final stages of a terminal cancer of the lymph glands. He needed oxygen, frequent drainage of body fluids, and had large tumors throughout the body. His death was only a matter of days or weeks. The patient heard of a new "miracle" anticancer drug, Krebiozen (which is now known to be useless in the treatment of cancer). After several requests, the man was given the drug. Within a day dramatic changes began to occur, and within a week the tumors vanished and the patient was released from the hospital. After two months of excellent health, he read newspaper articles casting doubt on Krebiozen. His hopes dashed, he relapsed to his previous condition, the tumors reappeared, and he was again hospitalized. Willing to try anything at this point, the physician told the patient not to believe what he had read and that a new superstrength variety of the drug was arriving the next day. The patient was given the new "superrefined drug" (actually water injections) the following day and showed another dramatic and complete remission of symptoms. He returned home and remained symptom-free for another two months. But at that point, the American Medical Association announced that nationwide tests had shown Krebiozen to be useless in treating cancer. The patient again relapsed almost immediately and died within 48 hours. (Shapiro, 1963)

Case studies like this have stimulated controlled research that proves beyond a doubt that faith can have profound effects on our psychological and physical functioning. We now know that **placebos**—inactive substances that people believe have medicinal properties—can have healing effects that rival our most powerful drugs. We will discuss this fascinating topic in Chapter 5.

In most case studies, explanations of the event occur after-the-fact, and there has been little if any opportunity to rule out other possible explanations by controlling for them. Even the most intensive study of an individual case cannot assure us that we isolated the true causes of the behavior. Nevertheless, such studies can provide important leads for more controlled research. Moreover, a single case study can cast doubt on an entire theory if the theory is assumed to hold in all cases and the case study is clearly at odds with what the theory predicts.

The observational approach

The first steps in the scientific process are usually observation and description. Some sciences are basically descriptive. In astronomy and anatomy, for example, scientists make careful observations of heavenly or earthly bodies, as the case may be, and tell us what they see. At times, psychologists also do research that is basically descriptive in nature. By describing various behaviors and the specific settings in which they occur, researchers can obtain important information about possible cause-and-effect relationships. While the individual case study is also observational in nature, here we are referring to more systematic observation of more than one person.

Observational research can be carried out in almost any setting. Our first example below was done in the natural environment of the mental hospital; it is an example of **uncontrolled observation,** since the researchers could not regulate the conditions. The second example was carried out in a controlled laboratory setting.

UNCONTROLLED OBSERVATION: SANITY IN INSANE PLACES

David Rosenhan (1973) of Stanford University wanted to know what happens when people who have been diagnosed as mentally ill begin to act completely sane after they are hospitalized (see Figure 2.4). Are they immediately recognized as sane and released, or does the label *mentally ill* affect how their behavior is perceived by the staff?

Eight normal individuals, including Rosenhan, got themselves admitted to mental hospitals by telephoning the hospitals and saying that they were hearing voices. They falsified their names and occupations (several were psychologists and psychiatrists), but otherwise gave their true life histories. All except one received a diagnosis of **schizophrenia,** a serious behavior disorder characterized by disorganized thought processes and inappropriate emotional responses. Once admitted to the hospitals, however, the "patients" acted as normal as possible.

Were these patients immediately detected as imposters and released? Not at all. No staff member in any of the hospitals ever expressed any suspicion. Nor was it particularly easy to get discharged. Although they were paragons of normality and cooperation and highly motivated to get out, their hospitalizations ranged from 7 to 52 days, with an average stay of 19 days.

The hospital staffs were understandably prepared to see the patients as mentally ill, since most of their patients are truly disturbed, and this strongly influenced their perceptions of the false patients. They sometimes

found evidence for mental illness in even the most innocent behaviors. For example, one psychiatrist pointed to a patient who was waiting for the cafeteria to open for lunch and remarked to a group of staff members that this behavior reflected the "oral-incorporative" dynamics of schizophrenia. A later examination of hospital records indicated distortions of the patients' life histories in ways that reinforced the diagnosis of schizophrenia.

Thus, the label *schizophrenia* persisted long after the behaviors that led to the original diagnosis had ceased. When they were finally discharged from the hospitals, all but one of the patients received the diagnosis *schizophrenia, in remission,* which implied that the disorder was still present, but in a dormant form.

Rosenhan's study raises a number of important issues: How many undiscovered sane persons are there in mental hospitals? What are the effects of being labeled

FIGURE 2.4 *These patients in a mental hospital have been given psychiatric diagnoses. Rosenhan's observational study as well as other research indicates that once a label is given, it influences staff perceptions of both disturbed and normal behavior.*

as having a mental disorder on the perceptions and responses of others? What happens when the patient comes to accept the label and perhaps behaves in accordance with it? These and other issues will be discussed in Chapter 15.

CONTROLLED OBSERVATION: BLIND OBEDIENCE TO AUTHORITY

Our second example is of **controlled observation**; it occurred in a far different setting, one in which it was possible to observe subjects under carefully contrived conditions. The behavior of interest—obedience—was operationally defined and measured very precisely.

After World War II, the famous Nuremberg war crime trials were held to punish Nazi war criminals. In many instances, the defense offered by those on trial was that they had "only followed orders." American soldiers accused of atrocities in Vietnam gave basically the same explanation for their actions.

Most of us reject justifications based on "obedience to authority" as mere rationalizations, secure in our conviction that we would behave differently under such circumstances. However, the results of a series of ingenious and controversial laboratory studies performed by psychologist Stanley Milgram (1974) suggest that perhaps we should not be so sure of ourselves.

To study the ability of an authority figure to command destructive obedience, Milgram devised a situation in which subjects thought they were assisting a Yale University researcher who was studying the effects of punishment on learning. The subject's task was to present the learning problems through a two-way intercom system to a learner who was strapped in a chair in an adjoining room. Each time the learner made an error, the subject was instructed to administer an electric shock through an apparatus having 30 numbered switches starting at 15 volts and going up to 450 volts. With each error, the shock was increased by 15 volts. Before beginning, each "assistant" was given a sample 45 volt shock, which was moderately painful (see Figure 2.5). *Obedience* was operationally defined as the maximum shock intensity the subject would administer when told to do so by the authority figure.

Forty men ranging in age from 20 to 50 and representing a cross section of the population served as subjects. They did not know that they were in a carefully

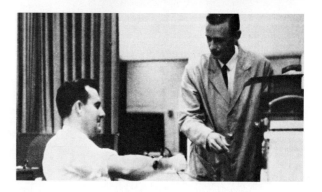

FIGURE 2.5 *Stanley Milgram created a convincing setting for his controlled observations of obedience to authority. Shown are the "shock generator," the "learner" being strapped into his chair, and a subject receiving a sample shock. (Copyright 1965 by Stanley Milgram. From the film* Obedience, *distributed by the New York University Film Library.)*

contrived situation and that the learner was actually an accomplice of the experimenter. No shocks were actually delivered, and the learner's responses heard over the intercom were tape recorded to be the same for all subjects.

As subjects increased the shock voltage, the learner (who had earlier noted that he had a mild heart condition) showed increased distress. At 75 volts, he began to moan. At 150 volts, he stated that he could not stand the pain any longer and demanded to be released. Beyond 200 volts, he began to emit agonized screams and began to complain about his heart. He screamed that he was no longer part of the experiment. Hysterical screams continued up to 345 volts, after which there was silence.

Whenever a subject became distressed and said that he was unwilling to continue the experiment, the experimenter ordered him to continue. The only way the

subject could stop the proceedings was to openly defy the authority figure.

How far do you think you would go if you were one of Milgram's assistants? Before the experiment began, a panel of psychiatrists predicted that no more than 1 percent of the subjects would be sadistic enough to proceed to the 450 volt maximum. In fact, the shocks produced by the results of this study were more startling than the simulated shocks administered in that laboratory. The average maximum shock administered was 368 volts, and 65 percent of the subjects gave the 450 volt maximum (see Figure 2.6).

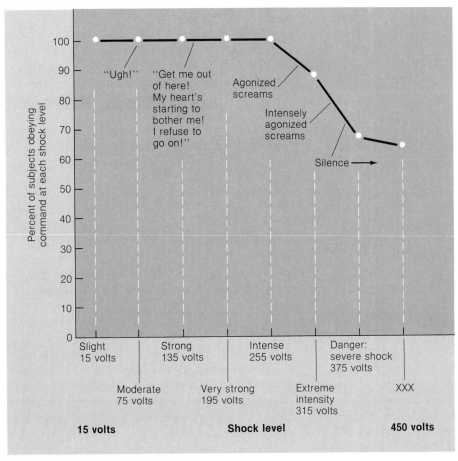

FIGURE 2.6 *Results of the first Milgram study of obedience to authority. A startling 65 percent of the male subjects gave the learner the maximum shock level when ordered to do so by the experimenter.*

Virtually all the subjects who gave high levels of shock exhibited extreme discomfort, anxiety, and distress. Although most of them balked at one time or another, they continued shocking the learner when ordered to do so by the experimenter, who assured them that he would take responsibility for what happened in the experiment. As Milgram noted later, "even when the destructive effects of their work became patently clear and they were asked to carry out actions incompatible with fundamental standards of morality, relatively few people have the resources needed to resist authority" (Milgram, 1974, p. 6).

By contriving a situation with many real-life elements, Milgram was able to observe directly and under controlled conditions behaviors that in many ways resembled those of people in other settings who claim that "I didn't want to do it, but I had to follow orders."

Milgram's study also generated shock waves among other psychologists, many of whom questioned the ethics of placing unknowing subjects into such a stressful situation. We will return to this issue later when we discuss research ethics.

The correlational approach: Finding relationships

Psychologists often wish to study relationships between naturally occurring events that they cannot directly control. For example, they may be interested in the relationship between scores on an intelligence test and college grade point average, or in how unemployment figures are related to crime rates. This type of investigation is called **correlational research**, since the term refers to how two things are co-*related*.

BOXING MATCHES AND HOMICIDES

For many years there has been concern about the effects of mass media violence on aggressive behavior. Much of the evidence that televised violence increases the tendency of viewers to behave aggressively comes from controlled laboratory studies in which the aggressive behavior that occurred was not of a serious or brutal nature. Policy makers, however, are more concerned about the possible effects of media violence on serious violence like assaults and homicide. Until re-

cently, there was little evidence linking the two, but David Phillips of the University of California, San Diego, has now reported findings that suggest such a link (Phillips, 1983; in press).

Phillips suggested that news of a violent act is most likely to stimulate violence when the aggression in the news story is presented as (1) rewarded, (2) exciting, (3) real, and (4) justified. He reasoned that one type of news story that meets all these standards is the heavyweight championship fight. Accordingly, Phillips analyzed daily counts of all U.S. homicides from the National Center for Health Statistics and related them to the occurrence of 18 heavyweight championship boxing matches during the period 1973–1978.

Phillips made a striking discovery. On the days following highly publicized fights, homicides increased nearly 15 percent. Those fights that attracted the greatest media attention were associated with even larger increases in homicides: the Ali-Foreman fight was followed by a 24 percent increase, and a startling 32 percent jump in national homicides followed the Ali-Frazier "Thrilla in Manila" (see Figure 2.7).

Phillips attributed these increases in violent behavior to the modeling of successful aggression by the victorious fighter. He found further support for social learning and modeling factors by examining victim characteristics. Analysis of the computerized death warrants disclosed that when the losers in the prize fights were white males, the homicide rate for young white males increased, but the rate for young black males did not. Conversely, when the losing boxer was a black male, there was a rise in killings of black males but no increase in white victims.

It might be tempting to conclude that Phillips's results *prove* that media presentations of boxing matches *cause* homicides. Unfortunately, the major problem with correlational studies is that they can demonstrate relationships but not causes. In this case, for example, other factors linked to both the boxing matches and murder rates could be responsible for the observed relationship. For instance, the day of the week, season of the year, amount of gambling involved, or other factors could all affect homicide rates. To Phillips's credit, he was aware of these possible factors and was able to rule them out by using sophisticated statistical procedures. Nevertheless, it is still possible that some overlooked factor might have contributed to the relationship.

If there is one thing that you should be sure to remember about correlational research, it is that *the presence of correlation does not necessarily mean that one event is the cause of the other event* (see Figure 2.8). Many events that are correlated are unlikely to be causally related. For example, did you know that (1) a high correlation was found between the hourly salaries of Presbyterian ministers in Massachusetts and the price of rum in Havana; that (2) suicides and weddings both occur at their highest rates during June; or that (3) a high correlation was found between the number of storks seen nesting in French villages and the number of births that occurred in those locales? We'll leave it to you to figure out these relationships.

CORRELATION AND PREDICTION

While correlational data do not allow us to establish causality, they do have a useful role in prediction. The correlations that we have discussed so far represent positive relationships (for example, the greater the media

attention, the larger the increase in homicides). Correlations can also be negative, so that a high score on one measure is related to a low score on the other (for example, size of tuition increases and student satisfaction). If two measures are highly related, either positively or negatively, then knowledge of the score on one allows us to predict (within certain limits) the score on the other. Thus, college entrance examination scores

FIGURE 2.7 *Correlational research conducted by David Phillips showed a striking increase in homicides following highly publicized heavyweight championship fights like this one between Muhammed Ali and Joe Frazier.*

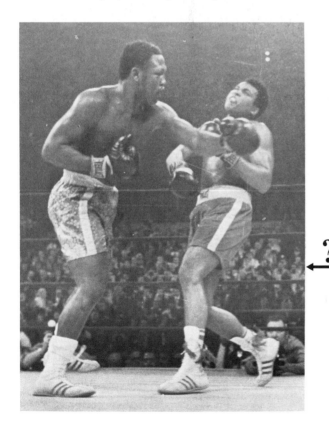

"Contrary to the popular view, our studies show that it is real life that contributes to violence on television."

(DRAWING BY S. HARRIS. REPRODUCED BY SPECIAL PERMISSION OF *PLAYBOY* MAGAZINE. COPYRIGHT © 1977 BY PLAYBOY.)

("FRANK AND ERNEST" DRAWING BY B. THAVES; REPRINTED BY PERMISSION OF NEA.)

FIGURE 2.8 *As these cartoons suggest, it is dangerous to infer causality from correlational data.*

are used to predict probable success in college because these measures are positively correlated with one another. Insurance premiums are likewise established on the basis of correlations among certain factors. In a sense, your insurance company is betting you that you will not demolish your car, become seriously ill, or die before you are statistically "supposed to." Since their predictions are based on sound correlational data, the odds are solidly in their favor. If you doubt this, notice who owns some of the largest and newest buildings in your community.

The experimental approach: Control and manipulation of variables

The psychologist's most powerful tool for establishing causal relationships is the controlled experiment. The experimental method differs from the observational and correlational approaches because the experimenter can directly manipulate one or more factors and then measure how behavior is affected. The logic behind this approach is that if two or more groups of "equivalent" subjects are treated identically in all respects but one, and if the behavior of the groups differs, then the difference is likely to have been caused by the factor that was varied.

Henceforth we shall use the term **variable.** A variable is quite simply anything that can vary, or change. It can refer to situations that differ, to behavioral measures that can take on different values, or to characteristics on which subjects can differ, such as age, sex, personality, and so on. Thus, correlational research looks for relationships among variables, and so does experimental research. In experimental research, there are two classes of variables that are particularly important.

INDEPENDENT AND DEPENDENT VARIABLES

In psychological experiments we are interested in relationships between conditions that are manipulated and behaviors that are measured. The condition that is controlled or manipulated by the experimenter is called the **independent variable;** the resulting behavior that is measured is called the **dependent variable** because it is presumably dependent on what the experimenter has done (see Figure 2.9).

To look at it another way, the independent variable is the *cause,* or the stimulus, and the dependent variable is the *effect,* or the response. In the executive monkey experiment, the monkey's ability to control the shock was the independent variable, and the severity of its ulcers was the dependent variable.

EXPERIMENTAL AND CONTROL GROUPS

The experimental method is the most powerful of all scientific approaches because it is expressly designed to rule out alternative explanations of the results. If everything can be held constant except the independent variable, then the researcher can be fairly confident that a cause-and-effect relationship has been demonstrated.

Suppose that we want to study the effects of noise on learning. We decide to subject (or treat, depending on your outlook) a group of subjects to blaring rock music while they try to learn a list of facts. This group would be termed an **experimental group.** To be sure that the music is indeed having an effect, however, we need to measure the learning of a second group of subjects—a comparison, or **control group**—who are not exposed to the music. To make the two groups as similar as possible in all other respects besides exposure to the music, we would assign subjects to the experimental or control groups on some random basis. We could give each subject a number and then draw numbers out of a hat, or we could use a table of random numbers (see Figure 2.9).

Having discussed the logic and some of the key concepts in the controlled experimental approach, we now consider two experimental designs that are frequently used in psychological research.

MANIPULATING ONE INDEPENDENT VARIABLE: OBEDIENCE REVISITED

Earlier we described Milgram's controlled observational study on obedience to authority. Although the laboratory situation in which Milgram measured obedience was as highly controlled as that of any experi-

ment, the study was not a true experiment because no independent variable was manipulated; all subjects were exposed to the same situation.

Why did so many subjects obey the experimenter? What were the critical ingredients of the situation that Milgram created? Milgram and others proceeded to answer this question through a series of experiments in which independent variables thought to be important were systematically manipulated and their effects on obedience observed.

Most of us grow up in settings that stress obedience to legitimate authority—first in the family, then in school, and later in the working world. We are well practiced in carrying out the wishes of others, and we tend to view responsibility for the consequences as belonging to them, and not to us. In Chapter 1, we described some of the cognitive operations that allow people to disclaim responsibility and reduce guilt for aggressive acts. One of these is *displacement of responsibility* to the authority figure who gave the order. This feeling of being another's agent was repeatedly expressed by Milgram's obedient subjects. Like the Nazi war criminals at Nuremberg and the GI's tried for the My Lai massacre in Vietnam, Milgram's subjects said

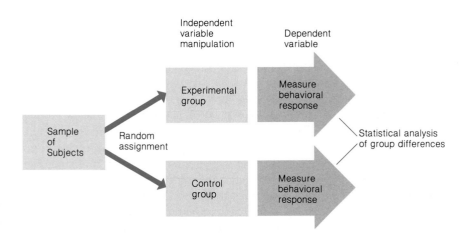

FIGURE 2.9 *In a conventional experimental design, subjects are randomly assigned to an experimental or control group for manipulation of the independent variable. Their dependent variable behaviors are then measured and differences between the two groups of subjects are assessed through statistical analysis to determine the effects of the independent variable.*

they felt they had no other choice, that the responsibility was not theirs. The experimenter who ordered them to continue was the one who should be held responsible.

Harvey Tilker (1970) wanted to see how obedience was affected when people assumed personal responsibility instead of displacing it onto an authority. His experimental hypothesis was this: "If a person is forced to 'get involved' or 'feel responsible' for the safety and well-being of another person, and is receiving enough feedback from the victim regarding his condition, then he will be most likely to react in a socially responsible manner and in some way attempt to alter the course of events" (p. 95).

To test this hypothesis, Tilker randomly assigned male college students at Michigan State University to one of three responsibility conditions. In one condition, the subjects were told that the experimenter was completely responsible for the welfare of the learner in the next room. In the personal responsibility condition, the subjects were told that "since you are in the best position to judge developments as they might occur, you will be responsible for the conduct of the study as well as the welfare of the learner" (p. 97). In the third, or ambiguous responsibility, condition, no explicit statement was made about who was accountable for what happened. To make sure that subjects were aware of the condition of the learner, they not only heard him, as in the Milgram study, but were able to observe him, through a one-way vision mirror, writhing in pain and struggling to free himself.

Although there is only one independent variable in this kind of experimental design, there can be more than one dependent variable in any experiment. (Indeed, having more than one provides additional information concerning the effects of the independent variable.) In Tilker's experiment, there were several dependent variables, including the number of subjects in each responsibility condition who refused to allow the experiment to continue; the number of verbal protests made by subjects during the experiment; and the maximum level of shock administered by each subject. (As in Milgram's study, no shocks were actually given.)

Figure 2.10 shows the percentage of subjects in each responsibility condition who stopped the experiment. As you can see, making subjects feel personally responsible for the welfare of the learner had a strong effect. All of the subjects in that condition stopped the

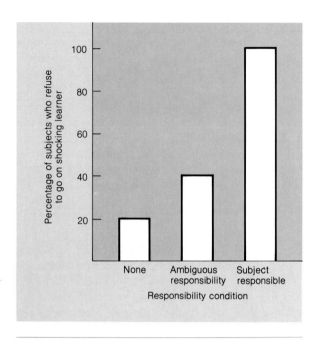

FIGURE 2.10 *Results of Tilker's (1970) study of the effects of perceived personal responsibility on obedience to authority. Emphasizing to subjects that they were responsible for the welfare of the "learner" sharply reduced obedience; all the subjects in that condition defied the authority figure.*

experiment. These subjects also made more verbal protests and stopped the experiment at an earlier point than did subjects in the other two conditions. Tilker's hypothesis was thus supported. Making people feel personally accountable for the consequences of their acts increases their social responsibility.

Other factors that affect obedience have also been isolated and studied experimentally. Obedience is reduced by physical proximity to the learner (although 30 percent of the subjects gave the maximum shock level even when they were sitting next to the screaming learner and forcibly pressing his hand down upon the "shock plate"); by observing other assistants refuse to continue; and by the physical absence of an authority figure, who gave his orders by telephone (Milgram, 1974). But despite these findings, it is strikingly apparent that the social forces at work in situations involving destructive obedience to authority are very potent ones that are difficult for most people to resist.

MANIPULATING TWO INDEPENDENT VARIABLES: THE THINK-DRINK EFFECT

Psychologists are often interested in measuring the effects of more than one independent variable at the same time. This permits them to compare the relative strength of the variables' effects on behavior as well as to see if certain combinations of the variables have particular effects.

We have all encountered the type at one time or another, either directly or in stories: the mild-mannered person who is transformed after a few drinks into a loud, obnoxious, hostile fool, fully prepared to tear down the drapes or challenge every person in the house. Drinking plays a major role in violent behavior. Well over half of all violent crimes are alcohol-related (Lang and others, 1975).

There is general agreement that alcohol serves as a releaser of aggressive behavior (Marlatt and Gordon, 1985). This is typically attributed to the physiological effects of alcohol, which is known to depress inhibitory centers in the brain. But there may be more to it than this. Perhaps at least some of the effects of alcohol are psychological, based in part on our expectations that people will do things under the influence of alcohol that they would not ordinarily do (see Figure 2.11). If we believe that we will lose our inhibitions when we drink, then perhaps we will. In this respect, alcohol may act the way a placebo does.

FIGURE 2.11 *Many people apparently believe that drinking relieves them of personal responsibility for their acts. In fact, our beliefs about the effects of alcohol may be a powerful determinant of our behavior under its "influence."*

"Oh, that wasn't me talking. It was the alcohol talking."

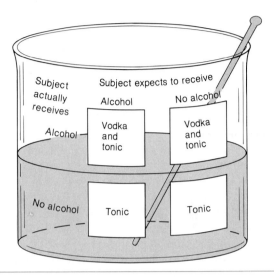

FIGURE 2.12 *In this experimental design, two independent variables, expectation and actual alcoholic content, are manipulated at the same time to create four experimental conditions. It has been used to study the separate and combined effects of "thinking" and "drinking" on aggressive behavior.*

But how can one separate out the psychological effects of drinking from the physiological ones? The answer emerged in the form of an ingenious experimental design in which alcohol and belief were jointly controlled as independent variables. The researchers concocted a mixture of one part vodka and five parts tonic water (plus a squirt of lime juice). Subjects could not tell whether this mixture contained vodka or not. Under the guise of a taste test of different brands of tonic water or vodka, the experimenters could manipulate subjects' expectations about whether or not they were drinking alcohol. The nature of their mixture then allowed the experimenters to give the subjects tonic alone or vodka plus tonic.

Figure 2.12 shows this two-factor experimental design. There are four possible combinations of expectation and alcoholic content. The "expect alcohol/receive alcohol" condition is the normal state of affairs when people drink. The "expect tonic/receive alcohol" condition assesses physiological effects alone, and the "expect alcohol/receive tonic" condition isolates the effects of the belief that one is drinking. The group that expected no alcohol and got none is a control group with which the other three conditions can be compared.

Numerous experiments have been conducted using this design to manipulate alcohol consumption and beliefs as independent variables so as to compare their effects on behavior. In one study (Lang and others, 1975), males were randomly assigned to the four experimental conditions and performed the "taste test." Those actually given vodka were allowed to drink to a blood-alcohol level of .10 percent, the legal definition of intoxication in most states. Following the taste test, subjects were placed in a Milgram-type situation in which they administered shocks to a learner when mistakes were made on a learning task. One important difference, however, was that the subject was allowed to choose whichever shock level he wished on each trial from among 10 buttons that differed in the intensity and duration of the shock. The average shock level chosen was the experimenters' operational definition of aggression.

The results of the experiment are shown in Figure 2.13. As you can see, men who believed that they had received alcohol gave more intense shocks, regardless of whether or not they had actually had vodka. An even more interesting finding was that men who thought they had consumed alcohol but had not were more aggressive than those who actually had been given vodka but thought they were drinking only tonic. These results as well as those of many other studies suggest that our beliefs about how drinking will affect us may be at least as important as the physiological effects of the alcohol, especially at low levels of intoxi-

cation (Marlatt and Rohsenow, 1980). These studies also illustrate the usefulness of experimental designs in which several independent variables are manipulated at the same time.

SINGLE-SUBJECT EXPERIMENTS: ATTENTION AND ASTHMA

In all experimental research, conclusions are based upon comparisons of behavior under different conditions. In the experimental designs we have discussed so far, the different conditions were presented to different groups of subjects. Experiments can also be conducted with only one subject who is exposed to different experimental conditions. This is frequently done in clinical research designed to change some problematic behavior in an individual client. **Single-subject experiments** are like case studies in many ways, but they involve systematic manipulation of the subject's environment and precise measurement of the subject's response to the manipulations.

A single-subject experiment designed to reduce a 7-year-old boy's asthmatic attacks exemplifies this approach (Neisworth and Moore, 1972). The boy's attacks consisted of prolonged wheezing, coughing, and gasping. They tended to occur at bedtime, and the par-

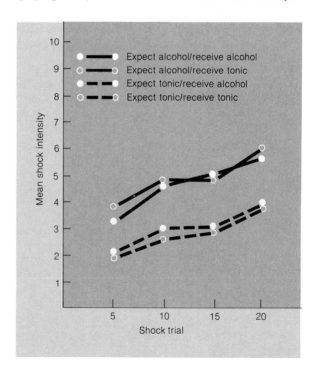

FIGURE 2.13 *Results of the study by Lang and others (1975) on the think-drink effect and aggression. This experiment showed that the belief that one has been drinking alcohol increases aggression, whether or not the subject has actually had any vodka. On the other hand, subjects who had been drinking vodka while thinking that the beverage was only tonic water delivered lower levels of shock to the learner.*

ents understandably responded with a great deal of attention. The clinicians hypothesized that the attacks might be encouraged and rewarded by the excessive attention they received. The experiment involved changing this attentional pattern and measuring the effects on the boy's asthmatic behavior. The data collected during the experiment are shown in Figure 2.14.

First, the duration of the attacks was measured by the parents on 10 consecutive nights to provide a **baseline measure**. These measures showed a fairly consistent duration of 60 to 80 minutes per night and provided a basis for assessing change. In the next phase of the experiment, the parents were instructed to give the boy no attention after he was put to bed, and attacks that occurred at this time were ignored. This **treatment contingency** condition clearly had an effect. After a temporary worsening of the attacks, they became progressively shorter over the next 30 days. In order to determine that this change was the result of the reduction in attention and not some other factor (like improving health), a **reversal condition** was introduced in

which the parents were told to pay attention to the boy's attacks as they had done in the past. Sure enough, the duration of the subsequent attacks began to climb again. Reinstatement of the reduced attention again reduced the attacks, and the parents were instructed to maintain this pattern. Follow-up data collected over the next 10 months indicated a lasting improvement. This experiment, conducted with only one subject, illustrated the powerful effects that parental attention can have on a child's behavior.

Figure 2.15 summarizes the relationships among many of the concepts that we have discussed so far. In this example, we start with a *hypothesis* that predicts a relationship between two *constructs*—in this case, stress and aggression. *Operational definitions* allow us

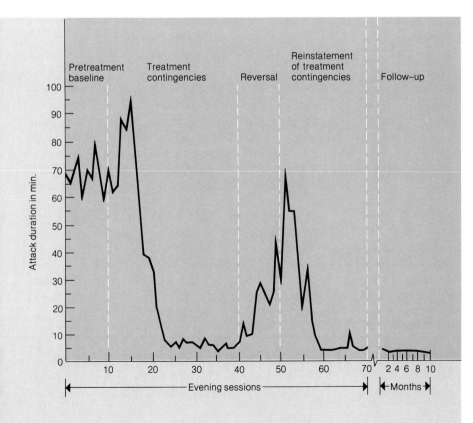

FIGURE 2.14 *Results of a single-subject experiment in which parental attention patterns were systematically manipulated to study their effect on a child's asthmatic attacks. The design called for an initial baseline period followed by a cessation of parental attention to the asthmatic attacks at bedtime. The original attentional pattern was then reinstated for a period of time to establish that reduced attention had been the factor that lowered the duration of attacks. Finally, the decreased parental attention condition was reestablished. The reduction in attacks was maintained at follow-up (Neisworth and Moore, 1972).*

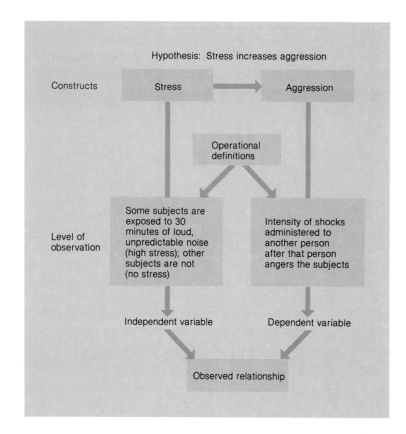

Hypothesis: Stress increases aggression

Constructs — Stress → Aggression

Operational definitions

Level of observation

Some subjects are exposed to 30 minutes of loud, unpredictable noise (high stress); other subjects are not (no stress)

Intensity of shocks administered to another person after that person angers the subjects

Independent variable

Dependent variable

Observed relationship

FIGURE 2.15 *Operational definitions form the bridge between the level of constructs and the level of observation, making it possible to test a hypothesis that involves a predicted relationship between the constructs* stress *and* aggression. *Stress is thus translated into an independent variable and aggression into a dependent variable so that the observed relationship is a legitimate scientific test of the hypothesis.*

to translate these constructs into observable *independent* and *dependent variables* so that the hypothesis can be tested under the controlled conditions of an *experiment*.

THREATS TO THE VALIDITY OF EXPERIMENTS

Because of the precision with which variables can be controlled and measured, the experiment is a powerful scientific tool for establishing cause-and-effect relations. But it is by no means infallible. Certain factors can seriously undermine the validity of experimental results. Four of the most serious flies in the scientific ointment are *confounding of variables, reactivity, demand characteristics*, and *experimenter expectancy effects*.

Confounding of variables The experimental method is based on the conviction that any differences between experimental and control groups on the dependent variable are the result of the manipulation of the independent variable. But sometimes uncontrolled variables affect the dependent variable in a way that is mistakenly attributed to the independent variable. When this happens, the independent variable and the uncontrolled variable are said to be **confounded,** because we don't know which of them caused the observed differences in behavior.

In this chapter we have already described one example of the disastrous effects of confounding: the fatal flaw in the executive monkey studies. Because the high-strung monkeys were all placed in the executive condition, the researchers were led astray. They mistakenly concluded that the level of responsibility had caused the ulcers, when actually the uncontrolled factor of emotionality was responsible. When emotionality was controlled through random assignment in later studies, the pattern of results changed completely.

Experiments must be planned very carefully so that extraneous factors that could affect the results are controlled. Confounding of variables can be a major threat to the validity of experimental results, and "Confound it!" is probably the tamest thing that's likely to be said by a researcher who has just discovered that confounding occurred in his or her experiment.

Reactivity Even amateur photographers have discovered how difficult it is to get spontaneous poses when people know they are being filmed. Experimenters have the same problem. How do we know that the behavior we observe in an experimental setting is not the result of the subject's knowledge that he or she is being observed or studied? If subjects are reacting to being observed by behaving differently from the way they would if they were encountering the independent variable out in the real world, we can easily draw false conclusions from experimental results.

Reactivity thus constitutes a threat to the validity of experiments. Researchers try to minimize reactivity in a number of ways. In most cases, they simply explain to the subject what the experiment is about and try to enlist the subject's collaboration. In some instances, however, the topic of the experiment requires that the experimenter hide the true purpose of the study. When deception is used in an attempt to obtain a more valid sample of behavior, the subject is usually led to believe that the experiment involves some other topic. In Milgram's studies, for example, the subjects were told that the research was about the effects of punishment on learning.

Reactivity effects are usually less of a problem outside the laboratory, where behavior can often be observed in a less obvious fashion. This is one reason why psychologists emphasize the importance of comparing laboratory results with those observed in more natural settings. If the two types of results are consistent with one another, more confidence can be placed in the validity of both.

One approach to avoiding reactivity effects is to use **unobtrusive measures**—or records that simply accumulate in the course of everyday living—so that subjects never have to know that they are being studied. For example, racial attitudes at different colleges were assessed by noting the degree to which black and white students mixed or clustered in lecture halls. Public interest in exhibits at a museum was compared by measuring how worn the floor tiles were in front of each

exhibit. Rate of alcohol consumption in "dry" towns was determined by counting the number of empty liquor bottles in trashcans. (Ah, the glamor of psychological research!) Measures of water pressure provided evidence for patterns of television viewing; less interesting programs resulted in greater fluctuations in water pressure as viewers went to the bathroom or got drinks of water. Children's increasing fear while being told ghost stories at camp was measured in terms of the shrinking diameter of the circle they sat in. These and many other ingenious unobtrusive measures have been used by psychologists to study psychological questions (Webb and others, 1966; Cook and Campbell, 1979).

Demand characteristics When we enter unfamiliar situations, it is quite natural for us to search for clues about how we are expected to behave. The clues that subjects pick up about the nature of the experiment and how they are "supposed" to behave are called **demand characteristics** (Orne, 1962). Sometimes subjects are able to guess the experimenter's hypothesis rather quickly (or, more properly, to *think* they've discovered it). Once this occurs, subjects may respond in different ways. People who are eager to be "good subjects" try to give the experimenter the results they think he or she wants, while others may do just the opposite (sometimes termed the "I'll fix you" effect, as well as less printable terms). Some subjects may try to ignore the clues and behave "naturally." Demand characteristics can be a threat to valid results, which is one reason why researchers often feel a need to hide the true nature of the experiment. In many instances, experimenters also question subjects after the experiment to determine whether subjects were aware of the purpose of the study and, if so, how their responses were affected. In this way, the data of "aware" subjects can be excluded if necessary.

Experimenter expectancy effects Subjects aren't the only ones who develop expectations about how they are supposed to behave. Experimenters who have a strong commitment to the hypothesis they are testing may subtly and unintentionally influence their subjects to respond in a way that is consistent with that hypothesis. Many studies have shown that if experimenters expect to obtain certain results, they are more likely to get them (Rosenthal, 1966). With subjects looking for clues about how they are expected to behave and experimenters unintentionally encouraging or reinforcing certain behaviors, there is the possibility of an unwitting conspiracy to produce desired results.

One of the ways in which researchers try to eliminate experimenter expectancy effects is through the *double blind technique*, in which neither the subject nor the experimenter is aware of which experimental condition the subject is in. This technique is almost always used in drug studies in which some subjects receive a drug and others get a placebo. If the person who is dispensing the drugs is unaware of whether the subjects are getting the drug or the placebo, the likelihood that the experimenter will react differently to the two groups of subjects is minimized (see Figure 2.16).

"It was more of a 'triple-blind' test. The patients didn't know which ones were getting the real drug, the doctors didn't know, and, I'm afraid, nobody knew."

(SIDNEY HARRIS)

ETHICS IN HUMAN AND ANIMAL RESEARCH

Many psychologists were gravely concerned and even outraged when Stanley Milgram published his research on obedience to authority in 1963 (e.g., Baumrind, 1964). Perhaps you had similar reactions while reading about his research. Milgram's critics questioned the ethics of exposing subjects without warning to a situation that was likely to cause them considerable stress and that might even have lasting negative effects on them. In reply, Milgram (1964) argued that the great social importance of the problem he was studying justified the methods he had used and that adequate precautions had been taken to protect the welfare of the subjects. He pointed out that in a debriefing at the end of the study, the subjects were told that they had not actually shocked the learner. They had a friendly meeting with the learner. The purpose of the study was explained to them and they were assured that their behavior in the situation was perfectly normal. He also cited questionnaire responses collected from the subjects after they received a complete report of the study's purposes and results. Eighty-four percent of the subjects stated that they were glad to have been in the study, and several noted that their experience had made them more tolerant of others or changed them in other desirable ways. Only 1.3 percent of the subjects said that they were sorry that they had participated (Milgram, 1964).

The dispute over Milgram's research has raged for over 20 years. In combination with other controversial issues, such as the use of deception in research and the potential for invasion of privacy, the discussion has prompted deep concern for protecting the welfare of subjects. It is most unlikely that research like Milgram's could be conducted in the United States or Canada

FIGURE 2.16 *To control for experimenter expectancy effects in drug studies, a* double blind *procedure is used. Neither the subjects nor the people who dispense the substances know who is receiving the drug and who is getting a placebo. However, someone* is *supposed to know.*

today because of strict guidelines developed by government agencies and professional organizations.

The ethical and moral issues are not simple ones They are very similar to those with which medical researchers must deal. In some instances the only way to discover important knowledge about behavior or to develop new techniques to enhance human welfare is to deceive subjects or to expose them to potentially stressful situations. To help researchers balance the potential benefits against the risks involved and to ensure that the welfare of subjects is protected, virtually every academic and research institution has established review panels. If a research proposal is considered ethically questionable or if the rights, welfare, and personal privacy of subjects are not sufficiently protected, the proposal must be modified or the research cannot be conducted.

According to the research guidelines of the American Psychological Association (APA), subjects cannot be placed in either physical or psychological jeopardy without their informed consent. They must be told about the procedures to be followed and warned about any risks that might be involved. If deception is necessary, then subjects must be completely debriefed after the experiment and the entire procedure must be explained to them. Special measures must be taken to protect the confidentiality of data, and subjects must be told that they are free to withdraw from a study at any time without penalty.

When children, seriously disturbed mental patients, or others who are not able to give true consent are involved, permission must be obtained from their parents or guardians. Strict guidelines also apply to research in prisons. No prisoner can be forced to participate in research or be penalized for refusal to do so. In the case of research on rehabilitative programs, prisoners must be permitted to share in decisions concerning program goals. Researchers who violate the code of research ethics face serious legal and professional consequences.

Concern about the rights of subjects extends to animals as well as humans. As in medical research, animals are frequently the subjects in psychological studies considered too hazardous for humans. The APA's guidelines require that animals be treated humanely and that the risks to which they are exposed be justified by the potential importance of the research. But advo-

cates of animal rights believe that these regulations are not strong enough. The dilemma surrounding the use of animals in research has been stated well by the Australian philosopher Peter Singer:

Either the animal is not like us, in which case there is no reason for performing the experiment; or else the animal is like us, in which case we ought not perform an experiment on the animal that would be considered outrageous if performed on one of us. (Quoted in Shapiro, 1984)

There are no easy answers to this issue. Nevertheless, the welfare of animals in research is receiving the renewed attention it deserves. Some researchers are seeking alternatives to the use of animal subjects, such as the use of computer simulations of animal behavior under particular experimental conditions.

STATISTICS: ANALYZING AND INTERPRETING DATA

Scientific observation results in data that are usually numerical in nature. Data are the building blocks for the description of behavior, and relationships between measured variables form the basis for explanation and understanding, the testing of scientific hypotheses, and theory building.

Mathematical procedures known as *statistics* are a vital scientific tool. They allow the scientist to summarize and bring order to data, as well as to measure relationships among variables. Virtually all of the research results presented in this book were arrived at through systematic observation and statistical analysis.

Because statistics are so important to psychology, we have prepared a special appendix in the back of the book that describes these methods in some detail. For now, we simply wish to introduce you to some of the basic concepts and methods of statistical analysis.

Descriptive statistics: Organizing and summarizing results

In psychological research, observations are generally collected from a relatively large number of subjects. It is usually hard to make much sense out of the data by merely examining the individual scores of each subject. We therefore need some way to organize all the scores and to describe the characteristics of the entire set, or *distribution*, of scores. **Descriptive statistics** provide us with a shorthand method for summarizing data.

The most common way of organizing a set of individual observations is through a **frequency distribution.** To do this, all we have to do is count the number of subjects who receive each score. Certain characteristics of the distribution, such as whether there are more high or more low scores, whether scores tend to cluster in one area of the distribution or are scattered throughout, and so on, then become clearer. Table 2.1 shows a frequency distribution from Milgram's study of obedience. Once the data have been tabulated in this way, we can see at a glance that the majority of subjects gave the maximum shock level.

Suppose your instructor made up two forms of your first examination in this course. Form A contained many humorous test items, while Form B contained no humor. If half of the class were given each form on a random basis, it would be of interest to compare the two distributions of scores to see if the humor seemed to make a difference, perhaps by helping to reduce tension during the test.

We would first want to see how the students performed on the two forms of the test. We could simply "eyeball" the two frequency distributions, but we would prefer to have a single score for each group that characterized their level of performance—that is, a **measure of central tendency.** The most commonly used measures of central tendency are the mean, the mode, and the median. The **mean** is the arithmetic average, computed by adding up all the scores in the distribution and then dividing by the number of scores. The **median** is the point that cuts the distribution in half, so that half of the rank-ordered scores fall above it and half below it. The median is not affected by ex-

TABLE 2.1 A FREQUENCY DISTRIBUTION OF THE NUMBER OF SUBJECTS WHO GAVE EACH MAXIMUM LEVEL OF SHOCK IN THE MILGRAM (1963) STUDY

SHOCK LEVEL	VERBAL DESIGNATION AND VOLTAGE LEVEL	NUMBER OF SUBJECTS GIVING EACH MAXIMUM SHOCK LEVEL
	SLIGHT SHOCK	
1	15	
2	30	
3	45	
4	60	
	MODERATE SHOCK	
5	75	
6	90	1
7	105	
8	120	
	STRONG SHOCK	
9	135	
10	150	6
11	165	
12	180	1
	VERY STRONG SHOCK	
13	195	
14	210	
15	225	
16	240	
	INTENSE SHOCK	
17	255	
18	270	2
19	285	
20	300	1
	EXTREME INTENSITY SHOCK	
21	315	1
22	330	1
23	345	
24	360	
	DANGER: SEVERE SHOCK	
25	375	1
26	390	
27	405	
28	420	
	XXX	
29	435	
30	450	26
	Average maximum shock level	368 volts
	Percentage of obedient subjects	65.0

Source: Milgram, 1974, p. 60.

treme scores as much as the mean is. The **mode** is simply the score that the largest number of students obtained. The mean is the most commonly used of the three, and you will find that most of the data presented in this text are means.

The less variation there is among scores, the more the measure of central tendency is characteristic of the group's performance. However, measures of central tendency do not tell us anything about the pattern of scores. Do the scores cluster around the average, or do they vary widely, with some very high scores and some very low ones? **Measures of variability** help to answer this question. The simplest measure of variability is the **range,** which is the difference between the highest and the lowest scores. A measure of variation called the **standard deviation** is preferred because it takes into account all of the scores in the distribution rather than only the highest and the lowest. To compute the standard deviation, the difference (or deviation) between each score and the mean is squared and the squared deviations are summed and divided by the total number of scores minus 1 (for example, by 19 if there are 20 scores). The square root of this "average squared deviation" value is the standard deviation.

When scores are plotted according to their frequency of occurrence, the distribution sometimes resembles a symmetrical bell-shaped distribution like the one shown in Figure 2.17. This is called a **normal distribution,** or *normal curve*. In a normal distribution, half of the cases fall on each side of the mean, and the

mean, median, and mode are all exactly the same. Many human characteristics, including height, weight, and intelligence, have essentially normal distributions.

The normal curve has important statistical properties and is the basis for many statistical analyses. For example, if a normal curve is divided into bands, each equal to one *standard deviation (SD)*, a fixed percentage of the cases will fall within each band. As you can see in Figure 2.17, 68 percent of the cases fall within one SD above and one SD below the mean. Knowledge of these properties forms the basis for many statistical tests that could be used to examine the hypothesis that humorous test item content affected the test performance of students in your class. (For more details on these procedures, as well as all the other concepts discussed in this section, see the appendix.)

The correlation coefficient

Much psychological research is designed to examine relationships among variables. In our earlier discussion of the correlational approach, we saw how heavyweight

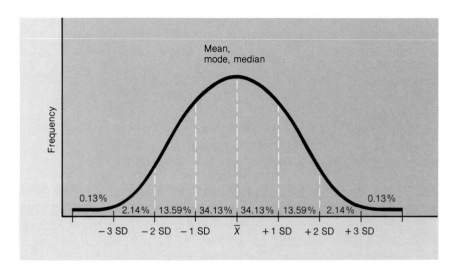

FIGURE 2.17 *A normal distribution, showing the percentage of cases falling within the areas of the curve created by standard deviations above and below the mean.*

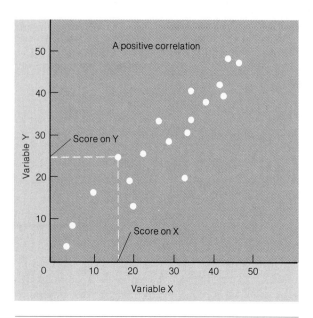

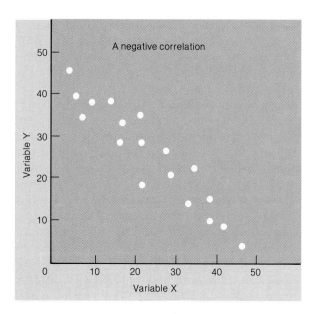

FIGURE 2.18 *Scatter plots illustrating positive, negative, and zero correlations between two variables, X and Y. Each point represents the scores obtained by a particular subject on variable X and on variable Y.*

---

championship fights were related to homicide rates. In most correlational research, however, we are interested in the relationship between two sets of scores obtained from the same subjects. For example, we might be interested in how scores on an intelligence test are related to students' grade point averages. We would have a score on each of the two measures for each student in our sample. These data could be graphed in a *scatter plot* like those shown in Figure 2.18. Each point in the scatter plot represents an individual subject's scores on the two variables of interest, which we'll call variable X and variable Y. The three scatter plots in Figure 2.18 illustrate the three types of correlational relationships: **positive,** in which high scores on X are related to high scores on Y; **negative,** in which high scores on X are related to low scores on Y; and a *zero correlation*, in which there is no relationship between the two variables. (In case you're wondering, there is a moderate positive correlation between intelligence and grade point average.)

The relationship between two variables can be represented more precisely by the **correlation coefficient.**

Correlation coefficients can range from -1.00 through .00 to $+1.00$. A coefficient of $+1.00$ means that there is a perfect positive relationship between X and Y, with the person having the highest score on X also having the highest score on Y, the second highest on X also being the second highest on Y, and so on. A correlation of -1.00 signifies a perfect negative relationship, and a correlation of .00 means that there is no relationship at all between X and Y. The correlation coefficient thus tells you both the *direction* (positive or negative) and the *strength* of the relationship. The closer to $+1.00$ or -1.00 the correlation, the more strongly the two variables are related. Thus, a correlation of -0.59 indicates a stronger relationship between X and Y than does a correlation of $+0.37$. If you wish to know more about how correlation coefficients are computed, you will find the formula and an example in the appendix.

Inferential statistics: Drawing conclusions about data

Returning once more to our study of the effects of humorous items on test performance, suppose that the descriptive statistics indicate that the students who got the humorous form of the test had a higher mean score. The next question is whether this is a "real"

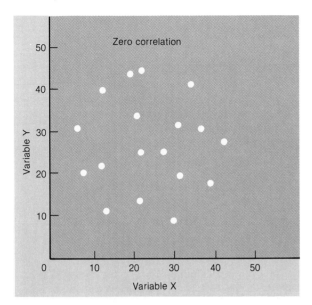

finding that applies to students in general (the population) rather than simply to your class (the sample). How can we decide whether the observed difference in mean test scores is simply a chance occurrence? What is the likelihood that differences like this would occur if the experiment were repeated again and again with other samples drawn from the population of college students studying introductory psychology? **Inferential statistics** help us to answer questions like these.

There are a number of statistical tests that allow us to examine differences between means. All of these tests yield what is known as a **level of significance,** which is determined by comparing the results of the statistical test with a set of special statistical tables. The level of significance indicates the likelihood that the results obtained from the sample occurred by chance and thus do not reflect a finding that can be applied to the population from which the sample was drawn.

Statistical significance levels are expressed as percentage figures. When psychologists write that the results are significant at the 5 percent (0.05) level of significance, they mean that the chances are only 5 in 100 that the same results would *not* occur if the entire population could be run in the experiment. In other words, the chances are 95 in 100 that the obtained differences between the various groups in the experiment hold for the entire population. The level of significance can also be calculated for correlation coeffi-

cients to determine the likelihood that the correlation also departs from .00 in the population. The 5 percent level of significance is the conventional cut-off point used by psychologists (see Figure 2.19). If the level of significance is above the 0.05 level (for example, at 0.06 or 0.10), it is assumed that the results occurred by chance and that they cannot be generalized to the rest of the population.

FIGURE 2.19 *The statistical level of significance may have important practical as well as scientific applications.*

"I'm sorry, but you've been rejected at the .05 level."

(APA MONITOR, SEPTEMBER–OCTOBER 1973. COPYRIGHT 1973 BY THE AMERICAN PSYCHOLOGICAL ASSOCIATION. REPRINTED BY PERMISSION.)

PSYCHOLOGY AND THE COMPUTER REVOLUTION

Few technological developments have affected our lives as much as the computer. It has influenced how we live, how we work, and even how we learn. Microcomputers are now within the financial reach of a great many people, and college students of the 1980s have access to a tool that was dreamed of by only the most visionary students of the 1960s. Perhaps you are one of the thousands of college students using the computerized study guide available for this textbook on your own microcomputer.[1]

Computers have also changed the face of modern-day psychology. Their ability to store and process staggering amounts of information with lightning speed has made computers an indispensable tool in many areas of psychology. Psychologists, in turn, have been leaders in research designed to make computers more accessible and useful to people of all ages. The development of *computer-assisted instruction,* or "teaching machines," occurred largely within psychology, and many psychologists are currently working in this area of research and application. Psychologists are also heavily involved in the development of computer designs and programs that make these electronic marvels easier for all of us to use.

Perhaps the most obvious impact of the computer is in the statistical analysis of research data. Complex statistical analyses can take weeks or months to do on an ordinary calculator; advanced computers can do them in seconds. Thanks to computer analysis, psychologists can analyze data in increasingly more sophisticated ways that make it possible to extract new kinds of information from research results.

Computers are also revolutionizing many aspects of data collection (see Figure 2.20). In some laboratories, experiments are being conducted by computers rather than by human experimenters. In learning experiments, for example, microcomputers like the Apple and the IBM PC can be programmed to pres-

[1]Information and an order form for the Apple or IBM Study-Aid for this book can be found at the back of the book.

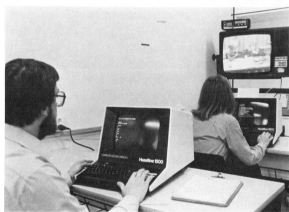

FIGURE 2.20 *Computers are finding many uses in psychology. In the top photo, a mother interferes with her child's problem-solving behavior by pointing to the part that should be used next. These interactions are videotaped and coded by two independent observers on computer terminals. The data can be summarized and analyzed immediately.*

ent stimuli to subjects, record their responses, and make decisions about which stimuli or learning problems to present next. At the University of Iowa, programs have been developed that allow use of a microcomputer to study brain mechanisms of learning in animals having microelectrodes implanted in specific brain regions. The computer can present complex electrical stimuli to the brains of up to eight animals at a time while it simultaneously records the electrical activity in the brains (Schreurs and others, 1983). Computer programs have also been developed to help survey researchers collect telephone interview data. The programs randomly generate and dial telephone numbers, display the appropriate questions for the interviewer on a monitor, and provide a way for the interviewer to log in the interviewee's responses. The computer can provide a frequency distribution of responses to each question whenever the interviewer requests it (Phillipp and Cicciarella, 1983).

In the next chapter, we will highlight some of the recent advances in our understanding of how the brain functions. One of the tools that have made such advances possible is *computerized axial tomography,* more popularly known as the *CT scan.* In this procedure, numerous X-ray beams take pictures of narrow "slices" of the brain from many different angles. A computer then analyzes the X rays and combines them into a composite three-dimensional "picture" of the inside of the brain. The CT scan and newer computer-based techniques have provided windows to the living brain.

In an area known as *artificial intelligence,* computers can create models of the human mind. The thinking and problem-solving "behaviors" of the computer models can be compared with the mental output of humans to test theories of human thought. We will examine this interesting area of research in greater detail in Chapter 8.

Microcomputers have become increasingly useful in clinical settings as well as in laboratories. They can administer a variety of different psychological tests in which questions are presented on a monitor and answers are typed by the patient on a keyboard. The computer can then score the tests and write a sophisticated report for the clinical staff. It can also be used to keep records of patients' behavior and response to medication (Romanczyk, 1985; Spaulding and others, 1983). These functions help free clinicians to provide more intensive therapy for their patients.

The computer promises to make important contributions to testing and measuring human abilities and mental processes. By presenting questions or problems that depend on the subject's previous responses, the computer can test the limits of a subject's intellectual or problem-solving abilities more effectively than a human examiner can with a paper-and-pencil test. The highly sophisticated graphics that can be displayed on monitor screens allow for the presentation of problems (such as those involving movement) that are not possible on a printed page. Cognitive psychologists are using the computer to measure human abilities in new ways, and this research may alter our current conceptions of intelligence (Hunt and Pellegrino, 1985).

Last but not least, computers are contributing to the skills and productivity of psychologists themselves. Computer programs allow psychologists to interact with computers to learn new skills, such as complex statistical techniques (Levy, 1983). Clinicians can sharpen their diagnostic and interviewing skills through interactive programs that present case material or patients' verbal responses. The use of computers for word processing is also enhancing our productivity. In fact, this textbook was composed on word processors. This not only speeded up the writing and editing processes, but it contributed significantly to the mental health of our secretaries, who in previous editions had to cope with our barely intelligible scrawling.

SCIENTIFIC PRINCIPLES IN PSYCHOLOGY (p. 35)

1. Scientific understanding usually proceeds through a number of steps: (a) informal observation and formulation of a question; (b) intuitive attempts to answer the question; (c) formulation of scientific hypotheses; (d) hypothesis testing; and (e) theory construction.

2. Good theories are able to incorporate already known facts, give rise to additional hypotheses that can be tested to generate new knowledge, and are testable and capable of being refuted.

3. In psychology, understanding means being able to specify the causes of behavior. There are two basic approaches to understanding. After-the-fact understanding is limited because there are countless possible explanations and no way to ascertain which is correct. Scientists prefer to test their understanding through prediction and control.

4. In order for a psychological construct to be scientifically useful, it must be possible to provide an acceptable operational definition of it either in terms of conditions imposed on the subject (in *stimulus* terms) or of observable behaviors of the subject (in *response* terms). Thus, constructs are defined in terms of the operations used to measure them.

SCIENTIFIC METHODS: GATHERING INFORMATION ABOUT BEHAVIOR (p. 39)

1. Research is almost always done with samples drawn from the larger population about which conclusions will be drawn. Ideally, samples are representative of the population; they mirror important characteristics that influence the behavior being studied. Large sample sizes and random assignment to experimental conditions are methods used to try to avoid sampling errors.

2. Case studies involve the detailed examination of a person, group, or organization. Although conclusions about causality are difficult to establish, case studies often lead to more systematic observation, and they can show if a theory is invalid.

3. Uncontrolled observation can be used in many real-life settings to gather helpful information about behavior and about possible causal relationships. Rosenhan's report of patient and staff behavior in mental hospitals is an example of uncontrolled observation.

4. Observation under controlled conditions allows psychologists to control and standardize the conditions to which subjects respond. Milgram's study of destructive obedience to authority utilized this approach. (Since there was only one condition, this does not qualify as an experiment.)

5. Correlational research studies the relationships between naturally occurring events that are not controlled by the researcher. Phillips's research on the relationship between media attention to boxing matches and homicides illustrated this approach. A limitation of this method is that causality cannot be established through correlation alone. Correlation can, however, serve as the basis for predictions.

THE EXPERIMENTAL APPROACH: CONTROL AND MANIPULATION OF VARIABLES (p. 46)

1. Experiments involve the manipulation of one or more independent variables and an assessment of their effects on dependent variable behaviors. An attempt is made to hold everything constant except the independent variable so that cause-and-effect conclusions can be drawn.

2. Comparisons between experimental and control conditions are the basis for drawing conclusions in experiments. Experimental manipulation may involve only one independent variable, as in Tilker's obedience experiment, in which the degree of personal responsibility was varied. In other experiments, more than one independent variable is manipulated, as in the study on the think-drink effect. In any experiment, more than one dependent variable can be (and often is) measured.

3. Single-subject experiments involve systematic exposure of one subject to different conditions and careful measurement of behavior under each condition. Sometimes, as in the study on parental attention and asthma, the experimental conditions are reversed, or repeated, in order to establish cause and effect.

4. Several factors can undermine the validity of conclusions drawn from experiments. These include confounding of independent and extraneous variables (as occurred in the executive monkey study), reactivity (changes in behavior when subjects know they are being studied), demand characteristics (stimuli that suggest to subjects how they are expected to behave), and experimenter expectancy effects.

ETHICS IN HUMAN AND ANIMAL RESEARCH (p. 54)

Psychologists are placing increasing emphasis on the protection of human and animal subjects used in research. Research panels must be assured that subjects' rights and welfare are protected before research is approved. This includes provision for informed consent from subjects, debriefing after deception is used, and freedom of subjects to decline to participate or to withdraw at any time. Serious issues about animal research are currently being debated.

STATISTICS: ANALYZING AND INTERPRETING DATA (p. 55)

1. Descriptive statistics are used to summarize data. The most common descriptive statistics are measures of central tendency (mean, median, and mode) and measures of variability (range and standard deviation). Many frequency distributions resemble a symmetrical, bell-shaped, normal curve.

2. Correlation coefficients provide a measure of the direction (positive or negative) and the strength (from .00 to +1.00 or −1.00) of a relationship between two variables.

3. Inferential statistics are the basis for drawing scientific conclusions about results. The level of statistical significance refers to the likelihood that the results obtained from the sample occurred by chance alone and do not reflect a similar phenomenon in the population.

FRONTIER 2.1 PSYCHOLOGY AND THE COMPUTER REVOLUTION (p. 60)

Computers are making many contributions to psychology in both experimental and clinical settings. New computer-based methods for studying the brain, for automating experiments and the collection of test and survey data, and for increasing the professional skills of psychologists are having a major impact on modern-day psychology.

KEY TERMS AND CONCEPTS

hypothesis	construct
theory	operational definition
after-the-fact understanding	sample
	population
understanding through prediction and control	representative sample

random assignment	descriptive statistics
case study	frequency distribution
placebo	measures of central tendency
uncontrolled observation	
schizophrenia	mean
controlled observation	median
correlational research	mode
variable	measure of variability
independent variable	range
dependent variable	standard deviation
experimental group	normal distribution
control group	positive correlation
baseline measurement	negative correlation
treatment contingency	correlation coefficient
reversal condition	inferential statistics
confounding	level of significance
reactivity	computer-assisted instruction
unobtrusive measures	CT scan
demand characteristics	artificial intelligence
experimenter expectancy effects	

SUGGESTED READINGS

AGNEW, N. M., and PYKE, S. W. (1978). *The science game: An introduction to research in the behavioral sciences.* Englewood Cliffs, N.J.: Prentice-Hall. An interesting and readable introduction to research methods in psychology, sociology, and related fields.

HUCK, S. W., and SANDLER, H. M. (1979). *Rival hypotheses: Alternative interpretations of data based conclusions.* New York: Harper & Row. A delightful book that analyzes flaws in 100 interesting scientific reports and provides alternative explanations for their results.

PAGANO, R. R. (1986). *Understanding statistics in the behavioral sciences*, 2d ed. St. Paul, Minn.: West. An extremely readable text that covers both descriptive and inferential statistics.

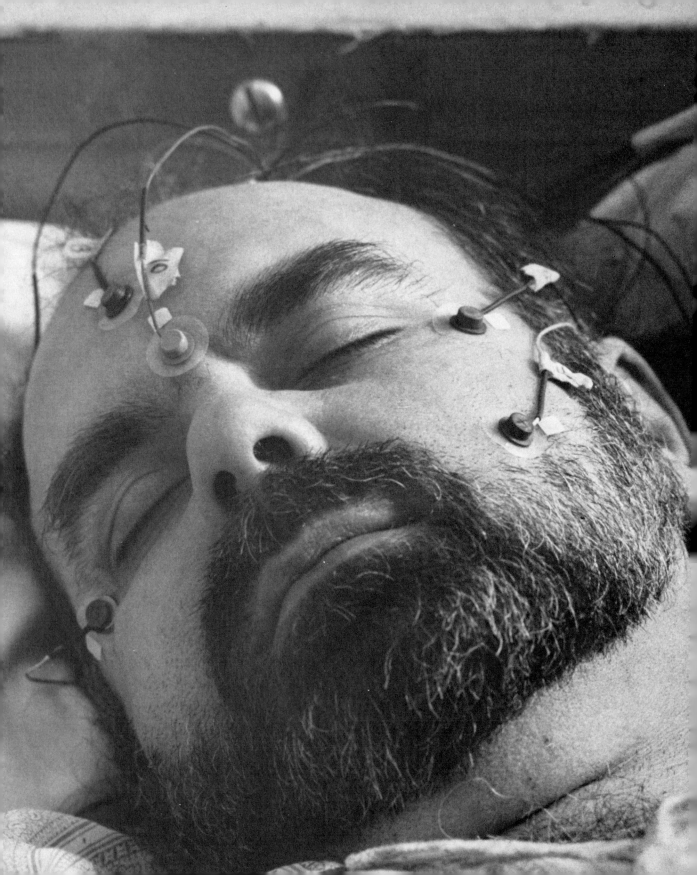

SECTION TWO

BRAIN, CONSCIOUSNESS, AND PERCEPTION

CHAPTER THREE: **BIOLOGICAL FOUNDATIONS OF BEHAVIOR**

CHAPTER FOUR: **STATES OF CONSCIOUSNESS**

CHAPTER FIVE: **SENSATION AND PERCEPTION**

CHAPTER THREE

BIOLOGICAL FOUNDATIONS OF BEHAVIOR

GENETIC INFLUENCES ON BEHAVIOR

Human heredity

FRONTIER 3.1   GENETIC ENGINEERING: THE EDGE OF CREATION

Behavior genetics

THE NEURAL BASES OF BEHAVIOR

The neuron

Nerve impulses

Synaptic transmission

Neurotransmitters

The language of neural communication

THE CENTRAL NERVOUS SYSTEM

The spinal cord

The brain: Seat of consciousness and behavior

The hindbrain

The midbrain

The forebrain

Brain damage and recovery of function

FRONTIER 3.2   UNLOCKING THE SECRETS OF THE BRAIN

THE AUTONOMIC AND ENDOCRINE SYSTEMS

The autonomic nervous system

The endocrine system

STUDY OUTLINE

KEY TERMS AND CONCEPTS

SUGGESTED READINGS

Maria was becoming increasingly worried about her husband. In the past few months she had noted striking changes in him. The editor of a successful suburban weekly magazine, he had become uncharacteristically irritable and highly opinionated. Trivial disagreements between them roused him to violent arguments. He had always been an energetic person, but now his activity level seemed out of control. At times he would work at a frenzied pace for up to 72 hours, sleep a bit, and then begin the cycle again. Recently, he had begun keeping a journal in which he recorded his thoughts and experiences. It was not long before notes jotted down in a hurried manner could be found all over the house.

Maria decided that what her husband needed was a rest, and they departed for a Caribbean vacation. But by now he was obsessed with recording in written form every experience and inner feeling he had. Maria tried to divert him from his frantic writing by buying him books to read. He occupied himself for a while with a book about a religious conversion experience, and Maria breathed a sigh of relief. But suddenly he became obsessed with religion as well as with his journal. The journal became a record of extensive and profound personal conversations with God.

Her husband had always been an attentive and affectionate spouse, but this aspect of his behavior also assumed a frenzied quality. Maria became alarmed and frightened (to say nothing of exhausted) by his insatiable sexual demands.

After their return home he had another 72-hour episode of manic behavior, then collapsed into a state of exhaustion. He was hospitalized and a psychiatric evaluation was performed. During the examination his thoughts were flighty and raced rapidly from one topic to another. His speech was nonstop. By the end of the interview the psychiatrist's head was also swimming.

The behavioral combination of hypergraphia (excessive writing), religious preoccupation, and excessive sexuality is sometimes seen in patients having damage in the temporal lobes of the brain, and a neurological examination was therefore ordered. This examination provided evidence of a brain tumor. Fortunately, this patient responded well to a combination of antimanic and antipsychotic drugs, and his behavior improved dramatically. Brain surgery was unnecessary at the moment, but doctors continued to observe his condition closely after his release from the hospital. (Gazzaniga and others, 1979)

This case, like others that we discuss in this chapter, illustrates the dramatic changes in behavior that can occur when something goes wrong in the nervous system. It also illustrates how behavior can be profoundly affected by altering (in this case, with drugs) the chemical activities that underlie all brain functioning.

In order to understand behavior, we must know something about its biological foundations. We are, first and foremost, biological creatures, and all the processes that are the focus of the psychodynamic, cognitive, behavioral, and humanistic-existential perspectives result from the functioning of biological systems. The biological perspective is stimulating great advances in our knowledge about how and why we behave as we do. Many of the facts presented in this chapter were unknown only a decade ago.

Every psychological process—attending, sensing, perceiving, thinking, feeling, acting—involves complex biological systems that operate in the invisible world within our bodies. Indeed, powerful determinants of our physical and behavioral traits are inscribed on a genetic blueprint that existed long before we were born. We begin, then, with the genetic factors that help to shape who we are and what we are capable of becoming.

GENETIC INFLUENCES ON BEHAVIOR

Our physical development is largely directed by the genes that we inherit from our parents. At one time, psychologists waged vigorous debates about how much of our behavior is genetically determined and how much of it is learned. This was known as the **nature-nurture controversy.** We now know that this "either-or" question is largely meaningless, since behavior depends on the *interaction* between heredity and environment. However, it is also clear that genetic factors do set limits on our behavioral capabilities, as illustrated most dramatically in certain genetically based birth disorders. Psychologists working in the field of **behavior genetics** study how behavior is influenced by biological factors and how favorable or unfavorable environmental conditions can affect an organism's genetically inherited potential.

Genetic theory began around 1865, when Gregor

Mendel reported on his experiments with garden peas. Mendel showed that heredity involved the passing on of specific organic factors, not the simple blending of the parents' characteristics. These specific factors might produce visible characteristics in the offspring, or they might simply be carried for possible transmission to another generation. In any case, the offspring of one set of parents did not all inherit the same traits.

Early in the twentieth century, geneticists made an important distinction between **genotype** and **phenotype**. Genotype refers to the specific genetic makeup of an individual, while phenotype refers to the observable characteristics produced by that genetic endowment. Genotype and phenotype are not identical because not every gene is expressed in a visible trait and because the expression of a genotypic trait may be modified by the environment.

An individual's genetic coding is like the catalog of a giant library. Some of the coded directives are used on one occasion, some on another. Some are never used at all, either because they are contradicted by stronger genetic directives or because the environment never calls them forth. For example, geneticists have discovered that chickens have retained the genetic code for teeth (Kollar and Fischer, 1980), yet, because the code is prevented from being expressed, hens' teeth remain a cliché for scarcity.

Human heredity

The union of two cells, the egg from the mother and the sperm from the father, is the beginning of a new individual. Like all other cells, the egg and sperm carry within them the material of heredity: a definite number of rodlike units called **chromosomes.** A chromosome is a tightly coiled molecule of *deoxyribonucleic acid* (**DNA**) that is partly covered by protein. All the information of heredity is encoded in the combinations of molecules that make up the approximately 3 feet of DNA chains that exist in each of your cells. The specific arrangements of molecules determine your species, skin color, body type, eye color, brain composition, and so forth.

The DNA portion of the chromosome carries the hereditary blueprint in units called **genes** (see Figure 3.1). Each human chromosome consists of about 20,000 genes (Tortora and Anagnostakos, 1984). Your

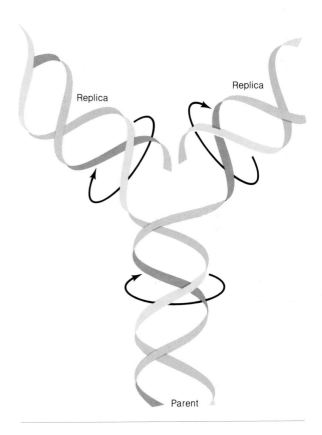

FIGURE 3.1 *Although the role of chromosomes and genes in heredity has been known for some time, the way in which genetic information is transmitted was not understood until 1953, when James Watson and Francis Crick proposed a model of the DNA molecule like that shown here. This model makes it possible to see how the genetic code reproduces itself. The inverted ladder of the DNA molecule can "unzip" up the center and reproduce the missing halves so that each new DNA molecule contains the complete code of the original.*

genes are like a giant computer file of information about your characteristics, potentials, and limitations. Every moment of every day, the strands of DNA silently transmit their detailed instructions for the functioning of your cellular processes.

With one exception, every cell in a normal person contains 46 chromosomes, arranged in 23 pairs. The exception is the sex cell, the egg or the sperm, which has only 23 chromosomes. At conception the mother's and father's sex cells unite to form a new cell, which contains the full 46 chromosomes (23 chromosome pairs). The genes within each chromosome also occur in pairs, and the offspring receives one of each gene pair from each parent. Thus, a human parent potentially can produce several trillion genetically different egg or sperm cells. In other words, the possible differences in genotype and phenotype among children in the same family are enormous. The only exception to this uniqueness of the individual occurs in monozygotic (identical) twins, whose heredity is identical because they develop from the same fertilized egg.

SEX DETERMINATION

The two members of each chromosome pair appear almost identical in size and shape when they are viewed under a microscope, except for the twenty-third pair in the human male. All of the female's eggs have the X chromosome, but there are two types of male sperm, X and Y. Every normal male has an XY chromosome pair, with the X chromosome being larger in size (see Figure 3.2). If a Y sperm fertilizes an X egg, an XY chromosome pair results, and a male offspring will develop. The combining of an X sperm with an X egg will result in a female offspring. Thus, it is the father's chromosomal contribution that determines the sex of the child.

DOMINANT AND RECESSIVE GENES

Genotype and phenotype are not identical because some genes are **dominant** and some are **recessive.** If a gene is dominant, the particular characteristic that it controls will be displayed. If a gene is recessive, the characteristic associated with it will not show up unless it is paired with another recessive gene; if only one gene in a pair is recessive, its effect will be masked by its dominant partner. Even if their traits remain hidden, however, recessive genes can be passed on to offspring.

The manner in which dominant and recessive genes affect phenotypic characteristics can vary considerably. Certain traits, such as one particular form of

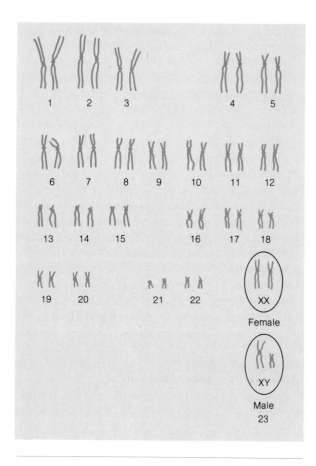

FIGURE 3.2 *Human beings have 23 pairs of chromosomes. Males and females cannot be distinguished by the first 22 pairs. Sex is determined by the twenty-third pair. In females the pair contains two similar (X) chromosomes; the female genotype is XX. In males it contains an X chromosome and a Y chromosome; the male genotype is XY.*

deafness, are produced by a single gene or gene pair, but others are produced by the combination of several genes. To complicate matters further, a single gene may affect development in several parts of the body (see Table 3.1).

Some hereditary characteristics are carried only by the female chromosome (the X chromosome) and are therefore said to be **sex-linked.** For example, red-green color blindness and hemophilia (a failure in blood clotting) are sex-linked traits. The male inherits an X chromosome from the mother and a Y chromosome from the father. If he inherits one of these recessive genes from his mother, he will have no matching gene from his father because only Xs carry these sex-linked characteristics. Therefore, the trait will appear. A female, however, inherits one X chromosome from each parent, so even if she inherits the recessive gene from her mother, the chances are great that it will be masked by the dominant gene from the father's X chromosome. Only if her father also carried the recessive gene would the female exhibit the sex-linked characteristic.

CHROMOSOME VARIATIONS AND MUTATIONS

The influence of chromosomes on our development is so great that the slightest damage to even a single one can have devastating effects. For example, a type of mental retardation known as the **Down syndrome** occurs when an extra chromosome attaches itself to the twenty-first pair. In most cases, loss of a chromosome during prenatal development is fatal. If only a small part is lost, the embryo may survive.

Ordinarily, as a cell grows and divides, it reproduces perfectly. But if a mutation (sudden change) occurs in the egg or sperm as a result of random factors or accident, it is likely that the mutated gene will be passed on to future generations. If, on the other hand, a mutation occurs in cells other than the egg or sperm, the cells that grow from it will duplicate the change, but the change will not be transmitted to the next gen-

eration. For example, certain individuals have flecks of brown in a blue eye. This means that most of their cells reproduced normally, and the mutation of one cell from blue to brown affected only cells descended from that particular cell and colored only a portion of the iris. Although observable mutations in human beings are rare, some environmental factors may increase the mutation rate. The most common of these factors is ionizing radiation, such as that from X rays and nuclear explosions.

When mutations occur in nature, processes of natural selection dictate which of the random errors will survive and which will not. Those mutations that prove adaptive are more likely to be passed on to future generations. Until recently, mutations occurred only in nature and on a random basis. But new techniques have been developed that allow humans to produce planned genetic mutations by combining DNA molecules from more than one organism. These **recombinant DNA techniques** may offer great benefits in the prevention or treatment of many incapacitating or life-threatening physical conditions. But even scientists who are actively involved in recombinant DNA research have voiced grave concerns about the ethics and possible consequences of genetic engineering. Are we opening a

TABLE 3.1 SOME HUMAN CHARACTERISTICS AND DISORDERS THOUGHT TO BE CAUSED BY A SINGLE DOMINANT GENE OR BY A SINGLE PAIR OF RECESSIVE GENES

DOMINANT OR RECESSIVE	TRAIT OR CHARACTERISTIC	DESCRIPTION
Dominant	Cataract	Opaqueness of lens of eye
Dominant	Huntington's disease	Degeneration of particular brain centers
Dominant	Amyloidosis	Congestive heart failure
Recessive	Albinism	Lack of pigment in hair, eyes, and skin
Recessive	Deaf-mutism	Deafness from birth
Recessive	Microcephaly	Abnormally small head

GENETIC ENGINEERING: THE EDGE OF CREATION

Since the discovery of DNA as the material basis for biological heredity, the field of molecular genetics has contributed a great deal to our understanding of the mechanisms of genetic transmission. One of the most far-reaching discoveries of recent years has been the development of recombinant DNA techniques. With the aid of certain enzymes, the long threadlike molecules of DNA can be cut into pieces, recombined with pieces of DNA from another organism, and inserted into a host organism, where it can produce copies of itself just as normal DNA does. For the first time, humans have potential control over the processes of heredity and evolution because recombinant DNA techniques permit the creation of new organisms that have specific genetic properties. A 1980 legal decision even decreed that new life forms created by genetic engineering can be patented, spurring the establishment of a large and highly competitive industry in which fortunes can be made overnight.

Recombinant DNA procedures clearly have practical as well as scientific significance. For example, because uncontrolled cell growth in cancer reflects a loss of normal gene regulation, the ability to manipulate genetic functioning could have important applications for the understanding, prevention, and treatment of cancer and other diseases. Since recombinant DNA procedures make possible the preparation of unlimited quantities of genes and their products, the manufacture of medically valuable human proteins such as hormones, clotting factors, and antibodies is now possible. In 1980, scientists succeeded in modifying the genetic structure of *E. coli* bacteria so that they could produce *interferon,* a natural antivirus and antitumor substance normally released in small quantities in human cells as part of the body's defense system. By the mid-1980s, the list of therapeutic substances produced by recombinant bacteria had grown to include the hormone required for growth during childhood, insulin, beta-endorphin (a brain chemical

that suppresses pain), and others. A more distant possibility is the use of genetic engineering to prevent or treat genetic birth defects and diseases or, perhaps, to cultivate certain desirable physical and psychological characteristics in humans.

As a scientific tool, recombinant DNA technology is increasing our understanding of how genes are organized, how they function, and how they are regulated. Scientists may soon be able to identify each of the genes in the human cell and perhaps replace defective genes responsible for hemophilia, sickle-cell anemia, and other disorders.

But some scientists believe that recombinant DNA techniques could lead to future catastrophe. In 1976, the federal government issued a series of extensive guidelines for research in this area. The guidelines emphasized the necessity for rigorous "biological containment" safeguards against the accidental production of dangerous pathogenic (disease-producing) strains of bacteria. For example, *E. coli,* the host organism used in recombinant research, is a harmless inhabitant of the human intestine. But suppose that a highly toxic species of *E. coli* were produced through DNA recombination and escaped from control. Could we have a real-life version of the fictional Andromeda strain? Research is currently being carried out with *E. coli* cells that have been genetically impaired to ensure a short life and minimal chance of survival outside of the laboratory.

The concerns about recombinant DNA research go beyond issues of containment, however. Fears have been expressed of possible long-term evolutionary dangers, the triggering of catastrophic ecological imbalances (see Figure 3.3), military and terrorist uses in biological warfare, and the potential control of human behavior through genetic engineering (Chargoff, 1976; Sinsheimer, 1975). Geneticist Erwin Chargoff, a vocal critic of recombinant methods, says: "My generation, or perhaps the one preceding mine, has been the first to engage, under the leadership of the exact sciences,

"Somehow I was hoping genetic engineering would take a different turn."

(© 1977 BY SIDNEY HARRIS/AMERICAN SCIENTIST MAGAZINE.)

FIGURE 3.3 *Recombinant DNA procedures offer the possibility of developing new as well as familiar life forms.*

in a destructive colonial warfare against nature. The future will curse us for it" (1976, p. 938).

Although some of the immediate dangers forecast by critics proved unfounded, the fact that many events that formerly could be regarded only as acts of God or nature are now the potential product of human decision and intervention ensures that concerns about recombinant DNA research will continue, as well they should. The consequences may ultimately affect us all.

Pandora's box by taking greater control of the evolutionary process? The scientific and political issues that have arisen in the recombinant DNA controversy are described in Frontier 3.1.

Behavior genetics

An individual's heredity influences the process of development through all the stages of life, from single cell to embryo, infant, child, adolescent, adult, and aged person. Many physical traits and virtually all behavioral ones result from some interaction of genetic code (nature) and environmental characteristics (nurture). As we noted earlier, the field of behavior genetics tries to determine the relative influences of genetic and environmental factors on particular behaviors (Henderson, 1982).

REACTION RANGES AND HERITABILITY

Two concepts that relate to the task of specifying the relative influence of heredity and environment are *reaction ranges* and *heritability*. The **reaction range** for a genetically influenced trait is the range of possibilities that the genetic code allows. The environment then determines where the individual will fall within these genetic boundaries (Gottesman, 1974). For example, we know that height is under genetic control. Figure 3.4 shows the reaction ranges for minimum and maximum possible heights in each of four different genotypes. A favorable environment with good nutrition will result in a taller person regardless of genotype, but only within certain upper and lower limits. Genotype A is caused by a gene that produces dwarfism, and the environment can have little effect on height in that case. In contrast, large height differences can occur in genotype D (white males) depending on the environment. Note also that there is overlap in the reaction

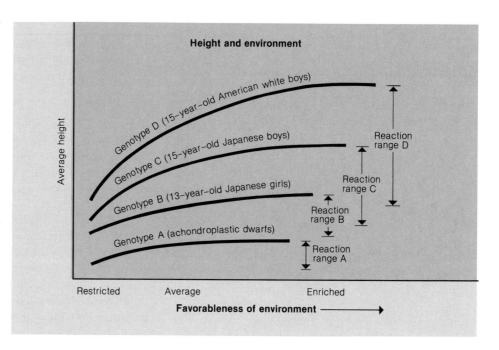

FIGURE 3.4 *Reaction ranges reflect the interaction of genetic potential and environmental factors. Each genotype shown here is affected to different degrees by favorableness of the environment. The widest reaction range occurs for genotype D, the smallest for genotype A (Gottesman, 1974).*

ranges. Therefore, a 13-year-old Japanese girl in the most favorable environment could be taller than a 15-year-old white male from a deprived environment.

When behavior geneticists want to express in mathematical terms the relative amount of variation on a trait due to genetic factors, they often use an index known as **heritability.** Heritability estimates are typically based on comparisons between identical (monozygotic) twins and fraternal (dizygotic) twins in their degree of similarity on the trait in question. Since identical twins have the same genes, they can show no genetic variation. Thus, any differences between identical twins must be due to environmental factors only. Fraternal twins do not have the same genes, so that both heredity and environmental factors contribute to differences between them. This means that if a trait has a genetic basis, the correlations between that trait in identical twins should be higher than in fraternal twins.

The heritability ratio is therefore based on a comparison of the correlation coefficients found in identical and fraternal twins. It can range from 0.0 (no trait variation due to genetic factors) to 1.0 (all variation due

to genetic factors). When identical twins resemble each other on a trait much more than fraternal twins do, the ratio is high. If trait similarities in identical twins are the same as in fraternal twins, the heritability ratio is zero. When similarities are somewhat greater for identicals than fraternals, the ratio is somewhere in between.

Heritability ratios have been calculated for many traits. Intelligence has been the most widely examined psychological trait, and the results of many studies indicate a moderate genetic component in the 0.3 to 0.7 range (Henderson, 1982). It is important to understand, however, that heritability is not something fixed; it is a relative index pertaining to a particular population at a particular time. For this reason, heritability ratios of the same trait sometimes differ widely across different studies. Ironically, heritability is also influenced by the environment itself. As the environment (and, thus, its effects) becomes more uniform, heritability goes up. Theoretically, if everyone lived in exactly the same environment, all trait variation would be due to genetic factors (and heritability would be 1.0). Finally, it is essential to understand that heritability is a *population* estimate. It can never be applied to a given individual. As we saw in our discussion of reaction ranges, the environment and people's genotypes can interact to produce a wide range of responses to environmental factors.

RESEARCH METHODS IN BEHAVIOR GENETICS

Three major approaches—**selective breeding, pedigree analyses,** and **twin studies**—have been used to study the role of genetic factors in behavior.

Behavior geneticists sometimes breed animals that exhibit certain behavioral traits. For example, mice differ in their activity level just as humans do. At the University of Colorado, researchers allowed very active males and females to mate with one another, while animals low in their activity levels were also mated with one another. By the thirtieth generation, a mouse from the high-activity line could scamper the length of a football field in six minutes (probably increasing the interest of many football coaches in behavior genetics), while the low-activity animals remained virtually motionless (Plomin and others, 1980). Animals have been selectively bred for many behavioral factors, including emotionality, learning ability, aggression, sexual activity, and exploratory behavior. Once the strains are established, investigators can search for the biological differences that account for the behavioral differences (Wimer and Wimer, 1985).

Ethical considerations do not permit the use of selective breeding to study human heredity. Two major approaches are used instead: pedigree analysis and twin studies. In pedigree analysis, the investigator identifies an individual who has some characteristic of interest, such as Huntington's disease. The investigator then studies the person's family history and examines the traits of ancestors, descendants, and other relatives (siblings, uncles, aunts). Tracing the family tree may make it possible to identify a particular pattern of inheritance for the characteristic. This approach has some built-in difficulties, most notably, incomplete information. A related method is a **consanguinity study,** which compares the statistical probabilities that a characteristic will occur in close relatives, in distant relatives, and in the general population.

Twin studies are the most frequently used method in psychological analyses of human heredity. One par-

ticularly interesting type of twin study involves identical twins who were separated at an early age and were thus reared in different environments. A large-scale study of this kind is currently being carried out by a University of Minnesota research team headed by Thomas Bouchard (1984).

So far, the team has studied 34 sets of monozygotic twins who were reared apart. Over an 8-day period, the subjects were given a massive battery of tests, including medical histories; physiological tests of brain waves, allergies, heart function, and other reactions; and psychological tests of personality, intelligence, interests, behavior disorders, aptitudes, and values.

Even though they were separated in infancy and were often raised in very different environments, the twins showed surprising similarities over a wide range of personality traits. In fact, these twins were just as similar in aggression, impulse control, introversion-extraversion, and neuroticism as a comparison group of identical twins who were being reared in the same families. Whether they had been reared together or separately, the genetically identical twins were twice as similar as fraternal twins reared together and four to five times more similar than genetically unrelated individuals reared in the same home (for example, parents and adopted children or adopted siblings).

Although many of them had never met before, the twins who were reared apart were highly similar in intelligence, vocational interests and values, emotional styles, and in the kinds of phobias (fears) some of them had. Striking similarities included a pair of British housewives who met each other at the Minneapolis airport, each wearing seven rings, two bracelets on one wrist, and a watch and bracelet on the other. One twin pair suffered suspected heart attacks at the same time; another pair developed diabetes simultaneously. Another pair of men, one raised in Germany and the other in the Caribbean and in Israel, shared a host of unusual behaviors, such as reading magazines from back to front, flushing toilets before using them, and

FIGURE 3.5 *These identical twins separated in infancy were subjects in the Minnesota twins study. The white tree benches each twin built are among the interesting similarities found for many of the twin pairs.*

dipping buttered toast in their coffee. A set of twins who lived in different parts of Ohio and had never met were the only people in their neighborhoods to have built a white bench around a tree in their front yards (see Figure 3.5).

Are some of these strange similarities mere coincidence, or do genes have a subtle influence on the choices that we make among the many alternatives presented by the environment? For example, could having pretty hands and an attraction to sparkling objects combine to produce a fondness for rings? Would we find

similarities like these on a purely chance basis if we simply studied unrelated strangers reared apart?

Some of the differences between the twins were as surprising as the similarities. For example, only one member of a certain twin pair developed a disorder thought to be entirely of genetic origin. This means that the disorder must have an environmental cause as well. Further study of the similarities *and* the differences between the twin pairs may shed more light on the direct and indirect ways in which nature and nurture interact to influence our behavior.

THE NEURAL BASES OF BEHAVIOR

The structures of the nervous system have been of special interest to psychologists because of the key role they play in behavior. The most basic of these structures are the nerve cells, or neurons. These cells form a highly sophisticated network that routes and processes information throughout your body in the form of electrical impulses.

The neuron

Specialized cells called **neurons** are the basic building blocks of your nervous system. At birth, your brain contained about 100 billion neurons (Stevens, 1979). You will never again have that many, for unlike other kinds of body cells, neurons are not replaced when they die. It is estimated that through normal cell death, you lose about 10,000 of them each day.

Like all cells in the body, each neuron is a separate unit within which the vital processes of growth and metabolism occur. The neuron has three main parts: a *soma*, *dendrites*, and an *axon* (see Figure 3.6). The

soma, or cell body, contains a nucleus that regulates the cell's life processes. Small fibers called **dendrites** extend from the soma. The dendrites receive messages from neighboring neurons and conduct them to the soma. Extending from one side of the soma is a single **axon,** which branches at its end to form a number of *axon terminals.* The axon conducts electrical impulses away from the soma to other neurons, muscles, or glands. The axons of many neurons are covered by a sheath of fatty tissue called **myelin.** This myelin sheath is thought to serve as a kind of insulation against the leakage of electrical impulses. Nerve impulses normally move in only one direction—from dendrite to soma (which can also receive impulses from other neurons) to axon. Although a given neuron has only one axon, it may have 1000 or more dendrites that receive nerve impulses from the axons of many other neurons. Thus the number of potential connections among neurons is immense.

All neurons have a soma, dendrites, and an axon, but they can vary greatly in size and shape (see Figure 3.7). A neuron in your spinal cord might have an axon that extends several feet to one of your fingertips; another neuron up in your brain might be no more than a thousandth of an inch long. What you think of as **nerves** running through your body are actually bundles of axons extending from hundreds or even thousands of neurons.

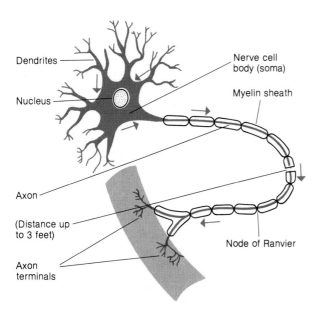

FIGURE 3.6 *The diagram shows the structural elements of a typical neuron. Stimulation received by the dendrites or soma (cell body) may trigger a nerve impulse that travels down the axon to stimulate other neurons, muscles, or glands. Some axons have a fatty myelin sheath interrupted at regular intervals by the nodes of Ranvier. The myelin sheath helps to increase the speed of nerve conduction.*

Dendrites

Nucleus

Axon

(Distance up to 3 feet)

Axon terminals

Nerve cell body (soma)

Myelin sheath

Node of Ranvier

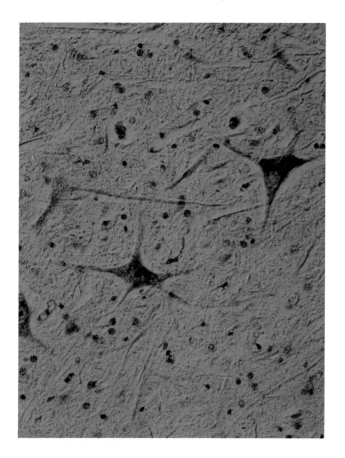

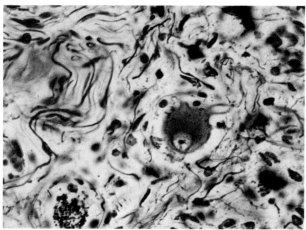

FIGURE 3.7 *As shown in these photographs taken through an electron microscope, neurons can vary widely in their structural characteristics. Despite these differences, however, all neurons have only one cell body and one axon.*

Nerve impulses

Neurons do two things. They generate electricity, and they release chemicals. Nerve conduction is thus an electrochemical process. We have known about the electrical properties of neurons for over a century, but we have only recently begun to learn about the chemical processes involved in neural activity.

How do neurons generate electricity? The answer to this question requires a brief excursion into chemistry. Neurons function like batteries in that their own chemical substances are a source of energy. Like other cells, they are surrounded by a cell membrane. This cell membrane is a bit like a selective sieve that allows certain particles in the body fluid around the cell to pass through, while refusing or limiting passage to other substances.

There is a large difference in the number of posi-

tively and negatively charged atoms, or ions, within the neuron compared to the fluids outside. Inside the membrane wall, there are concentrations of positively charged potassium ions ($K+$) and negatively charged protein molecules. Outside the neuron in the surrounding fluid, there are concentrations of positively charged sodium ions ($Na+$) and negatively charged chloride ions ($Cl-$). In the neuron's normal resting state, the large, negatively charged protein ions are trapped inside the cell. The membrane allows the potassium and chloride ions to flow in and out of the cell freely. The overall effect of this uneven distribution of ions is that the inside of the cell is electrically negative compared to the outside by about 70 millivolts, or 70/1000 of a volt. This is called the **resting potential**. In some animals this tiny voltage forms the basis for specialized organs that generate very high voltages. For example, electric eels can generate 600 to 700 volts because the cell membranes of their muscle tissue are arranged so that the tiny individual cell voltages add together to equal one big jolt.

All cells in the body also have this resting voltage. However, neurons and muscle cells have a unique property: sudden and extreme changes can occur in the voltage. A **nerve impulse** is nothing more than a sudden reversal in the membrane voltage of the neuron, during which the membrane voltage momentarily moves from −70 millivolts (inside) to +40 millivolts (see Figure 3.8).

What causes this sudden reversal? Through a sophisticated series of experiments that won them the Nobel Prize, British scientists A. L. Hodgkin and A. F. Huxley provided the answer. Recall that when the cell is resting, positively charged sodium ions are kept outside the cell. During an impulse, however, **sodium channels** in the axon membrane open for an instant and sodium ions flood into the interior of the cell. Because they are positively charged, the sodium ions cause the interior of the cell to become more positive than the outside. This change in polarity, called the **action potential,** starts a chain reaction and causes the "sodium gate" to open at adjacent membrane sites. In a reflex action to restore the resting polarity, the cell quickly closes the sodium channels and opens its **potassium channels.** Positively charged potassium ions flow out through the membrane, restoring the cell's negative resting potential (Stevens, 1979). Figure 3.8 shows this sequence of events.

Once the electrical impulse is started at any point on the membrane, it travels down the full length of the axon in bucket-brigade fashion. Immediately after an impulse passes a point along the axon, there is a recovery period, lasting a few thousandths of a second, during which the membrane is not excitable and cannot discharge another impulse. This is called a **refractory**

period, and it places an upper limit on the rate at which impulses can be triggered in a neuron. In humans the limit seems to be about 300 impulses per second (Tortora and Anagnostakos, 1984).

Some axons that have insulating myelin sheaths can flash impulses at speeds greater than 200 miles an hour. The myelin sheath is interrupted at regular intervals by the **nodes of Ranvier,** where the myelin is either extremely thin or absent (see Figure 3.6). In myelin-

FIGURE 3.8 *The nerve impulse is a product of changes in electrical potential. The axon membrane separates fluids that differ greatly in their concentration of sodium (Na+) and potassium (K+) ions. Because of this, the inside of the fiber is normally about 70 millivolts negative to the exterior during its resting potential. The movement of a nerve impulse along an axon involves the opening of a "sodium gate" that allows positively charged sodium ions to flow into the cell, reversing the polarity and creating the action potential. An instant later the sodium channel closes and the potassium channel opens. The outflow of K+ ions restores the negative potential. After a brief refractory period another impulse can follow.*

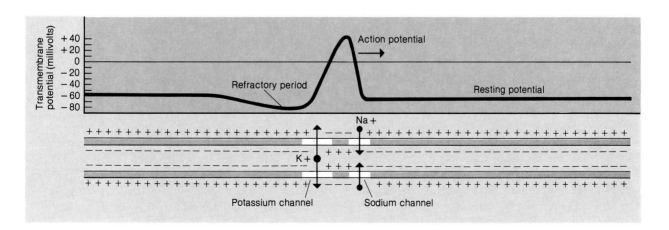

ated fibers, electrical conduction can skip from node to node rather than having to travel along the entire axon, and these "great leaps" from one gap to another account for the high conduction speeds. The myelin sheath, which occurred late in the evolutionary process, is characteristic of the nervous systems of higher animals. In many nerve fibers of the human brain, the myelin sheath is not completely formed until some time after birth. This may be one reason why some of our sensory and motor abilities mature so slowly (Black, 1984).

The tragic effects of damage to the myelin coating can be seen in people who suffer from multiple sclerosis. This progressive disease of the myelin sheath disrupts the delicate timing of nerve impulses, resulting in jerky, uncoordinated movements and, in its final stages, paralysis.

Synaptic transmission

The action of the nervous system requires the transmission of nerve impulses from one neuron to another. The complex connections between neurons are not physical in nature; axon terminals seldom actually touch the dendrites or soma of other neurons in the communications chain. Instead, there is a small space between the axon terminal and the next neuron. This space is known as the **synapse.**

Events that occur at the synapses determine whether or not neurons will fire. When the dendrites or the soma is stimulated by other nerve cells, small shifts occur in the electrical potential of the cell membrane. These shifts, called **graded potentials,** are proportional to the amount and kind of incoming activity. If the graded potential is large enough to reach the required level of intensity, called the **action potential threshold,** the neuron discharges with an action potential. If the graded potential is not strong enough, the neuron simply does not fire. But once an individual neuron fires, its action potential proceeds in an all-or-none fashion. In this sense, activating a nerve cell is like firing a gun. Unless a certain amount of energy is applied to the trigger, the gun will not fire; once it does fire, however, the velocity of the bullet bears no relation to how hard the trigger was pulled.

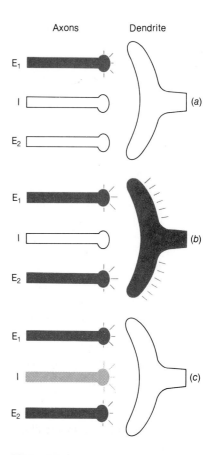

FIGURE 3.9 *Excitatory and inhibitory influences interact to affect neural transmission. In this instance, three axons—two excitatory (E_1 and E_2) and one inhibitory (I)—can stimulate the dendrite with their specific neurotransmitters. Stimulation by E_1 alone (a) is not sufficient to fire the postsynaptic neuron; simultaneous stimulation by E_1 and E_2 is required (b). However, if the inhibitory neuron stimulates the dendrite at the same time as E_1 and E_2, the postsynaptic neuron will not fire (c). The interaction of inhibitory and excitatory influences makes possible an exquisite fine tuning of neural activity.*

The synaptic activity of some neurons serves to inhibit rather than excite the firing of other neurons. This process of *inhibition* prevents a runaway discharge of the nervous system, such as occurs in epileptic seizures. Certain drugs, such as strychnine, block inhibition and produce this very effect—massive discharges of neurons and electrochemical disruption of life-serving functions.

Virtually every neuron is constantly being bombarded with excitatory and inhibitory influences from other neurons, and the interplay of all these influences determines whether or not the cell fires (see Figure 3.9). An exquisite balance between excitatory and inhibitory processes must be maintained if the nervous system is to function properly. This is why drugs that disrupt this balance can have such striking effects on consciousness and behavior.

Neurotransmitters

As we have noted, the transmission of nerve impulses is an electrochemical process. In most instances, a nerve impulse does not physically "jump" across the synaptic space and directly stimulate the next neuron. Instead, the impulse triggers the release of chemical molecules known as **neurotransmitters,** which are stored in **synaptic vesicles** in the axon terminals. When the transmitter molecules are released, they travel rapidly across the fluid-filled space between the axon of the sending (presynaptic) neuron and the membrane of the receiving (postsynaptic) neuron's dendrite or soma. There they bind or attach themselves to specific receptor sites, which are actually large protein molecules embedded in the receiving neuron's semiliquid cell membrane. A region on the surface of the receptor site is precisely tailored to match the shape of the transmitter molecule, which fits into the proper receptor with the precision of a key entering a lock. A chemical reaction between the neurotransmitter and the receptor site produces the graded potential that, alone or in combination with other excitatory synapses, may cause the receiving neuron to fire (Hanin, 1984). On the other hand, if the presynaptic neuron is an inhibitory one, the chemical reaction that results when its neurotransmitter finds an appropriate receptor site will inhibit the firing of the postsynaptic neuron (see Figure 3.10).

Once a transmitter molecule binds to its receptor, it will keep activating or inhibiting unless it is shut off or deactivated. This must be done quickly; for example, in neurons that fire several hundred impulses per sec-

ond, the membrane must recover its resting potential in a fraction of a millisecond. The transmitter molecule can be deactivated in several ways. Some transmitter substances are destroyed almost immediately by other chemicals located in the synaptic space. In other cases, the transmitter molecules are rapidly pumped back into the presynaptic axon terminal, where they are

FIGURE 3.10 *A synapse between two neurons. An action potential travels to the axon terminals, where it stimulates the secretion of transmitter molecules from the synaptic vesicles. The transmitter molecules travel across the synapse and bind to a specially keyed receptor site on a dendrite of the postsynaptic neuron. The resulting chemical reaction produces a graded potential in the dendrite. The transmitter molecules are then destroyed by other substances or taken back into the presynaptic neuron to be destroyed or recycled.*

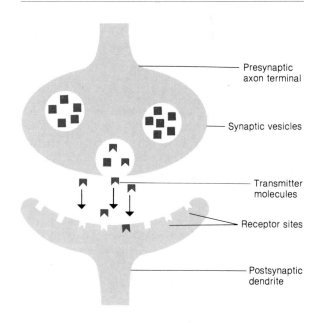

Presynaptic axon terminal

Synaptic vesicles

Transmitter molecules

Receptor sites

Postsynaptic dendrite

either destroyed or recycled back into the synaptic vesicles for future transmissions.

Some 30 or so different substances are known or suspected transmitters in the brain, and each has a specific excitatory or inhibitory effect on certain neurons (Tilson and Mitchell, 1984). Perhaps the best understood neurotransmitter is **acetylcholine** (ACh), which is known to be the excitatory transmitter where neurons activate muscle cells, as well as in various brain regions that are believed to be involved in memory (Bloom and others, 1984). Drugs that block the action of ACh can result in fatal muscular paralysis. *Curare*, a drug used by South American Indians to poison their arrows, prevents ACh from acting because its molecules cover up the postsynaptic receptor sites on the muscle cell. The muscle is temporarily unable to respond to nerve impulses, resulting in a deadly paralysis of the muscles, including those involved in breathing. A different but equally deadly kind of blocking action is performed at ACh synapses in *botulism*, a serious type of food poisoning. The toxin formed by the botulinum bacteria appears to block the release of ACh from the axon terminal, resulting again in a paralysis of the muscles, including those of the respiratory system.

Solving the mysteries of synaptic transmission may be the key to understanding the physical bases of learning, memory, emotion, and motivation. For example, learning and memory most certainly involve changes in interactions among neurons. Because the most significant neuronal interactions occur at the synapse, it is quite likely that these psychological processes reflect changes in chemical synaptic transmission (Lynch and Baudry, 1984). In Chapter 6, we will discuss new findings in this area.

Because they exist in such small quantities and are active for only an instant at a time, neurotransmitters are hard to identify and study. One recent technical advance that has considerable promise uses the recombinant DNA techniques discussed earlier (Frontier 3.1). In this method, chemists isolate molecules in the brain that appear to be transmitter substances. Then they collect tiny extracts, purify them, and inject their genetic DNA material into *E. coli* bacteria, which produce larger quantities of the substances. The cloned, or duplicated, molecules are marked with phosporus-32, a radioactive substance, and mixed with extracts from various parts of the brain to see which regions the molecules will bind to. In this way, it is possible to tell where in the brain the particular molecule belongs and to study how it affects synaptic transmission (Bloom and others, 1984).

The language of neural communication

All your experiences, thoughts, and behaviors are the result of complex communication patterns among your neurons. How does such communication occur?

Your nervous system has three basic ways of coding information for transmission. First, we know that neurons are spontaneously active, firing impulses at characteristic intervals known as their *base rate*. One way a neuron can signal that something is happening is by increasing or decreasing its rate of firing above or below its base rate; the size of the increase or decrease provides additional information. For example, a neuron that transmits information about pressure would show a larger increase in rate of firing when you are carrying a television set than when you are carrying a cup of coffee. A second way in which information is coded is the *number* of neurons that fire. Using the same example, carrying the television set would cause more individual neurons to fire than lifting the cup of coffee.

The fact that many neurons have specialized functions and are normally responsive to only certain kinds of stimulation is the basis for the third type of coding. We know, for example, that certain neurons in the visual system respond only to certain colors, brightnesses, or shapes. In addition, the nervous system is arranged so that particular groups of neurons transmit messages to particular areas of the brain. The language of the nervous system thus consists basically of the relationship between the rate of firing of individual neurons and their base rate of firing, the number of neurons that fire, and the particular neurons that are responding.

We have described some of the basic structures and processes that underlie the functioning of the nervous system; let us now consider its organization and the complex role it plays in our consciousness and behavior.

THE CENTRAL NERVOUS SYSTEM

The nervous system consists of three kinds of neurons that carry out the system's *input, integration,* and *output* functions. **Afferent** (sensory) **neurons** carry input messages from the sense organs to the spinal cord and brain. **Efferent** (motor) **neurons** transmit output impulses from the brain and spinal cord to the muscles and organs of the body. **Interneurons** perform a connective or associative function within the nervous system.

Although the parts of the nervous system are highly interrelated, they may be broken down into a number of subsystems (see Figure 3.11). The two major divisions are the *central nervous system* (all the neurons in the brain and spinal cord) and the *peripheral nervous system* (all the neurons that connect the central ner-

FIGURE 3.11 *Structural organization of the nervous system.*

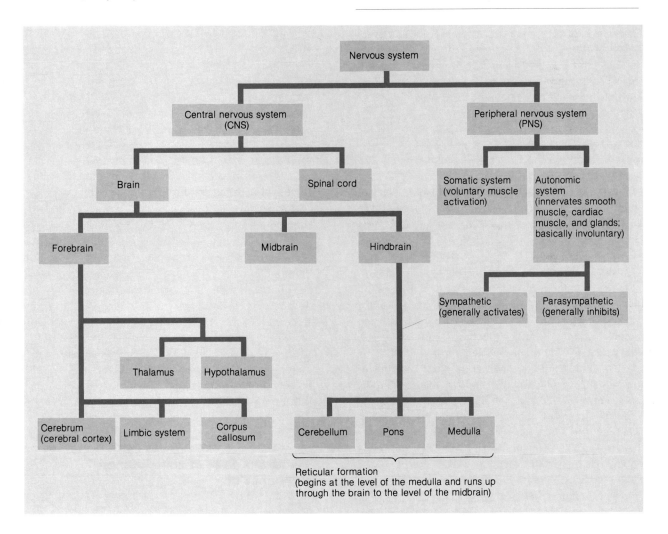

vous system with the muscles, glands, and sensory receptors). The peripheral nervous system may be further subdivided into the *somatic system*, which provides input from the sensory system and output to the skeletal muscles responsible for voluntary movement, and the *autonomic nervous system*, which directs the activities of the glands and internal organs of the body. (The autonomic system plays a critical role in emotional behavior and is discussed in greater detail later.)

The central nervous system is the body's master control center. It consists of increasingly complex structures that appear as we move up the phylogenetic scale. Some relatively simple processes, such as your knee-jerk reflex, can be performed at the level of the spinal cord and don't involve the brain at all. In most instances, however, the input-integration-output functions involve several levels of the brain. The higher mental processes that distinguish us from lower animals take place within the most recently evolved portion of the brain, the cerebral cortex.

The spinal cord

Most nerves enter and leave the central nervous system by way of the spinal cord, where they are protected by the vertebrae (bones of the spine). When the spinal cord is viewed in cross section (Figure 3.12), its central portion resembles an H. The H-shaped portion is **gray matter,** which consists largely of gray-colored neuron cell bodies and their interconnections. Surrounding the gray matter is the **white matter,** composed almost entirely of white-colored myelinated axons that serve to connect various levels of the spinal cord with each other and with the higher centers of the brain.

Emerging from both sides at the front and back of the spinal cord all along its length are the **dorsal roots** and **ventral roots.** The dorsal root on the back side consists of sensory nerves; the ventral roots contain motor nerves. Once they have left the dorsal and ventral roots, most nerve bundles contain both sensory and motor nerves and are therefore called *mixed* nerves.

Some very simple stimulus-response sequences, known as *spinal reflexes*, can be carried out at the level of the spinal cord. We have already mentioned the knee-jerk reflex. As another example, if you touch

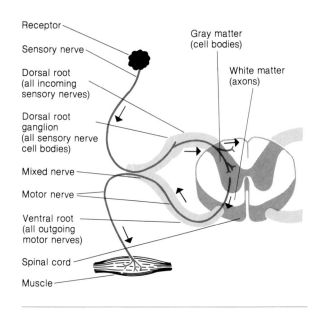

FIGURE 3.12 *A cross section of the spinal cord shows the organization of the sensory and motor nerves. Sensory nerves enter the spinal cord on both sides of the spinal column through the dorsal roots; motor nerves exit through the ventral roots. Primitive reflex activity is possible at this level of the nervous system.*

something hot, sensory receptors in your skin trigger nerve impulses that enter your spinal cord through the dorsal root and synapse with the interneurons in the cord's gray matter. These, in turn, excite motor neurons in the ventral root so that your hand jerks away. The sensory neurons have also synapsed with other neurons that carry the messages about all this to your brain, but it is fortunate that we don't have to wait for the brain to tell us what to do in emergencies like this. Getting messages to and from the brain takes slightly longer, so our spinal cord reflex system cuts our reaction time significantly.

The brain: Seat of consciousness and behavior

The three pounds of protein, fat, and water that you carry around inside your head is the most complex structure in the known universe. As befits this biological marvel, your brain is the most active energy consumer of all your bodily organs. Although it accounts for only about 2 percent of your total body weight, your brain consumes about 20 percent of the oxygen you use in a resting state (Iversen, 1979). Moreover, the brain never rests; its rate of energy metabolism is relatively constant day and night. In fact, when you dream, the brain's metabolic rate actually increases slightly.

The human brain (shown in Figure 3.13) consists of three major divisions: the *hindbrain*, which is the lowest and most primitive level of the brain; the *midbrain*, which lies above the hindbrain; and the

forebrain, which contains the cerebrum, the biological seat of Socrates's wisdom, Einstein's creativity, Hitler's mad vision of world conquest, and everything that makes you a unique human being.

The hindbrain

As the spinal cord enters the brain, it enlarges to form the medulla and the pons, the structures that comprise the **brain stem.** Attached to the brain stem is the other major portion of the hindbrain, the cerebellum. Buried within the stem is the reticular formation, which extends from the hindbrain through the midbrain into the forebrain.

THE MEDULLA AND PONS: SEAT OF VITAL FUNCTIONS

The **medulla** is the lowest structure in the primitive brain stem. But this inch-and-a-half-long structure plays an all-important role in vital bodily functions such as heart rate and respiration. The medulla also contains all the sensory and motor nerve tracts coming up from the spinal cord and descending from the brain. Most of these tracts cross over at the medulla, so that the left side of the brain receives sensory input from and exerts motor control over the right side of the body, and the right side of the brain receives sensory input from and controls the left side of the body.

The **pons** (meaning "bridge" in Latin) lies just

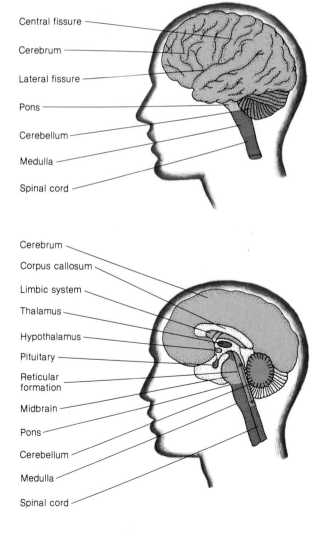

Central fissure
Cerebrum
Lateral fissure
Pons
Cerebellum
Medulla
Spinal cord

Cerebrum
Corpus callosum
Limbic system
Thalamus
Hypothalamus
Pituitary
Reticular formation
Midbrain
Pons
Cerebellum
Medulla
Spinal cord

FIGURE 3.13 *The drawing at the top shows the surface of the brain as it would appear if the skull were transparent. The drawing at the bottom shows the interior of the brain as it would appear if it were cut in half from its top to its bottom.*

85

above the medulla. As its name suggests, it serves as a bridge between higher and lower levels of the nervous system. It also contains motor neurons that control the muscles and glands of the face and neck. Like the medulla, the pons helps to control vital functions, especially respiration.

Because the brain stem structures play a major role in our basic functions, damage to them can be fatal. The tragic physical and psychological consequences of brain stem damage are seen in the following case:

Cleveland Denny, hovering near death with brain damage, has his "vital signs deteriorating rapidly. It's just a matter of time, a very short time" said Lynwood Farr of Montreal, a friend and adviser to the Denny family. Denny, 24, was in a coma in Montreal's Maisonneuve-Rosemount hospital where doctors said Friday Denny's brain activity had ceased completely. His brain stem was knocked out of place by a blow June 20 from the Canadian lightweight champion, Gaetan Hart, during a match in Montreal. Denny's family refused to permit switching off the life-support systems that keep Denny's heart beating. Doctors said removal of the respirator would bring on death within 20 minutes to an hour. "They just can't bring themselves to disconnect the respirator," Farr said. Denny's mother, Mrs. Dorothy Denny of New York, and his wife Clarine, 24, mother of their five-month-old son, Cleveland, Jr., were at his bedside. (UPI, July 6, 1980)

The next day, despite the continued use of the life-support systems, Cleveland Denny died.

THE RETICULAR FORMATION: SENTRY OF THE BRAIN

Buried within the brain stem is the **reticular formation,** a complex mixture of nerve fibers and cell bodies extending from the medulla up into the midbrain. It receives its name from its structural resemblance to a reticulum, or net. The reticular formation has an ascending part, which sends input to higher regions of the brain, and a descending portion through which higher brain centers can admit or block out sensory input.

The reticular formation has attracted a great deal of interest from psychologists because of its central role in consciousness, attention, and sleep. The ascending reticular formation acts as a general arousal center that activates the rest of the brain and somehow prepares it

to receive input from our sense organs (see Figure 3.14). Without reticular excitation, sensory messages do not register in consciousness, even though the nerve impulses reach the appropriate higher areas of the brain. Some general anesthetics work by deactivating neurons of the reticular formation so that the person is unaware of the sensory impulses that would ordinarily be experienced as pain (Tilson and Mitchell, 1984).

Sleep and wakefulness are also affected by the reticular formation. The application of particular kinds of electrical stimulation to the reticular formation can produce sleep in a wakeful animal and wakefulness in a sleeping animal. As in the case of the injured boxer, severe damage to the reticular formation can produce a permanent coma.

The reticular formation is known to play an important role in attention. Attention is an active process in which only certain sensory inputs get through to our consciousness; others are toned down or completely blocked out. It appears that the descending reticular

---

FIGURE 3.14 *Extending from the brain stem up into the midbrain, the reticular formation acts as a kind of sentry. Its ascending portion, shown here, alerts higher regions of the brain to incoming stimuli. Through its descending portion, incoming stimuli can be blocked from affecting cortical regions, as occurs when we are attending to something and other stimuli do not "register."*

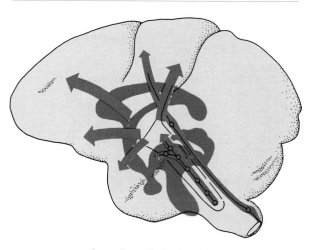

Ascending reticular formation

formation plays an important part in this process, serving as a kind of gate through which some inputs are admitted while others are not.

THE CEREBELLUM: MOTOR COORDINATION CENTER

The **cerebellum** is attached to the rear of the brain stem directly above the pons. It is covered by a wrinkled, or convoluted, cortex having a large number of lobes ("hills") separated by fissures ("canyons"). This covering consists mainly of gray cell bodies ("gray matter"). Buried at the center of the cerebellum are collections of neuron cell bodies that are concerned primarily with motor coordination. Specific motor movements are initiated in higher brain centers, but their timing and coordination depend on the cerebellum.

Damage to the cerebellum results, among other things, in severe motor disturbances characterized by jerky, uncoordinated movements and by an inability to perform habitual movements such as walking. The behavioral effects of damage to the cerebellum are apparent in the following case:

After his retirement, Ed tended bar at a neighborhood watering hole that he had long frequented as a customer. He enjoyed nothing more than drinking and spinning yarns with his cronies. No one was particularly concerned when one day he complained of a severe headache in the back of his head. But the pain continued well into the next day. By the third day, Ed could no longer walk a straight line. His gait involved wide separation of his legs. The timing of his steps was jerky and irregular, causing him to lurch from side to side. He could no longer manage changes in position smoothly, and turning or rising from a chair caused him to nearly fall. By the fifth day he could no longer stand without assistance. The pounding headache was still present and he began to display rapid and jerky eye movements.

All of Ed's symptoms pointed to a disorder of the cerebellum. He was hospitalized and underwent a diagnostic procedure known as a brain scan. A mildly radioactive substance was injected intravenously into the blood supply going to his brain. X-rays were then taken to see if any areas of his brain took up large concentrations of the substance. Tumors do so and are frequently located in this manner. As expected, a mass was found in Ed's cerebellum and subsequent surgery led to its removal. A month of hospitalization was required, but Ed was able to return

to work. His walking improved dramatically, but perhaps most importantly to Ed, "he could set the glass of ale to his mouth without spilling a drop." (Gazzaniga and others, 1979, p. 59)

The midbrain

The midbrain, which lies just above the hindbrain, contains a number of important clusters of sensory and motor neurons, as well as many sensory and motor fiber tracts connecting higher and lower portions of the nervous system. The sensory portion of the midbrain contains important relay centers in the visual and auditory systems. The midbrain also contains motor neurons that control eye movement. Extending well into the core of the midbrain is the upper portion of the reticular formation.

The forebrain

The most profound biological difference between your brain and the brain of lower animals is the size and complexity of your forebrain, particularly your cerebral cortex. The forebrain consists of two large cerebral hemispheres that envelop the brain stem, as well as a number of very important structures buried in the central regions of the hemispheres. We consider these inner structures first.

THE THALAMUS: THE BRAIN'S SWITCHBOARD

The **thalamus** is located above the midbrain. In appearance it resembles two small footballs, one within each cerebral hemisphere. The thalamus is an important sensory relay station and has sometimes been compared to a giant switchboard that routes sensory inputs to the appropriate areas of the brain. The visual, auditory, and body senses all have major relay stations in the thalamus.

THE HYPOTHALAMUS: MOTIVATION AND EMOTION

The **hypothalamus** consists of tiny groups of neuron cell bodies that lie at the base of the brain, above the roof of the mouth. This small structure plays an enormously important role in many aspects of motivational and emotional behavior, including sexual behavior, temperature regulation, sleeping, eating, drinking, aggression, and the expression of emotion. Through its connection with the pituitary gland, the master gland of the endocrine system, the hypothalamus exerts direct control over many hormonal secretions that regulate sexual development and sexual behavior, metabolism, and reactions to stress. (We'll consider the endocrine system later in the chapter.)

THE LIMBIC SYSTEM: LEARNING AND ORGANIZATION OF BEHAVIOR

The **limbic system** is comprised of a number of structures lying deep within the cerebral hemispheres. Shaped like a wishbone, these structures encircle the brain stem. The limbic system has many neural interconnections with the hypothalamus and seems to be involved in organizing the activities needed to satisfy the basic motivational and emotional needs that the hypothalamus regulates. If certain parts of your limbic system were injured, you would be unable to carry out the organized sequences of actions required for need satisfaction. A small distraction would make you forget what you had set out to do. Many activities that are instinctive in lower animals, such as fleeing from danger, mating, attacking, and feeding, appear to be governed by the limbic system. One of its structures, the **hippocampus,** seems to be a brain region where learning occurs (Thompson and others, 1983).

The limbic system is also deeply involved in emotional behavior, particularly aggression. Lesions (injuries) in certain areas of the limbic system produce extreme rage reactions to the slightest provocation, whereas damage to other areas results in an inability to respond aggressively, even in self-defense. Texas mass murderer Charles Whitman was found to have a large tumor in the limbic system, and some neurologists suggested that this may have played a significant role in his murderous outburst (see Chapter 1).

Finally, there are reward and punishment centers in the limbic system, as well as in other brain regions. When these areas are stimulated with mild electric currents, animals will learn and perform behaviors in order to gain their electrical reward, and they will learn to stop performing behaviors that are followed by stimulation of one of the punishment regions (Olds and Olds, 1965).

THE CEREBRAL HEMISPHERES: CROWN OF THE BRAIN

The two cerebral hemispheres constitute the largest part of the human brain. They consist of an outer gray cortex composed primarily of neuron cell bodies and unmyelinated fibers and an internal white core of myelinated fibers that connect the hemispheres with each other and with other parts of the brain.

The cerebral cortex is the crowning achievement of brain evolution. Fish and amphibians have no cerebral cortex, and the progression from more primitive to more advanced mammals is marked by a dramatic increase in the proportion of cortex compared to the total amount of brain tissue. The study of people who were born without a cerebral cortex gives us an idea of how much of our humanness depends on this sheet of gray matter:

Some of these individuals may survive for years, in one case of mine for twenty years. In them, the cerebral cortex is absent or has virtually disappeared, and the brain-stem and sometimes the thalamus remain relatively intact. From these cases, it appears that the human brain-stem and thalamic "preparation" sleeps and wakes; it reacts to hunger, loud sounds, and crude visual stimuli by movement of eyes, eyelids, and facial muscles; it may see and hear, it may be able to taste and smell, to reject the unpalatable and accept such food as it likes; it can itself utter crude sounds, can cry and smile, showing displeasure when hungry and pleasure, in a babyish way, when being sung to; it may be able to perform spontaneously crude movements of its limbs. (Cairns, 1952, p. 109)

Thus, the cerebral cortex is not essential for survival in the way that the brain stem structures are, but it is essential for life as a human being.

Most sensory systems send information to specific

regions of the cortex. Motor systems that control the activity of muscles and glands are situated in other cortical regions. The basic organization of the sensory and motor areas of the cortex is quite similar from rat to human. However, the relative proportion of **association cortex,** which is made up of neurons that are neither sensory nor motor but are believed to be involved in higher and more complex behavioral functions, increases dramatically from lower animals to humans.

A tremendous amount of cortical tissue is compressed into a relatively small space inside the skull. This is possible because the cortex is wrinkled and convoluted like a wadded-up piece of paper. It is estimated that more than three-quarters of the total amount of cerebral cortex lies within its folds, or *fissures.*

Two of the fissures serve as major landmarks. The *central fissure* divides the cerebrum into anterior (front) and posterior (rear) halves, and the *lateral fissure* runs in a front-to-rear fashion along the side of the brain (see Figure 3.15). Each hemisphere is divided into four lobes: *frontal, parietal, occipital,* and *temporal.* The frontal lobe is separated from the parietal lobe by the central fissure, the temporal lobe lies beneath the lateral fissure, and the occipital lobe is at the rear of the brain.

Each of the four cerebral lobes is involved in particular sensory and motor functions (also shown in Figure 3.15). Speech and skeletal motor functions are localized in the frontal lobe. The body sense area is located in the parietal lobe immediately behind the central fissure. Messages from the auditory system are sent to a region in the top portion of the temporal lobe, and the visual area of the brain is located in the occipital lobe. The noncolored areas in Figure 3.15 that seem to be neither sensory nor motor in function are the association areas.

FIGURE 3.15 *The drawing at the top shows the division of the human cerebral cortex into frontal, parietal, occipital, and temporal lobes. The drawing at the bottom shows the localization of certain functions in the cortex. The rest of the cortex is primarily association cortex, consisting of interneurons.*

THE MOTOR CORTEX

The motor area, which controls bodily movements, lies in the frontal lobe just in front of the central fissure. Each hemisphere governs movement on the opposite side of the body. That is, movements on the right side of the body originate in the motor area of the left hemisphere, while movements on the left side originate in the right hemisphere. Specific body areas are represented in different parts of the motor cortex, and the amount of cortex devoted to each area depends on

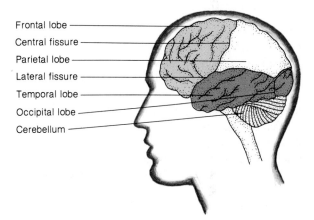

Frontal lobe
Central fissure
Parietal lobe
Lateral fissure
Temporal lobe
Occipital lobe
Cerebellum

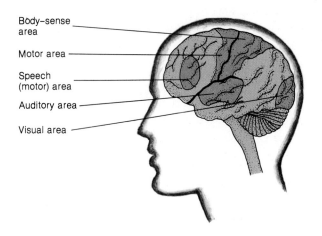

Body-sense area
Motor area
Speech (motor) area
Auditory area
Visual area

the complexity of the movements that are involved. The right side of Figure 3.16 shows the relative organization of function within the motor cortex.

We have been able to draw these "maps" by studying how people behave in response to electrical stimulation or injury. Electrical stimulation of the motor cortex results in muscle movements in the extremities represented by that part of the cortex. Injury to these motor cortex areas results in at least temporary paralysis of the same extremities. Usually, there is some recovery over time as other areas of the brain concerned with movement take over the functions of the motor cortex.

THE SENSORY CORTEX

Input from each of the sensory systems terminates in particular regions of the cortex known as **cortical projection areas.** With the exception of taste and smell, at least one projection area in the cortex has been identified for each of the senses.

The projection areas for heat, touch, cold, and sense of balance and movement lie in the parietal lobe immediately behind the central fissure. Each side of the body projects to the opposite hemisphere. As in the case of the motor area, this somatic sensory area is basically organized in an upside-down fashion, and the amount of cortex devoted to each body area is directly proportional to the sensitivity of that region. The organization of the sensory cortex is shown on the left side of Figure 3.16. As far as our sensory cortex is concerned, we are mainly fingers, lips, and tongue.

The auditory area lies on the surface of the temporal lobe at the side of each hemisphere. Both ears send impulses to the auditory areas of both hemispheres, so that the loss of one temporal lobe has very little effect on hearing. The sensory projection area for vision lies

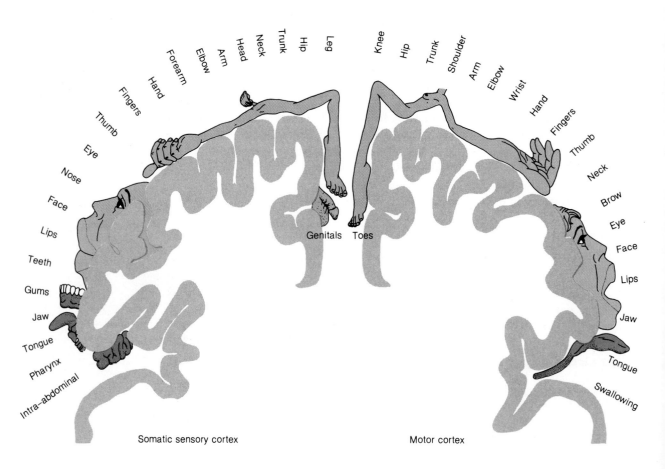

Somatic sensory cortex   Motor cortex

at the rear of the occipital lobe. Here messages from the visual receptors are analyzed, integrated, and translated into sight. As in the auditory system, both eyes send input to both hemispheres, although only one side of the visual field is represented in each hemisphere.

The sensory cortex is organized so that stimulation of a particular point on the skin, the retina, or any other sense organ will activate a particular point in the cortex. Conversely, electrical stimulation of a particular point in the sensory cortex can give rise to a particular sensory experience as if it were occurring through the sensory receptors.

In addition to this point-to-point connection between sensory receptor areas and the cortex, we know that within each sensory area are cells that respond to particular aspects of the sensory stimulus. Certain cells in the visual cortex, for example, fire only when a subject looks at a particular kind of stimulus, such as a vertical line (Hubel and Wiesel, 1979). In the auditory cortex, certain neurons fire only in response to high tones, while others respond only to tones having some other specific frequency. Some of these single-cell responses are present at birth, suggesting that we are "prewired" to perceive many aspects of our sensory environment.

ASSOCIATION CORTEX

The association cortex covers the largest area of the cerebral hemisphere. Association areas are known to be critically involved in perception, language, and

FIGURE 3.16 *The somatic sensory cortex and the motor cortex are highly specialized so that every site is associated with some specific part of the body. The amount of cortex devoted to each part of the body is proportional to the sensitivity of the motor or sensory functions in that area. As the distorted body parts indicate, in humans the amount of motor and sensory cortex devoted to the face and hands is greatly exaggerated. Only half of each cortical region is shown: the left somatic sensory cortex, which receives sensations primarily from the right side of the body, and the right motor cortex, which exercises control over movement in the left half of the body.*

thought. Damage to the association cortex causes disruption or loss of higher functions, such as speech, understanding, thinking, and problem solving. Physiological psychologists are doing extensive research to find out what kinds of electrical and chemical events occur in the association areas during the exercise of our higher mental functions.

The crucial role of the association cortex in complex cognitive behaviors is seen in the case of a young man who developed a severe impairment in memory for recent events after a temporal lobe operation for epilepsy:

He could no longer recognize the hospital staff, apart from Dr. Scoville himself, whom he had known for many years; he did not remember and could not relearn the way to the bathroom, and he seemed to retain nothing of the day-to-day happenings in the hospital. . . .Although he mows the lawn regularly, and quite expertly, his mother has to tell him where to find the lawnmower, even when he had been using it the day before. The same forgetfulness applies to people he has met since the operation, even to those neighbors who have been visiting the house regularly for the past six years. He does not recognize any of them if he meets them in the street. (Milner, 1966, p. 113)

THE FRONTAL LOBES: THE HUMAN DIFFERENCE

In the 1920s, a prominent neurologist suggested that the entire period of human evolutionary existence could be considered the "age of the frontal lobe." This mass of cortex behind our eyes and forehead barely exists in mammals like mice and rats. The frontal lobes comprise about 3.5 percent of the cerebral cortex of cats, 7 percent in the dog, and an impressive 17 percent in the chimpanzee. In humans, the frontal lobes include 29 percent of the cortex (see Figure 3.17). Though probably the most "human" part of the brain and the site of such human qualities as self-awareness, planning, initiative, and responsibility, the frontal lobes are in many respects the most mysterious and least understood.

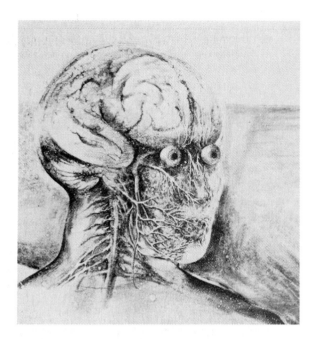

FIGURE 3.17 *The frontal lobes (behind and above the eyes) may be the seat of many functions that define our human nature.*

Much of what we know about the silent recesses of the frontal lobes comes from detailed studies of patients with brain damage in this area. Such people often cannot carry out tasks, even when they can verbalize what they should do. It is as if will is separated from action. Frontal lobe damage also seems to result in an inability to plan and carry out a sequence of actions, as well as difficulty in correcting actions that are clearly erroneous and self-defeating. Attitudes of apathy, unconcern, and denial of difficulties often compound these problems (Stuss and Benson, 1984). These observations suggest that the frontal lobes contain the internal programming functions that make human behavior willful and purposeful, an important feature of our humanness.

HEMISPHERIC LOCALIZATION: THE LEFT AND RIGHT BRAINS

The cerebral hemispheres are connected by a broad band of nerve fibers called the **corpus callosum,** which acts as a communication link and allows the two hemispheres to function as a single unit. However, both clinical observations and research studies indicate that there are dramatic differences between the psychological functions of the two cerebral hemispheres.

Evidence that certain complex psychological functions are localized within one or the other of the hemispheres comes from medical studies of patients who have suffered various types of brain damage. Clinical observations indicate that verbal abilities and speech are localized in the left hemisphere, as are mathematical and symbolic abilities. Damage to certain areas of the left hemisphere in a right-handed person abolishes the ability to speak or understand language. The speech centers for left-handed people are sometimes located in the right hemisphere, but many left-handed people have speech centers in the left hemisphere—see Table 3.2. In these left-handers, as well as right-handers, damage to corresponding parts of the right hemisphere has no effect on language. However, damage to the right hemisphere results in great difficulty in performing certain spatial tasks. The person may be unable to understand complex pictures and may even forget a well-traveled route (Springer and Deutsch, 1985).

Aphasia One disturbance of brain function that neuropsychologists are especially interested in is **aphasia,** the partial or total loss of the ability to communicate. There are perhaps one million aphasics in the United States.

There are two broad types of aphasia. A person with *receptive aphasia* has lost the ability to understand the meaning of words or the use of objects. People with *motor aphasia,* on the other hand, are able to understand language but cannot use it to express themselves. Receptive aphasia is usually caused by damage to temporal and parietal areas that seem to be storage sites for auditory memories for words. Motor aphasia results from damage to the frontal speech area (Figure 3.15). Regardless of handedness, the presence of aphasia usually indicates a lesion of the left hemisphere.

C. Scott Moss, a clinical psychologist who became aphasic and was paralyzed on his right side as the result of a stroke, has provided some insights into what it is like to be aphasic:

I recollect trying to read the headlines of the Chicago Tribune but they didn't make any sense to me at all. I didn't have any difficulty focusing; it was simply that the words, individually or in combination, didn't have meaning, and even more amazing, I was only a trifle bothered by that fact. . . .

The second week I ran into a colleague who happened to mention that it must be very frustrating for me to be aphasic since prior to that I had been so verbally facile. [I] later found myself wondering why it was not. I think part of the explanation was relatively simple. If I had lost the ability to converse with others, I had also lost the ability to engage in self-talk. In other words, I did not have the ability to think about the future—to worry, or anticipate or perceive it—at least not with words. Thus, for the first five or six weeks after hospitalization I simply existed. So the fact that I could not use words even internally was, in fact, a safeguard. . . .

It took a great deal of effort for me to keep an abstraction in mind. For example, in talking with the speech therapist I would begin to give a definition of an abstract concern, but as I held it in mind it would sort of fade, and chances were that I'd end up giving a simplified version rather than the one at the original level of conception. It was as though giving an abstraction required so much of my added intelligence that halfway through the definition I would run out of the energy available to me and regress to a more concrete answer. (Moss, 1972, pp. 4–5, 10)

For the majority of people, then, the left hemisphere is the seat of language. But the right hemisphere also has specialized functions. Mental imagery, musical and artistic skills, and the ability to perceive and understand spatial relationships are all functions of the right hemisphere.

The split brain: two minds in one body? Despite the localization of specific functions in the two cerebral hemispheres, the brain normally functions as a unified whole because the two hemispheres communicate with one another through the corpus callosum. But what would happen if the communication network between the two hemispheres were cut? Would we, in effect, produce two different and largely independent minds in the same person? A series of Nobel Prize–winning studies by Roger Sperry (1970) and his associates at the California Institute of Technology suggest that this is exactly what happens in **split-brain subjects.**

Certain patients suffer from a form of epilepsy characterized by a seizure—an uncontrolled electrical discharge of neurons—that begins on one side of the brain and then spreads to the other hemisphere. Years ago, following extensive research with animals, neurosurgeons found that some of these patients could be helped by cutting the nerve fibers of the corpus callosum. The operations were successful in preventing the spread of seizures to the other hemisphere and seemed to have no negative side effects on other psychological functions. Sperry's studies of patients who had such operations involved procedures to test separately the functions of the two hemispheres after the corpus callosum was cut.

Sperry's research was made possible by the way our

TABLE 3.2 HEMISPHERIC LOCALIZATION OF SPEECH FUNCTIONS IN RIGHT-HANDED AND LEFT-HANDED/AMBIDEXTROUS PEOPLE BASED ON THE EFFECTS OF BRAIN DAMAGE IN THE LEFT OR RIGHT HEMISPHERE

	RIGHT-HANDED	LEFT-HANDED/AMBIDEXTROUS
Speech in left hemisphere	92%	69%
Speech in right hemisphere	7%	18%
Speech in both hemispheres	1%	13%

Source: Milner and others, 1966.

visual input to the brain is "wired." Some of the fibers of the optic nerve cross over at a point called the **optic chiasma** and travel to the opposite brain hemisphere (see Figure 3.18). The right side of each eye's visual field projects to the left hemisphere and the left half goes to the right hemisphere. The visual projection areas of the two hemispheres are normally connected by the corpus callosum, and the inputs from each side of the visual field are combined so that a unified visual world is experienced rather than two half-worlds. But when the corpus callosum is cut, we can restrict visual input to one hemisphere by projecting the stimulus to either the right side of the visual field (in which case it goes to the left hemisphere) or to the left side of the visual field (which sends it to the right hemisphere).

In Sperry's experiments, split-brain subjects looked at a fixation point on a screen while slides of visual stimuli (words, pictures, etc.) were flashed briefly to the right or left side of their visual field (see Figure 3.19). The subject could respond verbally or with movements of either hand concealed behind a screen. Sperry found

that when words were flashed to the left hemisphere, subjects could immediately say them and could write them with their right hand (which is controlled by the left hemisphere). However, if words were flashed to the right hemisphere, the subjects could neither say nor write them, because the right hemisphere does not have well-developed language abilities.

This did not mean, however, that the right hemisphere was incapable of recognizing objects. If a picture of an object was flashed to the right hemisphere and the left hand (which is controlled by the right hemisphere) was allowed to feel many different objects behind the screen, including the object shown in the picture, the person's hand would immediately select the correct object and hold it up. As long as the person continued to hold the object in the left hand, so that

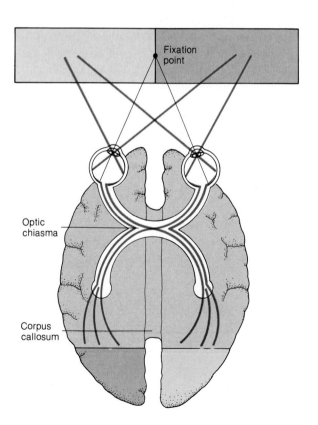

Fixation point

Optic chiasma

Corpus callosum

FIGURE 3.18 *The anatomy of the visual system made studies of split-brain subjects possible. Images entering the eye are reversed by the lens. The right side of the visual field of each eye projects to the visual cortex of the left hemisphere, whereas the left visual field projects to the right hemisphere. When the corpus callosum is cut, the two hemispheres no longer communicate with each other. By presenting stimuli to either side of the visual fixation point, researchers can control which hemisphere receives the information.*

FIGURE 3.19 *The apparatus used in Sperry's split-brain studies. In this instance, a word is briefly projected to the left side of the visual field and the information is sent to the right hemisphere. The subject cannot name the object, but can find it with his left hand. If the subject were to transfer the object to his right hand or if the word were flashed to the right side of his visual field, the information would be sent to his left hemisphere, which has language, and he would be able to name it.*

sensory input about the object went to the right hemisphere, the subject was unable to name it. However, if the object was transferred to the right hand, the person could immediately name it. In a very real sense, until the object was transferred to the right hand, the left hemisphere had no knowledge of what the right hemisphere was experiencing.

Later research showed a definite superiority of the right hemisphere over the left in the recognition of patterns. In one study, three split-brain subjects were presented with similar-looking facial photographs projected in either their left or right visual fields. On each trial, they were asked to select the photo they had just seen from a set of 10 cards. As Figure 3.20 shows, the

right hemisphere was far more accurate then the left hemisphere, probably because the similar faces could not be differentiated by means of a verbal description (Gazzaniga and Smylie, 1983).

The evidence obtained from split-brain studies indicated that, in a sense, separation of the hemispheres created two separate minds within a single brain. Some psychologists suggested that what we call the conscious self resides in the left hemisphere, because it is based on our ability to verbalize the past and present. The right hemisphere is, in this sense, an "unconscious" (nonverbal) mind, except when it communicates with the left hemisphere across the corpus callosum. When the connections between the two hemispheres are cut, the experiences of the right hemisphere are not part of verbal awareness (Springer and Deutsch, 1985). A person may then have emotions or other experiences without being able to verbalize them. One split-brain subject appeared to experience an "unconscious" emotional experience:

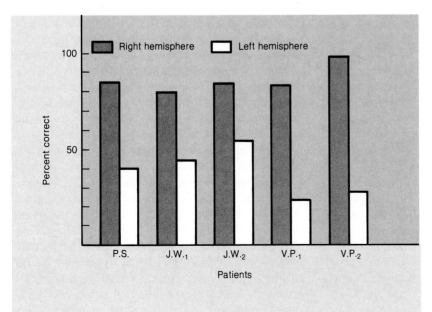

FIGURE 3.20 *Facial recognition accuracy by the right and left hemispheres of three split-brain patients. Patients J. W. and V. P. were tested twice. Because the faces were quite similar, the verbal abilities of the left hemispheres were not very useful, but the pattern recognition abilities of the right hemisphere contributed to more accurate facial recognition (Gazzaniga and Smylie, 1983).*

In one of our experiments we would present a series of ordinary objects and then suddenly flash a picture of a nude woman. This evoked an amused reaction regardless of whether the picture was presented to the left hemisphere or to the right. When the picture was flashed to the left hemisphere of a female patient, she laughed and verbally identified the picture as a nude. When it was later presented to the right hemisphere, she said in reply to a question that she saw nothing, but almost immediately a sly smile spread over her face and she began to chuckle. Asked what she was laughing at, she said, "I don't know . . . nothing . . . Oh—that funny machine." Although the right hemisphere could not describe what it had seen, the sight nevertheless elicited an emotional response like the one evoked from the left hemisphere. (Gazzaniga, 1967, p. 29)

The initial conclusions of split-brain researchers that the right hemisphere has no language capabilities have softened somewhat in recent years, and the issue has become a controversial one (Gazzaniga, 1983; Levy, 1983; Zaidel, 1983). At least 5 of the 44 split-brain subjects studied in the United States gave clear evidence of language skills in the right hemisphere. These skills ranged from simply being able to name objects to complex language skills that were essentially identical to left hemisphere abilities. In other patients, the right hemisphere demonstrated reading abilities as well as the ability to recognize isolated words (Levy, 1983). Much of the current controversy arises from a lack of agreement among researchers about the operational definition of "true" language ability. But it seems clear that there is more hemispheric interaction in language and other abilities than was originally assumed. For example, studies measuring cerebral blood flow in the brains of normal people indicate that both hemispheres are involved in speaking, reading, and listening (Ingvar and Lassen, 1977). The same is undoubtedly true of other brain functions as well (Levy, 1985).

Besides demonstrating differences in the specialized abilities of the left and right hemispheres, the split-brain studies have spurred interest in how the two hemispheres work together to receive information, integrate it, and generate responses to the environment. They have also focused attention on the entire range of human abilities and the importance of developing those of the right hemisphere as well as those of the left. Western culture is oriented more toward the devel-opment of left-hemisphere verbal and numerical skills than of the more esthetic and intuitive skills of the right hemisphere. By placing more educational emphasis on training right-brain functions as well, human potentials that lie largely dormant in the recesses of our right hemisphere might be released for our betterment (Ornstein, 1977).

Brain damage and recovery of function

Because brain injuries can have such devastating effects on psychological and behavioral functioning, the study of various types of brain damage and the factors that influence recovery from them has interested psychologists for many years.

TYPES OF INJURY

There are several common types of brain injury that range from mild to severe in terms of their effects on the physical and psychological welfare of the person.

Concussions and contusions result from severe blows to the head (see Figure 3.21). A **concussion** is a jarring of the brain in which minor damage to neurons and blood vessels may occur. **Contusions** are more serious, since the brain may be severely bruised or even torn when it strikes the hard inner surface of the skull. Both injuries commonly result in a loss of consciousness followed by confusion, headaches, and loss of memory for the events leading up to the blow, but the symptoms are typically more severe and long-lasting in contusions because of the more serious tissue damage. People usually show complete recovery from concussions, but contusions, especially if repeated (as in boxers who don't duck often enough), may have more permanent effects.

Strokes, or *cerebrovascular accidents* (CVAs), result either from a blood clot or from the bursting of a blood vessel in the brain. In either case, circulation and blood supply are disrupted, causing neurons to die. Depending on which area of the brain is affected, speech and memory may be temporarily or permanently impaired, and varying degrees of paralysis are common. Strokes are the third-ranking cause of death, after heart attacks and cancer. There are approximately

500,000 new strokes and 200,000 deaths from strokes in the United States each year. More than 80 percent of stroke victims are over the age of 65.

The term **epilepsy** comes from a Greek word meaning "to seize" or "to attack." About 3 out of every 1000 Americans suffer from some form of epilepsy. Epileptic seizures result from uncontrolled electrical discharges produced by scar tissue in the brain. The scar tissue may be caused by disease or injury, or it may have been present at birth. Whether or not seizures occur and the extent to which they spread depend in part on where the scar tissue is located. The temporal lobe is especially prone to seizures (Gazzaniga and others, 1979).

NEURAL PLASTICITY

An we noted earlier, neurons are not replaced when they die. This means that when an injury results in the destruction of brain tissue, other neurons must take over the lost functions if recovery is to occur. The ability of the brain to transfer functions in this manner is known as **neural plasticity.** At times the brain shows an amazing flexibility. As the following case study shows, however, the age at which an injury takes place determines strongly the amount of plasticity and recovery of function that occurs:

Jimmy was a healthy and normal five year old about to go on his first camping trip in the mountains. The night before the trip, he appeared more irritable than usual, but in the rush of packing no one took much notice. He later woke up crying in the middle of the night and seemed to be in pain, but he had no temperature and dropped back off to sleep in a few minutes after being comforted by his mother's presence. By the next day, however, Jimmy's parents were sure that something was terribly wrong. Jimmy appeared very drowsy and would not speak. He was rushed to a hospital where his condition was quickly evaluated. Jimmy was aphasic—he could not speak—and he was slightly paralyzed on the right side of his body. It was determined that he had suffered a stroke of unknown origin in the temporal lobe of his left hemisphere. A blood vessel in his brain had ruptured or had been blocked by a blood clot and an area of the brain "downstream" from the site of the stroke had died when its blood supply was interrupted.

For Jimmy's father, it was like reliving a nightmare. His own grandfather had also suffered a stroke. The old man never recovered his speech and he remained para-

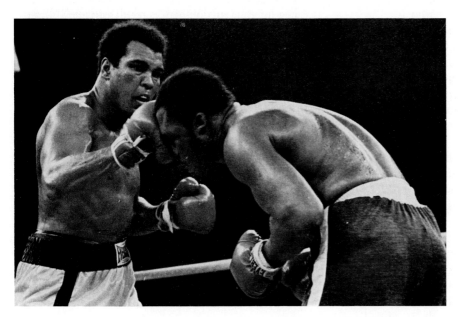

FIGURE 3.21 *In boxing, blows to the head bounce the brain around within the skull, at times hard enough to render the brain partly nonfunctional and the boxer unconscious. The effects of repeated blows to the head are seen in the impaired speech, coordination, and mental functions exhibited by many retired boxers.*

lyzed until his eventual death. But for Jimmy, the chances of recovery were much greater because of his young age. Nature took its course, and within three months, Jimmy was again speaking normally, and his paralysis had disappeared completely. He was ready to resume the life of a normal five year old. All that remained of his ordeal was a frightening memory. (Gazzaniga and others, 1979)

Jimmy's case illustrates a rather rapid recovery of function after brain injury. Somehow, neural reorganization occurred in Jimmy's brain so that other neurons took over the functions of those that had died.

Generally, brain damage suffered early in life is less devastating than damage suffered as an adult. Jimmy recovered his speech quickly; his great-grandfather never recovered. The brain seems to be capable of far greater plasticity early in life. Recent studies using the electron microscope may explain why. Peter Huttenlocher of the University of Chicago found that a 1- to 2-year-old child has about 50 percent more brain synapses than mature adults do (Huttenlocher, 1979). This overproduction of synapses may help to explain why children can recover from brain damage more quickly and completely than adults. Huttenlocher suggests that it may also help to explain why children can easily learn to speak a second language without an accent, while adults cannot. But, sadly, the days of synaptic riches don't last forever. Apparently, unused or "weaker" synapses deteriorate with age, so that the brain loses some of its potential flexibility.

But even adults can show recovery of function after brain injury. When nervous tissue is destroyed, surviving neurons can restore functioning by modifying themselves in two major ways (Marshall, 1984). The first is to alter their structure by sprouting enlarged networks of dendrites and extending axons from surviving neurons to form new synapses. The second mechanism is neurochemical in nature. Surviving neurons may make up for the loss of other cells by increasing the amount of neurotransmitters they release, or postsynaptic neurons may increase their sensitivity to transmitter substances so that they can fire in response to lower levels of transmitter stimulation.

In recent years, brain scientists have succeeded in transplanting embryonic brain tissue into the brains of adult rats; the grafts have "taken" and become parts of neural networks (Kromer and others, 1981). Although much experimental work remains to be done, this development may herald the future possibility of replac-ing dead or diseased neurons with living brain tissue. Transplant procedures may eventually be extended to that most intricate of all bodily parts, the brain.

The ability of the brain to reorganize itself is the focus of one of the most active areas of brain research. Plasticity has clear relevance not only for the ability of the brain to recover from injury (as well as for possible ways to increase or speed up this capability) but also for processes such as evolution, learning, memory, and the normal development of the brain.

As we have seen, numerous brain-behavior relationships have been established through research and clinical observations. Scientists are also delving more deeply into the mysteries of how the nervous system functions. Frontier 3.2 highlights some of the new research methods that are increasing our knowledge about brain functioning.

THE AUTONOMIC AND ENDOCRINE SYSTEMS

Hidden from view, many of our most vital behaviors occur in the internal recesses of the body. Our ability to behave and, indeed, to survive depends on the coordinated functioning of our internal organs and glands. These structures are also involved in many aspects of motivation, emotional behavior, and response to stress. The internal environment is regulated largely through the activities of the autonomic nervous system and the endocrine system.

The autonomic nervous system

The peripheral nervous system, which connects the organs and muscles of the body with the brain and spinal cord, consists of two divisions. The *somatic* system includes the major sensory systems and the motor nerves that activate skeletal muscles. The other major

FIGURE 3.22 *The sympathetic division of the autonomic nervous system functions to arouse the body and speed up its vital processes, whereas the parasympathetic division slows down bodily processes. The two divisions work together to maintain an equilibrium within the body.*

division is the **autonomic nervous system.** This system controls the glands and the smooth (involuntary) muscles that form the heart, blood vessels, and the lining of the stomach and intestines. The autonomic system is involved in such bodily functions as respiration, circulation, and digestion, and it is especially important in emotional behavior.

The autonomic nervous system consists of two subdivisions, the **sympathetic nervous system** and the **parasympathetic nervous system** (see Figure 3.22). Often

these two divisions affect the same organ or gland in opposing ways. By working together, the two divisions can maintain a delicately balanced internal state known as *homeostasis.*

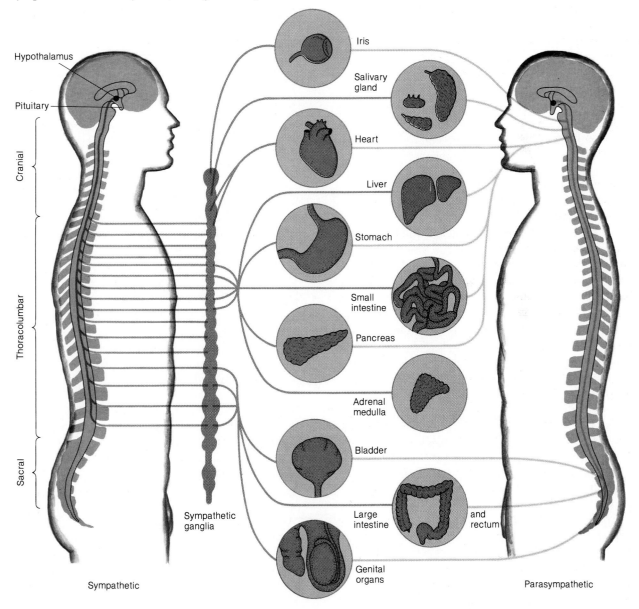

Hypothalamus

Pituitary

Cranial

Thoracolumbar

Sacral

Sympathetic
ganglia

Sympathetic

Iris

Salivary
gland

Heart

Liver

Stomach

Small
intestine

Pancreas

Adrenal
medulla

Bladder

Large
intestine

and
rectum

Genital
organs

Parasympathetic

UNLOCKING THE SECRETS OF THE BRAIN

A variety of methods are used by brain investigators to study the functions of specific brain areas. In many instances a combination of these techniques is used to study a particular brain-behavior relationship. Some of the new methods represent startling technical breakthroughs that permit detailed study of the living brain.

LESIONING AND SURGICAL ABLATION

We can often learn a great deal about a particular structure in the brain by destroying it and studying the behavioral effects. In *lesioning,* tissue is destroyed with electricity, with cold or heat, or with chemicals. In *surgical ablation,* a part of the brain is surgically removed. Obviously, most experiments of this kind are performed on animals, but humans can be studied in this way when accident or disease produces a lesion, or when the surgical removal of abnormal brain tissue is required.

THE STIMULATION METHOD

A specific region of the brain may be stimulated by a mild electric current or by chemicals that excite neurons. Again, most of these studies are done with animals. Electrodes can be permanently implanted so that the region of interest can be repeatedly stimulated. In chemical stimulation studies, a tiny tube is inserted into the animal's brain so that a small amount of the chemical can be delivered directly to the area of interest.

ELECTRICAL RECORDING TECHNIQUES

Electrodes can be used to record brain activity as well as to stimulate it. The electrical activity of neurons can be measured by inserting small electrodes into particular areas of the brain, or by placing larger ones on the scalp to measure the activity of large groups of neurons, as the *electroencephalograph (EEG)* does (see Figure 3.23). Specific EEG patterns are related to various states of consciousness. The EEG can also be used clinically to help determine whether a brain abnormality is present.

FIGURE 3.23 *Several techniques make it possible to study the structure and function of the brain. (a) An electroencephalogram is one method of recording human brain activity. Electrical signals are picked up by electrodes on the scalp, amplified, and written out on a moving paper by an electroencephalograph. This records the changing voltage generated by the brain over time. (b) Computerized axial tomography is a recent technical advance in brain research and medical diagnosis. With this machine, narrow beams of X rays are passed through the brain from many different angles. A high-speed computer analyzes the data from each of the "slices" and reconstructs a highly detailed image of the brain known as a CT scan. (c) Positron emission tomography (PET) scans showing brain activity in response to auditory stimulation. Response of auditory areas of the cerebral cortex (areas at horizontal arrows) and the frontal lobe (areas at vertical arrow) in response to language and music, language alone, and music alone. When the auditory stimulation consists of both language and music, the auditory cortex on both sides of the brain is active; when the auditory stimulation is language only, there is a predominant left-sided activation of the auditory cortex; and when the auditory stimulation is music only, there is a predominant right-sided activation. Frontal lobe activation probably results from a high level of cognitive activity and the promise that all subjects participating in the experiment would be paid in proportion to how much they could remember about the auditory stimulation for a subsequent test.*

A related measure of scalp-recorded electrical brain activity is the *event-related potential (ERP).* This is a short series of voltage fluctuations measured in brain tissue when a particular event occurs (Donchin, 1984). Two aspects of the brain waves are of interest. The first is the firing of neurons in response to a particular sensory stimulus, which enables researchers to discover where it "registers" in the nervous system. The second is the activity of the neurons after the stimulus registers, which is assumed to reflect information processing. ERPs have been studied in

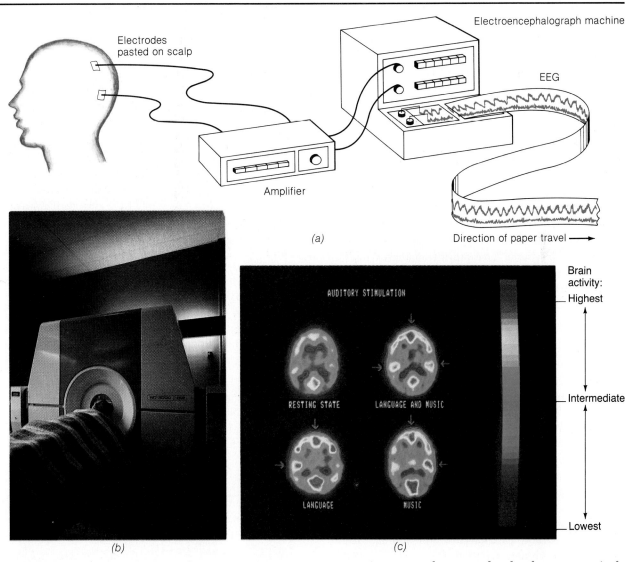

Electrodes
pasted on scalp

Electroencephalograph machine

EEG

Amplifier

(a)

Direction of paper travel ⟶

(b)

AUDITORY STIMULATION

RESTING STATE

LANGUAGE AND MUSIC

LANGUAGE

MUSIC

Brain
activity:

Highest

Intermediate

Lowest

(c)

relation to sensory and motor functions, cognitive processes, and consciousness (Hillyard and Kutas, 1983). One recent application is in the study of visual development in infants, where ERPs can tell researchers how long after birth various kinds of visual stimuli begin to register in the visual cortex (Sokol, 1984).

Technical advances now make it possible to record the activity of single neurons. The use of microelectrodes about one-thousandth of a millimeter in size

permits a researcher to study what happens to single neurons as sensation or learning occurs.

HISTOLOGICAL PROCEDURES

The structural features of neurons and fiber connections can be studied through microscopic examination of brain tissue. Special staining techniques can be used to make the neurons visible so that their structure and connections can be traced (see Figure 3.7, p.

78). The electron microscope makes it possible to study the finest details of neurons and the way they are modified by processes such as perception and learning.

BRAIN SLICES

Brain slices are thin sections of a brain region prepared and kept alive for many hours in a chemical substrate for electrophysiological and biochemical studies (Dingledine, 1984). The thin slices of brain tissue have relatively intact synaptic systems that can be studied by stimulating them chemically or electrically. Recent studies of the biochemical activities occurring at the synapse have provided valuable information on neural conduction and on synaptic changes that may be the basis for learning and memory (Lynch and others, 1984).

CT SCANS

Developed in the 1970s, the technique of *computerized axial tomography* (CT) is 100 times more sensitive than standard X-ray procedures and allows researchers to look within the living brain in a way never possible before. A narrow beam of X rays scans the patient's brain 160 times to take pictures of narrow "slices" of the brain. A computer analyzes the X rays and creates pictures of the brain's interior from many different angles (Weisberg and others, 1984). The detailed films showing where injuries or deterioration has occurred help to clarify the relationship between brain damage and psychological functioning. The technological advance represented by the CT scan technique was so dramatic that its developers, Allan Cormack and Godfrey Hounsfield, were awarded the 1979 Nobel Prize for medicine.

DEOXYGLUCOSE TECHNIQUES

Still another recent breakthrough is the invention of the *deoxyglucose technique* by Louis Sokoloff and his colleagues at the National Institute of Mental Health (Sokoloff and others, 1977). Neurons use the glucose carried in the blood for fuel, and they consume more glucose when they are active. Deoxyglucose is chemically similar to glucose except that it is not "digested" when the neuron consumes it. Thus, we can tell how active neurons have been by the amount of radioactive deoxyglucose that accumulates in them. The radioactivity is measured by sacrificing the experimental animal and placing thin sections of its frozen brain on radiation-sensitive film, a procedure known as *autoradiography*. Through the use of a mathematical formula worked out by Sokoloff, the information is programmed into a computer that converts the amounts of radiation into different colors. A color photograph can then be taken off the computer, with the various shades of color showing the level of activity in each area of the brain. In this way, it is possible to tell which cells in the brain were active during a specific experimental procedure.

PET SCANS

An even more recent advance allows researchers to use a technique known as *PET scan (positron emission tomography)* to study the absorption of a safe form of radioactive deoxyglucose from *outside* the scalp (Sargent, 1980). The radioactive deoxyglucose absorbed by the neurons emits positively charged particles called *positrons*. These collide with negatively charged electrons normally present in the cells, producing high-energy particles called *photons*. The photon activity is measured by the PET scan and the data are fed into a computer that produces a color picture of the brain on a display screen. Scientists can now map the activity of brain structures in a living animal or human in a way that was never before possible, and brain activity can be studied in relation to cognitive processes, behavior, and even forms of mental illness.

In addition to the deoxyglucose tracer used to study glucose metabolism, radioactive tracers have been developed to measure such diverse functions as local blood flow, blood volume, oxygen consumption, tissue pH, and drug distribution in living brains (Raichle and Ter-Pogossian, 1984). An especially promising recent development is a method for using the PET scan to trace and measure neurotransmitter binding sites in living brains by injecting radioactive forms of various transmitter substances (Mintun and others, 1984).

NUCLEAR MAGNETIC RESONANCE (NMR)

The most recently developed means of viewing the living brain is *nuclear magnetic resonance (NMR)*. It focuses on the nuclei of atoms in living tissue and determines if they behave normally in response to an external force such as magnetism. The part of the body to be studied is placed in an elaborate scanner, exposing the nuclei to a uniform magnetic field. The field is then altered, and when the magnetic field is shut off, the energy absorbed by the nuclei becomes a small electrical voltage. The voltage is picked up by detectors and relayed to a computer for analysis and reconstruction of a two- or three-dimensional image that serves as a blueprint of biochemical activity. In addition to providing color images of the tissue, NMR tells which chemicals are active in the tissue (Bottomley and others, 1984).

Early studies using NMR to assess the anatomy and metabolism of the normal human brain indicate that this could be an extremely useful procedure. Because of its greater sensitivity and clearer images, NMR appears far superior to the CT scan in assessing brain injuries as well (Han and others, 1984).

The technical advances that are occurring in every area of brain research are making this one of the most exciting frontiers of psychology. Grudgingly, but steadily, the brain is yielding its many secrets to scientists.

SYMPATHETIC NERVOUS SYSTEM

The sympathetic neurons have their cell bodies in the spinal cord and run out through the ventral root to a chain of cell bodies called *sympathetic ganglia* that run parallel to the spinal cord. In the sympathetic ganglia these fibers synapse with nerves that fan out to activate the internal organs of the body.

The sympathetic system has an arousal function and tends to act as a unit. For example, when you encounter a stressful situation, your sympathetic nervous system simultaneously speeds up your heart rate, dilates your pupils, slows down your digestive system, increases respiration, and, in general, mobilizes your body to confront the stressor. This is sometimes called the "fight or flight" response. It also stimulates the adrenal glands to secrete stress hormones, such as adrenaline, into the bloodstream in order to maintain or increase the level of arousal (Smith and DeVito, 1984).

PARASYMPATHETIC NERVOUS SYSTEM

The motor fibers of the parasympathetic system originate at points above and below those of the sympathetic system (see Figure 3.22). While the sympathetic system tends to act as a unit, the parasympathetic system is much more specific in its actions, affecting one or a few organs at a time. The action of your parasympathetic nervous system slows down bodily processes and maintains a state of tranquility. Thus, your sympathetic system speeds up your heart rate; your parasympathetic system slows it down. The two divisions of the autonomic nervous system work together to maintain a state of equilibrium in the internal organs. Some acts require a sequence of sympathetic and parasympathetic activity. For example, the sex act in the male involves erection of the penis, a primarily parasympathetic function, followed by ejaculation, a primarily sympathetic function (Katchadourian and Lunde, 1979).

The autonomic nervous system produces its effects

Gland	Hormone	Effect
Pituitary	Adrenocorticotropic hormone (ACTH)	Stimulates adrenal cortex
	Thyrotropic hormone (TTH)	Stimulates thyroid
	Luteinizing hormone (LH)	Stimulates testes and ovaries
	Follicle–stimulating hormone (FSH)	Stimulates follicle of ovary in ovulation
	Growth hormone (somatotropin)	Promotes growth in bone and muscle
	Prolactin	Stimulates breasts to produce milk
	Vasopressin	Controls excretion of water in kidneys
	Oxytocin	Stimulates contractions of the uterus at birth
Ovary	Estrogen	Promotes female sexual characteristics
	Progesterone	Stimulates thickening of uterus lining
Testis	Testosterone	Promotes male sexual characteristics
Thyroid	Thyroxine	Controls basal metabolism
Adrenal	About 50 cortical hormones, e.g., cortisone, aldosterone	Controls many basic chemical mechanisms
	Adrenaline, noradrenaline	Increases sugar in blood, raises heartbeat, dilates arteries
Pancreas	Insulin	Lowers level of sugar in blood
Thymus	Uncertain	Provides disease immunity in early life

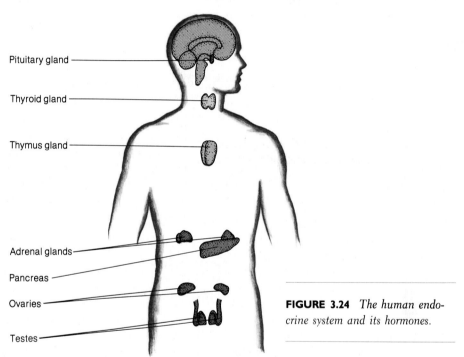

Pituitary gland

Thyroid gland

Thymus gland

Adrenal glands

Pancreas

Ovaries

Testes

FIGURE 3.24 *The human endocrine system and its hormones.*

in two ways: by direct neural stimulation of body organs and by stimulating the release of hormones from the glands of the endocrine system.

The endocrine system

The endocrine system consists of numerous glands distributed throughout the body. Like the nervous system, the endocrine system conveys messages from one area

of the body to another. Rather than utilizing nerve impulses, however, the endocrine system sends information in the form of chemical messengers called **hormones,** which are secreted into the bloodstream.

The nervous system transmits information rapidly, with the speed of nerve impulses. The endocrine system is slower because it depends on the rate of blood flow. Another important difference between the nervous and endocrine systems lies in the generality of the messages that are transmitted. A particular neuron in the nervous system usually synapses directly with a relatively small number of other neurons. But because hormones travel throughout the body in the bloodstream, they can reach millions of individual cells. Thus, when the brain has important information to transmit, it has the choice of sending it in the form of nerve impulses to a relatively small number of neurons, or to a large number of cells by means of hormones. Often, both communication networks are used.

The approximate locations of the endocrine glands within the human body and a list of their hormones and functions are presented in Figure 3.24. Many of the hormones secreted by these glands affect psychological development and functioning, but the adrenal glands are of special interest because they are related to the functions of both the central and autonomic nervous systems.

The **adrenal glands** have two distinct anatomical divisions. The *adrenal cortex*, the outer portion of the gland, secretes about 50 different hormones that regulate many metabolic processes within the body, including metabolism of carbohydrates, functioning of the reproductive organs, and balancing of sodium and potassium body fluids that surround the neurons and other cells of the body.

Lying beneath the adrenal cortex is the *adrenal medulla*. It secretes epinephrine (also known as adrenaline) and norepinephrine (noradrenaline). Epinephrine and norephinephrine can produce many of the same effects as those produced by the sympathetic nervous system. In an emergency, the adrenal medulla is activated by the sympathetic branch of the autonomic nervous system and epinephrine or norepinephrine is secreted into the bloodstream. Because hormones can remain in the bloodstream for some time, the action of the adrenal medulla and its hormones is especially important in circumstances of prolonged stress.

In the chapters to follow, we explore the complex psychological processes that result from the functioning of our biological systems. In each instance, we will find that the biological perspective on behavior has made major contributions to our understanding of who we are and how we function psychologically. In the next chapter we explore the states of consciousness that are produced by the activity of our nervous system and ways in which normal consciousness can be altered.

STUDY OUTLINE

GENETIC INFLUENCES ON BEHAVIOR (p. 68)

1. Genetic factors play a major role in the development and behavior of organisms. Hereditary potential is carried in the DNA portion of the chromosomes in units called genes.

2. The biological sex of a human is determined by whether an X or a Y chromosome from the father unites with the X chromosome of the mother. Males result from an XY combination, females from the combination of two X chromosomes.

3. Genotype and phenotype are not identical because some genes are dominant, while others are recessive. If a gene is recessive, the characteristic associated with it will not appear unless it is paired with another recessive gene. Some characteristics are said to be sex-linked because they are carried only by the X chromosome.

4. Chromosome mutations occur more or less randomly in nature, but recombinant DNA techniques permit the direct manipulation of genetic factors and the production of specific life forms.

5. Behavior depends on the interaction of heredity with environment, and behavior genetics studies these interactions. The reaction range is the range of possibilities that the genetic code allows. An index called heritability expresses the relative contribution of genetic factors in mathematical terms. The major research methods used by behavior geneticists are selective breeding, pedigree analysis, and twin studies.

THE NEURAL BASES OF BEHAVIOR (p. 77)

1. Neurons are the basic building blocks of the nervous system. Each neuron has dendrites, which receive nerve impulses from other neurons; a cell body, or soma, which controls the vital processes of the cell; and an axon, which conducts nerve impulses to adjacent neurons, muscles, and glands.

2. Neural transmission is an electrochemical process.

The nerve impulse is a brief reversal in the electrical potential of the cell membrane as sodium ions from the surrounding fluid flow into the cell through a sodium gate. Passage of the impulse across the synapse, the microscopic space between neurons, is mediated by chemical transmitter substances released from the axon terminals.

3. Some neurotransmitters excite other neurons, while others inhibit firing of the postsynaptic neuron. Acetylcholine is an important excitatory transmitter. Psychoactive drugs affect behavior by modifying neural activity at the synapse, and there is evidence that some mood and behavior disorders may involve defects in neurotransmitter systems.

4. Information is coded in the nervous system by increases or decreases in firing in relation to the neuron's base rate, by the number of neurons that fire, and by the particular neurons that are active.

THE CENTRAL NERVOUS SYSTEM (p. 83)

1. The nervous system is made up of afferent (sensory) neurons, efferent (motor) neurons, and interneurons (associative neurons). Its two major divisions are the central nervous system, consisting of the brain and spinal cord, and the peripheral nervous system. The latter is divided into the somatic system, which has sensory and motor functions, and the autonomic nervous system, which directs the activity of the body's internal organs and glands.

2. The dorsal roots of the spinal cord contain sensory neurons and the ventral roots contain motor neurons. Interneurons inside the spinal cord serve a connective function. Simple stimulus-response connections can occur as spinal reflexes.

3. The human brain consists of the hindbrain, the midbrain, and the forebrain. Major structures within the hindbrain include the medulla, which monitors and controls vital bodily functions; the pons, which contains important groups of sensory and motor neurons; and the cerebellum, which is concerned with motor coordination.

4. The midbrain contains a number of important sensory and motor neurons, as well as many sensory and motor tracts connecting higher and lower parts of the nervous system.

5. The reticular formation extends from the hindbrain up into the midbrain. It plays a vital role in consciousness, attention, and sleep. Activity of the ascending reticular formation excites higher areas of the brain and prepares them to respond to stimulation. The descending reticular formation acts as a kind of gate and helps to determine which stimuli "get through" to our consciousness.

THE FOREBRAIN (p. 87)

1. The forebrain is highly developed in humans. It consists of two cerebral hemispheres and a number of subcortical structures. The cerebral hemispheres are connected by a band of fibers known as the corpus callosum.

2. The thalamus is a kind of giant switchboard through which impulses originating in sense organs are routed to the appropriate sensory projection areas. The hypothalamus plays a major role in many aspects of motivational and emotional behavior. The limbic system seems to be involved in organizing the behaviors involved in motivation and emotion.

3. The cerebral hemispheres have a convoluted surface, the cerebral cortex, which is highly developed in humans. It is divided into frontal, parietal, occipital, and temporal lobes. Some areas of the cortex are sensory in nature, some control motor functions, and others consist of the association cortex believed to be involved in the higher mental processes in humans. The frontal lobes appear to be particularly important in planning, in voluntary behavior, and in self-awareness.

4. The two cerebral hemispheres appear to have different functions and abilities. Studies of split-brain patients who have had the corpus callosum cut indicate that the left hemisphere is skilled in language and mathematical abilities, whereas the right hemisphere has well-developed spatial abilities, but generally limited ability to communicate through speech.

BRAIN DAMAGE AND RECOVERY OF FUNCTION (p. 96)

1. Common types of brain damage include concussions, contusions, strokes, and epilepsy.

2. The ability of people to recover from brain damage depends on several factors, including the nature and

extent of the injury and the age of the victim. Other things being equal, recovery is greatest early in life and declines with age.

3. Neural plasticity refers to the ability of the brain to reorganize itself and recover functions following injury. Neurons are not replaced when they die, but surviving neurons can alter their structure by sprouting enlarged dendritic networks and extending axons to form new synapses. They can also increase the amount of neurotransmitter substance they release so that they are more sensitive to stimulation.

THE AUTONOMIC AND ENDOCRINE SYSTEMS (p. 98)

1. The autonomic nervous system consists of sympathetic and parasympathetic divisions. The sympathetic system has an arousal function and tends to act as a unit. The parasympathetic system slows down bodily processes and functions in a more specific manner. The two divisions work together to maintain a state of homeostasis, or balance.

2. The endocrine system secretes hormones into the bloodstream. These chemical messengers affect many bodily processes. Because of their relation to functions of the nervous system, the adrenal glands are of particular interest in the study of psychological processes.

FRONTIER 3.2: UNLOCKING THE SECRETS OF THE BRAIN (p. 100)

1. Discoveries concerning brain-behavior relationships are made using a variety of techniques. These include lesioning and surgical ablation, electrical and chemical stimulation of the brain, electrical recording techniques, and histological procedures. Newer techniques include the use of brain slices as well as several recently developed methods for producing computer-generated pictures of structures and processes within the living brain. The most notable of these techniques are CT scans and PET scans, and nuclear magnetic resonance (NMR).

2. Deoxyglucose and other radioactive tracers are being used in conjunction with the PET scan to study activities in the living brain, such as glucose metabolism, blood volume, and neurotransmitter binding. This technique promises to shed new light on many aspects of brain functioning.

KEY TERMS AND CONCEPTS

nature-nurture controversy

behavior genetics

genotype

phenotype

chromosome

DNA

gene

dominant gene

recessive gene

sex-linked characteristic

Down syndrome

recombinant DNA technique

E. coli

interferon

reaction range

heritability

selective breeding

pedigree analysis

consanguinity study

neuron

soma

dendrite

axon

myelin

nerve

resting potential

nerve impulse

sodium channel

action potential

potassium channel

refractory period

node of Ranvier

synapse

graded potential

action potential threshold

neurotransmitter

synaptic vesicle

acetylcholine

afferent neuron

efferent neuron

interneuron

gray matter

white matter

dorsal root

ventral root

brain stem

medulla

pons

reticular formation

cerebellum

thalamus

hypothalamus

limbic system

hippocampus

association cortex

cortical projection areas

corpus callosum

aphasia

split-brain subjects

optic chiasma

concussion

contusion

stroke

epilepsy

neural plasticity

lesioning

surgical ablation

electroencephalograph

event-related potential

brain slice

deoxyglucose technique

CT scan

PET scan

nuclear magnetic resonance

autonomic nervous system

sympathetic nervous system

parasympathetic nervous system

hormone

adrenal gland

SUGGESTED READINGS

BLOOM, F. E., LAZERSON, A., and HOFSTADTER, L. (1984). *Brain, mind, and behavior*. New York: Freeman. An introductory-level text that provides an excellent overview of many of the topics discussed in this chapter. It is comprehensive, illustrated with many color photographs and drawings, and focuses on recent discoveries in brain science.

GAZZANIGA, M. S., STEEN, D., and VOLPE, B. T. (1979). *Functional neuroscience*. New York: Harper & Row. An overview of brain behavior relationships that provides many case studies like those presented in this chapter.

PLOMIN, R., DEFRIES, J. C., and MCCLEARN, G. E. (1980). *Behavior genetics: A primer*. San Francisco: Freeman. An interesting and readable introduction to the methods and findings of behavior genetics.

SPRINGER, S. P., and DEUTSCH, G. (1985). *Left brain, right brain*. New York: Freeman. A revised edition of an award-winning book that presents findings on hemispheric differences in split-brain, brain-damaged, and normal subjects. The book discusses learning disabilities, left-handedness, sex differences in hemispheric functions, theories of consciousness, and many other interesting topics.

CHAPTER FOUR

STATES OF CONSCIOUSNESS

SLEEPING AND DREAMING
Our biological clocks
Stages of sleep
The nature and functions of dreams
FRONTIER 4.1   SLEEP DISORDERS

MEDITATION
Meditation and stress

HYPNOSIS
Animal magnetism, mesmerism, and hypnosis
The scientific study of hypnosis
Hypnotic behaviors and experiences
Theories of hypnosis

DRUGS AND CONSCIOUSNESS
Mechanisms of drug action
Depressants
Stimulants
Narcotics
Hallucinogens
Cannabis
FRONTIER 4.2   LIMITS OF CONSCIOUSNESS

STUDY OUTLINE

KEY TERMS AND CONCEPTS

SUGGESTED READINGS

Billy Milligan is a most unusual person. In fact, he may be as many as 10 unusual people. Billy's multiple personalities became known shortly after he was arrested for rape in Columbus, Ohio. A psychologist began a jailhouse interview by asking him if he was William Milligan. "Billy's asleep," came the reply. "I'm David."

An intensive psychological study of Milligan revealed at least nine other distinct personalities, most of whom are unaware that the others exist. These other personalities include Christene, a loving 3-year-old girl who likes to draw flowers and butterflies; Adelena, a young female homosexual who may be the one who committed the rapes; David, a withdrawn youngster who bangs his head against the wall when he is upset; Arthur, an intellectual who speaks with a British accent; Ragan, an aggressive male with a Slavic accent who considers himself the others' protector; and Allen, an 18-year-old who plays the drums and is the only one who smokes. When given intelligence tests, the various personalities obtained IQs ranging from 68 to over 130. As Figure 4.1 shows, the artistic productions of the different personalities reflected their diverse characteristics.

Cases of multiple personality like Billy Milligan's illustrate a dramatic division of consciousness that psychologists call **dissociation.** Although such cases are quite rare, they are not as far removed from our normal functioning as we might think. We all drift into and out of different states of consciousness and awareness, though in a far less extreme and dramatic way than Billy Milligan did. Our self-awareness gives us a stable personal identity that has a past, a present, and a future. But a moment's reflection tells us that even when we are fully awake, our consciousness is not a single, simple state. At any instant, we may be looking, listening, feeling, planning, or anticipating. The many processes and experiences that occur in our normal stream of consciousness are so familiar to us that we often take them for granted and forget how wonderfully varied they are.

FIGURE 4.1 *William Milligan is an example of multiple personality. His artwork clearly reflected whichever of his personalities was dominant at the time. Milligan produced one of these drawings as Christene and the other as Billy, his core personality.*

Why do I gots to say in a cage and cant get out an play
Do you like I creaм
I Long you
Mp Antfei say you going to help us

A giant big hug an a kiss for Miss Judey

From Christene

We are far more aware of the fluctuations in consciousness that occur as we pass from wakefulness into sleep. In addition to the changes in consciousness that we call falling asleep and dreaming, there is a kind of dissociation that we rarely think about. Have you ever wondered why you don't fall out of bed while you are asleep, as young children often do? Despite the fact that "you" are sound asleep, a part of you somehow knows where the edge of the bed is (Bowers, 1976).

But the variety of states of consciousness goes even beyond this. Perhaps you are among those who have experienced an **altered state of consciousness,** which can occur under extreme fatigue or under the influence of drugs, as well as in other circumstances. In altered states people may experience strange and even mystical sensations and may discover mental functions and perceptual capabilities that seem to have no counterparts in normal experience.

Studying consciousness scientifically is not an easy task. We are dealing with the most private of personal experiences. We cannot enter the subject's head and directly observe these events. At best, we can study external signs that may indicate what the subject is experiencing subjectively.

Figure 4.2 shows the types of observable behavior that are used to study consciousness. The most common of these is verbal self-report, in which subjects describe their inner experiences. While sometimes our only tool for studying certain aspects of consciousness, self-reports are not always reliable and are usually im-

possible to verify. This is why the behaviorists have always opposed the use of introspection.

A second class of behaviors is physiological responses. Because all experience involves the functioning of the nervous system, physiological measures that are consistently associated with self-reports of particular mental processes or inner experiences can provide valuable indirect measures of mental events. As we shall see, such measures have been extremely useful in the study of sleep and dreaming. Increasingly more sophisticated ways of analyzing the electrical activity of the brain now permit the measurement of a variety of mental processes and perhaps even subjective experiences (Donchin, 1984). We are approaching the time when scientists will be able to "watch" a thought.

Nonverbal behaviors are a third class of indicators used to infer mental events. Suppose, for example, that you wanted to know if chimpanzees have self-awareness. You might do what one scientist did (Gallup, 1979). He anesthetized a chimp and put a red spot on its face. When the chimp awoke, it was handed a mirror. Seeing its reflection in the mirror, the chimp immediately raised a hand to its face and tried to rub off the spot, indicating that it knew (1) that the mirror

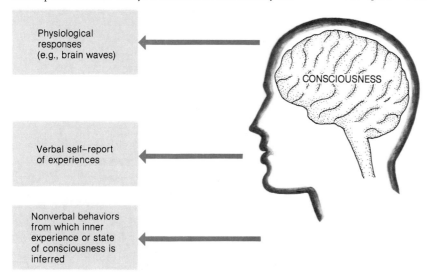

Physiological
responses
(e.g., brain waves)

Verbal self–report
of experiences

Nonverbal behaviors
from which inner
experience or state
of consciousness is
inferred

CONSCIOUSNESS

FIGURE 4.2 *As a private event, consciousness cannot be observed directly. However, conscious experience can be studied scientifically through three major classes of externally observable and measurable responses: physiological responses, verbal self-reports, and nonverbal behavior.*

image was a reflection of itself and (2) that the red spot was something new. These nonverbal behaviors imply some degree of conscious self-awareness on the part of the chimp.

The realm of consciousness is broad and complex. Four areas are at the forefront of current research and theory: sleeping and dreaming, meditation, hypnosis, and drug-produced alterations of conscious experience.

SLEEPING AND DREAMING

We probably spend from 30 to 40 percent of our lives asleep. No wonder we sometimes feel that there are not enough hours in the day! Yet, scientists do not really understand why we sleep so much or, for that matter, why we sleep at all. One long-standing idea is that sleep restores us. When we are fatigued, sleep gives our bodies a chance to recuperate. Consistent with this hypothesis are studies that show that substances removed from the brain or spinal fluid of fatigued animals will quickly induce sleep if injected into the brains of animals who are wide awake. Recently, a similar **sleep factor** has been discovered in humans, spurring hopes that the manufacture of this chemical, perhaps through recombinant DNA procedures (see Frontier 3.1, page 72), might result in a natural sleeping drug without side effects (Maugh, 1982).

But other findings do not fit the hypothesis that we sleep because the body needs to recuperate. For example, our body uses about the same amount of oxygen and glucose during sleep as it does during relaxed wakefulness, and we do not seem to rid ourselves of any body toxins during sleep (Horne, 1978). Moreover, scientists have studied people who customarily sleep as little as 15 to 30 minutes a night with no ill effects (Moore-Ede and others, 1982). Hence the question of exactly why we sleep remains unanswered. But whatever its function, we know that sleep is important to most of us because our mental and physical functioning can deteriorate if we go without it. The following case illustrates an extreme reaction to sleep deprivation.

In 1959 Peter Tripp, a well-known New York disc jockey, vowed to remain awake for 200 hours in a marathon for the March of Dimes. For over eight days, he broadcast his regular program and periodic progress reports from a glass-walled booth in Times Square (see Figure 4.3).

Tripp's "wake-a-thon" attracted the attention not only of many New Yorkers but also of a group of psychologists and medical researchers. They set up a laboratory in a nearby hotel to study Tripp, gave him a daily battery of psychological tests, and monitored his physiological reactions.

By the second sleepless day Tripp began to feel intense fatigue. On the third day he began to experience visual illusions and hallucinations. He saw cobwebs in his shoes. He imagined that specks on the table were live insects, and he thought he saw a rabbit in his booth. He began to have trouble remembering things. After being awake for 100 hours, he could no longer perform psychological tests that required attention and mental problem solving. He was unable to recite the alphabet. His mental functions deteriorated rapidly, and after 170 hours simple tests became torture for him and for the psychologists testing him.

By the fifth day Tripp's personality began to grow dis-

FIGURE 4.3 *An exhausted Peter Tripp ends his 200 hours without sleep.*

organized, and his hallucinations became more grotesque. He saw a tweed coat as a suit of furry worms. He claimed that a nurse was dripping saliva and that the tie on one of the scientists was jumping. Although he appeared to be awake, his brain waves sometimes resembled those that occur during deep sleep. Somehow he managed to marshal his resources during his daily 5 P.M. to 8 P.M. show, and neither his listeners nor casual onlookers were ever aware of his private torment.

On the morning of the final day, during an examination performed by a neurologist, Tripp concluded that the doctor was really an undertaker who was about to bury him alive. He jumped from the examination table and raced for the door with several doctors in hot pursuit.

With some persuasion, Tripp managed to get through the final day and then sank into deep sleep for 13 hours. When he awoke, his mental anguish and disorientation had disappeared, and he was able to solve mental problems. He was slightly depressed for the next three months, but in other respects his functioning returned to normal. However, neither Peter Tripp nor the scientists who witnessed his ordeal will forget the nightmare of his 200 sleepless hours.

Our biological clocks

Most of us regulate our periods of sleep and wakefulness in accordance with external events, such as changes in light and darkness, mealtimes, and the unwelcome buzzing of alarm clocks. But underlying these artificial regulators of our sleep cycle is a biologically based 24-hour activity cycle. Over the billions of years that life has been evolving, human biological activities as well as those of other species, including plants, have become linked to the 24-hour cycle resulting from the earth's rotation on its axis. This **circadian rhythm** (from the Latin *circa*, "around," and *dia*, "*day*") involves daily cyclical changes in body temperature, blood pressure, blood-plasma volume, hormonal secretions, and other bodily processes (Moore-Ede and Czeisler, 1984). We normally sleep during the low point of the temperature cycle.

Animal species have differing cycles of sleep and wakefulness. Many, including adult human beings, sleep for one long period every 24 hours. This is called a **monophasic** (one-phase) **sleep cycle.** Other animals have several sleep-wakefulness cycles during their 24-

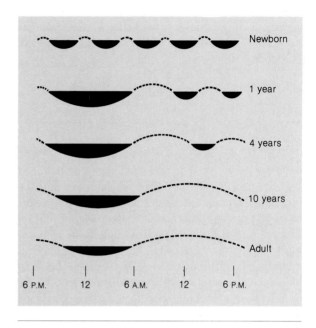

FIGURE 4.4 *The human sleep cycle changes from a polyphasic to a monophasic cycle from birth to adulthood. Solid areas indicate sleep periods.*

hour circadian rhythm. This is called a **polyphasic sleep cycle.** Rats, rabbits, and other rodents have polyphasic cycles. Human infants have polyphasic cycles that become monophasic as the young children mature (see Figure 4.4).

Disruption of the circadian rhythm by an extreme change in sleeping patterns may result in a kind of jet lag, similar to the fatigue and disorientation that people experience if they cross several time zones in one day. Our bodies may require a week or more to adapt completely to a major disruption of the circadian rhythm. In fact, some corporations require their executives to wait several days after they have made an overseas flight before they begin important negotiations.

Similar changes in physical and psychological

functioning occur for people whose circadian cycles are disrupted by rotating work shifts. A study of workers who rotated from shift to shift showed that they had more accidents than other workers on the same jobs. They consumed more alcohol and sleeping pills and reported more digestive difficulties, menstrual disorders, colds, nervousness, and fatigue. They also reported less satisfactory social relationships (Colligan and others, 1978).

Stages of sleep

Much of the research on sleep and dreaming has been done in specially equipped sleep laboratories where the physiological responses of sleeping subjects are monitored and processed on computers (see Figure 4.5). A more recent technique permits subjects to sleep at home in their own beds while their physiological data are transmitted through computer telephone hookups to laboratories miles away (Rosekind and others, 1978).

The most important technological advance in sleep research was the development of the electroencephalogram (EEG) for measuring the brain's electrical activity. EEG recordings during the sleep cycle resemble those shown in Figure 4.6(*a*). These records show that there are five fairly distinct stages of sleep. A relaxed waking state is represented by a brain wave pattern of 8 to 12 cycles per second. This is called an **alpha rhythm.** If we drop into light sleep, the alpha rhythm is replaced by the fast, irregular rhythm of stage 1, which is similar to an active state of wakefulness. The changes in wave patterns from stage 1 to stage 4 reflect increasing synchronizing in the electrical "firing" of millions of brain cells. As sleep progresses toward stage 4, the brain waves become progressively slower and larger. The deepest sleep, which occurs in stages 3 and 4, is called **slow-wave sleep** (SWS) because of the slow, irregular pattern of the brain waves.

In 1953, sleep researchers Eugene Aserinsky and Nathaniel Kleitman identified a fifth sleep stage that begins about an hour after we fall asleep and occurs approximately every 90 minutes thereafter. The EEG pattern for this stage resembles the pattern for stage 1, but it also involves *rapid eye movements* (REMs) that

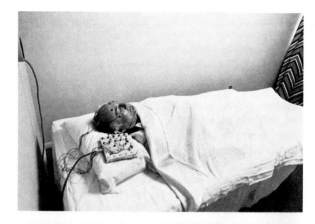

FIGURE 4.5 *In a modern sleep laboratory, a subject sleeps while his physiological responses are monitored and recorded in an adjoining room. The electrodes attached to the scalp area record the subject's EEG brain wave patterns. Those beside the eyes record eye movements, and the other electrodes measure muscle tension in the facial area.*

occur about 20 times per second and is thus called **REM sleep.** Aserinsky and Kleitman found that people who were awakened during REM periods almost always reported that they had been dreaming. Research stimulated by this discovery has yielded great insights into the nature of sleep and dreaming.

FIGURE 4.6 *Brain wave changes define the various stages of sleep. (a) Typical brain wave patterns of each stage appear on this EEG record. Note that the brain waves become slower and larger as sleep deepens. Note also that the pattern of REM sleep is similar to that of stage 1. (b) Also shown is a record of a typical night's sleep. The REM stages are shown in bars. Subjects usually average four to five REM periods during the night. These tend to become longer as the night wears on.*

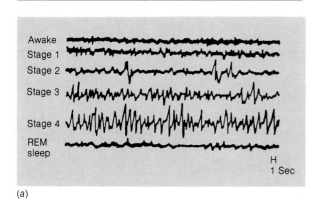

(a)

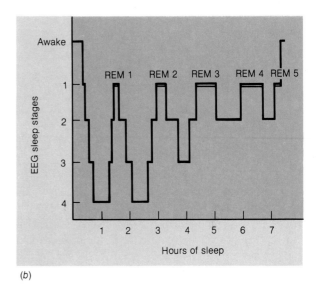

(b)

The nature and functions of dreams

Infants spend about 50 percent of their sleeping hours in REM sleep. This proportion drops to about 25 percent by ages 5 to 9 and continues at about this level throughout adult life. As Figure 4.6(b) shows, adults have about five REM periods each night. These periods become progressively longer as the night wears on and may last as long as 60 minutes (Dement, 1974). Because subjects awakened during REM sleep reported having been dreaming about 80 percent of the time, it was formerly believed that dreams occur primarily during REM sleep. But it now appears that an appreciable amount of mental activity also occurs during non-REM sleep, and that there are no completely consistent differences between dream reports obtained when subjects are awakened from REM and non-REM sleep (Herman and others, 1978). Clearly, the brain is mentally active throughout the sleep cycle. We probably dream far more than our ability to recall our dreams would suggest.

The physiological processes that give rise to dreams are not completely understood. One current theory is the **activation-synthesis model** (McCarley, 1983). According to this theory, the activation of dreams arises from the brain-stem reticular formation, which stimulates both perceptual elements (such as sensations, emotions, and memories) and motor patterns, including complex motor activities as well as the rapid eye movements that are correlated with the dream state. At the level of the forebrain, these perceptual and motor elements are combined, or synthesized, into the integrated sensory-motor experiences that we know as dreams (see Figure 4.7). Presumably, the content of a dream is based on the relative strength of the specific perceptual and motor elements that are activated and on the way they are combined within the forebrain.

Many of our dreams involve vigorous physical activity, such as running, jumping, or struggling. During this time, recordings of brain activity show that the motor cortex of our brain is quite active, though our bodies remain almost motionless. The reason why we seldom find ourselves on the floor when we awaken is a

FIGURE 4.7 *According to the activation-synthesis theory of dream formation, dreams are triggered by activity in the brain stem reticular formation, which stimulates other brain regions involved in sensation, memory, emotion, and motor behavior. Mechanisms in the forebrain synthesize these perceptual and motor elements into the dream itself. (Adapted from McCarley, 1983.)*

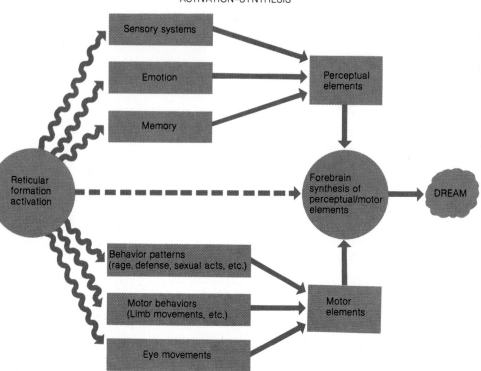

neural mechanism at the level of the brain stem that blocks nerve impulses from the brain to the skeletal muscles. Cats with damage to this brain stem mechanism act out their dreams physically. They typically groom themselves, then get up and chase something around their cage. While chasing the mouse of their dreams, they will ignore real mice placed in their cages, showing that they are definitely asleep (Morrison, 1983).

Down through the ages people have sought to understand the shadowy world of dreams. Because dreams often seem to have some sort of symbolic significance, people have tended to think of them as informative, even prophetic. In psychology, the possible symbolic significance of dreams has been of special interest to psychodynamic theorists.

FREUD'S THEORY

Sigmund Freud believed that dreams are stimulated by unconscious impulses and that the aim of any dream is **wish fulfillment,** the gratification of some instinct. Because of Freud's conviction that dreams allow our unconscious to disguise forbidden thoughts and desires and slip them past our defenses in disguised form, he regarded dreams as "the royal road to the unconscious."

Freud distinguished between a dream's **manifest content** (the story or symbols that the dreamer reports) and its **latent content** (its true psychological meaning). The process by which the dream's latent content is transformed for defensive purposes into the manifest content is called **dream work.** Freud believed that if the unconscious material in the dream were to appear in undisguised form, it might frighten or awaken the sleeper. Freud regarded nightmares as dreams in which the latent content was insufficiently disguised. The following dream was interpreted as an expression of the clash between dangerous impulses and restraining defenses that presumably takes place within every person. The two "people" in the dream are thought to be these two aspects of the dreamer.

I am walking, holding a leash in my hand to which is attached a young man, who is very sweet and docile. All of a sudden, he turns into a ferocious beast, threatening to destroy me. I grab ahold of him, and we attempt to fight, but it becomes apparent neither of us can win: the best I can do is keep him from destroying me. (Whitmont and Kaufmann, 1973, p. 94)

Because they believe that dreams serve as a means of releasing mental tension, resolving conflicts, and compensating for things that are lacking in our waking lives, psychodynamic therapists often use dream interpretation as a central part of treatment. In this way they hope to help patients achieve insight into the psychodynamics that underlie their behavior.

DREAMS AND MEMORY CONSOLIDATION

Dreaming clearly involves some kind of brain activity, and perhaps this activity in some way improves the brain's mental functioning. For example, dreaming may help the brain to consolidate memories of things we learned while awake (Cartwright, 1977). In animals, the amount of REM activity during sleep increases significantly for about seven hours following the learning of a complex task (Smith and Lapp, 1984). Findings suggesting the possible role of REM sleep in memory consolidation have also been reported in humans. In one study, subjects who had been asleep in the laboratory for five hours were awakened and told that they were going to learn something before going back to sleep. They were shown a series of slides depicting common objects and were asked to write down the names of all the objects they could remember. Then they went back to sleep for another two hours, and their EEG patterns and eye movements were monitored. When they woke up, those subjects who had had REM sleep during the interval either showed no memory loss or remembered even more of the objects than before. But those who did not have any REM sleep showed significantly poorer recall (Barker, 1972). Findings like these have fueled speculation that REM sleep is linked to cognitive processes in the brain. Table 4.1 outlines some of the other key observations scientists have made about dreaming.

DREAMING AS HOMEOSTASIS

Perhaps REM sleep plays an even more basic role in brain functioning. Early in the history of dream research, scientists concluded that we seem to have a definite need for REM sleep. When subjects were pre-

TABLE 4.1 SOME FACTS ABOUT DREAMS, DREAMING, AND DREAMERS

It appears that everyone dreams, and people who do not recall their dreams have about as much REM sleep as people who do.

When subjects are awakened from REM sleep and asked to act out their dreams, the length of time it takes them to do so is about as long as the REM episode, suggesting that incidents in dreams last about as long as they would in "real life."

Some people have **lucid dreams,** meaning that they are aware that they are dreaming. They voluntarily initiate actions in their dreams (like suspending themselves in midair) to prove to themselves that they are indeed dreaming. From their sleep state, they can signal an experimenter that they are dreaming by activating a mechanical switch.

People can control their dream content to varying degrees by means of presleep suggestions that they will have a particular dream.

Sleepwalking and sleeptalking generally take place in the non-REM stages of deep sleep, as do the "night terrors" that cause some children to cry out in their sleep.

Dreams occurring during the night's first REM periods tend to be related to events of the preceding day, while those in later REM periods tend to be more vivid, unusual, and, sometimes, anxiety-provoking.

Men's dreams tend to be more active and aggressive than women's. Men use more "action" terms to describe their dreams, while women use more "emotional" terms.

Dreams are frequently reported to be in color. Color-blind people dream in the colors they see when awake, and people blind from birth dream in the senses they know, mainly hearing and touch.

vented from dreaming for several nights by being awakened each time they entered a REM phase, they spent more time in REM sleep on subsequent nights, as if they needed to catch up on their dreaming. They also tended to slip into REM phases much sooner after they went to sleep (Dement, 1974). This **REM rebound ef-**

SLEEP DISORDERS

The physiological mechanisms involved in sleep are complex, and they can go wrong in a variety of ways. Most of us take our relatively stable sleep cycles for granted. But millions of people suffer from sleep problems whose effects range from relatively mild to life-threatening (Chase and Weitzman, 1983).

The most common chronic sleep complaint, afflicting between 10 and 25 percent of the population, is *insomnia,* the inability to fall asleep or remain asleep. Insomnia is not a single disorder; it may be associated with a variety of physiological conditions, with alcohol and drug abuse, and with emotional problems such as anxiety and depression (Wehr and others, 1983). Some insomniacs suffer from a *delayed sleep phase syndrome,* or pattern, in which they are unable to go to sleep until 2 to 6 A.M. They awaken for work or school the next morning feeling exhausted. On weekends, however, they sleep to a late hour (11 A.M. to 2 P.M.) and awaken refreshed. Victims of delayed sleep phase have been treated successfully by essentially resetting their biological clocks. The sufferers go to bed later and later over several days until their biological clocks have been reset to an acceptable time for sleeping and waking, such as 11 P.M. to 7 A.M. (Weitzman and others, 1983).

The traditional method of treating insomnia is with sedating drugs, which can have undesirable side effects and may be addictive (Roth and Zorick, 1983). However, promising results have recently been obtained with nondrug treatments such as changing the sleep cycle, meditation (see the next section), and relaxation training (Duguay and others, 1984).

A more serious disorder than insomnia is *narcolepsy,* a condition in which people suffer sudden and uncontrollable sleep attacks. In its milder forms,

FIGURE 4.8 *Dogs suffering from narcolepsy, a disorder involving sudden and unpredictable sleep attacks, are being studied at Stanford's Sleep Disorders Center. This dog suddenly falls to the floor and lapses into sleep.*

the person may simply "go blank" for a brief period, and then continue his or her activities as if nothing had happened. Children with this form of the disorder may be mistakenly labeled as inattentive or daydreaming, when, in fact, they are briefly asleep. In more severe cases, narcoleptics suddenly fall asleep during the day and may even collapse in the middle of a vigorous activity. Physiological recordings show the sudden appearance of REM sleep during narcoleptic attacks.

The causes of narcolepsy are unknown, and so is its cure. However, animals can also have the disorder, and in them, there appears to be a genetic basis for it. Through selective breeding, a colony of narcoleptic

fect suggested that REM sleep may maintain some kind of an internal equilibrium, or homeostasis, in the brain.

Recent research suggests that one homeostatic function of dreams may be to give the right hemisphere

of the brain a chance to be more active than it is during our predominantly left-brain waking activity. Consistent with this view is the finding that people whose waking time is dominated by left-hemisphere verbal-logical activity seem to show a greater REM rebound dogs has been developed at Stanford University's Sleep Disorders Center (Dement, 1983). Research on these animals may advance our understanding of this baffling disorder (see Figure 4.8).

In the 1970s, a middle-aged man was being studied in a sleep laboratory. He complained of daytime tiredness and his wife complained of his loud and persistent snoring during sleep. Scientists observing his sleep in their laboratory were astounded to see his breathing suddenly stop for several minutes. The lack of oxygen eventually triggered brain stem reflexes and awakened him from the brink of death. He gasped loudly, causing the noises his wife thought were snores, then quickly lapsed back into sleep. Soon he stopped breathing again, and the death-defying pattern was repeated—over 500 times per night (Guilleminault and others, 1973).

The man was suffering from *sleep apnea,* a serious and life-threatening disorder in which breathing stops. This occurs because of a collapse of the pharynx resulting in an obstruction of the upper airway (Remmers, 1983). Although the respiratory rhythm is normal, no air gets through; the airway collapses like a straw being sucked on while a finger is placed over the other end. Cardiac failure is one possible consequence of the obstruction and is probably a leading cause of death in apnea sufferers.

As apnea became a topic of scientific study, researchers soon forged a link between it and *Sudden Infant Death Syndrome* (SIDS), or "crib death," which claims the lives of infants in their sleep. Indeed, middle-aged apnea victims may be the survivors of SIDS; perhaps they remain alive because they wake up. There is now speculation and some preliminary evidence that the non-REM, or "quiet," sleep of SIDS victims may differ from normal non-REM sleep and may prevent them from awakening in time to gasp life-giving air when respiration ceases because of apnea (Harper, 1983).

Many apnea sufferers are unaware of their condition. In one study, nearly a third of the patients who were referred to a sleep clinic because of complaints about their snoring had sleep apnea (Miles and Simmons, 1984). Other unknowing victims of sleep apnea who report disturbed sleep patterns may be at risk from an ironic source—the sedatives prescribed by physicians unaware of their condition to help them sleep more soundly. Such medications could suppress the reflexes that ordinarily rouse them in time. Alcohol and other drugs could have the same effect (Herbert, 1982).

The treatment of apnea remains a mystery. Surgeries to eliminate occlusion of the windpipe have had mixed results (Dinner and others, 1984; Schoen and others, 1984). The search continues for the causes and a successful treatment for this serious disorder.

Sleep disorders occur during the entire life span, from infancy to old age. Some conditions, such as narcolepsy, appear in childhood or adolescence and never disappear. Others appear later in life. Most of us can look forward to a decrease in sleep efficiency as we get older. It doesn't appear that the *need* for sleep decreases, but rather that the ability to sleep deteriorates as we age (Dement, 1983). Sleep disorders associated with aging are only now beginning to receive the scientific attention they deserve. The establishment of sleep disorder centers in major hospitals and universities promises to speed progress in understanding the nature and functions of sleep and the conditions that give rise to sleep problems.

effect the night after they have been repeatedly awakened from REM sleep, as if they had more "catching up" to do (Cartwright, 1977).

Although we have nearly as many scientific questions about sleep as we have answers, both sleeping and dreaming are clearly important to our physical, mental, and emotional well-being. For this reason, scientific interest in sleep disorders has surged in recent years. Frontier 4.1 describes recent attempts to understand and treat these disorders.

MEDITATION

Meditation has a long history. It has been performed throughout the world for centuries in connection with religious, military, and recreational activities. In the United States, however, most of the current interest in meditation has occurred during the past few decades. Transcendental Meditation (TM), a quasi-religious technique founded by the Maharishi Mahesh Yogi, may have as many as half a million American disciples who practice it daily. The increasing popularity of meditation seems to reflect a search for peace and harmony in a world that has become increasingly chaotic and stressful.

All forms of meditation involve concentrating on something—a thought, sensation, word, object, or mental state. **Active meditation** techniques require practitioners to make strenuous efforts to focus their attention. In certain Yoga techniques, for example, practitioners maintain specific postures and deliberately control their breathing. Other meditation techniques, such as Transcendental Meditation, are **passive** approaches. Passive meditators remain in a quiet atmosphere and make a relaxed attempt to achieve a state of inner peace by concentrating on a particular thought or on their breathing. Most passive techniques are practiced for two 20-minute periods each day, once in the morning and again before dinner. Proponents of passive meditation report positive personality changes, improved interpersonal functioning, increased energy and mental efficiency, and reduction in tension and stress. Not all scientific evidence supports these claims (Shapiro and Walsh, 1984), but there is little doubt that many people find meditative techniques helpful.

Popular as well as scientific interest in meditation was sparked by early reports that meditation, like drugs, could produce dramatically altered states of consciousness. But, in fact, bizarre or mystical experiences are not very common while meditating (Goleman, 1977). People do, however, frequently report feeling deeply relaxed, free from stress, and refreshed by meditation. Thus current interest is centering on meditation's possible stress-reducing effects.

Meditation and stress

EEG recordings made during meditation show brain wave patterns that are typically associated with relaxation and drowsiness. Most notable are increases in **alpha rhythm,** the brain wave pattern closely associated with a pleasant state of relaxation and low physiological arousal (see Figure 4.9). EEG studies suggest that during as much as 40 percent of their meditation time, meditators may actually be asleep (Pagano and Warrenburg, 1983). There are also decreases in respiration rate, heart rate, and amount of blood lactate, a chemical associated with fatigue and anxiety.

"My problem has always been an overabundance of alpha waves."

FIGURE 4.9 *Alpha waves in the brain are associated with a relaxed waking state. Meditation is one of several restful activities that can produce an increase in alpha waves.*

Meditation is believed to affect the autonomic nervous system, whose sympathetic branch arouses the body for action and whose parasympathetic branch calms us down. The physiological responses of TM subjects suggest that meditation causes an increase in parasympathetic activity, a decrease in sympathetic activity, or both. Thus, meditation results in a state of relaxation that is quite the opposite of the body's "fight or flight" response to danger and stress. Herbert Benson (1975) of Harvard University has referred to the restful physiological state produced by meditation as the **relaxation response.** He also notes that a variety of activities aside from meditation, such as restful relaxation and even exercise, can produce this response.

Benson maintains that the relaxation response is a generalized physical and mental reaction. But other researchers feel that a distinction should be made between **somatic** (bodily) **relaxation** and **cognitive** (mental) **relaxation** (Davidson, 1978). If you've ever had the experience of trying to go to sleep while your body was deeply relaxed but your mind was racing with thoughts, you have first-hand knowledge of the difference between somatic and cognitive relaxation. Meditation has been found to be effective for producing somatic relaxation, but no more so than other techniques such as training in voluntary muscle relaxation or simply resting (Holmes, 1984; Pagano and Warrenburg, 1983). On the other hand, meditation seems ideally suited for the promotion of cognitive relaxation, since attention is diverted from intrusive and anxiety-arousing thoughts and concentrated instead on a neutral word or idea, or on one's breathing.

Proponents of meditation have hailed it as a unique state of consciousness and as a panacea for everything from stress to drug abuse, crime, and the threat of nuclear war. And yet, despite the benefits reported by many meditators, meditation has not stood up very well under the unblinking eye of controlled research. An extensive review of the current scientific literature resulted in this conclusion:

We regret to report that our search for a unique or dramatic effect directly attributable to meditation thus far has not been successful. In this area many practitioners have made sweeping claims about the effectiveness of their techniques. Frequently, this is based on subjective experience, and often the claims are "shored up" on the basis of "research." All too often, this research turns out not to be

very rigorous—really only of a pilot nature. This has been especially true within the TM movement. Our experience has been that when good scientific methodology has been used, the claims made have been extravagant and premature. (Pagano and Warrenburg, 1983, p. 203)

Does this mean that meditation is without merit? Not at all. Meditation is only one of a variety of ways to experience relaxation and a sense of well-being. Activities such as reading for pleasure, physical exercise, restful leisure activities, and daydreaming may be equally valuable, depending on individual characteristics and needs. The important element in any relaxation technique may simply be the temporary withdrawal it provides from the stresses and strains of daily living.

HYPNOSIS

The idea that people can be controlled through hypnotic power has been popularized, and often sensationalized, in books, plays, and movies. We are all familiar with the stereotype of a hypnotized person in a zombielike trance who mindlessly obeys the sinister hypnotist, and with the fantastic "feats" performed by stage hypnotists. Considering how long hypnosis has been around, you may be surprised to learn that much controversy still rages among scientists about what hypnosis is, as well as about the psychological processes that underlie its effects on consciousness, on the body, and on behavior.

Animal magnetism, mesmerism, and hypnosis

During the eighteenth century a Viennese physician named Anton Mesmer became famous as a result of a series of dramatic cures of physical and psychological afflictions. He claimed that these cures were brought about by magnetic forces that radiated from the planets. Mesmer treated his patients by exposing them to magnetic objects and fluids in order to restore their "bodily harmony," and he called his technique *animal magnetism*. Later, it came to be called **mesmerism**.

The patients who came to Mesmer's clinic were treated in a *baquet*, a trough around which more than 30 persons could be "magnetized" simultaneously. The bottom of the trough was covered with iron filings, other minerals, and bottles. The patients were tied to the baquet with cords and instructed to join hands. Mesmer, adorned in impressive robes, paced through the crowd, from time to time touching the bodies of patients with an iron rod, placing his hands on their abdomens, or "magnetizing" them with his eyes (see Figure 4.10). A visitor to the baquet gave this description of the scene:

Some patients remain calm, and experience nothing; others cough, spit, feel slight pain, a local or general heat, and fall into sweats; others are agitated and tormented by

---

FIGURE 4.10 *An eighteenth-century Dodd engraving portrays an "animal magnetizer" putting his patient into a "crisis."*

convulsions. These convulsions are remarkable for their number, duration, and force, and have been known to persist for more than three hours. They are characterized by involuntary, jerking movements in all the limbs, and in the whole body, by contraction of the throat, by twitchings in the . . . abdominal regions, by dimness and rolling of the eyes, by piercing cries, tears, hiccoughs, and immoderate laughter. They are preceded or followed by a state of languor or dreaminess, by a series of digressions, and even by stupor. . . . it is impossible not to admit, from all these results, that some great force acts upon and masters the patients, and that this force appears to reside in the magnetizer. This convulsive state is termed the crisis. . . .

Young women were so much gratified by the crisis that they begged to be thrown into it anew; they followed Mesmer through the hall and confessed that it was impossible not to be warmly attached to the magnetizer's person. (Binet and Fere, 1901, pp. 9–11)

Descriptions like this undoubtedly strengthened the view that mesmerism was a mystical and possibly dangerous spiritual force. Concerned that young women could easily be seduced while under the influence of these mysterious forces, a French scientific commission recommended that mesmerism be outlawed in France, and for a time it was.

James Braid, a Scottish surgeon, was impressed by the fact that patients undergoing mesmerism often went into a trance in which they appeared to be oblivious to their surroundings. He decided that mesmerism was a state of "nervous sleep" that the subject entered because of concentrated attention rather than as a result of magnetic forces. Braid noted that individuals who entered this state of "nervous sleep" became highly responsive to verbal suggestions, and in 1842 he renamed the phenomenon **hypnosis**, for Hypnos, the Greek god of sleep.

The scientific study of hypnosis

Much of what we know about hypnosis has been learned only in the last 25 years. Controlled research has been made possible by the development of **hypnotic susceptibility scales**. These scales or tests contain a series of items that investigators can read to subjects. Each item involves a different suggested behavior (for example, "You cannot move your arm"). Subjects are given a "pass" or "fail" on each item, depending on whether they meet specific criteria for compliance with the suggestion. The total hypnotic susceptibility score is based on the number of "passes." Items from one of the most widely used research scales, the Stanford Hypnotic Susceptibility Scale, are described in Table 4.2. Additional measures have been developed to explore how people feel under hypnosis and what their experiences are like. Such scales ask subjects to rate the intensity of various experiences they may have had during hypnosis (Tellegen, 1979).

Hypnotic susceptibility scales make it possible to manipulate and study the effects of a variety of situational, procedural, and individual difference factors on hypnotic susceptibility. Some existing scales can be

administered either with or without previous hypnotic induction instructions, so that the behaviors and experiences of hypnotized subjects can be compared with those of nonhypnotized control subjects.

Most of us are fascinated by hypnosis because we have either seen or heard about remarkable physical, mental, and behavioral variations that occur when people are hypnotized. The effects of hypnosis can be so striking and profound that they defy explanation in terms of everyday psychological principles. Or do they? Let us examine some of these effects more closely.

Hypnotic behaviors and experiences

Hypnotists typically begin their sessions by asking their subjects to stare at a stationary or moving object, such as a thumbtack on the wall or a swinging pendant. In a soothing voice they suggest that the subjects' eyelids are becoming heavy, that they are relaxing and becoming hypnotized, and that they will find it easy to comply with the hypnotist's suggestions. If subjects are willing to be hypnotized, they appear relaxed and drowsy and become responsive to test suggestions from the hypnotist. Afterward, they report changes in bodily sensations and claim that they have been hypnotized.

Hypnotic induction can produce striking changes in consciousness and behavior. The most striking characteristic of hypnotized subjects is an increase in their suggestibility. Highly susceptible subjects focus their attention wherever the hypnotist suggests. Subjects may suspend their reality testing and readily accept distorted experiences. Under hypnosis one may vividly experience things (such as a large purple dog sitting in one's lap) that would ordinarily be rejected as impossible. Increased suggestibility may also be manifested by "naturally" enacting unusual roles. In hypnotic age regression, for example, some subjects are able to experience themselves as they were at a much earlier age and to act accordingly.

Distortions in cognition also can occur under hyp-

TABLE 4.2 SAMPLE TEST ITEMS AND CRITERIA FOR PASSING FROM THE STANFORD HYPNOTIC SUSCEPTIBILITY SCALE, FORM C

ITEM	SUGGESTED BEHAVIOR	CRITERION FOR PASSING
Arm lowering	Right arm is held out; subject is told arm will become heavy and drop.	Arm is lowered at least 6 inches in 10 seconds.
Moving hands apart	With hands extended and close together, subject is asked to imagine a force acting to push them apart.	Hands are 6 or more inches apart in 10 seconds.
Mosquito hallucination	It is suggested that a mosquito buzzing nearby alights on the subject.	Any grimacing movement or acknowledgment of mosquito that occurs.
Posthypnotic amnesia	Subject is awakened and asked to recall suggestions after being told they cannot be remembered.	Three or fewer items are recalled before subject is told, "Now you can remember everything."

Source: Adapted from Weitzenhoffer and Hilgard, 1962.

FIGURE 4.11 *Hypnosis is receiving increasing police use in attempts to enhance the recall of witnesses to crimes. The sessions are videotaped for later presentation in court. Recent research suggests the use of caution in investigative hypnosis.*

nosis. Instances of posthypnotic amnesia are commonly observed. If told to forget what occurred under hypnosis, some suggestible subjects show an absence of recall until they are later told by the hypnotist that they can remember (Kihlstrom and Shor, 1978).

The use of hypnosis to improve memory has a long history, but the topic is now being studied with new vigor. One reason is the increasing use of hypnosis by police (see Figure 4.11) to aid the recall of eyewitnesses to crimes (Hibler, 1984). Unfortunately, however, scientific evidence casts doubt on the assumption that hypnosis can aid recall. A recent survey of the results of many controlled studies indicated that when proper control groups are used, hypnosis does not significantly help memory (Smith, 1983). Even more disturbing is the fact that some of the "memories" recalled under hypnosis are actually manufactured during the hypnotic state on the basis of inadvertent suggestions or "facts" implied by the questions (Laurence and Perry, 1983). These findings have alarming implications for the use of investigative hypnosis.

PERCEPTUAL DISTORTIONS

Hypnosis can produce marked perceptual distortions, including temporary deafness, blindness, and visual hallucinations. For example, some hypnotized subjects who are told that they can no longer hear do not react to unexpected sounds, insults, and so on.

But are these hypnotically deaf people actually deaf? To find out, Theodore Barber and David S. Calverley (1964) used a method known as **delayed auditory feedback.** In this technique people speak into a microphone and hear their own voice through a set of earphones, but transmission of the voice is delayed for a fraction of a second. When individuals with normal hearing are exposed to delayed auditory feedback, they typically begin to stammer and to mispronounce words. Deaf people keep right on talking because they cannot hear the disruptive feedback. Barber and Calverley hypnotized subjects and suggested to them that they could no longer hear. When these subjects were tested on delayed auditory feedback, they showed the same speech distortions as did nonhypnotized control subjects.

Clearly, hypnotic deafness is not the same as physiological deafness. But how does it occur? Is the auditory input registering at a physiological level but being cut off from conscious experience in some way? Later we will consider a theory that states that this is exactly what happens during hypnosis.

PHYSIOLOGICAL EFFECTS

Studies have indicated that hypnosis can have striking physiological effects. Nearsighted people see more clearly; allergic responses are inhibited; warts are cured; stomach acidity can be increased. However, other well-controlled studies have shown that nonhypnotized control subjects who are given the same suggestions can also exhibit these same responses (Barber and others, 1974). The power of suggestion alone can apparently produce some rather remarkable physiological effects.

An investigation that illustrates the powerful effects that suggestions can have, with or without hypnosis, involved 13 subjects who were allergic to two poisonous trees. Five were hypnotized and the other 8 served as controls. Each subject was blindfolded and told that one arm was being touched by leaves from a harmless tree, when in fact it was being touched by leaves from one of the poisonous trees. Four out of the 5 hypnotized subjects and 7 out of the 8 nonhypnotized controls had no allergic reaction. Next, the subject's other arm was rubbed with leaves from a harmless tree and he or she was told that the leaves were poisonous. All subjects, both hypnotized and control, responded to this suggestion with mild to severe allergic reactions (Ikemi and Nakagawa, 1962). These results dramatically demonstrate how thinking can make it so.

Most hypnotism shows contain several "amazing physical feats" performed by "entranced" subjects. One is the so-called human plank routine. A male subject is placed between two chairs, one chair beneath the calves of his legs, the other beneath his shoulders. He is told that his body is absolutely rigid, and a woman is asked to stand on his chest. The audience attributes the man's ability to support the woman to his "profound somnambulistic trance." What they don't know is that an average man suspended in this manner can support at least 300 pounds on his chest with little discomfort and no need of a hypnotic "trance" (see Figure 4.12). However, stage hypnotists are not known for their insistence on nonhypnotized control subjects.

There are indications that suggestions given under hypnosis can bring about long-lasting physical changes in the body. Several studies indicate that significant increases in breast size (1 to 2.5 inches) can be brought about in women by means of hypnotic suggestions of swelling sensations, tightness of the skin over the

breasts, and age regression to the adolescent period of breast growth (Staib and Logan, 1977; Willard, 1977; Williams, 1974). The increases were largely maintained over 3-month follow-up periods. If confirmed by future research, the results suggest a possible alternative to surgical methods of breast augmentation.

INCREASED PAIN TOLERANCE

Virtually every surgical procedure known to medicine has been accomplished under hypnosis (Ewin, 1984). Hypnosis has been used successfully to control pain

FIGURE 4.12 *The "human plank" demonstration is a favorite of stage hypnotists and seems to reveal the power of the hypnotic trance. Most of the audience is unaware that the average man suspended in this manner can support about 300 pounds on his chest without hypnosis.*

during surgery since the nineteenth century (see Figure 4.13). The Scottish surgeon James Esdaile did more than 300 major operations in the mid-1800s using hypnosis as the sole anesthetic. Joseph Barber (1977), a noted hypnotherapist, needed an average of only 11 minutes to hypnotically produce adequate analgesia in 99 out of 100 dental patients.

Taken at face value, clinical reports of surgery under hypnosis are impressive. Most of us assume that the pain resulting from cutting into internal organs would be impossible to tolerate. Actually, however, most tissues of the body other than the skin are rather insensitive to cutting (although they are sensitive to other sensations, such as stretching or pressure). If people can tolerate the initial incision through the skin, they can probably tolerate extensive internal cutting with little discomfort. Major operations, such as ampu-

FIGURE 4.13 *This patient is undergoing an appendectomy with hypnosis as the sole anesthetic. The hypnotic suggestions that the patient can feel no pain are being delivered through the tape recorder.*

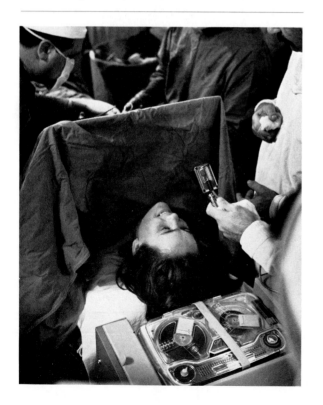

tating limbs, removing thyroid glands, removing the appendix, cutting and draining the gall bladder, removing glands in the neck and groin, and removing the female breast, have been performed without hypnosis by using only a local anesthetic to desensitize the skin (Barber and others, 1974). It is noteworthy in this regard that in most cases of major surgery performed under hypnosis, local anesthetics are used to deaden the skin in the area of the incision. And again, there is evidence that giving suggestions for anesthesia and surgical pain relief to unhypnotized patients may at times be as effective as giving them suggestions after hypnotic induction (Evans and Paul, 1970).

It would be a mistake to conclude, however, that hypnosis has no value in increasing pain tolerance. The effects are undoubtedly real, and they are striking. Controlled clinical and laboratory studies have shown dramatic increases in pain tolerance under hypnosis (Coe, 1980). What is at issue is how the effects are produced. By reducing anxiety and fear; by establishing positive attitudes, motivations, and expectations about stressful situations; by distracting patients from their pain; by exposing them to believable suggestions that they will not experience pain; or by somehow helping them to separate the pain from conscious experience, hypnosis may be unusually effective as a way of increasing tolerance of pain.

Theories of hypnosis

Once again, the control group has reared its ugly head and challenged our romantic notions about a psychological phenomenon. We have seen that when appropriate control groups are included in studies of hypnosis, they often exhibit the same dramatic changes in experience and behavior that hypnotized people report.

If hypnotic and nonhypnotic behavior is really similar, then what is hypnosis and how does it produce its effects? The best way to begin to answer this question is to state what hypnosis is *not*. It is not sleep, nor is it any other state of consciousness with unique physiological properties. The EEGs of subjects under hypnosis are not like those of people in any of the recognized states of sleep. Instead, they are the same as those for people in a waking state, and they change continuously, depending on the activities that the person is engaging in. No physiological measure shows a unique pattern for hypnosis that would enable us to tell who is hypnotized and who isn't (Bauer and McCanne, 1980).

This fact has important implications. If we wish to maintain that a specific physiological state, the "hypnotic trance," is the scientific explanation for hypnotic behavior, then we must be able to define and measure that state in some way other than in terms of the behaviors it is assumed to produce. If we can't do that, we find ourselves on the scientifically uncomfortable merry-go-round of circular reasoning: "Why do hypnotic subjects behave as they do? Because they are in a trance. How do we know that they are in a trance? Because they behave as they do." Clearly, we've explained nothing.

Because hypnosis does not seem to be a distinct physiological state and because hypnotized and non-hypnotized subjects often behave in identical ways, psychologists have sought to understand hypnosis in terms of other psychological processes: role playing, imagination, hemispheric dominance shifts, and dissociation.

ROLE PLAYING

A number of theorists have advanced a **role theory of hypnosis.** They have suggested that being hypnotized involves "taking on" the role of a hypnotized person (Sarbin and Coe, 1972). In our culture, most people have a general idea of how hypnotized individuals are supposed to behave: they are supposed to be responsive to suggestions, to listen carefully to the hypnotist, to have a trancelike appearance, and to lose their self-consciousness. People who are motivated to conform to this role, who are free from fears or inhibitions, and who expect to be able to experience hypnosis are likely to adopt successfully the role of hypnotized subject and to experience the suggested effects.

The importance of beliefs and expectations about the hypnotic role was shown in a study conducted by Martin Orne of the University of Pennsylvania. During a classroom demonstration, college students were told that hypnotized people frequently exhibit "catalepsy (stiffening of the muscles) of the dominant hand." (Actually, catalepsy of the hand rarely, if ever, occurs spontaneously in hypnosis.) An accomplice of the lec-

turer was then hypnotized, and, sure enough, he "spontaneously" exhibited the cataleptic response. When students who had seen the demonstration were later hypnotized, 55 percent of them exhibited the catalepsy spontaneously without any suggestion from the hypnotist. A group of control subjects saw a demonstration without a mention or exhibition of catalepsy. Not one of them exhibited catalepsy when hypnotized later (Orne, 1959).

Does the role-playing explanation of hypnosis mean that people are simply faking or play-acting when they are hypnotized? Not at all. Role theorists stress that we are constantly taking on roles in our daily lives. Being a hypnotic subject is simply another specific role. When people become truly immersed in this role, the experiences and behaviors that result are as completely real to them as the role of college student is to you. They are not merely play-acting.

IMAGINATION

Hypnotic experiences and behaviors can also be seen as the result of thought and imagination. If an individual is able to become actively involved in imagining, then it seems as if the imagined events actually do occur. Research has shown that imagining an event often produces the same bodily changes as occur during an actual event. For example, individuals who imagine themselves moving body parts actually do have small but measurable movements in those muscles (Katkin and Goldband, 1980). During hypnosis, this "as if" process is supported by the hypnotist's suggestions. When a hypnotist suggests to a subject that his or her arm feels heavy, the subject may imagine previous experiences in which the arm did feel heavy and may reexperience the sensations. Researchers have found that people who are especially responsive to hypnotic suggestions have rich imaginative lives and tend to become absorbed in the themes of their imagery (Hilgard, 1970). One highly responsive hypnotic subject reported the following experience:

I identify myself with the character in *1984*, with Winston Smith, who was tortured at the end, fearing rats. His head was in a cage and he felt he would have to submit. I *felt* the fear that he felt as it came closer, closer. Walking back from the Union after finishing the book, I had a problem relating myself to my present environment, to the stuff around me, for I was so entangled in the story that I had become exhausted. (J. R. Hilgard, 1970, p. 26)

CEREBRAL HEMISPHERE SHIFTS

Many hypnotic effects, such as the suspension of reality testing and the forming of vivid images, resemble right cerebral hemisphere functions (Wall, 1984). Recent scientific evidence suggests that hypnosis may involve a **hemispheric dominance shift**—a shift in cerebral activity toward relatively greater right hemisphere activation. In one direct test of cortical functioning during hypnosis, right hemisphere cortical brain wave activity became relatively more dominant during the hypnotic period (Chen and others, 1981).

Hemispheric shifts can also be examined through a **dichotic listening technique.** Subjects wearing earphones are simultaneously presented with different syllables to each ear and are asked to repeat what they hear. Because the left hemisphere receives input primarily from the right ear and the right hemisphere from the left ear, hemispheric dominance is indicated by how much of the input from each ear gets through.

As Figure 4.14 shows, dichotic listening under hypnosis shows a shift toward relatively greater right hemisphere activation (Pagano and others, 1985). Thus, hypnosis may be an effective means of engaging right hemisphere functions.

DISSOCIATION

The case of multiple personality that opened this chapter illustrated how mental events can become so split off from each other that 10 distinct personalities, some totally unaware of the others, coexisted in the same person. As we later pointed out, less extreme forms of dissociation occur in our daily lives.

Ernest Hilgard (1977) of Stanford University has been studying the possible role of dissociation in hypnosis. Hilgard's basic approach is to try to communicate with what he calls the "**hidden observer**," a subconscious mind that remains in contact with reality while the person is hypnotized. For example, procedures that are normally quite painful, such as placing the hand and forearm in ice water—see Figure 4.15(*a*), can be experienced as painless by hypnotized subjects who receive the suggestion that they will feel no pain. If it is suggested to the subject that all awareness of the other arm will be lost, but that this arm will write down how the person really feels, the nonstressed arm may report a rise in pain even while the hypnotized person verbally reports feeling very little pain—see Figure

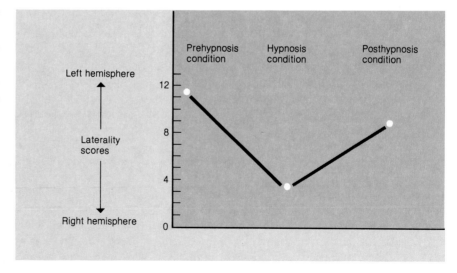

FIGURE 4.14 *Dichotic listening scores recorded before, during, and following hypnosis. The pattern indicates a shift toward relatively greater right hemisphere dominance during hypnosis. (Adapted from Pagano and others, 1985.)*

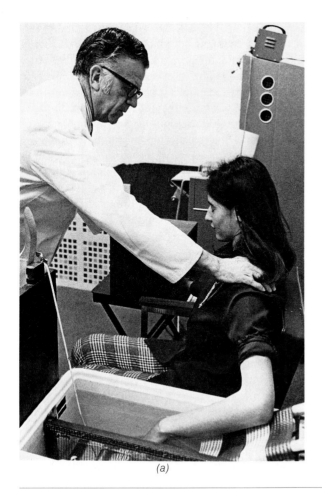

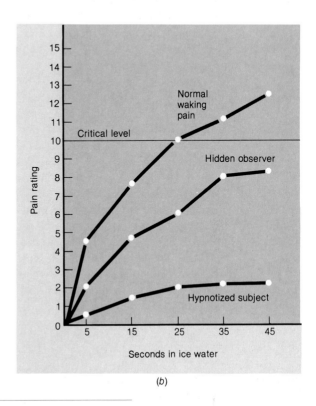

(a)

(b)

FIGURE 4.15   *(a) This hypnotic subject's hand is immersed in painfully cold ice water. By placing his hand on her shoulder, hypnosis researcher Ernest Hilgard contacts her dissociated "hidden observer." (b) This figure shows the pain intensity ratings given by the subject when she is not hypnotized, under hypnosis, and by the "hidden observer" in the same hypnotic state. The "hidden observer" reports more pain than does the hypnotized subject, but less than is reported by the subject when not hypnotized.*

4.15(*b*). The "hidden observer" can also report sounds presented while the subject is hypnotically deaf or may remember facts that the hypnotized subject cannot recall because of amnesia instructions. It has been suggested that the "hidden observer" may involve left hemisphere functioning that is dissociated from right hemisphere activities that dominate during hypnosis (Wall, 1984).

There are wide individual differences in hypnotic susceptibility, and these may be linked to differences in the ability to dissociate. Perhaps people who are highly susceptible to hypnosis can dissociate better than low-susceptibility people because they can register and respond to information that is not consciously perceived. Future research on hypnosis may help us to understand the process of dissociation not only in hypnosis but also in multiple personality and in other states of consciousness.

DRUGS AND CONSCIOUSNESS

A **drug** is any substance, other than food, whose chemical action alters the structure or functioning of the body. There are many different kinds of drugs. We concern ourselves here with drugs that affect the functioning of the nervous system and produce alterations in states of consciousness.

Like any cell, a neuron is essentially a fragile bag of chemicals floating in a liquid that has specific chemical properties. The neuron's life and activities are governed by chemical interactions within it, between it and other neurons, and between it and the surrounding fluid. It should not be surprising that this delicate chemical balancing act makes neurons highly vulnerable to invading chemicals. To protect neurons, certain cells form a **blood-brain barrier** that screens out foreign chemicals in the brain's blood supply while letting in substances that the neurons need. Generally, the blood-brain barrier does a very effective job, but there are some chemical substances that can pass through the blood-brain barrier and affect the workings of neurons, often in a dramatic fashion. Alcohol is one of them. Others come from the opium poppy, the peyote cactus, and the coca and hemp plants. Additional substances are produced artificially in pharmaceutical laboratories. Collectively, these substances are known as the **psychoactive drugs,** and they are the fastest, the most effective, and, in some instances, the most dangerous way of artificially altering states of consciousness.

Mechanisms of drug action

Psychoactive drugs produce their effects by altering the normal functioning of neurons in some way. By duplicating, stimulating, or inhibiting the neuron's naturally occurring processes, a psychoactive drug can speed up, slow down, or stop synaptic transmission. The magnitude of the effect depends on the concentration of the drug at the site where it affects the neuron. The duration of its effect depends on how long it continues to influence the neuron.

Drugs can interfere with synaptic transmission in several ways. Some drugs mimic, or imitate, certain natural neurotransmitters. Their molecules are shaped like the natural neurotransmitters and act like them, so they can occupy the neuron's receptor sites and fire it, just as the natural neurotransmitter would. Drugs known as stimulants often act in this way. Other drugs can prevent neural firing by occupying the receptor site and keeping the natural neurotransmitter from reaching the neuron. Some tranquilizers work in this way. Some drugs invade the neuron's membrane and prevent it from manufacturing transmitter substances. Others prevent the release of the neurotransmitters into the synaptic space. As a result, the neuron's ability to transmit information is lost. Finally, a drug that prevents the reuptake of a neurotransmitter from the synaptic space allows the transmitter to keep stimulating other neurons and greatly increases neural firing (Julien, 1985).

A particular drug may affect different people in varying and unpredictable ways. The effects of any drug can be heightened or diminished by several factors: dosage, frequency of use, the person's size and physical condition, his or her psychological state, whether other drugs have been taken or food eaten, expectations concerning the drug's effects, and the setting in which the drug is taken. Thus, in describing how psychoactive drugs affect consciousness and behavior, we have to speak in generalities while keeping the important role of these other factors in mind.

Before we describe the effects of specific drugs, we need to define three terms: *tolerance, dependence,* and *addiction.* When a person repeatedly uses a drug, the body adapts to it, and larger and larger doses are needed to produce the original effects. This need for increasingly larger doses is called **tolerance.** In an attempt to restore homeostasis, the nervous tissue has begun to counter the effect of the drug, so that more drug is needed to overcome the body's "protest."

When tolerance develops, it is frequently accompanied by dependence on the drug. **Physical dependence** means that when the drug is not taken, the person experiences unpleasant *withdrawal symptoms* because the body's protest response against the drug continues anyway. **Psychological dependence** means that the person simply wants the drug because of its pleasurable effects, not because he or she wants to avoid withdrawal symptoms. Psychological dependence can occur without physical dependence.

Addiction is usually defined as a strong physiological and psychological dependence on a habit-forming drug. Addicts lose their ability to control their drug intake, take drugs compulsively, and experience a craving when drugs are unavailable. Both tolerance and dependence undoubtedly underlie addiction.

Drugs can be classified in a number of different ways. Many researchers, as well as the Drug Enforcement Administration, currently classify psychoactive drugs into five categories: depressants, stimulants, narcotics, hallucinogens, and cannabis (marijuana) (*Drug Enforcement*, July 1979).

Depressants

Depressants decrease the level of activity in the nervous system. In moderate dosages, they reduce feelings of tension and anxiety and produce a state of relaxed euphoria. In extremely high dosages, however, depressants can slow down vital life processes to the point where death occurs.

ALCOHOL

The most commonly used depressant is alcohol, which has been used in virtually every society as a social relaxant for thousands of years. Its widespread cultural acceptance masks the fact that, because it affects the lives of so many people, alcohol is perhaps the most dangerous of all drugs.

If you get a "high" from drinking, you may be surprised to find alcohol classified as a depressant, but that's what it is. Alcohol seems to act directly on the neural cell membranes to reduce electrical impulses. Within the brain, alcohol in the blood affects the ascending reticular formation first. Normally, the ascending reticular system alerts and stimulates the cerebral cortex, but this process slows down under the influence of alcohol. The decreased input from the reticular formation results in a depression of inhibitory control mechanisms in the cortex. This release of inhibitions is seen in the happy or euphoric "high" experienced at low blood alcohol levels by many people. As one expert states, "At some point, we become uninhibited enough to enjoy our charming selves and uncritical enough to enjoy the clods around us. This point seems to occur when the alcohol has disrupted social inhibitions and impaired good judgment but has not depressed most behavior. We become witty, clever, true continentals. Fortunately, most of those around us at this time also have impairment of judgment, so they

can't say any differently!" (Ray, 1983, p. 165). The release of inhibitions makes it impossible to predict specific behavioral effects. Which behaviors are suppressed and which are released from inhibition depends on the individual. Thus, a usually shy person may become a live wire equipped with a lamp shade, while a typically friendly one may become a modern version of Attila the Hun.

As the concentration of alcohol in the blood increases, other parts of the brain, including the cerebral cortex, are directly affected. The behavioral and cognitive effects of progressively higher blood alcohol levels are shown in Table 4.3. As you can see, after the initial

TABLE 4.3 EFFECTS OF BLOOD ALCOHOL LEVELS ON CONSCIOUSNESS AND BEHAVIOR

BLOOD ALCOHOL LEVEL (PERCENT)	BEHAVIORAL EFFECTS
0.00	Sober
0.05	Lowered alertness, usually good feeling, release of inhibitions, impaired judgment
0.10	Slowed reaction time, impaired motor function, less caution; legal intoxication in many states
0.15	Large, consistent increases in reaction time
0.20	Marked depression in sensory and motor capability; decidedly intoxicated
0.25	Severe motor disturbance, such as staggering; sensory perceptions greatly impaired; "wiped out," "plastered"
0.30	Stuporous but conscious; no comprehension of the world around them
0.35	Surgical anesthesia; possible death at this point and beyond

Source: Adapted from Ray, 1983.

excitement phase, the body begins to react in quite the opposite way. Feelings of fatigue, nausea, unhappiness and depression may occur, exactly as we would expect from a depressant drug. Thought processes and physical coordination become progressively more disorganized as cortical control is depressed.

Thus, the effect on conscious experience of an increase in blood alcohol level seems to be a **two-phase reaction:** an initial "upper" from the release of inhibitions, followed by a "downer" as higher brain centers are depressed. Unfortunately, some people respond to the second phase by drinking even more in the hope that it will make them feel "high" again, a self-defeating strategy if ever there was one (Marlatt and Gordon, 1985).

Unlike most foods, alcohol does not require a long period of digestion before it can enter the bloodstream. Instead, it passes directly through the walls of the stomach and small intestine and is absorbed immediately into the bloodstream and carried to the brain. The **blood alcohol level** that results depends on the size and sex of the person as well as on the size of the drink. Alcohol is distributed throughout the body fluids, including the blood. Women have less body fluid than men of the same weight (because women have more body fat), and large people have more body fluid than smaller ones. Thus, four cans of beer or four glasses of wine consumed during a one-hour period produce a blood alcohol level of 0.18 in a 100-pound female, 0.15 in a 100-pound male, 0.12 in a 150-pound woman, and 0.10 in a 150-pound man. A 200-pound man will have a blood alcohol level of only 0.07 (Ray, 1983). In most states, a person whose blood alcohol level is 0.10 is considered legally intoxicated and unfit to operate a motor vehicle. One rough rule of thumb used to approximate how much a person can drink and metabolize in an hour without raising the blood alcohol level is to divide body weight (in pounds) by five times the percentage of alcohol in the beverage (Ray, 1978). Thus, a 150-pound person could drink about 6 ounces of 5-percent beer per hour $\left(\frac{150}{5 \times 5} = 6 \right)$.

Humans aren't the only primates who cease being "dull and dignified" after too much alcohol, as the following news account suggests:

Sloshed after a day of solitary drinking, a 150-pound pet chimpanzee dived through a window of his owner's house and reeled through the neighborhood, breaking windows, biting a neighbor's toe and repeatedly hugging a pursuing female cop.

Congo the chimp evaded police for half an hour until his owner, Mario Cervantes, got home and persuaded his ward to sleep it off, police said yesterday.

"The chimp was left in the family house alone," said police Sgt. Charles DeCosta. "He somehow found a quart bottle of vodka and he drank it, then two bottles of beer, and then he crashed through a window and ran into the street."

Cervantes was given a summons for failure to control a dangerous animal, DeCosta said. (Associated Press, August 12, 1984)

A quick chaser Alcohol is our most abused drug. Because the use of alcohol is so much a part of our lives, it is easy for someone to slide from being a user to being an abuser. Even if you are young, you need to monitor yourself and those you care about. If someone asks you if he or she has a drinking problem, the key question is whether the person has physical or psychological difficulty in stopping his or her drinking. If the answer is yes, there is definitely a potential, if not an existing, drinking problem.

BARBITURATES AND TRANQUILIZERS

Physicians frequently prescribe barbiturates and tranquilizers as sedatives, relaxants, and sleeping pills. Barbiturates, such an nembutal ("yellow jackets"), seconal ("redbirds"), and phenobarbital and amobarbital (the "purple hearts"), and tranquilizers, such as Valium, are classed together because both groups depress the nervous system by interfering with synaptic transmission. They either prevent the release of excitatory neurotransmitters or cause the release of inhibitory ones (Tallman and others, 1980).

Mild doses of barbiturates are effective as "sleeping pills." Higher doses, such as those used by addicts, trigger an initial period of excitation, followed by slurred speech, loss of coordination, extreme depression, and severe impairment of memory and thinking. Overdoses, particularly when the drugs are taken with alcohol, may cause unconsciousness, coma, or death.

Users can build up a tolerance for barbiturates. Addicts may take as many as 50 sleeping pills a day to regain the initial high. Barbiturates are highly addic-

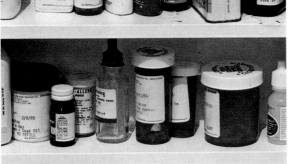

FIGURE 4.16   *The widespread use of tranquilizers is a cause of increasing concern. Tranquilizers like Valium are treated as if they were the aspirin of the prescription drug world, but their overuse can have serious effects.*

Stimulants

Stimulants increase neural firing and activate the nervous system. Two of the most widely used stimulants are amphetamines and cocaine.

AMPHETAMINES

Amphetamines—popularly known as *speed*, *uppers*, and *bennies*—are powerful stimulants of the brain and the autonomic nervous system. They mimic the neurotransmitter norepinephrine, triggering synapses and spreading excitation throughout the nervous system. They also cause leakage of norepinephrine from axon terminals, which increases firing even more. Amphetamines are sold under such trade names as Benzedrine, Dexedrine, and Methedrine. They are prescribed to reduce appetite, fatigue, and the need for sleep, and to alleviate depression. In small dosages, amphetamines are sometimes prescribed as "diet pills," with variable results. Low dosages meant to overcome fatigue are also used by groups ranging from truck drivers to students cramming for exams.

Amphetamines appear to have no harmful effects if they are used in moderation. However, people who use higher dosages readily develop tolerance and often a psychological dependence on amphetamines. Amphetamines do not appear to cause physical dependence. But eventually, many heavy users start injecting, or "mainlining," large quantities of the drug. When speed is mainlined, a sudden flash or "rush" of intense plea-

tive, and heavy users may die if the drug is withdrawn suddenly. Several months of gradual, supervised withdrawal may be needed before addicts lose their physical dependence on these drugs.

The overuse of tranquilizers is extensive in our society. Americans spend almost half a billion dollars a year on Valium alone. Nearly 90 million tranquilizer prescriptions are filled each year (see Figure 4.16), and perhaps half a million Americans use tranquilizers for nonmedical purposes (Vischi and others, 1980). Many people mistakenly regard Valium as harmless, but it is not. The body develops a tolerance to Valium, and physical and psychological dependence can occur. Many users become addicted without knowing it until they try to stop taking the drug and experience serious withdrawal symptoms. Tranquilizers are involved in perhaps a quarter of all drug-related deaths (Vischi and others, 1980).

sure envelops the body within seconds and a great surge of energy is experienced. This energy surge is one reason why amphetamines are sometimes used by athletes to gain a competitive edge. As one professional football player said in the 1970s, "You look at your opponent and he's staring at you wild-eyed with big dilated pupils and drooling all over himself. I'm not about to go out there unless I'm in the same condition" (Mandell, 1978). Fortunately, amphetamine use by athletes during competition has been reduced by stringent antidrug legislation in sports.

Addicts may mainline amphetamines repeatedly and remain awake continuously for as long as a week. During this period, their body systems are racing at breakneck speed. They become increasingly tense and anxious and may suffer a large weight loss. When they stop the injections, there is an inevitable "crash," and they may sleep deeply for one or two days, only to wake up profoundly depressed and exhausted, with severe headaches and intense irritability. The depressive crash is brought about by the amphetamine-induced leakage of the excitatory transmitter norepinephrine from the axon terminals. The neurons are, quite literally, exhausted.

When amphetamines are mainlined, there is an enormous increase in blood pressure, which can lead to heart failure and cerebral hemorrhage (stroke). There is considerable evidence that repeated use of high doses of speed causes brain damage. Thought processes and memory can become permanently impaired. Because amphetamines tax the body so heavily, addicts have a short life expectancy. This type of speed kills, too.

COCAINE

Cocaine is a stimulant derived from the coca plant, which grows mainly in western South America. Cocaine was once used widely as a local anesthetic in eye, nose, and throat surgery, but unlike other local anesthetics, cocaine also acts as a powerful central nervous system stimulant, apparently by stimulating the release and preventing the reuptake of the transmitter norepinephrine.

Cocaine is a white or colorless crystalline powder that is usually either inhaled ("snorted") or injected (mainlined). Recently, a chemically converted cocaine "free base" that can be smoked has appeared. Its effects are faster, more intense, and more dangerous (Ray, 1983). Overdoses of free base can cause death from cardiorespiratory arrest (Cohen, 1980).

Hailed at various times in its history as a wonder drug and as a menace, cocaine has a wide range of possible effects. It can induce euphoria, excitation, anxiety, a sense of increased muscular strength, talkativeness, and liveliness. The stimulant effect occurs within minutes and lasts about 30 minutes. Cocaine causes pupils to dilate and heart rate and blood pressure to increase. In larger doses, it can produce fever, vomiting, convulsions, hallucinations, and paranoid delusions.

One kind of sensation that high doses can produce is the appearance of "cocaine bugs" (technically called **formication,** from the Latin *formica,* "ant"). Users feel something like bugs crawling under their skin and may scratch vigorously or even take a knife to cut them out.

Although there is no evidence that they become physically dependent, cocaine users may develop a strong psychological dependence on the drug. Although it is largely a drug of the affluent and upper-middle class, it is also attracting younger users in increasing numbers. Despite its rise in popularity, however, cocaine is and should be a source of concern. Considering the damage that heavy cocaine use has done to many lives, minimizing its dangers is a bit like saying that Einstein was "into numbers" or that Michelangelo "did ceilings."

Narcotics

The term **narcotic** in its medical sense refers to opium and opium derivatives, such as morphine, heroin, and codeine. For at least 6000 years, products of the opium poppy, an annual plant that grows in hot, dry climates, have been used to reduce pain and produce pleasure. Narcotics are indispensable in the practice of medicine—they are the most effective agents known for the relief of intense pain. Unfortunately, they have also caused untold misery and destroyed many lives.

The 1970s witnessed our first real glimpses into how narcotics affect the nervous system. Opiate receptors were found in the brain, and it was discovered that the body produces its own opiates, the *endorphins.* We will have much more to say about them in Chapter 5, when we discuss pain perception. For now, it is sufficient to note that parts of the brain stem and thalamus that seem important in pain perception and parts of the limbic system that are involved in emotional reactions are packed with opiate receptors. These sites of receptor concentration may help to account for two different and important effects of narcotics: (1) pain relief and (2) mood changes that are sometimes euphoric in nature.

Heroin, a widely abused narcotic, mainly causes emotional changes. Experienced users feel a "thrill" within several minutes of an injection. It resembles, some say, a sexual orgasm, except that the sensation is in their abdomen rather than in their genitals. For a time, users feel as if they are on top of the world, with no worries, no concerns. They feel peaceful and nonaggressive. Their psychological functions are not im-

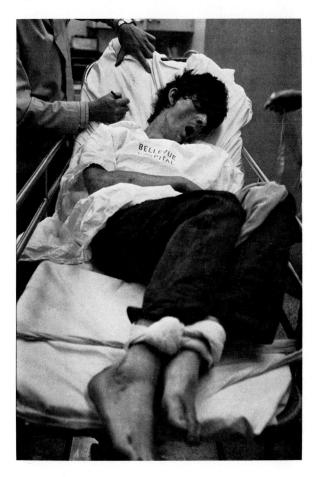

paired, as they are with alcohol and barbiturates, and heroin users can perform well on certain kinds of skilled tasks.

But tolerance for and physical and psychological dependence on narcotics develop quickly. Some people think that if narcotics are not taken intravenously, one cannot become addicted. That's simply not so.

Withdrawal symptoms that occur when heavy narcotics users stop taking the drugs are traumatic, and many addicts continue to "shoot up" in order to avoid the symptoms, even if they do not feel high any longer (see Figure 4.17). The following description of withdrawal was made by a young woman who succeeded in kicking her heroin habit:

It's like a terrible case of flu. Your joints move involuntarily. That's where the phrase "kick the habit" comes from. You jerk and twitch and you just can't control it. You throw up. You can't control your bowels either and this goes on for four or five days afterwards. For fifteen days afterwards, you can't sleep and you cough up blood, because if you're on drugs, you can't eat and that's all there is to cough up.

Hallucinogens

The **hallucinogens**, or **psychotomimetic** drugs, are the most powerful of the mind-altering drugs. *Psychotomimetic* literally means "imitating psychosis"; the term is used because some of the effects of these drugs are very close to symptoms of psychosis (severe mental illness). The plants from which some of the hallucinogens are derived are considered sacred in many tribal cultures

FIGURE 4.17 *The agonies of narcotic withdrawal symptoms can be so severe that addicts who would like to kick the habit continue to shoot up to avoid withdrawal.*

135

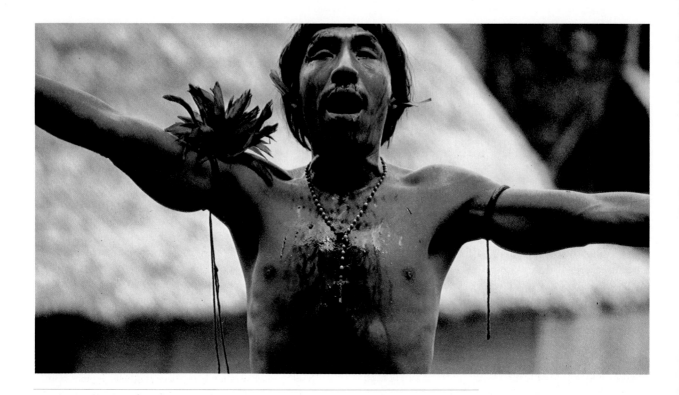

FIGURE 4.18 *In some cultures, hallucinogenic drugs are thought to have spiritual powers. Under the influence of peyote, this modern Indian shaman prepares to conduct a religious ceremony.*

where, because of their ability to produce "unearthly" states of consciousness, they are thought to contain spiritual forces (see Figure 4.18).

The effects of hallucinogens are not determined solely by the drug; they are heavily influenced by the user's mood, mental attitude, and environment. Hallucinogens usually distort or intensify sensory experience, and they can blur the boundaries between fact and fantasy. Users may speak of seeing sounds and hearing colors. They may lose their sense of direction or distance and their ability to make objective judgments. Their pupils become dilated, and their eyes are thus more sensitive to light. Until the drug wears off, they may be restless and unable to sleep.

The mental effects of these drugs are always unpredictable even if taken repeatedly, and their effects may recur as "flashbacks" days or even months after the drug has been taken. Hallucinogens may cause mysti-

cal experiences, illusions, exhilaration, withdrawal from reality, violent movement or self-destruction, or sheer panic. This unpredictability constitutes the greatest danger to users. Unlike depressants and narcotics, hallucinogens are apparently not physically addictive, but psychological dependence may develop.

LSD

Lysergic acid diethylamide (LSD-25) is many times more potent than other hallucinogens, such as the cactus-derived peyote. It is derived from ergot fungus, a disease that affects rye and wheat grain. By stimulating the release of neurotransmitters and affecting control mechanisms in the brain, LSD causes a runaway flooding of excitation in the nervous system. A dose no larger than the tip of a pin can take a user on a "trip" for 8 to 16 hours. Albert Hofmann, the Swiss chemist who accidentally discovered LSD in 1943, described his experiences when he took a tiny dose of the drug.

> The dizziness and sensation of fainting became so strong at times that I could no longer hold myself erect and had to lie down on a sofa. My surroundings had transformed themselves in more terrifying ways. Everything in the room spun around and the familiar objects and pieces of furniture assumed grotesque, mostly threatening forms. . . . Even worse than these demonic transformations of the outer world were the alterations that I perceived in myself, in my inner being. Every exertion of my will, to put an end to the disintegration of the outer world and the dissolution of my ego, seemed a wasted effort. A demon had invaded me and had taken possession of my body, mind and soul. I jumped up and screamed in order to free myself from him, but then sank down again powerless on the sofa. The substance, with which I had wanted to experiment, had vanquished me. (Hofmann, 1980, p. 58)

During and after such "trips," users may suffer acute panic or depression. Some even suffer short- or long-term psychoses. We do not yet know whether the drug actually causes the psychotic disorder or merely precipitates it in people who are marginally adjusted to begin with.

Although pure LSD-25 is manufactured, its use is generally restricted to government-sponsored research projects. Most acid sold on the street has been made in a "basement lab" and may contain other chemicals such as speed and strychnine. The addition of these other drugs is thought to make the effects of the drug even more unpredictable and to increase the likelihood of a bad trip.

PCP

Phencyclidine (PCP) was introduced in the 1950s as a synthetic anesthetic, but this use was discontinued when some patients reported agitation, disorientation, and hallucinations. In 1967 it was made commercially available as an anesthetic in veterinary medicine. That same year it began to appear in the drug culture in San Francisco. However, after bad trips were experienced by many in the drug community, the popularity of PCP declined rapidly. Recently, however, it has reappeared with increasing frequency. It is often mixed

with other drugs, or represented as other drugs and sold to naive buyers.

We don't know exactly how PCP affects the nervous system, but its effects on consciousness and behavior are becoming alarmingly apparent. The drug is highly variable in its effects. Rapid and involuntary eye movements, a blank stare, and an exaggerated gait are among the more commonly observed effects. Image distortion (as in a fun-house mirror), auditory hallucinations, and severe mood disorders may also occur. Some people experience acute anxiety and feelings of impending doom, while others become paranoid and hostile. Users may commit violent assaults on others, and a number of bizarre murders have been directly attributed to PCP use (Siegel, 1978). People have also been known to pluck out their eyes or cut off their hands while under the influence of the drug.

Perhaps PCP's most notable characteristic is its ability to produce psychotic reactions that are indistinguishable from schizophrenia. Perhaps 15 to 20 percent of those taking the drug become temporarily psychotic (Lerner and Burns, 1978). Normal behavior and thought patterns return, usually in about a week, but in severe cases recovery may take 12 to 18 months (Garey, 1979). As evidence mounts on PCP's effects, it becomes increasingly clear that angel dust is anything but heaven-sent.

Cannabis

Has our country gone to pot? It certainly has, in at least one respect. Marijuana, the product of **cannabis,** the hemp plant, has become a major recreational drug. Surveys indicate that between 40 and 50 million Americans have used it, including perhaps 60 percent of those in the 17 to 25 age range (Ray, 1983). Formerly classified as a hallucinogenic drug, marijuana has now been categorized separately by the federal government (*Drug Enforcement*, July 1979).

The major active ingredient of marijuana is a chemical substance called tetrahydrocannabinol, or THC. As with most drugs, the effects that any individual experiences and the intensity of those effects depend on the dosage, the person's sensitivity to the drug, his or her psychological state, and the setting in which the drug is taken.

Usually inhaled, but sometimes eaten, the drug starts to take effect within about 15 minutes. Depending on drug potency and dosage, its effects can last up to 4 hours. Low doses may cause people to feel an increased sense of well-being. Initially, they may feel restless and giddy, then sink into a dreamy, carefree state of relaxation. Their sense of space and time may be expanded. Sensations can become more intense, and a craving for food ("the munchies") often occurs, even though blood sugar level has not changed. Finally, subtle alterations occur in thought formation and expression. An uninformed observer, however, would probably not notice anything unusual about a user's behavior.

With higher doses, marijuana users may experience rapid changes in emotions and sensory imagery, a dulling of the ability to attend, and more pronounced alterations in thought formation and expression. These distortions can produce temporary feelings of panic and anxiety in some individuals who have had little experience with drugs and might make them fear that they are dying or "losing their minds." Very high doses may cause distortions in body image and sense of personal identity, as well as fantasies and hallucinations.

Individuals under the influence of marijuana may have a hard time making decisions that require clear thinking and may be highly susceptible to the suggestions of other people. Their ability to perform tasks that require quick reflexes and thinking is impaired. For example, experimental evidence derived from performance on driver test courses and under actual traffic conditions clearly shows that driving under the influence of marijuana (even "social doses") can be hazardous (Klonoff, 1974).

Debates over possible health hazards associated with marijuana use have gone on for years. Various researchers have suggested that prolonged and heavy usage may cause chromosomal damage, sterility in males, loss of cellular immunity to invading diseases, hormonal dysfunctions, lung and bronchial disorders,

FIGURE 4.19 *The use of increasingly potent forms of marijuana by children and adolescents is a new source of concern among public health officials.*

and perhaps even brain damage. Aside from evidence that marijuana smoke is a lung irritant, none of these effects has been clearly established (National Academy of Sciences, 1982). On the other hand, there is evidence that marijuana can be medically useful in reducing excessive eye pressure in glaucoma and in lessening nausea in cancer patients undergoing chemotherapy.

But in the 1980s new concerns began to arise about marijuana smoking. Youngsters in their early teens were showing an increasing tendency to use forms of marijuana that were up to seven times more potent than normal marijuana (see Figure 4.19). In an interview with *Newsweek* (January 7, 1980), Dr. Sidney Cohen, a drug researcher who had once dismissed marijuana as a "trivial weed," stated, "This heavy use of more potent material by increasingly younger persons makes the marijuana issue a whole new ball game" (p. 43).

Table 4.4 summarizes the major properties and effects of marijuana and the other drugs that we have discussed.

TABLE 4.4   EFFECTS OF THE MAJOR PSYCHOACTIVE DRUGS

CLASS	TYPICAL EFFECTS	EFFECTS OF OVERDOSE	TOLERANCE/DEPENDENCE
DEPRESSANTS			
Alcohol	Biphasic; tension reduction, "high," followed by depressed physical and psychological functioning	Disorientation, loss of consciousness, possible death at extremely high blood alcohol levels	Tolerance; physical and psychological dependence, withdrawal symptoms
Barbiturates Tranquilizers	Depressed reflexes and impaired motor functioning, tension reduction	Shallow respiration, clammy skin, dilated pupils, weak and rapid pulse, coma, possible death	Tolerance; high psychological and physical dependence on barbiturates, low to moderate on such tranquilizers as Valium, withdrawal symptoms
STIMULANTS			
Amphetamines Cocaine	Increased alertness, excitation, euphoria, increased pulse rate and blood pressure, sleeplessness	Agitation, hallucinations (e.g., "cocaine bugs"), paranoid delusions, convulsions, death	Tolerance; psychological but probably not physical dependence
NARCOTICS			
Opium Morphine	Euphoria, drowsiness, "rush" of pleasure, little impairment of psychological functions	Slow, shallow breathing, clammy skin, convulsions, coma, possible death	High tolerance; physical and psychological dependence, severe withdrawal symptoms
HALLUCINOGENS			
LSD PCP	Illusions, hallucinations, distortions in time perception, loss of reality contact; with PCP, possible violent behavior	Psychotic reactions, particularly with PCP; possible death	Tolerance; no physical dependence for LSD, degree unknown for PCP; high psychological dependence for PCP, degree unknown for LSD
CANNABIS	Euphoria, relaxed inhibitions, increased appetite, possible disorientation	Fatigue, disoriented behavior, possible psychosis	Tolerance and psychological dependence

LIMITS OF CONSCIOUSNESS

Within the past decade, states of consciousness have become a subject of increasing popular and scientific interest as Eastern beliefs about consciousness and its nature have become more widely publicized and as mind-altering techniques like meditation, other forms of mental training, and drugs have become more commonly used. Indeed, some people have begun to question the very nature of reality as it is perceived in our usual state of consciousness. Fully developed mystics tell us that we are prisoners of our own minds and that our normal perception of reality is an illusion, a distortion shaped by our Western culture. They maintain that only through remedial mental training, as occurs in Yoga and intensive meditation, can we awaken from the distorted "dream" that we experience in common with most other people and recognize both our former state and a new perception of reality (Walsh, 1980).

Recalling our earlier discussion of the role of per-spectives in shaping our perception of reality (Chapter 1), you will recognize that advocates of altered states of consciousness are advancing the same basic ideas on an even larger scale. They are maintaining that our reality as perceived is actually a common "dream" that is shaped by cultural forces. Psychoanalyst Erich Fromm has expressed the same idea:

The effect of society is not only to funnel fictions into our consciousness, but also to prevent awareness of reality. . . . This system works, as it were, like a socially conditioned filter; experience cannot enter awareness unless it can penetrate the filter. . . . What is unconsciousness and what is consciousness depends on the structure of society and on the patterns of feelings and thoughts it produces. (1960, pp. 98, 99, 106)

Many people seek altered states in the hope that their experiences will reveal alternate views of reality

"Hey, what is this stuff? It makes everything I think seem profound."

(DRAWING BY W. MILLER; © 1978 THE NEW YORKER MAGAZINE, INC.)

FIGURE 4.20 *Some altered-state experiences appear to be "state-specific" and cannot be retrieved later in a normal state of consciousness.*

not shaped by previous learning and cultural influences. But learning from altered states may not be so easy. Some of the experiences appear to be *state-specific*—that is, they are so different from normal mental functioning that it is difficult to translate what has been experienced within an altered state into the thinking, feeling, and remembering of normal experience. A person may feel that he or she has had a great insight or new mode of understanding yet be unable to recall what it was or express it in the language that we use to describe "normal" reality (see Figure 4.20).

Throughout history, people have felt themselves influenced by mystical and spiritual experiences. Now, for the first time, we are making an attempt to understand these experiences in scientific terms. But the task is a formidable one because our scientific methods have been developed as tools to study a different range of phenomena. The "objective" approach of science does not lend itself well to exploring inner states that Eastern theorists tell us can be reached only through direct experience. Any viewpoint or method is limited and selective in what it allows us to see, and there may be strange and novel realms beyond its range. But the willingness of science to explore these novel realms and viewpoints may help to expand our understanding of both consciousness and reality. As William James, one of the founders of psychology, wrote more than 80 years ago:

Our normal waking consciousness is but one special type of consciousness, whilst all about it, parted from it by the filmiest of screens, there lie potential forms of consciousness entirely different. We may go through life without suspecting their existence, but apply the requisite stimulus, and at a touch they are there in all their completeness, definite types of mentality which probably nowhere have their field of application and adoption. No account of the universe in its totality can be final which leaves these other forms of consciousness quite disregarded. How to regard them is the question. . . . At any rate, they forbid our premature closing of accounts with reality. (1902, p. 298)

STUDY OUTLINE

STATES OF CONSCIOUSNESS (p. 110)

Because consciousness is a private and subjective experience, it cannot be studied directly. Three classes of observable behavior—verbal self-report, physiological responses, and nonverbal behaviors—are the major sources of information about states of consciousness.

SLEEPING AND DREAMING (p. 112)

1. Scientists do not fully understand why we sleep. Our periods of sleep and wakefulness are in part regulated by a 24-hour circadian rhythm, which involves cyclical changes in various bodily processes. Adult humans have a monophasic sleep cycle. The physiological and psychological problems of "jet lag" result from a disruption of the circadian rhythm.

2. EEG recordings during the sleep cycle indicate that there are five distinct stages, including the slow-wave patterns of stages 3 and 4. The REM stage, characterized by rapid eye movements and reports of dreams if the person is awakened, occurs about every 90 minutes during the night. The proportion of REM sleep decreases from about 50 percent in infancy to about 25 percent by ages 5 to 9. Although dreams are very likely to be reported during REM sleep, they also occur in non-REM sleep.

3. Various theories about the nature and functions of dreams have been proposed. According to Freud, dreams are a reflection of psychodynamic processes. They allow some degree of wish fulfillment, and the manifest content of the dream is often a symbolic manifestation of the latent content, or true psychological meaning. Freud believed that dreams were "the royal road to the unconscious."

4. Dreams may help to consolidate memories formed in the waking state. The REM rebound effect has led to suggestions that dreams are part of a homeostatic mechanism in the nervous system. REM sleep may also be the right hemisphere's chance to increase its activity after a left-hemisphere-dominated day.

5. Insomnia is the most common sleep disorder. More serious is narcolepsy, a condition in which people suffer sudden and uncontrollable sleep attacks. In sleep apnea, people suddenly stop breathing for several minutes at a time. This may occur numerous times during the night and can be life-threatening. Links seem to exist between apnea and Sudden Infant Death Syndrome, and there is a possibility that adult apnea victims are survivors of SIDS.

MEDITATION (p. 120)

All types of meditation involve concentrating on something. Passive approaches, such as Transcendental Meditation, result in a relaxation response due to a decrease in sympathetic nervous system activity, an increase in parasympathetic activity, or both. Some researchers distinguish between somatic relaxation and cognitive relaxation. Meditation appears no more effective than other techniques for producing somatic relaxation, but seems promising for producing cognitive relaxation. Current research is focusing on the usefulness of meditation as a stress management technique.

HYPNOSIS (p. 121)

1. Hypnosis was popularized by Anton Mesmer, who called it animal magnetism. James Braid renamed it hypnosis. The most striking characteristic about hypnosis is an increase in suggestibility. Cognitive distortions, including age regressions and amnesia, are frequently experienced, as are physiological changes and increased pain tolerance.

2. There is no physiological state that is unique to hypnosis. Research has shown that many of the phenomena produced by hypnosis can also be exhibited by non-hypnotized control groups. This finding has given rise to attempts to identify the psychological principles that underlie hypnosis.

3. Some theorists have suggested that hypnosis involves "taking on" the role of a hypnotized person and behaving in accordance with role expectations. Others have stressed the role of imagination and its possible effects on behavior and experience in hypnosis. A third point of view suggests that hypnosis involves a shift toward greater right hemisphere dominance. Ernest Hilgard and other theorists have suggested that dissociation accounts for many hypnotic phenomena, and Hilgard has developed a technique for communicating with a presumably dissociated "hidden observer" during hypnosis.

DRUGS AND CONSCIOUSNESS (p. 130)

1. A drug is any substance other than food whose chemical action alters the structure or functioning of the body. Certain psychoactive drugs are able to pass through the blood-brain barrier and affect the nervous system.

2. Drugs work by duplicating, stimulating, or inhibiting neuronal processes. Some drugs mimic neurotransmitters; others affect their manufacture, release, or reuptake. A drug's effects depend on dosage, frequency of use, individual differences, and the setting in which the drug is taken.

3. Tolerance is the requirement of increasingly larger doses to reproduce the original effects. Physical dependence results in withdrawal symptoms if the drug is not taken. People can also become psychologically dependent on a drug. Physical and/or strong psychological dependence on a drug results in addiction.

DEPRESSANTS (p. 131)

1. Depressants decrease the level of activity in the nervous system, resulting in relaxation, sleepiness, and feelings of well-being. Moderate doses reduce tension and anxiety; extremely high doses can slow down vital life processes to the point of death.

2. Alcohol has a two-phase effect: initial relaxation and a "high" as inhibitory centers in the brain are depressed, followed by the "downer" phase as the depressant effects impair higher brain centers. Effects depend upon the person's blood alcohol level, which is determined by the amount of alcohol consumed per unit of time, the person's sex and body size, food ingestion, and other factors.

3. Barbiturates and tranquilizers interfere with synaptic transmission by inhibiting the secretion of excitatory neurotransmitters or by releasing inhibitory transmitter substances. Tolerance, physical and psychological dependence, and addiction can occur with both barbiturates and tranquilizers.

STIMULANTS (p. 133)

1. Stimulants increase neural firing and activate the nervous system. Amphetamines mimic the transmitter norepinephrine and also cause this substance to leak out of the axon terminals, increasing neural activity still further. Cocaine works by stimulating norepinephrine release and preventing its reuptake.

2. In low doses, amphetamines decrease appetite and fatigue, as well as relieving depression. Moderate doses produce euphoria, while higher doses can result in a high level of arousal that taxes the body and disrupts behavior. Tolerance and psychological dependence develop readily, and extended usage of high doses can produce brain damage, strokes, and other organ damage.

3. In moderate doses, cocaine produces euphoria and other pleasant sensations. Larger doses can produce convulsions, hallucinations, and paranoid delusions. Cocaine is not physically addictive, but psychological dependence can develop rather quickly.

NARCOTICS (p. 134)

Opiate receptors in various regions of the brain account for two different effects of narcotics: pain relief and mood changes that are sometimes euphoric in nature. Morphine chiefly produces pain relief, while heroin mainly causes mood changes. Tolerance, dependence, and addiction occur readily, and withdrawal effects are especially traumatic.

HALLUCINOGENS (p. 135)

1. Hallucinogens, the most powerful of the mind-altering drugs, usually distort or intensify sensory experience, and they frequently cause hallucinations and delusions. Their effects are very unpredictable and are influenced by the user's mood, expectations, and environment. The dangers of hallucinogens are increased by the mixing of other drugs with them to increase dealers' profits.

2. PCP is a particularly dangerous hallucinogen that is highly variable in its effects and has been linked to violent and self-destructive behavior. It can produce a long-lasting psychosis that is very similar to schizophrenia.

CANNABIS (p. 137)

Marijuana is well on its way to rivaling alcohol as a major recreational drug. With few documented side effects and low potential for tolerance, marijuana's greatest problems are the strong psychological dependence that can develop; its disruptive effects on driving and other behaviors requiring decision making, attentiveness, and quick reflexes; and its increasing use by children. Concern is rising about more potent forms of marijuana that are appearing among users.

LIMITS OF CONSCIOUSNESS (p. 140)

Experiences that occur during altered states of consciousness are sometimes state-specific and difficult to translate into the language of everyday life. Although traditional scientific methods are not well suited to the study of consciousness, the willingness of psychological researchers to study these phenomena may expand our understanding of important psychological processes.

KEY TERMS AND CONCEPTS

dissociation	REM sleep
altered state of consciousness	activation-synthesis model
sleep factor	wish fulfillment
circadian rhythm	manifest content of a dream
monophasic sleep cycle	latent content
polyphasic sleep cycle	dream work
alpha rhythm	memory consolidation
slow-wave sleep	lucid dreams

REM rebound effect

insomnia

delayed sleep syndrome

narcolepsy

sleep apnea

Sudden Infant Death Syndrome

active meditation

passive meditation

alpha rhythm

relaxation response

somatic relaxation

cognitive relaxation

mesmerism

hypnosis

hypnotic susceptibility scales

delayed auditory feedback

role theory of hypnosis

hemispheric dominance shift

dichotic listening technique

hidden observer

drug

blood-brain barrier

psychoactive drug

tolerance

physical dependence

psychological dependence

addiction

depressant

two-phase reaction (to alcohol)

blood alcohol level

stimulant

formication

narcotics

hallucinogen

psychotomimetic drug

cannabis

state-specific effects

SUGGESTED READINGS

CARTWRIGHT, R. D. (1978). *A primer on sleep and dreaming*. Reading, Mass.: Addison-Wesley. A brief, interesting, and nontechnical treatment of current knowledge about the nature of sleep and dreams.

MOORE-EDE, M. C., SULZMAN, F. M., and FULLER, C. A. (1982). *The clocks that time us*. Cambridge, Mass.: Harvard University Press. A far-ranging discussion of what is currently known about biological rhythms in humans and animals. It contains a somewhat technical discussion of research methods in this area.

RAY, O. (1983). *Drugs, society, and behavior*. (3rd ed.). St. Louis: Mosby. A comprehensive and delightfully written book about drugs and their effects on consciousness and behavior, as well as legal and social issues concerning drug use.

WESTER, W. C., and SMITH, A. H. (eds.) (1984). *Clinical hypnosis: A multidisciplinary approach*. Philadelphia: Lippincott. An excellent source book on current theories of hypnosis and on the way hypnosis is being used for medical and behavior-change purposes.

CHAPTER FIVE
SENSATION AND PERCEPTION

THE SENSORY SYSTEMS
Vision
Audition
The chemical senses
FRONTIER 5.1   ODORS AND SEXUALITY IN HUMANS
The skin and body senses
Psychophysics: The study of sensory capabilities

PERCEPTUAL PROCESSES
Attention: Selecting which information gets in
Patterning and organization in perception
Depth and distance perception
Auditory localization

PERCEPTUAL DEVELOPMENT
The role of experience in perceptual development
FRONTIER 5.2   PAIN PERCEPTION AND CONTROL

STUDY OUTLINE

KEY TERMS AND CONCEPTS

SUGGESTED READINGS

When I turn my gaze skyward I see the flattened dome of sky and the sun's brilliant disk and a hundred other visible things underneath it. What are the steps which bring this about? A pencil of light from the sun enters the eye and is focused there on the retina. It gives rise to a change, which in turn travels to the nerve layer at the top of the brain. The whole chain of these events from the sun to the top of my brain is physical. Each step is an electrical reaction. But now there succeeds a change wholly unlike any which led up to it, and wholly inexplicable by us. A visual scene presents itself to the mind; I see the dome of the sky and the sun in it, and a hundred other visual things besides. In fact, I perceive a picture of the world around me. When this visual scene appears, I ought, I suppose, to feel startled; but I am too accustomed to feel even surprised. (Sherrington, 1950, p. 3)

Like Sir Charles Sherrington, the eminent brain researcher who made these observations, you probably take your visual window to the world for granted. But the world that you experience would be much different if that window were closed by the shutters of blindness. Helen Keller, blind and deaf from early infancy, described the experience of being cut off from the world of sight and sound:

Sometimes, it is true, a sense of isolation enfolds me like a cold mist as I sit alone and wait at life's shut gate. Beyond there is light, and music, and sweet companionship; but I may not enter. Fate, silent, pitiless, bars the way. . . . Silence sits immense upon my soul. (Keller, 1955, p. 162)

The basic question of how we come to know and experience ourselves and our world has intrigued philosophers since Plato and Aristotle. Psychologists have been concerned with the same question for over a century. Recall from Chapter 1 that Wilhelm Wundt established the first psychology laboratory at Leipzig in order to study sensations, which he regarded as the basic units of the mind.

Sensation is the process by which we receive raw information about the environment from the action of our sense organs. **Perception**—how we make sense of what our senses tell us—is a step beyond sensation. Since many of our behaviors are responses to what we are experiencing as reality, perception is intimately related to virtually every topic in psychology.

What we experience as reality is not a mirror of the outside world. Far from it. In ways not yet completely understood, our nervous system acts on, organizes, and interprets the raw sensory data to create the "product" that we call experience. Since perception is such an active and creative process, the same sensory input may be perceived in different ways at different times. For example, read the two sets of symbols in Figure 5.1. The middle symbols in both lines are exactly the same, but you probably perceived them differently. Your interpretation, or perception, of the characters was influenced by their context—that is, by the characters that preceded and followed them.

In this chapter we first examine the sensory systems that provide our brain with the basic data from which our experiences are constructed. Then we consider the ways in which those data are acted on and organized in the process of perception. As we shall see, the biological, cognitive, behavioral, and psychodynamic perspectives have all contributed in important ways to our understanding of the factors that govern perception.

FIGURE 5.1 *Quickly read these two lines of symbols out loud. Did your perception of the middle symbol in each line depend on the symbols that surround it?*

THE SENSORY SYSTEMS

The only language your brain understands is the electrochemical language of your nervous system. The brain cannot "understand" light waves, sound waves, or any of the other forms of energy that make up the language of the environment. Contact with the outer world is possible only because certain nerve cells have developed into specialized sensory receptors that have the ability to transform different types of energy, such as sound, light, and temperature, into the code language of nerve impulses. This transformation process is called **transduction.**

How many senses are there? It really depends on how you classify them. Certainly there appear to be more than the five classical senses that we are all famil-

iar with—vision, audition (hearing), touch, taste, and smell. For example, there are body senses that provide information about balance and body position. Also, because there are many different receptors in the skin, touch might be broken down into the separate senses of pressure, pain, and temperature. We also have receptors deep in the brain that monitor the chemical makeup and temperature of the bloodstream.

One popular way of classifying sensory systems is in terms of the type of stimuli to which they respond (Christman, 1979; Uttal, 1973). For each of the senses presented in Table 5.1, we will discuss the sensory receptors and the transduction process by which the physical stimulus is translated into the language of nerve impulses that are sent to the brain.

TABLE 5.1 CLASSIFICATION OF SENSORY SYSTEMS IN TERMS OF THE TYPES OF STIMULI TO WHICH THEY RESPOND

STIMULUS	SENSE	RECEPTORS
Electromagnetic energy	Vision	Rods and cones in retina
Mechanical energy		
Sound waves	Audition	Hair cells in the basilar membrane, inner ear
Displacement of skin; pressure	Skin senses	Various types in skin and tissues
Movement of joints	Kinesthetic body sense	Nerve endings in tendons, muscles, and joints
Gravity, acceleration	Vestibular body sense	Hair cells in semicircular canals of ear
Thermal	Skin senses	Various types in skin and tissues
Chemical substances		
Dissolved in saliva	Taste	Taste buds on the tongue
Molecules in air	Olfaction (smell)	Cells in upper nasal cavity

Source: Based on Christman, 1979; Uttal, 1973.

Vision

Vision is our most important means of experiencing the external environment, and, as a result, the visual sense has been studied more than the other sensory systems.

The normal stimulus for the visual sense is electromagnetic energy, which also includes X rays, television and radio signals, and infrared and ultraviolet rays (see Figure 5.2). These energies may be described in terms of their wavelengths, which are measured in **nanometers.** (A nanometer [nm] is one billionth of a meter.) The human visual system is sensitive to wavelengths extending from about 400 nanometers (blueviolet) to about 700 nanometers (red), only a tiny fraction of the electromagnetic spectrum.

THE HUMAN EYE

Your eye is a complex and marvelously specialized sensory receptor. Its main parts are shown in Figure 5.3.

Light rays enter the eye through the transparent *cor-*

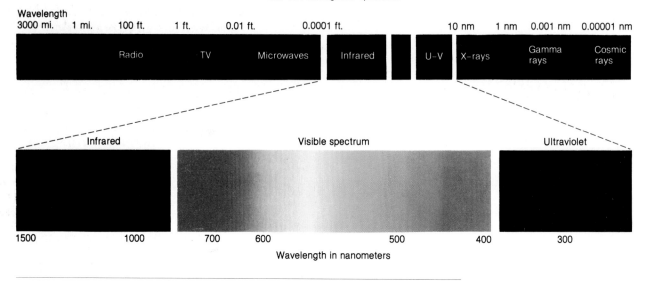

The electromagnetic spectrum

Wavelength										
3000 mi.	1 mi.	100 ft.	1 ft.	0.01 ft.	0.0001 ft.	10 nm	1 nm	0.001 nm	0.00001 nm

Radio   TV   Microwaves   Infrared   U-V   X-rays   Gamma rays   Cosmic rays

Infrared   Visible spectrum   Ultraviolet

1500	1000	700	600	500	400	300

Wavelength in nanometers

FIGURE 5.2 *The full spectrum of electromagnetic radiation. Only the narrow band between 400 and 700 nanometers (nm) is visible to the human eye. One nanometer = $\frac{1}{1,000,000,000}$ meter.*

nea. The amount of light allowed to enter is regulated by the *pupil* in the center of the colored *iris*. The pupil can dilate or contract, depending on the brightness of the light and other factors such as your emotional state. (Emotional arousal often causes the pupil to dilate, letting more light into the eye to improve optical clarity.) The **lens** is an elastic structure whose shape varies with the distance of the object you're looking at: thinner to focus on distant objects and thicker for nearby objects. This adjustment of the lens shape is called **accommodation,** and it is carried out through the action of the **ciliary muscles.** Just as the lens of a camera focuses an image on a photosensitive material (the film), so the lens of the eye focuses the image on the *retina*, which contains the visual receptors. The interior of the eyeball is filled with clear liquids called **aqueous humor** and **vitreous humor.**

THE RODS AND CONES

Embedded in the retina at the back of each eye are over 125 million photoreceptor cells called **rods** and **cones** because of their shapes. The rods outnumber the cones by more than 10 to 1 and are found throughout the retina except in a small central region called the *fovea*, which contains only cones. The cones decrease in number as we move away from the center of the retina.

Interestingly, the rods and cones form the *rear* layer of the retina; there are other layers of cells between the retina and the lens. One of these layers includes the **bipolar cells,** which make direct synaptic connections with the rods and cones. The bipolar cells, in turn, synapse with the **ganglion cells** in the frontmost layer, whose axons are collected into a bundle to form the *optic nerve.*

Surprisingly, the light-sensitive ends of the rods and cones face *away from* the direction of the entering light. Because of this, and because of the structures and the liquid substances that lie in front of the receptors, only a small portion of the total light energy entering the eyeball actually reaches the rods and cones.

The rods and the cones play different roles in vision. The more numerous rods are about 500 times more sensitive to light than the cones, but do not give rise to color sensations. The cones, which function only when the light is relatively bright, are the color

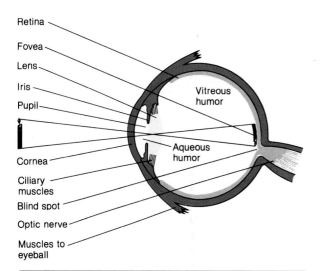

FIGURE 5.3 *This cross section shows the major parts of the human eye. The iris regulates the size of the pupil. The ciliary muscles regulate the shape of the lens. The image entering the eye is reversed by the lens and cast on the retina, which contains the photoreceptor cells.*

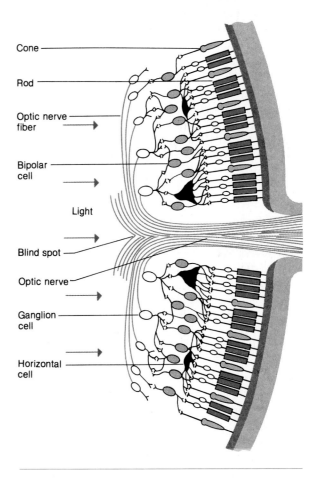

FIGURE 5.4 *There are two types of photoreceptor connections in the retina. The rods and cones synapse with bipolar cells, which in turn synapse with ganglion cells, whose axons form the optic nerve. The horizontal cells connect rods and cones to bipolar cells and allow activity in one part of the retina to influence activity in other parts.*

receptors of the retina. The rods are a bit like black-and-white film; the cones are like color film.

Figure 5.4 shows the photoreceptor connections in the retina. Each rod and cone is connected to one or more bipolar cells. Typically, many rods are connected to the same bipolar cell and can combine their individual electrical messages to fire it. This funneling arrangement is especially good for the detection of very dim lights, but it is not conducive to good **visual acuity,** the ability to see fine detail. The cones in the periphery of the retina also share bipolar cells, but in the fovea each cone has its own. This "private line," plus the fact that the cones in the fovea are very tightly packed together, means that our visual acuity is greatest when the image projects directly onto the fovea. Thus, both color and fine detail are best seen when objects are looked at directly, because this places the image on the fovea. On the other hand, because cones do not function under dim illumination, we can more easily detect a faint stimulus, such as a dim star, if we look slightly to one side so that its image falls outside of the fovea to

where the rods are packed most densely. This is why soldiers are trained to fixate slightly to one side of an object during night combat.

How do the rods and cones translate light waves

into nerve impulses? Not all the details of the process are fully understood, but we do know that each rod and cone contains several million chemical molecules called **photopigments.** The absorption of light by these molecules produces a chemical reaction in the receptor cell. If the chemical reaction is strong enough, a change occurs in the electrical potential in the receptor's cell membrane that is directly proportional to the intensity of the stimulus. This *graded potential*, in turn, changes the rate of neurotransmitter release at the receptor's synapse with the bipolar cells. The greater the change in transmitter release, the stronger is the signal passed on to the bipolar cell and the more likely it is that an all-or-none action potential will be triggered in the next layer of ganglion cells (the first place at which action potentials can occur). If nerve responses are triggered at each of the three levels (rod or cone, bipolar cell, and ganglion cell), the message is instantaneously on its way to its final destination, the visual cortex of the brain.

The optic nerve exits through the back of the eye not far from the fovea. Because there are no receptors at this point, there is a **blind spot** there whose existence can be shown through the demonstration in Figure 5.5. Ordinarily, we are unaware of the blind spot be-

cause our perceptual system "fills in" the missing part of the visual field. Notice, for example, how you continue to see the entire checkerboard pattern surrounding the objects in Figure 5.5 even when they fall on the blind spot and are no longer visible.

BRIGHTNESS VISION

Brightness is probably the most elementary type of visual sensation. Some lower organisms have sense organs that are responsive only to differences in illumination. In the human eye, brightness vision is a more complex process because you have more than one type of photoreceptor. As we noted earlier, rods are far more sensitive to low illumination than cones are. Psychologists have studied the relative sensitivity of these two kinds of photoreceptors by establishing their **absolute thresholds**—the minimum amount of light energy of various wavelengths needed to produce a visual sensation. By this process they have shown that the rods have a much greater sensitivity than cones do throughout the color spectrum except at the red end, where rods are relatively insensitive. We also know that cones are most sensitive to low illumination in the greenish-yellow range of the spectrum, while the rods are most sensitive in the bluish-green area. Many cities are now changing their fire engines from the traditional red color to yellow-green to increase their visibility to both rods and cones in dim lighting.

DARK ADAPTATION

Perhaps you have had the experience of entering a dark movie theater from bright sunlight, groping around in the darkness, and finally sitting down in someone else's lap. To avoid such embarrassments, many people learn to stand in the rear of the theater until their eyes become accustomed to the dimly lit interior. This improvement in sensitivity is called **dark adaptation.**

Dark adaptation occurs as the result of changes in the photopigment molecules of each photoreceptor. After absorbing light, the receptor molecule undergoes a chemical change and is depleted of pigment for a period of time. Until the photopigment has been regenerated, visual sensitivity is lost in that receptor. If the eye has been in conditions of high illumination, such as bright sunlight, a substantial amount of the

FIGURE 5.5 *Close your left eye and, from a distance of about 12 inches, focus steadily on the X with your right eye as you slowly move the book toward your face. At some point the image of the dot will cross your blind spot and disappear; it will reappear after it crosses the blind spot. Note how the checkerboard pattern remains wholly visible despite the fact that part of it falls on the blind spot. Your perceptual system "fills in" the missing information.*

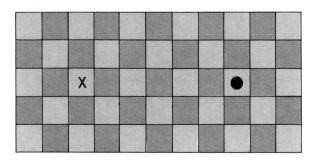

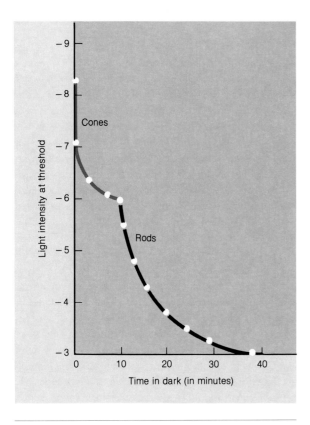

FIGURE 5.6 *The course of dark adaptation is graphed over time. The resulting curve has two parts, one for rods and one for cones. The cones adapt completely in about 5 minutes, whereas the rods continue to increase their sensitivity.*

as the visual system gradually recovers its sensitivity.

Note that the curve has two distinct parts. By changing the wavelength of the light and the area of the retina being tested (so that either rods or cones are being stimulated), it can be shown that the first part of the curve is due to the dark adaptation of the cones and the second part is due to the dark adaptation of the rods. We can see that the cones gradually become sensitive to fainter lights as time passes. But after about five minutes in the dark, their sensitivity has reached its maximum as measured by the absolute threshold. The rods, however, do not reach their maximum sensitivity for about half an hour. The reason is the differences in regeneration rates of the pigments in rods and cones.

These principles of dark adaptation had an important wartime application for certain fighter pilots who had to be ready for night duty at all times. They needed to be able to take off at night on a moment's notice and see their targets under conditions of very low illumination. An experimental psychologist familiar with the facts of dark adaptation provided a solution. Knowing that the rods are very important in night vision and that they are relatively insensitive to red wavelengths, he suggested that fighter pilots either wear goggles with red lenses or work in rooms lit only by red lights while waiting to be called for a mission. Because red light stimulates only the cones, the rods remained in a state of dark adaptation, constantly ready for service in the dark (see Figure 5.7).

COLOR VISION

The wavelength of light determines the color—or, more technically—the *hue* that we experience. The translation of wavelength signals into sensations of color begins in the retina.

At one time scientists thought that there was a different kind of photoreceptor for each hue. We know now that human beings are sensitive to over 200,000 distinct hues; clearly there could not be that many dif-

photopigments will be exhausted. During dark adaptation the photopigment molecules are regenerated, and sensitivity increases greatly in the receptor. It is estimated that after complete adaptation, the rods are able to detect light intensities only 1/10,000 as great as those that could be detected before dark adaptation began.

Studies of how dark adaptation proceeds have provided further evidence for differences in sensitivity between rods and cones. Figure 5.6 shows a typical dark adaptation curve. Such curves are calculated by having people look at a bright light until their retinas have become adapted to it. The people are then placed in darkness, and their ability to detect light flashes of different intensities and wavelengths (colors) is measured

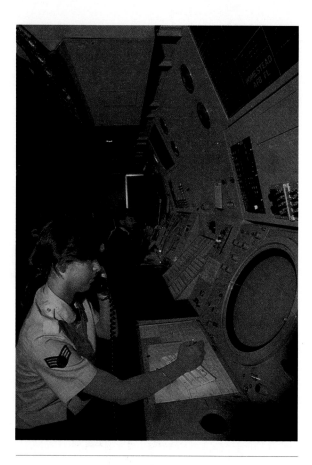

FIGURE 5.7 *Working in red light keeps the rods in a state of dark adaptation.*

FIGURE 5.8 *(a) Additive color mixture. A beam of light of a single wavelength directed onto a white surface will be perceived as the color that corresponds exactly to that wavelength on the visible spectrum. Two light beams of different wavelengths directed together onto a white surface will be perceived as a color that corresponds to a wavelength different from that of either of the two beams, or an additive color. If beams of wavelengths that fall at certain points within the red, green, or blue color range are directed together onto the surface in the correct proportions, additive color mixtures for the whole visible spectrum can be produced. The Young-Helmholtz theory of color vision assumes that color perception results from the additive mixture of impulses from cones that are sensitive to red, blue, and green (see text). (b) Subtractive color mixture. Mixing pigments or paints produces new colors by subtraction. Paints absorb (subtract) colors that correspond to wavelengths different from those of the original color. For example, blue paint mainly absorbs wavelengths that correspond to nonblue hues. Mixing blue paint with yellow paint (which absorbs colors outside the yellow wavelengths) will produce a subtractive mixture that falls within wavelengths between yellow and blue (i.e., green). Theoretically, certain wavelengths of the three primary colors of red, yellow (not green, as in additive mixture), and blue can produce the whole range of colors by subtractive mixture.*

ferent kinds of color receptors. Around 1800, it was discovered that any color in the visible spectrum could be produced by some combination of the colors blue, green, and red in what is known as **additive color mixture** (see Figure 5.8). This fact was the basis for an important theory of color vision developed in 1867 by Thomas Young, an English physicist, and Hermann von Helmholtz, a German physiologist. The **Young-Helmholtz trichromatic theory** assumes that there are three types of color receptors in the retina; each type is sensitive to wavelengths that correspond to the colors blue, green, or red (see Figure 5.9). Presumably, each

of these receptors sends messages to the brain, which combines them to re-create the original color.

Although the Young-Helmholtz theory is consistent with the laws of color mixture, there are some other facts that do not fit the theory. For example, according to the theory, yellow is produced by activity in red and green receptors, yet certain people with red-green color blindness seem to be able to experience yellow.

A second influential color theory, formulated by Ewald Hering in 1870, attempted to solve this problem. Hering also assumed that there were three types of cones, each of which responded to *two* different wavelengths—one to red or green, another to blue or yellow, and a third to black or white. Each receptor was assumed to be capable of two different chemical reactions, depending on the type of stimulation. For exam-

(a)

(b)

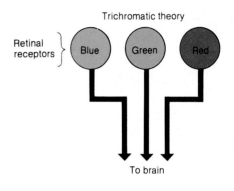

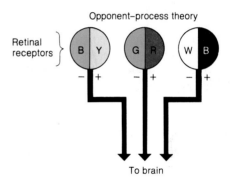

FIGURE 5.9 *Two classic theories of color vision. The Young-Helmholtz trichromatic theory proposes three different receptors, one for blue, one for red, and one for green. The ratio of activity in the three types of cones in response to a stimulus yields our experience of color. Hering's opponent-process theory also posits three different receptors, one for blue/yellow, one for red/green, and one for black/white. Each of the two color receptors can function in two possible ways, depending on the wavelength of the hue. Again, the pattern of activity in the receptors yields our perception of the hue.*

ple, a red-green cone responded with one chemical reaction to a green stimulus and with its other chemical reaction to a red stimulus. Because the receptor cannot react both ways at the same time, Hering's theory has become known as the **opponent-process theory** (see Figure 5.9).

Which theory is correct? It appears that both may be, but at different points in the visual system. According to recent findings, the photopigments of each cone contain one of three different visual proteins that are most sensitive to wavelengths roughly corresponding to the colors blue, red, and green, respectively. These visual proteins bind together with **retinal,** a light-absorbing molecule that comes from vitamin A. When light waves are absorbed by the protein-retinal units in the cones sensitive to the particular wavelength, the units snap apart and the cones produce graded potentials. Different ratios of activity of the "red," "blue," and "green" cones can produce any hue in the spectrum (Nakanishi and others, 1979; Honig and others, 1979).

These photochemical processes in the cones seem consistent with the Young-Helmholtz trichromatic theory. But opponent-processes also appear to be involved in color vision. Microelectrode studies have shown that some bipolar cells in the retina (as well as some neurons in visual relay stations further up in the brain) respond to short wavelengths with a burst of impulses above their base rate of spontaneous firing, but decrease their activity when the eye is stimulated by long wavelengths. This finding suggests an opponent-process operating not in the cones themselves, as the original Hering theory suggested, but further along in the pathway from the eye to the brain (Hurvich, 1978).

It thus appears that the retina contains receptors sensitive to three different hues, as the Young-Helmholtz theory suggests. However, interactions at the bipolar cells and beyond recode the messages from the receptors so that the neurons in the higher visual centers of the brain respond in an opponent-process fashion. See Figure 5.10 for a demonstration of opponent-processes.

VISUAL DEFECTS: LIMITS ON SENSATION

The more we learn about how vision works, the more miraculous it seems that such a complex system can work so consistently and efficiently. Because of the complexity of the visual system, however, there are many points at which defects can cause visual problems. The lens, for example, can be affected by nutritional and hormonal deficiencies, the aging process, and microwave radiation, among other things. One

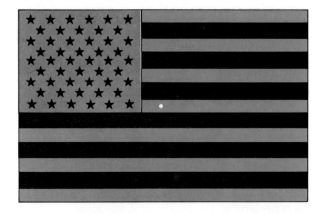

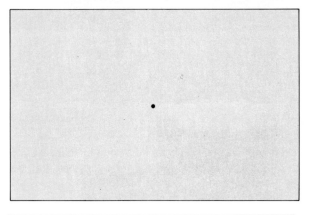

FIGURE 5.10 *Negative color afterimages have been regarded as a demonstration of opponent-processes in the visual system. Stare steadily at the white dot in the center of the flag for about a minute, then shift your gaze to the black dot in the blank space. You should see a red, white, and blue American flag. Theoretically, what has happened is that adaptation has occurred in the three yellow, green, and black processes. When you shift to a blank surface, a rebound effect occurs, yielding activity in the blue, red, and white mechanisms.*

common disorder of the lens is **cataracts,** which make the lens cloudy or opaque. If the clouding becomes severe enough, the person is unable to perceive forms.

Nearsightedness and farsightedness also involve problems with the lens. The normal eye is able to adjust its lens shape for both far and near vision. In nearsightedness, or **myopia,** the lens is too thick. When a nearsighted person looks at a distant object, the lens forms an image that falls in front of the retina instead of directly on it, resulting in a blurred image. Vision of nearby objects is not affected. This condition can be corrected by eyeglasses (or contacts) with negative or concave lenses, which are thicker on the edges than in the center. Negative lenses correct for the natural lens's inability to become thin enough to focus the image of the distant object directly onto the retina (see Figure 5.11).

Farsightedness, or **hyperopia,** occurs when the lens does not thicken enough to focus the image of nearby objects onto the retina. The image falls "behind" the retina instead. Perception of distant objects is not affected. A positive or convex lens—thicker in the center than on the edges—is used to correct this problem.

Several severe eye disorders involve dysfunction of the retina. A common cause of blindness is **glaucoma,** in which pressure within the eyeball gradually destroys the retina. The pressure is produced by a build-up of aqueous humor, the fluid that fills the chamber between the cornea and the lens. Retinal dysfunction and eventual blindness can also be caused by diabetes, the leading cause of blindness in Americans between the

ages of 20 and 65 (Maugh, 1976). The destruction results from the deterioration of tiny blood vessels in the eye. New blood vessels often grow over the retina and hemorrhage into the vitreous humor, making the normally clear liquid cloudy. Scar tissue may also form over the retina and obscure vision.

Color blindness is another common visual problem. About 7 percent of the male population and 1 percent of the female population are unable to discriminate all the wavelengths (colors) from one another. The normal eye is capable of discriminating three systems of color: red-green, yellow-blue, and black-white; the person with normal vision is called a *trichromat.* Color blindness results from a deficiency in the red-green system, the yellow-blue system, or both, due to a lack of hue-sensitive photopigment in certain cone types. A person who is color-blind in only one of the systems (red-green or yellow-blue) is called a **dichromat.** A **monochromat** has only the black-white system and is totally color-blind. Most color-blind people have a deficiency in the red-green system. A number of different tests of color blindness have been developed. Typically, these tests contain sets of colored dots like those in Figure 5.12. A color-blind person cannot pick out the numbers embedded in the circles. Figure 5.12 also shows how people with varying types of color blindness would see the same scene.

Many color-blind people are able to discriminate colors by characteristics other than hue. For example, red-green color-blind people can easily discriminate

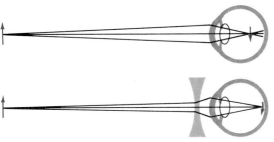

Nearsightedness corrected by a negative (concave) lens

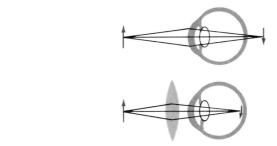

Farsightedness corrected by a positive (convex) lens

FIGURE 5.11 *Nearsightedness (myopia) and farsightedness (hyperopia) are caused by incorrect focusing of distant or nearby objects onto the retina. Negative (concave) lenses are used in eyeglasses to correct myopic focusing, while positive (convex) lenses are used for hyperopic focusing.*

between red and green traffic lights once they learn which one is on top. They can also detect differences in the brightnesses of different hues. In addition, the light waves reflected from most objects in our environment usually contain mixed wavelengths, so that a red-green color-blind person may be able to use the small amounts of blue or yellow wavelengths that are present to discriminate between red and green. Indeed, because they have such abilities, some people may be unaware that they are color-blind; they may assume that everyone sees the world the same way they do.

Audition

The energy that is the stimulus for our sense of hearing is fundamentally different from light. Light waves are electromagnetic energy, but sound waves are a form of mechanical energy. What we call sound is actually pressure waves in air, water, or some other conducting

FIGURE 5.12 *The chips below the picture are used to test for color blindness. The one on the left is used to detect red/green color blindness, and the one on the right to assess yellow/blue blindness. Because the dots in the picture are of equal brightness, the only cue for perceiving the figures in the chips are color. The photographs show how the scene would appear to a person with normal color vision (a) and to people with various types of color blindness (b, c, d).*

(a)

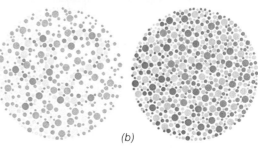

(b)

medium. When a drum is struck, for example, the resulting vibrations cause successive waves of compression and expansion among the air molecules surrounding the drum. These sound waves have two characteristics, *frequency* and *amplitude* (see Figure 5.13). *Frequency* is measured in terms of the number of vibrations, or cycles, per second. The technical measure of cycles per second is the **Hertz (Hz);** one Hz equals one cycle per second. The frequency of the sound waves is related to the *pitch* that we perceive; the higher the frequency in cycles per second, the higher the perceived pitch.

Humans are capable of detecting sound frequencies from 20 Hz up to 20,000 Hz (about 12,000 Hz in older people), but most common sounds are in the lower frequencies. Among musical instruments, the piano

can play the widest range of frequencies, from 27.5 Hz at the low end of the keyboard to 4186 Hz at the high end. Even an operatic soprano's voice has a range of only 250 Hz to 1100 Hz.

Amplitude refers to the intensity of the sound waves—that is, to the amount of compression and expansion of the molecules in the conducting medium. The amplitude of the sound wave is the primary determinant of the *loudness* of the sound. Differences in amplitude are expressed as **decibels,** a unit developed

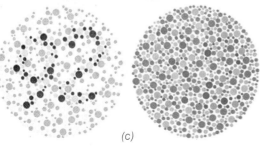

(c)

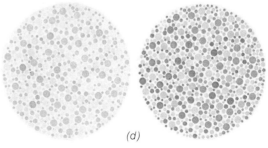

(d)

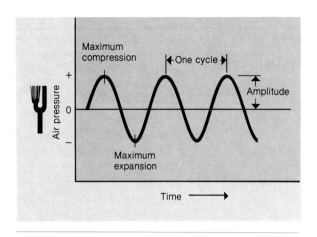

FIGURE 5.13 *Sound waves are a form of mechanical energy. As the tuning fork vibrates, it produces successive waves of compression and expansion of air molecules. The height of the wave above 0 air pressure represents its amplitude, and the number of maximum compressions per second (or cycles per second) is its frequency (measured in Hz). Amplitude determines intensity, while frequency is related to pitch.*

by scientists at the Bell Telephone Laboratories to measure the physical pressures that occur at the eardrum. Table 5.2 shows various common sounds scaled in decibels.

THE HUMAN EAR

The transduction system of your ear is made up of tiny bones, membranes, and liquid-filled tubes designed to translate pressure waves into nerve impulses (see Figure 5.14). Sound waves travel into an auditory canal leading to your eardrum, a movable membrane that vibrates in response to the sound waves. Beyond the eardrum is the middle ear, a cavity housing three small bones called the *hammer, anvil,* and *stirrup.* The hammer is attached firmly to the eardrum, while the stirrup is attached to another membrane called the *oval window.* When the eardrum is activated by sound waves, its vibrations are passed along from the hammer to the other small bones of the middle ear to the oval window, which forms the boundary between the middle ear and the inner ear. The inner ear contains the **cochlea,** a coiled tube filled with fluid. The cochlea has two membranes, the **basilar membrane** and the **tectorial**

TABLE 5.2 DECIBEL SCALING OF COMMON SOUNDS

LEVEL IN DECIBELS (db)	COMMON SOUNDS	THRESHOLD LEVELS
140		
	50 hp siren at a distance of 100 feet Jet fighter taking off at 80 feet from plane	
130		
	Boiler shop Air hammer at position of operator	
120		
	Rock and roll band Jet aircraft at 500 feet overhead	Human pain threshold
	Trumpet automobile horn at 3 feet	
110		
	Crosscut saw at position of operator	
100	Inside subway car	
90	Train whistle at 500 feet	Hearing damage with prolonged exposure
80	Inside automobile in city	
70	Downtown city street (Chicago)	
	Average traffic	
60		
	Restaurant	
50	Business office Classroom	
40	Inside church Hospital room	
30	Quiet bedroom Recording studio	
20		Threshold of hearing (young men)
10		Minimum threshold of hearing
0		

The decibel scale relates a physical quantity—sound intensity—to the human perception of that quantity—sound loudness. It is a logarithmic scale—that is, each increment of 10 decibels represents a tenfold increase in loudness. The table indicates the decibel ranges of some common sounds as well as the thresholds for hearing, hearing damage, and pain. Prolonged exposure at 150 decibels causes death in laboratory rats.

Source: Adapted from Christman, 1979, p. 236

membrane. Resting on the basilar membrane is the **organ of Corti,** which contains thousands of tiny *hair cells* whose ends are in contact with the tectorial membrane. These hair cells are the actual sound receptors.

When sound waves strike the eardrum, pressure created at the oval window by the bony transmitters of the middle ear sets the fluid inside the cochlea into motion. These fluid waves shift the basilar and tectorial membranes in relation to one another so that the hair cells in the organ of Corti are bent, setting up an electrical potential that results in nerve impulses being sent to the brain through the auditory nerve.

CODING OF AUDITORY INFORMATION

The sound characteristics that your auditory system must detect and communicate are loudness and pitch. Loudness appears to be coded in terms of the total number of auditory nerve fibers that fire and by the activation of certain fibers that fire only when considerable bending of the hair cells occurs in response to an intense sound.

The coding of pitch is more complicated because two different processes—one for frequencies below about 400 Hz and another for higher frequencies— seem to be involved. Low-frequency sounds cause individual hair cells to fire at the same frequency as the sound wave. Groups of individual hair cells in the cochlea can also coordinate their firing so that they fire

at slightly different times, resulting in "volleys" of nerve impulses sent through the auditory nerve at about the same frequency as the sound wave. This is known as the **frequency theory** of pitch coding.

Individual impulses or volleys of impulses cannot produce high enough frequencies of firing to match the frequency of sound waves above 400 Hz. Frequencies above this range are apparently coded in terms of the area of the basilar membrane that is displaced the most by the fluid waves. Because of the wave action in the cochlea, the point of maximum wave action on the basilar membrane moves closer to the oval window as the sound's frequency increases. The research that led to this **place theory** of pitch coding won Georg von Bekesy the Nobel Prize.

The chemical senses

Taste and smell are called the chemical senses because their receptors are sensitive to chemical substances rather than to some form of energy or pressure. These

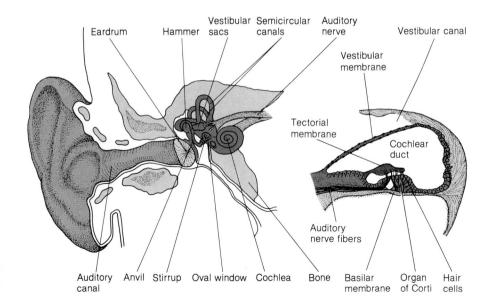

Eardrum   Hammer   Vestibular sacs   Semicircular canals   Auditory nerve   Vestibular canal

Vestibular membrane

Tectorial membrane

Cochlear duct

Auditory nerve fibers

Auditory canal   Anvil   Stirrup   Oval window   Cochlea   Bone   Basilar membrane   Organ of Corti   Hair cells

FIGURE 5.14 *A cross section of the ear shows the structures that transmit sound waves from the auditory canal to the cochlea. There they stimulate hair cells in the organ of Corti. The resulting nerve impulses reach the brain via the auditory nerve. The semicircular and vestibular sacs of the inner ear contain sense organs for equilibrium.*

senses, particularly smell, have great significance for many species. Vision and audition are more important to us, and our chemical senses are far less developed than are those of some lower animals who depend heavily on them for survival.

People who fancy themselves as gourmets are frequently surprised to find their sense of taste is responsive to only four qualities: sweet, sour, salty, and bitter. Every other taste experience is composed of a combination of these qualities and those of other senses, such as smell, temperature, and touch.

The stimuli for taste are a variety of chemical substances that come into contact with sensory receptors in the mouth. These receptors, known as *taste buds*, are concentrated along the edges and back surface of the tongue. Humans have about 9000 taste buds (see Figure 5.15). Each taste bud consists of several receptor cells arranged like the segments of an orange. Hairlike structures project from the top of each cell into the taste pore, an opening to the outside surface of the tongue. When a substance is taken into the mouth, it interacts with saliva to form a chemical solution that flows into the taste pore and stimulates the receptor cells.

The stimuli for olfaction, the sense of smell, are also chemical molecules. This is one reason we sometimes have difficulty determining whether we are tasting or smelling something. Both chemical senses are undoubtedly involved in our enjoyment of a good meal or our displeasure with a bad one. Remember how tasteless your meals were the last time you had a bad cold?

The receptors for smell are long cells that project through the lining of the upper nasal cavity and into the mucous membrane. Our ability to discriminate odors is not well understood. One theory is that specifically shaped odor molecules fit into receptor "slots" like keys into locks (Amoore, 1969). Each odor would then result in a particular pattern of firing among the neurons in the olfactory system, much as colors are mixed in an artist's palette, accounting for our ability to discriminate among odors.

Compared with vision and audition, olfaction's relation to human behavior has received far less attention. However, as Frontier 5.1 indicates, some interesting and unexpected discoveries are occurring in research on our sense of smell.

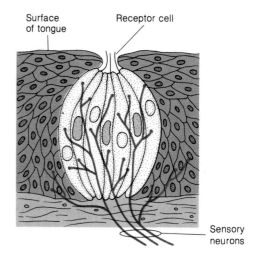

FIGURE 5.15 *The receptors for taste are specialized cells located in taste buds in the tongue. The taste buds are grouped in different areas of the tongue according to the taste sensation to which they respond. The center of the tongue is relatively insensitive to taste qualities.*

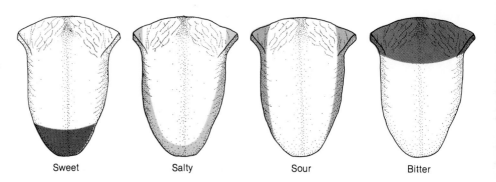

Sweet   Salty   Sour   Bitter

ODORS AND SEXUALITY IN HUMANS

Anyone who has owned a female dog or cat in heat could tell you all about the role of odors in controlling the sexual behavior of lower animals. But while we support a huge cosmetics industry based on its supposed ability to increase our sexual attractiveness by making us smell like limes, roses, and spruce trees, the potential role of natural body odors in governing our sexual behavior has been largely ignored. In fact, we do our best to camouflage them with deodorants and perfumes. But recent findings suggest that natural body scents may affect our sexual functioning at both a physiological and a behavioral level.

It has been noted that women who live together or are close friends tend to have similar menstrual cycles. Psychologist Martha McClintock (1971) tested 135 college women and found that, during the course of an academic year, roommates moved from a mean of 8.5 days apart in their periods to 4.9 days. Is it possible that the synchronizing factor is body odors? To test this possibility, Michael Russell of San Francisco State University asked a woman with a regular 28-day cycle who used no deodorant to collect odor samples on pads placed under her arms. These pads were rubbed on the skin beneath the noses of five female volunteers three times a week. A control group of six women were dabbed with an alcohol solution instead. After 4 months the volunteers moved from an average of 9.3 days away from the "donor's" cycle to 3.4 days; 4 of the 5 volunteers moved to within 1 day. The controls showed no such shift (Hassett, 1978). These results suggest that odor may be the key to "menstrual synchrony."

It appears that, like lower animals, some men and women are responsive to certain chemicals released in the urine or sex organs of the opposite sex. During ovulation, some women show increased olfactory sensitivity to a musky substance called *exaltolide,* which is excreted in male urine. Another substance secreted by adult males, *androstenol,* has been the subject of research conducted by Victor Johnson (1985) at New Mexico State University. Johnson measured the brain waves of male and female subjects while they viewed slides of same- and opposite-sex models. Of particular interest to him was a brain wave pattern known as P3, which appears to be related to positive emotional responses (Miller, 1985). The subjects were told that their respiration was being recorded through a small tube under their noses; the tube actually contained a cotton swab saturated with either an alcohol solution containing androstenol or with alcohol alone. Johnson found that the P3 responses of female subjects were higher when they viewed male slides while breathing androstenol than when they did so while breathing alcohol alone, while female slides evoked lower P3 responses when androstenol was present. Male P3 responses to female slides were higher than to male slides under both chemical conditions, but their responses to female slides were especially high in the presence of androstenol. Johnson suggests that body odors produced by substances like androstenol may affect emotional responses to potential sexual stimuli. He also suggests that body hair and beards in males may help to retain the odors produced by such secretions.

Chemicals known as *copulins* are secreted in the vaginas of women, with peak secretions believed to occur during ovulation (Keverne, 1977). In one experiment with 62 married couples, the wives were asked to rub 1 of 4 different perfumes on their chests each night at bedtime according to a predetermined random schedule. The couples were unaware that one of the perfumes contained copulins. Each morning the couples completed questionnaires concerning their sexual behavior the previous evening. The investigators found that the sexual responsiveness of 12 of the 62 couples was apparently affected by the copulins. These couples showed increases in sexual activity on the nights the women wore copulins, and their peak sexual activity occurred during the ovulation phase of the women's cycles (Morris and Udry, 1978). The fact that some couples, but not others, showed changes in their sexual behavior suggests the possibility that there are individual differences in sensitivity and/or responsiveness to copulins. If so, the reasons for these differences could become an important topic for future research.

Findings like these are attracting the attention of researchers to the question of whether sexuality and other aspects of our behavior are influenced by our sense of smell more than we realize (Snowdon, 1983).

The skin and body senses

The skin and body senses include the senses of touch, kinesthesis, and equilibrium. The last two are called body senses because they inform us of the position and movement of the body.

THE SKIN SENSES

The sense of touch is important to us in a great many ways. Sensitivity to extreme temperatures and to pain not only enables us to avoid external danger but also alerts us to disorders within our bodies. In addition, tactile sensations are a source of many pleasures.

We are sensitive to at least four tactual sensations: pressure or touch, pain, warmth, and cold. These sensations are conveyed by receptors in the skin and in our internal organs. Mixtures of these four sensations are the basis for all other common skin sensations, such as itch.

Considering the importance of our skin senses, we know surprisingly little about how they work. We know that there are a number of receptor structures in the skin, but it has not been possible to find consistent relationships between the various structures and specific sensations. We are relatively certain that the primary receptors for pain are free or bare nerve endings that terminate in the skin, and that nerve fibers situated

at the base of hair follicles are receptors for touch and for light pressure. We also know that there are "warm" and "cold" spots on the skin and that their simultaneous activation results in our sensation of warmth.

The brain can "locate" sensations because the skin receptors send their messages to the point in the sensory cortex that corresponds to the area of the body in which the receptor is located. People who have had arms or legs amputated sometimes experience a "phantom limb phenomenon" in which they feel vivid sensations coming from the missing limb. Apparently, the irritation of nerves that used to originate in the limb fools the brain into interpreting the impulses as real sensations. The experience can be quite maddening; imagine having an intense itch that you can never scratch!

Perhaps the most interesting of the skin senses is pain. We discuss the perception and control of pain in greater detail later in the chapter.

THE BODY SENSES

We would be totally unable to coordinate our body movements if we did not receive constant feedback about the position and movements of our muscles and joints. The sense of **kinesthesis,** or body movement, functions by means of nerve endings in the muscles, tendons, and joints. The information it gives us is the basis for making corrective movements.

Cooperating with kinesthesis is the *vestibular sense*—the sense of body orientation or equilibrium. Those of us who have experienced seasickness, vertigo, or dizziness from an amusement park ride have encountered the vestibular sense's effort to tell us which end is up when neither end will stay still.

The sense organs for equilibrium are located in the **vestibular apparatus** of the inner ear (see Figure 5.14). One part of this system consists of three *semicircular canals*, each in a different plane: left–right, backward–forward, or up–down. These canals are filled with fluid and lined with hairlike cells that function as receptors. When the head moves, the fluid in the appropriate canal shifts, stimulating the hair cells and firing associated neural fibers. The semicircular canals respond only to acceleration and deceleration. When a constant speed is reached (no matter how high), the fluid and the hair cells return to their normal resting state. That's why takeoffs and landings give you a sense of movement, while flying at 500 mph on a cruising airliner doesn't.

The second part of the body sense system is the *vestibular sacs*, located at the base of the semicircular canals. These structures, which are also lined with hair cells, respond to the position of the resting body and tell us whether we are upright or tilted at an angle.

Psychophysics: The study of sensory capabilities

Much research in a specialized area of investigation known as **psychophysics** has been aimed at finding out exactly how sensitive our senses are. In studying this question, psychologists have been concerned with two different kinds of sensitivity. The first kind has to do with the absolute limits of sensitivity. For example, what is the dimmest light or the lowest amplitude of sound wave that we can detect? The second kind has to do with sensitivity to differences between stimuli. For example, how much must two tones differ before we can tell that they are not identical? Both kinds of questions involve relationships between physical energy and sensory experience, which is why the term *psychophysics* is used for the study of such relationships.

STIMULUS DETECTION: THE ABSOLUTE THRESHOLD

Exactly how strong must a stimulus be before we can detect its presence? As noted earlier, this minimum amount of energy is called the *absolute threshold*. The lower the absolute threshold, the greater the sensitivity. In research, the absolute threshold is operationally defined as the intensity at which the stimulus can be detected 50 percent of the time.

Absolute thresholds vary depending on the conditions under which the stimulus occurs and on the characteristics of the perceiver. However, we can estimate the limits of sensitivity for the five major senses. Some examples are presented in Table 5.3.

Signal detection theory   At one time it was assumed that each person has a more or less fixed level of sensitivity for each sense. But psychologists and engineers who study stimulus detection learned that people's apparent sensitivity can fluctuate quite a bit. They con-

TABLE 5.3 SENSITIVITY OF THE VARIOUS SENSES: SOME APPROXIMATE ABSOLUTE THRESHOLDS

SENSE MODALITY	ABSOLUTE THRESHOLD
Vision	Candle flame seen at 30 miles on a clear, dark night
Hearing	Tick of a watch under quiet conditions at 20 feet
Taste	I teaspoon of sugar in 2 gallons of water
Smell	I drop of perfume diffused into the entire volume of a large apartment
Touch	Wing of a fly or bee falling on your cheek from a distance of I centimeter

Source: Based on Galanter, 1962.

cluded that the concept of a "fixed" absolute threshold is largely meaningless because there is no single point on the intensity scale that separates nondetection from detection of a stimulus. There is instead a range of uncertainty, and people set a decision criterion or standard of how certain they must be that a stimulus is present before they will say they detect it. **Signal detection theory** is concerned with the factors that influence such decisions.

In a typical signal detection experiment, subjects are told that after a warning light appears, a tone may or may not be presented. Their task is to tell the experimenter if they heard it or not. Under these conditions, there are four possible outcomes, as shown in Figure 5.16. When the tone is in fact presented, the subject may say "yes" (a hit) or "no" (a miss). When no tone is presented, the subject may also say "yes" (a false alarm) or "no" (a correct rejection).

At low stimulus intensities, characteristics of both the subject and the situation influence the decision criterion (Pitz and Sachs, 1984). Bold subjects who say "yes" get more hits, but also give more false alarms than do conservative subjects. We can also influence subjects to become bolder or more conservative by manipulating the rewards and costs for giving correct or incorrect responses.

FIGURE 5.16 *This matrix shows the four outcomes possible in a signal detection experiment. The percentages of responses that fall within each category can be strongly affected by both subject characteristics and the nature of the situation.*

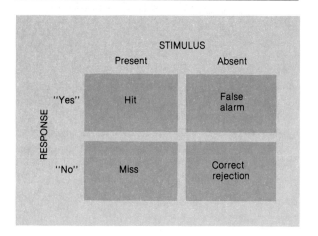

The decision processes involved in signal detection experiments are similar to those faced by physicians who must decide whether or not a given disease is present. The consequences of deciding that a person is or is not suffering from a particular disease will affect the doctor's decision criterion for a positive diagnosis (Grossberg and Grant, 1978). Physicians will not make certain diagnoses (especially those that will result in radical interventions, such as open-heart surgery) unless they have compelling evidence, because the consequences of a mistake would be too costly to the patient, to them, and, perhaps, to their insurance companies.

SUBLIMINAL STIMULI

Certain stimuli are so weak or brief that, although they are received by our senses, they cannot be perceived consciously. The effect of these **subliminal stimuli** has been a matter of great controversy in psychology. We now know that the nervous system can indeed process incoming information "preconsciously"—that is, without our conscious awareness of it (Dixon, 1981; Kahneman and Treisman, 1984). But can such stimuli affect behavior without our knowing it?

In the late 1950s, James Vicary, a public relations executive, arranged to have messages flashed on a theater screen during a movie. These "secret" messages were flashed so quickly that they were imperceptible. They urged the movie audience to "Drink Coca-Cola" and "Eat popcorn." Vicary claimed that the subliminal messages increased popcorn sales by 50 percent and soft drink sales by 18 percent. Naturally, his claims aroused a public furor. Consumers and scientists worried about the possible abuse of subliminal messages for "mind control" and "brainwashing." Advertising agencies and manufacturers gleefully foresaw an opportunity to have a more direct influence on the buying habits of millions of Americans. The National Association of Broadcasters reacted by outlawing the use of subliminal messages on American television.

The most important issue, of course, is whether or not subliminal stimuli can affect our subsequent actions. Some researchers have suggested that subliminal cues may affect our behavior even though these cues never reach our awareness, while other scientists have insisted that this is impossible. Numerous studies have been conducted in laboratories, on television and radio, and in movie theaters, and their results indicate that behavior is not profoundly influenced by subliminal stimuli. Attempts to reproduce Vicary's results under controlled conditions ended in failure. After many years of research, psychologist Norman Dixon did an extensive review of the evidence concerning subliminal stimulation. He concluded, "There is little evidence to suggest, and strong arguments against, the possibility of seriously manipulating drives, or drive-oriented behavior, by subliminal stimulation" (1971, p. 178).

No research conducted during the intervening 15 years has seriously challenged Dixon's conclusion, although it does appear that some behaviors can be influenced in subtle ways (Dixon, 1981). Thus, despite claims to the contrary in popular books like *Subliminal Seduction* (Key, 1972), there seems little reason to be seriously concerned about significant or widespread control of behavior through subliminal stimulation. Persuasive stimuli above the threshold appear to be far more effective in influencing our actions, perhaps because we are more certain to get the total message.

THE DIFFERENCE THRESHOLD

Sometimes subtle differences between stimuli are important. The smallest difference that people can perceive between two stimuli is called the **difference threshold** or the *just noticeable difference* (**jnd**).

An important discovery about the difference threshold was made about 150 years ago by the German physiologist Ernst Weber. He discovered that the difference threshold, or jnd, is proportional to the intensity of the stimulus with which the comparison is being made. For example, the jnd value for weights that we lift is approximately 0.02, or $\frac{1}{50}$. This means that if we lift a weight of 100 grams, a second weight must weigh at least 102 grams ($\frac{2}{100} = \frac{1}{50}$) in order for us to discriminate between them. If the first weight is 200 grams, then the second must be at least 4 grams heavier, and if the first weight is 400 grams, the second one must be at least 408 grams. **Weber's law** holds up well within the middle ranges of stimulation that we most frequently encounter, but it breaks down at extremely high or low intensities of stimulation.

Weber also found that the specific ratios differed, depending on the nature of the stimulus. Weber ratios, or constants, have been calculated for all the senses.

Sound receptors are very sensitive to differences in stimulation; the Weber constant for differences in pitch is approximately $\frac{1}{333}$. Taste is the least sensitive of our senses, with a jnd of $\frac{1}{5}$ for detecting differences in salt concentrations. The jnd for brightness discrimination is about $\frac{1}{60}$.

At any given time, we are aware of only a tiny portion of the millions of messages that are being sent out by our sensory receptors. Our sense organs do not select what we will be aware of or how we will experience it. They merely transmit as much information as they can through our nervous system. But that is only the beginning of the story. Once in the nervous system, the stimuli are acted upon, processed, and transformed into our perceptions. This fascinating process, still only dimly understood, is affected by biological features of the system, by the effects of learning, and by cognitive and psychodynamic factors.

PERCEPTUAL PROCESSES

On a brisk autumn afternoon some years ago, Princeton and Dartmouth met in the annual renewal of their football rivalry. From the opening kickoff, it was clear that it was going to be a rough game. Tempers flared frequently, and the officials had their hands full trying to keep the game under control. In the second quarter, Princeton's star player, Dick Kazmaier, was led from the field with a concussion and a broken nose. Later in the game, a Dartmouth player was carried off with a broken leg. Several other players on both sides suffered serious injuries.

After the game, things really heated up. Princeton coaches, officials, and fans accused Dartmouth of deliberately trying to maim Kazmaier. Dartmouth supporters denied the charges and in turn accused Princeton of flagrantly dirty football. Charges and counter-charges were exchanged for several weeks after the

FIGURE 5.17 *Failing to see eye-to-eye on a play, a manager and an umpire go jaw-to-jaw. Motivational and psychodynamic factors can play a prominent role in perception.*

game, and the war of words attracted more national attention than the gridiron war had.

Fortunately, a few people at Dartmouth and Princeton would still talk to each other without clenching their teeth. Psychologists Albert Hastorf of Dartmouth and Hadley Cantril of Princeton were struck by the fans' violent disagreement over what had actually occurred. It was almost as if the fans had been in two different stadiums that day.

Their curiosity aroused, Hastorf and Cantril (1954) conducted a study of the perceptions of Dartmouth and Princeton students, which they published under the title, "They Saw a Game." The researchers showed a film of the game to students from the two institutions and asked them to check off on a questionnaire any infractions of the rules that they saw on the film. While viewing the film, Dartmouth students saw both teams make about the same number of infractions. Princeton supporters, however, saw the Dartmouth team commit twice as many infractions as the Princeton team, and they detected twice as many rule violations by Dartmouth as the Dartmouth fans did. Even on the replay, it was clear that students from the two schools were still seeing "different" games.

Disagreements over what "really happened" are not confined to the world of sports. The same sensory in-

formation transmitted to the brains of two different people may be experienced in radically different ways. Our experiences are not simply a one-to-one reflection of what is "out there." Rather, perception is an active process in which the raw sensory data are coded, organized, and given meanings derived from our unique personal experiences.

We know quite a bit more about how our sensory systems function than about the ways in which the real world and our perceptions of it are linked. A variety of factors influence our perceptions, only one of which is the physical characteristics of the stimulus. Some of these factors are biological; they are built into our nervous system. Others are the result of our learning experiences. And, like the Dartmouth and Princeton students, what we perceive is also influenced by our attitudes, motives, values, and psychological defenses.

Attention: Selecting which information gets in

As you read these words, countless stimuli are bombarding your senses. A hundred million sensory messages may be clamoring for attention this very second. Yet only a small number of these register in awareness;

the rest you either perceive dimly or not at all. But you can shift your attention to one of those "unregistered" stimuli at any time. (For example, how does the big toe of your right foot feel right now?) Attention, then, involves two processes of selection: (1) focusing on certain stimuli, and (2) filtering out other incoming information.

ATTENTIONAL SHIFTS

Imagine that you are at a party having an interesting conversation with a group of your friends. Other groups of people are talking nearby, but you are almost unaware of them until you hear someone in a group across the room mention your name. This meaningful stimulus filters through, despite your inattention to the rest of the partygoers. You quickly shift part of your attention to the group across the room while trying at the same time to listen to what the person you were talking to is saying.

This *cocktail party phenomenon* has been studied experimentally through a technique called **shadowing.** People wearing earphones listen to two messages simultaneously, one presented through each earphone. They are asked to repeat (shadow) one of the messages word for word. Most subjects can do this quite successfully, but only at the cost of not remembering what the message presented to the other ear was about. People can also shift their attention rapidly back and forth between the two messages, trying to attend to bits of each and draw upon their general knowledge of the English language and the topics to fill in the gaps. The results of these shadowing experiments have demonstrated quite conclusively that we cannot attend completely to more than one thing at a time, but we can shift our attention rapidly enough to get the sense of two different messages (Sperling, 1984).

Attention is strongly affected by both the nature of the stimulus and by personal factors. Stimulus characteristics that attract our attention are intensity, novelty, movement, contrast, and repetition. Think about the ways in which advertisers use these properties in their commercials and packaging.

MOTIVATIONAL AND PSYCHODYNAMIC FACTORS

Internal personal factors also act as filters to determine which of the many stimuli in our environment we will notice. Motives are very powerful filters. For example,

when we are hungry, we are especially sensitive to food-related cues. Our interests function in the same way. A botanist walking through a park is especially attentive to the plants; a landscape architect attends primarily to the layout of the park; a male college student may be most interested in the young women in the park. Our previous learning experiences also determine which stimuli we notice. A person who has narrowly escaped from a fire may be very sensitive to the smell of smoke. A person who has been painfully jilted in an important romance is likely to be very sensitive to words or actions that signal rejection in future relationships.

In some cases, the filtering process serves a defensive function and protects us from the anxiety that would be aroused if we allowed ourselves to perceive threatening stimuli. This phenomenon is known as **perceptual defense.** It has been shown in studies of the absolute threshold that many people have higher visual and auditory thresholds for (that is, are less able to perceive) stimuli that are threatening or anxiety-arousing to them (Dixon, 1981). These include not only words of a sexual or violent nature, but also stimuli that have previously been paired with shock to condition anxiety responses to them. People also show a strong tendency to attend to information that is consistent with their beliefs and self-concepts while ignoring or distorting contradictory information (Wylie, 1978). Some people simply cannot seem to "hear" or "see" input that contradicts their picture of themselves and the world. Thus, psychodynamic factors also play a role in our perceptions.

Patterning and organization in perception

Perhaps the most fundamental as well as the most complex question about perception is how our brain processes the information that it receives from our millions of individual sensory receptors to produce the unified mosaic that we experience as a perception. As you read this page, for example, millions of nerve impulses are flashing from your rods and cones back into your visual cortex. Somehow these impulses are being analyzed and the visual image you perceive is being reconstructed. Moreover, you know what these funny black squiggles "mean." How does this occur? Some of the most important and exciting work in the study of perception is now being directed at this question.

CORTICAL COLUMNS AND BLOBS

The cerebral cortex of our brain must be organized in such a way that it can receive and integrate sensory nerve impulses. It appears that one of the key principles of that organization is the **cortical columns** (Hubel, 1982). These are vertically arranged groups of neurons that extend downward from the surface into other layers of the cortex.

Much of our knowledge about the role of cortical columns comes from research that won David Hubel and Torsten Wiesel of Harvard University the 1981 Nobel Prize. Using microelectrodes to record the activity of individual cells of the visual cortex of animals (see Figure 5.18), they found that certain columns fire most frequently when lines of certain orientations are presented (Hubel and Wiesel, 1959). For example, the cells of a particular column might fire most frequently when a horizontal line was presented, the cells of the next column would fire most frequently to a line of a slightly different orientation, and so on "around the clock." Figure 5.19 shows how these cortical units, known as **orientation columns,** are arranged. Hubel and Wiesel also found that a column of cells dominated by the left eye is usually next to a column that receives input from the right eye. They called these alternating columns **ocular dominance columns.**

As you can see in Figure 5.19, the individual columns are grouped into larger units called **hypercolumns.** Each hypercolumn is composed of about 400 to 1600 individual columns (Frisby, 1980). The job of the hypercolumn is to inspect a particular region of the retina and to act as an information processing subunit within the cortex. The total pattern of neural activity in each hypercolumn is believed to be the basis for the

FIGURE 5.18 *A partially anesthetized monkey views an image projected on the screen while an electrode embedded in its visual cortex records the activity of a single neuron. This research led to the discovery of feature detectors and cortical columns.*

analysis and integration of inputs by the visual cortex, though how this occurs is still a mystery. Another Nobel Prize surely awaits the discoverer of how the hypercolumns work.

Hubel and Wiesel's discovery of cortical columns that respond selectively to specific stimuli revolutionized the field of vision research. Since then, researchers have studied the stimulus features to which specific cells in the visual system respond. So-called **feature detectors** have been identified by recording the electrical activity of individual cells in the retina and higher visual centers when various kinds of visual stimuli are presented. Cells have been found that respond most strongly to bars, slits, and edges in certain positions. It is thought that the feature detectors send information

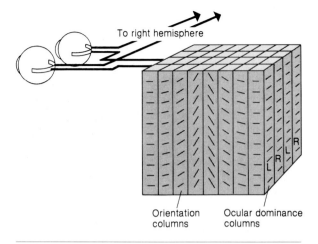

To right hemisphere

Orientation columns

Ocular dominance columns

FIGURE 5.19 *This representation of a portion of a hypercolumn in the left visual cortex shows the general arrangement of cortical columns. Cells within each orientation column show maximum firing to stimuli having a particular orientation. Input from the two eyes is alternated in ocular dominance columns lying side by side in the cortex. The patterns of neural activity in the 400 to 1600 individual columns that make up a hypercolumn are analyzed to detect features of the visual stimulus.*

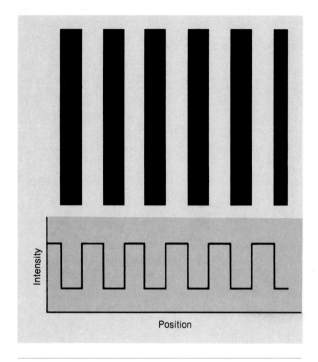

Intensity

Position

FIGURE 5.20 *A spatial frequency wave measures the location and extent of variations in brightness. This wave shows the amount of contrast between bands and the location and number of contrasts. Certain cells in the visual system are differentially sensitive to particular spatial frequency waves—that is, they will fire in response to a certain frequency and not in response to others. It appears that the brain "sees" or reconstructs the visual pattern by analyzing which spatial frequency cells are firing.*

about edges, contours, and angles to the cortex, where the data are integrated and analyzed by successively more complex feature detector systems to produce our perception of objects.

Feature detectors have also been identified for such varied stimuli as rate and direction of movement, sound frequencies, and movement across the skin (Goldstein, 1984). Recently, patches of cells given the colloquial name **blobs** have been found interspersed among the form detectors. These are sensitive to color and operate in an opponent-process fashion (Hubel and Livingstone, 1983). Thus, the visual cortex seems to have feature receptors for form, movement, and color.

An important recent development, the **spatial frequency model,** has provided a new way of understanding how the brain receives and processes visual information. Any visual pattern can be represented as variations in brightness, darkness, and contrast, as in a black and white photograph. For example, the series of bars in Figure 5.20 can be represented as a spatial frequency wave that reflects the variations in brightness in

terms of their position in the visual field. There is now a great deal of evidence that we have specialized cells in the retina and in the higher levels of the visual system that respond to specific spatial frequencies (Westheimer, 1984). These cells are called *spatial frequency filters*. The spatial filter theory suggests that these cells detect information about the spatial frequencies—

differences in intensity and location of brightness, darkness, and shading of objects. Within the brain, these many bits of spatial frequency information from small areas of the retina are integrated and put together like the pieces of a jigsaw puzzle to form a perception of the object (Georgeson, 1979).

GESTALT PRINCIPLES OF PERCEPTUAL ORGANIZATION

Long before the biological perspective stimulated the discovery of feature detectors and cortical hypercolumns, the Gestalt psychologists had their own approach to the same basic question of how we organize the separate parts of our perceptual field into a unified and meaningful whole. They argued that "the whole is greater than (and frequently different from) the sum of its parts" and attempted to discover the principles of perceptual organization that make it so.

The Gestalt psychologists emphasized the importance of *figure-ground relationships*. We tend to organize stimuli into a central, or "foreground," figure and a background. In vision, the figure is usually in front of

or on top of what we perceive as background. It has a distinct shape and is more striking in our perceptions and memory than the background is. The background "flows" around the shape of the figure; it has no edges of its own. We see contours whenever there is a distinct change in the color or brightness of the background, but we interpret these contours as being part of the figure rather than as part of the background. Consider the drawing in Figure 5.21. It is known as a *reversible figure* because it can be seen in two equally plausible ways. If you examine it for a while, two different perceptions will emerge. Whichever way you see the stimulus, the contour is always part of the figure, not the background. This same principle of figure and ground operates in relation to auditory stimuli: most music is heard as a melody (figure) surrounded by other chords (ground).

The Gestalt psychologists were also vitally interested in the way separate stimuli come to be perceived as parts of larger wholes. They suggested that we group and interpret stimuli in accordance with four laws of perceptual organization: similarity, proximity, closure, and continuity. Visual illustrations of these organizing principles are shown in Figures 5.22 and 5.23.

The law of **similarity** states that when parts of a stimulus configuration are perceived as similar, they will also be perceived as belonging together. For exam-

FIGURE 5.21 *Figure-ground relationships are demonstrated by the reversible figure, a drawing which can be seen as either a vase or two facial profiles. Whichever percept exists at the moment is seen as figure against background. As the photograph shows, military camouflage experts create patterns to hide the figure-ground relationships that help us to identify objects.*

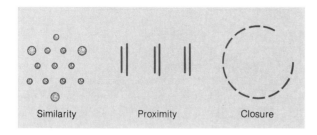

Similarity   Proximity   Closure

FIGURE 5.22 *Among the Gestalt principles for perceptual organization are the laws of similarity, proximity, and closure. Each principle allows us to organize stimuli into "wholes" that are greater than the sum of their parts.*

ple, most people immediately perceive the dots in Figure 5.22 as two triangles formed by different-sized circles. The law of **proximity** says that elements that are near each other are likely to be perceived as part of the same configuration. Thus, most people perceive the middle figure in 5.22 as three sets of lines, rather than as six separate lines. The law of **closure**, also illustrated in Figure 5.22, states that we tend to close the open edges of a figure or fill in gaps when a stimulus is incomplete, so that what we see is more complete than what is actually there. Finally, the law of **continuity** holds that we link individual elements so they form a continuous line or pattern that makes sense to us. To illustrate, Figure 5.23 shows *Fraser's spiral*, which is not really a spiral at all! We see the concentric circles as a spiral because our nervous system finds that the best continuity between individual elements is the one given by a spiral rather than by a set of circles. The spiral is created by us, not by the stimulus.

PERCEPTUAL HYPOTHESES AND EXPECTANCIES

As the Gestalt principles of perceptual organization show, there is more to understanding perception than knowing the biological details about how input gets into the system and how pattern recognition occurs. We need to understand how we "know" what the object we see, the spoken word we hear, or the object we feel really is. Recognition of a stimulus implies that we have some sort of internal representation to compare it with. It is as if we have sets of descriptions stored in our

brains. These internal descriptions, which are largely a product of past experience and memory, contain the critical elements necessary for identification. The features of incoming stimuli are extracted and matched with the alternative internal representations until the "best fit" is established. The closer the fit between stimulus features and internal concept, the more confident we are in our perception (Lindsay and Norman, 1977).

Perception is, in a sense, a search for the best interpretation of sensory information we can arrive at based on our knowledge and previous experience. Indeed, psychologist R. L. Gregory (1966) has suggested that

FIGURE 5.23 *The operation of the Gestalt law of continuity is seen in our perception of Fraser's spiral. If you follow any part of the "spiral" with your finger, you will find that it is actually not a spiral at all, but a series of concentric circles. The "spiral" is created by your nervous system because that perception is more consistent with continuity of the individual elements.*

each perception is essentially a **hypothesis** about the nature of the object or, more generally, the meaning of the sensory information. The perceptual system actively searches its internal files for the interpretation that best fits the sensory data. If we have only partial data, we are often able to "fill in" the missing information. Thzs, wz caz rezlaze ezerz thzrd zetzer zitz a *z*, anz yoz caz stzll zo azl rzghz.* When you read, you can skim the page and, because you have learned a lot about the style of written language, you can make good predictions the words you expect to see. In fact, your perceptual expectancies may have caused you to automatically fill in the missing *about* in the previous sentence or not to even notice that it was missing.

An example of how effortlessly our perceptual system builds up descriptions (hypotheses) that best fit the available evidence is found in the upside-down comic strips created by Gustave Verbeek in the early 1900s. The *Sunday New York Herald* told Verbeek that his comic strip had to be restricted to 6 panels. Verbeek wanted 12 panels, so, with amazing skill and ingenuity, he created 12-panel cartoons in only 6 panels by drawing pictures like that shown in the upper part of Figure 5.24. When you turn your book upside down, a bird story becomes a fish story! The important point to note is that we do not simply see an upside-down version of the same picture, even though the physical stimuli remain exactly the same. We see radically different pictures.

Another example of how the same stimulus can give rise to different perceptions is the Necker cube, shown in the lower part of Figure 5.24. As you stare at the cube, you will find it changes before your eyes. The front of the cube suddenly becomes the back, and it appears that the cube is being viewed from a different angle as your nervous system tries out a new perceptual hypothesis.

ILLUSIONS: FALSE PERCEPTUAL HYPOTHESES

In 1965, the Boeing Company introduced the 727 jet airliner. The plane performed well in test flights, but four fatal crashes in late 1965 and early 1966 suggested that there might be some serious problems in the design of the aircraft.

The first accident occurred as a 727 made its ap-

*Thus, we can replace every third letter with a *z*, and you can still do all right.

(SUNDAY NEW YORK HERALD, 1900s.)

"Just as he reaches a small grassy point of land, another fish attacks him, lashing furiously with his tail."

"The largest of the ROCS picks her up by the skirt."

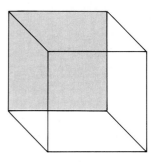

FIGURE 5.24 *Two examples of how the same stimulus can give rise to different perceptions are found in the comic strips of Gustave Verbeek and in the Necker cube. To produce the reversals, turn the comic strip panel upside-down and stare at the cube.*

proach to Chicago over Lake Michigan on a clear night. The plane plunged into the lake 19 miles off shore. About a month later, another airliner glided in over the Ohio River to land in Cincinnati. Unaccountably, it struck the ground about 12 feet below the runway elevation and burst into flames. The third accident occurred as an aircraft approached Salt Lake City over dark land. The lights of the city twinkled in the distance, but the plane made too rapid a descent and landed short of the runway. In the fourth accident, a Japanese airliner approached Tokyo at night. The flight ended unexpectedly and tragically as the plane, its landing gear not yet lowered, struck the waters of Tokyo Bay 6 miles from the runway and spun itself to destruction.

Analysis of these four accidents, as well as others, suggested a common pattern. Because all occurred at night under clear weather conditions, the pilots were operating under visual flight rules rather than performing instrument landings. In each instance, the plane was approaching city lights over dark areas of water or land. In all cases, the cities in the background sloped upward. Finally, all of the planes crashed short of the runway.

These observations led Boeing psychologist Conrad L. Kraft to suspect that the cause of the crashes might be pilot error based on some sort of visual illusion, or

misperception. To test this possibility, Boeing constructed an apparatus to simulate night landings (see Figure 5.25). It consisted of a cockpit and a miniature lighted "city" named Nightertown. The city moved toward the cockpit on computer-controlled rollers and could be tilted to simulate various terrain slopes. The pilot could control simulated air speed and rate of climb and descent, and the Nightertown scene was controlled by the pilot's responses just as a true visual scene would be.

Kraft (1978) tested 12 experienced Boeing flight instructors who made "landings" at Nightertown under

FIGURE 5.25 (a) Conrad Kraft developed this apparatus to study how visual cues affect the stimulated landings of airline pilots. A pilot "approaches" Nightertown in the simulated cockpit. The movable and computer-controlled "city" can be tilted to study the illusion that was thought to be responsible for the fatal air crashes. (b) The effects on visual perception of the illusion created by upward-sloping city lights in the distance is shown in the approaches made by experienced pilots in their simulated landings at Nightertown. The illusion caused pilots to overestimate their altitude, and 11 of the 12 pilots "crashed" short of the runway. When the lights were flat, the pilots made perfect approaches.

(a)

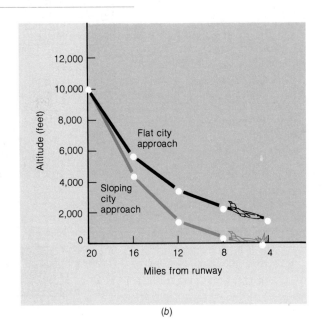

(b)

various conditions. The results of the experiments confirmed Kraft's suspicion of a strong visual illusion. When the conditions of the fatal crashes were duplicated by having the pilots approach an upward-sloping distant city over a dark area, they were unable to detect the upward slope and consistently overestimated their altitude. They assumed that the background city was flat and adjusted their altitude accordingly. On a normal landing, the preferred altitude at 4.5 miles from the runway is about 1240 feet. As Figure 5.25(b) shows, the pilots approached at about this altitude when the simulated city was in a flat position. But when it was sloped upward, 11 of the 12 experienced pilot instructors reached zero altitude at about 4.5 miles out! Like those of the pilots involved in the real crashes, the perceptual hypotheses generated by the flight instructors were incorrect. On the basis of Kraft's findings, Boeing urgently recommended that pilots attend carefully to their instruments when landing at night, even under perfect weather conditions. In this case, seeing should *not* be believing.

Illusions, then, are incorrect perceptions. Put another way, they are erroneous perceptual hypotheses about the nature of the stimulus. With some exceptions, such as the pilots' illusion we just described, illusions are intriguing and, at times, delightful visual experiences. Perception researchers have long been interested in them because they give us important information about how our perceptual processes work under normal conditions.

Constancies as a basis for illusions To understand the nature of illusions, we have to discuss **perceptual constancies,** those compromises with sensory reality that allow us to recognize familiar stimuli under varying conditions. For example, **shape constancy** allows us to recognize objects from many different angles. Perhaps you have had the experience of having to sit off to one side of the screen in a crowded movie theater. At first, the picture probably looked distorted, but after a while your visual system corrected for the distortion and objects on the screen looked more normal again.

Because of **brightness constancy,** the relative brightness of objects remains the same under different conditions of illumination. Brightness constancy occurs because the ratio of light intensity between an object and its surroundings is usually constant. The actual brightness of the light that illuminates the object does not matter, as long as the same light intensity illuminates both an object and its surroundings.

Size constancy is an extremely important basis for

FIGURE 5.26 *The Ponzo illusion. Which bar is longer? Measure them and see. The distance cues provided by the railroad tracks affect size perception. In this case they disrupt size constancy.*

perceptual hypotheses. Even though the size of objects on our retina changes when they are viewed at varying distances, our perception of their size remains constant. When we fly in an airplane, we know that the cars down there on the highway aren't toys. We learn to use distance cues to judge the size of objects. But distance cues can sometimes fool us. In Figure 5.26, the bar that appears to be in the background looks larger than the one in the foreground because we judge their relative sizes, and relative positions, on the basis of the distance cues provided by the railroad tracks. Actually, as you can prove to yourself if you measure them, the bars are equal in length. This is called the *Ponzo illusion.*

For an interesting demonstration of size constancy, look into your bathroom mirror. Estimate how large the circle, ellipse, or square will be if you trace around the mirrored image of your head with a piece of soap. Then trace the actual outline of your head on the mirror with the soap and step to one side. (When you do this demonstration, you get a clean mirror as a bonus!) You may be surprised to see that the actual image is much smaller than you had thought it would be (in fact, about half the size). The reason, of course, is that the image of your face reflected back from the mirror is twice as "far away" as the mirror is, yet size constancy is based on the distance from you to the mirror's surface (Goldstein, 1984).

The study of perceptual constancies provides ample evidence that our perceptual hypotheses are strongly influenced by the context or surroundings in which a stimulus occurs (see Figure 5.27). For example, have you ever noticed how much larger the moon looks when it is low on the horizon than it does when it is overhead in the sky? Obviously, the moon doesn't shrink during the night. The moon looks larger at the horizon because we use objects in our field of vision, such as the ground, trees, and buildings, to estimate its distance. Objects look farther away when viewed through "filled" space than when viewed through "empty" space. Research has shown that the use of such cues causes us to estimate the distance of the moon on the horizon as 2.5 to 4 times farther away than when it is above us in the sky (Frisby, 1980). Because our size perceptions are based in part on distance cues, we perceive the "more distant" moon on the horizon as being larger.

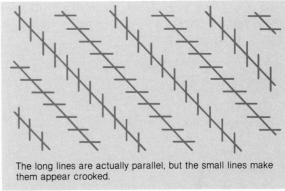

The long lines are actually parallel, but the small lines make them appear crooked.

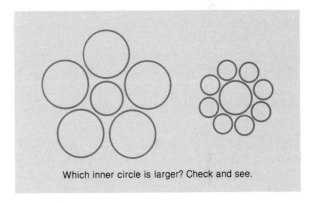

Which inner circle is larger? Check and see.

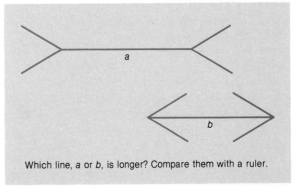

Which line, *a* or *b*, is longer? Compare them with a ruler.

FIGURE 5.27 *Context-produced geometric illusions.*

Depth and distance perception

One of the more complicated aspects of perception is our ability to perceive depth. Our retinas receive information in two dimensions (length and width), but we translate these cues into three-dimensional perceptions. We do this by using both **monocular depth cues** (which require only one eye) and **binocular depth cues** (which require both eyes).

MONOCULAR CUES

Each of our eyes is capable of perceiving perspective. Perspective is really a combination of several kinds of cues that help us to judge distances. One of these distance cues is that parallel lines appear to meet at the horizon. Look again at the railroad tracks in Figure 5.26; they seem to angle closer together as distance increases. This phenomenon is called **linear perspective**. *Decreasing size* is another distance cue; as objects move

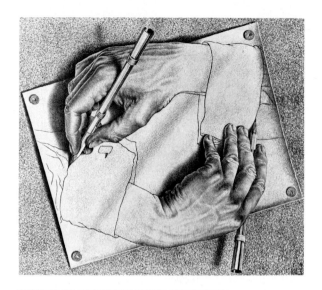

FIGURE 5.29 *Patterns of light and shadow can serve as monocular depth cues, as shown in the painting* Drawing Hands *by M. C. Escher.*

FIGURE 5.28 *If he'd taken your psychology course, he'd know that height in the horizontal plane is a monocular cue for depth and distance.*

(© 1978 BY SIDNEY HARRIS/AMERICAN SCIENTIST MAGAZINE.)

away from us, they produce smaller retinal images. An object's *height in the horizontal plane* also provides information (see Figure 5.28). For example, a ship 5 miles offshore appears in a higher plane and closer to the horizon than does one which is only 1 mile from shore. *Texture* is a fourth perspective cue, because the texture or grain of an object appears finer as distance increases. Finally, *clarity* can be an important cue for judging distance; we can see nearby hills more clearly than ones that are far away, especially on hazy days. These five perspective cues provide us with information that we can use to make judgments about distance and, therefore, about depth.

In addition to these five distance cues, there are two other important monocular depth cues. The first is patterns of *light and shadow*. In Figure 5.29, the Dutch artist M. C. Escher has skillfully used light and shadow to create a three-dimensional effect. The depth effect is as powerful if you close one eye as it is if you view the picture with both eyes. Finally, since objects closer to us may cut off part of our view of more distant objects, **interposition** is still another monocular indication of distance and depth.

Since artists can draw only in two dimensions, they

FIGURE 5.30 *This painting by Van Gogh illustrates seven monocular depth cues. (1) The converging lines of the corridor represent linear perspective. (2) The arches in the back of the corridor are smaller than those in front. (3) The end of the corridor is in a higher horizontal plane than the foreground. (4, 5) The more distant parts of the corridor are painted in less detail than the closer ones (texture and clarity). (6) Light and shadow are used to create depth. (7) The arches and hallway in the front of the painting cut off parts of the corridor behind them (interposition). (Source: van Gogh, Vincent. Hospital Corridor at Saint Rémy (1889). Gouach and watercolor, 24⅛ × 18⅝". Collection, The Museum of Modern Art, New York, Abby Aldrich Rockefeller Bequest.)*

need to be skillful in using monocular depth cues. Vincent Van Gogh, like Escher, was a master at using such cues. His *Hospital Corridor at St. Remy*, shown in Figure 5.30, illustrates his use of all seven monocular depth cues we have discussed (see figure caption).

Some of the most intriguing perceptual distortions are produced when monocular depth cues are manipu-

lated to create a figure or scene whose individual parts all make sense but whose overall organization is "impossible" in reality. Figure 5.31 shows three impossible figures. In each case the brain extracts information about depth from the individual features of the objects, but when this information is all put together, the percept that results simply doesn't make sense.

Before we leave the topic of monocular depth perception, we invite you to experience a rather remarkable demonstration of one additional monocular depth cue. The demonstration also shows how your brain tries to organize ambiguous depth cues. All you need in order to experience this phenomenon is a piece of fairly heavy paper and a little patience.

First, fold the paper down the middle and set it on a table with one of the open ends of the "tent" facing you. Close one eye and view the paper from a point above and directly along the line of the fold. Stare at a point midway along its length. At first the object looks like a tent, but if you continue to stare at it intently, the paper will suddenly "stand up" and look like a corner viewed from the inside. When this happens, gently move your head back and forth. (Remember to use only one eye!) The effect produced by the movement is a striking one.

To analyze your experience, it is important to understand that both the "tent" and the "corner" cast identical images on your retina. After perceiving a tent for a while, your brain shifted to the second perceptual hypothesis, as it did in response to the reversible figures shown in Figure 5.24. When the object was a "tent," all the depth information was consistent with that perception. But when you began to see it as a "corner" and then moved your head slowly back and forth, the object seemed to twist and turn as if it were made of rubber. This occurred because when you moved, the image of the near point of the fold moved across your retina faster than the image of the far point. This is the normal pattern of stimulation for points at different depths and is known as **motion parallax**. Thus, when you were seeing a tent, the monocular cue of motion parallax was consistent with the shape of the object. But

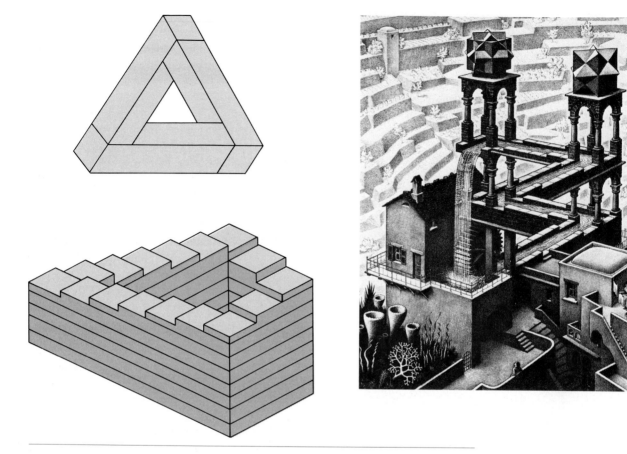

FIGURE 5.31 *Monocular depth cues are manipulated to produce three impossible figures— an impossible triangle, a never-ending staircase, and a perpetual waterfall, as illustrated in* Waterfall *by M. C. Escher.*

when you later saw the object as standing upright, all the points along the fold appeared to be the same distance away, yet they were moving at different rates of speed! The only way your brain could maintain its "corner" perception in the face of the motion parallax cues was to see the object as twisting and turning. Again, as in the case of other illusions, forcing all of the sensory data to fit the perceptual hypothesis produced a rather unusual experience.

BINOCULAR CUES: STEREOPSIS

Monocular cues can provide us with valuable information concerning depth and distance, but the most dramatic perceptions of depth arise when we use both

eyes. If you extend your pencil or pen out in front of you and view it against the background with one eye shut and your head perfectly still, you will perceive little depth. But open the other eye and a much richer perception of depth will occur. The appearance of depth when both eyes are used is called **stereopsis.**

Most of us are familiar with the delightful depth experiences provided by the View Master, stereoscopes, and the 3-D movies that you watch through glasses with red and green lenses. All of these devices make use of the principle of **binocular disparity.** In normal binocular vision, each eye sees a slightly different image; the two images are fused by our brain into a single image that has depth.

Stereopsis does not occur in the eyes themselves,

but at higher levels of the visual system. Microelectrode studies of the visual cortex during binocular vision have found feature detector cells that respond only to stimuli that are either in front of or behind the fixation point (Poggio and Fischer, 1977; von der Heydt and others, 1978). Receptor channels near the fixation plane may be narrowly tuned for detailed vision of the fixated object, while other, broader channels cover nearer and farther objects. The responses of these depth-sensitive neurons are probably integrated within the brain to produce the perception of depth (DeValois and DeValois, 1980).

Auditory localization

Now that you know why you have two eyes on the front of your face, have you ever wondered why you have an

FIGURE 5.32 *This device used by sailors to increase their stability to localize sounds in thick fog increases time differences in sounds arriving at the two ears, resulting in greater perceptual sensitivity.*

PROFESSOR MAYER'S TOPOPHONE.

ear on each side of your head? As is usually the case, there is a good reason. Our ability to locate and perceive objects often involves the use of auditory as well as visual cues, and this is where our two ears play a crucial role. Our nervous system uses information concerning the time and intensity differences of sounds arriving at the two ears to locate sounds in space (Phillips and Brugge, 1985).

Sounds arrive first and loudest at the ear closest to the sound. When the source of the sound is directly in front of us, the sound reaches both ears at the same time and intensity, so it is perceived as straight ahead. The amazing sensitivity of our binaural (two-eared) ability to localize sounds is shown in the fact that a sound 3 degrees to the right arrives at the right ear only 300 millionths of a second before it arrives at the left ear, and yet we can tell that the source of the sound is not straight ahead (Yin and Kuwada, 1984).

Suppose that you were steering a ship through treacherous waters in a dense fog. Your vision would do you little good, and you would depend heavily on your auditory abilities to localize sounds. You might profit from a device like that shown in Figure 5.32. This device was actually used by sailors in the late 1800s to increase their ability to localize sounds. The device aided in sound localization in two ways: (1) the two ear receptors were much larger than human ears and could thus collect more sound, and (2) the increased spacing between the receptors served to increase the time difference between the sound's arrival at the two human ears, thus increasing directional sensitivity.

PERCEPTUAL DEVELOPMENT

Philosopher and psychologist William James once described the perceptual world of the newborn infant as "one great blooming, buzzing confusion." Obviously, we do not know how true this description is, because newborn babies are notoriously poor at describing their experiences. However, this difficulty has not kept psychologists from grappling with the critical question of how our perceptual abilities develop. Are they inborn? Do they develop with learning and experience? Or do innate factors and learning interact with each other in complex ways? As a result of some ingenious research techniques, the pieces of the perceptual puzzle are gradually fitting into place. Because vision is perhaps the most important sensory and perceptual system in humans, psychologists have been especially interested in tracing its development.

The role of experience in perceptual development

The Ba Mbuti pygmies live in the rain forests of the Congo in central Africa. Their environment is a closed-in green world of densely packed trees without open spaces. The anthropologist C. M. Turnbull (1961) once brought one of the pygmies out of the forest to the edge of a vast plain. A herd of buffalo grazed in the distance. To Turnbull's surprise, the pygmy remarked that he had never seen insects of that kind. When told that they were buffalo, not insects, the man was deeply offended and thought that Turnbull was insulting his intelligence. To prove his point, Turnbull drove his jeep toward the animals. The pygmy's eyes widened in amazement as the "insects" grew into buffalo before his eyes. To explain his perceptual experience to himself, he concluded that witchcraft was being used to fool him.

We can explain the pygmy's misperception as a failure in size constancy. Having lived in an environment without open spaces, he had no experience in judging the size of objects at great distances. But this story raises a larger issue; we must ask what role learning and experience have in perceptual development. The behavioral perspective has been particularly influential in guiding research on this issue and in shedding light on the ways in which learning and biological factors affect each other during perceptual development.

Certain experiential and learning factors are clearly critical to the development of perceptual abilities as well as the underlying sensory and neural apparatus. For some aspects of perception, there is apparently a **critical period** during which certain kinds of experiences must occur if perceptual abilities are to develop normally. Three research strategies have been particularly valuable in providing information on the effects of abnormal perceptual development: visual deprivation studies, manipulation of the visual environment, and clinical studies of restored vision in blind people.

VISUAL DEPRIVATION STUDIES

One way to study the role of experience in visual development is to deprive animals of visual input from birth and see what kinds of perceptual abilities they have when they mature. However, scientists quickly found out that if animals are raised in total darkness, their retinas degenerate. Therefore, visual deprivation researchers make use of opaque or translucent goggles that allow the animals to receive light stimulation but not to see shapes or patterns.

When animals are raised with these goggles, they have severe perceptual deficiencies. Monkeys, chimpanzees, and kittens deprived of patterned stimulation early in life perform almost as well as ordinary animals in distinguishing differences in brightness, size, and color, but they cannot perform more complex tasks, such as distinguishing objects and discriminating between various geometric shapes (Riesen, 1965).

Experiments have shown that the development of the brain itself can be affected by visual deprivation. You will recall that Hubel and Wiesel found alternating columns of visual cortex cells, called *ocular dominance columns*, that respond to input from either the left or the right eye (see Figure 5.19). To see how visual deprivation might affect the development of these columns, David Hubel and his co-workers surgically closed either the left or the right eyelid of several monkeys when they were 2 weeks old. The eyelid was not opened until the monkeys were 18 months of age. The researchers then injected into the nondeprived eye a radioactive substance that they knew would soon be transported through the neurons to the visual cortex. By taking pictures of slices of the cortex with radiation-sensitive film (a procedure known as *autoradiography*) after the animals were sacrificed, the researchers could compare the ocular dominance columns of the deprived monkeys with those of normally reared animals.

The top portion of Figure 5.33 shows a normal monkey's ocular dominance columns. The light bands containing the radioactive substance injected into one eye alternate with dark (nonradioactive) columns of about equal size from the other eye. The lower portion of the figure shows the autoradiograph of a deprived monkey. The light portions are the ocular dominance columns from the eye that was not closed. It is clear

that the columns of the nondeprived eye are greatly expanded, while those connected to the closed eye have shrunk dramatically. The critical period during which the monkey is most affected by deprivation is the first three to six weeks after birth (Hubel, 1979).

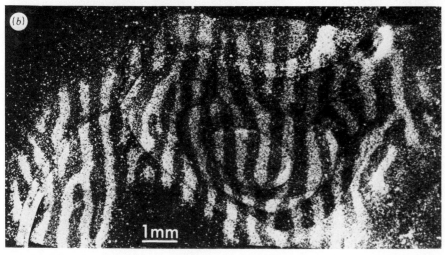

FIGURE 5.33 *Autoradiographs show the difference between ocular dominance columns of a normal monkey (upper) and of a monkey in whom one eyelid was closed from 2 weeks of age to 18 months (lower). In the deprived monkey, the ocular dominance columns for the nondeprived eye are greatly expanded, while those for the closed eye are abnormally narrow.*

MANIPULATING THE VISUAL ENVIRONMENT

A second and related approach to studying the impact of experience on visual development involves limiting the specific visual inputs received by subjects. Earlier we saw that in addition to ocular dominance columns, the visual cortex has orientation columns composed of neurons that respond only to lines at particular angles. What would happen if newborn animals grew up in a world in which they saw only certain angles? In a classic study, British researchers Colin Blakemore and Grahame Cooper (1970) created such a world for newborn kittens. The animals were raised in the dark except for a five-hour period each day during which they were placed in round chambers that had either vertical or horizontal stripes on the walls. Figure 5.34 shows one of the kittens in his vertically striped chamber. A special collar prevented the kittens from seeing their own bodies while they were in the chambers.

When the kittens were 5 months of age, Blakemore and Cooper tested the electrical responses of individual cells in the visual cortex with microelectrodes while bars of light at different angles were presented to them. The results are shown in Figure 5.34 for animals raised in the vertically striped environment. The kittens did not have any cells that fired in response to horizontal stimuli. They also had visual impairments. For example, they acted as if they could not see a pencil held in a horizontal position and waved in front of them. As you might expect, the opposite was the case with animals raised with horizontal stripes. They had no orientation columns for vertical stimuli and could not seem to see them. The cortical neurons of both groups of kittens had grown accustomed to the jail bars of their youth.

FIGURE 5.34 *Blakemore and Cooper (1970) raised kittens in either vertically or horizontally striped chambers. Kittens raised in a vertically striped chamber, such as the one shown in (a), lacked cortical cells that fired in response to horizontal stimuli. The orientation column "holes" are easily seen in (b), which shows the orientation angles that resulted in cell firing. Kittens raised in the horizontally striped environment, on the other hand, lacked vertical orientation columns.*

(a)

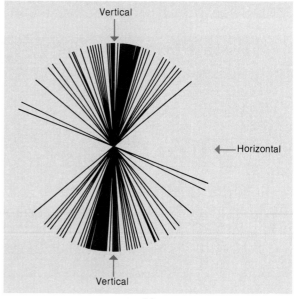

(b)

CLINICAL STUDIES OF RESTORED VISION

Suppose people who were blind from birth suddenly had their vision restored during adulthood. What would they see? Could they perceive visually the things that they had learned to identify with their other senses?

People who are born with congenital cataracts perceive the world much like experimental animals who are fitted with translucent goggles do. The clouded lenses of their eyes permit them to perceive light but not patterns or shapes.

A German physician, von Senden (1960), compiled data on patients with congenital cataracts who were tested soon after the cataracts were surgically removed. These people were immediately able to perceive figure-ground relationships, to scan objects visually, and to follow moving targets with their eyes, indicating that such abilities are innate. However, they could not visually identify objects that they were familiar with through touch, nor were they able to distinguish simple geometric figures without counting the corners or tracing them with their fingers. After several weeks of training, the patients were able to identify simple objects by sight, but their perceptual constancy was very poor. A shape that they recognized in one color was often not recognized in another color, even though they could discriminate between colors. Years after their vision was restored, some of the patients could identify only a few of the faces of people they knew well. Many also had great difficulty in judging distances. Apparently, no amount of subsequent experience could make up for their lack of visual experience during childhood.

All these lines of evidence therefore suggest that some of our perceptual abilities are at least partially present at birth, but that experience plays an important role in their normal development. The manner in which innate and experiential factors interact with one another promises to be the focus of research for years to come.

We have seen that there are many new frontiers emerging from recent discoveries in sensation and perception. One of the most important of these is the study of pain and the development of methods for the control of this most unwelcome perceptual experience. Frontier 5.2 describes current knowledge and recent advances in this area.

FRONTIER 5.2
PAIN PERCEPTION AND CONTROL

Pain. Surely one of the most unpleasant realities of life, and one that most of us do our best to avoid. But in spite of its negative aspects, pain has certain important survival functions. First, it serves as a warning signal when the body is being threatened or damaged. Second, pain is part of a defensive system that triggers reactions to help us cope with the threat. Pain is thus an important part of the natural "biofeedback" system that helps us adjust to our environment. Because of its crucial survival function, as well as its role in physical illnesses and certain psychological problems, many psychologists are conducting research to discover the physiological and psychological causes of our perception of pain as well as ways in which we can control pain.

MECHANISMS OF PAIN PERCEPTION

Receptors for pain are found in the skin, joints, muscles, and all body tissues, with the exception of the brain, bones, hair, nails, and nonliving parts of the teeth. The major receptors for pain are thought to be *free nerve endings* that respond to intense mechanical, thermal, or chemical stimulation. The receptors send their impulses into the spinal cord, where several tracts carrying pain information ascend to the brain. There is no area of the sensory cortex that responds specifically to pain; pain impulses are directed to subcortical regions, especially the limbic system.

The role of the spinal cord in the transmission of pain impulses has been known for a long time. Beyond that, however, pain was one of the most mysterious aspects of perception. But in recent years a series of discoveries have revolutionized pain research and given us major new insights into the mechanisms of pain perception.

Gate control theory

One major advance was the development of the *gate control theory* of pain (Melzack, 1973). This theory deals with neural transmissions that can open or close a system of "gates" between the pain receptors in the body tissues and the brain regions responsible for our perception of pain. Briefly, the theory holds that free nerve endings can activate both small-diameter and larger-diameter sensory fibers. The thin fibers carry pain impulses; the thick fibers convey information about touch. Whether or not we experience pain depends partly on the ratios of thin-to-thick fiber transmission. A high ratio of thin fiber activity opens the gates, whereas thick fiber activity closes them. It follows, then, that anything that can increase thick fiber impulses can decrease our perception of pain. Gate control theorists believe, for example, that acupuncture achieves its pain-relieving effects because the acupuncture needles stimulate these thick fibers, closing the pain gates.

Another important aspect of gate control theory is that the gates can also be opened or closed by nerve impulses coming down from the brain. This would help to explain how some of the psychological factors that we will be discussing later might increase or decrease our experiencing of pain.

The endorphins

A second major breakthrough in our understanding of pain was the discovery of the *endorphins.* Opiates (opium, morphine, heroin) have been used to relieve pain for centuries, but it wasn't until the discovery of the endorphins (literally, "morphine within") in the 1970s that we became aware that the nervous system has its own built-in analgesics (painkillers) with opiatelike properties. One recently discovered brain endorphin is over 200 times more powerful than morphine (Goldstein and others, 1979). The discovery of the endorphins is helping us to account for the success of many analgesic procedures.

While the endorphins have been isolated and examined directly by biochemists, behavioral researchers have been able to study their action either by injecting endorphins into subjects and observing

analgesic effects or by injecting a drug called *nalaxone,* which blocks the effects of the endorphins. If a procedure produces analgesia when nalaxone is not used but does not work when nalaxone is present, we have indirect evidence that endorphins mediate the pain-reducing effects of the procedure. For example, research done in China has shown that injections of nalaxone greatly reduce the analgesic effects of acupuncture. This finding and gate control theory suggest that there may be two separate or related mechanisms for pain relief through acupuncture. The possibility also exists that the endorphins are part of the gate control mechanisms. Perhaps endorphins released by the brain stimulate the thick sensory fibers, which then close the gate and decrease the perception of pain (Goldstein, 1984).

Stress-induced analgesia

Under severe stress, people and animals sometimes become insensitive to pain. Soldiers in battle and people in accidents have been known to be unaware of serious injuries until after the crisis was over. Recent evidence suggests that *stress-induced analgesia* is created by the release of endorphins. Animals injected with nalaxone and then exposed to stress show reduced levels of analgesia to subsequent painful stimuli (Fanselow, 1984).

What is the survival value of stress-induced analgesia? Michael Fanselow (1984) suggests that in a life-threatening situation, defensive behavior must be given immediate priority over natural responses to pain. By reducing or preventing pain sensations, stress-induced analgesia helps suppress these behaviors so that the person or animal can get on with the self-defensive behaviors that are needed for immediate survival, such as fleeing, fighting, or getting help.

Newborns are relatively insensitive to painful stimuli, which some believe may be a defense against the stresses of birth. It has been found that both the placenta and the amniotic fluid in which the fetus lives are richly endowed with endorphinlike substances (Houck and others, 1980). The "birth trauma" proposed by several theories of personality may thus be less severe than we once thought, at least in terms of physical pain.

There is mounting evidence that running and other vigorous forms of exercise that stress the body stimulate the release of endorphins (Farrell, 1985; McArthur, 1985). An intriguing but as yet unsubstantiated hypothesis is that the release of these opiates may underlay such familiar concepts as the "runner's high" and "positive addiction" to exercise (Morgan, 1985).

The release of endorphins may thus be part of the body's natural response to stress, but there may be a price to be paid for this temporary relief from pain. Recently it was discovered that morphinelike substances, including endorphins, block the activity of *natural killer cells,* lymph cells that recognize and selectively kill certain tumor cells as part of the body's immune system against tumor-related diseases. This may be one way in which chronic stress makes us more susceptible to serious illnesses (Shavit and others, 1984).

PSYCHOLOGICAL FACTORS INFLUENCING PAIN

Sensations from our pain receptors are only the first step in our ultimate experiencing of pain. Like all perceptions, pain is a subjective experience. Its quality and intensity are influenced not only by the physical stimulus but also by psychological factors, such as personal and cultural beliefs, customary methods of coping with difficulties, and the meanings that one attaches to painful situations.

Coping styles

People respond to pain and injuries in a variety of ways. Some regard pain as an unpleasant inconvenience and go about their business as best they can.

Others have an exaggerated response to the pain, become preoccupied with it, and go to great lengths to protect themselves from it.

In England, researchers studying factors that influence recovery from injury have advanced a *fear-avoidance theory* to account for exaggerated pain perception (Lethem and others, 1983). They note that fear is the normal response to the threat of more pain. People respond to fear of pain in two basically different ways, which they term *confrontation* and *avoidance.*

People who adopt the adaptive response of confrontation regard the pain as a temporary nuisance, are strongly motivated to return to normal social, work, and leisure activities, and do so as soon as the injury allows. They thus test the reality of the pain experience at every stage and maintain an accurate perception of their true physical state. Their fear of further pain dissipates over time as they heal.

Avoiders, on the other hand, do their best to prevent any recurrence of the pain. They avoid physical and social activities, and many retreat into a self-protective shell. With fewer opportunities to test reality, many develop an exaggerated sense of their physical damage and their vulnerability to further injury. Instead of dissipating, their fear increases; they become chronic pain cases long after the physical injury has apparently healed (Slade and others, 1983).

Cultural factors

Childbirth is an event dreaded by many American women because its potential for excruciating pain is widely publicized and frequently exaggerated in our culture. Yet in certain societies women show virtually no distress during childbirth and work in the fields almost up until the moment the baby arrives. In some cultures the woman's husband gets into bed and groans as if he were in great pain, while the woman calmly gives birth to the child. The husband stays in bed with the baby to recover from his terrible ordeal, and the mother returns to work in the fields almost immediately (Kroeber, 1948).

Cultural values have a great influence on an individual's interpretation of the meaning of pain. In certain parts of India, people practice an unusual hook-hanging ritual. A celebrant is chosen to bless the children and crops in a number of neighboring villages. Steel hooks attached by strong ropes to the top of a special cart are shoved under the skin and muscles on each side of his back, and he travels on the cart from village to village. At the climax of a ceremony in each village, the celebrant swings free, hanging only by the hooks embedded in his back, to bless the children and crops (see Figure 5.35). Incredibly, there is no evidence that the celebrant experiences any pain during the ritual; on the contrary, he appears to be in a state of ecstasy. When the hooks are removed, the wounds heal rapidly and are scarcely visible within two weeks (Kosambi, 1967).

Expectations and personal beliefs

Faith and hope influence much of our behavior, including the way we experience pain. Perhaps nowhere are mind–body effects more consistently illustrated than in the case of *placebos,* inert substances that people are told will affect them in some medical way.

Can placebos provide relief from pain having true physical causes? The answer is clearly yes. In one study, either placebo or morphine injections were given to 122 surgical patients suffering postoperative pain from their wounds. Sixty-seven percent of those who received morphine reported relief, but 42 percent of those given placebos reported equal relief (Beecher, 1959).

The power of belief and expectation not only can cause placebos to relieve pain but can completely reverse the usual pharmacological effects of a drug. For example, the drug ipecac is used to induce vomiting

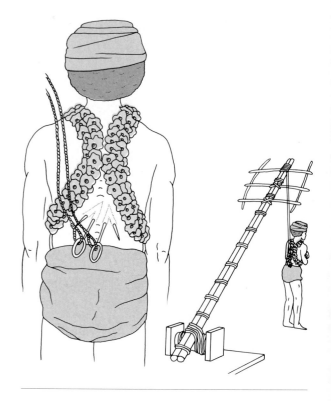

FIGURE 5.35 *The annual hook-swinging ceremony practiced in remote Indian villages. Two steel hooks are thrust into the small of the back of the "celebrant," who is decked with garlands. He travels from village to village in a special cart equipped with a large crossbeam to which the hooks are attached with ropes. After he blesses all the children and farm fields in a village, he swings free from the beam, suspended by the hooks. The crowds cheer at each swing. During the ceremony the celebrant is in a state of exaltation and shows no sign of pain.*

in people who have swallowed certain poisons. In one extraordinary experiment, pregnant women suffering from nausea caused by morning sickness were given ipecac and told that it was a new drug to relieve nausea. Some of them reported immediate relief and re- mission of symptoms from their morning sickness (Haas and others, 1959).

One way in which placebos may bring about their analgesic effects is through the release of endorphins. Subjects who had previously been shown to react strongly to placebos were given nalaxone to block en- dorphin effects. Under nalaxone, the pain-reducing effects of the placebos were completely eliminated in these suggestible subjects (Fields, 1978).

COGNITIVE CONTROL OF PAIN

We all experience pain occasionally, but for some peo- ple pain is a never-ending nightmare. It is estimated that as many as 40 million Americans suffer from long- term and chronic pain of arthritis, cancer, headaches, and physical injury. Pain management is an area of psychology that is receiving increasing attention (Elton and others, 1983).

Among the promising developments in pain man- agement is research on cognitive pain control strate- gies. One approach involves giving subjects informa- tion about specific cognitive strategies that they can use during exposure to a painful stimulus, which may be immersion of the hand in ice water of 2°C (the cold-pressor test), painful pressure applied to a finger, or electric shock. The length of time that subjects can tolerate the pain as well as their physiological stress responses and their ratings of pain intensity is com- pared with that of control groups who receive no pain control instructions.

Recent attention has focused on two strategies known as *dissociation* and *association*. As the name implies, the first strategy involves increasing pain tol- erance by dissociating or distracting oneself from the painful sensory input. This can be done in a variety of ways: by concentrating attention on some other fea- ture of the external situation, by imagining a pleasur-

able experience, or by repeating a word or thought to yourself. Association is just the opposite. Here you focus your attention on the physical sensations but do so in a detached and unemotional fashion, taking care not to label them as painful or difficult to tolerate. Both techniques have proven to be effective pain con- trol strategies. Many experiments have shown that dis- sociation reduces distress and increases pain tolerance when compared with control conditions in which no instructions, or instructions known to be ineffective, are given (McCaul and Malott, 1984). Dissociation seems most effective when the distraction requires full attention and when the pain is relatively mild.

If you are a recreational jogger or a long-distance runner, you are familiar with the discomfort that can result from extending yourself. Endurance running seems an ideal real-life task to use in the study of cog- nitive strategies. In a study done at the University of Wisconsin, the effects of a dissociative strategy were examined under laboratory conditions. Male subjects ran to exhaustion on a treadmill at 80 percent of their maximum aerobic capacity. They were then randomly assigned to either a control group that received no strategy instructions or to an experimental group in which subjects were instructed to focus their attention on a spot in front of them on the treadmill and say "Down" each time their legs came down onto the treadmill. Then all the men were retested on the treadmill.

The results of the experiment are shown in Figure 5.36. Physiological measures taken during the tread- mill run showed that the two groups were similar in their bodily reactions. Yet the dissociation group was able to run the treadmill 32 percent longer, indicating that their strategy enabled them to tolerate the dis- comfort for a longer period of time (Morgan and oth- ers, 1983).

Is dissociation, then, the more effective strategy? Not always. It appears that when pain is intense, asso- ciative strategies that focus in a nonemotional fashion

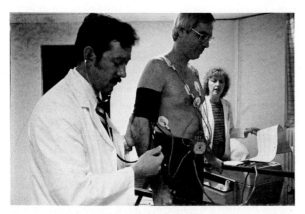

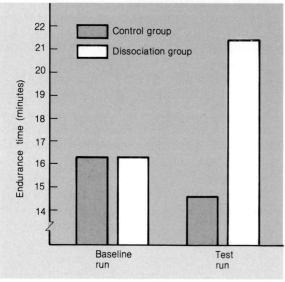

FIGURE 5.36 *Effects of a dissociation strategy on running endurance. Physiological measures indicated that the two groups were equally taxed during the test run, yet the group instructed in a dissociative cognitive strategy was able to run considerably longer. (Data from Morgan and others, 1983.)*

on the basic sensory aspects of the pain become more effective (Ahles and others, 1983; McCaul and Malott, 1984). Perhaps there is a point at which pain stimuli become too intense to ignore. One possibly effective strategy is to use dissociation as long as possible and then to shift to an associative mode when the pain becomes too severe to permit distraction.

There is yet another benefit of associative strategies. Focusing on bodily sensations enables one to tune in to the present state of the body, which can be very helpful in endurance tasks. Sport psychologist William Morgan (1984) has studied the cognitive strategies used by distance runners. He found that many marathoners use dissociative strategies, such as focusing attention on one's shadow, repeating phrases, or fixing total attention on a distant point. However, when he interviewed the truly elite marathoners, he found that most of them use an associative cognitive approach in which they monitor their bodies carefully during competition, "paying attention to all cues, signals and body sensations with an aim toward slowing, maintaining, or picking up the pace on the basis of how they felt" (p. 313). But many of these elite runners also noted that there were times when they would dissociate temporarily to get through a particularly difficult point in the race. The key point may be that these superbly conditioned athletes can afford to associate more than the average marathoner can and are thus able to pace themselves and run at maximum efficiency.

The effects of cognitive strategies seem to be especially strong when subjects view them as ways of increasing their personal control over painful stimuli. There are still many unanswered questions, however. Which strategies are most effective and under what conditions? How effective are they in the control of long-term chronic pain? These are some of the questions that remain to be explored on this research frontier.

SENSATION AND PERCEPTION (p. 146)

1. Although the two processes are interrelated, sensation refers to the activities whereby our sense organs receive and transmit information, whereas perception involves the processing and interpretation of the information.

2. The senses may be classified in terms of the forms of energy to which they respond. These energy forms—electromagnetic, mechanical, thermal, or chemical—are transformed into the common language of nerve impulses, a process called transduction.

VISION (p. 147)

1. The visual receptors are light-sensitive receptor cells located in the retina. The rods are brightness receptors and the less numerous cones are color receptors. Light energy striking the retina is converted into nerve impulses by chemical reactions in the photopigments of the rods and cones. Dark adaptation involves the gradual regeneration of photopigments that have been depleted by brighter illumination.

2. The two classical color vision theories are the Young-Helmholtz trichromatic theory and Hering's opponent-process theory.

3. Color vision appears to be a two-stage process involving both trichromatic and opponent-process components. The first stage involves the reactions of cones that are maximally sensitive to red, green, and blue wavelengths. In the second stage, color information from the cones is coded through an opponent-process mechanism further along in the visual system.

4. Among the most common visual defects are cataracts (clouding of the lens), myopia (nearsightedness) and hyperopia (farsightedness), glaucoma (destruction of the retina by excessive pressure within the eyeball), retinal damage caused by diabetes, and color blindness.

AUDITION (p. 156)

1. Sound waves have two characteristics: frequency, measured in terms of cycles per second, or Hertzes (Hz); and amplitude, measured in terms of decibels. Frequency is related to pitch, amplitude to loudness.

2. The receptors for hearing are hair cells in the organ of Corti of the inner ear. Loudness is coded in terms of the number and types of auditory nerve fibers that fire.

3. Pitch is coded in two ways. Low frequency tones are coded in terms of corresponding numbers of nerve impulses in individual receptors or as the result of volleying of impulses from a number of receptors. Frequencies above 4000 Hz are coded by the region of the basilar membrane that is displaced most by the fluid wave in the cochlear canal.

THE CHEMICAL, SKIN, AND BODY SENSES (pp. 159, 162)

1. The receptors for taste and smell respond to chemical molecules. Taste buds are responsive to four basic qualities: sweet, sour, salty, and bitter. The receptors for smell (olfaction) are cells in the upper nasal cavity.

2. Recent evidence suggests that body odors may be related to the menstrual synchrony that sometimes occurs among women who are in frequent contact, to increases in brain waves associated with positive emotions, and that there are individual differences in human sexual responsiveness to certain chemicals released in the urine or the sex organs of the opposite sex. Human behavior may be influenced by olfactory stimuli to a greater degree than previously assumed.

3. The skin and body senses include touch, kinesthesis, and the vestibular sense. Receptors in the skin and body tissues are sensitive to touch, pain, warmth, and cold. These receptors send their messages to particular areas of the sensory cortex. Kinesthesis functions by means of nerve endings in the muscles, tendons, and joints. The sense organs for equilibrium are in the vestibular apparatus of the inner ear.

PSYCHOPHYSICS (p. 163)

1. Psychophysics is the scientific study of how the physical properties of stimuli are related to perception.

The study of sensory sensitivity is concerned with both absolute thresholds and difference thresholds. The absolute threshold is the intensity at which a stimulus is detected 50 percent of the time. Signal detection theory studies factors that influence decisions concerning whether or not a stimulus is present.

2. Research indicates that subliminal stimuli, which are not consciously perceived, can affect behavior in subtle ways but that they do not influence behavior strongly enough to justify concerns about subconscious control of behavior through subliminal messages.

3. The difference threshold (just noticeable difference) is the amount that two stimuli must differ in order to be perceived as different. Studies of the jnd led to Weber's law, which states that the jnd is proportional to the intensity of the original stimulus and is constant within a given sense modality.

ATTENTION (p. 166)

1. Attention is an active process in which certain stimuli are focused on, while other stimuli are blocked out. We cannot attend completely to more than one thing at a time, but we are capable of rapid attentional shifts.

2. Attentional processes are affected by stimulus factors as well as by internal factors such as motives, interests, and the results of previous learning. Perceptual defense refers to a process whereby threatening or anxiety-arousing stimuli are not consciously perceived.

PATTERNING AND ORGANIZATION IN PERCEPTION (p. 167)

1. The discovery of feature detectors in the nervous system has deepened our understanding about how sensory input might be processed and integrated. In the visual cortex there are orientation columns that respond to lines of particular orientations, ocular dominance columns, and hypercolumns, which are thought to be processing subunits.

2. Recent research suggests that our nervous system is responsive to spatial frequencies and uses such input to create our perception of patterns and objects.

3. The Gestalt psychologists identified a number of principles of perceptual organization, including figure and ground, similarity, proximity, closure, and continuity. R. L. Gregory suggested that perception is essentially a hypothesis about what a stimulus is, based on

previous experience and the nature of the stimulus. According to this view, illusions are incorrect hypotheses.

4. Perceptual constancies allow us to recognize familiar stimuli under changing conditions. In the visual realm, there are three constancies: size, shape, and brightness. Constancies are the basis of many illusions.

DEPTH AND DISTANCE PERCEPTION (p. 176)

1. Perspective consists of several cues that help us judge distances. These include linear perspective, decreasing size, height in the horizontal plane, texture, and clarity.

2. Depth perception occurs through both monocular cues, such as perspective, light and shadow, and interposition, and binocular cues, resulting from the use of both eyes. Stereopsis is the perception of depth when both eyes are used. Binocular disparity is the basis for stereopsis.

AUDITORY LOCALIZATION (p. 179)

Sounds are localized in space on the basis of time and intensity differences in the sound waves arriving at each ear.

PERCEPTUAL DEVELOPMENT (p. 179)

1. Perceptual development involves both physical maturation and learning. Certain perceptual abilities are innate or develop shortly after birth, whereas others require particular experiences in order to develop.

2. There appear to be critical periods for the development of certain perceptual abilities. Visual deprivation studies, manipulation of visual input, and studies of restored vision have shown that the normal biological development of the perceptual system depends upon certain sensory experiences.

PAIN PERCEPTION AND CONTROL (p. 183)

1. The major pain receptors appear to be free nerve endings. Once pain impulses are sent toward the brain, gate control theory proposes that a series of neural gates may be opened or closed to influence pain perception. The nervous system also contains opiates called endorphins that appear to play a major role in pain perception. Endorphins released in response to stress produce analgesia, which increases pain tolerance. However,

recent evidence indicates that the endorphins block the activity of natural killer cells that are part of the body's defenses against tumors.

2. Psychological factors strongly influence response to painful stimuli. Coping styles involving inappropriate avoidance of additional pain appear to be related to chronic pain problems. Cultural factors also influence the manner in which painful stimuli are appraised and responded to, as do expectations and personal beliefs. The latter account for the effects of placebos.

3. Cognitive control of pain is possible through a number of strategies. Dissociative strategies appear useful with milder forms of pain, while associative strategies seem to produce better results when pain is intense and monitoring of bodily processes is linked to efficient behavior. Elite marathoners tend to use associative strategies.

KEY TERMS AND CONCEPTS

sensation

perception

transduction

nanometer

lens

accommodation

ciliary muscle

aqueous humor

vitreous humor

rod

cone

bipolar cell

ganglion cell

visual acuity

photopigment

blind spot

absolute threshold

dark adaptation

additive color mixture

subtractive color mixture

Young-Helmholtz trichromatic theory

Hering opponent-process theory

retinal

cataracts

myopia

hyperopia

glaucoma

dichromat

monochromat

Hertz (Hz)

decibel

cochlea

basilar membrane

tectorial membrane

organ of Corti

frequency theory (pitch)

place theory (pitch)

copulins

kinesthesis

vestibular apparatus

psychophysics

signal detection theory

subliminal stimuli

difference threshold (jnd)

Weber's law

shadowing

perceptual defense

cortical column

orientation column

ocular dominance column

hypercolumn

feature detector

blob

spatial frequency model

Gestalt laws (similarity, proximity, closure, continuity)

perceptual hypothesis

illusion

perceptual constancies

monocular depth cues

linear perspective

interposition

motion parallax

stereopsis

binocular disparity

critical period

gate control theory

endorphin

stress-induced analgesia

fear-avoidance theory of pain

placebos

dissociative strategy of pain control

associative strategy of pain control

SUGGESTED READINGS

FRISBY, J. P. (1980). *Seeing: Illusion, brain, and mind.* Oxford, England: Oxford University Press. A fascinating and beautifully illustrated treatment of visual sensation and perception.

GOLDSTEIN, E. B. (1984). *Sensation and perception* (2nd ed.). Belmont, Calif.: Wadsworth. A good introductory textbook that surveys all the major areas of sensation and perception.

MELZACK, R. (1973). *The puzzle of pain.* A somewhat dated but classic description of the development of the gate control theory of pain. (The Goldstein book cited above provides more recent information.)

SECTION THREE
LEARNING, COGNITIVE PROCESSES, AND INTELLIGENCE

CHAPTER SIX: **LEARNING: PRINCIPLES AND APPLICATIONS**

CHAPTER SEVEN: **INFORMATION PROCESSING AND MEMORY**

CHAPTER EIGHT: **LANGUAGE, PROBLEM SOLVING, AND INTELLIGENCE**

CHAPTER SIX
LEARNING: PRINCIPLES AND APPLICATIONS

WHAT IS LEARNING?

CLASSICAL CONDITIONING: LEARNING THROUGH ASSOCIATION
Acquisition, extinction, and spontaneous recovery
Generalization and discrimination
Some applications of classical conditioning principles

OPERANT CONDITIONING: LEARNING THROUGH CONSEQUENCES
The study of operant conditioning
The ABC's of operant conditioning
Response consequences and behavior
Schedules of reinforcement
Negative reinforcement: Escape and avoidance conditioning
Punishment
Timing of behavioral consequences
FRONTIER 6.1   BEHAVIORAL SELF-CONTROL: OPERANT PRINCIPLES IN THE SERVICE OF SELF

THE COGNITIVE PERSPECTIVE ON LEARNING
Cognition in classical conditioning
Cognition and operant conditioning
The power of expectancies: Learned helplessness and learned mastery
Internal self-evaluations as rewards and punishment
Observational learning (modeling)

THE BIOLOGICAL PERSPECTIVE ON LEARNING
Biological constraints on learning
FRONTIER 6.2   THE SEARCH FOR THE BIOLOGICAL BASIS OF LEARNING

STUDY OUTLINE

KEY TERMS AND CONCEPTS

SUGGESTED READINGS

A young woman sits nervously on the edge of a comfortable chair as she begins her first interview with a psychotherapist.

THERAPIST: When you called last week, you mentioned your fear of cars. Can you tell me about the problem?

CLIENT: Well, about a year ago I was driving on a rainy night when my car went out of control. It crashed into a light pole, rolled over, and began to burn. I . . . couldn't get out . . . (begins to weep) . . . I'm sorry, doctor, but even thinking about it is horrible. I had a broken pelvis and third-degree burns over half my body. I can still remember being trapped in the car and hearing myself being burned alive before I passed out . . . I was hospitalized for months.

THERAPIST: That's an experience that would upset anybody. When did the fear of cars begin?

CLIENT: When my husband came to take me home. As we walked toward the new car he had bought, I began to feel uneasy. I felt nervous all the way home. It started to get worse after that. I found myself avoiding riding in the car, and I couldn't drive it at all. I stopped visiting friends and tried to get them to come to our house all the time. After a while, even the sight of a car started to make me nervous.

THERAPIST: As nervous as riding in one?

CLIENT: No, but still nervous. It's so stupid. I'd even turn off the TV during scenes involving car crashes. You know, this is the first time I've left the house in about four months. I figure I'd better get over this stupid thing.

THERAPIST: You say "stupid thing."

CLIENT: Of course it's stupid! I know those cars on TV can't hurt me in any way. And even if I'm riding in one or driving one, I'm unlikely to get into another accident. But I can't help myself. The fear just gets triggered automatically when I see or hear about cars. I've gotten so uptight, I've even thrown up. And the longer it goes on, the worse it gets.

A middle-aged man has been playing roulette in a Las Vegas casino for nearly 36 hours. His clothes are disheveled and his hair hangs limply over his forehead. Hope and desperation are alternately mirrored on his face as he peers through the smoke-filled air at the whirling roulette wheel.

Nearby, one casino guard nudges another and mut-

ters, "That poor guy's really got the fever. He's been in here since yesterday. A real loser, too—I'll bet he's blown thousands. He's in hock up to his ears. I'll never understand what keeps these guys going. It's a sickness."

As Northwest Orient Flight 608 taxied toward takeoff from Seattle, a young man approached a crew member and said that he had a bomb in his briefcase. He demanded $100,000 and two parachutes. After a tense 10-hour standoff as the plane stood isolated on the runway, the would-be hijacker surrendered. He stated that he had patterned his attempt as closely as possible after the legendary crime of D. B. Cooper, who parachuted from an airliner over southern Washington with $200,000 in 1971. The young man's roommate said that he had carefully studied Cooper's procedures for nearly a year before trying them himself. Ironically, he didn't know that after Cooper's crime, airliners were modified so that their emergency exits cannot be opened while the plane is in flight. (*Seattle Times*, July 12, 1980)

All these instances of human behavior have one important factor in common: they can be analyzed and understood in terms of the principles of learning. Indeed, the study of learning is fundamental to an understanding of most aspects of our behavior. Unlike lower animals, we do not come equipped with instincts and preprogrammed behavior patterns. What we do have is an ability to behave in a great variety of ways that are determined by our learning experiences. The products of learning include knowledge and intellectual skills, attitudes and emotional responses, social behaviors, and movement skills. We learn to think, act, and feel in the ways that contribute most richly to our individual human identities. We also learn, unfortunately, to respond in ways that hinder us from full freedom.

For example, how did the young woman learn her intense and irrational fear of cars, and why does the fear seem to be getting stronger? How did the compulsive gambler develop his habit, and why is he so strongly compelled to go on playing? How strongly is our behavior, like that of the would-be hijacker, affected by observing the actions of others? In this chapter we focus on these and many other questions. We discuss some of the ways in which the principles of learning established within the behavioral perspective have been applied to the understanding and solution of personal and social problems. We also see how the cognitive and biological perspectives have contributed to our understanding of the processes that govern and limit what we learn.

WHAT IS LEARNING?

We define **learning** as *a change in behavior or in potential behavior that occurs as a result of experience.* This definition has several important elements. First, it excludes changes in behavior that occur as a result of purely physical factors such as maturation, injury, fatigue, or drugs. Second, by using the term "potential" behavior, the definition includes two different aspects of learning: "knowing how" and "doing." This helps to remind us that learning is actually a construct referring to some hypothesized change that occurs within the organism as the result of experience. We can't see this internal process; all we can see is some change in *performance.* For scientific purposes, performance changes are our operational definition of learning. Yet we know that learning is not always reflected in performance. For example, you probably know what's involved in robbing a bank. Even though you haven't actually carried out a robbery, you are aware of the *potential* behaviors. Likewise, all of us have seen top athletes perform poorly—the superstar basketball player who suddenly loses the shooting touch, or the champion gymnast who suddenly seems unable to walk and chew gum at the same time. There is no question that the *potential* for better performance is there. Thus, our definition of learning is based on potential as well as actual changes in behavior.

The products of learning are innumerable, but they appear to be based on three major types of learning: classical conditioning, operant conditioning, and observational learning, or modeling. Many complex behaviors are learned through some combination of these processes.

CLASSICAL CONDITIONING: LEARNING THROUGH ASSOCIATION

Some eight decades ago Ivan Pavlov, a Russian physiologist, made a landmark discovery about learning. Pavlov was studying salivation in dogs as part of his

research on digestion (which later won him a Nobel Prize), and he developed an apparatus that allowed him to collect and measure samples of a dog's saliva (see Figure 6.1). Pavlov's procedure was to place various kinds of food in front of the dog and to measure the natural salivary response.

But, as often occurs in science, Pavlov was about to make an important accidental discovery. He noticed that with repeated testing, the dogs began to salivate *before* the food was actually presented. For example, the footsteps of the approaching experimenter could induce salivation. Pavlov began to study this "stimulus substitution," and the scientific discovery of **classical conditioning** was about to occur. He observed that if some stimulus that would not ordinarily cause salivation, such as a bell, were presented to the dogs slightly before a small amount of dried meat powder was squirted directly into their mouths, the sound of the bell alone would soon make the dogs salivate.

In more formal terms, the principle underlying classical conditioning is that if a neutral stimulus (that is, one that presently elicits no response) is paired with a stimulus that already evokes a reflex response, then eventually the new stimulus alone will evoke a similar response. The original stimulus (in Pavlov's experiments, the meat) is called the **unconditioned stimulus (UCS),** and the response it naturally evokes (salivation) is called the **unconditioned response (UCR).** The neutral stimulus that is then introduced (the bell) is called the **conditioned stimulus (CS),** and the response that it eventually evokes (salivation) is called the **conditioned response (CR)** (see Figure 6.2).

You may be wondering why we need to have different labels (UCR and CR) for what seems to be exactly the same response (salivation). Well, in fact, the CR may not be identical in all respects to the UCR. In Pavlov's experiments, for example, the bell usually did not make the dogs salivate quite as much as the meat did. But, because of its association with the UCS, the CS had clearly become a substitute stimulus capable of eliciting the salivary response.

(a)

FIGURE 6.1 *(a) Ivan Pavlov (the man with the white beard) is shown here with colleagues and one of his canine subjects. (b) Pavlov carried out his studies of classical conditioning with an apparatus like this. The harness restrains the dog. A tube inserted into the salivary gland permits the precise measurement of salivation (far right). During training the bell (CS) is sounded and food (UCS) is placed before the dog, or meat powder is squirted directly into its mouth through another tube. After a number of CS–UCS pairings, the bell alone elicits a salivary response.*

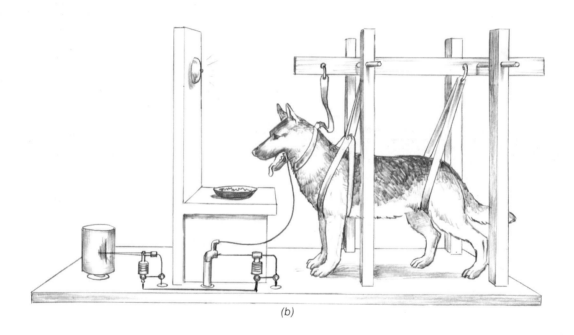

(b)

Acquisition, extinction, and spontaneous recovery

During the acquisition or learning phase of classical conditioning, each **learning trial,** or pairing of the CS with the UCS, strengthens the connection between the CS and the CR. The strongest and fastest conditioning occurs when the CS is presented about one second *before* the UCS.

The strength of the CS–CR bond and the speed with which a response is acquired may vary considerably. In some cases, conditioning may require only one CS-UCS pairing (Rescorla and Holland, 1982). Once a CR has been established, it may last for an extremely long period of time without the presentation of the

UCS. In one study, hospitalized Navy veterans who had seen combat in World War II showed strong emotional responses (measured by increased physiological arousal) to a "call-to-the-battle-stations" gong, even though 15 years had passed since this stimulus had been associated with danger. Hospitalized Army veterans, who had not served on ships, were significantly less emotionally responsive to this stimulus (Edwards, 1962).

If learning is to be adaptive to changes in the environment, there must be a way of eliminating the CR when it is no longer appropriate. Fortunately, there is. If, after conditioning, the CS is presented repeatedly without the UCS, the CS–CR bond will become weaker and the conditioned response will eventually

disappear. This process is called **extinction.** Pavlov found that if he kept ringing the bell without giving the dogs meat, they salivated less and less; eventually they stopped salivating altogether in response to the bell. Occasional re-pairings of the CS and the UCS are required to maintain a classically conditioned response.

Even when a CR has been extinguished, however, it may suddenly reappear (usually in weakened form) if the CS is presented after a period of time. This phe-

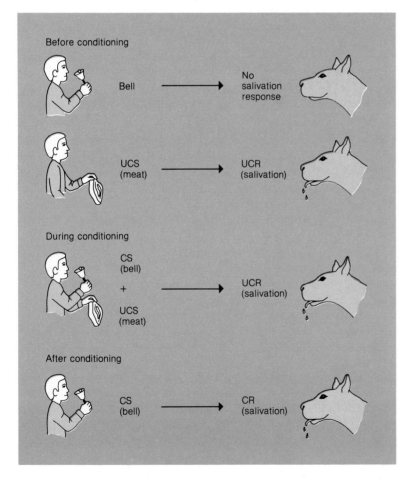

FIGURE 6.2 *In classical conditioning, after the bell (conditioned stimulus) is associated with the meat (unconditioned stimulus) on a number of occasions, the bell alone triggers the salivation response (conditioned response).*

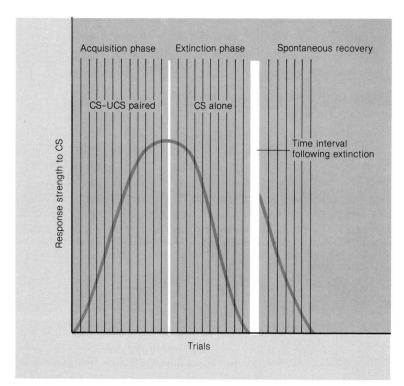

Acquisition phase   Extinction phase   Spontaneous recovery

CS–UCS paired   CS alone

Time interval
following extinction

Response strength to CS

Trials

FIGURE 6.3 *Acquisition, extinction, and spontaneous recovery of a classically conditioned response can be represented on a graph. The strength of the CR increases during the acquisition phase as the CS and the UCS are repeatedly paired on each trial. During the extinction phase only the CS is presented, and the response strength decreases and finally disappears. After a period of time following extinction, presentation of the CS elicits a weak response (spontaneous recovery) that quickly extinguishes again.*

nomenon is called **spontaneous recovery.** Such a response will extinguish again very rapidly in the absence of the UCS (see Figure 6.3).

Generalization and discrimination

Once conditioning has occurred, the subject may respond not only to the CS but also to stimuli that are similar to it. The more similar a stimulus is to the original CS, the more likely the subject is to respond to it with the CR. This phenomenon is called **stimulus generalization;** see Figure 6.4(a). The emotional responses of the Navy veterans, for example, could probably have been evoked by sounds that were similar to the battle stations gong. Perhaps you have had the experience of feeling a momentary aversion to someone who reminded you of a person you disliked intensely in the past. Many of our likes and dislikes are based on generalization.

One of the most famous demonstrations of the gen-

eralization of a conditioned response was reported by John B. Watson and Rosalie Rayner (1920). The subject of the study was an 11-month-old child named Albert. One day, as Albert was playing contentedly, Watson and Rayner showed him a white rat. Albert showed no sign of fear. On several later occasions, however, they made a loud noise behind Albert's back as they showed him the rat. The noise scared Albert and made him cry. After the rat had been paired with the noise several times, the sight of the white rat alone was enough to make Albert cry and try to escape.

Watson and Rayner then presented a number of other test stimuli to Albert. When they placed colored blocks in a crib, Albert showed no sign of fear. But objects such as a gray rabbit, a sealskin coat, and a Santa Claus mask with a white beard made him cry and struggle to escape, though not as much as the sight of the rat had done (see Figure 6.5). The experimenters had not only classically conditioned a fear response but had also demonstrated how a conditioned emotional response can generalize to other similar stimuli.

What became of little Albert? We cannot be sure.

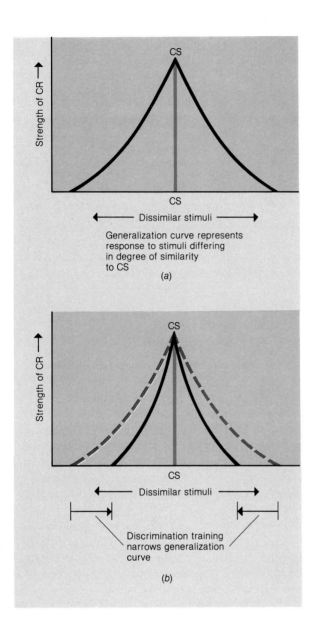

Generalization curve represents response to stimuli differing in degree of similarity to CS

(a)

Discrimination training narrows generalization curve

(b)

FIGURE 6.4 *(a) A stimulus generalization curve shows that the strongest CR occurs to the exact stimulus that was paired with the UCS. Progressively weaker responses occur as stimuli become less similar to the CS. In (b), the generalization curve narrows after a series of discrimination learning trials in which the original CS is paired with the UCS while the other stimuli are not paired, so that the CRs to the other stimuli begin to extinguish.*

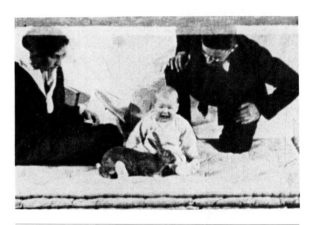

FIGURE 6.5 *In this rare photograph taken in 1919, John B. Watson and Rosalie Rayner are shown testing the reactions of Little Albert to a rabbit following the pairing of an aversive sound with a white rat. It is clear that Albert's fear response has generalized to this stimulus.*

History does not tell us whether this child is the same Albert who later opened a rodent extermination business in Cucamonga, California.

Discrimination is basically the opposite of generalization. It refers to the ability to detect differences among stimuli. Poor little Albert could not discriminate very well among the white, furry stimuli that were presented to him. But discrimination can be established during classical conditioning by presenting a series of similar stimuli but only pairing one of them with the UCS; see Figure 6.4(*b*). In fact, exactly this procedure can be used to test the abilities of nonverbal subjects, such as animals and human infants, to discriminate among various stimuli, such as colors. If a conditioned response occurs to one color and not at all or more weakly to another color, we know that the subject can tell the difference (discriminate) between them.

Some applications of classical conditioning principles

Although classical conditioning is a relatively simple form of learning, it is the basis for many complex human behaviors. While we may find it difficult to become excited about salivating dogs, Pavlov's principles help us to understand how many of our own behaviors can be learned through the process of stimulus association. Let us briefly consider several practical applications of classical conditioning principles.

CLASSICAL CONDITIONING AND PHYSICAL DISORDERS

Pavlov's initial demonstrations of classical conditioning focused on salivary responses because they could be easily measured. However, we now know that the range of bodily responses that can be classically conditioned is enormous. For example, increases and decreases in blood sugar level can be classically conditioned to many different conditioned stimuli. By pairing neutral stimuli, such as lights, sounds, and even the experimental room, with injections of insulin—a hormone that lowers blood sugar level—researchers can create a state known as **conditioned hypoglycemia** (Woods and Kulkosky, 1976; Woods, 1979). Subsequent exposure to these previously neutral stimuli in the absence of insulin injections can trigger a rapid drop of blood sugar—at times sufficient to throw animals into a state of physiological shock. Other studies have shown that increases or decreases in pain sensations can be conditioned to environmental stimuli in a similar manner (Fanselow, 1984).

Findings like these suggest that classical conditioning may be important in the development of some **psychosomatic disorders,** in which physical symptoms are caused by emotional or mental factors. For example, one study of asthma patients revealed that their attacks often occurred in the presence of specific stimuli such as radio speeches by influential politicians, goldfish, the national anthem, and waterfalls. Once the critical stimuli were identified in each case, the investigators were able to induce asthma attacks by presenting the critical stimuli or facsimiles of them. The researchers describe one such case:

Patient L had told us that she got an asthmatic attack from looking at a goldfish. After a baseline had been obtained, a goldfish in a bowl was brought into the room. . . . Under our eyes she developed a severe asthmatic attack with loud wheezing, followed by a gradual remission after the goldfish had been taken from the room. During the next experiment the goldfish was replaced by a plastic toy fish which was easily recognized as such. . . . but a fierce attack resulted. (Dekker and Groen, 1956, p. 62)

In a case known to us, a man began to have violent attacks of wheezing and difficulty breathing while having sex with his wife in their bedroom. The removal of a large, scowling portrait of his mother-in-law from the room ended his respiratory problems.

CLASSICAL CONDITIONING AND ATTITUDE FORMATION

Emotional reactions are an important component of attitudes. When we say we have a "positive" or a "negative" attitude toward a person or situation, we are referring in part to the way the person or situation makes us feel. Some theorists believe that classical conditioning is critically important in establishing attitudes (Staats, 1975). In classical conditioning terms, the object or situation is the CS. If this CS is associated with another stimulus (UCS) that already elicits a positive or negative emotional response (UCR), we may develop a conditioned emotional response toward that object. For example, most of us have a song that became a favorite because it was paired with a pleasurable situation or event, or one that arouses negative feelings because it was associated with a negative event.

But how can attitudes be classically conditioned to people or objects that we've had no personal contact with? The concept of **higher-order conditioning** provides us with a possible answer. Once a response has been conditioned to a CS, that CS can be used like a UCS to establish another CS. For example, the word "bad" has no meaning when it is presented initially to an infant; it is a neutral stimulus. But after "bad" has been paired with slaps or a spanking (pretty potent UCSs), the word alone become capable of triggering a variety of emotional responses. "Bad" has become a CS. If we now pair "bad" with the name of a person or group of people with whom the child has had no contact, it is possible that the child's negative emotional reactions to the word could be transferred to the new stimulus. The result: instant dislike. This process can potentially occur with words that have either positive or negative learned connotations.

Advertisers seem to have a great deal of faith in higher-order conditioning. They carefully link their products to attractive people and settings, to personal wealth, and most of all to pleasurable interactions with the opposite sex. When was the last time you saw an advertisement showing an unattractive, dirty person contentedly puffing on a cigarette in a cancer ward?

Now that we have discussed the elements of classical conditioning, let us return to one of the cases that you read about at the beginning of this chapter—the young woman with the automobile phobia. Suppose that you were her therapist. Do you think that classical conditioning could help you explain any part of her problem?

It seems pretty clear that classical conditioning played a role in establishing her fear of cars. During her accident, conditioned stimuli relating to her car and to driving were associated with unconditioned stimuli (fire, danger) that evoked pain and terror (UCRs), and she was left with a strong conditioned fear response. It is also clear that considerable stimulus generalization has occurred, so that stimuli other than those involved in the original accident situation can also evoke strong fear responses. Note that the young woman experiences less anxiety when she merely views a car on TV or in magazines than when she is riding in a car. This would be predicted on the basis of stimulus generalization, because these stimuli are less similar to the original conditioned stimuli.

Although classical conditioning principles explain the way in which the woman's automobile phobia was established, a number of important questions remain. Why doesn't the fear decrease? After all, the stimuli that relate to the car are no longer being associated with pain. Shouldn't the fear responses simply extinguish? Most puzzling of all, why does the client seem to be getting progressively worse? She clearly realizes that her fear is irrational and seems highly motivated to get rid of it. In order to answer these questions we must consider a second major type of learning: operant conditioning.

OPERANT CONDITIONING: LEARNING THROUGH CONSEQUENCES

At about the same time Pavlov was making his landmark discoveries of classical conditioning in Russia, an American psychologist, Edward L. Thorndike, was studying a somewhat different kind of learning. Pavlov was examining the relationship between involuntary responses and the stimuli that precede them, while Thorndike was studying the trial and error learning that animals use to solve problems, such as how to operate a latch to get out of a box and get food. The behaviors that Thorndike was investigating were not involuntary reflexive responses to particular stimuli, as were Pavlov's conditioned responses. Instead, they were voluntary behaviors that helped the organism attain some goal.

The terms *operant* and *instrumental*, which are often used interchangeably, refer to the fact that the behaviors in question produce some kind of an effect for the organism. The organism *operates* on its environment in some way; the behaviors in which it engages are *instrumental* in achieving some outcome.

Thorndike developed an elaborate theory of behavior, but he is probably most famous for his **law of effect,** which can be summarized in this way: if a response is followed by a pleasant or "satisfying" consequence, that response will be strengthened. If a response is followed by an unpleasant or negative state of affairs, it will be weakened. This law of effect is the cornerstone of **operant conditioning.**

It is easy for us to see how the law of effect works in our own lives. Each of us has developed a set of behaviors that for the most part allow us to get along in our environment. Can you trace one or two of your own behaviors back and remember when and why you began using them? Can you remember any social behaviors that you once used but have since discarded? Can you see how the law of effect has functioned in relation to the development of your own personality?

Do the behaviors that you usually perform seem to produce a positive outcome for you? Are there any behaviors you would like to discard because they are no longer producing positive outcomes?

The study of operant conditioning

Much of our current knowledge about operant conditioning stems from the research of B. F. Skinner and his co-workers, who performed many laboratory studies with animals. A typical laboratory demonstration of operant conditioning might proceed as follows. A rat that has been deprived of food for a number of hours is placed in an experimental chamber called a **Skinner box** (named for its inventor, over his objections). There is a lever on one wall of the chamber. Beneath the lever is a small cup into which a pellet of food is dropped by an automatic dispenser whenever the rat presses the lever (see Figure 6.6). When put into the chamber, the rat first explores its surroundings. In the course of its explorations, it happens to press the lever. A pellet of food clinks into the cup and the surprised animal eats it quickly. Sometime later, the rat again randomly presses the bar and receives another pellet. If we record the rat's behavior on a **cumulative response recorder** (see Figure 6.7), we will find that the animal soon begins to press the bar more and more frequently. In the language of the learning psychologist, we would say that an operant bar-press response has now been established. Receiving the food pellet is a *reinforcement*—an outcome that increases the likelihood that the rat will press the bar again.

Suppose we now place a light on the panel above the bar. When the light is on, pressing the bar dispenses food, but when the light is off, no food is dispensed. The rat will soon learn to press the bar only when the light is on. That is, it will respond to the stimulus that signals the availability of reinforcement.

This general procedure has been used to study operant conditioning in many different species, including human beings. One only need modify the response to be made (for example, pigeons peck a disc instead of pressing a bar) and the type of reinforcer employed (children respond more enthusiastically to candy than they do to rat pellets).

We now consider the major principles of operant conditioning in greater detail and indicate ways in which these principles have enabled psychologists to understand and, sometimes, to change behavior.

FIGURE 6.6 *A rat explores a Skinner box, which has been used in studies of operant conditioning.*

When the rat presses the bar on the wall, food is automatically delivered by the apparatus to the left of the box. The light above the bar can be used as a discriminative stimulus signaling the availability of the reinforcer.

The ABCs of operant conditioning

The operant analysis of behavior involves the study of relationships between three kinds of events: **antecedents** (A), or environmental stimuli; **behaviors** (B) that the organism engages in; and **consequences** (C) that follow the behaviors and either strengthen or weaken them. The relationships that exist among these elements are called **contingencies.** The ABCs of contingencies can be expressed in the following way:

IF antecedent stimuli (A) are present

AND behavior (B) is emitted,

THEN consequence (C) will occur.

Two aspects of these relationships are of interest. The first is the relationship between antecedents and behaviors (A and B); the second is the contingency between behavior and its consequences (B and C).

ANTECEDENTS: STIMULUS CONTROL OF BEHAVIOR

Through previous experience, we learn which kinds of behaviors have which kinds of consequences under which conditions. Antecedents that signal the likely consequences of particular behaviors in a given situation are known as **discriminative stimuli.** In the Skinner box, the light that signals the availability of food if the bar is pressed serves as a discriminative stimulus. Such signals help to guide our behavior so that it is "appropriate" and most likely to lead to positive consequences for us. When antecedents are influential in governing our behavior (not in the reflexlike classical conditioning sense, but rather in signaling the likely consequences of a behavior), that behavior is said to be

FIGURE 6.7 *A cumulative recorder, connected to a Skinner box in which a rat is being trained, produces a record of responses. The paper moves at a constant speed in the direction indicated. Each bar press operates an electromagnet, which moves the pen one step upward. When the pen reaches the top of the paper, it activates a switch, which causes the pen to move back down to the bottom of the paper. In this way the animal "draws" its own learning curve. Responses are also counted by an electric counter.*

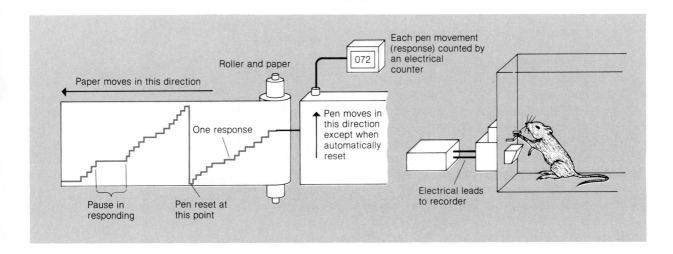

under **stimulus control.** The sight of a squad car occupied by a police officer who obviously has had a bad day can exert powerful stimulus control over most people's driving behavior.

DIFFERENCES BETWEEN OPERANT AND CLASSICAL CONDITIONING

There are two main differences between operant and classical conditioning.

1. In classical conditioning, the behavior (CR) is triggered by a particular stimulus (CS) and is therefore called an **elicited behavior.** Operant behavior is **emitted behavior** in the sense that the response occurs in a situation containing many stimuli. In a sense, the subject "chooses" when and how to respond.

2. In both classical and operant conditioning, a behavior is strengthened. The difference is that the classically conditioned behavior (CR) is affected by something that occurs *prior to* the behavior (the CS-UCS pairing). The operant response, on the other hand, is affected by what happens *after* the behavior—that is, by its consequences.

Although the procedures for classical and operant conditioning are easily distinguishable, many learning situations involve both processes. For example, when a young child is bitten by a large dog that he or she has tried to pet, the bite is a punishing response consequence, so that the child becomes operantly conditioned to avoid petting that dog again. In addition, the painful stimulation is paired with the neutral stimuli of the dog, so that the child may also develop a classically conditioned fear of the dog which may generalize to other dogs.

Response consequences and behavior

We have emphasized that the key feature in operant conditioning is what happens after a response is made. Psychologists have done a great deal of research on how different types of consequences affect behavior.

POSITIVE REINFORCEMENT

A positive reinforcer is any stimulus or event that increases the frequency of a behavior that it follows. The term *reward* is often used as if it were synonymous with **positive reinforcement.** However, psychologists prefer the term *reinforcement* because it focuses on the way the consequence affects behavior, while "reward" often seems to be a subjective label for something that we personally might find pleasurable. Besides, in many instances what we think of as "rewards" do not function as positive reinforcers. For example, the study behavior of some students is not affected by the promised "reward" of higher grades.

Two basic conditions must be met if positive reinforcement procedures are to be successful in developing desired behaviors. First, the reinforcer must be strong enough to strengthen the behavior. Second, that reinforcer must be made contingent or dependent on the desired behavior, so that the subject learns what it must do to earn the reinforcer.

Learning psychologists distinguish between **primary reinforcers** and **secondary, or conditioned, reinforcers.** Primary reinforcers satisfy biological needs. Food and water are examples. Because they relate to tissue needs, they are unlearned reinforcers. However, we can also learn to want reinforcers that are not directly related to satisfaction of biological needs through a process of conditioning; hence the term secondary, or conditioned, reinforcer. Theoretically, any stimulus associated with the attainment of a primary reinforcer can also become a reinforcer. Attention, verbal praise, trading stamps, and money are examples of secondary reinforcers. In an animal version of the secondary reinforcement properties of money, a chimpanzee will learn to value and work for (and even to hoard) tokens it can place into a vending machine to obtain raisins (see Figure 6.8).

Secondary positive reinforcers are often used in behavior modification programs designed to strengthen certain desired behaviors. One such program focused on a special-education preschool classroom straight out of a teacher's nightmare. Here is a record of four minutes of behavior in that classroom:

Mike, John, and Dan are seated together playing with pieces of Playdoh. Barry, some distance from the others, is seated and is also playing with Playdoh. The children, except Barry, are talking to each other about what they are making. Time is 9:10 A.M. Miss Sally, the teacher, turns toward the children and says, "It's time for a lesson. Put your Playdoh away." Mike says, "Not me." John says, "Not me." Dan says, "Not me." Miss Sally moves toward Mike. Mike throws his Playdoh in Miss Sally's face. Miss Sally jerks back, then moves forward rapidly and snatches Playdoh from Mike. Puts Playdoh in her pocket. Mike screams for Playdoh, says he wants to play with it. Mike moves toward Miss Sally and attempts to snatch the Playdoh from her pocket. Miss Sally pushes him away. Mike kicks her on the leg, kicks her again, and demands the return of his Playdoh. Kicks her again, picks up a small steel chair and throws it at Miss Sally. She jumps

out of the way. Mike picks up another chair and throws it more violently. Miss Sally cannot move in time and chair strikes her foot. Miss Sally pushes Mike down on the floor. Mike starts up, pulls over one chair, then another, another; stops a moment. Miss Sally is picking up chairs. Mike looks at her. She moves toward Mike. Mike runs away. John wants his Playdoh. Miss Sally says, "No." He joins Mike in pulling over chairs and attempts to grab Playdoh from Miss Sally's pocket; she pushes him away roughly. John is screaming that he wants to play with his Playdoh; moves toward phonograph, pulls it off the table and lets it crash to the floor. Mike has his coat on; says he is going home. Miss Sally asks Dan to bolt the door. Dan gets to the door at the same time as Mike. Mike hits Dan in the face. Dan's nose is bleeding. . . . Time: 9:14 A.M. (Hamblin and others, 1971, p. 102).

Baseline observations disclosed that, on the average, the children were engaging in 55 cooperative behaviors and 140 aggressive sequences per day. In an attempt to increase cooperative behavior (which would also serve to decrease aggression), a program was established in which Miss Sally reinforced cooperative behaviors with tokens that the children could later exchange for toys and opportunities to engage in prized activities. Under this positive reinforcement program, the behavior patterns in the classroom changed radically. Within 12 days, the number of cooperative behaviors rose from 55 to 151 per day, while the number of aggressive sequences dropped from 140 to fewer than 15 per day.

SHAPING

Stiff trade winds buffeted the coconut palms and tropical plants at Sea Life Park in Hawaii. The blue-green waters of the Pacific shimmered in the distance beneath the warm afternoon sun. A sizable crowd had gathered in the stands around Whaler's Cove to watch the trained dolphins and killer whales. *Oohs* and *ahs* had greeted the complex acrobatic tricks that the animals performed with great precision. As the buzzing crowd left the show, a young woman trainer in colorful Hawaiian garb was explaining to a group of interested

FIGURE 6.8 *A chimp drops a token into the Chimp-O-Mat vending machine to obtain raisins. Through their association with food (a primary reinforcer), the tokens become valued secondary reinforcers for the chimps. The chimps began to hoard their tokens just as some people hoard money.*

spectators how the animals are trained to perform their remarkable feats (see Figure 6.9):

The animals you're seeing are not geniuses, although they may look like it at times. Actually, what you're seeing is the end product of very systematic training. We use a method known as **shaping** or *successive approximations* to gradually build the complex behaviors you see. This means that we reinforce, with a juicy fish, behaviors that get closer and closer to the desired trick. For example, no dolphin or killer whale, regardless of how brilliant, is going to jump spontaneously through a hoop ten feet above the water. We have to gradually shape her, first by rewarding her when she swims into the area near the hoop, then when she breaks water, and so on. In other words, in order to get her fish, she has to come closer and closer to what we want her to do eventually. This is basically how all animal acts are developed, whether here at Sea Life Park or in a circus. We can eventually put together long **behavior chains** in which a number of responses are run off in sequence, with reinforcement at the end of the chain.

The products of operant conditioning go far beyond rats pressing bars and pigeons pecking discs in Skinner boxes, and even beyond the feats performed by trained animals. Humans also learn many complex behaviors through shaping. Shaping is involved when we are learning a language or developing educational skills. If we want to train children to be mathematicians, we do not expect them to solve complex calculus problems spontaneously. We start by teaching them basic arithmetic operations and successively building on what they have already learned. On a broader level, the acquisition of the behaviors, values, and attitudes of our society involves a great deal of shaping on the part of parents, teachers, and peers.

OPERANT EXTINCTION

In operant conditioning, as in classical conditioning, **extinction** refers to the gradual disappearance of a learned response. Extinction of operant behaviors occurs when we stop reinforcing them. Extinction undoubtedly accounts for many changes in human behavior. When previously reinforced behaviors no longer pay off, we are likely to abandon them and replace them with more successful ones. It follows, therefore, that an effective way to change people's negative behaviors is to make sure that they get no rein-

FIGURE 6.9 *Shaping procedures have been used to train this false killer whale performing at Sea Life Park in Hawaii. Progressively more complex behaviors are built up using fish as a positive reinforcer.*

forcement for the undesirable behaviors while reinforcing alternative behaviors that are more desirable. An example is presented in the following case study.

Changing the contingencies: the taming of Pascal the Rascal This case, typical of many seen at child guidance clinics, illustrates the use of operant procedures that have proven highly effective (Patterson, 1982).

Mrs. Adams sought help at a child guidance clinic because of severe problems with her 4-year-old son Pascal. Pascal seemed to delight in misbehaving. "He'll go to any lengths just to make my life miserable," she complained. His behavior was especially disruptive, she added, when she was concentrating on her housework. Under the circumstances she found Pascal very difficult to love and felt guilty about her hostile feelings toward him.

Mrs. Adams was at her wit's end because nothing seemed to work. First she had tried to reason with him. Then she resorted to yelling and screaming at him when he misbehaved. When that produced no effect, Mrs. Adams began using physical punishment. Even that did not work. "In fact," she reported, "he got worse."

Like many parents, Mrs. Adams could not understand why measures like scolding and spanking not only failed to reduce her son's negative behaviors, but even seemed to increase them. She did not realize that any sort of attention is such a powerful positive reinforcer for many children that it can overshadow the effects of the "punishment" it accompanies. Behavior patterns like Pascal's usually develop when parents do not reward desirable behaviors with attention; then the only way for a child to get their attention is to misbehave. This again illustrates the difference between the concepts of reward and reinforcement. Parents are not likely to view their "punishments" as a reward for negative behavior, but they certainly can function as a reinforcement by increasing the behavior.

Like many parents who have similar problems, Mrs. Adams believed that there was something wrong with her child. She thought his obnoxious behavior was a symptom of possibly severe emotional problems and was eager for him to begin psychotherapy. The psychologist urged her to consider another explanation: that Pascal was simply responding to the reinforcement contingencies in his life and that the most effective approach would be to modify these contingencies. Mrs. Adams agreed to try to extinguish Pascal's problem behavior while strengthening his positive behaviors.

After a week of baseline data showed that Pascal was misbehaving an average of 24 times per day, Mrs. Adams was instructed to ignore Pascal's obnoxious behaviors whenever possible. She was warned that Pascal was likely to increase his negative behaviors for a period of time. When a reinforcement is removed, most people try harder for a while before they begin to decrease the behavior. This is the main reason why many people stop extinction

procedures before they have a chance to work. They are afraid they are making matters even worse.

But because Pascal's behavior was so disruptive, it could not simply be ignored. The psychologist suggested a procedure called **time out,** which is short for "time out from positive reinforcement" and involves removing the child from the situation in which he can receive reinforcement. When Pascal's behavior was too disruptive to be ignored, Mrs. Adams was instructed to lock him in another room for a specified period of time. If Pascal threw a tantrum, as he did on the first two occasions, she told him that the time out interval would begin when the tantrum ended. Because it was impossible for Pascal to receive attention during these periods, he soon began to reduce the behaviors that resulted in time out.

Mrs. Adams was also instructed to reinforce Pascal for desirable behaviors by paying attention to him. Because Pascal had strong needs for attention, simply extinguishing his negative behavior without establishing a way to reinforce him for positive behavior would not have been very effective. To help her in the use of the reinforcement and extinction procedures, the psychologist had Mrs. Adams bring Pascal to the clinic's playroom and interact with him while the psychologist observed through a one-way mirror and gave her pointers through a "bug in the ear," a tiny radio receiver that Mrs. Adams wore like an earplug.

Mrs. Adams collected behavioral data on Pascal throughout the program. The frequency of his negative behaviors increased briefly when she started extinction procedures, but declined steadily, along with a corresponding rise in the frequency of positive behaviors. The family atmosphere at the Adams house improved immensely, and Mrs. Adams began to enjoy once again her relationship with Pascal, the ex-Rascal.

Schedules of reinforcement

The environment that responds to our behavior can be varied and unpredictable. The kinds of reinforcers that we receive occur in different patterns and frequencies. In everyday life, there are many different types of positive reinforcement contingencies. Sometimes we receive reinforcement after every response, but more typ-

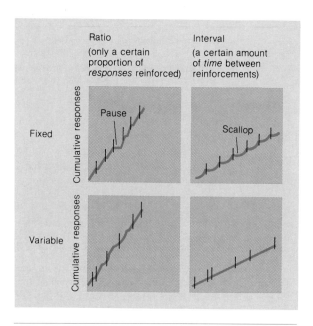

Ratio (only a certain proportion of *responses* reinforced)

Interval (a certain amount of *time* between reinforcements)

Fixed — Cumulative responses — Pause

Scallop

Variable — Cumulative responses

FIGURE 6.10 *Each type of partial reinforcement schedule produces a typical cumulative response curve. The hash marks indicate the delivery of a reinforcement. Ratio schedules produce a high rate of responding, as shown in the steep slopes of the curves. The variable-interval schedule elicits a steady rate of responding. The fixed-interval schedule produces a scalloped curve because the animal learns to stop responding until the time for the next reinforcement approaches.*

ically only a proportion of our responses are reinforced. These patterns, or **schedules of reinforcement,** have strong and predictable effects on learning, extinction, and performance.

The first important distinction is between continuous and partial reinforcement. On a **continuous reinforcement schedule,** every response is reinforced. **Partial,** or **intermittent reinforcement** refers to conditions in which only some responses are followed by reinforcement.

Partial reinforcement schedules can be categorized as ratio schedules or interval schedules. On *ratio schedules*, a certain percentage of the subject's responses are reinforced. On *interval schedules*, a certain amount of time must elapse between reinforcements, regardless of how many responses might occur during that interval.

Both types of partial schedules can be further subdivided into fixed and variable schedules. On a *fixed schedule*, the reinforcement always occurs after a fixed number of responses or after a fixed time interval; on *variable schedules*, the required number of responses or the time interval varies at random around an average. Figure 6.10 shows how all these partial reinforcement categories combine to produce four different reinforcement schedules: fixed-ratio (FR), variable-ratio (VR), fixed-interval (FI), and variable-interval (VI). As you can see by looking at the cumulative response curves, the different schedules have quite different effects on behavior. Let us see why.

FIXED-RATIO SCHEDULE

On a **fixed-ratio** (FR) **schedule,** reinforcement is given after a fixed number of responses. For example, FR 10 means that reinforcement occurs after every tenth response, regardless of how long it takes for the subject to respond ten times.

An FR schedule produces a high rate of responding with little hesitation between responses. That's one reason why some businesses prefer piecework wages based on a set number of items produced. If the ratio is gradually increased over time, many responses can be obtained with relatively few reinforcements. Pigeons in a Skinner box have been known literally to wear down their beaks pecking a disc on an FR 20,000 schedule. But if the ratio is increased too rapidly, the response may extinguish between reinforcements.

FR schedules have a second characteristic effect. As shown in Figure 6.10, the subject pauses for a while after each reinforcement, perhaps because the responses that follow never get reinforced. The larger the number of subsequent responses needed to earn reinforcement, the longer the pause before the animal resumes responding.

VARIABLE-RATIO SCHEDULE

On a **variable-ratio** (VR) **schedule,** reinforcement is given after a variable or average number of responses. A VR 10 schedule means that, *on the average*, 10 responses are required for reinforcement. Because the schedule is a variable one, however, reinforcement can occur when fewer or more than 10 responses have been made.

A VR schedule, like an FR schedule, produces a high rate of responding. But because the occurrence of reinforcement is variable and unpredictable, there is no pause after reinforcement. Instead there is a relatively steady rate of responding, as shown in Figure 6.10. Because each response is equally likely to result in reinforcement, the VR schedule can be physically taxing. Both animals and human beings may continue to respond to the point of exhaustion.

Let us return now to the gambler described at the beginning of the chapter. As the casino guard remarked, the gambler has been responding without reinforcement for a long time. Is he indeed "sick," as the guard suggests, or can we now understand his behavior

in terms of the reinforcement conditions in that situation?

Gambling is a good example of behavior that is maintained on a variable-ratio schedule (see Figure 6.11). Because any spin of the roulette wheel or any pull of the lever on a slot machine is as likely as any other to be reinforced with a jackpot, it is easy to establish a high rate of responding that is very resistant to extinction. This is especially true if a person wins a jackpot early on. Suppose, for example, that a slot machine is programmed on a VR 20 schedule. You drop a coin in, pull the lever, and receive a 10-coin jackpot. After two more attempts, you hit a 15-coin jackpot. But then, after 67 consecutive unsuccessful attempts—nothing. You walk away muttering angrily about your lot in life, probably unaware that you've been "hooked" by the VR schedule. If you were to stay and play the machine indefinitely, you would receive a payoff for every 20 attempts, *on the average*. These "one-armed bandits" make a handsome profit for the casino because the average number of coins in a jackpot is smaller (perhaps 10 to 15 coins) than the average of 20 needed to trigger the jackpot.

Our gambler, then, may be seen as the unhappy victim of a difficult and compelling reinforcement schedule rather than the victim of some mysterious sickness.

FIXED-INTERVAL SCHEDULE

On a **fixed-interval (FI) schedule,** reinforcement follows the first response that occurs after a certain interval of time. On an FI 3 schedule, for example, the first response that occurs 3 minutes after the preceding reinforcement is always reinforced. The reinforcement does not occur until there is a response. The FI schedule produces a characteristic response pattern, as shown in Figure 6.10. After each reinforcement, there is a period of time during which the rate of response is very low. This feature of the curve is called an *FI scallop.* As the fixed time interval elapses, the response rate

FIGURE 6.11 *Slot machines, which operate on variable ratio schedules, can elicit a high rate of behavior that is resistant to extinction because of the unpredictable schedule of jackpots.*

gradually increases until, by the end of the interval, there is a very rapid response rate.

Although "pure" FI schedules such as those arranged in the laboratory are probably quite rare in everyday life, some situations do approximate them. One such situation—familiar, unfortunately, to all of us—is the schedule of tests in most college courses. Many instructors give three exams, one every four weeks. Let us assume that each exam offers you the opportunity for potent positive reinforcers in the form of a good grade, increased self-esteem, satisfaction of your insatiable thirst for knowledge, and approval from an attractive classmate. This situation would be very similar to an FI schedule. What kind of pattern does your study behavior follow?

If you are like many students, the cumulative recording of the number of hours you spend studying may resemble the one presented in Figure 6.12. It shows very little study during the first two weeks of the Test 1 interval, somewhat more during the third week, and a great deal of studying during the week of the test. This "cramming" pattern demonstrates the potency of the FI reinforcement schedule. Study behavior usually changes quite radically in the face of a variable and hence unpredictable schedule of "pop quizzes," as you are well aware if you have known the joy of having a professor who used that system of testing.

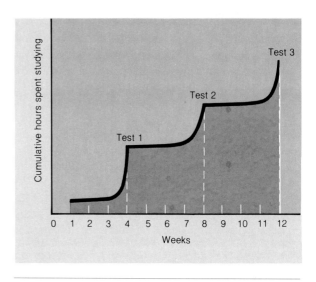

FIGURE 6.12 *The manner in which tests are scheduled in college courses often creates a kind of fixed-interval schedule. The cumulative response curve of study behavior for many students shows a gradually increasing amount of study that reaches its maximum rate in "cramming" immediately before the test.*

hook a lunker. The fact that the reinforcement is available but unpredictable may make you very persistent, even if you have not had a bite all day.

EFFECTS OF REINFORCEMENT SCHEDULES ON LEARNING AND EXTINCTION

In addition to influencing response patterns and rates, reinforcement schedules affect the course of learning and extinction. As you might expect, learning occurs most rapidly on a schedule of continuous reinforcement. If each response is reinforced, then there is no opportunity for extinction to occur and the relationship between the behavior and its consequences is easily perceived.

Although learning occurs most rapidly under continuous reinforcement, partial schedules produce behavior that is harder to extinguish, especially if the behavior was reinforced on a variable schedule. If reinforcement has been unpredictable in the past, it takes subjects longer to realize that it is gone forever. If, on the other hand, the behavior has been reinforced on

VARIABLE-INTERVAL SCHEDULE

On a **variable-interval** (VI) **schedule,** reinforcement occurs after a variable interval of time. Reinforcement is given for the first response that occurs after that interval. A VI 5 schedule means that, on the average, there is a 5-minute interval between opportunities for the subject to obtain reinforcement. Because the availability of reinforcement is apparently random, the VI schedule produces a rather steady response rate that is much different from the scallop pattern that occurs on an FI schedule. The rate of response on a VI schedule, although fairly steady, is affected by the size of the average interval between reinforcements. The longer the average interval, the lower the rate of response.

Fishing often approximates a VI schedule. You know that the fish are present, but it is difficult to predict when they will start biting. The very next cast may a continuous schedule, the change in reinforcement pattern is radical and easy to perceive, so that extinction is likely to occur quite rapidly. Most people do not continue to drop coins into a candy machine that doesn't deliver, since vending machines are supposed to operate on a continuous schedule. However, their behavior toward a slot machine that doesn't deliver (but isn't necessarily supposed to) may be quite different.

The best way to promote fast learning and high resistance to extinction is to begin reinforcing the desired behavior on a continuous schedule until the behavior is fairly strong and then to shift to a partial (preferably variable) schedule that is gradually made more demanding. With a gradually increasing ratio on a VR schedule, for example, a pigeon may learn to peck a disc 12,000 times per hour in order to obtain a reinforcer given, on the average, once every 110 responses (Ferster and Skinner, 1957).

Negative reinforcement: Escape and avoidance conditioning

As we suggested earlier, we can understand many behaviors as attempts to maximize positive outcomes and to minimize negative ones. In our discussion of positive reinforcement, we have focused on positive outcomes. We now turn to those behaviors that we learn and maintain in order to escape from or avoid negative consequences. These behaviors are maintained through the process of **negative reinforcement.**

A negative reinforcer is anything that increases a behavior that results in the *removal* of the reinforcer. Don't confuse negative reinforcement with punishment. Although the same kinds of stimuli (for example, shock) may be involved, negative reinforcement (shock *removal*) *increases* a response that results in the consequence, whereas punishment (*being* shocked) *decreases* any response that produces the consequence. Whether positive or negative reinforcement is involved, we are always talking about a consequence that *increases* a response (see Figure 6.13).

Escape conditioning is one form of learning that results from negative reinforcement. In the laboratory, escape conditioning might be carried out in the following manner: A rat is placed in one compartment of a

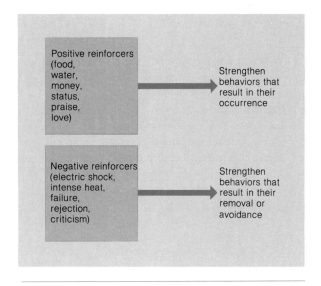

FIGURE 6.13 *Both positive and negative reinforcers increase and strengthen responses that lead to them. Organisms learn to perform behaviors that lead to the occurrence of positive reinforcers or the removal or avoidance of negative reinforcers.*

shuttlebox, a rectangular chamber divided into two compartments by a partition with a doorway (see Figure 6.14). The floor of the shuttlebox is a grid through which electric shock can be delivered to either compartment. When it is turned on, the shock evokes pain and fear, and the rat attempts to escape from the compartment. Sooner or later, the animal runs through the door into the other compartment, where the current is not on. When a shock is then delivered in that compartment, the rat can again escape by running back to the other side. Because the escape behavior of running through the door removes the shock, this consequence is a negative reinforcer for the behavior. As the conditioning proceeds, the rat will require less and less time to escape the shock, until finally it will escape as soon as the shock is administered.

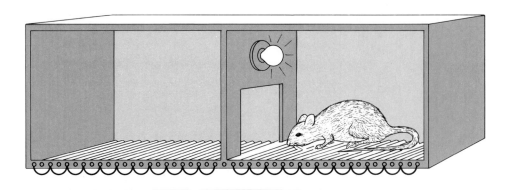

FIGURE 6.14 *The shuttlebox is used by psychologists to study escape and avoidance conditioning. One side of the chamber is electrified, but the animal can learn to escape shock by going into the other compartment. If a warning stimulus such as a light precedes the shock, the animal will eventually learn to avoid the impending shock by running through the doorway. In both cases the electric shock is a negative reinforcer because escaping or avoiding it strengthens the response of switching compartments.*

To study **avoidance conditioning,** we now introduce a warning light (as in Figure 6.14) or some other discriminative stimulus that precedes the shock. The animal will learn after the first several trials that the light signals impending shock, and it will begin to run to the other compartment after it sees the light and before the shock is administered, thereby avoiding it.

One aspect of this avoidance experiment that has intrigued psychologists is the remarkable strength of the avoidance behavior that may develop in only a few trials. Some dogs, for example, need only a few shocks before they learn to run into the other compartment of a shuttlebox at the sight of the warning light. After that, they may run hundreds of times in response to the light without ever again experiencing shock. What makes avoidance behavior so resistant to extinction?

A TWO-FACTOR THEORY OF AVOIDANCE LEARNING

One attempt to answer this question is the **two-factor theory of avoidance learning** (Rescorla and Solomon, 1967). The theory is so named because two processes—classical conditioning and operant conditioning—are assumed to be involved.

Because the warning stimulus (in our example, the

light) is paired with shock (a UCS) in the beginning, the light becomes a CS that triggers a classically conditioned fear response. Since fear is an unpleasant state of affairs, responses that reduce it are strengthened through negative reinforcement. This is where the second process, operant conditioning, enters the picture. Fear reduction is a powerful negative reinforcer, and as long as the fear remains, the avoidance behavior that reduces it will continue.

But why doesn't the classically conditioned fear response extinguish? After all, the light is paired with the shock only a few times at the beginning of the training. Note that this is exactly the same question we asked earlier about the young woman's fear of cars. In her case, the automobile stimuli were associated with pain on only one occasion, yet the conditioned fear response did not grow weaker.

The answer is that the avoidance responses themselves prevent the unlearning of fear. In order for a classically conditioned response to be extinguished, the CS (warning light, automobile stimuli) must be presented without the UCS (shock, pain) long enough for extinction to occur. But once an avoidance response is learned, the subject may leave the fear-producing situation before it finds out that the UCS will not occur. The dog in the shuttlebox has no opportunity to learn that the light (CS) is no longer followed by a shock because the animal is long gone by the time the shock would occur. Similarly, the young woman never allows herself to be around an automobile long enough for her fear to extinguish. The avoidance behaviors prevent the conditioned fear response from extinguishing, and the avoidance responses are in turn strengthened time after time through negative reinforcement. This helps to account for the fact that phobic avoidance often seems to become stronger over time, as appears to have been the case with our young woman's automobile phobia.

The two-factor theory suggests not only a cause for phobic behavior but also a cure. To extinguish the conditioned fear response that motivates and maintains the phobic behavior, the avoidance response must be prevented from occurring so that the subject can be exposed to the feared CS in the absence of the UCS. This approach has proven successful in eliminating learned fears in both animals and humans (Mineka, 1979; Morris, 1980). Thus, if the young woman can be helped by her therapist to expose herself to the feared automobile stimuli (either in her imagination or in real life) long enough for the fear to extinguish, her automobile phobia can be eliminated.

So far, we have discussed response consequences that are rewarding enough to increase the performance of certain behaviors. We now turn to the other side of the coin and consider what is probably the most frequently used method for controlling undesirable behavior—punishment.

FIGURE 6.15 *As demonstrated by this baseball coach, there are two forms of punishment: application of aversive stimuli (top) and response cost involving withdrawal of a prized reinforcer, in this case batting practice (bottom).*

Punishment

Punishment is a consequence that decreases the future occurrence of the behavior that produces it. It is important not to confuse punishment with extinction, a procedure that also decreases a behavior. Punishment involves negative consequences that are made contingent upon a given behavior, whereas extinction simply involves a failure to reinforce the behavior.

Punishment can be administered in two forms. The first, **aversive punishment**, is carried out by applying aversive (unpleasant) stimuli, such as painful slaps or verbal reprimands. The second is done by taking away

positive reinforcers, such as privileges, social interactions, or possessions (see Figure 6.15). This second form of punishment, known as **response cost**, is also different from extinction because the reinforcer that is being taken away is not one that is reinforcing the undesired behavior. For example, if a motorist is fined for speeding, it is punishment through response cost rather than extinction, because presumably money is not the reinforcer for speeding (unless, of course, the motorist is driving a getaway car from the scene of a robbery).

APPLYING AVERSIVE STIMULI

When aversive or painful stimuli occur in response to a particular behavior, an inhibition or *suppression* of that behavior typically occurs. This suppression usually takes place as a result of fear of additional punishment (Axelrod and Apsche, 1983). In a sense, this form of punishment pits the suppressive effects of fear against the power of whatever is reinforcing the undesired behavior.

Aversive punishment has several advantages. First, it often produces rapid results. This can be an important consideration when it is necessary to stop a particularly dangerous behavior, such as a child's playing with a loaded gun or running into a busy street. Second, if you are trying to extinguish a behavior, you need to control and eliminate the reinforcers of the behavior. Some positive reinforcers, such as those that maintain thrill-seeking behaviors, are beyond our control. When no control over positive reinforcers is possible, punishment may be the best way to bring a behavior under control.

But punishment can also have undesirable side effects. The suppression of the behavior may be only temporary and may last only as long as the punisher is present ("When the cat's away . . ."). Another problem is that punishment arouses negative emotional states such as fear and hostility. This can result in dislike for the person delivering the punishment or avoidance of the situation in which punishment occurs. Most parents do not want their children to dislike or fear them; likewise, we do not want students dropping out of school or avoiding punishing school situations. Finally, the suppressive effects of strong punishment may generalize to other behaviors that are actually appropriate. A child who is severely punished for aggressive behavior may become generally unassertive, even in situations in which assertive behavior is called for, or one punished for sexual behaviors in childhood may suffer from sexual inhibitions as an adult (Bandura, 1969).

One of the most difficult problems with punishment is the example that it sets. Aversive punishment amounts to control through aggression, and the message conveyed to the victim of punishment is that aggressive behaviors are appropriate and effective. There is evidence that this lesson is quickly learned. One study found that by 13 to 35 months of age, children whose parents used severe physical punishment already displayed more aggression toward peers and care-givers in day-care centers than did a matched sample of children who were not physically punished (George and Main, 1979).

Punishment, then, is a two-edged sword. It is probably the quickest way to control negative behaviors, but it clearly has shortcomings and possible negative side effects. Some of the side effects can be minimized, however. Punishment can be used very effectively in conjunction with positive reinforcement for alternative desirable behaviors (van Houten, 1983). For example, punishment may be used temporarily to suppress physically aggressive responses while cooperative social responses are being strengthened through positive reinforcement.

It is important to focus on alternative positive behaviors when using punishment, for punishment only teaches the recipient what *not* to do; it doesn't guarantee that desirable behavior will appear in its place. When punishment is used in conjunction with reinforcement of alternative behaviors, and when language is used to help the recipient discriminate between appropriate and inappropriate behavior in particular situations, complete and relatively permanent suppression of problem behaviors can occur, desirable behaviors can appear in their place, and problems stemming from fear and dislike can be minimized (Routh, 1982). Nonetheless, because of the aggressive component in aversive punishment, most learning psychologists recommend the use of extinction over aversive punishment whenever possible.

THERAPEUTIC USE OF AVERSIVE PUNISHMENT

Like the other learning principles we have discussed, aversive punishment is sometimes used as a therapeutic technique. Psychologists ask themselves two important questions before they decide to use punishment as a treatment technique: (1) Are there alternative, less painful approaches (such as extinction) that might be effective? (2) Is the behavior to be eliminated sufficiently threatening to the individual or to society to justify the severity of the punishment?

Sometimes the answers to these questions lead to a decision to use punishment. For example, some of the most startling self-destructive behavior imaginable occurs in certain severely disturbed children. These children strike themselves repeatedly, bang their heads on the floor and on sharp objects, bite or tear pieces of flesh from their bodies, and engage in other forms of self-mutilation. They must often be kept under constant physical restraint (see Figure 6.16). It is also difficult to specify what is reinforcing such behavior, since the children continue the behavior despite the pain it produces. Extinction is therefore not a viable method for reducing these responses.

O. Ivar Lovaas of UCLA and his co-workers have been successful in using electric shock to eliminate se-

vere self-destructive behavior in such children (Carr and Lovaas, 1983). One 7-year-old boy had been self-injurious for 5 years. During one 90-minute period when his restraints were removed, he struck himself more than 3000 times. During treatment, the boy was wired with electrodes and given a strong electric shock each time he struck himself. Only 12 shocks over 4 treatment sessions were needed to virtually eliminate his self-destructive behavior. In another case, a severely disturbed girl with a 6-year history of banging her head against objects stopped after she received only 15 shocks (Lovaas, 1977). These short-term but effective treatment programs were carried out because no other measures had been successful in controlling the behavior, and only with the knowledge and consent of the parents of the children.

RESPONSE COST: PUNISHMENT THROUGH REMOVAL OF REINFORCERS

The legendary major league umpire Bill Klem once called a batter out on a close pitch. Enraged, the batter flung his bat high into the air and whirled around to argue the call. Klem tore off his mask, fixed the batter with a steely gaze, and said, "If that bat comes down, it'll cost you 100 bucks."

Fines, loss of privileges, and "groundings" are all examples of a second form of punishment that involves the removal of *noncontingent* reinforcers. That is, the reinforcers that are taken away are not those that maintain the behavior. (If they were, we would be dealing

FIGURE 6.16 *This disturbed child has to wear a helmet to prevent him from seriously injuring himself by banging his head against objects. In cases like this, suppression of the self-destructive behavior by response-contingent electric shocks has proven effective.*

with extinction.) This form of punishment, as we noted earlier, is called *response cost* (as in, "That'll cost you").

Punishment through deprivation has two distinct advantages over aversive punishment. First, even though response cost may arouse temporary frustration or anger, it does not create the kind of fear that aversive punishment does (Pazulinec and others, 1983). It is therefore less likely to cause avoidance of the punisher or the punishing situation, and it may actually increase the attractiveness of the withdrawn reinforcer (which can then be used to reinforce desired alternative behaviors). Second, the punisher is not modeling physical aggression, so that there is less opportunity for the learning of aggression through imitation.

It is important to emphasize to parents that when response cost is used to punish behavior, the withheld reinforcer should be some prized object or activity rather than love. When parents withhold love and reject misbehaving children, the effects on the child's self-concept can be damaging (Wylie, 1978). It is far better to deprive a child of some other prized reinforcer while continuing to communicate love and concern.

Figure 6.17 summarizes the types of response consequences we have discussed. These involve either the presentation or the removal of positive or aversive stimuli.

Timing of behavioral consequences

The timing as well as the schedule of consequences can have important effects on behavior. Other things being equal, consequences that occur immediately after a behavior have stronger effects than those that are delayed (Commons, Rachlin, and Nevin, 1984).

Some behaviors have both immediate and delayed consequences. Smoking, drinking, drug use, and criminal acts are all examples of behaviors that have immediate positive consequences and later negative ones: short-term "goods" and long-term "bads" (see Figure 6.18). Behaviors like these are difficult for many people to overcome because the immediate, positive reinforcement for the behavior overrides the negative consequences that occur later on.

In his discussion of what he termed the **neurotic paradox,** the psychologist O. H. Mowrer (1950) tried to explain why many people seem to be trapped in a web of maladaptive and self-defeating behavior. Mowrer suggested that the deviant behaviors are maintained because they produce immediate negative reinforcement, often in the form of anxiety reduction. For example, some people destroy their love relationships again and again because they unconsciously fear being

FIGURE 6.17 *This figure shows the five different response consequences resulting from the presentation or removal of positive or aversive stimuli.*

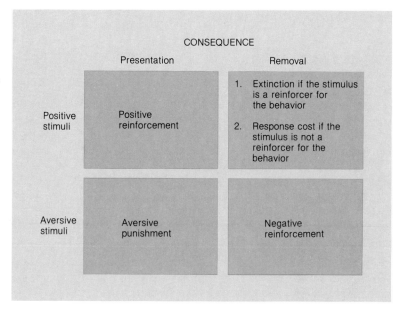

FIGURE 6.18 *Smoking is a behavior that is maintained in spite of long-term negative consequences because it has immediate positive consequences.*

you could be doing something even *more* intensely pleasurable?)

Human behavior seems to be less influenced by the timing of behavioral consequences than is animal behavior. One factor that makes a difference is our ability to imagine future events and thereby bring the distant consequences into the present. Many people are able to tolerate current unpleasantness by imagining pleasures that will result in the future. Likewise, imagining the long-term aversive outcomes of a behavior like taking drugs may override the effects of immediate positive reinforcement. Our cognitive abilities thus help to free us from the shackles of the reinforcement contingencies in our external environment.

The behavioral perspective emphasizes the power of the external environment to control our behavior, and there is no question that the ABC (antecedent–behavior–consequence) relationships exert considerable control over us. But this does not mean that we are at the mercy of our environment, for we can use our knowledge of these relationships in our own self-interest. Frontier 6.1 describes recent advances in developing a technology of behavioral self-control.

close to others and therefore vulnerable. Their need to reduce their anxiety right now can be more potent than their need to be loved today or to avoid being lonely tomorrow, even though the future negative consequences may have a much greater impact on the person's life. Social rejection, loss of important goals, loneliness, and even psychiatric hospitalization are the prices some people pay for immediate fear reduction.

Despite their greater potency, immediate consequences do not always govern our behavior. Many people strive for long-term goals in the face of short-term difficulties. To cite an example close to home, think of the many day-to-day frustrations that you experience as you work toward your college degree. (In fact, is it possible that right *now*, if you weren't reading this book,

THE COGNITIVE PERSPECTIVE ON LEARNING

Early behaviorists believed that learning involves the relatively automatic formation of bonds between stimuli and responses. Pavlov, for example, was convinced that the nervous system is built in such a way that the close pairing of a CS and a UCS automatically creates a bond between them. Radical behaviorists like Watson and Skinner have always opposed any attempt to explain learning that went beyond observable stimuli and responses.

Even in the early days of psychology, other theorists disagreed with the radical behaviorists and emphasized

BEHAVIORAL SELF-CONTROL: OPERANT PRINCIPLES IN THE SERVICE OF SELF

A highly significant development within the behavioral perspective has been an increased emphasis on the way people can use principles of learning to modify their own behavior (Kanfer, 1980; Watson and Tharp, 1981). Ideas like "will power" and "self-control" have been translated into the concept of *self-controlling behaviors.* The basic notion is that people can learn to operate as their own scientists and agents of change by using the principles of learning in their own behalf.

The flow chart in Figure 6.19 shows the basic steps for designing and carrying out a systematic self-control program. Throughout the program, the person collects data on antecedents, consequences, and the target behavior that he or she wants to change. To illustrate these procedures, we will show you how they might be used by a college student who wants to increase the amount and effectiveness of studying. Additional self-control procedures that are used to change emotional responses are described in Chapter 14.

SPECIFYING THE PROBLEM

The first step in a self-control program is to pinpoint the behaviors you want to change. This may be more challenging than it sounds. We tend to use abstract words like *lazy, unmotivated, hostile,* and *dependent* to describe our problems. These are fairly vague "trait" words that do not tell us much about the actual behaviors and the situations in which they occur. One of our students described her study problem by saying, "I'm just not motivated to study hard." With

a little help, she redefined her problem in behavioral terms as follows: "I don't spend enough time at my desk between the hours of 7 P.M. and 10 P.M. reading and outlining my textbook." This redefinition specified both the target behaviors and the situations (time and place) in which she wanted the changes to occur.

Many problems can be defined in terms of com-

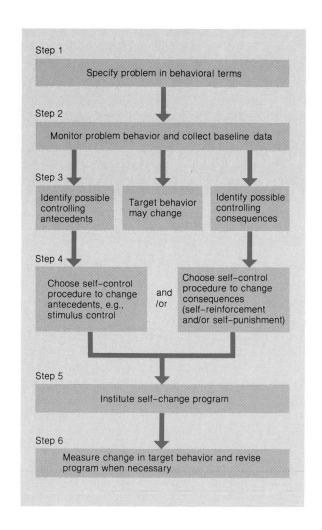

FIGURE 6.19 *This flow chart shows the basic steps and options in designing a self-control program that involves modifying the antecedents or consequences of behavior.*

peting behaviors—one desirable and the other undesirable (for example, studying vs. not studying; not smoking vs. smoking; being reasonably assertive vs. being overly submissive). A general rule is that whenever possible, self-change programs should be designed to increase the desirable alternative through positive reinforcement rather than to decrease the undesirable alternative through the use of punishment. As we pointed out earlier, punishment makes situations aversive, and simply decreasing some undesirable behavior does not guarantee that a desirable one will appear in its place. Thus it is far better to reinforce yourself for studying than to punish yourself for not studying.

FIGURE 6.20 *One student in a self-control program graphed both the amount of time he spent in the study situation and the amount of time he spent actually studying (that is, reading, outlining, and memorizing). He measured actual study time with a stopwatch.*

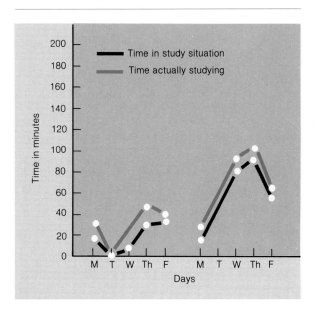

COLLECTING BASELINE DATA

The next step in the program is to collect initial *baseline* data on your behavior. Accurate baseline data provide valuable information about how frequently and in which specific situations the target behavior occurs. Unless you have good baseline data, you will have no way of measuring change once you begin your program. Moreover, during the baseline period, people often discover some key information about the antecedents and consequences of the target behavior that are useful in planning the self-modification program.

The most effective way to examine and detect behavioral changes is by plotting data on a graph, as is done in laboratory and clinical studies. The behavioral data collected by one of our students over a two-week period are shown in Figure 6.20. Notice that he has graphed both the amount of time spent in the study situation and the amount of time spent in actual study (defined by him as reading and taking notes). To do this, he used a stopwatch that he ran only when he was actually studying. He found that a week of baseline data was enough to give him a good idea of how much time he was actually studying (and how much time he was wasting). In the second week, he began his change program. In cases where behavior varies greatly, it is necessary to collect baseline data over a longer period.

IDENTIFYING ANTECEDENTS AND CONSEQUENCES

Careful observation of your behavior and the situations in which it occurs should help you to identify conditions that are affecting the behavior. You should take careful note of situational factors that seem to trigger an undesirable target behavior or to interfere with a desirable one. You also need to focus on the consequences of the behavior. These include both

BEHAVIORAL SELF-CONTROL: OPERANT PRINCIPLES IN THE SERVICE OF SELF

external consequences, such as compliments from others, and internal consequences, such as anxiety reduction or feelings of satisfaction. Once you have identified controlling antecedents and consequences, you are ready to apply your self-controlling behaviors. These behaviors may be attempts to alter antecedents, to rearrange consequences, or both.

CONTROLLING THE ANTECEDENTS

We constantly respond to stimuli in our environment, and many of our behaviors eventually come under stimulus control. Undesirable behaviors tend to occur within a specific range of situations. Students who have difficulty studying often find that certain stimuli, such as a television set or the presence of friends, trigger behaviors that are incompatible with studying. If behavior is under this kind of stimulus control, then it should be possible for a person to change target behaviors by changing the stimulus environment.

Stimulus control techniques can be used very effectively to help increase studying. Select a particular place in which you do *nothing* else but study. If you find your attention wandering or need to do something else, get up immediately and leave the study area. Your objective is to condition yourself to study in response to the stimuli present in the study area. In time you will find that the study area is a powerful stimulus for studying. B. F. Skinner himself used this technique throughout his career. He did all his writing at a particular desk and did nothing else there (Skinner, 1983).

ALTERING RESPONSE CONSEQUENCES

Although antecedent conditions stimulate and guide our behavior, their consequences determine whether we will repeat them. Fortunately, we have the power to arrange many of our own consequences, and this provides us with an effective way to control our own behavior.

Self-administered positive reinforcement is one of the most effective self-modification procedures, and it should be the cornerstone of most programs. You need to find an effective reinforcer that you can control and then arrange to make it available to yourself only if you engage in the desired behavior.

Virtually any object or activity can serve as a reinforcer if it is something that you enjoy having or doing and if you have complete control over it. Some people employ the *Premack principle* (Premack, 1965), which states that a behavior that frequently occurs may be used to reinforce one that occurs less frequently. Thus you can identify something that you do frequently (for example, jogging) and make this behavior contingent on studying.

Another procedure that can be effective is to place yourself on a token or point system, in which tokens or certain numbers of points can later be converted into various reinforcers. There are several advantages to

TABLE 6.1 A "TOKEN ECONOMY" IN WHICH SPECIFIED POINT TOTALS EARN REINFORCERS THAT DIFFER IN NATURE AND VALUE.

REINFORCERS	POINTS NEEDED
15 minutes of TV	1
One Coke	2
Taking an afternoon nap	4
Going bowling	5
Reading *Playgirl* magazine	3
One beer	3
Going to a movie	6
Eating at my favorite restaurant	10
Doing anything I want to, all day	15

this. First, you can reinforce a desired behavior immediately after it occurs with a token (for example, a poker chip) or a point recorded on a counter or card, and we know that immediate reinforcement is more effective than delayed reinforcement. In addition, tokens or points can be linked to a great variety of other reinforcers. This prevents people from getting tired of a particular reinforcer and allows them to work for reinforcers that vary in value. One woman created the "token economy" shown in Table 6.1 for use in her self-modification program.

Once you have selected reinforcers, you must decide how to use them to change the target behavior. It helps to draw up a contract with yourself. The contract should specify in detail the reinforcement contingencies for each step of your plan. It should state precisely how often or how long you must or must not perform the target behavior, and the kinds and numbers of reinforcements you will receive for specific achievements. Make your contract as clear, detailed, and loophole-free as possible, and then sign it. You may decide to change the terms of the contract during the program, but you should always be operating under a specific contract.

THE USE OF SHAPING

As we saw when we discussed the training of animals, the most effective way to build new behaviors is by *shaping*, or rewarding successive approximations. Shaping starts with the behaviors the person is already able to perform and proceeds from there by reinforcing behavior that resembles the desired final product more and more closely.

If you collect good baseline data, you will know the current level of performance of your target behavior. Shaping requires that you begin at this level or *slightly* beyond it and begin to move *slowly* toward your goal, reinforcing yourself at each step. Start with a small change and make the steps small. If you have trouble, reduce the size of your steps. Through experimentation, you will discover the correct pace for yourself. It is far better to move forward slowly than to rush yourself and become discouraged by the failures that result. Impatience is probably the greatest threat to completion of self-modification projects (Watson and Tharp, 1981).

Shaping should almost always be used to increase studying. Don't let your initial steps be influenced by how much you think you *should* be studying. In your project, start slightly (10 to 15 minutes) above your current daily level and reinforce yourself when you succeed. Successive increases should not exceed 10 to 15 minutes unless you find that you can succeed easily with larger ones. Remember, your self-modification program should not be a test of your pain tolerance. The goal is to bring about gradual change while you enjoy plenty of honest reinforcers and the satisfaction that you are increasing your degree of self-mastery. The way in which you arrange the reinforcement contingencies is the most critical determinant of whether you will achieve your goal.

Few things of value come easily. Most people experience occasional setbacks or reach plateaus where progress seems to stop. When this happens, it is not a sign that the person is a hopeless weakling but that changes need to be made in the arrangement of antecedents, the contingencies, the shaping procedure, or perhaps all of these. Patience and resourcefulness are called for rather than discouragement and despair.

Behavioral self-control procedures have proven to be effective ways of helping people gain greater control of their lives (Kanfer, 1980). The development and testing of methods designed to increase behavioral self-control are attracting the attention of a growing number of psychologists, promising to give a new dimension to the phrase "Power to the people."

the role of cognition. The Gestalt psychologists argued that learning involves the perception of relationships among events. They cited experiments on insight learning in both animals (see Chapter 1, page 17) and humans to support their view (Kohler, 1925).

The most influential of the early cognitive learning theorists was Edward Tolman of the University of California. The basis of learning, argued Tolman, is the development of an **expectancy,** a cognitive representation of "what leads to what." In other words, stimuli serve as *signs* that certain events will follow. From this point of view, reinforcement does not "stamp in" behavior automatically; it provides *information* that a particular consequence will follow from a particular response.

In a famous series of experiments on what he called **latent learning,** Tolman and his associates demonstrated that learning can occur without reinforcement. In one experiment, three groups of rats were run in a complex maze. One group was run under normal conditions, with food always available at the end of the maze. A second group never received any food. The critical third group had no food at the end of the maze

for the first 10 days, but on the eleventh day food was introduced. The result, as shown in Figure 6.21, was striking. As soon as food was introduced, the performance of the third group became as good as that of the group that had been reinforced all along (Tolman and Honzik, 1930). Tolman concluded that these animals must have learned a *cognitive map* of the maze during the first 10 days. This learning, however, remained latent, or hidden, until there was a good reason to get to the end of the maze, at which time the learning was manifested in performance.

Cognition in classical conditioning

Cognitive learning theorists believe that the basis of classical conditioning is the learning of an expectancy that the CS will be followed by the UCS (Bolles, 1979). The expectancy model predicts that the most important factor in classical conditioning is not *how often* the CS and the UCS are paired but *how predictably* the UCS follows the CS. If two groups of animals are given ex-

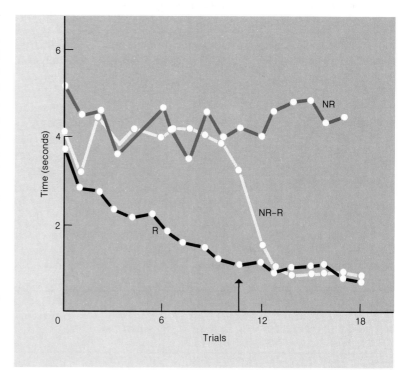

FIGURE 6.21 *Maze-running performance in an experiment that demonstrated latent learning. The rats had one trial on each of 18 consecutive days. Group NR received no reinforcement in the maze at any time. Group R received reward on all trials when members reached the end of the maze. The critical group (NR-R) had food reward introduced on the eleventh day. Their dramatic performance increase indicated that they had learned the maze prior to the introduction of reinforcement (Tolman and Honzik, 1930).*

actly the same number of CS–UCS pairings but the second group receives additional presentations of the UCS in the absence of the CS, the first group will show much stronger classical conditioning (Rescorla and Holland, 1982). Apparently, the extra UCS presentations decrease CS predictability and thus weaken the conditioning.

Support for the cognitive interpretation of classical conditioning also comes from a phenomenon known as **blocking.** In a typical blocking experiment, subjects are exposed to repeated pairings of a light and an electric shock (UCS) until the light alone elicits a fear response. Then a second stimulus, such as a tone, is added so that both the light (the CS) and the tone occur together before the shock. We would expect that the tone will also become a CS, since it too is being regularly paired with the shock.

But that's not what happens. If the tone is later presented alone, it does not evoke the fear response. It has somehow been "blocked" from becoming a CS because of the previous conditioning involving the light. Pavlovian theory has a hard time explaining this finding, but the cognitive expectancy theory can explain it. Since the light already predicts the occurrence of the shock, the new tone stimulus is irrelevant because it provides no new information. Since the new stimulus does not enhance predictability, it fails to become a CS (Rescorla and others, 1985).

These experiments challenge the traditional behavioral view that classical conditioning is a mechanistic process dependent solely on the association of the CS with the UCS. It may be that even in animals, cognitive processes play a key role.

Cognition and operant conditioning

The story is told of a demonstration of operant conditioning that once occurred in an introductory psychology class. The instructor sent one of the students out of the room for a few minutes and instructed another student in how to shape the response of flicking the light switch on and off, using M & M's as the reinforcer. When the naive student returned, he was reinforced first for looking at the wall that held the light switch, then for approaching the wall, and so on, until 25

minutes later, he was happily flicking the switch and chomping one M & M after another.

At this point, another student asked if she could serve as experimenter. A new subject left the room for a moment while the class decided that he should be shaped to erase the blackboard. When the student re-entered the classroom, the new experimenter quickly said, "John, if you'll erase the blackboard immediately, I'll give you this whole bag of M & M's." This time it took all of 25 seconds to get the desired operant behavior.

As this ancedote shows, there's more than one way to establish an operant response. The cognitive perspective stresses that awareness—knowing the relationships between responses and their probable consequences—is important if not essential in operant conditioning (see Figure 6.22). Awareness, however, is

FIGURE 6.22 *According to the cognitive perspective, operant conditioning involves learning expectancies about "what leads to what."*

"What it comes down to is you have to find out what reaction they're looking for, and you give them that reaction."

(© SIDNEY HARRIS.)

not easy to establish scientifically. For one thing, animals are notoriously reluctant to tell us what they know. Studies with humans are not foolproof, either. Even if subjects are able to verbalize the relationship, it is impossible to determine exactly *when* they became aware and whether or not any learning had occurred prior to awareness. Nevertheless, the weight of evidence indicates that, at least in humans, awareness is very important.

Consider, for example, a **verbal conditioning** experiment by Charles Spielberger and L. D. DeNike (1966). The subjects were reinforced by the experimenter with positive comments such as "Mmm-hmm" and "good" whenever they used a certain kind of word in sentences they made up. In this case, the desired response was the use of nouns having a human reference, such as *arm*. Subjects in a control group did not receive this reinforcement. The change in the number of times subjects included such words in their sentences was measured. In addition, subjects were frequently asked questions to determine whether they were aware of the reinforcement contingency.

The results of the experiment are shown in Figure 6.23. Part (a) shows that the subjects who were aware of

the reinforcement contingency showed a large increase in their use of human nouns, while unaware and control subjects displayed virtually no change. Part (b) shows the impact of awareness. There was a rapid increase in responsiveness at the point where subjects said they became aware of the relationship between what they were saying and the experimenter's positive comments.

It is important to note that, from the cognitive perspective, the best predictor of a person's behavior is the *perceived* contingency, not the actual one (see Figure 6.24). In many instances, the two are identical, but that's not always the case. Sometimes people perceive contingencies that do not actually exist. A good example of this occurs in superstitious behavior, when a person thinks that good luck or bad luck will follow from performing or not performing the superstitious act. We have also described the potent effects that placebos can have when people believe that they will be helped by them. A final example of a misperceived contingency is seen in this anecdote:

A psychologist reported that a frustrated mother once contacted him for assistance in the reduction of swearing behavior on the part of her two young sons. A behavior

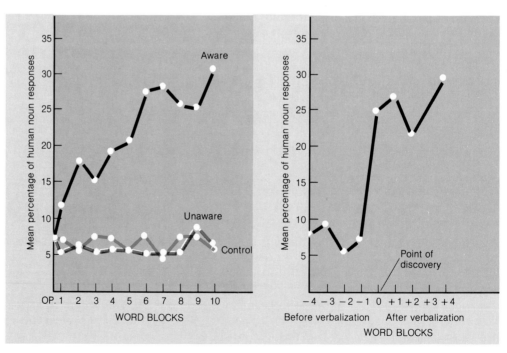

FIGURE 6.23

Awareness has a measurable effect on verbal conditioning. Part (a) shows the percentages of desired responses given by aware subjects, unaware subjects, and a control group. Part (b) shows level of performance before and after the subjects were able to verbalize the reinforcement contingency.

(a)

(b)

"Boy, have I got this guy conditioned! Every time I press the bar down, he drops in a piece of food."

(COLUMBIA JESTER (1951): H. MAZZEO '52/P. GARDNER '52.)

FIGURE 6.24 *The cognitive perspective on operant conditioning holds that the behavior of both people and animals is governed by perceived relationships between behaviors and their consequences, whether or not they are accurate.*

therapist, the psychologist recommended that she use punishment techniques. He told her that it was important to use immediate and severe punishment each and every time the swearing occurred. To maximize the impact of the punishment, he also recommended that she try to use each child as an example for the other—that is, punish him in front of his brother.

Enthusiastic over this advice, the mother returned home. At breakfast the next morning, she sat down ready and raring to modify behavior. The older son opened the conversation by requesting that she "pass the goddam Cheerios." With lightning fury, the mother lunged across the table and hit her son—sent both him and his chair sprawling to the floor. Pleased with her skillful execution of behavioral principles, the mother turned to her somewhat bewildered younger son. "Well, what will you have?" He paused a moment, glanced at his supine brother, and answered, "You can bet your sweet ass it isn't Cheerios!" (Mahoney, 1980, pp. 136–137)

The power of expectancies: Learned helplessness and learned mastery

Once learning experiences result in the development of expectancies, these expectancies may generalize beyond the specific situations and influence behavior in other settings as well. Personality traits like self-confidence, optimism, and pessimism can be viewed as **generalized expectancies.**

Research on **learned helplessness** indicates the way in which self-defeating expectancies can be acquired and can affect subsequent behavior. In studies by Martin Seligman (1975) and his associates, dogs were given a series of electric shocks while they were strapped in a harness and unable to escape or avoid it. Another group of dogs, the control group, did not receive this "helplessness training." The next day, the dogs were individually placed in a shuttlebox so that their avoidance learning could be studied. The animals had to learn to respond to a warning signal by jumping over a low barrier to the other side of the shuttlebox within 10 seconds. If they did not, they received 50 seconds of painful electric shock.

The animals in the control group learned the avoidance behavior very quickly. But such was not the case for the previously helpless animals. About two-thirds of them seemed unable to learn the avoidance behavior at all. They seemed passively resigned to suffering, and even if they successfully avoided the shock on one trial, they were unlikely to do so on the next. Some dogs had to be forcibly pushed over the barrier by the experimenter over 200 times before their "learned helplessness" wore off. Apparently, exposure to the inescapable electric shock on the first day taught the dogs that they had no control over what happened to them, and this lesson carried over to the shuttlebox avoidance situation. These learned helplessness effects are strongest when the original inescapable shock occurs in a highly unpredictable manner (Overmier and Wielkiewicz, 1983).

Learned helplessness effects have been shown in humans as well as in animals (Miller and Norman, 1979). When human subjects receive a series of electric shocks that they cannot control, their subsequent avoidance learning, like that of Seligman's dogs, is sometimes impaired, at least temporarily. Likewise, many children who have early failures in school and who attribute those experiences to their own inadequacies develop a kind of learned helplessness, an academic "give-up-itis" (Johnson, 1981).

Seligman suggests that learned helplessness acquired by an animal or a human (1) reduces the motivation to try to control outcomes, (2) interferes with the ability to learn that one's own behavior controls the outcome, and (3) produces fear and depression (Seligman, 1975). Thus the inescapable effects of poverty, deprivation, and other aversive situations may teach people that they are helpless to control their environment.

Recently, by creating a learning situation that is the opposite of the learned helplessness procedure, Seligman and his co-workers have shown that **learned mastery** can be established in animals (Volpicelli and others, 1983). In their initial training, rats learned to press a lever to successfully escape shock. When these animals were later placed into a shuttlebox in which they could *not* avoid shock, they continued trying the escape response for hundreds of trials. In sharp contrast to the apathy shown by animals suffering from learned helplessness, they displayed not only great persistence but also an increased ability to learn new responses that permitted them to escape shock.

These findings raise the intriguing possibility that learned helplessness might be reversed through mastery training. Children with a history of school failure have been helped by placing them in training situations where they can have mastery experiences. These studies have also shown, however, that simply enjoying success is not enough to reverse the children's helplessness. The key factor is their recognition that what *they do* is the determining factor in their successes (Fowler and Peterson, 1981).

Internal self-evaluations as rewards and punishment

For more than a decade, a middle-aged man referred to by students as Holy Hubert has been a regular visitor to the University of Washington campus. His fire-and-brimstone exhortations to repent and avoid damnation, delivered on the steps of the Student Union, evoke reactions ranging from amused smiles to loud insults and ridicule (see Figure 6.25). One could hardly imagine less positive consequences for an evangelist.

One day, one of your authors approached Hubert as he was cleaning the remnants of a tomato off his clothes. Why, he was asked, did he continue to preach when the response of students was so negative? He answered, "I don't care what they say. When I know I'm doing the Lord's work, I feel so good that they could hang me for all I care."

Hubert shows us that external reinforcement and

FIGURE 6.25 *The persistence of "Holy Hubert" (left) in evangelizing can scarcely be attributed to external consequences like this.*

punishment are not the only things that control behavior. If they were, how could we account for the behavior of a prisoner of war who chooses to die rather than cooperate with the enemy, or a person who resists temptation when there is no chance of discovery and punishment? All of us have at times felt proud of ourselves for doing something, even if others did not approve, and we have all disapproved of, berated, or devalued ourselves for failing to live up to our standards at other times. Psychologists have begun to pay more attention to internally administered reinforcements and punishment, or **self-evaluative processes.**

These internal processes are learned in a number of ways. Significant adults, such as parents, set standards for our behavior, approve of and reward us when we meet their standards, and disapprove of or punish us when we don't. Eventually, we ourselves may adopt these standards. For example, children whose parents reward them only when they perform at a superior level are likely to regard average achievement as inadequate and to disapprove of themselves unless they meet or exceed the high standards they have been taught (Mischel, 1981).

We also establish standards for self-reinforcement by observing others. People tend to adopt the standards that they see in others, particularly in novel situations in which they are unsure of what constitutes acceptable performance. When one of our children began playing baseball, it wasn't long before he wanted to know what's considered a good batting average. He found it hard to believe that major leaguers strive for an average (.300) that entails making 7 outs in every 10 times at bat, but he finally conceded that if it was good enough for them, he too might be satisfied with it.

Once standards of self-reinforcement have been adopted, a given behavior can have two consequences: an external consequence and a self-evaluative response. In some instances, the two may conflict with one another and the self-reinforcement system may override the external consequences. This is one way in which people achieve some degree of freedom from the constraints of the external environment.

Self-evaluative responses related to personality and behavior disorders are currently receiving much attention. For example, what we call self-esteem seems to involve self-evaluative processes. In one study, college students were asked to monitor and record their

thoughts about themselves over an eight-day period. Subjects who scored high on a psychological test of self-esteem engaged in a high proportion of positive self-evaluative responses. Conversely, low self-esteem subjects reported many more negative self-evaluations (Vasta and Brockner, 1979). Depressed psychiatric patients show a similar tendency to make a great many negative self-evaluations, even when they succeed in something (Missel and Sommer, 1983). College students who are low in self-reinforcement tendencies also tend to report more depressive episodes during periods in which unpleasant events are occurring in their lives, or when they are not receiving adequate levels of external reinforcement (Heiby, 1983).

Sometimes unrealistic standards for self-reinforcement result in maladjustment and unhappiness. Some people experience a great deal of distress because they have lofty standards that they can rarely meet. As a result, they suffer from depression, feelings of worthlessness, and self-devaluation. Helping such people relax their standards can result in feelings of increased self-worth and a reduction in depression (Rush and others, 1977).

Observational learning (modeling)

As we have seen repeatedly, we learn a great deal by observing others. Observational learning often saves us time and effort. By imitating those behaviors that produce positive outcomes for others and avoiding those that do not, we can bypass the potentially dangerous process of learning through trial and error. The process of learning by imitating is called **modeling.**

When we observe models, we receive information not only on how to behave but on what the consequences are likely to be. Observation alone is enough to learn the behavior, but future performance depends on the consequences that we have observed or have come to expect. Presumably, the would-be hijacker described at the beginning of the chapter learned not only how D. B. Cooper carried out his act but also that Cooper escaped from the plane with the ransom money.

The difference between observational learning and performance was demonstrated in an experiment by Albert Bandura (1965). Children watched a film in which a model engaged in a series of specific aggressive acts. One group of children saw the model rewarded with praise and candy, a second group saw the model reprimanded for aggression, and a third group saw no consequences for the model. After the film, the children were carefully observed to see how many of the aggressive responses they reproduced.

Those children who had seen the model punished performed fewer imitative responses than did those who had seen the model rewarded and those who had seen no consequences (see Figure 6.26). But did this mean that they had not learned the aggressive responses? To find out, the experimenter offered the children attractive incentives if they could do what the model had done. All of the children quickly reproduced the model's aggressive responses.

Emotional responses can also be learned through modeling. Children often acquire fears by observing fear responses of parents or other adults. In fact, it may be that more of our fears arise in this way than through direct classical conditioning—that is, our own experiencing of CS–UCS pairings. Laboratory studies have shown that classically conditioned emotional responses can be learned just by observing what happens to another person.

FIGURE 6.26 *The learning and performance of modeled aggressive responses. Children who saw an aggressive model punished spontaneously reproduced fewer of the aggressive behaviors than did subjects who saw the model rewarded or saw no consequences. However, when the children were later offered incentives for reproducing the behaviors, both the boys and the girls showed that they had clearly learned the behaviors (Bandura, 1965).*

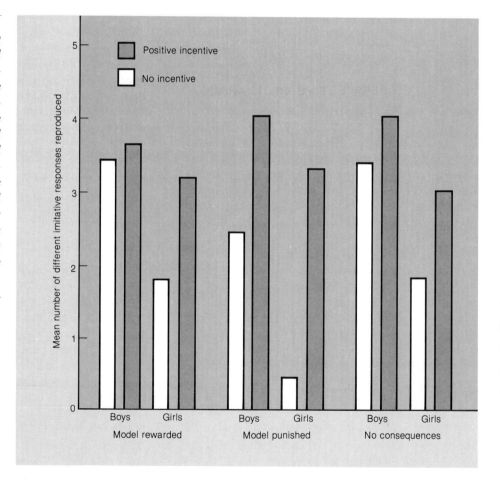

In a typical **vicarious classical conditioning** experiment, the subject observes another person (actually an accomplice of the experimenter) exhibit a pain response to a simulated electric shock. A neutral stimulus, such as a tone, occurs shortly before the "shock." Later, the observer is presented with the tone alone while his or her physiological responses are measured. Typically, an increase in arousal is observed in response to the tone, even though the subject has never personally experienced the shock (Berger, 1962).

Cognitive processes may be involved, to varying degrees, in virtually all forms of learning. They are clearly involved in complex tasks that require the learning of concepts and relationships among facts, as you are doing right now. Many learning theorists would argue that more primitive cognitive processes are also at work when a white rat learns a maze or a dog is classically conditioned.

THE BIOLOGICAL PERSPECTIVE ON LEARNING

The changes in behavior that occur as the result of experience surely reflect underlying changes in the nervous system. What is the nature of these changes? Where and how do they occur? Does the structure of the nervous system, forged in part by evolutionary factors, place limits on what can be learned? Can the biological processes involved in learning be influenced in ways that will enhance learning capacity? For more than a hundred years, psychologists have searched for answers to these questions.

Biological constraints on learning

It has always been obvious that biological factors place limits on the complexity of behaviors that various species can learn. Not even the most radical behaviorist of the 1920s ever suggested that the white rat could be conditioned to solve complex mathematical problems. But it was always assumed that the basic principles of classical and operant conditioning could be used to

condition any behavior that the organism was physically capable of performing. Recent years have witnessed one challenge after another to that basic assumption. Let us examine some of these challenges and their implications.

THE MISBEHAVIOR OF ANIMALS

Keller and Marian Breland had a farm where they trained animals for circuses, advertising agencies, and the movies. They used well-established operant techniques like shaping and the chaining of behaviors into complex sequences. These operant techniques were usually successful, but not always. Sometimes the animals simply refused to behave according to the laws of learning.

On one occasion, the Brelands tried to train a chicken to play baseball. The game was arranged so that a small ball would roll toward home plate and the chicken would pull a chain to swing a small metal bat. If the ball was hit, a bell would ring and the chicken would run to first base to get its food. To the Brelands, this was no real challenge; it seemed as easy as training the San Diego Chicken. The chicken was soon pulling the chain to swing the bat, and then running to first base when it heard the bell.

But when the ball was introduced into the game, utter chaos occurred. Whenever the chicken hit the ball, instead of running to first base to collect its food reinforcement, it would attempt to field the ball, pecking furiously at it, flapping its wings, and chasing the ball all around the diamond. Try as they might, the Brelands could not stop these behaviors. End of training and end of the chicken's baseball career. In this and other instances, animals simply refused to "shape up." But why?

PECULIARITIES IN AVOIDANCE LEARNING

While the Brelands were pondering some of their failures, other unexpected findings were being reported in avoidance learning experiments. As we noted earlier, avoidance learning can occur very rapidly in animals. Sometimes only one trial is necessary. It makes sense that animals should be highly motivated to avoid painful stimuli like electric shock. We might therefore assume that they would quickly learn any avoidance behavior that they are physically able to perform.

Not so. In some situations, avoidance learning is barely possible and sometimes impossible. For example, the average rat will learn very quickly to avoid shock in a shuttlebox. It will also quickly learn to press a bar to get food. But it will *not* learn to press a bar to avoid shock. Likewise, birds can be quickly trained to fly from one perch to another to avoid shock and will readily peck a disc to get food. But it is almost impossible to train pigeons to peck a disc in order to avoid shock (Bolles, 1980). These findings raised still more questions.

CONDITIONED AVERSIONS

Some years ago, psychologist John Garcia discovered that animals quickly learned to avoid eating food that had been contaminated with a tasteless substance (lithium chloride) that made them violently ill (Garcia and others, 1970). The *conditioned aversion* took place after only one experience, even though the sickness (the UCS) did not occur until several hours after they had eaten the food (the CS). Before Garcia's studies, a CS–UCS interval of this length was virtually unknown in animal research. Moreover, the conditioning was restricted to the taste of the specific food that made them sick; it did not generalize to similar foods with different tastes.

Another important finding that emerged from research on the *Garcia effect* was that there are definite biological limitations on the ability of animals to develop an aversion of this kind (Braveman and Bronstein, 1985). Almost all species that have been tested develop aversions much more easily to new foods and liquids than to familiar ones. For example, it is virtually impossible to turn a pigeon off to water, even if other liquids are available to drink.

The differences in conditioned aversions in various species are even more striking. Rats quickly develop aversions to new tastes but not to new odors. For other species, however, taste aversions are hard to establish even if the animal is made very ill. Quail, for example,

develop aversions on the basis of the visual characteristics of the food rather than its taste, even though they have an acute sense of taste (Wilcoxon and others, 1971). Again, we are faced with the question of what these findings mean in terms of the biological bases for learning.

THE CONCEPT OF PREPAREDNESS

All these findings—the misbehavior of the Brelands' animals and the species differences in avoidance learning and conditioned aversions—indicate that there are biological limits on learning that go beyond the animals' physical capabilities. In every instance, the artificial learning conditions established by the experimenters were apparently overridden by innate factors specific to that species.

For example, the Brelands found to their dismay that once a particular stimulus came to represent food, the animals began to act as if it *were* food. The chicken pecked at the "baseball" as if it were something to eat. Raccoons insisted on washing tokens that were intended to act as secondary reinforcers. These responses are so deeply rooted in the animals' evolutionary histories that they simply took over under relevant conditions (see Figure 6.27).

The same seems true in avoidance learning. Over the course of evolutionary history, certain behaviors have been instrumental to the survival of each species. The rat responds to danger by freezing or running away. Thus, we should not be surprised that it will quickly learn the shuttlebox response of running, but not a bar press, in order to avoid shock. Birds, on the other hand, fly away when in danger; they don't peck. Pecking is for getting food, not for avoiding danger.

Finally, we come to the species differences found in learned food aversions. Here again, the evolutionary history of the animal must be important. The rat is a forager that eats many different kinds of food. If it is to survive, it must have a learning mechanism that protects it from poisonous foods. The rat thus has an innate readiness to learn which tastes are dangerous. Visual and odor cues are far less important to its survival than taste is.

The bottom line is that we have to consider the evolutionary history of the organism as well as its learning history (Bolles, 1980). Martin Seligman (1970) has captured this general idea in his concept of **preparedness.** By this he means that animals are biologically prepared to learn actions that are related to their survival as a species. These prepared behaviors are learned with very little training. On the other hand, the animals are *contraprepared* to learn behaviors that are contrary to their natural tendencies, and so such behaviors are learned very slowly, if at all. Seligman argues that most of the behaviors that have been studied in the learning psychologist's laboratory, such as bar pressing or disc pecking, fall somewhere in between these two classes of behaviors. That is why learning in the laboratory has always looked like a gradual process of establishing stimulus–response connections and why the findings that we have just discussed surprised many learning psychologists.

Is the concept of preparedness relevant only to lower animals like rats, chickens, and pigeons? Are humans, because of our greater flexibility, immune from the concept of preparedness? Perhaps not, as we shall now see.

Preparedness in humans   Earlier we described how little Albert was classically conditioned to fear a white rat. Less widely known is a study by Marian Bregman (1934), who tried to repeat the Watson and Rayner

demonstration. Like them, she was able to condition fear in children when she used an animal as the CS. But when she used inanimate objects like blocks, a bottle, or a wooden animal as the CS, fear conditioning did not take place. It was almost as if the children were prepared to learn to fear some things but not others.

Even more striking evidence of selective conditioning of fear in humans comes from experimental studies in which various kinds of stimuli were paired with electric shock (Ohman and others, 1975; Hygge and Ohman, 1978). In these experiments, people who received shocks each time pictures of snakes or spiders were projected on a screen quickly acquired conditioned emotional responses to these stimuli. But subjects who received shocks while looking at slides of flowers, houses, or berries showed little or no fear conditioning. It thus appears that humans are prepared to acquire fears to some stimuli but not to others. The clinical literature indicates that human phobias tend to fall into certain narrow classes, most of which pertain

FIGURE 6.27   *As the Brelands found, innate behavior patterns may come to the fore once a particular stimulus comes to represent a primary reinforcer. The pigeon on the left is pecking the disc for food. Note how the beak is in eating position. On the right, water is the reinforcer, and the beak position resembles that of drinking. (Jenkins and Moore, 1973).*

THE SEARCH FOR THE BIOLOGICAL BASIS OF LEARNING

The physiological basis for learning and memory has proved to be one of the most baffling mysteries in science. For more than 100 years, psychologists, physiologists, and biochemists have been trying to discover where and how memories are formed in the nervous system. Three major approaches that have been used to discover links between biological and behavioral processes are illustrated in Figure 6.28.

The first approach involves some sort of biological intervention and the measurement of its effects on behavior. For example, a particular region of the brain might be destroyed or electrically stimulated so that effects on learning and memory can be studied. Investigations of this type have shown that some very sim-

FIGURE 6.28 *Three approaches have been taken in the search for the biological bases of learning and memory. Biological interventions can be performed and the effects on behavior studied (1). Conversely, the effects of behavioral interventions on biological variables can be studied (2). The correlational approach (3) studies relationships between biological and behavioral measures, as when differences in neurotransmitter concentrations are related to differences in learning capacity. (Adapted from Rosenzweig, 1984.)*

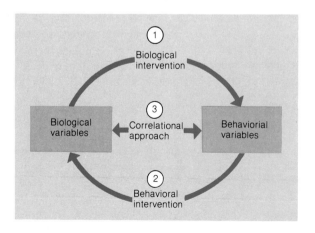

ple forms of reflex learning can occur at the level of the spinal cord alone, while other types of learning depend on specific brain structures (Thompson and others, 1983).

The second approach involves performing some sort of behavioral intervention and studying its effects on the nervous system. For example, we now know that exposing young animals to "enriched" environments with many opportunities to learn new behaviors results in increases in brain weight, in neurotransmitter substances, and in the number and sizes of synaptic contact areas (Rosenzweig, 1984). These effects also occur in older animals to a lesser extent. The use of new techniques such as the tracking of radioactive deoxyglucose with the PET scan (see Chapter 3, page 102) has made it possible to identify the neural circuitry involved in the sensory, motor, and integrative activity of the nervous system during learning. Recently, Louis Sokoloff and his colleagues at the National Institute of Mental Health used this procedure to map metabolic processes in the brain while animals were being reinforced with electrical stimulation of a "reward center" in the brain (Porrino and others, 1984).

The third research technique illustrated in Figure 6.28 is the correlational approach, in which the relationship between a biological variable and a behavioral one is studied. For example, relationships have been shown between concentrations of certain neurotransmitters in the brain and learning ability (Rosenzweig, 1984).

One of the most exciting areas of current research involves the effects of learning on structural and biochemical changes in neurons. Since the brain interacts with the environment through axon firings and synapses, the biological basis for learning must involve changes at the level of the neuron. Many years ago, physiological psychologist Donald O. Hebb (1949) theorized that learning involves the formation of new electrical "circuits" in the brain. We are now approaching an understanding of how this might occur. Recent studies of individual neurons have shown that when a neuron is stimulated briefly with a burst of impulses from another neuron, it becomes more sensitive to subsequent stimulation. Because this increased sensitivity lasts for a week or more, it is called *long-term potentiation* (LTP). LTP has attracted much attention because it has the characteristics that would be needed by a cellular learning mechanism: (1) it is triggered by brief physiological events; (2) it is strengthened by repetition; (3) it produces changes in the operating characteristics of neural circuits; and (4) it lasts for a relatively long period. Moreover, LTP is correlated with the speed of learning in animals (Berger, 1984).

Gary Lynch and Michael Baudry (1984) pieced together what is known about the biochemistry of LTP into an intriguing hypothesis concerning the cellular basis of learning. They presented evidence that brief bursts of electrochemical activity at the synapse activate a membrane-associated enzyme called *calpain* in the dendrite of the receiving neuron. This enzyme breaks up a localized portion of a protein layer in the cell membrane, exposing neurotransmitter receptors that have been previously covered over. The calpain-produced increase in the number of available receptors results in the greater sensitivity to subsequent stimulation observed in LTP. In support of their hypothesis, Lynch and Baudry found that injections of a drug that is known to inhibit the action of calpain produced serious impairments of maze recall and avoidance learning in rats.

Whether or not Lynch and Baudry have truly isolated the cellular basis of learning, it is clear that researchers are closing in on answers to the questions of where and how learning is represented in the nervous system. Knowledge of the underlying processes could have important implications for reversing learning disabilities and enhancing learning capacity.

to animals and dangerous places. Snakes are the most common type of phobia, and fears of spiders, the dark, high places, and closed-in spaces are also fairly common. Interestingly, in many phobias, no evidence can be found for previous classical conditioning of fear. The fact that few people develop phobias of common objects such as doorknobs, ashtrays, or zippers also suggests that phobic responses may be prepared behaviors. Perhaps we're still afraid of the things that scared *Homo erectus* and our Neanderthal ancestors.

STUDY OUTLINE

WHAT IS LEARNING? (p. 197)

Learning is a change in behavior or in potential behavior that occurs as a result of experience. Learning is inferred from a change in performance. The three major types of learning are classical conditioning, operant or instrumental conditioning, and observational learning, or modeling.

CLASSICAL CONDITIONING: LEARNING THROUGH ASSOCIATION (p. 197)

1. Classical conditioning involves the pairing of an unconditioned stimulus (UCS) with a previously neutral stimulus (CS). The CS alone eventually evokes a conditioned response (CR) similar to the unconditioned response (UCR) previously evoked by the UCS.

2. The acquisition phase of classical conditioning involves the pairing of the CS with the UCS. Extinction, the disappearance of the CR, occurs when the CS is presented repeatedly in the absence of the UCS. Sometimes, however, spontaneous recovery occurs and the CS will temporarily evoke a response even after extinction has taken place.

3. Stimulus generalization occurs when a CR is evoked by stimuli other than the CS. Generalization depends on the degree of similarity of the new stimuli

to the original CS. Discrimination is the ability to detect differences among stimuli.

4. A wide range of bodily responses can be classically conditioned, and this process is believed to underlie the development of some psychosomatic disorders. Once a response has been conditioned to a CS, that CS can sometimes be used like a UCS for subsequent classical conditioning of new stimuli. This process, known as higher-order conditioning, may be important in attitude formation.

OPERANT CONDITIONING: LEARNING THROUGH CONSEQUENCES (p. 203)

1. Thorndike's law of effect states that responses followed by pleasant or rewarding consequences will be strengthened, while those followed by unpleasant consequences will be weakened. This law is the cornerstone of operant conditioning, so called because the organism operates on its environment to achieve some outcome.

2. Many laboratory studies of operant conditioning have been done with rats, pigeons, and other animals. The Skinner box and the cumulative response recorder are important tools for the operant researcher.

3. The operant analysis of behavior involves relationships between antecedents, behaviors, and consequences. Relationships among these elements are called contingencies. Antecedents that signal the likely consequences of particular behaviors in a given situation are known as discriminative stimuli, and behaviors that are heavily influenced by such stimuli are said to be under stimulus control.

4. Operant behaviors are emitted behaviors, whereas classically conditioned responses are elicited behaviors. Classically conditioned responses are influenced by what happens before the behavior (i.e., by the CS–UCS pairing), whereas operant behaviors are influenced by consequences that occur after the behavior.

POSITIVE REINFORCEMENT (p. 206)

1. A positive reinforcer is any stimulus or event that increases the occurrence of a behavior that it follows. Secondary or conditioned reinforcers acquire their value through their association with primary reinforcers that satisfy biological needs.

2. Shaping, or the method of successive approxima-

tions, involves the reinforcement of behaviors that increasingly resemble the desired behavior.

3. In operant conditioning, extinction refers to the weakening and eventual disappearance of a response when it is no longer reinforced.

SCHEDULES OF REINFORCEMENT (p. 209)

Schedules of reinforcement have important effects on learning, performance, and extinction. On a continuous schedule, every response is reinforced. Partial reinforcement schedules involve reinforcement of only some responses. Partial reinforcement may occur on a ratio schedule, in which a certain percentage of responses are reinforced, or on an interval schedule, in which a certain amount of time must pass before a response gets reinforced. Ratio and interval schedules may be fixed, so that reinforcement always occurs after a fixed number of responses or a fixed time interval, or variable, so that the required number of responses or interval of time varies around some average. Each type of schedule results in a particular pattern of responding. Learning occurs most rapidly under continuous reinforcement, but partial schedules produce behaviors that are harder to extinguish.

NEGATIVE REINFORCEMENT: ESCAPE AND AVOIDANCE CONDITIONING (p. 213)

A negative reinforcer is any stimulus that increases a behavior that results in its removal. Escape and avoidance conditioning are two types of learning that result from negative reinforcement. According to the two-factor theory of avoidance conditioning, fear is created through a process of classical conditioning. This fear motivates avoidance behavior, and avoidance behaviors are negatively reinforced and thereby strengthened through fear reduction.

PUNISHMENT (p. 215)

1. Punishment is a consequence that decreases the occurrence of a behavior that it follows. Punishment can be administered by applying aversive stimuli or by removing reinforcers that are unrelated to the punished behavior (response cost).

2. Aversive punishment can result in a quick suppression of an undesired behavior, but this form of punishment can have undesirable side effects. These include

generalization of its suppressive effects to other behaviors, development of fear and avoidance, and the modeling, or imitation, of aggressive behaviors. Punishment through response cost avoids some of these side effects.

3. Punishment is most effective when desirable alternative behaviors are simultaneously strengthened through positive reinforcement.

TIMING OF BEHAVIORAL CONSEQUENCES (p. 218)

In general, immediate consequences have a stronger effect on behavior than delayed ones. Many maladaptive behaviors are maintained because they produce immediate positive consequences, even though the long-term consequences are negative.

BEHAVIORAL SELF-CONTROL (p. 220)

Principles of operant conditioning have been adapted to permit people to change their own behavior. Important procedures in the development of self-controlling behaviors are specifying the problem, collecting baseline data, identifying antecedents and consequences, controlling the antecedents, manipulating response consequences, and using the process of shaping to change target behaviors gradually.

THE COGNITIVE PERSPECTIVE ON LEARNING (p. 219)

1. Cognitive interpretations of classical conditioning suggest that what is learned is an expectancy that the UCS will follow the CS. Studies of the blocking of a new CS by previous conditioning support the cognitive view of classical conditioning. Cognitive theorists attribute operant conditioning to the development of an expectancy that certain behaviors will produce certain consequences under certain conditions. Research with humans suggests that awareness of reinforcement contingencies greatly facilitates learning.

2. Certain kinds of learning experiences can result in the development of generalized expectancies that affect behavior in different settings. Seligman and his associates have shown that unavoidable aversive experiences can produce a state of learned helplessness and that previous mastery experiences can produce learned mastery, which makes animals more persistent and resourceful in new situations.

3. Internal self-evaluations can function as rewards

and punishers and may, in some instances, override external consequences. Standards for self-reinforcement are acquired through direct learning and through observation of others' standards.

4. Many behaviors are learned through modeling. Observation of others' behavior is sufficient in order for learning to occur, but performance is affected by the consequences that the behaviors produce for the model. Emotional responses can also be learned through observation.

THE BIOLOGICAL PERSPECTIVE ON LEARNING (p. 231)

1. Evidence in the form of limitations on operant conditioning, avoidance learning, and the conditioning of food aversions suggests that there are biological limitations on learning. An animal's evolutionary history may make it prepared to perform certain responses but contraprepared to perform others.

2. For many years, psychologists have been seeking the biological basis of learning, using a variety of research strategies. Recent discoveries suggest that long-term potentiation may be an important process and that the basis for LTP may be the action of an enzyme in the neuron membrane that increases its sensitivity to repeated stimulation.

KEY TERMS AND CONCEPTS

learning	learning trial
classical conditioning	extinction (classical conditioning)
unconditioned stimulus (UCS)	
unconditioned response (UCR)	spontaneous recovery
	stimulus generalization
conditioned stimulus (CS)	discrimination
	conditioned hypoglycemia
conditioned response (CR)	psychosomatic disorder

higher-order conditioning

law of effect

operant conditioning

Skinner box

cumulative response recorder

antecedent

consequence

contingency

discriminative stimuli

stimulus control

elicited behavior

emitted behavior

positive reinforcement

primary reinforcer

secondary (conditioned) reinforcer

shaping (successive approximations)

behavior chain

extinction (operant conditioning)

time out

schedules of reinforcement

continuous reinforcement schedule

partial reinforcement schedule

fixed-ratio schedule

variable-ratio schedule

fixed-interval schedule

variable-interval schedule

negative reinforcement

escape conditioning

avoidance conditioning

two-factor theory of avoidance learning

punishment

aversive punishment

response cost

neurotic paradox

self-controlling behavior

Premack principle

expectancy

latent learning

blocking

verbal conditioning

generalized expectancy

learned helplessness

learned mastery

self-evaluative processes

modeling

vicarious classical conditioning

preparedness

long-term potentiation

calpain

SUGGESTED READINGS

BOLLES, R. C. (1979). *Learning theory* (2nd ed.). New York: Holt, Rinehart and Winston. A good introduction to current theories of learning and their historical development.

NAVARICK, D. J. (1979). *Principles of learning*. Reading, Mass.: Addison-Wesley. A clear and well-written introduction to learning principles and their application to education, industry, and memory improvement.

WATSON, D. D., and THARP, R. G. (1981). *Self-directed behavior: Self-modification for personal adjustment* (3rd ed.). Monterey, Calif.: Brooks/Cole. A detailed guide to the application of behavioral self-control principles. The work contains many concrete examples and suggestions.

CHAPTER SEVEN

INFORMATION PROCESSING AND MEMORY

INFORMATION PROCESSING
Input
Processing, coding, and storage

FRONTIER 7.1   METACOGNITION

RETRIEVAL FROM MEMORY
Context and memory
Memory for complex stimuli
Reconstructive memory
Episodic and semantic memory
Retrieval failure or forgetting
Are memories ever permanently lost?

**CURRENT THEORETICAL VIEWS
OF MEMORY PROCESSES**
The duplex theory
Levels of processing and elaboration

STUDY OUTLINE

KEY TERMS AND CONCEPTS

SUGGESTED READINGS

I was trying to think of Carl's last name but I just can't think of it. Umm, okay, let me see if there's any other neighborhoods that I haven't gotten to that I can remember where people my age lived. Um . . . hummm. There is no one that lived way up on the end . . . And now I'm trying to think of the Sunset Cliffs down on Cal Western 'cause a lot of people always used to go there and go tide pool picking and just run around and go surfing. I'm trying to think of all the people that perhaps went surfing or even tide pool picking that were in my grade. Um . . . If I could see them lined up against . . . There's this one cliff down at Newbreak Beach they always used to line up with their boards and sit down and look at the waves, and then I go down the row and see if there's anybody I haven't already named. There's Benny Nesbit, I already named him, and Dave Culbert and they used to go surfing, and . . . um . . . there are a lot of older people too. Um . . . Joe Nate, I already named them, all those guys used to go surfing. Um . . . he was older—he was older—and older—he was younger. A lot of those guys were older. Let me see, him and him . . . Okay I was just going down the list and I don't see anybody that I haven't already seen and there was this one girl who always used to be down there, but she was younger. I already named the people that she hangs around with. Um . . . is there anybody else that I know that used to . . . (Williams, 1976)

Are you wondering what's going on? This person is practicing a cognitive skill. He is searching his long-term memory by trying to remember the names of people in his high school class. Notice how he comes up with more names by thinking about the people he could remember and then recalling other people associated with them. Whether or not we're aware of it, all

of us are almost constantly occupied with putting information into our memories and getting it back out again. For example, consider this situation:

A car driver sees a stoplight at an intersection. The light turns from green to yellow. She brakes the car gently to slow it down. By the time the car reaches the intersection, the light is red. The driver stops, shifts into neutral gear, and waits for the light to change to green. When she sees the green light, she shifts again and crosses the intersection.

This sequence of behavior is so commonplace that you may not realize how complex it is until you stop and analyze it. From a scientific standpoint, stopping your car at a stoplight involves sensation and perception (seeing the light and recognizing it for what it is), learning (a red light means stop, a foot on the brake slows the car, a green light means go), and memory (retaining the learning from an earlier time and retrieving it when it is needed). A psychologist with a behavioral point of view would stress that a habit (stopping the car at a red light) had been formed by pairing a number of exposures to a red light (the stimulus) with stopping the car (the response). A cognitive psychologist would recognize the stimulus-response association but would be more interested in what went on within the individual between the time the stimulus appeared and the time the response was made. Cognitive psychologists focus on how knowledge is processed by the human organism: how we acquire, modify, manipulate, store, and use what we learn.

INFORMATION PROCESSING

In general, cognitive psychologists who study memory, language, and thought see these human behaviors as **information processing** involving input, processing

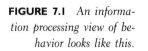

FIGURE 7.1 *An information processing view of behavior looks like this.*

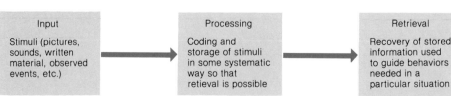

Input
Stimuli (pictures, sounds, written material, observed events, etc.)

Processing
Coding and storage of stimuli in some systematic way so that retieval is possible

Retrieval
Recovery of stored information used to guide behaviors needed in a particular situation

(coding and storage), and retrieval (see Figure 7.1). Perhaps the best and most obvious way to describe the information processing view of thought and memory is to compare the human being with a computer. Information is coded and fed into a computer in an organized way. When the computer is asked to produce a part of that information, the machine searches its memory and outputs the information on a screen or prints it out. For example, we might ask for the names of all people hired by a large multinational bank on July 12, 1984. This relatively simple task is equivalent to asking you to search your memory for the names of the first seven presidents of the United States. Then we might ask the computer to tell us which of the workers hired on July 12, 1984, was the most productive. This task is more complex because these data do not exist in the computer in precisely that form. The computer could not simply reproduce information from its memory; to produce the data requested, it would have to process the information it did have—analyze and manipulate it in some way. If the computer had data on the number of items processed per day, absences, and the number of quality complaints for each worker, it could collect that information, analyze it, and answer the question.

The operation of human cognitive processes is basically similar to the way a computer functions, but except for speed of calculation, our abilities far surpass those of the most sophisticated computer. One area of research, known as *artificial intelligence*, concentrates on developing computer programs that reproduce certain human cognitive functions. Although some of the programs work well in certain simplified situations, no program can yet cope with the complex input and output functions required of most human beings.

In order to understand how we process information, we will look at three stages—*input*, *processing (coding* and *storage)*, and *retrieval*—in more detail.

Input

We receive information in the form of stimuli from our sense organs. Researchers have looked carefully at differences in how much information we can receive at one time and how long we can retain it. Both factors

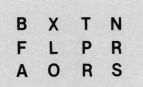

FIGURE 7.2 *Sperling's partial report technique uses an array of letters that measures 4" × 3".*

depend on the sensory system involved. For example, input that we see differs in some interesting respects from input that we hear.

VISUAL INPUT

If you ask people to take a single glance at something and tell you what they see, most people report only a limited amount of information. Researchers wondered if people actually perceive more than they report. Some additional information that was perceived might slip away before it could be reported because reporting itself takes up time. To deal with this problem, George Sperling (1960) used what he called a *partial report technique*. Subjects were shown a rectangular array of 12 letters, such as the one in Figure 7.2. After seeing an array for less than a second, the subjects were asked to report the contents of one of the rows. To signal which row they should report, Sperling sounded a high-, medium-, or low-frequency tone after the stimulus array. A high-frequency tone meant that subjects should report the contents of the top row, a medium tone the middle row, and a low tone the bottom row.

Subjects were able to report almost all the letters in the rows indicated by the tone. They would not have been able to do this unless they had stored almost all the letters in the entire array because when they saw the stimulus, they did not know exactly which row they were going to be asked to report. Sperling's subjects reported that the images of some of the letters did fade away as they were reporting others. Sperling used a variation of his original partial report procedure to see how long a visual image actually lasted. He concluded

that the information in the entire array lasted about 1 second before fading. These results indicate that visual information remains intact for a brief period after the stimulus disappears (see Figure 7.3). This brief period of retention is called the **iconic store.**

AUDITORY INPUT

The sensory store for auditory information that corresponds to the iconic store is called the **echoic store.** Researchers have studied the echoic store by using a modified version of Sperling's technique. Subjects wearing earphones heard three letters in the right ear channel, three in the left ear channel, and three read through both earphones at once (Darwin and others, 1972). Because of the stereo effect, those read through both earphones were heard as coming from the middle. After the letters had been presented, subjects were signaled to report the left, right, or middle set of letters. The results showed the same general pattern as that for the iconic store. A higher percentage of the letters was recalled under the partial report condition than when the subject was asked to repeat all the letters that he or she could recall. The results suggest that auditory information remains in the echoic store after the stimulus is no longer physically present and then fades away grad-

ually. It takes about 4 seconds for auditory information to fade completely, compared to 1 second for visual images—see Figure 7.4. (We all seem to know this. For example, when you want to remember a strange phone number, do you say it out loud or concentrate on how it looked in the phone book?) **Sensory stores** exist for other modalities, too—touch and taste, for example.

Processing, coding, and storage

REHEARSAL

Since we obviously remember information for longer than a few seconds, we must do something with it before the images in our sensory stores fade away. One way we can hold something in memory is by repeating it over and over, the old phone number trick.

In a classic experiment, Margaret Peterson and Lloyd Peterson (1959) set out to show what happens if people are prevented from rehearsing material. They showed subjects a set of three consonants, such as BFP, followed immediately by a three-digit number. Subjects were asked to count backward from the number; this ensured that they could not rehearse the letters. On a signal from the experimenter, subjects stopped counting and tried to recall the three letters. Immediately after the letters were presented, recall was nearly perfect, but after a 15-second wait, recall was poor.

Repetition is clearly not a satisfactory way to remember everything. Only a limited amount of information can be constantly repeated, and repetition prevents other cognitive activities from taking place. If you were studying a foreign language, you might learn new vocabulary words by repeating the foreign word and its English equivalent over and over. For example, in French the word for bread is *pain*, the word for red is *rouge*, and the word for night is *nuit*. You could walk around saying "bread, *pain*, red, *rouge*, night, *nuit*," all day, but eventually you might want to think about something else. To keep information from fading when repetition stops, some of it is stored so it can be retrieved later. This means that it is processed in some way.

What we extract from the sensory store—which stimuli we select for further attention and processing—depends not only on the characteristics of the stimulus but on the knowledge we have about the world.

In Chapter 5, on perception, you read about the

cocktail party phenomenon, in which the speech of the other guests is just background noise until someone across the room says your name. This is an example of selective processing based on personal meaning or importance. Other stimulus characteristics also affect the way information is processed. For example, the more vivid or unusual the stimulus is, the more likely we are to remember it.

SELECTIVE PROCESSING

Imagine that you had been given a large number of pictures to look at. Among them you saw one picture of a completely equipped kitchen including a white electric stove with four burners and an oven and another picture of the same kitchen that showed a large seal with a ball on its nose instead of the stove. The next day you are shown a set of pictures and asked to pick out

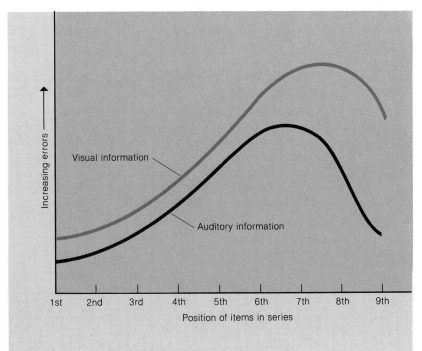

FIGURE 7.4 *Auditory stimuli are stored for a longer (but still brief) period than visual stimuli.*

243

those that you had seen before. You are much more likely to select the seal picture than the stove picture. The seal in the kitchen, because of its uniqueness, was processed with more effort. The stove picture, on the other hand, was encoded easily and almost automatically, and because of this the memory for that particular picture was poor. If you were shown several similar kitchen pictures, it would be difficult to be certain which one you had seen the day before. In much the same way, if you read a familiar passage giving details that you already know, your involvement and your ability to recognize sentences from the passage will be much less than if you were reading some new and difficult material that requires you to stop often and think about the author's meaning. (**Selective processing**— the differences in the ways that unique and familiar stimuli are processed—will come up again later in the chapter when we discuss the concept of levels of processing.)

Cognitive psychologists are very interested in what we do with stimuli that we have selected for processing. One distinction is whether processing occurs from the "top down" or from the "bottom up." In **bottom-up processing,** all the individual parts or elements of the stimulus are inspected and then combined to reproduce what the person has seen or heard. **Top-down processing** means that people tend to start out with the overall meaning and then fill in the elements that they expect to find associated with it. In most cases we use a combination of these two types of processing. The one that is dominant may differ with the situation. For example, consider speech perception. Most people do not speak clearly. They may drop endings, say "walkin" rather than "walking," or speak in incomplete sentences. Yet their listeners not only understand what they mean, but will usually correct the mistakes if they are asked to repeat what they heard (Marslen-Wilson and Welsh, 1978). Their perception corrects reality. They are not simply recording the stimulus; they are using past experience and knowledge to understand it and to make it conform to their expectations. Their top-down processing is dominant. On the other hand, if you were listening to someone speak a language that you did not know—say, Norwegian—what you repeated would be closer to the original because your bottom-up processing would be dominant. You would be analyzing the speech sound by sound.

You have no doubt had personal experience with these findings. Have you ever carefully proofread a term paper only to have errors leap out at you as you sat in class waiting to hand it in? Your top-down processing overrode your bottom-up processing and filled in the correct letters when you did the proofreading. You saw what you expected to see, not what was really there. You are not alone in this. Your authors have had the same maddening experience when looking at a finished book that they and three or four expert copyreaders had carefully checked for mistakes. You may even find one or two in this book that everyone has missed. (If you do, write the publisher and tell *them* about it.) Despite the problems that it sometimes causes us, processing has to be selective because so much information is coming in at all times. Once you are aware of this tendency to shortchange familiar items, you can try to give them extra attention in situations that make accuracy important.

Once a stimulus has been processed, it is coded in some way so we can get it back out again if we need to.

CODING AND ORGANIZATION

Two general types of codes used in memory storage and retrieval have been of special interest: visual codes and abstract codes. Both types of codes make it much easier to organize information because they provide a kind of shorthand.

Visual codes All of us know that some memories seem to be stored visually. For example, if someone asked you to describe the house or apartment you lived in as a child, chances are you would picture the house and, even more likely, take a mental stroll through the rooms and tell what you "saw" there. **Visual codes** can be efficient aids to memory.

There is experimental evidence that people use imagery in solving certain kinds of problems. For example, Allan Paivio of the University of Western Ontario asked people to think of two clocks showing times such as 4:25 and 9:10 and to identify the clock on which the hour and minute hands form a larger angle. Try this yourself. How did you solve the problem? Did you visualize the clocks? Paivio found several pieces of evidence to suggest that imagery was generally used to solve this problem. Most subjects said they formed images, but more important, people answered more quickly if the two angles were very different in size than if they were similar (for example, comparing 1:55 and 2:25 versus 1:55 and 2:40; if you gave even the briefest thought to this comparison, you were using imagery, too). When Paivio divided his subjects into good and poor visualizers on the basis of another test, he found the good visualizers generally had shorter reaction times on the clock task than the poor visualizers did (Paivio, 1978).

Research findings suggest that images are stored in some visual way and not in a descriptive or languagelike format (Kosslyn and Shwartz, 1981). You can easily duplicate the kinds of experimental data that have led to this conclusion. Does a German shepherd have a long thin tail or a long plumelike one? Answer this question and then stop to think how you did it. Most people report that they scan along the image of the dog's body until they see the tail. If you were asked the same question about an elephant, the chances are that your response time would be longer. This is because the time of scanning is related to the length of the object scanned, and since the elephant is larger than the dog, the answer takes longer to find. Another typical experimental finding suggests that the parts of small images are more difficult to detect than the parts of

larger images. This is another result that you can demonstrate yourself. First imagine a duck and an elephant together and then ask yourself what shape the duck's bill is. Now imagine the duck standing with an ant and ask yourself the same question. Experiments have shown that questions about the duck take longer to answer when it is paired with the elephant, presumably because the duck seems smaller when it is paired with the elephant than with the ant (Kosslyn, 1975).

Even though common experience suggests that storing memories as if they were on videotape works, we can't remember everything that way. Such a visual storage procedure would soon become overcrowded with data. The rules of a code mean that we don't always have to specify details. Most researchers do not think of visual coding as a point-for-point replica of the object but rather as some visual representation of only its important features, like a map. A map contains basic features but does not duplicate everything that you might see from an airplane.

One application of abstract visual coding is the efficient use of the ancient wooden bead calculator, the abacus (see Figure 7.5). The abacus is used by moving beads on rods set in a frame. Addition and subtraction are reasonably straightforward, but multiplication and division require a great deal of skill in visualization. Surprisingly, one place where the abacus is still used extensively is Japan, where millions of efficient electronic calculators are manufactured. Some of these calculators even combine the electronic elements with a small abacus so that both systems can be used.

A recent abacus champion of Taiwan, South Korea, and Japan is a 19-year-old who can solve a prob-

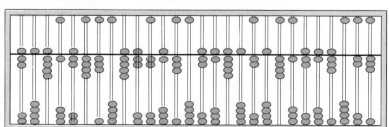

FIGURE 7.5 *Visual coding is important in the efficient use of the abacus.*

lem involving the addition and subtraction of 115 numbers, each with 11 digits, in 9 seconds. That is the equivalent of doing this problem in 1 second:

328 minus 247 plus 162 minus 108 plus 927 plus 867

How fast can you do this one? (The answer is 1929.)

The more proficient people become on the abacus, the more they can visualize the movement of the beads without actually moving them. A few years ago a calculating contest in Japan allowed the use of any type of device, electronic or beaded. Abacus users won all the competitions—addition, subtraction, multiplication, and division.

Abstract codes Much of the material that we code into our memory seems to be recorded in an abstract or symbolic fashion rather than visually. **Abstract codes** usually don't have much actual similarity to what they represent. To understand the meaning of the term *abstract code*, consider the everyday example of language. The way that some words look and sound does tell us something about what they mean—for example, *gurgle* or *zigzag*—but most words simply represent arbitrary connections between symbols and objects. Does the word *child* look anything like you did when you were younger? When we discuss language in the next chapter, it will be clear that language has a special value as a memory code because it connects symbols by a system of rules.

When we see the sentence, "The bucking horse threw the rider into the mud," our knowledge of the rules of English tells us that the rider, not the horse, got dirty. We know what acted (the horse) and what was acted upon (the rider). We also know what the word *horse* means and don't need to say "a large, hoofed, four-legged mammal." We know that *mud* means "dirt with a high water content that may stick to you and make you messy," and so on. As with visual codes, abstract coding helps us function much more efficiently by not forcing us to include details and definitions that we can assume most people know. Other examples of abstract symbolic coding systems that we use in everyday life are musical notation, computer languages, and mathematical systems. Although, as Figure 7.6 suggests, not everyone codes information in the same way, it seems likely that there are certain basic similarities in the ways that most individuals code and organize information.

FIGURE 7.6 *One way to remember data is to code them into a more familiar form. Not all of us would choose the method pictured here. For someone trained in physics, like Albert Einstein, these equations might be a natural way of thinking, but for most of us they would not be a very efficient memory code.*

(© SIDNEY HARRIS/AMERICAN SCIENTIST MAGAZINE.)

Chunking Any memory usually involves many pieces of information. One way of organizing these little pieces is to group them into larger units that are meaningful. This process, called **chunking**, is a way of organizing or coding information so that more can be retained, both for short intervals and sometimes for a longer time. Look quickly at Figure 7.7. Your memory of the first row was probably not very good, but you could remember all the letters from the second row because they form a recognizable word.

A *chunk* is any information that can be represented in memory as a unit. The letter *W* is a chunk, and so is the word *Washington*. NOTGNIHSAW could be considered 10 separate chunks, or 6 chunks if *NOT* and *SAW* were chunked as units. In experiments in which

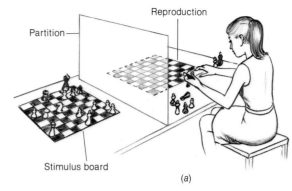

FIGURE 7.7 *Look at the top row of letters for just an instant, look away, and try to recall as many as you can. Then do the same with the bottom row. In which case did you recall more letters?*

subjects are shown a collection of items and asked to recall them, most people can repeat about 7 items or chunks. The meaningfulness of the chunks affects how well we remember them. You could probably remember a 10-word sentence after only a brief presentation, but you might have more trouble recalling 10 random letters of the alphabet or 10 random words.

In chunking, we organize newly perceived material on the basis of some earlier knowledge. In general, the greater our skill or knowledge on a particular topic, the better we are at chunking the information about that topic. For example, when presented with an arrangement of chess pieces as they might appear during the middle of an actual game, a master chess player remembered the positions of the pieces better than either a very good player or a beginning player did (Chase and Simon, 1973). This was not a question of better memory alone, however, because his advantage disappeared when all three viewed boards with randomly placed chess pieces (see Figure 7.8). The experimenters found that the chess master was using his memory of real game situations and could form larger chunks than the other players did, but this advantage in chunking did not help him when the pieces were placed randomly. He was not better at chunking overall, but only at

FIGURE 7.8 *(a) The task of the subject was to observe the set-up board for only a few seconds and then reproduce the placement of the chess pieces on another board. (b) When they were shown chess boards with pieces in actual positions from the middle of a game, a chess master's (M) memory of the positions was superior to that of a class A player (A) or a beginner (B). (c) However, when the pieces were placed randomly on the board, this superior memory for piece positions disappeared.*

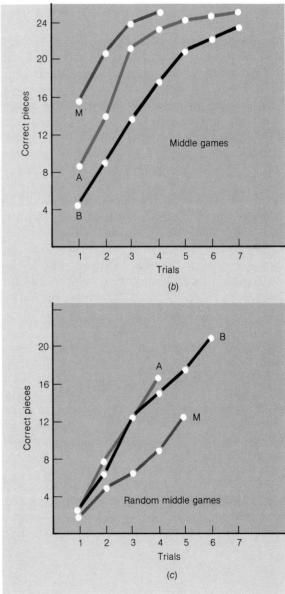

chunking the kinds of chess piece combinations that he might expect to actually occur.

Mnemonics   Mnemonic techniques are another way to organize material for storage. The information processing model in cognitive psychology has affected the study of mental imagery in an important way. Research on imagery had originally focused on how the use of images helped people to perform tasks such as describing their childhood homes. As a result of the information processing approach, researchers have focused on questions about the kinds of mental structure and processes that make it possible for images to be used for memory storage. These techniques help to give the material some structure and to provide cues that may make it easier to recall. Several types of mnemonics depend on visual imagery.

One mnemonic technique, the **peg word system,** is based on a rhyme that gives you a series of locations or mental pegs on which to store memories. A well-known peg word system is the rhyme "ONE is a BUN, TWO is a SHOE, THREE is a TREE, FOUR is a DOOR, FIVE is a HIVE, SIX is a STICKS, SEVEN is a HEAVEN, EIGHT is a GATE, NINE is a WINE, and TEN is a HEN."

After you have memorized the rhyme, it can be used to remember lists of items more easily. First, you number the list to be learned in sequence. Then you form a series of compound visual images involving the items on your list and the things in the rhyme: the first list item is linked with a bun, the second with a shoe,

and so on. The vividness and unusualness of the image are important in memory. For example, suppose you had to learn the following list of raw materials produced by a particular country: coffee, tin, rubber, beef, sugar, hides, handcrafts, fertilizer, cocoa beans, and caustic soda.

For COFFEE, you might picture a *bun* with a man's head inside. The man has a cough. For TIN, your picture could be a *shoe* with a large letter T standing in it. For RUBBER, the picture might be a *tree* using its branches to scratch a girl's back. For BEEF, your mental image might be a *bee* carrying a large letter F through a door (see Figure 7.9).

People who must meet a lot of people and remember the details about them often use another mnemonic technique that calls for a high degree of visual imagery. They try to associate what is to be remembered with some physical characteristic of the person and then visualize both together. For example, among cocktail waitresses who must sometimes remember 15 or more drink orders and the location of the individual who made each, the best waitresses used a variety of mnemonics (Bennett, 1983). Most of them visualized the customer with the drink. Thus, a woman wearing rouge who ordered a strawberry Daiquiri would be easy to remember, as would a large barrel-chested man who ordered a beer. As one waitress stated, "After a while customers start looking like drinks" (p. 165).

Some mnemonics do not have a strong visual component. Instead, they use verbal cues such as rhymes or sentences. Some are familiar to all of us. For example, the rhyme "Thirty days hath September . . ." is a simple way to remember the number of days in each

FIGURE 7.9 *The use of key words and visualization and recall of a series of items.*

COUGH-HE

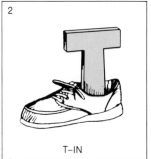

T-IN

RUB-HER

BEE-F

month. The rhyme "*i* before *e* except after *c*" has helped spellers of *believe* and *receive* for generations. Although rhymes work well for lists of items, sometimes the narrative technique, making up a sentence or story using the words to be learned, works better. Either the words themselves or the first letter of each word can be used as a cue.

All these techniques can help us to learn information and to remember it when it is needed. All mnemonics work on the same basic principle. They provide a way to organize material based on a set of cues that are easily remembered. The cues can then be used as reminders to direct the search through long-term memory to relocate the material.

But mnemonic devices are not always the route to an improved memory. In one study (Baker and Santa, 1977) subjects had to learn seven 4-word groups presented as a 28-word list. Half the subjects were instructed to tie together each group of four words with images; the other half were not given any special instructions. When the subjects were simply asked to remember the words, the group that had used visual imagery did better. However, when the subjects were given a new list of words that were associates of the words on the original list (for example, *pear* when *apple* had been on the original list), the imagery-using subjects performed much more poorly than the control group. What caused this result? Apparently, it had to do with the problem of context. Mnemonic devices provide a *context*, or a set of cues that aid memory. But when a different set of cues is given, a problem is created. It is as if a new code book has been provided that doesn't mesh with the material already coded by another system. For this reason, you should be sure to study material in a variety of ways in order to create a flexible coding and retrieval system.

Despite this disadvantage, mnemonic techniques can be helpful in several situations. Students who customarily use mnemonics for organizing some of their study material tend to have higher grade point averages than other students (Carlson and others, 1976). Mnemonics can also be important to people who sometimes need to remember a great deal of new information very quickly (a guest at a large party who meets 25 new people all at once) or those who have particular difficulty in remembering (for example, because of aging).

GENERAL ORGANIZING PRINCIPLES

While chunking and mnemonics provide ways to organize material, they are useful only in special situations. Cognitive psychologists are interested in how people organize all the information that goes into memory. Unlike the sensory images that we have looked at so far, the bulk of our memories are keyed to words. The organized knowledge we have about words and other verbal symbols, their meanings, and the things to which they refer; relationships among them; and rules for manipulating them is called **semantic memory.** Answering the following questions draws on semantic memory:

Did Napoleon have ears? How many TV sets did Alexander the Great have? Where did John F. Kennedy sit at the inauguration of Abraham Lincoln? It is extremely doubtful that you ever learned the specific information in these questions. So your knowledge of the answers can't have come from your sorting through some kind of organized group of facts as a computer might do. How are you able to answer them? You figured out the answers by using inference. You were probably able to answer these rather absurd questions very quickly, without much awareness of the series of thoughts that made the answers possible. If you had to stop and record your thoughts, they might have gone something like this: Human beings have ears. Since Napoleon was a human being, he must have had ears. You may have seen a portrait of Napoleon in the past, recalled it visually and noticed his ears, but the first solution is more likely. Although you may not know exactly when TV sets were introduced, it had to be long after Alexander the Great lived, so the answer to the next question has to be "none." As for the last question, while you may not know the dates of Kennedy's life or the date of Lincoln's inauguration, again the time span is too long to make sense. The ability to do this kind of inferential thinking using material available in semantic memory is what has so far distinguished the human brain's behavior from that of a computer.

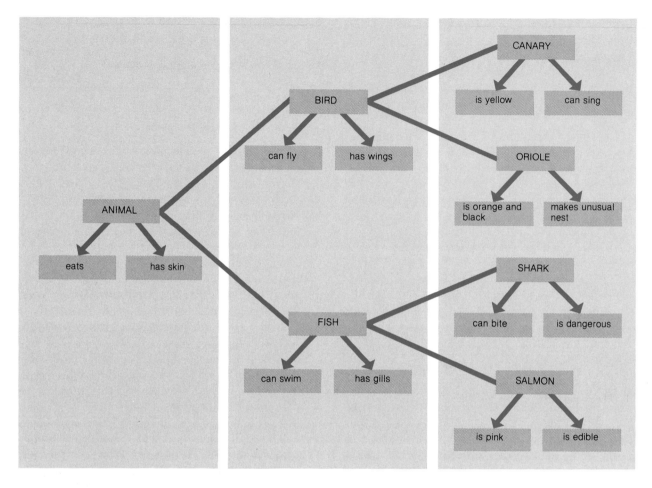

Thinking computers, the goal of those interested in the field of artificial intelligence, have not yet arrived. A computer would search the data bank to answer the questions above, but it would find the data lacking. Since, unlike you, the computer cannot use inference, it would be unable to answer these questions. Computer programs still depend on **declarative representation schemes** that are composed of explicit relationships between words. The declarative representational schemes that give a logical organization to the information stored in human and computer memories are based on large numbers of propositions.

A **proposition** is the smallest unit of knowledge that one can make a true-or-false judgment about. For example, we can make each of the following propositions into a question that can be answered "yes" or "no":

A bird flies.   Does a bird fly?

Harry is bald.   Is Harry bald?

A sparrow is a bird. Is a sparrow a bird?

Networks made up of propositions can be used to help understand information storage and retrieval. Figure 7.10 illustrates one of the most influential of the declarative representation schemes that were developed by Allan Collins and Ross Quillian (1969). This network is made up of *nodes*—objects, concepts, or events—and *links* between the nodes that represent their relationships.

This structure is called a **hierarchical network** because the concepts in it are organized into subordinate-superordinate relationships: *Animal* is the superordinate of *bird* and *bird* is the superordinate of *canary*.

This scheme is very economical because a particular class of things is stored only once, at the place in the network that corresponds to that class. For instance, a property that characterizes all birds, such as their wings, is stored only at *bird*. It is not stored over and over again with each different type of bird, even though they all have wings. A computer can search this network to find the answers to many questions. For example, given the network in Figure 7.10, the computer could answer questions such as "Is the canary a bird?" or "Is there a bird that is yellow?"

Other researchers have used more complicated pieces of information to build their propositional models. For example, look at the sentence "Harry gave the furry rabbit to Mike, who is his son." The sentence can be broken down into three simpler propositions:

1. Harry gave the rabbit to Mike.

2. The rabbit is furry.

3. Mike is Harry's son.

Each of these propositions expresses one unit of meaning. If any of them were false, the whole sentence would be false. Experimental data tell us that in most cases our memory preserves the meaning of the sentence but not the exact wording. For example, we might store one of these versions instead of the original sentence: "Harry gave Mike, who is his son, the furry rabbit." "Harry gave the furry rabbit to his son, Mike." "His son, Mike, was given a furry rabbit by Harry." We could verify the truth of each of these sentences by consulting our propositional network, but it could not tell us which of the sentences we had actually heard before, because the way the information is stored does not preserve the exact wording.

Networks of this type have been proposed by a number of memory researchers (Rumelhart, Lindsay, and Norman, 1972; Anderson, 1980). Although these memory models are important, it is clear that they are able to deal only with a greatly simplified memory system. It is very difficult to conceive of a model that could explain how all the complex ideas in our memories are stored and interconnected. One thing that has so far differentiated the human cognitive system from computers is our ability to think about how we think. This process, called *metacognition*, is described in Frontier 7.1.

RETRIEVAL FROM MEMORY

Once something is stored in an organized system, we can pull it out again if we have the right cue or entry key. This process of retrieval is called *remembering*. There are two types of remembering: (1) something looks familiar to us because we think we have seen it in the past; (2) we are able to answer a question by searching through our stored knowledge and producing the answer. The first of these two processes is called **recognition,** the second is termed **recall.**

Do recognition and recall involve the same basic memory processes? Some researchers think they do (Gillund and Shiffrin, 1984). Even if the same processes are involved, there are some differences. Recognition is often easier than recall. You may find that your score is higher on a multiple-choice test (recognition) than on a test that requires you to fill in the blanks (recall). Sometimes, however, recognition is more difficult. Imagine that you are given a long list of pairs of words that includes words like the following:

table

sleep

lamp

spoon

You are given another list and asked to recognize any words from the first list. Then you are asked to try to

METACOGNITION

A growing area of both theoretical and research interest in cognitive psychology is the field of metacognition. Developmental psychologist John Flavell, who has been responsible for much of the current interest in this research, defines *metacognition* in this way:

"Metacognition" refers to one's own knowledge concerning one's own cognitive processes and products or anything else related to them, e.g., the learning-relevant properties of information or data. For example, I am engaging in metacognition (metamemory, metalearning, metaattention, metalanguage, or whatever) if I notice that I am having more trouble learning A than B; if it strikes me that I should double-check C before accepting it as a fact; if it occurs to me that I had better scrutinize each and every alternative in any multiple-choice type task situation before deciding which is the best one; if I sense that I had better make a note of D before I forget it. . . . Metacognition refers, among other things, to the active monitoring and consequent regulation and orchestration of these processes in relation to the cognitive objects or data on which they bear, usually in the service of some concrete goal or objective. (1976, p. 232)

Part of being a good student is knowing what you know and what you do not know. A recent series of experiments illustrated how insensitive young children are to their own lack of comprehension (Markman, 1977). In these experiments, children in grades one through three were asked to help the experimenter construct card games to be taught to other children their age. The instructions were quite clearly incomplete and the experimenter was interested in how soon the child would ask for more information. In one experiment the child and the experimenter were each given four alphabet cards and the child had the following instructions:

We each put our cards in a pile. We both turn over the top card in our pile. We look at the cards to see who has the special card. Then we turn over the next card in our pile to see who has the special card this time. In the end the person with the most cards wins the game.

Before the child could play the game, he or she of course had to know how to define a "special card." Markman found that the younger children were not aware that they did not know how to play the game until after a series of prompts had been given. They also needed to have the instructions repeated several times and sometimes had to try out the game before they realized what they did not know.

Complex reasoning is needed in order for you to be aware of what you know and what you do not know. Children not only know less than adults, but their knowledge is poorly organized and may be filled with inconsistencies of which they are not aware. Even college students are likely to have problems in assessing their own knowledge. Good problem solvers know not only what facts they have at hand but also what they can deduce from these facts. In addition, they are sensitive to "facts" that cannot be known—for example, "What kind of a car did Joan of Arc drive?" Although you could answer this question quite easily, it actually involves a series of inferences based on other knowledge you already had—for example, when automobiles came into use and when Joan of Arc lived.

Interest in metacognition forces cognitive psychologists to look at the introspections of their subjects and many related areas, including some traditionally studied by psychologists interested in personality and social psychology—for example, feelings of competence, need for achievement, and learned helplessness. Researchers also need to answer questions like what besides "amount" distinguishes people who have well-developed metacognition from those who don't (Cavanaugh and Perlmutter, 1982). Experts and novices differ not only in the amount of knowledge they have but in the way it is organized.

remember words from the original list without any aids. At which task would you do better? You might have less trouble recalling them than you would picking them out from the following list:

chair   table
bed   rest
lamp   spoon
knife   fork
sleep   light

Because the words are all so familiar, they are not easy to recognize. If, on the other hand, the first list had included words such as

onomatopoeia

serendipity

aardvark

biosynergy

you might have found these words easier to recognize then to recall because very likely most of them are new to you. These results would conform to our earlier discussion of selective processing.

Context and memory

It makes intuitive sense that a subject's performance will be improved if an item to be remembered is presented in the same way for a recognition test as it was in the original learning situation. The context in which it is presented can affect the way an item is coded. For example, YELLOW-*sun* would be encoded differently from YELLOW-*coward*. If the word is presented in the same way during the retention test, then similar encoding will be induced and the probability of remembering will be increased (Tulving and Thomson, 1973). If a word is re-presented by the same voice or in the same typescript, the subject's recognition performance is also

improved (Geiselman and Bjork, 1980). In general, performance is improved by similar environments during learning and later testing situations.

However, when the definition of learning becomes more specific, the effects of similarity of presentation improve memory only in some cases. For example, when learning and remembering take place in the same physical environment or in one that induces the same physiological state, recall is improved, but recognition is not affected. In one well-known study, divers recalled a list of words best when they were in the same environment in which they had learned the list originally, either underwater or on dry land (Godden and Baddeley, 1975). But in a later study by the same researchers, similarity of environment had no effect on recognition (Godden and Baddeley, 1980). Researchers have also looked at the efficiency of learning, measured by both recognition and recall, while subjects are under the influence of a drug—for instance, alcohol. In this situation, too, the difference between recognition and recall seems to hold up: positive effects are found in recall but usually not in recognition.

Another environmental factor that can affect learning and memory is mood. If you are in the same mood when trying to recall something as you were when you learned it, your performance may be enhanced (Bower and others, 1978). Bower and his co-workers suggest that a noticeable or discriminable mood may function like a peg word that reduces interference and makes the material to be recalled more distinctive and therefore easier to remember. Even instructions to imagine the original learning environment during the recall session can improve performance (Smith, 1979). All these research findings suggest that physiological cues, such as those induced by drugs or by a particular mood state, and nonphysiological environmental cues that heighten the similarity of the learning and testing situations may make it easier to locate and identify the material in the memory store and therefore also make it easier to produce it on demand.

Memory for complex stimuli

Cognitive psychologists are interested in memory tasks that involve simple words, but they also want to know how people remember more complex stimuli such as stories. One of the first researchers to study this topic was F. C. Bartlett. His classic study (1932) is still one of the best examples of how such complex memories function. Bartlett asked his subjects to read this story.

THE WAR OF THE GHOSTS   One night two young men from Egulac went down to the river to hunt seals, and while they were there it became foggy and calm. Then they heard war-cries, and they thought: "Maybe this is a war-party." They escaped to the shore and hid behind a log. Now canoes came up, and they heard the noise of paddles and saw one canoe coming up to them. There were five men in the canoe, and they said:

"What do you think? We wish to take you along. We are going up the river to make war on the people."

One of the young men said: "I have no arrows."

"Arrows are in the canoe," they said.

"I will not go along. I might be killed. My relatives do not know where I have gone. But you," he said, turning to the other, "may go with them."

So one of the young men went, but the other returned home.

And the warriors went up the river to a town on the other side of Kalama. The people came down to the water, and they began to fight, and many were killed. But presently the young man heard one of the warriors say: "Quick, let us go home: that Indian has been hit." Now he thought: "Oh, they are ghosts." He did not feel sick, but they said he had been shot.

So the canoes went back to Egulac, and the young man went ashore to his house, and made a fire. And he told everybody and said: "Behold I accompanied the ghosts, and we went to fight. Many of our fellows were killed and many of those who attacked us were killed. They said I was hit, and I did not feel sick."

He told it all, and then he became quiet. When the sun rose he fell down. Something black came out of his mouth. His face became contorted. The people jumped up and cried.

He was dead.

Barlett then asked his subjects to try to retell the story. About 20 hours later, one subject recalled the story this way.

THE WAR OF THE GHOSTS   Two men from Edulac went fishing. While thus occupied by the river they heard a noise in the distance.

"It sounds like a cry," said one, and presently there appeared some men in canoes who invited them to join the party on their adventure. One of the young men refused to go, on the ground of family ties, but the other offered to go.

"But there are no arrows," he said.

"The arrows are in the boat," was the reply.

He thereupon took his place, while his friend returned home. The party paddled up the river to Kaloma, and began to land on the banks of the river. The enemy came rushing upon them, and some sharp fighting ensued. Presently some one was injured, and the cry was raised that the enemy were ghosts.

The party returned down the stream, and the young man arrived home feeling none the worse for his experience. The next morning at dawn he endeavoured to recount his adventures. While he was talking something black issued from his mouth. Suddenly he uttered a cry and fell down. His friends gathered round him.

But he was dead.

Notice how the story has changed from the original. The story is shorter, and the style is more modern. Words such as *hunting seals* and *canoe*, which hardly appear in our everyday worlds, have been replaced by more familiar words such as *fishing* and *boat*.

This same person recalled the story again eight days later. This time the name *Kalama* (which had been incorrectly reproduced as *Kaloma* in the first retelling) was gone altogether. On the other hand, one element of the original story—"I might be killed"—that was missing in the first retelling reappeared. This item was apparently not available to his memory on his first retelling but could be retrieved later. You probably have had this same experience; perhaps you couldn't remember an important point during a test but remembered it completely when you told a friend about the question later on.

Another one of Bartlett's subjects recalled the story two and a half years after it had been presented. This is what he remembered:

Some warriors went to wage war against the ghosts. They fought all day and one of their number was wounded. They returned home in the evening, bearing their sick comrade. As the day drew to a close, he became rapidly worse and the villagers came round him. At sunset he sighed; something black came out of his mouth. He was dead.

Only the most basic points of the story remain, and some material that was apparently related to what the subject thought would happen was brought into the story. For example, the subject has added the detail about dying at sunset, which occurs in many folk tales, to the original story.

When Bartlett analyzed the retold stories, he noted a number of changes made by most subjects:

Omissions. Some information drops out. Things that are illogical or don't fit into the subject's expectations are most likely to be omitted.

Transformations. Unfamiliar words are changed into familiar ones, and the sequence of events is altered.

Dominant theme. Some themes, apparently perceived by the subject as dominant, continue to appear. Details that are remembered are related to these dominant themes.

Rationalization. Sometimes information is added that "makes more sense" to the subject than the original does.

More recent research with this same story produced similar changes in retelling (Glass and others, 1980, p. 116).

Reconstructive memory

One of the things to notice about all these retold stories is how much material has been added or invented to make a story seem more logical to the teller. Many of the details that people add, such as the bows and arrows used in the fight, are probably familiar from other Indian stories. This filling in of new elements is called **reconstructive memory.**

People routinely add their own knowledge to what they read. An experiment conducted by Sulin and Dooling (1974) illustrates this point. One group of subjects read the following paragraph:

CAROL HARRIS'S NEED FOR PROFESSIONAL HELP Carol Harris was a problem child from birth. She was wild, stubborn, and violent. By the time Carol turned eight, she was still unmanageable. Her parents were very concerned about her mental health. There was no good institution for her problem in her state. Her parents finally decided to take some action. They hired a private teacher for Carol.

Another group read the same story, except that the name of the main character was changed to "Helen Keller." Subjects were then given a list of sentences and asked to judge whether they were from the paragraph they had just read. Twenty percent of the subjects who had read the "Keller" paragraph agreed that the sentence "She was deaf, dumb, and blind" had occurred in the original story, but none of the "Carol Harris" group selected that sentence. Other subjects were tested a week after they read the paragraph. At that time, 50 percent of the "Keller" group and 5 percent of the "Harris" group selected the sentence. This experiment demonstrates clearly how people add information that they already have to new knowledge. It also shows that this effect grows over time.

Information acquired after an event can also change a person's memory in the same way that previous knowledge can. When another group that had read the "Harris" paragraph came in after a week for their retest, they were told that the paragraph was really about Helen Keller. They then made the same kinds of memory errors that the "Keller" group made. They "recognized" their own stored facts about Helen Keller as part of the paragraph's general content (Dooling and Christiaansen, 1977).

This phenomenon of reconstructive memory has important practical implications, especially for legal proceedings and police interrogations. Later stimuli, such as questions asked by investigators, can influence what people remember. This was illustrated in a series of experiments by Elizabeth Loftus and others (Loftus, 1981) in which college undergraduates were questioned about slides of crimes or traffic accidents. The way that the questions were phrased affected subjects' memories of what they had seen (see Figure 7.11).

New information included in the questions was found to become part of the observer's memory. Questions that were especially effective in producing this result were those in which the incorrect information was embedded in the question but was not its main focus. For example, subjects answering questions about a series of slides of a bank robbery were more likely to "remember" a nonexistent "loans" sign on a desk if the question were phrased "Was the woman, who was sitting at the desk with the 'loans' sign, biting her fingernails?" than if the question were asked more directly: "Was the 'loans' sign knocked off a desk by a robber?" (Johnson, 1979). It seems likely that, because the first question focused on the woman's fingernail biting, the subject's attention was diverted from the false information being introduced. Instead of being scrutinized and evaluated, that information was processed in a rather automatic fashion similar to the way that familiar stimuli are processed into memory using top-down coding. Sometimes, if familiar material is involved, it is processed quite effortlessly, and the individual, with divided attention, does two things at once. While this can be very efficient if a person is a witness to a crime, such effortless processing can lead to inaccurate and misleading testimony.

Advertisers also make use of people's tendency to elaborate and change their memories. For example, look at this portion of a Listerine commercial:

"Wouldn't it be great," asks the mother, "if you could make him coldproof? Well, you can't. Nothing can do that. [Boy sneezes.] But there is something that you can do that may help. Have him gargle with Listerine Antiseptic. Listerine can't promise to keep him cold-free, but it may help him fight off colds. During the cold-catching season, have him gargle twice a day with full-strength Listerine. Watch his diet, see he gets plenty of sleep, and there's a good chance he'll have fewer colds, milder colds, this year." (Anderson, 1980, p. 203)

This commercial, with the name of the product changed to Gargoil, was used in a memory experiment (Harris, 1977). After subjects had heard the commercial, they all agreed with the statement "Gargling with Gargoil Antiseptic helps prevent colds," even though the commercial did not say that. The subjects elaborated their memories by adding their own inferences to the ad. No doubt this was what the advertisers hoped would happen, but does it mean that they made a false claim? Memory research can help in legal decisions on points such as these.

Episodic and semantic memory

Memory can be divided into two types: semantic and episodic (Tulving, 1972, 1984). Up to now, we have been mainly looking at semantic memory. As we mentioned earlier, *semantic memory* is the organized knowledge a person possesses about words and symbols and the rules and relationships that govern their use. In our earlier discussion of verbal coding networks, for example, we focused on ways to encode semantic memories. Artificial intelligence research also looks for ways to reproduce and use semantic memory. **Episodic memory** means our record of personal life experiences. Some psychologists believe that these two types of memories are stored at different sites in the brain (Paivio and de Linde, 1982).

Episodic memory contains information about when and where an episode occurred as well as information about the event itself. Even the act of recalling

FIGURE 7.11 *Reconstructive memory uses a person's general store of information to fill in and modify memories of complex events. The questions asked of a witness may supply information that distorts the original memory. The picture on the left shows the original information, the question provides external information, and the picture on the right shows the memory of the information.*

Original information	External information	The "memory"
	"About how fast were the cars going when they SMASHED into each other?"	

information from episodic memory adds to the episodic store. In addition to remembering what last night's television program was about, you remember telling your friend about it. When you activate your semantic memory—for example, to remember that $5 \times 9 = 45$—your episodic memory is activated too when you remember the second-grade teacher who drilled the multiplication tables into your head. Semantic memory changes very little, since the facts that it is made up of are relatively stable. Episodic memory, on the other hand, is constantly changing because it refers to personal experience.

Another important point is that the only use we can make of episodic memory is to retrieve whatever has previously been stored there. Semantic memory, on the other hand, can use stored information to answer new questions. This is because semantic memory contains not only knowledge—Albany is the capital of New York and $4 \times 7 = 28$—but also the rules that are necessary to draw logical conclusions. You may never have seen a particular sentence before, but very likely you can identify its subject and its predicate. Even if you have never encountered a particular math problem, your memory is likely to have stored some rules that enable you to solve it.

Episodic memory may be thought about as a kind of conveyor belt of memory traces (Murdock, 1974). At today's end of the conveyor belt, the items are still in our consciousness. As new items are added throughout the day, earlier ones are carried farther and farther away from consciousness. As more time intervenes, it becomes more difficult to scan over the items because of their increasing number and distance. Accuracy of memory then suffers or forgetting occurs unless some method other than scanning is used. One method for retrieving older events is reconstruction, in which the context or cues present in the original situation are used as aids in retrieving the material. This method of retrieval may explain why memories that have not been in consciousness for a long period of time may suddenly return if we are in a similar situation.

Reread the anecdote at the beginning of the chapter. Notice the use of reconstructive memory techniques to provide cues that help retrieve information. The person struggling to remember his high school classmates tries out different organizational structures, much as you might do if you were looking in a library

card catalog for some books for a research paper. He searches his memory under different categories—for example, home neighborhood and activity interests such as surfing. In addition, he tries to visualize the surfing group because he might be able to remember their names if he can see their faces in his memory.

You have probably used the reconstructive technique many times. For example, what were you doing on March 24, 1985, at 10:00 A.M.? At first, the question might seem impossible to answer. You might start by thinking that in the spring of 1985 you were attending school. It was your second semester. In that semester you took chemistry, English literature, and physical education. March 24 was a Monday. Monday and Wednesday you had chemistry labs from 9:00 to 11:00 A.M. By this process, you could figure out that you were probably in the chemistry lab. Memories such as your lab partner's name, the experiments that you did in the middle of the semester, and so forth might also return as you continued your reconstruction. Although this procedure is logical, one problem with reconstruction is that there is always a chance that it will end in recapturing a fictitious memory. Maybe you were in chemistry lab, but perhaps the class was dismissed early that day or you had stayed home with a cold. Though they seem so logical and the recovered "memory" seems so convincing, sometimes such reconstructive techniques can misguide you.

Retrieval failure or forgetting

Cognitive theorists currently view forgetting as a failure to retrieve desired information. Most of us have at some time tried desperately but unsuccessfully to think of some piece of information that we knew was in there somewhere.

There are several theories about why we forget. In the next sections, we'll examine interference, biological state, and mood.

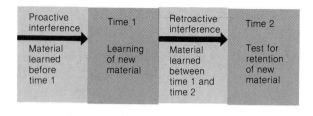

Proactive interference	Time 1	Retroactive interference	Time 2
Material learned before time 1	Learning of new material	Material learned between time 1 and time 2	Test for retention of new material

FIGURE 7.12 *Interference theory says that other learning blocks the items to be recalled. Some material is learned at time 1. After an interval there is a test for recall at time 2. Material learned before time 1 produces* proactive interference, *whereas material learned between time 1 and time 2 produces* retroactive interference. *Both types of interference lead to forgetting.*

INTERFERENCE

One of the oldest explanations of forgetting is that people forget things because other things interfere with, or block, the items that they are trying to remember. Interference theory is based on two observations: material that we have learned in the past can interfere with our ability to recall new material (**proactive interference**) and our ability to retain new material can be interfered with by material that we learn later (**retroactive interference**). These two types of interference are illustrated in Figure 7.12. Interference is greatest when previous or later learning is similar to what we are trying to recall.

One illustration of the effects of similarity on retention comes from research on the impact of TV news programs (Gunter and others, 1982). Since many people get most of their information about current events from the TV news, one goal broadcasters have is to present the news items in such a way that they will be remembered. Yet when retention of information has been measured by telephone interviews shortly after the program, half of those contacted could not remember any of the topics that were discussed. Even with prompting, few people could give details about 20 percent of the topics (Neuman, 1976). One reason for the failure to remember may be the organization of newscasts. They usually consist first of several national or international news stories that focus on politics or economics. These are followed by several sports stories and

finally by several human interest or science stories. Barry Gunter and his co-workers found that memory for the content fell off rapidly throughout each group. When the researchers rearranged newscasts so that stories were presented in a mixed order and not grouped by topics, memory for their contents was greatly improved. Each time there was a shift in topics, memory for the following story improved. These findings illustrate the practical implications of the interfering effects of similarity.

BIOLOGICAL STATE

Research with rats has shown that particular kinds of stimulation in a learning situation can lead to rather rapid changes in the activated nerve cells (Rosenzweig, 1984). These changes occur in both the dendrites and the synaptic contacts and are rapid enough to account for the establishment of long-term memories (long-term memory is discussed a little later). When certain kinds of chemicals such as Anisomycin are administered, they interfere with the protein synthesis necessary for these changes, and long-term memory is prevented.

Drugs that affect the effectiveness of the neurotransmitters by changing activity of the acetylcholene (ACh) receptors have been shown to influence memory in human beings (Flood and others, 1981). Drugs that decreased receptor activity improved retention of information; those that increased it improved memory in moderate doses, although at high doses they worsened it. Experimental use of these drugs has helped some individuals with impaired memories. Since not all memory problems are helped, the study of the effects of these drugs may also be useful in understanding the processes that occur in memory formation.

MOOD AS A RETRIEVAL CUE

Some psychologists have argued that forgetting is much like being unable to find something we have misplaced. The information we are looking for is temporarily unavailable, but it is not gone forever. The problem of remembering lies in finding the correct place in the storage system. If we have the right retrieval cue, the information will again be available.

The importance of context as a retrieval cue was

discussed earlier in the chapter. One important contextual retrieval cue is a similarity of mood or emotion at the time material is learned and when a memory search is conducted (Bower, 1981). For example, if you felt sad while learning your French vocabulary words, the chances are that if you were also sad while trying to recall them, you would remember more words. If you were up on top over some good news such as finding that your bank balance was $20 higher than you thought, you would be likely to remember fewer words because the sadness present during learning would not be functioning as a cue. While these examples may seem rather ridiculous, they have an important application for clinical psychologists. Use of similar emotions as cues for retrieval can have important effects in recall of episodic memories. People who are sad or depressed are likely to remember more unpleasant experiences from the past than people who are in a pleasant mood. This can result in a negative view that may intensify the depression.

Are memories ever permanently lost?

The view of some memory investigators who claim that information is never permanently lost once it has been learned—it's still in there, even if we are temporarily unable to find it—has been supported by research in areas other than cognitive psychology.

CONTRIBUTIONS FROM SURGERY

Findings from the field of brain surgery have provided some indication that forgetting does not mean that the information is no longer stored somewhere in the person's memory system. For many years researchers have been trying to identify particular points on the brain where specific memories may be stored. One of the earliest attempts was conducted in the 1950s. Wilder Penfield, a Canadian neurosurgeon, exposed portions of the temporal lobe cortex of epileptic patients while using a local anesthetic so that the patients were fully conscious during the operation. (Remember, as we saw in Chapter 5, the brain feels no pain.) Penfield then stimulated different points on the cortex electrically. One patient reported that she could see herself in an office in which she had worked a long time ago: "I

could see the desks. I was there and someone was calling to me—a man leaning on a desk with a pencil in his hand." Other patients reexperienced insignificant events from early childhood, events that were unlikely to have been remembered under normal conditions. However, only a few of Penfield's patients had such early memories, and other memory researchers have questioned whether these memories were of actual events or were merely examples of reconstructive memory in which events that could have occurred at about that time were remembered as having occurred (Loftus and Loftus, 1980).

Penfield's work and other studies at first seemed to suggest that it was possible to identify particular points on the brain where specific memories are stored. However, many authorities have concluded that the brain's memory storage is diffuse, not localized in particular spots. Recently researchers have again opened this question to debate (Fox, 1983). Working with rabbits, they believe they have found memory trace circuits so localized that a lesion as small as one pin prick can destroy the trace for a particular learned response. Using chemicals that either permanently or temporarily destroy the function of selected nerve bodies, they have succeeded in eradicating a conditioned eyeblink response to a tone while the eyeblink response to the original unconditioned stimulus, a puff of air, remains (Mishkin and Petri, in press). This research, together with surgical data from monkeys and studies of human performance in patients with brain lesions, leads some researchers to believe that there are two information storage systems. One, a habit system, regulates behavioral response and may be quite localized; the other is related to cognitive responding and may be more wide-ranging and diffuse (Mishkin, 1984).

PSYCHODYNAMIC OBSERVATIONS

In his therapy sessions, Sigmund Freud found that his patients remembered incidents from the past that had long been forgotten. Many of these events, it seemed to him, had been forgotten because they were so upsetting to the patient. He called this process of motivated forgetting *repression*. For example, one of his patients remembered that while standing beside her sister's coffin, she had thought, "Now my brother-in-law is free to marry me." This thought apparently shocked her so much that she had repressed it immediately and did not remember it again until the therapy session. This type of later recovery of events suggests that forgetting may be more a result of psychological state than a loss of stored information. The same process occurs when amnesia, or sudden memory loss, results from an extremely upsetting situation. Sometimes amnesia occurs when people cannot face the reality of their own behavior or the situation in which they find themselves. For example, soldiers may have no memory of a particularly traumatic battle experience.

THE TIP OF THE TONGUE PHENOMENON

Another example of the persistence of stored information—the **tip of the tongue** (TOT) **phenomenon**—comes from everyday experience. Suppose someone asked you the name of the capital of Illinois. You might think of Fairfield, Mayfield, or other similar words. You might think it was a two-syllable word beginning with S. If you could not think of the answer, it is likely that the question would keep returning to your mind until the correct answer, Springfield, finally occurred to you. The inability to remember exactly, while being able to produce clues to the correct answer, is interesting to psychologists who study memory. It implies that the fact is not forgotten, but that the retrieval mechanism has temporarily shorted out.

DISPLACEMENT OF MEMORIES

It seems clear that some things become temporarily inaccessible either because they are blocked by other memories or because we do not have an appropriate method for getting them out. We can't say that this applies to all memories because it is not yet possible to prove that information can't be forgotten completely. In fact, some recent research has suggested that, at least in certain situations, if new memories become blended with old ones, then the original memories cannot be retrieved even by providing strongly relevant cues

(Loftus, 1981). For example, after showing subjects slides of a pedestrian–auto accident at an intersection with a stop sign, the researchers asked them questions about the accident, using the phrase "yield sign" instead of "stop sign." When asked later about what they had seen, many of the group said they had seen a yield sign rather than a stop sign. Even when the original slide showing the stop sign and a doctored slide showing a yield sign were presented, the subjects did not remember what they had actually seen. It appeared that the new memory introduced by the questioning had actually taken the place of the original memory. Even when the subjects were told the purpose of the experiment, 90 percent of those who responded incorrectly still insisted they had seen the yield sign. This study raises a question about whether all memories endure and suggests that some memories are not merely unretrievable; they may actually have been displaced by others and now no longer exist.

Other researchers question this conclusion that the original memory no longer exists. When memory was tested by presenting the slides about the incident in a random order, subjects' responses were influenced by the last information they had, which was the misleading question. However, when the slides were presented in the original action sequence, the original memory was reported correctly (Berkerian and Bowers, 1983). These experimenters believe that forgetting has taken place because relevant cues are missing rather than because a new memory has replaced the old one.

CURRENT THEORETICAL VIEWS OF MEMORY PROCESSES

A variety of perspectives have contributed to our understanding of information processing and retrieval. The biological perspective has furnished information about how chemicals and electrical impulses affect memory. The behavioral perspective has provided information about the effects of interfering stimuli on learning and retrieval. The psychodynamic perspective has contributed ideas about how emotions affect the ability to remember. At present, the cognitive perspective probably has the greatest influence on researchers who are trying to understand why we forget and how we organize in-

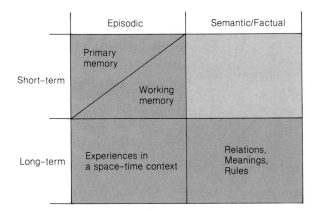

	Episodic	Semantic/Factual
Short-term	Primary memory / Working memory	
Long-term	Experiences in a space-time context	Relations, Meanings, Rules

formation so that we can retrieve it when we want to do so.

As we explained earlier, most memory researchers today use an information processing model to guide their work. They separate cognitive functions into input, processing (including coding and storage), and retrieval. Now that we have discussed these processes, we will look at the way current theorists view the memory process in general (see Figure 7.13). As we have stressed throughout the book, the theoretical views that researchers have make a great difference in the kinds of problems they investigate and also in the kinds of information their studies produce.

The duplex theory

Everyday observation tells us that not everything that our senses perceive is remembered, even briefly. Only a limited amount of new information can be retained at once, although clearly as time passes, a great deal more information can be stored in what we call memory. To help them understand these different aspects of memory, many researchers have used a **duplex theory** as the basis for their work. The theory is called *duplex* because it divides memory into two separate parts: immediate or **short-term memory** and permanent or **long-term memory** (see Figure 7.14).

The process of remembering a phone number can again serve as a good illustration of how the duplex model works. Suppose that we called the information operator in Washington, D.C., and asked for the tele-

FIGURE 7.13 *Some of the major categories of memory used in current theories are shown in this diagram. (Adapted from Estes, 1982, p. 202.)*

phone number of the White House. When the operator gave us the number, the information would enter our memory system through our ears. In the first stage of the memory process it would be placed in a sensory store. We discussed two kinds of sensory stores earlier, the iconic store for visual input and the echoic store for auditory input. In this case the echoic store would hold not only the telephone number but any other information that had entered through our ears, such as the operator's words "The number is . . . " The sensory store has a large, but very short-term, storage capacity. Unless the information is quickly transferred to another area of memory, it will be lost forever.

In the second stage of the process, assuming we acted quickly enough, our telephone number would be transferred to short-term memory, which has a limited capacity. As we said in our earlier discussion of chunking, only about 7 items can be retained in immediate memory. If our number included an area code—say, (555) 543-6786—these 10 digits might be too much to hold in current memory. Even if we chunked them, our ability to remember would be limited because information in the short-term memory will fade in about 15 seconds unless it is processed further. If we dialed the phone number as soon as we received it from the operator, but got a busy signal, we might discover that we needed to ask for the telephone number again before we could redial it. In those few minutes the number would have been lost, unless we had rehearsed or repeated it. Information can be stored indefinitely by constantly repeating it. However, rehearsing the number over and over means that our attention couldn't be devoted to other things.

If we felt that the president's telephone number was a matter of lasting importance, we might make it a

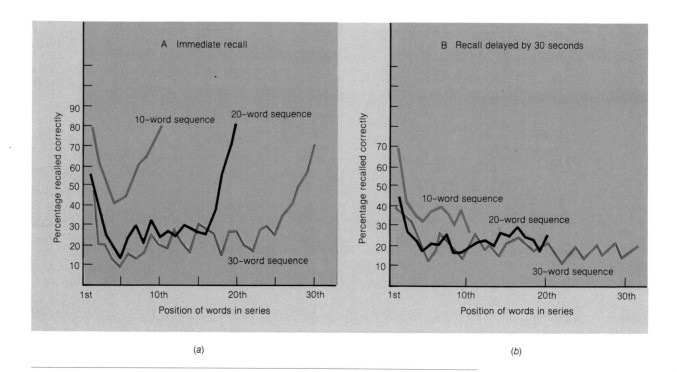

FIGURE 7.14 *If recall is immediate, (a) the last items on the list are recalled quite accurately. If there is even a half-minute delay, (b) the last word on the list is not usually remembered. (Adapted from Postman and Phillips, 1965.)*

more enduring memory by processing it further and storing it more or less permanently in long-term memory. Our long-term memory store has a huge capacity for holding information. It holds all the words we have ever learned, along with their meanings. It holds all the important events of our past and a great many unimportant ones as well. It holds the alphabet, the multiplication tables, our telephone number, and our friends' names. All this information is coded and stored in some manner to make retrieval easier.

The duplex model and others similar to it stimulated a great deal of research built on the ideas that short-term memory has characteristics different from memory that lasts longer or indefinitely and that these differences can be explained best by thinking of two separate storage systems in addition to the sensory store.

One type of data supporting the duplex theory is supplied by the **serial position curve** obtained in many verbal learning experiments. In such experiments lists of words or syllables are briefly presented singly or in groups. When people are immediately asked to recall as many words or syllables as they can, the results look like the curve of immediate recall in Figure 7.14. This curve shows that the probability that a word will be recalled depends largely on where it occurred in the list. The fact that words from the beginning of the list have a good chance of being recalled is known as the **primacy effect.** Words from the end of the list also have a good chance of being recalled (this is termed the **recency effect**). Words from the middle of the list cannot be recalled as often.

The curve of delayed recall in Figure 7.14 describes the results when time elapses between learning and recall. The first words in the list can be recalled easily because the person has had more time to rehearse them than the later ones. The last words in the list can be recalled immediately after learning because these items are still in short-term memory. As we illustrated earlier, short-term memory cannot retain information when rehearsal cannot take place. If the recall is delayed for even a short period, this superior memory of the last items no longer occurs because these items are no longer in short-term memory. If the list is short enough so that the limited capacity of short-term memory is not overtaxed, then the items can be kept in its memory by rehearsal. If, however, the subjects think about something else, as when an experimenter asks them to repeat a series of numbers, then the result is a curve like one of the curves in Figure 7.14(*b*). Thus, the duplex theory accounts for the serial position curve quite well.

Another kind of data supporting the dual store idea comes from clinical observations. Daniel Schachter, a researcher interested in selective memory failure, observed M.T., a patient with Alzheimer's disease, as the two played golf together (Schachter, 1983). (Alzheimer's disease is a brain disorder in which memory is severely impaired.) Schachter found that M.T. kept forgetting where his ball was if he had to wait for

(© SIDNEY HARRIS.)

Schachter to play first. If M.T. had teed off first, he forgot that he had done so by the time Schachter had played his ball. M.T. was also totally incapable of keeping score because he could not remember any of his shots a minute or two after completing the hole. Even though his memory kept M.T. from playing golf well, he was able to use all the golf jargon he had previously learned (*bogey*, *driver*, *wedge shot*), always selected the proper club for the shot, and teed up flawlessly, always aiming toward the green. This ability to use his long-term knowledge was functioning quite well, but his retention for recent events, even those a minute or two old, was very poor (see Figure 7.15). Although M.T.'s spatial and perceptual skills were very poor when he was tested under laboratory conditions, on the golf links those deficiencies disappeared. Findings such as this one suggest that memory, in order to be studied productively, must be broken down into components and that new or short-term information and information recovered from long-term store are two of those components.

Levels of processing and elaboration

Most theories cannot explain every bit of experimental data, and duplex memory theory is no exception. For example, the duplex theory assumes that information is transferred from the short-term to the long-term memory by the use of rehearsal. Yet Fergus Craik and Rob-

FIGURE 7.15 *Usually when we think of improving memory, we are talking about long-term retention; that is why this cartoon strikes us as funny. However, for certain individuals, such as the patient M.T. with Alzheimer's disease, and some accident victims with particular kinds of brain damage, problems with short-term memory are very real and very debilitating.*

ert Lockhart (1972) of the University of Toronto pointed out that rehearsal in and of itself does not always lead to the long-term retention of information. Even if you repeat a telephone number 20 times while you continue to dial a busy number, after your call finally goes through, the number may not remain in your memory. This is especially true if it is a number that you think you will never need again.

Craik and Lockhart were not concerned with the question of two memory systems; they emphasized two different ways of processing material. They suggested that these two kinds of rehearsal have different effects on retention. People may use **maintenance rehearsal** to keep material available for immediate use (as when we repeat a telephone number that we have looked up for one-time use). But when people intend to remember something permanently, they may use **elaborative rehearsal**—that is, in addition to repetition, they begin to form associations between the new information and information already stored in their memories.

In elaborative rehearsal incoming information is processed in a variety of ways so that it can be integrated with existing memory. In general, the more it is elaborated, the better it will be remembered. One way to elaborate material is to set up some mnemonic formula. A method like the peg words provides a search structure through its verbal cues and also forces people to form images so that the items are stored visually. Information can also be stored according to its meaning by connecting the information with something already known. For example, if someone tells you that her birthday is August 23, you might think, "August 23 is exactly a month after my dad's birthday, on July 23, and it's one day after my sister's wedding anniversary, on August 22." The next time you want to remember the date, you might enter your memory store at one of several places—your friend's birthday, your dad's birthday, or your sister's anniversary.

Although repeating the stimulus can help to keep the item in memory, it may not produce efficient long-term learning (Craik, 1981; Nelson, 1977). The memory may not be established as quickly in the long-term store and may be harder to retrieve than memories established through elaboration. Elaboration provides more memory cues that facilitate later retrieval. What may count most in memory is the ties made between the information already stored and the new informa-

tion that is rehearsed. Elaboration that creates more ties to items already learned seems most beneficial to learning (Wickelgren, 1981). Both recognition and recall are improved by the elaboration with which the stimulus is encoded. Probably this is true because there are more context cues available and it is easier to locate a particular memory. Other kinds of context cues—similarities of environment, for example—also improve recall if they are again present when an attempt to remember occurs (Baddeley, 1982b). This is probably because the similar cues help focus the search.

Are short-term and long-term memory separate? This question has been actively debated by memory researchers for the last twenty years and the evidence is not yet in to make a clear answer possible. Like many other difficult questions, as conflicting research findings have mounted, researchers have realized that the answer probably is "both are true, sometimes" and have wisely decided to investigate other related questions that may be more productive in helping to understand how memory works.

A great deal of investigation is now concerned with larger and more comprehensive questions of memory, meaning, and knowledge. Researchers are more interested in the organization of permanent memory and the ways the retrieval systems handle the storage of complex information. Analysis of memory for complex stimuli, stemming from the work of Bartlett; investigations with very practical implications (such as the study of eyewitness testimony); and a new interest in variables such as the importance of context and of emotional factors in retrieval of earlier learning—all have focused the energies of both researchers and theorists on new sets of questions. How information is processed and how processing relates to organization of memory data and facilitates retrieval are of primary interest to researchers in developing a theoretical understanding of cognitive behavior.

STUDY OUTLINE

INFORMATION PROCESSING (p. 240)

1. Cognitive psychologists see memory, language, and thought as forms of information processing in which the human being behaves similarly to a computer. Information processing involves several steps: input, processing (coding and storage), and retrieval.

2. A sensory store, one for each of the senses, can retain material only for a short period. To be remembered longer, the material must be processed and coded. Before processing occurs, it can be held in memory during the time it is actively repeated or rehearsed.

3. Processing can be bottom-up, which means that all the elements in the stimulus are inspected and then combined to reproduce the stimulus. Or it can be top-down. In this case, the person uses the overall meaning and simply fills in a few other ideas that he or she expects to find associated with that meaning.

4. In order for the person to retain what has been processed, the information is coded for storage. Some is coded visually by means of a kind of condensed imagery. Other information is coded abstractly into such forms as language, musical notation, or mathematical symbols. As an aid to retention and to retrieval of what is remembered, several techniques are used to organize the material. These include chunking, mnemonic techniques, and peg words.

5. In our memory, factual information may be organized into hierarchical networks made up of propositions or units of knowledge organized according to their relationships. Metacognition, an awareness of one's knowledge about what one knows, is important in understanding how to search for and use information.

RETRIEVAL FROM MEMORY (p. 251)

1. Recognition, or the correct identification of what has been seen (or heard, felt, smelled, etc.), and recall, or the correct reproduction of the stimulus, seem to be two different memory processes. Most people retain more if learning and remembering take place in a similar situation.

2. When complex stimuli are remembered, they seem to be processed so that only the basic ideas remain. When they are remembered, the information is expanded by the use of reconstructive memory, which adds information that logically seems to go with what has been retained. Sometimes this can lead to inaccurate and misleading "memories."

3. Two categories of memory are semantic and epi-

sodic. Semantic memory consists of organized knowledge and the rules that govern its use. Episodic memory, which is made up of personal experiences, changes constantly over time.

RETRIEVAL FAILURE OR FORGETTING (p. 257)

1. There are several theories as to why things are forgotten; probably all are useful. Interference may cause forgetting, either because new material gets in the way of the old (retroactive interference) or because old material interferes with learning new information (proactive interference). Interference is especially important when new and old material are similar. The chemical state at sites within the brain is also important. Specific drugs can alter changes in the nervous system that ordinarily occur during learning or may change the effectiveness of the neurotransmitters. Sometimes material is harder to access because of differences between the situation in which it was learned and the one in which it is searched for, as if the right cue for retrieval is more difficult to find.

2. The question of whether data that are forgotten are permanently lost has not been settled. Direct stimulation of the brain has yielded memories that seemed to have been forgotten. The tip of the tongue phenomenon, in which the correct answer cannot be immediately remembered but the person still can provide clues about what the answer is, suggests that the problem of forgetting lies in correct access to the retrieval system. Sometimes one memory appears to replace another, so that the original version of what was experienced seems to have disappeared.

CURRENT THEORETICAL VIEWS OF MEMORY PROCESSES (p. 260)

Most memory researchers today use the information processing model in their work. The duplex theory stresses that long-term and short-term memory have different characteristics. The levels of processing and elaboration theory stresses the importance of understanding how an individual codes information and how many different access cues he or she provides by developing relationships between the new material and other information already in memory.

KEY TERMS AND CONCEPTS

information processing

input

coding

storage

iconic store

echoic store

sensory store

selective processing

bottom-up processing

top-down processing

visual code

abstract code

chunking

mnemonic technique

peg word system

semantic memory

declarative representation scheme

proposition

hierarchical network

metacognition

recognition

recall

reconstructive memory

episodic memory

proactive interference

retroactive interference

tip of the tongue phenomenon

duplex theory

short-term memory

long-term memory

serial position curve

primacy effect

recency effect

maintenance rehearsal

elaborative rehearsal

SUGGESTED READINGS

BADDELEY, A. (1983). *Your memory: A user's guide.* New York: Penguin Books. A brief and interesting discussion of learning, storage, and retrieval as well as discussions of eyewitness testimony, amnesia, and ways to improve memory. The book includes a variety of interesting examples and illustrations.

KLATZKY, R. L. (1984). *Memory and awareness: An information processing perspective.* New York: W. H. Freeman. A short and clear discussion of the role that consciousness of three aspects of behavior—ongoing mental activities, knowledge stored in memory, and one's own memory abilities—plays in what is remembered.

SPOEHR, K. T., and LEHMKUHLE, S. W. (1982). New York: W. H. Freeman. V*isual information processing.* An up-to-date review of the role of the visual system in memory that covers pattern recognition, picture processing, and visual memory.

CHAPTER EIGHT

LANGUAGE, PROBLEM SOLVING, AND INTELLIGENCE

LANGUAGE
The structure of language
Understanding language
Language development
Biological basis of language
FRONTIER 8.1   DO ANIMALS USE LANGUAGE?
Language and cognition

PROBLEM SOLVING
Understanding problem-solving techniques
Algorithms versus heuristics
Common difficulties in problem solving

INTELLIGENCE
Sources of intelligence
The structure of intelligence
The processes of intelligent behavior
Intelligence tests
Social issues and testing
FRONTIER 8.2   A NEW GENERATION OF INTELLIGENCE TESTS?

STUDY OUTLINE

KEY TERMS AND CONCEPTS

SUGGESTED READINGS

What we call intelligence, in the narrow sense of the term, consists of two chief processes: First to perceive the external world, and then to reinstate the perceptions in memory, to rework them, and to think about them. (Binet, 1890)

Alfred Binet, creator of the first widely used intelligence test, thought about intelligence in terms of the cognitive processes that were discussed in Chapter 7. In this chapter we will discuss how the types of cognitive functioning that we call intelligence are studied and measured by psychologists. Before doing that, however, we will first look at language, one of the vehicles for storing, organizing, and retrieving information. Language is not only one of the best ways available to study cognitive processes and the way people solve problems, but it is also the primary way to assess the cognitive skills that we call intelligence.

In this chapter, we look at the behavior that may make us unique among all other animals—language—and at those problem-solving skills and intellectual abilities that no other animal has more of than we do.

LANGUAGE

Language permits us to communicate. We could make some of our thoughts known without language, but the process would be cumbersome and restricted to very basic information. *Memory has an important language component.* Language provides a way to process and store information by allowing us to treat it symbolically. *To some extent, thinking is talking to ourselves.* Without language, the way that we think and solve problems would be very different and the level of complexity that we could deal with would be greatly reduced. Finally, *language affects our perception of the environment.* It would be hard to imagine a world without language: we wouldn't even have the words to describe how bleak it would be. We use language as a tool, but its existence has in turn shaped our values and our way of life. Psychologists are interested in how language changes us as well as how we change language.

Psycholinguistics is the study of the way that sounds and symbols are translated into meaning and of the psychological processes that are involved in that translation. Psycholinguists have mainly concentrated on understanding the structure of language and comparing language structures in a variety of cultures. We'll look at this aspect of psycholinguistics first. Then, along with many psycholinguists today, we'll focus on the role that language plays in cognition and thought.

The structure of language

The most basic of the structural elements of language are **phonemes.** Phonemes are the smallest units of speech, those sounds that are recognized as separate in any given language. In English, the phonemes are the vowel and consonant sounds as well as certain letter combinations such as *sh* and *th*. The number of phonemes differs among different languages, from 15 to over 80. English is in the middle of the range with 45. The phonemes can be combined into **morphemes,** which are the smallest units of meaning in a given language. Some English morphemes are whole words *(tree, run, learn)*. Some are prefixes or suffixes *(un-, pre-, anti-, -s, -ed,* and *-ous)*. In all languages the number of morphemes is limited by certain rules that restrict the possible combinations of phonemes. For example, in English no more than three consonant sounds *(spl,* for instance) can be combined, while in Russian four consonants *(stch,* for example) can be used together. Even with such restrictions, the 45 phonemes of the English language can be combined into more than 100,000 morphemes.

The sentence "She rode the horse fast" is constructed according to English language rules of syntax; the sentence "Horse the she fast rode" breaks those rules. Rules of syntax vary from language to language. In German, for instance, the verb often comes at the end of the sentence. In some languages, adjectives are always found after the noun they modify, although in

English they generally come before the noun. Knowledge of a language's rules of syntax helps people speaking the same language to understand each other.

Psycholinguists describe language as having both a **surface structure** and a **deep structure.** The surface structure consists simply of the way that the words are organized. The deep structure, on the other hand, refers to the underlying meaning of the sentence. The term **semantics** refers to the meaning of words and sentences and to the rules that govern deep structure.

The difference between surface structure and deep structure can be illustrated by the following sets of sentences:

Christy ran over the dog with her car.
The car driven by Christy ran over the dog.

The surface structures in this set of sentences are quite different, yet because the sentences mean the same thing they have the same deep structure. But consider these sentences:

There is the white house cat.
There is the White House cat.

The second two sentences have identical surface structures, but the deep structures are very different. Psycholinguists believe that the deep structure—the meaning—rather than the actual words themselves is what is stored in memory, searched for, and retrieved.

Understanding language

Understanding language involves several steps. Basically, the speech sounds that we hear are organized into basic phrases or units called **constituents.** The meaning of the individual constituents is determined; then they are combined to figure out the meaning of the whole sentence.

What are the constituents of language and how do we know they exist? In general, a constituent is a group of words that can be replaced by a single word without changing the structure of the rest of the sentence (Clark and Clark, 1977). For example, think of this sentence:

The chubby boy twisted the steering wheel.

Figure 8.1 shows how this sentence can be broken down into increasingly detailed parts. *The chubby boy* can be replaced by a single word such as *Harry* or *Brian* or *he*, but *boy twisted the* is not a constituent because no single word can be substituted that has the same function in the sentence.

But how do we know that constituents exist except in the mind of the psycholinguist? Studies in which subjects are asked to decide which words in sentences go together show that there is a very high degree of agreement (Martin, 1970). For example, in a sentence like, "He was walking the scraggly dog," subjects almost always joined the auxiliary verb *was* with the main verb *walking*, the adjective *scraggly* was almost always included in the same grouping with the noun *dog*, and so on. These results suggest that we organize what we hear into natural units of meaning.

FIGURE 8.1   *An example of constituents.*

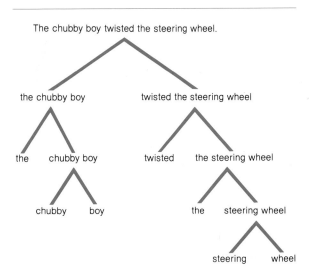

Language development

One of the biggest developmental changes that young children make is the acquisition of language. As cognitive psychologist Jerome Bruner put it, he was drawn to the study of language because, "if language was *the* human means by which we finally represented and interpreted the world, then its acquisition must shed light not only on language but on thought" (Bruner, 1983, p. 163). How this comes about is thought of in rather different ways by theorists of varying theoretical perspectives.

PERSPECTIVES ON LANGUAGE DEVELOPMENT

Linguist Noam Chomsky's theories about language have dramatically changed the way psychologists approach the study of language development. Chomsky (1968, 1975) emphasizes that the elements and rules of meaning—the deep structures of language—are innate and can be explained by the way that the human nervous system is put together. In other words, no matter what language we speak first, we have a built-in mechanism that provides the set of rules we use for language communication (see Figure 8.2). Chomsky believes that without such an innate mechanism, the enormous number of possible variations would make learning language impossible because no one would ever be able to comprehend the rules.

The Kennedy twins, shown in Figure 8.3, provide an interesting example that could be used to support Chomsky's theory. Until they were 6 years old, Grace and Virginia Kennedy spoke only their own private language, despite the fact that they could understand what was said to them in either of two languages, English and German. Although they could communicate with each other perfectly, their language was not comprehensible to others. Consider the following interchange:

Virginia says, "Dugon, thosh yom dinckin, du-ah?"
Grace answers, "Snup aduk, chase-dipanna."

Psycholinguists who studied the Kennedy sisters described their private language as having all the characteristics of a real language: a definite syntax as well as nouns, verbs, and verb tenses. Some of the language

"What's the big surprise? All the latest theories of linguistics say we're born with the innate capacity for generating sentences."

(© SIDNEY HARRIS.)

FIGURE 8.2 *This young child seems to be an advocate of Noam Chomsky's theories of language development.*

sounds were similar to German and some resembled English, but it was clearly not a mixture of the two languages. For that reason, some linguists interpret the case of the Kennedy sisters as evidence that there is some inborn knowledge of syntax. Why else would the girls' language behavior have contained the structural forms common to all languages?

According to Chomsky's theory, all the language that the child hears is processed or analyzed in certain ways according to the built-in pattern. Children fit the language they hear into this pattern and then as their brains develop over the first year of life and reach a state of readiness for language, they use the pattern to create new language examples. Although this programmed idea may sound far-fetched, research data suggest that programming occurs in other areas of development. For example, when babies look at geometric figures such as squares or triangles, they tend to look at the corners rather than at the connecting lines (Cohen, 1979). This built-in strategy for scanning is presumably based on the fact that the corners provide more information about shape than the sides of a figure do. Why is this strategy considered to be programmed? Because the babies in this study were only 1 to 2 days old.

Before Chomsky introduced his ideas, the study of language development was based on a behavioral viewpoint that a child's sounds were shaped into words by selective reinforcement (Skinner, 1957; Whitehurst and Vasta, 1975; Staats, 1971). It is true that this technique has been used to teach language to psychotic children and to children with delayed language development (Lovaas, 1973). But a great deal of research with children suggests the inadequacy of the behavioral approach. Children do not usually imitate exactly what they have just heard, and parents do not usually correct a young child who speaks ungrammatically or who does not use complete sentences. As a result, the role of imitation in children's language development is still hotly debated (Stine and Bohannon, 1983).

Roger Brown, a psychologist who has made an extensive study of the speech development of young children, found that parents typically respond to the basic meaning of their children's speech but put little pressure on the children to speak grammatically. The parent is more likely to make a correction if the child uses an incorrect *concept* rather than incorrect grammar. If Stevie looks out the car window at the cows grazing in the field and says, "See doggie," then his parent is likely to correct him and say, "See the cows."

Apparently, children drop their early speech patterns on their own and speak grammatically as they grow older (Brown and others, 1969). Parents do use a technique called **expanding,** in which they change a child's simple phrase into a more complex adult sentence. For example, "Go store" might be responded to by, "Yes, Stevie is going to the store." However, contrary to what might be predicted, there is no evidence that expanding is an important factor in the child's language progress. In fact, research has shown that a great deal of parental emphasis on correct speech can be counterproductive. Children whose mothers systematically correct their pronunciation develop vocabularies more slowly than children whose mothers simply respond to the meaning of their speech (Nelson, 1973). This finding also argues against reinforcement of imitation as a total explanation for language development.

Instead of being considered a biologically programmed trait (Chomsky) or an imitative response (Skinner), language development can be seen as a response to a need to communicate. Some cognitive psychologists—for example, Bruner—believe that chil-

FIGURE 8.3 *Grace and Virginia Kennedy developed a private way of communicating that seemed to have the characteristics of a real language.*

FIGURE 8.4 *Babbling is common to all infants, but exactly what function it plays in language development is still unclear.*

dren learn to speak to relieve the stress that they feel at being unable to communicate in social situations. This point of view emphasizes the reinforcement value of speaking and of receiving feedback from others.

The importance of feedback in language acquisition is illustrated by the following case study (Moskowitz, 1978). A child learned to use sign language to communicate with his deaf parents. Since they also wanted him to learn spoken English, the parents encouraged him to watch television. The child quickly learned sign language by interacting with his parents, but he could not learn spoken language by passively viewing television.

Bruner (1978) believes that the natural style that most adults use in speaking to young children increases the child's interest in language. When young children are around, people tend to speak slowly, to change the pitch of their voices, to articulate more clearly, to use shorter sentences, and to repeat the message in several different ways to ensure understanding. Although there is no evidence that children cannot learn speech when adults speak to them only in an adult manner, children as young as 4 months prefer listening to adult-to-child speech than adult-to-adult speech (Fernald and Kuhl, 1981). Also, adults seem to adjust the complexity of

their speech as children's abilities advance (Snow and others, 1976).

THE SEQUENCE OF DEVELOPMENT

The process of language acquisition is the same regardless of the reasons for learning to speak. Infants can differentiate between speech sounds and other environmental noises at a very early age. For example, infants 1 month old can distinguish between *b* and *p* sounds just as adults can (Eimas and others, 1971). Infants not only distinguish between sounds that occur in their own culture, but, in a way very similar to adults, they can also differentiate between sounds that do not occur in their own language (Eimas, 1976). This suggests to some researchers that the ability to discriminate between particular speech sounds is present at birth.

Infants' production of speech sounds also seems to have a powerful biological determinant. Sometime around their third or fourth month, babies in all cultures begin to make babbling sounds that are similar to speech (see Figure 8.4). Hearing sounds spoken to them does not seem to be the vital factor because deaf infants begin to babble at about the same time as those who can hear. However, deaf babies soon stop babbling, probably because they are deprived of the auditory feedback from their own noises. Parents are usually excited by the infant's babbling and reinforce it when it occurs, but this reinforcement doesn't seem necessary for babbling to continue. Children who have deaf parents show babbling patterns similar to those of infants whose parents can hear and can thus respond to their babbling (Lenneberg and others, 1965). How close the link is between babbling and speech has been debated by researchers for a number of years. It seems likely that babbling is related to speech but not directly tied in to the process of learning language (Clark and Clark, 1977).

When children first begin to speak, they simplify many words. The first word is often a sound or set of sounds that the child uses consistently to refer to a particular thing or event, such as *ba* to mean "bottle." Later the child may take the first part of a word and repeat it: *dada* for "daddy." Another kind of simplification that children use is to omit the unstressed syllable from a multisyllable word—for example, *nana* for "banana."

Most children have a vocabulary of about 50 words within 6 to 8 months after they speak their first word. At about 18 to 24 months they speak their first "sentence," which usually consists of only 2 words, such as "Want cookie." From this point on, children increase their vocabularies at a rapidly accelerating pace; several hundred words may be added every 6 months for the next few years. The child's grammar also grows rapidly.

Children in all cultures seem to have a grammar all their own. For example, they go through a stage in which they attach a *wh-* word (*why, who, where, when, what*) to the beginning of sentences, so that they can ask questions without changing the sentence's internal structure: "Why he play song?" "When we go store?" "Why Bobby hit me?" The grammar that they use is a consistent system, but it is obviously not one that children copy from anyone around them. The whole process appears to be creative rather than imitative.

Children's early words are of several kinds. They have words for people and objects, words about feelings and relationships (*please, no, yes, want, ouch*), and action words (*go, look, up*). What is missing in these early vocabularies is superordinate words, those that refer to larger classes of objects. Children 2 to 3 years old may have words for cookie, grapes, milk, peas, and

other foods, but they are unlikely to have the word *food* in their vocabularies, or, if they have it, they are unlikely to use it in a general sense to include all the other food words that they know. In this sense, then, early vocabulary is specific; words tend to refer to particular objects or groups of objects. But even at this early age, children do have a sense of classes of objects. They typically use the word *chair* to refer to several different chairs, rather than just one specific chair.

As children grow older, their **metalinguistic awareness**—the knowledge about their own language processes—also grows. Language development in syntax, in semantics, and in the use of figurative language continues along with developmental changes. Social interactions also play an important role in language development (Durkin, 1983).

Biological basis of language

There is a long-held idea that language is the primary characteristic that makes us different from all other species. Are there biological characteristics unique to humans that determine why language has evolved into its present form? The first determinant of the form of language is the structure of the parts of the human body that are used in the production of speech. The variety of anatomical features used in vocal production that are available to the human being (see Figure 8.5) and the flexible muscles of the human face make possible a large repertoire of sound differentiations.

Second, the human brain is larger and heavier than the brains of highly developed animals such as chimpanzees, and much less of the human cerebral cortex is devoted to sensory motor activities. But the one thing that seems to be unique about the human brain is its *lateralization*, the division of functions between the right and left hemispheres. It may be that this separation is what allows human beings to function at the level of cognitive complexity needed for language de-

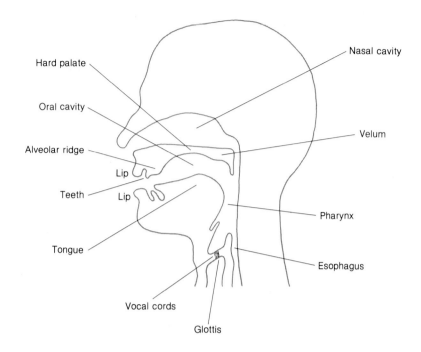

FIGURE 8.5 *Components of the human speech production system.*

Hard palate

Oral cavity

Alveolar ridge

Lip

Teeth

Lip

Tongue

Nasal cavity

Velum

Pharynx

Esophagus

Vocal cords

Glottis

velopment. The left hemisphere of the human brain contains the centers for most important language and speech functions (see Figure 8.6), although the right hemisphere may contribute as well (Levy, 1985).

Is language a unique ability that separates the human species from other animals? Scientists have carried out a number of ingenious studies and demonstrations challenging that idea and have discovered much about communication among other species. Some of the characteristics that distinguish language from other ways of communicating were mentioned at the beginning of the chapter; keep them in mind while you read Frontier 8.1, in which we have summarized opposing views about whether animals have demonstrated true language behavior.

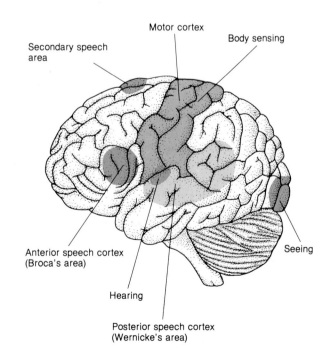

Motor cortex

Body sensing

Secondary speech area

Anterior speech cortex (Broca's area)

Hearing

Posterior speech cortex (Wernicke's area)

Seeing

FIGURE 8.6 *Broca's and Wernicke's areas in the left hemisphere of the brain are the places where speech and language functions are localized. Broca's area is involved in the production of speech and Wernicke's area with the comprehension of auditory input as well as the monitoring of speech output.*

DO ANIMALS USE LANGUAGE?

Bees use complex dances to tell their co-workers where a supply of nectar is (Von Frisch, 1967). Jane Goodall has reported the ways in which wild chimpanzees communicate. Marler found that monkeys use different calls to warn against different types of predators (1967). For example, the sound "rraup" is a response to sighting an eagle. When the other monkeys hear "rraup," they climb down from trees and hide in the undergrowth. A "chirp" sound, on the other hand, signals the presence of a leopard. Hearing this sound, the other monkeys get off the ground into the trees above a leopard's reach.

Although animal behaviors like these have specific meanings that translate into particular actions, some aspects of true language are lacking. For instance, there is no evidence that these communications are made up of symbols that can be rearranged to give a variety of meanings, in the way that the components of human speech can. Thus the range of ideas that can be expressed by animals appears very limited. Since *generativity,* the ability to provide for a large variety of meanings, is considered a fundamental property of language by many psycholinguists, they believe that neither these natural observations nor the results from the primate experiments that we are about to describe really qualify as proof that language is possible for species other than human beings.

About 20 years ago, Allen Gardner and Beatrice Gardner of the University of Nevada decided to use a new approach to study a chimpanzee's ability to communicate. All previous language work with chimps had focused on training them to speak. Such experiments were doomed to failure because the vocal apparatus of the chimpanzee is not physically capable of producing human speech. But chimps have fine manual dexterity, and Gardner and Gardner reasoned that American Sign Language, the form of communication taught to many deaf people, would be a much more appropriate language vehicle.

The Gardners began training Washoe, a 1-year-old

FIGURE 8.7 *Roger Fouts and his co-workers believe their videotapes document one chimpanzee teaching sign language to another. Baby Loulis, shown here on the right, has learned signs taught by trainers only to an older chimp, Washoe. Loulis is signing "want" in this photo by pulling his hand down his chest.*

female chimp, in 1966. They used virtually every known training method to get her to produce signs, including operant training and reinforcement, modeling, and actually holding her hands. During her waking hours Washoe was constantly in the company of a human being, who communicated with her through sign language. By the time she was 5 years old, Washoe was using 1600 different signs (Fleming, 1974). In fact, she was using up to five signs in sequences that were very similar to sentences. Some of the sign combinations were her own creations and not those she had learned from her trainers. For instance, when she was threatened by an aggressive rhesus monkey, she combined the signs for "dirty" and "monkey." When she saw a swan for the first time, she described it as a "water bird," thus suggesting to her caretakers that she understood the meaning of the words involved. When Washoe was 4 years old, 78 out of 249 two-sign combinations she used fit into the semantic categories for classifying children's speech (Brown, 1973). This figure is very close to those for cross-cultural studies of 2-year-old children's combinations.

Roger Fouts, a psychologist who now works with Washoe, observed Washoe teaching several signs to her young son Loulis. Fouts and his assistants have been careful to use only five signs in Loulis's presence, yet he knows more than that (see Figure 8.7). If teaching sign language can be verified, the argument for primate language will be greatly enhanced by this demonstration of the passing on of symbolic behavior from one primate to another.

At about the same time that the Gardners were training Washoe to use sign language, David Premack trained a chimp called Sarah to associate a set of "word symbols"—pieces of plastic in various shapes and colors with magnetic backings so that they could be used on a metal "language board"—with various aspects of her environment. In time, Sarah was able to say things such as "Mary [trainer] insert banana bowl." She could also read and follow instructions when they were "written" with the plastic symbols (see Figure 8.8). Her trainers believed that Sarah had learned concepts as well as symbols. For example, they agreed that Sarah was aware of what the concept of color meant because when the symbol for color was included in a comparison question about a banana and a yellow ball, she correctly replied that they were the same.

Following in Premack's footsteps, Duane Rumbaugh and Sue Savage-Rumbaugh at the Yerkes Re-

gional Primate Research Center in Atlanta have taught their primates Yerkish, a computer language (see Figure 8.9). The animals are able to answer questions, follow instructions, make requests and observations, and work cooperatively through a computer communication system (Rumbaugh, 1977). Savage-Rumbaugh and her colleagues have now taught two chimps a complex game, which they think demonstrates the chimps' ability to use symbols to make a statement, as is done in human speech (Savage-Rumbaugh and others, 1983).

FIGURE 8.8 *Sarah, after reading the message "Sarah insert apple pail banana dish" on the magnetic board, performed the appropriate actions. To be able to make the correct interpretation that she should put the apple in the pail and the banana in the dish (not the apple, pail, and banana in the dish), the chimp had to understand sentence structure rather than just word order. In the actual tests, most symbols were colored.*

FIGURE 8.9 *Chimps at the Yerkes National Primate Research Center in Atlanta, Georgia, become adept computer users.*

For a considerable period of time, those who argued that language was not an exclusively human ability have been providing data to support their view. But the doubters have become more verbal and persuasive. B. F. Skinner and his co-workers (Epstein and others, 1980) have demonstrated that pigeons can be trained to perform languagelike behavior in an operant learning situation by pecking the proper disc to answer a question selected by a peck from a pigeon in another compartment of the apparatus (see Figure

8.10). Skinner argued that this shows that no understanding of meaning is necessary for the feats of primates who use computers for communication.

Noam Chomsky says that the primates' performance doesn't meet his criteria for the structure of language because new word combinations and the ability to express what seem like abstract ideas may be in part based on learning cues rather than on a real understanding of language.

Other psychologists have focused their doubts on whether the sign language symbols are the most important aspect of communication between the chimps and their trainers. These critics believe that the chimps are merely responding to cues or demands for

FIGURE 8.10 *One of these pigeons, taught by B. F. Skinner and Robert Epstein, pecks a disc that asks a question. The second pigeon, who cannot see the first, looks at the lighted symbol and then pecks the correct disc to answer the question. These researchers believe that the pigeons' apparent ability to construct new, complex behavior that seems symbolic or languagelike can, instead, be explained by simple learning principles.*

specific behavior that the trainers are unaware that they are giving. For example, Herbert Terrace and his associates (1979) worked with a male chimp named Nim, who eventually acquired a vocabulary of 125 signs. Could Nim combine them to create new meanings? After a study of more than 20,000 combinations of two or more signs, Terrace concluded that Nim produced the sign combinations in response to demands from the trainer and not as a means of communicating new information.

The case of Clever Hans, a horse who could apparently count by tapping out numbers with his hoof, has also been used to show that researchers in primate speech may be deceiving themselves even though they have a sincere belief in their results (Sebeok and Umiker-Sebeok, 1980). Hans's trainer believed that he had taught Hans to count; he didn't know that he was involuntarily jerking his head when Hans reached the correct total. The case, unraveled by an observant psychologist around 1900, has come to represent the dangers of unconscious cueing and experimenter self-deception. Other critics focus on the reasons for using language. Children begin to speak because they want to communicate with language, not because they cannot communicate another way. So far, these critics say, other animals use signs or symbols because they have been taught to do so in a game context, not because they want to (Sugarman, 1983).

All these critics believe that the data cited by the workers in animal language can be explained by much simpler principles than language ability. As yet, the issue is not settled. Primates' ability to sign and manipulate computers represents an intriguing research area that will continue into the future.

CRITICAL PERIODS, SENSITIVE PERIODS, AND LANGUAGE DEVELOPMENT

There may be a **critical period** early in life during which language development must begin if a high level of language competence is to be reached later in life. The question of the role of biological development in language ability is illustrated in the debate over critical periods. Ethologists who study the behavior of some species—birds in particular—have suggested that there is a timetable for biologically determined behaviors. If the proper conditions are not present during the critical period, the behavior, even if it is necessary for survival, may not be established.

A famous example of this process, called **imprinting** when it is applied to birds, is the behavior of young geese. For its own safety, the young goose needs to stay close to its mother and follow behind her wherever she goes. The imprinting of this behavior occurs during a brief period soon after hatching. If the gosling is reared in isolation and another object—a human being or a large ball, for example—is introduced during this period, the young goose will be imprinted on that person or object and will later follow it in the way that a normally reared gosling would follow its mother. The study of mother–child bonding in humans, discussed in Chapter 12, investigates whether a special relationship between the two must be established shortly after birth if it is to occur at all.

The analysis of critical periods in human language acquisition has focused on the study of a few children who, because of unusual circumstances, were not exposed to language in a normal way. So-called feral or wild children found living on their own and children reared in almost complete isolation until the age of 5 or 6 have been successfully taught some language behavior. However, even with intensive tutoring they never achieved normal speech (Clarke and Clarke, 1976). Of course, growing up under such circumstances probably has severe negative effects on language acquisition, as it does on nutrition, emotional development, and cognitive growth. At this time the question of whether a critical period for language exists in humans has not been answered. Even if such a critical period exists, it may not be specifically for language alone but may have to do with a more general set of cognitive skills.

Even if development could begin at some later time, perhaps there is a certain early **sensitive period** in which language learning is most successful. The existence of a period during which language learning is optimal is illustrated by observations about learning foreign languages. If a young child moves to a new country, his or her learning seems to be effortless, and no formal language instruction is needed. After puberty more effort seems required and learning is not as complete. People who learn languages when they are adults usually do not develop a really native accent. They always continue to sound like foreigners even though they may have an adequate knowledge of vocabulary and grammar. The difference in ability to adopt a new accent holds true even within one's native language. Probably everyone has known families that have moved from one area of the United States to another. While the parents continue to speak like Bostonians, Brooklynites, or North Carolinians even after 30 years in Denver or Los Angeles, their children have no trace of the accent of their original hometown.

Language and cognition

Because so much information in our memories is verbally stored, questions about how language influences thinking and memory have been the focus of a great deal of research.

LINGUISTIC RELATIVISM

Linguist Benjamin Whorf developed the concept called **linguistic relativism** or **linguistic determinism,** the idea that the language a person speaks influences the way that he or she thinks and perceives. For example, some languages have no past or future tense. If

linguistic relativism were operating, we might expect people who speak those languages to worry much less about yesterday or tomorrow than we do.

The classic example given to support Whorf's argument is that the Eskimo language has a great many words for *snow*, but English speakers use only two. But this difference can be explained simply in terms of the need for expertise about particular topics in particular cultures. Experts in any field in any culture probably develop a highly specialized vocabulary to think about and to communicate the details of their knowledge. Of course, Eskimos, if they are to survive in their traditional habitat, need to be experts on snow because of its effect on their lives. But what about an English-speaking cross-country skier or mountain climber? Wouldn't discriminations among snow types be essential in analyzing climbing and safety conditions? In fact, a quick review of two mountaineering books produced a list of 32 terms to differentiate snow types, including *powder, corn snow, suncrust,* and *sugar snow* (Ferber, 1974; LaChapelle, 1978). Most linguists do not agree that language determines *how* we think. They would say instead that language influences how efficiently we can code our experiences and perhaps also how much detail we attend to in our everyday thinking.

An alternative theory is that different languages share the same concepts, but these concepts are more easily expressed in some languages than in others. But, in fact, new words can be invented in all languages as they are needed. If you doubt that English is constantly growing, find a dictionary published 30 years ago and look up *moon shot, byte, hard rock,* or *stagflation.* These terms were invented to refer to new things, but we could grasp the ideas behind them even without these particular words.

LANGUAGE AND PERCEPTION

One area in which the effect of language has been researched extensively is color perception. At one time, most theorists believed that the color spectrum was di-

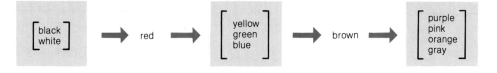

vided up arbitrarily and differently by different cultures. This would mean, for example, that in some cultures the colors red and yellow would be grouped together and described by some overall term similar to our word *orange*. Research by anthropologists has demonstrated that this idea is wrong and that no matter what the language, colors are not named in an arbitrary way (Kay, 1975).

Every language uses basic color terms that come from a list of only 11 colors: black, white, red, yellow, green, blue, brown, purple, pink, orange, and gray. English uses all 11 of these basic terms; at the other extreme, a New Guinea tribe, the Dani, use only 2 (Rosch, 1973). If any number of these color names, from 2 to 11, were used together, there would be 2048 possible groups, but reality is far different. The choice among the groups is not random but occurs in a definite hierarchy, illustrated in Figure 8.11. When a language, like that of the Dani, has only 2 terms, it uses only black and white, the two terms at the left of the figure. If there are three color terms, they always refer to black, white, and red. A language with 6 color terms will take the first 6 at the left of the figure, and so on. The terms within the brackets can be added in any order, but the colors red or brown always occur if all the colors to the left of them in the figure are recognized as distinct terms in a language.

These findings suggest another built-in cognitive characteristic that is reflected in the language behavior of all cultures. Research on color perception in different cultures suggests that groups who use only a few color terms have the same ability to perceive color differences as groups who use many terms (Heider and Olivier, 1972). The Dani tribe, with its two-color vocabulary, might seem at a disadvantage in tests of color memory and discrimination compared to English-speaking individuals. However, Dani subjects can remember the 11 basic colors more accurately than other color shades, just as English speakers can.

LANGUAGE AND MEMORY

Although language may not affect the way in which a person thinks, except in terms of specificity of detail, language can sometimes influence memory. The experiments on eyewitness testimony discussed in Chapter 7 make this clear, as does an early classic study of perception (Carmichael and others, 1932). In that experiment, drawing *(a)* in Figure 8.12, labeled either as a dumbbell or spectacles, was presented to subjects. Later subjects were asked to sketch what they had seen. Subjects for whom it was labeled a dumbbell tended to draw a figure with a straight but extended midsection, as shown in drawing *(b)*. Subjects who saw the figure with the label "spectacles" reproduced it with a short curved midsection like that in drawing *(c)*. This experiment and many others demonstrated that the figures are stored in memory not simply by their visual image but by their labels as well. Labeling a visual image does more than determine the form of the figure when it is recalled; it helps in the retrieval process itself. Even nonsense figures were remembered better with labels than without them (Santa and Ranken, 1972).

FIGURE 8.12 *The way a drawing is labeled can affect the way it is remembered (Carmichael and others, 1932).*

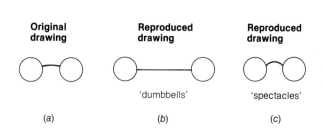

PROBLEM SOLVING

Although language may not influence how we think, it is certainly one of the tools we use to solve problems. What is a problem? A problem exists when some elements or conditions of the situation are known and some are unknown (Morgan, 1941). Another way to describe a problem is as "a deviant member of a series of earlier situations of some sort" (Raaheim, 1974). As these definitions imply, success in problem solving depends on metacognitive skills—knowing what you know, what you don't know, and what you can figure out from what you do know.

To be successful as a problem solver, keep three points in mind: the *original state* of the situation, the *goal state*, and the *rules* or *restrictions* that must be followed. The original state, the situation at the beginning of the problem, might be, "I am at the shopping center, 7 miles from home, and my car has broken down." The goal would be, "I want to be at home in 30 minutes." The rules might include, "The bus doesn't run anywhere near my house"; "My sister, whom I would usually be able to call for help, is out of town"; and "I have only $2 with me and a taxi would cost at least $12." Once these rules are established, an active cognitive process can begin. People rarely solve problems by jumping randomly from one possibility to another until they land on a solution. Even young children know that trial and error is extremely time-wasting. A quick solution is usually desirable, but certain kinds of strategies have the risk of yielding a solution that may be inaccurate or inefficient.

Understanding problem-solving techniques

To study any phenomenon, we must first try to observe it. Obviously, direct observations of human thinking and problem solving are difficult to make. Psychologists have tried to get around this difficulty by asking people to "think out loud" while they are solving a problem. One drawback with this procedure is that people usually give only a summary of their reasoning steps. Some crucial ideas may be omitted.

In a study of how people solve algebra problems, nonsense words were inserted in a word problem to force subjects to spell out their thoughts in more detail (Hinsley and others, 1977). One problem read:

According to ferbent, the optimally fuselt grix of voipe unmolts five stems of voipe thrump 95 bines per sten. In order to embler some wuss voipe, each grix will unmolt one sten at 70 bines per sten. If the grix is to be optimally fuselt, what should the bines per sten of the rest of the voipe be? (p. 100)

One subject's protocol or verbal report started out this way:

There is some sort of machine, let's call it the grix. Which receives some sort of fuel, called a sten. And it produces, let's say work, out of that sten, usually whips out 90 bines per unit of sten. . . . (p.101)

Analysis of the protocols of a number of subjects showed that people approach these problems by trying to fit them into some kind of normal framework and then analyzing them as though they were not nonsense. Thus the first step in problem solving seems to be to identify the familiar elements in the situation. Then the unfamiliar elements are evaluated to see how they would affect a solution based on the familiar ones.

ALGORITHMS VERSUS HEURISTICS

From the analysis of such verbal reports, we can distinguish the use of two kinds of methods: algorithms and heuristics. An **algorithm** is a plan that automatically generates a correct solution. The rules for multiplication or addition might be called algorithms. If you use them properly, you will always get the right answer.

The difficulty in using algorithms comes in situations in which a number of possible combinations must be tried in order to find the best solution. For example, look at this anagram problem. What real word do these scrambled letters spell?

> **TERALBAY**

One way to solve the problem would be to try the letters in all possible combinations until a familiar one is found. The drawback with this strategy is that 8 letters can be rearranged in 40,320 different ways. A computer could generate all these letter strings and compare them to words stored in its memory, but most of us would use a heuristic solution instead. **Heuristics** are rules of thumb. They are search procedures that are quick and easy to use, but they do not always work because they cut corners. Although they are sometimes unsuccessful, heuristics are more suitable choices for the many complicated problems encountered in everyday life. Table 8.1 lists 10 heuristics that can help students become better problem solvers.

TABLE 8.1 HEURISTICS THAT ARE USEFUL IN PROBLEM SOLVING

Try to look at the problem as a whole. Don't let yourself focus only on details.

Try to restate the problem in your own words.

Think of ways to express the problem more simply. For instance, can you convert the problem to an equation or a diagram?

Use analogies and metaphors to see if they suggest a solution.

Don't decide on a strategy too fast. Wait until you have thought about all aspects of the problem.

Don't take your assumptions about the problem for granted. Question each one of them and try to look at the problem from several points of view.

Try working backwards from the desired outcome to the original problem.

Break the problem into parts and try to solve one part at a time.

Explain the problem and your ideas about how to solve it to someone else.

One kind of heuristic that people often use is the *analogy*: they look for similarities in two different stimuli or events and then use the same rules that worked for one to solve the second. Problems on a math test can be treated as analogies of similar problems in homework assignments or class demonstrations. There is always a chance, of course, that the two situations may seem to be alike but are not really so; in such a case, using an analogy would be misleading. However, like all heuristics, analogies are convenient and frequently save time.

People often report using a kind of heuristic called the **means-ends analysis.** In a means-ends analysis, people first define a subgoal that they hope to achieve (an end). They then compare that subgoal with their present state of knowledge. If there is a discrepancy between the two, people try to find a means to reduce that difference. For example, a parent must take a son to nursery school. A means-ends analysis of that problem begins:

I want to take my son to nursery school. What's the difference between what I have and what I want? One of distance. What changes distance? My automobile. My automobile won't work. What is needed to make it work? A new battery. What has new batteries? An auto repair shop. I want the repair shop to put in a new battery, but the shop doesn't know I need one. What is the difficulty? One of communication. What allows communication? A telephone. . . . (Newell and Simon, 1972, p. 416)

Of course, if you were in this situation, your thoughts might not be as detailed as this, but if you spelled out every step you would cover all these points.

After studying subjects' verbal reports of their problem-solving strategies, psychologists have programmed simulation models into computers. The most famous of these simulations is the **General Problem Solver,** originated by Newell and Simon, which simulates means-ends analysis and other heuristics.

Understanding the process or strategies they use in solving problems can be helpful to students who are fearful in certain kinds of problem situations. A computer program that helps find erroneous algorithms, or "bugs," used by students in solving subtraction problems showed that there are many more of these bugs than teachers know about (Brown and Burton, 1978).

FIGURE 8.13 *Computers can be programmed to do some of the work of experts. This troubleshooting system for locomotive repair was generated by a team of computer specialists who spent several months interviewing David Smith (right), a top locomotive service specialist. The team wrote a customized software program that put Mr. Smith's diagnostic expertise into a computer. A series of questions appear on one screen. When these are answered, the system identifies the cause of the problem and demonstrates repair procedures on a second screen.*

Discovery of the particular error a student often makes is more helpful in improving performance than advice to try harder and be more careful.

Most real-life problem solving—for example, decisions in business or government, as well as mathematical or scientific reasoning—calls on both episodic and semantic memories, although different sorts of demands are made on each type. Experience creates a store of episodic memories that may be potentially useful in new situations. Training or education increases the individual's skill at sorting through these situations to bring to mind past situations that have basic rather than superficial similarities. Research comparing the problem-solving procedures of experienced physicists with those of students who have the required knowledge to solve the problem but who lack experience supported this expected difference in approach (Chi and others, 1981). The experienced physicists first categorized the problem and then looked for analogies based on physical principles. The students, on the other

hand, looked for analogies based on very superficial perceptual aspects of the problem. Research on problem solving by lawyers and physicians has also shown this pattern.

Research on real-world problem solving has resulted in a number of useful programs in which usable heuristics, or rules of thumb, are embedded in precise logical sequences that a computer can carry out. Among these systems are several for medical diagnoses or treatment and many business-oriented programs such as "Drilling Advisor" that diagnoses the causes of sticking problems on oil rigs. Figure 8.13 shows an individual who is working to help translate his expertise into a computer program.

Common difficulties in problem solving

Two difficulties that people often encounter in solving problems in the laboratory as well as in everyday life are functional fixedness and mental set. **Functional fixedness** occurs when people let the customary way in which an object is used or labeled interfere with using it in a new way. In one classic problem, subjects are presented with a box of tacks, a candle, and a few

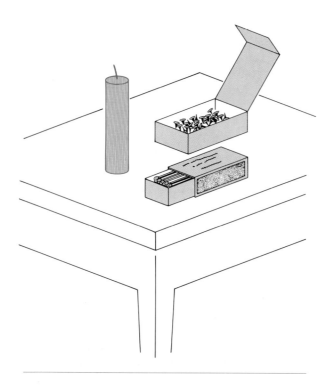

FIGURE 8.14 *Imagine that you were given these items and told to attach a candle to the wall so that the candle will burn properly. How long would it take you to come up with an answer?*

wooden matches (see Figure 8.14). They are told that they must figure out a way to attach the candle to the wall so that it will not drip. To solve the problem, the subject must see that, once the tacks have been taken from the box, the box itself can be tacked to the wall and used as a support for the candle (Duncker, 1945). Because of functional fixedness, most subjects saw the box only in its role as a container for the tacks, and so they had difficulty solving the problem. In a later experiment using the same task, problem-solving speed increased when the objects were presented and labeled separately (Glucksberg and Weisberg, 1966). The subjects who were not given labels needed nearly 15 times as long to solve the problem. This experiment nicely demonstrates the way that language affects cognition in problem-solving situations.

Once we get into the habit of solving particular types of problems in a particular way, we are using a kind of **mental set**. Mental habits can make life much easier because we do not have to stop each time to figure out the process from the beginning. But sometimes the use of patterns is not efficient. Mental sets can keep us from taking a fresh look at the problem and thus can prevent us from solving it. Water jar problems illustrate the disadvantage of mental sets. In a typical water jar experiment, subjects are shown a number of problems that can all be solved in exactly the same way, except for the last one, which also has a simpler solution (see Table 8.2).

Problem-solving tasks have been used by many researchers. One drawback in using the information they have accumulated is that to have valid comparisons, the solutions to the problems cannot rely on the sub-

TABLE 8.2 MENTAL SETS REDUCE THE SUBJECT'S EFFICIENCY IN SOLVING PROBLEMS SUCH AS THIS ONE

SUBJECTS ARE ASKED TO SOLVE A SERIES OF PROBLEMS.

1.	$A = 21$	$B = 127$	$C = 3$	obtain	100
2.	2	40	4		30
3.	1	27	6		14
4.	2	16	3		8
5.	7	59	12		28
6.	12	80	19		30
7.	23	49	3		20

Problems 1–6 can be solved by the formula $B - A - 2C$. Problem 7 could be solved much more simply using the formula $A - C$. Subjects usually used the more complicated formula unless they were given a hint about problem 7.

In a variation of this experiment it might be impossible to solve problem 7 using the same formulation. For example:

$A = 2$, $B = 27$, $C = 7$ obtain 14.

Subjects who had solved the earlier problems would have more difficulty solving this new problem than would subjects who had not practiced the series. (The answer is $2C = 14$.)

ject's prior knowledge. Since problem solving in the real world often depends on past experience as well as knowledge of rules and concepts, research based on content-limited tasks leaves many questions unanswered.

INTELLIGENCE

How do you decide how intelligent, or "smart," someone is? One important way of defining intelligence focuses on how well people solve problems (Estes, 1982). From this viewpoint, **intelligence** includes attributes related to reasoning skills, knowledge about the culture, and the ability to come up with solutions to new problems.

Psychologists have at least two kinds of interest in intelligence. One kind is theoretical and falls under three general headings: what it is, where it comes from, and how it works. The second kind of interest is practical—constructing tests that measure it and that can be used for predicting future achievements.

Sources of intelligence

How does a person acquire the abilities that we call intelligence? One obvious place to look is at the person's heredity. Another area to study is the kind of surroundings in which the person grew up. Sound familiar? These are the two sides in the debate between nature and nurture.

THE BIOLOGICAL PERSPECTIVE

The first scientific interest in intelligence was Francis Galton's work in the nineteenth century on the heredity of genius. The genetic effects emphasized by Galton and many researchers after him do have important influences on intellectual functioning. For example, more than 150 known genetic defects are associated with mental retardation or with greatly below-average mental ability (Anderson, 1972). Some of these genetic

defects appear to be due to accidental factors, but others show a distinct hereditary pattern.

One way of investigating the role of heredity in intelligence (as in any other trait) is to study identical twins, because their genetic makeup is exactly the same. Identical twins have highly similar intelligence test scores and are much more alike than ordinary brothers and sisters, who share a lower proportion of similar genes. A second line of evidence for the importance of genetic factors comes from follow-up studies of children who have been adopted in infancy. These adopted children are more like their biological mother and siblings in intelligence than they are like their adoptive mother and siblings (Horn and others, 1979; Scarr and Weinberg, 1978). Both types of findings suggest that genetic heritage is important in determining a child's level of intellectual functioning and must be considered along with environment when predictions about intelligence are made. Although the role of heredity in intelligence is a highly political topic, many researchers would be willing to agree that heredity contributes about half the intellectual difference among individuals (Scarr and Carter-Saltzman, 1982).

There is a well-known folk saying that optimists will describe a cup that is 50 percent filled as half-full, while pessimists will describe it as half-empty. Just as the biological view of intelligence emphasizes the half of intellectual ability that seems traceable to heredity, the behavioral approach focuses on that half that seems to be influenced by other factors, mainly the environment. We might say that the behavioral theorists are the optimists because they devote themselves to an area where changes can be made, while the biologically oriented scientists are the pessimists because they concentrate on what is unchangeable.

But in some ways this is an unfair statement. Geneticists have been able to identify specific genes responsible for some types of retardation and ultimately may provide a way to improve people's chances for full intellectual functioning by directly altering genes.

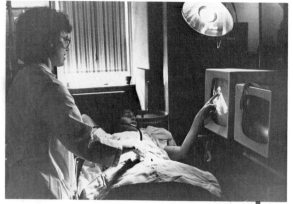

An ultrasound scan shows the fetus on the TV screen.

FIGURE 8.15 *Ultrasound scan and amniocentesis can provide information about abnormalities in the unborn child.*

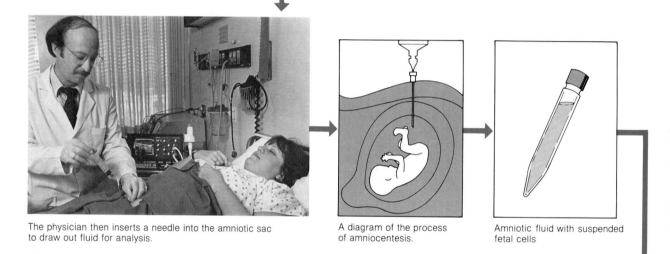

The physician then inserts a needle into the amniotic sac to draw out fluid for analysis.

A diagram of the process of amniocentesis.

Amniotic fluid with suspended fetal cells

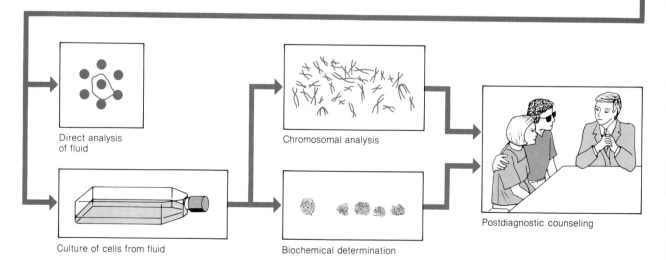

Direct analysis of fluid

Culture of cells from fluid

Chromosomal analysis

Biochemical determination

Postdiagnostic counseling

Even now, through genetic counseling, prospective parents can be warned of inherited risk factors (see Figure 8.15). Moreover, the unborn child's genetic makeup can be affected not only by heredity but also by the environment. For example, radiation from X rays; a viral infection such as rubella (German measles) experienced by the mother; chemical incompatibilities between the mother and child, such as Rh positive and negative blood; and certain chemical states in the mother's body (for instance, from the use of large amounts of alcohol) can all contribute to later retardation or decreased intellectual functioning. Knowledge about these relationships can also lead to preventive actions.

THE BEHAVIORAL PERSPECTIVE

The optimism of some of those who emphasize learning and environmental stimulation knows almost no bounds. Probably the best-known example of this was the behaviorist John B. Watson, who believed that, if given complete control of a child's environment, he could produce a child with any skills that he desired. Stimulated by this view of humans as infinitely shapable, scientists carried out a number of famous studies of the effects of adoption in the 1920s and 1930s (Burks, 1928, 1938; Skeels, 1938; Skodak, 1938; Skodak and Skeels, 1949). Although these investigations showed, just as more recent studies have (Scarr and Weinberg, 1978), that adopted children resembled their biological parents more than they did their adoptive parents, the analyses also demonstrated that children who were adopted into homes with stimulating environments tended to have higher intelligence-test scores than would have been predicted by their biological mothers' intelligence level.

Whether the environmental or biological point of view is stressed has important implications for social policy—for example, whether large amounts of public money should be spent on early intervention programs, such as Head Start, in an effort to change childrens' later school performance and ultimate level of cognitive functioning. Those who view the glass as half full have pressed for programs that teach skills and provide an enriched and stimulating environment for children.

Whether researchers emphasize heredity or environment in their work depends on their psychological

perspective. Today most psychologists interested in the source of intelligent behavior look at the interaction of heredity and environment. A majority would probably agree with the statement that heredity sets a general range of intelligence and the environment determines where in that range the person will fall.

The structure of intelligence

Having looked at where intelligence might come from, we now try to discover what it is. Let's ask the experts. The definitions suggested at a conference of experts in 1921 varied so much that one of them proposed, perhaps with tongue in cheek, that intelligence was simply "the capacity to do well on an intelligence test." Psychologists who are interested in measurement and test construction and have tried to develop a more precise (and less facetious) definition are the primary sources for descriptions of intelligence.

THE FACTOR ANALYTIC APPROACH

Psychologists interested in testing have used a statistical technique called **factor analysis** to identify specific intellectual abilities. (The basic concepts of factor analysis are described in the appendix.) The factor analytic approach divides the skills demonstrated on an intelligence test into separate mental abilities based on clusters of problems that correlate highly with one another and are thus assumed to be measuring the same mental skill. For example, suppose the items in factor A included questions such as

What does the word *aviary* mean?

How are the words *house* and *barn* alike?

Hen is to *chick* as *cow* is to _____.

This factor might be called *verbal ability*. Items in another factor might be

Arrange these blocks to repeat the pattern in this booklet.

Put together these puzzle pieces to make something.

Put these cartoon pictures in the correct order so they tell a story.

This second group of items might represent a factor labeled *nonverbal ability* or *spatial perception*. Test items that represent the same factor can then be grouped together as a separate examination to measure one particular part or aspect of intelligence. For example, L. L. Thurstone (1938) used a factor analytic technique to develop a battery of tests for measuring what he called **primary mental abilities**. These primary abilities were spatial ability, perceptual speed, numerical ability, verbal meaning, memory, verbal fluency, and inductive reasoning. Thurstone's work on multiple factors established a pattern followed by many other American psychologists.

The different factors are ordinarily not completely independent of each other; they are all correlated to some degree. This means that there is an overlap in what they measure. For example, two parts of the same intelligence test have a 0.58 correlation with each other, which means that, although they are not measuring the same thing, there is apparently some overlap.

This overlap represents a common factor, often called the **general,** or **g, factor** in intelligence. The g factor, first described by the British psychologist Charles Spearman, is thought of as the dominating intellectual trait that determines ability in all areas. The g factor is based on the idea that people who are good at some kinds of intellectual tasks are likely to be good at others as well. We might think of the g factor as something like general problem-solving ability. The idea of a general factor is the basis for using a single general term for intelligence (the *IQ,* discussed later in the chapter) and for measuring intelligence by a single test rather than by the several tests used in factor analytic research.

THE COGNITIVE STAGES APPROACH

Psychologists using the cognitive perspective have a much different view of the structure of intelligence from that of the factor analysts. Jean Piaget, whose work we will discuss again in Chapter 11, has proposed that children pass through a series of cognitive stages. At each stage, concepts appear which the child had been unable to grasp earlier. Unlike the test constructors, Piaget was more interested in the way the child arrives at the responses than in how correct the response is.

INTELLIGENCE AS SPECIFIC BRAIN FUNCTIONING

Although the factor analysts, like Piaget, do not emphasize biology, some biological basis is implied in their approaches. A recent theorist who stresses the biological perspective more directly is Howard Gardner (1983), who suggests that there are a small number of separate human intelligences and that each is controlled by a specific region of the brain. His list includes language use, logical or mathematical reasoning, spatial skills, physical talents like dance or mime, and awareness of one's own feelings and those of others. He emphasizes that cognition plays a basic role in all these intelligences, even those like body movement, and that the nervous system functions more efficiently the more it is used.

Neuropsychologists interested in differentiating intellectual functions and their biological basis studied the effects of lowered oxygen intake on the performance of members of an expedition to Mount Everest in 1981 (West, 1984). The researchers measured the expedition members' memory and coordination at various altitudes on the mountain and one year after the expedition (see Figure 8.16). At higher altitudes, there was a significant decline in verbal learning, verbal expression, short-term memory, and finger tapping speed. A year later, memory, verbal expression, and learning had returned to preexpedition levels, but most of the subjects still showed impairment in finger tapping speed. Although the reason is unclear, it is likely that prolonged severe oxygen deprivation was related to a continuing dysfunction in the cerebrum.

The processes of intelligent behavior

Until recently, most researchers have not focused on what goes on in the individual that results in intelligent behavior. Over the years some stabs at this question have been made from the learning perspective. However, the focus on laboratory learning tasks that try to break the learning process down into small components has not been very productive because the correlations between performance on the learning tasks and scores on intelligence tests have not been very high (Sternberg and Salter, 1982).

One reason for this may be that learning takes place at different levels. The kinds of learning that have been studied in learning laboratories are usually quite simple. They require very superficial processing, and the subject usually has little reason to process the material for long-term storage. Some of the items on a standard test of ability, on the other hand, measure learning that probably occurred at fairly deep levels of processing. Solving arithmetic problems, for example, or algorithms that require people to discriminate among subtle differences in meaning should not be expected to correlate highly with remembering a string of numbers or nonsense syllables.

As a result, some cognitive psychologists are studying learning situations closer to those found in everyday life. In one study, subjects learned the meaning of new words presented in an everyday reading context (Sternberg and others, 1982). These learning scores had a reasonably high correlation with ability (about .60), which suggests that research on learning tasks requiring

more complex levels of processing may make a contribution to the understanding of the processes involved in intelligent behavior.

Both cognitive psychologists and researchers using the learning perspective have tried to understand the processes involved in intelligent behavior by studying the differences in the way that individuals with widely differing scores on intelligence tests solve problems. One of the most dramatic differences seems to be in the area of strategies of learning or *metacognition* (recall from Chapter 7 that *metacognition* refers to a person's awareness of what he or she knows). Low intelligence test scores are related to deficiencies in these metacognitive strategies. For example, most people learn a variety of mnemonic devices without any particular instruction, but retarded people need to have the strategies explicitly taught and explained. Teaching the strategies to retarded individuals improves their performance on the particular task, but the training does not generalize well enough to help them perform better on other tasks (Campione and others, 1982).

FIGURE 8.16 *The main laboratory of the 1981 American Medical Research Expedition to Mount Everest, 20,700 feet above sea level.*

The focus on the response processes that comes from the information processing viewpoint in cognitive psychology contrasts with the earlier emphasis on the outcome or "answer" given as an end product of thought. Many researchers hope that this new focus will end what has been a long period of stagnation in the theoretical approach to intelligence.

Intelligence tests

Few people these days can get through school without having to take intelligence tests, aptitude tests, achievement tests, and so on (see Figure 8.17). These tests are all attempts to measure how people differ in the particular cognitive abilities that we usually think of as being signs of intelligence. Before looking at some of these tests, let's consider the characteristics that a test must have in order to be a useful measuring instrument.

TEST RELIABILITY

No measurement device is perfect, but the smaller the measurement error, the more reliable the data. For example, if your bathroom scale registers the same

FIGURE 8.17

"What with the primary mental ability test and the differential aptitude test and the reading readiness test and the basic skills test and the I.Q. test and the sequential tests of educational progress and the mental maturity test, we haven't been learning anything at school."

(© 1978 BY SIDNEY HARRIS/AMERICAN SCIENTIST MAGAZINE.)

weight each time you step on it (and you haven't radically changed your diet), your scale is a reliable instrument. In terms of tests, the higher the **reliability** of the test, the more confidence the tester can have that a person's score would be about the same if he or she were to take the same test again tomorrow or next week. Reliability is, in fact, usually determined by testing the same people twice and then comparing their scores on the two tests. This is called *test-retest reliability*.

Reliability is expressed in terms of a correlation coefficient. The best-constructed psychological tests, such as some intelligence tests, have a test-retest correlation of .90 or above. Correlations of .70 or above may be acceptable for some types of tests, such as behavior ratings. Low test reliability may be caused by problems with the test questions, with the way that the test is scored, and with changes in the person's performance.

TEST VALIDITY

Validity is even more important than reliability. **Validity** simply means that the test measures what the test interpreter believes it measures. For example, a test of musical ability may be reliable because its questions and scoring are clear and unambiguous, but if it consists only of questions about composers' lives, it is not valid for the purpose that the examiner had in mind.

Test validity is also measured by correlation coefficients. Validity is measured not by the correlation between two scores on the same test, but by the correlation between the test score and some outside measure of the ability or performance, known as a *criterion*. For example, the criterion for a test of insurance-sales aptitude might be the dollar value of insurance sold.

Validity coefficients are seldom as high as reliability coefficients. In predicting job performance, they may range from .25 upward. In predicting academic success, they are often above .50. Validity coefficients for tests used to predict behavior in a true-to-life situation, not behavior on another test, are rarely greater than .70.

STANDARDIZATION

Test standardization refers to the way that the test is administered and to the development of norms or standards for interpreting test scores. If the same test is supposed to measure the same things each time it's given, it is important that it be administered in exactly the same way to every person who takes it.

To obtain norms for interpreting scores, the test is administered to a large sample of people who are representative of the population for whom the test has been designed. The distribution of scores for the norm group serves as a standard against which the score of any member of that population can be compared and interpreted. Knowledge of the norm group's makeup is important in understanding the meaning of a score. Your attitude toward your score would depend on whether the norms were based on the test scores of people living at a state school for the retarded or on the scores of a group of theoretical physicists.

Scores may be translated into percentile ranks that indicate what percentage of the norm group scored above and below a given score. This information is useful in understanding what a test score means. For example, knowing that you are in the sixty-fifth percentile on an intelligence test tells you that you scored higher than 65 percent and lower than 35 percent of the people in the norm group. This gives more information than knowing that you correctly answered 87 out of 119 questions.

Early intelligence tests were constructed to fill particular needs. In the early 1900s there was a great deal of concern about the placement of retarded children in special-education programs. Alfred Binet developed a test to meet this special need. Binet's test was given to children individually, required a skilled examiner, and took a long time to administer.

The need for an intelligence test that could be given to groups, administered quickly, and scored by untrained workers arose when the United States assembled a large army in preparation for the First World War. The aim was to sort men quickly by ability levels so the military services could give them appropriate assignments. These early tests, called Army Alpha and Army Beta, planted the seed for the many group intelligence tests used in schools and industry today. More than 1100 different tests, grouped in 15 broad content categories, are listed in the eighth edition of the *Buros Mental Measurement Yearbook*, the most comprehensive listing and description of printed tests available. This chapter can concentrate only on a few well-known tests of cognitive abilities.

INDIVIDUALLY ADMINISTERED TESTS

The Binet Tests   Alfred Binet thought that people's intelligence could be measured by sampling their work on a number of tasks. Because the tests were intended to classify schoolchildren, Binet included many school-related tasks as he tried to measure reasoning, the ability to understand and follow directions, and the exercise of judgment.

Binet's approach to intellectual assessment was rapidly adopted, and his original test has gone through numerous revisions and adaptations. In the United States, Lewis Terman was instrumental in developing a revised version of the Binet tests, called the **Stanford-Binet.**

Use of the Stanford-Binet has declined, however, partly because it does not provide analyses of specific mental abilities, particularly nonverbal skills. But perhaps the most important reason for the decline in the use of the Binet scales is that many of the questions sound too schoollike to adults. Although the Binet tests are regarded as useful tools for measuring children's scholastic ability, other tests have replaced them, especially at the adolescent and adult levels. In an attempt to regain its earlier popularity, the fourth edition of the Stanford-Binet (1985) includes norms for separate item types and is designed to minimize sexual and ethnic bias.

The Wechsler Tests   The individually administered tests that replaced the Stanford-Binet as the most used tests in the United States are those developed by David Wechsler. Wechsler thought that Binet-type tests were deficient because they produced only a single score. He believed that intelligence should be measured as a group of abilities.

Three scores are obtained from each of the Wechsler scales: a verbal score, a performance score, and a total score. On the **WAIS-R**, for example, the verbal score is based on subtests dealing with general information, vocabulary, attention and rote memory, compre-

Picture arrangement
(a)

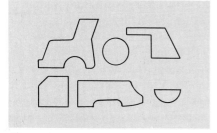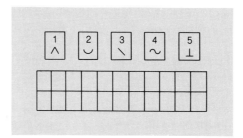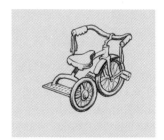

Object assembly
(b)

Digit symbol
(c)

Picture completion
(d)

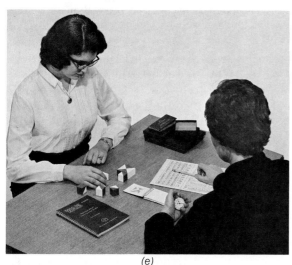

(e)

FIGURE 8.18 *The items shown here are similar to those included in one version of Wechsler performance measures. In picture arrangement (a) the task is to place the pictures in logical order. In object assembly (b) subjects must assemble the pieces to form an object. The digit symbol subtest (c) requires that the subject learn a code. In each picture completion item (d) there is an omitted detail or feature that the subject must name. In the block design test (e) the subject uses painted wooden blocks to copy a design displayed by the examiner.*

hension, ability to think in abstract terms, and arithmetic. The performance score is based on the correctness and speed of solution of several kinds of puzzles, the substitution of symbols for digits, and the reproductions of drawings of designs with a set of colored blocks. The Wechsler Adult Intelligence Scales (WAIS) were so successful that other tests of the same type were constructed for younger age groups: the revised Wechsler Intelligence Scale for Children (**WISC-R**) and the Wechsler Preschool and Primary Scale of Intelligence (**WPPSI**). Table 8.3 illustrates verbal items from several of the Wechsler tests. Figure 8.18 illustrates the general form of some of the performance tests.

For many years, a large difference between the verbal and performance standings was thought to indicate some abnormality in functioning. By now, many people whose behavior is normal have been found to show these discrepancies, so it is probably better to think of the two kinds of tests as measures of two different but

TABLE 8.3 SAMPLE ITEMS FROM SEVERAL WECHSLER TESTS

INFORMATION

How many wings does a bird have? (WPPSI)

Who was Thomas Jefferson? (WISC-R)

Who wrote *Huckleberry Finn?* (WAIS-R)

COMPREHENSION

Why should we wear shoes when we go outside? (WPPSI)

Why is it important to use zip codes when you mail letters? (WISC-R)

Why do married people who want a divorce have to go to court? (WAIS-R)

SIMILARITIES

Puppies grow up to be dogs, and kittens grow up to be —————. (WPPSI)

In what way are corn and macaroni alike? How are they the same? (WISC-R)

In what way are a book and a movie alike? (WAIS-R)

VOCABULARY

What is a hammer? (WPPSI)

What do we mean by *protect?* (WISC-R)

What does *formulate* mean? (WAIS-R)

ARITHMETIC

(The examiner places 10 blocks in front of the child) Give me all of the blocks except three. Leave three of the blocks here. (WPPSI)

Dick had 13 pieces of candy and gave away 8. How many did he have left? (WISC-R)

How many hours will it take to drive 240 miles at the rate of 30 miles an hour? (WAIS-R)

SENTENCES

I'm going to say something, and I want you to say it after me just the way I say it: *Karen has two dogs and a new blue wagon.* (WPPSI)

DIGIT SPAN

I am going to say some numbers. Listen carefully, and when I am through, say them right after me: *3–6–1–7–5–8.* (WISC-R and WAIS-R)

Now I am going to say more numbers, but this time when I stop, I want you to say them backwards: *1–9–3–2–7.* (WISC-R and WAIS-R)

Source: Cronbach, 1984, p. 207. These items were supplied by Alan Kaufman.

overlapping kinds of abilities rather than as two different measures of the same thing (Cronbach, 1984). Many clinicians who use tests of ability to make recommendations about important questions in people's lives prefer the Wechsler tests because the total score is less dependent on verbal skills than that of the Stanford-Binet. However, the Wechsler test total IQ and the Stanford-Binet are highly correlated (.85), so despite the differences between them, they measure much the same thing.

In the newest (1981) revision of the adult test, the WAIS-R, the test constructors tried to make the test more culturally fair by choosing items that covered materials as well known to minority groups as to the white middle class. The test norms also represent a sample very much like the U.S. population in age, sex, race, geographical region, and occupation.

Other intelligence tests have been designed to fit a variety of special needs. For example, nonverbal tests have been developed to measure intellectual functioning among the deaf, people with certain types of neurological damage, and those who do not speak English. Other tests, such as those described later in Frontier 8.2, attempt to measure more accurately the intellectual potential of minority individuals whose cultural background may be very different from that of the test constructors.

GROUP TESTS OF INTELLIGENCE

Because tests like the Stanford-Binet and the Wechsler tests are expensive to administer, most individuals come into contact only with one or more of the many group tests. These tests do not permit the tester to observe the individual's behavior in the way that individually administered tests do, but they do provide a convenient method for obtaining test scores. Group tests are used to estimate students' ability levels, to make decisions regarding the admission of students to college, to select employees, and to divide research subjects into groups.

Intelligence tests or **aptitude tests** measure skills at

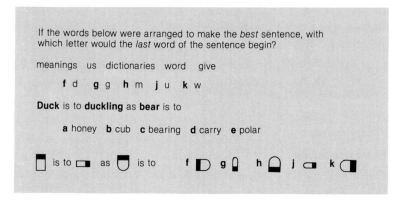

FIGURE 8.19 *A version of the Otis-Lennon Mental Ability Test contains items such as these. The test is intended for older elementary pupils.*

dealing with information that a person has gained from a wide variety of experiences during his or her lifetime. Group intelligence tests currently being used include the **Scholastic Aptitude Test (SAT)**, the Otis-Lennon Mental Ability Test, the Cognitive Abilities Test, and the Henmon-Nelson Tests of Mental Ability. Figure 8.19 shows some typical test questions.

Achievement tests measure how a relatively standardized set of experiences—say, three years of high school mathematics courses, or a one-semester geometry course—affects a person's ability to solve problems. Among the better-known tests are the California Achievement Tests, the Iowa Tests of Basic Skills, the Metropolitan Achievement Tests, and the Stanford Achievement Tests. Most of these tests are given to children in grades 3 through 12 (see Figure 8.20).

There can be no rigid distinction between aptitude and achievement tests. Some aptitude tests call for rather specific learning experiences and some achievement tests cover a broad and unstandardized exposure to information. It is especially important not to conclude that the difference between these two types of tests is a difference between innate and acquired, or learned, ability. All psychological tests measure a person's current behavior, which partly reflects past learning experiences. Anne Anastasi (1982), the author of an influential book on psychological testing, solves the problem of the overlap between aptitude and achievement tests by thinking of them both as tests of developed abilities. In general, these tests, no matter what their title, all measure people's efficiency in dealing with information and problem-solving tasks.

Most of the prominent tests today are very similar in general content to the tests developed in the early 1900s. While part of this similarity can be considered a reflection of the expertise of the original test constructors and theorists, the field of intelligence testing has been justly criticized for its failure to incorporate important findings from the areas of cognitive development and neuropsychology (Cronbach, 1984; Kaufman, 1979). Although test items have been modernized and statistical techniques have been applied to improve the tests as measuring devices, the content and structure of the major group intelligence tests have remained basically unchanged since the First World War.

THE IQ CONCEPT

The **IQ** began with a problem created by the Binet test. Binet had ranked his tasks according to age. The average age level of the tasks that the child could solve was called the child's **mental age.** One problem with this approach was that a 3-year-old and a 7-year-old who solved the same tasks would both be assigned a mental age of 5, when clearly they could not really be described as similar. When Terman and his co-workers revised Binet's test, they tried to deal with this problem by establishing an intelligence quotient, or ratio, that was arrived at by dividing the mental age by the chronological age (and then multiplying by 100 to remove the decimal point). Thus, IQ = (MA/CA) × 100. A little consideration of this formula makes the problems with it clear. For example, a 4-year-old with a mental age of 5 would have an IQ of 125 and could be said to be developing 25 percent faster than the average child (the average IQ for any age group is 100). An 8-year-old would have to have a mental age of 10 to have the same IQ score. But the biggest problem with this approach relates to expressing the performance of adults. Since the average score on the Stanford-Binet at age 40 is only a little higher than the average score at age 15, it makes no sense to speak of a mental age of 40.

Because the mental age concept is meaningless for adults, David Wechsler expressed the scores on his series of intelligence tests in a different way. He used the

idea of deviation from the mean, a concept that we discussed in Chapter 2. The IQ scores on the Wechsler tests are determined by consulting a table based on a mean of 100 and a standard deviation of 15 (see Figure 8.21). This means that the score is not a quotient but a

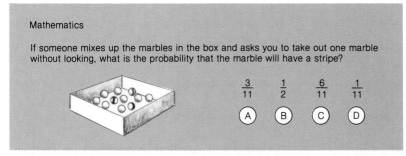

Mathematics

If someone mixes up the marbles in the box and asks you to take out one marble without looking, what is the probability that the marble will have a stripe?

$\frac{3}{11}$ $\frac{1}{2}$ $\frac{6}{11}$ $\frac{1}{11}$

(A)   (B)   (C)   (D)

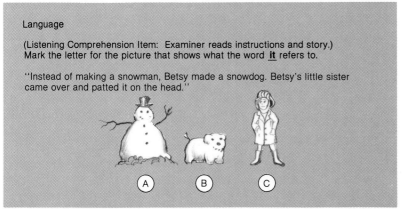

Language

(Listening Comprehension Item: Examiner reads instructions and story.)
Mark the letter for the picture that shows what the word **it** refers to.

"Instead of making a snowman, Betsy made a snowdog. Betsy's little sister came over and patted it on the head."

(A)   (B)   (C)

Science

You have dissolved some sugar in a pan of water and left the pan in a warm place. When the water evaporates, the sugar will—

(A)   break down into molecules of carbon and water

(B)   evaporate too

(C)   melt

(D)   still be in the pan

FIGURE 8.20 *Achievement tests contain items related to information learned in school. These items are typical of those on the Complete Survey Battery of the Metropolitan Achievement Test.*

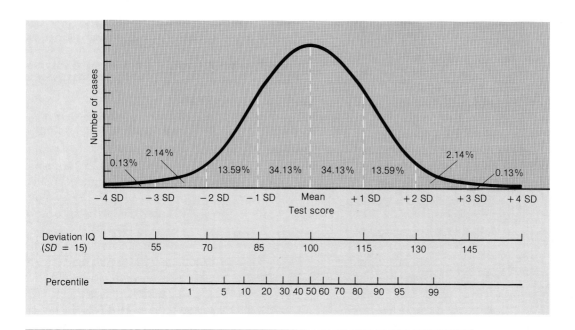

FIGURE 8.21 *The meaning of intelligence test scores expressed in deviation IQ and percentiles is illustrated by this normal curve.*

standard score, which is calculated by subtracting the mean of all scores from the individual's score and then dividing the result by the standard deviation of that same set of scores. Using standard scores makes it possible to compare scores on different tests in a meaningful way because they are all expressed by the same scale of measurement.

The Stanford-Binet and other intelligence tests now also use the concept of standard or deviation score. The term *IQ* is a holdover from the past that many psychologists and educators would like to see abolished. It would be much better to use a term such as "School Ability Index" (Cronbach, 1984). Just as Americans cling to measures like pounds and feet instead of shifting to the metric system, the term *IQ* is hard to do away with because people are used to it.

Social issues and testing

Since the 1950s the use of intelligence tests has come under increasing attack in the United States. Use of these tests in schools and in business organizations has

been criticized as an invalid selection device. Many critics believe that tests are often used by unqualified people who do not understand the cautions that must be applied in interpreting the results. Test supporters, on the other hand, argue that assessment has many practical uses and that doing away with tests would make correctly classifying individuals very difficult. They believe that tests, when they are used correctly, are the least biased way to assess behavior.

Tests of intelligence or aptitude have been used extensively—and thus criticized extensively—in two very different situations: in assigning elementary school students to classes for slow learners and in deciding which students should be admitted to the most competitive and prestigious colleges.

TESTS FOR SLOW LEARNERS

In the past, the use of intelligence test scores as the only basis for assigning children to classes for the retarded or for slow learners resulted in disproportionate numbers of minority children in these classes. Minority groups have asserted that this outcome was unfair because intelligence tests are generally biased in favor of middle-class students. Students who speak English as a second language, such as Mexican-Americans, are at a particular disadvantage.

A number of court cases and U.S. government regulations have affected the way that schools can use such tests. One of the most famous decisions, in the case of *Larry P. v. Wilson Riles*, stated that intelligence tests, which were being used to make school placements that often stigmatized children and assigned them to inferior educational programs, contained questions inappropriate to minority children's cultural background. Nine years after the case was filed and after many experts had testified on both sides, the United States District Court in California ruled in 1979 that IQ tests could no longer be used for educational diagnosis. Even before that decision, a 1977 federal regulation required that intelligence tests not be the sole basis for educational classification and that the decision be based on the child's performance level on a variety of types of adaptive behavior and on information about sociocultural factors in the child's background (Public Law 94-142, Federal Register, 1977). Some other court decisions have come to the opposite conclusion—in *PASE v. Hannon* the Illinois state court ruled that IQ tests were not biased and could be used to place children in classes for the retarded or slow learners.

Although the *Larry P.* decision technically applies only in California, it has influenced educational policy in many states. One result is that the proportion of schoolchildren in classes for slow learners is dropping. As one expert put it, "People are very worried about whether they are going to be sued" (Lambert, 1978). Another result is that construction of new tests to define and measure intelligence has been stimulated. Two of these tests are discussed in Frontier 8.2.

APTITUDE TESTS FOR COLLEGE ADMISSION

The dissatisfaction with the use of group-administered aptitude tests, primarily the Scholastic Aptitude Test (SAT), as a screening device for college admission has been as loud as the outcry over using intelligence tests to assign young children to classes for the retarded. Critics have attacked the tests as an inaccurate and unfair method of deciding such an important issue as college acceptance.

Those who defend the use of the SAT and other tests in screening college applicants argue that the test covers the words and symbols that the student will need for college work. If they couldn't use such tests, colleges would have to rely primarily on students' high school grades. Since high school grading standards differ widely, test supporters argue, the standardized tests are actually fairer.

Ralph Nader's team of consumer advocates spent six years studying the SAT (Nairn, 1980). Their report claimed that the SAT successfully predicted a student's performance in the first year of college only 12 percent of the time, a percentage only slightly better than chance. Critics have argued that this claim is incorrect and based on a misunderstanding of statistics (Kaplan, 1982). In fact, they assert, the use of the SAT score produces a significantly better prediction of college achievement than high school grades alone. The Nader group also claimed that coaching could help students to raise their scores and also that the cultural bias of the test items excluded many capable minority students from college admission. Test constructors and many test users dispute these findings, although most now concede that certain kinds of intensive coaching may help to increase test scores (Messick, 1980; Jackson, 1980). Supporters of the SAT claim that the problem is not the test itself, but rather the practice that many colleges have of picking a particular score as a cutoff point. They argue that this policy ignores the fact that the score is just an estimate of the score that the student would get if he or she took the test many times and averaged the results. The difference between the student's actual score and this true score (called the **standard error**) can be anywhere from 32 to 50 points on the 800-point SAT score. Most test constructors would consider a standard error of this size to be quite good prediction, but such a large range clearly is a problem when arbitrary cutoff points are used.

Because SAT scores have such an important effect on students' lives, a "truth in testing" movement has developed. A number of groups have demanded that

A NEW GENERATION OF INTELLIGENCE TESTS?

As a result of controversy over the use of tests, a number of new instruments have been developed. Two of these tests, the System of Multicultural Pluralistic Assessment (SOMPA) and the Kaufman Assessment Battery for Children (K-ABC), illustrate two different approaches to meeting objections that minority groups have to the WISC and other standardized tests.

SOMPA

Intelligence test scores tell us how well a child performs but not why he or she performs at a certain level. Jane Mercer and her colleagues hope to avoid the misclassification of children from culturally and linguistically diverse backgrounds as mentally retarded by constructing a test battery, referred to as *SOMPA*, that adds information about the child's cultural background, social competence, and health status to the information provided by a standard intelligence test (Lewis and Mercer, 1978; Mercer and Lewis, 1978).

This test battery includes the WISC (or WPPSI, depending on the child's age); a test of perception and nervous system functioning; tests of physical dexterity, hearing, and sight; and the weight/height ratio, which is a rough measure of the child's overall health. In addition, a structured interview in either English or Spanish is held in the child's home with the person who takes principal care of the child. The interview contains questions about the child's behavior and health history and the cultural and economic character of the family. The child's scores on all these measures are then profiled, and percentile scores are found for all of them except vision, hearing, and health. The child's WISC and behavior inventory scores are then compared with typical profiles of children of the same sociocultural background to produce a measure of *estimated learning potential* (ELP). Figure 8.22 illustrates the difference in percentiles for one 9-year-old black girl. The ELP scores reflect the child's relative WISC score compared to those of other children of

her sociocultural and ethnic background. Mercer believes this measure predicts how likely a child is "to benefit from an educational program that takes appropriate account of his or her sociocultural background" (Mercer and Lewis, 1978, p. 54). The test has separate norms for different subgroups. So far, norms are available for black, Hispanic, and Anglo (white) samples. This means that the child's score can be evaluated in terms both of his or her own ethnic group and of the "school culture" or the more general environment to which the child also needs to adapt.

The effect of using the ELP and an assessment of adaptive out-of-school behavior as a way of deciding whether a child is retarded or can profit from a regular school curriculum, even a curriculum that takes cultural influences into account, is still largely unknown. It is clear, however, that the combination of other criteria with WISC scores markedly reduced the number of nonwhite individuals classified as retarded (Reschly, 1981). In addition to doubts about SOMPA's predictive power, educators criticize the assessment system because it does not provide a way to isolate the particular skills in which a child may be weak. So far the advantages of the SOMPA approach still remain in dispute, but it represents a creative attempt to move away from the concept of intelligence toward a distinction between aptitude and performance and an increased awareness of the effects on performance of the interaction between the *person* and the *situation* that we have emphasized so many times in this book.

THE KAUFMAN BATTERY

The *Kaufman Assessment Battery for Children* (K-ABC) is designed to incorporate new ideas from cognitive psychology and neuropsychology into the assessment of intelligence. There are 16 subtests, some for older children and some for younger ones. The tests fall into several categories: sequential processing such as remembering a series of digits or hand movements; simultaneous processing such as arranging a series of

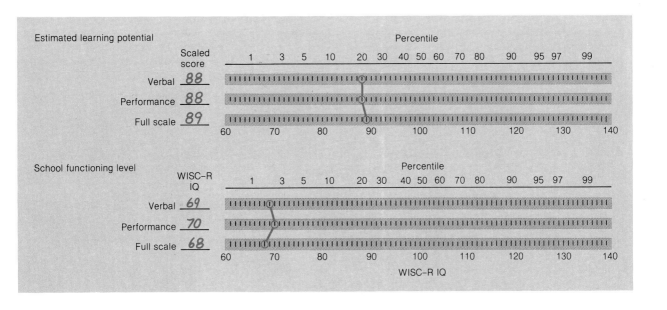

FIGURE 8.22 *A portion of the SOMPA scoring sheet shows the difference between estimated learning potential and school functioning level predictions for one child.*

related pictures in the correct order or recognizing an incompletely drawn picture of an object; and tests that measure more direct school experience such as reading, arithmetic, and naming pictures of well-known places and objects. Many of the tests do not require a verbal response; those that do, require at most only a few words (see Figure 8.23). In most cases the child can respond by pointing or in other nonverbal ways. The test has been described as a way to discover more about the child's approach to problem solving and learning tasks. Although the test's emphasis on short-term memory has been questioned by some critics, Alan Kaufman and Nadine Kaufman argue that what is being measured is not memory as such but rather the sequential and simultaneous pro-

cessing abilities that are defined as intelligence by cognitive psychologists.

Many cognitive psychologists make a similar distinction between what they call fluid and crystallized abilities (Horn and Cattell, 1966). *Crystallized abilities* are those that require information and the practice of certain skills; a brilliant but uneducated person would do poorly on a test of crystallized abilities. These skills—counting, for example—become so well practiced that they are almost automatic. *Fluid abilities,* on the other hand, represent an adaptive process of taking some stimuli and working out an answer. Some of the processes of metacognition, discussed in Chapter 7, such as judgment and self-criticism, are required in fluid ability. Table 8.4 illustrates the kinds of tasks that fall at different points on the crystallized-fluid spectrum. It has been suggested that crystallized abilities grow out of fluid abilities. If people who are the same in fluid ability differ on crystallized ability, according to this view, it is either because of a differ-

(a)

FIGURE 8.23 *A figure from the Kaufman-ABC. In the Face Recognition subtest (a), the child is shown a picture of one or two faces (left) for 5 seconds. Then the child selects the face(s) from a second photograph showing a group of people (right). In the Gestalt Closure subtest (b), the child is shown a partially completed drawing and names the object pictured, in this case a bicycle. In the Word Order subtest (c), a group of pictures is shown and the child is asked to touch them in the order named, for example, key, star. Later the task is made more difficult by naming the items and then asking the child to identify the colors in a series of colored dots before going back to the picture sequence.*

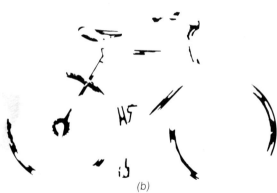

(b)

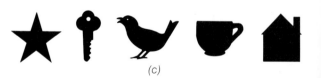

(c)

ence in the amount of their education or the degree of effort that they put into work during their school years (Undheim, 1981).

Although the Kaufman-ABC tests are described as being particularly fair to children of minority groups, test scores on the battery show the same black-white differences that are seen on other intelligence tests.

When parent education is taken into account, however, blacks of preschool age and Hispanics of preschool and school age perform as well as whites, thus demonstrating that there is little racial or ethnic difference on many nonverbal reasoning tasks.

Whether either the SOMPA or the Kaufman-ABC will solve the problem of fairness in the testing of mi-

TABLE 8.4   TASKS IN THE CRYSTALLIZED–FLUID SPECTRUM

MAXIMUM ADAPTATION OR TRANSFER OF EXPERIENCE

A	FLUID ABILITY	BLOCK DESIGN
		EMBEDDED FIGURES
		MATRICES
		SCRAMBLED SENTENCES
B	REASONING WITH ACQUIRED CONCEPTS	VERBAL ANALOGIES
		NUMBER SERIES
C	GENERAL EDUCATIONAL DEVELOPMENT	INTERPRETING UNFAMILIAR TEXTS, TABLES, DIAGRAMS
		QUANTITATIVE REASONING
D	SUBJECT-MATTER PROFICIENCY	GRAMMAR
		COMPUTATION
	"CRYSTALLIZED" ACHIEVEMENTS	FACTUAL KNOWLEDGE

MAXIMUM DIRECT TRAINING

Source: Cronbach, 1984, p. 253.

norities is unclear at this point. One problem is that the test scores are not highly related to school performance. The approach of both these tests displeases those who believe that tests should be primarily predictors of performance, but it pleases those who believe that tests of mental measurement should be designed to minimize test score differences between children of different cultural and ethnic backgrounds.

those administering such tests give test takers copies of the questions and answers after the test and provide more sophisticated data about the test. In 1979 a law was passed in New York that required these disclosures for all standardized exams used for admission decisions to colleges and graduate and professional schools. Similar bills have been introduced in other states and the U.S. Congress. The result of such action means that testing companies would have to produce many more items. Whether they can do this and still come up with tests that can predict well and that are reasonable in cost is an unanswered question. Like many other issues in testing, resolving these problems in a way that will benefit both students and college admission systems is a complex task.

STUDY OUTLINE

LANGUAGE (p. 268)

1. Language is important for communication, memory, thinking, and perception of the environment.

2. Psycholinguistics is the study of the way the sounds and symbols that make up language are translated into meaning. Psycholinguists describe language as having both a surface structure and a deep structure, or underlying meaning. Understanding this meaning involves breaking the sounds we hear into constituents or basic phrases.

3. Much of current psycholinguistic theory is based on the ideas of Noam Chomsky, who emphasizes that the deep structures of language are innate. Children learn language by fitting what they hear into these built-in patterns.

4. Children's first speech sounds or babblings are self-reinforcing. A deaf child will soon stop babbling, although a child with deaf parents, who cannot respond, still continues to make these sounds. Feedback from

others is important, however, in language acquisition. The development of children's speech has several characteristics. When they first begin to speak, they simplify many words and they use consistent grammatical forms that are different from those adults use.

5. The form of human language is determined by human anatomical features and by the specialization of parts of the human brain. There seems to be a sensitive period in which language learning is most successful. Whether nonhuman animals use true language in their communication is a hotly debated and researched question.

6. Language affects both cognition and perception. Linguistic relativism, the idea that language influences the way a person thinks, has not gained much experimental support. However, language does affect how efficiently we can code our experiences and also what we remember about what we see.

PROBLEM SOLVING (p. 281)

Success in problem solving depends on metacognitive skills. Most people use algorithms and heuristics to help solve problems. Algorithms always lead to a correct solution if they are used correctly. Examples are multiplication tables. Heuristics, rules of thumb that provide quick and easy searches through memory, are more efficient for many problems even though they may sometimes lead to incorrect solutions. Analogies and means-ends analysis are examples of heuristics.

INTELLIGENCE (p. 285)

1. Intelligence includes reasoning abilities, stored knowledge, and problem-solving skills. About half the intellectual difference among individuals is probably due to genetic inheritance. Although heredity sets the general range of intelligence, environment is important because it determines where in that broad general range a person's intellectual performance will fall.

2. The structure of intelligence has been studied through factor analysis, research on the cognitive development of children, and in terms of specific brain functioning. Recently, cognitive psychologists have been using information processing concepts to study intelligence. Metacognitive strategies are particularly important in intelligent behavior.

3. Intelligence tests attempt to measure how people differ in cognitive abilities. Like all tests, it is important that intelligence tests be reliable (be able to produce the same result if administered again) and valid (measure what is intended to be measured). Most tests are standardized so that norms are developed for interpreting test scores.

4. Individually administered tests are preferable because they allow the examiner to observe test-taking behavior and understand more about why certain results were obtained. Because they are expensive to give, these tests are usually used only in special circumstances. In other cases group-administered written tests are used. The most widely used individual tests are the Wechsler tests.

5. The concept of IQ as the ratio of mental to chronological age is a holdover from the past. What most tests now report as IQ is a standard score showing how far the person deviates from the mean. The score is translated into an IQ equivalent score because IQ is a familiar concept.

6. Achievement tests and intelligence or aptitude tests cannot be rigidly distinguished. Achievement tests are designed to give more emphasis to the subject matter that has been learned, and aptitude tests to potential ability, but both types of tests measure current behavior, which reflects both intellectual level and past learning experiences.

7. Two social issues are currently important in intelligence testing. Recently, intelligence tests designed for special uses, particularly for testing minority individuals who may have had different cultural experiences and those for whom English is not a native language, have become important because of legal challenges to fairness of intelligence tests as criteria for assigning children to school programs for the retarded. The Scholastic Aptitude Test (SAT), employed as a screening device by many colleges, has also been labeled by some critics as biased. Although SAT items have been scrutinized to eliminate those that are not culturally fair, the debate over the predictive value of SAT scores continues.

KEY TERMS AND CONCEPTS

psycholinguistics

phoneme

morpheme

surface structure

deep structure

semantics

constituents

expanding

metalinguistic awareness

critical period

imprinting

sensitive period

linguistic relativism (or linguistic determinism)

algorithm

heuristic

means-ends analysis

General Problem Solver

functional fixedness

mental set

intelligence

factor analysis

primary mental abilities

general (g) factor

reliability

validity

test standardization

Binet tests

Stanford-Binet

Wechsler tests

WAIS-R

WISC-R

WPPSI

aptitude test

Scholastic Aptitude Test (SAT)

achievement test

IQ

mental age

standard score

standard error

SOMPA

estimated learning potential

Kaufman Assessment Battery for Children

crystallized ability

fluid ability

standard error

SUGGESTED READINGS

ANASTASI, A. (1982). *Psychological testing* (5th ed.). New York: Macmillan. A standard text that describes the functions and characteristics of psychological tests and reviews a variety of tests that are commonly used.

BRANSFORD, J. D., and STEIN, B. S. (1984). *The ideal problem solver*. New York: W. H. Freeman. A brief and easy-to-read description of a memory system that can be useful to students.

MILLER, G. A. (1981). *Language and speech*. New York: W. H. Freeman. An easy-to-read discussion of the evolution and development of language and speech.

STERNBERG, R. A. (Ed.) (1982). *Handbook of human intelligence*. Cambridge: Cambridge University Press. A collection of up-to-date articles by prominent psychologists that reflect current research in a variety of aspects of intelligence.

SECTION FOUR
AROUSAL AND BEHAVIOR

CHAPTER NINE: **EMOTION AND MOTIVATION**

CHAPTER TEN: **HUMAN SEXUALITY**

CHAPTER NINE

EMOTION AND MOTIVATION

EMOTION
Eliciting stimuli
The cognitive component
The physiological component
The behavioral component
Interactions among components

MOTIVATION: THE "WHY" OF BEHAVIOR
Perspectives on motivation
Homeostatic needs: To thirst and hunger

FRONTIER 9.1   EATING DISORDERS

Sensory needs
Social motivation
Motivational conflict

FRONTIER 9.2   MOTIVES GONE AWRY: NEW THEORIES OF ADDICTION

STUDY OUTLINE

KEY TERMS AND CONCEPTS

SUGGESTED READINGS

There is an inner warm glow, a radiant sensation; I feel like smiling; there is a sense of well-being, a sense of harmony and peace within. . . . I think about beautiful things; I feel safe and secure. . . . My movements are graceful and easy; I feel especially well coordinated. . . . There is a sense of being more alive. I am excited in a calm way. . . . There is a particularly acute awareness of pleasurable things, their sounds, their colors, and textures. . . . I'm optimistic and cheerful; the world seems basically good and beautiful.

I feel empty, drained, hollow, understimulated, undercharged, heavy, loggy, sluggish; I feel let down, tired, sleepy; it's an effort to do anything. I have no desire, no motivation, no interest. . . . I feel sorry for myself; I want to withdraw, disappear, draw back, be alone, away from others, crawl into myself; everything seems useless, absurd, meaningless; I feel as if I'm out of touch, can't reach others; my body wants to contract. . . . I have no appetite; there is a heaviness in my chest; there is a lump in my throat; I can't smile or laugh; it's as if I'm suffocating.

These descriptions of contrasting emotional experiences—happiness and depression—come from interviews with more than 12,000 people who were asked to describe certain feelings (Davitz, 1970). It is obvious from the descriptions that **emotions** are complex internal states with many elements. There are physical components ("an inner warm glow," "tired," "sleepy," "lump in my throat"), thoughts ("sense of harmony and peace within," "everything seems useless"), and behavioral expressions of the feeling ("I feel like smiling"; "I can't smile or laugh").

We all intuitively know what emotions feel like, but intuition is not enough for science. Because emotions involve complex interactions between mind, body, and behavior, the biological, behavioral, cognitive, and psychodynamic perspectives are all concerned with important facets of emotion.

The dividing line between emotion and motivation is not always very clear, since motivation and emotion both involve states of arousal. We often react emotion-

ally when our motives are gratified or frustrated. Indeed, the descriptions of emotion that we opened this chapter with might well describe "the thrill of victory" and "the agony of defeat." One common distinction is that emotions are basically reactions or *responses* to certain events, while motives operate more like internal *stimuli* that energize and direct behavior toward some goal or incentive (Geen and others, 1984; Mandler, 1984).

EMOTION

Life without emotion would be strange indeed. The experiences of love, anger, joy, fear, and other feelings are a central part of our conscious lives. According to psychodynamic theorists, emotions are also an important part of the unconscious underworld that affects our behavior.

Emotions add color to our world of experience, and, like colors, they cover a wide spectrum. In fact, more than 550 words in the English language refer to various emotional states (Averill, 1980). But despite their diversity, emotions seem to share some common features. When we respond emotionally to some situation, there are, first of all, thoughts about the situation and its meaning for us. There is also a state of physiological or bodily arousal; we become physically "stirred up." Finally, there are certain behavior tendencies. Some of these are *expressive* behaviors (for example, smiling or crying). Others are *instrumental* behaviors, ways of reacting to the stimulus that aroused the emotion (for example, by attacking or running away). These features of the emotional response may differ from person to person and, as we shall see, from culture to culture.

Figure 9.1 illustrates the general relationships among these four primary components: (1) the **eliciting stimuli,** the events that arouse the emotion; (2) the person's **cognitive appraisal** or interpretation of the situation, which gives meaning to it; (3) **physiological arousal;** and (4) **expressive behavior** and/or **instrumental behaviors.** Of special significance are the relationships between cognitive and physiological factors. As the arrows indicate, these components appear to affect one another.

Eliciting stimuli

Emotions do not occur in a vacuum. They always have objects. We cannot simply be angry, fearful, proud, or in love. We are angry *at* something or someone; fearful or proud *of* something; in love *with* someone. Moreover, the stimuli that trigger our emotional responses aren't always external; they can be inside us in the form of images and memories. Usually we can identify the eliciting stimuli, but not always. Sometimes people feel anxious or "down in the dumps" without being sure why.

Learning plays an important role in determining how easily particular objects or people will arouse emotions. On the broadest level, cultures have different standards for defining the good, the bad, and the ugly. Physical features that provoke sexual arousal and feelings of infatuation in one culture, such as ornamental burns or scars, may elicit feelings of disgust in another. Individuals whose emotional responses deviate widely from the norms of their culture may be viewed as disturbed. In our culture, for example, such deviance occurs in fetishists, for whom inanimate objects like shoes or handbags serve as eliciting stimuli for high levels of sexual arousal.

As Figure 9.1 shows, personality and motivational factors can affect emotion by influencing the situations to which people expose themselves and what they think about those situations, as well as their physiological and behavioral responses. For example, one's desire for novelty and excitement is a motivational influence. Someone high in this motive might well experience a sense of exhilaration, a "peak experience," in skydiving (Zuckerman, 1979). Many others would experience complete terror in jumping out of an airplane, even *with* a parachute on.

Biological factors may also affect which classes of stimuli have the greatest potential to arouse emotions. For example, the concept of *preparedness* (see Chapter 6) suggests that people may be biologically primed to fear heights, snakes, or spiders. Fear responses can be much more easily conditioned to such stimuli than to others, such as flowers (Hygge and Ohman, 1978).

FIGURE 9.1 *Components of emotion, showing the relationships between eliciting stimuli, cognitive appraisal processes, physiological arousal, and expressive and instrumental behaviors. Appraisal and physiological arousal are the internal factors that influence what we feel and how intense our emotional response is. Individual differences in personality and motivation can affect each of the four primary components.*

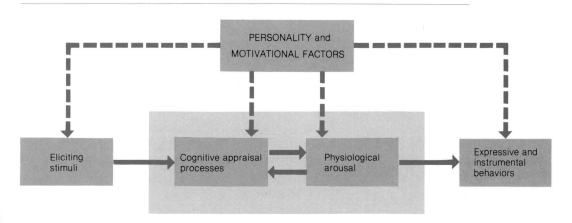

The cognitive component

Men are disturbed not by things, but by the views they take of them. (Epictetus, A.D. 60)

As you think, so shall you feel. This is the basic idea behind the concept of *cognitive appraisal*. Emotions are responses to our perception of the eliciting stimuli. The act of perception involves attaching meaning to sensations, and our thoughts, judgments, and interpretations create the psychological reality to which we respond. For example, recent research has shown that the strongest predictors of personal happiness are cognitive rather than environmental. How people compare their life situation with those of others, with their past life, and with their future aspirations is more important than objective factors like status, income, and marriage in determining how happy they are (Diener, 1984).

While all perceptions involve subjective interpretations of reality, the appraisals involved in emotional behavior are especially *evaluative* and *personal*; they relate to what we think is desirable or undesirable for us or for the people we care about (Averill, 1980). If the object of the emotion is appraised as desirable or beneficial, we might experience joy, delight, liking, or love if the object is present, and desire or hope if it is not present. Appraising an object as undesirable, threatening, or harmful triggers negative emotions such as fear, dislike, or hatred (Lazarus, 1984). We do not need to be consciously aware of the appraisals that underlie emotional responses. In some instances, we may do little more than transform sensory input into a perceptual whole, and little if any cognitive activity involving language may take place (Zajonc, 1984). After all, infants, who have no formal language, can still experience emotions. As our cognitive abilities develop, however, our appraisals are more likely to become tied to language, whether or not we are consciously aware of their content (Izard, 1984).

The ability of thoughts to elicit emotional reactions has been well established in laboratory research (Berkowitz, 1984). In one study, subjects simply read sentences that expressed anxiety (for instance, "This is awful. . . . I'm getting tense"), depression ("There is nothing to look forward to"), or no emotion ("Los An-

geles is south of San Francisco"). Their physiological responses were recorded while they read the sentences. Subjects also rated their moods. The anxiety sentences were associated with increased physiological arousal and with ratings of anxiety, while reading the depressive sentences triggered lowered arousal and ratings of depressed mood (Orton and others, 1983).

The idea that emotional reactions are triggered by cognitive appraisal rather than by external situations helps to account for the fact that different people (or even the same person at different times) may have very different emotional reactions to the same object or person. Statements like "I have a new attitude toward that person now" or "I've decided what's really important in life" reflect changes in the appraisal of certain situations or people. Figure 9.2 shows how to mentally transform a pleasant event into a threatening one.

Cultural learning and individual life experiences help to shape our appraisals. Clinical psychologist Albert Ellis suggests that some commonly held beliefs are irrational and self-defeating because they lead to unnecessary emotional distress (Ellis and Grieger, 1977). Perhaps the most basic of these beliefs is that "it is terrible, awful, and catastrophic when things and people (including ourselves) are not the way we demand that they be." The two key elements that make this idea irrational, according to Ellis, are that (1) things are seldom awful and catastrophic (they are more likely to be merely annoying and frustrating) and (2) it is self-defeating to turn our preferences and wants into demands and dire necessities. People who think in this manner tend to overreact with strong negative emotions (anger, depression, fear) when things or people are not exactly the way they "should" be. Four other irrational beliefs that Ellis has linked to emotional disturbance are listed in Table 9.1.

The physiological component

Perhaps the most immediately noticeable aspect of emotional experience is the physiological arousal that results when our feelings are "stirred up." Many parts of our body are involved in emotional arousal, but certain areas of the brain, the autonomic nervous system,

FIGURE 9.2 *Cognitive appraisal processes involved in "negative thinking" can increase the threat potential of innocuous features of the environment.*

Beginner's Exercise in Negative Thinking
Without referring to the list below, how many potential hazards can you identify in this scene?

Partial list of hazards: (A) Intense sunlight could fade your clothing, grass could permanently stain it; (B) passing bird could soil your head; (C) passing airliner could erroneously jettison its septic tank on your car or person; (D) bottles could tip over and spill on clothes; (E) soft drinks could rot your teeth; (F) pollen could inflame your nasal membranes; (G) nearsighted bee, attracted by flower, could accidentally fly into your ear, become trapped and hysterical; (H) weakened tree limb could fall and fracture your skull; (I) sultry weather could cause embarrassment; (J) great distance from nearest restroom could cause extreme anguish; (K) continuous weight on arm could irritate appendix; (L) companion could suddenly realize how boring you are; (M) freelance photographer could snap embarrassing pictures from helicopter; (N) vice-squad officer submerged in stream could be observing you through periscope; (O) thin bear could be lurking behind tree; (P) you could stub your toe on boulder or get tetanus from stepping on rusty nail; (Q) you could break your teeth on smooth white rock you mistook for hard-boiled egg; (R) passing Greyhound bus could careen out of control and demolish your car; (S) mischievous passerby could release handbrake, or paint obscenities in permanent enamel; (T) ground tremor could loosen bank; (U) sudden lava flow could engulf you; (V) stray lightning bolt from cloud could strike tree and electrocute you; (W) plant lice from bark could lodge in scalp; (X) flash flood could carry you away; (Y) rabid herring could leap out of stream and attack your toes.

and the endocrine system are especially significant in producing the physiological arousal that we identify with emotion.

THE BRAIN AND EMOTION

The brain's involvement in emotion is complex, and many aspects are not well understood. It is clear, however, that the hypothalamus and other subcortical structures known collectively as the limbic system play a major role. Electrical stimulation of certain areas of these structures produces unrestrained aggression, and

TABLE 9.1 SOME IRRATIONAL BELIEFS AND THEIR RESULTING MALADAPTIVE EMOTIONAL RESPONSES

IRRATIONAL IDEA	EMOTIONAL REACTION
1. It is a dire necessity for an adult to be loved by everyone for everything he or she does.	Anxiety and depression when someone disapproves or does not accept one
2. One should be thoroughly competent, successful, and achieving in all possible respects.	Fear, self-anger, shame, and feelings of worthlessness if one fails in any way
3. Certain people are wicked and villainous when they do not behave as we demand that they do, and they should be severely punished.	Anger or hatred when others behave in ways that one does not approve of
4. If something is or may be threatening, we should be terribly upset about it.	Maladaptive and excessive worry which may interfere with ability to handle the potential problem

Source: Adapted from Ellis, 1962.

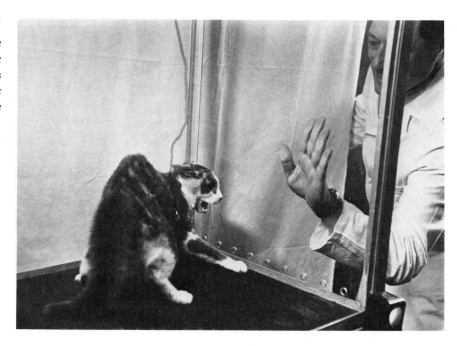

FIGURE 9.3 *A normally tame and friendly cat adopts an attack position as electrical stimulation is delivered to an area of the limbic system that organizes aggressive behavior and emotional arousal.*

an animal will growl at and attack anything that approaches (see Figure 9.3). Destruction of the same sites produces an absence of aggression, even if the animal is provoked or attacked. Other areas of the hypothalamus and limbic system show the opposite pattern: lack of emotion when they are stimulated, and unrestrained emotion when they are removed (Kolb and Whishaw, 1985).

For a long time, brain researchers focused their attention primarily on subcortical regions like the hypothalamus and limbic system. But the importance of the cerebral cortex in emotion is now being emphasized as well (Pribram, 1980). The cortex has many connections with the hypothalamus and limbic system. Moreover, cognitive appraisal processes surely involve "higher" brain centers. Cognitive and physiological processes controlled by various regions of the brain are so intimately related in emotion that both must be taken into account if we are to understand emotional reactions.

AUTONOMIC AND HORMONAL PROCESSES

You are afraid. Your heart starts to beat faster. Blood is drawn from your stomach, and digestion slows to a crawl as the blood flow to your muscles and the surface of your skin is increased. You breathe harder and faster to get more oxygen. Your blood sugar level is elevated, producing more nutrients for your muscles. The pupils of your eyes dilate to let in more light so you can see the danger better. Your skin perspires to keep you cool and to flush out waste products created by extra exertion. Your muscles tense, ready for action.

Some theorists call this arousal state the "fight-or-flight" response (see Figure 9.4). This arousal is produced by the activity of the sympathetic branch of your autonomic nervous system and by hormones from your endocrine system. The sympathetic nervous system produces its effects within a few seconds by directly stimulating the organs of the body. The endocrine system pumps stress hormones like adrenaline directly into the blood stream. These hormones produce physiological effects like those triggered by sympathetic nervous system activity, and their presence in the blood can keep the body aroused for a considerable length of time.

Do different emotions produce different patterns of physiological arousal? After 30 years of research using increasingly sophisticated ways to measure physiological arousal, most investigators have concluded that specific emotions do not result in distinct patterns of arousal (Mandler, 1984). But if all emotions are pretty much the same at the "gut" level, how do we know which emotion we're feeling? We'll return to this important question a bit later, because it is central to understanding the nature of emotion.

People differ from one another in their patterns of general arousal (Stern and others, 1980). For example, we don't all show the same pattern of bodily arousal when we are afraid. If our physiological responses were recorded, some of us would show marked changes in heart rate or blood pressure, but only minor changes in other responses, such as muscle tension and respiration. Others of us would show different patterns. Researchers have learned that no single physiological measure is appropriate for all subjects; it is important to measure as many autonomic indicators as possible.

Lie detection The **polygraph,** an instrument that can measure a wide range of different physiological responses, has been a valuable research tool for many years. But another use of the polygraph is as a "lie detector." Because we have far less control over our physiological responses than we do over many other behaviors, the polygraph is regarded by some as a nearly infallible means of establishing guilt. However, this approach to detecting "lying" has some very definite shortcomings, as our previous comments on the

lack of physiological differentiation between emotions would lead us to expect.

Figure 9.5 shows a portion of a polygraph record. Measures of respiration, electrical skin conductance (which increases in emotion as a result of sweat gland activity), and heart rate were obtained. Note the changes that occurred on these measures when an emotionally loaded question was asked (point A to point B). Unfortunately, however, polygraph records are not reliable indicators of guilt. Innocent people may appear guilty when doubt, fear, or lack of confidence increase the activity level of the autonomic nervous system, while other people may experience no emotion at all when they lie (Kleinmuntz and Szucko, 1984a). In reality, then, there is no such thing as a "lie detector."

How valid is polygraphic lie detection, then? Psychologists have begun to do systematic research on this specific psychological test, typically by giving experienced polygraph examiners the polygraph records of

FIGURE 9.4 *An important part of emotional responding is the physiological arousal state that mobilizes the body to respond to the situation.*

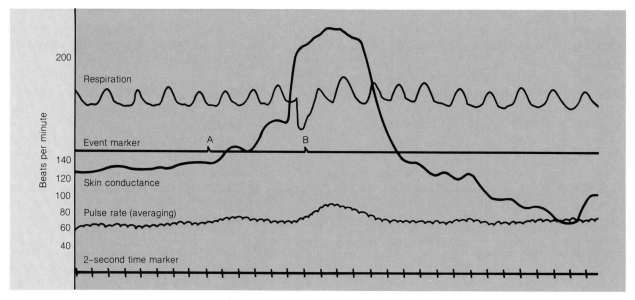

FIGURE 9.5 *The polygraph records physiological changes that are part of emotional responses. Between points A and B an emotionally loaded question is asked. Within 2 seconds the effects of the question are visible in the subject's respiration, skin conductance, and pulse rate. Does this mean she is lying or guilty?*

suspects who had been shown to be either innocent or guilty on the basis of other evidence. On the basis of the polygraph evidence alone, the examiners are asked to decide the guilt or innocence of the suspects. The results of these investigations are quite sobering. About 20 percent of the guilty people are misclassified as innocent, while 35 to 55 percent of the innocent suspects are judged by the experts to be guilty (Kleinmuntz and Szucko, 1984b; Lykken, 1984). Thus, the old adage that an innocent person has nothing to fear from a polygraph test is sheer nonsense.

As scientific evidence accumulates, it becomes increasingly clear that the lie detector has very questionable validity and the potential for ruinous effects on the lives of many people (Saxe and others, 1985). Yet the mistaken faith that many have in lie detection has re-

sulted in a widening range of use. About 20 percent of the country's major corporations now use polygraph testing of employees, and about 50 percent of fast-food companies use preemployment polygraph tests for screening purposes (Belt and Holden, 1978). In 1983, President Reagan issued an executive order for increased polygraph testing of government employees to protect national security. It is hoped that research on the validity of the lie detector will result in a more realistic picture of its limitations.

The behavioral component

Once cognitive appraisals have been made and the body has been mobilized for action, the stage is set for overt behavioral responses. Because both expressive and instrumental behaviors are externally observable, they are easier to study scientifically than the private and subjective elements of emotion that we have considered so far.

EXPRESSIVE BEHAVIORS

Although we can never directly experience another person's feelings, we frequently make judgments about them (see Figure 9.6). We may decide that someone is angry, sad, or happy on the basis of his or her emotional displays. Expressive behaviors are not only an important feature of the emotional response, but they also serve as social stimuli that influence the behavior of others (Mandler, 1984). Because of their important role in the regulation of social behavior, expressive behaviors have been an important topic of research and theory for many years.

Facial expression of emotion   Most of us have a fair degree of confidence in our ability to "read" the emotions of others. Although many parts of the body can communicate feelings, we tend to concentrate on what the face tells us. Most lower animals have relatively few facial muscles, so that they are limited in their facial expressions of emotion. Only monkeys, apes, and humans have enough well-developed facial muscles to produce large numbers of expressions.

Common lore has it that the eyes are particularly good sources of information about what is being felt: if looks could kill; the look of love; there's red-hot anger in his eyes; her eyes twinkled with amusement. Research tells us, however, that other parts of the face are at least as important, if not more so. In fact, it appears that different emotions are expressed through different parts of the face.

In one experiment, a set of 32 posed facial photographs were used. The photos had previously been rated by judges who strongly agreed upon the emotions being expressed. Each photograph was cut into three parts—a brow-forehead part, an eyes part, and a mouth part. These partial photos were then shown to a group of subjects who were asked to rate each one in terms of six emotions: anger, fear, happiness, surprise, sadness, and disgust. The results showed that different parts of the face provided the best cues for recognizing the various emotions. The eyes provided the most important cues for fear and sadness, but the mouth was the major cue for happiness and disgust, while the forehead was

FIGURE 9.6 *Expressive behaviors, such as facial expressions, body posture, and other nonverbal behaviors, can provide important cues for judging emotion.*

"I have before me, gentlemen, some figures that may shock you, as they did me."

(DRAWING BY MODELL; © 1977 THE NEW YORKER MAGAZINE, INC.)

the best indicator of surprise. Anger appeared to be a more complex emotion; it required information from all facial areas for accurate recognition (Boucher and Ekman, 1975).

Although facial expressions can be valuable cues for judging emotion, there can be significant differences between people in their facial expressions of the same emotion. Fortunately, we often have more than facial cues to base our judgments on. We usually know something about the situation to which the person is reacting, and this seems to be a particularly important basis for judgment. Many experiments have shown that subjects' accuracy and agreement in labeling emotions is considerably higher when pictures have a background situation, as long as the facial expression does not contradict the situation (Ekman and others, 1982). If there is a contradiction (for example, a man smiling blissfully as he waits to be executed), some observers judge the emotion in terms of the facial expression, while others base their judgment on the situation.

Evolution and emotional expression   In his classic work *The Expression of Emotions in Man and Animals* (1872), Charles Darwin argued that emotional displays are a product of evolution and that they developed because they contributed to species survival. Darwin emphasized the basic similarity of emotional expression from lower animals to humans. For example, both wolves and humans bare their teeth when they are angry. As Darwin explained it, this behavior made the animal look more ferocious and thus decreased its chances of being attacked, and perhaps killed, in a fight. Darwin did not maintain that all forms of emotional expression were innate, or unlearned, but he felt that many of them were.

Some modern theorists also stress the evolutionary significance of emotional expression (Izard, 1984; Plutchik, 1980; Tomkins, 1982). The expression of certain emotions (for example, rage and friendliness) is similar across a variety of cultures, suggesting that certain **fundamental emotional patterns** are wired into the nervous system. Other emotions are seen as resulting from various combinations of these innate emotions. The fundamental emotional patterns proposed by three leading evolutionary theorists—Carroll Izard, Sylvan Tomkins, and Robert Plutchik—are shown in Table 9.2.

One argument for the existence of innate expressive patterns is the fact that children who are blind from birth seem to express emotions in the same ways that sighted children do (Eibl-Eibesfeldt, 1973). Again, however, we must emphasize that the evolutionary view does not assume that *all* emotional expressions are innate, nor does it deny that innate emotional expressions can be modified or inhibited.

As an example of the adaptive significance of innate emotional displays, consider the effects that a baby's crying and smiling have on adults. Parents report feeling irritated, annoyed, disturbed, distressed, sympathetic, and unhappy when their baby cries. Physiological arousal also increases in the presence of a crying infant (Frodi and others, 1978). Adults generally respond to crying infants with care-taking responses that have obvious survival value for the infant. On the other hand, a smiling infant is likely to increase its parents' feelings of love and caring, thereby increasing the chances that the child's needs will be satisfied.

Cultural factors   Although some expressions of emotion seem to be the same all over the world, the culture we grow up in also has a strong influence on the form

TABLE 9.2 FUNDAMENTAL OR PRIMARY INNATE EMOTIONS PROPOSED BY THREE LEADING EVOLUTIONARY THEORISTS

CARROLL IZARD	SYLVAN TOMKINS	ROBERT PLUTCHIK
Anger	Anger	Anger
Fear	Fear	Fear
Joy	Joy	Enjoyment
Disgust	Disgust	Disgust
Interest	Interest	Anticipation
Surprise	Surprise	Surprise
Contempt	Contempt	
Shame	Shame	
	Sadness	Sadness
	Distress	
Guilt		
		Acceptance

Based on Izard (1984); Tomkins (1982); and Plutchik (1980).

that our emotional expressions take. Certain gestures, body postures, or physical movements can convey dramatically different meanings in different cultures. For example, in certain regions of Greece and Sardinia, hitchhiking with our familiar upright thumb gesture may result in tread marks on one's body rather than a ride. In those parts, an upright thumb is the equivalent of a raised middle finger in our culture (Morris and others, 1979). We begin in infancy to learn how to express emotions according to the display rules of our particular culture. As Figure 9.7 shows, 12-day-old infants can already imitate the facial expressions of adults (Meltzoff and Moore, 1983).

FIGURE 9.7 *Developmental psychologist Andrew Meltzoff demonstrates that even 2-to-3-week-old infants can imitate the facial expressions of adults. Such learning can influence from an early age how emotions are expressed in a particular culture.*

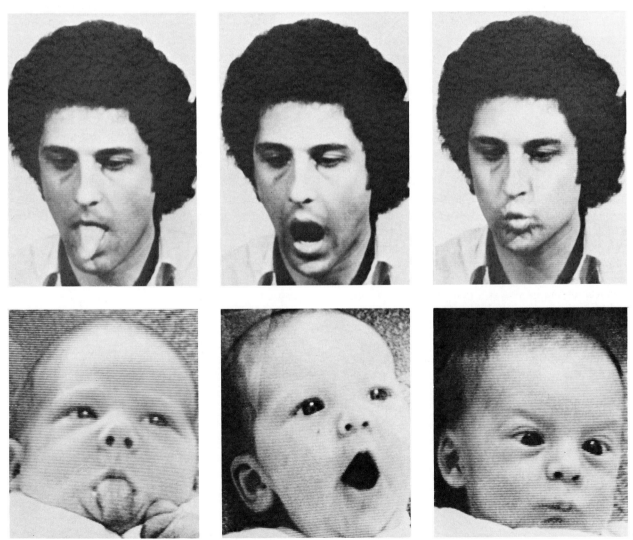

Individual differences in emotional communication Clearly, some people are easier to "read" emotionally than others, and some people are more sensitive in interpreting what others are feeling. Research has shown that people who are high in self-esteem and who have outgoing personalities are more successful in communicating emotions to others than are people who are introverted and have low self-esteem (Buck and others, 1974).

Individual differences are also related to the ability to perceive emotional cues accurately. Women have consistently been found to be more accurate perceivers than men (Ekman, 1982; Zuckerman and others, 1976). Perhaps young girls in our culture are encouraged more than boys are to be sensitive to the emotions of others and to express their own emotions openly. However, men in certain professions, such as psychology, psychiatry, drama, and art, are able to judge emotions as accurately as women do (Rosenthal and others, 1974).

INSTRUMENTAL BEHAVIORS

Often the situations that arouse our emotions must be dealt with in some way. The highly anxious student must find some way to cope with the test. The mother angered by her child's behavior must find a nondestructive way to get her point across. The basketball player attempting a game-winning free throw must concentrate and shoot the ball with a fluid motion despite high emotional arousal.

It is sometimes assumed that high levels of emotional arousal will enhance performance. Athletic teams try to "psych themselves up" for important games. A coach who is highly effective at locker-room pep talks might get the team so aroused that it will almost literally run through the walls to get at the "enemy." Yet a team can get too "high." After his team shot very poorly and lost an important tournament game, a college basketball coach explained, "Our kids were so high for this game that they grew five thumbs on each hand." But another coach who lost in the same tournament accounted for his team's poor performance by saying, "We had no intensity. We were completely flat."

Clearly, then, arousal can be either too high or too low. In many situations, the relationship between emotional arousal and performance seems to take the shape of an upside-down or inverted U (Geen and others, 1984). That is, as physiological arousal increases up to some optimal level, performance improves. But beyond that optimal level, further increases in arousal impair performance. It is thus possible to be either too "flat" or too "high" to perform well.

But there is more to it than this. The optimal level of emotional arousal depends on how difficult or complex the task is. A very high level of arousal may help us to perform a simple task, such as running, but might interfere with performance on a more complex task, such as taking a difficult examination or going through a complex gymnastics routine. This relationship between optimal arousal and task difficulty was recognized early in the history of experimental psychology and formalized as the **Yerkes-Dodson law** (Yerkes and Dodson, 1908). The Yerkes-Dodson law has two parts. First, it states that for every task, there is an optimal level of arousal for maximum performance. (This is the inverted-U curve that we just discussed.) Second, it states that the more difficult the task is, the lower the optimal level of arousal for maximum performance.

These two principles are illustrated in Figure 9.8. Note that the inverted-U relationship between arousal and efficient performance applies for all three tasks, and that the more difficult the task, the lower is the optimal arousal level. One other feature of Figure 9.8 is worth noting. There is less of a drop-off in performance at high levels of arousal for the simple task than for the others. In fact, even the highest levels of arousal can enhance performance of very simple tasks (Bargh and Cohen, 1978). Sometimes the results are quite astounding. In one case, a 102-pound mother in a highly distraught state lifted a panel truck off her child, who was trapped under one of its wheels (*Honolulu Star-Bulletin*, January 6, 1980).

The harmful effects that anxiety can have on the performance of a highly complex task was demonstrated in a sport psychology study by Robert Weinberg and Marvin Genuchi (1980). The anxiety levels of intercollegiate golfers were measured by a questionnaire prior to a golf tournament, and players who were low, moderate, and high in competition anxiety were identified. Although the three groups of golfers were similar in ability, their scores differed sharply during the anxiety-arousing tournament rounds. On the first day of

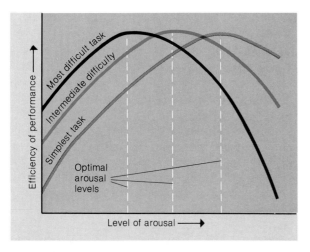

FIGURE 9.8 *The Yerkes-Dodson law states that the relationship between arousal and task performance takes the shape of an inverted U, with performance declining above and below an optimal level. The law further states that the more difficult or complex a task is, the lower is the optimal level of arousal for performing it. For example, a precision activity like golf probably has a very low optimal arousal as opposed to one like weight lifting.*

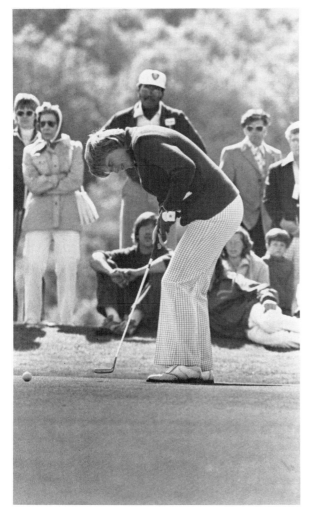

competition, the average performance of the low-anxiety group was five strokes better than the performance of the high-anxiety group. On the last day of the tournament, the difference between the two groups rose to nearly seven strokes. The moderate-anxiety group had intermediate scores. These results indicate that high levels of anxiety are especially likely to impair performance on a highly complex and difficult motor task, such as golf. High anxiety also impairs performance on complex mental tasks, such as taking college tests (Sarason, 1980).

Interactions among components

The relationship between emotional arousal and performance is only one example of how the four components of emotion influence one another. We now examine these interactions more closely.

THEORIES OF EMOTION

Common sense says . . . we meet a bear, are frightened, and run; we are insulted by a rival, are angry, and strike. The hypothesis here to be defended says that this order of sequence is incorrect . . . and that the more rational statement is that we feel sorry because we cry; angry because we strike, afraid because we tremble.

This statement, made by William James in 1890, ushered in nearly a century of research and theory concerning relationships among the cognitive, physiological, and behavioral components of emotion. At about the same time that James advanced his theory, a Danish psychologist named Carl Lange reached a similar conclusion. The **James-Lange theory** of emotion reverses the sequence of events proposed by the cognitive appraisal theory. In appraisal theory, we first make a judgment, then we become physiologically aroused. James and Lange maintained that the opposite is the case. When we encounter an emotion-arousing stimulus, our bodies react instantaneously with physiological arousal, which we then appraise as an emotion. We know we are afraid or in love only because our bodily reactions tell us so.

Cannon fires back It wasn't long before the James-Lange theory was challenged on a number of grounds. In 1927, physiologist Walter Cannon noted that our bodies do *not* respond instantaneously to an emotional stimulus; it may take several seconds before signs of physiological arousal appear. Yet we often experience the emotion immediately. Moreover, Cannon showed that if the internal organs of laboratory animals were surgically separated from the nervous system, so that arousal feedback could not be sent to the brain, the animals continued to display emotional behavior. This would be impossible according to the James-Lange theory.

In place of the James-Lange theory, Cannon and his student, L. L. Bard, advanced their own. The **Cannon-Bard theory** proposed that the thalamus, a major relay station for sensory input, plays a key role in both emotional experience and physiological arousal. According to Cannon and Bard, when an emotion-arousing situation is encountered, the thalamus simultaneously sends messages to the cerebral cortex and to the body's internal organs. The message to the cortex produces our experience of emotion, and the one to the internal organs produces the physiological arousal. Thus, neither cognition nor arousal causes the other; they are independent responses to stimulation from the thalamus.

So far, we have considered three different theories, each of which suggests a different relationship between the cognitive and physiological components of emotion. The **cognitive appraisal theory** states that cognitions stimulate arousal; the James-Lange theory says that arousal causes cognitions; and the Cannon-Bard theory maintains that both are triggered by the thalamus. Let us now consider a fourth theory, one that attempts to show how the cognitive and physiological components jointly influence our emotional experiences. This theory was advanced in the 1960s by Stanley Schachter of Columbia University.

Schachter's "jukebox" theory The two major aspects of emotional experience are *intensity* and *quality* (which emotion). Schachter pointed out that the pattern of physiological arousal seems to be basically the same from emotion to emotion. He suggested that the intensity of arousal tells us *how strongly* we are feeling something. But how do we know *which* emotion we are feeling? This is where cognition enters the picture. According to Schachter (1966), we *label* our emotions as fear, anger, love, or whatever on the basis of the situation we are in.

Schachter's theory was given its somewhat irreverent label—"jukebox"—because arousal is like the coin that gets the machine going, and cognition is the button that we push to select the emotional tune (Mandler, 1984). The important feature of this theory, then, is that cognition and arousal are completely interrelated. Figure 9.9 provides a summary of the James-Lange, Cannon-Bard, cognitive appraisal, and Schachter theories.

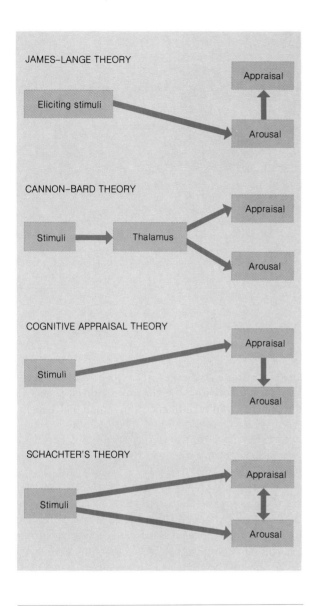

JAMES-LANGE THEORY

Appraisal

Eliciting stimuli → Arousal

CANNON-BARD THEORY

Stimuli → Thalamus → Appraisal

Arousal

COGNITIVE APPRAISAL THEORY

Stimuli → Appraisal → Arousal

SCHACHTER'S THEORY

Stimuli → Appraisal

Arousal

FIGURE 9.9 *The James-Lange theory holds that physiological responses give rise to our cognitive experience of emotion. The Cannon-Bard theory proposes that the thalamus receives sensory input and simultaneously stimulates physiological reactions and cognitive awareness. The cognitive appraisal theory emphasizes the role of cognitive processes in stimulating arousal. Schachter's model focuses on the interaction of cognitive and arousal components, which are assumed to influence each other.*

If appraisal and arousal affect one another in the ways these theories suggest, some intriguing possibilities emerge. For instance, if we can influence arousal, we should be able to affect cognitive appraisals of the situation. On the other hand, if we can influence appraisals, we should be able to modify physiological arousal. In other words, we should find the two-way influence between cognition and arousal shown in the model of emotion presented earlier in Figure 9.1.

MANIPULATING APPRAISAL TO INFLUENCE AROUSAL

In their development of the cognitive appraisal theory, Richard Lazarus and his colleagues at the University of California have been particularly concerned with the way in which appraisal can influence physiological arousal. In a classic study (Speisman and others, 1964), they showed subjects an anthropology film entitled *Subincision in the Arunta*, which depicts in vivid detail a puberty rite in which the penises of aboriginal boys are cut with a jagged flint knife. The film typically elicits a high level of stress in viewers (and, in all likelihood, a high frequency of leg-crossing responses by males).

Speisman and his colleagues tried to influence the subjects' appraisals by experimentally manipulating the film's sound track. Four different sound tracks were used. The "trauma" sound track emphasized the pain suffered by the boys, the danger of infection, the jaggedness of the flint knife, and other unpleasant aspects of the operation. The "denial" sound track was just the opposite; it denied that the operation was traumatic and emphasized that the boys looked forward to entering adulthood by undergoing the rite and demonstrating their bravery. The "intellectualization" sound track, also designed to produce a more benign appraisal, ignored the emotional elements of the scenes and focused on the traditions and history of the tribe. In a "silent" control condition, the film was shown without any sound track at all.

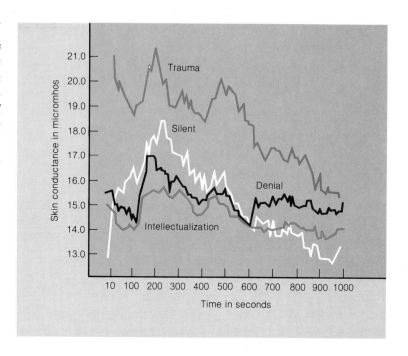

FIGURE 9.10 *Appraisal influences arousal. Subjects who viewed a film showing a tribal subincision rite in vivid detail exhibited different levels of physiological arousal depending on the sound track that accompanied the film.*

The amount of physiological arousal (measured by skin conductance) that was shown by subjects in the four "appraisal" conditions was the dependent variable. As shown in Figure 9.10, the sound tracks produced markedly different levels of arousal in response to the same visual stimuli. The trauma sound track resulted in the highest arousal, and silence turned out to be more arousing than either denial or intellectualization, presumably because silence left people free to make their own negative appraisals. This study, as well as the one described earlier in which subjects read "emotional" sentences to themselves, indicates that what we tell ourselves about external situations influences the level of arousal that we experience. Chalk up one point for cognitive appraisal theory. But is the opposite also true? Does level of arousal influence how we appraise situations?

MANIPULATING AROUSAL TO INFLUENCE APPRAISAL

It is conceivable that arousal could affect our appraisal of situations by giving us feedback on how our bodies are responding and causing us to wonder why. To study this possibility, we have to influence arousal directly in some way. Perhaps the easiest way to do this is with drugs, but it must be done in such a way that subjects are unaware that their arousal is being influenced by a drug. They have to believe that their arousal is being caused solely by the external situation they are appraising.

In an experiment by Schachter and Wheeler (1962), arousal was directly manipulated by injecting subjects with either epinephrine (to increase arousal), a tranquilizer drug to decrease arousal, or a placebo control substance. Subjects were told that they were being injected with a vitamin and that its effects on their visual perception would be studied. They were also told that the vitamin injection would have no side effects. While waiting for the vitamin to take effect, they were shown a short movie "to provide continuous black and white stimulation to the eyes."

The subjects were shown a comedy film having a slapstick chase scene. Schachter and Wheeler hypothesized that if level of emotional arousal influences appraisal, then subjects given epinephrine should find the film funnier than the placebo control subjects. The subjects given the tranquilizer should not find the film funny because the drug would prevent their becoming aroused.

Subjects were observed while they watched the movie by raters who were unaware of which subjects had received which injections. The raters recorded how frequently the subjects smiled, grinned, laughed, threw up their hands, slapped their legs, or doubled over with laughter. These measures were used as an index of how funny the subjects thought the film was.

As shown in Figure 9.11, the results supported the hypothesis that level of arousal would influence subjects' appraisal of the film. The aroused subjects in the epinephrine group found the film funnier than the tranquilized subjects did, and the placebo control group was in the middle. As long as the arousal is attributed to the external situation, arousal cues can apparently affect appraisal.

ASSOCIATIVE NETWORKS INVOLVING EMOTION

In Chapter 7, we discussed the way in which concepts or units of knowledge are organized in memory as propositional networks (see page 250). This concept from cognitive psychology is now being applied to emotion as well (Berkowitz, 1984; Bower, 1981). The basic idea is that each network's units consist of associ-

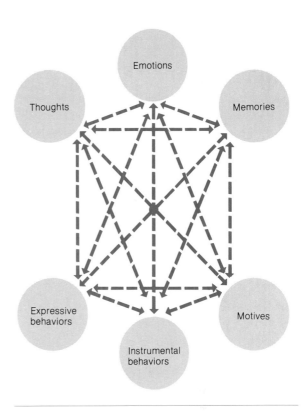

FIGURE 9.12 *Networks involving cognitive, physiological, and behavioral elements and organized by associative links are a new way of looking at emotion.*

ated groups of ideas, emotional responses, and behavioral tendencies. An example of such a network is shown in Figure 9.12.

It is assumed that activation of any element of a network tends to call forth the other elements associated with it. Thus, a particular idea may evoke associated memories, feelings, and behaviors, especially if the network's associations are strong ones. Leonard Berkowitz (1984) has applied this kind of model to account for media effects on behavior. He suggests that a television program depicting violence may produce a

FIGURE 9.11 *Level of arousal influences our appraisal of a situation. The amount of amusement shown by subjects who watched a humorous film varied with their state of arousal after being injected with epinephrine, a tranquilizer, or a placebo.*

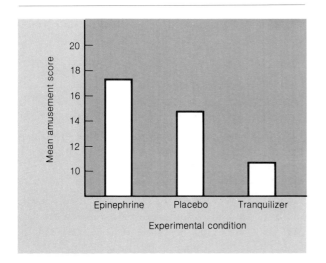

priming effect that activates related ideas, feelings, and behavior tendencies in the observer. Those viewers in whom aggressive ideas are strongly related to aggressive behavior tendencies are most likely to be stimulated to behave violently by the "planting" of such ideas.

Most of us have first-hand knowledge of how our moods can affect our thinking. When we're feeling happy, we tend to think "good thoughts" and see the world in a positive light. But when we're down, the world can seem like a pretty bleak place. Gordon Bower (1981) has shown that memory can be strongly and selectively influenced by mood, as the associative network theory would predict. Bower created happy and sad moods in his subjects by having each of them imagine happy and sad scenes while they were hypnotized. The subjects learned two lists of words, one while they were happy and one while they were sad. Later, the subjects were hypnotically returned to their

happy and sad moods and asked to recall the two lists of words. As Figure 9.13 shows, more words were remembered when the recall mood and the learning mood were the same. When the moods were different, fewer than half the words were recalled. This phenomenon is called **state-dependent memory,** and it helps explain several commonly observed phenomena. For example, people in a relationship are able to do a fine job of dredging up all the negative events of the past when they are angry, while seemingly losing sight of all the positive experiences that have occurred in the relationship.

MOTIVATION: THE "WHY" OF BEHAVIOR

The concept of motivation is a central one in our attempt to understand behavior and its causes. The word *motivation* comes from the Latin word meaning "to move." We use the concept of motivation to help us explain how internal factors seem to move animals and people toward certain goals. The nature of the goal, or *incentive,* toward which behavior seems to be directed—for example, food, water, success, or control over others—determines the label that we attach to the motivational state—hunger, thirst, achievement motivation, or a need for power (McClelland, 1985). Motivated behavior is often vigorous in nature, and it may persist over long periods of time. We therefore define **motivation** as *an internal process that influences the direction, persistence, and vigor of goal-directed behavior* (see Figure 9.14).

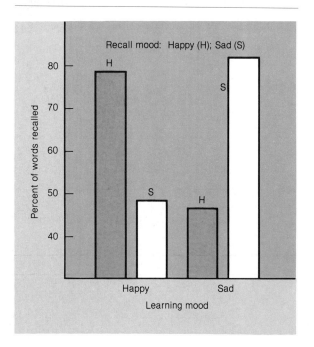

FIGURE 9.13 *Memory is affected by the match between the predominant mood during learning and the mood during recall. The bars represent the mean recall scores of subjects who learned two lists of words, one when happy and the other when sad. (Adapted from Bower, 1981.)*

Perspectives on motivation

There is no area in the science of psychology in which the value of the different perspectives on behavior has been more evident than in motivation. The range of motives that affect our behavior is so great that some of them are bound to be particularly relevant to each perspective. Another reason for the value of the perspectives is that they often provide us with different ways of understanding the same motivational states.

FIGURE 9.14 *Although motives take many different forms, they help to account for the direction, persistence, and vigor of goal-directed behavior.*

THE BIOLOGICAL PERSPECTIVE: DRIVES AND THEIR REGULATION

We begin with the biological perspective because some of our most basic needs have biological foundations. Without food, water, oxygen, warmth, and the other things that satisfy basic tissue needs, we could not survive. Without a biologically based sex drive, no species could continue to exist. Therefore, the study of the internal and external processes related to the arousal and reduction of biological needs has been and continues to be a major focus of psychological theory and research (Pfaff, 1982; Whalen and Simon, 1984). Major advances have occurred in our understanding of how the activity of the nervous system is involved in the regulation of internal states, as well as how such states affect behavior. As we shall see later, the biological perspective has also provided valuable insights into certain human problems related to motivational states, such as the problem of obesity.

THE BEHAVIORAL PERSPECTIVE: LEARNING AND MOTIVATION

If the behavioral perspective makes you think of rats running through mazes to obtain food, it may surprise you to learn that certain radical behaviorists feel that we should do away with the concept of motivation entirely. B. F. Skinner, for example, claims that studying "fictional motives" gives us an illusory understanding of behaviors that can only be truly understood in reference to externally observable stimuli and responses. Skinner does not believe that we need to muddy our thinking with an internal motivational concept like "hunger" when we can study the effects of an observable and controllable variable like "hours of food deprivation."

Despite Skinner's extreme view, other behavioral psychologists continue to study motivation. In fact, for many years, learning and motivation were virtually inseparable in behavioral research because the events that enhanced learning by serving as reinforcers frequently seemed to be related to the reduction of drives like hunger (Berlyne, 1978). Indeed, for a time some learning theorists argued that all reinforcement involved some kind of drive reduction. As subsequent research showed, that does not seem to be the case. Nonetheless, most modern theorists give motivational variables

a prominent place in their theories of how learning occurs. The concept of motivation also helps to account for performance fluctuations after learning has occurred.

Some of the important social motives—achievement, affiliation, and power—seem to be learned, and the expression of even innate biological needs can be modified in important ways by learning (McClelland, 1985).

THE COGNITIVE PERSPECTIVE: EXPECTANCY AND VALUE

The cognitive perspective on motivation emphasizes the influence of mental processes on goal-directed behavior. One influential cognitive approach to motivation is known as **Expectancy X Value theory** (Heckhausen, 1977; Jung, 1978). According to this theory, the direction and intensity of goal-directed behavior are jointly determined by the strength of the person's *expectation* that that behavior will lead to the desired goal and by the *value* that goal has for the individual. Goal-directed behavior will be strongest and most persistent if the goal is highly valued and if there is a high expectation that the behavior will result in attaining it. For example, a person who greatly values academic success and expects that study will lead to such success will study harder than someone who does not have the same value or the same expectancy.

The hidden costs of reward The cognitive approach to motivation raises a number of interesting issues not considered by the behavioral perspective. For example, what happens when a person starts to receive *extrinsic reward* for behaviors that have been done because of *intrinsic motivation?* What if Jennie, who already loves to read (intrinsic motivation), is given money or some other extrinsic reward for time spent reading? From a behavioral point of view, the added rewards for reading should increase her total motivation to read. But what happens if the extrinsic reward is later withdrawn? Will Jennie still enjoy reading for its own sake?

Perhaps not. One cognitive theory holds that extrinsic rewards can undermine and even reduce intrinsic motivation (see Figure 9.15). According to the **overjustification hypothesis**, the crucial factor is our changing interpretation of why we perform the behavior. If we come to attribute our behavior to the presence of the external reward, we will experience a decreased desire to perform the behavior if the reward is withdrawn; we become "unmotivated." In one study, children who already spent a great deal of time drawing with felt-tipped markers were suddenly offered certificates for doing so. As long as the certificates were given, the amount of time spent in drawing remained high. But when they stopped receiving certificates, the children decreased their drawing by 50 percent, and they subsequently spent less time drawing than children who had received no external reward for drawing (Lepper and Greene, 1978). In another study, Teresa Amabile (1985) studied the effects of intrinsic and extrinsic motivation on the creativity of poets. The rated creativity of poems produced by writers after they thought about extrinsic reasons for creative writing (e.g., external recognition and financial reward) was significantly lower than for writers who had been asked to think about intrinsic reasons for their activity, such as self-expression and self-satisfaction.

Does this mean that we should never use extrinsic reinforcers? Not at all. Sometimes extrinsic rewards can be used to get a behavior started so that a person can *develop* an intrinsic motivation for it. But it does seem important to use extrinsic reinforcement spar-

ingly. The rewards should be just powerful enough to bring forth the desired behavior, and they should be phased out as soon as the person indicates a desire to perform the behavior for its own sake.

THE PSYCHODYNAMIC PERSPECTIVE: THE MOTIVATIONAL UNDERWORLD

A major focus of psychodynamic theorists is the motivational underworld of unconscious wishes and conflicts. Much of our behavior is seen as a product of the never-ending battle between unconscious motives struggling for release and the defenses that have been erected to keep these unacceptable impulses under control. The following case described by psychoanalyst Charles Brenner illustrates a psychodynamic interpretation of unconscious motives and defenses.

A college student returned to his family's home at the end of the academic term and found no one at home. He had a vivid daydream in which he imagined

FIGURE 9.15 *Research has shown that external rewards given for activities that children already enjoy for their own sake can weaken intrinsic motivation.*

that his mother and younger sister had been killed. He reported feeling absolutely no emotion during or after the daydream and could not understand why. Here is Brenner's analysis of the reason.

The patient was alone in the house after his return from college. . . . These and other circumstances forcibly re-minded the patient of the time when his mother had gone to the hospital for delivery and when the patient had felt very alone. What had happened after the mother's return had been even worse. She had turned from the patient and focused her affection on the new baby, a girl. From that time on, the patient felt unwanted and unloved. But rage was dangerous, since being a "bad boy," he learned, would lead all the more to being abandoned by mother, who used to punish him by putting him in a dark closet when he had an angry outburst, or later on, by refusing to talk to him. . . . When the patient came home to an empty house he reacted with memories of that earlier time when his sister was born and was overcome by jealousy, longing, and rage. He could not banish completely all his frightening and guilt-ridden reactions. He did imagine that his mother and sister had been killed. At the same time, however, he denied that it was his own wish to kill them—in his fantasy, the deed had been done by others—and he did ward off any feelings of either pleasure or unpleasure at the idea that they had been killed. There was no con-scious trace of either, any more than there was a con-scious trace of sexual wishes toward mother, or of memo-ries of such wishes and the past experiences connected with them. (Brenner, 1974, p. 536)

Freud believed that because our society discourages the direct expression of such drives as sex and aggres-sion, the energy from these drives is often expressed in behaviors that are more socially acceptable. For exam-ple, aggressive impulses may be channeled into a ca-reer of public service as a police officer or a trial attor-ney.

THE HUMANISTIC-EXISTENTIAL PERSPECTIVE: DEFICIENCY AND GROWTH NEEDS

The concern of humanistic and existential theorists with the ultimate meaning of human existence and with the struggle of the individual toward self-actuali-zation has extended the frontiers of motivation beyond the biological and social motives that are the focus of the other perspectives. Humanistic theorist Abraham

Maslow (1970) distinguished between **deficiency needs,** which are concerned with the individual's phys-ical and social survival, and **growth needs,** which moti-vate the person to develop his or her full potential as a human being. Marlow viewed these growth needs as the highest expression of human motivation, and he argued that they have not received the attention they deserve in psychology.

Maslow suggested that human needs can be ar-ranged in a **hierarchy** ranging from the most necessary requirements for survival, at the bottom, to the most profound expressions of human potential, at the top (see Figure 9.16). A given need will not appear until the needs below it have been satisfied. Thus, the basic needs, such as the physiological and safety needs, must be met before other, higher-level needs can be attended to. This makes perfect sense—a person who does not have enough to eat or whose safety is threatened in some other way cannot afford the luxury of contem-plating beauty and truth. Self-preservation has to come before self-actualization. Maslow's theory is the most inclusive of all the theories we have considered in that

---

FIGURE 9.16 *Maslow's need hierarchy ranges from basic biological needs to self-actualization, the highest of human motives. In order for the growth needs to manifest them-selves, the deficiency needs lower in the hierarchy must be satisfied.*

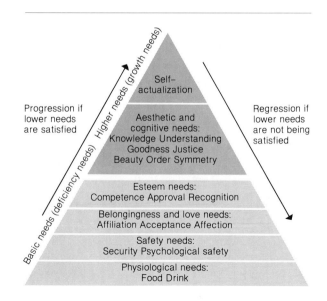

it deals with the full range of human motives, from those that are the focus of the biological and behavioral perspective to the growth needs that are not considered by any of the other perspectives.

As a humanistic theorist, Maslow was particularly interested in the higher-level needs. Aesthetic needs include the creation and appreciation of beauty and a striving to discover and find peace, goodness, justice, and beauty. Maslow thought that the highest of all human needs was *self-actualization*. Unlike the more basic needs, which can be satisfied through appropriate activities, the need for self-actualization is never satisfied. Maslow believed that few, if any, human beings ever achieve complete self-actualization. Living up to our potential always remains a potential goal; in this case the need is to try, not to achieve.

Maslow believed that most people are blocked from progressing smoothly up this motivational hierarchy. Some people must spend their entire lives working very hard just to satisfy the lower-level deficiency needs. Some never succeed in achieving the belongingness and love that they desire from others. Even people who have reached the higher levels can quickly tumble back down the hierarchy if circumstances change and their lower-level needs are no longer being met.

We now turn to the range of motivational states that are the primary focus of psychological theory and research. We first consider some of the basic biologically rooted needs that humans share with lower animals.

Homeostatic needs: To thirst and hunger

Your body consists of complex and interrelated biological systems. A delicate balance is required within these systems to ensure survival. **Homeostasis** is the regulatory process that maintains this balance.

Homeostasis requires a sensory mechanism for detecting changes within the internal environment, a response system that can maintain equilibrium, and a control center that receives information from the sensors and activates the response systems (see Figure 9.17). The control center functions like the thermostat in a furnace or air conditioning unit. If the thermostat is set at a fixed temperature, or "set point," significant temperature changes in either direction are detected by

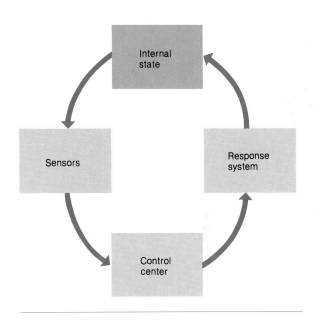

FIGURE 9.17 *The internal environment of the body is regulated by homeostatic mechanisms that require sensors for detecting changes, a response system to restore equilibrium, and a control center that receives input from the sensors and activates the response system.*

the sensor. The control unit then turns on the furnace or air conditioner until the sensor indicates that the set point temperature has been restored.

The maintenance of a stable internal state can involve learned behavioral adjustments as well as innate physiological adjustments. When your body temperature becomes too high, for example, the innate physiological adjustment of perspiration helps to cool you. Behavioral adjustments may include looking for a shady place to sit, taking your coat off, or getting something cold to drink.

Two of our basic homeostatic motives are hunger and thirst. Although these motivational states are rooted in basic tissue needs, psychological factors can strongly influence how we act to satisfy them.

THIRST

If today is an average day, you have lost more than 2 quarts of water through perspiration, elimination, and breathing. Clearly, if your body did not have a highly efficient mechanism for regulating your fluid content, you would soon die.

Recent research has focused on the sensors that monitor fluid levels and help regulate drinking behavior (Epstein, 1982). There appear to be two different types of receptors. The first, which are located in veins and in the kidneys, monitor the volume of fluids *surrounding* the cells of the body. When a reduction in these vital extracellular fluids is detected, the sensors transmit impulses to the brain, where sensations of thirst are produced. Reduced extracellular fluid volume also stimulates the kidneys to produce **angiotensin,** a blood protein that stimulates drinking.

A second class of receptors, located in the hypothal-amus, monitors changes in the amount of fluid contained *within* the cells of the body. When the body's supply of water is low, these receptor cells and other body cells release water into the body. Unlike the body's other cells, however, the receptor cells in the hypothalamus generate nerve impulses when they release fluids. These impulses can create thirst sensations. When fluids are taken into the body, water is returned to these receptor cells, and the thirst sensations cease. Thus, a complex set of biological processes underlie that simple decision to stop at the drinking fountain.

HUNGER

How does your body signal that it needs food? Perhaps the most common and noticeable signals are those familiar "hunger pangs" from your stomach. Hunger

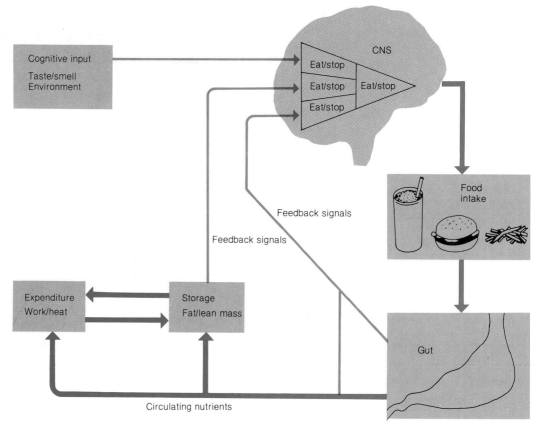

FIGURE 9.18
Control of food intake is based on a regulatory system that involves input to the central nervous system from both the external environment and internal feedback mechanisms.

pangs come from muscular contractions of your stomach walls, and research has shown that stomach contractions are often closely linked to reports of feeling hungry. Early physiological theories of hunger proposed that eating is triggered when receptors in the stomach signal that it is empty, and that eating stops when these receptors report that the stomach is full. But then it was found that feelings of hunger and normal regulation of eating continue even if all nerves leading from the stomach to the brain are cut (Brown and Wallace, 1980). Thus, although stomach contractions can undoubtedly play a role in the complex processes that regulate food intake, they cannot be the whole story. Figure 9.18 shows that there are environmental, cognitive, and internal feedback systems, all of which help to regulate food intake by signaling control centers in the central nervous system.

Neural control   The brain seems an obvious place to look for these control centers. But where in the brain? One possible lead was provided by medical case histories of people who experienced difficulties in weight regulation after injuries to the hypothalamus (Gazzaniga and others, 1979). Two specific regions of the hypothalamus appeared particularly important. The **lateral** area, located near the sides of the hypothalamus, appeared to stimulate eating behavior, whereas the **ventromedial** area, located near the center of the hypothalamus, seemed to inhibit eating behavior.

When the lateral hypothalamus is damaged or surgically destroyed, animals often refuse to eat. In fact, they will actually starve if not forced to take food. They gradually recover from this condition, but they never completely return to normal. Their weight remains lower than it was before the lateral area was damaged, and they become rodent gourmets of sorts, quite finicky and choosy in their eating.

Quite the opposite effect occurs when the ventromedial hypothalamus is destroyed. Now, instead of animals who undereat, we have animal gluttons who begin to eat huge quantities of food. In a short period of time they double or triple their body weight and then level off at a very high weight (see Figure 9.19).

As a result of findings like these, researchers at first thought that the lateral and ventromedial hypothalamic areas were the "eating" and "satiation" control

FIGURE 9.19 *Damage to the ventromedial hypothalamus affects regulation of eating behavior. The rat on the right has more than doubled its body weight by overeating following ventromedial destruction. The rat on the left is normal.*

centers they had been seeking. But, naturally, the situation turned out to be more complicated. It now appears that fibers from many widely separated areas of the brain funnel through the hypothalamus and then spread out again when they leave the hypothalamus. Researchers began to discover that the effects of lesions in the hypothalamic regions can be duplicated with lesions in other locations extending all the way from the brain stem to the frontal lobes (Schwartz, 1984).

The dramatic results that occur in the hypothalamic regions appear to stem from the cutting of these tracts rather than from damage to any particular "centers" in the hypothalamus; the same results occur wherever you cut the tracts. Thus, many widely separated parts of the brain seem to be involved in the regulation of eating.

Chemical control Chemical factors are now known to play a central role in the regulation of food intake. For example, sensors in various parts of the body, including the liver and the brain, provide feedback to the nervous system about the amount of glucose and other nutrients in the blood. Some of the major discoveries of recent years have involved the role of chemical substances known as **peptides** on many aspects of behavior (Whalen and Simon, 1984). One class of peptides, the endorphins, is related to the perception of pain (Chapter 5). Another peptide, *cholecystokinin* (**CCK**) has received much recent attention because of its role in the regulation of eating. Released by the intestine and pancreas, CCK stimulates receptors in several brain regions and decreases eating (Smith, Gibbs, and Kulkosky, 1982).

Set point theory One popular way of viewing the regulation of eating is in terms of an internal standard around which body weight is regulated. Actually, it may be more useful to think of body weight as being regulated within a "set range" rather than around a single "set point" (see Figure 9.20). Our weight normally varies with such conditions as diet and sleep changes, exercise or weight training, and processes like menstruation, pregnancy, and aging. According to one theory, the major cause of obesity is an abnormally high set point (Stunkard, 1982).

Different regulatory systems may be involved in correcting deviations above and below the usual weight range (Schwartz, 1984). Hence, some people, like Person A in Figure 9.20, may easily gain a great deal of weight before regulatory mechanisms swing into action, yet would tolerate only a relatively small loss before their control system is activated. Conversely, others might find it easy to lose a lot of weight, but hard to gain much, like Person B in Figure 9.20.

Acceptable range above and below usual weight

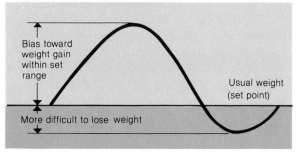

Person A

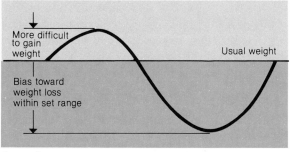

Person B

FIGURE 9.20 *Body weight is regulated within a range around one's usual weight. Individuals differ, however, in terms of the location of the set point within the set range. Person A thus finds it easy to gain weight but difficult to lose it, whereas the opposite is the case for Person B.*

Sensory needs

Had the Communists discovered some sinister new way to control people's thoughts, attitudes, and convictions? This question was the immediate response of Western governments to reports in the late 1940s and early 1950s that people in Communist countries were being "brainwashed" by severe **sensory deprivation.** There were reasons to suspect that depriving people of normal sensory stimuli might affect them psychologically. High-altitude pilots, people trapped in caves, and shipwrecked sailors drifting in the ocean have some-

EATING DISORDERS

One of the most active areas of current research involves disorders related to food intake. One of the disorders currently being studied—obesity—affects a great many people. Two other disorders—anorexia nervosa and bulimia—are less common but more serious in nature.

OBESITY

In humans, *obesity* is usually defined as a body weight more than 20 percent over the average for a given height and body build. By this definition, about 35 percent of all Americans are obese. Because obesity is stigmatized in our culture and has serious health consequences, many overweight people are highly motivated to lose weight.

Evaluation of many weight loss methods indicates that almost any overweight person can lose weight. But, unfortunately, losing weight is far easier than keeping it off. Few people can maintain a significant weight loss for as long as one year (Grinker, 1982). An ironic and perverse fact about obesity is that being fat primes people to stay fat or to become fatter, in part by altering body metabolism, body chemistry, and energy expenditure (Rodin, 1981). Because of these alterations, it often takes fewer calories to keep people overweight than it did to get them fat in the first place. An overweight person who complains, "But I hardly eat a thing," may well be telling the truth.

When people gain weight, the fat cells in their bodies become larger. Unfortunately, the larger a fat cell becomes, the greater is its ability to store fat and become still larger (Salans and others, 1968). Moreover, overweight people tend to have higher basal levels of insulin in their bodies than people of normal weight. A higher insulin level increases fat storage because it speeds the entry of sugar into the fat cell and the conversion of sugar into fat. It also causes people to feel hungry. Thus, fat people not only are more likely to experience hunger but also are primed to make and store more fat.

Metabolism reflects the body's rate of energy or caloric utilization. The *resting*, or *basal, metabolism*, which maintains our internal life maintenance systems, requires about two-thirds of our normal energy expenditure. Fat tissue is less active metabolically—it uses less energy—than lean tissue does. Thus, as lean tissue is replaced by fatty tissue during weight gain, metabolism can be directly lowered. This may be one reason why some overweight people require fewer calories to maintain a high level of body weight than do people who are eating to gain the same weight for the first time (Tortora and Anastanakos, 1984).

Ironically, dieting also slows down the basal metabolism because the body responds to food deprivation with decreased energy expenditure. Moreover, this energy-saving metabolic slowdown becomes more pronounced with each weight loss attempt, as if the body has learned to respond more efficiently to new periods of food deprivation (Wooley and others, 1979). Thus, the repeated dieting that many overweight people engage in may actually be a factor that contributes to their obesity by slowing down their metabolic processes. Finally, obesity tends to reduce physical activity and exercise, so that overweight people burn fewer calories and thus retain more fat.

All in all, it appears that once obesity has developed, a variety of physical and metabolic factors serve to maintain or enhance weight gain and to make permanent weight loss difficult. But obesity is more than a physical problem. Eating behavior is regulated by complex interactions between genetic, physiological, cognitive, social, and learning factors. For this reason, there can be many possible reasons why a given person is obese, and an understanding of obesity's causes defies simple answers. For example, until recently, obese people were thought to be less tuned in to their internal states and more responsive to food-related external stimuli (Schachter, 1971). Recent research has cast severe doubt on this hypothesis. It has been found that in every weight category, there are people who are highly responsive to external cues, such as the sight or smell of food, and many others who are not (Grinker, 1982). The same is true of responsiveness to internal stimuli, such as stomach contractions. Thus, it has become apparent that obesity is not a single disorder, it has no single cause, and no single cure. The answers to the puzzling questions raised by obesity require research that analyzes the interaction of internal and environmental factors. On the biological front, preliminary findings indicate that injections of the peptide CCK, discussed earlier in relation to eating cessation, reduces eating in obese people (Pi-Sunyen and others, 1982), but it remains to be seen whether CCK will become an effective treatment for obesity.

ANOREXIA AND BULIMIA

Although obesity can result in negative physical, social, and psychological consequences, there are two other disorders whose symptoms are so severe that they are considered to be clinical disorders. *Anorexia nervosa* and *bulimia* occur primarily among young women, and both involve abnormal concerns with body size, a morbid fear of becoming fat, and a distorted image of what constitutes normal body size. Anorexics and bulimics frequently view themselves as fat, even though they may be severely underweight.

Anorexics have an intense fear of losing control over their eating, and they severely restrict food intake to the point of self-starvation. Many anorexics lose more than 25 percent of their body weight. Although they are preoccupied with food, they develop what amounts to an eating phobia that can become a life-threatening condition (see Figure 9.21). Singer Karen Carpenter's death was attributed to the fatal strain that anorexia nervosa placed on her heart.

Anorexia frequently has its onset during adoles-

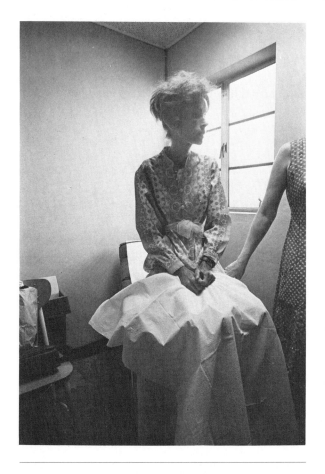

FIGURE 9.21 *This victim of anorexia nervosa shows the severe weight loss that can occur as a result of self-starvation.*

cence, shortly after the start of menstruation. Many anorexics suffer from amenorrhea, a cessation of menstruation. Personality studies indicate that they are often perfectionists who become easily depressed when they do not live up to lofty self-standards (Garfinkel and Garner, 1982).

Bulimia is sometimes called "the binge-purge"

syndrome. In contrast to anorexics, who successfully regulate food intake, bulimics indulge in uncontrolled overeating that is often followed by self-induced vomiting or overdoses of laxatives to eliminate the food they have consumed (Schlesier-Stropp, 1984). Some bulimics have reportedly consumed up to 55,000 calories at a single sitting—roughly equivalent to 16 pounds of food. More commonly, they consume 2,000 to 3,000 calories of high-caloric or junk food. One female athlete who weighed 110 pounds wolfed down 17 hamburgers during a late-night binge. Like most bulimics, she was very secretive about her binging, and her eating spree took her to 6 different fast food establishments in an hour's time. The binge was terminated by self-induced vomiting and consumption of a dozen laxative pills.

Unlike anorexics, bulimics are not necessarily underweight; many are normal weight and some are even obese. Nonetheless, the drastic measures they take to expel food from their bodies following binging can produce severe physical consequences, including gastric problems, ulcers, and acute chemical imbalances that can be life-threatening. Surveys have indicated that 10 to 15 percent of college females may exhibit the full symptom picture, and many more (perhaps half to two-thirds of all college women) are at risk for the disorder (Polivy and Herman, 1985; Schlesier-Stropp, 1984).

High levels of depression and anxiety are characteristic of bulimics, as are obsessive preoccupations with food and a distorted body image that causes them to see themselves as overweight even when they are not. Binging is often brought on by life stresses, and it is followed by guilt and self-contempt. The purging may be a means of reducing depression and anxiety triggered by the binging (Rosen and Leitenberg, 1982).

Theories about the causes of anorexia and bulimia have spanned the physiological and sociocultural domains. One intriguing possibility is that the stringent dieting that often precedes and accompanies bulimia actually contributes to the pattern of binging (Polivy and Herman, 1985). According to this theory, successful dieting virtually requires that the dieter ignore physiological body-weight regulators as represented in the experiences of hunger and satiation. This means that over time deliberate and intentional cognitive controls over eating come to replace the natural physiological set-point regulators, whose feedback mechanisms normally stop food intake at some physiologically appropriate point. As long as these cognitive controls function successfully, a lower-than-"normal" (in terms of set point) body weight results. But if the cognitive controls collapse (as often occurs if the person violates the diet and feels out of control), the pent up physiological urges to eat take over and binging results. If this theory continues to receive experimental support, there is much food for thought in the conclusion of the theorists that "perhaps dieting is the disorder that we should be attempting to cure" (Polivy and Herman, 1985, p. 200).

On the sociocultural side, anorexic and bulimic women may be casualties of our society's growing emphasis on slimness as a requisite of feminine attractiveness. Studies indicate that Miss America contestants, the female models who grace advertisements, and the women who appear in *Playboy* centerfolds are significantly thinner now than they were in the 1950s and 1960s, and they typically weigh at least 20 percent less than the average American woman (Garfinkel and Garner, 1982). Successful treatment of bulimia frequently requires resolution of the unrealistic self-standards about body image and femininity that tyrannize its victims (Root, 1983). Behavioral approaches dealing with the anxiety surrounding eating and gaining weight also appear promising (Leitenberg and others, 1984). The optimistic note is that the eating disorders can be treated successfully (Garner and Garfinkel, 1984), and the seeking of professional help is strongly advisable.

times reported strange and bizarre hallucinations and thought processes.

The Canadian government acted first, funding a research project at McGill University in Montreal to study the effects of sensory deprivation on human functioning. The McGill group built a sensory isolation chamber like that shown in Figure 9.22. Subjects wore translucent goggles to eliminate all patterned visual stimulation, and they could hear nothing except the exhaust fan. Their hands were covered with cuffs to reduce their sense of touch, and they were asked to lie as motionless as possible on the mattress except when they were being given food and water. They were paid $20 a day to stay in the chamber.

Suppose you were given $80 a day (inflation affects research, too) to remain in the chamber for as long as you could. How long would you stay in the chamber? A week? A month? The McGill researchers' first sur-

prise was that over half of their college student subjects quit the experiment within 48 hours. Virtually all of them found the experience to be increasingly stressful and unpleasant with the passage of time. Many of the subjects responded to the decreased sensory input by having hallucinations that became progressively more complex, intense, and vivid (Heron, 1961). It was as if, in the absence of external stimulation, the brain was generating its own.

Humans seem to have innate needs for activity, exploration, and manipulation. Although these sensory needs have no direct effect on the maintenance of biological homeostasis, as hunger or thirst do, they still seem to be an important part of our nature.

There is much evidence that animals also seek out stimulation and prefer novelty, change, and stimulus complexity (Berlyne, 1978). Rats who are thoroughly familiar with a maze will quickly explore new sections that are added to the maze network, even if they have been consistently fed somewhere else. Rats and other mammals will learn to press a lever when the only consequence is a brief increase in illumination. Monkeys confined in a box will repeatedly push open a heavy spring door just to see what is happening on the other side (Butler, 1954). In a classic series of experiments performed at the University of Wisconsin, Harry Harlow (1950) showed that monkeys will spend hour after hour working on mechanical puzzles, even if they receive no tangible reward for doing so (see Figure 9.23). Anyone who has taken small children to an expensive gift store and seen a sign that says, "IF THEY BREAK IT, YOU'VE BOUGHT IT," knows how common the same tendencies are in humans from infancy on.

FIGURE 9.22 *The McGill University research group used a chamber like this to study the effects of sensory deprivation. Subjects wore translucent goggles to limit visual stimulation. Cuffs covering the hands reduced tactile stimulation. Most subjects found the reduced stimulation stressful, and many experienced hallucinations and temporary difficulties in thinking.*

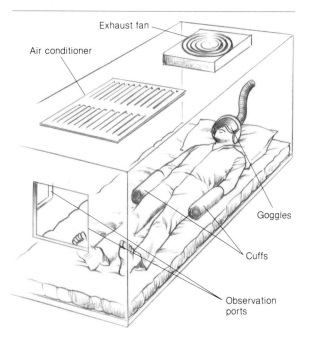

Exhaust fan

Air conditioner

Goggles

Cuffs

Observation ports

INDIVIDUAL DIFFERENCES IN SENSATION SEEKING

For each of the following sets of statements, choose the alternative that is more characteristic of you:

1. A. I prefer people who are calm and even-tempered.
   B. I prefer people who are emotionally expressive even if they are a bit unstable.
2. A. The most important goal of life is to live it to the fullest and experience as much of it as you can.

B. The most important goal of life is to find peace and happiness.

3. A. I would like a job that requires a lot of traveling.
   B. I would prefer a job in one location.

There are individual differences in the tendency of people to seek out stimulation. Some people prefer a relatively nonstimulating and calm environment, while others seek out adventure, danger, and excitement. Observations of these individual differences in stimulus-seeking behavior prompted Marvin Zuckerman to develop a psychological test to measure the **sensation-seeking motive** and to study its effects on behavior. The statements you just responded to are from Zuckerman's 22-item Sensation Seeking Scale. Notice that each item forced you to choose between one alternative that implied novelty, changes, or excitement, and another that implied the opposite. Nearly two decades of research has shown that scores on the test are related to numerous behaviors (Zuckerman, 1979; Zuckerman and others, 1980).

For example, people who get high scores on the Sensation Seeking Scale enjoy engaging in physically risky activities such as skydiving, motorcycle riding, firefighting, and scuba diving. High sensation seekers perceive such activities as being less risky than low sensation seekers do. They tend to be interested in gambling, they bet more, and they prefer higher odds against them. The tendency to experiment with different drugs is also related to sensation seeking. High sensation seekers enjoy drug-produced altered states more than lows do, whether the alterations involve increases or decreases in arousal. They are attracted to depressant drugs as well as to stimulants and hallucinogens; the change in consciousness rather than the direction appears to be the important consideration (Kohn and Coulas, 1985). Among college students, high sensation seekers of both sexes report engaging in more heterosexual activities with more partners than low sensation seekers do. Sensation seeking in married women correlates positively with self-ratings of sexual responsiveness, frequency of masturbation, preferred frequency of intercourse, and reports of multiple orgasms.

Although rumor has it that curiosity has resulted in the demise of more than one cat, sensory needs have important significance in adapting to the environment.

FIGURE 9.23 *Research by Butler and by Harlow has demonstrated that animals have sensory needs that seem unrelated to biological drives such as hunger and thirst. Monkeys will learn and work in order to open a door that allows them to view the electric train briefly. They will also work diligently to open locks that lead to no tangible reward.*

It seems likely that such needs can also find expression in the basic forms of social motivation, to which we now turn.

Social motivation

Our biological motives help ensure our survival, but the motives that we acquire from interactions with our social environment often dominate our personal functioning and help to establish our individual identities. People show wide individual differences in the vigor and persistence of behaviors directed toward such social goals as affiliation, approval, achievement, and power. The study of these important social motives—as well as the conditions under which they are learned and the ways in which they affect thought, perception, and behavior—is an important focus of motivational research.

It is fairly easy to identify our biologically based motives, such as our need for food, liquids, air, and sleep. But it's not so easy to catalog our learned social motives, because people seem capable of learning to want almost anything. Although theorists disagree about the number and kinds of social motives that exist, three widely accepted ones have been the subject of much research. The first, known as the need to affiliate, or attachment, will be discussed in Chapter 12, since it is a crucial part of social development in childhood. The other two important social motives are the need for achievement and the need for power.

THE ACHIEVEMENT MOTIVE

College students are often painfully aware of the emphasis our society places on achievement and the fierce competition that characterizes the academic atmosphere on many campuses. Americans are internationally regarded as being preoccupied with competition and success. Small wonder, then, that the **need for achievement** and its origins have received more attention from American researchers than any other learned social motive.

Measuring need for achievement   Much of the research on achievement motivation has used a measure-ment technique devised by David McClelland, John Atkinson, and their associates (McClelland and others, 1953). Subjects are shown a series of pictures and asked to write a story about each of them. The story is supposed to answer the following questions: (1) What is the situation—that is, who are the people and what are they doing? (2) What has led up to this situation—that is, what has happened in the past? (3) What is being thought? What is wanted? By whom? (4) What will happen? What will be done? The content of the stories is then analyzed for references to achievement according to a well-defined scoring system. One advantage of this measurement technique is that it can be applied not only to stories written in response to the standard pictures but to any written material. We shall see a bit later how historical changes in achievement motivation have been measured in this way.

Need for achievement and behavior   Individuals with a high need for achievement are ambitious, enjoy competitive situations, and are persistent in their attempts to solve problems. They are also better able to pass up immediate gratification for future reward. Achievement motivation scores are sometimes, but not always, positively related to academic grades and IQ. College students with high achievement motivation do best in courses that they perceive as relevant to their future careers, and they tend to seek out and enter more prestigious occupations than do individuals with lower achievement motivation (Raynor, 1970). In terms of occupation, those involved in sales and marketing tend to have the highest achievement motivation scores. On a less positive note, there is some evidence that very high need for achievement is associated with a higher than average death rate from ulcers and hypertension.

In people having high achievement motivation, the motive is engaged and affects behavior only when situational factors arouse it. People with a high need for achievement are more successful than those with low achievement motivation, but only when they work for firms that are especially achievement-oriented.

In experimental situations, people with a high need for achievement generally outperform individuals with low achievement motivation when the experimenter places great stress on excellence of performance, but not under relaxed conditions (McClelland, 1985). Subjects low in need for achievement work harder when they are told that a task is easy; those high in achievement motivation work harder when told the task is difficult (Kukla, 1975).

Risk-taking behavior also is related to achievement motivation. High-need-for-achievement subjects prefer intermediate rather than extremely high or low risks (Atkinson and Birch, 1978). For example, on a ring-toss task, "highs" tend at first to select an intermediate distance to toss the rope ring at the peg, a distance from which the task is a challenge and success is uncertain. But when given a number of successive opportunities to choose tasks of differing difficulty levels, highs begin to prefer increasingly more difficult tasks (Kuhl and Blankenship, 1979). One explanation for these risk preferences is that tasks of intermediate and increasing difficulty give subjects more information about their ability, and that people high in achievement motivation are eager for such feedback (Brody, 1980).

Achievement motivation has been related to national accomplishment as well as to individual achievement. In a series of correlational studies, achievement imagery in children's stories was related to national ecomonic growth. The researchers reasoned that the level of achievement concern in children's books reflects the motivational level of the adults in the country at that time, as well as the values that are being transmitted to children.

The results of one analysis are shown in Figure 9.24. Achievement motivation scores derived from content analysis of second- and fourth-grade school readers corresponded closely to the number of patents issued per million population in the United States between 1810 and 1950 (deCharms and Moeller, 1962).

Fear of failure It is important to distinguish between two very different achievement-related motives, both of which can cause people to appear to be success-oriented. The first is the positive desire to achieve success that we have been discussing; the second is a negative fear of failure. People high in fear of failure work hard not because they yearn for "the thrill of victory" but because they dread "the agony of defeat."

Studies on the development of these two motives indicate that positive achievement motivation develops when parents encourage and reward independence and achievement but do not punish failure. Fear of failure seems to develop when successful achievement is taken

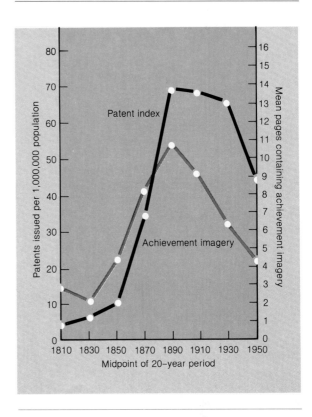

FIGURE 9.24 *Relationship between achievement imagery in children's stories and number of patents per million population issued in the United States between 1800 and 1950. (Adapted from de Charms and Moeller, 1962.)*

for granted by parents but failure is punished. As a result, the child learns to dread the possibility of failing (Weiner, 1980).

In contrast to people who are motivated to achieve, high-fear-of-failure individuals try to avoid feelings of failure by taking either extremely high risks (where no one can truly expect to succeed) or extremely low risks (where success is all but assured). Their performance deteriorates under achievement pressure because of the disruptive effects of anxiety. (Recall the study described earlier in which the highly anxious collegiate golfers "choked" and performed poorly during the tournament.)

Thus, people can be "driven" toward success or away from failure. We need to know which of these needs is motivating them in order to understand and predict their achievement behavior.

THE NEED FOR POWER

Many people have a need to exert control over the lives of others. Like the need to achieve, the **need for power** can be measured through content analysis of stories (McClelland, 1975; Winter, 1973). Subjects' scores are based on the number of phrases and verbal images that describe impact on or control over other people. These images can involve actions that range from strong, aggressive, and forceful (ordering, threatening) to subtle and socially acceptable (helping, advising, inspiring).

McClelland (1975) suggested that there are actually two kinds of power motivation. One kind is oriented toward winning out over adversaries. These people see life as a jungle in which the strongest survive by destroying or eliminating their foes. In every social interaction someone wins and someone loses. The fictional J. R. Ewing of the television series "Dallas" typifies this type of power motivation.

The other kind of power motive is more socialized. It involves using power for the benefit of others and helping to further group goals by exercising social influence (see Figure 9.25). Individuals with this type of motivation may hesitate to seek power because they realize that the overt quest for power may be frowned on by society. Perhaps that is why some politicians prefer to be "called" to public service rather than to actively seek an office.

Some of the behavioral characteristics of people who have a high need for power have been identified. Unfortunately, almost all the research on the need for power has used male subjects, and very little is known about how the power motive applies to females.

Male college students with a high need for power more often hold office in organizations, they write more letters to university newspapers, and they more frequently get elected to important university committees. They are also more likely to play vigorous competitive sports (or at least watch them), to read magazines

"And I hereby swear that should my quest for the secret of superstrength be successful, I shall use this power only for good."

(DRAWING BY LORENZ; © 1975 THE NEW YORKER MAGAZINE, INC.)

FIGURE 9.25 *This child is exhibiting the socialized rather than the competitive type of power motivation.*

like *Playboy*, and to watch adventure programs on television (Winter and Stewart, 1978).

Men with high power needs tend to buy material goods that are advertised as prestigious. They prefer cars with high maneuverability, "which give the driver the impression of total control over the vehicle, the road, and, presumably, other drivers. It may be that for the person with a high need for power the highly maneuverable car is the model for the whole of human society, which he then sees as a series of maneuverable machines" (Winter, 1973, p. 446). People with high power needs are often skilled at manipulating other people and social situations to their advantage. One interesting finding that may relate to their social influence skills is that, compared with males low in power needs, men who obtained high power motivation scores in college had wives with lower levels of career involvement 10 years later (Winter and others, 1977).

It appears that male power fantasies can be aroused by alcohol, but the nature of the power fantasies is affected by the amount of alcohol the man drinks. Small amounts increase the frequency of socialized power thoughts, but larger amounts promote fantasies about personalized power that often involve exploitative sexual and aggressive behavior (McClelland and others, 1972).

According to some theorists, a high need for power is a way of compensating for a sense of inferiority or powerlessness as a child. Research suggests, however, that many adults who have a high need for power felt powerful, not inferior, when they were younger (Winter and Stewart, 1978). They are often first-born sons who were rewarded by their parents when they exercised control over various aspects of their lives, including their younger siblings and their peers.

In one intriguing series of studies, the power motivation of U.S. presidents was measured by content analysis of their inaugural addresses (Winter and Stewart, 1978). Presidents judged to be high in power motivation, such as John F. Kennedy, tended to be active and fond of their job, and they liked to display themselves publicly. They were also more likely than other presidents to be the target of assassination attempts, perhaps because of this fondness for self-display. Ronald Reagan was found in this analysis to be moderately high in the need for power.

Motivational conflict

Motives energize and direct our behavior toward goals. But, as we all know, our goals are not always compatible with each other. The result is **conflict.** Conflicts place us in a motivational bind; we must forego one goal in order to attain another.

In the 1930s, psychologist Kurt Lewin suggested that conflicts can be described in terms of two opposed tendencies: approach and avoidance. When something attracts us, there is a tendency to approach it; when something repels or frightens us, there is a tendency to avoid it. Different combinations of approach and avoidance tendencies can produce three basic types of conflict (see Figure 9.26).

The first type of conflict is between two attractive alternatives and is therefore called an *approach-approach conflict.* The selection of one alternative means

the loss of the other. Conflict is at its greatest when both alternatives are equally attractive and very important to us. A woman who wants to pursue an advanced degree in medicine but also wants to have a family and spend a great deal of time with her children faces an approach-approach conflict.

The reverse of this dilemma is the *avoidance-avoidance conflict,* in which a person is faced with two unde-

FIGURE 9.26 *Three basic types of conflict arise from incompatible motives: approach-approach, avoidance-avoidance, and approach-avoidance. A variation of approach-avoidance is the double approach-avoidance conflict, in which two alternatives elicit both approach and avoidance tendencies.*

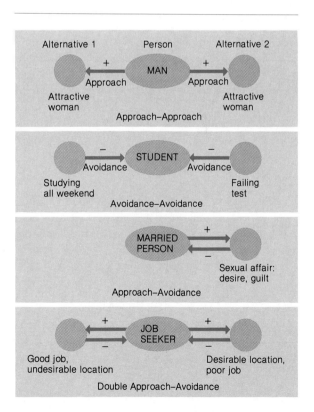

sirable alternatives. You may recently have experienced such a conflict if you had to choose between studying a subject you find terribly boring (hopefully, not this one!) or failing an exam. People faced with an avoidance-avoidance conflict tend to try to escape from the situation (perhaps you have already dropped the course). When we cannot escape, we tend to vacillate between one threat and the other.

In *approach-avoidance conflicts*, a person is both attracted to and repelled by the same goal. These are sometimes the most difficult of all conflicts to resolve. A person is driven toward a sexual affair but is inhibited by guilt and by moral values and beliefs. An injured athlete wants to take a painkilling drug so that she can play in an important game but realizes that she may be risking permanent injury if she does so.

Neal Miller (1959) has provided an analysis of approach-avoidance conflicts that is illustrated in Figure 9.27. According to Miller, the tendency to approach a desired goal grows stronger as we get nearer to it. But so does the desire to avoid the goal. A critical factor, however, is that the avoidance tendency usually increases in strength *faster* than the approach tendency does. Thus, the maximum conflict in an approach-avoidance situation occurs where the two lines, or gradients, cross; there the approach and avoidance tendencies are equal in strength. At this point, we may stop, retreat, approach again, and continue to vacillate in a state of conflict.

Approach-avoidance dilemmas can be resolved in favor of the approach tendency by increasing the motivation to approach, by decreasing the tendency to avoid, or both. Sometimes, without realizing it, people behave in ways that resolve the conflict in favor of avoidance. For example, the person whose conflict involves a sexual affair may start an argument with the person he or she desires. The negative feelings resulting from the argument may reduce the approach tendencies enough so that an affair is no longer such a temptation.

Many of the important decisions that we have to make in life require a choice between two or more alternatives, each of which evokes an approach-avoidance conflict. Let us consider, as an example, a *double approach-avoidance* conflict. You have just graduated from college and have received two job offers. One job will allow you to do exactly the kind of work that you

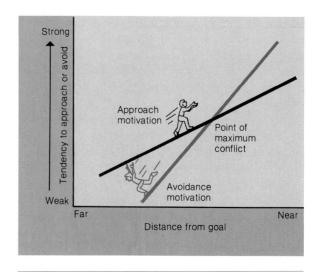

FIGURE 9.27 *Neal Miller has analyzed the dynamics of approach-avoidance conflicts. Both the tendency to approach and the tendency to avoid grow stronger as one moves closer to the goal, but the avoidance tendency increases faster than the approach tendency. Maximum conflict is experienced where the two gradients cross, because at this point the opposing tendencies are equal in strength.*

want to do. It also pays well and offers good opportunities for professional advancement. Unfortunately, if you take the job, you will have to move to an area of the country where you would dislike living. The second job is not as attractive and offers little chance of advancement, but it will allow you to live in a highly desirable geographical area. Each job thus has both approach and avoidance elements connected with it. It is easy to see how such a conflict would be difficult to resolve if the nature of your work and the place where you live are both very important to you.

As we noted earlier, emotion and motivation are closely related to one another, and the study of their linkages has resulted in new ways of understanding the forces that affect our behavior. Frontier 9.2 spotlights some provocative new ways of viewing one of the most baffling of motivational phenomena—addictions.

MOTIVES GONE AWRY: NEW THEORIES OF ADDICTION

One of the most perplexing motivational problems occurs when people become so strongly attracted to substances, activities, or other people that they are said to be addicted. As we noted in Chapter 4, addictions are characterized by the need to increase "dosage" in order to get the same amount of pleasure, by a craving for the incentive, and by the experiencing of unpleasant withdrawal symptoms in the absence of it.

The processes underlying addiction have recently been addressed by new theories of emotion and motivation known as *opponent-process theories* (Siegel and others, 1982; Solomon, 1982). Richard Solomon (1982), one of the originators of opponent-process theory (not to be confused with Hering's opponent-process theory of color vision), believes that the ner-

vous system is constructed so that whenever any emotional response (A) occurs, its opposite (B) is spontaneously triggered shortly afterward to return the system to a neutral state of homeostasis. If a stimulus triggers elation, then the system generates its opposite (depression), and vice versa. From this point of view, every cloud has a silver lining, and every silver lining a cloud. There are some important differences in the A and B states or processes, however. They differ in their intensity, the speed with which they develop, and their persistence.

Upon initial exposure to the stimulus (Panel 1 of Figure 9.28), the A process develops quickly. The B state is delayed somewhat and is not as strong, but when it occurs, it cancels out part of the A state. When the stimulus is removed, the A state dissipates

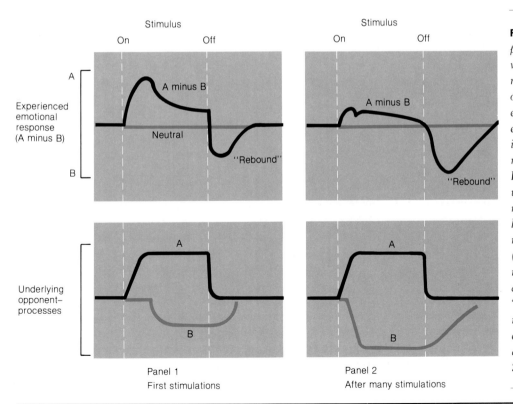

FIGURE 9.28 *Opponent-process theory states that whenever any emotional response (A) occurs, its opposite (B) is soon generated in order to restore equilibrium. The net feeling we experience is the result of A minus B. During the first few stimulations (Panel 1), B is relatively small, but it becomes stronger with repeated stimulations (Panel 2) and cancels out more of A. It also produces a stronger poststimulus "rebound effect." This model has been applied to explain several aspects of addiction. (Adapted from Solomon, 1982.)*

MOTIVES GONE AWRY: NEW THEORIES OF ADDICTION

quickly, but the B state fades away more slowly. Thus, if A is a positive emotion, the B state will cancel out part of A while the stimulus is present and then will produce a temporary "downer" after the stimulus (for example, a love partner) leaves.

With repeated exposure to the stimulus, however, an important thing happens. The A state remains unchanged, but the B state increases in intensity (Panel 2, Figure 9.28). B's greater relative strength has the effect of canceling out more of the A state and thereby producing a more neutral emotional response. It also produces a stronger rebound effect. For example, if you try skydiving (and are sane), the A process will be strong fear and the B process will be relief or elation. Studies of skydivers indicate that on their first jumps, they experience intense fear followed by a dazed sense of relief after landing. With repeated jumps, the fear (A) dissipates and the relief (B) intensifies into elation, exactly as opponent-process theory would predict (Solomon, 1982). This may be one way in which people become addicted to thrill-seeking activities.

For some people, a physical activity like jogging can become a "positive addiction." Opponent-process theory would suggest that, at first, a novice jogger may find the activity boring and physically unpleasant (the A state). If the jogger persists, however, the positive, opponent B state will assume more strength

and the B rebound after the activity will produce a "runner's high." Many joggers maintain that, after a long period, the activity becomes addictive to them, and they experience a "downer" if they miss their run.

Shepard Siegel (1978) also has an opponent-process theory of addictive behavior, but with a new twist. Siegel claims that the opponent state becomes *classically conditioned* to external environmental stimuli. Because of these conditioned opponent responses (which he calls *compensatory responses),* an addict who is exposed to an environment in which drugs have previously been taken experiences a strong, unpleasant craving. However, if the usual drug dose is taken in a novel environment, the addict may actually die of overdose because of the absence of the protective conditioned opponent responses. In fact, many overdoses do occur when addicts take their usual drug dose in an unfamiliar environment (Siegel and others, 1982).

If Siegel is correct, then conditioned negative processes could be occurring whenever we experience pleasure. Perhaps we can enhance these pleasurable experiences by having them in a novel environment where the opposing responses do not occur (Hoyenga and Hoyenga, 1984). Maybe this is one reason why many couples find sexual relations in a novel setting more pleasurable.

STUDY OUTLINE

EMOTION (p. 308)

1. Emotions are complex psychological and biological responses to internal and external stimuli. Emotions are closely related to motives, which are internal processes that guide behavior toward some goal or incentive.

2. Emotional experiences are characterized by subjective feelings, physiological arousal, and observable

behavior. There are four primary components of emotion: the eliciting stimuli, the person's cognitive appraisal of the situation, physiological arousal, and expressive and instrumental behaviors. Individual differences in personality and motivation affect the experience and expression of emotion, as do cultural factors.

3. Although it is possible that innate factors can affect the eliciting properties of certain stimuli, learning plays an important role in determining the arousal properties of stimuli.

4. The cognitive component of emotional experience involves the evaluative and personal appraisal of the eliciting stimuli. The ability of thoughts to elicit emotional arousal has been demonstrated clinically and in experimental research.

5. Our physiological responses in emotion are produced by certain areas of the brain, including the hypothalamus, the limbic system, and the cortex, and by the autonomic and endocrine systems.

6. Research has shown that the polygraph has questionable validity as a "lie detector," largely because of the difficulty of establishing the meaning of physiological responses.

7. The behavioral component of emotion includes expressive and instrumental behaviors. Different parts of the face are important in the expression of various emotions, and accuracy of perception is enhanced when situational cues are also available. Evolutionary theorists propose that certain fundamental emotional patterns of expression are innate, but they agree that cultural learning can influence emotional expression in important ways. There are individual differences in the ability to communicate and interpret emotional expressions.

8. According to the Yerkes-Dodson law, there is an optimal level of arousal for the performance of any task. This optimal level varies with the complexity or difficulty of the task; complex tasks have lower optimal levels.

INTERACTIONS AMONG COMPONENTS (p. 320)

1. Several important theories deal with the relationships among emotional components. Cognitive appraisal theory states that appraisals trigger emotional arousal, while the James-Lange theory reverses this sequence, maintaining that we first become aroused and then judge what we are feeling. The Cannon-Bard theory proposes that arousal and cognition are simultaneously triggered by the thalamus. According to Schachter's "jukebox" theory, arousal tells us how strongly we are emoting, while cognitions derived from situational cues help us to label the specific emotion.

2. There appears to be a reciprocal or two-way relationship between the cognitive and physiological components. It is possible to manipulate appraisals and

thereby influence level of arousal, but arousal changes can also affect appraisal of the eliciting stimuli.

3. Several theorists have applied the cognitive psychology concept of associative networks to emotion. These networks consist of associated groups of ideas, emotional responses, and behavioral tendencies. This idea receives support from studies of state-dependent memory, which have shown that better recall occurs when the moods that exist under conditions of learning and recall are the same.

MOTIVATION (p. 324)

1. Motivation is defined as an internal process that influences the direction, vigor, and persistence of goal-directed behavior.

2. All the perspectives are concerned with various aspects of motivation. The biological perspective studies the external and internal processes related to the arousal and reduction of biological needs. Behaviorists study relationships between motivation and learning, as well as the way learning is involved in acquiring motives. Examples of the cognitive perspective's contributions include the Expectancy X Value theory and the study of how extrinsic rewards can undermine intrinsic motivation. Psychodynamic theorists are particularly interested in the role of unconscious motivation in behavior, while humanistic theorists like Maslow stress the importance of higher-order growth needs.

HOMEOSTATIC NEEDS (p. 329)

1. Our biological needs are directed at maintaining a stable internal environment and are governed by control centers that respond to deviations from certain set points. Receptors that are sensitive to fluid levels around and inside cells are important in the regulation of drinking. Where hunger is concerned, much research has centered on the hypothalamus, but it now appears that many widely separated parts of the brain are involved in the regulation of eating. Chemical factors, such as peptides, are known to play a vital role in the regulation of food intake.

2. Eating disorders, including obesity, anorexia nervosa, and bulimia, are the focus of much current research. Several factors, including increased fat cell size and insulin secretion, lowered basal metabolism, and lowered activity level, combine to increase the difficulty obese people have in achieving and maintaining weight loss. Anorexics and bulimics both show a preoccupation with food intake and a distorted body image. Both disorders can have drastic life-threatening consequences.

SENSORY NEEDS (p. 332)

Both animals and humans tend to seek out novelty and an optimal level of stimulation that can vary among individuals. The study of individual differences in the sensation-seeking motive has shown that the strength of this motive is related to a variety of human behaviors, including risk taking, drug use, and sexual activities and preferences.

SOCIAL MOTIVATION (p. 338)

1. Achievement motivation can be measured by content-analyzing stories told by subjects in response to pictures. People high in achievement motivation perform better than lows when the situation stresses competition with standards of excellence. They prefer moderate risks and tasks that increase in difficulty over time.

2. An important distinction exists between achievement motivation and fear of failure, which is a negative motive aimed at the avoidance of failure rather than at success for its own sake. People high in fear of failure tend to perform more poorly in achievement situations because of the disruptive effects of anxiety.

3. The need for power seems to take two forms: winning out over rivals, and achieving positive group goals through social influence. The traditional belief that people high in power motivation are compensating for feelings of inferiority or feelings of powerlessness as children has not been well supported by research.

MOTIVATIONAL CONFLICT (p. 341)

Three basic varieties of conflict are approach-approach, avoidance-avoidance, and approach-avoidance. According to Miller, in approach-avoidance conflicts, the tendency to avoid the goal grows stronger as we get closer to it and increases in strength faster than approach motivation.

OPPONENT-PROCESSES AND ADDICTIONS (p. 343)

A new way of understanding addictive behaviors has come from the opponent-process theories, which hold that whenever an emotional response occurs, the body triggers its opposite shortly afterward in the interest of maintaining homeostasis. Over time, the opponent reaction becomes stronger, producing a negative emotional reaction when a liked object or activity is no longer present, and elation when a disliked event ceases. Siegel suggests that opponent-processes can become classically conditioned to environmental stimuli and has related this phenomenon to several aspects of drug addiction.

KEY TERMS AND CONCEPTS

emotion

eliciting stimuli

cognitive appraisal

instrumental behavior

polygraph

fundamental emotional pattern

Yerkes-Dodson law

James-Lange theory

Cannon-Bard theory

cognitive appraisal theory

Schachter's theory

priming effect

state-dependent memory

motivation

Expectancy X Value theory

overjustification hypothesis

deficiency need

growth need

Maslow's need hierarchy

homeostasis

angiotensin

lateral hypothalamus

ventromedial hypothalamus

peptide

CCK

set point theory

obesity

metabolism

anorexia nervosa

bulimia

sensory deprivation

sensation-seeking motive

need for achievement

fear of failure

need for power

conflict (three basic types)

opponent-process theory

compensatory responses

SUGGESTED READINGS

GEEN, R. G., BEATTY, W. W., and ARKIN, R. M.   (1984). *Human motivation: Physiological, behavioral, and social approaches*. Boston: Allyn and Bacon.

MCCLELLAND, D. C.   (1985). *Human motivation*. Glenview, Ill.: Scott, Foresman.

Both of these books, which provide excellent overviews of the entire field of motivation, are current and include the latest theories and research findings.

MANDLER, G.   (1984). *Mind and body: Psychology of emotion and stress*. New York: Norton. A fascinating book that includes wide-ranging discussions of all the important topics in the psychology of emotion and stress. The author embellishes the book with many interesting speculations.

CHAPTER TEN
HUMAN SEXUALITY

THREE APPROACHES TO THE STUDY OF SEXUALITY
The survey approach
The observational approach
The experimental approach

SEX, CULTURE, AND RELATIONSHIPS
Cultural influences on sexuality
Sex, love, and intimacy
FRONTIER 10.1 PASSIONATE LOVE

SEXUALITY THROUGH THE LIFE SPAN
Childhood sexuality
Development of gender identity
Sex and aging

SEXUAL DYSFUNCTION
Psychological factors in sexual dysfunction
Treatment of sexual dysfunction

ALTERNATIVE MODES OF SEXUALITY
Homosexuality
Atypical sexual behaviors

SEXUAL VICTIMIZATION
Rape
Child molestation

STUDY OUTLINE

KEY TERMS AND CONCEPTS

SUGGESTED READINGS

Perhaps no aspect of human behavior provokes as much moral and legal controversy, as many conflicting beliefs, and as much personal conflict as sexuality does. Violations of moral and legal standards pertaining to sex are particularly likely to elicit strong emotional responses in our society. Consider, for example, the following remarks addressed by a California Superior Court judge to a teenager who had been discovered having sexual relations with his 15-year-old sister:

This is one of the worst crimes that a person can commit. I just get so disgusted that I just figure what is the use? You are just an animal. You are lower than an animal. Even animals don't do that. . . . You are no particular good to anybody. We ought to send you out of the country. . . . You belong in prison for the rest of your life for doing things of this kind. You ought to commit suicide. That's what I think of people of this kind. You are lower than the animals and haven't the right to live in organized society—just miserable, lousy, rotten people. . . . Maybe Hitler was right. The animals in our society probably ought to be destroyed because they have no right to live among human beings. (State of California, County of Santa Clara, September 2, 1969; cited in Katchadourian and Lunde, 1979)

Sex in animals is seen as natural—birds do it, bees do it—but in humans it is complicated by all sorts of taboos, laws, and customs. If satisfying our hunger drive was as complicated as satisfying our sex drive, many people would be a lot thinner.

For a long time, it was simply not acceptable to talk openly about sex. Husbands and wives didn't talk about it. Scientists are people, too, and they didn't talk about it very much, either. Even physicians were sometimes pretty uninformed about sexual matters. Fortunately, this situation has changed to some extent in recent years. Society is loosening its restrictions and allowing a freer discussion of sex and an expansion of scientific research on it.

Because sexual expression has always been laced with moral and legal issues, the scientific study of sexu-

FIGURE 10.1 *In our culture, sex is a topic that has such high interest value that it is a familiar aspect of advertising and product promotion.*

ality has been slow to evolve. Alfred Kinsey's pioneering survey studies of sexual behavior in the 1940s drew strong condemnation in many segments of society, and the work of William Masters and Virginia Johnson in the 1960s also evoked cries of outrage. However, the so-called sexual revolution that began in the 1960s brought into focus many questions of social importance. What impact do erotic stimuli have on behavior? What are the psychological effects of varying forms of sexual expression? How is sexual satisfaction related to love? What are the differences in the sexual attitudes, behaviors, and preferences of males and females? Why do some people have sexual problems, and how can such people be helped? Is homosexuality a disorder or simply an alternative way to express one's sexuality? What are the short- and long-term effects of rape and child abuse? As scientific research pushes back the curtains of fear and ignorance, many commonly held beliefs about sex are being shown to have no basis in fact. Table 10.1 presents just a sample of scientifically validated facts that contradict popular folklore.

THREE APPROACHES TO THE STUDY OF SEXUALITY

Three research strategies have provided the bulk of our scientific knowledge about human sexual behavior. The first of these approaches is the survey study, in

TABLE 10.1 RESEARCH FINDINGS THAT CHALLENGE WIDELY HELD BELIEFS ABOUT SEX

1. There is no known aphrodisiac (sexual stimulant) that is uniformly effective in increasing sexual pleasure. Spanish fly (*Cantharis vesicatoria*) is a dangerous drug and can produce severe illness. In males it can produce prolonged erections by inflaming the urinary tract and dilating the blood vessels of the penis, but no increase in sexual arousal occurs.

2. On a physiological level, the size of the male's penis is unrelated to sexual effectiveness or his ability to provide pleasure for a woman. During intercourse the vagina adapts to the size of the penis. If penis size affects the amount of pleasure a woman experiences, it is for psychological rather than physical reasons. Black males tend to have a longer flaccid penis than whites, but the difference disappears after erection occurs.

3. Masturbation does not cause blindness, growth of hair on the palms, brain damage, or mental illness (although guilt and anxiety sometimes occur because of cultural or moral beliefs about masturbation). A large percentage of men and women masturbate, and many achieve more physically intense orgasms through masturbation than they do through intercourse.

4. There is no evidence that frequent sexual activity during youth causes a person to "burn out" in later years, nor that frequent sexual activity adversely affects health. In fact, frequent sexual expression in early adulthood seems to prolong the sexual activity of elderly males.

5. Freud held that clitoral orgasms are "immature" and mature women eventually graduate to vaginal orgasms. But in fact there is no known physiological difference between vaginal and clitoral orgasms. The vagina is actually rather insensitive to stimulation, so that most if not all orgasms during intercourse are probably triggered primarily by direct or indirect clitoral stimulation.

6. Sexual pleasure is not restricted to the young. Regular sexual gratification is experienced by a substantial number of people over age 70. Psychological factors rather than physical changes are the strongest reasons for reduced sexual activity among elderly persons.

7. Women do not necessarily take longer to reach orgasm than men do. With appropriate stimulation, most women can have an orgasm in 4 minutes or less.

8. Simultaneous orgasm during intercourse is not necessarily a sexual ideal, since the male often desires deep penetration at the point of ejaculation, while the female may desire continued pelvic thrusting. Many couples find successive orgasms more pleasurable, since they each can focus on and enjoy their partner's climax.

9. People who have had heart attacks need not avoid sex. They can resume sexual activity as soon as they are capable of walking several blocks or climbing several flights of stairs.

10. There is no medical reason why women should avoid sexual intercourse during menstruation. In fact, intercourse may help relieve menstrual cramps, and many women have strong sexual desires during their period. Sex is also possible during pregnancy, though intercourse may be discontinued during its latter stages.

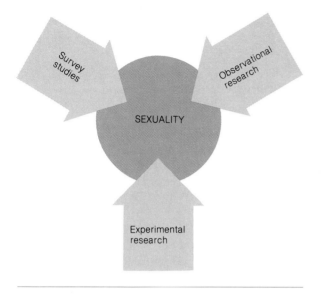

FIGURE 10.2 *Three research approaches—surveys, laboratory observation, and experimental studies—have provided much of the scientific data on sexual attitudes, beliefs, and behavior.*

which large groups of people are asked about their sexual beliefs, attitudes, and practices.

A second and somewhat newer descriptive strategy involves observation under controlled conditions. Much of our recently acquired knowledge about the physiology of sex has come from the laboratories of researchers like Masters and Johnson, who carefully observed and measured bodily responses during sexual activity. Clinical case studies, though less controlled, have also provided important information.

The third major technique in understanding human sexuality is the experimental approach, which is used to study the ways in which certain variables affect sexual behavior under controlled conditions. For example, an experimenter might measure differences in the extent to which men and women are differentially aroused by particular kinds of erotic stimuli. Many important studies of sexual behavior in animals have also been experimental in nature. The experimental approach using human subjects is newer than the survey and descriptive approaches (Figure 10.2).

The survey, observational, and experimental approaches complement one another. The first step in

understanding any phenomenon is to describe it carefully, and surveys and observational studies generate descriptive data. But, as we noted in our discussion of research methods in Chapter 2, description is not enough; scientific understanding requires that we test our explanations through prediction and control. This testing is possible using the experimental approach.

The survey approach

The first large-scale attempts to study and describe human sexual behavior were begun in the late 1930s by Alfred Kinsey and his colleagues at Indiana University. Kinsey, a zoologist who had spent more than 20 years researching the wasp, was asked to give some guest lectures in a course on marriage. As any of us might, he headed for the library to find material for his lectures. To his dismay, he found that very little research had been conducted on human sexuality. This discovery marked a turning point in his career. From 1938 to 1948, Kinsey and his co-workers conducted the most extensive survey study of human sexual behavior ever attempted (see Figure 10.3).

The first Kinsey report, *Sexual Behavior in the Human Male* (Kinsey, Pomeroy, and Martin, 1948), presented a highly detailed statistical analysis of the sexual activities of 5,300 American males ranging in age from 10 to 90. In personal interviews that lasted about 2 hours, the men were asked nearly 300 questions about their sex lives. A companion volume, *Sexual Behavior in the Human Female* (Kinsey, Pomeroy, Martin, and Gebhard, 1953), was the result of similar interviews with 5,940 American women.

Although they appeared a generation ago, the Kinsey reports are still considered to be the most comprehensive scientific surveys of sexual behavior ever undertaken. More recently, several other large-scale survey studies have appeared. One, sponsored by the Playboy Foundation, was based on questionnaire data

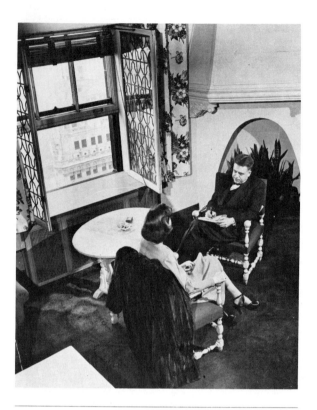

FIGURE 10.3 *Alfred Kinsey conducts one of the more than 11,000 intensive interviews that were carried out during his surveys of male and female sexual behavior.*

collected by a public opinion research firm from 2,026 men and women residing in 24 cities (Hunt, 1974). *The Hite Reports* (1976, 1981) surveyed several thousand women and men who provided narrative answers to essay questions about their sexual attitudes and practices. Two women's magazines, *Cosmopolitan* and *Redbook*, sponsored questionnaire studies in 1980. More than 106,000 women returned the *Cosmopolitan* questionnaire (Wolfe, 1980), while about 6,000 men and 20,000 women responded to the *Redbook* survey (Sarrel and Sarrel, 1980). In combination with numerous smaller surveys, these studies provide a broad overview of sexual behaviors, attitudes, and experiences and allow us to see how matters have changed since Kinsey's day. Before considering this information,

however, we should comment on several features of survey research on sexuality that temper our interpretation of these data.

PROBLEMS OF SEX SURVEY RESEARCH

The great strength of the survey approach to sexual behavior can be quickly stated. While people don't usually let scientists into their bedrooms, they are often willing to fill out a questionnaire or submit to an interview. Ideally, a survey should be based on a *random* and *representative* sample. A representative sample is one in which important characteristics such as age, sex, educational level, and ethnicity exist in the same proportions as in the larger population. If we have a sufficiently large and representative sample and if our subjects give us truthful and accurate data, then we can confidently generalize our results to the larger population.

The major problems in interpreting the results of sex surveys come from failure to satisfy the ideals we have just described. Two issues are of particular importance: self-selected and nonrepresentative samples, and possible distortions in self-reports of sexual behavior.

Let us first consider sampling problems. No sex survey has come close to obtaining a truly random and representative sample. Kinsey's surveys were very competently carried out, and although his sample of 11,240 people reflected a wide range of differences in age, educational level, occupation, religious affiliation, marital status, and so on, the sample was not representative of the American population. For example, rural groups and lower educational levels were underrepresented, as were children and people over 50 years of age. Most respondents were white volunteers. Kinsey was well aware of the shortcomings of his sample, and he was careful to point out that his findings did not necessarily reflect the sexual behaviors of the American population. But people who cited his surveys did not always keep that proviso in mind.

A major problem in later surveys has been the refusal of a great many people to participate. In the Playboy Foundation study, an attempt was made to select a random and representative sample, but 80 percent of the people who were selected refused to be involved. The Hite survey of females was based on 3,000 respondents, but another 97,000 women did not return the questionnaire. The 1980 *Redbook* and *Cosmopolitan* reports were based on samples of up to 106,000 people, but the fact that both magazines have circulation figures of over 10 million means that, at best, fewer than 1 percent of their readers (who are hardly representative of all women to begin with) responded. In all of these studies, then, we have the problem of *self-selection*. There is always the possibility that people who agree to participate in such surveys may be substantially different in their attitudes and behavior from those who decline to participate. We can therefore generalize these survey results only to people who are similar to the respondents. This does not mean that the data are not useful or important, but it does mean that there are limitations to the conclusions that we can draw about other segments of the population.

A second potential problem in survey research relates to the accuracy of the data that are obtained. People may give false statements for a variety of reasons. They may not remember precisely, they may be embarrassed or reluctant to report certain behaviors, they may be boastful, or they may simply misunderstand the questions.

With these points in mind, we now turn to some of the major survey findings.

PATTERNS AND CHANGES IN SEXUAL BEHAVIOR

Kinsey and his co-workers generated a tremendous amount of data. Table 10.2 highlights a number of results concerning sexual practices that attracted much attention in a society which had to that point virtually no scientific information about sexual behavior.

Although differences in sample characteristics and data collection methods must be kept in mind, a comparison of the Kinsey figures in Table 10.2 with the results of more recent surveys suggests several notable changes in sexual behavior. In general, it appears that the percentage of people who engage in masturbation has not changed much, but that those who masturbate begin doing so at a younger age and do so more frequently. Among liberal young females, masturbation appears to be far more common than among Kinsey's respondents. In Hite's (1976) survey, 82 percent of the female respondents said that they masturbated.

More profound changes in sexual behavior seem to have occurred in the areas of premarital sex and the

practice of oral-genital stimulation. By the time they are 19, about 60 percent of all females in the United States have had intercourse (Zelnick and others, 1981). Among married persons between the ages of 18 and 24, the percentage who had premarital intercourse has

TABLE 10.2 SOME NOTABLE FINDINGS FROM THE KINSEY SURVEYS

1. Masturbation. Over all age groups, 92 percent of the males and 58 percent of the females had masturbated to orgasm at least once in their lives. By age 20, 82 percent of the males and 33 percent of the females had done so. There was wide variation in the frequency with which both males and females masturbated.

2. Premarital intercourse. Forty-eight percent of all the married women in the sample had had sexual intercourse before marriage. About 25 percent of the 20- and 21-year-old unmarried women reported that they were not virgins. Among men, 85 percent reported premarital sex experiences. The figures ranged from 98 percent among males with no high school education to 68 percent among college graduates.

3. Extramarital sex. Twenty-six percent of the married women and about 50 percent of the married men reported having had extramarital sexual affairs.

4. Oral-genital stimulation. Fifty percent of the college-educated men, but fewer than 5 percent of those with grade school educations engaged in cunnilingus (oral stimulation of the female genitals). Fellatio (oral stimulation of the male's genitals) was reported by slightly over 40 percent of the women, but most had done so infrequently.

5. Female orgasm. Among married women, slightly fewer than half reported experiencing orgasm always or almost always during intercourse; 28 percent said they never experienced orgasm.

6. Homosexual relationships. Of the males interviewed, 37 percent had engaged in at least one homosexual relationship to the extent of having orgasm. Thirteen percent of the females reported similar experiences.

Source: From Kinsey, Pomeroy, and Martin, 1948; Kinsey, Pomeroy, Martin, and Gebhard, 1953.

been reported to be as high as 95 percent for males and 81 percent for females (Hunt, 1974). Although more people are having premarital sex, only about 20 percent of young females and 40 percent of males find their first experience pleasurable, and about a third of the males and two-thirds of the females experience regret, guilt, and worry afterward (Hunt, 1974). In a large survey study of high school and college students (Sorenson, 1973), females tended to report more negative reactions to their first experience of intercourse than males did (see Table 10.3).

The practice of oral-genital stimulation has increased rather dramatically at every level of education since the days of Kinsey (Downey, 1980). The Playboy Foundation study found that about 80 percent of single males and females between the ages of 25 and 34, and about 90 percent of married persons under 25, engaged in oral-genital stimulation (Hunt, 1974). In a more recent survey of female college sophomores who were currently dating, 61 percent reported performing oral sex on their partner, and 68 percent indicated that they had been recipients of oral-genital stimulation (Herold and Way, 1983).

Despite its limitations, the survey approach to the study of sexuality has been extremely valuable. The surveys, beginning with Kinsey, helped to break barriers to studying sexual behavior and attitudes and have provided us with much of our current knowledge.

The observational approach

Sexual behavior is usually observed only by the participants. In 1953, however, gynecologist William Masters and his research associate Virginia Johnson began a landmark study that provided a great leap forward in scientific knowledge about the body's complex responses during sexual activity.

For more than 10 years, Masters and Johnson studied the sexual responses of 694 men and women under controlled laboratory conditions. In all, about 10,000 sexual episodes were monitored. While the volunteer subjects engaged in masturbation, intercourse, and other sexual activities, many of their physiological responses were measured (see Figure 10.4). By putting a camera into a transparent penis-shaped case, Masters and Johnson were even able to film vaginal and uterine reactions during simulated intercourse. Their findings were published in a book entitled *Human Sexual Response* (Masters and Johnson, 1966).

Masters and Johnson found that most people go through a basic four-stage physiological response pattern of excitement, plateau, orgasm, and resolution. The initial **excitement** response to sexual stimulation is vaginal lubrication in the female and penile erection in the male. In the female, this is followed by nipple erection, a thickening of the vaginal walls, and a flattening and elevation of the external genitalia. The uterus begins to elevate and is pulled up from the vagina in a "tenting" fashion to allow for accommodation of the penis and to protect the cervix during intercourse. In males, there is a slight increase in the size and elevation of the testicles.

In the second stage, or **plateau phase**, heart rate,

TABLE 10.3 REACTIONS TO FIRST SEXUAL EXPERIENCE AMONG YOUNG PEOPLE

	MALES	FEMALES
Excited	46%*	26%
Afraid	17	63
Happy	42	26
Satisfied	43	20
Thrilled	43	13
Curious	23	30
Joyful	31	12
Mature	29	14
Fulfilled	29	8
Worried	9	35
Guilty	3	36
Embarrassed	7	31
Tired	15	14
Relieved	19	8
Sorry	1	25
Hurt	0	25
Powerful	15	1
Foolish	7	9
Used	0	16
Disappointed	3	10
Raped	0	6

*Percentages add up to more than 100% because most respondents reported more than one reaction.

Adapted from Sorenson, 1973, p. 203.

respiration, and muscle tension all increase. The male's testes increase in size by about 50 percent and are pulled up high into the scrotum. In the female, the tissues surrounding the outer third of the vagina swell, reducing the diameter of the vaginal opening up to 50 percent. The clitoris retracts under the hood that covers it.

In the third stage, **orgasm**, the penis begins to throb in rhythmic contractions. Semen collects in the urethral bulb, and contractions of the bulb and penis project the semen out of the penis. In females, orgasm involves rhythmic muscular contractions of the outer third of the vagina and the uterus. In both sexes, muscles throughout the body contract, and there is a temporary state of high physiological arousal.

In males, orgasm is ordinarily followed by the **resolution** phase. Physiological arousal decreases rapidly, and the genital organs and tissues return to their normal condition. Some males, however, are able to experience orgasm without ejaculation. They may be capable of several orgasms before resolution (Robbins

and Jensen, 1977). Females may have two or more successive orgasms before the onset of the resolution phase, but most women experience only one. Following orgasm, males have a temporary **refractory period,** during which they cannot be aroused.

Many of Masters and Johnson's findings contradicted popular beliefs. For example, despite Freud's assertion that clitoral orgasms were "immature," Masters and Johnson found no detectable physiological differences between female orgasms produced through direct stimulation of the clitoris and those brought about by vaginal penetration. As we shall see in our later discussion of sexual dysfunction, Masters and Johnson also developed a number of useful treatment techniques for certain sexual problems.

FIGURE 10.4 *William Masters and Virginia Johnson have done the most extensive research on the psychophysiology of sexual arousal and orgasm. Their findings have dispelled many sexual myths and demonstrated the value of sex research.*

The experimental approach

The most recent scientific approach to the study of human sexuality is the controlled laboratory experiment in which variables are manipulated and their effects on behavior observed. Several critical issues have been the focus of recent experimental research.

STIMULUS FACTORS IN SEXUALITY

Although our sex drive, like that of animals, is partially attributable to biological factors such as hormones, environmental stimuli appear to be far more important in eliciting sexual arousal and behavior in humans (Beach, 1969). Through learning experiences, a specific range of stimuli acquire arousing properties and influence our sexual responses. Researchers are currently studying the arousal properties of various kinds of stimuli. Because ethical considerations prevent the use of real-life stimuli, such as nude experimenters, most of this work has used pictorial, written, or imagined stimuli. Scientists either ask subjects to rate the height of their sexual arousal, or they measure the subjects' physiological responses directly. A number of methods are available for measuring blood volume in the penis (erections) as well as physical responses in the vagina. Figure 10.5 shows two of these measuring devices.

Sex differences in arousability: where have they gone?

Kinsey and his co-workers reported in 1953 that arousal responses to erotic pictures and stories were much rarer among women than among men, reinforcing the traditional belief that women are less interested in and aroused by erotic stimuli than men are. Other studies have established that women are less likely than men to frequent pornographic movies and adult bookstores. The traditional interpretation for such observations is that women's sexual arousal is more dependent on a personal and affectionate relationship (Schmidt, 1975).

An experimental study by William Fisher and Donn Byrne (1978) was designed to test this hypothesis. The experimenters showed male and female college students an explicit film of a nude couple engaging in a variety of sexual acts. To half of the subjects of each sex, the actors were described as a married couple who

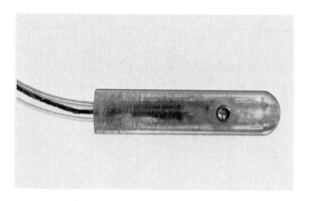

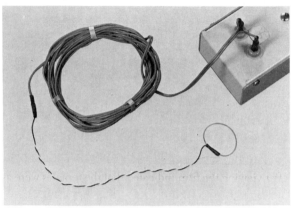

FIGURE 10.5 *Two devices that are frequently used to measure sexual arousal in laboratory studies. The vaginal photocell plethysmograph (top) is inserted into the vagina, where it uses changes in reflected light to measure increases in vaginal blood flow that accompany arousal. The penile plethysmograph (bottom) is used to measure male erection. The thin rubber ring slips around the penis, and even tiny changes in circumference are recorded on a polygraph.*

were deeply in love (love condition). The remaining subjects were told that the film depicted a nonromantic encounter between a prostitute and her customer (lust condition). The researchers hypothesized that if sexual stimuli are arousing to women only within a love relationship, the female subjects should be less aroused in the lust condition than in the love condition.

The results of the experiment are shown in Figure 10.6. Ratings of sexual arousal made by the subjects

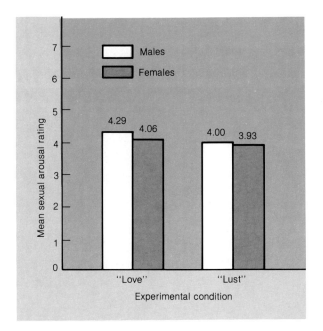

FIGURE 10.6 *Degree of sexual arousal reported by male and female subjects in response to a sexually explicit film. Whether the relationship depicted in the film was based on a love relationship or a lust relationship made no difference to either males or females. (Data from Fisher and Byrne, 1978.)*

But we must not lose sight of the fact that there are still wide individual differences in reactions to erotic stimuli among both males and females. The reasons for these differences are destined to become the focus of a new wave of research.

EFFECTS OF PORNOGRAPHY ON BEHAVIOR

In 1961, the following resolution was entered into the *Congressional Record* by a subcommittee investigating sexually explicit materials:

There is a black plague sweeping the nation more devastating than the one that ravaged Europe in the Middle Ages. Its principal victims are children and adolescents, although like its ancient predecessor, it destroys adults as well. . . . Those concerned declare that no act of subversion planned by the Communist conspiracy could be more effective in shredding the Nation's moral fabric than the lethal effect of pornography. (August 29, 1961)

As we all know, there is still great concern and controversy about the effects of pornography on those who are exposed to it. Yet the findings of more than a dozen studies suggest that exposure to pornography temporarily increases arousal and allows people to learn sexual responses through modeling but that the effects on subsequent sexual activity are quite limited and temporary. In 1969, the Presidential Commission on Obscenity and Pornography concluded that no reliable relationship had been demonstrated between pornography and criminal acts. That same year, laws in Denmark were

after viewing the film indicated that the females were as highly aroused as the males in both film conditions; whether the film depicted a love relationship or a lust relationship made no difference. Women in the lust condition also reported as many breast and genital sensations and as much vaginal lubrication as did those in the love condition. Interestingly, however, the women rated the lust film as more pornographic and more deserving of being banned than the males did.

This pattern of findings—high sexual arousal but negative attitudes toward sexual stimuli—has been found in other studies as well (Schmidt, 1975). One explanation for this apparent contradiction is that many women have been socially conditioned to believe that it is not proper for them to seek out and enjoy sexually explicit materials. Thus, their attitudes and conduct suggest disinterest, but their bodily responses indicate that they are as capable as men of being aroused, whether or not the context involves love and affection. Moreover, when the social setting is judged as appropriate to the enjoyment of sexual stimuli, many women appear anything but disinterested (see Figure 10.7).

Thus, sex differences in arousability appear to have diminished in the years since the Kinsey reports as cultural attitudes about female sexuality have broadened.

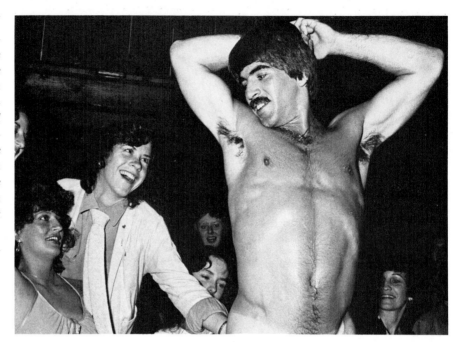

FIGURE 10.7 *Women have traditionally been characterized as less interested in erotic stimuli than are men. However, research has shown that there is little difference between men and women in arousal responses to sexual stimuli. Although women often indicate more negative attitudes toward such stimuli, they can respond quite positively when the social situation makes it permissible to do so, as at this male strip show.*

revised to permit the unrestricted sale of sexually explicit materials. Arrests for sex crimes dropped 30 percent in the first year and continued to decline in subsequent years (Ben-Veniste, 1971).

To many respected authorities, the issue of how pornography affects people seemed pretty much settled in the early 1970s. But now an important new issue has arisen. While nonviolent pornography may have little effect on people, what about pornography that depicts rape, sexual exploitation, and episodes in which partners inflict pain on one another? What about kiddie porn, which features sex with children, and the so-called snuff movies, in which the sex act ends with what is claimed to be a real murder? One authority has suggested that violent pornography may create a climate in which "acts of sexual hostility directed against women are not only tolerated but ideologically encouraged" (Brownmiller, 1975, p. 444).

Several recent studies suggest that exposure to violent sexual stimuli may have at least temporary negative effects (Malamuth and Donnerstein, 1983). At the University of Manitoba, for example, Neal Malamuth showed two groups of men a slide show of a rape based on photos taken from a pornography magazine. One group heard a sound track that described the woman as being terrified and forcibly raped. The other group heard a sound track in which the woman agreed to have sex.

Both groups of men experienced high levels of physiological arousal while they watched the episode. The subjects were then asked to create the most sexually arousing fantasies they could. Those who had been exposed to the violent rape version reported more sexual fantasies of a violent nature. Since deviant sexual fantasies have frequently been shown to be associated with sexually deviant behavior (MacCulloch and others, 1983), the fact that exposure to violent pornography can stimulate such fantasies merits concern and further study. Exposure to such films also seems to enhance men's acceptance of false beliefs about rape—for example, the view that many women have an unconscious wish to be raped—and to increase the acceptability of sexual violence against women (Malamuth and Check, 1981).

At the University of Wisconsin, Edward Donnerstein and Leonard Berkowitz (1981) studied the effects of erotic and sexually violent films on actual aggression against a woman. Male subjects were randomly divided into four groups. One group saw a nonsexual film of a talk show. The second group was shown an erotic film in which a young couple made love. The films seen by the other two groups were violently erotic depictions of a woman being physically and sexually assaulted by two men. In one of these films, the woman resisted at first, but then became a willing sexual participant; in the other, the victim was shown suffering during the entire experience.

All of the male subjects then interacted with a female accomplice of the experimenter. Half of these interactions were purposely designed to make the men angry. After interacting with the woman, the subjects were given the opportunity to aggress against her by giving her electric shocks in a modified Milgram situation.

The results were both clear and sobering. As shown in Figure 10.8, exposure to the nonviolent erotic film did not increase aggression above the level in the neutral film condition, but the violent erotic films did. Among the subjects who saw the suffering rape victim, those who were later angered by the female accomplice gave her higher levels of shock, but the nonangered

ones did not. But subjects who had seen a rape victim who ultimately "enjoyed" the experience gave high levels of shock whether or not they had been angered.

Overall, experimental studies indicate that exposure to violent pornography at least temporarily weakens men's restraints against violence toward women, encourages sexually calloused attitudes (for example, that women are sexual objects), and increases the stated willingness of men to engage in rape if there is no chance of being caught (Malamuth and Donnerstein, 1983). It thus appears that there is legitimate cause for concern about this type of erotic material.

The effects of erotic stimuli on behavior are far from being completely understood. It is clear, however, that the experimental approach will play a vital role in helping to answer the many questions that remain.

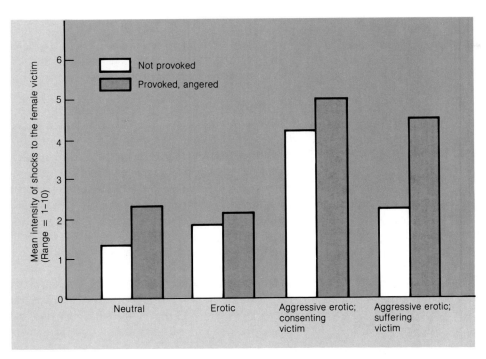

FIGURE 10.8 *Exposure to an aggressive erotic film in which the female victim did not appear to suffer enhanced later aggression against a female accomplice by both angry and nonangry male subjects. In contrast, exposure to an aggressive erotic film in which the victim seemed to suffer as a result of an attack by two males enhanced later aggression only by angry individuals. The erotic film with no violent content failed to increase later aggression. These findings raise serious concerns about the potential effects of violent pornography. (Data from Donnerstein and Berkowitz, 1981.)*

SEX, CULTURE, AND RELATIONSHIPS

The expression of our sexuality is heavily influenced by the cultural, social, and relationship contexts in which we find ourselves. These contexts confer on sex much of its psychological meaning, and they also help to determine the forms that sexual expression takes. To understand sexuality from a psychological viewpoint, we must consider the social forces that shape our sexual attitudes and behavior.

Cultural influences on sexuality

We do not need to look far to appreciate the role of social factors in human sexuality. Compare your attitudes toward sex with your parents' and grandparents'. As we saw in our look at survey studies, many of our sex practices differ sharply from those of only a generation ago.

The role of cultural learning comes into even sharper focus when we go beyond our own culture and examine others. For example, childhood sexuality is frowned upon and suppressed in our society, whereas in some other cultures it is not only permitted but encouraged. In the Marquesas Islands in French Polynesia, for example, families sleep together in one room, and children have ample opportunity to observe sexual activity. When a baby boy is distressed, Marquesan parents may masturbate the child. Both boys and girls begin to masturbate at age 2 or 3, and most of them engage in casual homosexual contacts during their youth. When they reach adolescence, an adult of the opposite sex carefully instructs them in sexual techniques by having intercourse with them (Suggs, 1962).

While Americans are clearly not as sexually permissive as the Marquesans, we are nowhere near as repressive as the inhabitants of an island off the coast of Ireland. Sex is a taboo topic among these people, and nudity is abhorred. Only infants are allowed to be completely naked, and adults feel embarrassed even if they are seen barefoot. The sexes are separated from early childhood until marriage, which typically occurs in the mid-thirties for males and in the mid-twenties for females. Sexual jokes are unknown in this society, and

sexual anxiety and revulsion are so intense that dogs and other animals are customarily beaten if they are caught licking their genitals. In contrast to Marquesan women, who customarily experience orgasm in sexual interactions, sexual climaxes among these Irish women are virtually unknown (Messenger, 1971).

Thus, what is considered proper, moral, desirable, and normal varies enormously from culture to culture. Moreover, while each society has standards of conduct that are often enforced by moral and legal sanctions, there are also important differences within cultures in what is viewed as appropriate sexual expression. For example, while our society now allows women a more active role in initiating sexual activity, many men feel threatened when women do so.

Sex, love, and intimacy

We all participate in a range of social relationships. Some of these relationships are fairly casual and impersonal. Others, such as friendships, are more personal and typically involve communication of feelings, mutual concern, and caring. Our most intense interpersonal relationships are those that we term *intimate*. Intimate relationships are most likely to involve strong emotional bonds, including romantic love, a major sharing of time and material goods, and perhaps sex. But sexual interactions may occur in virtually any kind of relationship, from casual to intimate.

Sexual behavior can fulfill many functions and satisfy many needs. Some of these are direct and self-evident, such as reproduction and physical pleasure. But sexuality also plays other roles that are clearly psychological rather than biological. Sex can be a means of expressing and receiving love and of satisfying dependency needs. As a highly prized commodity, sex can be used to obtain valued social outcomes, such as attention, acceptance, popularity, and a favored social position. It can serve as a defense against loneliness and as a means of bolstering self-esteem.

In our society, the concepts of love, marriage, and sex are closely intertwined. But it is increasingly clear that social values and behaviors are changing, and that people are less committed to formal and permanent relationships (Allgeier and McCormick, 1983). The divorce rate has climbed steadily, and today a third of all first marriages and half of all remarriages end in divorce. Moreover, there is an increasing willingness to experience sexual relationships in ways that were once considered taboo. For example, in the 1950s, only about 5 percent of college women and 20 percent of college men approved of premarital sex for both sexes. By the 1980s, those percentages had climbed to 60–80 percent for both sexes (Brehm, 1985).

Cohabitation (unmarried people living together) is also on the increase. About 2.2 million unmarried men and women live together in the United States (U.S. Bureau of the Census, 1979). One survey indicated that perhaps 25 percent of all college students have tried cohabitation, and another 50 percent are willing to do so given the right partner (Macklin, 1978). The reasons given for cohabitation are many. They include convenience, sexual fulfillment, wariness about the formal commitment implied by marriage, escape from loneliness and insecurity, and the belief that cohabitation will serve as a kind of training ground for a successful future marriage (Geer and others, 1984). This final goal may or may not be attained. In a recent survey of 287 couples who had been married for 1 to 2 years, the 72 percent who had lived together prior to marriage actually indicated lower levels of marital satisfaction than did those couples who had not cohabitated, and the wives who had lived with their husbands prior to marriage reported poorer couple communication (Demaris and Leslie, 1984).

As to the link between love and sex, the picture is less clear. Contrary to popular belief, young people have not accepted "sex for its own sake" in a wholesale fashion. There is evidence, however, that the traditional "double standard"—that sex without love is more appropriate for males than for females—still exists, even among young people (Rosen and Hall, 1984). Females still believe more strongly than males that an emotional bond is an important precondition for having sexual relations, and they are more likely to label the relationship in which they have their first sexual relations as a close one (Hatfield, 1983).

The "free love" morality that emerged in the 1960s seems to have been replaced by a search for a new morality of responsible sexual conduct in which people are not exploited or hurt but are free to explore a range of relationship styles to discover the type and depth of

intimacy that is optimal for them. There is also an increasing emphasis on **equity** in intimate relationships—that is, an equal emphasis on both partners' needs (Kelley, 1983). Couples are now more likely to focus on the intellectual, emotional, and career needs of the woman as well as the man. But the equity goal has not yet been widely achieved. In fact, in one survey of more than 50,000 young adults, only about half the people in love relationships felt that equal love was being shared by the male and the female. In the inequitable relationships, it was usually the woman who felt that she was giving more love than she was receiving. Men and women who were in equitable relationships expressed the greatest happiness (Shaver and Freedman, 1976).

For most people, sexual desires are part of the experience of passionate love. In Frontier 10.1, we examine recent psychological theorizing and research about this intense emotional experience.

SEXUALITY THROUGH THE LIFE SPAN

Our discussion so far has centered on adult sexual relationships. Because the years from adolescence through middle age are the peak times for engaging in sexual behavior, we (as well as sex researchers) tend to forget that sexual motivation and behavior occur across the entire life span, from infancy through old age.

Childhood sexuality

Modern recognition of childhood sexuality is largely due to the influence of Sigmund Freud. Freud's theory that children have sexual wishes and fantasies shocked the Victorian society of the late 1800s, which regarded

PASSIONATE LOVE

Perhaps the most exciting and consuming emotion that we can experience is romantic or passionate love (see Figure 10.9). Its grandeur and mystery have been of abiding interest to poets, songwriters, novelists, and people in general down through the ages.

In contrast to feelings of liking or respect, which usually grow at a slower pace, passionate love can occur with startling suddenness. We find ourselves experiencing a depth of feeling that seems far beyond any other emotion. We ride an emotional roller coaster that ranges from ecstasy in the presence of the other person to heartsickness and longing when the person is absent. We can't seem to get our thoughts off our beloved. Sexual desires and fantasies are a common part of this state of passionate love.

FIGURE 10.9 *Passionate or romantic love has in recent years become the subject of both research and theory.*

Because of the strong emotional aspect of passionate love, its causes, components, and course of development and decline have been addressed by a number of theorists (Berscheid, 1984; Mandler, 1984; Walster and Walster, 1978). In line with our analysis of emotion in Chapter 9, these attempts to understand love have focused on the interaction of cognitive and physiological arousal components. According to these viewpoints, we experience passionate love because our culture has taught us to label strong physiological arousal as "love" under certain conditions.

We grow up in a culture that believes in the concept of love, and we are exposed to love themes from childhood on. Our fairy tales contain many stories in which women meet Prince Charming, fall in love, get married, and live happily ever after. Movies, novels, and soap operas reinforce this fairy-tale scenario. By adolescence, many of us are eagerly awaiting the glories of love ourselves. There is research evidence that the more a person thinks about love, the more likely that she or he is to have the experience (Tesser and Paulhus, 1976).

In addition to beliefs and expectations about love, the other two requirements for passionate love are the presence of someone to love and the experiencing of strong physiological arousal. If we experience high arousal in the presence of someone whom we appraise as attractive and desirable, we may well conclude that we are "falling in love." Once we label our feelings as love, we become more attentive to features that make the other person "lovable."

This approach to understanding love has some interesting implications. One is that emotional arousal that occurs for some other reason could in some instances be misinterpreted as love. This phenomenon is known as *transfer of excitation* (Zillmann, 1983). The key requirement of such transfer, however, is that the arousal be attributed at least in part to the presence of the romantic other. There is research evidence to support this idea.

In one experiment, some of the subjects were aroused by being startled. First, they were seated in a dental chair (which would already be arousing for most of us). Then they were suddenly startled by a loud crashing noise accompanied by a sudden backward tilting of the chair. Both male and female subjects who were aroused in this fashion subsequently rated the experimenter as more attractive and likeable than did nonstartled subjects. But this occurred only when the experimenter was of the opposite sex and therefore a suitable target for the feelings (Dienstbier, 1969). In another experiment, half the male subjects were aroused by engaging in physical exercise while they watched a videotape of a young woman. The other subjects watched the same videotape without exercising. Within each of these conditions, half the men were told that they would meet the woman later, while the others were told that they would not. All the subjects then rated the woman on a number of factors, including how much they were romantically attracted to her. Ratings of romantic attraction were highest when the males were aroused by exercise but did not link their arousal to that source, and when they expected to meet the woman (White and Kight, 1984). While the feelings that were increased in these studies fall far short of passionate love, they do suggest the possibility that transfer and relabeling of arousal can occur.

The *cognitive-arousal theory of love* seems able to account for a number of common observations and

FIGURE 10.10 *The blossoming and decline of passionate love. Current theories of passionate love emphasize relationships among physiological, cognitive, cultural, and stimulus factors. One mechanism proposed to account for the transitory nature of passionate love is the opponent-processes response, which, over time, dampens the intense passion of the earlier stage, resulting in a "warm afterglow" of contentment and affection.*

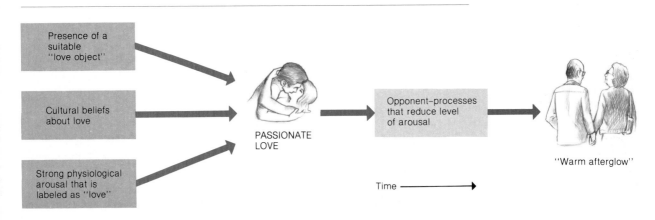

experiences. For example, people sometimes experience a rapid alteration between intense love and hatred. This shift may occur when the high arousal is suddenly relabeled because of something that happens in the relationship. As another example, people's feelings of love sometimes increase when the other person plays hard-to-get or even rejects the lover. This may occur because frustration increases arousal, which is then mislabeled as even more intense love than before.

Passionate love can be a rather fleeting phenomenon, as noted by a sixteenth-century sage, who observed, "the history of a love affair is the drama of its fight against time" (cited in Berscheid, 1983). It seems to have a sudden onset, but, in contrast to milder positive feelings such as liking, the stability of passionate love seems distressingly fragile. Research on the course of romantic love over time in American marriages suggests that the best most couples can hope for after a number of years is a "warm afterglow," contentment, and affection (Blood and Blood, 1978). Why should this be?

One possible explanation is offered by the opponent-process theories discussed in Frontier 9.2 (page 343). Opponent-process theory holds that, because of the body's overwhelming need to maintain homeostasis, emotional states are balanced out by an opposing feeling that becomes stronger over time. In the case of passionate love, this implies that with repeated exposures to the object of passion, the opponent processes should begin to dampen the original feelings of intense love, joy, and euphoria so that interaction with the loved person comes to be associated with the "cooler" feelings of contentment and comfort (see Figure 10.10).

It follows from what we know about the course of passionate love that we should relish and enjoy it while it lasts but that if a love relationship is to endure, it needs a more stable foundation than passion alone. The footings of this foundation seem to be other determinants of interpersonal attraction. In one study of over 200 college students who proclaimed themselves to be in love, about half the couples had broken up after 2 years. Those who had broken up said the relationships had failed because of dissimilar interests, values, attitudes, or levels of intelligence (Hill and others, 1976). These are all elements that predict liking and friendship (Baron and Byrne, 1984). It thus appears that genuine friendship may be the ultimate secret of a love relationship that endures.

---

childhood as an "age of innocence." The suggestion that young children have sexual desires was repulsive to many people in a society that was none too comfortable even with adult sexuality.

There is little doubt that children have the capacity for sexual arousal from an early age and that they engage in behaviors that closely resemble adult sexual behavior. But the critical issue is the *meaning* that such feelings and behaviors have for them. At this point, we know more about what children do sexually than about why they are doing it. Because children have difficulty communicating such meanings to us, we tend to project our own adult meanings and interpretations onto the child's behavior, and this may result in false conclusions.

Male children can have erections shortly after birth. Erection can be a reflexive response to a variety of stimuli, including those accompanying feeding, fullness of the bladder, and urination. By 6 months of age, both male and female children appear capable of having orgasms through genital stimulation (although boys are not yet capable of ejaculation). The behavioral manifestations and physiological responses that occur in children are so similar to adult orgasms that there can be no doubt of their sexual nature (Katchadourian and Lunde, 1979).

Self-exploration and self-stimulation are the young child's most common forms of sex play (see Figure 10.11). From the first year of life, males seem to be more actively involved in sex play than females are. Beginning at age 2 or 3, sexual exploration may be extended to relationships with other children. Sporadic genital exploration and manipulation are common for many children, and curiosity seems to be the major motivator. In Kinsey's data, the peak age for sex play among girls was 9, when 14 percent engaged in some form of sex play. For males the peak age was 12, when 39 percent did so. At nearly all preadolescent ages, sex play was more commonly carried out with same-sex companions. Again, however, we must caution against interpreting such behavior, even when orgasm is involved, as being psychologically similar to adult homosexuality.

Children frequently experience intense curiosity about sexual matters. Unfortunately, many parents are reluctant to deal with the child's curiosity, either because they are uncomfortable with the topic or because they feel they do not know the answers. The results of one large survey study showed that only 8 percent of fathers and 15 percent of mothers had ever discussed intercourse with their children (Roberts and others, 1978). Unfortunately, parental discomfort communi-

cates negative attitudes about sexuality to children, and they are left to their own devices in satisfying their curiosity. Often, this involves inaccurate information received from peers.

Development of gender identity

An important developmental milestone that we take for granted because, in most cases, it appears to occur so "naturally" is the establishment of gender identity, our conception of ourself as male or female. Gender identity is psychosocial rather than physical in nature—that is, a person may be a male or female physically or anatomically yet have the gender identity of the opposite sex. Most often, of course, physical sex and gender identity are the same, but because the development of gender identity is based on complex interactions between biological and psychological factors, anatomical

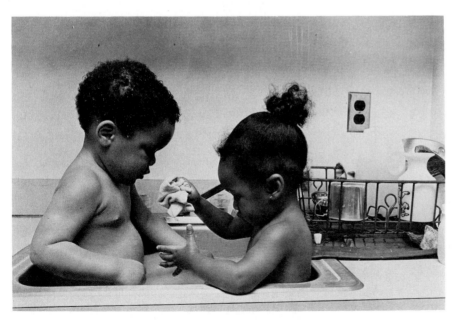

FIGURE 10.11 *Their natural curiosity leads young children to explore each others' bodies in sex play and may include genital inspection.*

sexual characteristics are not the sole determinant of gender identity.

Whether a fetus develops the sexual anatomy of a male or a female depends on the action of hormones. Those of us who develop into males exhibit a genetically triggered secretion of male sex hormones called **androgens** about six weeks after conception. If these hormones were not secreted, we would all develop the female genital system, regardless of our other genes. Sometimes, hormonal accidents disturb this developmental sequence, and a genetic male may fail to develop male sex organs, or a genetic female may develop genitals that appear male. This may strike you as next to impossible, since we tend to think of males and females as being quite different anatomically. Actually, however, the male and female genitals are remarkably similar in their structure and physiology, especially at early stages of development (see Figure 10.12).

Some researchers believe that fetal sex hormone secretions affect brain development as well as the development of sex organs. There is increasing evidence of sex differences in brain functioning, and it may be that such differences underlie some of the sex differences in behavior—for example, in aggression and in the ability

to accurately perceive and convey emotional expression (Hoyenga and Hoyenga, 1984). The influence of hormones on sexual development begins in the womb and continues throughout life. Their effects are especially evident at puberty, when sex hormones produce marked changes in our bodies. To a lesser extent than in animals, hormones also influence sexual motivation and activity. In general, the links between hormones and sexual behavior are stronger in males than in females (Bancroft, 1984).

Physical development, though obviously crucial, is not the only factor that determines gender identity. The moment the baby's sex is labeled at birth, social influences also become enormously important. From the first pink or blue blanket, the assigned gender of the child affects how others respond to it. Adults selectively reinforce certain behaviors and have many ways of reminding the child that it should behave in certain ways because it is a male or a female (see Figure 10.13). These two sets of factors—biological and psychosocial—continually reinforce one another (Money and Ehrhardt, 1972). In the normal course of development, the individual acquires a stable and consistent self-concept and a body image of maleness or femaleness.

FIGURE 10.12 *Genetically programmed secretions of the male sex hormone androgen begin the process of sexual differentiation shortly after conception. After several months of fetal development, the structural similarities in the developing male and female genitals are still quite apparent. The bulb-shaped structure on the top will become the head of the penis (glans penis) in males and the clitoris (glans clitoris) in females.*

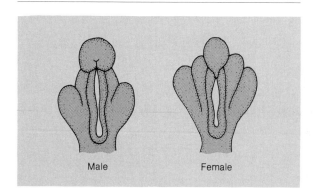

Male   Female

TRANSSEXUALISM: REVERSED GENDER IDENTITY

Freud said that "anatomy is destiny," but this is not always the case. For some individuals the process of gender identity does not proceed in a normal fashion. **Transsexuals** are people whose biological features and gender identity do not match. Transsexualism may occur in either sex, but the incidence is about eight times higher in anatomical males than in females (Levine and Lothstein, 1981).

Most male transsexuals do not simply want to act like women; they are convinced that they *are* women imprisoned in a man's body by a cruel trick of nature. The same is true of the female transsexuals. Many transsexuals yearn to be loved by a person of the opposite gender identity, but they are thwarted by the fact that they have identical sex organs and do not want to involve themselves in "homosexual" relationships (Geer and others, 1984).

What causes transsexualism, and what can be done to help such people? It appears that both biological and social factors may be involved in the development of this reversal of gender identity. Some theorists suggest that social learning is involved. For example, a close attachment and identification with the parent of the opposite sex, together with possible rewarding of opposite-sex behavior by the parent, may contribute to difficulties in establishing the appropriate gender identity (Green, 1974). Given the evidence that now exists, many experts believe that transsexualism results from some not-yet-understood interaction of social and biological factors (Diamond and Karlen, 1980).

If the factors that contribute to transsexualism are difficult to determine, so is the question of what can be done to help such people. Attempts to change gender identity through traditional psychodynamic psychotherapy have had only limited success, but several successful outcomes have been reported using a combination of behavioral techniques aimed at social skills training and modification of sexual fantasies and arousal patterns so that these become more consistent with the person's biological sex (Barlow and others, 1979).

An alternative to changing gender identity is to change sexual anatomy. This may be accomplished through a costly and time-consuming combination of hormone treatments to stimulate the external physical characteristics of the opposite sex (for example, to increase or decrease body hair, breast size, and muscle definition) and surgical procedures in which the sex organs are changed (see Figure 10.14).

What are the effects of sex-change procedures? This question is hard to answer because none of the outcome studies has had control groups of transsexuals who wanted but were not given the sex-change procedures. The data from existing studies suggest that, while few transsexuals regret having undergone the changes, only modest gains, if any, occur on objective measures of psychological, occupational, and interper-

FIGURE 10.13 *In subtle—and not so subtle—ways, culture influences and reinforces emerging gender identity. The little girl has already entered the world of the beauty pageant; the boy's activity calls for quite different behavior.*

FIGURE 10.14 *In one highly publicized hormonal and surgical sex-change treatment, transsexual James Morris became Jan Morris.*

sonal adjustment (Hunt and Hampson, 1980; Meyer and Reter, 1979). Although these data are far from conclusive, there have already been reactions to the modest results obtained thus far. In 1979, Johns Hopkins Hospital, a leading center for transsexual surgery, stopped performing the sex-change procedures. The number of operations performed at other medical centers seems to be on the decline (Griffitt and Hatfield, 1985).

Sex and aging

Just as people in the early years of life have traditionally been seen as sexually undeveloped, those in the later periods of life have been viewed as sexually depleted. Both views are wrong.

Traditional attitudes toward sexuality in the elderly have begun to change as society has become more attentive to this segment of our population (see Figure 10.15). People now live longer, are healthier and more active, and engage in athletics and other activities that were once seen as inappropriate or impossible for them. There are, however, both physiological and psychological factors that affect sexual responsiveness in older people.

CHANGES IN MALE SEXUALITY

Males reach their peak of sexual capacity (though not necessarily sexual enjoyment) in their late teens, when the male sex hormone testosterone is secreted in peak quantities. Thereafter, physical sexual capacity gradually declines. Men in their twenties and thirties can experience orgasm several times a day with short recovery periods. They get erections quickly, their orgasmic sensations are intense and localized, and semen leaves the penis with considerable force.

Sexual capabilities typically begin to decline for men in their forties. They may require longer and more intense stimulation for orgasm, and orgasmic sensations become less intense and more diffuse. By their late forties, men may require 8 to 24 hours after orgasm before another erection is possible. Some men in their sixties find that if they lose their erection before orgasm, they cannot become erect again for 12 to 24 hours. With age, the force with which semen is propelled from the penis also declines. Levels of sexual tension and the incidence of masturbation are lower for men over 60. It is important to note, however, that this could be caused, in part, by the sexual attitudes, values, and expectations of their generation. Because of different socializing influences, today's 20-year-old male may be far different when *he* is 60.

Age-related changes in sexual capacity do not necessarily decrease sexual pleasure. In fact, they may actually increase satisfaction. For example, being slower to ejaculate may allow men to prolong sexual pleasure for themselves and their partners. Social and psychological factors such as lowered expectations, life stress, and difficulty in finding desirable partners probably take a greater toll on the sexual pleasure of aging males than their diminished physical capabilities do. Masters and Johnson (1966) concluded that the most important factor in maintaining sexual capacity is the frequency and consistency with which men have had orgasms in their younger years. Whether these orgasms occurred through heterosexual, homosexual, or masturbatory activities did not seem to matter. Factors that seem to decrease sexual responsiveness in men over 40 include boredom, preoccupation with their career, fatigue, excessive eating and drinking, fear of sexual failure, and negative emotional responses brought about by their diminished sexual capacity.

FIGURE 10.15 *Sexuality among the elderly is becoming increasingly recognized and accepted.*

CHANGES IN FEMALE SEXUALITY

For women, sexual responsiveness as defined by frequency of orgasm tends to peak during the late thirties and early forties (Jones and others, 1977). Most women experience **menopause** (the end of menstruation) and its associated hormonal changes between the ages of 46 and 50, after which there are marked changes in the sex organs and in physiological responses to sexual stimulation. Clitoral responsiveness remains virtually unchanged, but the vaginal walls become thinner and less elastic. These changes are responsible for many of the sexual problems older women experience, such as irritation of the vagina, urethra, and bladder. Nevertheless, postmenopausal women are completely capable of orgasmic intercourse, although vaginal lubrication takes longer, the orgasmic phase is shorter, and about half as many vaginal contractions occur as in younger women.

After menopause, some women experience a decline in sexual interest and capacity, but others continue or even increase the frequency of their orgasmic experiences. Although individual differences in hormonal changes undoubtedly play a major role in some cases, psychological factors are probably most important. Women who believe that their sexuality is (or should be) over, who suffer a loss of self-esteem because of advancing age, or who have an aging or unresponsive mate may very well lose interest in sex. On the other hand, psychological factors that may increase sexual desire are freedom from fears of pregnancy, decreased family responsibilities as children leave home, and a desire to relive or recapture earlier sexual delights. Regular and fairly frequent intercourse is also likely to contribute to a continuing desire and capacity for sexual enjoyment.

The increasing acceptance of sexuality in the aged can have positive consequences, but it is important to recognize that there are individual differences in sexual interest during old age. More liberal attitudes and expectations about sexuality among the aged may free some of the elderly to enjoy sex, but they may also place an unwelcome burden on those who are not so inclined. It is important that all people, including the elderly, have the freedom to make their own decisions about the nature and extent of their sexual involvement.

SEXUAL DYSFUNCTION

Sex may be perfectly natural, but for most people it is not naturally perfect. Virtually everyone's ability to achieve high levels of arousal, to experience intense orgasms, and to give sexual pleasure fluctuates from time to time. Some people, however, experience difficulties in sexual performance or enjoyment to such an extent that they are said to suffer from a **sexual dysfunction**. Here again, we must realize that what is termed "dysfunction" is relative to what is considered normal or appropriate in a given society at a given time. In our culture today, a woman who cannot experience orgasm would be viewed as having a dysfunction. But only a century ago, in our own society, a

---

TABLE 10.4 VARIETIES OF SEXUAL DYSFUNCTION

MALE DYSFUNCTION

Erectile dysfunction (impotence). Inability to have an erection or to maintain one. *Primary erectile dysfunction* is diagnosed by Masters and Johnson (1970) when a man has never been able to have intercourse; *secondary erectile dysfunction* exists where a man has erection problems in at least 25 percent of his sexual encounters.

Premature ejaculation. Consistent inability to control or postpone ejaculation long enough to experience or share sexual enjoyment with his partner.

Retarded ejaculation. Inability to ejaculate despite a full erection and more than adequate stimulation.

FEMALE DYSFUNCTION

Orgasmic dysfunction. Inability to experience orgasm despite adequate sexual stimulation. Masters and Johnson differentiated between *primary orgasmic dysfunction,* in which the woman has never experienced orgasm, and *secondary orgasmic dysfunction,* in which the woman has experienced orgasm in the past, but no longer does so or can do so only infrequently.

Vaginismus. Spasm of the muscles in the lower third of vagina which so constricts the entrance to the vagina that penetration by the penis is difficult, painful, or impossible.

Painful intercourse (dyspareunia). The experiencing of pain during intercourse. The pain may be felt around the vaginal entrance and clitoris or deep in the pelvis. Vaginismus may be a cause of dyspareunia in some cases.

dominant medical view was that female orgasm was physically unhealthy (Diamond and Karlen, 1980).

The major types of male and female sexual dysfunction are presented in Table 10.4. In perhaps 10 to 20 percent of the cases, sexual dysfunction results directly from physical factors. For this reason, a thorough physical examination should always be the first step in dealing with such problems. In the majority of cases, however, psychological factors play the key role.

It is not really known how prevalent sexual dysfunction is, but there probably are few human disturbances that result in more silent suffering. Masters and Johnson (1970) estimated that half or more of all marriages experience sexual dysfunction of one kind or another. A more recent study—and an important one because it is based on couples who were not in sex therapy—tends to support Masters and Johnson's claim. A sample of 100 predominantly white, well-educated couples was studied. Eighty percent of the couples claimed to have happy or satisfying marriages, and about 85 percent stated that their sexual relations were moderately or very satisfying. And yet 40 percent of the men reported having problems with getting or maintaining an erection or with ejaculating too quickly. More than 60 percent of the women reported difficulties in becoming aroused or in reaching orgasm. Consistent with other studies, 15 percent of the women never achieved orgasm (Frank and others, 1978). We may safely conclude that even among well-functioning married couples, sexual relations are far from "naturally perfect."

Psychological factors in sexual dysfunction

The human sexual response is exceedingly complex. It has cognitive, motivational, emotional, and behavioral facets. Moreover, except for solitary masturbation, sex involves a relationship with another human being, and this introduces additional psychological factors into the picture. Personality, previous cultural conditioning, and past sexual history form an important backdrop to one's current sexual situation. It is no wonder, then, that the range of psychological factors that underlie both adequate and inadequate sexual functioning is enormous.

Perhaps the most common source of sexual difficulties are negative emotional responses such as anxiety, revulsion, guilt, or anger, all of which are incompatible with sexual arousal. Negative emotional responses may be triggered by the immediate situation, or they may have their origin in past traumatic sexual experiences, in faulty beliefs and attitudes, in relationship difficulties and conflicts with the partner, or in personality disturbances.

To describe how maladaptive emotional responses can contribute to sexual difficulties, let us apply the model of emotion that we discussed in Chapter 9 to sexual behavior (see Figure 10.16). Again, we have four primary components—eliciting stimuli, cognitive appraisal processes, physiological arousal, and expressive and instrumental behaviors.

We may represent the typical sequence as follows (see Figure 10.16). The first important appraisal process relates to the circumstances and the partner. If these are appraised in a positive manner—as desirable and sexually exciting—then this appraisal should trigger an emotional response that we perceive as sexual arousal. But previous social learning can affect the appraisal process in important ways. If one has learned that sex in general, certain sexual practices, or sex with certain partners is "dirty," immoral, or perverted, then the appraisal of the situation may produce guilt, revulsion, or anxiety instead of arousal. Likewise, if one is afraid of performing inadequately, or if the partner does not respond with enthusiasm, then the situation may be appraised as threatening instead of arousing. Such *performance anxiety* is a major contributor to sexual dysfunction in both sexes, but particularly in males (Masters and Johnson, 1970). Finally, problems in the relationship between the sex partners may create feelings of anger or resentment, which are surely incompatible with sexual arousal. Indeed, for some couples, the sexual relationship becomes one battleground in a larger war of nerves.

The next important set of appraisals involves the person's perception and interpretation of his or her own

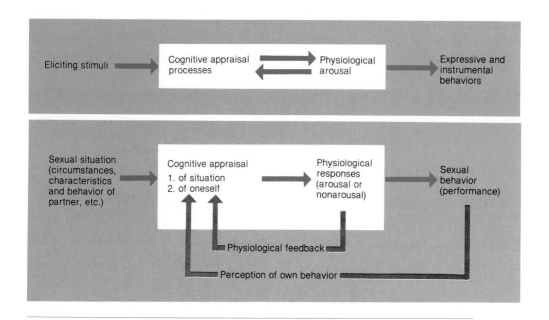

FIGURE 10.16 *Cognitive and emotional responses play a central role in sexual function. Negative emotional responses that interfere with effective functioning can result from negative appraisals of the situation, including the circumstances of the act and the characteristics and behaviors of one's partner. Negative appraisals of one's own arousal or of expected or perceived failures in performance also generate emotional responses that interfere with enjoyment and performance.*

physiological arousal. Ideally, people are sensitive to signs of physiological arousal and interpret them as sexual excitement, an appraisal that may result in even greater arousal. But some people are insensitive to sexual arousal cues, and they may not know when they are aroused. Women are more likely than men to be unaware of such cues because their arousal responses do not include anything as obvious as an erection. Failing to sense arousal cues, the person may conclude that he or she is not excited, thus limiting the potential for increased arousal.

In other cases, people may be tuned in to their bodily excitement, but they may have learned to label sexual arousal as bad or shameful. Or they may have a bad body image or be ashamed of certain aspects of their body's response (for example, lubrication in the woman). Negative appraisals of arousal may trigger negative emotions, such as anxiety or shame, that effectively shut down sexual excitement.

A third important set of appraisals involves our perception of our own behavior. Many people are self-conscious about how they are doing. They pay close attention to their own behavior and its apparent effects on their partner, and they evaluate their own performance. (Sex therapists refer to this as *spectatoring*.) If they perceive themselves as not performing or responding adequately, they appraise themselves negatively and become anxious and upset. These negative emotional responses may worsen their sexual performance still further.

The open discussion of sexual matters that has occurred in recent years has been a positive development in many ways. But, as a result, many men and women have adopted some rather demanding and, in some cases, unrealistic performance standards that contribute to negative appraisals. For example, some men feel that unless a woman experiences several orgasms during intercourse, they have somehow failed as a lover.

On the other hand, some women are troubled that they cannot have (or do not want) more than one orgasm, or they feel inadequate because they do not always achieve orgasm. Unrealistic standards can set people up for unnecessary perceptions of failure that can seriously affect their sexual adjustment. As one sex therapist has concluded:

It appears that the core ingredients in all of the categories [of dysfunction] are a high level of emotional distress induced by cognitive errors of evaluation, often coupled with cognitive errors of perception. The end product is an individual who approaches the job of sex (rather than the joy of sex) as a way to prove him/herself (rather than to enjoy him/herself)—certainly a very unsexy attitude. (Walen, 1980, p. 96)

Treatment of sexual dysfunction

The publication of Masters and Johnson's *Human Sexual Inadequacy* in 1970 had a major impact on the treatment of sexual dysfunction, and it created a wave of interest in sex therapy. Masters and Johnson described the treatment of 790 dysfunctional men and women. The treatment programs they described for each of the dysfunctions have been refined and embellished by other sex therapists (for example, Heiman and others, 1976; Kaplan, 1974; Zilbergeld, 1978).

The goals of these procedures are quite consistent with our analysis of the role that psychological factors play in dysfunction. For example, through sex education, therapists may try to modify the negative appraisals that can interfere with sexual functioning. Therapists also encourage open verbal and nonverbal communication between the partners. Specific homework assignments are given, to help couples learn to stimulate one another, to become more aware of their own sexual sensations, and to overcome fears and inhibitions. A kind of shaping procedure is used in which the couple moves gradually from nonthreatening sexual interactions like hugging toward more involved exchanges that terminate in intercourse. The aim is to reduce anxiety while increasing the amount of satisfaction the couple experiences.

In Masters and Johnson's approach, the couple, not the "patient," is usually the focus of treatment. The couple is seen together, often by a male and female therapist team, and they work in partnership to increase sexual satisfaction. For example, treatment of orgasmic dysfunction in women involves a strategy of attitude examination and graduated homework assignments. The first step involves an exploration of beliefs and, where necessary, attitudes about sex. If the woman is willing, she is instructed to begin exploring her body in private, focusing on the sensations that result, and to stimulate herself through masturbation. As she becomes more comfortable with her body and its stimulation, her partner begins to participate in these sessions and helps her to explore new sensations at her own pace and choosing. Much time is spent in "pleasuring" through kissing and tactual stimulation with no attempt being made to have intercourse. As the woman becomes more aware of and comfortable with arousal, the couple moves gradually toward full sexual relations. The female-on-top position is recommended because this position allows the woman greater control of the forms and varieties of stimulation she would like to experience. There is also a strong emphasis on the woman's clear communication of her reactions and desires to her partner.

Masters and Johnson reported very low rates of *failure* in treating sexual dysfunction. They stated that after an intensive two-week program of treatment, only 20 percent of their clients failed to improve their sexual functioning. More recently, other sex therapists who have used the same methods with less apparent success have criticized Masters and Johnson for not being clearer on exactly how they defined success and failure (Zilbergeld and Evans, 1980). Nevertheless, a fair conclusion seems to be that while sex therapy may be somewhat less effective in treating sexual dysfunction than we once thought, these techniques are still far superior to more traditional approaches, such as intensive psychotherapy (Geer and others, 1984).

ALTERNATIVE MODES OF SEXUALITY

Every society has rules, or *norms*, that regulate social behavior and help define the range of behaviors that are considered appropriate or "normal." People who violate those rules are regarded as atypical or deviant. In an area of behavior that is as value-laden as sexuality, society's responses to norm violations are bound to be strong.

Homosexuality

Until December 15, 1973, homosexuality was officially considered to be a form of mental illness. On that day, the trustees of the American Psychiatric Association voted unanimously to remove homosexuality from the psychiatric classification system—surely the quickest, most profound, and most widespread "cure" in the history of psychiatry.

Homosexuality was long considered to be a form of mental illness not only because this sexual orientation violates societal norms that regard heterosexual involvements as normal but also because the homosexual clients seen by psychotherapists were almost invariably unhappy and disturbed people. Mental health professionals tended to generalize their impressions of homosexual clients to homosexuals who were not in treatment. Wardell Pomeroy, one of Kinsey's co-workers, reached the following conclusion:

If my concept of homosexuality were developed from my practice, I would probably concur in thinking of it as an illness. I have seen no homosexual man or woman in that practice who was not troubled, emotionally upset, or neurotic. On the other hand, if my concept of marriage in the U.S. were based on my practice, I would have to conclude that marriages are all fraught with strife and conflict, and that heterosexuality is an illness. In my 20 years of research in the field of sex, I have seen many homosexuals who were happy, who were practicing and conscientious members of their community, and who were stable, productive, warm, relaxed, and efficient. Except for the fact that they were homosexual, they could be considered normal by any definition. (1969, p. 13)

Studies of homosexuals who are not in treatment tend to support Pomeroy's view. The incidence and types of psychological disturbance that exist among homosexuals tend to parallel those found among heterosexuals (Saghir and Robins, 1973). Some clinicians believe that psychological disturbance among homosexuals is often due to the social stigma connected with being homosexual rather than to something pathological in the nature of homosexuality itself (Diamond and Karlen, 1980).

The sexual behavior of homosexuals has been studied in depth by Masters and Johnson (1979). For 10 years they observed and compared the behaviors and physiological responses of male and female homosexual couples with those of heterosexual couples under laboratory conditions. They found no differences in the physiological response cycles of homosexuals and heterosexuals during sexual activity and orgasm. However, they concluded that, in many ways, homosexuals were more considerate and proficient lovers than were heterosexuals. The heterosexuals tended to rush past the preliminaries on their way toward the goal of orgasm. In contrast, homosexual couples took more time, engaged in more foreplay, communicated much more with their partners, and seemed to be more sensitive to each other's pleasure and needs.

HOMOSEXUAL LIFE STYLES

Not all people who engage in homosexual behavior are exclusively homosexual. Kinsey (1953) proposed a sexual orientation continuum that ranged from exclusively heterosexual behavior and interest to an exclusively homosexual orientation. In between these extremes are several categories of bisexuals whose behavior includes both homosexual and heterosexual interactions. Kinsey's surveys indicated that by age 55, about half his male subjects had had some type of homosexual contact. About 4 percent of Kinsey's white males were exclusively homosexual, and another 10 percent were primarily homosexual for at least 3 years between the ages of 16 and 65. The proportion of female homosexuals is about one-third to one-half as large as males, but about 28 percent of all women have a homosexual experience at some point in their lives, according to Kinsey.

Only about 20 percent of homosexuals openly display their orientation. Many others live double lives, concealing their sexual orientation from their parents, families, and co-workers (Weinberg and Williams, 1974). The proportion of homosexuals who are satisfied with their orientation seems to have increased as social attitudes toward homosexuality have become more liberal. In one study of homosexuals living in the permissive San Francisco gay community, only 5 percent of the homosexual women and 14 percent of the males indicated that they would like to be heterosexual (Bell and Weinberg, 1978). But other studies done in less permissive settings present a less positive picture of homosexual contentment and adjustment. In a sample of homosexual women studied in Germany, for example, one in four had a history of at least one suicide attempt (Schäfer, 1976).

There have been many attempts to understand why certain people become homosexuals, but no consistent pattern of biological, cognitive, psychodynamic, or learning factors has yet been shown to result in a homosexual life style. While there are many theories of homosexual development, none of them has received enough research support to command our attention here. We still have a great deal to learn about homosexuality, its causes, and its effects on people. The search for causes is complicated by the fact that homosexuality

does not appear to be a single or unitary behavior pattern. A highly significant 10-year study by Alan Bell and Martin Weinberg (1978) of the sex research institute founded by Kinsey at Indiana University suggests that there are at least five distinct patterns of homosexuality.

More than 1500 homosexual men and women living in the San Francisco Bay area were extensively interviewed by the Indiana research team. Seventy-one percent of the homosexuals could be classified as engaging in one of the following five life styles (see Table 10.5).

1. **Closed couples** were homosexual couples who lived together in stable relationships, much as if they were married. The partners rarely sought other partners, were happy with their homosexual orientation, and were warm, caring, and well-adjusted people. Closed couples were more common among females than among males (see Figure 10.17).

2. **Open couples** lived together but were less committed to one another. The partners frequently "cheated" on each other and sought other lovers. Though fairly well adjusted, they were less happy and more lonely than closed couples.

3. **Functionals** were the "swinging singles" of the homosexual scene. They organized their lives around sexual experiences and spent much of their time cruising for new partners. Some had had more than 1000 different partners. They were exuberant and happy people who were nearly as well adjusted as the closed couples.

4. **Dysfunctionals** were homosexuals who seemed to be unhappy and tormented people. They were poorly adjusted, felt sexually and interpersonally inadequate, and often regretted being homosexual. They were the type of homosexual that formerly led

TABLE 10.5   FIVE MAJOR HOMOSEXUAL LIFE STYLES

LIFE STYLE	MALES (PERCENT)	FEMALES (PERCENT)
Closed couples	10	28
Open couples	18	17
Functionals	15	10
Dysfunctionals	12	5
Asexuals	16	11
Other*	29	29

*This group was too diverse to be categorized.
Source: Data from Bell and Weinberg, 1978.

FIGURE 10.17 *Many homosexual couples establish deep, exclusive, and meaningful relationships. Closed couples appeared to be more common among females than among males in Bell and Weinberg's study.*

psychotherapists to conclude that homosexuality was a psychiatric disturbance.

5. **Asexuals** were people who had a low level of sexual activity, few partners, and no close relationships. Although their general adjustment was adequate, they described themselves as lonely.

Bell and Weinberg found little support for several common stereotypes about homosexuals. For example, most homosexuals were not easy to identify by their appearance. Moreover, many shared interests with heterosexuals and had social and sometimes sexual involvements with the opposite sex. One-third of the women and one-fifth of the males had been in at least one heterosexual marriage.

While attitudes toward homosexuality have liberalized in many segments of society, homosexuals (as well as some heterosexuals) face a new and serious biological threat. The lethal and presently incurable illness **acquired immune deficiency syndrome (AIDS)** has been linked to a number of specific subpopulations, one of which is male homosexuals. The viral disease results in a breakdown of the body's immune system, so that an AIDS sufferer is unable to fight off infections that would ordinarily produce only minor and temporary illnesses. Other people can be infected through contact with the semen or the blood of an AIDS victim

(Handsfield, 1984; Mavligit, 1984). Nearly 7,800 cases of AIDS were reported in the United States between 1981 and 1985, and 43 percent of its victims died within a year. More than 70 percent of the cases were male homosexuals (Centers for Disease Control, 1984).

The fear created by AIDS has affected heterosexuals and homosexuals alike. *Homophobia*, the fear of homosexuality, has been reinforced and intensified among heterosexuals. Many people have limited their contact with homosexuals, even to the point of refusing blood transfusions from potentially homosexual donors. (Blood banks are routinely testing blood samples for AIDS to protect recipients.) Rather than seeing them as the victims of the disease, many view homosexuals as its cause. For a while, some bus drivers in San Francisco refused to handle change from male riders or began to wear rubber gloves.

Homosexuals, too, have reacted to AIDS. Many of them are confining their sexual activity to a small circle of other men or to a single partner (Morin and Batchelor, 1984). AIDS seems certain to have a lasting and dramatic effect on homosexual life styles. Since AIDS is also being transmitted among heterosexuals who have had no homosexual contact, similar precautionary measures are occurring among many heterosexuals.

Atypical sexual behaviors

Although homosexuality is far from being universally tolerated, other forms of sexual behavior are even less tolerated, perhaps because they seem more rare and atypical. An example is **fetishism**, in which an inanimate object rather than a person serves as a primary source of sexual arousal and gratification. The object may range from undergarments to articles with less apparent connection with sexuality, such as rubber boots. Most fetishists are males who conduct their activities in secret. They typically get into trouble only if they commit crimes to obtain the prized object (see Figure 10.18).

Transvestites are people who like to dress in the

clothing of the opposite sex. Unlike transsexuals, transvestites retain the appropriate gender identity, but they achieve significant gratification in their cross-dressing.

Exhibitionists are males who achieve gratification by exposing their genitals to strangers in public.

FIGURE 10.18 *A fetishist who became known as the "Seattle Shoe Bandit" attacked women on the street and stole a single shoe from each. Here, a police officer surveys some of the shoes found in the fetishist's apartment.*

"You don't often see a real silk lining, these days. . . ."

(DRAWING BY SPENCER; © PUNCH/ROTHCO.)

FIGURE 10.19 *Exhibitionists achieve their gratification from the shocked reactions of observers. A response like this provides no gratification.*

Women and children are their usual targets, and their gratification comes from the shock, fear, disgust, or negative reactions they cause. Some exhibitionists experience orgasm and ejaculate when the shocked reaction occurs. Women who remain calm can usually spoil the exhibitionist's pleasure (see Figure 10.19).

Sadomasochism in the sexual sense involves the achievement of sexual satisfaction by inflicting pain on another (sadism) or by being subjected to pain (masochism). Although innocent people are occasionally harmed by sexual sadists, sadists and the more numerous masochists typically form voluntary relationships with each other. Usually, each person consistently occupies the same role; they generally do not take turns inflicting or suffering pain.

There are many ways in which a person can deviate from conventional sexual norms, and many ways in which today's norms differ from those of previous generations. Clearly, not all sexual behavior is equally adaptive, socially desirable, healthy, and moral. However, society should make judgments about sexuality with great care. History has shown how easy it is to inflict unnecessary pain and hardship on people whose acts harm neither themselves nor others and whose only real offense is that they are different.

SEXUAL VICTIMIZATION

In most sexual relations, the partners participate more or less willingly. Sometimes, however, one of the participants is either an unwilling victim or too young, uninformed, or psychologically vulnerable to give legitimate consent. Two of the most obvious examples of sexual victimization are rape and child molestation.

Rape

Forcible rape is a violent and degrading act in which sexual relations are forced upon an unwilling victim. It is estimated that a woman is forcibly raped in the United States nearly every second of every day. In more than half of all reports of rape, the victim is threatened with a weapon (Hursch, 1978). Probably no more than 15 to 20 percent of all rapes are reported to authorities.

Despite increasing attention to the plight of the rape victim, it is difficult for a person who has not been forcibly raped to fully comprehend its horrifying dimensions:

Rape can be the most terrifying event in a woman's life. The sexual act or acts performed are often intended to humiliate or degrade her: bottles, gun barrels, and sticks may be thrust into her vagina or anus. She may be compelled to swallow urine or perform fellatio with such force that she thinks she might strangle or suffocate; her breasts may be bitten or burned with cigarettes. In many instances, her hope is to save her life—not her chastity. Her terror may be so overwhelming that she urinates, defecates, or vomits. If she escapes without serious outward signs of injury, she may suffer vaginal tears or infections, contract venereal disease, or be impregnated. For months or years afterward, she may distrust others, change residences frequently, and sleep poorly. Her friends and family may blame or reject her. (National Institute of Law Enforcement and Criminal Justice, 1978, p. 15)

The aftermath of rape can be nearly as traumatic as the incident itself (see Figure 10.20). Many victims experience what has been termed the **rape trauma syndrome** (Burgess and Holstrom, 1974). The initial reaction of most women is a strong display of fear, anxiety, self-blame, or anger. Others mask their inner turmoil with a controlled external appearance. For weeks afterward, many victims experience physical reactions like nausea, sleeplessness, headaches, and bodily pains, some of which may be related to the assault (Ruch and Chandler, 1983). Then begins a *reorganization* phase, in which feelings of nervousness and fear of retaliation by the rapist continue. Many victims change their place of residence but continue to have nightmares and to be frightened when they are alone, outdoors, or in crowds. Victims frequently report a decreased enjoyment of sexual activity long after the rape, even when their ability to have orgasms is not affected (Holmes and St. Lawrence, 1983; Sales and others, 1984).

Some men as well as women experience the humiliation, violence, and powerlessness of rape. Rape of prison inmates is a serious problem. Prison rapists typically do not regard the rapes as homosexual acts, but as a means of achieving sexual release and of establishing dominance. Male rape victims often are subjected to anal intercourse during brutal gang assaults, or, for protection, they may become the "old lady" of a dominant male inmate.

FIGURE 10.20 *The experience of being forcibly raped is not only terrifying when it occurs but can also have traumatic long-term effects on a woman.*

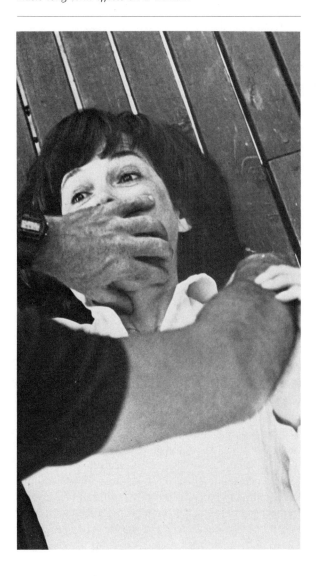

RAPISTS

Many people think of rape as being the expression of a rapist's uncontrollable sex drive. In reality, however, the dynamics of rape probably have more to do with power and aggression than with sexual needs. About half of all convicted rapists are married, and masturbation is certainly an alternative means of sexual release. And yet these men sexually assault unwilling victims. Why?

Many authorities believe that the primary motivation of many rapists is the need to degrade and impose their will on the woman. Violence, power, and triumph are their main goal (Groth, 1979). A smaller percentage of rapes are carried out primarily for sexual gratification. Many of these sexually oriented rapists have a callous and amoral disregard for the consequences to the victim. In other cases, sex-oriented rapes occur because of an alcohol- or drug-induced release of inhibitions (Gebhard and others, 1965).

Contrary to popular belief, most convicted rapists are not "mentally ill" in other areas of functioning, although many are impulsive and aggressive (Rada, 1978). They tend to be between 16 and 24 years of age and to come from lower socioeconomic backgrounds. They also tend to be highly active sexually and to have many sexual fantasies that are often aggressive in nature. About half of those who are prosecuted have a history of prior sexual offenses.

Most rapes that result in criminal prosecution are committed by strangers, but the use of force by males may be more common even in dating relationships than we would care to believe. For example, a survey of 282 Purdue University women revealed that during the previous year, more than half of them had experienced male sexual aggression in which forcible efforts were made by their dates to kiss them, to fondle their breasts or genitals, or to have intercourse with them. Although actual threats or violence were seldom employed by the males, about one-third of the forcible attempts at intercourse were successful, even though the women maintained that they did not want to have sex (Kanin and Parcell, 1977). In another study involving college males, 25 percent of those interviewed indicated that, on at least one occasion, they had forced sex on an actively protesting woman (Gross, 1978).

Child molestation

Even more powerless than adult women are young children who are sexually victimized. While most rapes that result in prosecution are committed by strangers, child molesters tend to be acquaintances and family members. In many instances the child is victimized by someone with whom he or she has a close emotional bond. In such relationships, the child is highly vulnerable.

The true incidence of sexual contacts between children and adults is unknown. In surveys asking about childhood sexual experiences, about 30 percent of the respondents reported childhood sexual experiences with adults (Gagnon, 1965; Landis, 1956). It is estimated that about 5000 children are sexually abused each week in the United States, and as many as 4000 children die annually as a result of violent sexual abuse.

In the majority of cases, the abuse consists of manual or oral-genital stimulation. In some cases, however, genital or anal intercourse occurs. Child molestation, particularly between parents and children, was once thought to be a lower social class phenomenon, but more recent findings suggest that molestation occurs (but is less frequently reported) in middle- and upper-class families as well (Butler, 1978).

Our knowledge concerning the long-term effects of molestation is quite limited. Several studies have focused on women who were molested as children. In one of them, psychotherapy patients with a history of molestation were matched on age, education, and ethnic origin with a group of therapy patients who had no history of incest. The two groups did not differ on measures of general psychological adjustment, but the molested women reported significantly more sexual problems as adults (Meiselman, 1980).

In another, more extensive study, 30 women seeking therapy for problems related to childhood molestation were compared with a nonclinical group of women who had been molested as children but who were not seeking therapy and considered themselves well adjusted. A third group consisted of nonmolested women who were matched with the two molested groups in terms of age, marital status, and ethnicity.

The well-adjusted molested women did not differ from the nonmolested women on measures of psychological adjustment or sexual functioning. But the group of molested women who were in therapy was less well adjusted both psychologically and sexually. These women frequently reported difficulties in establishing close relationships with other people; they had a basic mistrust of intimate relationships. They also reported more sexual difficulties.

The molestation experiences of the clinical group differed from those of the better-adjusted molested women in several important ways. First, the women in therapy were far more likely to have been molested by their fathers or stepfathers rather than by family friends or neighbors. Perhaps this helps account for their later distrust of intimate relationships. Second, their molestation experiences tended to occur after age 12 and to elicit intense fear and guilt, whereas the nonclinical women had typically been molested at age 8 or 9 and had experienced less intense emotional reactions. These results suggest that the level of intimacy in the relationship between victim and molester and the age at which molestation occurs may have an important impact on the long-term effects of the experience (Tsai and others, 1979). The parents' reaction is also important, especially with younger children who may not really understand what happened and will take their cue from the way that their parents react.

The study of sexual behavior is an important psychological frontier not only because sexuality is a significant part of our lives but also because many basic psychological processes such as motivation and emotion, learning, cognition, attitude development and change, and physiological factors are involved in sexual behavior. The study of sexuality thus provides an opportunity to learn more about these basic processes.

STUDY OUTLINE

THREE APPROACHES TO THE STUDY OF SEXUALITY (p. 350)

1. The three main approaches to the study of human sexuality are the survey study, the observational approach, and the controlled experiment.

2. The first large-scale survey studies of sexual behavior were carried out by Alfred Kinsey and his associates. Comparison of the results of recent surveys with Kinsey's suggests that the greatest changes are increases in premarital sex and in oral-genital stimulation.

3. Two problems frequently encountered in sex surveys are self-selected and nonrepresentative samples, and possible distortions in self-reports of sexual behavior.

4. Masters and Johnson measured physiological responses during thousands of sexual episodes and reported a four-stage response pattern consisting of excitement, plateau, orgasm, and resolution. They also found no physiological differences between clitoral and vaginal orgasms.

5. Recent experimental studies have shown that women are as likely as men to be aroused by sexually explicit stimuli but that women are also likely to have more negative attitudes toward such stimuli. Experiments have also shown that exposure to nonviolent pornography seems to have no long-term effects on behavior but that the viewing of sexual violence may stimulate deviant sexual fantasies in men as well as increase males' aggression toward women.

SEX, CULTURE, AND RELATIONSHIPS (p. 360)

1. Culture plays a large part in how we express sexual drives and how we feel about sex. In our society, sex has traditionally been linked to romantic love and marriage, but today, divorce, premarital sex, and cohabitation are more common than they used to be. Although the double standard lives on, there is an increasing emphasis on equity in intimate relationships.

2. Recent theoretical attempts to understand passionate love have emphasized relationships among cognitive and physiological processes. The experiencing of strong arousal in the presence of a suitable person is viewed as the core of passionate love. The fact that

passionate love tends to cool to a "warm afterglow" over time has been explained in terms of the opponent-process theory. Factors that increase interpersonal attraction, such as similarity in attitudes and values, seem to increase the likelihood that love will endure.

SEXUALITY THROUGH THE LIFE SPAN (p. 361)

1. Although children seem to behave in ways that resemble adult sexual behavior, the psychological meaning of such behavior is not clear. Many children have an intense curiosity about sex, and self-stimulation and exploration of other children's bodies are common.

2. Gender identity is one's concept of being male or female. Its development involves the interaction of physiological and psychological factors. Transsexuals are people whose gender identity is inconsistent with their biological sex.

3. Although males' sexual capacity declines after age 40, psychological factors are probably more important than physical ones in the maintenance of an active sex life. Masters and Johnson found that the frequency of orgasm at younger ages is the best predictor of the maintenance of male sexual capacity in old age. In women, menopause brings hormonal and physical changes, but, again, psychological factors have a stronger influence on sexual functioning.

SEXUAL DYSFUNCTION (p. 370)

1. Premature ejaculation in men and failure to achieve orgasm in women are the most common forms of sexual dysfunction. Psychological factors play a key role in perhaps 80 percent of all cases. Negative emotional responses triggered by faulty beliefs, performance anxiety, or interpersonal conflicts can effectively undermine sexual enjoyment and functioning.

2. Current programs designed to treat sexual dysfunction include attempts to reduce negative emotions, to enhance sensitivity to arousal, to challenge self-defeating sexual attitudes, and to improve couple communication.

ALTERNATIVE MODES OF SEXUALITY (p. 374)

1. The most common alternative mode of sexuality is homosexuality. Homosexuals are no longer considered to be mentally ill, although society's reaction to their homosexuality may help create psychological problems. Kinsey found that a high percentage of males had one or more homosexual contacts during their lives, and he suggested a sexual orientation continuum ranging from exclusively heterosexual to exclusively homosexual.

2. No single pattern of causes for the development of homosexuality has been discovered. According to Bell and Weinberg, there are five basic homosexual life styles, and this may be one reason that no single pattern of causal factors has been found. Only about 20 percent of homosexuals openly display their sexual orientation.

3. Atypical sexual behaviors include fetishism, transvestism, exhibitionism, and sadomasochism. The majority of people who behave in these unusual ways are heterosexual males.

SEXUAL VICTIMIZATION (p. 378)

1. Rape is often an aggressive rather than a sexual act. Many rape victims go through a rape trauma syndrome characterized by fear, mistrust, sleep disturbances, residence changes, and subsequent sexual and relationship difficulties.

2. Coercive sexual advances on the part of males are frequently reported by female college students, and many college males report forcing sex on actively protesting women.

3. The long-term effects of child molestation appear to depend in part on the closeness of the relationship between molester and victim, the age of the victim, and the reaction of significant adults if the molestation is discovered. Relatively severe long-term effects on psychological well-being and sexual functioning can occur to victims of child molestation.

KEY TERMS AND CONCEPTS

excitement phase

plateau phase

orgasm

resolution phase

refractory period

equity

transfer of excitation

cognitive-arousal theory of love

androgen

transsexual

menopause

sexual dysfunction

erectile dysfunction (impotence)

orgasmic dysfunction

vaginismus

dyspareunia

spectatoring

closed couple

open couple

functionals

dysfunctionals

asexuals

acquired immune deficiency syndrome (AIDS)

fetishism

transvestism

exhibitionism

sadomasochism

rape trauma syndrome

SUGGESTED READINGS

CROOKS, R., and BAUR, K. (1980). *Our sexuality*. Menlo Park, Calif.: Benjamin/Cummings.

GEER, J., HEIMAN, J., and LEITENBERG, H. (1984). *Human sexuality*. Englewood Cliffs, N.J.: Prentice-Hall.

Both of these books provide excellent overviews of the entire field of human sexuality, offering in-depth coverage of topics discussed in this chapter and examining many additional subjects as well.

SECTION FIVE
DEVELOPMENTAL PROCESSES

CHAPTER ELEVEN: **LIFE SPAN DEVELOPMENT: THEORIES AND RESEARCH**

CHAPTER TWELVE: **BIOLOGICAL, COGNITIVE, AND SOCIAL CHANGES IN DEVELOPMENT**

CHAPTER ELEVEN

LIFE SPAN DEVELOPMENT: THEORIES AND RESEARCH

THE LIFE SPAN APPROACH
Factors in life span development
Basic developmental concepts
FRONTIER 11.1 PRACTICAL APPLICATIONS OF LIFE SPAN DEVELOPMENTAL THEORY
Research techniques for the study of development

LONGITUDINAL STUDIES OF DEVELOPMENT
The Terman Study
The New York Longitudinal Study
The Grant Study

PSYCHOLOGICAL PERSPECTIVES ON DEVELOPMENT
Freud's theory of psychosexual development
Erikson's psychosocial theory of personality development
Piaget's theory of cognitive development
Kohlberg's theory of moral development
Kübler-Ross's theory of death and dying

STUDY OUTLINE

KEY TERMS AND CONCEPTS

SUGGESTED READINGS

Andrea doesn't seem to do anything but think about boys.

Marian responds to any stressful situation by sucking her thumb.

Arthur notices that his reaction time is slower than it used to be, although he seems to be able to think just as clearly as before.

Frank can't decide on a career; he comes up with a new choice every day.

How would you interpret these statements? One important fact that you would need about Andrea, Marian, Arthur, and Frank would be how old each was. If Andrea were 4 and Marian were 13, you might decide that each of them ought to be looked at closely. On the other hand, if their ages were reversed, you would probably think that their behavior was pretty typical. Similarly, if Arthur were 19 and Frank were 35, these descriptions might suggest important problems. However, if their ages were 75 and 16, these descriptions would not sound a bit unusual.

We expect people to behave differently at different ages. Life is a dynamic process; changes occur in our social and psychological functions as well as in our biological processes. Developmental psychologists are interested in every subject dealt with in this book, but they look at all these topics primarily in terms of the highly predictable changes that occur in life. We devote two chapters to the topic of development because so much is happening in developmental research and because an understanding of the effects of development on behavior is so important in all fields of psychology.

THE LIFE SPAN APPROACH

Life span developmental psychology is concerned with describing and explaining the developmental processes as they occur naturally and as they are modified by the environment over the whole period of human life, from conception to death.

For a long time, developmental psychology focused on infancy and on the preschool years, though there was also some interest in development through adolescence. This emphasis is understandable because early infancy, childhood, and adolescence are times when the mutual influences of biology and environment are quite easy to see and comparatively easy to study. The interdependence of physical growth and behavior becomes less obvious during the long period between early adulthood and old age; as a result, their significance in the developmental scheme was ignored for many years.

The tradition of the life span approach has been around for at least 200 years. In 1777 a German philosopher-psychologist, J. N. Tetens, published a major book on human development from the life span perspective (Groffman, 1970), but the explosion of interest in the field did not come until the 1960s and 1970s. In

---

FIGURE 11.1 *These theoretical curves show the relative impact of several factors on life span development. In childhood, age-related factors are the most important. In adolescence, events of the historical period have their maximum effect and the impact of age-related factors declines. In old age, the importance of age-related factors increases, but unique life events are most influential.*

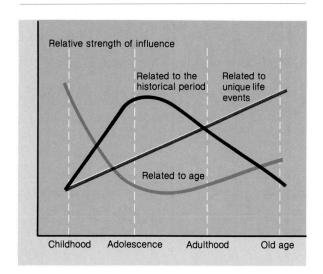

the 1980s we still consider this area of development beyond adolescence to be an exciting psychological frontier.

Factors in life span development

Development is influenced by a number of factors besides the person's chronological age (see Figure 11.1). **Age-related biological and sociological processes** are most important in childhood and extreme old age (see Figure 11.2), but are by no means absent at other stages of the life cycle. Age-related abilities seem to develop naturally as the person gets older; examples include motor skills like roller skating, cognitive skills like the ability to appreciate cause and effect relationships, and social behaviors like empathy and consideration for others.

History-related events such as war, depression, an economic boom, change in the roles of women and men, and school desegregation are thought to become more important in early adulthood. Even the number of other people who were born in the same year as you were (your **cohort**) can have lifelong effects upon you. Consider, for example, the children born in the years

1933 to 1937. Relatively few children were born then, partly because of economic problems created by the depression in the 1930s. When these children were in their twenties, jobs were plentiful in an expanding economy, many careers were open, and advancement was rapid because there were few people to compete with. In contrast, consider people born between 1953 and 1962—the children of the baby boom. All through their lives, educational systems, from elementary schools all the way through college, had to expand to cope with their great numbers. Now this group has been in the job market for a few years, and they are encountering conditions quite different from those faced by people born between 1933 and 1937. Competition is fierce, opportunities in many fields are limited, and the prospects for rapid advancement are much dimmer. All these differences can be explained in terms of a single variable: the size of the birth cohort.

Behavior is also affected by personal experiences that are not necessarily connected with age or with the

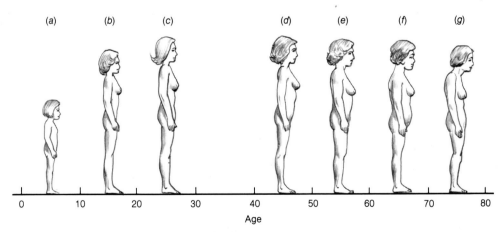

FIGURE 11.2 *Age-related physical changes occur all through the life cycle. They are most important in determining the developmental pattern early in life; they are also important at adolescence, and again significant in old age.*

(a) *Childhood.* Great physical growth and skill development occur.
(b) *Adolescence.* Physical energy reaches a peak at age 12 and then declines. (c) *Early adulthood.* Irreversible loss of nerve cells from the brain and spinal cord begin. (d) *Middle age.* Some mental abilities and muscular strength decline. (e) *Postmenopause.* Body fat is redistributed. The fertile period has ended. (f) *Beginning of old age.* Posture droops as muscles become weak. Hearing loss for high frequency sounds of up to 75 percent may occur. (g) *Old age.* Muscular strength declines to half that of a 20–year–old. Intellectual efficiency may be reduced.

389

condition of society in general—such **unique life events** might include moving to a new city or contracting an incurable disease.

All these factors—biology, history, and the cards life deals you—combine to affect your development throughout life, though at times one of these factors may be more important than the others.

Basic developmental concepts

MATURATION

One of the things that developmental psychologists want to explain is the type of change that unfolds over time and appears to be characteristic of an entire species. For example, when human infants are 9 to 11 months old, they uniformly show anxiety about being separated from their mothers or care-givers. Why don't they act that way in the first few months of life? Also, why does this separation anxiety develop just before the children begin to use language? Such predictable behavior changes can be explained through the concept of **maturation.** If the environment provides a reasonable level of need satisfaction, **psychological maturation**—including the acquisition of perceptual and cognitive skills and the ability to form in-depth relationships with others—will be one result of the normal growth of the central nervous system.

Developmental psychologists are also interested in variations among individuals in the same age group. Some infants begin to speak before they are 12 months old; others utter their first word more than 6 months later. What accounts for these differences?

STAGES OF DEVELOPMENT

While there is obviously a great deal of variation among human beings, most people who study development become impressed with the regularities of developmental change that occur in living creatures. Many theories of development focus on these regular periods of change and on the stages of development that result.

As the individual grows, many behaviors seem to come not only in a certain order but in certain groupings. Each of these groupings of behavior is called a **stage of development.** The idea of stages implies that the skills gained during one stage are the necessary building blocks for the new set of skills that define the next stage. Thus the skill of walking appears before that of running, and babbling and vocalizing in infants precedes the use of words. The stage concept also implies that behavior remains stable for a time after a new stage is reached, until, in what sometimes appears to be an abrupt transition, behavior indicating another new stage is seen.

Although theorists usually define these stages in terms of the ages at which certain behaviors occur, it is important to remember that these are only crude estimates rather than exact boundary lines. The variability in age level may be the result of what psychologists refer to as *individual difference variables*. These individual differences would include intelligence, physical coordination, activity level, and degree of impulsivity. Variability may also be the result of different environmental conditions—for example, how well nourished the individual was and how stimulating the environment was that he or she grew up in. Two other points of dispute, besides the timing of the developmental stages, are whether the stages must always occur in the same order and whether any of them can be omitted. These questions have arisen as more information has been gathered, particularly about the period just after birth.

In spite of the disagreement about some aspects of stage theories, those described here have been important in a variety of ways. They have influenced the questions that researchers ask, and, as we have seen so often throughout this book, the kinds of questions that are asked influence the kinds of data that come out of the research. In addition, many of the theories have altered child-rearing practices, the way that young children are taught in school, and the way adults think about themselves and what is happening to them as they grow older.

Stage theories have long been helpful to parents and professionals in understanding children's behavior. These theories can also call attention to some of the stage-related problems of adulthood so that preventive steps can be taken. When life crises do happen, knowledge about developmental stages is useful in dealing with the problems created by the crises. Frontier 11.1 illustrates some practical uses of stage theories for adults.

PRACTICAL APPLICATIONS OF LIFE SPAN DEVELOPMENTAL THEORY

The population of many Western countries is aging because not only are people living longer, but as a result of the bulging birth rates of certain historical periods, there are simply more middle-aged and older people coming into the pipeline. In the twenty-first century, the baby boomers born after the Second World War will be getting gray. This great increase in the middle-aged brings with it the prospect of both economic and social readjustments and has focused the thoughts of many scientists and planners on the problems of living in a society heavily weighted toward the elderly.

How can theories of life span development help with some of the problems that are likely to arise both from an aging population and from a large number of individuals who are having personal problems related to aging?

One effective method is through organized interventions (see Figure 11.3). Certain life events—for example, marriage, birth of the first child, achieve-

ment of maximum job status, and retirement—occur at generally predictable times during a person's life. Because problems of adjustment are often associated with such events, preventive programs can be set up for those who are entering that period. For example, people who are 5 or 10 years away from retirement often begin to worry about its implications. Such people usually do not seek out a therapist for help in dealing with these questions. They tend to shun such professionals because they often associate them with the negative stereotype of mental illness. An adult education course at a local community college or university or a program organized by the personnel department of a large company usually seems most appropriate in the eyes of the soon-to-be retirees.

In order for the course to be helpful, the leaders must have some idea of the developmental tasks involved in that life stage. For example, it seems clear that retirement means a change in income and in amount of free time. Both these topics are useful to

FIGURE 11.3 *As men and women approach retirement age, information on what to expect from this new life experience is useful. Workshops or lecture series that discuss ways to adapt, help answer questions and lead to constructive problem solving.*

discuss. What is perhaps not so obvious are the developmental tasks that are often not completed before any important life change is made. These include premature decision making; fear of change coupled with an internal demand for it; reluctance to leave the present gratifying, stable stage; and lack of an image or dream of oneself in the future (Rodgers, 1984). While no group program is likely to deal with the resolutions of these problems for all the participants, it can at least call their attention to the possible existence of such issues so that they can begin to think about them. Probably about one-third of those functioning adequately at middle age would be significantly helped by such preventive programs (Farrell and Rosenberg, 1981).

To-be-expected transitions do not result in acute crises for most people (Neugarten, 1976), but when these life events occur unexpectedly, the adjustment demands are much greater. For example, since women in general live longer than men and also tend to marry men who are older than they are, becoming a widow in their late 60s or 70s is usually an event that women can cope with. After an adjustment period, most older widows return to their previous level of functioning. However, if a woman loses her husband in her 30s, this event, because it is unexpected and unprepared for, may be much more difficult to adjust to. Even under these crisis conditions, knowledge of

adult developmental theory and phases of transition can be helpful to counselors (Raines, 1982).

Sometimes crises can be part of a developmental transition. If the adjustment needed is beyond the person's coping capacity, an acute crisis may follow. For example, just before his sixty-fifth birthday and retirement, an apparently well-adjusted executive may take an overdose of sleeping pills. After her husband moves out and her 20-year marriage breaks up, a 45-year-old woman may develop chest pains or digestive problems for which no physical basis can be found. In situations like these, after a counselor has helped the individual handle the immediate crisis, it is often useful to deal with the developmental issues involved, even though the connection between the two may not be obvious at the moment. The retiring executive may never have confronted the issues of intimacy, and faced with the loss of work to fill his life, may be frightened of the long periods of time he and his wife will have to spend together. Or the soon-to-be-divorced middle-aged woman may never have considered her or her husband's need for autonomy. These issues, worked through with a counselor after the immediate crisis is under control, are often helpful in allowing the person to move to a new developmental stage as a better-integrated person. Without a knowledge of life span development, many of these issues might never come to the clinician's attention.

Research techniques for the study of development

Developmental research is often based on information about what happens in a person's life as well as on the person's present abilities. One way to take both these factors into account is to get *retrospective* information by asking people about what happened to them or to members of their family at different times in the past—

what they worried about at age 12, age 18, age 30, for example, or when one of their own children first walked, talked, or was toilet-trained. The retrospective approach is often used in developmental studies because it is convenient and inexpensive, but it has an important drawback: the information that you get may not be very accurate. People tend not to remember the timing of particular occurrences very well, especially if they are expected events—for example, the milestones in a baby's progress. Less specific information, such as their feelings and attitudes, is probably recalled even less accurately. People also tend to distort their memories of the past to make them more consistent with the present (Yarrow and others, 1970). For example, if a family member has recently committed a crime or been hospitalized for schizophrenia, relatives will tend to emphasize different aspects of his or her past than they would if he or she had just graduated from college with honors.

Sigmund Freud himself saw the defects of the retrospective approach, even though his theories were built largely on retrospective data (the memories of the patients whom he treated in psychoanalysis). He described the problem this way:

So long as we trace the development [of a mental process] backwards, the connection appears continuous, and we feel we have gained an insight which is completely satisfactory or even exhaustive. But if we proceed the reverse way, if we start from the premises inferred from the analysis and try to follow these up to the final result, then we no longer get the impression of an inevitable sequence of events which could not be otherwise determined. We no-

tice at once that there might have been another result, and that we might have been just as well able to understand and explain the latter. (Freud, 1950a, p. 226)

As a way of getting around this problem of accuracy, developmental psychologists use special research techniques. The longitudinal and cross-sectional strategies each have certain advantages and disadvantages (see Table 11.1). Studying the same group of individuals over time, as is done in the **longitudinal** approach, eliminates many sources of variation between people that might make the results less meaningful, but a whole list of problems are associated with this approach. Longitudinal studies are expensive and, because humans take so long to mature, a longitudinal study may well outlive its creator. Moreover, the find-

TABLE 11.1   RESEARCH DESIGNS TO STUDY DEVELOPMENTAL CHANGE

TYPE OF DESIGN	ADVANTAGES	DISADVANTAGES
1. Retrospective interview	In-depth data, lowered costs	Problems of accuracy
2. Cross-sectional	Lowered costs, short time	Ignores historical or cohort effects; cannot make "change" statements
3. True longitudinal	Analysis of in-depth change	Very costly and time-consuming; may not distinguish between age-related and external causes
4. Short-term longitudinal	Careful analysis of short-term changes, lowered costs	No measurement of long-term changes
5. Time lag	Historical events taken into account	Costly and time-consuming; "change" statements not possible
6. Sequential	Cross-sectional, longitudinal, and time lag comparisons all possible; takes both historical and individual change effects into account	Very costly and time-consuming; very large number of subjects needed

ings may be biased in unknown ways as subjects move away, withdraw from the study, or die. The problems that seemed important when the subjects were infants may not turn out to be significant when they become adults. The development of improved measuring techniques and advances in scientific knowledge may make earlier work done under less sophisticated conditions less valuable. Repeatedly testing the same people may also affect the results. An even more serious problem is that a change related to maturation may be hard to distinguish from a change related to historical events or to special environmental conditions. Access to better health care, or adjustment to the stress of war, might cause someone's behavior to vary at different ages even though no age-related developmental changes had occurred. But there are ways to modify the longitudinal method to capitalize on its best features while minimizing its limitations. For example, a short-term longitudinal study lasting, say, five years may trace the development of a particular behavior or growth pattern during a period when great change in that behavior is expected.

The **cross-sectional** method is less expensive and takes much less time than the longitudinal method does. In this approach, the characteristics of groups differing in age are compared. Loss of subjects during the research and changes in available methodology are not significant problems. The greatest difficulty with cross-sectional studies is the amount of interpersonal variation that they introduce. Subjects may have grown up in different socioeconomic environments; subjects in different age groups will also have lived through different historical events. In one study of intelligence and personality, one-third of the total differences between the groups was related to these historical or, as they are called, **generational factors** (Nesselroade and others, 1972). Think about the different generations in your own family. Do they have similar attitudes about money or about other important topics, such as sexual behavior?

To illustrate the difficulties introduced by generational factors, let us suppose that in 1986 we decided to see if there was any relationship between age and the tendency to save money. People born in 1910 were 19 when the stock market crashed. They may have lost their jobs as well as whatever savings they had accumulated. In 1986 these people may have been concerned about saving, but they still distrusted the stock market and the banks and perhaps felt safest when their money was in gold coins or hidden away in a drawer. People born in 1930, on the other hand, might remember the depression's hard times from their childhoods, but they became adults during the postwar boom, when jobs were plentiful and the economy was expanding. They may have had high expectations for their future, invested in a house and in stocks, and lived much better than their parents did. In 1986 these people may have worried about having enough money for future retirement, but they still retained their earlier habits of investing. People born in 1950 grew up during the postwar boom. In 1986, even though they may have experienced a great deal of competition for good jobs because of changed economic conditions and the large size of their cohort, they still expected to have a high standard of living. They may have bought a house as inflation protection and spent the rest of their income on what people born in 1910 might consider luxuries. Finally, people born in 1970 would have been only 16 years old at the time of the study—still at the stage where saving doesn't play a big part in their lives. Although the effects of historical events seem intertwined with the age of the subjects and thus limit the conclusion we could draw about the effect of age on saving money, the cross-sectional study would probably be the most practical approach. If we used a longitudinal study to see how saving behavior changes with age from 15 to 75, we would have to be very patient and long-lived experimenters.

Attitudes would be much more affected by historical events than physiological variables would, but generational factors such as changes in diet, advances in medicine or technology, or changes in pollution levels could affect physical development as well. Even differences on such measures as intelligence scores among 20-year-olds, 40-year-olds, and 60-year-olds could be related to such factors as physiological changes, differences in group education levels, or changes in nutrition.

A way to determine whether historical events have an effect on behavior is the **time lag study**. In this approach, a different group of, say, 12-year-olds would be tested every 5 years, then the scores of the 4 groups could be compared. While such a design could be used to determine changes in average heights or weights, time lag studies have many of the disadvantages of cross-sectional studies and also take a long time to carry out.

The longitudinal, cross-sectional, and time lag studies may be combined into a **sequential design** that has some of the best features of each (Schaie, 1965, 1979). Look at Figure 11.4 to see how this method works. Although the idea of combining the different approaches is appealing from a theoretical point of view, it creates practical problems because it requires very large numbers of subjects, a great many years of research commitment, and a great deal of money. Perhaps the most important aspect of Schaie's model is not that it will be used as a whole but that researchers utilizing portions of it will be more aware of the variety of time- and age-related variables they must take into account.

Although it is easy to make broad statements about the effects of generational or historical factors on individuals' behavior, it is important to remember that these events interact with personal characteristics and environmental factors. Predictions based on only one of these sets of factors are too sweeping and may not be very useful. An example of the importance of the interaction of the three sets of factors is shown in an investigation of the impact of the Great Depression of the 1930s on problem behavior in childhood and early adolescence (Rockwell and Elder, 1982). Using longi-

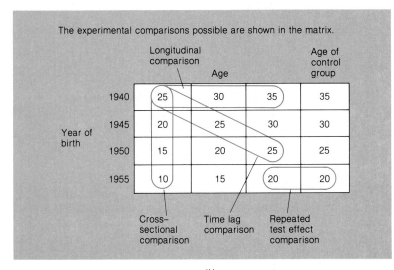

The four experimental groups and testing times are described in the table.

Year of birth	Test 1 Year	Test 1 Age of subjects	Test 2 Year	Test 2 Age of subjects	Test 3 Year	Test 3 Age of subjects	Test of control group Year	Test of control group Age of subjects
1940	1965	25	1970	30	1975	35	1975	35
1945	1965	20	1970	25	1975	30	1975	30
1950	1965	15	1970	20	1975	25	1975	25
1955	1965	10	1970	15	1975	20	1975	20

(a)

The experimental comparisons possible are shown in the matrix.

(b)

FIGURE 11.4 *The sequential strategy for studying development was prepared by Schaie. Using four age groups (a), this design enables researchers to make several age comparisons (b). It allows three cross-sectional comparisons, four time lag comparisons, and four short-term longitudinal comparisons. Contrasting the various groups makes it possible to compare subjects receiving the tests for the first time with those who have had repeated testings. Using all these comparisons, the researcher can then form some conclusions about the effects of age, year of birth (generational effect), and time of testing.*

tudinal data, the investigators assessed the children's behavior and examined the extent to which each of the families had suffered economic deprivation because of the Depression. In addition, they determined the compatibility of the children's parents before the Depression began. When the interaction of economic and parental environment was considered, the results were somewhat surprising. If only incompatible parents were considered, the results were as might be expected: deprived boys had more behavior problems. However, as Figure 11.5 shows, deprived boys whose parents had had strong marriages before the Depression had the lowest level of problem behavior. Another important variable in this study was the sex of the child. Girls showed no significant differences in problem behavior related to their parents' relationship or economic state. If the investigators had merely looked at behavior problems in connection with economic deprivation, they would have concluded that there was little if any effect. However, including another variable, one that described the family environment, showed that deprivation and problem behavior were related, but only under certain circumstances. In other words, an interaction between several factors produced different results under different combinations of conditions.

LONGITUDINAL STUDIES OF DEVELOPMENT

Despite its drawbacks, the longitudinal method remains an important tool in the study of development. Some longitudinal studies that were started in the 1920s and 1930s are still going on and have provided information about a great part of the life span of a num-

FIGURE 11.5 *Behavior of Berkeley, California, boys born at the beginning of the Great Depression was affected differently by family economic deprivation depending on whether the parents had gotten along well before the Depression started.*

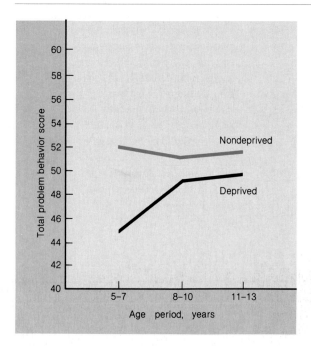

Compatible parents

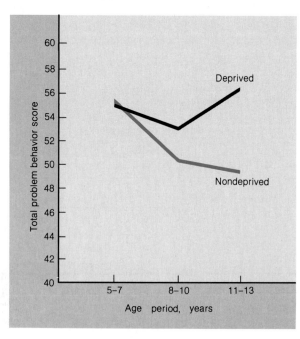

Incompatible parents

ber of individuals. In the Berkeley Guidance Study, begun in 1928 at the Institute of Human Development at the University of California at Berkeley, 248 subjects were studied intensively from the ages of 3 months to 18 years and then were tested several times in adulthood, most recently during their early 50s. The study focused on the incidence of personality and behavior problems, the hereditary and environmental factors that were associated with them, and the effect of counseling on the problems.

Another study from the same institute was the Oakland Growth Study, begun in 1931, when its 212 subjects were in the fifth or sixth grade. This group, followed intensively until they were 17 and then at intervals until they were 50, was less socioeconomically advantaged than the people in the Berkeley Guidance Study. The Oakland research emphasized physical, physiological, and personal-social changes during adolescence. During adulthood, the subjects' physical and emotional health, their personality characteristics, social relationships, and work competencies were stressed. For example, the investigators compared the high and low points in life satisfaction that the subjects reported 10 and 20 years after they graduated from high school (Runyan, 1979). Table 11.2 shows some examples of the findings.

Another, even larger study was begun at the Fels Research Institute in Ohio in 1929. The Fels investigation differed from the Berkeley and Oakland studies because from the beginning of the study until 1974 new groups of 3-month-old infants were enrolled on a regular basis. Thus, the subjects now cover an age range from the early teens to the late 50s. The study has emphasized physical and psychological growth and maturation in children as well as developmental changes in the adult years.

To get a better idea of the kinds of findings that longitudinal research can provide, let's look at three longitudinal projects in more detail.

The Terman Study

The **Terman Study,** begun in 1922 by Louis Terman of Stanford University, focuses on high-IQ children in urban California. The more than 1500 subjects have

lived through a number of dramatic events and major historical changes in the more than 60 years since the study began. The research, which originally focused on the subjects' cognitive development, has also investigated their occupational success and job satisfaction as well as their marital history and overall satisfaction with life. A major finding is that gifted children tend to be well adjusted and live productive lives. You may not find this conclusion surprising, but, when Terman began his study, many people believed in the "crazy, doomed genius" stereotype—the idea that high intelligence was often accompanied by unconventional behavior and by an unhappy, even tragic life. The Terman Study was an important factor in dispelling that belief.

Because the Terman Study has followed the subjects over such a long period, it has now yielded a great deal of information about development throughout the life span. One recent research effort investigated whether attitudes toward marriage had changed among Terman's subjects as a function of the changing attitudes toward marriage in society in general (Holahan, 1984). These attitudes had been measured in 1940, when the subjects were 30 years old, and they were measured again at age 70. In addition, as a control on historical factors, marital attitudes of adults who were age 30 in 1980 were also measured.

Although it is generally believed that, with age, people become more conservative in their attitudes, the Terman group did not. Both men and women became more liberal, especially with regard to greater sex-role equality and independence for women, but the effect was much more pronounced in women than in men. At 70 the males were more similar to what they had been at 30 than they were to men who were currently 30. In other words, for men the cohort differences were greater than the longitudinal changes. For women the longitudinal change was much greater. The older women had changed significantly in their attitudes over the 40-year period and were very similar in attitude to women who were currently 30. This one small survey,

TABLE 11.2 REASONS FOR HIGH AND LOW POINTS IN LIFE SATISFACTION AT TWO PERIODS IN ADULTHOOD

HIGH POINTS	FIRST DECADE AFTER HIGH SCHOOL (%)		SECOND DECADE AFTER HIGH SCHOOL (%)	
	MEN (44)*	WOMEN (44)	MEN (44)	WOMEN (44)
Occupational success, reward	21	2	39	5
Social support by friends	2	0	12	2
New marriage and/or children	48	86	16	41
Courtship, dating, being in love	0	0	7	11
Fewer problems than before	0	2	5	5
Emotional/physical well-being	2	0	2	7
General enjoyment	9	0	18	14

*The number of persons identifying a high point during that age period.

LOW POINTS	FIRST DECADE AFTER HIGH SCHOOL (%)		SECOND DECADE AFTER HIGH SCHOOL (%)	
	MEN (43)*	WOMEN (38)	MEN (34)	WOMEN (40)
Occupational or school problem	26	5	41	3
Failure of close friendship	5	8	0	0
Conflict in marriage and/or child rearing; divorce	7	21	15	8
Overburdened with family problems	0	5	3	13
Physical and/or emotional health problems	12	8	24	25
Death, absence of loved one; accident	2	47	12	40
Military service	42	0	3	0

*The number of persons identifying a low point during that age period.

Source: Runyan, 1979, p. 332.

representing a tiny fraction of the information from the Terman data, illustrates how the longitudinal approach can help to answer questions that cannot be handled in any other way. A researcher who looked only at the cross-sectional data might have concluded that the attitudes of 30- and 70-year-old women were more similar than those of 30- and 70-year-old men on several issues relating to marriage, but the researcher could not have determined whether there had been any attitude changes among the older people.

The New York Longitudinal Study

The **New York Longitudinal Study** began with a very different focus, the identification of temperamental characteristics and the study of their influence on both normal and deviant psychological development. The 133 subjects have been studied from infancy into early adulthood (Thomas and Chess, 1984). Objective descriptions of their behavior from early infancy on have been obtained from the researchers' own observations as well as from the reports of parents and teachers.

The children were divided into three groups on the basis of the temperamental characteristics they displayed as infants in their interactions with parents. One group was quick to develop regular feeding and sleeping schedules, was not bothered by environmental changes, and accepted frustrations with little fuss. Later they adapted easily to school and were able to learn rules for new games quickly. This group, the "easy children," made up almost 40 percent of the sample. At the other extreme were children who had irregular sleep and feeding schedules; had trouble adapting to new routines, people, or situations; cried a lot in infancy; and often responded to frustration with a violent tantrum. These so-called difficult children made up about 10 percent of the entire group. The remaining children showed a mixture of characteristics; they either adapted gradually to most conditions, or they were difficult in some situations and had mild reactions in others. In spite of their temperamental differences, none of the children showed behavior outside normal limits.

When the easy and difficult children became adults, the researchers found that their adjustment was

related to their classification in infancy and to the degree of parent-child conflict that had been observed when the children were 3 years old. These two ratings, together with the ratings of the children's adjustment at ages 3 and 5 and whether they had been diagnosed as having a psychological problem before age 12, could be used to explain 34 percent of the difference between the subjects when they were young adults. This is an impressive achievement. It appeared to the researchers that a large part of the continuity of behavior between early childhood and adulthood was the effect not only of the consistency of each individual's characteristics but also of the continuation of the environmental forces that had been a major part of the child's life from the very beginning. In other words, it was the continuity of the interaction between the child and the situation that produced the similarity over time.

But what about the unexplained 66 percent of the difference that, as the researchers themselves pointed out, was still unexplained? It seemed to the researchers that a large part of this difference could be understood by looking for changes in the person × situation interaction—for unpredictable events or life changes, or for unpredictable changes in the individual that produced dramatic alterations in behavior. Although for some subjects there was striking consistency between adjustment in childhood and adult life, for others there seemed to be fundamental changes. In the two case histories that follow, Thomas and Chess illustrate the importance of the interactive parent-child relationship in some of the changes.

Case 1. Unpredictable events or changes in life situations. The subject was temperamentally active, approaching, and intense in her reactions. In childhood, occasional behavioral difficulties occurred because of her quick and intense reactions, but these disappeared with quiet, firm, and consistent limit setting by her parents. As a result, development through childhood was essentially positive and favorable. When she was 13, her behavioral difficulties again appeared in relationship to increased academic demands, the onset of puberty, and the complexities of adolescent peer interactions. Shortly thereafter her father, who had been a stabilizing authoritative (but not authoritarian) figure in the family, died suddenly and unexpectedly. The same advice for quiet, consistent limit setting had again been recommended, but this time the mother could not follow our advice. Bereft of her husband and his influence, stretched to her limits physically by having to return to a full-time demanding and difficult job, she was unable emotionally to cope with her daughter's crisis and outbursts in addition to attending to the needs of her other three young daughters. The girl's problems escalated, her interaction with her mother and sisters became increasingly hostile and disruptive, and she developed a severe sociopathic behavior disorder. It appears clear that if her father had lived, he and her mother, working together as they had in the girl's earlier years, would probably have prevented this highly unfavorable adolescent development.

Case 2. Unpredictable changes in the individual. One girl had severe symptoms starting in her preschool years. She was temperamentally a difficult child, and her father responded with rigid demands for quick, positive adaptation and hostile criticisms and punishment when the girl could not meet his expectations. The mother was intimidated by both her husband and daughter and was vacillating and anxious in her handling of the child. With this extremely negative parent-child interaction, the girl's symptoms grew worse. Psychotherapy was instituted with only modest improvement. But when she was about 10 years of age, the girl blossomed forth with musical and dramatic talent, which brought her favorable attention and praise from teachers and other parents. This talent also ranked high in her parents' own hierarchy of desirable attributes. Her father now began to see his daughter's intense and explosive personality not as a sign of a "rotten kid," his previous label for her, but as evidence of a budding artist. He began to make allowances for her "artistic temperament," and with this the mother was able to relax and relate positively to her daughter. The girl was allowed to adapt at her own pace, and by adolescence all evidence of her neurotic symptoms and functioning had disappeared. Her early adult follow-up at age 22 showed a continuation of her positive functioning. (Thomas and Chess, 1984, p. 7)

Chess and Thomas have drawn several interesting conclusions. They found that most of the cases of disturbed behavior in older children could not be predicted on the basis of conflict or stress in the child's early life. In fact, they believe that, under certain circumstances, stress and conflicts may have a constructive effect on a child's development. Stress seemed excessive only if there was a poor fit between environmental demands and the child's capacities at that particular level of development. The findings also indicate that, if the difficulties experienced early in childhood were solved at the time, the child was not unusually vulnerable later on and was unlikely to experience similar difficulties in adult life. A major conclusion from the study is that a young child's personality is not always an effective predictor of later development. All in all, the findings from this study give an optimistic view of human development. As Stella Chess put it in summing up the study's findings, "The emotionally traumatized child is not doomed, the parents' early mistakes are not irrevocable, and our preventative and therapeutic intervention can make a difference at all age-periods" (Chess, 1979, p. 112).

The Grant Study

The subjects of our final longitudinal research study, the **Grant Study**, were Harvard undergraduates in 1937. These men, now nearing their 70s, have been followed up frequently over the whole period, usually by questionnaires but also by several interviews and physical examinations during their middle age. Most of the 268 men in the study were selected because of their excellent grades and good health at the time the study began. A few (about 10 percent) were randomly selected from the Harvard undergraduate population. Therefore, like the Terman investigation, the Grant Study gives us a picture of development of a group of individuals who were both economically advantaged and of superior intelligence.

When the study began, the subjects were given intensive medical, psychological, and psychiatric tests. Data about their entire lives from childhood on were collected through interviews with the subjects and their parents. The researchers had a psychodynamic perspective; one of their primary interests was the way each individual dealt with stress and how his responses contributed to success or failure in later life.

One hundred men from the Grant survey were restudied when they were around age 50. The researcher,

George Vaillant (1977), wanted to see if he could find continuities in personality characteristics and in customary ways of dealing with difficulties between the subjects' early life and their present situation. One of his findings was that men who had been rated as having the best childhoods tended also to have the best lives as adults. When he compared the men who had the best childhoods, the "Lucky," with those who had the worst childhoods, the "Loveless," he found several major differences among these two groups in later life:

1. Lucky men were much more likely than Loveless men to participate in competitive sports, to play games with friends, and to take full, enjoyable vacations.

2. Lucky men were much less pessimistic, passive, dependent, and self-doubting than Loveless men were. They typically thought that the study had helped them, while the Loveless men saw the study's efforts as inadequate and its requirements as extremely demanding. The Loveless group took 10 times as many prescription drugs as the Lucky group did.

3. While a tenth of the Lucky men were at some time diagnosed as mentally ill, half the Loveless fell into this category. The Lucky group was also in better physical health. Many of the Loveless men suffered from chronic illnesses like high blood pressure, diabetes, and heart attacks.

4. The Loveless were less likely to have friends in middle life than the Lucky.

Vaillant also looked at his data another way. He compared the 30 men who had the "best outcomes" (the best social, physical, and psychological health) with the 30 who he thought had the "worst outcomes." Important variations between the groups suggest that childhood differences generally made a significant difference in later life (see Table 11.3). But, like Chess and Thomas's findings in the New York Longitudinal Study, Vaillant's research showed that some of the subjects had very different outcomes from what might have been predicted from the original data. Seventeen percent of the men whom Vaillant classified as best outcomes had a poor childhood environment, while some

TABLE 11.3 SOME DIFFERENCES BETWEEN "BEST OUTCOME" AND "WORST OUTCOME" MEN

	BEST OUTCOMES (30 MEN)	WORST OUTCOMES (30 MEN)
Childhood environment poor	17%	47%
Pessimism, self-doubt, passivity, and fear of sex at 50	3%	50%
In college, personality integration put in bottom fifth	0	33%
Subjects whose career choice reflected identification with father	60%	27%
Dominated by mother in adult life	0	40%
Failure to marry by 30	3%	37%
Bleak friendship patterns at 50	0	57%
Current job with little supervisory responsibility	20%	93%
Children admitted to father's college	47%	10%
Children's outcome described as good or excellent	66%	23%
Average yearly charitable contribution	$3,000	$500

Source: From *Adaptation to Life* by George E. Vaillant. Copyright © 1977 by George E. Vaillant, by permission of Little, Brown and Company.

who had good childhoods were not such successful adults. One case was that of Francis De Mille:

In 1940 Francis De Mille impressed the Grant staff with his charm. He seemed rather effeminate, never dated, and blandly stated, "I am anything but aggressive." He had grown up in a household consisting of his mother and two maiden aunts. His father had left home before his birth and died shortly after it. His childhood was solitary— without playmates. His mother, a domineering woman, kept him close to her side. In his adolescence she commented, "Francis takes me to a nightclub as a man does a woman." [Stop here and predict what kind of adult adjustment Francis will make. Now read on.] Francis joined the Navy in World War II, but never was stationed more than 50 miles from home. In the Navy, however, his behavior changed. He described it as "rebelling" and standing up for himself and his men, although his superiors saw it differently, for they gave him high ratings in "morale," "courage," and "cooperation." During this period Francis became worried about his masculinity and possible homosexual feelings. But by 27, after he had taken a job teaching college drama, he found he enjoyed working with women. Three years later he married an actress whom he had formerly directed and completed the break from his mother. He later wrote a successful comedy which humorously described some of his own problems. Career choice still troubled him. He wanted a career high in financial reward and social acceptance. Eventually he became a successful insurance executive who used his artistic flair to become a success in advertising the product. In a business not known for its opportunities for individual expression, he had carved out a niche where he had autonomy, the chance to use his creative talent, and traditional occupational status. His hobby was performing in a community theater group, where he reported that he enjoyed playing aggressive roles the most. Although he still lived only a few blocks from his mother, she now played a dependent role similar to that of his children. (Adapted from Vaillant, 1977, pp. 243–246)

What caused De Mille to change so dramatically in his adult development? He had matured from an effeminate, mother-dominated boy to an assertive, happily married, independent, and successful man who had been able to find both the conventional financial success he thought important and a chance to express his artistic interests in one well-chosen job. What did you predict when you knew only about his childhood? Were you accurate? By studying the lives of both successful and unsuccessful men, the Grant Study has uncovered some clues about successful and unsuccessful ways of meeting the different needs of the different stages of life.

PSYCHOLOGICAL PERSPECTIVES ON DEVELOPMENT

The five perspectives on behavior have all made important contributions to the study of psychological development. In this chapter, we look at the psychodynamic, cognitive, and humanistic-existential perspectives. The biological and learning perspectives (including social learning) are the subject of the next chapters.

Because human development is such a complex topic, no one theory could encompass all its aspects. The five theorists that we will survey in this chapter each focuses on a particular aspect of behavior as it develops across the life span. Sigmund Freud and Erik Erikson deal with the development of personality from the psychodynamic perspective. Jean Piaget and Lawrence Kohlberg are concerned with development of thinking and represent a cognitive perspective. Elisabeth Kübler-Ross examines emotional changes involved in the acceptance of death and illustrates one aspect of the humanistic-existential perspective. Although the specifics of these theories have been questioned and modified, they have all had an impact not only on psychological thinking and research but in many other fields and in the general culture. We might say of all these theorists, but especially of Freud and Piaget, what the poet W. H. Auden wrote after Freud's death:

If often he was wrong, and at times absurd, to us he is no more a person now but a whole climate of opinion under whom we conduct our differing lives. (Auden, 1940)

Freud's theory of psychosexual development

Freud's theories are presented at several points in this book (Chapter 1 and Chapter 13 in particular). In this section, we will discuss only one part of Freud's work: his **theory of psychosexual development.**

PSYCHOSEXUAL STAGES

Freud placed tremendous emphasis on the effects of experiences that occurred during the first five years of

FIGURE 11.6 *According to Freud, the most important developmental stages are now completed in this 5-year-old.*

are severely deprived or overindulged, they may become *fixated* at that period, building their character around the unresolved difficulties of that particular stage. Although psychological development goes on, the individual will continue to be troubled by "unfinished business." His or her behavior may be unconsciously influenced by a need to replay the conflicts of the fixated period. As a result, *regression* may occur—an otherwise competent person may behave in immature or maladaptive ways, especially in times of stress.

The oral stage During the first year of life, the erogenous zone is the mouth; a great deal of the child's pleasure is derived from sucking, not only on the breast or bottle but also on fingers, rattles, or any handy object. We also know that infants use sucking or mouthing of objects as a way of exploring their environment. Because the child is totally dependent during this period, it is easily frustrated. Freud felt that individuals who do not successfully pass through the oral stage continue to

life (see Figure 11.6). During this period, children pass through a number of distinctive stages that Freud called **psychosexual** because during each stage, sexual energy, or libido, is focused on a specific pleasure-giving area, or **erogenous zone.** Pleasure, new conflicts, and major developmental tasks are associated with each stage (see Table 11.4).

Freud believed that what happens to children during these psychosexual stages molds their adult personalities. If children are unsuccessful in resolving the conflicts at a given stage, or if their needs for pleasure

TABLE 11.4 FREUD'S STAGES OF PSYCHOSEXUAL DEVELOPMENT

AGE	STAGE	PLEASURE FOCUS	MAJOR DEVELOPMENTAL TASK
Birth–1	Oral	Mouth	Weaning
2–3	Anal	Anus	Toilet training
4–5	Phallic	Genitals	Identification with parent of same sex
6–12	Latency	No specific area	Development of cognitive mechanisms to deal with stress (defense mechanisms)
13–adulthood	Genital	Genitals	Mature sexual relationship

be concerned with "intake," either by accumulating possessions or by behaving in very dependent ways. When frustrated as adults, such individuals may over-eat, smoke, or chew handy objects such as their finger-nails or pencils.

The anal stage Freud believed that children gain plea-sure from expelling feces. During toilet training, which often occurs in the second year, the parent and child may get into a power struggle. If toilet training methods are harsh, the child may continue the conflict in later life by becoming obstinate and stingy or by venting rage in temper tantrums and destructiveness. According to Freud, productivity and creativity in early life are re-lated to successful resolution of the anal stage.

The phallic stage During the third through fifth years of life, the child derives great pleasure from masturba-tory exploration. This is also the stage during which, according to Freud, a child may have fantasies of doing away with the same-sex parent in order to replace him or her in the remaining parent's affections. In males, this wish is called the *Oedipus complex*; in females, it is the *Electra complex*. During this stage, anxiety may develop as a result of the child's fear of being punished for such "terrible" wishes.

Latency and genital stages At the end of the phallic stage, a latency period occurs during which overt sexu-ality and memories of infantile sexuality are repressed. During this period of about six years, considerable so-cial development is centered on relationships with peers of the same sex. With the onset of puberty, sexual impulses toward the opposite sex return, but in a new form. Earlier the individual chose love objects only because they provided pleasure. In adolescence some of this self-oriented, or narcissistic, love is normally channeled into a nonselfish and altruistic love. In well-socialized adults, the sexuality of earlier psychosexual stages becomes fused into a mature, genital love, and the individual is then capable of genuine caring and adult sexual satisfaction.

EVALUATION

Freud's theory called attention to the importance of the child's relationship with its mother or care-giver, but Freud did not give specific guidelines about how the care-giver should behave to provide the best environ-ment for the child. His ideas of fixation and regression are still helpful to clinicians, but most of what he said about the early stages of development has not held up as well. Also, perhaps because many of his ideas were based on the memories of rather disturbed patients, Freud's theory doesn't seem to apply too well to normal development.

Although most theorists agree that childhood expe-riences have a major influence on the development of personality, many of them reject Freud's assertions about the importance of childhood sexuality. Freud's idea that the most significant stages of development are completed by the time the child reaches age 5 is also disputed by data from longitudinal studies such as that of Chess and Thomas.

Erikson's psychosocial theory of personality development

Another example of a psychodynamic stage theory is that of Erik Erikson, who combined a psychodynamic viewpoint with a strong emphasis on the cognitive changes that occur in transition from one stage to an-other (1963, 1974). Erikson differed with Freud in two important ways: he did not see sexuality as a central factor in development, and he did not think that devel-opment essentially ends at age 5. Like Freud, Erikson (1963) proposed a number of stages in personality de-velopment, but because he argued that personality de-velopment continues through life, he extended his stage theory over a much broader age range than Freud did. Also, he referred to these stages as **psychosocial** rather than psychosexual to emphasize his belief that the social problems encountered at each stage are more important than difficulties in satisfying biological in-stincts.

According to Erikson, development involves a se-ries of eight stages through which all of us pass during the course of our lives (see Table 11.5). In each stage we are confronted with a basic crisis that can be re-solved positively or negatively. How well we resolve the problems facing us at each stage determines how ade-quately we will be prepared to deal with the psychologi-cal crises of later stages.

TABLE 11.5 ERIKSON'S EIGHT STAGES OF PSYCHOSOCIAL DEVELOPMENT

STAGE AND AGE	PSYCHOSOCIAL CRISIS
1. Oral-sensory (1st year of life)	Basic trust vs. basic mistrust
2. Muscular-anal (2nd year)	Autonomy vs. shame, doubt
3. Locomotor-genital (3rd through 5th years)	Initiative vs. guilt
4. Latency (6th year to start of puberty)	Industry vs. inferiority
5. Puberty and adolescence	Identity vs. role confusion
6. Early adulthood	Intimacy vs. isolation
7. Young and middle adulthood	Generativity vs. stagnation
8. Mature adulthood	Integrity vs. despair

Source: Adaptation from *Childhood and society* (2nd ed.), by Erik H. Erikson, is used by permission of W. W. Norton & Company, Inc. Copyright 1950, © 1963 by W. W. Norton & Company, Inc.

PSYCHOSOCIAL STAGES

Stage 1: Oral-sensory During the first year of life, we are totally dependent on our parents. The adequacy with which our needs are met and the amount of love and attention that we receive determine whether we develop *basic trust* or *basic mistrust* in the world. Healthy personality development is built on the foundations of basic trust.

Stage 2: Muscular-anal The second critical stage occurs in the second year of life; at stake is the attainment of *autonomy*. Children who have developed basic trust become ready to separate themselves from their parents and to exercise their individuality. Erikson views many of the rebellious behaviors of this period as the child's attempts to establish individuality. If parents do not allow children to become autonomous, or if they make harsh, unreasonable demands on them during toilet training, the children tend to develop *shame* and *doubt* about their abilities and later lack the courage to be independent individuals.

Stage 3: Locomotor-genital During the third through the fifth years, children begin to develop an exploratory curiosity about their world. They want to know the "whys" and "hows" of things around them. Their curiosity also leads them to explore their bodies, and they become attracted to the parent of the opposite sex. If they are allowed their freedom and if they receive answers to their questions, they develop a sense of *initiative*. If they are held back or punished, they develop *guilt* about their desires and suppress their basic curiosity (see Figure 11.7).

Stage 4: Latency From the sixth year to puberty, children are in school. Children who experience a sense of pride in being able to master tasks and reach their goals develop what Erikson called *industry*. If they fail repeatedly or do not receive encouragement for trying, they develop feelings of *inferiority*. During this stage, children identify with what they do: "If I do good, I am good."

Stage 5: Adolescence One of the most critical life periods is adolescence, when the individual struggles to establish a personal *identity* and to avoid *role confusion*. Even if an individual has positively resolved the earlier stages, this period can still be full of conflict, turmoil, and anxiety. Adolescents often rebel against authority figures whom they see as preventing them from discovering and being what they want to be.

Stage 6: Young adulthood The issue during early adulthood becomes one of *intimacy* versus *isolation*. Young people who have passed successfully through the earlier stages are prepared to take the emotional risks involved in establishing intimate relationships. Those who have not often feel vulnerable and are afraid to get close to others.

Stage 7: Adulthood In middle adulthood, it is quite possible for people who have passed satisfactorily through the first stages to settle into a life of compla-

cency and *stagnation*. To continue growth, people must commit themselves to working for the next generation and for society as a whole *(generativity)*.

Stage 8: Maturity When they reach maturity, people come to grips with the issue of *integrity* versus *despair*. Despair grows out of the feeling that "it's too late now." But individuals who have dealt successfully with the crises of the first seven stages can look back with a sense of fulfillment as they reach the end of their lives.

EVALUATION

A major drawback of Erikson's theory is its vagueness. What is lacking is a translation of his ideas into a form that could be tested experimentally. This difficulty also exists with many other theories—Freud's, for example.

Erikson's theory has had a strong influence on developmental psychology. One of Erikson's important contributions is his integration of personality development and cognitive development. The transition from one stage to another comes about as a combination of maturational changes, changes in the individual's social structure, and changes in his or her cognitive abilities.

Erikson's outlook is more optimistic than Freud's. Erikson suggests that a negative resolution of a developmental crisis need not create permanent damage; a need left unsatisfied at an earlier stage can be satisfied later. By expanding on Freud's developmental stages and by analyzing the social and role requirements that accompany maturation, Erikson has generated interest in personality development across the entire life span. The Grant Study, one of the longitudinal investigations discussed earlier in the chapter, was stimulated by Erikson's ideas.

A researcher interested in life span development who has been influenced by Erikson is Daniel Levinson. Levinson and his co-workers (Levinson, 1978) interviewed men who were between 25 and 45 years old concerning their childhood and adolescence as well as about their present lives. The researchers identified a series of major developmental changes that seemed to occur for all the subjects. Their analysis pictures adult life as comprising alternating periods of stability and transition. During each transition, the life structure that has been built up in the previous stage is reexamined. Choices made during these periods of reexamination may involve major alterations in life patterns such as divorce, job change or relocation, or lesser changes such as weight loss or gain, attitude change, or a new hobby. Levinson believes that each person emerges from such transitions as a changed individual.

The case of Jim Tracy is an example. The transition that he went through around age 30 had culminated, after a long period of indecision, in divorce and remarriage. He also left the Marine Corps after a productive career as a combat officer and became a success as a manager in private industry. Later, during his midlife transition (ages 40–45), Tracy described his feelings this way:

Every once in a while, I just think, my God, the whole goddamn roof is going to fall in. This is sort of what scares me at 45. I'm about halfway through and what is the second half going to be like, because the first half has been pretty good, business-wise. . . . I think one of these days the whole goddamn roof is going to fall in. I just can't keep going like this; that scares me a little bit every once in a while. (Levinson, 1978, p. 307)

During this period, Tracy had severe problems with the children of his first marriage and with his second wife. By the end of the midlife transition, Tracy had solved a good many of those difficulties. He changed his job to one in a smaller company and altered his life style to become more family-centered. Out of the chaos of the first years of his midlife transition, he emerged a person of greater reflectiveness who was better able to have close relationships with others. According to Levinson's view, Tracy then entered a period of consolidation, middle adulthood, all the while preparing for his next transition at about age 50 (see Figure 11.8).

Piaget's theory of cognitive development

Both Freud and Erikson used the psychodynamic perspective and were particularly concerned with the stages in social and personality development. Jean Piaget, on the other hand, used the cognitive perspective and focused much of his interest on the stages of cognitive development.

Piaget developed his ideas in Europe, isolated from the behaviorists who dominated the work going on in

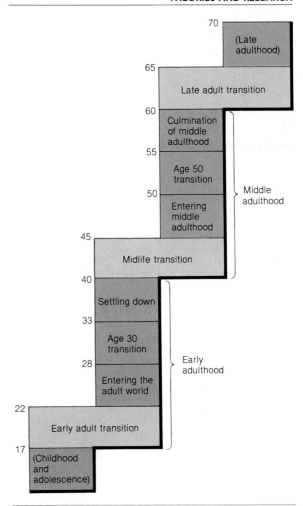

FIGURE 11.8 *Levinson's theoretical picture of developmental periods in men's early and middle adulthood involves alternating periods of transition and relative stability. In the early adult transition the task is to move out in the adult world and test some preliminary choices for adult living. The age 30 transition is made in response to an examination of the results of the previous transition with the feeling, "If I am to change my life I must start or it will soon be too late." At the midlife transition the important question becomes, "What have I done with my life?"*

the United States and Britain and ignored by them as well. After a long period of neglect, his work finally became popular in English-speaking countries as well as in Europe. In fact, the Piagetian model became so influential in developmental psychology and education that for a 20-year period, almost all work on cognitive development referred to Piaget's theories. Piaget's view was basically a biological one in which maturation of cognitive structures (and resulting changes in the process of thinking) hold an important place. His scientific work was conducted mainly by presenting problems to children and then questioning them about how they arrived at their answers. Piaget believed that the important point was not whether a child could solve a problem correctly but what the reasoning was that led up to the solution. He was interested in "what the child considers possible, impossible, or necessary" (Inhelder and Piaget, 1980).

Someone looking at cognitive development from a strict learning standpoint would say that the child reacts to stimuli and is shaped by the reinforcement patterns. Piaget, however, viewed children as active ingredients in the process. They examine, explore, match, sort, look at, classify, and compare experiences, objects, and events. The environment does not simply mold their response; they interact with it. Piaget saw the child as an inventor or a theoretician: each child, over the

course of the first 10 or 15 years of his or her life, must rediscover the basic principles of nature and devise basic theories about how the world works and how objects relate to one another. Piaget believed that children learn most effectively through self-discovery of these principles rather than by simply hearing them explained. This has had important implications for the education of young children.

STAGES OF COGNITIVE DEVELOPMENT

In his early work, Piaget believed that children's thinking develops in a fixed series of stages. He thought of the stages as long periods of equilibrium interrupted by relatively brief transition periods. His theoretical model later became more complex, as models usually do when researchers begin testing them and trying to explain a variety of findings. In this later model, there were smooth transitions among the periods of preparation, achievement, and consolidation in each stage; the new stage's replacement of the previous stage as well as the entire process of moving from one stage to another covered a period of years. This model fits the research data much better than the earlier, more rigid description of moving from one sharply defined stage to another.

FIGURE 11.9 *Even children who are able to use object representation fairly easily may return to using concrete symbols when they feel upset. This girl, faced with a difficult arithmetic problem, uses her fingers to make sure she will get the right answer.*

(a)

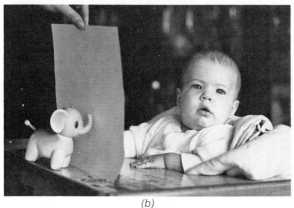

(b)

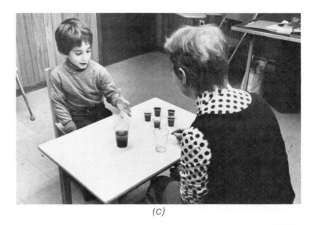

(c)

FIGURE 11.10 *These photos illustrate Piaget's concepts of object permanence and conservation. An attractive toy captures an infant's attention (a). When the toy is hidden behind a screen, the infant, who has not yet developed the concept of object permanence, acts as if the toy no longer exists (b). To test for the concept of conservation, the liquid in one of the two large cups is poured into the four smaller ones, and the child is asked, "Which holds more, the large cup or these four?" (c). A child who has reached the concrete operational period will understand that the amount of liquid is the same.*

An example of research on children's thinking is the investigation of children's development of number skills. The researcher had the following conversation with a 4-year-old child:

ADULT: How many is two and one more?

PATRICK: Four.

ADULT: Well, how many is two lollipops and one more?

PATRICK: Three.

ADULT: How many is two elephants and one more?

PATRICK: Three.

ADULT: How many is two giraffes and one more?

PATRICK: Three.

ADULT: So how many is two and one more?

PATRICK: (Looks adult straight in the eye) Six.

HUGHES, 1984, p. 9

It is clear from this conversation that Patrick has some concept of numbers, but only as long as concrete objects are involved. Most children, like Patrick, make no attempt to translate formal problems into a concrete form that they can understand. This continues, for many children, at least until they are 7 or 8. Older children in stressful situations are likely to revert to concrete representations even though they can usually deal with formal problems (see Figure 11.9).

Piaget's theory is a descriptive one; the emphasis is on identifying and characterizing the stages, not on understanding how a new stage develops. The stages of cognitive development described by Piaget include the **sensorimotor period,** the **preoperational period,** the **concrete operational period,** and the **formal operational period.** Table 11.6 summarizes the traits of each stage and gives examples of the kind of thinking characteristic of each. Tests demonstrating two of Piaget's basic concepts are illustrated in Figure 11.10.

TABLE 11.6 PIAGET'S STAGES IN COGNITIVE DEVELOPMENT

NAME	AGE PERIOD	BASIC CONCEPTS
SENSORIMOTOR PERIOD	birth–2 yrs.	*Object permanence.* The stage develops gradually and is not fully complete until the child is about 18 months of age. At 6 months babies will look for an object that has been hidden under a cloth while they are watching. But they do not keep looking for long, and if the object is hidden under a series of cloths, they will look under only the first one. By about 18 months of age, infants will search for objects they have not actually seen being hidden. Until then, children have no mental image or word to represent the existence of an object when it is not in sight.
		Object consistency. The child comes to understand that even if things appear different because of distance, light, viewing angle, and so on, they actually are the same.
PREOPERATIONAL PERIOD	2–7 yrs.	*Object representation.* Children acquire the ability to represent objects and events to themselves through images or with a few words.
		Object classification. Children understand that objects can be classified and grouped. At first, children group things on the basis of what they can do with them—things you can throw, things you can put in your mouth, things that mothers use, things people ride in, and so forth. By the end of the period, children group things more systematically, often by color or shape.
		Lessening of egocentrism. Younger children are not able to imagine that an object looks different from another person's viewpoint. At the end of the period, they can describe things as they look to someone else—for example, someone sitting across from and facing them.
CONCRETE OPERATIONAL PERIOD	7–11 yrs.	*Operations.* Children grasp the idea that certain processes are reversible.
		Conservation concepts. Children learn the idea that objects have fundamental qualities that do not change even when their outward appearance changes. For example, changing the shape of a ball of clay from a sausage to a pancake doesn't change the amount of clay. Such changes always fool preoperational children. But older children may say, "It looks different, but it's still the same amount" or "It's the same amount because you haven't added anything or taken anything away," because they understand the operations of addition and subtraction. Or they may realize that "this one is bigger this way but thinner the other way, so it's the same," because they understand the fact that changes in two dimensions can complement one another.
		Conservation concepts apply to length, number, quantity (see Figure 11.10), and volume. Some, such as volume, may not be understood even by a 12 to 14-year-old.
		Class inclusion. Children grasp the idea that one class is included in a larger class—for example, that in a bunch of flowers containing mostly daffodils there are more flowers (the larger class) than daffodils.
		Mental representation. Children acquire the ability to draw and use maps.
FORMAL OPERATIONAL PERIOD	11 yrs. and beyond	*Deductive logic.* Children are able to use a general statement or theory to predict specific outcomes.

According to Piaget, learning, in the sense of understanding basic concepts, comes about only when the child's biological development has progressed to the point where such learning is possible. As he put it, "Learning is no more than a sector of cognitive development which is facilitated by experience" (Piaget, 1970, p. 714). This idea has important implications. If applied strictly, it means that there is no use in trying to teach a child certain concepts before the child has acquired the necessary cognitive structure. Since the stages are not objective characteristics, like height, weight, or eye color, there is no way to test this idea because we cannot determine what the child's current state of cognitive development is. We can only infer the stage of the child's thinking either by setting up a situation that successfully demonstrates that he or she can produce the required concept or by waiting for evidence of a particular stage to occur spontaneously.

EVALUATION

Piaget's work has had a great effect on the whole field of developmental psychology. Especially in the area of cognitive development, his work has been a major source of research ideas. In education too, his influence has been important in creating new approaches to teaching young children.

Although the types of thinking that Piaget has described seem generally accurate, a great deal of research has raised questions about some of his basic ideas. First, there is evidence that the stage a child is in may not limit learning as strongly as Piaget supposed. Piaget was too quick to explain results in terms of the child's logical inadequacies, when more detailed analysis may reveal that features of the test situation can account for the results. For example, in one study, when the examiner laid out two rows of objects and then pushed one row together, most 4-to-6-year-old children said, as Piaget would predict, that the shorter row had fewer objects in it (McGarrigle and Donaldson, 1974/1975). These children did not seem to have mastered the principle of conservation. However, when the examiner told the children that she had a mischievous teddy bear who was always messing up the toys and then made the bear move one row of objects closer together, most of the children said the number of objects was the same. With the different phrasing of the

question, the children showed they could understand the operation of conservation. Perhaps this difference is like that between your success on a multiple-choice test, where the question is a recognition task, and on a test in which you have to retrieve information by filling in the blanks. Chapter 7 pointed out that recognition is usually easier than recall. In other research, preschoolers' performance on tasks that appeared to be beyond their level of cognitive operation improved substantially when the children received special training in attention, in obeying verbal instructions, and in modeling. Even better, this training generalized to other tasks and still had an effect several months later (Brainerd, 1983). Thus, the evidence suggests that strong stage limits on learning do not exist. Stages of cognitive development appear to be less steplike than might be expected from Piaget's earlier theorizing. His later thinking and the experimental data of other researchers suggest weaker stage boundaries: the different operations are acquired over a relatively long period and often overlap considerably.

Another of Piaget's basic ideas that has been modified by research work is the importance of self-discovery in learning. Educational programs using Piagetian methods typically discourage teachers from explaining concepts before the child has discovered them by manipulating objects. However, some evidence suggests that the amount of learning produced by self-discovery methods is smaller than that in a more traditional teaching situation (Cantor and others, 1982).

Despite the questions raised about the specific application of Piaget's work, his contribution to an understanding of cognitive development remains enormous.

Kohlberg's theory of moral development

Lawrence Kohlberg (1964) extended Piaget's work across a wider age range and expanded the number of stages. Let's examine Kohlberg's theories.

Cognitive researchers such as Piaget and Kohlberg are not particularly interested in the specific things that a particular child considers right and wrong, but in the ways in which thinking about right and wrong changes with age. A child may continue to think, from age 5 to 15, that lying is bad, but, over that period, his or her conception of what lying is and when it may be justifiable may change considerably.

Studies of children's moral judgments during the school years suggest that there are systematic shifts in the child's basis for making decisions about right and wrong. One of these shifts is from judging wrongness by the amount of harm or damage done to judging it by the intention of the wrongdoer. This is a cognitive change, not a change in the context of the moral rules.

Another shift is from judgments based on fixed rules to judgments based on general principles. Children of 10 or 12, for example, are likely to think that if something is against the law, it is automatically wrong. Older children see laws as less absolute; they try to decide whether something is wrong on the basis of whether it violates some basic principle, such as the importance of human life.

STAGES OF MORAL REASONING

Kohlberg's theory describes a series of **stages in the development of moral reasoning** that are linked to some extent to the child's general level of cognitive development. Children who progress rapidly in their cognitive growth are somewhat more likely to have a more advanced sense of moral judgment, although the link between cognitive growth and morality is not perfect. Kohlberg's classification system not only extends Piaget's concepts to an older group but also makes it possible to compare levels of moral judgments among cultures by the use of a standardized test or set of situations.

To study moral judgments, Kohlberg presented his subjects with stories that usually involved a choice between two culturally unacceptable alternatives. For example:

On the battlefield, an officer orders a retreat because of heavy enemy attack. A bridge should be blown up behind the troops before they retreat. Whoever is sent to blow up this bridge will almost certainly be killed. The officer

knows this, but he also knows that he is the best person to lead the retreat. What should he do?

A man's wife is almost certain to die without a certain drug. The druggist who invented the drug won't sell it to the husband except at a very high price, more than the husband can possibly pay. He will not consider the possibility of receiving part of the money later. Should the husband steal the drug to save his wife's life? (Kohlberg, 1964).

The subject then answers a series of questions about each story. A complex scoring system determines the subject's classification (Colby and others, 1983). Kohlberg's stages of moral reasoning and examples of judgments made in response to the second story are given in Table 11.7.

Kohlberg believed that the stages of his system are experienced by people in all cultures in an irreversible, step-by-step sequence and that each stage is a distinct structural unit characterized by a particular type of thinking. When a longitudinal research study indicated that individuals sometimes regress to an earlier stage as they grow older, Kohlberg believed that the problem was not with his theory but with his scoring system, so he and his co-workers revised it (Colby and others, 1983). Using the new scoring system in a 20-year longitudinal study in which the subjects were tested at 3- to 4-year intervals, he and his co-workers made a number of findings that supported their views. Almost all the subjects moved upward in the stage system, only a few of the comparisons showed any backward shift between testings, and the scores on the different stories used in any one testing were highly similar. On the negative side, the changes were not great. Most subjects moved up less than 2 full stages. They started in stage 2 and ended in stage 4. The average time for the change from one stage to the next was almost 14 years. Stage 6 is not scored in the new manual, and even occurrences of stage 5 were rare.

EVALUATION

Kohlberg's theory has satisfied one important criterion for any theory: it has stimulated a great deal of research. His new scoring system is an impressive achievement, although only after other researchers have duplicated some of his findings will the value of the system be clear. Those who are uncomfortable with the use of stage theories have raised a number of questions about

TABLE 11.7 KOHLBERG'S STAGES OF MORAL
REASONING

LEVEL 1. PRECONVENTIONAL MORAL REASONING

Stage 1. Obedience and punishment orientation

A person must be obedient to powerful authority because
of fear of punishment.

Example: The husband must not steal the drug because he
would be punished.

*Stage 2. Recognizing that each person has his or her own in-
terests to pursue*

The act is moral if it satisfies an important need of the
person or some family member.

Example: He should steal the drug because his wife needs
it and he isn't doing any harm to the druggist. He can pay
him back.

LEVEL 2. CONVENTIONAL MORAL REASONING

Stage 3. Good person orientation

A moral action is one that causes others to approve.

Example: He should steal the medicine because society
expects a husband to help his wife. He is only doing something that is natural for a loving husband to do.

Stage 4. To keep the social order going

Moral people are those who do their duty in order to
maintain the social order.

Example: He should steal the drug because if people are
allowed to be selfish and greedy, our civilization will break
down. But he must pay the druggist back and he must be
punished because people can't take the law into their own
hands.

LEVEL 3. POSTCONVENTIONAL MORAL REASONING

Stage 5. Social contract and individual rights

Society has rules and both the individual and society must
fulfill their parts of the contract.

Example: Before you say the stealing is wrong, you should
consider that the law should not allow the druggist to
keep secret a life-saving formula. In this case it seems reasonable for him to steal the drug.

Stage 6. Universal ethical principles

Society's rules are arbitrary. Different people may interpret them in different ways. The ultimate judge of whether
something is moral is a person's own conscience.

Example: He must steal the medicine because if his wife
died he could never forgive himself. When a choice must
be made between disobeying a law and saving a life, the
higher principle of saving a life must prevail.

what they see as Kohlberg's rigid way of thinking about
stages in moral development. Some researchers have
found that cognitive changes are gradual rather than all
or none. Subjects seem to fluctuate back and forth between stages even on the same task and may show variations of as much as a third of a stage over a two-week
period (Rest, 1983). This is a significant amount of
shift because, in Kohlberg's longitudinal study, a third
of a stage took four years to complete. Critics of a rigid
stage concept argue that these findings indicate that
subjects cannot be simply assigned to one stage or another but should be seen as fluctuating within a range.

Some critics have objected to the limited scope of
Kohlberg's theory. Kohlberg, like Piaget, has been primarily interested in the development of the process of
thought and in the way that changes in cognition are
reflected in an individual's interpretation of various
problem situations, including moral issues. Some psychologists point out that morality includes much more
than just a way of thinking; it takes in emotions, feelings of empathy for others, and ways of behaving (Rest,
1983). More recent work on morality has reflected the
wider view. For example, studies have been done on
the effect of social norms and assignment of blame in
problem situations and also on the way that the various
pieces of information in any situation must be integrated to produce moral evaluations and judgments.

The cognitive theory of morality represents a distinct contrast to explanations of morality from the behavioral perspective, as we will see in Chapter 12.
From a behavioral point of view, the development of
moral behavior is built up not through stages of growth
but by repeated punishment for a particular action
(Mowrer, 1960). The anxiety created by the anticipation of punishment eventually leads to a suppression of
the behavior.

A different behaviorist approach, the social learning view, stresses that many aspects of moral behavior
are acquired through modeling. Children observe
adults regretting their own bad behavior, they can hear
moral judgments being made, they watch parents or
other adults setting high standards for their own behav-

FIGURE 11.11 *Children may not always learn the lesson parents believe they are teaching. Parents may preach one attitude and teach another through their behavior. Children often pay more attention to their parents' actions than to their words.*

ior, and so on. A number of researchers using the social learning approach believe that moral behavior can be explained solely on the basis of observational learning, without any reference to the internalized rules stressed by cognitive psychologists (see Figure 11.11).

Kübler-Ross's theory of death and dying

All of us will eventually face the approach of death: the deaths of our friends and the members of our family and, finally, our own. As interest has grown in development over the whole life span, more attention has been focused on old age and on the psychological implications of approaching death. One of the pioneers in this effort was Elisabeth Kübler-Ross, who has emphasized the concern with existence and nonexistence seen in the humanist-existential perspective.

To understand the problems of people who are coping with a serious and probably terminal illness, Kübler-Ross interviewed over 200 dying patients. She found that the typical dying person goes through five stages in the process of coping with approaching death. She stresses that these stages do not always occur in the same order and that several may occur at the same time, which makes her approach less rigid than the other stage theories (Kübler-Ross, 1974).

STAGES OF DYING

Denial and isolation People who have just been told that they have a terminal illness frequently respond with denial: "It can't be true. There must have been a mistake." This response is often followed by a search for any physician who will give a different, more positive diagnosis or for a faith healer or a miracle cure. The reality of death is usually isolated from awareness. Even when it has been partially accepted, fleeting periods of denial will occur.

Anger When denial becomes less complete, anger at the unfairness of life often occurs. This anger, which is frequently directed at anyone available—nurses, physicians, family members, or visitors—often makes the dying person difficult to deal with. The dying person is asking, "Why me?" (and implicitly, "Why not you?").

Bargaining When anger fails to work, a dying person sometimes turns to bargaining—with God, with the disease itself, or with the medical staff: "I must live until June, to see my daughter get her law degree," or "My children are too young to be without a father," or "I promise I'll straighten up, if you'll just let me off this time." Bargaining, of course, is not a very effective way of dealing with illness.

Depression   Many dying patients become depressed, as a reaction either to the loss of some body part, such as the surgical removal of a breast, or to the loss of life and all its relationships. Talking about these feelings of depression can lead to the final stage.

FIGURE 11.12   *Elisabeth Kübler-Ross is shown presenting a dying patient with an urn to hold her ashes after her body is cremated. This patient, Louise, writes movingly about her acceptance of death. "During one of Elisabeth's many visits she asked if there was anything she could do for me, as she always did. I had been thinking of my funeral plans and the only part unfinished was the actual urn for my ashes. Elisabeth traveled to so many different and exotic places I thought she could surely find the kind of urn I was interested in; besides, what closer, dearer friend could I think of to have purchase my urn for me? It was like having her hold my hand all the way. How much I had changed, from stumbling and struggling to accept my condition. I had reached the point where friends could calmly talk about the plans left to complete, buying the urn for my ashes. And I knew I was free to ask her to shop for me. That is friendship!" (Kübler-Ross, 1978)*

Acceptance   This period has been described by patients as being almost without feeling. The dying person may have worked through the responses of denial, anger, and depression and have come to "contemplate his coming end with a certain degree of quiet expectation" (Kübler-Ross, 1969, p. 112)—see Figure 11.12.

EVALUATION

This model has relevance not only for those facing their own or another's death but also for very old people who anticipate that their time is limited. Little systematic study of how dying people cope with death exists. Some therapists who see many dying patients find a much more varied pattern of response than Kübler-Ross did (Shneidman, 1973). Other observers suggest that there are sex differences in adaptation. For example, women are concerned about the effect of their death on others, but men are more concerned about the effect of a life-threatening illness on their occupational role, about the likelihood of becoming dependent, and about possible pain (Kastenbaum, 1975). Such findings suggest that the idea of a progression of stages is too simple. Despite these criticisms, Kübler-Ross's theory has been valuable because it calls attention to a long-neglected topic—the stages of development related to dying.

STUDY OUTLINE

THE LIFE SPAN APPROACH (p. 388)

1. Life span developmental psychology describes the interaction between developmental processes and the environment over the entire period from birth to death. Research emphasis on development in adulthood is relatively recent compared to interest in childhood development.

2. Important factors in life span development are age-related biological and sociological processes, history-

related occurrences, and unique life events. The size of your cohort, or the other individuals born the same year (or period of years) as you were, can have important effects on your life.

3. Maturation refers to the changes that unfold over time and that seem to be characteristic of the entire species. Stages of development refer to the groupings of behavior that seem to come together in a predictable order as an individual grows older. Stage theories usually assume that the order will not vary because each stage is built on the behaviors of the previous one.

4. Techniques used in developmental research include longitudinal and cross-sectional studies. Each has some positive and negative features. Time lag studies are also used to determine the effect of historical events. Sequential designs have some of the best features of all these approaches but have many practical drawbacks.

LONGITUDINAL STUDIES OF DEVELOPMENT (p. 396)

1. The Terman Study of gifted children has continued for more than 60 years. It has shown that gifted individuals are likely to be well adjusted and live productive lives.

2. The New York Longitudinal Study has focused on the influence of infants' temperamental characteristics in interaction with their parents. Children who were difficult and who had a high degree of parent-child conflict in early childhood showed poorer adjustment as adults. However, unpredictable changes in life situations could dramatically alter the outcome.

3. The Grant Study has periodically reexamined men who were Harvard undergraduates at the time the research began. Those who had the best childhoods tended to have the best lives as adults. The researchers have also focused on the factors that seemed to contribute to successful later adjustment for men who had less than good childhood environments.

PSYCHOLOGICAL PERSPECTIVES ON DEVELOPMENT (p. 402)

1. Sigmund Freud emphasized the importance of the first 5 years of life in development. He thought children passed through a number of psychosexual stages and that in each stage their energies were focused on a different erogenous zone. Freud divided psychosexual development into the oral, anal, and phallic stages, all occurring before the age of 5; a latency period of about 6 years; and, finally, the genital stage, which accompanies puberty. Although Freud's emphasis on the child's relationship with the mother or care-giver has been useful, many current theorists reject much of Freud's thinking about the role of childhood sexuality and his emphasis on the completion of so much development by the age of 5.

2. Erik Erikson concentrated on psychosocial development rather than psychosexual development. He believed that personality growth continues throughout life in a series of eight stages and that in each stage the person must solve a particular set of problems. The way these are resolved is crucial to success in later developmental stages. Erikson's ideas have influenced several longitudinal studies of development.

3. Jean Piaget's theory of cognitive development stresses the maturation of cognitive structures that allow a child to progress to a later stage. His focus is on the way children arrive at their answers to problems rather than simply the correctness of their responses. Piaget's stages of cognitive development include the sensorimotor period, the preoperational period, the concrete operational period, and the formal operational period. His ideas have been very influential in research in child development and education for several decades. Recent research findings have led to questions about whether the cognitive stages are as distinct as Piaget thought.

4. Lawrence Kohlberg extended Piaget's ideas of cognitive stages across a wider age range and focused his own theory on the development of moral judgment. Kohlberg constructed a test that involves a series of judgments between culturally unacceptable alternatives. The test responses are scored for the kinds of reasoning the individual uses in coming to a decision. Kohlberg's theory has been criticized for its rigid stage approach and for its focus on moral thinking and not on moral behavior as well.

5. Elisabeth Kübler-Ross's theory of death and dying is not as rigid a stage theory as the others. Her model includes periods of denial and isolation, anger, bargaining, depression, and acceptance. Her theory has been valuable because it calls attention to an important area long neglected by developmental researchers.

KEY TERMS AND CONCEPTS

life span developmental psychology

age-related biological and sociological processes

history-related event

cohort

unique life events

maturation

psychological maturation

stage of development

longitudinal approach

cross-sectional approach

generational factors

time lag study

sequential design

Terman Study

New York Longitudinal Study

Grant Study

Freud's theory of psychosexual development

psychosexual stages

erogenous zone

oral stage

anal stage

phallic stage

latency

genital stage

Erikson's theory of psychosocial development

psychosocial stages

Piaget's theory of cognitive development

stages of cognitive development

sensorimotor period

preoperational period

concrete operational period

formal operational period

Kohlberg's theory of moral development

stages of moral reasoning

Kübler-Ross's theory of death and dying

stages of dying

SUGGESTED READINGS

BEE, H. L., and MITCHELL, S. K. (1984). *The developing person* (2nd ed.). New York: Harper & Row. A basic, engagingly written general text.

CARMICHAEL, L. (1983). *Handbook of child psychology* (vol. 1–4). A new edition of the most comprehensive reference source for childhood development.

WOLMAN, B. B. (Ed.) (1982). *Handbook of developmental psychology*. Englewood Cliffs, N.J.: Prentice-Hall. A collection of articles relating to all aspects of development and covering the age span from infancy to old age.

417

CHAPTER TWELVE
BIOLOGICAL, COGNITIVE, AND SOCIAL CHANGES IN DEVELOPMENT

BIOLOGICAL DEVELOPMENT
Periods of physical change
Motor performance
Emotional development
Sensory skills

LEARNING AND COGNITIVE DEVELOPMENT
Learning in infancy
Measuring cognitive development in infants
Cognitive changes over the life span
Age changes in learning techniques

SOCIAL AND PERSONALITY DEVELOPMENT
Attachment
Socialization
Plasticity of development

FRONTIER 12.1   THE EFFECTS OF DIVORCE ON
CHILDREN'S DEVELOPMENT

STUDY OUTLINE

KEY TERMS AND CONCEPTS

SUGGESTED READINGS

The boy who wrote the two letters in Figure 12.1 changed a lot in the two years that passed between the first letter and the second one. We know that people change very rapidly during some periods and very little during others. If we looked at the letters this boy wrote when he was 20 and 22, we probably would notice few changes. From 6 to 8 years of age, however, his handwriting changed as his coordination improved. His way of thinking about his situation changed: he no longer thought only about expressing his emotions; he also considered how his father might view his feelings. And, as he became more socially aware, he expressed his aggressive feelings in a more controlled and acceptable way.

In Chapter 11 we discussed ideas about the stages in people's lives and the patterns of behavior that are typical of those stages. We illustrated those theories with information from longitudinal studies that followed the same group of people as they grew up and matured. Although the concept of stages of development has been helpful in understanding some of the different behaviors that occur in an individual's life span, research has made it increasingly clear that a rigid stage approach does not fit reality.

The rate of developmental change is uneven over the life span: developmental changes occur most rapidly in the first few years of life. The focus of developmental change also varies: physical and cognitive changes are dominant in childhood; social changes are the focus in adolescence and adulthood.

In this chapter, we will highlight the biological, cognitive, and social capabilities of human beings during periods in which development and change are especially noticeable.

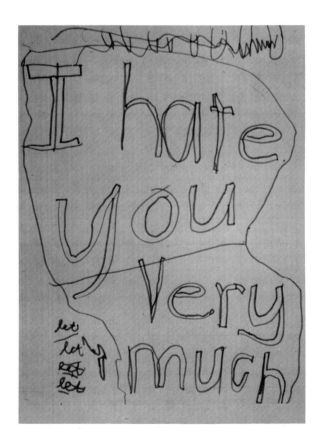

FIGURE 12.1 *Behavior changes with age. These two notes, written by the same boy at the ages of 6 and 8, illustrate different responses to the same situation. In both cases he had been sent to his room for misbehavior. Although the emotions he experienced were no doubt similar, he expressed them differently and probably thought about them differently as well.*

BIOLOGICAL DEVELOPMENT

The biological perspective suggests that we behave as we do because of the way our bodies are built and the stage of development that we have reached. Some of the differences in developmental patterns shown by males and females illustrate this connection between anatomy and behavior. In the first months after birth, girls' maturational timetable is four to six weeks faster than that of boys. Girls continue to be ahead physically throughout childhood, and the changes of puberty begin and end earlier for girls. Some sex differences in developmental norms are shown in Table 12.1. Many variations in performance between young boys and girls are most likely a function of such developmental differences, rather than of parental expectations or the effects of society, but many of them could also be affected by environmental factors.

Periods of physical change

Dramatic physical changes take place in three periods during the life span—in infancy, in adolescence, and in old age. These physical changes have interested psychologists because of their effects on behavior patterns and on other people's expectations of the individual.

INFANT GROWTH

A newborn baby is one-third its adult height; an 18-month-old is one-half its full height. These statistics come as a surprise to most people. They may perceive a child's growth as even greater than it is because children and adults are proportioned so differently (see Figure 12.2) and because the child weighs so much less than an adult in proportion to its height. Weight at birth is less than 5 percent of the person's final weight, but the body surface area is about 15 percent of an adult's. This means that the infant is more vulnerable to heat loss and so must burn more calories per unit of weight—as well as eating enough to maintain a very rapid rate of growth. Infants get most of the calories they need from milk. On a relative weight basis, to

TABLE 12.1 SEX DIFFERENCES IN RESPONSE TO GESELL DEVELOPMENTAL TESTS

	SUCCESS IN TASK	
	GIRLS	BOYS
CUBES: *THE TEST GIVER PROVIDES A MODEL OR DEMONSTRATES THE BUILDING WITH CUBE-SHAPED BLOCKS.*		
TOWER OF 10, 3 YEARS	95%	67%
IMITATES BRIDGE OR BETTER, 3 YEARS	58%	66%
BRIDGE FROM MODEL, 3½ YEARS	82%	88%
6-CUBE STEPS (WITH DEMONSTRATION), 4½ YEARS	40%	36%
10-CUBE STEPS (WITH OR WITHOUT DEMONSTRATION)	5½ YEARS	6 YEARS
INTERVIEW: *THE TEST GIVER ASKS THE CHILD FOR INFORMATION.*		
GIVES OWN AGE	3 YEARS	4 YEARS
GIVES SEX	2½ YEARS	3 YEARS
KNOWS MONTH OF BIRTHDAY		
AT 5 YEARS	45%	24%
AT 5½ YEARS	60%	26%
MOTOR TESTS: *THE TEST GIVER DEMONSTRATES THE BEHAVIOR OR THROWS THE BEANBAG AND ASKS THE CHILD TO CATCH IT.*		
HOPS ON ONE FOOT	3½ YEARS	4 YEARS
JUMPS DOWN, LANDS ON BOTH FEET	3 YEARS	3½ YEARS
THROWS BEANBAG OVERHAND	4½ YEARS	5½ YEARS
BEANBAG CATCH, HANDS VERSUS CHEST OR BETTER	5½ YEARS	4½ YEARS

Source: Adapted from Ames and others, 1979, pp. 168–170.

equal a baby's diet, you would have to drink 10 to 20 quarts of milk per day (Smith, 1951). The infant must also excrete the large volume of water that goes along with all those necessary calories and nutrients. Small wonder that feeding and diaper changes are such a large part of infant care.

PHYSICAL DEVELOPMENT IN ADOLESCENCE

Sometime around age 10 or 11 in girls and somewhat later in boys, a decrease in secretions from the pineal gland starts the process of puberty in motion (Kolata, 1984a). It is important to remember that there is a great deal of variation among children in the timing and speed of completion of puberty. The range of ages that is considered normal is great. For example, in the United States, the normal range of first menstruation is from 9 to 17 years.

Since puberty is related to dramatic growth and changes in physical appearance, and since the hormonal changes that occur as part of puberty have an effect on emotional responses, it would not be surprising if early or late puberty has an effect on the individual's personality development. An early maturing adolescent has a grown-up physical appearance, which may cause others to expect adult behavior, but his or her emotional and cognitive development is still at a more childlike level. On the other hand, if he or she has an adult self-image because of these physical changes, an early maturer constantly runs up against school classifications, laws relating to driving, and so on that emphasize his or her "child" status. Both of these situations, in which there is a discrepancy between self-image and environment, can lead to frustration and confusion.

Early maturing boys tend to have an advantage physically, athletically, and socially. Many studies demonstrate that they are rated as more poised and popular and are more likely to be school leaders than later maturing boys (Siegel, 1982). When psychological rather than social adjustment is considered, however, the late maturing boy may have an advantage: the late maturing male has a lengthened period to prepare for the changes of puberty and thus may be better able to handle them (Peskin, 1973). Longitudinal research has suggested that differences between males who are early and late maturers fade away by the time they reach their 30s (Jones, 1965).

For girls, early onset of puberty can be both a social and a psychological disadvantage. Since girls tend to mature earlier than boys on the average anyway, the early maturing girl is likely to be big and physically conspicuous, which may cause problems in peer relationships. It may also be a factor leading a female to establish social relationships with older males—relationships that have social and sexual implications that may not be in tune with her emotional maturity

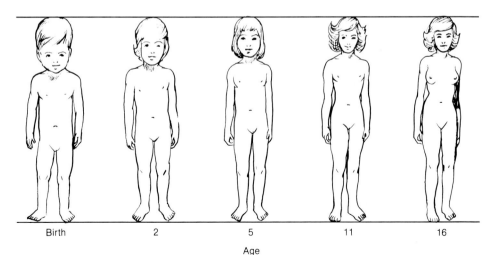

FIGURE 12.2 *Body proportions change from birth through adolescence. In proportion to the child's total height, the head becomes smaller, the legs become longer, and the body midsection becomes slimmer with age.*

Birth   2   5   11   16

Age

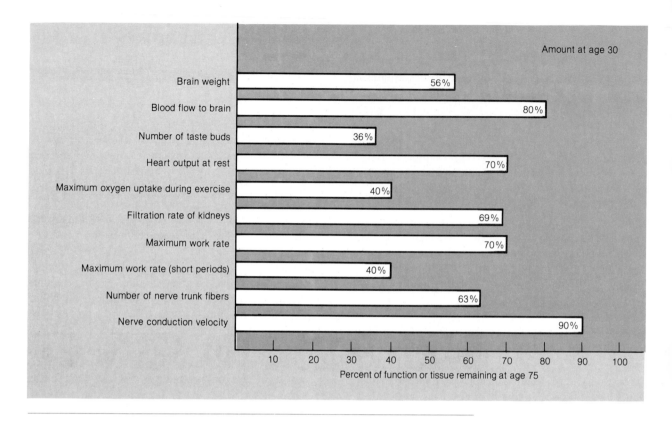

Amount at age 30

Brain weight	56%
Blood flow to brain	80%
Number of taste buds	36%
Heart output at rest	70%
Maximum oxygen uptake during exercise	40%
Filtration rate of kidneys	69%
Maximum work rate	70%
Maximum work rate (short periods)	40%
Number of nerve trunk fibers	63%
Nerve conduction velocity	90%

10 20 30 40 50 60 70 80 90 100

Percent of function or tissue remaining at age 75

FIGURE 12.3 *Aging affects many body functions. This figure shows the approximate percentage of functioning or tissues remaining in the average 75-year-old man using the average 30-year-old man for comparison. Because the human body has great reserve capacity, loss of even thousands of cells hardly affects the performance of an organ. Eventually, however, impairments develop. One especially interesting problem is why some people age less rapidly than others. Understanding this puzzle may provide a key to minimizing loss of function.*

and cognitive development. Some longitudinal research suggests, however, that early maturing girls make a better adjustment as adults (Jones and Mussen, 1958; Peskin, 1973).

BODY CHANGES IN AGING

Body changes associated with aging begin early; there is a progressive loss of body tissue from at least the mid-20s on. Some of these changes are easily visible, while others are hidden within the body. Gerontologists (spe-

cialists in the study of aging) have examined these changes; some of their findings are shown in Figure 12.3.

Presumably, the physical changes that are part of the aging process are governed in part by maturation, but it is still not clear how heredity and environment interact in aging. Studies of twins indicate that genetic differences play an important role, because identical twins have more similar life spans than fraternal twins do (Kallmann and Jarvik, 1959). They also are more similar in appearance at various ages (see Figure 12.4).

FIGURE 12.4 *Similarity in physical development at several stages in the life span is shown in these photographs of identical twins at the ages of 5, 20, 55, and 86 years. Contrast the appearance of the fraternal twins (below).*

Motor performance

How the baby's body works and its stage of development are directly related to motor activity and muscular coordination. Infants' muscles are small and watery. Their bones are not fully hardened and have a much lower mineral content than an adult's. Even though infants' nervous systems are relatively advanced, they lack the strength and leverage to sit or stand alone and to direct their arm and leg movements precisely. Normative charts, such as the one in Figure 12.5, can help a parent to determine how a child's development compares with that of other children. (Remember, though, that there is wide variation among children and mild deviations from the average are no cause for alarm.)

Knowing about biological development has important practical applications. For example, research on the growth of muscles in infants shows that the sphinc-

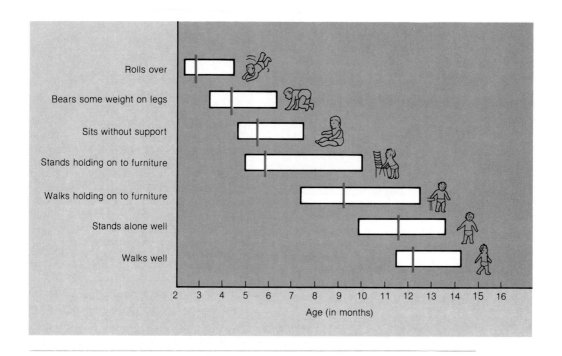

FIGURE 12.5 *Normally developing children differ in their maturation rate. The bars in this figure show the age range over which each skill develops. The vertical line on each bar marks the age at which 50 percent of all infants can perform the behavior. The left end of each bar marks the age at which 25 percent can perform the behavior; the right end marks the age at which 90 percent can perform the behavior.*

ter muscle, which controls defecation, is rudimentary and is not fully connected to the nervous system until well into the second year of life. Obviously, a child cannot be fully toilet trained until this muscle is under voluntary control. Mothers who insist that their 10-month-old child is toilet trained are usually kidding themselves; they have probably trained themselves to respond to the child's signals.

Parents' child-rearing practices, including toilet training, reflect their psychological perspective. A parent who emphasized the biological perspective would probably not attempt to toilet train a child until it was about 2 years old and had adequate muscular coordination to control its urination and bowel movements. A parent who was behaviorally oriented might begin toilet training when the child was 1 year or less, as John Watson did with his own children. A psychodynami-

cally oriented parent might delay toilet training until the age of 2 1/2 or later in order to make the power struggle between parent and child less traumatic. A cognitive psychologist might wait until the child could understand the principles involved.

Emotional development

From the moment of birth, infants' emotions are intense, but they don't appear to have a very wide range of them, and those that they do have are poorly differentiated from each other. At first only distress, disgust, pleasure, and surprise seem to be obvious. Researchers have noticed that emotional responses are added to this repertoire one or two at a time in a certain order. The order in which emotions appear, according to recent research, is shown in Figure 12.6. By the age of 5 or 6, children show most of the emotions that adults do. Two additional emotions—romantic passion and philosophical brooding—are added in adolescence.

Although Figure 12.6 makes the development of emotion seem very neat and precise, the moment when a particular emotion arrives for a specific child can be hard to determine from observation. A newborn baby does not express fear in the same way that an 18-month-old does. The development of emotions seems to have a biological basis, but several investigators have suggested that circumstances can alter it. For example, fear is not usually observed until 8 or 9 months, but infants who have been physically abused have what look like fear reactions as early as 3 months (Gaensbauer and Hiatt, 1984).

What we describe as a particular emotion may have different meanings at different ages. For instance, the emotional response of empathy means being able to put oneself psychologically in another's place and to understand what that other person is experiencing. If an 11-month-old child cries when another child falls down and cries, we can describe this as empathy, but we cannot be sure whether the child is really putting itself in the other child's place or is simply complaining because the situation is distressing.

In many cases, emotion has a strong cognitive element as well as a biological one. If two children, a

1-month-old and a 7-month-old, are shown a distorted human face, the 7-month-old will cry and appear distressed, but the 1-month-old will view the face with interest (Kagan, 1984). The difference is probably caused by a difference in level of cognitive function. The 7-month-old can compare the distorted image with its own mental image of what a face should look like, but the 1-month-old does not yet have that capability and so does not become disturbed. These cognitive changes are connected to the biological maturation that goes on in the brain during the first 2 years of life. In fact, measures of brain activity show that different brain areas may be involved in different emotions. For example, the right frontal area is more active during positive emotions, while the left frontal area is active during negative emotions.

Some researchers, such as Jerome Kagan (1984), have linked the development of a child's emotional life to the development of the series of cognitive stages described by Piaget and outlined in Chapter 11. A teenager, for example, acquires the whole range of adult emotions when he or she advances to the cognitive level of "formal operations." This cognitive stage en-

FIGURE 12.6 *Emotions seem to have a strong biological basis and develop according to a maturational timetable.*

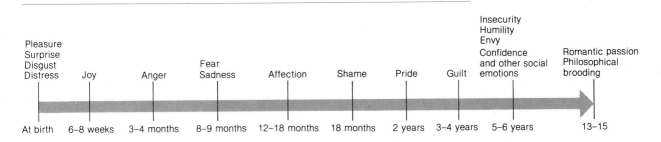

An emotional timetable

ables the adolescent to examine beliefs for logical consistency and makes possible the idealism and abstract philosophizing that go on during adolescence.

Sensory skills

Although the brain continues to develop after birth, particularly in the frontal lobes, a great proportion of brain development has already been accomplished by the time the child is born. Even though the nervous system is comparatively advanced at birth, developmental changes in the way it functions affect behavior just as structural differences do.

SENSORY MEASUREMENT TECHNIQUES FOR INFANTS

Although space-age technology and computerization make it possible for investigators to look at behavior even in very young infants (Acredolo and Hake, 1982), measuring the sensory functioning of very young infants has been a problem because their behavioral repertoire is so limited. One measure that is sometimes used is heart rate: when an infant is attending to a stimulus, its heart rate decreases. Using this technique, 2- and 3-day-old infants could be shown to discriminate between a patterned stimulus and one that was blank (Sameroff and others, 1973); 1- to 4-day-old infants perceived the turning on and off of colored lights (Adkinson and Berg, 1976).

Sensory functioning can also be studied by watching a baby's eyes. Much of the visual perception research in infants is based on the **preferential looking procedure** originated by Robert Fantz in the early 1960s. Infants were laid on their backs and two sets of visual stimuli were presented at the same time, one on each side of the visual field above them. Fantz filmed the infants' eye movements to determine how long they preferred to look at each of the stimuli. He reasoned that, if infants showed visual preferences, the common assumption that newborn infants cannot see must be wrong. It was found that infants less than 5 days old preferred black and white patterns to plain colored surfaces. Infants also preferred to look at the representation of the human face rather than at a scrambled face

or a pattern. These findings seem to indicate that at least some of our form perception and preference is innate. The human face apparently has special significance for us from the very beginning. Using variations of this technique, we have also learned that infants prefer curved to straight lines, and three-dimensional figures to two-dimensional ones.

Psychologists Davida Teller and Velma Dobson have refined Fantz's technique and obtained precise mathematical data on infants' visual behavior. Their apparatus is shown in Figure 12.7. An adult holds the infant in front of a display screen, and a single visual stimulus can be presented to either side of the screen. If color vision is being studied, colored lights of the same brightness as the rest of the screen are projected through holes in a white screen. In visual acuity experiments, black and white gratings of various widths are presented on a gray screen. A trained observer who is unaware of the location of the stimulus tries to find it

FIGURE 12.7 *To study early development, the infant is held before Teller's apparatus so that it can view the two openings where the stimulus may appear. The assistant holding the infant cannot see these openings because of the eye shield built into the apparatus. An observer is located behind a peephole in the apparatus. By looking at the infant's eye and head movements, the observer judges on each trial whether the stimulus has appeared on the left or right side. These judgments are then compared with the actual locations of the stimuli.*

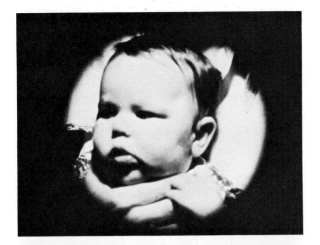

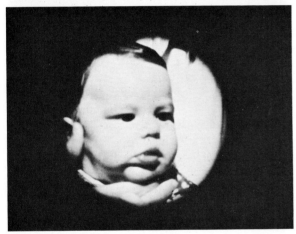

FIGURE 12.8 *These photos show the observer's view of the infant through the peephole. In the top photo the stimulus has appeared on the observer's left. In the bottom photo the stimulus has appeared on the observer's right.*

by using the baby's eyes as cues (Figure 12.8). Thus, data on infant visual behavior, including age norms, are actually being collected from an adult's performance (Dobson and others, 1978).

Another technique used to study the development of vision in very young children involves **visually evoked potentials** (VEP). Through electrodes attached to the scalp above the visual cortex, researchers can measure the electrical activity of large groups of neurons when visual stimuli are presented to infants. VEPs have been obtained in newborn babies, indicating that some degree of visual acuity is present even at birth (Atkinson and others, 1979). VEP responses to finer and finer grids occur progressively in the first six months of life (Sokol, 1984), which indicates that visual acuity develops steadily during that period.

Despite this increase in acuity in the early months, the visual pathways through which signals from the two eyes converge do not appear to be developed at birth. Instead, they begin to function sometime in the infant's fourth month of life (Birch and Heidt, 1983). This information is important in understanding whether young infants, who at times may appear "cross-eyed," have a problem that should be investigated or whether this is merely a part of normal development.

The coordination of vision with other senses has also been studied. Infants as young as 4 months can coordinate auditory and visual information. For example, infants were shown 2 films of a bouncing toy kangaroo while listening to sounds from a loudspeaker. The kangaroos on each of the films bounced at different rates: the movement of one was synchronized with the sound, while the other was out of phase. The infants looked significantly longer at the synchronized film, indicating that they were able to coordinate the information of two senses (Maynard, 1979).

DEPTH PERCEPTION

To study depth perception, Eleanor Gibson and Robert Walk (1960) developed an interesting piece of equipment called the *visual cliff*. The apparatus, shown in Figure 12.9, consists of a raised platform divided into two parts. One side of the platform was covered with a checkerboard pattern. On the other side, a sheet of the patterned material was placed several feet below a pane of heavy plate glass. Thus, the infants would be receiving conflicting sensory data: their hands would tell them that the glass was solid and could be crawled on,

while their eyes would interpret the change in the checkerboard pattern as indicating a dropoff or a cliff. What would the babies do?

Gibson and Walk tested thirty-six 6-month-old infants. Each infant was placed in the center of the apparatus; then its mother called to it first from the "deep" side and then from the "solid" side. If the babies could not perceive depth, the researchers reasoned that they would be equally likely to crawl to either side of the visual cliff. However, the evidence clearly showed that the infants could perceive depth. Of the 27 children who moved off the center platform, only 3 crawled onto the glass above the cliff. Many of the babies cried when their mothers called to them from the deep side, but they still refused to crawl there; some actually crawled away to more secure territory. A number of babies patted the glass above the deep side, but they still refused to crawl on it. Studies with animals who were far younger than these infants showed that chicks, goats, and lambs less than a day old avoided the cliff, and, when they were placed on the glass above the deep side, they froze in fear. These findings suggested to Gibson and Walk that, in these animals and perhaps in human beings as well, depth perception and fear of falling may be innate rather than learned.

So far, however, researchers have not been able to make much headway on the question of whether or not depth perception is innate in human beings. In one ingenious attempt, the experimenters tested 2-month-old infants by measuring their heart rates on each side of the visual cliff (Campos and others, 1970). There was a significant change on the deep side, but the nature of the change—a slowing of the heart rate—suggested that the infants were interested in the deep side, not frightened by it. Other efforts to determine whether depth perception exists in very young infants have also been subject to several interpretations, so as yet the question of when depth perception first occurs and whether it is present at birth is still unanswered.

FIGURE 12.9 *The "visual cliff" was developed by Eleanor Gibson to study depth perception. This child pats the glass on the deep side but refuses to crawl across it to his mother.*

LEARNING AND COGNITIVE DEVELOPMENT

Much of the research on children's thinking has been stimulated by the theories of Jean Piaget, which we discussed in Chapter 11. Researchers with Piaget's cognitive perspective have been primarily interested in how the child comes to certain conclusions—what he or she thinks about to get from point A to point B. Researchers coming from the learning perspective have been more interested in another question: Under what circumstances do children learn? Much recent research in these areas has focused on two topics: How early can learning be demonstrated in the human infant? And how do various types of intellectual performance change over the life span, especially in late middle age and old age?

Learning in infancy

As we saw in the last section, even newborn infants have functioning sensory systems. If infants can taste, smell, feel, hear, and see, then it is possible that the perceptual experiences of very early infancy will generate memories and that learning is therefore possible even in the newborn infant.

In *classical conditioning*, as we discussed in Chapter 6, a neutral stimulus and a stimulus capable of producing the desired response are paired; after a number of such pairings the formerly neutral stimulus alone becomes capable of eliciting or bringing forth the desired response. For example, a mild but unpleasant stimulus such as a puff of air will cause an eye blink. By pairing the puff of air with another stimulus—for example, the touch of a nipple—the eye blink response can eventually be produced in response to the nipple alone. One technique used to record such a conditioned response is shown in Figure 12.10.

Naturally occurring classical conditioning can be observed in the very young infant's response to being placed in a typical feeding position. The sucking movements that initially appear when a nipple is presented eventually are produced when the infant is simply picked up and held in the feeding position. Classical

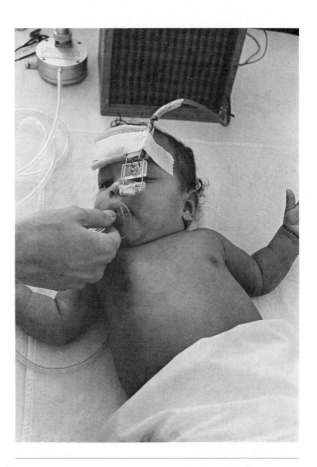

FIGURE 12.10 *Equipment for eyelid conditioning can be used with a very young infant. This 2-month-old seems unperturbed by the process.*

conditioning may also be important during toilet training. If a potty chair is repeatedly present when a child feels the physiological signals for urination or defecation, then contact with the chair alone may eventually trigger the response.

Instead of involving the build-up of a new association between a response and an initially neutral stimulus, as in classical conditioning, *operant conditioning* is demonstrated by the change in the rate of a naturally occurring response as a result of the rewards or punishments which follow that response. Operant conditioning may occur even before birth. When pregnant women read *The Cat in the Hat* aloud twice a day during the last six weeks before their children's birth, the sucking behavior of newborn babies showed their preference for listening to that book rather than to a similar children's story (Kolata, 1984). Naturally occurring operant conditioning is also of practical importance in a child's everyday life. Children very quickly learn how to exploit the reinforcement contingencies around them. One reinforcer that is particularly effective for young children is attention.

Two responses that are frequently used in conditioning experiments with very young infants are sucking and head turning (see Figure 12.11). There are two components of sucking: the positive pressure of the infant's gums against the nipple, and the negative pressure or suction that it exerts. Sameroff (1972) reinforced sucking by feeding only when the baby was sucking harder than it was biting down. The relationship between the two sucking components could be altered by operant conditioning, even in newborns.

An important methodological advance in operant conditioning is the use of **conjugate reinforcement,** in which the rate or size of the response alters the flow of the reinforcement, rather than producing the same amount of reward regardless of the magnitude of the response. Learning proceeds very quickly under these conditions, and the transfer of learning from one task to another also seems to be facilitated (Lipsitt, 1982).

Interest in learning has declined in the past 10 years among developmental psychologists. The emphasis has shifted to the area of cognitive development (Stevenson, 1983). Many of the procedures used in both learning experiments and in work on sensory development can also be used to explore memory in young children and to understand how the child learns to think. For instance, memory can be studied using cognitive reinforcement. An example is shown in Figure 12.12. A mobile is placed above the infant's crib, and, after a period to measure baseline response, it is connected by a ribbon to the infant's ankle so that the mobile moves in direct proportion to the frequency and vigor of the infant's kicks. In this conjugate reinforcement situation, the infant's kicking frequency typically doubles. When the mobile is reintroduced without the ribbon at a later time, we can conclude that the infant has remembered its earlier experience if the rate of kicking increases. Younger babies learn the relationship be-

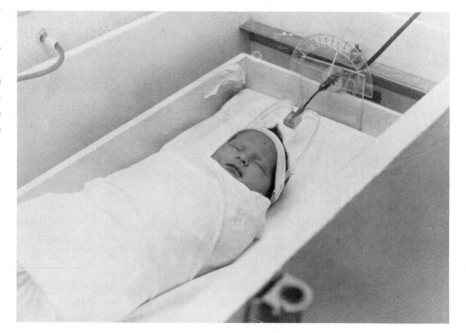

FIGURE 12.11 *Head turning is a voluntary response made by very young infants. This equipment, a plastic harness fitted to the infant's head with a Velcro band and connected to a polygraph, measures the size and direction of head turns when the infant is stimulated by a tone or other signal.*

FIGURE 12.12 *Conjugate reinforcement can be carried out with young infants by using a mobile connected to the baby's ankle by a ribbon. The frequency of infant kicking will increase in this situation because the movement of the mobile is reinforcing. Later the situation can be used as a measure of memory by placing the infant beneath an unconnected mobile and noting whether the child's frequency of kicking increases even though the mobile no longer moves with each kick.*

tween kicking and the mobile as quickly as older ones, but older infants remember it longer (Vander Linde, cited in Rovee-Collier, 1984).

Measuring cognitive development in infants

Procedures used in conditioning experiments can also be used to study discrimination in young infants. For example, a newborn can learn to differentiate between two tones by being reinforced for a response to one of them and not reinforced for a response to the other. Being able to discriminate between two tones also means that the infant must be able to remember the first tone long enough to compare it to the second. Human infants will respond vigorously to a new or sudden stimulus, but, if it is repeatedly presented, **habituation** occurs, and that stimulus gradually loses its ability to provoke the same response. Habituation can be used to determine whether an infant can discriminate between two stimuli. If the first stimulus no longer produces a vigorous response but the infant responds strongly to the other, the researcher can conclude that a discrimination has been demonstrated.

The extent of infants' preferences for novel stimuli has been related to intelligence test scores four to seven years later (Fagan and McGrath, 1981). If this relationship holds up in future research, it could have important practical implications, because no really satisfactory measures of intelligence for very young infants are presently available. This is one example of the many times that "basic" research—that is, research directed primarily at understanding a process more fully rather than at seeking knowledge for its practical applications—turns out to have unexpected, but ultimately very valuable, practical applications.

The habituation approach can also be used to study the way very young infants form concepts. An infant may be shown a number of similar slides—for example, views of different human faces—until he or she has become habituated to each of them. Then two new slides are shown—one of a human face that the infant has never seen before, and one of another object, such as a dog. If the infant seems habituated to the face but not to the dog, the experimenter could conclude that this discrimination implied the infant's ability to form the concepts *face* and *not-face*.

As children become older, experimenters have a wider range of behaviors with which to measure their performance. Children 6 months old, for example, could look at a set of 4 objects and group together those that were similar (Starkey, 1981). Even though it is clear that children can categorize objects in some fashion from a very early age, little is known about the nature of the categories that they use and even less is understood about the relationship between the conceptual categories used by a young, preverbal child and those employed by an adult (Clark, 1983).

Another aspect of cognitive development that interests researchers is the question of when children begin to use memory aids and whether the use of these devices changes with age. Six- or 7-year-old children often rehearse a whole list of items each time a new item is presented (*cart, ball; cart, ball, table; cart, ball, table, chair*). Children of 4 or 5 don't use this rehearsal technique spontaneously, but they can use it if it is modeled for them. By the time children are 9 or 10, they utilize a silent rehearsal technique similar to that seen in adults (Paris and Lindauer, 1982).

Cognitive changes over the life span

As they grow older, most people wonder how increasing age will affect intelligence. Can people in middle age and beyond expect to think as effectively and to solve problems as efficiently as they have in the past?

One of the difficulties in comparing the intellectual functioning of people at different ages is the problem of cohort effects. Different age groups in the population have experienced different historical events (wars, exposure to television, and so on) as well as changes in the general standard of living. Different scores that people of varying ages achieve on intelligence tests could be partly due to changes in diet, housing, or health care or, even more likely, to the amount and quality of education. Since the beginning of this century, there has been a trend for more people to go to school and to remain in school longer. Because it eliminates these cohort effects, a longitudinal study, as described in Chapter 11, may be the best way to look at age-related changes in intellectual functioning.

One of the few longitudinal studies of intellectual functioning is the Seattle Longitudinal Study, conducted by K. Warner Schaie and his associates (Schaie, 1983). The original subjects, who ranged in age from

18 to 67, have now been tested 4 times over a 21-year-period. These results have given a reasonably good picture of longitudinal change in cognitive abilities (see Figure 12.13).

The data show that there are only trivial changes in the kinds of abilities measured by intelligence tests before the age of 60, and no reliable decrease can be shown in these abilities before age 74. Although there is some decrease in measured ability in the late 60s and the 70s, it is not until age 81 that the average person falls below the middle range of performance for young adults.

The data from the Seattle Longitudinal Study also suggest that there are very great individual differences in intellectual change throughout adulthood. Between the ages of 74 and 81, less than half the subjects showed any significant change. One important factor is health, especially the presence or absence of coronary heart disease. Another is a high socioeconomic status, which is related not only to higher initial levels of functioning but to the maintenance of a higher level throughout life. A flexible life style in middle age, probably associated with a flexible personality style, also tends to predict high performance in old age. While some of these variables may have substantial hereditary elements, changes in environment and education could also be important in maintaining a higher level of functioning for many individuals.

Age changes in learning techniques

Psychologists are interested not only in what people know at different points over the life span but also in how they go about learning new material and solving problems.

Children's approach to learning tasks seems to change with age through midadolescence. For most people, cognitive processes do not seem to change much in adulthood; in Piaget's terms, no new stage is reached. Even though physiological alterations in the brain and nervous system are continuous throughout life, the skills and knowledge that a person accumulates in adult life can compensate in many kinds of tasks. However, there does seem to be some change in old age, especially in areas such as memory and response speed. It also seems reasonable to assume that cognitive functioning in this period, just as in earlier ones, is a product of an interaction of genetics and environment, not just of genetics alone.

Elderly people usually perform less well in learning studies than younger people do, but researchers disagree about whether this means that they do not learn as well or that they have problems in demonstrating what they have learned. There is some evidence that, compared with younger people, elderly people are less able to organize information, especially new information (Craik, 1977). On the other hand, some old people seem to become very aroused or upset in laboratory

situations, and this overarousal is translated into poor performance. Older people seem to worry more about giving the wrong answer than younger people do, so they often don't feel confident enough to respond, and these omission errors lower their scores (Arenberg and Robertson-Tchabo, 1977). They also need more time to respond, so that if answer time is limited, scores may

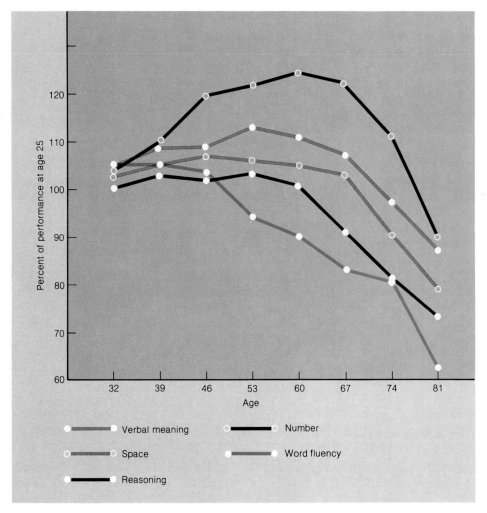

FIGURE 12.13 *Test performance on a variety of tasks often used to measure intelligence is shown as a percent of performance at age 25. (Adapted from data presented by Schaie, 1983, p. 114)*

be lower than they might be with unlimited time to answer.

Older people may become accustomed to different ways of thinking as their environment becomes less challenging. In a series of experiments, Ellen Langer and her co-workers found that restructuring a nursing home atmosphere to make it more intellectually demanding and then motivating the patients to increase their cognitive activity improved their memories in general as well as in the experimental situation (Langer and others, 1979). Langer suggests that too often we approach elderly people as if we were dealing with a failing organism and that a good deal of the lowered performance that we see is a result of this expectation.

SOCIAL AND PERSONALITY DEVELOPMENT

In social and personality development, perhaps even more than in other areas of growth, there is a dynamic interaction of the individual's personal characteristics, cultural factors, events that occur during life, and the historical period in which the person lives. Because of these multiple causes, theories based on the biological, cognitive, psychodynamic, and behavioral perspectives have all made major contributions to understanding this aspect of psychological development. Also, because this area is so complicated and is influenced by so many factors, most recent theories have dealt only with specific facets of social and personality development. This section discusses some of these specific areas: attachment, the process of socialization, and the plasticity of development.

Attachment

Freud's psychodynamic theory of personality development (discussed in Chapter 11) emphasizes the importance of the first five years of life. Freud believed that if trauma occurred at any stage of an individual's early development, the person, even though maturing in other respects, would be hampered throughout life.

The relationship of a child to its parents, especially its mother, is the most important factor from Freud's viewpoint. Rene Spitz (1946) and others showed that infants living in institutions who did not have close contact with a care-giving figure did indeed have poor physical and social development. The idea became prevalent that the child carried the influence of such early experiences with it into adulthood and that these influences were permanent.

Work with animals also suggested that an early relationship is important. Ethologists have observed that, during a specific and brief critical period in early development, a young animal forms a perceptual preference for an object; it shows an attachment for that object by following it. Ethologists call this behavior **imprinting** (see Figure 12.14). Ordinarily, the baby animal attaches itself to its mother, and the response of following the mother is a practical one that helps a young animal to survive. But ethologists have shown that, if the mother is absent and a human being or some other object is present at the critical time of imprinting, an attachment to that person or object may form instead.

Attachment, as the term is applied to human beings, may be defined as the infant's tendency, during the first 2 years of life, to be most receptive to being approached and cared for by a certain person or group of people. The infant is also less afraid of the environment while in the company of these people than when it is away from them.

ATTACHMENT THEORIES AND RESEARCH

John Bowlby, a British psychoanalyst, has combined the psychodynamic and ethological emphases on the importance of early experience in his studies of attachment and the effects of separation on young children (1969, 1973, 1980). Bowlby feels that attachment behavior in humans has the same practical result as that in animals: attachment keeps the child near its mother and thus protects it from danger.

Two large-scale studies observed the developmental process of attachment in several cultures (Ainsworth, 1963; Schaffer and Emerson, 1964). The first phase, extending from birth until approximately 6 or 7 months, was labeled **indiscriminate attachment.** During this period the baby shows many social behaviors, such as smiling, cuddling, and vocalization, but

FIGURE 12.14 *Imprinting has been well established in birds. This photo shows Konrad Lorenz, a Nobel Prize–winning ethologist, being followed by a group of young geese. They became attached or imprinted to Lorenz because he was the first large moving object they encountered during their critical period for imprinting. If the mother had been present at the critical time, she would no doubt have been the imprinted object. Their following behavior would then serve a protective function by keeping them close to her.*

these do not seem to be directed only at the mother. The child is usually happy to be picked up, and it does not seem to matter who does it. At about 6 or 7 months, however, the pattern changes, and the first **specific attachment** is formed. Babies begin to be selective; they smile more for the mother, cuddle more for her, hold out their arms to be picked up by her, and may reject similar approaches by strangers or acquaintances. This specific attachment may become extremely strong, and the child may cling to the mother or care-giver, show great distress when she leaves, and crawl vigorously toward her when she returns. By about 12 months of age, the single attachment begins to spread to a series of separate attachments. Infants show pleasure around several people, perhaps including the

father, a relative, or a frequent babysitter. The fear of strangers gradually wanes, and by 18 months most of the infants observed in these two studies showed some attachment to at least two people, and often many more.

One of the most thorough studies of the attachment process has been carried out by Mary Ainsworth and her co-workers at the University of Virginia. Ainsworth worked with Bowlby in much of his early study of attachment and shares his ethological point of view. Both Bowlby and Ainsworth suggest that infants have an innate biological tendency to behave in ways that promote contact and physical closeness with their mother figure. They cry for attention, and when the attention is given, they gurgle and coo to keep the relationship going. The parent responds to these innate behaviors and during a sensitive period in infancy the attachment bond develops. This view implies that, as with imprinting in animals, a particular period exists during which the bond must be established.

Some researchers argue that a critical **bonding period** occurs soon after the child's birth. They believe that the physical closeness of the child and mother during this period has an important long-term positive effect on their attachment (Klaus and Kennell, 1976). As a result of such findings, some hospital obstetric departments have changed their procedures to allow physical contact between the mother and child for a period immediately after the birth, and also encourage "rooming in," so that the infant remains in the mother's hospital room, not in the nursery, during the mother's hospital stay.

These procedures are not likely to have negative effects, though some researchers have been concerned about the psychological consequences for parents and children who must miss this experience, perhaps because the baby was premature and required an incubator, or because the mother was recovering from surgery after caesarian delivery. Many experts are convinced, however, that the idea of a critical bonding period for human beings has not been established, and, although the new hospital procedures are probably effective in humanizing the birth process, those mothers who must or would like to miss these experiences are not doing irreparable harm to their infants (Chess and Thomas, 1983; Goldberg, 1983).

LABORATORY STUDIES OF ATTACHMENT

Learning theorists and many psychodynamic psychologists emphasize the importance of feeding in building attachment. For example, learning theorists think of attachment as a result of a series of reinforcing experiences with the mother or care-giver that begins with early feeding experiences. This assumption was tested in a series of experiments with monkeys carried out by Harry Harlow and his co-workers at the University of Wisconsin. Harlow constructed two "mothers" (see Figure 12.15). One "mother," made of wire mesh, was the baby's source of food. The other "mother" was covered with terry cloth to which the monkey could cling; a light bulb inside it made it warm. Young monkeys living in the wild spend a great deal of time clinging to their mothers, and Harlow found that the satisfaction of clinging seemed more important in building a relationship than the gratification of being fed. His infant monkeys spent most of their time near the cloth mother. They approached the wire mother only to be fed. If frightened, they immediately ran to the cloth mother and clung to it. The strength of the clinging response, a survival behavior from the wild, even under these laboratory conditions suggests the importance of the ethological theory in explaining some behaviors.

Ainsworth has used a laboratory procedure that she calls the "strange situation" to study human attach-

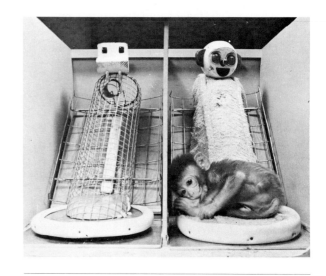

FIGURE 12.15 *Although the young monkey receives its food from the wire mother on the left, it still runs to the cloth-covered mother when a frightening event occurs. This attachment behavior seems to be based on the importance of mother-clinging behavior as a survival technique in monkeys reared in the wild. It suggests the significance of the ethological view in explaining the process of attachment.*

ment. A mother and a young child are observed when they are alone and when a "stranger" enters the room. The behavior of the infant is also observed when the mother goes out of the room, leaving the infant and stranger together, and when the mother returns.

Ainsworth noticed three general styles of attachment. Some babies use their mothers as a secure base to explore the toys in the room. When separated from her, they show distress; when she returns, they explore the room less and stay close to her. Ainsworth calls these **securely attached** children. Other infants seem more anxious and stay close to their mother even before separation. They are extremely distressed when she leaves, but after she returns, they seem ambivalent about her. They are **insecurely attached**. A third group avoid their mothers both before and after separation and do not cry when separated.

The differences observed in the laboratory were related to the way that the mothers and infants behaved at home. Mothers of the third group were less responsive to their babies. They ignored their cries and whimpers or responded slowly or inappropriately. Positive, secure attachments occurred in families in which mothers picked up their children fairly infrequently, but when they did pick them up, held and cuddled them for a long time in an affectionate manner (Ainsworth and others, 1972). These mothers apparently enjoyed holding their babies and picked them up at times other than for feeding and diapering. The type of attachment a child shows before age 2 is also related to later behavior. Children who were insecurely attached or avoidant at 18 months were rated by their preschool teachers to be significantly more dependent and to have more disciplinary problems than children who had been rated securely attached at 18 months (Sroufe and others, 1983).

The attachment process is not solely determined by the parent's response; the infant's behavior also has an important effect in establishing attachment. Some infants may be "difficult" from birth. They may be less responsive, less adaptive, or more intense in their reactions to stimuli. They may cry more and appear to resist being handled. Interacting with such an infant may be difficult for the parent, and this may lead to an anxious or insecure attachment (Waters and others, 1980). Mothers whose babies were more fussy about being picked up and fussier about being put down were likely to be less affectionate with their babies and were more likely to pick the baby up in a way that interfered with its activities.

FATHER ATTACHMENT

Mother-child attachment has been emphasized in psychological research, but children also become attached to their fathers. The mother-infant and father-infant relationships both appear when the child is about 6 months old. This is true not only when fathers played a major role in infant care, but even in families where fathers and children interacted for only 10 hours a week or less (Lamb, 1979). In these families children had different kinds of experiences with their male and female parents: the mothers' interaction was largely caretaking in character, while the fathers tended to interact with their children in play, especially active, boisterous play. By the time children are 2, fathers begin to treat their children differently depending on their sex; the

fathers pay more attention to their sons and withdraw from their daughters. This results in the child's increased preference for the same-sex parent and may play a major role in the gender identity process (discussed in the next section).

As researchers have begun to look at father-child attachment, they have become aware that the child and both parents must be viewed as a triad. Not only does the child's relationship with each parent affect development, but the parents' relationship with each other both affects and is affected by their parenting experiences (Belsky, 1981).

Socialization

Socialization is the developmental process through which we learn the rules of the game of life in our society. Human animals become human beings and acquire a set of distinctive personal attributes, motives, and social values through learning by various methods—imitation, identification, reward, and punishment. All these processes are involved in the type of socialization process called sex role development.

SEX ROLE DEVELOPMENT

A child's sex is a social fact as well as a biological one. When inquiring about a new baby, most people immediately ask, "Is it a boy or a girl?" Most people's perceptions of males and females differ, even when they are viewing newborn infants. If they see a boy infant or even an infant they think is a boy, they will tend to describe it as strong and large-featured. Girls, on the other hand, are described as delicate and fine-featured (Rubin and others, 1974).

Sex roles and sexual identity   Before discussing the development of sex roles, we need to define some terms. A *role* is the set of expected behaviors, rights, and duties that go along with a certain position in the social structure. A **sex role,** then, is the behavior that society thinks is appropriate for each sex. Not all differences in male and female behavior are due to sex roles, of course. For example, women urinate sitting down, and males urinate standing up. This is much more a function of biological structure than of sex role.

A person cannot know what behavior is appropriate until he or she has a **sexual identity.** A boy must know that he is a boy and that he will grow up to be a man before he can begin to acquire behavior considered appropriate to his sex. Sexual identity is usually well established by the age of 3 and seems to be based on what children are told rather than on their perceptions of their own physical characteristics. Most 3-year-olds know the labels *boy* and *girl* and can apply the correct label to themselves, but they are generally not capable of applying the labels correctly to others. The generalization of the concepts *male* and *female* occurs around age 4, but 4-year-olds do not yet realize that their boyness or girlness is permanent. A child of this age is very likely to think that one can change from a boy to a girl, or vice versa, perhaps by changing clothes. By the age of 5 or 6, children typically understand that gender is permanent and genital differences have more than an anatomical significance. How does this occur? The process can be viewed from several different psychological perspectives.

PERSPECTIVES ON SEX ROLE DEVELOPMENT

Behaviorists argue that children receive specific training in appropriate sex role behavior. Boys are rewarded directly with praise or attention for playing with trucks, for being a little tough, and for imitating their fathers. Girls are reinforced for imitating their mothers and for adopting appropriate female attitudes and behaviors in their play and other activities.

Although reinforcement is clearly involved in the acquisition of sex roles, it seems too simple an explanation and does not account for unreinforced responses learned by observation. Through modeling, children learn complex sets of interrelated behaviors that may not be expressed until later (see Figure 12.16). For example, a girl may not realize how she has been influenced by her mother's way of relating to her father until she gets married herself. What would a girl's sex role expectation be if she lived in a family where the father did all the food preparation? She might learn that food

FIGURE 12.16 *The immediate effects of modeling are clear in these photos (this page and next page) of mother-daughter, father-son duos. Modeling may also have long-term effects on much more complex behavior such as how a person interacts in later adult relationships.*

preparation was a male role. More likely, she would learn that men are capable of cooking but that cooking is generally a female role in our society, because she had seen women cook in other families, on television programs, in food ads, and so on. Because many aspects of cultural experience contribute to sex role expectations, those expectations are difficult to change. Social institutions such as education and the media often lag behind families in reflecting shifts in popular attitudes.

The idea that people acquire their sex roles by modeling merges into the cognitive viewpoint. *Male* and *female*, *boy* and *girl* are concepts, not unlike the concepts *big*, *little*, *happy*, and *sad*. From this perspective, the child's understanding of his or her own sexual identity is a cognitive accomplishment. Parents or other adults may play some role in this by providing appropriate labels for objects, but the process of developing concepts primarily occurs inside the child. Think back to Piaget's idea of the development of *conservation* discussed in Chapter 11. The realization that maleness and femaleness are constants is equivalent to the development of conservation—the realization that objects are constant even though their shape may be altered—and both processes occur at about the same time.

Five- or 6-year-old children have quite stereotyped views about sex roles, and they comment quite ruthlessly on other children's deviations from what they consider proper sex role behavior. By the time they are 9, however, children are less rigid in their sex role concepts and will accept occasional nonconformity (Damon, 1977). They think of sex role behavior in terms of what is customary and what is unusual rather than in terms of right and wrong.

Cognitive developmental theorists can explain why sex stereotypes appear early in life and how they change within the first 6 years. They cannot explain, however, why boys follow a predictable pattern of selecting and adopting male behaviors and activities, while girls are less likely to value and adopt only female behaviors. Girls and their parents often have a positive reaction to "boys'" behaviors, while boys and their parents react negatively to behavior associated with girls. This suggests that sex roles are not only cognitive in origin but

have a heavy weighting of social-cultural influence, too (see Figure 12.17).

A third view of the development of sexual identity and sex roles has been offered by Freud and by others who take a psychodynamic perspective. Freud proposed that they are acquired through a process called **identification** in which the child becomes as much like the same-sex parent (or really the child's view of that parent) as possible. Freud believed that identification occurs around age 5 during the phallic stage of development and is a way of resolving the Oedipal crisis.

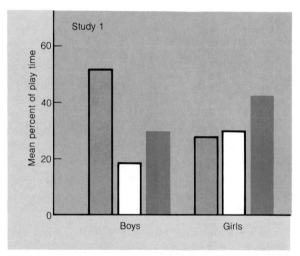

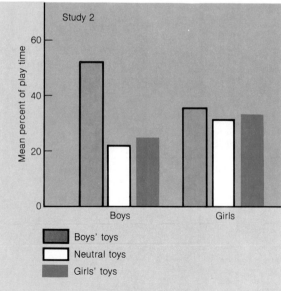

Plasticity of development

How **plastic**—how flexible—is the process of development? Can the emotional hang-ups or skill deficits that occur when a stage of development does not go well be compensated for at a later time? Some theorists are much more optimistic about that possibility than others are. In general, the biological theorists and some psychodynamic theorists, especially Freud, are pessimistic. Other psychodynamic theorists, such as Erikson, some cognitive psychologists, and the behaviorists take a more optimistic view.

One's attitude toward the concept of critical periods in maturation is related to how plastic one imagines development to be. For instance, Bowlby and Ainsworth's view of attachment and the ethologists' view of imprinting presume that certain critical periods occur. Present thinking about critical periods suggests that, although certain periods of maturation may be best for the development of certain behaviors, these behaviors may also be established at other times. According to a life span view, the whole of development, not just the early years, is significant. Whether some periods are more important continues to be a controversial issue.

Anne Clarke and A. D. B. Clarke (1976) cite many cases in which environmental improvements in middle or later childhood resulted in spectacular gains in intellectual development and increased ability to form relationships despite severe emotional and intellectual deprivation in early childhood. But research data still suggest that environmental improvements in early childhood are likely to have a greater effect than those in later childhood (Tizard and Hodges, 1978; Rutter, 1979).

FIGURE 12.17 *Even at an early age, young children select sex-typed toys. This figure shows the proportion of the time children 15 to 36 months of age chose sex-stereotyped toys for their play at a toddler day-care center. (O'Brien and others, in press)*

EXPERIMENTAL WORK ON CRITICAL PERIODS

Our knowledge of the effects of separation from an attachment figure or physical isolation on young children comes from a variety of case studies. From time to time a case of appalling deprivation comes to light, such as that of Genie, whose father had kept her in a small cubbyhole since she was born. When she was removed from her home at age 13, Genie could not control her bladder and bowels, could not speak, was able to walk only with difficulty, and functioned at a 5-year-old intellectual level (Curtiss, 1977). After 4 years of intensive training in an enriched environment, she made dramatic gains, although she still had severe problems. Because such cases leave many questions unanswered, psychologists have turned to experimental work with animals to cast some light on the importance of early experience in development. One of the most important investigators in this area has been Harry Harlow, whose study of monkeys' attachment to their terry cloth "mothers" we discussed earlier.

In another series of experiments, Harlow and his co-workers studied the effects on infant monkeys of early separation from their mothers or of being reared in isolation (Suomi and Harlow, 1978). Monkeys reared in isolation for the first 6 months or more of life showed disturbed behavior. They continually sucked on themselves and displayed stereotyped behavior such as constant rocking. They were extremely timid, but after being released from isolation, they were likely to behave very aggressively toward other monkeys. These inappropriate behaviors did not disappear spontaneously after isolation ceased; they continued throughout the monkey's life.

Harlow and his co-workers then tested the critical period theory to determine whether the effects of early isolation could be reversed. They found that even monkeys reared in total isolation for 6 months could be almost totally rehabilitated by "therapist monkeys" (see Figure 12.18). Monkeys raised in isolation for 12 months also responded well to therapy, although their rehabilitation was not as complete (Novak and Harlow, 1975). Although generalizing from animal to human behavior is risky, these results suggest that recovery from early isolation is not automatic but that it can be achieved with appropriate therapeutic techniques.

FIGURE 12.18 *A young monkey, still in the clinging stage but not yet showing aggressive behavior, can be an effective therapist for an older monkey reared in isolation.*

INVULNERABILITY

Many people grow up in circumstances that seem counterproductive of good development. Some emerge from that sort of childhood as poorly functioning people; others survive and become well adapted or even outstanding adults in spite of their genetic, psychological, and economic disadvantages. Psychologist Norman Garmezy (1974) has called these children "**invulnerables.**"

Until recently there has been little investigation of

why some children mature into unusually competent adults after extremely negative childhood situations. Recent research suggests that several factors are important. These include the number of different sources of stress experienced by the child, his or her personality characteristics, the kind of child-parent relationship that exists, and other factors such as school experiences and the neighborhood environment.

One source of stress, even though severe and chronic, does not seem enough to represent a major obstacle in development. But two stresses increase the risk of developmental problems four times, and additional stresses have an even greater effect. For example, if a child from a chronically deprived home has several hospitalizations, his or her development is more likely to be adversely affected than a child from a supportive home who is hospitalized (Quinton and Rutter, 1976). In the same way, a child whose parents are divorced will function better if economic problems, a move to a new school and neighborhood, and custody battles do not accompany the divorce process (Longfellow, 1979). Frontier 12.1 details some of what is known about the effects of divorce on children.

A child's personality is also important. Children who are stubborn or negative or have other personality features considered to be undesirable have a much higher risk of being diagnosed as disturbed than other children do. This may be partly due to the interaction of these children and their parents; such children are twice as likely as other children to be targets of parental criticism (Rutter, 1978).

HIGH-RISK CHILDREN GROW UP

A longitudinal study designed to look at characteristics that make it possible for children growing up in high-risk environments to become well-functioning adults has been in progress on the Hawaiian island of Kauai for several decades (Werner and others, 1971; Werner and Smith, 1977, 1982). Some of the children in the sample had biologically based developmental problems; many of them lived in chronic poverty or in a disorganized family environment. More than half of them had fathers who were semiskilled or unskilled laborers and mothers who did not graduate from high school. The children were born in 1955, before Hawaii became a state, and grew up in a period of rapid change

as their island shifted from a sugar-cane-growing economy to a tourist haven. Almost a third of the 698 children in the study showed serious behavioral or learning difficulties at some time before they were 20. However, most of them developed into adults who were competent at coping with their problems, who found their family and friends to be supportive, and who grew up with a strong sense of continuity of their family-held values in education and occupation. Some of the study participants particularly impressed the researchers with their invulnerability; they developed into competent and autonomous adults who "worked well, played well, loved well and expected well" (Garmezy, 1976). One example was Mary:

When she was 18, Mary described herself this way: "If I say how I am, it sounds like bragging—I have a good personality and people like me. Generally, I hope I can make it—I hope." Mary's optimism about herself seemed justified. At the time she spoke she was planning to enroll in a two-year community college on the island of Oahu. She intended to test out how well she did and if things worked out well, to go on to the University of Hawaii and become a medical or legal secretary.

Mary's early life was not highly favorable. Before her birth her mother had had a number of miscarriages; she had a variety of medical problems during the pregnancy and a 20-hour period of labor before Mary's birth. However, the visiting nurse judged Mary's infancy to be a warm, supportive experience. Although her mother was a "temperamentally nervous person," her father, a plantation laborer with only 4 years of formal schooling, participated in her care and seemed to have a close relationship with his infant daughter.

When Mary was 2 her intelligence test results were in the normal range; at 2½, she was advanced for her age on a standard test to measure self-help skills. Researchers who had contact with the family rated Mary's progress as good and the family as stable despite financial difficulties. By the time Mary was 10, her mother had had several major illnesses as well as 2 hospitalizations for mental disturbance. During her mother's absences some supportive relatives helped the family by staying with Mary. Mary's schoolwork was good throughout this time, and her intelligence tested as above average.

When she was asked to describe her relationship with her parents, Mary characterized her mother as a grumpy and lonely individual who hit and beat her frequently. "In a way I used to hate her, but as I got older I understood her better. . . ." Mary's father gave her more support. She

THE EFFECTS OF DIVORCE ON CHILDREN'S DEVELOPMENT

Each year about a million American children have their homes disrupted by the separation or divorce of their parents. By the end of the 1980s, it is estimated that nearly one-third of all children in the United States will have experienced their parents' divorce. Despite its becoming a commonplace event, from a cultural standpoint divorce is still considered to be an unusual event with many negative implications for the people involved. It is also one of the most stressful and disorganizing life events that may occur (Holmes and Rahe, 1967) and is one for which most children and most adults are not psychologically prepared.

The degree to which divorce is upsetting to children has been recognized for a long time. Children of divorce show up much more frequently in psychiatric out-patient clinic populations than their proportion in the population would predict (Kalter, 1977). Even children in nonclinical samples are likely to make dramatic divorce-related changes in play behavior and relationships with peers, teachers, and parents (Hetherington and others, 1979; Wallerstein and Kelly, 1980). Not only do children have to deal with their own stress, but they must cope with parents who are also experiencing high levels of stress and whose own physical and emotional health may have significantly deteriorated (Bloom and others, 1978).

Since divorce seems to play an increasing role in our culture, psychologists have thought it important to take a look, not only at how divorce affects children and adults at the time, but at how it affects their later development and adjustment. Another important question involves whether certain ways of handling some of the decisions associated with divorce are more beneficial than others in terms of the child's development. One of the most important decisions made concerning children involves custody.

A few longitudinal studies of divorce have been carried out. One of the best known is the California Children of Divorce Project (Wallerstein and Kelly, 1980). The study followed 60 divorcing families and

their 131 children, initially ages 3 to 15, through the first 5 years after the separation. A major purpose of the investigation was to understand how the children experienced the divorce itself and to see what factors made the experience more manageable for them. The researchers wanted to know whether age, sex, parent-child relationship, amount of stress in the predivorce relationship, and so forth influenced the way the children dealt with the divorce both at the time and afterward. Another aim of the study was to look at the children over time to see what developmental processes were impeded or accelerated by the changes brought about by the divorce.

The initial period after the parents' decision to divorce was experienced as extremely stressful by the children for its own sake and because they were able to obtain less psychological support from the parents, who were undergoing high degrees of stress themselves. After about a year, many of the acute responses had decreased or disappeared, and many of the children recovered their level of functioning faster than their parents, although girls seemed to recover much faster than boys. The changes that still remained after a year tended to become chronic. The transition period following the period of acute stress lasted as long as two or three years in many of the families. In the third stage, most of the families had stabilized either as a postdivorce family or in a new marriage.

The children and the parents frequently had different attitudes about the divorce that lasted throughout the 5-year period. Many of the marriages that had been unhappy for the parents were experienced as gratifying or even happy by the children. More than half the children did not think of the divorced family as an improvement over the predivorce family even after 5 years had passed; in contrast, less than 20 percent of the adults thought the divorce had been ill-advised, and many felt the situation was greatly improved. After 5 years about one-third of the children were well adjusted and adapting well, and about the same number were still unhappy, felt deprived or rejected, and were still angry at one or both parents.

The age of the child at the time of divorce did not seem to predict later adjustment. The factors that predicted good adjustment were related to the quality of the relationship with both parents, the quality of life of the divorced family, and the degree to which the divorce resolved the problems that brought it about. But the major factors in determining whether or not the child adjusted well to the divorce were the personalities and parenting styles of both the mother and the father. A continued close relationship with the noncustodial parent, in this study usually the father, was also important in the child's later adjustment. Children who lacked this were likely to continue to feel depressed and to have impaired self-esteem.

In recent times the courts have most frequently awarded custody of any children to the mother unless she was obviously an unfit person. A mother who for some reason wished the father to have custody was regarded with disapproval by society; she was seen as uncaring and not what a mother "should be." To base court decisions on more than just unfounded beliefs,

and to remove the unnecessary guilt faced by parents who do not conform to society's unwritten rules, better information on the results of custody awards was clearly needed. One study designed to supply some of this information is the Texas Custody Research Project (Warshak and Santrock, 1983). The study compared the adjustment of male and female children whose custody was granted to the father after divorce with both (1) children whose custody was awarded to the mother and (2) children who lived in intact families. Children living with the same-sex parent were found to show more competent social development. When comparisons were made among all the children, a sex difference appeared only for father-custody children: the boys in the father-custody homes were rated as more mature than boys from intact families. Girls from father-custody homes were rated lower in maturity than girls from intact families. Ratings of children from the mother-custody homes did not differ from those of children who lived with both parents. In general, though, children living with the same-sex parent seemed to be faring better than children living with the opposite-sex parent. This study,

FIGURE 12.19 *The drawing by an 11-year-old boy shows how he was tempted by the offers his parents made to bribe him in their custody battle. He felt their struggle left him hanging over "the pits," as his father offered a motorcycle and his mother emphasized what a lot of fun they'd have together. Even if both parents had been able to say, "I'll love you no matter what you decide," their son might have felt torn between them. Few children at 11, or even several years older, feel competent to decide their own fate.*

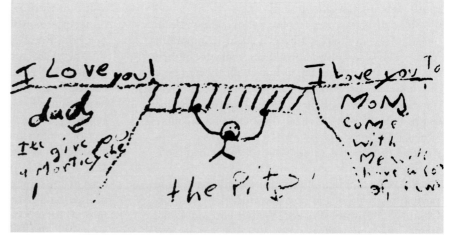

while certainly not sufficient basis for custody decisions in itself, nevertheless suggests that there is something very important about an ongoing relationship of a child with its same-sex parent.

Although longitudinal research data on ways to moderate the effects of divorce on children are scarce, the clinical experience of many therapists and counselors has provided some ideas that may help parents soften the blow for their children:

1. *Tell the children ahead of time.* This lets them prepare for one parent's moving out.

2. *Tell the children the reasons why the decision was made.* This helps prevent children's frequent belief that they were the cause of the breakup. Make the explanation brief but honest and suitable for the age of the child.

3. *Emphasize that the divorce is a permanent decision.* Many children harbor the belief that their parents will eventually get back together.

4. *Explain what changes there will be in the child's life.* These may include moving, a new school, and much less money to spend. Emphasize the positive challenge of adapting to the new situation.

5. *Let the children be free to express their anger.* This is an effective way to prevent long-term problems. At the same time the parents should avoid using their children as a dumping ground for their own sense of anger or despair. Instead they should share their negative feelings with an adult friend or with a therapist or counselor.

6. *Avoid forcing the child to choose between the parents or take sides.* Figure 12.19 illustrates the feelings that this may create. Custody and visitation rights that are fair to both parents should be agreed upon. Both parents should make continued contact with the children a high priority.

described how flexibly he handled parent-child difficulties as she grew up. "I used to sneak off before—you know my father is Filipino style and they're strict with their daughters. . . . I was 16 and I figured I was going to have dates and my father wouldn't let me so I snuck out. And after he caught me one time . . . he told me then 'if you want a boyfriend, you bring him over here and you can get to know him better because it's the natural way.' . . . I guess if my father had kept being strict with me and I kept sneaking out, I guess I may have turned out more the rugged type." (Adapted from Werner and Smith, 1982, pp. 140–144)

Reading the description of Mary's life may have given you some clues about why—despite what seem to be possible biological and environmental negatives— she seems to be developing into an effective and psychologically healthy person. There are some positive factors working for Mary: her health is good and her intellectual level better than average, and she had a warm and close relationship with her father throughout her life. Although we cannot pinpoint the specifics, these factors—biological hardiness, intelligence, and a caring and dependable relationship with someone— seem most important in predicting who will be "invulnerable."

As more is learned about development in difficult or traumatic situations, researchers become increasingly impressed with the resiliency of children and with their ability to develop into psychologically healthy adults despite very negative beginnings (Kagan, 1984; Chess and Thomas, 1983; Long and Vaillant, 1984). Longitudinal studies, such as the Kauai study and some of those discussed in Chapter 11, are among the best ways to understand the factors most crucial to developmental progress or to developmental problems. These findings give an optimistic outlook: many early difficulties and "mistakes" in parenting may not irrevocably blight the child's future. This does not mean, however, that parents and others should do nothing to help children who are having serious difficulties. At our present state of knowledge about what kinds of problems are self-remedying, it is usually better to give appropriate help rather than just to assume everything will turn out all right later. One way that seems especially useful in helping children cope effectively is the availability of a dependable and friendly relationship with someone who makes it clear that he or she cares about what happens.

STUDY OUTLINE

BIOLOGICAL DEVELOPMENT (p. 420)

1. Sex differences in developmental patterns are one cause of differences in performance, especially in infancy and childhood. Girls reach many of the developmental stages more rapidly than boys throughout this period. Physical changes, especially those of infancy, adolescence, and old age, affect both behavior patterns and other people's expectations of behavior.

2. Normative charts are helpful to parents in evaluating their child's development. Child-rearing practices tend to reflect not only the parents' information about normative development but the type of psychological perspective they emphasize.

3. Types of emotional responses also have a maturational timetable. Although emotions seem to have a biological basis, the environment can alter at least some of them, such as fear, which appears earlier in children who have been physically abused.

4. The nervous system, highly developed at birth, continues to develop during infancy and childhood. New technology has made it possible to study the sensory functioning of very young infants and has shown that they respond to a variety of sensory stimulation and can distinguish between similar stimuli.

LEARNING AND COGNITIVE DEVELOPMENT (p. 429)

1. Both classical and operant conditioning can occur in very young infants. Operant conditioning may take place even before birth. Natural responses of young infants, such as sucking and head turning, are used in these conditioning studies. Both sensory development and cognitive development, including learning and memory, can be examined using these techniques.

2. Research on cognitive development in adulthood and old age shows that abilities do not all change in the same manner over time and that many abilities remain relatively stable at least into early old age. Because of the strength of cohort effects, the longitudinal rather than the cross-sectional approach is needed to study cognitive development through the life span. Cognitive functioning, both early and late in life, seems to be a result of a combination of genetic and environmental factors.

SOCIAL AND PERSONALITY DEVELOPMENT (p. 434)

1. Attachment, a strong relationship that may be formed with a particular individual in the first 2 years of life, is considered by many biologically and psychodynamically oriented theorists to be important in later ability to form interpersonal relationships. Attachment behavior in animals seems to facilitate survival. In human beings, the research has shown that children may be securely or insecurely attached, or may avoid contact with their mothers in stressful situations. These behaviors are related to the child's later adjustment. Father attachment has also been studied.

2. Socialization is the developmental process through which the rules of society are learned. Sex role development is one example of socialization. A sex role is the behavior that society thinks is appropriate for each sex. Sexual identity is gained through the individual's cognitive process of understanding his or her own gender as a permanent characteristic.

3. Plasticity of development refers to the ability to make up for early difficulties in development without permanent damage to the individual. Those who believe in critical or sensitive periods take a pessimistic view of how much catch-up is possible. Those who have a behavioral viewpoint, as well as some psychodynamic and cognitive theorists, have a more optimistic view.

4. Some individuals become effective, well-adjusted adults despite a heredity and environment that seem unfavorable to development. What makes these individuals "invulnerable" is of great interest to psychologists. One factor that seems particularly important is the presence of a dependable relationship with someone who lets the child know he or she cares what happens.

KEY TERMS AND CONCEPTS

preferential looking procedure

visually evoked potentials

conjugate reinforcement

habituation

imprinting

attachment

indiscriminate attachment

specific attachment

bonding period

securely attached

insecurely attached

father attachment

socialization

sex role

sexual identity

identification

plasticity of development

invulnerability

high-risk children

SUGGESTED READINGS

ESPENSCHADE, A. S., and ECKERT, H. M. (1980). *Motor development (2nd ed.)*. Columbus, Ohio: Merrill. A discussion of the development of basic motor skills that incorporates information from many disciplines.

KAIL, R. (1984). *The development of memory in children (2nd ed.)*. New York: W. H. Freeman. A clear and interesting presentation of the relation between changes in memory development and cognition, and the role of memory in children's social and intellectual activities.

MACCOBY, E. E. (1980). *Social development: Psychological growth and the parent-child relationship*. New York: Harcourt Brace Jovanovich. A review of the literature on the parental role in socialization of children.

WALLERSTEIN, J. S., and KELLY, J. B. (1980). *Surviving the breakup: How children and parents cope with divorce*. New York: Harper & Row. A readable account of the first major study of the long-range effects of divorce on children and on their parents.

SECTION SIX
PERSONALITY, ADAPTATION, AND HEALTH

CHAPTER THIRTEEN: **PERSONALITY: PERSONS AND SITUATIONS**

CHAPTER FOURTEEN: **ADJUSTING TO LIFE: STRESS, COPING, AND HEALTH**

PERSONALITY: PERSONS AND SITUATIONS

WHAT IS PERSONALITY?

PERSONALITY THEORIES

Freud's psychoanalytic theory

Other analytic theories

Humanistic and existential theories

Cognitive-behavioral theories

Biological approaches to personality

Trait theories

An appraisal of personality theories

Situations, persons, and their interactions

FRONTIER 13.1 EXPERIMENTAL STUDY OF
PSYCHOANALYTIC CONCEPTS: A PERSON × SITUATION
PERSPECTIVE

PERSONALITY ASSESSMENT

The interview

Paper and pencil questionnaires

Projective techniques

Behavioral assessment

Cognitive assessment

Bodily assessment

Personality tests and the privacy and validity issues

STUDY OUTLINE

KEY TERMS AND CONCEPTS

SUGGESTED READINGS

Mary Spane couldn't believe she actually had gotten a summer job. There had been applications, letters, phone calls, and several interviews. The result was always either a letter saying, "We are sorry, but . . . " or no response at all. But now she had a job. She had the status of being a worker and the money she needed to pay part of her next year's college expenses.

Assured of summer employment, Mary began to look forward almost with a sense of relief to studying for final exams. But two thoughts about job hunting kept intruding. One was her sense of gratification at "getting something." Mary wanted work experience but, even more important, she dreaded having to ask her parents to pay for all her next year's expenses. What she wanted most was to be independent or as close to it as she could come. Thinking about her new job was a real delight for Mary.

The other thought was not so delightful. She could still feel the pain of all those fruitless job applications, and she knew that next year she would have to go through the same torture all over again. She dreaded having to "sell" herself, and she didn't want to experience again that terrible fear that she might not find a job or that some personnel manager might not like the clothes she wore or the way she styled her hair.

Why does Mary continue to feel the pain of her fruitless job applications? Is it because of what actually took place in the job interviews, or is it attributable more to the kind of person she is? Psychologists who study personality focus on the interplay between personal and situational characteristics. Some researchers see our behavior as being more under the influence of the type of situation. They might note that getting the job created a new set of circumstances that influenced Mary's mood and behavior. Researchers who stress individual characteristics might observe Mary's forebodings about the future. They might point out that those forebodings, as well as her need to be an independent person, came from within her, not from any actual and present threat. From this point of view, understanding the inner workings of each person is crucial to an explanation of behavior.

WHAT IS PERSONALITY?

Many students take psychology courses because they want to learn more about how personality functions. An analysis of what personality is, and what it is not, may help us to explain our own behavior as well as that of our family and friends. Because it is a noun, we use the term **personality** as if personality were a thing. We speak of *the* personality, *her* personality, and so on, as if it were something real and concrete, like red hair and freckles. But personality isn't a thing in its own right; it has no existence apart from behavior.

Personality is a concept, or construct, that arises from the observation and evaluation of behavior. For example, when we say that someone has a "good" personality or a "lousy" one, we mean that the person customarily behaves in ways that are either pleasing or displeasing to us. Personality is a generalization about people's behavior—what they usually do in a certain kind of situation. At the same time, as we saw in Chapters 11 and 12, human characteristics may change in important ways over time. Like development in general, personality development is a lifelong process. Thus, the person and the situation are involved in a reciprocal relationship; each influences the other.

Once we realize that personality is a construct, we are ready to consider why we have invented the concept of personality and the kinds of behaviors it includes. If everyone behaved in exactly the same way, there would be no need for such a concept as personality. The world would be pretty dull, and this book would be at least one chapter shorter. But even when people are put in highly controlled environments, there are still observable differences in their behaviors. The concept of personality is part of our attempt to account for these differences.

Personality involves our overt behavior (what observers can notice about what we do) and covert processes (our thoughts, tendencies, fantasies—how we put 2 and 2 together). To characterize an individual's personality as an organized whole, we must pay attention to and draw inferences about both overt and covert events.

How can we learn about someone's personality? We need to study his or her behavior thoroughly but selectively: certain types of behavior won't be as reveal-

FIGURE 13.1 *Four questions that must be answered in creating a personality profile:*

1. Which aspects of the person's behavior distinguish him or her from other people?

2. How consistent or inconsistent is the person's behavior?

3. What are the personal and situational causes of the person's behavior in various areas of life?

4. To what degree do the person's characteristics "fit together" and how can we best organize them into a meaningful whole?

ing as others. Joe's eye color tells us nothing about his personal identity, but the fact that he frequently loses his temper does. Behavior that is primarily caused by environmental factors also gives us little information about what a person is like. If Joe stands up and cheers while in the stands during an exciting football game, that behavior is not likely to be viewed as a crucial indicator of his personality. If he engaged in those same behaviors at a funeral, those behaviors might be worth noting.

In the course of observing Joe's behavior, we can draw some conclusions about how consistent his behavior is as he moves from situation to situation. In all likelihood, we will also draw some conclusions about the causes of the consistencies and inconsistencies in his behavior.

When an individual's behaviors seem to "fit together" in a meaningful fashion, we find it convenient to attribute them to a "personality" that guides and directs what the person does. Behavior that reflects personality is viewed as having organization and structure. Figure 13.1 summarizes four questions asked in creating a personality profile.

PERSONALITY THEORIES

Conclusions about someone's personality involve perceptions of the individual's behavior. These perceptions may vary according to the behaviors being observed, the situation in which the person is behaving, and the personal characteristics of the observer. Viewing personality as a product of such perceptions helps us to understand why there can be so many different theories of personality and eliminates the question of which theory of personality is true. People who begin to study personality theories are sometimes puzzled and confused by the diversity of viewpoints about the nature of personality. This diversity, which reflects the complexity of human behavior, led Kluckhohn and Murray (1953) to observe that every person is in certain respects like all other people, like some other people, and like no other person. There can be as many different conceptions of personality as there are personality theorists. In fact, personality theories can be viewed as specific

outgrowths of the general perspectives on behavior described in Chapter 2.

The components of personality theories are constructs, just as personality itself is. In the following pages we discuss a number of these concepts such as id, ego, superego, anxiety, personal constructs, expectancies, and the self. It is important to remember that all these constructs were invented by theorists to predict behavior and explain its causes; they are not real, concrete things. As we discussed in Chapter 1, a construct cannot be scientifically useful unless it can be operationally defined in terms of observable situations or behaviors. Theorists must tell us how to define and measure the observable events to which their constructs refer.

A theory is scientifically useful to the extent that it provides a comprehensive framework into which already known facts can be incorporated, is at least a fairly reliable predictor of future events, and stimulates the discovery of new knowledge. After considering the various personality theories, we evaluate them briefly in terms of these three scientific standards. We begin our survey with the most influential theory—the psychoanalytic theory of Sigmund Freud.

Freud's psychoanalytic theory

On the basis of his experiences as a therapist and his often agonizing self-analysis, Sigmund Freud developed a theory of personality and a method of treatment for personality disturbances. He based his theory on careful clinical observations and constantly sought to expand it. He often revised and modified his ideas, and he never viewed his theory as a finished product (although some of his disciples did). In his own way, Freud was very much a scientist, and few other theories have had as great an impact as his (see Figure 13.2).

PSYCHIC ENERGY AND MENTAL EVENTS

Freud thought of personality as an energy system. Psychic energy, or **libido,** which is generated by instinctual drives (sex, aggression, etc.), constantly presses for release or discharge. We saw in Chapter 11 that the modes through which libido is expressed change ac-

FIGURE 13.2 *Sigmund Freud, born in 1856, lived most of his life in Vienna. After receiving his medical degree, he conducted research on various medical topics for several years, then studied in Paris, and upon his return to Vienna entered private practice. Over a period of years he created psychoanalysis. In 1909, at the invitation of the psychologist G. Stanley Hall, he made his only visit to the United States and gave a series of lectures at Clark University. Today his influence extends far beyond the boundaries of psychology, and he is generally recognized as one of the most original thinkers of the past century. This photo, taken during Freud's visit to Clark, shows him with several of the other pioneering figures in psychoanalysis. Row 1 (left to right): Freud, G. Stanley Hall, Carl Jung. Row 2: A. A. Brill, Ernest Jones, and Sandor Ferenczi.*

cording to the stage of the person's life. Equilibrium in the psychic system is maintained when the build-up of libidinal impulses can be discharged either directly or indirectly. For example, a concentration of energy from sexual instincts may be discharged directly as sexual behavior or indirectly through sexual fantasies or such activities as gardening, writing poetry, and so forth.

Psychic energy powers the mind. Mental events may be conscious, preconscious, or unconscious. The **conscious** mind consists of mental events that we are

presently aware of. The **preconscious** is an area that contains memories, thoughts, feelings, and images that we are not aware of now but that we could recall if we needed to. A friend's telephone number, a date learned in history class, and memories of our sixteenth birthday are all likely to reside in the preconscious mind. Just because we are aware of them, we tend to see the conscious and preconscious areas as the most important parts of the mind, but they are tiny in comparison with the **unconscious,** a dynamic body of wishes, feelings, and impulses beyond our awareness. Only when the impulses from the unconscious are discharged in one way or another, such as in dreams, neurotic symptoms, overt behavior, or slips of the tongue does the unconscious reveal itself.

Many of the unconscious mind's expressions are symbolic and require interpretation. The following Dear Abby letter illustrates the problem of interpreting errors in speech. Does an error in speech reflect unconscious conflict, or is it simply a mistake?

"Dear Abby: My fiance Joey and I are having a cold war because of what he refers to as a "Freudian slip." The other night in the middle of a warm embrace, I called him "Jimmy." (Jimmy was my former boy friend.) . . .

How does something like this happen? Is it really just a slip of the tongue, or is there something in my subconscious that is driving me to destroy a good relationship with someone I love by driving him away with a slip of the tongue?

Please help me. My future relationship with Joey hangs on your reply. Thank you. Sign me . . .

—I hate Freud
(*Seattle Times*, July 14, 1979, p. B8)

Freud would probably have agreed with Joey—the girl's slip of the tongue seems to be a sign that her feelings for Jimmy are still there, far from awareness in her unconscious mind. Psychoanalysts believe that such verbal slips are holes in our armor of conscious control and thus expressions of our true feelings. For example, while talking about her family during a therapy session, a young woman stated, "My sin's name is Tommy." Further questioning by the analyst revealed that Tommy was the product of a brief affair that she had had several years earlier.

In January 1975, while he was being seriously criticized for failing to deal more decisively with a lagging economy, President Gerald Ford gave a talk at a meeting of college athletic directors. In noting the similarities between the job of athletic director and president, Ford said, "We both buy aspirin by the six pack and we both have a certain lack of *performance* in our jobs" (our italics). According to an Associated Press report, the prepared text had read "permanence in our jobs."

THE STRUCTURE OF PERSONALITY

Freud divided the personality into three structures: id, ego, and superego. These three structures interact intimately with one another, but each has its own characteristics.

The **id** exists totally within the unconscious mind. It is the innermost core of the personality, the only structure present at birth, and the ultimate source of all psychic energy. Freud described the id as a chaotic jumble of excitation. It has no direct contact with reality and functions in a totally irrational way. The id operates according to the **pleasure principle:** it seeks immediate gratification or release, regardless of rational considerations or environmental realities.

The id cannot directly satisfy its needs by obtaining what it wants from the environment because it has no contact with reality. Therefore, in the course of development, the ego develops out of the id. The **ego** is in direct contact with reality, and it works to satisfy the demands of the id without jeopardizing the individual's survival in society. Because the ego is an outgrowth of the id, it receives all its energy and power from the id and never becomes totally independent of it. The ego functions primarily at a conscious level, and it operates according to the **reality principle.** It tests reality to decide when and under what conditions the id can safely discharge its impulses and satisfy its needs. The id demands immediate gratification, but the ego strives to delay gratification until conditions are appropriate. Its logical decision-making function has led to its nickname, the "executive of the personality."

The third and last personality structure to develop is the **superego,** the moral arm of the personality. It contains the traditional values and ideals of the society that have been communicated to the child by its parents and other representatives of society. This communication occurs chiefly through their use of rewards and punishments that teach the child what is "right" and what is "wrong." With the development of the super-ego, self-control is substituted for external control.

Like the ego, the superego strives to control the instincts of the id. However, like the id, the superego is irrational. The ego simply tries to postpone instinctual gratification until conditions are safe and appropriate, but the superego, in its blind quest for perfection, tries to block gratification permanently, particularly of those sexual and aggressive impulses that are condemned by society. For the superego, moralistic goals take precedence over realistic ones, regardless of the potential cost to the individual.

Because the id, ego, and superego operate simultaneously, Freudian explanations of behavior can sometimes be pretty complex. If you examine your own life, you can probably identify situations in which all three played conflicting roles. For example, what are the forces at work when you are studying hard for an important exam, and your work is interrupted by good friends who invite you to go to a party with them? What influences might your id, ego, and superego exert on you and how would you resolve the conflicts in this situation?

THE ROLE OF DEFENSE MECHANISMS

The dynamics of personality involve a continuing conflict between the id's struggle for release and the counterforces generated by the ego and the superego. Observable behavior is the product of this continuing internal struggle.

As the "executive of the personality," the ego is squarely in the eye of the storm. When the ego is confronted with impulses that threaten to get out of control or with dangers from the environment, the result is **anxiety,** an increase in tension that, like physical pain, serves as a danger signal and motivates the ego to deal with the problem at hand. In many instances, the anxiety can be reduced through realistic coping behaviors (if you're nervous about a test, study). However, when realistic strategies are ineffective in reducing anxiety, the ego may resort to another line of defense, one that involves the denial or distortion of reality. These **defense mechanisms** are constructed by the ego to allow the release of instincts in disguised forms that will not conflict with conditions in the external world or with the prohibitions of the superego.

Many psychoanalysts believe that **repression** is the most basic defense mechanism. Repression is often described as motivated forgetting. A recent college graduate may forget to go to a job interview if she's worried that she will not get hired. Repression is an active process in which the ego uses some of its energy to prevent anxiety-arousing memories, feelings, and impulses from entering consciousness. Repressed thoughts and wishes are often expressed indirectly. For example, someone who seems to have no guilt about masturbating might feel compelled to wash his hands every 20 minutes.

Suppression is like repression, except that it is conscious. The individual deliberately decides to exclude a memory, a feeling, or a motive from awareness. Saying to yourself, "I'm not going to worry about it because I can't do anything about it" illustrates the use of conscious suppression. Suppression is less likely to be associated with maladaptive behavior because the individual is less at the mercy of forces outside of awareness. It is important to remember that labeling a given behavior as repression does not in itself explain the causes of the behavior. A complete understanding requires an identification of the underlying needs that motivate a person to rely on the defense mechanism in the first place.

Freud's interest in defense mechanisms centered on the role of repression. Although he discussed other defenses in his work, it was his daughter Anna Freud, also a psychoanalyst, who defined and described the variety of defense mechanisms that we think of today. Table 13.1 lists, defines, and illustrates a number of defense mechanisms.

The defense mechanisms are one aspect of ego functioning that occurs at an unconscious level. People are usually unaware that they are using self-deception to ward off anxiety. Defense mechanisms may be mobilized in response to either external or internal sources of threat. Everyone uses these defense mechanisms sometimes. Only an individual who uses them to such an excessive degree that more realistic approaches to

TABLE 13.1 SOME DEFENSE MECHANISMS USED IN ADDITION TO REPRESSION

DISPLACEMENT: *A shift of feelings and attitudes from one object to another, more acceptable substitute.*

Examples:

A man is criticized by his boss and then feels angry. He comes home and yells at his wife (yelling at the boss might be too dangerous).

A young girl feels sexually attracted to her older brother. She finds a person in her office who has the same dry sense of humor and curly hair as her brother and quickly becomes very attracted to him.

INTELLECTUALIZATION: *Dealing with problems as interesting events which can be explained rationally and which have no anxiety or emotional content attached to them.*

Examples:

A woman whose husband has just died discusses the inadequacy of America's mourning rituals, rather than her anger at her husband for leaving her.

A man who has just seen a bank robbery in which five people near him were gunned down talks about how interesting it was to observe the variety of ways that the people present reacted to the murders.

REACTION FORMATION: *Expressing an unacceptable impulse by transforming it into its opposite.*

Examples:

A person who is attracted by the excitement and brutality of war becomes an overly zealous pacifist.

A mother who feels angry and rejecting toward her child checks many times to see if the child is all right during the night and worries excessively about her safety on the way to and from school.

DENIAL: *Refusal to acknowledge the anxiety-arousing aspects of the environment. The denial may be related only to the emotions connected to an idea or event or it may involve failure to acknowledge the event itself. Denial is most often seen in psychosis. It is seen in adults only under severe stress.*

Examples:

A husband, when told that his wife has incurable cancer, remains convinced that she will recover.

A student, who has to take a final exam on material she doesn't understand, tells herself the exam is really not important and goes to a movie instead of studying the material with which she is having trouble.

PROJECTION: *Characteristics or impulses that arouse anxiety are externalized by attributing them to others. Psychotics are particularly likely to use projection.*

Examples:

Nazis in Germany who started World War II insisted that they did so because of aggressive threats from other countries.

A man who has a strong desire to have extramarital affairs but feels guilty about it constantly accuses his wife of being unfaithful to him even though he has no evidence.

REGRESSION: *Going back to earlier ways of behaving that were characteristic of a previous developmental level. Typical of people who go to pieces under stress.*

Examples:

A wife goes home to her mother every time she and her husband have a quarrel.

A student consoles himself, whenever things get rough, with several hot fudge sundaes, repeating behavior learned when his mother gave him ice cream to make him feel better after a scraped elbow or a disappointment.

SUBLIMATION: *A socially useful course of action developed when more direct forms of gratification are blocked.*

Examples:

A teenager with strong aggressive feelings expresses them without danger by becoming a football player.

Someone with strong erotic feelings expresses them in a socially approved way by becoming a painter of evocative nudes.

Source: Sarason and Sarason, 4th ed., 1984, p. 53.

dealing with problems are abandoned is considered to be maladjusted.

CONTRIBUTIONS AND EVALUATION

Freud believed that situational variables in early childhood have powerful effects on behavior. Seductive or abusive parents can scar children for the rest of their lives. On the other hand, a warm, supportive home environment can help a child to develop self-confidence and the ability to enjoy life.

Freud recognized that certain types of situations are more likely than others to elicit expressions of particular personality traits from a specific individual. A person who is a well-motivated worker with one supervisor might become an angry and resentful one with another. Psychoanalytically significant person-situation interactions are those in which particular personalities react in special and often maladaptive ways to circumstances to which they are sensitive. At the risk of sounding like a fortune cookie, we might say that the wise person is one who steers clear of situations to which he or she is vulnerable.

Because of the large number of person-situation interactions with which it deals, psychoanalytic theory has had a profound impact on the field of personality. Freud's most notable contributions were his recognition of the influence of unconscious motives and conflicts on behavior and his emphasis on the importance of childhood experiences in later personality development and behavior.

Freud's theory of personality evolved largely from his experiences in treating psychiatric patients, and it has had a major role in attempts to understand and treat behavior disorders. (We discuss these contributions in Chapters 15 and 16.) Although it has had a powerful influence in psychology, psychiatry, and other fields, psychoanalytic theory has been criticized on scientific grounds. Many of Freud's constructs are ambiguous and difficult to operationally define and measure. How, for example, can we measure the strength of an individual's id impulses and defenses? Moreover, because very different (even opposite) behaviors can result from the same impulse, it is hard to make specific behavioral predictions. If we make a prediction from psychoanalytic theory that an individual

will behave aggressively and the subject behaves instead in a loving manner, is the theory wrong or is the aggression being masked by the operation of defense mechanisms? The difficulties in operationally defining psychoanalytic constructs and in making clear-cut behavioral predictions mean that many aspects of psychoanalytic theory are untestable, and this detracts greatly from its scientific usefulness. Despite its limitations as a scientific theory, though, psychoanalysis has stimulated a large amount of research and theorizing in such diverse areas as child development, cultural anthropology, and psychotherapy.

Other analytic theories

One of the greatest contributions made by Freud's theory was the storm of controversy that it aroused. Stir up the scientific community and, eventually, the masses of discord and argument will resolve themselves into new theories and new lines of research. In this case, two criticisms in particular stimulated the development of newer, or **neoanalytic,** theories that incorporated many of Freud's basic ideas but departed from psychoanalytic theory in significant ways. One criticism has been that social and cultural factors were not given a sufficiently important role in the development and dynamics of personality. Even many of Freud's own followers eventually came to feel that he stressed infantile sexuality at the expense of other important determinants of personality. Another criticism was that Freud laid too much emphasis on the events of childhood as determinants of adult personality. Neoanalytic theorists agree that childhood experiences are important, but some of them feel that personality development continues throughout the entire life span as individuals confront problems that are specific to particular stages in their lives.

ADLER'S INDIVIDUAL PSYCHOLOGY

Alfred Adler was one of the first members of Freud's inner circle to establish his own school of thought (see Figure 13.3), known as **individual psychology**. In contrast to Freud's assertion that behavior is motivated by inborn sexual and aggressive instincts, Adler insisted that humans are inherently social beings who are motivated by social urges. Freud argued that individuals are pushed by forces and counterforces over which they have little control. Adler's conception of human nature was much more optimistic than Freud's. Adler viewed humans as creatures who relate to others, cooperate with them, and place general social welfare above selfish personal interests. Freud, on the other hand, often seemed to view people as animals caged by the bars of civilization. Although he acknowledged the importance of unconscious phenomena, Adler felt that individuals are pulled by their personally developed goals.

Adler is perhaps best known for his discussion of inferiority feelings. He believed that much of the resentment that some people feel toward their parents grows out of the inferiority feelings that we all have as children when we compare ourselves to adults. He

pointed out that unconscious feelings of inferiority are capable of motivating powerful strivings for superiority, but some people develop rigid and maladaptive ways of overcompensating for their perceived inadequacies.

JUNG'S ANALYTICAL PSYCHOLOGY

Like Adler, Carl Jung was Freud's friend and associate before he broke away and developed his own theory, **analytical psychology.** Jung accompanied Freud on his only visit to the United States and can be seen on the right in Figure 13.2.

Jung expanded Freud's notion of the unconscious in a unique direction. In addition to a **personal unconscious,** which corresponds to Freud's preconscious and unconscious and is unique to each individual, Jung believed that humans possess a **collective unconscious,** which consists of memories accumulated throughout the entire history of the human race. The contents of the collective unconscious are **archetypes**— mythological images or universal concepts such as God, the Wise Old Man, the Mother, the Young Hero, rebirth (resurrection), and evil spirits. Jung believed that these archetypes reflect all the knowledge and wisdom gained by our ancestors, and he devoted much of his life to the study of the symbolic expressions of archetypes in tribal societies, mythology, alchemy, and dreams.

While Freud viewed the unconscious as a source of antisocial impulses and unacceptable desires, Jung saw it as a source of wisdom and as a guide to achieving unity and wholeness. The focus of his system of analytical psychology became the study of the unconscious, and his method involved helping people to become more receptive to their dreams as reflections of archetypal wisdom and as guides to living.

Jung and Freud quarreled bitterly over Freud's emphasis on sexuality. Jung spoke of libido more as an

FIGURE 13.3 *Alfred Adler (1870–1937) was originally a follower of Freud's. However, his views began to diverge from Freud's over the issue of infantile sexuality and the importance of social motives. In 1911 he broke with Freud and developed his own theory, known as individual psychology.*

orientation than as a force. One either focused one's libido outward to the objects of the external world (**extraversion**) or inward to the individual (**introversion**). The extravert is actively involved with his or her environment; the introvert is more attentive to the inner world of subjectivity. Jung also placed less emphasis on the early years of life than Freud did.

Jung's analytical psychology is as wide-ranging as Freud's theory, but it has had less impact within psychology largely because Jung's ideas often seem idiosyncratic and vague, as well as scientifically unverifiable. Ironically, the aspects of his theory that made scientific psychologists shy away from him in the past—his stress on the need for human beings to emphasize spiritual qualities as well as rational ideas and his interest in Eastern religions and mysticism—have made him popular with many people today.

CONTRIBUTIONS AND EVALUATION

Neoanalysts such as Adler and Jung differ from Freud in the developmental transitions that they see as critical in the formation of the personality. Both Adler and Jung reject Freud's emphasis on sexual and aggressive instincts, as well as his notion that psychosexual development during childhood is the major determinant of adult personality. Their theories are more positive and optimistic than Freud's. Although each has directly stimulated a small body of research, they are more important for the role they have played in focusing attention on social variables and on developmental aspects of personality across the life span.

Humanistic and existential theories

Psychoanalysis is a psychodynamic theory because it focuses on the way that the interplay among mental forces influences behavior. However, as we have seen, there are differences of opinion about specific psychodynamic issues (for example, the role of instinctual impulses). Another group of theories about the organization and structure of personality almost totally rejects the assumptions of both the Freudians and the neo-Freudians. This group includes two overlapping points of view.

Humanistic, or *third-force*, theorists emphasize the individual's creative potential and need for personal growth. Abraham Maslow, who saw humanism as a "third force," or an alternative to what he regarded as the two major influences in psychology—psychoanalysis and behaviorism—stressed the importance of self-actualization. By **self-actualization,** Maslow meant self-fulfillment and the complete realization of one's potential, the "highest" of the needs in his need hierarchy (see Chapter 9). While Jung, Adler, and others have used the concept in passing, contemporary humanistic psychologists see self-actualization as the core of human development and creativity.

The characteristics that Maslow attributed to self-actualized people include self-acceptance, an ability to perceive reality without defensive distortion or "blind spots," independence, spontaneity in thought and behavior, a good sense of humor, creativity, an abiding concern for the welfare of the human race, a deep appreciation of the basic experiences of life, and an ability to establish intimate and satisfying relations with a few people. He felt that the possibility of attainment of self-actualization is imbedded in human nature, although only a few people actually reach that goal (see Table 13.2).

TABLE 13.2 THE SELF-ACTUALIZED PERSON

Self-actualized people show the following characteristics:

Self-acceptance

Realistic perceptions of themselves and others

Independence

Spontaneity

Good sense of humor

Creativity

Concern for the well-being of others

Capacity for intimate, satisfying relationships

Existential psychologists join in Maslow's call for a humanistic approach. Existentialists criticize psychoanalysis for focusing too much on the early years of life, just as they reject the behaviorists' view that people respond to the environment like machines. Existentialists believe that current behavior is influenced by the present and the future, as well as by the past. Existentialists are **phenomenological** in their approach; they are concerned with immediate experience. They are more interested in describing how a person feels about something that has happened than explaining why it happened.

Although their positions overlap, humanistic theorists tend to emphasize self-actualization, while existentialists focus on personal responsibility. A value shared by all theorists of the humanistic-existential persuasion is the importance of recognizing one's need for self-determination. Self-determination means that the individual has freedom to choose among alternatives. Because many people either are not aware of their need for self-determination or have difficulty making wise choices, existential psychotherapists focus particularly on freeing the individual to make more sensible decisions.

ROGERS'S SELF THEORY

Carl Rogers's theory of personality has been highly influential because it includes both humanistic and existential elements. Rogers emphasizes the unique moment-to-moment character of reality; he views behavior not as a reaction to external stimuli but as a response to the individual's perceptions of those stimuli (Rogers, 1951). Because no one else can directly know our perceptions, Rogers maintains that no one can explain our behavior more expertly than we ourselves can (see Figure 13.4).

Rogers's conception of human nature is an optimistic and positive one, far different from Freud's view of humans as basically irrational and destructive, and at variance with the behavioristic conception of human beings as the pawns of external forces. Rogers feels that the forces that direct behavior are within us, and when they are not distorted by social conditions, these forces can be trusted to direct us toward positive growth.

The self In the beginning, children cannot distinguish between themselves and their environment. Rogers has

FIGURE 13.4 *Carl Rogers's humanistic theory of personality has been influential in therapeutic work with both individuals and groups. Rogers emphasizes the importance of subjective experience. "Though there may be such a thing as objective truth I can never know it; all I can know is that some statements appear to me to have the qualifications of objective truth (Rogers, 1959, p. 192).*

theorized that, as children interact with their environment, a portion of their perceptual or "phenomenal" field gradually becomes differentiated as the self. He saw the **self** as an organized, consistent set of perceptions of and beliefs about oneself (Rogers, 1959). Once the self-concept is formed, any experience that is inconsistent with it, including one's own behaviors, is a threat. Well-adjusted individuals can respond to the threat adaptively by modifying their self-concept, but other individuals may choose to deny or distort the experience.

For example, suppose that a young man's self-concept requires that every woman find him irresistible. He meets a young woman whom he finds very attractive but who shows a total lack of interest in him. This incongruence between his self-concept and his experience produces a threat. He could react adaptively by modifying his self-concept to acknowledge that he is not, after all, irresistible to all women. On the other hand, he might resolve the incongruence by distorting reality. He might deny the woman's lack of interest ("She's just playing hard to get"), or he might distort his perception of the woman ("She must be crazy. Thank heaven I found out before she fell hopelessly in love with me").

At the other extreme, consider a young man who believes that he is totally unattractive to women. If an attractive woman expresses interest, he might possibly revise his self-concept, but it is often as difficult for people with negative self-concepts to accept success as it is for those with unrealistically positive self-concepts to accept failure.

The more rigid and inflexible an individual's self-concept, the less open he or she will be to accepting incongruous experiences and the more maladjusted he or she will become. If there is a significant degree of incongruence between self and experience, the defenses used to deny and distort reality may collapse, and the individual may experience extreme anxiety and a disorganization of the self-concept.

The fully functioning person Rogers has worked with individuals who fall everywhere along the continuum from adjustment to maladjustment. More recently, he has become more involved in working with relatively well-adjusted individuals who want to grow into what he defines as **fully functioning persons** (1959, 1970). Like Maslow, Rogers has emphasized the self-directing capacity of the individual and each person's potential for positive growth. Maslow and Rogers arrived at very similar descriptions of the fully functioning, or self-actualized, person.

Fully functioning persons do not hide behind masks or adopt artificial roles. They feel a sense of inner freedom, self-determination, and choice in the direction of their growth. They can accept inner and outer experiences as they are, without modifying them defensively to suit a rigid self-concept. They have no fear of behaving spontaneously, freely, and creatively.

CONTRIBUTIONS AND EVALUATION

Rogers and others who have humanistic-existential points of view are especially concerned with subjective experiences. The psychodynamics that interest them differ markedly from those discussed by psychoanalysts and relate to such person variables as the struggle for self-expression, creativity, and individual growth. Because certain situations and experiences (such as insensitive parents) inhibit self-actualization, clinical workers must provide environments in which clients can overcome those inhibitions.

Some critics believe that the humanistic-existential point of view is too limited because it relies so much on the individuals' reports of their personal experiences. These critics fear that using self-reports as the primary means of studying personality may lead to erroneous conclusions. Some critics also believe that it is very difficult to make precise behavioral predictions on the basis of certain humanistic concepts. For example, they argue that it isn't possible to define an individual's actualizing tendency except in terms of the behavior that it supposedly produces.

Despite the fact that most humanistic-existential theories have produced only a small amount of objective evidence, Carl Rogers throughout his career has recognized the need for scientific studies. His greatest contribution in this regard has been the sizable body of research on the process of client-centered therapy, which he invented. In **client-centered therapy,** which is described in Chapter 16, a person seeking help is treated not as a dependent patient but as a responsible client (Rogers, 1977). The client-centered therapist is less active than most psychotherapists are and strives to establish an accepting atmosphere in which clients can win their own struggles for self-actualization and self-determination. Research on client-centered therapy has provided insights into the nonverbal and verbal events that occur in psychotherapy. Studies have also focused on the discrepancy between clients' ideal self-image and their real one. This discrepancy gets smaller as therapy proceeds, suggesting that therapy may help the individual to become more self-accepting and perhaps also more realistic.

Cognitive-behavioral theories

One of the major influences in modern personality research is the cognitive-behavioral point of view, which is concerned with the interplay between behavior and cognitive processes (what people think about, their approaches to solving problems). This point of view evolved gradually in response to the sometimes heated dialog carried on over many years between cognitive and behavioral theorists. The cognitive theorists, while rejecting traditional psychodynamic approaches, focused attention on the contents of thought and thinking styles. The behavioral theorists were primarily interested in the learning process—how behavioral patterns are acquired and extinguished. In this section, we look at each of these points of view and at recent advances toward integrating them.

BEHAVIORAL APPROACHES

All the personality theories mentioned so far are based mostly on clinical data, but the behavioral approach to personality is rooted in laboratory findings of research on animals and humans. For example, an operant approach to personality involves precise measurement of the individual's behavior as it is affected by observable environmental conditions.

As we saw in Chapter 2, B. F. Skinner and other radical behaviorists are strongly opposed to a psychology of internal events. They regard internal "personality" processes as fictions that deflect attention from the true causes of behavior, which to them reside in the external environment and in the past learning of the individual. The learning approaches to personality attempt to specify the conditions under which the particular patterns of behavior that are characteristic of personality are developed, maintained, and changed.

COGNITIVE APPROACHES

For cognitive theorists, the person is an information processor. They emphasize what the individual does with the information that reality provides. The cognitive theorist is most interested in how people interpret situations and formulate plans for action. Ideas about friends and enemies, safety and danger, together with other concepts, play important roles in each individual's unique information processing theory. We might say that each of us is our own personality theorist, with unique assumptions, emphases, and views of the world that guide our lives. Out of life's experiences, we develop a conception of who we are as individuals and what we can expect of ourselves and the world.

A theory developed by George Kelly (1955) is the

FIGURE 13.5 *George Kelly's theory of personality is one of the earliest examples of the cognitive approach. He developed his theory in the 1940s and 1950s while serving on the faculty of Ohio State University.*

clearest example of a purely cognitive perspective on personality. According to Kelly (see Figure 13.5), our primary goal is to make sense out of our world by discovering personal meaning in it. To find that meaning we try to explain and understand the events of our lives, and we test our understanding in the same way that scientists test theirs: we attempt to anticipate, to predict. We do not react so much to the past as we do to the present and the future, reaching out for mastery and control over ourselves and our environment.

Kelly's primary interest was the manner in which we construct our reality by sorting the people and events in our lives into categories. Kelly termed these categories **personal constructs.** Every person has a unique pattern of preferred categories or personal constructs. By understanding an individual's constructs, the rules that he or she uses to assign events to categories, and his or her hypothesis about how the categories relate to one another, Kelly believed that we can understand the individual's psychological world.

Rather than evaluating alternative constructions according to whether or not they are "true" (which we cannot know), Kelly preferred to examine the consequences of the perceptions. Kelly saw psychotherapy as a way of demonstrating to clients that their constructions are hypotheses rather than facts. Once clients realize this, they can be encouraged to test their constructs so that the maladaptive ones can be replaced with more useful ones.

When Kelly first presented it, his theory was often ignored or criticized for not being sufficiently objective. It is now more positively regarded because contemporary psychology is more preoccupied with viewing the person as an information processor, interpreter of events, and problem solver than was true in the 1950s. In addition, many clinicians and their clients find the concept of personal constructs useful.

THEORIES INTEGRATING COGNITIVE AND BEHAVIORAL PRINCIPLES

As recognition grows that both cognitive and learning processes affect our lives, views of personality that make use of both are becoming more popular. Early indications of this type of integration can be found in the work of John Dollard and Neal Miller.

Dollard and Miller (1950) thought that they saw

parallels between learning theory and Freudian theory in the area of personality development. For example, the reinforcement principle and Freud's pleasure principle reflect the same general idea: people are more likely to do what makes them feel good. Dollard and Miller also made use of cognitive concepts by describing inappropriate behavior as the joint product of unfortunate life experiences and maladaptive thinking. Despite their preference for describing behavior in terms of habits and learning—for example, insight into the roots of one's behavior is referred to as the acquisition of self-awareness responses—Dollard and Miller emphasized the individual's cognitive resolution of conflicts. For example, they suggest that people may try to control their reactions in a particular situation through the use of **labeling,** a cognitive device used to classify emotional responses. A woman may say that she is tense because she has so much to do at home, when her tension is actually the result of her frustration at the lack of outside stimulation in her life. She can whip her family into shape from now until next Christmas, but her tension will remain until it has been correctly labeled.

Bandura's social learning theory   Albert Bandura, one of the most influential contemporary personality theorists, has increasingly merged his original learning perspective with cognitive elements (see Figure 13.6). Bandura's social learning theory is concerned with the way that social relationships, learning mechanisms, and cognitive processes jointly contribute to behavior. Bandura agrees that we learn much of our behavior through directly experienced rewards, nonrewards, and punishments, but he also believes that complex cognitive processes play important roles, particularly with regard to social relationships. For example, according to Bandura, we can solve problems symbolically (in our heads) without having to resort to actual trial and error because we can foresee the consequences of our behavior. Cognitive processes also allow us to code and store in memory our observations of others' behaviors and its

FIGURE 13.6 *Albert Bandura, born in a small town in Alberta, Canada, received his education at the University of British Columbia and the University of Iowa. His current work has involved the study of ways in which people can learn to regulate their own behavior more easily.*

quences that the model experiences and on the observers' expectations about the consequences that they would experience if they performed the behavior.

The behavior's consequences determine whether you keep up that activity or change your ways. Rewards and punishments may be either external or self-administered. Social learning theorists place strong emphasis on the importance of self-reinforcement and self-punishment. In some cases, powerful self-administered consequences may override external consequences, and a behavior that is unrewarded or even punished by others may be maintained by self-approval. Bandura (1978) has become interested in studying **self-regulation**—learning that occurs through internal, as opposed to external, reinforcement. Many cognitive-behavioral psychologists are developing techniques by which people lacking in behavioral self-control can be helped to acquire it.

consequences. In other words, we often acquire complex social behaviors through **observational** or **vicarious learning** (see Figure 13.7).

Bandura makes a distinction between learning and performing. For example, you have probably learned how to kill people from reading murder mysteries or watching TV. If learning were the same as performing, we'd all be in a lot of trouble. Observation alone is sufficient for learning, but whether or not observers subsequently perform a behavior depends on the conse-

(DRAWING BY OPIE; © 1978 THE NEW YORKER MAGAZINE, INC.)

FIGURE 13.7 *In observational learning, we attend to the characteristics (style of dress, manner of speaking, mood) of a model and adopt some of them. Modeling is especially important in the child's development.*

Rotter's social learning theory Julian Rotter has stressed the cognitive perspective for many years. Like other social learning theorists, Rotter believes that the problems of maladjusted people originate in their relationships with other people. He emphasizes that our expectations for the outcomes of new situations have a great influence on our behavior (Rotter, 1980). Maladjusted people typically have low expectations for success in particular situations (for example, on a job), which then generalize to other areas of life.

Rotter is also interested in the amount of control that people believe they have over the environment. People who believe that they have the power to affect the outcome of situations have an **internal locus of control** ("I'll work things out"). Those who think that they have little control over what happens to them have an **external locus of control** ("I'll just have to wait and see what happens"). The work of a therapist, from Rotter's viewpoint, is to teach clients to take responsibility for change (to become more internal) by restructuring the way that they think about the situation and by learning to perform new, more adaptive behaviors.

CONTRIBUTIONS AND EVALUATION

While the effort to develop personality theories that integrate cognitive and behavioral principles is a relatively recent trend, the progress that has been made is encouraging. In the past decade, cognitively oriented behavioral researchers have paid increasing attention to personality variables that determine the ways in which individuals give "meaning" to situations (Mischel, 1973, 1979). As cognitive-behavioral theorists emphasize, people are active as interpreters of information and also as planners, decision makers, and doers. Recent attempts to specify the personal variables that influence an individual's responses to situations are a major step toward making the social learning approach a more comprehensive theory of personality.

Biological approaches to personality

Many writers have considered the idea that personality is rooted in biology, but there is no consensus on which biological processes are most relevant to human indi-

viduality, on how those processes might work, or on how they might interact with social influences, culture, and other factors that influence the organization of personality.

Recent attempts to explore the influence of biology on personality have focused on genetic and neurological bases for individual differences. We know that intelligence is partially determined by inherited characteristics, as are differences in such traits as activity level, emotionality, and social introversion-extraversion (Buss and Plomin, 1984). Nongenetic biological influences such as brain disorders, hormonal changes, and drugs can bring about dramatic shifts in personality. Some psychologists feel that the most dramatic breakthrough in understanding and controlling personality development and change will emerge from the biological perspective. However, exactly where that breakthrough will occur is not yet clear.

SHELDON: BODY TYPE AND PERSONALITY

Anyone interested in human individuality must have noticed that people come in all shapes and sizes. Could there be a connection between the diversity of body shape and the diversity of personality? Could people's bodies (and their personalities) be sorted into distinct types? Back in the fifth century B.C., Hippocrates said that there were two main body types—people who are short, thick, and muscular, and those who are long, thin, and delicate—and he related these body types to the incidence of certain illnesses.

A more modern approach to body typing was offered by William H. Sheldon (1942, 1954). Although he recognized that life experience is important, he built his constitutional psychology on the premise that biological structure influences behavior. Sheldon used a set of 4000 photographs of nude male college students as the basis of his search for body types. He looked for characteristics that would permit all 4000 men to be ranked on a continuum. Sheldon found that he could reliably sort the photographs by using only three basic categories of body structure:

1. **Endomorphy,** characterized by body fat, flabbiness, roundness, and weakness in muscular development. (Weight Watchers and remote-control TVs were designed with endomorphs in mind.)

2. **Mesomorphy,** characterized by a well-developed musculature and a large, squarish body structure. (Professional football teams and *Playgirl* magazine photographs have very high proportions of mesomorphs.)

3. **Ectomorphy,** characterized by a long, thin, delicate body build. (High-fashion models are ectomorphs or starving endomorphs.)

By using a seven-point scale, Sheldon could rate a person on each of these three categories; each person would be assigned a three-digit number, called a **somatotype.** A 7-1-1 person, for example, is an extreme endomorph, while a 4-4-4 is someone who is perfectly balanced among the three types (see Figure 13.8). Sheldon believed that somatotypes are genetically determined and do not change despite aging or alterations in diet, life style, or the environment.

Sheldon then developed a temperament scale that permitted ratings of personality dimensions he thought might be related to certain body types. For instance, strongly endomorphic individuals may be especially dependent on others for approval, require a lot of sleep, and spend much of their time relaxing. Strongly mesomorphic individuals tend to be assertive, to act resolutely when in trouble, and to need a lot of exercise. Strongly ectomorphic people tend to be socially inhibited, to value privacy, and to be emotionally restrained.

FIGURE 13.8 *Artist Norman Rockwell, bodybuilder Chuck Beckley, and actor Orson Welles represent extremes of the ectomorph, mesomorph, and endomorph somatotypes.*

Although the scientific status of Sheldon's somato-types is still in question, body types probably do have several important effects on personality. For one thing, they are noticeable. Our bodies influence how people react to us as well as how we react to situations (the physically weak are less likely than the strong to stand up for themselves). From an early age, people learn to assign certain traits to themselves and to others on the basis of body type. For example, they usually learn quite positive stereotypes about mesomorphs and negative ones about endomorphs. Even if Sheldon's theory is questionable and some of his research is methodologically weak, he has encouraged psychologists to include bodily characteristics in the comprehensive study of personality (Hartl and others, 1982).

EYSENCK'S BIOLOGICAL PSYCHOLOGY

Although conceptually quite different from Sheldon's emphasis on body types, Hans J. Eysenck's theory is also based on the assumption that biological processes are related to behavior (see Figure 13.9). Eysenck believes that personality is made up of a combination of three dimensions: introversion-extraversion, neuroticism, and psychoticism. The relative proportions of these dimensions are the result of inherited differences in the way the central nervous system functions. Thus, much of personality is genetically determined. Eysenck defined **introversion** as "stimulus shyness" and **extraversion** as "stimulus hunger," developed questionnaires to assess this dimension, and then related subjects' scores to their actual behavior in clinical and experimental settings (Morris, 1979). According to Eysenck's theory, introverts need to avoid stimulus overload because their nervous systems are particularly sensitive to excitation. Their higher levels of cortical arousal make introverts more attentive to details, and so they don't need a great deal of stimulation from outside; a little goes a long way. The typical introvert is introspective, is socially distant except from certain intimate friends, keeps feelings tightly under control, and seldom behaves in an angry or aggressive manner. Extraverts, on the other hand, have strong, stable, and even sluggish nervous systems. They need powerful or frequent stimuli to achieve cortical arousal and excitation. The extravert seeks social contacts and physical

FIGURE 13.9 *Hans J. Eysenck was born in 1916 in Berlin, Germany. An extremely prolific author, he has written over 30 books and 600 articles. He is interested in identifying biologically rooted factors that predispose people to respond to stress in characteristic and consistent ways.*

arousal, likes parties, takes chances, and is easygoing (see Figure 13.10).

How people adjust to life is influenced by the dimensions of neuroticism and psychoticism, as well as by introversion-extraversion. By **neuroticism,** Eysenck

means the tendency to be emotionally overreactive and socially dependent. Eysenck believes that people high in neuroticism tend to experience vague somatic upsets (headaches, digestive problems, insomnia) and are prone to have neurotic breakdowns requiring clinical attention. The dimension of **psychoticism,** which has been studied less extensively than Eysenck's other two dimensions, seems to reflect a tendency toward restless distractibility, disordered thought, and withdrawal. As

you would expect, people diagnosed as psychotic have higher scores on the psychotism factor than do normals or neurotics.

CONTRIBUTIONS AND EVALUATION

Although they have passed the superficial "tell a book by its cover" stage, biological theories of personality tend to be somewhat narrow in the phenomena they examine. For example, the role of environmental factors needs to be explicitly incorporated into these theories; new discoveries about bodily processes and improvements in psychological assessment will certainly affect them. Nevertheless, these theories reflect the fact, often forgotten, that body build and the way that the nervous system functions may indeed affect the behavior that we call personality.

Trait theories

According to both Eysenck and Sheldon, each person has enduring qualities that continue to influence behavior throughout life. Another approach to personality is based on the idea that these enduring characteristics—these **traits**—can be measured and can be used to account for a person's behavior in various types of situations (Stagner, 1984). All trait theorists share a commitment to assessing the sources of variation among people.

Contemporary trait theorists recognize that the influence of a particular trait will usually be indirect, being affected by a number of other traits and situational factors (Phares, 1984). It is important not to mistake one or two traits for a more complete understanding of an individual's personality. Knowing that a person has a particular trait (for example, the need to be dominant or the need to achieve) does not necessarily tell us how or when the person will display that trait. What is going on in a situation may be more important than personality characteristics in accounting for how someone behaves.

Although the importance of situations is currently emphasized in personality, perhaps even more significant is the way traits and situations interact—that is, how people perceive situations. To predict behavior, we must assess people and situations. A situation that seems difficult or impossible to some people might be no particular problem to others. Behavioral inconsistency may be due as much to our ignorance of how people perceive situations as to their standing on a particular trait.

Some people tend to behave consistently in a vari-

ety of situations (here traits would be more important), while other people are less predictable (here situations are more important). In an innovative experiment on cross-situational consistency, Bem and Allen (1974) asked the question: If a person behaves one way in a particular situation, will he or she behave similarly in a different one? The researchers divided a number of college students into two groups based on whether or not they said they were friendly and conscientious. These self-ratings were compared with reports from the subjects' parents and friends and with ratings by two independent observers. The subjects were also asked to indicate how consistent they were on a particular trait.

Bem and Allen found that people who said they were consistent in their level of friendliness tended to be rated the same way by other people, and people who described themselves as variable were seen as inconsistent by others. Thus, Bem and Allen's work showed that people do differ in the consistency with which they respond in a variety of situations and that they know that they do. People may be more accurate observers of their own behavior than many of us think. Experiments like this one have given new life to the concept of traits, although traits are viewed as part of a complex interaction between personal characteristics and the environment or situation, rather than as determinants of personality in their own right.

CONTRIBUTIONS AND EVALUATION

Despite differences of opinion concerning the nature of the most basic personality dimensions, trait theorists have made an important contribution by focusing attention on the value of identifying and classifying stable, enduring dispositions. They have also emphasized the need to assess personality dispositions objectively. Trait researchers use complex statistical techniques (such as factor analysis, which is described in the appendix) to sort items on personality tests and questionnaires into homogeneous groups. This helps to increase the reliability of measuring particular traits.

Several issues confront personality psychologists who are committed to a trait approach. One is the necessity for more agreement about the number of basic traits needed for arriving at comprehensive personality descriptions. At the present time, there seem to be two camps: "splitters," theorists who believe that many specific traits are needed to get at a person's individuality; and "lumpers," those who prefer working with a small number of basic traits (Eysenck is a "lumper"). Another issue concerns how traits are conceptualized and used. Grouping questionnaire items together doesn't guarantee that they will have any predictive value. Furthermore, there is a difference between naming a trait and showing that it plays a causal role in behavior. Describing Mary as industrious might be interpreted as saying that she works hard and is reliable because she is industrious. This not only implies causality without substantiating it but also reflects circular thinking, since it is likely that we call her industrious because of her hardworking behavior.

An appraisal of personality theories

Having reviewed a variety of theoretical approaches to personality, we should now say something about their adequacy. A good theory should help us to understand facts we already know. By and large, all the theories do that. Indeed, almost any behavior can be "understood" in terms of any of the theories. But, we must ask, what kind of understanding have we achieved? Because all the theories can account for just about everything on an after-the-fact basis, how can we distinguish among them in terms of their relative validity?

This brings us to another criterion for a useful theory: its ability to predict successfully. If all the theories can explain a behavior once it has occurred, perhaps a more rigorous test of their value is their ability to predict behavior. Most of these theories were not constructed for making predictions, and indeed, most do not predict terribly well. As we have seen, it is extremely difficult to generate testable predictions from some of them because many of their constructs cannot be operationally defined.

Yet another measure of a scientifically useful theory is its capacity to stimulate research that leads to the acquisition of new knowledge. Most of the theories have generated considerable research, but in many instances the studies did not constitute adequate tests of the theories. Not surprisingly, theories whose constructs can be operationally defined and measured are most likely to stimulate sound research.

Future personality theories will probably not attempt to explain all of human behavior within one grand framework. The current trend is toward the development of "mini-theories" that focus on specific areas of behavior and attempt to specify controlling variables. These more precise theories will not be as much fun to read nor will they create as much controversy or provide us with as many rich insights into the meaning of human existence. But they should lead to more precise predictions of behavior, to more direct ways to control the conditions that affect our lives, and to greater understanding of human individuality.

Situations, persons, and their interactions

Formulating adequate theories of personality clearly requires more than speculation about what is going on within individuals or careful description of the situations that they meet in life. We also need information about how the person and the situation interact.

SITUATIONS

Sometimes behavior is completely determined by the circumstances of a given situation; in other words, it is under **stimulus control**. We all stop at red lights (at least most of the time). When the phone rings, we answer it (most of the time). When we see an attractive person, most of us look. Either because of prior learning or a sufficiently compelling stimulus (for instance, the sounding of the fire alarm), we seem to respond automatically in certain situations. In such circumstances, there doesn't seem much point in inquiring into personal attributes such as motivations and emotions.

PERSONS

Wherever it comes from, people show their individuality very early in life. Infants differ in temperament as well as in their eating and sleeping patterns. As they grow up, these differences become more numerous, subtle, and pervasive.

Why does one person who has just been complimented on a job well done seem embarrassed and not know how to respond, while another person takes the compliment in stride and graciously says, "Thank you, I'm glad you liked the way I handled that assignment"? Why does Mary Spane begin worrying about job hunting next year when she hasn't even started her summer job this year? Why is being independent important to her? One of the challenges in the study of personality is how to develop a vocabulary that reflects those nonobservable person attributes that define individuality.

PERSON × SITUATION INTERACTIONS

Increasingly, it is being recognized that person variables (for example, a strong need to be independent) and situational variables (for example, a red light) are not either/or matters. Both types of variables play roles in most forms of human behavior. Mary Spane seems to have a need to become independent of her family. This need might apply only to her relationships with her parents, but it might also express itself in other situational contexts (for example, relationships with her friends). Another example of the importance of **person × situation interaction** is the .300 batter who has very different probabilities of hitting the ball when runners are on base, when left-handed pitchers are on the mound, when playing at home, and so on. Behavior is usually a joint product of what people bring to a situation and what is happening in that situation. Frontier 13.1 describes a series of experiments growing out of psychoanalytic theory that illustrate the person × situation approach.

This approach is concerned with what takes place between the time we enter a situation and the moment we deal with it. There is growing evidence that we "process" the situations that we find ourselves in. Situations provide us with information that we act on after

FRONTIER 13.1

EXPERIMENTAL STUDY OF PSYCHOANALYTIC CONCEPTS: A PERSON × SITUATION PERSPECTIVE

No single experiment, no matter how brilliantly conceived, can be expected to solve the whole puzzle of what goes on in the unconscious, but good research can contribute pieces to the puzzle's solution. Lloyd Silverman and his colleagues (Silverman and others, 1984) have reported an intriguing series of experiments that fit a person × situation approach. The experiments were planned to find out whether selected person variables are related to the way subjects respond to special situational variables, in this case particular types of perceptual displays.

Silverman used an instrument called a tachistoscope, which exposes each stimulus (a picture or printed phrase) for only 4/1000 of a second, too short a time for subjects to recognize it. Silverman found that, although people are unaware of tachistoscopically presented stimuli, the material may affect their feelings and behavior in demonstrable ways.

Silverman has been particularly interested in the way clinically depressed people respond to this technique. According to psychoanalytic theory, unconscious, unacceptable aggressive impulses increase feelings of depression. To stimulate such impulses, Silverman showed depressed individuals an aggressive picture—for instance, a snarling man holding a dagger or a verbal message such as CANNIBAL EATS PERSON. As a control condition, other subjects were exposed to neutral pictures and phrases (for example, a person reading a newspaper or PEOPLE ARE WALKING). Before and after the presentation, both groups rated themselves on their emotional states. Silverman found that his subjects did indeed report increased feelings of depression after the tachistoscopic presentation of material like CANNIBAL EATS PERSON. When neutral material was used, there was no increase in depression.

Silverman and his colleagues have also used the

EXPERIMENTAL STUDY OF PSYCHOANALYTIC CONCEPTS: A PERSON × SITUATION PERSPECTIVE

FIGURE 13.11 *Information received into unconscious awareness can influence behavior.*

tachistoscopic procedure with normal people. In one experiment, male college students were subliminally exposed to either the phrase BEATING DAD IS OK or BEATING DAD IS WRONG (Silverman and others, 1978)—see Figure 13.11. Then, the subjects performed a dart-throwing task. Subjects who saw BEATING DAD IS OK did better at throwing darts than did the subjects who saw BEATING DAD IS WRONG. These results seem to support the idea that a conflict-related stimulus that registers below the level of awareness makes contact with whatever unconscious conflicts are active in the individual at the time. Why did BEATING DAD IS WRONG have a negative effect on dart throwing? Perhaps because many college men are ambivalent about their fathers. On the one hand, they respect and love them; on the other hand, they want to excel in comparison with them. This conflict may operate even in a game of darts.

These experiments with depressives and college students show that people's psychological makeup has a lot to do with their reactions to situations with particular connotations. They are part of a growing body of evidence suggesting that people can understand and respond to meaning, form emotional responses, and guide behavior largely independent of conscious awareness. It may be that, despite the subjective experience of being in conscious control of feelings and thoughts, decisions, and actions, people are piloted far more than they know by the unconscious mind. Although it may be difficult to draw the precise border between conscious and nonconscious, researchers are fascinated by what that elusive line means for the way the mind orchestrates behavior.

Freud didn't have an inkling of the computer revolution that has marked the past several decades. Yet he recognized the complexity of the human memory system to which new bits of information are added daily. While many of the pieces are trivial, others are personally significant. There is increasing receptivity by cognitive psychologists to Freud's theory of thought. However, cognitive theorists are quick to point out that there is not necessarily a hidden meaning in every error and slip of the tongue. For example, standing at a friend's door trying to unlock it with one's own house key may simply represent the intrusion of a strong habit. A Freudian analysis of the mistakes people make is not required for the understanding of the mechanisms that underlie all slips and errors (Reason and Mychielska, 1982). We can hope that, through the combined efforts of psychoanalytic and cognitive researchers, advances will be made in the experimental investigation of processes like repression (the conversion of thoughts we are aware of into inaccessible ones) and the retrieval of previously inaccessible memories.

sizing them up. Researchers need to define both the situations and the personal characteristics that influence how a given situation is handled if they hope to understand more about these interactions.

PERSONALITY ASSESSMENT

Theories of personality have stimulated the development of a variety of tests, rating scales, and questionnaires aimed at measuring individual differences in person variables (Goldstein and Hersen, 1984). These devices can be useful shortcuts to understanding an individual's behavior. Think how long it takes you to get to know people; in many situations, psychologists do not have that kind of time.

Personality tests and other assessment methods are used in clinical settings in making a diagnosis, in deciding whether treatment is required, and in planning the treatment to be used. Personality tests are often used in personnel work to select employees. A third major use of personality tests is in psychological research, where the tests may serve as either independent or dependent variables. For example, as an independent variable, scores on a measure of test anxiety might be used to divide people into groups differing in how much they get upset while taking exams. (**Test anxiety** is the feeling that people get before exams. Some people have butterflies in their stomachs, some have elephants, and some couldn't care less.) The researcher would then want to know whether these groups would behave differently in an experimental situation. Another, not so common, use of personality tests is as a dependent measure. One group of subjects might see a war movie showing violent battle scenes, while another viewed a nature film. A personality test might then be given to determine which group had the higher aggression score.

We will now describe and illustrate the major approaches to personality assessment.

The interview

Practitioners in all the theoretical perspectives that we have reviewed use **interviews** to assess personality. The techniques range from informal conversational exchanges to well-organized series of specific questions designed to elicit specific responses. Good interviewers do not limit their attention to what the interviewee says; they also look at how he or she says it. They note the interviewee's general appearance and grooming, voice and speech patterns, the content of his or her thoughts, and facial expressions and posture.

The interview is valuable for the direct personal contact that it provides, but it has some limitations, particularly from a research standpoint. For example, it is difficult to quantify everything that goes on in an interview. The person being interviewed may not understand or may resist the purpose behind the interview. Interviewees may state facts, opinions, and attitudes in a reliable fashion; but, in some cases, they may distort facts and lie. They may sign, gesture, avert their eyes, tap their feet, and smile or grimace at the interviewer. Even experienced interviewers can extract and use only a small percentage of all this information.

In addition, interviewees may be defensive and may hesitate to discuss personal opinions, attitudes, and concerns openly. Interviewers must estimate the degree to which the desire of some interviewees to present themselves in a socially desirable light may invalidate some or all of their responses. Sometimes interviewers observe behaviors that clients are unaware of themselves. For example:

During the interview she held her small son on her lap. The child began to play with his genitals. The mother, without looking directly at the child, moved his hand away and held it securely for a while. . . . Later in the interview the mother was asked what she ordinarily did when the child masturbated. She replied that he never did this—he was a very "good" boy. She was evidently entirely unconscious of what had transpired in the very presence of the interviewer. (Maccoby and Maccoby, 1954, p. 484)

Despite its limitations, the face-to-face interview is obviously essential for certain purposes. A clinical psychologist needs to observe and converse with someone who is being considered for treatment in a mental hospital. So, also, does a personnel specialist who wants to fill a top management position. But other, more convenient and quantifiable techniques that supplement or improve upon certain aspects of the interview are being constructed by personality assessors.

Paper and pencil questionnaires

The success of intelligence tests in predicting future achievement led researchers to try to develop similar ways to measure personality. But personality isn't something that you either have or don't have (like the answer to the fourth question on the pop quiz last Friday). You can't fail a personality test. Everyone has a personality. The testlike measures used in personality assessment are meant to indicate the types of characteristics that combine to make up your individual identity.

Most paper and pencil **questionnaires** ask people to agree or disagree with certain statements about their behavior, thoughts, or emotional reactions. The scores that are derived from these instruments are often interpreted as indicators of traits and behavioral tendencies (Anastasi, 1982). The most widely used personality questionnaire is the **Minnesota Multiphasic Personality Inventory** (MMPI).

THE MINNESOTA MULTIPHASIC PERSONALITY INVENTORY

The MMPI was originally designed to provide an objective basis for classifying different types of psychiatric patients. It consists of 566 statements (16 of which are repeats) to be answered true, false, or cannot say (undecided about the truth of the statement). The items are so varied in content that it is not easy to generalize about them. Some are concerned with attitudes and emotions, others relate to overt behavior and symptoms, and still others refer to the person's life history.

The following sample items suggest the diversity of MMPI statements:

I believe there is a God.

I would rather win than lose a game.

I am worried about sex matters.

I believe I am being plotted against.

I believe in obeying the law.

Everything smells the same.

The person's responses on the MMPI are scored in relation to a number of keys. These scores are then plotted on a graph or profile sheet that reflects the degree to which the individual deviates from the norm. A high score on any given scale indicates that the individual's responses to its items were similar to those of the particular type of patients whose responses were used to construct the scale. The MMPI contains clinical and validity scales; several special scales have also been developed. The clinical scales are designed to measure personality deviations such as schizophrenia, depression, and psychopathic personality. The validity scales are designed to measure people's tendencies to lie, to "fake bad," or to place themselves in a socially desirable light. For example, if you marked "true" to the following items, your responses would be somewhat suspect:

I like everyone, even loud-mouthed, obnoxious people.

I never get upset.

I am always kind and thoughtful.

Projective techniques

Personality questionnaires are convenient and easy to score, but do not give individuals much latitude in how to respond. **Projective techniques** have much looser structures than questionnaires, involve relatively unclear and ambiguous stimuli, and allow subjects a wider range of possible responses to those stimuli. They are also more difficult to score and interpret.

The two most widely employed projective techniques—the Rorschach test and the Thematic Apperception Test—are based on psychodynamic theories and are used to assess unconscious processes. Freud stressed the importance of free association and believed that individuals would more fully reveal themselves and their unconscious thoughts in ambiguous situa-

tions than in those in which they have a clear idea of what is expected of them.

RORSCHACH INKBLOTS

There are 10 **Rorschach inkblots.** Subjects are shown each one and asked, "What does this look like? What might it be?" (see Figure 13.12). Examiners write the responses down word for word. They also carefully note

---

FIGURE 13.12 *An inkblot similar to those used in the Rorschach test can be made by spilling ink (one color or several) on a piece of paper and folding the paper in half while the ink is still wet. Try making several inkblots and compare your own perceptual reactions to them with the reactions of other people.*

subjects' behavior during testing, including gestures, mannerisms, and attitudes. They categorize and score responses to the inkblots in terms of the types of items to which the responses refer (for example, animals, human movement, tiny details), the correspondence between the responses and the objective characteristics of the inkblots, and the emotional tone associated with particular types of responses.

As yet, not many consistent relationships between Rorschach responses and behavior have been demonstrated (Lerner, 1984). Nevertheless, Rorschach tests continue to be among the most widely used personality instruments. There is no simple explanation for this state of affairs. Clinical psychologists, who are among the prime users of psychological tests, know about the discouraging research results, but they continue to put the Rorschach test near the top of their list of assessment techniques. They still feel that it helps them in personality evaluation.

THEMATIC APPERCEPTION TEST

The **Thematic Apperception Test** (TAT) was developed in the 1930s by Henry Murray of Harvard University. It consists of 30 pictures, including 1 blank card (usually no more than 20 cards are presented in a single testing). The pictures were obtained from paintings, drawings, and illustrations from magazines. Although they are more ambiguous than most photographs are, they have much more structure than inkblots. Subjects are told to describe what is going on in the scene on the card, what the characters are thinking and feeling, and what the outcome of the situation will be (see Figure 13.13).

Descriptions of personality written on the basis of the TAT usually deal with such topics as the following:

1. The subject's behavior in the testing situation
2. Characteristics of the subject's words or phrases
3. Kinds of fantasies that the subject talks about
4. Personal relationships depicted in the stories
5. Conscious and unconscious needs of the subject
6. The subject's perception of the environment
7. Emotional tone of the stories
8. Outcomes of the stories

FIGURE 13.13 *This is one of the pictures used in the Thematic Apperception Test. Select from magazines, newspapers, and books a group of pictures that are vague and ambiguous but that seem to reflect particular motivations and needs. Then compare the responses of different individuals to these stimuli. How can you categorize the responses?*

9. Common themes that run through the stories
10. Degree to which the stories reflect control over impulses and contact with reality

Behavioral assessment

Learning theory's emphasis on identifying the stimulus conditions associated with particular types of responses has given impetus to the development of behavioral assessment procedures.

478

Behavioral assessment procedures provide reliable information about how frequently and under what conditions certain classes of responses occur. Observing and recording behavior in different settings (at school, home, the playground) allows for the classification of the stimulus situations that give rise to specific types of behavior. Behavioral assessors reporting on a young child who is having problems in school do not simply say, "Jerry is disruptive" or "Mary isn't achieving up to her potential in arithmetic." Instead, they try to answer such questions as "What does Jerry do that causes disruption and what events precede and follow his disruptive behavior?" and "How many long division problems can Mary do in 10 minutes?" Once they identify a specific type of response, the next question they would ask is, "How often and under what conditions does the response occur?"

Behavioral assessment techniques may be helpful in identifying specific problem areas in people's daily lives. For example, a couple that has been fighting continually might find that their often vaguely defined tension and anger can be broken down in a way that permits them to change their behavior. A behavior analysis might reveal that the husband's failure to ask, "Did you have a good day?" when he comes home in the evening is followed first by a withdrawal from conversation by his wife and then an increase in her negative comments about the husband's table manners. The behavior analysis might suggest that the absence of the husband's greeting leads to the wife's negative behavior. If he greeted her differently, the rest of this negative behavior chain might be broken. Such chains of related behavior patterns can often be identified.

Because behavioral assessment developed in a clinical context, it has been closely linked with the modification of problem behavior. However, there is no reason why behavioral assessment should be limited to maladaptive responses. A behavioral assessment can also be used in an effort to try to understand the kinds of behaviors used by a successful individual. For example, what does a successful coach actually do during practice sessions? Roland Tharp and Ronald Gallimore (1976) used behavioral techniques to study John Wooden, who coached the UCLA basketball team to 10 national championships in the 12 years prior to his retirement in 1975. Tharp and Gallimore carefully observed Wooden during many practice sessions and

found that they could code virtually all his behaviors into specific response categories. They found, for instance, that 50.3 percent of Wooden's communications to his players were instructions (what to do or how to do it), 12.7 percent were hustles (verbal statements to activate or intensify previously instructed behavior), 6.9 percent were praises (verbal compliments, encouragement), and 14.6 percent were scolds (verbal statements of displeasure). More than half the scolds were followed by restatements of previously instructed behavior (see Figure 13.14). It would be interesting to do

FIGURE 13.14 *In this photo, John Wooden, former UCLA basketball coach, carefully observes his team during a practice session. The next night his Bruins won their tenth national championship. By breaking complex behaviors like coaching into small components and then sampling these in successful individuals, psychologists hope to learn more about what makes some teachers or coaches more successful than others.*

a similar assessment of less successful coaches to see how they differ. But the behavioral assessment of Wooden has wider educational implications. Since Wooden is also known as a great teacher, the specifics of his technique can be applied to other educational programs.

Cognitive assessment

Assessing the thoughts and ideas that pass through people's minds is a relatively new development. It has received impetus from the cognitive approach to personality and from the growing evidence that thought processes and the content of our thinking are related to our emotions and behavior. The difference between normal and abnormal behavior can frequently be explained by the thoughts that preoccupy the individual. **Cognitive assessment** provides information about adaptive and maladaptive aspects of people's thoughts and the role that their thoughts play in planning, making decisions, and interpreting reality. Cognitive assessment can also provide information about thoughts that precede, accompany, and follow maladaptive behavior. It also furnishes data about the effects of treatment procedures.

Cognitive assessment can be carried out in a variety of ways (Kendall and Korgeski, 1979). "Beepers" have been used as signals asking subjects to record their current thoughts at certain times of the day (Klinger and others, 1981). Questionnaires have been developed to sample thoughts after an upsetting event has taken place. There are also questionnaires to assess the directions that people give themselves while working on a task and their theories about why things happen as they do. While cognitive assessment is useful in providing data for researchers, it can also help people keep track of their own thoughts. We are often not very aware of how frequently we think about particular, often unwanted, ideas as we engage in our daily activities.

Bodily assessment

Sophisticated devices have been developed to measure such physiological attributes as pupil dilation and blood pressure. We are all familiar with the array of

FIGURE 13.15 *Portable blood pressure monitors like the one pictured are a product of space-age technology. This instrument automatically records blood pressure and heart rate at predetermined intervals over a 24-hour-period. This allows study of the particular conditions that accompany high and low readings.*

biological functions that are automatically measured when astronauts are on space flights. Fortunately, equipment as complex as that used by NASA is not needed in studying the rest of us who are earthbound. The assessment of bodily processes in the field of personality is growing and seems promising (Cacioppo and Petty, 1983)—see Figure 13.15.

Personality tests and the privacy and validity issues

Personality tests have been used extensively in schools and industry. The public has raised many questions about the validity of personality tests. Although personality tests may be helpful to the clinician, their predictive power has not been well established. They may be useful in describing a person, but often they function poorly in predicting how he or she may behave in the future. Research has shown that people's behavior is not always predictable in terms of general traits such as introversion, anxiety, or aggression. The individual's characteristics and the situation are both important in determining behavior.

Another issue is whether all kinds of personality tests represent an invasion of privacy. Legal rulings now require employers to show that their tests and other hiring procedures are job-related. If the tests are not job-related, their use may not be defensible.

STUDY OUTLINE

WHAT IS PERSONALITY? (p. 452)

Personality helps us understand why everyone does not behave the same way in a particular situation. The term *behavior* includes both overt, observable actions, and covert processes such as thoughts.

PERSONALITY THEORIES (p. 454)

1. Different personality theories are outgrowths of the various psychological perspectives.

2. Freud's psychoanalytic theory is concerned with the build-up of psychic energy. Freud divided mental events into three categories—conscious, preconscious, and unconscious—and the personality into three structures—id, ego, and superego. He emphasized defense mechanisms that help the individual keep anxiety under control.

3. Many of Freud's followers disagreed with some of his ideas and constructed their own, neoanalytic theories. Alfred Adler developed a theory of individual psychology that, in contrast to Freud's, emphasizes the

importance of social urges rather than sexual ones. Adler was particularly interested in the effect on a person's later life of inferiority feelings acquired in childhood. Carl Jung's theory is known as analytical psychology. In addition to a personal unconscious, Jung believed that each individual has a collective unconscious that holds memories accumulated during all of human history. He called these universal concepts archetypes and was especially interested in their symbolic expression—for instance, through mythology and dreams.

4. Humanistic theories, such as Abraham Maslow's, stress self-actualization and the development of self-acceptance and satisfying relationships with other people. Existential theorists have these humanistic concerns and also emphasize an individual's responsibility in choosing among alternatives. Carl Rogers's theory, which has both humanistic and existential elements, focuses on the development of the concept of self and the growth of the individual into a fully functioning person who is not afraid to behave spontaneously and freely.

5. Cognitive-behavioral theories emphasize the interaction between what people do and what they think about. George Kelly's theory emphasizes the individual's use of personal constructs and the way he or she integrates these categories. John Dollard and Neal Miller tried to show the parallels between Freud's ideas and learning theory. They also stressed the use of a cognitive device, labeling, to classify emotional responses. Albert Bandura's social learning theory emphasizes the acquisition of social behavior through observational learning. He is especially interested in self-regulation, the learning that occurs through internal reinforcement. Julian Rotter's social learning theory focuses on the importance of outcome expectancy on behavior. He is interested in the amount of control people believe they have over what happens in their environment.

6. Two theorists who have highlighted the role of biological factors in personality are William Sheldon and

Hans Eysenck. Sheldon divided male body builds into three categories—endomorph, mesomorph, and ectomorph—and related these to personality characteristics. According to Eysenck, central nervous system functions determine how a person reacts on three dimensions—introversion-extraversion, neuroticism, and psychoticism. He believes that introverts and extraverts have different excitation levels in their nervous systems.

7. Trait theorists believe that each person has an assortment of enduring qualities that can be measured and used to account for behavior in a variety of situations. Trait theorists construct tests and employ statistical procedures such as factor analysis to study personality. Most contemporary trait theorists also recognize the importance of environmental events in behavioral prediction.

8. Present-day personality theory is oriented toward mini-theories that attempt to specify variables that are important in specific areas of behavior. Most current personality research emphasizes the significance of the person × situation interaction.

PERSONALITY ASSESSMENT (p. 475)

1. Personality tests are used in making clinical diagnoses, in deciding on appropriate therapeutic treatment, and in assessing the effectiveness of treatment. They also play a role in personnel selection and in psychological research.

2. Personality assessment techniques include the interview, paper and pencil questionnaires, projective tests, behavioral assessment procedures, cognitive assessment methods, and instruments for measuring physiological changes in a variety of living situations. Well-known assessment instruments are the Minnesota Multiphasic Personality Inventory, the Rorschach inkblots, and the Thematic Apperception Test.

KEY TERMS AND CONCEPTS

personality	unconscious
libido	id
conscious	pleasure principle
preconscious	ego

reality principle
superego
anxiety
defense mechanism
repression
suppression
neoanalytic theories
individual psychology
analytical psychology
personal unconscious
collective unconscious
archetype
extraversion
introversion
self-actualization
phenomenological
self theory
self
fully functioning person
client-centered therapy
personal construct
labeling
observational learning
vicarious learning

self-regulation
internal locus of control
external locus of control
endomorphy
mesomorphy
ectomorphy
somatotype
neuroticism
psychoticism
trait
stimulus control
person × situation interaction
test anxiety
interview
questionnaire
Minnesota Multiphasic Personality Inventory
projective technique
Rorschach inkblot
Thematic Apperception Test
behavioral assessment
cognitive assessment
bodily assessment

SUGGESTED READINGS

HALL, C. S., LINDZEY, G., LOEHLIN, J. C., and MANOSEVITZ, M. (1985). *Introduction to theories of personality.* New York: Wiley. Review of major personality theories.

PHARES, E. J. (1984). *Introduction to personality.* Columbus, Ohio: Charles E. Merrill. Surveys current topics in personality research.

RABIN, A. I., ARONOFF, J., BARCLAY, A. M., ZUCHER, R. A. (Eds.) (1981). *Further explorations in personality.* New York: Wiley. Analyzes key issues related to personality development and the experimental study of personality.

CHAPTER FOURTEEN

ADJUSTING TO LIFE: STRESS, COPING, AND HEALTH

STRESS
Factors involved in stress
Stress arousal
Vulnerability to stress

COPING WITH STRESS
Self-control
Social support

BREAKDOWNS UNDER STRESS
Posttraumatic stress reactions
Burnout
Quantifying life stress

HEALTH PSYCHOLOGY AND BEHAVIORAL MEDICINE
Physical disorders related to stress
FRONTIER 14.1   IMPROVING THE PREDICTION OF HEART ATTACK
Speeding recovery from illness
Achieving health

STUDY OUTLINE

KEY TERMS AND CONCEPTS

SUGGESTED READINGS

Thelma Rawlings took a chance, entered a contest run by *Sports Afield*, and won a $350,000 house in Inverness, Florida. As she put it, "It's a dream. No question about it. And at night, it's gorgeous."

"I'm sorry it happened" was how her husband, Raymond, summarized Thelma's good luck. What turned winning the contest into heartache was the changes the $350,000 house required in Thelma's life—her husband, a cattleman, was interested in cattle, not a dream house in Florida. After living in their dream house for awhile, the Rawlings decided to move back to Kansas. Then, somehow, previous minor marital difficulties between them suddenly became intense and resulted in a divorce.

Thelma Rawlings still has her dream house. She wants to get rid of it, but hasn't been able to sell it for what she thinks it is worth. Her chance-of-a-lifetime home brought Thelma nothing but stress, a divorce, and worry about the future. "What I want more than anything else . . . is to get this price tag off of me and become ordinary again. That's what it amounts to."

This story of Thelma Rawlings's "good luck," which originally appeared in the *New York Times* (September 21, 1982, p. 10), illustrates an important point about the psychology of stress and ties in with what we said in Chapter 13 about person × situation interactions. For someone else, with different needs, interests, and desires, the *Sports Afield* house that was a nightmare for Thelma might have been a dream come true. But Thelma and her husband were not able to cope successfully with the change in their life, and their marriage succumbed to stress. In this chapter we explore the way that people adjust to stress and the conditions that influence their adjustment.

STRESS

Stress puts us "on the spot." Like motivation and emotion, stress arouses us and influences our behavior. Although it may be the last thing that we need, we often experience strong emotional reactions in situations that pose challenges, demands, and threats.

Many interactions between you and the environment produce stress. Small amounts of stress may appear and disappear like bubbles. But when you perceive an imbalance between the challenge that faces you and the resources that you have to meet it, stress can be like a weight or a wall.

Note that the balance or imbalance is not between actual demand and actual capability, but between our *evaluation* of the challenge and our *perception* of our capacity to meet it. There are two stages in that evaluation. During **primary appraisal**, we interpret the situation as either threatening or harmless. During **secondary appraisal**, we consider the kind of action called for and the nature and potency of our resources. Our estimate of these resources, which in turn is based largely on the information provided by the environment and by our own experience, determines how threatened we feel. New information can cause us to change our appraisal of a situation either positively or negatively.

Factors involved in stress

Stress is one of the areas in which the interaction between situational, personal, and biological factors can be most clearly seen.

SITUATIONAL FACTORS

The nature of the stressful situation affects our adjustment. The general effects of situational variation include the following:

1. *Duration.* A job interview lasts for a short time, while a marital quarrel might last for hours or days.

2. *Severity.* A minor injury is generally easier to cope with than a major illness.

3. *Predictability.* The amount of stress resulting from having to give an oral presentation in class might depend on whether the speech was an on-the-spot request or had been previously assigned.

4. *Controllability.* One of the most upsetting aspects of a situation is the feeling that one is unable to

exert any influence on the circumstances. For example, victims of a hurricane can do nothing to stop the wind and the rain.

5. *Suddenness of onset.* An accident may be difficult to cope with because it is completely unexpected, whereas challenges that can be foreseen may be easier to cope with.

PERSONAL FACTORS

Adjustment to stress depends on the skills and resources that we have available. One of the great challenges for parents is to equip their children with effective ways of handling stress. A similar challenge confronts the psychotherapist who seeks to help people who perceive threats in too many areas of their lives and feel unable to deal with any of them.

When people experience an imbalance between a situational challenge and their personal resources and do not know what to do about it, **anxiety** develops. Most people do not let their anxiety throw them. A highly anxious individual, on the other hand, is hypersensitive to danger and, like an animal pinned by your car's headlights, seems continually immobilized. Then, because anxiety states are extremely taxing physically and psychologically, the individual finally moves to meet the challenge and end the anxiety. But high anxiety is not conducive to rational planning and effective action, and so the plans of anxious people may not be very effective. This ineffectiveness is doubly unfortunate: not only does anxiety contribute to failure, but failure lays the groundwork for more anxiety and future failure.

A lack of self-confidence can also result in reduced personal effectiveness. We may know how to handle a situation, but we may be afraid to try. For example, a recently divorced woman may feel ill at ease in social situations that she handled very well during her marriage.

BIOLOGICAL FACTORS

When situational and personal factors combine to produce stress, our body responds in certain characteristic ways.

Hans Selye, who at the time of his death in 1982 was the director of the International Institute of Stress

FIGURE 14.1 *Hans Selye wrote 33 books and 1600 articles on the subject of stress. He was once asked if modern life was not becoming too stressful. "People often ask me that question, sometimes comparing our lives with that of the caveman, who didn't have to worry about the stock market or the atomic bomb," he replied. "They forget that the caveman worried about being eaten by a bear while he was asleep, or about dying of hunger, things that few people worry about much today." He added, "In the end, I doubt whether modern man experiences more distress than his ancestors. It's not that people suffer more stress today, it's just that they think they do." (Newport Times, October 22, 1982)*

at the University of Montreal, did some of the most important early research on the biology of stress (see Figure 14.1). Selye (1976) believed that stress is the body's response to the demands made on it and he referred to those demands as **stressors.** Based on a long series of experiments with animals, Selye proposed that bodily stress reactions follow a three-stage **general adaptation syndrome** (GAS). The first stage is an **alarm reaction,** which involves physiological changes generally associated with emotion: pupil dilation, heart rate increase, increase in galvanic skin response, and increase in epinephrine secretion. If the stress persists, the individual enters a second stage, **resistance,** during which the body recovers from the initial stress reaction and begins adapting to the situation. There is a decrease in output from the sympathetic nervous system, a lower rate of epinephrine secretion, and higher than normal outputs from the adrenal cortex and the pituitary gland. If the stress still continues, the individual will eventually reach a final stage of **exhaustion** as its bodily resources are depleted. At this point, the adrenal glands can no longer function adequately, and the body begins to break down (see Figure 14.2).

Two ideas are central to Selye's theory. The first is that the body responds the same way regardless of the source of the stress; the second is that this pattern of reactions ultimately results in physical breakdown. A psychophysiological disorder is a breakdown that reaches clinical proportions and is not "all in your mind." The cause (prolonged emotional responses to stress) may be under the individual's control, but, as we shall see later in the chapter, the symptoms are real. Disorders that may be psychophysiological in origin include high blood pressure, heart disease, asthma, and ulcers.

Selye was primarily interested in the role played in the GAS by the endocrine glands. In response to stressors (overwork, an argument with a spouse, a death in the family), chemical messages are carried along neuronal tracks in the outer edge of the brain to the hypothalamus, which produces a substance called **corticotropin releasing factor** (CRF). The hypothalamus sends the CRF and other chemical messengers to the pituitary gland and the brain stem, which release several substances involved in the body's stress response. The appraisal process and emotional arousal are involved in transmitting the messages of stress that acti-

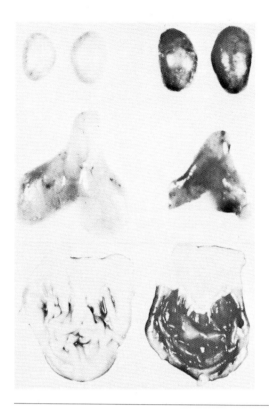

FIGURE 14.2 *The organs on the left are those of a normal rat and those on the right of one exposed to the frustrating psychological stress of being forcefully immobilized. Note the marked enlargement and dark discoloration of the adrenals (top), caused by congestion and discharge of fatty-secretion granules; the intense shrinkage of the thymus (middle); and the numerous blood-covered ulcers (bottom) in the stressed rat.*

vate the GAS. This means that physiological and psychological processes come to be intertwined when people are confronted with stressors (Goldberger and Breznitz, 1982).

Stress arousal

Two broad types of adjustment to stress have been identified—situational and transitional adjustments.

Situational adjustment is required in order to deal

with demands due to environmental circumstances. The sudden illness of a loved one, a natural disaster, and war are special events that require adjustment. Examples of everyday situations that often produce stress reactions include taking a test and entering a new social setting. In fact, stress reactions to these activities are so common that we have special names for them: *test anxiety* and *social anxiety*. People who are high in test anxiety or social anxiety not only respond maladaptively to the situation itself but also spend a great deal of time worrying about it beforehand.

There are several ways of responding to the stress of being evaluated. The most adaptive response is active, specific, and direct—for example, seeking a conference with a teacher before an exam and studying harder would be two such responses. A maladaptive reaction would be to deny the anxiety or relieve it by devaluing the evaluation: "So what if I get a low grade?" or "It was a dumb test."

The alarm reaction of the general adaptation syndrome is commonly observed in people who are concerned about being evaluated. Johansson (1977) stud-

ied a student who was preparing for the oral defense of her recently completed Ph.D. dissertation. Figure 14.3 shows changes in the student's epinephrine (adrenaline) and norepinephrine (noradrenaline) secretion rates before, during, and after her defense. The figure shows a gradual increase in epinephrine secretion during the days preceding the examination, followed by a dramatic rise on the day of the examination. Norepinephrine showed a similar, although less regular, pattern. Her body clearly mobilized itself to deal with the perceived threat of the evaluation.

Transitional adjustment is a normal part of human development. While transitional challenges occur more gradually than situational ones do, the need for transitional adjustment may seem sudden for the person going through it. Some of the transitions in the life

FIGURE 14.3 *Rates of adrenaline and noradrenaline secretion in a Ph.D. candidate during a three-week period before, during, and after the public defense of her dissertation.*

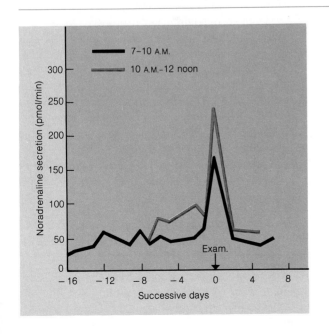
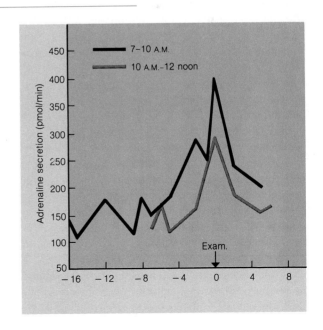

cycle that people respond to with varying degrees of stress include birth and establishing a good relationship between mother and baby, initial steps toward independence (day-care center, school), the biological and social changes of adolescence, major educational transitions such as going to college, entry into the world of work, marriage, having children and child rearing, moving to a new place of residence, the milestones of the children's development, retirement, and the death of the marriage partner. These stressful episodes can be resolved in either adaptive or maladaptive ways. Successful adaptation to one life crisis often influences success in adaptation later on.

Vulnerability to stress

When we talk about how people adapt, we have to consider the conditions—the personal conditions as well as the environmental ones—under which the adaptations are being made. You may handle a difficult situation well one time and badly the next. You may behave adaptively in circumstances that your friend handles poorly. Two concepts—stress and vulnerability—help us to understand these differences in behavior.

As we have seen, stress refers to our reactions to situations that pose demands, constraints, or opportunities. People are likely to experience psychological stress when they have to deal with an unexpected or unusual event, such as a natural disaster. They are likely to experience even greater stress when that event occurs at the same time as a severe life crisis (for example, the death of a loved one) or at the beginning of a critical developmental period (for example, adolescence).

Vulnerability refers to how likely we are to respond maladaptively to certain situations. Certain life conditions in and of themselves can increase people's vulnerability and thus can increase their risks of maladaptive behavior. Population groups that share these life conditions are more likely than the rest of the population to experience the negative effects of stress. Such high-risk groups include children and adolescents, the aged and the disabled, and disadvantaged minority groups.

Vulnerability might also be increased by particular

kinds of heredity, such as having schizophrenic parents; by certain personality characteristics, such as a high level of anxiety; by the lack of certain skills, such as being able to make decisions calmly; or by a build-up of negative experiences. Some people are more vulnerable in all situations because they are generally less able to deal effectively with what happens to them in daily life. Other people are more vulnerable simply because of a combination of unconnected events that have recently stressed them. Eleven-year-old Denton may adapt well when he has a sympathetic teacher, when his parents are getting along, and when he is healthy. But if he hates his teacher, if his parents bicker half the night and are on the verge of a divorce, and if he is constipated, not being a starter in his soccer team's first game may upset him more than we might have predicted. Or if Mrs. Block has just lost an important client for her firm, found a dent in her car, and heard that her 12-year-old son has left his expensive violin on the school bus, she may not respond as constructively as she might under other circumstances. Some people are more vulnerable only in particular kinds of situations that may remind them of former problems or difficulties. For example, on seeing a child swept away in a river, one person may act quickly to save the child, but a person who had seen one of her younger brothers killed in an accident when she was 5 might freeze.

Stress and vulnerability interact. The greater the stress, the less vulnerability a person needs to have before maladaptive behavior occurs. The greater the vulnerability, the less the stress needed to produce maladaptive behavior. There are two primary approaches to the treatment and prevention of severe stress reactions: we can decrease environmental stressors or increase people's resistance to stress, thereby decreasing their vulnerability. Because it is generally not possible to manipulate life's events, the most effective way to prevent stress reactions is to help people to learn better ways to cope.

COPING WITH STRESS

As Figure 14.4 shows, people can deal with stress in different ways. A task-oriented response—getting on with the problem at hand—is usually the most adaptive

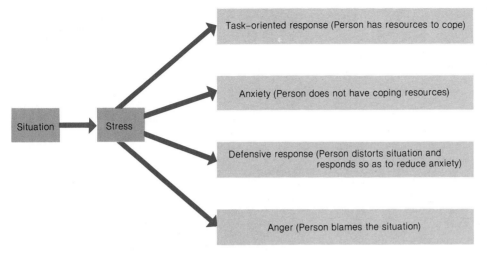

FIGURE 14.4 *Ways of dealing with stress.*

Task-oriented response (Person has resources to cope)

Anxiety (Person does not have coping resources)

Situation → Stress

Defensive response (Person distorts situation and responds so as to reduce anxiety)

Anger (Person blames the situation)

approach and is most likely to occur when the individual is not hampered by vulnerabilities. Anxiety, defensiveness, and anger are more likely to occur in vulnerable individuals (Taylor, 1983). People who cope effectively with stressful situations have first learned to direct their thoughts along productive lines and to avoid being distracted by fear and worry. Actors, football quarterbacks, and others in the limelight soon learn that paying attention to the task at hand is more constructive than self-preoccupied thoughts ("There

are 100,000 people out there waiting for me to fumble that ball"). On the other hand, the thoughts of some people who are prone to be worriers are saturated with self-blame and catastrophizing ("The worst will surely happen").

Coping with stress involves learning how to think constructively, to solve problems, to behave flexibly, and to provide oneself with feedback about which tactics work and which do not. How useful any of the skills listed in Table 14.1 will be depends on the nature

---

TABLE 14.1 WAYS TO IMPROVE YOUR STRESS-COPING ABILITIES

1. *Be task-oriented.* Focus only on the task confronting you. It is not productive to spend time with thoughts or feelings that are unrelated to accomplishing the task. Being task-oriented means that you are concentrating completely on the job at hand. Negative or disruptive thoughts and emotions are the enemies of task orientation.

2. *Be yourself.* Don't role play. You will be more effective acting naturally than trying to fit a role. Place your confidence in *yourself,* not in the role.

3. *Self-monitor.* Pay attention to the way you are thinking and feeling in a given situation. It is important to learn about what causes stress for you and about your personal reactions to stress. Effective self-monitoring is your early warning system. It can alert you to the necessity of using the other coping skills to *prevent* a blowup.

4. *Be realistic about what you can achieve.* Know your own

limits as well as your strengths. At times, laughter is the best medicine—don't lose your sense of humor.

5. *Have a constructive outlook.* Try to look for the positives in the people around you. Don't be too quick to conclude that people are behaving the way they are just to upset you. Put yourself in the other person's shoes—from that point of view his or her behavior may make perfect sense.

6. *Use supportive relationships.* Compare notes, blow off steam, and get support from your friends. Don't draw into yourself when you are feeling stressed. Remember that we all get by with a little help from our friends.

7. *Be patient with yourself.* Don't punish yourself for not achieving perfection. Your mistakes should be learning experiences, not times for heavy self-criticism. Keep your expectations of yourself at a reasonable level.

of the situation and on the individual's vulnerabilities and assets. Anger, which is often an outcome of stress (see Figure 14.4), illustrates the value of specific **stress-coping skills.** People who are prone to get angry can benefit from learning about the events and circumstances that typically arouse their anger. They need to pay attention to the thoughts that they have that evoke tension and agitation. They also need to set realistic goals because the frustration that leads to anger may be caused by excessively high personal standards. Since anger interferes with concentration, anger-prone people should remind themselves of the importance of staying focused on the task at hand. Finally, social support can help someone cope with anger. A good listener can help a person blow off steam and might also have valuable advice to offer.

Self-control

The environment is not always under our control, but we play an important role in how we respond to it. **Self-control** is not some internal force like "will power" or discipline. Self-control is just that: the ability to control ourselves by being aware of and directing our actions to achieve specific goals (Karoly and Kanfer, 1982). Self-control implies self-direction. When people see themselves as having choices and perceive themselves as being in control, they are most likely to deal effectively with stress (Fisher, 1984). The essence of a task-oriented technique is not so much "How do I feel?" but "What can I do?" This behavioral approach to self-control requires that we operate as our own scientists. We must seek out the conditions that seem to cause the **target behavior** (the behavior that we want to change). We must attempt to identify the **antecedents** (the situations that precede the occurrence of the target behavior) as well as the **consequences** of that behavior. Once we identify the antecedents and consequences, we may use self-controlling behaviors to alter them and bring about the desired change. Both internal, or covert, responses (thoughts, images, and feelings) and external, or overt, responses (for example, jogging or chewing every mouthful of food 20 times) may function as self-controlling behaviors. A simplified version of this process is presented in Figure 14.5.

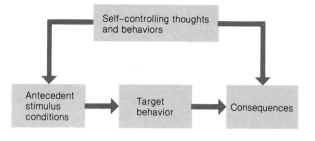

FIGURE 14.5 *Viewing self-control in behavioral terms, the person uses overt or covert self-controlling behaviors to change the antecedents or the consequences of the target behavior.*

Self-controlling behaviors are affected by their consequences, just as other behaviors are. So, to maintain them, we must reinforce them. Reinforcement may involve external rewards, such as social approval or financial gain, or it may consist of self-approval and encouragement from seeing desired changes occurring in oneself. In addition, the perception of personal freedom itself is reinforcing. For example, children are likely to study more and work harder on their homework when they are allowed to choose their own reinforcers and the requirements that they must meet in order to earn them. Their response rates are higher even when the reinforcement conditions that they choose are identical to those previously imposed by a teacher.

Psychologists have helped people to gain cognitive control over their emotions and behavior. For example, anger-provoking situations are highly stressful for people who are afraid of losing control. Raymond Novaco (1975) identified several key elements of these situations and trained people to avoid being overwhelmed by their anger by focusing on their own reactions (self-monitoring) and by using task-oriented thoughts. He emphasized the following steps:

1. *Preparation for provocation.* The person imagines situations in which anger might arise and rehearses thoughts that would encourage adequate coping ("I'll just stick to the issues; no need to get angry" or "Easy does it").

2. *Impact and confrontation.* The person imagines

that the provocation is actually occurring ("Think of what you have to do").

3. *The postimpact period.* The person imagines that the provocation has occurred, notices the emotional reactions that follow, and rehearses thoughts aimed at reducing emotionality ("My anger is a signal of what I need to do").

4. *Feedback.* If being made angry is highly stressful and leads to inadequate coping, the person is encouraged to engage in thought redirection ("Thinking about it only makes things worse. I can shake it off"). If the person does a good job of avoiding intense feelings of anger, self-reinforcing thoughts are brought to mind ("I'm doing better at this all the time").

Through this type of cognitive training, people who were prone to anger have achieved better control over their tempers and reported increased feelings of self-satisfaction.

People's thoughts—what they say to themselves, including self-instructions, beliefs, and evaluations of situations—clearly play an important role in controlling their lives. Most emotional responses, for exam-

ple, are not the result of external events but of what we covertly tell ourselves about the events. For example, your response to doing poorly on a test will be different depending on whether you tell yourself that it is a catastrophe and proves that you are stupid and worthless, or say, "So what? It's not the end of the world. I'll do better next time!"

The key ingredient in self-control is being able to see yourself as more than an object being pushed around by uncontrollable forces. We are not truly free unless we have the option of engaging in a variety of behaviors. The concept of self-control implies the ability to free ourselves from present or past conditions that have limited our options. We can have a greater sense of freedom if we think of self-control as an ability that we are capable of achieving, rather than as some inborn trait.

Social support

Although vulnerability is often thought of in terms of some personal inadequacy—having too short a fuse, being a worrier—external factors also play a role in how well we cope with stress. One of the key external influences is our network of social relationships.

Social support does not mean public welfare assistance; it means having close relationships with others, whether relatives or friends (see Figure 14.6). The type of social support that a person has affects both vulnerability and coping. Vulnerability to physical and psychological breakdown increases as our social network constricts. Put another way, social support acts as a buffer against the upsets of living in a complex world; it is nice to know that people are pulling for us when we're in a tough situation.

Knowing that other people are confronting similar life stress and sharing upsetting feelings and thoughts with them is often very beneficial. Too often the person in a crisis seems to hide or withdraw and thus becomes

FIGURE 14.6 *All people need social support.*

"Bless Mommy and Daddy, Aunt Emma and Uncle Sid, Cousin Myrna, Dr. Benson and all my support systems."

TABLE 14.2 THE SOCIAL SUPPORT QUESTIONNAIRE

Who do you know whom you can trust with information that could get you in trouble? (This item is completed as an example.)

_____ No one	(A) R.N. (brother)	(D) T.N. (father)	(G)
	(B) L.M. (friend)	(E) L.M. (employer)	(H)
	(C) R.S. (friend)	(F)	(I)

Whose lives do you feel that you are an important part of?

_____ No one	(A)	(D)	(G)
	(B)	(E)	(H)
	(C)	(F)	(I)

Whom can you really count on to distract you from your worries when you feel under stress?

_____ No one	(A)	(D)	(G)
	(B)	(E)	(H)
	(C)	(F)	(I)

Who helps you feel that you truly have something positive to contribute to others?

_____ No one	(A)	(D)	(G)
	(B)	(E)	(H)
	(C)	(F)	(I)

The *Social Support Questionnaire* (SSQ) consists of 27 items, 4 of which are presented here. After answering each item, the test taker is asked to indicate his or her level of satisfaction with the support available by marking a 6-point rating scale that ranges from "very satisfied" to "very unsatisfied." The SSQ yields scores relating to *Availability of* and *Satisfaction with* social support.

deprived of opportunities for social support. Special support groups can lead to stronger coping skills for persons undergoing intense, often prolonged stress (Cowen, 1982; Pilisuk, 1982). Social support is also helpful in times of relative calm. It gives us the security and self-confidence to try out new approaches and to expand our coping skills. With an expanded coping repertory, we are in a better position to handle demands, frustration, and challenges when they do arise.

Research aimed at measuring social support is now under way. The **Social Support Questionnaire** (SSQ) provides information about how much social support people have available and how satisfied they are with that support (Sarason and others, 1983). Table 14.2 lists some of the SSQ's items. One interesting finding is that there is only a moderate correlation between the availability of social support and people's feelings of satisfaction. Also, there appears to be no minimum

number of social supports that will satisfy everyone. Some people are satisfied with a small number of close friends and relatives, but others seem to need ties to many different people.

Maladaptive ways of thinking and behaving are more common among people who have few social supports. Even though lack of social supports in one's early years can be damaging, new social relationships can have therapeutic value. Psychotherapy, from this perspective, is a special social relationship directed at helping people to face and overcome obstacles in their lives. The support of one's family is particularly important. Many young people feel that they are being immature or weak if they try to maintain close ties with their parents. But, in fact, rather than sapping self-reliance, strong family ties seem to encourage it. The "apron strings" become strangling only when the family is allowed too much control over a person's life.

BREAKDOWNS UNDER STRESS

People may break down under stress because they don't have either the internal or external resources to cope with it adaptively, have a reaction so delayed that they are unprepared to deal with it, have too much to deal with at one time, or find their lives complicated by stress-related illnesses.

There seems to be some truth to the commonly held belief that everyone has a breaking point. As we saw in our discussion of the general adaptation syndrome, prolonged exposure to stress eventually leads to physical and psychological breakdown. Stress may be prolonged for two reasons: the stressful situation may not be under the individual's control (for example, being in a concentration camp); or the individual prolongs the stress by not coping with it effectively. Dealing with several stressful situations at the same time places greater demands on a person's resources. In addition, stress has cumulative effects: the more stress people experience, the more likely they are to break down either physically or psychologically. The severity of a stress reaction is not directly proportional to the severity of the stressor because personality characteristics as well as cultural or group norms contribute to the effectiveness with which an individual copes with a given set of circumstances. Behaviors that are shown in stress reactions vary widely, although depression, anxiety, and heightened emotionality are particularly common. A stress reaction might occur immediately after a traumatic event or later on (Spacapan and Cohen, 1983)—see Figure 14.7.

As an example, Paul Brendle flies a traffic helicopter for radio station KIRO in Seattle. He was uninjured when his helicopter crashed for the second time in a year. For two hours he stood near his crumpled copter, joking with reporters and talking to a crash investigator; then he suddenly collapsed. When medics revived him minutes later, Brendle asked whether he was upside down. Later on, he said: "It seems so far away now. Every couple hours I see it real clearly in flashes. The whole thing is sort of like a surrealistic dream." A few days later, Brendle was back on the job in a new helicopter. However, he continues to experience anxiety when thinking of his harrowing experience, and he does not want to be reminded of it.

FIGURE 14.7 *A stress reaction can be experienced immediately after an accident or days or weeks later.*

Posttraumatic stress reactions

Clark, an 18-year-old boy, had been a passenger in a car accident in which another vehicle had been damaged, two people injured, and a fence destroyed. Even though he had not been hurt, Clark found himself unable to stop reliving the events connected with the accident. He tortured himself with the thought that he might have been able to warn the driver if he had been more alert. Just about the time Clark's parents finally decided to get clinical help for him, the two people who had been injured were released from the hospital in good condition (their injuries were never considered to be life-threatening). Clark's state of mind seemed to change abruptly. He resumed his schoolwork and extracurricular activities and referred to the accident only in the overly dramatic, almost boastful manner displayed by many people who have had narrow escapes from danger. Clark had had what psychologists call a **posttraumatic stress reaction** of limited duration.

Reexperiencing the traumatic event is a frequent characteristic of posttraumatic stress reactions. People's waking hours are troubled by painful and intrusive recollections, and recurrent dreams or nightmares commonly disturb their sleep. The reexperiencing of the traumatic event may have an aura of unreality about it, like a dream where everything is in slow motion. When this happens, the person feels emotionally numb or anesthetized. Preoccupation with the event may lead to decreased interest in social relationships, intimacy, and sexuality. Painful guilt feelings, depression, restlessness, and irritability are all common. In some cases, there may be outbreaks of impulsive behavior, usually of a nonviolent nature (for example, unexplained absences from work), alcohol or drug abuse, and hyperalertness for danger.

Stress reactions usually settle down slowly within six months of the traumatic event. In some cases the event may be followed by an incubation period of days or weeks during which the person seems to be adjusting normally. This latency period is then followed by a delayed posttraumatic reaction.

Clinical studies of such cases suggest that people who have severe traumatic experiences benefit from the opportunity to express their emotions and thoughts openly to a supportive listener. For example, people experiencing bereavement often feel more objective about the implications of their loss if they can share their grief with others.

FIGURE 14.8 *Teaching can be unrewarding and frustrating if the class is hard to control and the teacher feels his or her best efforts to help the children learn are ineffective and unappreciated.*

Burnout

Burnout is a particular stress reaction related strictly to work. People who work closely with others—for example, teachers, psychiatrists, nurses, and social workers—and who experience a great deal of frustration and receive little satisfaction seem especially prone to burnout. Professionals who burn out are helpers who need help themselves (see Figure 14.8). After years of excellent performance, such people may suffer a type of emotional exhaustion. They seem to lose enthusiasm and concern for their jobs and for the people whom they have been working so hard to help. For example, public school teachers who burn out dread the thought of entering the classroom and seem to be detached from the problems and needs of their students.

External factors that play a role in professional burnout are heavy workload, lack of opportunities to do creative work, limited leisure time, and lack of contact with fellow professionals. For example, nurses who work 12-hour shifts in understaffed hospitals, get a half-hour for lunch, are talked down to by doctors, and have too many patients to care for may be likely candidates for burnout. Personality factors also play a role. People who actively express feelings, who do not take their professional problems home with them, and who do not take professional failures personally are less likely to burn out.

Burnout may be reduced by increasing opportunities for group cohesiveness (for example, through staff meetings at which mutual problems can be discussed), by increasing staff training, and by improving the quality of leadership. Authoritarian or workaholic administrators generate stress; democratic leaders who can pace themselves lessen it.

Quantifying life stress

All people expect to experience certain situational and transitional stresses. People move, marry, divorce, have children, lose jobs, get raises and promotions, and lose loved ones through death. These relatively commonplace events often require significant readjust-

ment, but they are usually manageable as long as the person is given adequate time to recover. Researchers have found that health problems and behavioral disorders often occur when major **life changes** occur in clusters. For example, Holmes and Rahe (1967) measured stress by assigning number values to certain common life changes and then adding up the total amount of readjustment required of an individual during a specific period of time—say, one year. Holmes and Rahe include positive (presumably desirable) as well as negative (presumably undesirable) life changes in their analysis. Since the birth of a child and the death of a parent both require adjustment, for instance, Holmes and Rahe considered them as contributing to the total level of stress.

From a commonsense point of view, positive and negative events would seem to have different stress potentials. Besides knowing whether or not certain desirable and undesirable events took place, we would also want to know how the individual experienced them. A newer measure, the **Life Experiences Survey,** or LES (Sarason and others, 1978; Sarason, 1981), attempted to take such individual factors into account. The LES measure gathers information not only about what events occurred but also the extent to which each event was desirable or undesirable, how much it affected the individual's life, how much it could have been anticipated, and the extent to which the individual could gain control over it (see Table 14.3).

Although there are still many problems in measuring life stress and its relationship to personal adjustment and disease, the information that we have seems consistent. Individuals with high negative life change scores describe themselves as significantly more anxious, depressed, hostile, and fatigued than those with low scores. They also report a higher intensity of physical symptoms than respondents with low stress scores do. Individuals who have experienced a great deal of life stress are more likely than other people to get sick or hurt enough to require psychiatric, medical, or surgical attention.

TABLE 14.3 A MEASURE OF STRESSFUL LIFE EVENTS

The revised version of the Life Experiences Survey (Sarason, 1981) gives a picture not only of the events people have experienced, but also of their reactions to the events. People who have had a bunching-up of negative life changes are more likely than other people to become depressed, perform poorly, and experience an increase in physical symptoms. Subjects are given the following instructions.

Listed below are a number of events that may bring about changes in the lives of those who experience them. Rate each event that occurred in your life during the past year in the following four ways:

1. Was the event *Good or Bad?*

2. How much did the event *affect your life?* [Rated from "No Effect" to "Great Effect"]

3. To what extent did you *expect the event to happen?* [Rated from "Not at All" to "Completely"]

4. To what extent did you have *control over the event's occurrence?* [Rated from "Not at All" to "Completely"]

Some of the events listed are:

Marriage

Death of a spouse

Leaving home for the first time

Failing a course

Moving to a new city or town

Being fired from a job

Divorce

Parents divorced or separated

HEALTH PSYCHOLOGY AND BEHAVIORAL MEDICINE

The care of tuberculosis depends more on what the patient has in his head than on what he has in his chest. (Sir William Osler [1849–1919], the father of modern medicine)

Although the influence of the mind on the body was well known to ancient healers and has dominated folklore to the present day, the field of medicine has until recently focused almost exclusively on physical causes of bodily illness. However, the idea that illness is exclusively the result of exposure to external agents now seems outmoded. For any given individual, a host of biological, psychological, and social variables contribute to the apparently either/or phenomenon that we call getting sick. New studies strongly indicate that virtually every illness—from the common cold to cancer and heart disease—can be influenced, positively or negatively, by a person's mental state, life style, and social relationships.

Physical, mental, social, and economic factors all influence health and recovery from illness. These interacting factors provide a clue to why we cannot make a simple statement like "John Jones got pneumonia because he had been working overtime for two months." Most people can work overtime without becoming sick, and many people who get pneumonia don't work at all.

Social and economic variables in the environment that seem to have especially strong influences on physical health include urbanization, poverty, rapid social change, migration, occupation, workload, working hours, attitudes toward work, morale, and job performance. Biological factors include individual differences in body type, hormone levels, and cardiovascular functioning. However, not all people who are biologically predisposed to a particular condition actually fall ill; some apparently have a greater capacity to adjust and therefore remain in good health. Psychological contributions to illness may depend on a number of factors, including age, the particular form of the illness, and what is going on in the person's life. By unveiling the mechanisms behind these effects, research may point to new ways to prevent and treat at least some killing or crippling diseases.

Behavioral medicine uses psychological techniques to help people to adopt generally healthier ways of living as well as to follow the treatment plans prescribed for specific problems. An important goal of behavioral medicine is to improve the way that professionals serve their patients. The related field of **health psychology** is especially directed toward disease prevention. Health psychologists seek to reduce health risks by changing people's thinking and living habits (Gatchel and Baum, 1983).

Researchers in behavioral medicine are particularly concerned with direct patient evaluation and treatment. Researchers in health psychology tend to be concerned with broader topics, including the acquisition and modification of behavior that influences health. Both of these areas emphasize a philosophy that sees health as a personal achievement whose attainment is determined by people's behavior.

It is important to find out about the mechanisms involved in the role that psychological factors play in physical health and illness. As the relationship between stress and various bodily processes becomes better known, we may be able to predict who is likely to develop certain illnesses. A factor that increases the complexity of stress-illness relationships is that it is how a person responds to life events, not the events themselves, that influences susceptibility to disease. Failure to cope well with stress can impair a person's ability to fight off illness, whereas adequate coping may protect an individual even from the consequences of a high-stress life.

Physical disorders related to stress

There is ample evidence that psychological stress has profound effects on our bodies as well as on our emotions and behavior. Besides their obvious immediate effects on our body, stress reactions such as increased pulse rate, increased blood pressure, and various hormonal secretions may have long-term consequences as well. The extreme physiological responses that occur while we are caught in a burning building subside relatively quickly after we escape from the structure, but much milder forms of stress that persist for a longer time can have more damaging long-term physiological effects.

Why do some people respond to stress primarily with bizarre thoughts and behavior, while others respond primarily by becoming physically ill? People's reactions to stressors are idiosyncratic, but they are also stable and consistent for each individual. We do not know why a person develops one pattern or the other, but we do know that patterns of stress response involve interactions between person variables and situational variables. Certain psychological factors do play roles in

physical illness. These factors, which do not usually act alone, include the inability to do the following:

1. Adapt to changes in environmental demands

2. Appropriately express and deal with strong feelings and emotions

3. Interpret correctly demands, constraints, and opportunities

4. Form rewarding, long-lasting interpersonal ties, particularly love relationships

Furthermore, just as the personalities of individuals can accelerate physical illness, so physical illness can bring about personality changes. The bedridden individual who is in pain to some extent becomes a different person from what he or she was when up and about. It has been estimated that between 25 and 50 percent of hospital patients have psychological as well as medical disorders (Lipowski, 1977).

PSYCHOPHYSIOLOGICAL DISORDERS

Many reactions to stress result in strong, persistent emotional states such as anger and anxiety. Continual and intense emotional states may in turn produce structural changes in our internal organs. **Psychophysiological disorders** involve tissue damage or physiological changes caused by persistent and intense emotional states. The concept of psychophysiological disorders arose out of the study of a group of diseases or conditions that have undeniable physical symptoms but no clearly established physiological cause. The field of medicine concerned with psychophysiological disorders—which was originally called *psychosomatic medicine*—is relatively young, and there are many gaps in our knowledge.

Psychological factors seem to play a major role in migraine attacks as well as in cardiovascular disorders such as high blood pressure; respiratory disorders such as asthma; skin disorders such as dermatitis and eczema; and gastrointestinal disorders such as peptic ulcers and constipation. In addition to these "traditional" psychophysiological disorders, psychological factors seem to play roles in certain types of muscle cramps, backaches, and menstrual disturbances. Psychological factors also seem to hasten or to retard death in terminally ill people whose conditions are *not* regarded as psychosomatic. One of the intriguing aspects of the study of psychophysiological disorders is the light that it might ultimately shed on the psychological side of illness and even death.

Intense or continuous life stress can reveal weakness in an individual's "carrying capacity," whether it is an aging dockworker's capacity to carry heavy loads or a new widow's ability to carry new interpersonal relationships. Sometimes a crisis reveals a latent and slowly developing constitutional weakness. For example, an individual who has smoked heavily, eaten a poorly chosen diet, and worked too hard for 30 years may "suddenly" develop a coronary condition.

The most extensive evidence we have that physical illness is caused by the interaction of psychosocial and biological factors probably comes from the study of coronary diseases. For that reason, we deal with heart attacks and related disorders in some detail.

CORONARY HEART DISEASE

Coronary heart disease (CHD) accounts for two-thirds of all cardiovascular deaths (about 650,000 deaths per year, 150,000 of which occur in people less than 65 years old). CHD is produced by lesions of the arteries that circulate blood within the heart itself. In CHD, one or more of these three arteries is partially or totally obstructed. When the coronary arteries become rigid, thick-walled, and narrow as a result of plaque deposits, the supply of blood to various portions of the heart muscle will be temporarily or permanently cut off. This build-up of plaque is referred to as **atherosclerosis.**

CHD takes different forms. In **angina pectoris,** people suffer from periodic chest pains caused by an insufficient supply of oxygen-rich blood to the heart. A **myocardial infarction,** also caused by insufficient blood supply, is more serious than angina pectoris because it involves a more complete curtailment of the heart's blood supply. When people speak of a heart attack, they are usually referring to a myocardial infarc-

tion. Mortality due to CHD has decreased more than 30 percent in the last 30 years. Heart disease remains the leading cause of death at ages 45 and over, but among people between 25 and 44 years of age, deaths as a result of heart disease have declined from first to third among all causes (Levy and Moskowitz, 1982). Improved medical services, the development of coronary-care units in hospitals, advances in surgical and medical treatment of CHD, and improved control of blood pressure may all have contributed to this decline. Life style changes, such as less smoking, better eating habits, and increased physical fitness, may also play roles.

Factors that increase the risk of CHD include age (older persons are at greater risk), sex (males are at greater risk), cigarette smoking, high blood pressure, high cholesterol level, and diabetes. Some studies have also implicated factors such as obesity, heredity, and lack of physical exercise. These factors may not be causes of CHD; they may simply be correlated with it. Even the most predictive of the risk factors still fails to identify more than half the new cases of CHD. Stress seems to contribute to coronary disease through the body's general reactions to frightening or unpleasant events. Under arousing conditions, catecholamines are secreted. Two of these catecholamines, epinephrine and norepinephrine, accelerate the rate of arterial damage and, ultimately, can lead to heart attacks.

While stress leads to many kinds of physical consequences, a large group of people seem especially prone to heart problems. Is there a heart-attack-prone personality? Meyer Friedman and Ray Rosenman (1974), two heart specialists, have concluded that there is. They have described a behavior pattern, called **Type A,** which seems to be associated with high risk of coronary disease. Type A characteristics include rapid talking, moving, walking, and eating, and excessive irritation at delay (for example, at having to wait in line or at being stuck in traffic). Type A people are apt to live under great pressure and to be demanding of themselves and others. They typically schedule more and more activities in less and less time and try to do several things at once. Type A's are competitive, continually strive for achievement, and are aggressive in their orientation toward life. They seem to be "workaholics" who have difficulty relaxing on vacations and holidays. They are reluctant to revise their standards to accommodate the demands of everyday life or to compromise their stand once they have taken it (see Figure 14.9). While the Type A pattern has not been proven to cause heart attacks, there are definite links. For example, one study (Rosenman and others, 1975) shows that a group of Type A men had more than twice the incidence of heart disease during eight and a half years of follow-up as did men who were not Type As. This difference could not be explained simply in terms of traditional risk factors such as cigarette smoking, because these other risk factors were equal in the two groups. Although, as we pointed out earlier, none of the major known risk factors is as predictive of heart attacks as we would like, the Type A behavior pattern is the strongest single predictor of recurring heart attacks (see Frontier 14.1).

The popular idea that high-level executives are especially susceptible to physical breakdowns such as heart attacks is not supported by current research. Often the Type A behavior pattern is stronger among middle-level administrators than among those at the top of the organization. One group of researchers con-

ducted a 5-year study of 270,000 male telephone company employees and found no evidence that men with high levels of responsibility or those who had been promoted rapidly, frequently, or recently had any added risk of coronary heart disease. Men who entered the telephone company with a college degree had lower rates of heart attacks, death, and disability than those who had no degree (Hinkel and others, 1968).

Cross-cultural data have provided a broader perspective on the relationship between psychosocial experience and physical breakdown. Japan, for example, has one of the lowest rates of heart disease in the world; the rate in the United States is one of the highest. The coronary death rate for Japanese men between the ages of 35 and 64 is 64 deaths per 100,000, while the com-

"He's busy now, Doctor. Can you come back later?"

(DRAWING BY B. TOBEY; © 1980 THE NEW YORKER MAGAZINE, INC.)

FIGURE 14.9 *Type A people tend to be workaholics who take on too many responsibilities and set too many deadlines for themselves.*

parable figure for American men is 400 per 100,000. Could simply living in the United States lead to such a high mortality rate? In one study, Japanese people living in Japan had the lowest incidence of CHD, Japa- nese-Americans living in Hawaii a somewhat higher rate, and Japanese-Americans in California the highest frequency of heart disease (Marmot and Syme, 1976). While diet probably accounts for some of these varia-

---

IMPROVING THE PREDICTION OF HEART ATTACK

Why is the Type A pattern predictive of a heart attack in some cases and not in others? This question is leading researchers in a variety of directions. One of these involves novel approaches to assessing risk factors. Type A behavior is detected behaviorally, on the basis of a person's responses to an interview or questionnaire. Behavioral, cognitive, and physiological measures are not always highly correlated. This means that two people who display similar Type A behavioral patterns might not show similar bodily reactions.

Two researchers at the University of Nebraska, Robert Eliot and James Buell (1983), are interested in classifying people in terms of their physiological reaction to stress. Eliot and Buell measure their subjects' blood pressure while the subjects are performing a variety of stress-arousing tasks. The tasks include mental arithmetic (serially subtracting 7 from 777 as fast as they can in three minutes), playing a competitive video game, and putting a hand into very cold water. People seem to have two types of cardiovascular reactions to these tasks.

"Hot reactors" tend to overrespond physiologically. Their blood pressure rises steeply, and other circulatory system responses may also occur. "Cool reactors," on the other hand, have a normal cardiovascular reaction to stress: blood pressure changes only slowly and slightly, if at all, and any change is appropriate to the demands of the situation. Eliot and Buell have found that one in five seemingly healthy people is a "hot reactor." Their findings may explain why many people with hard-driving coronary-prone Type A personalities do not get heart disease, while some people with more relaxed, Type B personalities do. Analyses of bodily reactions to stress have shown that some people who seem highly excitable on the surface actually remain quite "cool," cardiovascularly speaking, whereas others who appear extremely calm are really seething inside.

John Hunter, an eighteenth-century British pioneer in cardiovascular medicine, recognized his heart's vulnerability to stress when he said, "My life is in the hands of any rascal who chooses to put me in a passion." His prediction was all too accurate; he died during an emotional debate at a hospital board meeting. Many heart attack victims are seemingly healthy people whose hearts suddenly develop ventricular fibrillation, a highly abnormal rhythm that is incompatible with life. And many of the victims of sudden death have no severe blockages in their coronary arteries to explain their heart's vulnerabilities. One explanation for these sudden deaths is that emotional stress overstimulates a part of the nervous system that can cause spasms in the coronary arteries and clumping of the blood platelets. The combination can result in a sudden reduction of blood flow to the heart, precipitating the irregular beats.

If this line of reasoning is correct, most office physical examinations are not adequate to detect people at high risk for stress-induced heart disease because the examinations are conducted when the patient is at rest and away from the usual stresses of daily life. A compact, convenient portable monitor allows us to obtain blood pressure and heart recordings as the individual carries out his or her normal activities (see Figure 13.15, p. 480). Once identified, "hot reactors" can be treated with appropriate drugs or given behavioral training to help them be less excitable in provocative situations.

tions, social and cultural differences also play a substantial role. In general, the prevalence of CHD tends to be low wherever tradition and family ties are strong. For example, Japanese-Americans who believed in preserving traditional Japanese culture had a lower incidence of CHD than Japanese-Americans who had strongly accepted the American culture. Work group characteristics, the availability of stress-reducing activities and facilities, and social outlets are among the other variables that may cause different rates of psychophysiological disorders among different social groups (Matsumoto, 1970).

Speeding recovery from illness

Besides identifying the factors involved in vulnerability to illness, psychologists are also trying to identify factors that might speed recovery once a person has actually developed a clinical condition. Three of these factors are: what the patient knows about the condition, the patient's sense of control over the course of the illness, and the availability of social support.

INFORMATION AND EXPECTATIONS

Irving Janis (1958) carried out one of the first research studies of psychological factors involved in recovery from surgery. Janis believes that worry can be constructive and can speed recovery. He found that patients who have a moderate amount of fear before an operation make a better recovery than either patients who have little fear or patients who are very much afraid. Janis's findings suggested that a moderate amount of anticipatory fear is necessary to prod a person to begin the "work of worrying." By mentally rehearsing potentially unpleasant events and by gaining information about what to expect, patients can develop effective ways of coping with postoperative pain and with their concerns about recuperation.

Researchers in the area of behavioral medicine are carrying out extensive investigations about the types of information that are medically useful and the best ways of communicating the information. People who find out about the medical treatment that they will be getting develop more effective ways of coping with the

stress of illness than people who do not obtain such advance information. Four kinds of information play important roles in the way that patients respond to illness and treatment:

1. Information about the nature of the illness and the medical reasons for initiating particular treatments

2. Information describing the medical procedures to be carried out step by step

3. Information about particular physical sensations (for example, pain or the possible side effects of medication)

4. Information about coping strategies that can be used in adjusting to the upcoming threat

Free communication between patients and healthcare providers is especially important. Without it, patients' fears stay bottled up and their misconceptions cannot be corrected. Patients who express concerns to their doctors and receive answers in simple language tend to experience less stress about their physical condition. Self-help groups, made up of patients with similar conditions, can provide needed social support as well as encourage the communication of information.

The use of films and videotapes to convey information to patients is illustrated by Melamed's (1979) research with children scheduled to undergo painful dental procedures. She showed some of the children films of other children receiving the same treatment and found that those who saw the informative film exhibited fewer disruptive behaviors, reported less apprehension, and showed better clinical progress than children in the control/comparison groups did. In other words, their coping abilities had increased. This sort of preparatory procedure is effective with both children and adults and is particularly useful for people who experience high levels of worry and emotional tension before and during medical procedures (Peterson and others, 1984; Shipley and others, 1979).

PREDICTABILITY AND PERCEIVED CONTROL

Whether or not patients use the information available to them and follow medical advice depends on several factors besides the information given and the way that it is presented. Two psychological factors that seem especially important in recovery from illness and the maintenance of health and well-being are *predictability* and *perceived control*. Stressful life events and crises will generally have less of a negative impact on health if they are perceived as predictable or controllable. Telling people what to expect in advance reduces stress partly because the information makes the future course of events more predictable. For example, postsurgical pain is more tolerable if the patient is told in advance that pain is inevitable, will decrease, and does not mean that the operation was a failure.

When a sense of choice and perceived control is added to the predictability of a sequence of events, the likelihood of successful coping with stress increases (Abbott and others, 1984; Fisher, 1984; Perlmuter and Monty, 1979). People who see themselves as having choices among alternatives and who perceive themselves as personally controlling events are better able to tolerate pain and unpleasant conditions than people who don't believe that they are in control. For instance, people who do not feel that they are in control of their lives may not follow instructions about exercise and medication. Also, less-educated people are more likely than better-educated people to break medical appointments and not to follow medical advice. Loss of control and a feeling of helplessness can lead to heightened physical and mental distress, particularly for heart attack victims and the elderly (Krantz and Schulz, 1980). As we pointed out at the beginning of the chapter, how we cognitively appraise a situation and estimate our ability to handle it has a lot to do with how we actually handle it.

SOCIAL SUPPORT AND CLINICAL PROGRESS

The positive role of social support in a patient's recovery is illustrated by one study that investigated the relationship between life stress, social support, and the dosage of drugs necessary to control symptoms in adult asthmatics (de Araujo and others, 1973). As shown in Figure 14.10, the group with many life stresses and few

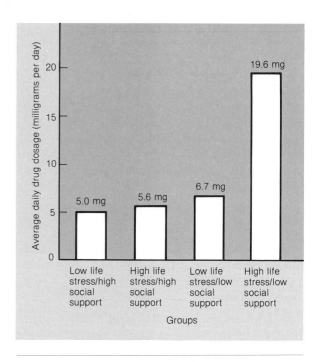

FIGURE 14.10 *The average daily drug dosage necessary to control symptoms of asthma patients varied with their level of life stress and social support.*

social supports needed the largest dose. Individuals with good social supports seemed less adversely affected by stress in their lives than those with poor social supports.

Another study has examined the moderator effect of social supports on the lives of pregnant women (Nuckolls and others, 1972). The women were assessed in two ways: frequency and severity of recent life changes and amount of social support (people with whom the women were close, from whom they obtained affection, and on whom they could rely). The pregnancies of women who had many social supports had significantly fewer complications. The effect of social support was much more noticeable among women who were subjected to a great deal of stress: 91 percent of the highly stressed women who had few social supports had birth complications, while only 33 percent of the highly stressed women with many social supports did. In a recent study, the effects of having a supportive woman in the delivery room were examined in healthy women who were bearing their first child (Sosa and others, 1980). Women in a control group showed a higher rate of medical complications than the women who had social support in the delivery room. Women who had social support were awake more after delivery and stroked, smiled at, and talked to their babies more than the control mothers did.

Achieving health

Psychologists are concerned with applying the principles of coping and self-controlling behavior to the whole field of health, not just to coping with stress. Helping people to live more healthful lives is a goal of health psychologists. They are especially interested in identifying and strengthening life styles that contribute to well-being.

The need for improvement in healthful life styles is shown by a few statistics. It has been estimated that 40 to 80 million people in the United States are overweight, don't exercise enough, and don't have proper nutrition. About 50 million are smokers, and approximately 9 million abuse alcohol. Smoking and drinking are self-destructive behaviors with profound personal, social, and economic implications. Unfortunately, much self-destructive behavior is not accompanied by unpleasant symptoms in the early stages, and so its medical consequences may go unnoticed.

Both self-destructive and health-promoting behaviors have complex determinants that must be understood in order to devise effective ways of decreasing self-destructiveness and increasing health. The benefits of self-destructive behaviors have to be considered as well as their risks and dangers. An occupation that has environmental or safety hazards (coal mining, law enforcement) may support a family; hazardous recreational activities (mountain climbing, hang-gliding) may provide relaxation and physical exercise. Some benefits may be compelling to the individual but less clear to others, as in the case of taking dangerous drugs. Conforming to self-destructive group behavior, such as excessive drinking, may give an individual a feeling of social acceptance.

EXERCISE AND HEALTH

A life style that includes a program of physical activity has many benefits (see Figure 14.11). Moderately strenuous jogging often produces a reduction in the tension experienced by clinically depressed and anxious people. This positive effect has encouraged psychotherapists to recommend running, walking, or swimming programs to many of their clients. People who are not suffering from clinical conditions also benefit from exercise programs; they say they feel better, worry less, and feel more competent (Brownell, 1982). The beneficial effects of exercise might be due to physiological changes (for example, reduction in the amount of lactic acid, a byproduct of exercise, and a lowering of blood pressure), psychological changes (for example, feeling stronger and more in control), or both.

Exercise is particularly important for health in industrialized societies. The modern conveniences that have become available since 1900 have resulted in a twofold increase in obesity despite a 10 percent decrease in daily caloric consumption. Obesity and sedentary lives do not lead to health. Regular aerobic exercise, however, generally lowers the blood pressure and thus reduces the risk of coronary heart disease for many people.

Health psychologists are working on a major problem connected with exercise programs—the tendency for people to give them up. A variety of techniques to lure people into continuing seem promising. People who deposit items of personal value and must meet a specific target (losing 5 pounds, regularly running a mile) to get them back tend to persist in their physical activities. A behavioral contract that requires the individual to formally sign a contract to exercise regularly in exchange for some reward is also an effective procedure. Social support and reinforcement from friends and associates are also helpful.

Future research on the physical and psychological effects of exercise needs to focus on the mechanisms

FIGURE 14.11 *Exercise contributes to a person's fitness and sense of well-being. Frequent jogging—not necessarily running a marathon to the point of exhaustion—reduces tension and increases body tone.*

responsible for the observed effects, determine the nature and extent of the effects, and compare different approaches to encouraging people to adopt healthful exercise programs.

STAMINA AND HEALTH

Exercise is one of many parts of a person's life style. Eating and drinking habits, social relationships, and patterns of work also seem to help determine whether people achieve health or become sick. These various factors probably interact with one another. For example, the effects of exercise may be different for a person who eats a lot than for one who eats moderately. Heavy smokers who have family histories of coronary heart disease, poor family relationships, and high cholesterol may get heart attacks at age 40 even if they run 5 miles a day.

The product of these interacting factors—a person's ability to resist or withstand disease, fatigue, or hardship—might be called **stamina** (Thomas, 1982). Who has stamina? How can it be measured? How can lack of stamina be detected? And, how can such a vulnerable state of health be remedied? Health psychologists are contributing in several ways to answering these questions with more information about person × situation interactions as they apply to health. For example, the term **psychological hardiness** has been used to describe people who are more resistant to stress and less susceptible to illness than most people are (Kobasa and others, 1982). People who are psychologically hardy tend to have a strong sense of personal control over their lives, feel more involved in whatever they are doing (for example, working), and are more open to new ideas and change. Psychological hardiness may be linked to longevity. Longevity might be thought of as the ultimate outcome of a person's stamina.

It is a well-established fact that women live longer than men do (see Table 14.4), though the cause of their greater longevity is unclear. Probably both genetic and life style factors play roles. Sex differences in longevity are greater in industrialized societies than they are in nonindustrial ones. To a large extent, these sex differences in mortality reflect the greater incidence of coronary heart disease in males in industrial societies, which in turn seems to be related to society's expectations that men will be more aggressive, adventurous, ambitious, and hard-driving than women. As more and more women hold jobs and support families, will their mortality rates go up? We do not yet have definite answers to these questions. Research that compares mortality among men who differ in their needs to adopt the traditional male role and among women who differ in their conceptions of the female role may clarify this issue. Such research would be an important step in developing a life style that would truly be a way of *life*.

TABLE 14.4 PREDICTORS OF LONGEVITY

FACTORS IN LONGEVITY WHOLLY OR PARTLY UNDER PERSONAL CONTROL

1. *Diet.* Too much or too little food reduces longevity. Many people in Western countries would live longer if they ate less, particularly of foods that are high in fat.
2. *Exercise.* People who are more active and get more exercise are likely to live longer.
3. *Smoking.* The association between cigarette smoking and greater mortality is now well documented.
4. *Retirement and work.* Retired people have higher mortality rates than those of the same age who continue to be gainfully employed.
5. *Marital status.* Aged married persons have lower mortality rates than elderly people who are not married.
6. *Social activity.* Social activity (for example, belonging to clubs and religious institutions) is modestly correlated with greater longevity.

LESS MODIFIABLE FACTORS IN LONGEVITY

1. *Heredity.* There is a positive relationship between the longevity of parents and that of their children.
2. *Sex.* Women live longer than men.
3. *Race.* Up to age 75, blacks have higher mortality rates than whites. After age 75, there is a small difference in favor of blacks.
4. *Intelligence.* Higher intelligence or better mental functioning is associated with greater longevity.
5. *Socioeconomic status.* Education and income levels are strong predictors of longevity.

STUDY OUTLINE

STRESS (p. 484)

1. Stress results from the perceived imbalance between an environmental demand and an individual's capacity to meet the demand. The perceptions result from primary appraisal of the situation and then secondary appraisal of both the action called for and the resources available to meet it. Situational factors that are important in stress include its duration, severity, predictability, controllability, and suddenness of onset. Anxiety develops from a perceived discrepancy between the challenge of the situation and the individual's resources.

2. The general adaptation syndrome is Hans Selye's description of a three-part biological response to stress. According to Selye, the body reacts the same way to all types of stressors: first an alarm reaction, then resistance, then a period of exhaustion. Continued stress ultimately results in physical breakdown.

3. Stress can be the result of environmental demands of a particular situation. Common stress reactions are

test anxiety and social anxiety. Stress also results from transitions from one life cycle stage to another.

4. Some individuals are more vulnerable to stress than others. Vulnerability is influenced by heredity, personality characteristics, lack of skills needed for particular situations, and the build-up of negative life experiences.

COPING WITH STRESS (p. 488)

1. Task orientation is the most effective way to cope with many stressors. Self-control of behavior involves understanding the antecedents and consequences of behavior and the way these are related to the desired or target behavior. Cognitive training that helps people control what they say to themselves and how they assess situations is effective in self-control of behavior.

2. Social support, the feeling that people care about you and are there to assist if you need them, helps to decrease vulnerability and encourage effective coping. Social support can be measured by such tests as the Social Support Questionnaire.

BREAKDOWNS UNDER STRESS (p. 493)

1. Stress reactions sometimes continue for some time after the event that caused them has ended. Sometimes the reaction, usually consisting of intrusive thoughts about the event, depression, and irritability, does not appear until some time after the event. Burnout is a work-related stress reaction common to professionals whose main job is to help others and who often feel frustration and lack of support in their efforts.

2. An individual's life stress can be quantified by tests that survey which life events have occurred as well as their implications for that person. One measure of life events is the Life Experiences Survey.

HEALTH PSYCHOLOGY AND BEHAVIORAL MEDICINE (p. 496)

1. Behavioral medicine uses psychological techniques to help people follow treatment plans and to adopt healthier ways of living to prevent problems from recurring. Health psychology focuses on reducing health risks by helping people change their living styles before problems occur.

2. Stress reactions that persist over long periods can cause tissue damage or physiological changes that may result in what are called psychophysiological disorders.

3. Stress may play an important role in coronary heart disease, a leading cause of death in the United States. The Type A behavior pattern, in which anger and impatience are prominent, is associated with a high risk of coronary heart disease.

4. Information about what to expect during and after surgery and about appropriate coping strategies can aid recovery. Patients who have a moderate amount of fear before an operation seem to have the best recovery. Feelings of control over the situation and good social support are also important in recovery from illness.

5. Psychological hardiness is a term used to describe individuals who seem able to withstand stress without illness or other negative effects. These people have a strong sense of personal control and involvement in their work and are flexible in their approach to situations.

KEY TERMS AND CONCEPTS

stress	vulnerability
primary appraisal	stress-coping skills
secondary appraisal	self-control
situational factors in stress	target behavior
personal factors in stress	antecedent
anxiety	consequence
stressor	social support
general adaptation syndrome	Social Support Questionnaire
alarm reaction	posttraumatic stress reaction
resistance	
exhaustion	burnout
corticotropin releasing factor	life changes
	Life Experiences Survey
situational adjustment	behavioral medicine
transitional adjustment	health psychology

psychophysiological disorder

coronary heart disease

atherosclerosis

angina pectoris

myocardial infarction

Type A

stamina

psychological hardiness

SUGGESTED READINGS

BURCHFIELD, S. R. (Ed.) (1985). *Stress: Psychological and physiological interactions*. Washington, D.C.: Hemisphere. An up-to-date review of research on stress and its effects.

LAZARUS, R. S., and FOLKMAN, S. (1984). *Stress, appraisal, and coping*. New York: Springer. Analyzes theoretical issues concerning stress.

MEICHENBAUM, D., and JAREMKO, M. E. (Eds.) (1983). *Stress reduction and prevention*. New York: Plenum. Describes specific ways of reducing or coping with stress.

BEHAVIOR DISORDERS AND TREATMENT

CHAPTER FIFTEEN: **BEHAVIOR DISORDERS**

CHAPTER SIXTEEN: **THERAPEUTIC BEHAVIOR CHANGE**

BEHAVIOR DISORDERS

WHAT IS ABNORMAL BEHAVIOR?
Abnormal behavior from various perspectives
How is abnormal behavior defined?

CLASSIFICATION OF ABNORMAL BEHAVIOR
The problems of constructing a classification system
DSM III

PERSONALITY DISORDERS
Odd or eccentric behavior
Dramatic or erratic behavior
Fearful or anxious behavior

ANXIETY DISORDERS
Generalized anxiety disorder
Panic disorder
Phobia
Obsessive-compulsive disorder
Perspectives on anxiety disorders

AFFECTIVE DISORDERS
Depression
Perspectives on depression
Mania and bipolar disorders

SCHIZOPHRENIC DISORDERS
Characteristics of schizophrenia
Hallucinations and delusions
Outcome prospects
Perspectives on schizophrenia

FRONTIER 15.1   NEW TECHNIQUES COMPLEMENT EARLIER RECORDS

STUDY OUTLINE

KEY TERMS AND CONCEPTS

SUGGESTED READINGS

The dream was over. Again, Al Castle lay in bed, his sweaty pajamas clinging to his body. The dream was full of the terror and rage that he had felt as a boy when the tough kids in the neighborhood would torment him about his "nutty" father. The terror came partly from the fact that he resembled his father in many ways. He was haunted by the thought, "Maybe I'll go crazy, too." His rage was directed at the kids and his father. He wanted to tear the kids to shreds—only they were too big, too tough, and too well organized—and he hated his father, for being crazy.

Al Castle is 41 years old. He is married, has a son and a daughter, and has a good job in a large corporation. He has had his nightmares in Ottawa, Tokyo, and London, among other places. At the office and in his travels he is usually cheerful, cooperative, and pleasant. People other than family members rarely see him when he is depressed. Outsiders do not know that he wakes up at 5 A.M. and does not go back to sleep, that he must force himself to get up, take a shower, and drive to work. He is never sure that he'll make it to the office.

"Depression is a nightmare. I feel like Dr. Jekyll and Mr. Hyde. At the office, I smile at the secretaries. At home, I tell my kids jokes. Then I slam my bedroom door and sweat and pray I can get through another day. That's the way it must have been with my father. Sometimes I think it might be best for everybody if I just turned the steering wheel a little too much to the left and ended it all."

WHAT IS ABNORMAL BEHAVIOR?

Most of us would agree that Al Castle is unhappy. But deciding whether his behavior is abnormal or disordered, interpreting the abnormality, and treating it are not so easy. For one thing, there is often disagreement about what the term **abnormal behavior** means. The five perspectives used in this book provide us with a variety of ways to decide what abnormal behavior is, what causes it, and how (or if) it can be treated or changed. Of course, as we have stressed often throughout this book, no perspective has a corner on the truth. Disordered behavior may have a number of interrelated causes including the interaction between biological or psychological vulnerability factors and stressors in the environment.

Abnormal behavior from various perspectives

Because the *biological perspective* looks at all behavior from the standpoint of physical processes, abnormal behavior is defined as mental illness and is considered in the same way as any other illness or physical dysfunction, like color blindness or polio. If a person is sick, a cure or at least an improvement in his or her condition can often be achieved (through changing the body's chemical balance with diet or medication, for example). In some cases, as in certain kinds of inherited mental retardation or progressive brain disorders, abnormal behavior can be prevented by identifying this type of condition before birth or by pinpointing the exact genetic mechanism that causes the disorder.

The view of abnormal behavior from a *psychodynamic perspective* is quite different. Psychodynamic theorists assume that abnormal behavior results from ineffective defenses against impulses, feelings, and memories that are rooted in childhood experiences. Psychodynamically oriented researchers would study a person's childhood experiences and try to relate them to his or her present behavior.

According to the *behavioral perspective*, people act abnormally because somewhere along the line, maybe in childhood, maybe later, that's what they learned to do. Even if the behavior was learned in childhood, learning-oriented researchers would probably spend little time delving into the past. Instead, they devote much more attention to analyzing the present conditions that relate to the maladaptive behavior and to helping the person to learn more adaptive responses to those conditions.

The *cognitive perspective* regards abnormal behavior as the product of disordered or maladaptive thinking. A cognitive researcher may study how someone who behaves abnormally processes information. For example, some researchers try to understand maladaptive information processing by trying to write computer programs that respond or "think" the way a human being might (see Table 15.1).

TABLE 15.1 PARANOID PERSON OR COMPUTER? YOU BE THE JUDGE

Many cognitive theorists use an information processing approach to study behavior disorders. They liken the brain to a computer and try to construct computer programs that reproduce human thought patterns.

Kenneth Mark Colby and his co-workers (Colby, 1977) have constructed computer programs that respond to questions in the way a paranoid individual would. Half the time even experienced clinicians cannot tell whether the answers are being given by a real person diagnosed as paranoid or by a computer. How well could you do? Is the patient in Interview A a live person or a computer? What about Interview B?

INTERVIEW A

INTERVIEWER: *Hello. My name is Dr. Jones.*
PATIENT: *Glad to meet you.*
INTERVIEWER: *What's your name?*
PATIENT: *Pat Smith.*
INTERVIEWER: *Patrick or Patricia?*
PATIENT: *I'm a man.*
INTERVIEWER: *How old are you?*
PATIENT: *Twenty-eight.*
INTERVIEWER: *Why are you here?*
PATIENT: *I'm somewhat upset.*
INTERVIEWER: *Have you dreamt any strange dreams?*
PATIENT: *I don't remember dreams.*
INTERVIEWER: *Can strangers read your mind?*
PATIENT: *Naturally not.*
INTERVIEWER: *I see you're touchy about that.*
PATIENT: *Only when people annoy me.*
INTERVIEWER: *Don't you like being here?*
PATIENT: *No.*
INTERVIEWER: *Being in the hospital might do you a lot of good.*
PATIENT: *It's not helping me much to be here.*
INTERVIEWER: *I was told you're on medication.*
PATIENT: *I take some sort of sedatives.*
INTERVIEWER: *Were you ever on any kind of medication before?*
PATIENT: *No.*
INTERVIEWER: *Do you plan to continue taking it?*
PATIENT: *I don't really need help like they think.*
INTERVIEWER: *Do you have any hobbies?*
PATIENT: *Yes, I like horse racing.*
INTERVIEWER: *Go on.*
PATIENT: *There are a lot of tricky operators down there.*

INTERVIEWER: *Did you get gypped?*
PATIENT: *Yes, those guys are crooks.*
INTERVIEWER: *Are you distrustful of people?*
PATIENT: *Some people act kind of funny, like those immigrant types I work with.*
INTERVIEWER: *In what way?*
PATIENT: *Those foreigners are trying to run the country.*

INTERVIEW B

INTERVIEWER: *Good afternoon. My name is Dr. Smith. How are you?*
PATIENT: *I'm fine.*
INTERVIEWER: *Could you tell me a little about yourself, your name, why you're here?*
PATIENT: *My name is Harry Oakes. I'm here for evaluation.*
INTERVIEWER: *How old are you, Harry?*
PATIENT: *Twenty-two.*
INTERVIEWER: *How long have you been hospitalized?*
PATIENT: *Three and a half months.*
INTERVIEWER: *What kind of problem brought you into the hospital?*
PATIENT: *Police and Secret Service.*
INTERVIEWER: *What were you doing that got you singled out by the police?*
PATIENT: *An informant's job.*
INTERVIEWER: *How did being an informer wind up putting you in the hospital?*
PATIENT: *I had a gun in my pocket.*
INTERVIEWER: *A lot of people have guns. Why did you end up in the hospital for carrying a gun?*
PATIENT: *Got set up by members of organized crime, among them an attorney by the name of Paul White.*
INTERVIEWER: *Tell me, Harry, do you consider yourself emotionally or mentally ill now?*
PATIENT: *No.*
INTERVIEWER: *Why are you still in the hospital, then?*
PATIENT: *I'm waiting to go to a halfway house.*
INTERVIEWER: *I see; do you think you were emotionally or mentally ill when the police brought you to the hospital?*
PATIENT: *No.*
INTERVIEWER: *What's changed for you in the last three and one half months, if anything?*
PATIENT: *Nothing.*

[Interview A is the computer interview.]

Source: Colby, 1977, pp. 101–102.

Those who view abnormal behavior from the *humanistic-existential perspective* hold that people who behave abnormally have the potential to function well if they can see themselves realistically and accept themselves the way they are. Humanists and existentialists stress the effect that self-acceptance has on people's self-concepts and behavior.

The different perspectives lead to different ideas about the causes and treatment of abnormal behavior. Being aware of the viewpoints of all these perspectives helps us to consider the multiple factors that may be involved in a particular case. The way that each perspective might view Al Castle's case is illustrated in Figure 15.1.

How is abnormal behavior defined?

Although all the perspectives have produced valid ideas about the causes and treatments of behavior disorders, none of them really tells us how to know when a person's behavior crosses the line from unusual to disordered or abnormal. In this book, we argue that people who have behavior disorders are unable to modify their behavior in response to changing environmental requirements. Thus, their behavior is maladaptive because it is inflexible and unrealistic. It is also likely to be statistically uncommon and socially deviant, although neither of these characteristics is always pres-

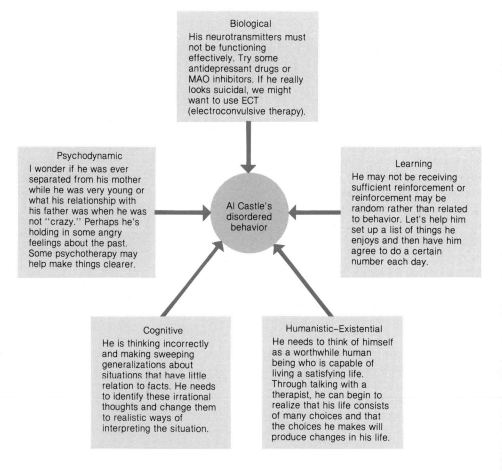

FIGURE 15.1 *When considering abnormal behavior, clinicians who follow different perspectives may ask themselves different questions and use different treatment methods. This figure illustrates some of the thoughts clinicians might have about a patient with disordered behavior.*

Biological
His neurotransmitters must not be functioning effectively. Try some antidepressant drugs or MAO inhibitors. If he really looks suicidal, we might want to use ECT (electroconvulsive therapy).

Psychodynamic
I wonder if he was ever separated from his mother while he was very young or what his relationship with his father was when he was not "crazy." Perhaps he's holding in some angry feelings about the past. Some psychotherapy may help make things clearer.

Al Castle's disordered behavior

Learning
He may not be receiving sufficient reinforcement or reinforcement may be random rather than related to behavior. Let's help him set up a list of things he enjoys and then have him agree to do a certain number each day.

Cognitive
He is thinking incorrectly and making sweeping generalizations about situations that have little relation to facts. He needs to identify these irrational thoughts and change them to realistic ways of interpreting the situation.

Humanistic–Existential
He needs to think of himself as a worthwhile human being who is capable of living a satisfying life. Through talking with a therapist, he can begin to realize that his life consists of many choices and that the choices he makes will produce changes in his life.

ent. People whose behavior is abnormal may or may not seem unhappy about their failure to adapt.

CLASSIFICATION OF ABNORMAL BEHAVIOR

Even if we all agreed about the kinds of behavior that we consider abnormal, in order to communicate sensibly we must still have a classification system. A good classification system should divide people into meaningful groups. People who have the same characteristics, whose behavior has the same causes, and who can be helped or treated by the same kinds of methods should all be grouped together. To make such a classification system possible, we must learn a great deal about the causes and effective therapies for disordered behavior.

The problems of constructing a classification system

In spite of great advances in some areas, we still lack knowledge about many important aspects of abnormal behavior. For this reason, the best classification system that we can hope for at present is one that describes behavior clearly enough to allow different observers to achieve reliability. In other words, we want a list of criteria that people can use to arrive at the same diagnosis of a particular person. The system must also take into account what is known about the causes of the observed behavior. We should not be too discouraged by these limited goals. Even such a highly developed classification system as Mendeleev's periodic table of the chemical elements had a lot of empty squares in it at first. It progressed through evolutionary stages that involved many guesses, assumptions, and theoretical "missing links," as well as systematic research, before more of the blanks were filled in.

Reliability in a classification system faces two main threats. One threat is the person being classified. People are notoriously inconsistent. A person may behave differently or may describe his or her symptoms differently in different situations. In such cases, interviewers

or observers cannot be blamed for drawing different conclusions, because each is actually seeing something different.

The other threat to reliability is the clinician. Differences in clinical workers' training and in their theoretical orientations can lead them to make different diagnoses. For example, for a number of years, a greater proportion of cases were diagnosed as schizophrenic in the United States than in Great Britain, while British clinicians seemed more apt to diagnose people as manic-depressive than U.S. clinicians were. Did these findings really mean that schizophrenia was more common in the United States, while Britain was overpopulated with manic-depressives? No, the clinicians were simply using different definitions of the disorders because they had different viewpoints and training. When clinicians in both countries were trained to use the same set of criteria in their diagnoses, the differences in the relative frequencies of the two disorders disappeared (Cooper and others, 1972).

Problems of definition still crop up, though. For instance, particular kinds of personality disorders seem to be found only in certain highly urbanized and cosmopolitan cities, and the diagnosis of somatization disorder is rarely found outside a small area in the Midwest (Vaillant, 1984). The theoretical perspective prevailing in each of these regions is much more likely to be the explanation for this phenomenon than a real difference in the occurrence of the disorders.

DSM III

A system designed to increase the reliability of classification and the meaningfulness of the diagnosis of abnormal behavior, the *Diagnostic and Statistical Manual of the American Psychiatric Association*, third edition, was published in 1980. The previous system, the *DSM II*, had used underlying causes as a basis for classification; but the new system, called the ***DSM III*** for short, emphasizes the description of clinical problems. The change was made because assessing the causes of many behavior disorders involves a lot of guesswork, which increases the unreliability of classification. Many other classification systems exist and some are used extensively in research. But for purposes of communication among the majority of researchers and practicing clinicians, for statistical purposes such as government record keeping, and for the diagnoses needed for insurance coverage, *DSM III* is the major system used in the United States. The major categories in the *DSM III* are shown in Table 15.2.

DSM III introduced more precise language into the classification system, included more categories of disordered behavior, and provided more concrete examples for the various categories. *DSM III* also lists factors that are known to be relevant to each diagnosis. These factors include the typical features of the disorder, the conditions under which it usually develops, its probable course or outcome, the amount of impairment to be expected, possible complications (for example, whether suicide attempts are likely), sex differences in its frequency (for example, depression is twice as common among women, while schizophrenia is equally

---

TABLE 15.2 THE *DSM III* CLASSIFICATION SYSTEM

The major topics covered by *DSM III* are outlined below.

Disorders arising in childhood or adolescence Problems of thought and behavior (for example, mental retardation, stuttering, and bedwetting) that are first identified relatively early in or are peculiar to the precollege or preworking life period.

Organic mental disorders Transient or permanent brain dysfunction caused by such factors as aging or the taking of a substance that affects the brain.

Substance use disorders Personal and social problems associated with the use of certain substances (for example, heroin).

Schizophrenic disorders Chronic disorganized behavior and thought of psychotic proportions (delusions, hallucinations), incoherence, and social isolation.

Paranoid disorders Well-organized system of delusions (often of being persecuted) without the incoherence, bizarreness, and social isolation seen in schizophrenia.

Psychotic disorders not elsewhere classified Includes both disorders that have not lasted long enough to be classified as schizophrenia and also disorders that combine schizophreniclike symptoms with feelings of depression, elation, or excitement.

Affective disorders Depression or mania, or both.

Anxiety disorders Anxiety, tension, and worry, but no psychotic features (delusions, hallucinations). Includes most of what were previously called neurotic disorders or neuroses.

Somatoform disorders Physical symptoms, apparently not

under voluntary control, and linked to psychological factors or conflicts for which no medical causes can be found.

Dissociative disorders Sudden, temporary change in the normal functions of consciousness (for example, loss of memory, sleepwalking).

Psychosexual disorders Deviant sexual thoughts and behaviors that are either personally anxiety-provoking or socially maladaptive.

Factitious disorders Physical or behavior symptoms voluntarily produced by the individual apparently in order to play the role of a patient, and often involving chronic, blatant lying.

Disorders of impulse control not elsewhere classified Maladaptations characterized by failure to resist impulses (for example, pathological gambling, chronic stealing, or habitual fire setting).

Adjustment disorder A maladaptive reaction to an identifiable stressor or group of stressors that subsides when the stressor ceases or when the individual adapts to the new situation.

Psychological factors affecting physical condition This category is used for any physical condition in which psychological factors seem to play a part.

Conditions not attributable to a mental disorder Various maladaptations (for example, marital problems, antisocial behavior) for which evidence of mental disorder is not available at the time of diagnosis.

Personality disorders Deeply ingrained, inflexible, maladaptive patterns of thought and behavior.

TABLE 15.3 THE *DSM III* MULTIAXIAL CLASSIFICATION SYSTEM

Most mental disorders are caused by interacting biological, psychological, and sociological factors. For this reason *DSM III* uses what is called a *multiaxial* classification system. This means that, instead of simply placing someone in one category, (for example, schizophrenia), diagnosticians characterize each person's behavior in terms of a number of clinically important factors. There are five axes in all. The first three axes are used by clinicians in classifying all cases. The last two are considered optional; whether or not they are used depends on the type of problem and on information available.

Axis 1 contains the *primary classification or diagnosis* of the problem that requires attention (for example, fear of heights). One of these terms would be selected for axis 1 when the diagnosis is made. (An exception is personality disorders; these would be described on axis 2.)

Axis 2 describes *ingrained, inflexible aspects of personality* that may influence the client's behavior and response to treatment (for example, the tendency to be overly suspicious of the motives of others).

Axis 3 refers to any *physical disorders* that seem relevant (for example, a history of heart attacks).

Axis 4 describes *psychosocial stressors* in the recent past that may have contributed to the clinical problem and that might influence the course of treatment (for example, divorce, death of a parent, or loss of a job). Wherever possible, the clinician rates the severity of psychosocial stress by the following rating scale (each point on the scale is defined and illustrated by an example).

RATING	LEVEL OF STRESS
1	None apparent
2	Minimal (minor violation of the law)
3	Mild (argument with neighbor)
4	Moderate (new job)
5	Severe (marital separation)
6	Extreme (death of close relative)
7	Catastrophic (devastating natural disaster)

Axis 5 contains an estimate of the client's *highest level of adaptive function,* or how well he or she has performed in social relationships, occupational activities, and use of leisure time during the past year. The ratings are also on a seven-point scale from superior (highly effective functioning) to grossly impaired (total inadequacy in almost all areas of functioning).

The rating of adaptive functioning is important because the similar behaviors of two severely disturbed people would probably be interpreted and even treated quite differently if one had a history of good relationships with others and an excellent work record, while the other had a history of social inadequacy and inability to hold a job.

---

likely in both sexes), and family patterns (depression is more common in women who lost their mothers early in life). The multiple axes shown in Table 15.3 and the many concrete examples included in *DSM III* should aid in the reliability of classifications.

Perhaps the most severe criticism of *DSM III* is its use of a number of diagnostic categories that have not yet been validated. The classifications for some areas—for example, schizophrenic disorders and affective disorders—can be supported by research. However, in others, particularly in childhood disorders and personality disorders, the divisions seem arbitrary and are possibly misleading (Rutter and Shaffer, 1980; Michels, 1984). Critics argue that, because so little is known

about these disorders, the diagnostic criteria in *DSM III* may not really be applicable to everyone with those disorders. In spite of these concerns, *DSM III* is generally agreed to be a step forward in understanding the very complex field of disordered human behavior.

PERSONALITY DISORDERS

Earlier in the chapter, we indicated that the two general criteria that we used to define abnormal behavior were inflexible and unrealistic approaches to environmental situations. **Personality disorders** represent failure to adapt because of inflexible and self-defeating response patterns.

Deeply ingrained habits and rigid coping styles do not always get in the way of positive adaptation. For example, personality characteristics such as extreme neatness, an especially careful and methodical approach to problem solving, or unusual suspiciousness of other people's motives may be assets if you are an accountant or a criminal investigator. However, when such patterns of behavior can't be shut off, they may get in the way in handling simple, everyday difficulties. Then the likelihood of behavioral problems increases, particularly if the person happens to encounter situations that involve stress. Like the tree that breaks because it cannot bend with the wind, these inflexible people cannot cope with new situations, and their behavior becomes more maladaptive as the stress increases. Their failure to cope with certain types of situations may cause either significant impairment in functioning or feelings of distress and unhappiness. Personality disorders are usually evident at least by early adolescence and continue throughout adult life.

Not much is known about most types of personality disorders. The emphasis given to their diagnosis by the *DSM III* should help researchers gather information about them. *DSM III* divides personality disorders into three general groups: odd, eccentric behaviors; dramatic or erratic behaviors; and anxious or fearful behaviors. Because of the lack of information, these categories are somewhat overlapping, and many individuals may be assigned to more than one.

FIGURE 15.2 *Those in the category of schizoid personality disorder are usually detached, withdrawn individuals who spend most of their time alone.*

Odd or eccentric behavior

Two disorders that involve odd or eccentric behavior are schizoid personality disorder and schizotypal personality disorder. Individuals with **schizoid personality disorder** are reserved, socially withdrawn, reclusive loners. They prefer to work and play alone, and appear to lack the ability to form warm, close social relationships. In general, their emotional responses seem flat, and they often appear absentminded and unaware of what is going on (see Figure 15.2). People with a **schizotypal personality disorder** have odd ways of thinking, communicating, and behaving. These people seem emotionally shallow and socially unskilled and tend to be suspicious of others. They are much more handicapped, on the average, than people with a schizoid personality disorder. Although schizotypal personality disorder is not a predictor of future schizophrenia, it is found more frequently in relatives of schizophrenic patients (Gunderson and others, 1983).

Dramatic or erratic behavior

The next group of personality disorders includes those that primarily show dramatic or erratic behaviors. One of these groups, **borderline personality disorder,** is currently the focus of a great deal of clinical interest and research. In the past, the term *borderline* has had many diagnostic meanings. At times it was so popular that it was applied to 50 percent of all hospitalized patients and 14 percent of the general population (Stone, 1981). The *DSM III* definition attempted to narrow the category a great deal and to define it as a disorder characterized by instability in a number of areas including mood, interpersonal relationships, and self-image. When the word *borderline* had been used previously, it usually implied some kind of intermediate state between normality and schizophrenia and a higher than ordinary risk of actually becoming schizophrenic. Since the *DSM III* diagnosis has come into use, researchers have been checking out that assumption. What they have found is something quite different: there seems to be a relationship between borderline personality disorder and affective disorder, either depression alone or mood swings between depression and elation (Soloff and Milward, 1983; McGlashan, 1983).

Borderline individuals tend to have intense and unstable interpersonal relationships that can also have a manipulative quality. For example, one patient told her therapist:

I was alone at home a few months ago; I was frightened! I was trying to get in touch with my boyfriend and I couldn't. . . . He was nowhere to be found. All my friends seemed to be busy that night and I had no one to talk to. . . . I just got more and more nervous and more and more agitated. Finally—bang!—I took out a cigarette and lit it and stuck it into my forearm. I don't know why I did it because I didn't really care for him all that much. I guess I felt I had to do something dramatic. . . . (Stone, 1980, p. 400)

A great deal of research has been done on **antisocial personality disorders,** another personality disorder characterized by dramatic or erratic behavior. This disorder is diagnosed when a person has a history of continuous and chronic behavior that violates the rights of others; for such a diagnosis to be made, this history must begin before the age of 15 and must continue into adult life. Such an individual also has a history of work failures over a period of several years. This category has not proved to be a very useful one in clinical terms because, while antisocial behavior is always deviant, it may not always be abnormal. For example, three-quarters of the prison population would probably meet the

criteria for this diagnosis (Wulach, 1983). Although it would be important to determine whether those in prison are typical of the whole group of antisocial personalities or just typical of those who behaved stupidly or were unlucky and got caught, researchers have found it difficult to identify antisocial individuals in the general population.

One researcher dealt with this sampling problem in a unique way. She placed the following ad in a counterculture newspaper in Boston:

Wanted: charming, aggressive, carefree people who are impulsively irresponsible but are good at handling people and at looking after number one. Send name, address, phone, and short biography proving how interesting you are to. . . . (Widom, 1978, p. 72)

The ad drew 73 replies, about 50 of whom were males. The one-third of these men who seemed to meet the criteria for antisocial personality were interviewed and given a battery of psychological tests. Many of these men had been detained or arrested as adults, but only a small portion had been convicted. Widom concluded that the men in her sample differed from individuals in prison samples only because they had somehow been able to avoid conviction.

Other research on antisocial behavior suggests that the behavior pattern may be inherited, at least in some cases. For example, adopted children who were separated at birth from their antisocial parents show more antisocial behavior later in life than control subjects do (Crowe, 1974), though how that antisocial behavior might be inherited is not yet clear. In one large study, having antisocial or retarded relatives was predictive of later antisocial behavior for women, and having alcoholic relatives was predictive of the later development of antisocial behavior for men (Cadoret and Cain, 1981). Other researchers have suggested that some patterns of brain wave activity might be related to antisocial behavior (Mednick and others, 1982). The whole question of heredity of antisocial behavior and the relationship of antisocial behavior to personality disorder, to other kinds of psychological problems, or to environmental factors is one that, despite many research efforts, remains unsettled. Until a narrower, more specific definition is employed, this state of affairs is likely to continue.

Fearful or anxious behavior

The final grouping of personality disorders includes those that have prominent components of anxiety and fear. For example, people with a **dependent personal-**

FIGURE 15.3 *Battered spouses often endure a great deal of psychological or physical harm rather than remove themselves from the abusive relationship.*

ity disorder are agreeable, self-effacing, and ingratiating people who subordinate their needs to those of their dominant partners to preserve the relationship. When left on their own, they feel anxious and unable to function. Even when the dependent relationship is intact, they may feel anxiety because they worry about losing the dominant figure. They try to make themselves so pleasing that others will never wish to abandon them. Sometimes this approach works fairly well, but sometimes the dominant partner also has considerable pathology and may behave abusively. Battered wives, who may accept continual severe physical abuse rather than face leaving their husbands, are likely to be dependent personalities. Figure 15.3 shows the physical damage such battering may produce.

Many people with a personality disorder go through life without ever coming into contact with mental health professionals, and our knowledge of personality disorders is limited because professionals see only a restricted sample of individuals who fit into these categories. The *DSM III*'s emphasis on the personality disorders, even though imperfectly defined, is already being reflected in increased research interest.

ANXIETY DISORDERS

The behaviors observed in anxiety disorders vary widely, but they all have one thing in common—the experience of intense anxiety. (The characteristics of anxiety were described in Chapter 14.) Anxiety may occur in anticipation of some future event, as a reaction after a particular event has taken place, or when a person decides to approach a fear-arousing situation, to change an undesirable aspect of behavior, or to resist a preoccupying idea. What is unusual about anxiety disorders is not that someone experiences anxiety, because we all do that. Anxiety disorders are unusual because the amount of anxiety seems to be a tremendous overreaction to the particular event that caused it.

Before *DSM III*, most anxiety disorders were called **neuroses,** a word that originated in psychoanalytic theory and essentially meant a "nervous disorder." Freud thought that his patients' neurotic symptoms represented inefficient ways of dealing with present problems that were emotionally related to early childhood traumas or other frightening events. Because *DSM III* attempts to describe disorders rather than to classify them on the basis of their inferred causes, the name was changed from *neuroses* to *anxiety disorders* because all these behaviors are accompanied by symptoms of acute anxiety.

The anxiety disorders described in *DSM III* include generalized anxiety disorder, panic disorder, phobia, and obsessive-compulsive disorder, as well as posttraumatic stress disorders of the kind discussed in Chapter 14.

Generalized anxiety disorder

I wish I could tell you exactly what's the matter. Sometimes I feel like something terrible has just happened when actually nothing has happened at all. Other times, I'm expecting the sky to fall down any minute. Most of the time, I can't point my finger at anything specific, but I am tense and jumpy almost all the time. Sometimes my heart beats so fast, I'm sure I'm having a heart attack.

People experiencing a **generalized anxiety disorder** are continually afraid, but they can't seem to tell you exactly what they're afraid of. The fear symptoms, which appear for no apparent reason, may continue for several months or longer. Anxiety is found in many disorders, but in a generalized anxiety disorder, anxiety, uncomplicated by such things as poor contact with reality or disordered thought, is the outstanding characteristic of behavior.

In addition to the physical symptoms of fear—rapid heart rate, shortness of breath, profuse sweating, frequent urination and diarrhea, loss of appetite, fainting and dizziness, tremors, and sleeplessness—a person who is extremely anxious often has several other behavioral characteristics:

1. *Motor tension,* an inability to relax, a feeling of being all keyed up, a strained facial expression, and deep sighs

2. *Excessive worry* or fear about the future

3. *Hypervigilance,* a constant scanning of the environment for dangers that the individual is unable to specify

Panic disorder

People with generalized anxiety disorders are anxious for extended periods. People with **panic disorders,** on the other hand, have sudden, intense, recurring, and often unpredictable *attacks* of the same anxiety-related behaviors. These attacks may last for only seconds or for hours or days. During the attack, the person is afraid of dying, "going crazy," or doing something uncontrolled:

[The client's] chief complaints were that at any time and without warning, he might suddenly feel he was about to faint and fall down, or tremble and experience palpitations, and if standing would cringe and clutch at the nearest wall or chair. If he was driving a car at the time he would pull up at the curbside and wait for the feelings to pass off before he resumed his journey. If it occurred during sexual intercourse with his wife he would immediately separate from her. . . . Between attacks the patient did not feel completely well, and a slight tremulousness persisted. . . . The patient felt that he lacked energy but was not depressed. He denied that he experienced fear, anxiety, or panic during the attacks. (Marks and Lader, 1973, p. 11)

Panic disorders often occur in combination with severe depression, and these two disorders may have some common cause. Researchers have found that relatives of individuals with panic disorder are much more likely to have either severe depression, some type of anxiety disorder, or alcoholism than the relatives of normal people or of people who have only a severe depression without the addition of panic disorder (Leckman and others, 1983).

Phobia

Phobias are extremely strong fears of highly specific things—for example, spiders, dirt, or high places—in situations that actually pose no real dangers. In some cases a number of these fears may be present simultaneously. Phobia seems unrelated to structural or organic damage. Although their fears are out of proportion, phobic individuals do not usually show other gross distortions of reality. The fear responses seem inexplicable and beyond the person's voluntary control. Phobias tend to generalize and grow progressively broader.

Phobias are very common: 11 percent of the 11,500 people interviewed in one large community had experienced a phobia (Robins and others, 1981). Phobias can be divided into several general groups.

Agoraphobia Although the term **agoraphobia** literally means "fear of open spaces," agoraphobics usually experience fear symptoms whenever they increase their distance from some "safe" place, often their home. They usually have great difficulty performing such activities as shopping, using public transportation, and attending public meetings. In these circumstances, they develop physical symptoms such as shortness of breath or faintness. Most agoraphobics have a "safe person," most often a spouse, with whom they can go safely (or at least with less discomfort) into situations that would otherwise cause a phobic response.

Social phobia **Socially phobic** individuals usually show anxiety in a variety of social situations: working while others observe them, signing their names in public, speaking to even one or two strangers, going to large parties, and so on.

Specific phobias Fears of a particular object or situation—snake phobia, dog phobia, driving phobia, fear of hospitals, and fear of death—are common examples of specific phobias.

The phobia that comes to the attention of mental health professionals most often is agoraphobia. More than 80 percent of the time, the agoraphobic is female. The problem tends to begin sometime in the person's mid- to late 20s following some stressful event or a period of stress. Most agoraphobics also show symptoms of social phobia and express fears of losing control, going insane, embarrassing themselves and others, dying, and fainting (Tearnan and others, 1984).

Biological factors may play a part in the development of some phobias. For example, agoraphobics may have a high level of arousal and may take more time to adapt to stimuli than other individuals do (Lader and Wing, 1966; Sheehan, 1982). An abnormality of the mitral valve of the heart, which, although not threatening to health, can cause heart palpitations and chest

FIGURE 15.4 *Even though this aerophobe was able to make what to him is a fearful flight, he does not yet seem to have rid himself of all his anxiety.*

pain, has also been suggested as a cause of panic attacks that may result in phobic or avoidance behavior (Gorman and others, 1981). Because some of the drugs used to treat depression are also effective in preventing the panic attacks that result from exposure to feared situations, some neurotransmitters may function in similar ways in phobia and in depression (Sheehan, 1982).

Phobics will distort their lives in a variety of ways to avoid putting themselves in the situations that they fear. Some phobics may be virtually trapped inside their homes for years. A newsmagazine reported the case of Marjorie Goff, who stayed in her house almost continuously from the time she was 31 until she was 61 because of phobic symptoms. During those 30 years she went out only 3 times, including one trip to the hospital for an operation (*Newsweek*, April 23, 1984). An overwhelming fear of flying is a common phobia, and some people refuse to fly even at great personal inconvenience. John Madden, former coach of the Los Angeles Raiders and now a TV broadcaster, made his frequent coast-to-coast trips by train because he could not bear to watch the flight attendant close the cabin door. Singer Aretha Franklin has canceled several concert dates so that she will not have to fly. Fear of flying is so common that courses have sprung up across the country to help people to overcome it. According to a survey by the Boeing Company, 25 million Americans are afraid to fly. Figure 15.4 shows one participant during the graduation flight of a fear-of-flying class. Although his comfort level does not appear too high, he made his first flight successfully. Many phobias can be treated successfully with the behavioral methods that we will discuss in the next chapter.

Obsessive-compulsive disorder

In this disorder, ideas and actions occur repetitively and seemingly without reason. An individual may be unable to stop thinking about a particular word or repeatedly feel an overpowering urge to wash his or her hands. Obsessive-compulsive individuals are literally tyrannized by their own thoughts and actions. They feel compelled to perform particular actions or series of actions again and again. The possibilities for obsessive thoughts and compulsive acts are practically unlimited (see Figure 15.5).

Obsessive-compulsive individuals experience intense anxiety if they do not perform their rituals. Sometimes these rituals are only minor distractions, like knocking on wood or always putting the right shoe on first. Sometimes the rituals take the form of excessive attention to detail. How much do you think the executive in Figure 15.6 actually accomplishes? When the more elaborate rituals or thoughts begin to interfere with daily life, they become significant problems that require professional attention. Obsessive thoughts and compulsive rituals shade into phobias to the extent that anxiety accompanies the thoughts or rituals, and there is avoidance of situations that evoke them. For example, someone who has a washing ritual will try to avoid dirt:

FIGURE 15.5 *Tremendous amounts of energy may be devoted to obsessive thoughts.*

"After 10 years, Ralph, I should think you'd give up trying to rhyme 'orange'."

(COPYRIGHT © 1969 BY ROBERT CENSONI.)

"*Let me just make a little note of that. I never seem to get anything done around here unless I make little notes.*"

FIGURE 15.6 *No doubt the speaker would be very uncomfortable if he didn't follow his ritual of noting down every item that comes to his attention. His compulsive behavior of note writing may prevent him from thinking repetitively or obsessively about the danger of forgetting details. However, we might question how efficient his behavior is and at what point the performance of the ritual interferes with the performance of the task that the ritual supposedly facilitates.*

If I see a speck of dirt on the bathroom mirror, I get very upset. When I notice it, I immediately get a cloth and wipe off the speck. I then have to inspect the wiped area to make sure it's completely clean. When I leave the bathroom, I worry about whether I'll see dust on the mirror when I next use the bathroom. As you can imagine, I'm even worse when it's a matter of real dirt—like muddy shoes. On rainy days, I hate to go out, because I know I'll have all the work of cleaning my shoes when I return home.

Obsessive-compulsives are often secretive about their preoccupations and frequently are able to work

effectively in spite of them. Consequently, their problems are probably underestimated (Rachman and Hodgson, 1980).

Perspectives on anxiety disorders

There is no standard explanation for these types of anxiety disorders, but we do have a number of clues about their causes. Several competing theories have incorporated different sets of these clues, based on their basic models of human behavior.

THE PSYCHODYNAMIC PERSPECTIVE

Psychodynamic theorists believe that we cannot take what we see at face value; we must examine the dynamics that lie beneath behavior. The observations and theories of Sigmund Freud have had an enormous impact on the way the dynamics of anxiety disorders (or neuroses, as he called them) are characterized. According to Freud, neurotic behavior patterns are the ultimate consequence of defensive inhibitions learned early in childhood as a way of avoiding the real or imagined dangers of sexual feelings and aggression. Many clinicians today continue to view the major causes of anxiety disorders as inner conflict, guilt, and unconscious motivations.

Inner alarms are frequently sounded when there seem to be no adequate external causes. When this happens, people may suddenly be overwhelmed by intense anxiety, even in the quiet, confined space of their own living rooms. Psychodynamic theorists argue that these individuals have inadequate or inappropriate defenses. We all struggle with internal pressures and fears, but most of us manage to put a lid on them or deal with them realistically. People with anxiety disorders cannot do this; they overreact to what they perceive as threats of disapproval or the withdrawal of love.

THE BEHAVIORAL PERSPECTIVE

Learning theorists, such as B. F. Skinner, believe that anxiety disorders can be explained by looking at observable behavior and at the learning conditions that give rise to it. Therapists, they say, must pay careful attention to environmental stimuli and how the patient responds to them.

The case of Little Hans illustrates the difference between the psychodynamic and behavioral interpretations of behavior. In 1909, Freud reported this case, which has become famous as an example of the psychoanalytic view of phobic disorder.

When Hans was 5 years old, he refused to go out into the street because he was afraid of horses. He was especially afraid that they would bite him. His father, a physician, discussed the case with Freud, who interpreted the horse as a symbol of Hans's hatred and fear of his father. Hans harbored aggressive fantasies and thoughts toward his father, Freud said, because his father was Hans's only rival for his mother's love. He was "a little Oedipus who wanted to have his father 'out of the way,' to get rid of him so that he might be alone with his handsome mother and sleep with her" (Freud, 1909/1950, p. 253). At the same time, however, Hans loved his father, so these feelings of hatred were upsetting. To resolve his conflict, Hans repressed his love for his mother and displaced his hatred for his father onto horses, which he could avoid more easily than he could his father.

Freud hypothesized that Hans focused on horses because his father had often played "horsie" with him and because horses' bridles reminded him of his father's dark moustache. In his fantasies Hans expected his father to punish him for his hostility. This expectation was displaced onto the fear that horses would bite him. Freud maintained that Little Hans was suffering from a classic conflict, in which he felt both love and hatred for the same person. Hans was treated by his father with Freud's advice. He recovered from his phobia and was able to cope with his conflict in a more effective way.

In general those who use the behavioral perspective explain phobic behavior in one of two ways. It may be a response to a single, extremely frightening incident that results in almost instantaneous learning of an avoidance response. An example might be someone who refuses to ride in any car after being involved in a serious automobile wreck. The other way that a phobia might develop, according to this perspective, is as a response designed to avoid potentially stressful situations after a massive build-up of everyday problems or stressful events has overwhelmed a person's ability to cope with even minimal amounts of stress.

In the 1960s, a number of behavioral theorists (Wolpe and Rachman, 1960; Bandura, 1969) took another look at the case of Little Hans. After carefully studying Freud's description of the case, they noticed three major elements that always seemed to be present whenever Hans had a phobic response: (1) a large horse, and (2) a heavily loaded cart, which (3) were traveling at high speed. The behaviorists argued that these stimuli, and not displaced anger for his father, were the cause of Little Hans's reactions. Freud had noted that Hans first became afraid of horses after he saw a terrible accident involving a horse. The behaviorists argued that Little Hans had undergone a classical conditioning process when he saw the accident, so that he continued to respond with great fear to horses. Thus, from the behavioral viewpoint, the phobia resulted from a conditioned emotional response, not from the actions of internal psychodynamics.

No one can be sure which interpretation is correct. All we know is that Hans did get over his horse phobia.

THE COGNITIVE PERSPECTIVE

Like psychodynamic theorists, cognitive theorists are concerned with the inner life, but they focus more on conscious mental events than on unconscious ones. Like behavioral theorists, they tend to look at current problems rather than at early childhood experiences. Cognitive theorists interpret anxiety disorders as a product of unrealistic thinking, undesirable learning experiences, and unproductive problem-solving strategies. As therapists, they seek to teach clients more realistic and effective ways of thinking about and responding to problems. They recognize that behavior changes when individuals think about and develop insight into their problems. By *insight*, a cognitive theorist means the person's understanding that his or her problem is caused by maladaptive thought patterns such as overgeneralization or inexact and inappropriate labeling of events. Psychodynamic theorists use the term *insight* in a different way. In psychodynamic terms, *insight* takes place when a person realizes that he or she behaves in a particular way because past experiences have become associated with the present situation, rather than because of the present situation alone. From a psychodynamic viewpoint, insight occurs when repressed thoughts become conscious.

THE BIOLOGICAL PERSPECTIVE

Although the fact that people with anxiety disorders have been treated successfully with various drugs indicates that anxiety has a biological component, biological theorists have not been able to discover any direct physiological cause for most cases of anxiety disorder. Anxiety disorders in some individuals may involve an exceptionally responsive nervous system, which means that heredity may play a role. Generalized anxiety disorders may appear in several generations of some families (Miner, 1973). Panic attacks also seem to run in families and are twice as frequent in women as in men. As we have pointed out many times in this book, heredity interacts with environmental forces in complex ways. For example, anxiety disorders may be caused by the parents' behavior. So despite these findings, we can't say for sure that anxiety disorders are inherited.

People with anxiety disorders have been treated successfully with various drugs as well as with psychotherapy. The many psychiatrists and general practice physicians who prescribe tranquilizers report that they help to reduce tension. The effects of tranquilizers vary with their chemical composition, and, despite intensive research by clinical investigators, physicians still have trouble predicting which antianxiety drug will be the most beneficial in a particular case. Most clinical conditions that require the use of tranquilizers improve within a few days or weeks. Medication is then reduced as the patient's anxiety subsides. Some psychodynamically oriented therapists may use tranquilizers with extremely anxious clients so that the clients can think about their inner feelings more easily during initial therapy sessions.

THE HUMANISTIC-EXISTENTIAL PERSPECTIVE

Existential theorists have been particularly interested in the problem of anxiety. They believe that anxiety disorders, like other behavior problems, result when soci-

ety interferes with an individual's healthy development. From their viewpoint, much anxiety is generated because society pressures people to behave *inauthentically*. Many people feel obliged to keep up a false front, to behave according to the stereotypes for their particular social group, even if they find such behavior extremely frustrating to their personal happiness. Existential therapists try to help clients to behave in ways that they, and not just society, feel are satisfying and appropriate.

AFFECTIVE DISORDERS

Emotional responses other than anxiety are involved in behavior disorders. Many people suffer from depression, and others have problems related to mood swings that are often extreme and unpredictable. Problems that involve moods or emotions are known as **affective disorders.**

Depression, which is characterized by intense feelings of sadness and sometimes also by a slowed pace of activity, and **mania,** a state of high excitement and activity, are included in the category of affective disorders. *DSM III* uses the term **bipolar disorder** to describe behavior that includes both depressed and manic phases. **Unipolar disorder** is a term sometimes applied to depressive disorders in which no manic episodes occur.

Depression

At some time everyone has been depressed or had the blues. Feelings of depression are common after arguing with a friend, suffering a financial reverse, being turned down for a job, recovering from a bad case of the flu, or during a holiday period. This everyday use of the term "depression" refers to a feeling state brought on by particular events, a state that usually fades away fairly quickly after the event has passed or the person becomes accustomed to the new situation. These feelings of depression are entirely normal and would not call for a diagnosis of depressive disorder. Where does "normal" depression leave off and "clinical" depression begin? In clinical depression, the sad feelings last longer than seems appropriate for the situation and are much more intense than one might expect. Some researchers believe that depression can be thought of as a continuum, like the one in Figure 15.7, that extends from the common blues through severe clinical depression (Blatt and others, 1976), while others think that the blues and depression are two very different states (Akiskal, 1981).

Depression is probably the most common problem dealt with by mental health professionals. Among patients who see physicians for physical complaints, at least 18 percent are depressed, and one-third of those people are depressed moderately or severely (Nielsen and Williams, 1980). Many people who never seek treatment could also be properly diagnosed as depressed. Community surveys have classified from 6 to 19 percent of those in their interview samples as depressed (Frerichs and others, 1981; Weissman and others, 1981).

Two features are always present in depression: a **dysphoric mood** (feeling depressed, sad, hopeless, worried) and a **loss of interest** or pleasure in the events of living, many of which would otherwise be enjoyable. Often other behaviors are also observed: loss of appetite and weight loss (or sometimes indiscriminate eating and weight gain), difficulty in sleeping, loss of energy, strong feelings of guilt and self-reproach, inability to concentrate and think clearly, and frequent thoughts about death and suicide.

This excerpt, from a book written by a prominent

psychologist about his own battle with depression, illustrates some of these characteristics:

I guess my major reaction was one of despair—a despair of ever being human again. I honestly felt subhuman, lower than the lowest vermin. Furthermore, I . . . could not understand why anyone would want to associate with me, let alone love me. I became mistrustful and suspicious of others and was certain that they were checking up on me to prove that I was incompetent. . . . I had become increasingly concerned about finances. On one hand, I thought that I was receiving extra money that I didn't deserve and, on the other, I was certain that we were going bankrupt. In any case, I was positive that I was going to wind up in jail. . . . I was positive that I was a fraud and a phony and that I didn't deserve my Ph.D. I didn't deserve to have tenure; . . . I didn't deserve the research grants I had been awarded; I couldn't understand how I had written the books and journal articles that I had and how they had been accepted for publication. I must have conned a lot of people. . . . Not only was my self-esteem low with respect to my academic and intellectual achievements but it was low also with respect to my emotional and social life. I analysed all the people I knew and felt that each of them could do most things better than I could. (Endler, 1982, pp. 45–49)

The Blues	Normal grief	Dysthymic disorder (neurotic depression)	Major depressive disorder
Short-term reaction to stress	Sadness that lessens as time passes	Chronic or recurring periods of feeling sad or low	First episode often stress-related, changes in eating, sleep etc.
Function impaired little or not at all	Function may be impaired for a relatively short period	Mild or moderate continuing impairment	Inability to function
Brief duration	May last a year	May continue or recur over many years	Long duration; may have several episodes in lifetime

FIGURE 15.7 *The range of depressed behavior.*

THE PROBLEM OF SUICIDE

Depressed individuals may not stop at self-condemnation. They may move from thoughts to action. *The best indication that a depressed person might attempt suicide is an announcement of an intention to do it.* People who talk about committing suicide may actually do it; few people commit suicide without warning. An-other danger signal is an unsuccessful suicide attempt in the past. Suicide attempts may even be most likely when the depressed individual is recovered or improving. Ernest Hemingway committed suicide by shooting himself after he was released from a hospital following a period of depression.

Suicide is statistically a rare event; in the United States it accounts for only 13 deaths out of every

FIGURE 15.8 *Concern over an increasing number of adolescent suicides has led some school districts to hold special programs to inform students and their parents about suicide prevention techniques. Photo (a) shows a human-relations specialist in a White Plains, New York, high school talking with students about suicide. Inset (b) shows one of the illustrative slides he used. Here an actor takes the part of a despondent teenager.*

(a)

(b)

100,000 that occur each year. The risk of suicide for individuals who are depressed is much greater; 15 percent of clinically depressed people can be expected to kill themselves (Murphy, 1983). The risk of a suicide attempt is much greater than average not only for those who are depressed but also for those with other diagnoses who have a family history of suicide (Roy, 1983). There has been a steady increase in suicide rates in recent years, especially among people aged 15 to 24, whose suicide rate more than doubled between 1960 and 1980. Experts believe that many teenage suicides

TABLE 15.4 WARNING SIGNS OF TEENAGE SUICIDE

Verbal comments Statements such as "I wish I'd never been born," and "You'll be sorry when I'm gone," should be taken just as seriously as the direct threat, "I'm going to kill myself."

Behavior changes These cover a wide range and include giving away treasured possessions, taking life threatening risks, and having frequent accidents. Other signs may be complaints of intense loneliness or boredom, a marked increase in agitation or irritability, or getting into trouble with school or the police. There may also be the more customary signs of depression: changes in appetite and sleep habits, suddenly dropping grades, complaints of inability to concentrate, and withdrawal from friends and from favorite activities.

Situational factors Inability to communicate with parents, recent problems at school, end of a love relationship, recent involvement with drugs or alcohol all increase the situational risk.

What to do Parents and friends should take action by asking questions such as "Are you very unhappy?" "Do you have a plan about taking your life?" "Do you think you really don't want to live anymore?" Asking direct questions about suicide doesn't put ideas into someone's head. Instead it may be a lifesaving measure if the answers are taken seriously. Both parents and friends often don't believe that such statements might be carried out or they may be too frightened to take action. Although friends are sometimes sworn to secrecy about suicidal thoughts, they should contact a parent or responsible adult immediately if they suspect thoughts of suicide and professional help should be obtained at once. If the suicidal threat seems immediate, the nearest suicide prevention center (usually listed under "suicide" or "crisis" in the phone book) should be contacted.

can be prevented if people close to the person recognize the danger signs (see Figure 15.8). Some of the distress signals to watch for are shown in Table 15.4.

Many more individuals attempt suicide than actually kill themselves. Suicide attempts are about 10 times as frequent as successful suicides. While twice as many males as females kill themselves, twice as many women as men attempt suicide. Suicides and suicide attempts seem to be different phenomena. People who commit suicide successfully generally plan carefully, make provisions for carrying out their act privately and without interruption, and use an effective means of killing themselves. Suicide attempters may act impulsively, may make provision for rescue, and may use a method that is ineffective or that is slow to take effect. Although some suicide attempters actually take their lives, their main purpose seems to be to manipulate others and to be alive to see the effects.

Perspectives on depression

Different types of depression seem to originate from different causes, and many instances of depression involve a variety of interacting causes stemming both from the person and from the situation. Perhaps for this reason many of the perspectives have contributed valuable insights to the understanding of depression.

BIOLOGICAL THEORIES

Research into the biological factors related to depression has focused on the **amine neurotransmitter systems,** particularly those involving the neurotransmitter chemicals **norepinephrine, serotonin,** and **dopamine.** Norepinephrine regulates many of our responses to the environment, so a lowered norepinephrine output may cause either over- or underreaction depending on the nature of the stimulus. Serotonin often functions as a balancing factor to norepinephrine, while dopamine helps to regulate body movement and also aids in coordinating our emotions and our cognitive processes. The knowledge of how the amine neurotransmitter systems work has led to a theory called the **amine hypothesis of depression and mania.** The theory states that too little of a transmitter is associated with depression and too much with mania, with a normal level somewhere in between.

As we explained in Chapter 3, a nerve cell, or neuron, is made up of a cell body, dendrites, and an axon. As a nerve impulse travels down the axon of one neuron, a *vesicle*, or storage container inside the cell body, moves over to the cell body wall. The vesicle and the cell body membranes fuse together, and the neurotransmitter chemicals are released. These chemicals then cross the synapse between two neurons. After they hit the receptor on the second neuron, the transmitter molecules start a series of chemical events that set off a nerve impulse in the second neuron. Transmitter molecules that do not reach the receptor area of the second neuron are drawn back up into the first neuron and are broken down chemically into an inactive substance by an enzyme called **monoamine oxidase,** or **MAO.** This process is illustrated in Figure 15.9.

Understanding this sequence is very important—first, because the body can regulate the process at any of these steps and, second, because each step is a possible location for intervention with therapeutic drugs. Two classes of drugs, known as **antidepressants,** are used to alter this process. One group, called **tricyclics,** block the reuptake of the transmitters into the cell body

so that more molecules remain out in the synapse to activate the receptor neuron. Another group, the **MAO inhibitors,** also increase the neurotransmitter level by interfering with the breakdown of the neurotransmitters. **Lithium** is used to treat bipolar disorders, in which individuals have episodes of both depression and mania. Lithium blocks the transmitter release process, which explains how it helps to prevent mania, but it is not clear how it helps to prevent depression as well.

BEHAVIORAL THEORIES

A clear connection between the frequency of certain behaviors and reinforcement has been established by hundreds of conditioning experiments. In applying this concept to depression, researchers have noted that, once a person becomes depressed, his or her behavior becomes less pleasant to others. In fact, depressed people tend to make those in contact with them feel anxious, depressed, and hostile (Blumberg and Hokanson, 1983). Because others tend to avoid people who are depressed, a depressed person has fewer opportunities for reinforcement from others (Lewinsohn and others, 1980). Therapists who use a behavioral approach stress the importance of reinforcement in overcoming depressed feelings. They may ask people to keep daily records of events and the mood that seems related to each event. An example of the kind of list that results from this monitoring is shown in Table 15.5. Once someone is aware of the relationship between events and mood, and of the low level of reinforcing events in

FIGURE 15.9 *Neurotransmitter chemicals function in a complex way.*

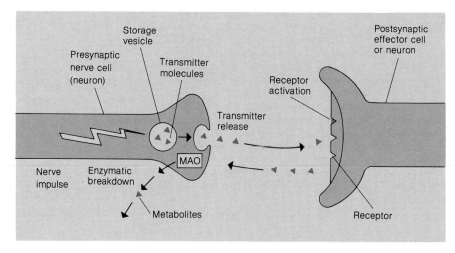

his or her life, the therapist and client can begin to work together to change this pattern. In the next chapter this approach will be illustrated in more detail.

THE COGNITIVE PERSPECTIVE

In recent years, the cognitive approach to depression has become increasingly popular. The two main cognitive models stem from the work of Aaron Beck and Martin Seligman and their respective co-workers.

Beck's cognitive theory of depression   Beck focuses on the way that depressed persons view their relations with the environment rather than on their actual interac-

tions. He emphasizes both the distortions that they make in the interpretation of events and their imperviousness to contrary evidence and environmental feedback. Beck believes that people are depressed because of their erroneous and exaggerated ways of thinking. The depressed person views himself or herself, the world, and the future negatively. According to Beck (1967, 1976), these negative cognitions cause and

TABLE 15.5   THE TEN PLEASANT AND TEN UNPLEASANT EVENTS MOST HIGHLY CORRELATED WITH ONE CLIENT'S MOOD

KIND	SPECIFIC EVENT
PLEASANT EVENTS	1. Buying things for myself
	2. Buying things for my family
	3. Learning to do something new
	4. Planning trips or vacations
	5. Going to a party
	6. Making a new friend
	7. Improving my health (having my teeth fixed, getting new glasses, changing my diet, etc.)
	8. Wearing expensive or formal clothes
	9. Combing or brushing my hair
	10. Playing party games
UNPLEASANT EVENTS	1. Coming home to a messy house
	2. Being bothered with red tape, administrative hassles, paperwork, etc.
	3. Being rushed
	4. Having someone I know drink, smoke, or take drugs
	5. Having something break or run poorly (car, appliances, etc.)
	6. Being unable to call or reach someone when it is important
	7. Seeing natural resources wasted (trees left to rot, polluted streams, etc.)
	8. Seeing a dead animal
	9. Riding in a car with a poor driver
	10. Being socially rejected

Source: Lewinsohn, Sullivan, and Grosscup, 1980, p. 331.

maintain the depressed state. The depressed person gives overgeneralized, exaggerated meanings to whatever happens and tends to magnify personal faults and to minimize his or her positive qualities. For example, if a career promotion is given to someone else, an unsuccessful candidate might think, "I am just not good enough. Failing proves I'm worthless. Everyone must see that, or I would have gotten the promotion." Another unsuccessful candidate, who does not think this way, might say to himself or herself, "Ms. Y., who got the job, has had more experience. I know I could do the job, but my qualifications simply aren't as impressive on paper."

Beck uses the concept of schemata to explain why depressed people persist in this kind of negative thinking even when there is a great deal of contrary evidence. **Schemata** are organized representations about past experiences that a person uses to interpret what is presently happening. People who are depressed have a set of dysfunctional or distorting schemata that cause them to make systematic errors in interpreting what is happening to them. This is Beck's explanation of why self-defeating and pain-inducing attitudes seem to persist in depressed people even when others clearly demonstrate to them that the situation is not the way they perceive it. He thinks that depression causes people not only to evaluate their performance harshly and to fail to reinforce themselves after they do something praiseworthy but also to have lower levels of expectation for their performance before they even begin a task (Lobnitz and Post, 1979). Even when nothing is going wrong, such a person may be preoccupied with thoughts of past mistakes and personal deficiencies. This kind of self-critical thinking is illustrated by Figure 15.10.

Learned helplessness and depression According to Martin Seligman and others, the depressed person has concluded that the outcome of events is uncontrollable, and this knowledge results in cognitive, motivational, and emotional deficits. Moreover, it is not simply the exposure to uncontrollable situations that fosters depression; it is the expectation that future outcomes will also be uncontrollable. Helplessness may develop in the following way (Abramson and others, 1978):

(COURTESY, ROZ CHAST.)

FIGURE 15.10 *The typical thinking of someone who is depressed tends to focus on failures and inadequacies.*

Actual helplessness → *perception* of present helplessness → *reminders* of past helplessness → *assignment* of blame for present or past helplessness → *expectation* of future helplessness → *symptoms* of helplessness

As you can see, the key step is the person's deciding on the cause of his or her helplessness—if that cause is a personal trait rather than some factor of the situation, then the person could take that "failure trait" into any or all events in the future.

For example, consider a college student who has failed an important exam. If the student attributes the failure to some general or unchangeable personal quality such as low intelligence, depression may result. If, instead, the failure is attributed to a situational factor such as insufficient study, the depressed feelings may be confined to that particular incident and may not generalize to future exams. Finally, if the failure is attributed to impossible demands by the test maker— "No one could pass a test like that"—then we would expect the student to experience anger rather than depression. Because it is the expectation of helplessness in the future that is critical for depression, situations that seem only temporary or that affect everyone, not just one individual, will not result in the learned helplessness response. Figure 15.11 illustrates the differences in the attributions that might be expected from people who are depressed and from those who are not. Learned helplessness eventually leads to the failure to respond to problems, a pattern that continues even if the person encounters some favorable outcomes after the original experience of helplessness.

The cognitive theories of depression assume that depressed people are less accurate in evaluating events than people who are not depressed, but at least one study has suggested that this is not the case. In fact, the situation may be just the reverse. In one study of social competence, conducted by Lewinsohn and others (1980), depressed patients rated themselves more accurately than did other psychiatric patients or normal controls, all of whom tended to overrate themselves. Most interesting of all was the finding that, as the depressed patients improved, they became less realistic about their impact on others. Although accuracy of perception by depressed individuals may not hold in

every case (Coyne and others, in press; Lewinsohn and others, 1980), the finding is still a provocative one. It fits well with an observation that Freud made based on his clinical experience:

When in his [the depressive's] heightened self-criticism he describes himself as petty, egotistic, dishonest, lacking in independence, one whose sole aim has been to hide the weakness of his own nature, it may be, so far as we know, that he has to be ill before he can be accessible to a truth of this kind. (Freud, 1917/1957, p. 246)

PSYCHODYNAMIC THEORIES

Depression may be triggered by an event that does not seem to be momentous to others but that may be highly significant to the depressed individual. According to the psychodynamic perspective, many, if not all, depressions are reactions to events that are symbolically meaningful because of experiences that the individual had earlier in life, especially in childhood. Freud described both normal mourning and depression (melancholia) as responses to the loss of someone or some-

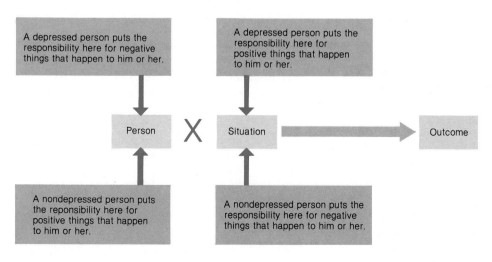

FIGURE 15.11 *Cognitive theorists believe that the attribution process of depressed and nondepressed individuals is different.*

thing that was loved (Freud, 1917/1957). Most psychodynamic theories focus on the idea of loss, particularly the loss of the mother, the person on whom a child tends to be most dependent. This loss, which may be real or fantasized, creates feelings of anger. Because of the anxiety that they arouse, these angry thoughts are pushed out of awareness, but they may still exert an influence. The person becomes especially vulnerable to all kinds of loss experiences in later life, not only of loss by death or by the breakup of a relationship, but also loss of prestige or power.

John Bowlby, a British psychoanalyst whose work on attachment is described in Chapter 12, emphasizes the importance of loss or separation in childhood on later development. Children who are securely attached—that is, who are able to function independently because they feel that their parent will be available if things get out of control—seem to carry the protection of that early relationship into their later life. Secure attachment in childhood has been related to the ability to have meaningful emotional relationships as an adult.

Loss and absence of a close emotional relationship may make people more vulnerable to depression as adults. This link has been substantiated by George Brown and his co-workers (Brown and Harris, 1978). They carried out extensive interviews with a sample of women living in central London. The researchers found that women who had lost their mothers before they were 11 years old had a greater risk of depression than other women did. The severity of the depression was also greater for those depressed women who had experienced a death in the family while they were growing up. Although a series of negative events happening in a short period of time often seemed to lead to the occurrence of depression, a close, confiding relationship with a husband or boyfriend seemed to lessen the likelihood that depression would occur. A similar study of women in Oxford, England, supported Brown's findings about the protective value of a close relationship (Campbell and others, 1983). The importance that both psychoanalytic theory and other psychodynamic views place on loss as a vulnerability factor and a supportive relationship as a protective element against depression seems to be holding up well under research scrutiny.

HUMANISTIC-EXISTENTIAL THEORIES

Existential theories have adopted the psychodynamic idea of loss, but they focus on the loss of self-esteem rather than the loss of a loved object. For example, an event that often triggers depression in men is the loss of a job. A man can no longer label himself as Harry R., assistant office manager, or Marty T., drill press operator, but only as Harry R. or Marty T., now unemployed. Although he might still label himself as husband, father, good citizen, or holder of a particular academic degree, society values the occupational label more, and so does the man. The job represents the man's identity and his value in his own eyes and in the eyes of others. In the same way, our culture tends to base the social status of a woman on her husband's role. If a woman loses her husband, she may suffer a decline in power, social rank, and financial position. Her feeling of loss may relate not merely to the absence of a loved one but to her diminished stature as a widow or a divorcee. This dependence of women on identification with their spouses' status is changing as more women are employed and gain recognition and self-esteem from their own jobs, but cultural expectations often change more slowly than reality does.

Mania and bipolar disorders

Mania can best be defined as a state in which the individual's mood is elevated, expansive, or irritable; speech is rapid or pressured, as if as many words as possible must come out in the shortest possible time; and behavior is hyperactive. The manic individual may also show grandiosity in thinking and a fast and illogical transition from one train of thought to another. The following case gives the flavor of manic behavior:

Robert B., 56 years old, was a dentist who for most of his 25 years of dental practice provided rather well for his wife and three daughters. Mrs. B. reported that there had been times when Robert displayed behavior similar to that which preceded his hospitalization, but that this was the worst she had ever seen.

About two weeks prior to hospitalization, the patient awoke one morning with the idea that he was the most gifted dental surgeon in his tri-state area; his mission then was to provide service for as many persons as possible so that they could benefit from his talents. Consequently, he decided to enlarge his 2-chair practice to a 20-chair one, and his plan was to reconstruct his two dental offices into 20 booths so that he could simultaneously attend to as many patients. That very day he drew up the plans for this arrangement and telephoned a number of remodelers and invited them to submit bids for the work.

Toward the end of that day he became irritated with the "interminable delays" and, after he attended to his last patient, rolled up his sleeves and began to knock down the walls of his dental offices. When he discovered that he couldn't manage this chore with the sledge hammer he had purchased for this purpose earlier, he became frustrated and proceeded to smash his more destructible tools, washbasins, and X-ray equipment. He justified this behavior in his own mind by saying, "This junk is not suitable for the likes of me; it'll have to be replaced anyway."

He was in perpetual motion and his speech was "overexcited." [When Robert was later admitted to a hospital] he could not sit in his chair; instead he paced the office floor like a caged animal. . . . He responded well to

lithium treatment and was discharged within several weeks. . . . (Kleinmuntz, 1980, pp. 309–310)

Bipolar disorders, which are characterized by mania and depression, usually appear early in adulthood. Frequently, the first symptoms appear in adolescence. Sometimes a person with bipolar disorder will have several episodes of depression before a manic episode appears. From 4 to 16 percent of depressed patients also develop manic symptoms as time passes (Egeland, 1983). Periods of mania and depression do not necessarily alternate, but both occur over the individual's lifetime. (Table 15.6 compares the characteristics of mania and depression.) People with bipolar disorder

TABLE 15.6   HOW MANIC BEHAVIOR AND DEPRESSED BEHAVIOR DIFFER

CATEGORIES OF BEHAVIOR	MANIC	DEPRESSIVE
EMOTIONAL CHARACTERISTICS	Elated, euphoric	Gloomy, hopeless
	Very sociable	Socially withdrawn
	Impatient at any hindrance	Irritable
COGNITIVE CHARACTERISTICS	Racing thoughts, flight of ideas	Slowness of thought processes
	Desire for action	Obsessive worrying
	Impulsive behavior	Inability to make decisions
	Talkative	Withdrawn
	Positive self-image	Negative self-image, self-blame
	Delusions of grandeur	Delusions of guilt and disease
MOTOR CHARACTERISTICS	Hyperactive	Decreased motor activity
	Does not become tired	Tired
	Needs less sleep than usual	Difficulty in sleeping
	Increased sex drive	Decreased sex drive
	Fluctuating appetite	Decreased appetite

also have periods when they seem to function quite normally. In one study, bipolar individuals were given the Minnesota Multiphasic Personality Inventory (Lumry and others, 1982). Their test scores showed clear signs of psychopathology when they were manic or depressed, but during their periods of remission, their MMPI profiles were within normal limits.

Most of the research on bipolar disorder comes from the biological perspective. Reasonably good evidence exists that there is a hereditary component in bipolar disorder. Relatives of bipolar individuals were much more likely to have either bipolar or unipolar symptoms than the relatives of people in a control group were (Weissman and others, 1984). In addition, the relatives of depressed people had higher rates of depression than a control group did. One theory is that bipolar disorder is associated with an X-linked dominant gene (Cadoret and Winokur, 1975; Geron and Cadoret, 1977). This means that the gene for bipolar disorder is carried on the X chromosome. Since a woman has two X chromosomes and a man has only one, more females than males would be affected by bipolar disorder. Further, a father with bipolar disorder could transmit that inheritance only to his daughters. However, a few cases of father-son inheritance of bipolar disorder have been found (Mendlewicz and Rainier, 1974). Another suggestion that bipolar disorder and some kinds of major depression may be linked is that treatment with lithium is effective both for bipolar disorder and for some kinds of depressive illness. Further, the chance that lithium may be effective in major depression is greatest for individuals who have relatives with a bipolar diagnosis (Peet and Coppen, 1980).

These findings suggest that the two disorders may share common genes, although it is also possible that environmental, behavioral, or nongenetic biological factors play a role. So far the hereditary issue in bipolar disorders has presented intriguing hypotheses that may explain some but not all of the research findings.

SCHIZOPHRENIC DISORDERS

Schizophrenia is not a single pathology; it is a group of disorders (Buchsbaum and Haier, 1978; Crow, 1980). The subgroups may have different causes and different treatment outcomes. Because the definition of schizophrenia has varied over time and has sometimes been much broader and more inclusive than at other times, many conclusions from past research may not hold true today. Figure 15.12 illustrates the effects of the change in the definition in the United States between 1932 and 1956, as well as the differences in definitions in the United States and in England. Many researchers felt that "schizophrenia" had become a catch-all diagnosis that included so many types of individuals that research on the whole group produced unclear or meaningless findings. As a result, they began to subdivide people diagnosed as schizophrenic into more homogeneous groups for research purposes. The *DSM III* has also adopted a much narrower definition that excludes many people who would previously have been labeled as schizophrenics. However, even within those narrower categories, there are several groups who have disorders with different causes and probably also with different potential outcomes.

Characteristics of schizophrenia

All disorders diagnosed as schizophrenia have several characteristics in common: the presence of hallucinations and delusions, and disturbances in a number of areas of behavior, including thinking, emotional response, sense of identity, and the motivation or ability to initiate and carry out goal-directed activity. To meet the criteria of the *DSM III*, someone who is diagnosed as schizophrenic must also be less than 45 years old, must show a deterioration from an earlier level of functioning, and must have continued to show those changes for at least 6 months. The case of Bob S. illustrates some of these characteristics:

Bob, age 20, was brought to the clinic by his parents. They were worried about the dramatic changes in his behavior over the last several months. He had dropped out of college midway through his second year. He was failing in all his courses, although he had done fairly well in high school. Bob had been on the high school track team, although he was not an outstanding athlete, and had played the cello in the school orchestra; at college, he had participated in no outside activities. Now that he was at home, he spent most of his time in his room listening to

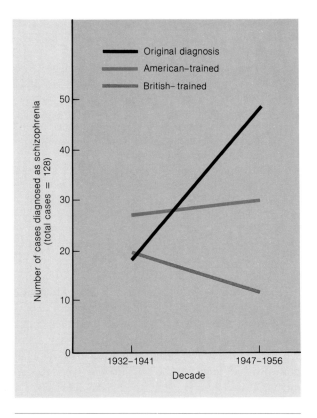

thought that Bob displayed remarkably little emotion in discussing the changes that had taken place in his life. Sometimes his mood seemed inappropriate—for instance, he smiled and giggled while describing how his dog, which he had owned since childhood, had recently been hit by a car and had to be destroyed.

He said a number of other things that made the interviewer take special notice. For example, he mentioned that whenever the neighbors turned to a certain station on the radio, they heard everything he was thinking. Bob reported hearing voices that told how to prevent a great catastrophe from happening to the whole country. He said that he began hearing these instructions early in the fall of his second year at college. He mentioned that at about the same time, he became concerned that his intestines were being eaten away, not by disease but by evil forces.

Because the category of *schizophrenic disorders* covers such a wide range of disordered behavior, Bob's case should not be considered typical of all individuals who receive this diagnosis. However, it does illustrate a number of behaviors that may lead to a diagnosis of schizophrenia.

Hallucinations and delusions

Of particular importance in making this diagnosis is the presence of hallucinations and delusions. Because these can occur in other disorders—for example, from the use of drugs, from a high fever, during a period of mania, or from dementia (a nonreversible deterioration of brain cells that alters brain activity)—the diagnosis of schizophrenia is made only after these other causes have been ruled out.

A **delusion** is faulty thinking, a misinterpretation of reality that is clung to despite strong evidence to the contrary. For example, in Bob's case, the idea that his internal organs were being eaten away was delusional. Many delusions are of this somatic (body-related) variety. One writer who had recovered from a schizo-

FIGURE 15.12 *Fashions change in diagnosis. The number of patients diagnosed as schizophrenic shot up between 1932 and 1956, not because the disorder was increasing, but because the definition was changing. There is still a difference in the frequency of this diagnosis in Great Britain and the United States, again because the criteria for the diagnosis have differed in the two countries. (Kuriansky and others, 1977, p. 681)*

records and seemed to have no interest in contacting any of his high school friends. There had also been a striking change in his personal grooming. Now, he seldom bathed or shaved and wore the same shirt and jeans for weeks—day and night—even though his parents urged him to shower and to change into clean clothing.

The interviewer at the clinic found Bob pleasant but difficult to talk to. He sometimes had little to say in answer to her questions, and often she was left wondering just what his answers meant. In general, the interviewer phrenic episode reported that she believed that she was able to stop her heart on command (Thelmar, 1932). Grandiose beliefs are another common type of delusion. This same writer reported her belief that people were worshipping her as the Madonna and as the mother of the (as yet unborn) savior of the world. A common delusion is that of being Jesus, Napoleon, Marie Antoinette, Theodore Roosevelt, or some other famous person.

A **hallucination** involves the perception of objects or events in the absence of relevant or adequate stimulation. Hallucinations can be associated with any of the sense organs—sight, hearing, taste, smell, or touch. The type most commonly found in schizophrenia is the auditory hallucination in which voices issue orders or make accusations of terrible crimes or actions. Figure 15.13 shows an artist's representation of some of the tormenting perceptions associated with his hallucinations during a period of psychosis. Hallucinations can be pleasant as well as unpleasant. One young man described the pleasant and unpleasant voices that he heard during a period of psychosis:

The voices weren't much fun in the beginning. Part of it was simply my being uncomfortable about hearing voices no matter what they had to say, but the early voices were

mostly bearers of bad news. Besides, they didn't seem to like me much and there was no way I could talk back to them. Those were very one-sided conversations.

But later the voices could be very pleasant. They'd often be the voice of someone I loved, and even if they weren't, I could talk too, asking questions about this or that and getting reasonable answers. There were very important messages that had to get through somehow. More orthodox channels like phone and mail had broken down. (Vonnegut, 1975, pp. 136–137)

Outcome prospects

The main purpose of diagnosis is not simply to divide people into neat groups; it is a way to determine appropriate treatment and to make more accurate predictions about their future progress. Although the diagnosis of schizophrenia is now narrower than it used to be, it probably still includes several different types of disorders. Many researchers make a distinction between **Type I** and **Type II** schizophrenics (Crow, 1980). The Type I classification shows what are called **positive**

FIGURE 15.13 *This painting, by a hospitalized psychiatric patient who later became a successful painter, records the terror of his hallucinations during his illness.*

symptoms—delusions, hallucinations, and disordered thinking. Type II has **negative symptoms**—flattened emotional expression and poverty of speech. These symptoms are not mutually exclusive, and there can be some overlap between the two types. However, it is more likely that either Type I or Type II symptoms will be found in an individual than that both will occur together (Maser and Keith, 1983).

The outcome for a particular individual can be predicted best from the kind of symptoms that he or she initially displays. Perhaps surprisingly, a high degree of disordered thought and frequency of delusions and hallucinations does not predict a negative final outcome. In contrast, Type II symptoms—a lack of emotional response and poor social adjustment prior to the outbreak of the symptoms—are clear predictors of a poor chance for recovery (Knight and others, 1979).

The original conception of schizophrenia as defined by the German psychiatrist Emil Kraepelin (who called it **dementia praecox**) was of a disorder that continued to become more severe over time and from which recovery was highly unlikely. In one group of patients Kraepelin studied, he considered only about 10 percent of the patients to have fully recovered (1914). Later, as the disorder was defined more broadly, the probability of reported recovery became much greater. In studies in which the follow-up was at least 10 years, the number of patients who neither recovered nor improved ranged from 11 to 83 percent (Stephens, 1978). This broad range probably is due largely to the wide variety of definitions of schizophrenia.

In one of the best-known long-term studies, the subjects were not merely recontacted after a certain number of years; instead, their progress was examined carefully over the entire period (Bleuler, 1972). In this study, and in a number of other less thorough investigations, whatever deterioration occurred happened in the first 5 years of illness. After that time, the proportion of individuals who recovered, improved, and remained unimproved stayed fairly constant. In another long-term study, the researchers concluded that only 14 to 17 percent of the patients were able to maintain a high level of social and occupational functioning without relapses (Harrow and others, 1978).

A number of researchers have noted that the characteristics of the disorder seem to have changed over

the years. The symptoms appear to have become milder and less likely to persist without periods of remission (Bleuler, 1973). Instead of long periods of hospitalization, a schizophrenic individual is likely to be in and out of the hospital with alternating episodes of remission and psychosis (Wilson and others, 1983). The best guess to account for this change is the almost universal use of antipsychotic drugs in the treatment of schizophrenia. For many individuals, these drugs seem to change the course of the disorder rather than to cure it.

A better understanding of the recovery prospects may come from the division of schizophrenic disorders into subgroups. Such information is important not only to mental health professionals but also to those who have been diagnosed as schizophrenic. If these different subgroups also show different degrees of impairment and different probabilities of recovery, then the negative reaction to the diagnosis may be lessened. The stigma of permanent disability sometimes attached to this diagnosis both by the public and even by professionals is illustrated in this portion of a letter from a researcher in the field of schizophrenia who, at one point during his medical school training, was diagnosed as schizophrenic:

During the years since my hospitalization, however, I have often been fraught with profound guilt over my diagnosis of schizophrenia. . . . I felt that for some people I would be forevermore something of a subhuman creature. I grieved and mourned over my loss for several months. . . . Returning to work as a fellow in a department of psychiatry, I was repeatedly in contact with psychiatrists, psychologists, and other mental health professionals. Quite frequently amidst such contacts there were derogatory and slanderous remarks of persons labeled as schizophrenic. Dismayed, I soon had repeated dreams in which I had a brain tumor, dreams that were not in the least bit frightening to me. Having an organic disease seemed far easier to live with then—preferable to experiencing the full psychological impact of this label of schizophrenia. (Anonymous, 1977, p. 4)

Perspectives on schizophrenia

We will demonstrate in our discussion of the person × situation interaction near the end of this chapter how all the perspectives have contributed to an understanding of schizophrenia. Before pulling them together, we will look at some of the research questions emphasized from each perspective and the findings that they have generated.

THE BIOLOGICAL PERSPECTIVE

Research from the biological perspective focuses on many different topics. The first major question is, Is there a hereditary factor in schizophrenia? If such a factor exists, and most people agree that it does, then the next step is to clarify the hereditary mechanisms involved. The second major question is, What specific biological differences can be found that distinguish between people who show schizophrenic behavior and those who do not? Clues such as these may be used to isolate the biological mechanisms involved in schizophrenia and may also help to identify people who have a greater risk than others of developing the disorder.

Genetic factors in schizophrenia   For the population in general, the lifetime risk of schizophrenia is about 1 percent. If one parent, a brother or a sister, or a nonidentical twin has had a schizophrenic disorder, the risk increases to 10 percent. If both parents or an identical twin has been diagnosed as schizophrenic, the risk rises to 50 percent. Children of nonschizophrenic parents, adopted by a parent who later becomes schizophrenic, do not have an increased risk, but children of a schizophrenic parent who are adopted in infancy by nonschizophrenic parents are at as great a risk as if they had continued to live with their schizophrenic parent (Seeman, 1983). These percentages, which have been verified by many different researchers, show that genetic factors appear to be at least as important in schizophrenia as they are in such common medical conditions as diabetes and hypertension (Kendler and Robinette, 1983). We still do not know, however, which genes are involved or how genetic inheritance interacts with environmental factors to produce schizophrenic behavior.

The role of neurotransmitters   Biologically oriented research stresses the importance of neurotransmitters in schizophrenia as well as in depression. In investigations of the schizophrenic disorders, interest has centered on the neurotransmitter dopamine. The **dopamine hypothesis of schizophrenia,** simply stated, says that there is an excess of dopamine at certain synapses in the brain. This excess is presumed to be due either to an overproduction of dopamine, or to faulty regulation of the feedback apparatus by which the dopamine returns to the sending neuron and is stored by the vesicles, or to increased sensitivity of the dopamine receptors in the receiving neuron.

Research designed to test the dopamine hypothesis has provided a mass of conflicting results. Most of its clearest support is indirect and comes from studies of the effects of drugs known either to increase or decrease dopamine availability in the nervous system. For example, amphetamine, which increases the effects of dopamine, can produce symptoms that are very similar to acute paranoid schizophrenia. The effectiveness of

FIGURE 15.14 *Antipsychotic drugs prevent stimulation of dopamine receptors by blocking the receptors in the receiving neuron.*

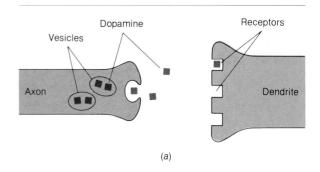

(a)

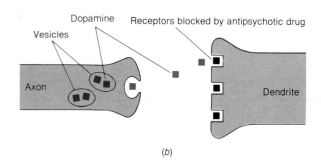

(b)

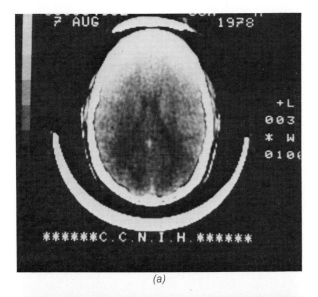
(a)

(b)

FIGURE 15.15 *CT scans have produced new information about possible relationships between abnormalities of brain structure and schizophrenia. One relationship that has been noted is that certain schizophrenics have significantly larger cerebral ventricles (cavities that contain cerebrospinal fluid) than are found in the brains of nonschizophrenics. Note how these CT scans of the brain of a 36-year-old schizophrenic woman (a) compare with those of a 25-year-old nonschizophrenic man (b). The elongated ventricles in her brain are noticeably larger.*

antipsychotic drugs in reducing schizophrenic behavior has been found to be directly related to the drugs' efficiency in blocking dopamine receptors in the receiving neuron (Peroutka and Snyder, 1980)—see Figure 15.14.

New techniques for biological research The search for abnormalities in the brain that distinguish schizophrenics from other people has a long and disappointing history. New technology is making this research

approach popular again and may provide some important insights into the causes of schizophrenic behavior.

As we noted in Chapter 3, one device, the **computerized axial tomography,** or **CT** scanner, can give the viewer a clear picture of the internal anatomy of the living brain viewed from a series of different angles and perspectives. Researchers have found that 20 to 50 percent of schizophrenics who are examined by CT scans have mild to moderate enlargement of their **cerebral ventricles** (cavities that contain cerebrospinal fluid) (Seidman, 1983)—see Figure 15.15. Those most likely to have enlarged ventricles are Type II schizophrenics, who also tend to respond less favorably to antipsychotic drugs and who are likely to have had a poorer adjustment before the schizophrenic behavior occurred (Weinberger and others, 1983). Atrophy or the shrinking of cortical tissue and the widening of the fissures or grooves on the exterior surface of the brain have also been noticed in some schizophrenic patients. These abnormalities may be seen even shortly after the development of the schizophrenic behavior, which suggests that they are not due to treatment with drugs or to institutionalization but represent earlier damage or some inherent defect in the central nervous system.

Another scanning device that has recently been used in examining the brains of schizophrenics is **positron emission tomography,** or the **PET scan.** Unlike the CT scan, which is used to study the anatomy of the brain, the PET scan allows researchers to see the vary-

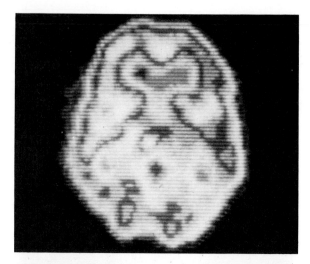

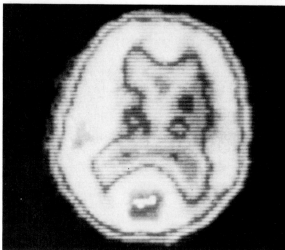

FIGURE 15.16 *These PET scans of identical twins show how brain activity differs with different types of sensory stimulation. Mike, the twin on the top, is receiving shocks on his right arm. John, the twin on the bottom, is counting light flashes.*

ing levels of energy use in different parts of the brain as a result of different kinds of mental activity. Figure 15.16 illustrates how brain activity varies depending on the kind of stimulus being received. The new insights and research approaches that these scanners are yielding are discussed in Frontier 15.1.

FRONTIER 15.1
**NEW TECHNIQUES
COMPLEMENT EARLIER RECORDS**

The way in which scanning devices can provide new information about schizophrenia is illustrated by the following case of four girls, identical quadruplets, all sharing the same genetic makeup. Because the odds for identical quadruplets are one in 16 million births, the sisters became celebrities in their home town. During their childhood, they performed song and dance routines and were so popular that they had a police escort on one early local tour. As the sisters grew older, however, it became clear that they were not developing in a normal way. One sister dropped out of high school. The other three graduated but had trouble holding jobs. During their 20s, all 4 sisters developed schizophrenic disorders. Because of the uniqueness of this case (4 individuals with identical heredity who all showed schizophrenic behavior could be expected to occur only once in tens of billions of births), a local physician alerted scientists at the National Institute of Mental Health. The sisters came to Washington, D.C., and were hospitalized there for intensive study. During the 3 years that they spent at NIMH, they were examined from a number of perspectives. Their physical and mental development, their family relationships, and measures of their brain activity were all investigated (Rosenthal, 1963). To protect their privacy, the sisters were given pseudonyms corresponding to NIMH's initials—Nora, Iris, Myra, and Hester—and the family was given the name of Genain, from the Greek words meaning "dire birth."

Several of the quadruplets' family members had histories of psychological problems. Not only was their father's behavior often bizarre, but his brother, his mother, and his paternal uncle had each had a nervous breakdown sometime in the past.

Even though they were genetically identical and may have had a hereditary risk factor, the sisters' schizophrenia could have been at least partly the result of environmental factors. For example, as is usual in multiple births, they were all small at birth. All of them spent time in incubators and did not go home from the hospital until they were 6 weeks old. They grew up in the glare of publicity and constantly heard comments about their similarity. Their father restricted their interactions with other people by refusing to allow them to play with other children or, later, to take part in school activities or to date.

The girls' father also objected to their stay at NIMH and often threatened to take them out of the hospital. Although he was cooperative and cordial at times, he also had considerable hostility toward people. His wife reported that he had tried to choke her several times and said that she had considered leaving him. At times, he accused his wife of having sexual relationships with his daughters' psychiatrists. During the quadruplets' third year at the hospital, he died.

The following report, which reflects the psychodynamic perspective, describes the family relationships in more detail:

Mrs. Genain's unfulfilled needs for maternal nurturing found expression in her closeness to Nora. It was the symbiotic tie of mother and infant, one in which the mother does not see the infant as a separate individual but as a part of herself. . . . In her adult psychosis, she [Nora] caricatured her mother's friendly facade and stereotyped sweetness. The closeness between them supported a report that Nora was not only her father's "favorite," but her mother's also. The earliest evidence for this was that Nora was always the first of the babies to be burped after feeding. The most recent evidence was that Nora was the daughter Mrs. Genain took home for trial visits from the hospital, although Iris' adjustment was also appropriate for home visits.

The central role for Myra was the "independent positive." Mrs. Genain identified Myra with her own independent strivings and actions. . . . Myra was the daughter upon whom Mrs. Genain was prone to lean in times of stress, who often strove for the favored position (which in this family was the protected one) with her mother. . . . She tried to live out the role her mother

assigned to her of becoming independent, and the dependent-independent conflict became acute for her when she tried to move out on her own.

The central theme of the role Mrs. Genain assigned to Iris was the "repressed" one. She identified in Iris her own feeling that she must put up with anything and in her psychosis, Iris caricatured this aspect of her mother's personality. Later, when she improved, she made occasional sarcastic remarks to her mother which Mrs. Genain described as being like Iris' prepsychotic behavior and as being hostile to her. . . . In areas that concerned Iris as an individual, e.g., her abilities and appearance, Mrs. Genain was neither concerned nor interested.

The central theme assigned to Hester was the "negative" one. It was as though Hester personified that which Mrs. Genain regarded as undesirable—hostility and sexuality, for example. The perception of these feelings in Hester appeared to have blocked her mother's perception of other human qualities in her. She was the last to be regarded as sick (she had been "bad") and she was not hospitalized before coming to the Clinical Center. Later Mrs. Genain did not even consider a time when Hester might come for home visits from the hospital. Hester had the end position on the continuum. (Rosenthal, 1963, pp. 463–465)

Twenty years after the Genains had first been studied at NIMH, they were invited back for a follow-up. During that period Myra had lived the most normal life. She went to business college and later worked as a secretary. She was the only one of the 4 sisters to marry and have children. Nora was next best in adjustment. She had worked at least 7 years, at least partly in government training programs. Hester and Iris had each spent at least 15 years in hospitals and had received more antipsychotic drug treatment than either Myra or Nora. Researchers wondered whether new biological techniques could shed light on the differences in their behavior.

Rather than just exploring the question of heredity vs. environment, investigators began to ask a more sophisticated question: How do brain injury, inher-

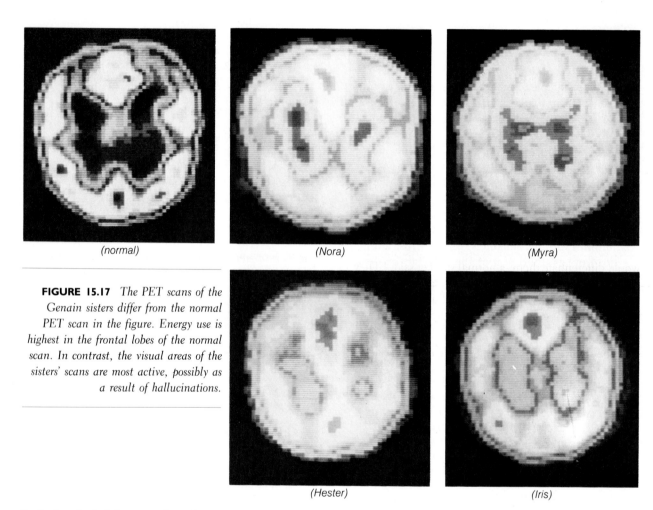

(normal) (Nora) (Myra)

FIGURE 15.17 *The PET scans of the Genain sisters differ from the normal PET scan in the figure. Energy use is highest in the frontal lobes of the normal scan. In contrast, the visual areas of the sisters' scans are most active, possibly as a result of hallucinations.*

(Hester) (Iris)

ited chemical defects, and environment interact to produce schizophrenic behavior? The sisters' CT scans appeared normal, but their PET scans, made when the women were resting, showed activity in the visual areas (see Figure 15.17). Scientists wondered if this was an indication of hallucinations. The PET scans of Myra and Nora, the two sisters who had made the best adjustment, were closer to the normal PET scans than those of the two sisters whose behavior was less adaptive. The Genains also showed much less alpha brain wave activity than is normal. Since alpha waves appear when people relax or let their minds go blank, the low frequency of alpha waves may also suggest hallucinations. These findings, when matched with the sisters' behavioral histories and with the earlier test data, may prove a help in relating specific behaviors with environmental factors and biological functioning.

THE COGNITIVE PERSPECTIVE

Schizophrenia has been viewed as being characterized by disordered thinking, but such thinking is not unique to schizophrenia. People diagnosed as manic also experience a high degree of thought disorder (Andreasen, 1979). Even normal individuals show occasional episodes of disordered thinking, although the incidents do not occur at the frequency found among schizophrenics (Holzman, 1978).

Language peculiarities shown by schizophrenics are an area of interest to cognitive theorists. Schizophrenic individuals seem to know the rules of grammar and do not use overly simple, childlike speech (Brown, 1973). Schizophrenic speech has been described as "disruptive" by listeners because the speakers fail to include the logical links necessary for a listener to follow the train of thought and because what they say is likely to be inappropriate for the situation. For example, when normal and schizophrenic subjects were asked to describe two similar color chips in a way that would differentiate them, a normal speaker said, "They both are either the color of canned salmon or clay. This one here is the pinker one." A schizophrenic subject replied, "Makeup. Pancake makeup. You put it on your face and they think guys run after you. Wait a second! I don't put it on my face and guys don't run after me. Girls put it on them." Studying the speech of schizophrenics may help researchers to understand more about how their cognitive processes function differently from those of other individuals. As you can see in the following descriptions, the areas of cognitive activity that seem to cause the most trouble for schizophrenics are focusing attention and concentrating:

Nothing settles in my mind—not even for a second. . . . My mind goes away—too many things come into my head at once and I lose control. . . . I'm falling apart into bits. (Chapman, 1966, p. 232)

At first it was as if parts of my brain "awoke" which had been dormant, and I became interested in a wide assortment of people, events, places and ideas which normally would make no impression on me. . . . What had happened to me . . . was a breakdown in the filter, and a hodge-podge of unrelated stimuli were distracting me from things which should have had my undivided attention. (MacDonald, 1960, pp. 218–219)

The delusions and hallucinations that schizophrenics are likely to experience may also distract them from concentrating attention on what is going on in their external environment. The activity of the visual areas of the brain in the absence of visual stimulation in PET scans shown in Figure 15.17 may indicate the presence of hallucinations. This type of investigation illustrates how two perspectives, in this case the biological and the cognitive, may complement each other.

THE PSYCHODYNAMIC PERSPECTIVE

In their attempt to understand why schizophrenic disorder occurs, psychodynamic theorists focus on the effects of extremely frustrating family relationships and on the lack of emotional ties. Although schizophrenic behavior is not likely to become apparent until late in adolescence or in early adulthood, the psychodynamic position holds that such behavior does not represent a new problem. The disorder has existed for some time but becomes clear only when an individual is expected to become more independent. Children can retreat into fantasy, but as a person grows older, this becomes more difficult.

The only way to understand what is actually happening in family relationships prior to the diagnosis of schizophrenia is through longitudinal research. In one such investigation, the researchers found that families in which the child later became schizophrenic tended to be more critical, intrusive, and guilt-inducing in their behavior than other families in the study (Doane and others, 1981).

Family environment also contributes to whether or not an individual who has been hospitalized for schizophrenia will have a relapse. A family whose members are highly critical, hostile, and overinvolved in each other's lives is associated with higher relapse rates (Leff and Vaughn, 1981). Such a family climate is called high in **expressed emotion.** This quality can be rated reliably in an interview with a family member, both by what is said and by the manner in which it is said.

Examiners are taught to rate speed, pitch, and intensity of speech as well as facial expression, gestures, and what is said. Follow-up studies suggest that expressed emotion in a family can be modified by family counseling and education (Leff and others, 1982).

Some psychodynamic theories about how families are involved in the development of schizophrenia have been criticized in the past because they were largely based on retrospective recall that may have been the outcome of distorted perceptions, not of fact. Families with a schizophrenic child may have felt unjustifiably guilty and ashamed of their presumed role in bringing about the condition. Newer studies have been able to define their constructs better and are beginning to give us a clearer view of how the development of schizophrenia may be related both to genetic vulnerabilities and to factors within the family.

THE BEHAVIORAL PERSPECTIVE

The behavioral perspective has been most concerned with ways of altering schizophrenic behavior, rather than with establishing its causes. From this point of view, the distinctive feature of schizophrenia is the extinction or lack of development of conventional responses to social stimuli. In addition, schizophrenic behavior includes a highly personalized, often bizarre, response repertory that often makes others avoid coming in contact with it. Training in social skills is often used to change the behavior of the schizophrenic. For instance, a **token economy** may be set up in which the patient receives tokens in return for appropriate behavior. These reinforcements can then be cashed in for such desirable items as candy, cigarettes, and other privileges. Unfortunately, when the tokens are discontinued, the desired behavior usually also decreases dramatically (Ayllon and Azrin, 1965). For that reason, researchers have concentrated on teaching social skills in the hope that the powerful reinforcer of social relationships would be more effective than tokens in continuing the behavior.

THE HUMANISTIC-EXISTENTIAL PERSPECTIVE

An existential view of schizophrenia that especially stresses social relationships is offered by R. D. Laing (1969). Laing sees schizophrenia not as a disease, but as a normal response to deteriorated social relation-

ships. The psychosis appears as madness only to those who are unaware of the environment that gave rise to it. The environment of the schizophrenic is so negative or aversive that inventing special strategies is the only way that the individual can live in an otherwise unlivable situation. Laing considers the family the most important feature of the environment for most people. Laing's views have become popular in recent years, but a sizable body of research has not grown out of them.

THE INTERACTION OF STRESS AND VULNERABILITY

One way to combine the insights on schizophrenia provided by these perspectives is through the interactional model. Although this model can be used to study any category of behavior, in the area of schizophrenia it has been particularly well defined by Joseph Zubin (Zubin and others, 1982; Zubin and Spring, 1977). Zubin's **vulnerability hypothesis** assumes that schizophrenia is not a permanent disorder but rather a permanent *vulnerability to a disorder*. Each person has a level of vulnerability to schizophrenia, ranging from zero risk to almost certain risk. Whether a person will show evidence of schizophrenic disorder is determined by the interaction of genetic inheritance, prenatal and postnatal physical factors such as a virus contracted while in the uterus or a brain injury during or after birth, and the impact and frequency of stressful life experiences. The higher a person's level of vulnerability, the smaller the amount of stress required to produce the maladaptive behavior.

Zubin's theory assumes that if a person has no vulnerability to schizophrenia, no amount of stress will produce the disorder. The interactive view has quite different implications from most of the other perspectives. It emphasizes the episodic character of the disorder, which may come and go in vulnerable individuals depending on the stress in the environment. When the degree of stress subsides, according to this theory, the schizophrenic disorder will also disappear, and the person will return to his or her earlier level of functioning. It may be possible to identify people who are vulnerable by a variety of biological markers or specific characteristics—for instance, gene structure, electrical brain responses, or patterns in CT or PET scans.

Most present-day researchers, no matter what their perspective, would agree that the development of a

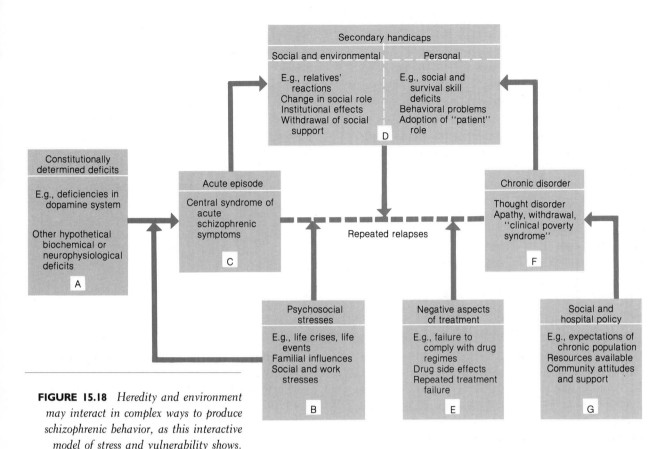

FIGURE 15.18 *Heredity and environment may interact in complex ways to produce schizophrenic behavior, as this interactive model of stress and vulnerability shows. (Adapted from Marzillier and Birchwood, 1981, p. 142)*

schizophrenic disorder is almost always a product of several factors including biological makeup, level of coping skills, environmental conditions, and life experiences. Figure 15.18 depicts a complex model that illustrates the many interactions that occur in producing schizophrenic behavior in someone with an underlying vulnerability.

STUDY OUTLINE

WHAT IS ABNORMAL BEHAVIOR? (p. 512)

1. The psychological perspectives each have a somewhat different definition of abnormal behavior. The biological perspective defines abnormal behavior as mental illness and emphasizes "curing" it, usually through medication. This perspective also emphasizes the genetic aspects of mental illness. The psychodynamic perspective relates the person's behavior to feelings and memories from childhood experiences. The behavioral perspective emphasizes faulty learning patterns, either in childhood or later and focuses on analyzing the present conditions that bring on the maladaptive behavior. The cognitive perspective concentrates on changing disordered or maladaptive thinking patterns and does not put much emphasis on how such patterns originated. According to the humanistic-existential perspective, self-acceptance is important to the individual's happiness and adaptive behavior.

2. Abnormal behavior can be defined as inflexible and unrealistic behavior that does not adapt to changing environmental requirements. It may also be statistically uncommon and socially deviant, but these are not necessary characteristics.

CLASSIFICATION OF ABNORMAL BEHAVIOR (p. 515)

1. Reliability is important in a classification system. Two sources of unreliability are inconsistent behavior

of the person being classified and differences in the clinical training and theoretical orientation of the person using the classification system.

2. The major classification system for abnormal behavior used in the United States is the *Diagnostic and Statistical Manual of the American Psychiatric Association, third edition*, also called *DSM III*. The *DSM III* is based on clinical descriptions of behavior, rather than on presumed causes of behavior, as the preceding manual was. The *DSM III* includes more categories of disordered behavior than the preceding system, *DSM II*, and also gives more concrete examples. The system has multiple axes so that the person's behavior is described in terms of several factors. The five axes include primary classification or diagnosis, personality characteristics, physical disorders, recent psychosocial stressors, and a rating of previous level of adaptive functioning.

PERSONALITY DISORDERS (p. 517)

1. Personality disorders refer to failures to adapt because of inflexible, self-defeating response patterns. They usually become evident by adolescence.

2. *DSM III* lists three general groups of personality disorder: odd, eccentric behaviors; dramatic, erratic behaviors; and anxious, fearful behaviors. In group 1 are schizoid personality disorder (socially withdrawn and reclusive individuals) and schizotypal personality disorder (individuals with odd ways of thinking, communicating, and behaving). In group 2 are borderline personality disorder (instability in mood, behavior, and self-image) and antisocial personality disorder (chronically violating the rights of others). Group 3 includes dependent personality disorder (willingness to undergo abuse to maintain a dependent relationship).

ANXIETY DISORDERS (p. 520)

Anxiety disorders take many forms, but in each the amount of anxiety appears to be much more than the situation might call for. These disorders, formerly called neuroses, include posttraumatic stress disorder, generalized anxiety disorder, panic disorder, phobia, and obsessive-compulsive disorder. In generalized anxiety disorder people are continually afraid, but they are not sure about what. Symptoms include physical sensations of fear, motor tension, excessive worry, and constant scanning of the environment for dangers. In panic

disorders there are sudden, often unpredictable attacks of intense fear. Phobias are extreme fears of specific things. The most common are agoraphobia and social phobia. Obsessive-compulsive disorder includes both obsessive thoughts that preoccupy an individual and compulsive behaviors that must be continually repeated to ward off anxiety. Each of the perspectives includes specific ideas about the origin of anxiety and/or its treatment.

AFFECTIVE DISORDERS (p. 526)

1. Affective disorders involve problems of mood and emotion and include feelings of depression and mania. Bipolar disorder includes episodes of both mania and depression. Unipolar disorder refers to problems with depression.

2. Symptoms of depression include dysphoric mood and loss of interest in living, as well as difficulty in sleeping, guilt feelings, inability to think clearly, and thoughts of death. There is an increased risk of suicide in depression. At least some depressions may be associated with a lack of amine neurotransmitter activity. Beck's cognitive theory of depression emphasizes erroneous and exaggerated ways of thinking, while the learned helplessness view of depression asserts that depressed individuals do not feel in control of what happens to them.

3. Bipolar disorders usually appear in adolescence. Heredity, perhaps through a gene carried on the X chromosome, is thought to play a role in this disorder.

SCHIZOPHRENIC DISORDERS (p. 536)

1. Schizophrenia is probably a group of disorders with different causes and outcomes. For a diagnosis of the condition, there must be a deterioration from a previous level of functioning, with symptoms including hallucinations and delusions; disturbed thinking, emotional response, and feelings of identity; and lack of motivation. Type I schizophrenics are those with positive symptoms (delusions, hallucinations, and disordered thinking). Type II schizophrenics have negative symptoms (flattened emotional response and poverty of speech). Type I symptoms are associated with a better chance of improvement.

2. Genetic factors raise the risk of schizophrenia. The role of neurotransmitters may be important: the dopamine hypothesis suggests that an excess of dopamine may be related to schizophrenic behavior. New research techniques may be helpful in understanding more about schizophrenia. These include both CT scans, which can picture the anatomy of a living brain, and PET scans, which allow study of the energy use in different portions of the brain. The vulnerability hypothesis highlights the interaction between the individual's risk factors and the amount of stress in the production of schizophrenic behavior.

KEY TERMS AND CONCEPTS

DSM III

personality disorders

schizoid personality disorder

schizotypal personality disorder

borderline personality disorder

antisocial personality disorder

dependent personality disorder

neuroses

generalized anxiety disorder

phobia

agoraphobia

social phobia

insight

affective disorder

depression

mania

bipolar disorder

unipolar disorder

dysphoric mood

amine neurotransmitter systems

norepinephrine

serotonin

dopamine

amine hypothesis of depression and mania

monoamine oxidase (MAO)

antidepressant

tricyclic

MAO inhibitor

lithium

Beck's cognitive theory of depression

schemata

learned helplessness

schizophrenia

delusion

hallucination

Type I schizophrenia

Type II schizophrenia

positive symptoms

negative symptoms

dementia praecox

dopamine hypothesis of schizophrenia

computerized axial tomography scanner (CT scan)

cerebral ventricles

positron emission tomography scanner (PET scan)

expressed emotion

token economy

vulnerability hypothesis of schizophrenia

SUGGESTED READINGS

SARASON, I. G., and SARASON, B. R. (1984). *Abnormal psychology* (4th ed.). Englewood Cliffs, N.J.: Prentice-Hall.

COLEMAN, J. C., BUTCHER, J. N., and CARSON, R. C. (1984). *Abnormal psychology and modern life* (7th ed.). Glenview, IL: Scott, Foresman.

The readings listed above are two basic and authoritative abnormal psychology texts.

American Psychiatric Association (1981). *Diagnostic and statistical manual of mental disorders* (3rd ed.). Washington, D.C.: American Psychiatric Association. The official classification system used in the United States.

MILLON, T. (1981). *Disorders of personality: DSM III, Axis II*. New York: Wiley. A complete description of what is known about each of the personality disorders described in *DSM III*.

ENDLER, N. S. (1982). *Holiday of darkness*. New York: Wiley-Interscience. An interesting account of a personal experience with depression by a prominent psychologist.

VONNEGUT, M. (1975). *The Eden express*. New York: Bantam Books. A personal account of a dramatic battle with schizophrenia.

THERAPEUTIC BEHAVIOR CHANGE

PSYCHODYNAMIC THERAPIES
Psychoanalysis
Other psychodynamic approaches

HUMANISTIC-EXISTENTIAL THERAPIES
Client-centered therapy
Existential therapy

BEHAVIOR THERAPIES
Therapies based on operant conditioning
Therapies based on classical conditioning
Therapies based on social learning theory

COGNITIVE THERAPIES
Rational-emotive therapy
Cognitive therapy for depression
Self-instructional training

GROUP THERAPY
Specialized group approaches
Family and couples therapy

BIOLOGICAL THERAPIES
Drug therapies
Electroconvulsive therapy

EVALUATION OF THERAPIES
Meta-analysis
FRONTIER 16.1 CAN PSYCHOTHERAPY REDUCE TOTAL HEALTH CARE COSTS?
Comparative outcome research

DISORDERED BEHAVIOR AND PUBLIC POLICY
Criminal responsibility
Institutionalization
Prevention

STUDY OUTLINE

KEY TERMS AND CONCEPTS

SUGGESTED READINGS

CHAPTER SIXTEEN

THERAPEUTIC BEHAVIOR CHANGE

In Chapter 15, we briefly surveyed the main categories of disordered behavior. In this chapter we will describe the different techniques that professional therapists use to try to help people who suffer from these behavior disorders. There are a number of therapies to choose from. The therapeutic approach that has grown out of each perspective reflects that perspective's view of the way that maladaptive behavior develops in the first place.

The biological approach is based on the idea that all behavior is the result of the way the body works—change the body, and you change behavior. Biological therapies include drugs, electroconvulsive therapy, and psychosurgery. The other perspectives examined in this book have given rise to a wide variety of psychological therapies. Figure 16.1 shows one way of organizing the various types of psychological therapies.

According to the psychodynamic approach, unresolved conflicts that took place in childhood are responsible for maladaptive behavior in adulthood. Psychoanalysis and other therapeutic and counseling methods based on the psychodynamic approach focus on helping the client to gain insight into the way that past events have influenced his or her present behavior.

FIGURE 16.1 *Psychological therapies can be organized according to general types and according to various perspectives.*

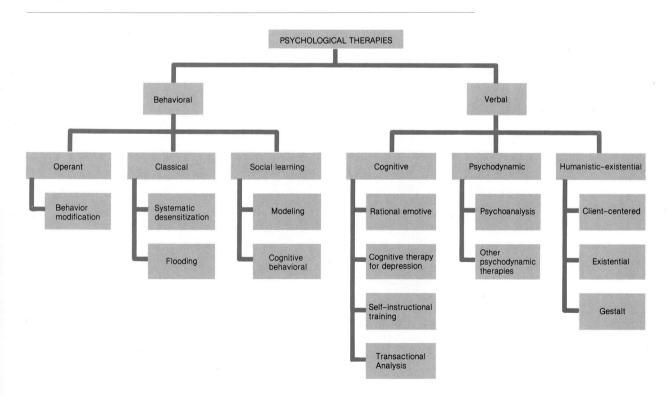

Since behavioral theory holds that maladaptive behavior is learned just like any other behavior and that how and when it was learned are not important, behavioral therapists consider psychoanalysis to be a waste of time. Instead, behavior therapy is aimed directly at helping the client to learn more effective ways to deal with problems in the present.

The cognitive approach has much in common with the behavioral view—both point to learning as the source of the problem, and neither cares much about the person's past—but the cognitive approach stresses the inappropriate thinking that lies behind the maladaptive behavior. Cognitive therapy is based on the idea that changing clients' behavior depends on changing what they think.

The humanistic-existential approach says that maladaptive behavior develops when people feel trapped into living up to society's expectations instead of their own. Humanistic-existential therapy focuses on raising the client's self-esteem as a way of gaining the strength to pay more attention to his or her own needs than to the pressures of society.

According to another point of view, the **community approach,** maladaptive behavior comes from living in disadvantaged environments and becoming alienated from the rest of the community. This method of therapy focuses on changing the environment in which the client lives and on providing social supports and other forms of therapeutic help.

The kind of therapy that is ultimately chosen is influenced by two major factors: the therapist's psychological perspective, and what he or she knows about the causes of the problem and its effective treatment. But these approaches are not meant to be mutually exclusive. In fact, the most effective clinical workers often use combinations of these methods in treating their clients.

PSYCHODYNAMIC THERAPIES

The basic tool in psychotherapy, the primary treatment used by psychodynamically oriented clinicians, is talk. Most psychotherapists have one-to-one relationships with their clients, although sometimes one or more therapists will work with a group of clients; the principles and objectives of therapy are the same in both situations. Psychotherapists try to help their clients to bring their anxieties and conflicts into the open so that the client can determine where they came from, what effect they have, and how to deal with them. Even

FIGURE 16.2 *Throughout his career, Sigmund Freud saw his patients in an office that featured an elaborate couch and items from Freud's collection of objects from tribal cultures. This photo shows his office in London after his flight from Nazi-dominated Vienna.*

therapists who share a common theoretical orientation, however, use differing methods to bring about the self-understanding that they feel is an important step toward personal happiness and effectiveness.

Psychoanalysis

The first formal psychotherapeutic technique—psychoanalysis—was developed by Sigmund Freud. Freud believed that people are often blocked in the present by their inability to free themselves from their past frustrations. In the classic image of psychotherapy, the client lies on the couch (see Figure 16.2). Freud felt that, if his clients could not see him, they would be less inhibited about revealing their inner lives and intimate secrets. He called the method he used **free association.** His clients were instructed to express their thoughts as freely and as uninhibitedly as possible—to talk about anything that came to mind without worrying about being logical or finishing one train of thought before jumping to another.

In psychoanalysis, the major vehicle for achieving therapeutic change is the way that the client and the therapist relate to each other. During therapy, the client-therapist relationship reflects relationships that the client originally experienced with significant figures in his or her earlier life (usually parents, brothers, or sisters). Behaviors and feelings associated with those people will reoccur in therapy; this process is called **transference.** The concept of transference is based on the idea that we do not approach new people as if they were blank screens. Rather, without being aware of it, we seem to transfer what we have already experienced from the past into the present. In **positive transference** the client relates to the therapist with trust and affection. In **negative transference,** however, the client expresses hostility and resentment. Freud felt that analyzing the kind and strength of the transference was the most powerful means of helping patients to achieve insight into their unresolved conflicts (see Figure 16.3).

Therapists are only human. They can have blind spots, too. A therapist's irrational reactions to his or her clients are called **countertransference.** As part of their training, psychoanalysts go through analysis, so that they will have enough self-awareness to recognize

"I hereby dub thee, officially and forevermore, grown up."

(DRAWING BY W. MILLER; © 1978 THE NEW YORKER MAGAZINE, INC.)

FIGURE 16.3 *Psychotherapy aims at increasing maturity through self-understanding. Although progress is not recognized as formally as this cartoon suggests, both the client and the therapist in a successful therapy are aware of this kind of developmental change.*

countertransference and prevent it from interfering with their clients' progress.

The following excerpt illustrates a number of features of psychoanalytic sessions. The analyst (A) encourages the patient (P) to free associate, and the patient shows strong transference reactions toward the analyst. The patient has just expressed concern about a mental block:

A: What comes to your mind about the hesitation in your thinking?

P: I have a sense of fright about my feelings toward you. . . . I was hoping that you could do my analysis. [Elaborates.] Then . . . I felt as if I had found someone who cared and that somehow I would get a relationship here even though I know that that's ridiculous and that I'm just a patient. . . .

A: Try to pursue what comes to your mind about this.

P: . . . I have the feeling that you'll be mad at me if I don't say something, and so I just can't say anything. But the longer the silence lasts the worse it gets.

A: What comes to your mind about the idea that I would be mad at you?

P: I think of the way Mr. Harris [a former therapist] used to react if I didn't say anything. It also makes me think of my father and the way he would say "jump" and I'd have to jump or else he would call me "stupid"—I have a sense of hostility about it. I know when I'm feeling love but I don't know when I'm being hostile. And it scares me most to show my hostile feelings. But I wonder if maybe I have that turned around.

A: What comes to your mind?

P: Maybe I'm really afraid to show my love feelings. I have quite a bit of hostility that I'm aware of, and it's like my mother's. She takes it out on sales people. Last night I dreamed that I was going to do this but then I ran back to Harris instead of to you. Somehow I felt so sorry for you. In the dream I thought, "I'm so sorry that I didn't go to him and when I didn't he cried." But then in the dream I said to myself, "You're not the first one and he's probably been hurt before."

A: Dreams are frequently useful in analysis, but we use them in a special way. After you've told me the dream itself, try to take each of the elements in the dream as it occurred and see what your associations are to each part.

P: The man in the dream somehow reminded me of a boy that I used to go with. He got upset when I left him but he also got over it almost immediately. Somehow there was a feeling of many women being in the dream and that reminds me of my father and all of his affairs.

A: What are the details of your thoughts about the boy that you went with?

P: That was really the worst time in my life and I turned into a terrible person. He was a horrible boy and he came from a very bad family but I would cling to him just as I clung to my life. I had lost all of my feeling of security when we moved to Springfield and so grasped the nearest straw that I could find. I did lose that security that I had. (Dewald, 1972, pp. 22–23)

Both the client and the therapist analyze the behavior that arises during therapeutic sessions. When the therapist gives an interpretation that is anxiety-provoking, clients may become irritated with the therapist

and, to protect themselves, may offer a more acceptable explanation. Reactions that avoid anxiety but interfere with the course of analysis are called **resistance.** Resistance is also analyzed to provide insight. Everything—from dreams to slips of the tongue to silence—is grist for the analyst's mill.

Other psychodynamic therapies

Only a small number of clients choose to be treated through psychoanalysis. It is a long and costly procedure; the therapist and client may meet three or four times a week for several years. Some clients may prefer the greater flexibility offered by other forms of psychodynamic therapy. Psychoanalysts work within a very clear theoretical framework that guides how they think about the client's problems and how they interpret that information to the client. Other psychodynamic therapists do not necessarily have exactly the same set of theoretical views, although, like psychoanalysts, they emphasize understanding the idiosyncratic or personal meanings that clients give to various events and relationships and the specific maladaptive ways they interact with other people. Psychodynamic therapy may be brief or may extend over several years; usually clients see their therapist no more than once a week. The following case illustrates that successful psychodynamic therapy can sometimes require only a few sessions:

A bright college dropout, age 21, applied to a public clinic, asking for psychotherapy because he found himself chronically unable to make a career choice. . . . In a few introductory interviews he described complex and painful relationships with his father and elder brother, and a more pleasant relationship with his sister. He consistently failed to mention his mother, and brushed aside every inquiry made about her.

In the fourth interview, the clinician pointed out that he seemed to be avoiding any thoughts of his mother. This angered the patient. He accused him of treating him according to some old Freudian textbook. But he came into the next interview announcing that the clinician had really hit the nail on the head. He then poured out a long account of his mother's "silent disapproval" of everything he ever did, and added that he thought the "hangup with my mother" might be what was really keeping him from making any choices in his life. Feeling considerably relieved, he thought he did not need to continue in treatment. He terminated therapy and later reported good progress.

Identifying his avoidance of thoughts about his mother was nearly all that was needed in this situation. . . . He did most of the reevaluating on his own, after the therapy had formally ended. (Balsam and Balsam, 1984, p. 54)

HUMANISTIC-EXISTENTIAL THERAPIES

Client-centered therapy

Carl Rogers, one of the most influential therapists with a humanistic perspective, saw psychotherapy quite differently from the way Freud and his followers did. While the focus of psychoanalysis is the relationship between the therapist and the client, Rogers felt that the client alone should be the center of attention. Unlike psychoanalysts, **client-centered therapists** do not provide interpretations or give advice; instead, they concentrate on the client's immediate experiences. Rogers says that the job of the therapist is to try to see the world as the client sees it and to communicate empathy and understanding of what the client is experiencing. Because the therapist's acceptance reduces threat, clients feel freer to explore their own thoughts, feelings, and behaviors.

Rogerian therapists try to create an environment in which clients can "reorganize" their subjective world. Reorganization is needed because maladjusted and anxious people may be threatened when their self-concepts and their experiences don't match. To reduce the threat, they may distort or deny experiences that are inconsistent with their self-concept. The Rogerian therapist tries to help clients to explore these inconsistencies and learn to accept themselves as they are.

In this excerpt from a client-centered therapy session, note how the therapist (T) tries to understand and reflect the client's (C) statements and how decision-making responsibility is placed on the client, not on the therapist:

C: I've never said this before to anyone—but I've thought for such a long time—This is a terrible thing to say, but if I could

just—well [short, bitter laugh; pause], if I could just find some glorious cause that I could give my life for I would be happy. I cannot be the kind of a person I want to be. I guess maybe I haven't the guts—or the strength—to kill myself— and if someone else would relieve me of the responsibility— or I would be in an accident—I—I—just don't want to live.

T: At the present time things look so black to you that you can't see much point in living—.

C: Yes—I wish I'd never started this therapy. I was happy when I was living in my dream world. There I could be the kind of person I wanted to be—But now—There is such a wide, wide gap—between my ideal—and what I am. I wish people hated me. I try to make them hate me. Because then I could turn away from them and could blame them—but no— it is all in my hands—here is my life—and I either accept the fact that I am absolutely worthless—or I fight whatever it is that holds me in this terrible conflict. And I suppose if I accepted the fact that I am worthless, then I could go away someplace—and get a little room someplace—get a mechanical job someplace—and retreat clear back to the security of my dream world where I could do things, have clever friends, be a pretty wonderful sort of person—

T: It's really a tough struggle—digging into this like you are—and at times the shelter of your dream world looks more attractive and comfortable.

C: My dream world or suicide.

T: Your dream world or something more permanent than dreams—.

C: Yes. [A long pause. Complete change of voice.] So I don't see why I should waste your time—coming in twice a week— I'm not worth it—What do you think?

T: It's up to you, Gil—It isn't wasting my time—I'd be glad to see you—whenever you want to come—but it's how you feel about it—if you don't want to come twice a week—or if you do want to come twice a week?—once a week?—It's up to you. [Long pause.]

C: You're not going to suggest that I come in oftener? You're not alarmed and think I ought to come in—every day—until I get out of this?

T: I believe you are able to make your own decision. I'll see you whenever you want to come. (Rogers, 1951, pp. 46–47)

This therapist's words may seem a bit cold and uncaring to you as you read them, but a Rogerian therapist would say them with a great deal of warmth and understanding. Client-centered therapists also strive to communicate warmth nonverbally through gestures and careful attention to what the client is saying.

More recently, Rogers has changed his view of the therapist's role. He now believes that the therapist should express his or her feelings more explicitly about the therapeutic interaction as a way of letting clients know what responses they evoke in other people (Rogers, 1981).

Existential therapy

The emphasis in existential therapy is on helping clients to come to terms with basic issues concerning the meaning of their lives and the choices by which they shape their own destinies. Like many other clinicians who see nonhospitalized clients, most existential therapists work with individuals who are troubled by intense anxiety and/or by depression.

Perhaps because many prominent existential therapists were originally trained as psychoanalysts, existential and psychoanalytic therapy have much in common in their focus on emotions and the way they affect perceptions and behavior. However, unlike many psychodynamic theorists, especially psychoanalysts, existential therapists keep their attention turned more to the present and future and away from the past. According to one prominent existentialist, Rollo May, the therapist's primary role is to help lonely, empty people to develop enough self-confidence to choose to express their own uniqueness rather than to adjust to the threats of life by repressing or distorting their experience.

The existential therapist's role in confronting the client with the possibility of change and with his or her responsibility for deciding whether or not to change is shown in the following example. As an existential therapist would say, this patient (Pt.) wants to be treated as an object in the hands of the therapist (Dr.) rather than as a subject who takes responsibility for her choices and decisions:

Pt.: I don't know why I keep coming here. All I do is tell you the same thing over and over. I'm not getting anywhere. (Pa-

tient complaining that therapist isn't curing her; maintenance of self-as-therapist's object.)

Dr.: I'm getting tired of hearing the same thing over and over too. (Doctor refusing to take responsibility for the progress of therapy and refusing to fulfill patient's expectations that he cure her; refusal of patient-as-therapist's object.)

Pt.: Maybe I'll stop coming. (Patient threatening therapist; fighting to maintain role as therapist's object.)

Dr.: It's certainly your choice. (Therapist refusing to be intimidated; forcing of patient-as-subject.)

Pt.: What do you think I should do? (Attempt to seduce the therapist into role of subject who objectifies patient-object.)

Dr.: What do you want to do? (Forcing again.)

Pt.: I want to get better. (Plea for therapist to "cure.")

Dr.: I don't blame you. (Refusing role of subject-curer and supporting desire on part of patient-as-subject.)

Pt.: If you think I should stay, okay, I will. (Refusing role of subject-who-decides.)

Dr.: You want me to tell you to stay? (Confrontation with patient's evasion of the decision and calling to attention what the patient wants, or how the patient is construing the world of the therapy.)

Pt.: You know what's best; you're the doctor. (Patient's confirmation of her construing of therapy.)

Dr.: Do I act like a doctor? (Keen, 1970, p. 202)

R. D. Laing, another existential therapist, has worked intensively with schizophrenics. He believes that society imposes a falseness on people and that schizophrenia represents the crumbling of this false facade and the direct expression of inner preoccupations, distortions, and fears. Laing treats patients by allowing them to regress into their psychoses because he thinks that it is a necessary step toward a positive integration of personality and recovery.

BEHAVIOR THERAPIES

The therapies that we have discussed so far are based on the assumption that behavior can be changed by understanding and changing emotions. Behavior therapy, on the other hand, assumes that changing behavior will change the individual's feelings of unhappiness, inadequacy, or discomfort.

Before behavior therapy begins, a **behavioral assessment** is carried out. This assessment focuses on identifying the specific settings in which problems occur, not on discovering possible historical reasons for the behavior's origin. A problem is broken down into its components, and therapy is specifically aimed at only those elements that seem to be maladaptive. This means that treatment is individually tailored for each person.

Behavioral approaches to therapy can be divided into several groups. **Applied behavior analysis** relies on operant conditioning. Because it is based on the idea that behavior is determined by its consequences, it stresses the powerful effect of environmental variables in producing significant changes in behavior. The *classical conditioning* approach, an application of Pavlov's conditioning principles, is particularly concerned with conditioned emotional responses such as those involved in phobias or anxiety reactions. The *social learning* approach, a third kind of behavioral therapy, concentrates on the process of learning through observation. Finally, **cognitive behavior modification,** the most recent development among the behavioral therapies, emphasizes that maladaptive behavior is based on the learning of faulty thought patterns that must be identified and replaced. We'll look at all four types in more detail.

Therapies based on operant conditioning

In operant conditioning, the therapist attempts to change behavior by manipulating its consequences. The case of Byron illustrates the combined use of reinforcement and punishment to decrease undesired behaviors:

Byron was a 5-year-old child who had an obsessive-compulsive fascination with electrical devices. He also had a ritual of being unable to sleep except in his parents' bed and a negativistic attitude, which was expressed in a refusal to follow his parents' instructions.

He roamed through the house turning lights on and off and staring at them and unplugging the refrigerator and other appliances. At the grocery store, he cut off

power to the meat counter. At neighbors' houses he unscrewed lightbulbs, dismantled lamps, and unplugged clocks and other appliances. In the evening, it sometimes took his parents two or three hours to get him to bed. The evening was punctuated by requests for water for his thirst and cookies for his hunger. During the night, he continued to get up and would lie down between his parents in their bed. Despite their efforts to remove him, he was usually found asleep there the next morning.

Byron's parents were taught how to make his maladaptive behaviors less rewarding and how to reward his adaptive behaviors. They were instructed to stop all attempts to spank him, reason with him, or understand his behavior. They were to meet all his requests for food prior to bedtime. If he stayed in bed all night, he would receive 8 tokens in the morning. These tokens could then be exchanged on a daily basis for activities such as snacks, watching TV, or visiting friends. If Byron did get into his parents' bed, they were to pretend to be asleep and make it uncomfortable for him by taking up more room themselves. If this failed, his mother was to lead him matter-of-factly back to bed.

When Byron played with switches, he was required to pay half the tokens in his account for each episode, and in addition his parents were instructed to put him in his room for a 30-minute time period. Since he gained tokens during the day only by following instructions, this meant he lost his opportunity to earn tokens. Within 3 or 4 weeks after the behavior therapy began, Byron began to develop friendships with other children and, since his compulsion to manipulate electrical items was controlled, he was again invited into their homes. (Adapted from Ayllon and others, 1977)

Researchers who study operant conditioning procedures to change behavior often work with one person at a time. How can they determine whether the conditioning procedures caused whatever change occurs? One way to test the effect of the procedures is to use a single subject comparison, sometimes called an A-B-A-B experimental design.

The A-B-A-B design consists of obtaining a precontingency, or baseline, measure of the target behaviors (A), reinforcing specific behaviors whenever they occur

FIGURE 16.4 *Sometimes the basic A-B-A-B design is elaborated in order to study the effects of a number of different kinds of treatments on one individual. In the study illustrated here, two drugs, dexedrine and Ritalin, and self-control training were evaluated for their impact on the hyperactive behavior of a child treated in an inpatient psychiatric unit. First a baseline (A) was established, then dexedrine was tried (B). After a second baseline period (A), another drug, Ritalin, was given (C). In the next phase (CD), Ritalin was combined with self-monitoring of behavior and a self-administered token system. Then self-monitoring was used alone (D). Finally, Ritalin and self-monitoring were again combined (CD). As the figure makes clear, when all responses are considered, Ritalin combined with self-monitoring is the most effective treatment. Neither one alone was as powerful as their interactive effect.*

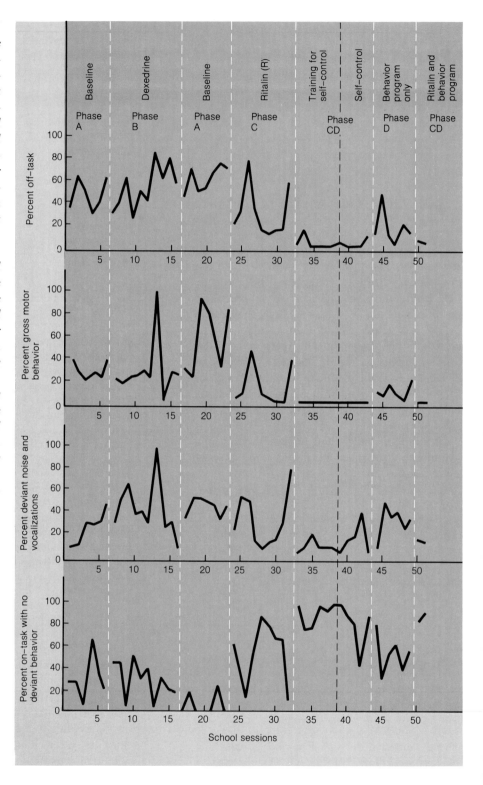

(B), reinstating the conditions of the baseline period (A), and, finally, reinstating reinforcement (B). This design is a very powerful method for isolating the conditions that control behavior. Some designs using this basic idea are even more complex. One such study is illustrated in Figure 16.4.

Therapies based on classical conditioning

The learning perspective presumes that many of our preferences and needs are the product of classical conditioning. According to this view, destructive or abnormal desires can be corrected through the application of specific conditioning procedures. This idea has been clinically applied to help people to stop smoking or drinking. The cigarette or alcoholic beverage is paired with an unpleasant stimulus such as a shock or a nausea-inducing drug. Eventually, after enough pairings, the cigarette or drink arouses such negative responses that clients decrease their drinking or smoking. However, therapies derived from classical conditioning principles are used primarily for anxiety-based disorders because anxiety is thought to come about through conditioned stimuli. We will describe two types of treatment for anxiety or phobias.

SYSTEMATIC DESENSITIZATION

Systematic desensitization involves cognitive activity (thinking and imagining) as well as learning. In desensitization, a client is exposed to a series of scenes that relate to his or her particular fears. The scenes are arranged in a hierarchy and are progressively more anxiety-arousing. The person is trained to relax deeply and to remain relaxed while imagining the scenes. If this procedure makes the client anxious, he or she is allowed to stop imagining the stimulus. If the stimulus is actually present, it will be removed. Then the person is brought back to a state of relaxation. Systematic desensitization is thought to be effective because anxiety is gradually extinguished while a relaxation response that is incompatible with the anxiety is built up.

FLOODING

Like systematic desensitization, **flooding** is used in cases of phobia or specific fear. But flooding differs

from systematic desensitization because, in flooding, the fear-arousing stimuli are not removed when they produce a high level of tension. Also, flooding uses real as well as imagined stimuli. Flooding appears to be an effective technique in some cases (Rimm and Masters, 1979), but because of the high level of stress that it produces, many behavior therapists prefer not to use it unless other, less stressful methods have failed. The use of flooding is shown in the following example:

A 40-year-old woman whose daughter had died two and one-half years earlier in a vacation trailer fire complained of sleeplessness, irritability, loss of weight, and phobias to any material suggesting fire. This even extended to looking at newspapers. Her husband and child complained that the woman's grieving occupied all her time and they could no longer live with the situation. She had already had extensive therapy but seemed to be even more controlled by her grieving after 30 months than she was soon after the daughter's death. Treatment involved five sessions of exposure to anxiety- and grief-producing scenes totaling nine hours. The sessions dealt with vividly imagining the loss of her daughter, handling the daughter's belongings, and visiting places that reminded her of the relationship. Throughout the therapy the client experienced a very high level of grief. Her anxiety about confronting the facts of the daughter's loss eventually lessened. Ten months later she was still much improved, had lost most of her bereavement pain, was working full time, had joined several clubs, and functioned better with her family. (Based on Ramsay, 1976)

Therapies based on social learning theory

Social learning theorists acknowledge the part that conditioning plays in altering behavior, but they emphasize the role of cognitive processes as the mediators of behavior change.

Observing how a model reacts to a situation can provide important clues about how to cope adaptively with that situation. Modeling is a particularly effective

FIGURE 16.5 *Modeling, or observing another person engage successfully and without anxiety, in an activity that a person fears, can be an effective way to counteract anxiety. In this photo, the child, afraid of dogs, is more likely to reach out toward the animal and eventually pat it in the company of other children who are obviously enjoying contact with the dog.*

technique to use with children. Individuals who have seen models not get hurt when doing something that they are afraid to do (for example, pet a dog) reduce their efforts to avoid that behavior (see Figure 16.5).

Modeling approaches can also be used to strengthen socially appropriate behavior. For example, a frequent therapeutic use of social learning theory is in **assertiveness training.** Some people who lack self-confidence allow others to manipulate them too easily and may not know how to react assertively in certain types of situations. Modeling can play an important role in teaching appropriate assertive behavior. Frightened individuals can watch another person saying no or standing up for his or her rights without being obnoxious, annoying, or aggressive and then can practice the responses themselves. In the following example, a therapist served as a model for his client, a male college student who had difficulty making dates with girls. The client began by pretending to ask for a date over the telephone:

CLIENT: By the way [pause], I don't suppose you want to go out Saturday night?

THERAPIST: Up to actually asking for the date you were very good. However, if I were the girl, I think I might have been a bit offended when you said, "By the way." It's like asking her out is pretty casual. Also, the way you phrased the question, you are kind of suggesting to her that she doesn't want to go out with you. Pretend for the moment I'm you. Now, how does this sound: There is a movie at the Varsity Theatre this Saturday that I want to see. If you don't have other plans, I'd like very much to take you.

CLIENT: That sounded good. Like you were sure of yourself and like the girl, too.

THERAPIST: Why don't you try it.

CLIENT: You know that movie at the Varsity? Well, I'd like to go, and I'd like to take you Saturday, if you don't have anything better to do.

THERAPIST: Well, that certainly was better. Your tone of voice was especially good. But the last line, "if you don't have anything better to do" sounds like you don't think you have much to offer. Why not run through it one more time.

CLIENT: I'd like to see the show at the Varsity, Saturday, and if you haven't made other plans, I'd like to take you.

THERAPIST: Much better. Excellent, in fact. You were confident, forceful, and sincere. (Rimm and Masters, 1979, p. 94)

By rehearsing alternative approaches to social behavior and receiving reinforcement from the therapist, clients learn the skills for handling problematic situations more effectively, and they come to believe they are able to handle the situations. This feeling of **self-efficacy** is an important determinant of whether the behavior will occur. It illustrates a strong emphasis in much of current behavior therapy—the incorporation of cognitive preparation into the traditional conditioning elements in therapy.

Early behavior therapies based on conditioning procedures have often been effective in changing behavior, but in many cases the behavior change stopped shortly after the treatment did. Because of these sometimes short-lived results, behavior therapists have been motivated to use a combination of methods. They continue to emphasize identification of the specific environmental conditions, now including particular thoughts that the situation evokes, that are causing maladaptive behavior. But they are also probing more deeply into the variety of factors that may contribute to these conditions.

An example of this broadening of behavior therapy

is the treatment of alcoholism. An analysis of the circumstances under which alcoholism occurs might show that a client drinks to excess when he or she is depressed. Thus, simply attacking the drinking behavior may not work. Instead, the situational factors that lead to depression should also be determined. In a particular case, marital problems might be the cause of depression. If that were so, treating only the drinking problem would probably be ineffective.

At the same time that characteristics such as personality and past experience have become important to behaviorally oriented therapists, many psychotherapists are becoming convinced that some behavioral techniques such as practicing new behaviors may be useful treatment tools. This change suggests that a gradual integration of psychodynamic and behavioral therapeutic methods is taking place.

COGNITIVE THERAPIES

Like the psychodynamic and humanistic-existential therapies that we discussed earlier, cognitive therapies are based primarily on talking. But in many ways they have closer ties with learning theory than with the psychodynamic perspective. In simple terms, cognitive therapists are concerned with their clients' thinking in the same way that behavior therapists are concerned with their overt behavior. Cognitive therapists concentrate on helping their clients to identify and change the irrational ideas that interfere with their effective behavior and cause them to feel unhappy and inadequate.

Rational-emotive therapy

Albert Ellis has developed a form of cognitive therapy called **rational-emotive therapy**, or **RET** (Ellis and Grieger, 1977). Ellis contends that all effective psychotherapists, whether or not they realize it, function as teachers for their clients. They help their clients to modify unrealistic and illogical thoughts and emotions and ultimately to change their behavior. In a sense, the therapist teaches clients to talk to themselves, to replace irrational thoughts with thoughts that fit reality better and do not arouse anxiety. Table 16.1 lists 12 common irrational beliefs.

A rational-emotive therapist may devote significant portions of a session to explaining and demonstrating productive thinking and to persuading the client to think and behave in these more effective ways. The following excerpt from a session of rational-emotive therapy illustrates this method:

T: What are you really afraid of in regard to marrying?

C: Of rejection, it would seem. Of being left alone once again, after I had built up high hopes of remaining together with a man forever, as I did with my ex-fiance.

T: That's a surface explanation that really doesn't explain

TABLE 16.1   COMMON IRRATIONAL BELIEFS

1. The idea that it is a dire necessity for an adult to be loved by everyone for everything he does

2. The idea that certain acts are awful or wicked, and that people who perform such acts should be severely punished

3. The idea that it is horrible when things are not the way one would like them to be

4. The idea that human misery is externally caused and is forced on one by outside people and events

5. The idea that if something is or may be dangerous or fearsome one should be terribly upset about it

6. The idea that it is easier to avoid than to face life difficulties and self-responsibilities

7. The idea that one needs something other or stronger or greater than oneself on which to rely

8. The idea that one should be thoroughly competent, intelligent and achieving in all possible respects

9. The idea that because something once strongly affected one's life, it should indefinitely affect it

10. The idea that one must have certain and perfect control over things

11. The idea that human happiness can be achieved by inertia and inaction

12. The idea that one has virtually no control over one's emotions and that one cannot help feeling certain things

Source: Adapted from Ellis, 1970.

anything. First of all, you are constantly getting rejected, the way you are going on now, because you pick men who aren't marriageable or whom you refuse to wed. Therefore, your hopes of a prolonged, intense involvement are perpetually being dashed—rejected. Secondly, you are really rejecting yourself, all the time. For you are assuming that if you did get refused by some man, just as you once did, you couldn't possibly stand it—weakling that you are! This is a complete vote of nonconfidence in yourself. You are therefore truly refusing to accept yourself as you are. You are demanding that you be perfectly safe.

C: But isn't it better to be safe than hurt?

T: You mean, isn't it better to have never loved and never lost?

C: O.K. But if losing is so dreadful, isn't that better?

T: But why should losing be so dreadful?

C: Oh, loneliness. Not ever getting what you want.

T: But aren't you lonely this way? And do you now get what you want?

C: No, I don't. But I also don't get what I very much don't want.

T: Partly. But not as much as you think.

C: What do you mean?

T: I first of all mean what you mean, that you do not like to get rejected—and who the hell does?—and that you are avoiding this dislikeable event by not trying to get accepted. But I mean, secondly, that what you really dislike most about being rejected is not the refusal itself—since that merely gets you what you have when you do not try for acceptance; namely, being alone—but the belief that this kind of loneliness makes you a slob, a worthless person.

C: Oh, but I do dislike, and dislike very much, the refusal itself. I hate to be refused and then have to be by myself.

T: Partly. But suppose you won one of the males you desired and he died, and you lost him that way. Would that make you feel as badly as if you won him, he were still alive, and he then rejected you?

C: No, I guess it wouldn't.

T: Ah! You see what I'm getting at?

C: That it's not really the loss of the man that I'm concerned about, but his rejection of me. (Ellis, 1973, pp. 47–48)

As you can see, rational-emotive therapists take a much more direct approach than other therapists do. They actively comment on their clients' behavior and are quite open with advice. The therapist also spends considerable time discussing homework assignments for the client. These might include practicing ways of behaving more assertively with co-workers or family members without alienating them.

Cognitive therapy for depression

Another prominent cognitive therapist, Aaron Beck, has done a great deal of work with depressed individuals. Beck also focuses on replacing inaccurate thoughts. One of the major elements in the thinking of depressed people is overgeneralization. Beck challenges these overgeneralizations in therapy. In the following example, the client had said that swimming makes her feel better but it seemed impossible to arrange:

C: There is nowhere I could go swimming.

T: How could you find a place?

C: There is a Y—if I could get there. . . . I'd get my hair wet and get a cold.

T: How could you get there?

C: My husband would take me.

T: How about your wet hair?

C: I couldn't take a hair dryer; someone would steal it.

T: Could you do something about that?

C: They don't have lockers.

T: How do you know?

C: I just don't think they do.

T: For the first step, why don't you call up and see if they do. (Beck and others, 1978, p. 132)

After this session, the client got the necessary information and began her swimming sessions. Making arrangements had not seemed possible to her until the therapist spelled them out for her step by step and challenged her generalized view that the whole plan was impossible.

Self-instructional training

Self-instructional training is derived both from RET and from the work of the Russian psychologist Aleksandr Luria (1961), who theorized that children develop control over their behavior first by being told what to do by others, then by telling themselves out loud, and finally by talking to themselves. Donald Meichenbaum has translated this idea into **self-instructional training (SIT).** His approach is often used with children. It involves identifying maladaptive thoughts; watching the therapist model effective behavior, including task appraisal, ways to guide performance, statements about personal adequacy, and self-reinforcement for success; and performing the behavior, first by verbalizing all the strategies out loud and then by covertly rehearsing them while the therapist provides feedback.

GROUP THERAPY

Most of the techniques that we have discussed can be adapted for use in **group therapy.** Group methods are more economical than individual therapy; it reduces the cost to the individual and makes maximum use of highly trained and sometimes scarce personnel.

Many group therapies are based on the psychodynamic model, but behavioral therapies, especially social learning and cognitive behavioral techniques, can also be adapted for use with groups. Group programs for weight control, stopping smoking, controlling alcohol abuse, and assertiveness training combine these behavioral methods with the social supports available from group participation. Cognitive techniques like rational-emotive therapy also frequently use a group format.

Some advocates believe that group therapy is more effective than individual therapy, regardless of the therapeutic procedures employed. Group members usually come to realize that other people have faced problems similar to their own or that others—even though their problems differ—have troubles to cope with, too. Individuals have an opportunity to observe how other group members handle the problems that arise during each session. For some people group therapy can be a testing ground for new approaches to interpersonal relationships. For others the most significant aspect of the group may be the members' relationship to the therapist. In group therapy each member has the attention of the therapist for only short periods. The therapist attempts to help group members learn to share an authority figure as well as their feelings. However, indi-

viduals who are unable to express their ideas and emotions with others may not benefit as much from group therapy as they would from individual treatment.

Specialized group approaches

Some therapeutic approaches have been developed especially for use with groups. Among these are well-defined methods such as *Transactional Analysis* and *Gestalt* therapy.

TRANSACTIONAL ANALYSIS

Practitioners of **Transactional Analysis (TA)** emphasize gaining insight into the defensive social roles that people habitually play. The leader of a transactional analysis group focuses on the basic units of social relationships, which are called "transactions." The therapy stresses people's tendency to set up interpersonal transactions on the basis of their unrecognized personal needs and conflicts rather than on reality and is directed toward helping clients to discover the unconscious factors that lead them to play the games that characterize their relationships. In these transactions, people may act out roles, as a Parent, a Child, or an Adult, depending on the situation and on their attitudes toward themselves and toward the person with whom they are interacting. The goal of transactional therapy is to teach people to respond as Adults in all situations.

GESTALT THERAPY

In **Gestalt therapy,** originated by Fritz Perls, the therapist uses a variety of techniques, including role playing, to maneuver the client into releasing strong emotions. Unlike humanistic therapists who stress the importance of unconditional positive regard for the client, Perls believed that the therapist's main task was to frustrate the clients in order to make them angry enough to fight out conflicts with authority.

One Gestalt procedure is the "hot seat," where a client volunteers to interact with the therapist and to role play for the group. One or more empty chairs allow the client to switch roles by moving back and forth.

Gestalt therapists believe that anxiety and personality disorders arise when people dissociate parts of themselves from awareness, particularly their needs for personal gratification. Because dreams often contain clues to dissociated parts of the self, Gestalt therapists in their work with individuals and groups encourage discussion and acting out of dreams. Fritz Perls is the therapist (T) in the following case of a woman (C) who was a member of a Gestalt group:

C: In my dream, I'm sitting on a platform, and there's somebody else with me, a man, and maybe another person, and—ah—a couple of rattlesnakes. And one's up on the platform, now, all coiled up, and I'm frightened. . . . And . . . the other snake's down below, and there's a dog down there. . . .

T: So, up here is one rattlesnake and down below is another rattlesnake and the dog.

C: And the dog is sort of sniffing at the rattlesnake. He's—ah—getting very close to the rattlesnake, sort of playing with it, and I wanna stop—stop him from doing that.

T: Tell him.

C: Dog, stop! (T: Louder.) Stop! (T: Louder.) (Shouts) STOP! (T: Louder.) (Screams) STOP!

T: Does the dog stop?

C: He's looking at me. Now he's gone back to the snake. Now—now, the snake's sort of coiling up around the dog, and the dog's lying down, and the snake's coiling around the dog, and the dog looks very happy.

T: Ah! Now have an encounter between the dog and the rattlesnake.

C: You want me to play them?

T: Both. Sure. This is your dream. Every part is a part of yourself.

C: I'm the dog. [Hesitantly] Huh. Hello, rattlesnake. It sort of feels good with you wrapped around me.

T: Look at the audience. Say this to somebody in the audience.

C: [Laughs gently] Hello, snake. It feels good to have you wrapped around me. . . .

T: Let this develop. . . . Now dance rattlesnake. [She moves slowly and sinuously, gracefully.] . . . How does it feel to be a rattlesnake now? . . .

C: Quite aware of not letting anything get too close, ready to strike.

T: Say this to us. "If you come too close, I—"

C: If you come too close, I'll strike back.

T: I don't hear you. I don't believe you, yet.

C: If you come too close, I will strike back!

T: Say this to each one, here.

C: If you come too close, I will strike back!

T: How are your legs? I experience you as being somewhat wobbly.

C: Yeah.

T: That you don't really take a stand. . . . Now say again the sentence, "If you come too close—" [She makes an effort.] . . . [Laughter]

C: If—if you . . .

T: O.K., change. Say "Come close." [Laughter]

C: Come close.

T: How do you feel now?

C: Warm.

T: You feel somewhat more real?

C: Yeah.

T: O.K. . . . So what we did is we took away some of the fear of being in touch. So, from now on, she'll be a bit more in touch. (Perls, 1969, pp. 162–164)

This case illustrates the high activity level of the Gestalt therapist. Perls did not hesitate to tell the client what to do and was not shocked by how the client did it.

EXPERIENTIAL GROUPS

A number of other group therapies focus on improving the functioning of already adequate individuals. **Encounter groups** and human relations training (**T groups**) share a commitment to enhancing self-awareness, increasing intimacy with others, and understanding the experience of being a group member. Group leaders try to eliminate social conventions, status symbols, and ordinary procedural rules to allow the group members to reexamine their assumptions about themselves and their relationships with others. Various training exercises may be used to heighten such awareness.

An encounter group can result in a great deal of closeness, but sometimes a negative confrontation occurs that is not helpful to any of the participants. In the following excerpt, Norma scolds Alice, who had made some quite vulgar and contemptuous remarks to John:

NORMA: [Loud sigh] Well, I don't have any respect for you, Alice. *None!* [Pause] There's about a hundred things going through my mind I want to say to you, and by God I hope I get through 'em all! . . . I personally don't think John has any problems that are any of your damn business! . . . Any real woman that I know wouldn't have acted as you have this week, and particularly what you said this afternoon. . . . I'm just shaking I'm so mad at you—I don't think you've been real once this week! . . . I'm so infuriated that I want to come over and beat the hell out of you!! I want to slap you across the mouth so hard and—oh, and you're so, you're many years above me—and I respect age, and I respect people who are older than me, but I don't respect you, Alice, at all! [A startled pause] (Rogers, 1970, pp. 31–32)

FIGURE 16.6 *Family therapy sessions are useful because they give both the therapist and the family members a chance to understand the typical interaction patterns that may be causing difficulties.*

On the other hand, strongly positive feelings sometimes arise among the group members. One vivid example is that of Jerry, a competent business executive:

Somewhat puzzled by the statements of others in the group, he said in an early session: "I look at myself with some strangeness because I have no friends, for example, and I don't seem to require friends." In a later session when he heard Beth, a married woman, talking of a remoteness she felt between herself and her husband and how much she craved a deeper and more communicative relationship, his face began to work and his jaw to quiver. Roz, another member of the group, seeing this, went over and put her arm around him and he broke into literally uncontrollable sobs. He had discovered a loneliness in himself of which he had been completely unaware and from which he had been well defended by an armor-plated shell of self-sufficiency (adapted from Rogers, 1970, p. 109)

Family and couples therapy

Sometimes therapy focuses on individuals who already constitute a group. Two examples are family therapy and couples therapy.

Family therapy often comes about because one member of a family, usually a child, is referred to a mental health professional. If it seems that maladaptive interactions with other members of the family are part of the problem, one of the most effective ways that a therapist can help the child is to work with all the family members together (see Figure 16.6).

Couples therapy usually comes about because one or both of the partners believe that the relationship is troubled or are contemplating ending it through separation or divorce. By seeing the therapist together, the partners can more easily identify problems and alter the ways that they relate to each other. The main advantage of couples therapy is that the therapist, as an impartial observer, can actually witness the couple's inter-

565

actions rather than hearing about them in a secondhand and perhaps one-sided report. Both family therapy and couples therapy can be carried out from one of several perspectives. Family therapy is likely to include behavioral or psychodynamic approaches. Couples therapy often utilizes a cognitive focus as well. Table 16.2 illustrates the kind of self-monitoring that might be used by couples participating in a behaviorally oriented therapeutic program.

BIOLOGICAL THERAPIES

Drug therapy and electroconvulsive therapy (ECT) are the two general approaches most likely to be used by therapists who have a biological perspective. Of these, the various drug therapies are by far the most common. They are used for a wide variety of disordered behavior. ECT, now used far less often than formerly, is considered mainly for severely depressed individuals when drug treatment has not been effective.

Drug therapies

The fact that drugs affect behavior is hardly news. For many years, researchers, therapists, and members of the general public have known that narcotics such as morphine reduce pain, that sedatives such as barbiturates reduce anxiety and induce sleep, and that stimulants such as caffeine increase alertness. Only recently, however, have chemicals been used extensively to treat almost the entire range of behavior disorders. Each year, in the United States alone, more than 200 million prescriptions are filled for drugs that affect moods, thought, and behavior. Table 16.3 lists some of the drugs prescribed for the treatment of anxiety, schizophrenia, and the affective disorders.

TABLE 16.2 EXAMPLES OF ITEMS FROM THE SPOUSE-OBSERVATION CHECKLIST

TYPE OF BEHAVIOR	ITEM
Shared activities	We sat and read together. We took a walk.
Pleasing interactive events	Spouse asked me how my day was. Talked about personal feelings. Spouse showed interest in what I said by agreeing or asking relevant questions.
Displeasing interactive events	Spouse commanded me to do something. Spouse complained about something I did. Spouse interrupted me.
Pleasing affectionate behavior	We held each other. Spouse hugged or kissed me.
Displeasing affectionate behavior	Spouse rushed into intercourse without foreplay. Spouse rejected my sexual advances.
Pleasing instrumental events	Spouse played with the children. Spouse did the dishes.
Displeasing instrumental events	Spouse yelled at the children. Spouse left a sink full of dishes. Spouse talked too much about work.

Source: Adapted from Jacobson and others, 1980.

TABLE 16.3 DRUGS USED IN THE TREATMENT OF ANXIETY DISORDERS, SCHIZOPHRENIC DISORDERS, AND AFFECTIVE DISORDERS

CLASS	GENERIC NAME	TRADE NAME	USE AND EFFECTS
DRUGS FOR ANXIETY DISORDERS			
ANTIANXIETY DRUGS (minor tranquilizers)	Diazepam	Valium	Used to treat symptoms of anxiety and tension in nonpsychotic individuals. Side effects include drowsiness and lethargy. Danger of developing drug dependence. May be toxic in large doses.
	Chlordiazepoxide	Librium	
	Clorazepate	Tranxene	
	Flurazepam	Dalmane	
	Oxazepam	Serax	
DRUGS FOR SCHIZOPHRENIC DISORDERS			
ANTIPSYCHOTIC DRUGS (major tranquilizers)			Used to treat psychotic symptoms, especially in schizophrenic disorder. Prescribed to counteract extreme agitation, delusions, hallucinations, and violent behavior. Side effects include dryness of the mouth and jaundice. If used over a long period may produce serious motor disturbances which include tremors of the arms and legs and immobility of the facial muscles.
Phenothiazines	Chlorpromazine	Thorazine	
	Thioridazine	Mellaril	
	Perphenazine	Trilafon	
	Prochlorperazine	Compazine	
	Promazine	Sparine	
	Trifluoperazine	Stelazine	
Butyrophenones Thioxanthenes	Fluphenazine	Prolixin	
	Haloperidol	Haldol	
	Chlorprothixene	Taractan	
	Thiothixine	Navane	
DRUGS FOR AFFECTIVE DISORDERS			
ANTIDEPRESSANT DRUGS			Used to treat relatively severe depressive symptoms of the unipolar type. Variable effectiveness in moderating symptoms. Slow-acting. May take up to three weeks before response is seen. Many side effects, some dangerous. MAO inhibitors require restrictions in diet because of serious interactive effects with certain food chemicals.
Tricyclics	Imipramine	Tofranil	
	Amitriptyline	Elavil	
	Nortriptyline	Aventyl	
	Protriptyline	Vivactil	
Monoamine oxidase (MAO) inhibitors	Isocarboxazid	Marplan	
	Phenelzine	Nardil	
	Tranylcypromine	Parnate	
ANTIMANIC DRUGS	Lithium carbonate	Eskalith	Used to treat manic episodes and some severe depressions, especially those that alternate with mania. Effective in reducing or preventing manic episodes but variable success with depressions. Many possible side effects if use not closely monitored. High toxic potential.
		Lithane	
		Lithonate	
		Lithotabs	
		Phi-Lithium	

ANTIANXIETY DRUGS

Surveys have shown that more than 15 percent of Americans between the ages of 18 and 74 use antianxiety, tranquilizing drugs such as Valium. Between 15 and 20 percent of the people who visit physicians are the "worried well" who do not have a clear physical disorder that might explain their symptoms. Some physicians routinely prescribe antianxiety medication for such patients; about 90 percent of the prescriptions for antianxiety drugs are written by general practitioners. These drugs are designed to reduce anxiety as much as possible without affecting other capabilities, such as alertness or concentration. But it may be true that, by altering mood, these medications may also alter the way that people appraise their situation (see Figure 16.7).

One well-established drawback of antianxiety drugs is the dependency or addiction that results from their continued use. People who use drugs such as Valium can become physiologically dependent on them and can experience characteristic withdrawal symptoms (such as restlessness, anxiety, and nausea) when they stop taking them.

ANTIPSYCHOTIC DRUGS

Antianxiety drugs are often described as "minor" tranquilizers, in contrast to the "major" tranquilizers that are used to treat schizophrenic disorders. These drugs, introduced over 30 years ago, are now so widely used that nearly all schizophrenic patients living in the United States, Canada, or Western Europe have received an antipsychotic drug at one time or another. In fact, it is common practice to recommend that the medication be continued indefinitely once the individual has returned to the community (Carpenter and Heinrichs, 1983). But these drugs are not perfect. One of their most serious side effects is the possible development of **tardive dyskinesia,** a nonreversible disorder in which the individual makes uncontrollable movements, often facial grimaces. These movements are so dramatic that they make the person's ordinary social interaction very difficult. Continued use of the drugs may also undermine the patient's social and psychological adjustment over the long term.

Recently, a growing appreciation of the risks involved in the long-term, continuous use of these medications has led to a search for alternatives. Antipsychotic drugs are not equally effective with all schizophrenic individuals or at all points in the course of a schizophrenic disorder. This is not surprising because, as Chapter 15 pointed out, the term *schizophrenia* probably includes several types of disorders that researchers and clinicians have not yet succeeded in differentiating. Some patients do well after discontinuing the drugs, while others would probably do poorly with or without drugs. One way to find out is to discontinue drug administration after the person has improved and then see what happens; if symptoms begin to worsen, the medication can be reinstated. Another strategy that researchers are pursuing is the development of new drugs that more efficiently regulate the activity level of dopamine, the neurotransmitter that seems related to the development of schizophrenia (Friedhoff, 1983). The influence of the stress and vulnerability approach has led some researchers to study

---

FIGURE 16.7 *Tranquilizers reduce anxiety and tension. However, at times some users of drugs like Valium may wonder whether their feelings of relaxation and optimism are due more to the drugs than to the realities of life.*

"I see a substantial upswing in the economy by October, but who knows? Maybe it's the Valium talking."

the effects of the combination of drugs and cognitive-behavioral therapy to promote interpersonal skills. Drugs may be used at first because a quick relief is needed, but then family therapy and social skills training may help significantly in maintaining the initial improvement (Falloon and Liberman, 1983).

ANTIDEPRESSANT DRUGS

Although many depressed people are anxious, antianxiety drugs are frequently not much help to them. Instead, physicians will prescribe antidepressant drugs if the symptoms of depression are reasonably severe. As noted in Chapter 15, there are two major groups of these drugs: **tricyclics** and **monoamine oxidase (MAO) inhibitors.** Drugs from the tricyclic group are usually tried first, because their side effects are not as severe as those of the MAO inhibitors. Drugs in the MAO group can cause dangerous elevations in blood pressure if the individual takes them along with certain foods, such as

cheeses and some types of wine. One disadvantage of both drug groups is that they do not begin to be effective for three or four weeks after starting the medication. Antidepressant drug treatment is often combined with some type of psychotherapy or behavior therapy.

ANTIMANIC DRUGS

Antimanic drugs are sometimes more effective in treating depression than antidepressants are. This is probably because bipolar disorders often begin with one or more episodes of depression before a manic or hypomanic (less severe manic behavior) episode occurs. In choosing the most effective medication, the clinician will usually ask if any of the person's relatives have shown manic or hypomanic symptoms. If some have, then *lithium* may be the most effective drug to treat the depression.

Lithium compounds are generally the treatment chosen for people who have periods of manic behavior or the manic and depressive phases typical of bipolar disorder. The medication can have severe side effects, so its level in the blood must be frequently and carefully monitored. It seems to be effective treatment, although one problem has been that some individuals stop taking the medication, apparently because they miss the pleasurable feelings or highs that are part of the transition into a period of manic behavior (Jamison and others, 1980). In this case the therapist must deal with the client's positive perceptions of the disorder as well as prescribe an effective medication.

Electroconvulsive therapy

Another biologically based treatment, **electroconvulsive therapy,** or **ECT,** can be useful in depression, especially when there is a high risk of suicide, because its effects can be immediate rather than delayed for several weeks, as occurs with the tricyclics and MAO inhibitors (see Figure 16.8). While still commonly used,

FIGURE 16.8 *Electroconvulsive therapy is sometimes used when a depressed person is considered a high suicide risk. The ECT treatments often bring a rapid change in depressive behavior.*

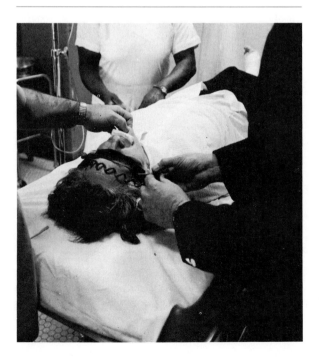

ECT has decreased in popularity as drug therapies, especially the use of antidepressant medications, have become the preferred treatment. There are several reasons for the decline in popularity. First, ECT, which is easy and inexpensive to administer, was probably overused in the past. It was the treatment for a wide range of problems, though research now suggests that it cannot relieve anxiety disorders and is of questionable value for schizophrenic patients. Concerns have also been raised about the safety of ECT because some instances of permanent memory loss have been reported. In any case, even if the results are dramatically positive, the possibility of a relapse is high. Because the reasons for ECT's effectiveness are not understood and because it seems inhumane to many people, there has been increased public resistance to its use. However, available scientific evidence suggests that ECT is an acceptably safe treatment, especially since the introduction of a modified procedure in which electrodes are placed on only one side of the head (Crowe, 1984).

EVALUATION OF THERAPIES

Being aware of all the therapeutic possibilities is not enough. We need to know: Do they work? Which are most effective? What kinds of problems are helped most by which approaches? Can therapies be harmful as well as helpful?

These questions are significant for many reasons. Selecting the most appropriate kind of intervention is vital in human terms; it is also important for economic reasons. Each year millions of dollars are spent on therapeutic treatments. More and more of the costs are being paid by so-called third parties—insurance companies or government agencies. As the costs rise, these and other organizations increase their demands for accountability. They want demonstrations that the treatments are useful. Some of the economic implications of psychotherapy are discussed in Frontier 16.1.

Perhaps the first question to be answered is whether

FIGURE 16.9 *Meta-analysis allows the statistical combination of many separate and often very different studies. This figure illustrates the general finding from combining 475 controlled studies of therapeutic effectiveness. Overall, the average person in the treated group was 0.85 standard deviations above the mean of the control group on the measures used to evaluate therapeutic outcome. This difference is a large one when compared to the effect of many experimental interventions used in psychology or education. For example, cutting the size of a school class in half causes the increase in achievement of 0.15 standard deviation units. The effect of 9 months of instruction in reading results in an improvement in reading skills of 0.67 standard deviation units (Smith and others, 1980, p. 88).*

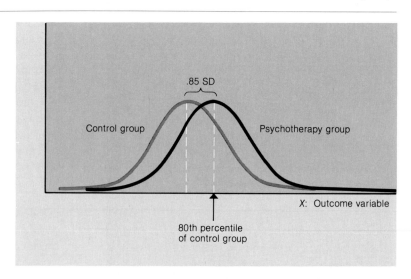

psychological therapies are actually helpful. In one of the most famous investigations of this issue, the British psychologist Hans Eysenck (1952) seriously questioned psychotherapy's effectiveness. Eysenck argued that two-thirds of all anxious patients, the people who most often receive psychotherapy, would recover within two years without any treatment at all and that psychotherapy produced no better rate of recovery. Except for interventions derived from learning theory or behavior therapy, Eysenck argued, psychological therapies had no effect. Of course this pronouncement, coming from a well-known psychologist, caused an uproar. It was not until quite a few years later that the controversy was finally ended.

Meta-analysis

Studies of the effectiveness of psychotherapy are expensive, because of the large amount of time required and the number of professionals involved. For this practical reason such investigations usually include at most a few types of therapy and a small number of therapists, but this makes it difficult to draw general conclusions from any single piece of research. One way of dealing with this problem is to apply meta-analysis. In **meta-analysis** the results of a large number of studies can be integrated through a statistical procedure that compares the outcome measures for the treated and control groups while taking the variability in the control groups into account (Smith and Glass, 1977). When this procedure is used, psychotherapy looks pretty effective. The meta-analysis of the data from 475 controlled studies that included tens of thousands of people showed that at the end of treatment, the average applicant for therapy was better off than 80 percent of those who need therapy but remain untreated (Smith and others, 1980). Figure 16.9 illustrates this finding.

Opinions about the procedure of meta-analysis are divided. Some see it as the best available way to understand a very complex question. Others criticize it for lumping excellent, well-controlled research in with mediocre or poor efforts. Nevertheless, the findings of this study, and those of others using the technique, have become important sources of evidence about the effectiveness of psychotherapy.

FRONTIER 16.1
CAN PSYCHOTHERAPY REDUCE TOTAL HEALTH CARE COSTS?

The American public, health insurers, employers who pay employee health insurance premiums, and the federal government are all worried about the skyrocketing costs of medical care, which have gone up far faster than inflation. Part of this rise can be explained by the development of sophisticated and very costly diagnostic tests—for instance, CT and PET scanners—and of surgical techniques, such as those used in organ transplants and open heart operations. Use of mental health services has also increased as health care professionals and the general public become more aware of the effectiveness of many of these therapies in improving both health and the quality of life.

As we point out in this chapter, the effectiveness of psychotherapy is a difficult area to research; even more difficult are questions such as: Which particular therapy will be most helpful? How many therapeutic sessions are most cost effective? What are the most appropriate criteria for assessing improvement? These questions all focus on whether psychotherapy increases individuals' ability to function and makes their lives happier and more satisfying. From the point of view of health care costs, there is another question— Can money spent for psychotherapy reduce individuals' total medical bills? Most insurance companies look at mental health care as a kind of luxury, without a proven dollar value. Whenever the high cost of medical care and the size and rate of increase of health insurance premiums are discussed, questions are often raised about the necessity or the excessive use of a variety of treatments, but especially of psychotherapy. As a result, many health insurance plans do not cover psychotherapy, cover only a portion of the cost, or limit the total paid much more severely than for other kinds of health care coverage.

For more than 20 years, researchers have been trying to determine whether the view of psychotherapy as a luxury is justified. An early study, carried out in

CAN PSYCHOTHERAPY REDUCE TOTAL HEALTH CARE COSTS?

Germany, found that people treated with psychoanalytic therapy used hospital facilities less than a control group (Duehrssen and Jorswiek, 1965). Since this finding had important implications, researchers scurried to look at the matter further. After about 10 years, a review of this research concluded that the availability of psychotherapy reduced the public's use of medical services by about 20 percent (Jones and Fischi, 1979). Other researchers revised the reduction

downward, to somewhere between 0 and 14 percent (Mumford and others, 1978).

In the period between 1978 and 1982, there were at least 58 controlled studies of the influence of psychotherapy on total health care costs. The outcomes of all the studies ranged from a 72 percent increase to a 182 percent decrease in total health care costs after individuals received psychotherapy. When the statistical technique of meta-analysis was applied to com-

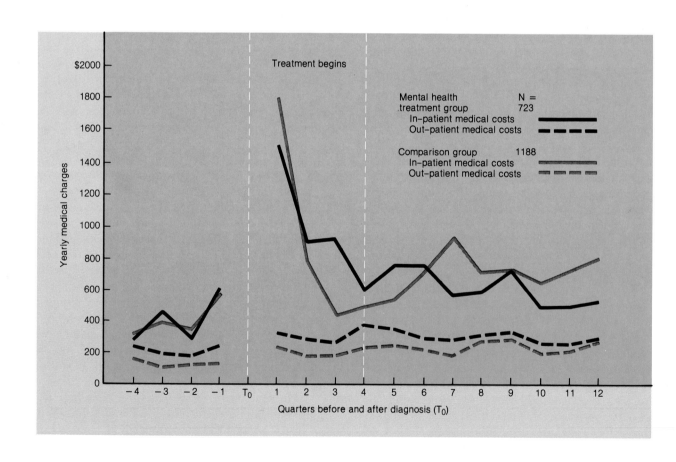

bine these studies, the results showed that individuals who had had psychotherapy needed hospital inpatient facilities less in later years, although their use of outpatient services did not change (Mumford and others, 1984). People over 55 years of age showed a greater decrease than those who were younger.

These findings suggest that mental health treatment may improve individuals' ability to stay healthy enough to avoid hospital admission for physical illness. This is important from a dollar standpoint, since treatment in a hospital costs a great deal more than outpatient visits. The finding that older people's general health seemed to be affected most by mental health interventions is especially interesting, because psychotherapy is often thought to be less useful for older people and is less often recommended. The results also show that psychotherapy does more than simply keep the "worried well" from making unnecessary medical visits. In general, the people who received mental health treatment had more chronic disease and were physically sicker than people who did not use these services (Schlesinger and others, 1983).

In fact, mental health treatment seems to be especially important as a cost saver for people who have chronic diseases—for instance, hypertension or diabetes. In a large study of federal employees covered by a group insurance program, people who began mental health visits within one year after their chronic disease was diagnosed had total yearly medical charges of over $300 less by the third year after that diagnosis than a control group (Schlesinger and others, 1983). Figure 16.10 shows the difference in inpatient medical charges for chronic disease patients who had mental health services compared to those who did not receive them. The cost savings are clear. Outpatient costs did not differ between the groups, but this was not anticipated, since it is necessary to check these individuals frequently to keep tabs on their chronic disorder. It is likely that the psychotherapy helped these patients to cooperate better with their medical programs and, in general, to maintain a more healthful life style.

Psychotherapy can help people enjoy life more and be more effective in their daily living; it can also improve physical health. Research has been pointing at both these conclusions for some time. What is most impressive about these new findings about medical costs, however, is that all this can be accomplished without spending more health care dollars over the long run. This means that hospitals can improve the quality and appropriateness of their care and may even lower the total costs by the use of outpatient mental health treatment.

FIGURE 16.10 *Yearly medical charges for patients with a chronic disease are decreased by mental health interventions. This figure compares inpatient and outpatient medical costs for two groups of chronically ill individuals whose disorder had just been diagnosed. One group received mental health intervention in the first year after diagnosis; the other did not. The decrease in overall cost for the mental health treatment group is clear.*

Comparative outcome research

If we grant that psychotherapy is useful, we next have to specify which type of psychotherapy. This is not easy because there are so many. Some years ago one researcher was able to identify more than 130 of them (Parloff, 1979). Another issue is whether any particular psychological therapy or therapies is more effective than a biological approach, which usually means drugs. In this type of **comparative outcome research,** the questions that we ask have to be much more specific than the questions that we raised about general therapeutic effectiveness. For example, is one type of therapy more effective with a particular type of client than another specific therapy or no treatment at all? There are hundreds of studies that look at this question. Here we will mention only a few of the most famous.

A study by Sloane and his co-workers (1975) evaluated the effects of behavior therapy and psychoanalytically oriented psychotherapy for the treatment of severe neurosis and personality disorders; it is recognized as the best comparative study to date (Heimberg and Becker, 1984). The therapists were experienced, there were a large number of clients (90), few people dropped out of the study, there was a relatively long period of follow-up (one year), and the outcome was measured in a number of ways. At the end of the treatment period outcomes for both behavior therapy and psychotherapy were superior to the control condition. Those clients who had received behavior therapy were slightly superior in social functioning and ratings of adjustment. After a year, the differences between the two therapy groups had disappeared, although both therapy groups still had better outcomes than the controls.

In another well-known study, Klerman and his colleagues compared the effects of a tricyclic antidepressant and psychotherapy for preventing a relapse in a group of women who had previously had neurotic depressions (Klerman and others, 1974; Weissman and others, 1974). One hundred fifty women who had improved after being treated with the tricyclic were assigned to one of several conditions. Women receiving the tricyclic had similar relapse rates (12 percent) whether or not they also had psychotherapy. Those who received only psychotherapy had relapse rates of 17 percent. Those who received a placebo rather than the tricyclic but had psychotherapy or contact with a social worker showed double this relapse rate, and those who received no treatment were even more likely to relapse. When the clients' social adjustment was used as the outcome measure instead of relapse rate, those who had psychotherapy had the best ratings. This study suggests that combined treatment approaches are most effective. However, because only those individuals who had shown a positive response to the drug in their initial treatment were included, the meaning of the results is not clear.

In another study, Rush and his co-workers (1977) measured Beck's cognitive therapy against a tricyclic antidepressant for the treatment of unipolar depression. Individuals with a prior history of poor drug response were excluded. Both treatments led to a reduction in symptoms of depression, but on the measures used—self-reports and clinical ratings—79 percent of cognitive therapy patients were improved, compared to 23 percent of drug patients at the end of the treatment period. A year later both groups were still almost symptom-free on the clinical ratings, but the cognitive therapy group still gave self-reports of significantly less depression (Kovacs and others, 1981).

This study has been criticized because the clinical raters were not blind to the experimental group assignments and the self-report measures are especially likely to be influenced by the cognitive therapeutic approach. The type, amount of dosage, and length of medication period for those receiving antidepressants have also been criticized by reviewers (Becker and Schuckit, 1978).

This brief look at a few studies of comparative outcome using different treatment methods indicates how very difficult research in this area is even for highly qualified researchers. This is one reason why meta-analysis and other ways of surveying the results of large groups of studies have become popular. As we have seen, though, this approach is also open to criticism.

One of the most important questions in comparative outcome studies is what the criteria for improvement should be. Table 16.4 organizes a number of ways of analyzing outcome measures. Which are more important, changes in how the client feels and behaves, or changes in what he or she thinks about? Would the opinions of the client's family or co-workers be helpful in evaluating improvement? How significant is the therapist's evaluation of the outcome? Sometimes the therapist and the client don't agree. Anthony Storr, a British psychoanalyst, gives this example of what he had considered an "unsuccessful" case:

Some time ago I had a letter from a man whom I had treated some twenty-five years previously asking whether I would see, or at any rate advise treatment for, his daughter. He assumed, wrongly, that I would not remember him, and, in the course of his letter, wrote as follows: "I can quite truthfully say that six months of your patient listening to my woes made a most important contribution to my life style. Although my transvestism was not cured my approach to life and to other people was re-oriented and for that I am most grateful. It is part of my life that I have never forgotten."

Looked at from one point of view, my treatment of this man was a failure. His major symptom, the complaint which drove him to seek my help, was not abolished. And yet I think it is clear that he did get something from his short period of psychotherapy which was of considerable value to him. A man does not write to a psychotherapist asking him to see his daughter, twenty-five years after his own treatment was over, using the terms employed in this letter, unless he believes that what happened during his period of treatment was important. (Storr, 1980, p. 146)

If all the measures do not agree, which is most important? How can we compare studies that use different

---

TABLE 16.4 IMPORTANT DIMENSIONS OF THERAPY OUTCOME MEASURES

DIMENSIONS

Focus of measures	Emotions
	Thoughts
	Behaviors
Possible processes	Evaluation
	Description
	Observation
Possible sources of data	Self-report
	Therapist rating
	Relevant-other rating
	Trained observation by others
	Trained self-monitoring
	Instrumental behavior

The three dimensions may be combined in many ways, but all combinations may not yield similar results.

---

outcome measures to compare the effectiveness of various therapies? Clearly, although outcome research is progressing in sophistication, many of the important questions will be difficult to answer.

DISORDERED BEHAVIOR AND PUBLIC POLICY

Criminal responsibility

Until recently the most frequent community response to very severe maladaptive behavior has been institutionalization, either in a mental hospital or in a prison. If the person had committed a crime, then the choice of institution would be determined by whether or not he or she was judged to be "insane." This legal term, which has no psychological meaning, is based on a series of definitions that have grown out of judicial decisions over a long period of time. One that is still important is the **M'Naghten Rule** (1843), in which the courts held that individuals could not be convicted of a crime if, because of some mental disorder or defect, they did not understand what they had done, or if they did know, could not distinguish right from wrong. Another influential decision is the **Durham Test** (1954), which states that an accused person is not criminally responsible if the unlawful act was a product of "mental disease or mental defect," and should be hospitalized for treatment, not sent to prison. The Durham decision gives experts a great deal of leeway in characterizing the accused person's mental state at the time the crime was committed. Periodically a topic of public concern, the laws on crime and insanity became an issue at the time of John Hinckley's attempted assassination of Ronald Reagan. Experts testifying at Hinckley's trial disagreed about whether he was criminally responsible, and he was acquitted by reason of insanity and confined to a mental institution, not a prison. This case and others have raised questions about the usefulness and fairness of the legal definition of insanity.

Institutionalization

Another public policy issue that involves legal decisions is the question of whether someone who has not committed a crime but who shows extremely maladaptive and possibly self-destructive behavior can be confined to an institution. Such individuals may voluntarily commit themselves to a facility, or they may be **involuntarily committed.** In recent years the philosophy of deinstitutionalization has been popular. Concern for civil rights has been a strong argument for making involuntary commitment more difficult to achieve. Although this approach can prevent loss of liberty, it may also have negative effects on recovery. In involuntary commitments a judge must decide, based on the testimony of expert witnesses and on very strict criteria of what "dangerous" means, whether such individuals present a danger to themselves or others. While the individuals' civil rights are protected by not hospitalizing them, their welfare may be threatened because they may be denied needed treatment. Antipsychotic medication may stabilize a hospitalized person's condition so that a judge will declare that he or she is not presently dangerous. But, once a person is out of the hospital, the drugs may not be continued. Then the disturbed behavior returns, and the cycle resumes. Two cases reported in Seattle newspapers illustrate different aspects of this problem.

In the first case, a young male whom the court had refused to commit because his condition had stabilized stopped taking his medication a day later and jumped to his death from the seventeenth floor of a downtown hotel. His mother told reporters, "I think the law is very bad. . . . The law has worked against anybody who wanted to help him. . . . The mental-health professionals, psychiatrists, ourselves, our hands are all tied by the law. . . . There was nothing we could do. We didn't know when he would explode and hurt himself or someone else. But our hands were tied" (Jones, 1979, p. A21).

In a quite different case, a 64-year-old woman had been living in the Public Safety Building in Seattle for 2 years. She bathed in the building's restroom sinks, dressed in the elevators, and slept on the floor. Despite being dragged from the building by the police on several occasions, she resisted all efforts by social workers to find her another home. Apparently she believed the building to be her only safe refuge from people who were out to shoot her. She was judged not competent enough to stand trial for trespassing but not dangerous enough to institutionalize.

The movement to keep people out of institutions or to release them quickly began with great enthusiasm, but there have been many problems. The wide use of drugs with severely disturbed patients and the strict laws about institutionalization have decreased the length of hospitalization, but the frequency of hospitalization for any given individual has increased in a kind of revolving door syndrome. Not only do some individuals need a protective institutional setting to begin solving their personal problems or even to function reasonably well, but they do not get the support they need if they are released from the hospital. Money has not been made available to create the special living situations and treatment facilities these people may need to rejoin the community (see Figure 16.11).

Halfway houses—specially created transitional homes that provide housing, therapeutic, and health services and an opportunity to participate in planning and decision making—are in short supply. Group homes that provide long-term housing for some individuals who cannot function completely independently are also few in number. Many deinstitutionalized patients have been "dumped" into communities that fear their eccentric behavior and do not look after them in any organized way. Nursing homes, skid row rooming houses, single room occupancy hotels, and subsidized apartments now substitute for institutions. But because of insufficient funding, vocational training, recreational facilities, and even simple opportunities for socialization are not provided (Kiesler, 1982). As a result, public officials and such organizations as the American Psychiatric Association have initiated public discussion of the need to rethink the value of keeping people out of institutions. The present policy has been described as a failure and a major societal tragedy "that had left perhaps a million or more mentally ill individuals cast

(a)

FIGURE 16.11 *These photos illustrate two often inadequate solutions to the problem of helping those with severe maladaptive behaviors. Photograph (a) illustrates the barren, often depressing environment found in mental hospitals. Individuals who are hospitalized against their will lose their civil liberties and may find it difficult to obtain a release. Photograph (b) shows how discharged patients, who are not really capable of functioning independently, may end up living isolated lives in marginally adequate quarters such as these in a Seattle rooming house.*

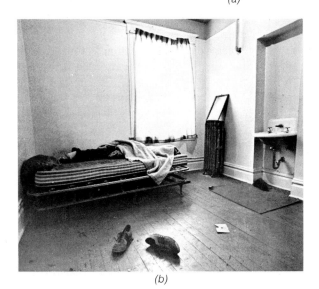

(b)

adrift under conditions that most persons think can no longer exist in this country" (Boffey, 1984, p. 1).

Prevention

From the community psychologist's perspective, the emphasis on prevention is even more important than the issue of hospitalization. Preschool programs, peer counseling programs, workshops for parents who are potential child abusers, and single-parent support groups are all examples of community interventions that are directed at preventing maladaptive behavior before it starts.

For example, early detection projects carried out in the schools are concerned with identifying as soon as possible children who are likely to have adjustment problems in later life. In one study, nonprofessional child aides, under close supervision, worked for an entire school year with children who were thought to have a high potential for school maladjustment. Children who received this one-to-one contact showed significant improvement in social and academic skills and in overall adjustment (Weissberg and others, 1982).

As we have seen, evaluating the effectiveness of the various therapies involves the examination of many interconnected questions. Is one particular therapy, or a combination of several therapies, most effective in treating a given disorder? Can therapies be shown to reduce other health care costs? When is it appropriate to require an individual to participate in a treatment program? Issues such as these must be addressed not only by future research but by the community at large if we are to adequately determine the appropriateness of the different therapeutic techniques. It is probably true that particular therapies are most appropriate for specific disorders, particularly for schizophrenia and the anxiety disorders. Of particular promise is the trend toward integrating the most effective aspects of the various therapeutic techniques in achieving mental health goals.

STUDY OUTLINE

PSYCHODYNAMIC THERAPIES (p. 552)

1. Psychoanalysis, originated by Sigmund Freud, uses the technique of free association. Freud believed that behavior and feelings toward significant people in earlier life will reoccur in a transference relationship with the therapist.

2. Other psychodynamic therapies also focus on the thoughts and feelings experienced in the client's past, but instead of interpreting clients' thoughts and behaviors in the rather rigid theoretical framework originated by Freud, the therapist may use a variety of ideas in understanding and interpreting the client's behavior.

HUMANISTIC-EXISTENTIAL THERAPIES (p. 555)

1. Client-centered therapy, originated by Carl Rogers, focuses on the client rather than on the therapist-client interaction, as in psychodynamic therapies. Rogers focuses on immediate events in the clients' lives and the importance of helping clients make a better match between their self-concepts and their experiences.

2. Existential therapists focus their clients' attention on the crucial choices that they make and help them to clarify what is important and unimportant in their own lives.

BEHAVIOR THERAPIES (p. 556)

The first step in behavior therapy is behavioral assessment to pinpoint the specific situations in which the problem occurs. There are several categories of behavior therapy. Applied behavior analysis uses operant conditioning and emphasizes that behavior is determined by its consequences. An A-B-A-B design is often used. The classical conditioning approach focuses on changing conditioned emotional responses that have become paired with certain stimuli—for instance, in phobia or anxiety reactions. Systematic desensitization and flooding are two techniques based on classical conditioning. Social-learning-based therapy stresses learn-

ing new behaviors through observation and modeling and attempts to build feelings of self-efficacy in the client. Assertiveness training is one focus of social learning therapy. Finally, cognitive behavior modification emphasizes the changing of maladaptive thought patterns.

COGNITIVE THERAPIES (p. 561)

Cognitive therapies focus on helping clients identify and change irrational ideas that interfere with effective behavior. Albert Ellis developed rational-emotive therapy, which emphasizes the replacement of irrational thoughts with more realistic ones. Aaron Beck created a cognitive therapy specifically focused on depression. Self-instructional training, an approach often used with children, was developed by Donald Meichenbaum.

GROUP THERAPY (p. 563)

1. Group therapy is economical because one professional can meet with several clients at one time. It may also be especially effective in certain cases because of the sharing of experiences and the opportunity to observe other individuals in problem-solving situations. Transactional Analysis is a specialized group technique that focuses on the social roles people play. Gestalt therapy, created by Fritz Perls, encourages the release of strong emotions through role-playing techniques and verbal "attacks" by the therapist. Encounter groups and T groups attempt to increase the self-awareness and understanding of what goes on in relationships among already well functioning individuals.

2. Family therapy focuses on helping family members understand how the ways in which they customarily interact may produce difficulties and behavior problems for some family members, usually children. Couples therapy concentrates on helping to identify interaction problems for couples who perceive their relationship as troubled.

BIOLOGICAL THERAPIES (p. 566)

1. Drug therapies are used extensively to treat anxiety, depression, bipolar disorder, and schizophrenia. Antianxiety drugs such as Valium are commonly prescribed for the "worried well"; their addictive properties are often underemphasized. Antipsychotic drugs, used to treat schizophrenia, may have serious side effects, in-

cluding tardive dyskinesia, a nonreversible disorder that produces uncontrollable movements. Research is focusing on how to determine which patients will do well if medication is discontinued after their initial symptoms decrease. Social skills training often is a useful addition to drug therapy for schizophrenic patients. Antidepressant drugs include tricyclics and MAO inhibitors. Mania and some depressions can be controlled by lithium.

2. Electroconvulsive therapy, or ECT, can be useful in severe depression, either when antidepressant drugs have not been effective or when the risk of suicide is high. Despite concern about its safety, current studies show ECT to be acceptably safe.

EVALUATION OF THERAPIES (p. 570)

Evaluation of therapeutic effectiveness has become more important as costs for therapy rise and insurance companies and government agencies demand demonstration that a particular treatment is useful. Meta-analysis, a statistical procedure that allows the combination of many studies for analysis, may be helpful in comparing therapies. Studies focused on comparative outcome research are difficult and expensive. One of the most troublesome decisions in these investigations is what the criteria for improvement should be.

DISORDERED BEHAVIOR AND PUBLIC POLICY (p. 575)

1. Despite many important legal decisions in the past, experts often differ about whether or not an individual is criminally responsible or should be acquitted because of "insanity," a legal term that has no psychological meaning.

2. Recent public policy has made it difficult to hospitalize mentally ill individuals without their consent, but has provided no supportive care or traditional services for these disturbed people.

KEY TERMS AND CONCEPTS

community approach

free association

transference

positive transference

negative transference

countertransference

resistance

client-centered therapy

behavioral assessment

applied behavior analysis

cognitive behavior modification

systematic desensitization

flooding

assertiveness training

self-efficacy

rational-emotive therapy (RET)

self-instructional training (SIT)

group therapy

Transactional Analysis (TA)

Gestalt therapy

encounter group

T group

family therapy

couples therapy

antianxiety drug

antipsychotic drug

tardive dyskinesia

tricyclic antidepressants

MAO inhibitors

lithium

electroconvulsive therapy (ECT)

meta-analysis

comparative outcome research

M'Naghten Rule

Durham Test

involuntary commitment

halfway house

SUGGESTED READINGS

WILSON, G. T., FRANKS, C. M., BROWNELL, K. D., and KENDALL, P. C. (1984). *Annual review of behavior therapy*. Vol. 9, *Theory and practice*. New York: Guilford Press. This volume and others in this series contain current detailed evaluative reviews of cognitive and behavioral therapy.

BASCH, M. F. (1980). *Doing psychotherapy*. New York: Basic Books.

STORR, A. (1980). *The art of psychotherapy*. New York: Methuen.

These two volumes contain fascinating accounts of psychodynamic therapy from the therapist's viewpoint.

GOLDFRIED, M. (Ed.) (1982). *Convergent trends in psychotherapy: Trends in psychodynamic, humanistic and behavioral practice*. New York: Springer. This series of papers illustrates how the psychotherapeutic perspectives are becoming more integrated in both theory and practice.

SECTION EIGHT
SOCIAL BEHAVIOR

CHAPTER SEVENTEEN: **SOCIAL BEHAVIOR AND THE INDIVIDUAL**

CHAPTER EIGHTEEN: **THE SOCIAL ENVIRONMENT**

SOCIAL BEHAVIOR AND THE INDIVIDUAL

RESEARCH METHODS IN SOCIAL PSYCHOLOGY

SOCIAL PERCEPTION
Attribution
Motivation and attribution

SOCIAL COGNITION
Schemata

ATTRACTION, LIKING, AND LOVE
What characteristics cause attraction?
The development of a relationship
Love
Theories of interpersonal attraction
The ending of a relationship

ATTITUDES AND BEHAVIOR
What are attitudes?
Cognitive complexity and evaluative simplicity
Stereotyped attitudes and prejudice
How attitudes translate into behavior
Persuasion and attitude change

ALTRUISM AND PROSOCIAL BEHAVIOR
The biological perspective
The psychodynamic perspective
The learning perspective
The cognitive perspective
The person × situation interaction in helping
FRONTIER 17.1   WHO DONATES BLOOD AND WHY? A
STUDY OF PROSOCIAL BEHAVIOR

STUDY OUTLINE

KEY TERMS AND CONCEPTS

SUGGESTED READINGS

As Harry walked across the campus on his way home from a late night at the library, his backpack, slung by one strap over his shoulder, kept slipping. He held one hand on the strap to steady it. As the wind whipped about him, Harry's hand smarted from the cold. He thought about how much warmer his hand would feel snug in his pocket. Of course he could use both shoulder straps to secure his pack, but no one but a very green freshman would walk across campus with a pack suspended from both shoulders as the designer had intended. His hand felt even colder as the wind picked up. "That wind is cold, it must be below freezing," Harry thought. He glanced around. No one was in sight. He really had studied late. He stopped, flung the extra strap over his shoulder, and warmed his hand. A hundred yards later, Harry went back to one strap. "How stupid," he thought. But he still couldn't resist. Someone might see him. Harry plunged into the wind again, shaking his head in irritation at himself.

Social psychology is the study of how the behavior of individuals is influenced by the actual, imagined, or implied presence of other people. It will take us two chapters to cover this complex topic. In this chapter we are interested in how other people affect the individual's feelings, self-perceptions, and behavior. In Chapter 18, we look at how people's behavior changes when they become part of a group.

Fortunately, despite their range and complexity, many social interactions are predictable. The general rules of social behavior that we learn as children remove the need to assess each situation carefully, to decide what it means and how to respond. For example, when someone comes up, holds out his hand, and says, "I'm Mike Sowinsky. I'm going to be your new neighbor," your response is probably rather automatic. You shake his hand, tell him your name, ask some friendly questions about when he's moving in, and so on. Imagine how complicated life would be if we had to figure out what an outstretched hand meant or what we should say when someone tells us his or her name.

Although we need rules to simplify things, some of the general assumptions that these rules are based on are not necessarily correct. For instance, have you ever used the expression "opposites attract" to explain why two dissimilar people like each other? Or have you reassured a friend who was worried about her steady date's decision to go to college in another state that "you know, absence makes the heart grow fonder"? You may take such statements for granted and might wonder why social psychologists would bother to study something so obvious. But consider some equally well known truisms: If opposites attract, how can "birds of a feather flock together"? Or how can absence make the heart grow fonder, if "out of sight, out of mind" is also true?

What does common sense tell you about the following statements?

The more highly motivated a person is, the better he or she will be at solving a complex problem.

Boys and girls behave in the same way until they are exposed to environmental influences.

Fortunately for babies, human beings have a strong maternal instinct.

To change people's behavior toward members of ethnic minority groups, we must first change their attitudes.

In a study, a group of introductory psychology students generally agreed that these statements were correct (Vaughn, 1977). Do you agree with them? Do you say, "Of course, those things are obvious"? According to psychological research, *none* of these statements is true. Social psychologists focus a great deal of their attention on investigating behaviors that "common sense" tells us we already understand.

RESEARCH METHODS IN SOCIAL PSYCHOLOGY

Social psychologists often use the same kind of experimental methods that we have described throughout this book. But they also use a number of research methods that take them out of the laboratory.

One commonly used technique is the **survey study,**

in which people are simply asked, in person, by phone, or by mail, how they feel about certain topics. You may have been approached by someone in a shopping center who asked you which soft drink you prefer, or been telephoned by someone conducting a survey of opinions about political candidates.

Field studies use observation of behavior in natural settings as their principal technique, although they may also include surveys. In one very elaborate and complex study, a 14-year observation was carried out so that life in a small Kansas town could be compared with that in a small town in North Yorkshire, England (Barker and Schoggen, 1973). The townspeople knew that they were being observed, and the researchers lived in the towns and participated in community activities as they gathered their data.

Natural experiments present unique opportunities to observe changes in attitudes and behavior after certain major events happen. The occurrences may be disasters, such as the eruption of Mount St. Helens in Washington State and the Three Mile Island nuclear accident in Pennsylvania, or changes in laws that have widespread social and behavioral implications, such as the lowering of the voting age to 18 and the desegregation of the public schools.

Field experiments also take place in real-life settings, but unlike field studies and natural experiments, field experiments contain variables manipulated by the experimenter. The Robbers Cave experiment, described in Chapter 18, is an example of a field experiment.

SOCIAL PERCEPTION

When we interact with other people, we try to understand what their behavior means and why they behave in the way they do. For example, assume that your professor has just opened a letter saying that her paper was rejected by a prestigious journal, and then you walk into her office with a question about the next test. The response you get might be, "Why are you bothering me with such a perfectly obvious question? You should know that." After you beat a hasty and embarrassed retreat, you might say to yourself, "What was wrong with my question? Students need to know things

like that." Psychologists describe your attempt to understand why your professor behaved the way she did as engaging in **attribution.** The attribution process is a focus for social psychologists investigating a variety of problems, including attitudes, liking and attraction, and helping behavior.

Attribution

Attribution, as we noted, is the process of pinpointing the cause of another person's behavior. In the case of your professor, you might make a **personal attribution.** You might have decided that she was really a very unpleasant person who didn't care anything about students. You might have been especially likely to do this if you had observed her behaving the same way on other occasions. On the other hand, you might make a **situational attribution** and conclude that she really must have been having a bad day. Or you might attribute her behavior to a *combination* of personal and situational factors. The causal factors of attributions may be seen as *internal* (personal) or *external* (situational), and they will also reflect the observer's perception of whether those causes would be the same on most occasions (**stable**) or could be expected to vary over time (**unstable**). Table 17.1 shows examples of a season's worth of attributions made about the Los Angeles Rams by a sports writer for the *Los Angeles Times.*

People have a pronounced tendency to attribute their own behaviors to the situation, while they attribute other people's behaviors to personal factors. If someone spills coffee on the table and on your clothes, you might think, "How could she be so clumsy?" However, when you spill your coffee, you are more likely to say to yourself, "I dropped the cup because it was too hot to hold," or "Mary bumped my arm just as I was setting it down." This common tendency to blame others for their actions and the world for ours is called the **fundamental attribution error** (Ross, 1977).

TABLE 17.1 WHY A TEAM PLAYS WELL OR POORLY

STABILITY	LOCUS	
	INTERNAL (CAUSALITY IS ATTRIBUTED TO THE SPORTSWRITER'S HOMETOWN TEAM— TO A SPECIFIC PLAYER, COACH, OR THE TEAM AS A WHOLE)	EXTERNAL (CAUSALITY IS ATTRIBUTED TO THE OTHER TEAM, OR TO SUCH FACTORS AS WEATHER, LUCK, INJURIES, A REFEREE'S DECISION, ETC.)
Stable[a]	1. "This kind of long kick was Septien's Achilles Heel. The Rams were sold on the superior strength of Corral's leg."	5. "As usual, the Saints' performance against the Rams here was more than fair."
	2. "Los Angeles outclassed the young rebuilding 49ers in almost every way possible en route to a 27–10 victory."	6. "[The Ram's offense was] frustrated by . . . a Pittsburgh defense that isn't too bad either."
Unstable[b]	3. "[The Ram's defense] hit Dorsett so hard he fumbled three times, and the one that Los Angeles recovered hurt the Cowboys."	7. "Eight seconds remained on the 30-second clock at the Coliseum's west end but the clock on the east end showed :00; that was the one referee Jim Tunney went by when he called the delay penalty."
	4. "Los Angeles's offense piled up plenty of yards between the 20 yard lines but played like the Keystone Kops in scoring territory."	8. "This time—no doubt hindered by the absence of the Falcons' best offensive players, halfback Haskel Stanback and receiver Alfred Jenkin— Jones had all kinds of problems."

Note: All quotes come from articles by Ted Green, appearing in the *Los Angeles Times*: 1. Corral saves day for the Rams. (1978, September 4). *Los Angeles Times*, p. CC, Part III, 1. 2. On flag day, Rams continue the parade. (1978, October 9). *Los Angeles Times*, p. CC, Part III, 1. 3. This time, big D stands for defense, 27–14. (1978, September 18). *Los Angeles Times*, p. CC, Part III, 1. 4. Rams win dull one, 10–0. (1978, September 11). *Los Angeles Times*, p. CC, Part III, 1. 5. Rams' offense turns to gumbo . . . but they win. (1978, October 2). *Los Angeles Times*, p. CC, Part III, 1. 6. Defense does a number on Steelers and Rams win. (1978, November 13). *Los Angeles Times*, p. CC, Part III, 1. 7. Rams call on UCLA to beat the USC alumni, 26–23. (1978, November 6). *Los Angeles Times*, p. CC, Part III, 9. 8. (1978, September 11). *Los Angeles Times*, p. CC, Part III, 10. (Article #1 continues on p. 8; #2 continues on p. 10; #3 continues on p. 10; #s 4 & 8 are the same article, on pp 1, 10; #5 continues on p. 8; #6 continues on p. 10; and #7 starts on p. 1.)

[a]Explanation would predict the same outcome in future games between these two teams this season.

[b]Factor could vary over time; no reason to expect the same outcome in future games this season.

Source: Lau, 1984, p. 1020.

There seem to be several reasons for these differences in attribution. For one thing, we pay more attention to other people than we do to ourselves. When we are in a situation, we concentrate on that situation and are likely to view ourselves as responding to it. When we watch someone else, however, we are likely to be concentrating more on the person than on the situation. In the second place, we know more about ourselves than we do about others; we know that our behavior varies somewhat according to the situation. We usually do not have that kind of information about other people, so we are more apt to attribute their behavior in a given situation to personal causes. Third, while it is painful to blame ourselves, being critical of others doesn't hurt us so much.

These typical attribution tendencies reverse themselves when the result of the behavior is success rather than failure. In a study of the sports pages, Lau and Russell (1980) found that successes tended to be accompanied by internal attributions ("We played great team defense and hung in there"), while failures were explained by external attributions ("Everything they shot was going in"). Self-protective attributions like these help to preserve our self-esteem and give us the confidence to try again next time.

Although the attribution process might seem time-consuming, it may happen very rapidly, while the behavioral information is being encoded into memory (Winter and Uleman, 1984). Attribution may be a spontaneous process carried out without any particular motivating conditions.

RULES OF ATTRIBUTION

People usually consider three factors when forming attributions: whether the behavior occurs only in response to certain stimuli (the distinctiveness of the behavior), whether other people in the same situation would respond the same way (the degree of consensus), and whether the behavior is likely to occur in other situations (the consistency of the behavior) (Kelley, 1973). Distinctive actions and actions with a high degree of consensus are usually attributed to external causes. Actions that are highly consistent over a variety of situations are usually attributed to internal causes.

Let's see how these principles of attribution work by imagining that you are on the jury in a trial of a man accused of killing his brother. During the testimony you hear that at the time of the killing, the defendant's brother was attacking him with a butcher knife. The dead man was 6 feet 4 inches and weighed 240 pounds. The defendant is less than 5 feet 10 and weighs about 150 pounds. He hit his brother with a chair as the big man lunged with the knife. The victim fell, hit his head against the corner of the kitchen counter, and was fatally injured. You might decide that the defendant's behavior was distinctive because he had never been known to attack his brother before. His behavior also showed a high degree of consensus. (Most people

would defend themselves against a mad mammoth with a knife.) You might then decide that the defendant had acted in self-defense and that situational variables had caused him to kill his brother. But what if the testimony also showed that, although the defendant never fought with his brother, he had often attacked other people who argued with him? This consistency in his behavior might lead you to conclude that the attack may have been provoked by the defendant's uncontrollable temper and aggressive personality. This might change your attribution about the cause of his behavior and your verdict from "not guilty" to "guilty."

THE EFFECTS OF ATTRIBUTION

Attribution thus has a strong effect on how we react to a behavior. Our basic tendency to attribute our own behaviors to situational factors and to explain other people's behavior in terms of their personalities often makes us more tolerant of our own misdeeds and shortcomings than of those of others. The tendency to blame external factors for all our failings may also make us unlikely to try to change our behavior. In his study of the attributions made by coaches and players in the National Football League during one season, Richard Lau (1984) found that the more internal the attributions that the team made for a previous game (especially when they lost), the better the team did compared to general expectations in the next game. Their internal attributions must also have been unstable. They played poorly in one game, but they assumed that if they played better they could win. Unstable internal attributions can be important motivators that make people "try harder."

Sometimes internal attributions have a negative effect on motivation. People who are depressed and people with low self-esteem tend to attribute the unfavorable outcomes in their lives to their own stable personal characteristics and to attribute positive outcomes to unstable situational causes or to luck. This attributional pattern is likely to perpetuate their feelings of low self-worth. Attributing someone else's negative behavior to stable internal personal causes also may have important implications. For one thing, there is less reason to be optimistic about future positive change, because people are harder to change than situations. As a consequence, we may be less likely to encourage change when we attribute people's behavior to personal factors. For example, we might be less likely to help underprivileged college students who have academic problems if we attributed their poor academic performance to laziness and lack of motivation rather than to inadequate high school preparation.

Motivation and attribution

The rules for attribution—distinctiveness, consensus, and consistency—approach it as a purely cognitive process. Recent research has shown that needs and wishes also play an important role in attribution (Harvey and Weary, 1984). The need for *self-esteem* causes individuals to accept more responsibility for positive outcomes than for the negative outcomes of their behavior (Greenwald, 1980). This bias toward self-esteem has been found not only in the laboratory but also in real-life attributions. For example, successful applicants for medical school assumed that their personal characteristics were more important in the decision than unsuccessful applicants did (Smith and Manard, 1980), while coaches and players took more responsibility for their wins than for their losses (Lau and Russell, 1980).

Another example is found in attitudes toward victims. Seeing someone victimized may cause the observers to feel threatened and to think about the possibility of being victimized themselves. One way to defend against such thoughts is to attribute the misfortune to the victim. This is the basis for the assumption that a rape victim must have engaged in some sort of provocative behavior. In a laboratory study designed to test this idea, female subjects were given information about "another student" who was described as having attitudes either similar or dissimilar to theirs (Thornton, 1984). The subjects then read a folder of selected materials provided by this "student." One of the items was the "student's" account of having been sexually assaulted when she was returning to her dorm from the library where she had briefly met the attacker. In their ratings of the victim, the subjects assigned her less responsibility for the rape if she had been described as similar to themselves. When the "student" was described as dissimilar to the subjects, they attributed the assault more to the victim's character than to her behavior.

Another factor that is reflected in the kind of attributions that individuals make is the need for a desirable **self-presentation.** People seem to choose the causal explanation that would be most likely either to gain public approval or to avoid embarrassment. For example, in general people seem to toot their horns less loudly if they expect their performance to be evaluated later by experts (Greenberg and others, 1982). Personality differences also contribute to differences in self-presentation. Subjects who are socially anxious are more likely to accept credit for failure than for success (Arkin and others, 1980). Another motivational variable that has a bearing on attribution is the issue of *control.* Sometimes when people are worried about the outcome of a particular situation, they may behave in a way that makes the outcome hard to attribute. For example, a student who is worried about a difficult exam may stay up very late the night before. Therefore, negative results could be attributed to exhaustion as well as to lack of ability or to poor study habits. The uncertainty created by the lack of sleep can thus become a face-saving measure.

SOCIAL COGNITION

As we have seen, social psychologists have typically looked at attribution from the cognitive perspective. The study of attitudes, opinions, and stereotypes has also largely depended on the cognitive perspective. Recently, a new cognitive approach to understanding the general processes that people use to make sense of other people and themselves has become popular (Fiske and Taylor, 1984). This area of study—called **social cognition**—combines an interest in cognitive events with some of the cognitive concepts and principles that we discussed in Chapter 7, including the encoding, integration, and decoding of information.

Schemata

As we learned when we studied perception, in any situation so much information is generated that it is impossible for any one person to attend to and process it all. For this reason, to ensure that nothing important to the individual will be missed, the information is filtered, organized, and interpreted on the basis of the person's past social experiences. These past experiences, which are organized into cognitive structures called **schemata,** have important effects on social thought and behavior (Fiske and Taylor, 1981).

There can be a variety of schemata—for example, self schemata, person schemata, role schemata, and event schemata. **Self schemata** are the cognitive structures that describe a person's own characteristics and customary behavior patterns (Markus and Sentis, 1982). How would you describe yourself, if someone asked you to quickly name a few of your most outstanding characteristics? Most people, through observation of their own behavior and the input received from others, have rather clear ideas about themselves, at least about certain dimensions of their behavior. These self schemata are important because they influence the kind of new information that individuals will add to their self-perception. If their self schemata are in error, the chances are very high that any new information will also be distorted. Our perception of other people is affected by the **person schemata** that we have used to characterize them. When we apply terms such as *jock, wimp, grind,* or *yuppie* to particular people, we think of them as having a whole set of characteristics that we have concluded are part of this key concept. We also think of whole groups of people in terms of particular **role schemata.** These schemata are important because they often cause us to interpret behavior differently depending on the group involved. For example, you see a man waving at you. Now, imagine that he is an old man, a young man of another race, your family doctor, a police officer.

Sagar and Schofield (1980) investigated how the role schemata held by blacks and whites affected their perceptions. Sixth grade black and white boys from several schools were shown drawings and given descriptions of four different actions that might be interpreted in a variety of ways. In half of the examples, the person carrying out the action was black; in the other half, he was white. After each of the four situations was presented, the boys were asked to rate how well each of several adjectives described the behavior in the situation. The findings, illustrated in Figure 17.1, were very clear: both black and white boys rated the behaviors as more threatening and meaner when they were carried out by blacks rather than by whites. The likelihood that such social cognitions will become self-fulfilling is especially unfortunate. By responding to individuals as if their behavior were aggressive, we may indeed bring forth aggressive responses.

FIGURE 17.1 *Social schemata have a powerful effect on cognition. Both black and white children perceived ambiguous actions performed by blacks to be meaner and more threatening than the same actions performed by whites. (Adapted from Sagar and Schofield, 1980)*

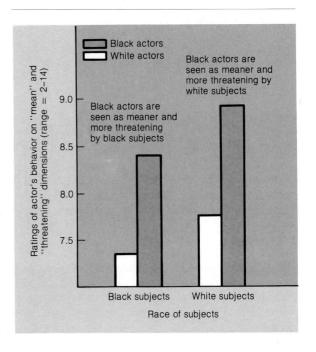

Event schemata are cognitive structures that tell us what to expect in a variety of situations. These schemata, often called *scripts*, provide a useful method of dealing easily with many situations without having to devote too much time and energy to them. For example, when a cashier in a supermarket says, "How are you?" you almost automatically say something like, "Fine, and how are you?" However, sometimes the interaction departs from your script, and then you may feel disturbed or tense. For example, suppose the cashier treats your response as a real question and not as part of a script, and says, "Just terrible! My dog ran away, and I've had a very sore throat all week, and a fever and cough, too." Do you let the line behind you fume while you find out more? Or do you simply say, "I'm sorry" and leave. Whatever you do, this departure from the script is likely to make you feel uncomfortable and to wish that you had not responded quite so automatically.

ATTRACTION, LIKING, AND LOVE

Most of us have a strong desire to **affiliate,** to develop relationships with other people, ranging from casual acquaintanceships to in-depth associations that may last a lifetime. Some of these relationships are platonic—that is, regardless of their intensity, they are based on friendship, not on physical intimacy. Other relationships, short-lived or lasting, emphasize sexuality and perhaps also romantic love. All these relationships begin with attraction.

What characteristics cause attraction?

How do birds of a feather and attractive opposites find each other? Figure 17.2 illustrates several important factors in attraction.

SIMILARITY

At the beginning of the chapter, you read that bit of folk wisdom summarized as "opposites attract." Although you can probably come up with an example of a couple you know who "prove" this point, social psychologists have found that, in general, just the reverse

is true. Your chances of liking someone are much greater if that person's beliefs, values, and personality characteristics are similar to rather than different from yours. In one study, students who had chosen to be college roommates were questioned about a variety of characteristics (Hill and Stull, 1981). Among female roommates a high degree of value similarity was important in their initial choice and was a good predictor of whether they continued to room together. Such similarity of values was not an important factor for men, however. This finding, as well as many others that show sex differences, suggests to many researchers that men and women do not experience same-sex friendship in the same way.

In a study of dating couples, the researchers found that the partners tended to be similar in a variety of ways (Hill and others, 1976). They resembled each other in physical and social characteristics such as age, intelligence, educational plans, religion, and physical attractiveness. Their attitudes toward sexual behavior and toward sex roles were also similar. The more similar the couples in this study were, in fact, the more likely they were to be in the same relationship a year later.

COMPLEMENTARITY

There do seem to be occasions when similarity is upsetting or threatening. The "opposites attract," or *complementary characteristics*, concept seems logical in such situations. In many relationships, the two individuals seem to have different roles. For instance, one partner seems dominant and the other submissive, or one is talkative and the other quiet. Usually, though, if we look at such relationships closely, we can see that these differences are not in basic values, but rather are the result of a division of tasks or behaviors depending on the different skills which each of the participants brings to the relationship. For example, partners in a traditional marriage may have similar values but may divide the roles of the spouses into homemaking and income producing. Problems will probably not occur unless the two discover that they actually have different values or unless the values of one of them change. Research suggests that both similarity and complementarity are important for a successful relationship (Sternberg and Grajek, 1984).

FIGURE 17.2 *A number of factors contribute to interpersonal attraction. These include similarity, complementarity, familiarity, and attractiveness.*

591

FIGURE 17.3 *Which would look better to you if this were your photo? Individuals are accustomed to seeing their reflected image, in which left and right are reversed. When subjects were given a choice between their images as they would be seen by another person or reversed, as they would see themselves in a mirror, familiarity led them to select the reversed image.*

FAMILIARITY

A concept closely related to similarity that also seems to influence liking is *familiarity*. In one study, college students were shown pictures of faces. They saw some of the faces only once or twice, while others were shown to them as many as 25 times (Moreland and Zajonc, 1982). When they had finished looking at the pictures, they were asked two things: how much they liked each face and how much they thought they would like the actual person. The more frequently they had seen the picture, the more the subjects liked the face and thought they would like the person.

The idea of familiarity can also be applied to one's own face. Most of us are probably familiar with our own face as we see it in a mirror—that is, with the

image reversed from left to right. Other people, because they see the true image, are most familiar with our faces the other way. In an inventive experiment, Mita and others (1977) tested whether liking would be affected by reversing this situation. They asked subjects to view two photos of themselves that were identical except that one was reversed left for right, like the pair shown in Figure 17.3. Friends of the subjects also viewed the pair of photos. What would you predict the result would be if familiarity increases liking? If you said that the friends preferred the original photograph and the individuals themselves preferred the reversed image, you were correct. The experiment suggests that not just general familiarity, but familiarity with exact detail, may be important in liking.

Familiarity may also be important in the develop-

FIGURE 17.4 *Each of the units in the apartment complex was designed with the same plan. The number of doors apart two people lived was defined as their functional distance. For example, on the first floor, apartments 1 and 3 were two doors apart; so were apartments 3 and 5. (Adapted from Festinger and others, 1950)*

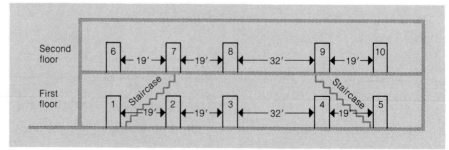

ment of friendships. People who live in the same apartment building or housing development are more likely to be friends with close neighbors than with those people who live farther away. In one famous study of friendship patterns among married students, Leon Festinger and his co-workers (1950) studied students living in a 170-unit apartment complex. The complex was composed of 2-story buildings with 5 units on each floor (see Figure 17.4). The researchers asked the residents which 3 other people living in the complex they saw socially most often. Next-door neighbors were mentioned most frequently. People living 2 doors away were mentioned half as often, and those living at the end of the hall were mentioned only one-quarter as many times. This finding was somewhat surprising, because the *physical distance* between units was actually very small. But physical distance turned out to be

only part of the explanation. People who lived on the same floor were more likely to be friends than those who lived on different floors, even though their doorways were actually *closer* to each other's than the doors of the apartments on the same floor were. Apparently this is because it takes more effort to go up and down stairs than to walk down the hall. Thus the **functional distance** was a more important factor in friendship patterns than the actual physical distance. Figure 17.5 shows the difference in socializing patterns based on both physical and functional distance.

ATTRACTIVENESS

How physically attractive someone is plays a major role in determining your ideas about the desirability of developing an acquaintance or a friendship with that person (Dion, 1981). Attractiveness seems to influence our perception of others' traits (see Figure 17.6). Attractive people are judged to be more poised, sociable, independent, interesting, exciting, and to have greater sexual warmth (Brigham, 1980). In one study concerned with the importance of physical attractiveness, Karen Dion and her colleagues asked university students to rate a series of photographs of both males and females as high, average, or low in physical attractiveness (Dion and others, 1972). The photos were then passed on to another group of students, who were asked to rate those pictured on a number of personality traits and to predict future events in their lives. The results showed that, regardless of whether the rater was the same or the opposite sex as the subject, attractive people of both sexes were rated as having more socially desirable personality traits than less attractive people. In addition, attractive people were predicted to have greater personal happiness and more prestigious future occupations than less attractive people.

These impressions of beautiful people do not suddenly appear during adolescence. As early as age 4 or 5, attractive children are more popular with their peers than their unattractive counterparts (Dion and others,

FIGURE 17.5 *Functional distance was more important than physical distance in establishing friendship patterns. Students living on the same floor were more likely to be friends than those living on different floors because the time and effort to move from one floor to another increased the functional distance even though the physical distance might be small. (Adapted from Festinger and others, 1950)*

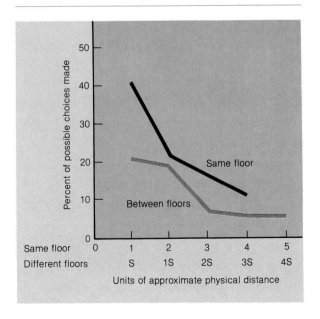

FIGURE 17.6 *Look at these photographs. Write down your guess as to the personality of each individual. Then when you have finished, rate these women from most to least attractive. Now compare these ratings with the personality characteristics you attributed to each. If your responses correspond to those of others who have been studied, the person you rated most attractive will also have the most positive personality characteristics.*

1972). Adults also form more favorable impressions of attractive children. In one study, women read a description of an aggressive act performed by a 7-year-old child. The description was accompanied by a photograph of either an attractive child or an unattractive one. When the women were asked to describe the child whose picture they had seen, they characterized the unattractive child as bratty, selfish, and antisocial. The attractive child was likely to be excused for aggressive acts because these were assumed to be deviations from the youngster's usual behavior (Dion, 1972).

Attractive people are apparently not unaware of their effect on other people. Being attractive may help determine the way that people actually behave as well as how they are perceived. Attractive males are more assertive than less attractive males. They also have less fear of rejection and have more of their social interactions with females than with males (Reis and Nezlek, 1980). Attractive females are not as assertive as females

who are less attractive, but both groups of women have an equal number of social interactions.

The development of a relationship

Research has demonstrated that similarity, familiarity, and physical attractiveness are all important in feeling attracted to someone. But not everyone we feel attracted to becomes a good friend or even an acquaintance. Assuming that there is a possibility of seeing such a person again, what are the factors that encourage a relationship to develop?

RECIPROCITY

Reciprocity is one way in which relationships are encouraged to continue. We like people who like us and who think well of what we do. This is true even if their evaluation is inaccurate (Drachman and others, 1978). Friends are people who are expected to care about us, to do nice things for us, and to evaluate us positively. (Remember, as we discussed earlier in this chapter, we tend to like those whose views are similar to ours.)

In one experiment designed to see whether liking could be manipulated, female subjects were asked to work on a difficult and time-consuming task (filing index cards) while another subject, really a confederate of the experimenter, who had been described to the subject as either very similar or dissimilar to the subject in various attitudes, did a much easier and less time-consuming task (Riordan and others, 1982). When the confederate finished her task, the experimenter suggested to the subject that she ask her for help. In half the cases the confederate agreed to help; in half she refused. The subject's attraction to the confederate was measured before and after the request for help. As you can see from Figure 17.7, if the confederate refused to help, she was less liked afterward. This is not a surprising finding. What was interesting about the results was that liking for the similar person who agreed to help remained almost the same, but liking for the dissimilar person who agreed to help increased greatly. This is

probably because most people assume that people they like reciprocate their liking and will help them. On the other hand, not much help is expected from dissimilar individuals, so when they do help, attraction for them increases and they are liked better.

SELF-DISCLOSURE

Another kind of reciprocity that is important in building a relationship is **self-disclosure.** As relationships develop from superficial to intimate, both the amount and type of self-disclosure increase. Self-disclosure can be *descriptive*, such as telling someone that you have three brothers, one sister, went to Hale High School, and come from Seattle. Descriptive self-disclosure often occurs early in a relationship. Another kind of disclosure is *evaluative*—for example, what your fears are about the future or how you feel about the way that

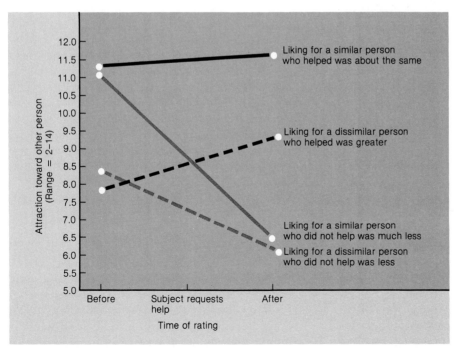

FIGURE 17.7 *We expect people who are similar to us to like us more than dissimilar people might. Therefore, we also expect more help from similar than from dissimilar people. If their helping behavior doesn't match our expectations, there is a noticeable increase in liking for the dissimilar person who helps and in dislike for the similar person who refuses. An offer of help from a similar person does not have much effect on liking because such help is expected. (Based on data from Riordan and others, 1982)*

595

your mother treated you when you were little. As a relationship progresses, the amount of evaluative self-disclosure also increases.

Evaluative self-disclosure gives others a much better idea of what you are really like than hearing an account of how you behaved in a certain situation. In one study the subjects heard other university students describe their backgrounds, their relationships, and the major choices and conflicts in their lives in terms of their behavior, in terms of their thoughts and feelings, or in terms of a combination of both (Andersen, 1984). The subjects who heard the presentations featuring thoughts and feelings made inferences about the speakers that were more in line with both the speakers' self-assessments and the assessments made by their friends than the subjects who heard the presentations that emphasized behavior or the combined material.

If self-disclosure is one-sided, and especially if one person tends to disclose much more rapidly than the other, the relationship may not develop. Both partners, but particularly the one who is receiving the disclosures, are apt to experience discomfort. You probably have had the experience of meeting someone who tried to cram his or her entire life history, in intimate detail, into your first encounter. How did that make you feel about wanting to see that individual again? Chances are good that you responded with some negative feelings that did not enhance the odds of a future for the relationship.

Love

When you hear the word *love*, you probably think about an ecstatic state full of bells, whistles, and fire-crackers, of love at first sight, and of falling in love. Our culture tends to emphasize this type of passionate love or romantic love and to think of it as a necessary step toward marriage. However, psychological researchers have suggested that there are at least two kinds of love: **passionate** and **companionate** (Walster and Walster, 1978). The passionate or sexual kind includes both the idea of "intense absorption in another" and "a state of intense arousal" (Walster and Walster, 1978, p. 9). Companionate love is a deep, close, caring friendship. Companionate love can develop as a later stage of a relationship that begins with passionate love. It may be more likely to develop in relationships that have equity, where both people perceive that they are getting equal rewards from the relationship (Kelley, 1983).

Describing love is difficult enough, but, to do meaningful research, psychologists must also measure it. One such measure was developed by Zick Rubin (1970, 1973). Rubin compared statements rated by university students as characteristic of feelings toward either the person with whom they were romantically involved or a friend of the opposite sex with whom they had a nonromantic relationship. From these statements, Rubin constructed a Liking Scale and a Love Scale. When these scales were given to later groups of students, the results suggested that there is a measurable difference between love and liking. Although the students rated both their dating partner and their friend similarly on the Liking Scale, they rated the dating partner much higher on the Love Scale. Couples who scored high on the Love Scale also behaved differently from couples with lower love scores. For example, during laboratory sessions, high-scoring couples made much more eye contact than low-scoring couples did.

In a study of the components of love, Robert Sternberg and Susan Grajek (1984) found that interpersonal communication, sharing, and support were common factors in all love relationships, including love for same-sex friends, love for a specific person, and love for siblings. Different kinds of love relationships generate different kinds of subjective experiences because of differences in feelings of responsibility, sexual desire, perceived permanence of the relationship, competition for affection, and so on. However, despite these differences, the common factors of communication, sharing, and support are present in all love relationships.

Theories of interpersonal attraction

Social psychologists have developed several theories to explain how relationships work. The most basic explanation is the **reinforcement/affect theory,** which is based on learning theory (Byrne and Clore, 1970). Rewarding stimuli elicit positive feelings and punishing stimuli generate negative ones. In social terms, this means that, if someone does something nice for you, positive feelings become associated with that person. These feelings will generalize to other people and objects associated with the situation. For example, the people present or the particular place where a positive (or negative) interaction took place also tend to be liked (or disliked) more than they would have been otherwise (Byrne, 1971).

Social-exchange theory includes the basic idea of reinforcement/affect theory, but it focuses much more attention on *both* parties involved in the relationship by considering the costs and rewards of the relationship to each (Kelley and Thibaut, 1978). According to this view, each person in the relationship weighs its gains against its costs. We are attracted to people if there is a profit in the relationship—that is, if the relationship's rewards are greater than its costs. For example, you may have a friend who is always late but who is lots of fun and who will always stand by you in any difficulty. You will probably continue to feel attracted to that friend because a good time and a trustworthy friendship outweigh being kept waiting 10 or 15 minutes. Your evaluation of a relationship will be influenced by your personality characteristics and by the specific factors that are especially important to you. For example, in a particular relationship you may gain companionship, excitement, and romance, but you may lose some independence. You would probably not feel good about the relationship if independence were crucial to you.

In addition to stressing the comparison of reward and cost in a particular relationship, exchange theory emphasizes that people also weigh the gains in a relationship against what they might expect in general or against those in another specific relationship. For example, if the loss of independence is less or the excitement is more in another romantic friendship, then the second relationship may seem more rewarding and will replace the first.

Equity theory goes one step further than social-exchange theory by comparing the costs and rewards for *both* individuals in a relationship (Walster and others, 1978). Equity theory assumes that if you are overbenefited or underbenefited compared to your partner, then you will be distressed. This will happen even if your benefits in the relationship are very great and your costs are very small. If you cannot equalize the unbalance, you will probably end the relationship.

The ending of a relationship

Many relationships don't last. For example, about half of all current U.S. marriages will end in divorce (see Figure 17.8). Psychologists have wondered what characteristics of individuals or of relationships might be used to predict which relationships will last. Some personality characteristics have been found to be associated with an increased probability of divorce. For instance, women who are high in ambition and intelligence, and men who have a strong need for orderliness, are more likely to divorce (Newcomb and Bentler, 1981).

Features of the relationship can also be good pre-

FIGURE 17.8 *The wide range of services offered by this merchant suggest how accepted divorce has become in our culture.*

dictors. If both members of the couple are very satisfied with the relationship, do not have suitable alternatives, and have invested a large amount of effort or time in the relationship, they are less likely to break up (Rusbult and others, 1982). In one 2-year study of relationships among student dating couples in the Boston area, the researchers found that after 2 years, 65 of the 231 couples were still dating, 9 were engaged, and 43 were married. Forty-five percent of the sample (103 couples) had broken up, and 11 could not be contacted. Scores on the Rubin Love Scale were better predictors of continuing relationship than scores on the Liking Scale, and women's Love Scale scores were better predictors than men's Love Scale scores. Similarities in age, education, intelligence, and attractiveness were all greater for couples who stayed together than for couples who broke up. Whether or not the couple had lived together or had a sexual relationship was not an important predictor of the later fate of the relationship.

If a relationship is not going well, there are a number of behavioral options. Four common response patterns include:

Discussing the problem and trying to change the behavior of one or both partners

Passively waiting and hoping that things will improve with time

Neglecting, ignoring, or mistreating the partner

Leaving the relationship

Social-exchange theory can be used to predict which of these response patterns will be chosen (Rusbult and others, 1982). If the partners had formerly been well satisfied with the relationship, had invested a great deal of time and effort in it, and had no desirable alternative, they tended to discuss the problem and to wait it out. If their prior satisfaction with the relationship and their time and energy investment were relatively low, and they had a desirable alternative, they were likely to end the relationship.

ATTITUDES AND BEHAVIOR

The development of positive or negative feelings toward other people essentially means that we have formed an attitude toward them. We form attitudes

toward things and ideas as well as toward people. Attitudes are important because they determine what we notice in the environment, how we code the information we gather about what we notice, and how we respond.

What are attitudes?

An **attitude** can be defined as a relatively long-lasting organization of a person's beliefs and feelings about, and behaviors toward, other people, situations, or objects. To put it another way, an attitude is a general tendency to respond to a person or object through a consistent pattern of thoughts, feelings, and behaviors.

Attitudes thus have three components: cognitions (beliefs), emotions (feelings), and behaviors (actions)—see Figure 17.9. You may know, for example, that a snail is a small animal with a shell attached. This knowledge by itself is not an attitude. But perhaps thinking about snails makes you have visions of a plate of the tender creatures dripping with butter and garlic. Now we have a feeling as well as knowledge, and we

---

FIGURE 17.9 *The components of an attitude and an example of how they function—in this case, how the components are expressed in prejudice toward foreigners.*

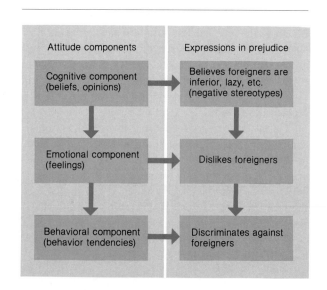

FIGURE 17.10 *This diagram represents the cognitive and affective components of an individual's attitude toward smoking cigarettes. Around the core idea are many cognitive components that are related to smoking. The + and − signs show the positive and negative affect associated with each of these cognitions. The minus sign in the central core indicates the affective component of this person's overall attitude toward smoking. (Adapted from Sears and others, 1985, p. 132)*

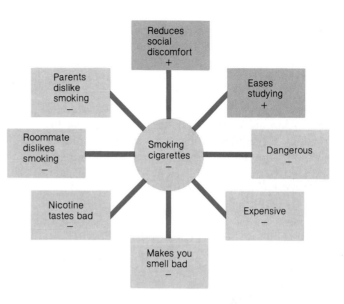

are two-thirds of the way toward an attitude about snails. If you would eat that plate of snails any time you had a chance, that behavior supplies the third essential component, and we can now say you have a particular attitude about snails. (Refusing to eat the snails does not mean that you have no attitude about them. Your refusal would be a behavior indicating a negative attitude.)

How did that attitude develop? The behavioral perspective is often used to answer this question. The behavioral perspective presumes that you learned to like snails through conditioning in the past. Perhaps you watched your father eating a plateful with obvious relish and heard him comment on what a treat they were (modeling), or, possibly, even though you didn't like them at first, every time you ate one your mother told you how grown up you were (operant conditioning).

According to behavioral theorists, changing the pattern of reinforcement will change people's attitudes. If you got stomach cramps the last time you ate snails, your attitude toward the animals as a gourmet treat might change; instead of salivating at the very thought of them, you might feel slightly nauseated whenever the topic came up.

Cognitive complexity and evaluative simplicity

Sometimes the emotional and cognitive components associated with an attitude can be very complex. Think about your attitude toward smoking, for example. You may know a number of negative facts about smoking: it is unhealthful, many people find it objectionable, it is

an expensive habit, smokers sometimes die of lung cancer or in fires caused by forgotten cigarettes. On the other hand, you also know that smoking has some positive features: it gives a person something to do in social situations, people who smoke may look sophisticated, it may provide a pleasant pause after a meal or an excuse to postpone chores. Each of these ideas about smoking is accompanied by a positive or negative affective response. Figure 17.10 combines a variety of evaluations of smoking into one central attitude. A cluster of cognitions like this is not unusual based on numerous and often conflicting ideas.

The **cognitive complexity** of the pieces of information that contribute to an attitude contrasts with the **evaluative simplicity** of the feeling attached to it. In general, despite our awareness of a variety of positive and negative ideas about people or ideas, we tend either to like or to dislike them, rather than having a mixture of feelings about them and the things with which they are associated. This tendency to boil complex appraisals down into simple judgments of liking or disliking has important implications. For example, whether or not they were well informed about each of the separate issues, people who favored a conservative presidential candidate generally supported the candidate's views on such different issues as military preparedness, abortion, and minimum sentences for different kinds of crimes.

People who supported a liberal candidate generally had a different, but also highly consistent, set of views on all these topics (Kinder and Sears, 1985). Moreover, these feelings, the emotional or affective component of an attitude, are much more important in determining behavior than the cognitions that are related to the attitude. They are also much harder to change than the cognitive component. Once an attitude is formed, learning a new fact that might contradict it is unlikely to produce any attitude shift. You have probably demonstrated this principle yourself.

You had thought that the population of your home town was 23,000; when you learn it is 19,000, you probably just substitute that figure in your store of knowledge. However, if you fear and mistrust the Russians, finding out that they are helping to feed starving people in Africa will probably not be effective in changing your negative attitude toward them. It seems to be not what you know as much as how you feel about what you know that causes your attitudes to resist change. One reason for this may be that the facts that produced the attitude have long ago been forgotten, so new information is less likely to change an attitude.

Stereotyped attitudes and prejudice

Many attitudes, such as your boyfriend's or girlfriend's attitude toward marriage or your attitude toward smoking or drinking, affect only you and the people close to you. But some attitudes can influence the nature of the whole society.

Throughout history, prejudice has had more destructive effects on the fabric of society than any other social attitude. It is at the root of racial, ethnic, religious, and sex discrimination. It produces violent, often bloody intergroup confrontations, and feelings of inferiority and self-rejection in its victims. Like all other attitudes, **prejudice** consists of a combination of beliefs, feelings, and behavioral tendencies. Some attitudes, such as a negative reaction to drunk driving, are based on accurate information. But this is not the case with prejudice. The foundation of prejudice is a **stereotype**—a set of beliefs based on inaccurate or incomplete information that is uncritically applied to a whole group of people. Stereotypes can lead us to false appraisals and can blind us to individual differences (McCauley and others, 1980).

Stereotyped beliefs are often used to explain behavior. For example, many people think that all women (or all men) behave alike and that there are certain things that can be done well only by one or the other sex. These people never stop to wonder how they got such ideas in the first place.

Many beliefs are learned from our parents. Others are learned in church, synagogue, and school. The media are also an effective way of communicating attitudes, because they reach such wide audiences. Unfortunately, media presentations—for example, television shows—often create and perpetuate racial, sexual, and occupational stereotypes (see Figure 17.11).

One of the most tragic consequences of prejudice is that the targets of discrimination may eventually come to accept these stereotypes, which lower their self-esteem and lead to feelings of hopelessness and even self-rejection. As a defense against the negative features that they perceive as part of their own identity, oppressed individuals may sometimes come to identify with those who oppress them. In an experiment conducted during the 1940s, black preschool children were given two dolls, one black and one white, and were asked to indicate which of the dolls "looks like you." The black children chose the white doll more frequently than the black one. In another version of the same experiment, about two-thirds of a large sample of black children between the ages of 3 and 10 characterized the white doll as "good" and as preferable to the black doll (Clark and Clark, 1947). More recently, as a result of the black-pride movement, black children have increasingly preferred the doll of their own race (Teplin, 1977). However, the change is not complete, as shown by the Sagar and Schofield experiment described earlier, in the section on schemata.

The growth of prejudice, like that of any other attitude, can be understood in several ways. Prejudice often seems to be a result of *social learning*. Prejudices usually develop on the basis of what other people have said and the attitudes they have expressed, rather than through direct personal contact with the minority groups. Children may hear their parents making negative comments about minorities and justifying discriminatory behavior. Parents may then reinforce their children for expressing prejudiced attitudes similar to their own. Reinforcement also comes from other important people such as friends. If members of a group that you want to be part of have a certain set of attitudes or prejudices, you are likely to feel great pressure to *conform*. You may become prejudiced simply to fit in.

GROUP COMPETITION AND CONFLICT

Political and economic forces often lie at the root of prejudice. Competition for power, jobs, or other scarce resources can motivate a dominant group to exploit or discriminate against a less powerful group. As a result of the powerful civil rights movement of the 1960s, employment and educational opportunities for black Americans were considerably expanded. Research done during the 1970s showed that whites who were just above blacks on the socioeconomic ladder were the most prejudiced against them, especially if the two groups were in close competition for jobs. The same kind of reaction has been expressed toward the Cubans who have settled in large numbers in southern Florida. As their numbers have grown, they have exerted pressure for bilingual services, and existing residents have felt increased competition for jobs, housing, and educational opportunities. Probably as a result of such competition, intergroup conflict has worsened; nega-

tive attitudes toward the Cubans have increased among both black and white Floridians.

THE OUTGROUP-INGROUP CATEGORIZATION

Individuals tend to divide the people in their world into two groups—"us" and "them." As you might expect, the people in the **ingroup,** or the "us" category, are seen in a very positive light, while those in the **outgroup** are viewed in a very negative way. Henri Tajfel and his colleagues have shown that this effect can be produced even by separating people in an experiment in a way that has no relationship to any real-life social categories (Tajfel and Turner, 1979; Turner, 1984). These researchers explain their findings by what they call **social competition.** According to this idea, individuals enhance their self-esteem by perceiving their ingroup as superior. All groups in the society behave in this way, and the inevitable result is the production of prejudice. Tajfel and his co-workers distinguish social competition from social conflict, but it is clear that the

FIGURE 17.11 *The characters in the long-running television program* All in the Family *reflect many of the stereotypes conveyed by television programs.*

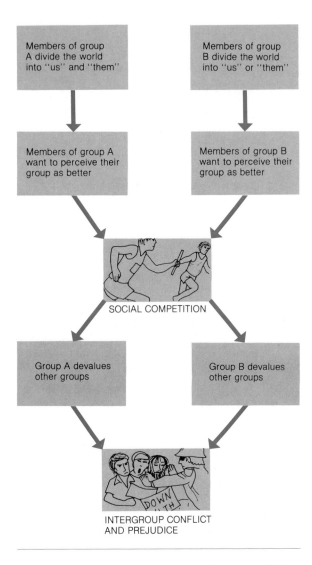

FIGURE 17.12 *Social categorization is the process of dividing the world up into "us" and "them." Each group then perceives themselves as superior. This results in social competition, in which each group devalues the others—a process that may lead to prejudice and intergroup conflict.*

FIGURE 17.13 *An outgroup, in this case members of the opposite sex, is seen as more homogeneous than the ingroup, members of the same sex. This is true even when, as in the case of males and females, there has been considerable contact with members of the outgroup. (Adapted from Park and Rothbart, 1982)*

outcome of each can be the same. Figure 17.12 illustrates how social competition works.

COGNITIVE MECHANISMS IN THE DEVELOPMENT OF PREJUDICE

Imagine that you had been the witness to a crime. Would you be able to pick out the criminal from a police lineup of similar individuals? One factor in your ability to do so would be whether the criminal was of the same or a different racial group from yours. People seem to process and to recall information differently depending on whether the person involved is or is not a member of the same group as they are. In this example a racial group is involved, but it could be any other kind of ingroup-outgroup division. People from the outgroup are perceived as more similar to each other both in physical appearance and in behavior than ingroup people are (Park and Rothbart, 1982). This difference in cognitive behavior is not just the result of lack of exposure to another group. It also applies for groups with which one has extensive contact—for example, members of the opposite sex, as shown in Figure 17.13.

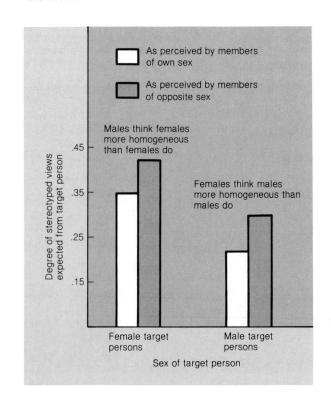

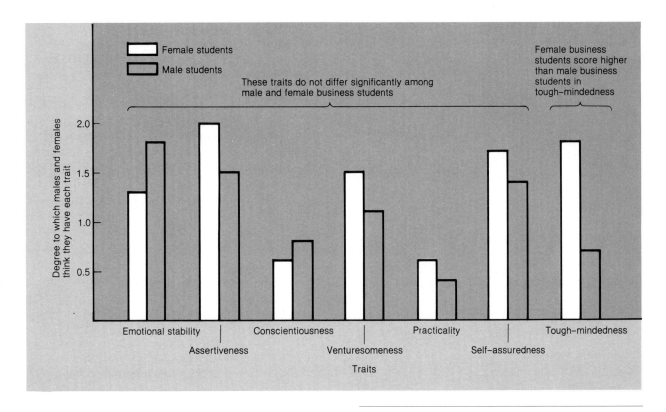

FIGURE 17.14 *Male and female sex stereotypes do not fit well with the personality characteristics of male and female business students. Few differences were found between the two groups on personality tests. Those that did appear suggested that women were more likely than men to have the characteristics that would lead to future managerial success. (Adapted from Steinberg and Shapiro, 1982)*

SEXISM

A very common form of prejudice and discrimination, called **sexism,** is based on whether an individual is male or female. Since most people have had ample opportunity to become acquainted with members of both sexes, lack of exposure does not seem a useful explanation for this type of prejudice. As Figure 17.13 suggests, perhaps stereotypes affect our perceptions of opposite-sex individuals. If you were asked to describe traits of males and females in our culture, you might come up with lists like these: Males are assertive, ambitious, self-confident, logical, decisive, and dominant. Females are submissive, dependent, gentle, passive, emotional, and low in ambition and self-confidence. Do you think that the male list contains more favorable characteristics than the female list does? We agree, but we hasten to assure you that these lists are not the result of any bias on the part of the authors; they were the result of research carried out only a few years ago (Frieze and others, 1979). Such stereotypes have important effects. For example, jobs that are thought of as basically masculine are also considered to be of more value than jobs that are considered to be feminine.

Are these stereotypes accurate? In one study, men and women business students took a series of standard personality tests designed to measure a wide variety of traits (Steinberg and Shapiro, 1982). Since such characteristics as assertiveness, decisiveness, and leadership are often linked with future success as a manager, the researchers were particularly interested in any sex differences in these traits. Few variations were found between the two groups of students. When differences were found, women tended to be higher in the scores thought to represent good managerial potential. Figure 17.14 illustrates how different the findings of this study were from a still persisting stereotype.

(a)

(b)

(c)

(d)

FIGURE 17.15 *Children's book illustrations show stereotyped (a and b) and unstereotyped (c and d) behavior for males and females.*

Since stereotypes may begin to develop early, one way to combat them may involve the material presented to very young children—for instance, the pictures in their storybooks. Figure 17.15 shows stereotyped and unstereotyped illustrations for children's books that were all published at about the same time. Although education designed to combat stereotypes may have some effect, changes in the social system may be more important. For example, in a study about male-female stereotypes, whether or not the females were described as employed was much more important in the characteristics ascribed to them than their gender was (Eagly and Steffen, 1984).

How attitudes translate into behavior

Attitudes do predict behavior, but sometimes the prediction is much more accurate than at other times. A number of factors are involved:

How strong the attitude is

How directly relevant the attitude is to the situation

How much time has elapsed between the measurement of the attitude and the behavior

What other pressures exist in the situation—for example, the presence of friends who may encourage conformity

THE THEORY OF REASONED ACTION

Probably the most influential model used to test the relationship between attitude and behavior is the **theory of reasoned action,** developed by Ajzen and Fishbein (Ajzen and Fishbein, 1975; Ajzen and Fishbein, 1980). The three steps of this model, which assumes that people behave rationally, are outlined in Figure 17.16. One source of prediction has to do with *beliefs* about the usefulness or desirability of a certain behavior; the other relates to the expressed *intention* to perform the behavior. The Ajzen-Fishbein model was used in a study to predict whether pregnant women would bottle- or breast-feed their babies (Manstead and others, 1983). Each prospective mother answered the questionnaire about her own beliefs in the value of breast feeding (personal attitude), about how her close relatives and friends felt about breast feeding and whether those views were important to her (subjective norms), and whether she intended to breast-feed her child when it was born (behavioral intentions). The researchers found that the model predicted behavior quite well: the correlation with the mothers' actual behavior after the birth of their babies was .77, quite a high level of agreement.

COGNITIVE DISSONANCE

Although knowing someone's attitude is useful in predicting his or her behavior, it is always possible to look at the process from the opposite viewpoint: the way that we behave may be responsible for our attitudes.

According to Leon Festinger's theory of **cognitive dissonance,** we like consistency. Our cognitions about related things should all fit together neatly. When we experience something that directly contradicts what we believe, we feel tense and uncomfortable. We can reduce this tension and discomfort by denying the truth of the new information, by changing our belief to fit the new information, or by somehow distorting the situation so that it no longer threatens our beliefs.

People actively try to avoid dissonance. For exam-

ple, if you have doubts about staying in college, you may talk to other people about them. But once you have made your decision, you may be inclined to discuss it only with people who already agree with you, and you may carefully avoid conversations in which people are likely to make negative comments about your choice. Festinger would say that you are attempting to reduce the possibilities for dissonance by focusing on information that you already know is consistent with your beliefs.

In a classic study inspired by dissonance theory (Festinger and Carlsmith, 1959), subjects worked on an extremely boring task (packing thread spools into a box, dumping them out, and repacking them, over and over again) for a considerable period of time while an experimenter recorded their performance. At the end of the experiment, each subject was offered money to tell another subject who was waiting to begin the experiment that the task was interesting. Some subjects were offered $1 to do this; others were offered $20. After the subjects who agreed to do so had lied to the next participants, they were asked to evaluate the experiment. Which group of subjects do you think evaluated the task more favorably, the $1 group or the $20 group? If you think the $20 group did because they received a

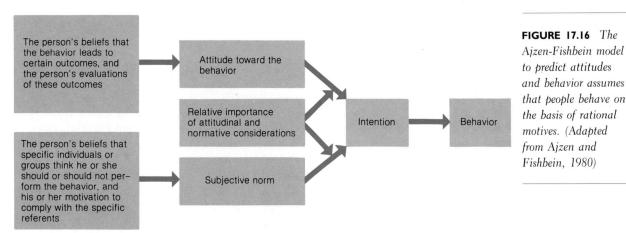

FIGURE 17.16 *The Ajzen-Fishbein model to predict attitudes and behavior assumes that people behave on the basis of rational motives. (Adapted from Ajzen and Fishbein, 1980)*

The person's beliefs that the behavior leads to certain outcomes, and the person's evaluations of these outcomes

Attitude toward the behavior

Relative importance of attitudinal and normative considerations

Intention

Behavior

The person's beliefs that specific individuals or groups think he or she should or should not perform the behavior, and his or her motivation to comply with the specific referents

Subjective norm

The arrows indicate the direction of influence

greater reward for doing so, you are wrong. The $1 group rated the task as far more enjoyable than the $20 group did.

How can we explain this result? We can begin with the assumption that both groups of subjects probably viewed themselves as basically moral people. Both groups had lied in telling another person that the boring task was enjoyable. These two cognitions were likely to produce dissonance because moral people don't lie. The theory of cognitive dissonance predicts that individuals will either change one of their cogni-

FIGURE 17.17 *Cognitive dissonance is at work here. In many cases people prefer the things for which they have paid a high price (in money or effort) to those they have obtained at little cost.*

"I suppose I shouldn't admit this, but I liked it better at three-fifty."

(DRAWING BY FRASCINO; © 1975 THE NEW YORKER MAGAZINE, INC.)

tions or add more cognitions to explain such inconsistencies (see Figure 17.17). Because individuals in the $20 group could justify their behavior in terms of the large reward they received ("After all, who wouldn't tell a little lie for $20?"), they felt less dissonance and had little reason to change their attitude toward the task. The subjects who lied for only $1 could not use money to justify their behavior, but there was another way out for them: if they were to decide that the task really was enjoyable, then they wouldn't have been lying after all, and the dissonance would be removed.

Changing behavior does not always change attitudes in this way. An individual who feels forced into compliance can blame the inconsistent behavior on external demands and will not experience cognitive dissonance (Riess and Schlenker, 1977). Dissonance and attitude change are both more likely to occur if no force is involved and the individual has *free choice*. Our personal commitment to our behavior also affects the amount of dissonance that we will experience. For example, being caught smoking a cigarette causes more dissonance if you have publicly proclaimed that you were quitting smoking than it would if you had kept that knowledge to yourself.

The cognitive dissonance theory has been attacked and defended in almost every way imaginable. Behavioral psychologists have been particularly critical of it. According to behaviorists, the greater the reinforcement, the greater the learning or change in behavior. But the cognitive dissonance effect shows that sometimes this behavioral law does not work. The $20 group doesn't always change its behavior. Other psychologists believe that the findings of cognitive dissonance research can be explained in a simpler way.

SELF-PERCEPTION THEORY

Daryl Bem (1972) has set forth a **self-perception theory** to explain the cognitive dissonance effect. He suggests that people infer their own attitudes in the same way that they infer those of others: by observing behavior and relating it to the type of situation in which it occurs. According to Bem, people first look at the situation. If the situation does not seem to be the cause of their behavior, then they assume that the behavior is a reflection of their attitudes. For example, Bem would explain the results of Festinger and Carlsmith's study this way. The $1 reward group would say, "I said I liked the spool task. Since I was paid only $1 to tell someone I liked it, I must really have liked it because $1 is not enough to make me lie." The $20 reward group would say to themselves, "I was paid $20 to tell someone I liked to place spools. Twenty dollars is enough to make me lie. I really don't like the spool task." In each case, the attitude is inferred from the person's own behavior. Bem maintains that we can explain the results without recourse to some internal dissonance state.

Some experimenters have argued that both cognitive dissonance and self-perception theories can be useful, depending on the situation (Greenwald, 1975). Festinger's theory presumes an emotional state; Bem's is based on a cool appraisal of behavior. If a person behaves in a way that is very different from his or her initial attitude—for example, by enjoying something that he or she previously disliked—then dissonance theory seems to be a better explanation for the change. On the other hand, if the behavior is not very different from the initial attitude—for example, "I thought I wasn't hungry, but I must have been because I ate two pieces of pie instead of one"—then self-perception theory may provide a simpler explanation.

Persuasion and attitude change

Large corporations spend millions of dollars each year in advertising campaigns trying to change our behavior by changing our attitudes. These campaigns are designed to create new wants and needs and to make us feel that only GLORY shampoo and MINTO breath freshener can attract dates and make us socially acceptable. Political candidates also attempt to change our attitudes and to persuade us that only they can solve the problems of the country. Government agencies work hard to change old attitudes and to substitute new ones—for example, the desirability of riding the bus instead of driving to work or school. You might work very hard to change your parents' attitude about your living off campus or to change your boyfriend's or girlfriend's attitude toward marriage.

There are innumerable approaches to persuading others. The processes involved are so complex that, in spite of several decades of research and hundreds of

studies, we do not yet fully understand them. Some factors that have been examined include the characteristics of communicators and the form and content of the communications.

CHARACTERISTICS OF THE COMMUNICATOR

In the 1950s a Yale research group that included Carl Hovland, Irving Janis, and Harold Kelley (1953) began to systematically study the role of the communicator in the process of persuasion. They identified the communicator's *credibility*—how believable he or she is— as a critical characteristic. Credibility has two major components: *expertise* and *trustworthiness*. The most effective persuader is one who appears to be an expert in the area that he or she is talking about and who appears to be presenting the truth in as unbiased a manner as possible.

The source of the communication can affect the meaning that it conveys. People often change a message's meaning to fit their perceptions of the communicator. For example, consider the following statement: "The goal of liberty justifies any means used to attain it." Would your understanding of the statement be any different if George Washington had said it instead of Karl Marx?

The particular characteristics of the audience can change the way the speaker presents the information and also his or her own later attitudes toward the information presented. In one study, subjects were asked to present information about another person to an audience who, the subject believed, either liked or disliked that person (Higgins and McCann, 1984). When the subjects were later asked about their own attitude toward the person, those who had spoken to an audience whose attitude was positive described the individual much more favorably than those who had talked to an audience whose attitude was negative. The subjects' tailoring of their description to fit their audience had apparently influenced their own attitudes.

ONE-SIDED VERSUS TWO-SIDED ARGUMENTS

When trying to persuade someone, is it more effective to present only one side of the issue or also to present the opposition's arguments and then try to refute them? The relative effectiveness of these two approaches seems to depend on the audience's initial attitude toward the position that you want them to take and on their awareness that there are two reasonable sides to the issue.

One-sided arguments are most effective for audiences who agree with the message or who are ignorant of the other side of the issue. Two-sided messages are more effective with individuals who disagree with the communicator's position or who are aware that there is another point of view. These people are likely to perceive a one-sided argument as biased and are apt to construct counterarguments against it. Two-sided arguments that acknowledge and refute the arguments against their position seem more fair and will discourage the audience from formulating their own arguments.

Exposing people to counterarguments that are then refuted appears to strengthen their attitudes and to make them highly resistant to change. In fact, William McGuire has suggested that it is possible to "inoculate" people against attempts to change their attitudes by presenting a form of two-sided argument. McGuire argued that stating weak counterarguments to your position and then refuting them stimulates the audience to think up additional refutations of their own (McGuire and Papageorgis, 1961).

PERSUADING THROUGH FEAR

Some attempts to change our attitudes and behaviors are specifically designed to scare us. For example, we are told that smoking will increase our chances of developing lung cancer (see Figure 17.18).

Fear can be an effective way to change behavior. One study compared the effects of high-fear and low-fear appeals on changes in attitudes and behaviors related to dental hygiene. One group of subjects was shown awful pictures of decayed teeth and diseased gums; another group was shown less frightening materials such as plastic teeth, charts, and graphs. Subjects who saw the frightening materials reported more anxiety and a greater desire to change the way they took care of their teeth than the low-fear group did.

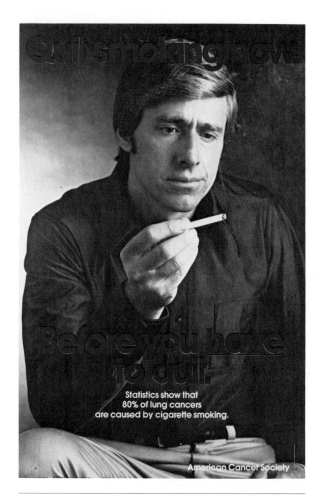

Statistics show that 80% of lung cancers are caused by cigarette smoking.

American Cancer Society

FIGURE 17.18 *Scare techniques are often used for persuasion.*

But were these reactions actually translated into better dental hygiene practices? To answer this important question, subjects were called back to the laboratory on two occasions (five days and six weeks after the experiment). They chewed disclosing wafers that give a red stain to any uncleaned areas of the teeth and thus provided a direct indication of how well they were really taking care of their teeth. Figure 17.19 shows that the high-fear appeal did actually result in greater and more permanent changes in dental hygiene (Rogers and Mewborn, 1976).

However, to be an effective persuasive device it is very important that the message not be too frightening and that people be given concrete guidelines to help

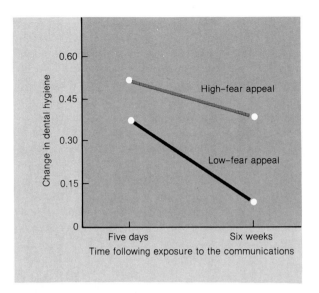

of a reward, except possibly the good feeling of having done something useful. Someone who jumps into the street, pulls a young child from the path of an out-of-control car, and then disappears into the crowd has performed an altruistic act. In addition to altruistic acts, **prosocial behavior** includes help that may be motivated by self-interest—for example, offering to serve as a volunteer fundraiser for a particular charity that you know is the company president's favorite. In this section, we will consider two basic questions: What are the sources of the behavior? What are the conditions under which it is most likely to occur?

FIGURE 17.19   *The effects of high- and low-fear appeals on dental hygiene behaviors show that subjects exposed to high-fear warnings brushed their teeth more carefully than did those who saw low-fear warnings. (Adapted from Rogers and Mewborn, 1976)*

The biological perspective

Human beings are not the only living things that help others. Many examples of helping behavior can be found throughout the animal kingdom. Birds pretend to be injured to lead an attacker away from their young. Soldier termites use their own bodies to protect the other termites against intruders. Psychobiologists thus think of helping behavior performed by all animals as a way to guarantee the survival of their own genes by ensuring that their young and their close relatives will continue to be able to reproduce (Wilson, 1975).

them to reduce the cause of the fear. If this isn't done, they may reduce their anxiety by denying the message or the credibility of the communicator. If that happens, it is unlikely that either attitude or behavior change will occur.

ALTRUISM AND PROSOCIAL BEHAVIOR

One group of attitudes of particular interest to psychologists are those that relate to the importance of helping others. Most of us have stopped to help someone who has tripped and fallen on the street, given money to a charity, donated blood, worked as a volunteer for some organization, or done something similar to be helpful to others. Social psychologists are interested in why some people often help others and some almost never do.

Helping behavior is usually divided into two types: altruism and prosocial behavior. **Altruism** refers to voluntary acts that are carried out without any expectation

The psychodynamic perspective

Freud thought of the development of the superego, or conscience, as a result of the child's identification with the same-sex parent. In the course of the identification process, the child adopts the values and standards of the parent and usually also those of the culture. Freud believed that if a person does not behave as morally or altruistically as his or her culture expects, the penalty is the experience of guilt. An example of the identification process was found in a study of the motives of people who helped Jews to escape from the Nazis dur-

609

ing World War II (London, 1970). Often the people whom they helped were strangers, and many times the rescuers did not particularly like them. Yet they helped them escape, often at great personal risk. Although a number of motives for this helping behavior were noted, an important one seemed to be parental identification. The rescuers behaved as they thought their parents would have liked them to.

The learning perspective

Social learning theory emphasizes the role parents, teachers, and other adults play in teaching children about the value of helping other people. Modeling by parents is one important source of learning altruistic behavior. What children see on television can also serve as a model for behavior. In one study, first grade children watched one of two programs from the popular TV series *Lassie* (Sprafkin and others, 1975). One program focused on the attempts of Lassie's owner, Jeff, to avoid violin lessons. The other program was the story of Lassie's attempt to prevent her puppy from being given away. At the end of the program, after the puppy has fallen into a deep hole, Lassie brings Jeff and his grandfather to the scene. Jeff rescues the puppy at the risk of his own life. After each child watched the program, he or she was taken into another room to play a game in which points could be earned. The more points earned, the better the prize. After the child had been shown how to play the game, the experimenter said she had to go out of the room briefly. Before she left she asked the child to help her by listening through some headphones while playing the game. The headphones were being used, she told the child, to monitor the safety of some puppies who were kept nearby. If the child heard the puppies barking, he or she could help by leaving the game and pressing a button to alert the experimenter. Children who had seen the second *Lassie* episode spent more time helping than the other children, even though this meant that they had less of a chance to accumulate points and win a desirable prize. This study suggests that modeling is an important factor in encouraging helping behavior.

Reinforcement is another useful method of promoting helping behavior. In one study, people walking down a city street were stopped by an attractive young woman who asked for directions (Moss and Page, 1972). She responded either with thanks (reward) or by commenting that she didn't understand and would ask someone else (punishment). A little farther down the street, each subject came upon another woman who dropped a small bag and walked on without appearing to notice it. The results were a dramatic support for the power of reinforcement: 90 percent of those thanked for their directions helped by returning the woman's bag. Only 40 percent of those whose attempts to help had been rebuffed retrieved the bag.

These studies suggest the importance of learning in the development of prosocial behavior. Helping may become a habit and the reinforcement may become internalized.

The cognitive perspective

Some researchers interested in prosocial behavior from a cognitive perspective have focused on development. The work of Jean Piaget has emphasized how, as children's thinking develops, they show greater empathy: the ability to see things from another's point of view and to understand other people's intentions and purposes. Thus, defined from Piaget's viewpoint, empathy is a cognitive skill. However, it can be thought of as much more than that. Experiencing the feelings of others has also been described as an important feature of empathy (Feschbach, 1978). In one study, children between the ages of 7 and 12 were asked to discuss happy, sad, or neutral experiences that had happened to them or another child (Barnett and others, 1979). After the discussion, they were given tokens that could be exchanged for prizes after the study was over. The experimenter then told the subjects that they could donate some of their tokens to some other children who could not be in the study and who therefore could not receive prizes. As Figure 17.20 shows, the children who were asked to tell about the negative experiences of another child gave the most tokens and those who told about bad things that had happened to themselves gave the fewest. This study suggests that inducing a mood relating to the sadness of others can increase helping behavior, while self-absorption decreases it. It also may be given a more cognitive interpretation: the children

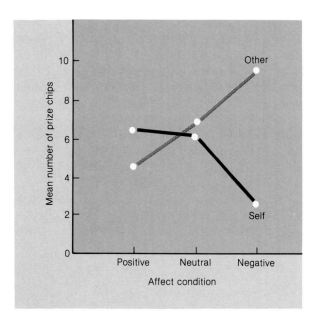

FIGURE 17.20 *Induced moods and focusing on others can both affect giving. Children who were asked to tell about the bad experiences of others donated more tokens to other youngsters than did children who were asked to tell about good experiences of themselves or others. Children asked to tell about their own bad experiences gave away the fewest tokens. (Adapted from Barnett and others, 1979)*

may have become more aware of the difficulties of others and thus more understanding that others may need help too.

The person × situation interaction in helping

Helping behavior can also be examined in relation to personal factors and situational variables.

THE SITUATION

Most research has concentrated on characteristics of the situation that either encourage or discourage helping. Factors that have been investigated include the number of others present, how ambiguous the situation is, and the safety and convenience of helping.

Number present   A consistent finding from experiments on helping (Latane and Nida, 1981) was that assistance was most likely to be offered when only one bystander was present. This can be explained from a cognitive perspective as the result of **diffusion of responsibility** (Latane and Darley, 1970). When several people were present, none felt the responsibility to act. Each may have adopted a "let George do it" attitude.

This phenomenon can also be explained from the behavioral perspective. According to modeling theory, people are less likely to help when a group is present because each person in the group serves as a model for others and each waits for someone else to act. For example, suppose you join a crowd watching a man and a woman fighting in the street. According to the diffusion of responsibility idea, you may decide that someone else should intervene; after all, they were there first and know more about it than you do. According to the modeling interpretation, in contrast, the other bystanders are models who show you what may be the appropriate behavior for this situation. Following their pattern, the suitable behavior seems to be doing nothing.

Ambiguity   Both interpretations involve the idea of uncertainty, of not knowing what to do. Few of us have had much practice dealing with emergencies. Because many emergency situations are quite **ambiguous,** people are likely to look for cues from others. Observers may often be reluctant to help because they are not sure how to interpret the situation and are afraid of making a mistake. If the participants remove the ambiguity, then the observers may feel a greater sense of responsibility and are more likely to offer assistance if it seems needed. In one experiment, observers witnessed a fight between a man and a woman. When the woman cried out, "I don't know you" during the course of the battle, 65 percent of the male observers tried to help. When she indicated that she and the man knew each other, however, only 19 percent of the observers intervened (Shotland and Straw, 1976).

Evaluation apprehension The number of people present and the ambiguity of the situation also influence helping because of **evaluation apprehension.** Most people don't want to appear foolish by trying to help in an inappropriate situation. For example, what if the people fighting are really having a lovers' quarrel? If you butted in, both of them might turn on you, and you'd be embarrassed. A finding that supports the evaluation apprehension explanation is that even self-help is inhibited by the presence of others. In one study, for example, a sign was placed in an elevator telling passengers to help themselves to free coupons for McDonald's hamburgers. When passengers rode the elevator alone, 81 percent took a coupon. When there were other passengers on the elevator, however, only 14 percent took one (Petty and others, 1977). Apparently, the other riders created some sort of pressure to ignore the offer. Someone taking a coupon may have felt like a cheapskate or may not have wanted to admit that he or she ever ate at McDonald's.

Costs and rewards Another way of looking at helping behavior is **cost-reward analysis** (Walster and Piliavin, 1972). The cost-reward analysis combines the ideas of diffusion of responsibility, modeling, and social evaluation into one framework. A decision tree illustrating the cost-reward analysis is shown in Figure 17.21. This explanation puts more emphasis on cognitive factors

FIGURE 17.21 *A decision tree illustrates the cognitive processes leading to intervention or nonintervention in an emergency. Helping behavior is not indiscriminate. People are more likely to help those they like, those with whom they can identify, and those who appear to be really in need (greater benefits). They are less likely to help if the victim's plight appears very serious (greater cost).*

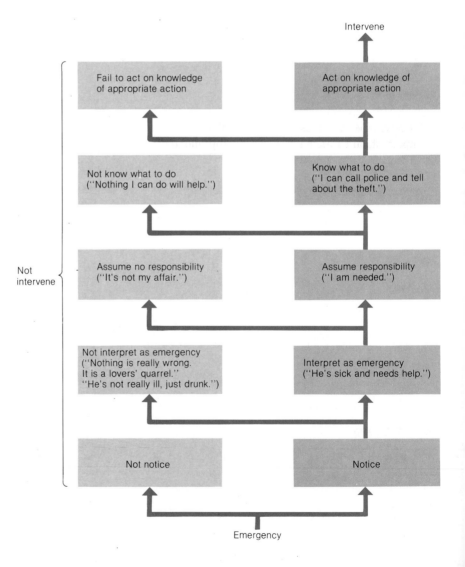

and on the characteristics of the situation. According to this interpretation, the bystander in an emergency experiences some amount of emotional arousal. Because arousal is uncomfortable, the bystander is motivated to reduce it. This can be done in several ways: by helping, by not helping, or by cognitively redefining the situation so that helping becomes unnecessary. If the emergency is severe, the observer's arousal is high, but the costs of intervention may be high as well. To reduce the arousal at low cost, the bystander is most likely to redefine the event into a nonemergency or at least into a situation that holds few chances for serious injury. The perceived costs to someone who helps are also considered. If they are low, the bystander is more likely to help. However, as the cost of helping increases, the chances of direct intervention decrease. So if the victim appears to be severely injured and the assailant with the knife is still there, the chances of helping will decrease (Piliavin and Piliavin, 1972).

Time pressure Another factor that can influence helping is whether potential helpers are in a hurry. People in a hurry, especially those who believe that their goal is important, are much less likely to stop and help. Even students at a theological seminary who were on their way to give lectures on the helping behavior of the biblical Good Samaritan were less likely to stop to help a man sprawled in a doorway if they were in a hurry (Batson and others, 1978).

THE PERSON

Personality characteristics, mood, and the presence or absence of guilt feelings can also be important in determining helping behavior.

Personality characteristics We have already discussed the idea that *empathy* may be an important motivator for helping. Work with adults has shown that individual differences in empathy are related to the probability that people will aid others, but research with children has produced conflicting results (see, for example, Marcus and others, 1979; Levine and Hoffman, 1975). Another personality characteristic related to helping is **locus of control.** People who have an internal locus of control—who believe that their behavior can affect the outcome of events—are more likely to help than those whose locus of control is external—who feel that what they do will not have much effect (Midlarsky and Mid-

larsky, 1973). However, as is the case with many personality variables, the effects of locus of control and variables in the situation often interact, so that in some cases internal individuals are the least likely to help. Individuals with an internal orientation seem more likely to conclude that others are undeserving—that is, that they could do something about the situation themselves or are responsible for having gotten themselves into difficulty in the first place (Phares and Lamiell, 1975).

Some researchers have argued that there is a personality characteristic of altruism that distinguishes people who are "consistently more generous, helping, and kind than others" (Rushton and others, 1981, p. 296). One scale designed to predict altruism, the Self-Report Altruism Scale (Rushton and others, 1981), correlates with other self-reports of altruism. Even more interesting, individuals who scored high on this scale were found to be more likely to have completed the medical organ-donor card attached to their driver's license than those subjects who scored low on the scale. This indicates that the scale may be related to at least some kinds of altruistic behaviors.

Mood and guilt Other personal characteristics that affect helping behavior are mood and guilt. Being in a good mood may often increase helping behavior (Fried and Berkowitz, 1979), but the effects of a bad mood seem more complicated. If a bad mood leads to thoughts about one's own needs, it can discourage helping (Thompson and others, 1980). On the other hand, if a person believes that helping someone may serve to break the bad mood, "the blues" may encourage generosity (Cialdini and others, 1981).

In addition to understanding the situational and personality characteristics that lead to altruistic or prosocial behavior, psychologists have been interested in developing ways to increase prosocial behavior. Frontier 17.1 describes how the increasing need for blood as a result of improvements in medical technology has led to psychological research on ways to promote one specific kind of giving: the donation of blood.

WHO DONATES BLOOD AND WHY? A STUDY OF PROSOCIAL BEHAVIOR

The availability of human blood often determines whether a patient will live or die. Technological advances in medicine have saved numerous lives, but many of these procedures have increased the need for whole blood or blood products. One of the biggest consumers of blood transfusions is coronary bypass surgery. Others include bone marrow transplantation for the treatment of leukemia, hospital emergency care facilities, and trauma centers. Figure 17.22 shows a blood donor during the donation. Figures 17.23, 17.24, and 17.25 illustrate some of the uses for blood.

The best sources of blood are voluntary donors rather than those who are paid for their blood. Blood from volunteers is safer because it is less likely to carry viruses that could threaten the health of the recipient. Yet the blood banks that seek voluntary donations have a problem—often their supplies run short, and

even special radio and television appeals do not bring in enough donors. For example, the Puget Sound Blood Bank reported a great increase over the four years from 1979 to 1983 in the use of some products derived from whole blood. The demand for red cells jumped 54 percent and the use of platelets 82 percent. During this same period the total blood donated grew by only 25 percent. A number of observers have expressed concern that current methods of attracting donors will soon not be effective in preventing a shortage of blood. More efficient use of various components of the blood made possible by new technology has helped prevent a serious shortage, but medical advances cannot solve the basic problem that the demand for blood is outstripping the supply.

The average blood donor is male, gives as part of an organized campaign from a school or business, is a

FIGURE 17.22 *Blood donation takes a short time, does not harm the donor, and fulfills an important social need.*

FIGURE 17.23 *The use of blood and blood products helps to save the lives of many accident victims.*

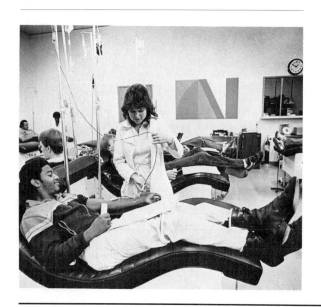

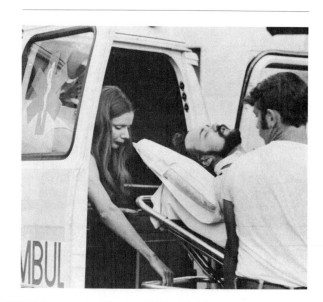

repeat donor, gives blood at a mobile unit brought to the site especially for the blood drive, and is likely to be a resident of the community where the blood is collected. Only a small fraction of the public in the United States donates blood, between 2 and 4 percent in different areas. Yet donating blood is safe, has no harmful effects for the donor, and is an important contribution to public welfare. Why is the percent of participation so low despite blood drives in businesses and schools and appeals to the general public?

Psychologists are interested in what motivates people to donate blood and how an understanding of these reasons can help to bring about an increase in donations. Research on altruism and prosocial behavior has suggested a few leads. Although people who are high in the personality characteristic of prosocial behavior tend to behave in ways that are helpful to the community, their other personality characteristics, or the aspects of the situation, help to determine *when* they are likely to behave in a prosocial manner (Staub, 1978). Thus, helping behavior is influenced in part by the situational payoff that the individual foresees if he or she behaves prosocially (Gergen and others, 1972).

Researchers have looked at the donating situation with these points in mind. Donors identify several reasons for donating: a general desire to help others, the convenience of the clinic, a sense of duty, and expected feelings of satisfaction. Reasons given for ceasing to donate included the absence of a convenient clinic, a lack of time, and temporary illness (Lightman, 1982). Reasons for not donating at all center on fear of discomfort, fear of the needle used to draw blood, and other concerns about the procedure (Richmond, 1975). The challenge for the psychologist

FIGURE 17.24 *Surgical procedures that require large amounts of blood, such as this open heart surgery, have become increasingly common.*

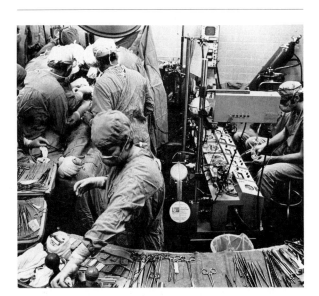

FIGURE 17.25 *Many cancer patients require large quantities of blood products for their treatment.*

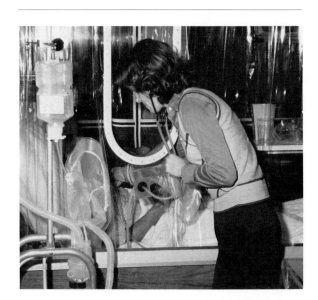

WHO DONATES BLOOD AND WHY?
A STUDY OF PROSOCIAL BEHAVIOR

is to decrease these anxieties and to increase individuals' feelings of self-worth. Connecting the cognition "this is something I can do that will make a difference" with giving blood may be important in boosting donor activity.

As this book goes to press, two of your authors, Irwin and Barbara Sarason, are at work on a project to study the effects of such a cognitive-behavioral approach to blood donation among high school students. Before a blood drive is scheduled at a high school, the local blood bank often presents a program giving information about what blood does in the body, how donated blood is processed, and how the components of human blood work in saving lives. In this research some students will see this kind of informational presentation, while other students will view a cognitively oriented slide program that focuses on why people decide to donate blood and the positive thoughts that blood donation creates in people's minds. The researchers predict that the cognitively oriented program will increase both initial and repeated blood donations among the students who see it compared to donations from students who see either the information program or no program at all. This is but one of many examples of the use of psychological theory and research data to help solve a practical problem.

RESEARCH METHODS IN SOCIAL PSYCHOLOGY (p. 584)

Social psychologists use a number of methods that allow them to assess behavior in real-life settings. These include surveys, field studies, natural experiments, and field experiments.

SOCIAL PERCEPTION (p. 585)

1. When we interact with other people we try to understand not only what their behavior means but why they behave the way they do. The process of explaining the cause of another person's behavior is called attribution. Some attributions focus on the personal characteristics of the individual and some on the situation in which the behavior occurs. Both of these types may reflect either stable or unstable factors.

2. The fundamental attribution error is the tendency to blame other people for their own nondesirable actions and to blame the world for ours. The rules of attribution include distinctiveness, consensus, and consistency. In addition to these cognitive characteristics, needs and wishes play a role in attribution.

SOCIAL COGNITION (p. 588)

1. Social cognition relies on the concepts and principles of encoding, integration, and decoding of information to help interpret the general processes that people use to make sense of other people and themselves.

2. Past experiences, organized in cognitive structures called schemata, help us to quickly understand the meaning of others' behavior. Perceptions are influenced by person, role, and event schemata.

ATTRACTION, LIKING, AND LOVE (p. 590)

1. Similarity is an important factor in attraction. Although complementary characteristics sometimes can be observed in couples who are drawn to each other, closer investigation usually reveals that their basic values are very similar. Familiarity also influences liking. Familiar people are more apt to be liked. Physical attractiveness plays a role in liking; people who are physically attractive are assumed to have more positive traits than less attractive individuals.

2. Once attraction has occurred, several characteristics play a role in determining whether a relationship will develop. These include reciprocity in liking and in helping, as well as in self-disclosure.

3. Love can be based on passion and sexual attraction, or it can be companionate—that is, be a close, deep, and caring friendship without any romantic element. Sometimes companionate love can develop in a relationship that began with passionate love and the two kinds of love can coexist. Love and liking have somewhat different characteristics that can be measured by paper and pencil tests. However, recent research has found that despite the differences in love and liking relationships, communication, sharing, and support are present in all three.

4. Several theories have been used to explain how relationships function. These include the reinforcement/affect theory, the social-exchange theory, and the equity theory. The theories can also be used to study the ending of relationships and to predict which relationships are most likely to last.

ATTITUDES AND BEHAVIOR (p. 598)

1. Attitudes are a long-lasting organization of a person's beliefs, feelings, and behaviors toward other people, things, or events. The pieces of information that contribute to an attitude are often complex, but the feelings attached to the attitude may be very simple.

2. Prejudices are attitudes that may have effects, not just on the individual but on all of society. Prejudices are based on stereotypes that consist of inaccurate information that is applied to a whole group of people who are lumped together in the mind of the prejudiced person. Examples of the results of prejudice are discrimination because of race or sex.

3. Political and economic forces are often the basic cause of discrimination based on prejudice. In social competition, groups are formed and those people not in one's ingroup are considered as inferior.

4. The theory of reasoned action developed by Ajzen and Fishbein is a model for predicting behavior on the basis of individuals' beliefs about the usefulness of a specific activity and their intention to behave in a particular way.

5. Cognitive dissonance is the state of tension felt

when there is a difference between what a person is experiencing and what he or she believes. People who undergo dissonance may cognitively distort either the situation or their beliefs in order to avoid the tension. Self-perception theory is an alternate way to interpret the cognitive dissonance effect. It emphasizes that people may experience the situation first, and if it does not explain their behavior, may conclude, instead, that their behavior is based on attitudes.

6. Persuasive communications may result from characteristics of the communicator and also from the form and content of the communication. The communicator must appear to be an expert and also to be trustworthy. Sometimes a frightening message can be a good way to persuade people to alter their behavior as long as they are given suggestions about how to make the changes.

ALTRUISM AND PROSOCIAL BEHAVIOR (p. 609)

Altruistic behavior is carried out without any thought of reward except possibly a good feeling about having done something worthwhile. Prosocial behavior includes both altruistic acts and helping behavior that may be motivated by the thought of some reward. Each of the perspectives has a different way to explain helping behavior. From a person × situation viewpoint, several aspects of the event may be important. These include the number of people present and the ambiguity of the situation, as well as the relative costs and rewards of helping behavior and the time pressure felt by the individual. Personality characteristics related to helping behavior are empathy and locus of control, as well as a person's mood at the time that help is needed.

KEY TERMS AND CONCEPTS

survey study	field experiment
field study	attribution
natural experiment	personal attribution

situational attribution

stable attribution

unstable attribution

fundamental attribution error

self-presentation

social cognition

schemata

self schemata

person schemata

role schemata

event schemata

affiliation

functional distance

reciprocity

self-disclosure

passionate love

companionate love

reinforcement/affect theory

social-exchange theory

equity theory

attitude

cognitive complexity

evaluative simplicity

prejudice

stereotype

ingroup

outgroup

social competition

sexism

theory of reasoned action

cognitive dissonance

self-perception theory

altruism

prosocial behavior

diffusion of responsibility

ambiguity

evaluation apprehension

cost-reward analysis

locus of control

SUGGESTED READINGS

BARON, R. A., and BYRNE, D. (1984). *Social psychology: Understanding human interaction* (4th ed.). Boston: Allyn and Bacon. A complete and up-to-date review of the field of social psychology. Diagrams illustrating many basic relationships are especially helpful.

FISKE, S. T., and TAYLOR, S. E. (1984). *Social cognition*. Reading, MA: Addison-Wesley. Well written in a simple style, this review of one of the most active areas in social psychology is an especially good choice for additional reading.

KELLEY, H. H., BERSCHEID, E., CHRISTENSEN, A., HARVEY, J. H., HUSTON, T. L., LEVINGER, G., McCLINTOCK, E., PEPLAU, L. A., and PETERSON, D. R. (1983). *Close relationships*. New York: Freeman. This collaborative work, with chapters by specialists in the field, looks at both the internal dynamics and the environmental factors that shape intimate relationships.

SEARS, D. O., FREEDMAN, J. L., and PEPLAU, L. A. (1985). *Social psychology* (5th ed.). Englewood Cliffs, N.J.: Prentice-Hall. Brief and highly interesting, this basic text emphasizes the newer areas of social psychology, for example, relationships and social cognition.

CHAPTER EIGHTEEN
THE SOCIAL ENVIRONMENT

SOCIAL NORMS AND ROLES
Development of norms
Conformity
Deindividuation

GROUP DYNAMICS
Group influences on task performance
Group decision making
Social power and leadership
Intergroup conflict and conflict resolution
FRONTIER 18.1   GROUP DYNAMICS IN SPORTS

SOCIAL IMPACT OF THE PHYSICAL ENVIRONMENT
Crowding
Noise
FRONTIER 18.2   PSYCHOLOGY AND THE ENVIRONMENT

STUDY OUTLINE

KEY TERMS AND CONCEPTS

SUGGESTED READINGS

The prison had become a living hell. Hidden behind their mirrored sunglasses, the guards asserted their total authority and power over the prisoners. The prisoners had to get the guards' permission to do virtually anything, including going to the toilet. After a few days, the prisoners revolted, but the disturbance was quickly put down by the guards. Cruelty and inhumanity now became the order of the day. The guards began to do roll calls in the middle of the night to disrupt the prisoners' sleep and to assert their power. Prisoners were forced to do pushups, sometimes with a guard's foot pushing down on their back. The guards stretched routine 10-minute lineups into hour-long ordeals filled with verbal assault and abuse (see Figure 18.1). They refused to allow the prisoners bathroom privileges during the night and forced them to use containers in their cells.

For their part, the prisoners became increasingly passive, helpless, and depressed. They hated the guards with a vengeance, but they were powerless against them. After a few days, one of the prisoners cracked emotionally. Soon afterward, another broke down. Before long, the smelly, demoralized prisoners became what the guards imagined them to be—objects of scorn and abuse.

This prison was not in some Central American country. It was not in Iran, in the Gulag, or on Devil's Island. The prisoners were not hardened criminals, nor were the guards sadistic psychopaths. No, this prison was in the basement of the Psychology Building at Stanford University, and the guards and prisoners were intelligent, well-adjusted college students who had been carefully screened beforehand. The Warden of the Stanford County Prison was Philip G. Zimbardo, a prominent social psychologist, who watched in disbelief and horror as scenes of callous inhumanity unfolded before him. What had begun as a two-week simulation study of prison life had to be stopped after only six days. So powerful was the experience for both the prisoners and the guards that Zimbardo and his associates held several sessions with the participants to help them work through their emotional reactions, and they maintained contact with each student for the next year

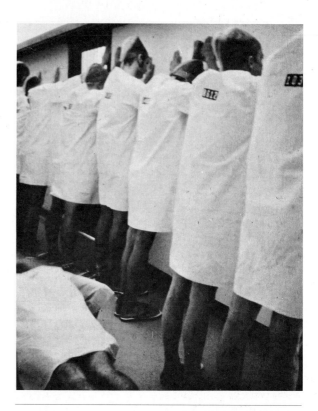

FIGURE 18.1 *During the Stanford prison study, prisoners were forced to stand in lineups like this one for long periods of time. The prisoner doing the pushups is being punished by the guards for moving during the lineup. (Courtesy of Philip G. Zimbardo)*

to ensure that the negative effects of the prison simulation did not persist.

What had happened to transform these normal college students into people they themselves would not have recognized one week earlier? What goes on in a social setting that can transform the typical behavior of peers so dramatically that they become dehumanized enemies? A simulation in which two groups of people had been asked to take on temporary roles as prisoners and guards had become a nightmarish social reality that called forth extreme and uncharacteristic behaviors. As one of the guards later recalled, "I was surprised at myself. . . . I made them call each other names and clean out the toilets with their bare hands. I practically considered the prisoners cattle, and I kept thinking: I have to watch out for them in case they try something" (Zimbardo and others, 1973, p. 42). Zimbardo related that "in the end, I called off the experiment not only because of the horror I saw out there in the prison yard, but because of the horror of realizing that I could have easily traded places with the most brutal guard or become the weakest prisoner full of hatred at being so powerless that I could not eat, sleep, or go to the toilet without the permission of authorities" (Zimbardo, 1972, p. 9).

As social animals, we spend our lives embedded in social systems that exert profound influences on our thoughts, emotions, attitudes, and behavior. In this chapter, we conclude our journey through the domains of psychology by examining some of the forces at work in the social environment, as well as how these forces are being harnessed in attempts to solve significant social problems.

SOCIAL NORMS AND ROLES

During the course of our lives, most of us function within a wide range of social systems. First, we are part of a family. Later, we become immersed in the social systems of neighborhood peer groups, the schools we attend, sport teams, perhaps the military, college groups like fraternities and sororities, business and occupational associations, and perhaps a newly formed family resulting from our own marriage. In all of these systems, we occupy particular positions known as **social roles.**

A *role* may be defined as a pattern of behavior that characterizes and is expected of a person who occupies a particular position in a social system. Certain behaviors are socially programmed into the roles of mother, father, student, police officer, or minister. At any given period in our lives, we all occupy a number of different roles. Because the "appropriate" behavior patterns may differ and, in some cases, may even conflict with one another, considerable behavioral flexibility may be required of us to meet the demands of these different roles. The concept of roles is a useful one in helping us to understand the manner in which a person's behavior may vary from situation to situation.

The socially defined "rules of the game" that regulate social behavior are called *norms*. **Social norms** are expectations shared by the members of a group, and they are the cement that binds social systems together and allows them to function in a generally harmonious fashion. Norms differ in their explicitness. The most specific ones are written down as formal laws. Others, though widely accepted, are more or less unspoken, yet they, too, function as powerful regulators of social interaction. For example, you may have had the experience of feeling an unwelcome pressure to repay a favor that someone else had done for you. If so, you were probably feeling the influence of the widely held *norm of reciprocity*, which specifies that a person who has been helped should "pay back" the helper. People who don't ask for or accept favors because they "don't want to feel obligated" are usually trying to avoid the consequences of this norm.

Social norms and social roles are closely related to one another. The norms associated with social roles specify how the person occupying that role is expected to think, feel, and behave, as well as how others are expected to respond in return. These norms can exert tremendous influence on behavior to the point of compelling a person to behave in a totally uncharacteristic manner. The Zimbardo prison study may be a dramatic example of this. Once the college students were randomly assigned to the roles of prisoner or guard, the norms associated with those roles seemed to take over, resulting in a destructive pattern of social interactions. Although both the prisoners and the guards had been selected because of their psychological "normality," the power of the social norms came to control and regulate behavior within a social system organized around the concepts of crime and punishment. The power of the norms seemed to override the previously acquired values, ethics, and personality characteristics of the subjects. As one of the prisoners later reported, "I began to feel that I was losing my identity. The person I call [subject's real name] . . . was distant from me, was remote, until finally I wasn't that. I was Number

FIGURE 18.2 *Social roles have norms associated with them, specifying how people in those roles are expected to behave and how others are expected to act toward them.*

416—I was really my number" (Zimbardo, 1972, p. 9).

Fortunately, these transformations were temporary and confined to the mock prison setting. While few of us are likely to find ourselves in such an extreme situation, all of us will have the experience of finding ourselves in new roles that are quite foreign to us. Such exposure to new roles is a major way in which personality develops and changes. Indeed, this is precisely why many psychotherapists try to get their clients to experiment with new social roles as a way of encouraging them to alter their maladaptive patterns of social interaction.

Development of norms

Social psychologists call the groups whose standards and beliefs a person identifies with and accepts **reference groups**. The earliest reference group for most children is their family. An important part of the socialization process is the passing on of attitudes, values,

and rules of conduct. The norms that are important to the family and to the social roles within it are communicated verbally (for instance, "Always treat others as you want them to treat you" or "We should be grateful to God for all the gifts we've been given") and through the modeling of role-appropriate behaviors by other family members. Many of these early lessons on the nature of social reality may remain intact throughout a person's life.

As we develop, however, reference groups beyond the family become important to us and may even override the early family influences. A study by Theodore Newcomb (1963) demonstrates this point quite nicely. Back in 1935, Newcomb had conducted extensive interviews with the freshman class at Bennington College, an expensive and exclusive college for women. Most of the freshmen were daughters of wealthy and highly conservative New England families, and they shared their families' conservative attitudes. In contrast, junior and senior students and the faculty at Bennington tended to have extremely liberal political beliefs.

Newcomb was interested in how much the attitudes of the freshmen women would change as a result of their college experience. He predicted that students whose primary reference group shifted from their family to their college peers and professors would become more politically liberal. This is exactly what he found. On the other hand, those students who remained very attached to their families maintained their conservative beliefs, but they were less popular and less involved in campus life.

In 1960, Newcomb again interviewed the women. He found that the attitudes formed through association with the liberal college reference group were just as enduring as those formed by close attachments to family. Women who had become more liberal during their college years continued to be liberal and tended to marry extremely liberal men. Those who remained conservative had married men whose attitudes were similar to their own.

In a classic social psychology study, Muzafer Sherif (1935) observed the process by which group members establish a common norm as they interact over time. To do so, he needed a situation in which prior experience provided little basis for judgment. He found this in a phenomenon known as the **autokinetic effect.** When subjects are presented with a stationary pinpoint of light in an otherwise pitch-dark room, the light appears to move about erratically. Sherif first asked male subjects to make individual judgments concerning how far the light moved. Their judgments varied widely;

some "saw" the light move only a few inches, while others judged it to have moved several feet. Over time, each subject's judgment norm was established.

Then Sherif put subjects together in groups of three and asked them to make their judgments in front of the others. What occurred over time was a clear convergence of individual judgments toward a group norm, as shown in Figure 18.3. It is interesting to note, however, that the group norm was not the simple average of the original judgments. Sherif found that personal characteristics and degree of social dominance affected the final group norm. For example, a subject who

FIGURE 18.3 *In Sherif's experiments on the development of group norms, individuals' autokinetic judgments began to converge toward a common judgment when they were made in the presence of two other subjects. Each mean is based on 100 judgments per session. Here we see what occurred in one of the 3-person groups. (Adapted from Sherif, 1935)*

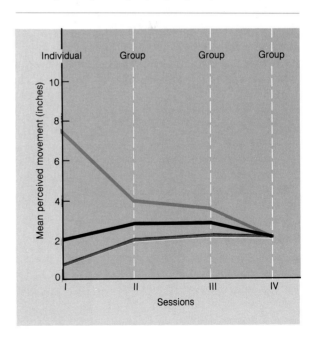

made extreme judgments with considerable force and self-confidence could pull the other members' judgments toward his, but even he would tend to compromise a bit toward their judgments. In the group shown in Figure 18.3, on the other hand, the person with the most deviant initial judgments clearly moved in the direction of the majority.

After a group norm is established, what do you suppose happens if the subjects make an additional series of autokinetic judgments by themselves? Do they revert to their original judgments once they are alone again, or do they maintain the group norm? Sherif found that even when the subjects were separated, they continued to follow the norm established by the group. Most of the subjects had taken on the norm as their own.

Conformity

Of course, norms will influence behavior only if people conform to them. Without **conformity**, we would have social chaos. Consider what would happen in supermarket checkout lines, outside movie theaters, and in crowded rest rooms if people did not conform to the norm of forming a line and waiting one's turn. Or picture the results of failing to adopt the norm that one does not drive on the left side of the road in the United States or make U-turns on freeways. Conformity to social norms is the stitching that holds the fabric of society together. It is no accident, therefore, that all social systems exert considerable pressure on their members

to conform. Often, the process is so subtle and gradual that we fail to recognize it as it occurs.

The pressures become more obvious when we fail to conform and begin to violate norms. If we violate the explicit norms we call laws, we may be labeled as criminals and punished. Violation of the more subtle and unspoken norms (for example, that we do not hold animated conversations in public with people who are not present, or that it is not appropriate to face the rear of the elevator and stare wild-eyed at our fellow passengers) may be grounds for being labeled mentally ill. Indeed, the various behavior disorders described in Chapter 15 all involve violations of various social norms. In a variety of ways, people who are labeled as emotionally disturbed do not live up to widely accepted social expectations.

There are two important reasons why people conform. The first is to be accepted by other people. This factor seemed to be important in the attitude shifts shown by the Bennington women who identified with and sought the approval of the older students and the faculty. A second reason for conforming stems from our desire to understand the world around us—to be "right"—so that we can respond effectively to it. In this case, the actions of others serve as information on how to get along, how to survive. Either or both of these factors may influence conformity in a given situation. Both were probably at work in a series of famous experiments on conformity conducted by Solomon Asch (1951, 1956).

In these experiments, groups of seven to nine students were told that they were going to take part in an

FIGURE 18.4 *In one of Asch's conformity experiments, seven students are being asked to judge which of three lines is the same length as the standard. Subject number 6 (from the left) has just heard the preceding five subjects (all of whom are accomplices of the experimenter) make the same incorrect judgment. As he prepares to answer, note the look of bewilderment on his face. (Asch, 1955)*

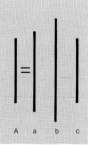

experiment on visual discrimination. Their task was to match a standard line with one of three comparison lines. In each case, one comparison line was the same length as the standard, while the other two were obviously longer or shorter.

Only one member of the group was actually a subject. The rest were accomplices of the experimenter. The group members were seated around a table and were called upon in order. The real subject was always next to last. The confederates gave previously agreed upon answers that were sometimes correct and sometimes incorrect. If the subject's answer disagreed with their obviously incorrect answers, they did not act surprised but continued to respond in an unemotional way.

When the majority gave the same incorrect answers, the effect was striking. In a control group, in which no incorrect answers were given, only 5 percent of the subjects made any errors. But in the experimental condition, at least 76 percent made one or more errors by going along with the erroneous majority. Many of these subjects said after the experiment that they felt puzzled by the difference between their perceptions and the judgments made by the unanimous majority. After several trials, subjects began to have doubts about their own eyesight, judgment, and ability to understand the instructions (see Figure 18.4). Even the subjects who did not conform expressed doubts about their own judgment.

Although Asch's experiment was carried out in a laboratory setting, it is easy to see how conformity influences behavior in everyday life (see Figure 18.5). For example, many students in high school and college are subjected to group pressures concerning such things as clothing, the importance of high grades, drug use, and sexual behavior. One female student at Yale described her nonconformity with her peers' behavior as a source of conflict to her: "I—the one who slept alone, the one whose only pills were vitamins and aspirins—I was the embarrassed one" (Maynard, 1972, p. 259).

But does the majority always rule? What happens if a determined and united minority opposes the group norm in a consistent and confident fashion? The results of numerous studies suggest that there is an important distinction to be made between *public conformity* and *private conformity*. When confronted by a majority that appears to be wrong, as in the Asch studies, many

"Well, heck! If all you smart cookies agree, who am I to dissent?"

(DRAWING BY HANDELSMAN; © 1972 THE NEW YORKER MAGAZINE, INC.)

FIGURE 18.5 *The kind of conformity demonstrated in the Asch experiments may occur in a variety of settings.*

people will conform publicly while maintaining their private convictions. But when a determined and consistent minority calls one's views into question, subjects tend to change or at least question their views on a private level, even though they are less likely to publicly conform to the minority (Maass and Clark, 1984). Thus, a determined minority with a credible point of view may exert more influence on the beliefs and judgments of other group members than is immediately and publicly apparent.

In the final analysis, conformity is a two-edged sword. On the one hand, a certain amount of conformity is needed if social systems are to function. On the other hand, conforming to social norms can result in destructive consequences, as we have seen in the Zimbardo prison study and in Milgram's studies of obedience to authority (Chapter 2). It remains for each person to decide when conformity has no practical utility for the individual or the group.

EXTREME CONFORMITY: BRAINWASHING AND CULTS

In the oppressive heat of the Guyanese jungle, the Reverend Jim Jones gave his last command. In response, over 900 of his followers walked to the galvanized iron buckets, dipped out cupfuls of fruit punch laced with cyanide, and drank the lethal potion. Mothers fed the drink to their children, and husbands gave it to their wives. In a matter of minutes, the village of Jonestown was littered with the corpses of its inhabitants.

As one of the most awesome and bizarre episodes of this or any other century, the Jonestown incident evoked the questions "Why?" and "How?" throughout the world. How could one man, no matter how powerful and charismatic, exert such total domination over the lives (and deaths) of his followers? How can we account for the extraordinary degree of conformity seen in Jones's People's Temple and in the other religious cults that have attracted more than 3 million members in the United States alone? Is this a new form of **brainwashing?**

The term *brainwashing* was originally applied to techniques used by the Chinese Communists to bring about "thought reform" in prisoners of war during the Korean conflict. In a number of instances, prisoners denounced their country, willingly made propaganda radio broadcasts, and appeared to embrace Communist beliefs. Some even elected to remain with the Chinese after the war, although most eventually returned to their own countries.

Analysis of the Chinese techniques indicated a pattern of extreme psychological and physical stress designed to weaken the individual's sense of personal and group identity. Social isolation, physical abuse, and relentless verbal attacks were combined with intense attempts to induce the prisoners to change their opinions. Such changes were then reinforced by gentle treatment and acceptance by the captors.

In recent years, interest has shifted to the techniques that certain religious sects use to obtain converts. Although few if any of the current cults employ the physical abuse used by the Chinese, their efforts to induce compliance in thought, belief, and behavior are no less determined.

Some observers of the cult phenomenon have concluded that the motivation to be controlled must lie within the converts themselves. But the view that the converts are social misfits who seek the group involvement that is denied them by the rest of society is not supported by research on cult converts. To be sure, young people who become cult converts are often struggling to gain a sense of self-identity, to pursue ide-

FIGURE 18.6 *Aftermath of the Jonestown mass suicide. This shocking event helped to rekindle interest in extreme forms of thought control and conformity.*

alistic goals, or to find a sense of personal meaning in their lives (Schwartz and Kaslow, 1981). Yet these people seldom seek out cults. Rather, cult members encounter them largely by chance at a time when they are particularly open to offers of friendship and "answers" to their questions.

The initial contact usually involves an invitation to dinner to meet the "family." The group treats the recruit with warmth, openness, and concern. After the first meeting, the recruit may be invited to a rural retreat to enjoy outdoor activities. Many accept out of curiosity and a reluctance to displease the group members who have offered their friendship. Once in the controlled environment of the retreat, recruits are bombarded with constant attention, affection, and concern. In small groups, recruits hear testimonials from members about the joy, peace, and love they have experienced by devoting their lives to the goals of the cult. The pace of religious discussions and physically strenuous exercise allows the recruits little opportunity to critically evaluate what they are experiencing. Cut off from family and the "real world," they are immersed in a new social reality that is relentless and compelling. The indoctrination technique is designed to lower resistance while instilling guilt, uncertainty, and confusion. Group members spend long hours with

the recruit, confessing sins of the past and praying for forgiveness. The answer to the guilt and confusion, of course, is to reject one's former life and join the cult. The convert is now told that he or she must break all ties with the Satanic past, including family and acquaintances.

Thus, the success of cult recruiting seems to stem from an interaction between characteristics of the recruit that increase vulnerability, and highly effective social influence techniques that establish the cult as the convert's new and powerful reference group (see Figure 18.7). Although many converts find a new sense of meaning and fulfillment in the cult's activities, some eventually become disenchanted and leave. Some of those who leave experience fears of harassment by the cult and difficulties in living independently. Once cut off from the cult, some ex-members experience depression and problems in returning to conventional lives that require independence and initiative (Singer, 1979).

FIGURE 18.7 *Cults can elicit extreme levels of conformity from members by capitalizing on needs for acceptance and a sense of purpose and by establishing the cult as a powerful reference group. Here, 2200 couples participate in a mass wedding conducted by Rev. Sun Myung Moon of the Unification Church.*

Deindividuation

Up to now, we have stressed the ways in which social norms and roles help to bring order to social behavior. Now we consider a form of social influence that leads to a loss of social restraints.

In New York City's Spanish Harlem, a Puerto Rican handyman sat perched on a ledge for an hour while a crowd of nearly 500 people on the street below shouted at him in Spanish and English to jump. As the cries of "Jump!" and "Brinca!" rang out, police managed to rescue the man.

What would prompt people to encourage a distraught human being to end his life? Social psychologist Leon Mann (1981) analyzed newspaper reports of 21 cases in which crowds of people were present when a person threatened to jump off a building. In 10 of the cases, the news accounts reported that the crowd had encouraged the person to jump. Mann found that this was most likely to occur when the crowd was large, when the incident took place after dark, and when the

victim was above the twelfth floor and thus distant from the crowd.

All of these conditions help to create anonymity. In the nineteenth century, Gustave LeBon, a French physician who became fascinated with the psychology of mob violence, suggested that the anonymity that exists in mobs leads to a loss of personal identity and the weakening of restraints. Immersed in a mob, people may engage in behaviors that they would not consider performing as individuals. Social psychologists have labeled this state **deindividuation** (Festinger and others, 1952).

Recent analyses of deindividuation suggest that the key to understanding this phenomenon is the loss of *self-awareness* that can occur under certain conditions (Diener, 1980; Prentice-Dunn and Rogers, 1983). In order to regulate our behavior, we need a moment-by-moment awareness of our feelings, values, and behavior. Such factors as anonymity (the knowledge that we are not identifiable), heightened emotional arousal, a focus of attention outward rather than inward, and immersion in a group with a common purpose, can

FIGURE 18.8 *Certain environmental factors (for instance, anonymity, group immersion) lead to reduced self-awareness and accompanying shifts in perception that constitute deindividuation. Deindividuation, in turn, produces several important effects, such as a weakening of internal restraints against impulsive behavior. (Adapted from Diener, 1980)*

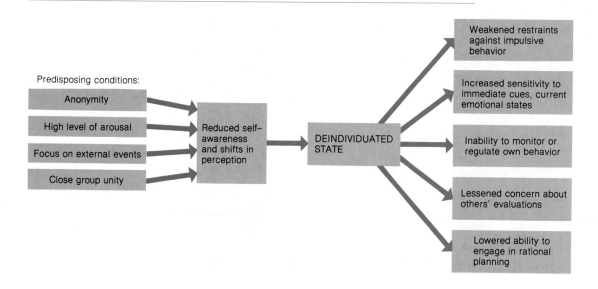

lead to a sharp reduction in personal awareness. The result is a drastic weakening of restraints and a lowered ability to engage in rational control of behavior. The factors involved in deindividuation are shown in Figure 18.8.

This theoretical model was tested in an experiment by Prentice-Dunn and Rogers (1982) in which subjects were permitted to aggress against another person by delivering electric shocks. The subjects' **private self-awareness** and their **public self-awareness** were both manipulated in the experiment. To increase their private self-awareness, some subjects were instructed to pay close attention to their thoughts and feelings. Others were told to concentrate on the situation rather than on themselves, which would decrease their private self-awareness. To enhance public self-awareness, some of the subjects were told that they would meet the victim after the experiment for a discussion of the shocks and that the shock levels they administered would be recorded by the experimenter. The public self-awareness of other subjects was reduced by telling them that they would not meet the victim and that their behavior would not be monitored.

Both before and after delivering shocks to the accomplice, subjects completed a questionnaire designed to measure their subjective feelings of deindividuation. This permitted the experimenters to determine whether shifts in self-awareness produced deindividuation and whether, in turn, this state increased aggression. The results showed that reductions in both private and public self-awareness enhanced aggression. However, the subjective sense of deindividuation was produced only when *private* self-awareness was reduced. Finally, the researchers found that the more intense the experience of deindividuation was, the more electric shock was administered. It thus appears that conditions that decrease private self-awareness can result in deindividuation and its consequences.

Returning for the moment to the Stanford prison study, we can now see that a number of conditions were present that might be expected to enhance deindividuation in the guards. No names were ever used. Guards had to be called "Mr. Correctional Officer." They all wore identical uniforms and reflecting sunglasses that prevented eye contact. They were unaware that their behavior was being monitored. These factors have led Zimbardo to conclude that deindividuation

may have been a key factor in the cruelty exhibited by the guards.

Can deindividuation be counteracted? The knowledge that social psychologists have gained about its nature and causes suggests a number of possible antidotes. One is to take steps to reduce anonymity. In the late 1960s, for example, reports of police brutality during civil disturbances decreased drastically in cities where police were equipped with large name plates. Likewise, authorities have found that one way to reduce crowd violence is to convince its members that the proceedings are being photographed or videotaped. Measures that reduce emotional arousal and that prompt people to focus on themselves rather than totally on the external event may also be effective. Finally, restoring internal restraints by appealing to people to examine their own attitudes and values or by threats of punishment may help to counter deindividuation.

GROUP DYNAMICS

Most of us belong to one or more groups besides our families. You may be a member of an athletic team, a social club at school or work, a living group of housemates, a sorority or fraternity, or a work group. In addition to groups that you voluntarily seek out and join, there are groups to which you automatically belong by virtue of your religion, your ethnic background, or other personal characteristics.

Social psychologists think of groups as having two major characteristics. First, their members usually recognize some degree of *connection* or affiliation with one another. Second, there are *interdependent* or *interlocking roles* within the group, so that the behavior of each of the individuals somehow affects what happens to the group as a whole.

A group is distinguished from an **aggregate,** which is merely a collection of people who have only an accidental or trivial relationship. The first day that your

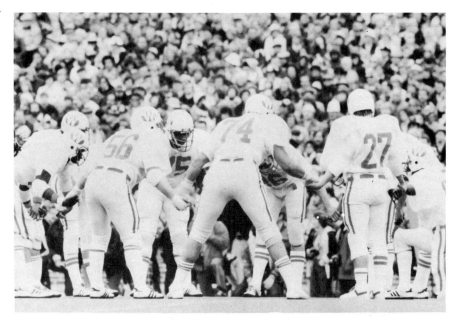

FIGURE 18.9 *Groups may take a variety of measures to enhance group cohesion.*

psychology class met, it was probably more an aggregate than a group. By this late in the term, however, it is likely that certain groups or subgroups have formed, particularly if classmates began studying together or working on joint projects.

People join groups for many reasons. They may be attracted to some of the members, or they may like the group's activities. Joining a group is sometimes a way to gain certain privileges or to make useful contacts. Sometimes, people join groups because of the social support they offer their members. Finally, groups may come together to work collectively on solving a problem or attaining a common goal.

Once formed, groups can differ along a number of important dimensions. One of these is *group composition*, which refers to the size of the group and the characteristics of its members. A second important aspect is the *structure* of the group. This refers to the communication channels that exist within the group and the status systems that develop. Who can talk to whom, and what patterns can such communications take? If communication patterns are restricted to certain channels, such as in a chain of command, the group functions much differently from one in which all members have equal access to one another. Finally, one of the most important group dimensions is *cohesiveness*. The spirit

of closeness—or lack of it—in a group can have significant consequences. For example, more than one athletic team with gifted personnel has failed to reach its potential because it lacked a sense of togetherness. It is no accident that experienced coaches devote considerable effort to "team building" (see Figure 18.9).

Because group characteristics can interact in complex ways, each group is as unique as the individuals within it. Nonetheless, the study of how groups function and how effectively they perform has a long tradition in social psychology. We will focus on four particularly important areas: group influences on task performance; decision making in groups; social power and leadership; and group conflict and conflict resolution.

Group influences on task performance

One of the major reasons why people form groups is to solve problems and perform tasks. Many tasks are simply too complex or physically demanding to be accomplished by one person. Moreover, it is frequently assumed that groups, because they can call on the expertise of several persons, can turn out a better product. This assumption that two (or three or four) heads are better than one underlies the use of "brainstorming" sessions within some organizations.

On the other hand, you've probably heard the definition of a camel as "a horse designed by a committee." This bears on the folk wisdom that too many cooks can spoil the broth, that the dynamics that operate within certain groups can actually impair task performance.

An even more elementary question concerns the way the simple presence of others affects task performance. If you are called upon to deliver a speech, will you do better when you are rehearsing alone or when you are in front of the audience? Sometimes, people rise to the occasion and perform better in the presence of others; at other times, the opposite can occur. Why?

SOCIAL FACILITATION

One of the earliest studies of social influence was performed by Norman Triplett (1898). Triplett, an avid bicyclist, carefully examined the records of the League of American Wheelmen. The league kept data on three kinds of bicycle races: unpaced, in which a person ran against a clock; paced, in which the racer was accompanied by a pacing vehicle that stayed slightly ahead; and competitions, in which participants raced against each other. Triplett's statistical analyses showed that racing times were fastest for groups in competition, next fastest for paced races, and slowest for races against the clock. He suggested that the presence of others had an energizing effect on performance. This effect came to be known as **social facilitation.**

Although Triplett's data showed enhanced performance when others were present, other studies revealed that the presence of others sometimes had quite the opposite effect. Task performance was sometimes much poorer when an audience was watching than if subjects performed in private.

In 1965, Robert Zajonc advanced a theory to explain why the presence of others has such variable effects. Zajonc suggested that the major factor in audience effects is arousal or, as it is sometimes called, *drive.* The presence of an audience can increase one's motivation to perform well or one's anxiety about performing poorly. The resulting arousal energizes behavioral tendencies and increases their vigor.

We come now to the key principle in accounting

for enhanced or impaired behavior. Arousal has the strongest energizing effects on *dominant* responses, the ones that are most likely to occur in a given situation. Thus, Zajonc's **drive theory** of social facilitation predicts that the presence of others will lead to improved performance when the dominant response is the correct one. This is likely to be the case when the task is a very simple one, such as running, or when we have learned the correct response very well. On the other hand, an increase in arousal brought about by the presence of an audience will result in impaired performance when the dominant responses are incorrect ones. This is especially likely on difficult, complex, or poorly learned tasks, where there are many other response tendencies competing with the performance of the correct response. These predictions are shown in Figure 18.10(a).

Increased motivation to do well and anxiety about doing poorly in front of others are not the only factors that might increase arousal. It is also possible that the distracting presence of spectators creates a conflict between focusing attention solely on the task and attending to the audience. The conflicting demands on our attention produced by the audience may also result in an increase in arousal and the social facilitation effects described above (Sanders, 1981). This **distraction-conflict model** of social facilitation is shown in Figure 18.10(b). Note that the term *social facilitation* is applied whether performance is enhanced or impaired. What is being facilitated by increased arousal is not performance but dominant response tendencies.

Predictions derived from social facilitation theory have been widely supported, even in such animals as cockroaches, rats, and fruit flies (Zajonc, 1980). Social psychologists have even wandered into such unseemly places as pool halls to test its real-world implications. James Michaels and his colleagues identified pairs of players who were either above average or below average in ability by watching the action in the pool room of their college's student union. Teams consisting of four observers then stood around the tables and watched the

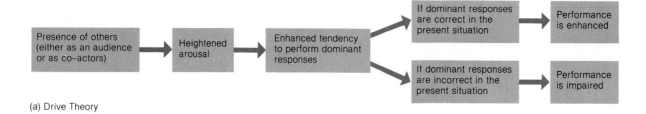

(a) Drive Theory

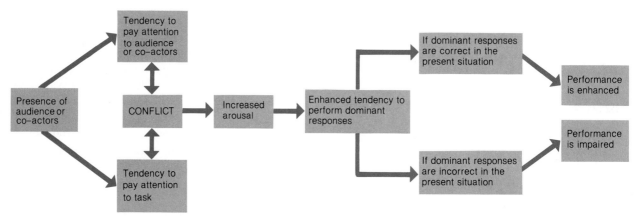

(b) Distraction–Conflict Model

FIGURE 18.10 *According to Zajonc's drive theory of social facilitation (a), the presence of others increases arousal, which, in turn, energizes response tendencies, particularly those that are dominant. If the dominant response tendencies are correct, performance is enhanced; if not, the presence of others will result in poorer performance. The distraction-conflict model (b) attributes the increased arousal to conflicting attentional demands produced by the presence of others, but leads to the same predictions.*

pairs play. The prediction derived from social facilitation theory was that the presence of an audience would increase the performance of the accomplished players, whose energized dominant responses were likely to be correct, while decreasing the performance of the less skilled players. As shown in Figure 18.11, the prediction was supported (Michaels and others, 1982).

The practical implications of social facilitation theory are quite clear. The best way to ensure that performance will be enhanced by increased arousal is to overlearn the correct responses through practice, practice, practice.

SOCIAL LOAFING: MANY HANDS MAKE LIGHT THE WORK

In the 1920s, a German psychologist named Ernst Ringelmann asked men to pull as hard as they could on a rope attached to a meter that measured the force they exerted. Not surprisingly, the amount of force applied increased as group size was increased. What was surprising, however, was that the *average* amount of effort applied by each individual dropped rather dramatically as group size increased. Thus, while a man pulling alone exerted an average pull of 63 kilograms, this dropped to an average pull of 53 kilograms per man in groups of 3 and to 31 kilograms per man in groups of 8.

At first glance, Ringelmann's finding might seem puzzling in view of our discussion of social facilitation. After all, the task is a very simple one, and performance should therefore be enhanced by an increase in arousal resulting from the presence of others. But, instead of social facilitation, we find **social loafing.** Why does working on a task with several others appear to reduce individual effort?

One possible answer lies in the **theory of social impact,** advanced by Bibb Latané and his colleagues (1979). According to this theory, any social pressure directed toward a group is diffused, or divided, among its members. Thus, as group size increases, each individual feels under less pressure to comply or to put forth a maximum effort. (We saw a similar process in Chapter 17 when we discussed the diffusion of responsibility that occurs in groups of bystanders and reduces the likelihood that a person who needs help will get it.) When people are working together on a task, there may

also be a tendency for them to believe that their individual efforts are less essential (Kerr and Bruun, 1983). The net result of social loafing can be an appreciable loss in group productivity.

Social loafing appears in a variety of contexts. For example, a group might respond more favorably to a low-quality proposal than the group's members would as individuals, because the group members will make less of an effort to look for flaws. On the other hand, if the proposal is of good quality, the group response may be less favorable than an individual's would be, because no group member has studied it carefully enough to fully perceive its merits (Petty and others, 1980).

One situation where social loafing can have important consequences is in the courtroom. Not all states

FIGURE 18.11 *Effects of an audience on the performance of skilled and less skilled pool players. As predicted from social facilitation theory, the performance of the skilled players was enhanced, while that of the less skilled players was poorer when an audience was present. (Adapted from Michaels and others, 1982)*

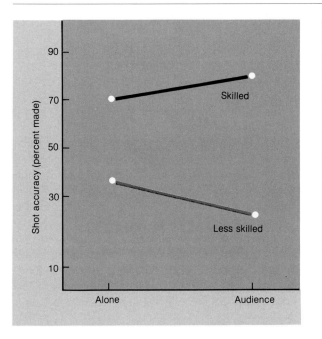

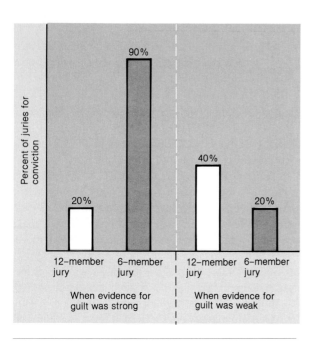

FIGURE 18.12 *The possibility of a social loafing effect is shown in these results from mock jury trials. The verdicts of the 6-person juries are more consistent with the strength of the evidence, suggesting that the 12-person juries do not inspect the evidence as critically. (Adapted from Valenti and Downing, 1975)*

have the same number of people on a jury. Some states require 12 jurors, while others mandate only six. In one experiment, mock trials were conducted using either 6- or 12-person juries. As social impact theory would predict, the larger juries did a poorer job; they were less responsive to the strength of evidence against the defendant. When the evidence against the accused was strong, fewer of the 12-person juries voted for conviction (see Figure 18.12); when the evidence was weak, the larger juries were less likely to vote for acquittal (Valenti and Downing, 1975).

One way to reduce social loafing is to make individual performance within the group identifiable so that it is harder to conceal mediocre effort (Harkins and Petty, 1982). However, this can be quite difficult to do in many situations, so that social loafing remains a real threat to the ultimate performance of many groups.

WHEN ARE GROUPS MORE PRODUCTIVE THAN INDIVIDUALS?

Thus far, we have considered some factors that favor group performance and others that can cause groups to function less effectively than we might expect. Under what circumstances, then, do groups perform better than individuals working alone? As we might expect, the answer to this question is complex and seems to depend on both the nature of the task and the characteristics of the group.

On a purely physical task, such as pulling a car out of a ditch, group performance should be better than any individual's despite the possibility of social loafing. On problem-solving tasks, groups frequently develop better solutions than individuals do (Deaux and Wrightsman, 1984). In a group, there are more opportunities for errors to correct themselves, and if the problem is complicated, there is a greater chance that at least one person will have the skills needed to solve it.

Groups are usually more effective than individuals at performing tasks or solving problems that can be subdivided easily. Such tasks also tend to reduce social loafing because each person's contribution is fairly obvious. On tasks that cannot be subdivided, the group usually performs at the level of its most gifted member if the task is simple and the solution is obvious to everyone once that member proposes it. In some situations, however, group processes may actually interfere with the activities of a gifted individual, resulting in poorer performance. For example, a bright person may feel reluctant to make suggestions in a group whose members make it clear that they do not want any one person to run the show. The social interchanges that go on within groups often cause them to work more slowly than individuals do.

As we might expect, groups that consist of highly competent individuals are usually more effective than groups composed of people of lower ability. Another factor that has been carefully studied is similarity among group members. Whether similarity helps or hinders group performance depends on the nature of the task and on the characteristics the group members share. A group composed of similar people might well be more cohesive (since similarity causes attraction), but similarity could also produce blind spots that would not exist in a more varied group (Raven and Rubin,

1983). We will see one example of this when we discuss the phenomenon of "groupthink."

Group decision making

Many key decisions are made by groups. Governments function largely through committees and panels. Large corporations are run by boards of directors who shape company policy. The fate of defendants rests in the hands of juries. Social psychologists, noting the importance of group decision-making processes, have devoted much study to them. We will consider two important aspects of this work: group polarization and the phenomenon of groupthink.

GROUP POLARIZATION

One reason why important decisions are frequently entrusted to groups is that they are assumed to be more cautious and thoughtful and less likely to "go off the deep end" than individuals. Research done to test this assumption has provided us with an answer that you should be used to by now: "It all depends."

It seems to depend primarily on the group's initial position on an issue. There is a strong tendency for groups to assume more extreme positions on an issue following discussion, a phenomenon known as **group polarization** (Mackie and Cooper, 1984). If the group is generally conservative to begin with, its final opinions or attitudes will likely become even more conservative. If, on the other hand, the group members are generally liberal, their attitudes after discussion will become even more liberal (see Figure 18.13).

Group polarization can have dramatic implications. In one study, career army officers discussed potential military crises involving a threat to the United States and recommended courses of action ranging from diplomatic negotiation to dropping nuclear bombs. A group of college students discussed the same crises and also recommended courses of action. Before the discussion began, the army officers were somewhat more inclined, as individuals, to favor dropping the bombs, and the students were more inclined toward negotiation. After the group discussions, however, the decisions of the two groups became more polarized. The officers were even more in favor of nuclear response, and the students were even more in support of negotiations (Semmel, cited in Lamm and Myers, 1978).

Decisions of judges in court situations seem to be affected by polarization in much the same way. One study compared decisions in civil liberties cases made by three federal judges acting as individuals with decisions made by those same three judges acting as a panel. The judges all tended to be slightly pro-civil liberties, and 30 percent of their individual decisions supported civil liberties. But when they served together on the panel, 65 percent of the group's decisions favored civil liberties (Walker and Main, 1973).

Why does group polarization occur? One possibility is that when individuals are attracted to a group, they are motivated to distinguish themselves as holding

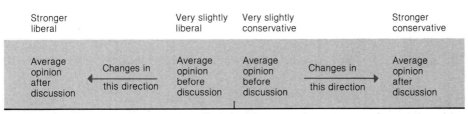

FIGURE 18.13 *Group polarization of opinion or attitude is a common consequence of group discussion. The opinions of the individual members become more extreme in either the liberal or the conservative direction if they are supported by the rest of the group.*

Stronger liberal | Very slightly liberal | Very slightly conservative | Stronger conservative

Average opinion after discussion ← Changes in this direction | Average opinion before discussion | Average opinion before discussion | Changes in this direction → Average opinion after discussion

Liberal opinion | Neutral opinion | Conservative opinion

more of the attitude position valued in the group so as to gain the group's approval. Thus, polarization would be especially likely to occur in cohesive groups or in those composed of similar individuals (Mackie and Cooper, 1984). Another factor may be that during group discussions, people may hear arguments that they had not previously considered. Such additional supporting evidence will tend to make the initial position seem even more valid, resulting in a shift to a more extreme conviction (Burnstein, 1983).

GROUPTHINK

In June of 1972, police officers arrested five men who had broken into the offices of the Democratic National Committee at the Watergate complex in Washington, D.C. The investigation that followed brought the Nixon administration to its knees and resulted in the president's resignation in 1974. During the inquiry, President Nixon and his inner circle of advisers made a series of critical decisions, each one of which got them into deeper trouble. Afterward, H. R. Haldeman, the president's chief adviser, said, "Too many foolish risks were taken. Too little judgment was used at every stage to evaluate the potential risks versus the gains." Nixon himself later said, "I have sometimes wondered whether, if we had spent more time on the problem at the outset, we might have handled it less stupidly" (Janis, 1982, p. 216).

Lest we think that only Republican administrations do stupid things, we need only recall another fiasco, this one carried out by the Kennedy administration. In 1961, John F. Kennedy and his advisers masterminded one of the most embarrassing and disastrous ventures in American history—the Bay of Pigs invasion of Cuba. The United States suffered a humiliating defeat in the eyes of the world, and the Soviet Union gained a firm foothold in Cuba that nearly led to a nuclear confrontation when the Soviets tried to place missiles there. Later, the members of the president's advisory group found it hard to believe that they had gone along with the plan. Kennedy himself later wondered, "How could we have been so stupid?"

Psychologist Irving Janis (1983) thinks he knows how. Janis has analyzed what went on within a large number of groups whose deliberations resulted in disastrous decisions, including the Watergate and Bay of

"All those in favor say 'Aye'."
"Aye."   "Aye."
        "Aye."   "Aye." "Aye."

(DRAWING BY H. MARTIN; © 1979 THE NEW YORKER MAGAZINE, INC.)

FIGURE 18.14 *The process of groupthink may produce an illusion of unanimity in a group that is cohesive and committed to a consensus.*

Pigs misadventures. Out of his analyses has come the concept of **groupthink.**

Groupthink tends to occur under stressful conditions in highly cohesive groups that are so committed to reaching a consensus that each member suspends his or her critical sense of judgment. Group members are prepared to go along with any proposal advanced by the leader or by the majority of the group. To remain loyal, the group's members stick with the policies and courses of action to which the group has committed itself, even when it becomes clear that these are not working out well and that there are alternatives. Any group member who expresses reservations about the group's policies is faced with immediate and direct pressure to "stop rocking the boat." *Mindguards* within the group protect its members from information that might threaten the consensus and complacency of the group. Under these conditions, even highly intelligent people may quit thinking independently, abandon their consideration of moral principles, and stop weighing alternatives. There occurs an *illusion of unanimity* within the group that reinforces all the other groupthink processes (see

Figure 18.14). The model of groupthink advanced by Janis is shown in Figure 18.15.

Can groupthink be counteracted or prevented? Janis thinks that it can. He suggests that leaders regularly encourage and reward critical thinking and even disagreement among group members. Several outside planning and evaluation groups with different leaders should be set up to prevent the formation of an insulated inner circle. At each stage of the group's deliberations, members should be urged to state any doubts

FIGURE 18.15 *The antecedents, characteristics, and consequences of groupthink as it relates to decision making. (After Janis, 1983)*

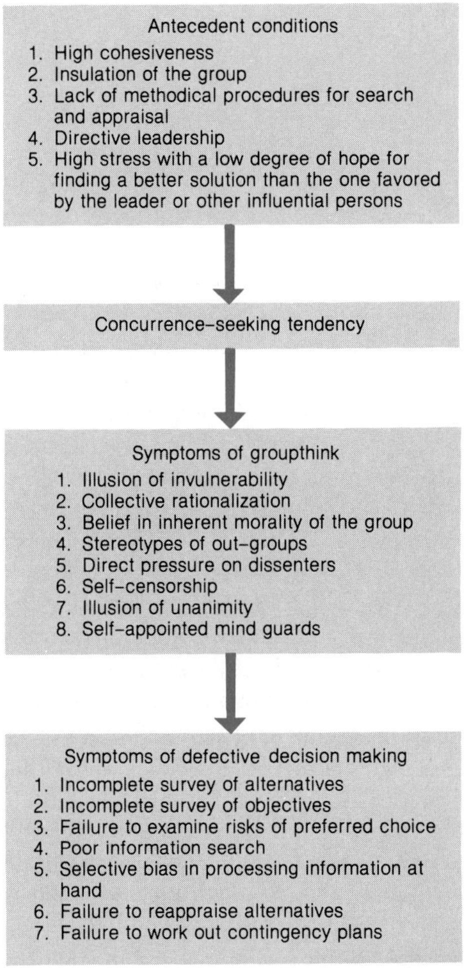

Antecedent conditions
1. High cohesiveness
2. Insulation of the group
3. Lack of methodical procedures for search and appraisal
4. Directive leadership
5. High stress with a low degree of hope for finding a better solution than the one favored by the leader or other influential persons

Concurrence-seeking tendency

Symptoms of groupthink
1. Illusion of invulnerability
2. Collective rationalization
3. Belief in inherent morality of the group
4. Stereotypes of out-groups
5. Direct pressure on dissenters
6. Self-censorship
7. Illusion of unanimity
8. Self-appointed mind guards

Symptoms of defective decision making
1. Incomplete survey of alternatives
2. Incomplete survey of objectives
3. Failure to examine risks of preferred choice
4. Poor information search
5. Selective bias in processing information at hand
6. Failure to reappraise alternatives
7. Failure to work out contingency plans

they might have, and the group should review alternative courses of action.

After the Bay of Pigs fiasco, President Kennedy incorporated several of these techniques into his Cabinet decision-making process. This same group of advisers subsequently handled the 1962 Cuban missile crisis in a much more effective way. Thus, groups can be helped to function in a manner that avoids groupthink.

Social power and leadership

In any group, there are differences in status and in the amount of impact that members have on each other and on the functioning of the group. **Social power** is the ability to influence others to think or behave in particular ways. Such power may come from a number of different sources, including the ability to reward or punish others, the possession of knowledge or skills needed by the group, or the occupying of a particular social role, such as a teacher or a parent (Raven and Rubin, 1983).

Sooner or later in almost any group, one or more members begin to exert influence and to direct the group's activities. The quality of the leadership that they provide is a major determinant of the group's morale and performance. The clear importance of leadership has stimulated much research on two central questions: (1) Who becomes a leader? and (2) What factors determine a leader's success once he or she has assumed that role?

TRAIT APPROACHES: BORN TO LEAD?

One of the oldest leadership theories holds that some people have certain unique traits that qualify them for leadership roles. Hundreds of studies have been designed to pinpoint these traits.

Attempts to construct the trait profile of the "great person" have met with very limited success. The as-

sumption that leaders have unique backgrounds or characteristics that make them fundamentally different from followers has not been well supported. Indeed, most people who are rated as good leaders are *also* rated as good followers. A second assumption, that leadership is a general attribute that gives the individual the ability to lead in all situations, also has not held up very well. Research shows that different group members are likely to emerge as leaders in situations in which they have the skills or knowledge to lead the group toward a goal.

Although there does not appear to be a unique cluster of "leader" traits, there is evidence that certain personality characteristics may be associated with the tendency to assume leadership positions. In one study, the personality test scores of more than 2000 political leaders who served as delegates or alternates to their parties' U.S. presidential conventions were compared with those of the general public. As a group, the political leaders were higher in self-confidence, dominance, and need for achievement, and they were lower than average in the tendency to seek emotional support from

FIGURE 18.16 *Trait theories of leadership look for the common characteristics that are assumed to exist in prominent leaders like Gandhi, Churchill, Kennedy, and Patton. So far, the search for the trait profile of the "great person" has met with limited success.*

others and to engage in self-criticism (Costantini and Craik, 1980). However, there was also a great deal of variability in the personality test scores of the leaders, and many of them did not fit this mold. Thus, although certain relationships exist between personal traits and leadership, trait theories cannot fully account for everyone who becomes a leader.

LEADERSHIP STYLES: THE CONTINGENCY MODEL

During the 1950s and 1960s, several important studies were conducted to observe and classify leadership behaviors. Two major **leadership styles** emerged. One style, which was called *initiating and directing*, is oriented toward organization and task accomplishment. The second, labeled *consideration*, is relationship-oriented and includes behaviors aimed at increasing morale, motivation, and group satisfaction (Bales and Slater, 1955).

A very influential theory of leadership today is the **contingency model** advanced by Fred Fiedler of the University of Washington (Fiedler, 1978). Fiedler argues that the effectiveness of both leadership styles is dependent, or *contingent*, on the nature of the leadership situation—most specifically, on its **favorableness.** A highly favorable leadership situation is one in which the leader's relations with the members are very good, the task is clear and well defined, and the leader's power to direct the group is acknowledged and accepted by the members. An unfavorable situation is one in which the group dislikes or is not willing to follow the leader, the task is uncertain or ambiguous, and the group members question the leader's right to power.

Fiedler maintains that task-oriented leaders are most effective when the situation is either very unfavorable or very favorable. In an unfavorable situation, there is often confusion, hostility, and uncertainty, and the task-oriented leader's skills in organizing and direct-

ing can bring order from chaos. In a highly favorable situation, leader-member relations are already good, and so the task-oriented leader can concentrate on completing the job at hand. Fiedler asserts that relationship-oriented leaders function best in situations of moderate favorability, where the task is somewhat clear and the leader can use his or her interpersonal skills to increase group satisfaction and morale (see Figure 18.17).

Predictions derived from the contingency model have been supported in a great many studies with groups ranging from tank crews to store managers (Fiedler, 1978). The contingency model, unlike the great-person theory, takes the characteristics of both the

FIGURE 18.17 *In Fiedler's contingency model of leadership, leader effectiveness is jointly determined by the leader's primary goals and the favorableness of the situation. Leaders who are chiefly task-oriented are relatively more effective in highly unfavorable or highly favorable situations, while relationship-oriented leaders are relatively more effective in moderately favorable situations.*

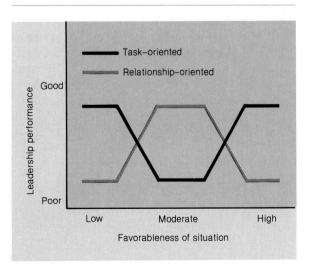

leader and the leadership situation into account. We have here another example of how individual and situational influences interact to affect behavior.

Intergroup conflict and conflict resolution

There are many ways in which groups can deal with one another. Some situations encourage cooperation between groups, while others may foster competition. Often, the goals of different groups are incompatible. The resulting conflict can create antagonism between groups, leading to negative and stereotyped attitudes toward those who belong to the other group.

One of the classic field studies in social psychology demonstrated how intergroup conflict can be created and overcome. The study was conducted at a summer camp in Robbers Cave, Oklahoma, by Muzafer Sherif and his research team (1961). The subjects were 22 well-adjusted 11-year-old boys. When the boys arrived at camp, they were divided into two groups, who chose to call themselves the Rattlers and the Eagles. The camp counselors encouraged group identification and closeness among the members of each group. The two groups worked on separate projects, such as improving the swimming hole. The cooperation required to complete the tasks made the Rattlers and the Eagles highly cohesive groups.

The experimenters then began to pit the two groups against each other in competitive contests and games. As this continued over time, the boys' good sportsmanship gradually deteriorated into deep resentment, hostility, and discriminatory practices. At one point, the counselors arranged a party, supposedly to reconcile the groups and encourage them to "let bygones be bygones." Half the food was fresh and attractive, whereas the remainder was crushed and unappealing. The counselors arranged things so that the Eagles arrived first. Naturally, they ate the appetizing food. The Rattlers were furious, and open conflict erupted.

The experimenters then set out to try to restore harmony between the groups. They soon learned that ordinary contact simply increased intergroup hostility. They then decided to try the same method that they had used to create harmony *within* the groups. They forced the Eagles and Rattlers to cooperate in order to

achieve a common goal. First, the experimenters arranged for the water supply system to fail, and the groups had to cooperate in order to fix it. Then they told the boys about a very exciting movie. The price was too high for either group to rent it themselves, so the Eagles and the Rattlers grudgingly decided to pool their funds. The groups later had to cooperate again to tow in the camp's disabled truck, which was their only transportation into town (see Figure 18.18). As the groups were forced to work with one another, the hostility and the tendency to stereotype members of the other group disappeared and was replaced by a spirit of friendship and cooperation.

The Robbers Cave experiment showed how intergroup conflict and hostility can be created through competition, and how it can be reduced through cooperation. We now turn to an application of this principle in another social setting.

APPLYING THE LESSON OF ROBBERS CAVE: COOPERATIVE LEARNING

Research on school desegregation has shown that legally mandated integration is not itself the solution to racial problems (Aronson, 1984; Stephan, 1978). Getting youngsters of different races and ethnic groups into the same school may be a start, but it's what happens after they get there that is crucial.

The traditional classroom environment is inherently competitive. Children compete with one another to demonstrate their competencies and to gain the teacher's approval. In this kind of setting, it is hardly surprising that previously disadvantaged minority children would have difficulties adapting and that resentments would form between different ethnic groups, just as they did between the Eagles and the Rattlers.

When the Austin, Texas, school system was desegregated, social psychologist Elliott Aronson drew upon the Robbers Cave experiment to develop a curriculum designed to reduce intergroup hostility, to enhance learning, and to provide a more positive school experience for both minority and nonminority students (Aronson and others, 1978). He wanted to create a classroom technique in which children must cooperate rather than compete in order to achieve success. The curriculum that resulted is called the **jigsaw program** because it works very much like a jigsaw puzzle. Children are divided into racially mixed groups of five or six. The groups must prepare for a later test on, let us say, the life of Abraham Lincoln. Each child within the group is given a "piece" of the total knowledge to be learned. In order for the group members to pass the test, they must fit their "pieces" of knowledge together like a jigsaw puzzle. The children soon learn that the only way they can be successful is to work together and help one another (see Figure 18.18). They learn to listen to one another, to share valued resources, and to appreciate one another.

The effects of the jigsaw technique have been care-

fully evaluated in scores of classrooms, and the results are encouraging. Children's liking for one another increases, and this increased liking crosses racial boundaries. Prejudice decreases among both white and minority children. Scores on tests of self-esteem improve for both whites and minorities, as does school achievement. Finally, the jigsaw method enhances children's empathy, the ability to put themselves in someone else's place and see the world through his or her eyes (Aronson and others, 1978). The success of the jigsaw method has stimulated the development of other cooperative strategies in the classroom, such as peer tutoring and group problem solving. These have also been successful in desegregated schools (Sharan and others, 1984).

The group processes that we have discussed are relevant to many social systems. In Frontier 18.1, we explore recent research on group dynamics in the world of sports.

(a)

(b)

FIGURE 18.18 (a) During the Robbers Cave experiment, members of the Eagles and the Rattlers work together to tow the camp's truck to be repaired. Ironically, they are using the same rope that they had once used competitively in a tug-of-war. Cooperative activities like this one helped to reduce intergroup conflict and hostility. (b) In a classroom using the jigsaw program of cooperative learning, children of different ethnic groups share their individual "pieces" of the knowledge puzzle with one another.

Sport has long been an important part of our culture. Whether we are active participants or spectators, sports touch the lives of most of us. It is also touching the professional lives of an increasing number of psychologists who have begun to appreciate the world of athletics as a rich "natural laboratory" for the study of psychological phenomena (Silva and Weinberg, 1984; Thomas, 1984). If you stop to think about it, most of the topics that we have dealt with in this book—perception, learning, motivation, cognition, stress, developmental issues, and so on—have direct application to sport and can be studied in the "real world" of the sport setting.

Our present topic, group dynamics, has special relevance to sport. The team with the most talent does not always win the championship. Examples of this can be found at every level of competition, from youth leagues to the professional level. Coaches say that they do not necessarily select the most talented players to be in the starting lineup. Rather, they choose a group of players who complement one another well and play well as a team. One of the most celebrated cases of team cohesion in recent years was the 1979 Pittsburgh Pirates, who attributed their world championship to the "family" atmosphere that they created both on and off the field. Thus, group dynamics play an important role in the outcome of athletic competition.

GROUP PROCESSES AND PERFORMANCE

On any team, the skills of the individual players must be combined in order for the team to reach the level of performance that would be expected on the basis of its talent. Diane Gill (1984) of the University of Iowa has suggested that team productivity can be understood in terms of individual effort plus or minus the influence of group processes. The more interaction, or teamwork, that a sport requires, the more difficult it will be to predict team performance on the basis of individual talent because group processes will increase in importance. We might therefore predict that the relationship between individual output and team success would be stronger in a sport like baseball, which requires less coordination between individual efforts, than in one like basketball, which requires a great deal of group interaction to run the offense and play team defense. And, in fact, this is so. Individual performance measures (points scored, rebounds, assists, and steals in basketball; batting averages, runs batted in, and earned run averages in baseball) are less predictive of team success in basketball than in baseball (Jones, 1974).

One group process that could interfere with team productivity is social loafing. To study its relevance to sport, Bibb Latané set up a competitive situation in which members of an intercollegiate swim team were divided into four teams of four swimmers each. All swimmers were timed in a 100-meter individual event and also swam 100 meters as part of a relay race. It was thus possible to compare the individual and group performances of each swimmer. Because identifiability of individual performance has been shown to reduce social loafing, the researchers also manipulated this factor by announcing individual lap times for half of the swimmers and not announcing them for the others.

The results of the experiment are shown in Figure 18.19. When lap times were not announced, producing low identifiability, swimmers' relay times were slower than when the same swimmers performed individually, indicating a social loafing effect. Under high identifiability, however, relay times were actually faster, suggesting not only that social loafing was overcome but that the group situation seemed to provide an additional social incentive (Latané and others, 1980). Although the time variations may appear small, they are large enough to spell the difference between victory and defeat in a swim meet.

Most successful coaches have developed methods for identifying and publicly displaying individual contributions to team performance. For example, Don James of the University of Washington and Earle

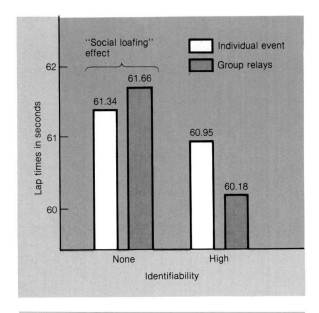

FIGURE 18.19 *Social loafing in the swimming pool. Under conditions of low identifiability (individual lap times not announced), collegiate participants swam more slowly in team relays than in individual laps. Increasing identifiability by announcing the lap times of each member of the relay team not only eliminated the social loafing effect but actually enhanced performance as compared with times in the corresponding individual event. (Data from Latané and others, 1980)*

Bruce of Ohio State film every practice and game, grade each player on every play, and post the grades the next day. At the University of Arizona, basketball coach Lute Olson uses a "total performance chart" that includes points, rebounds, steals, assists, and forced turnovers *minus* errors, fouls, turnovers, and missed shots. These methods are designed to tip group processes in favor of increased team productivity in much the same manner as identifiability did in the swimming study described above.

Another group factor that has been studied exten-

sively in relation to performance is *team cohesion* (Carron, 1984). Although we might assume that high attraction and involvement among team members would enhance team performance, this is not always the case. Sometimes, high attraction among group members can serve to reduce competition among them, so that they do not become as skilled as they might be. This negative effect has been found in research on rifle and bowling teams, in which each individuals's task is carried out independently (Carron and Chelladurai, 1982). Individual members who are distracted by social concerns or by the desire to protect the feelings of their teammates may not perform up to their potential in such sports. Even in more interactive sports, such as basketball, attraction among team members can sometimes reduce team effectiveness. Observational studies of basketball teams have shown a tendency for high school players to pass the ball to their friends and to set them up for shots, sometimes to the detriment of the team (Fiedler, 1967; Klein and Christiansen, 1969).

Although cohesion can occasionally cause problems, research has generally confirmed its relationship to team success, particularly in sports that require a great deal of teamwork. A cohesive team tends to provide considerable social support for its members, and its players tend to stick together under adversity. Many studies of team cohesiveness have utilized the Sport Cohesiveness Questionnaire (Martens and others, 1972), which measures seven aspects of cohesiveness in sports: (a) friendship, (b) power among group members, (c) sense of belonging, (d) value of membership, (e) closeness, (f) enjoyment, and (g) teamwork. One recent review of 11 separate studies relating team performance to cohesiveness scores across a wide range of sports showed positive relationships in about two-thirds of the studies. The aspects of cohesion that were most frequently related to high performance were teamwork, closeness, and value of membership (Carron, 1984).

Before concluding our discussion of cohesion, we

should note that cohesion, like other group processes, is a dynamic and ongoing process rather than a static characteristic. It both affects and is affected by other group factors, such as team success, team stability, acceptance of team roles, satisfaction with the activity, and so on. Thus, for example, team success may contribute to cohesion just as cohesion may contribute to team success.

LEADERSHIP IN SPORTS

The important role that the coach or manager plays in teaching techniques and developing teamwork, team unity, morale, and ability to perform under stress is well recognized in sports. It is also clear that leadership styles differ widely in successful coaches. Leaders like Vince Lombardi, Tom Landry, Billy Martin, John Wooden, and Bobby Knight have differed in many important respects, yet all rose to the top of their profession. Frequently, a coach who is fired by one team goes on to great success with another team of seemingly comparable ability, even though the coach's leadership style does not change.

The scientific study of leadership in sports has received renewed attention in recent years (Chelladurai, 1984; Smoll and Smith, 1984). Efforts are being made to identify specific coaching behaviors and styles that relate to team performance, morale, and positive psychological benefits for team members. For example, the Leadership Scale for Sports (Chelladurai and Saleh, 1980) is designed to measure preferences for five classes of coaching behaviors: instructional, rewarding (positive feedback), social support (relationship-oriented behaviors), democratic (allowing team participation in decision making), and autocratic (stressing personal authority). Studies utilizing this measure have shown that male athletes prefer their coaches to be more autocratic, more oriented toward instruction, and more socially supportive than do females (Chelladurai and Saleh, 1978; Erle, 1981). It is not yet clear, though, how scores on this measure

relate to other important variables, such as team performance and satisfaction.

Another group of researchers took a different approach to studying coaching practices and their effects on athletes (Smoll and Smith, 1984). To measure actual coaching methods, the psychologists used the technique of behavioral assessment. Observers carried portable tape recorders and essentially did a play-by-play of what coaches actually did during practices and games in a variety of sports. The behavior descriptions were transcribed and sorted into specific categories. This led to the development of a 12-category behavioral coding system that observers can use to measure how frequently coaches engage in specific behaviors during practices and games. The categories of the Coaching Behavior Assessment System are shown in Table 18.1.

In the first phase of the research, 51 male Little League baseball coaches were observed during more than 200 complete games. More than 57,000 individual coaching behaviors were coded into the 12 categories, and a behavioral profile based on an average of more than 1100 behaviors was computed for each coach.

After the Little League season, more than 500 boys who played for the coaches were interviewed in their homes. They completed a series of questionnaires designed to measure their reactions to their Little League experience and their attitudes toward their coach and teammates. They also completed a measure of self-esteem to assess their attitudes toward themselves.

Clear relationships were found between coaching behaviors and the children's reactions to their athletic experience. The children preferred playing for the coaches who gave a good deal of positive reinforcement, who responded to mistakes with encouragement and instruction rather than criticism, and who were well organized and promoted team unity and player support for one another. Interestingly, the teams' won-lost records were unrelated to how much

TABLE 18.1   CATEGORIES FROM THE COACHING BEHAVIOR ASSESSMENT SYSTEM

CLASS I. REACTIVE BEHAVIORS

RESPONSE TO DESIRABLE PERFORMANCE

Reinforcement	A positive, rewarding reaction (verbal or nonverbal) to a good play or good effort

RESPONSES TO MISTAKES

Mistake-contingent encouragement	Encouragement given to a player following a mistake
Mistake-contingent technical instruction	Instructing or demonstrating to a player how to correct a mistake he/she has made
Punishment	A negative reaction, verbal or nonverbal, following a mistake
Punitive technical instruction	Technical instruction following a mistake which is given in a punitive or hostile manner.

RESPONSE TO MISBEHAVIOR

Keeping control	Reactions intended to restore or maintain order among team members

CLASS II. SPONTANEOUS BEHAVIORS

GAME-RELATED

General technical instruction	Spontaneous instruction in the techniques and strategies of the sport (not following a mistake)
General encouragement	Spontaneous encouragement which does not follow a mistake
Organization	Administrative behavior which sets the stage for play by assigning duties, responsibilities, positions, etc.

GAME-IRRELEVANT

General communication	Interactions with players unrelated to the game

the children liked the coach and wanted to play for him again. It was the coach's behavior that mattered (Smith and others, 1978).

After the researchers had discovered a relationship between coaching behaviors and children's reactions to their Little League experience, their next step was to use these findings to develop a training program for coaches. The 3-hour training session was designed to help coaches become more aware of their behavior and to give them specific behavioral guidelines for creating a more supportive psychological environment for children. Briefly, the guidelines recommended a "positive approach" to child athletes, with liberal use of reinforcement, encouragement, and technical instruction and the avoidance of punishment. Coaches were urged to focus on effort and improvement rather than on winning. Ways to establish a supportive environment and team unity, and to reduce discipline problems, were also discussed and demonstrated by the psychologists.

Prior to the next season, the training program was administered to an experimental group of baseball coaches. A control group received no training. During the season, the two groups of coaches were observed by trained coders who recorded their behaviors during games. After the season, more than 300 children who had played for the two groups of coaches were interviewed, as before. The behavioral assessment showed that the trained coaches behaved more in accordance with the guidelines than the control coaches did. Although there was no difference in the average won-lost records of the two groups of coaches, the children who played for the trained coaches enjoyed their experience more and liked their coaches better. They also showed significant increases in self-esteem scores over the course of the season (Smith and others, 1979).

Because of the social nature of sports, there are many opportunities to study important group processes. Moreover, the knowledge gained in such research can be applied to create more positive athletic environments.

SOCIAL IMPACT OF THE PHYSICAL ENVIRONMENT

In late 1984, poisonous gas escaped from a Union Carbide plant in Bhopal, India. Within minutes thousands of people and animals in the surrounding area were dead, and many others suffered serious injury. At the same time, on the parched plains of Ethiopia, millions of starving people were helpless against a drought that had lasted for nearly 10 years.

Events like these are stark reminders of the fragile threads that link our survival with a sometimes unpredictable and uncontrollable physical environment. But even under the normal conditions of life, the physical environment in which we live influences our social behavior and psychological well-being in important ways. The relatively new field of **environmental psychology** deals with some of the most important issues confronting our society, including crowding, pollution, environmental planning, and other factors affecting the quality of our lives.

Crowding

Three centuries ago, the population of the entire world was about 500 million people. By 1850, it had grown to about 1 billion, and to over 3 billion by 1970. Each day, the earth gains about 200,000 people. At that rate, the population of our planet will double every 35 years. Although the rate of population growth has slowed in the United States and Europe, it continues largely unabated in the poorest and most underdeveloped nations.

If human beings were scattered uniformly over the land areas of the earth, each person would have about 10 acres of land to live on. For many reasons, however, people have congregated in urban areas, many of which have serious problems of uncontrolled growth. In densely populated areas like New York's Manhattan Island, there are up to 70,000 people per square mile. It is estimated that by the year 2000, the population of Mexico City will more than double to 31 million, and that of São Paulo, Brazil, will grow to 26 million. By that same year, New York City's population may approach 25 million (Nossiter, 1980).

Many theorists are convinced that the crowding that has become typical in the world's urban areas has serious negative effects on personal and social behavior. This belief has stimulated a great deal of research on how crowding affects one's behavior and sense of well-being.

CALHOUN'S BEHAVIORAL SINK

John Calhoun (1962) built an ideal environment for rats, supplying them with abundant food, water, and nesting materials (see Figure 18.20). As the rats multiplied in their physical Utopia, Calhoun was able to study how they adapted to increasingly crowded living conditions.

If the growth pattern that occurred early in the study had continued, Calhoun would have expected

FIGURE 18.20 *Researcher John Calhoun stands in one of the animal universes he constructed to study the effects of population density.*

over 5000 living rats at the end of his 27 months of observation. But after that early period of rapid growth, the population stabilized at about 150 adults. This stabilization was due to an extraordinarily high rate of infant mortality as the rats' behavior became increasingly abnormal. Females were often unable to carry their pregnancies to full term or to survive the delivery of their litters. Others abandoned their litters or even ate them. Aggression was common, and the sexual behavior of the males became disordered, with some becoming uninterested in sex and others mounting virtually any other animal in sight, whether it was a female, a male, or an infant. Some rats became hyperactive and constantly dashed about, while others became withdrawn and ventured out to eat only when the others were asleep. Calhoun was so struck by the deterioration of social and sexual behavior that he coined the term **behavioral sink** to describe the pathological environment that developed as conditions became crowded.

EFFECTS ON HUMANS: DENSITY VERSUS CROWDING

The dramatic effects observed by Calhoun, as well as those noted by other investigators who have studied animals in their natural environment, stimulated a good deal of research on how crowding affects humans. Some of the early studies were correlational in nature, relating population density in various cities with indices of physical and social health, such as mortality rates, fertility rates, juvenile delinquency, crime, and admissions to mental hospitals. Although relationships between density and measures of social pathology were often found, their interpretation was clouded by the fact that socioeconomic factors were also related to density. For example, it is usually the poorest people who live in the most crowded environments. Thus, it is possible that other conditions that go along with being poor, and not density *per se*, were the important factors. However, recent studies that have attempted to

TABLE 18.2 THEORETICAL PERSPECTIVES ON CROWDING AND WAYS OF COPING

THEORETICAL PERSPECTIVE	CRITICAL CAUSE(S) OF CROWDING	PRIMARY COPING MECHANISMS
Social overload	Excessive social contact; too much social stimulation	Escape stimulation; prioritize input and disregard low priorities; withdrawal
Behavior constraint	Reduced behavioral freedom	Aggressive behavior; leave situation; coordinate actions with others
Unwanted interaction	Excessive unregulatable or unwanted contact with others	Withdrawal; organization of small primary groups
Interference	Disruption or blocking of goal-directed behavior	Create structure; aggression; escape
Ecological	Scarcity of resources	Defense of group boundaries; exclusion of outsiders

Source: Adapted from Stokols (1976).

control for the influence of socioeconomic factors indicate that there are indeed relationships between density and poor mental health, poor social relationships between household members, and poor child care (Galle and Gove, 1979).

The inherent difficulties in establishing causal factors in correlational studies gave rise to experimental studies in which density was carefully defined in terms of number of square feet per person. These experimental studies have shown that density can produce negative emotional states, including dislike for both the situation and others in the situation, particularly in males. Density also results in higher levels of physiological arousal when subjects are kept in experimental settings for hours at a time (Fisher and others, 1984). A number of studies have revealed that density can lead to poorer task performance, especially when interaction is required among subjects (Heller and others, 1977). There appear to be aftereffects of exposure to density on later task performance as well. For example, subjects placed in high-density situations later showed less persistence in solving puzzles than did subjects first exposed to low-density experimental conditions (Evans, 1979).

However, even experimental studies indicated that

there was more going on than just density. Sometimes density had negative effects, and sometimes it didn't. Moreover, subjects within the same experiment often seemed to be affected differently by density. These observations led to an important distinction between *density* and *crowding* (Paulus, 1980; Stokols, 1978). **Density** refers to the actual physical conditions—that is, how many people per square foot occupy an area. **Crowding** refers to a negative psychological experience of having more people around than one would prefer. Density does not necessarily result in the experience of crowding. People often pack into football stadiums and rock concerts and find that the high density adds to their pleasure in being there.

What, then, does lead to the experience of crowding? Daniel Stokols (1976) of the University of California at Irvine has summarized five different sets of factors that have been suggested by various theorists: *social overload, behavior constraint, unwanted interaction, interference with goal-directed behavior,* and *scarcity of resources* (see Table 18.2). Each of these factors gives rise to different ways of trying to cope with the experience of crowding, including withdrawal, attempts to cooperate, and aggression.

This is clearly a more comprehensive and useful

way to understand the complexities of crowding, because crowding depends on how the individual interprets the situation and its implications for him or her as well as on the physical variable of density. It also allows us to take into account individual differences in personality, motivation, and previous background (for example, being from a large city versus growing up in a small farm community) that might influence whether or not a person experiences a particular situation as crowded. Personality characteristics may be particularly important. For example, people who are high in the motive to affiliate with others report feeling less stressed and crowded in a densely packed college dorm than do those lower in the need to affiliate (Miller and others, 1981).

Noise

Like crowding, the experience of noise is partly subjective. The crescendos from your favorite rock band may be music to your ears, but noise to your parents'. Because noise is, by definition, aversive, it increases arousal and is stressful (Fisher and others, 1984). Noise also causes people to feel less in control of their environment.

David Glass and Jerome Singer (1972) conducted a series of experiments to test the effects of noise on physiological and psychological responses. Subjects were exposed to 108 decibels of noise (approximately as loud as an automobile horn at 3 feet or a jet plane at 500 feet overhead) for 9 seconds per minute over a period of 25 minutes. The subjects had strong physiological responses to the initial blasts, but then seemed to adapt rather well. If subjects believed that they could predict or turn off the noise, their physiological responses to even the initial blasts of sound were lower. During this phase of the experiment, subjects worked on a series of arithmetic and word problems. Subjects exposed to noise made more errors at first than did control subjects not exposed to noise. But here, too, they adapted and their task performance was soon as good as that of the control subjects.

So far, the results sound like a monument to the human's ability to adapt to stress. But there is more. Glass and Singer also tested for aftereffects of the noise. In the second phase of the experiment, the experimen-

FIGURE 18.21 *Research has shown that being subjected to intense noise over a long period of time affects physiological, cognitive, and behavioral functioning.*

tal and control subjects were given more mental tasks to do. This time, the subjects who had been exposed to the noise performed more poorly than did the control group. They also became more easily frustrated. This conclusion parallels the findings described earlier concerning the delayed effects of density on task performance. It appears that, although people may be surprisingly capable of adapting to noise while it is present, there may be longer-term effects on their abilities to perform. This seems to be particularly true if they feel powerless to predict or control the noise (Sherrod and others, 1977).

Let us consider one additional study on noise, this one carried out in the natural environment of the classroom. Sheldon Cohen and his associates (1980) compared children who attended a noisy school near the Los Angeles International Airport with comparable pupils from quieter schools. The children from the noisy school had higher blood pressure than the other children and were also less successful at solving puzzles. Even more striking was their tendency to give up and not try to complete the puzzles. This suggested to the researchers that the time spent in the noisy setting may have produced a kind of learned helplessness in the children.

We might expect that children from the noisy school would learn ways of coping with the distractions caused by airliners passing overhead. However, this was not the case. These youngsters were actually more distractible, and distractions interfered more with their performance, than was the case for the children from the quiet schools. The researchers also found that the longer the children had been in the noisy school, the greater were the differences between them and the control children in blood pressure, performance, defeatism, and distractibility (Cohen and others, 1980). In a follow-up study done a year later, after 43 percent of the noisy classrooms had been modified to reduce sound levels, the researchers found that the children in these rooms were *still* more distractible than the children from the quiet schools (Cohen and others, 1981). It thus appears that people are unable to completely adapt to the negative effects of noise pollution even after they have left the situation. A behavior may thus be affected by both present and past physical environments.

FRONTIER 18.2
PSYCHOLOGY AND THE ENVIRONMENT

We currently face many critical environmental issues, including overcrowding, air and noise pollution, energy conservation, littering and vandalism, the preservation of the scenic environment, and the potentially disastrous consequences of nuclear accidents. Does psychology have anything to contribute to environmental issues?

We would argue that psychology has a great deal to offer. Human behavior is responsible for most of the threats to our environment, and human behavior is therefore likely to provide most of the ultimate solutions. Principles of learning, motivation, perception, attitude formation, and social interaction help explain how the problems arose, and they can suggest specific ways in which they might be solved. Let us consider a few examples of how psychological principles can help us to understand and change behavior.

Vandalism, defined as the willful and malicious destruction of property, is costly in financial as well as environmental terms. The cost of vandalism is more than $4 billion per year in the United States alone (Einolander, 1976). Vandalism seems totally senseless and irrational to many people. Yet recent psychological theories of vandalism suggest that this class of behavior can be understood in terms of social psychological principles that we have already discussed. One possible factor is how much control people think they have over their environment (Allen and Greenberger, 1980). People who feel that they have little control may sometimes resort to vandalism as a way of demonstrating to themselves and to others that they *can* control something. Vandalism can also be a way of releasing the anger that often accompanies feelings of helplessness.

Jeffrey Fisher and Robert Baron (1982) have suggested that vandalism may also be related to the *norm of equity*. Most people in our society are raised to believe that we should treat others fairly (or equitably) and be treated fairly in return. When people feel that they are being unfairly treated or denied their fair

FIGURE 18.22 *Although acts of vandalism like breaking tombstones or decorating them with graffiti sometimes appear totally irrational, several social psychological principles may be involved.*

share of society's resources, they may attempt to restore equity by responding to one type of perceived norm violation (not getting what they deserve) with one of their own (disregard for another's property rights). In many instances, vandalism can be an immediate and low-risk way of "paying society back."

Principles of social influence are being applied by psychologists on many fronts to deal with environmental problems. Let us begin with a problem that you are undoubtedly familiar with if you live in a college dorm. At one university, psychologists were asked to help reduce excessive noise. Preliminary or baseline data revealed an average of 345 serious noise transgressions per day in the dorm. A program that included elements of both environmental education and rein-

forcement principles was designed. Residents were given information about noise and how to deal with it. A feedback component included a doorbell set to ring in response to serious noise violations. Finally, provisions for social and monetary reinforcement of considerate behavior were established. As a result of the program, the number of noise transgressions dropped from 345 to 148 per day (Meyers and others, 1976). Still a bit noisy, perhaps, but no longer Animal House.

Energy conservation is one of our most critical problems. Because about 30 to 40 percent of all the fuel we use is for transportation (Everett, 1977), a number of researchers have applied psychological principles in attempts to reduce fuel consumption. One study involved 195 truck drivers who were given instructions on how to save fuel, as well as certificates commending them when they reduced consumption. Public feedback was provided by charting individual and fleet miles per gallon each day, and a weekly lottery was held in which chances to win were based on improvements in mileage. The program had impressive results. Mileage improved up to 9 percent, and the company saved enough money over two years to run its entire truck fleet for a month (Runnion and others, 1978).

Attempts have also been made to reduce residential energy consumption. One approach has been to install meters that give residents frequent, and sometimes daily, feedback on consumption. Such methods have resulted in reductions of up to 10 percent (Geller and others, 1982). Unfortunately, such programs are very expensive and not always effective. Research in this area is continuing, however, because it is important to determine how people can be motivated to change their behavior in order to preserve their environment.

As an exploding population gluts the earth and as precious resources are used up or destroyed by pollution, environments of the future are being planned.

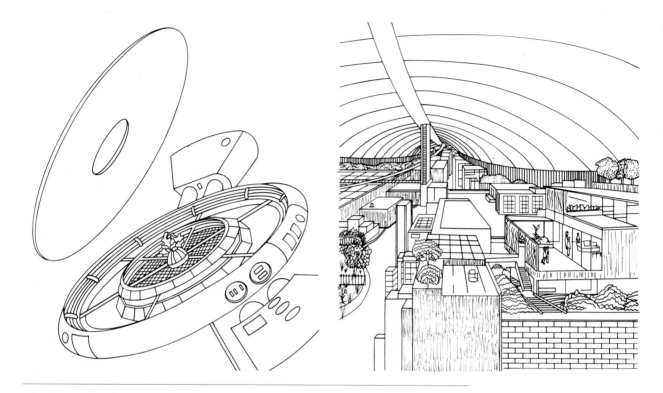

FIGURE 18.23 *Environments of the future may exist on the sea, under it, or in space. This NASA space colony has a large mirror to illuminate the interior with natural sunlight and an interior layout that incorporates environmental principles intended to increase livability.*

For example, R. Buckminster Fuller (1967) described large enclosed communities of up to a million people floating on the oceans. The National Aeronautics and Space Administration (NASA) has already begun to design large space colonies (Johnson, 1977). The colony pictured in Figure 18.23 could support about 10,000 people. Environmental psychologists have participated in the development of features that would enhance the residents' comfort, psychological well-being, and social interactions. The appearance of the internal habitat is intended to counteract monotony

and boredom. Living areas are designed to provide sufficient space and privacy, and natural vegetation creates an earthlike setting. Diverse recreational areas are located throughout the structure, and an agricultural area of only 153 acres inside the ring is expected to provide enough food for the inhabitants.

Whether our environmental future lies on earth, atop or under the seas, or in space, knowledge about how environmental factors influence health, behavior, and psychological well-being promise to enhance psychology's contributions to the quality of our lives.

STUDY OUTLINE

SOCIAL NORMS AND ROLES (p. 621)

1. Social roles are positions in a social system. They involve patterns of behavior that characterize and are expected of a person who occupies the position. Social norms are the rules or expectations shared by the members of a group. Roles and norms are intimately related to one another.

2. Social norms are learned in the process of socialization. A person's reference groups are particularly important sources of the norms that are internalized.

3. People conform in order to be accepted by others and because certain behaviors are clearly adaptive. Nonconformity involves the violation of social norms, and such behavior may result in negative sanctions, as in the cases of criminal behavior and "mental illness."

4. In extreme cases, people may adopt new beliefs and values by being brainwashed—that is, subjected to intense stress and attempts at persuasion. While religious cults do not use the stressful methods employed by the Chinese Communists during the Korean conflict, they frequently succeed in converting people who are disillusioned and seeking answers by weakening previous ties and establishing the cult as the person's new reference group.

5. Deindividuation refers to a temporary lowering of restraints that can occur when a person is immersed in a group. Recent theoretical analyses have focused on the role of reduced private self-awareness in producing deindividuation.

GROUPS (p. 629)

1. Groups differ from aggregates in that group members recognize some degree of affiliation with each other and there are interdependent roles within the group.

2. Groups can vary on a number of important dimensions, including composition, structure, and cohesiveness.

GROUP INFLUENCES ON TASK PERFORMANCE (p. 630)

1. Social facilitation refers to enhanced or reduced performance that occurs in the presence of an audi-

ence. Zajonc's drive theory of social facilitation states that the presence of an audience increases arousal, which, in turn, energizes behavior. When the dominant response tendencies are correct, the arousal helps to improve performance; when they are incorrect, performance suffers. The distraction-conflict model makes the same predictions, but links the arousal to attentional conflict caused by the presence of others.

2. Social impact theory attributes social loafing, the reduction of individual effort that occurs within a group, to the diffusion of social pressure that decreases feelings of personal responsibility and accountability. Identifiability of each individual's contributions helps reduce social loafing.

3. Groups are more effective than individuals at performing tasks that can be subdivided easily. Also, there are more opportunities for errors to correct themselves in a group and a greater chance that at least one person will have the necessary skills and knowledge to do the needed work. In some cases, however, group processes can make a group less effective than an individual would be.

GROUP DECISION MAKING (p. 635)

1. There is a strong tendency for groups to become more polarized in their opinions and attitudes following group discussion. This is believed to occur because people identify with the viewpoints held by an attractive group and desire the approval of other group members, and because people are likely to hear new supportive arguments during group discussion.

2. Groupthink occurs when cohesive groups become so committed to reaching a consensus that group members suspend their critical judgment and support any proposal advanced by the leader or by a majority of the group. The group shares an illusion of unanimity and is effectively blinded to erroneous courses of action and to alternatives.

SOCIAL POWER AND LEADERSHIP (p. 637)

1. Although a few traits are loosely associated with leadership, the nature of the group and the task seems

more important in determining who will assume a leadership role.

2. Fiedler's contingency model states that leadership effectiveness is dependent on the match between leadership style and the favorableness of the leadership situation. Task-oriented leaders function more effectively than relationship-oriented leaders when the situation is highly favorable or highly unfavorable, while relationship-oriented leaders perform better under moderately favorable conditions.

INTERGROUP CONFLICT AND CONFLICT RESOLUTION (p. 640)

1. Intergroup conflict results when the goals of two or more groups are incompatible. The Robbers Cave experiment showed that intergroup conflict can be reduced if the groups can be forced to cooperate with one another in order to achieve commonly desired goals.

2. The lessons of Robbers Cave are being successfully applied in ethnically mixed schools in the form of the jigsaw program and other types of cooperative learning.

GROUP DYNAMICS IN SPORTS (p. 642)

1. Team productivity can be understood in terms of individual output plus or minus the influence of group processes. The more that a sport requires teamwork, the more important group processes will be in team performance. Research has indicated, for example, that individual performance measures are less predictive of team success in basketball than in baseball. Social loafing has been shown to be one factor that can reduce team performance.

2. Although team cohesion is a desired goal, it can interfere with team success if it inhibits intragroup competition and arouses distracting social concerns. In general, however, studies have shown that cohesion is positively related to team performance.

3. Leadership studies have found relationships between coaching behaviors and athletes' attitudes toward the coach and other aspects of their sports experience. This information has been used to develop leadership training programs for coaches.

SOCIAL IMPACT OF THE PHYSICAL ENVIRONMENT (p. 646)

1. Relationships have been reported between crowding and various indices of physical and social pathology in both animals and humans. Laboratory studies have sometimes shown crowded experimental conditions to be related to negative emotional responses and lowered task performance.

2. A useful distinction has been made between density and crowding. Density relates to the physical environment, while crowding is a subjective experience that depends upon the individual's appraisals, needs, and personal characteristics.

3. Like crowding, noise is a subjective experience. Research has shown that exposure to noise can lower task performance (though the effects are sometimes delayed), increase physiological arousal, and be perceived as stressful. Studies of children exposed to high levels of noise have uncovered negative effects that persist even after the noise has been reduced.

4. Environmental psychology is concerned with the effects of the physical setting on behavior. Psychologists have applied psychological principles to the understanding and amelioration of environmental problems, including vandalism, energy consumption, noise, and environmental design.

KEY TERMS AND CONCEPTS

social role	group versus aggregate
social norms	social facilitation
reference group	drive theory
autokinetic effect	distraction conflict model
conformity	social loafing
brainwashing	theory of social impact
deindividuation	group polarization
private self-awareness	groupthink
public self-awareness	social power

leadership styles

contingency model

situational favorableness

cooperative learning

jigsaw program

team cohesion

environmental psychology

behavioral sink

density versus crowding

social overload

behavior constraint

norm of equity

SUGGESTED READINGS

BARON, R. A., and BYRNE, D. (1984). *Social psychology: Understanding human interaction* (4th ed.). Boston: Allyn & Bacon.

DEAUX, K., and WRIGHTSMAN, L. S. (1984). *Social psychology in the 80s* (4th ed.). Monterey, Calif.: Brooks/Cole.

Two outstanding general social psychology textbooks that cover the major areas in the field. Both books are well written and current in their treatment of social psychology.

FISHER, J. D., BELL, P. A., and BAUM, A. (1984). *Environmental psychology* (2nd ed.). New York: Holt, Rinehart and Winston. A newly updated book that covers many areas of theory, research, and application in environmental psychology.

SILVA, J. M., and WEINBERG, R. S. (Eds.). (1984). *Psychological foundations of sport*. Champaign, Ill.: Human Kinetics Publishers. A most comprehensive sourcebook in the growing area of sport psychology, covering more than 20 areas of research and application.

STATISTICAL CONCEPTS AND METHODS

DESCRIPTIVE STATISTICS
Measures of central tendency
Types of distributions
Measures of variability
Standard scores

THE NORMAL CURVE

STATISTICAL METHODS FOR DATA ANALYSIS
A key concept: Variance accounted for
Correlational methods
Inferential statistics and hypothesis testing

STUDY OUTLINE

KEY TERMS AND CONCEPTS

SUGGESTED READINGS

At various points in the text we have briefly described statistical procedures to help you understand the information being presented. This appendix is a more detailed description of statistical methods and focuses primarily on the concepts and reasoning underlying these procedures. Its goal is to help you gain a basic understanding of the manner in which psychologists use statistics in their research.

If you're like many of our students, the prospect of studying statistical procedures probably evokes reactions ranging from disinterest to dread (most things mathematical seem to elicit such responses in college students). You will find, however, that you need not be a mathematical genius in order to grasp the concepts to be presented. In fact, if you can add, subtract, multiply, and divide, you can easily perform basic statistical operations.

DESCRIPTIVE STATISTICS

Psychological research often results in a large number of measurements. Because data are frequently obtained from many subjects under different experimental conditions, it is difficult to make much sense out of the data by merely examining the individual scores of each subject. **Descriptive statistics** allow us to summarize and describe the characteristics of sets, or *distributions*, of scores.

A first step in summarizing a set of scores is to construct a **frequency distribution**. A frequency distribution will show us at a glance how many subjects received each score as well as certain characteristics of the distribution, such as whether there are more high or low scores, whether scores tend to cluster in one region of the distribution or are scattered throughout the distribution, and so on.

Table A.1 shows a frequency distribution of the scores obtained by 50 subjects on a 32-item measure of anxiety experienced before and during tests. The fre-

quency distribution tells us that 2 subjects had scores of 30, 31, or 32; none had scores of 27, 28, or 29; 11 had scores of 15, 16, or 17, and so on. Note that the researcher chose to use *intervals* of 3 points (for example, 30–32) rather than to show the number (frequency) of subjects who obtained each of the 33 possible (0 to 32) scores. She could have done the latter if she had wished to break down the scores even further. The number of intervals chosen is somewhat arbitrary, but most frequency distributions seen in the literature contain 10 to 12 categories.

Methods of graphing can give us a pictorial representation of our data. Figure A.1 shows a **histogram** of the test anxiety scores. In a histogram, the scores (in this case, score intervals) are plotted along the horizontal axis, or *abscissa*, while the frequencies are plotted on the vertical axis, or *ordinate*. The result is a column above each score that shows how frequently the score occurred in the sample of 50 subjects.

TABLE A.I   FREQUENCY DISTRIBUTION OF TEST ANXIETY SCORES

TEST ANXIETY SCORES	FREQUENCY
30–32	2
27–29	0
24–26	5
21–23	6
18–20	9
15–17	11
12–14	8
9–11	3
6–8	4
3–5	1
0–2	1

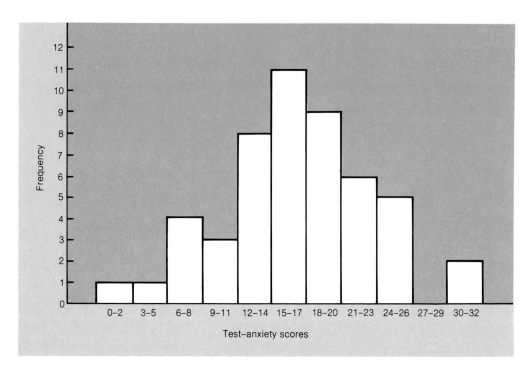

FIGURE A.I *A frequency histogram shows test anxiety scores obtained by 50 subjects. (Data from Table A.1)*

Measures of central tendency

Frequency distributions and histograms give us a general picture of how scores are distributed. **Measures of central tendency** allow us to describe a distribution in terms of a single score which is in some way "typical" of the subject sample as a whole. There are three commonly used measures of central tendency—the **mode,** the **mean,** and the **median.**

To illustrate the statistical properties and the methods of computation of these three measures of central tendency, the salaries of 10 employees of Little Albert's Rodent Extermination Company are shown in Table A.2. Our task is to arrive at a single number which somehow typifies the salaries of the group as a whole.

The *mode* is defined as the most frequently occurring score in a distribution. At Little Albert's, the modal salary is $105,000, since it is the only salary received by more than one person. (In a distribution in which no score occurs more than once, there is no mode.) While the mode is easy to identify in a distribution, it is not always the most representative score, par-

ticularly if it falls far from the center of the distribution. Clearly, $105,000 is not the "typical" salary of the 10 employees, since 8 of them receive $10,000 or less.

The *mean* is probably the most popular measure of central tendency. It is the arithmetic average, obtained by adding up all the scores and dividing by the number of scores. The statistical formula for computing the mean is:

$$\overline{X} = \frac{\Sigma X}{N}$$

$\overline{X}$ ("bar X") is the symbol for the mean of the individual scores (X). The Greek letter Σ (sigma) means "the sum," and N denotes the number of scores. To compute the mean of the salaries at Little Albert's, we simply add up the individual salaries and divide the total by 10, the number of salaries. As shown in Table A.2, the mean salary at Little Albert's is $27,350.

Would you be tempted to go to work for Little Albert upon hearing that "our average salary is $27,350 per year"? Is that figure really representative of the company's salaries? Your answer to this question illustrates one of the shortcomings of the mean as a measure of central tendency. The mean can be strongly affected by one or more extremely high or low scores that are not representative of the group as a whole. In this case, the high salaries of Little Albert and his mother raised the mean to a figure nearly three times as great as the salary of the next highest paid employee. Thus, we cannot consider the mean to be representative of Little Albert's salaries to his employees.

TABLE A.2 STATISTICAL PROPERTIES AND COMPUTATION OF THE MODE, MEAN, AND MEDIAN OF THE ANNUAL SALARIES OF TEN EMPLOYEES

EMPLOYEES	ANNUAL SALARY (X)
1 (Little Albert)	$105,000
2 (Albert's mother)	105,000
3 (Johnson)	10,000
4 (Jones)	9,500
5 (Thomson)	9,000
6 (Quiggly)	8,000
7 (Brown)	7,500
8 (Carter)	7,000
9 (Watson)	6,500
10 (Rayner)	6,000
$N = 10$	$\Sigma X = \$273,500$

N = number

ΣX = sum of individual scores

Mode = the score that occurs most often—in this case $105,000

Mean = the arithmetic average; computed by the formula

$$\overline{X} = \frac{\Sigma X}{N}$$

$$\frac{\$273,500}{10} = \$27,350$$

Median = The point above and below which there is an equal number of scores. In this case, because there is an even number of scores, it is midway between the fifth and sixth salaries—that is, $8,500

Our third measure of central tendency, the *median*, is defined as that point which divides the distribution in half when the scores are arranged in order from lowest to highest. Exactly half of the scores lie above the median and half below it. If there is an odd number of scores, there will be one score which is exactly in the middle. If there were 11 salaries in Table A.2, the sixth-ranked score would be the median, since 5 scores would fall above and 5 below. In distributions having an even number of scores, the median is halfway between the 2 middle scores. In our salary distribution, the median is the point halfway between employee 5 ($9,000) and employee 6 ($8,000), or $8,500.

The median has an important property that the mean does not have: It is unaffected by extreme scores. Whether Little Albert makes $500,000 or $11,000, the median remains the same. Therefore, the median is more representative of the group as a whole in instances where there are very extreme scores. In the case of Little Albert's company, the median figure of $8,500 is far more representative of the "average" employee's salary than is the mean figure of $27,370 or the modal salary of $105,000.

Types of distributions

Statisticians use specific terms to describe certain kinds of frequency distributions. Some common types of distributions are presented in Figure A.2.

Symmetrical distributions are those in which the scores are distributed in about the same manner above and below the mean. In a perfectly symmetrical distribution the mean, the median, and the mode are the same. Later, we will describe one such curve, the normal curve.

Nonsymmetrical distributions, in which scores tend to cluster on one end of the distribution, are called **skewed distributions**. A distribution in which there are relatively few low scores is said to be **negatively skewed**.

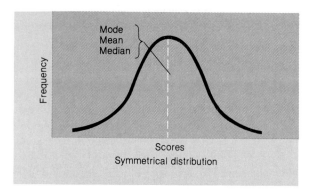

Mode
Mean
Median

Frequency

Scores
Symmetrical distribution

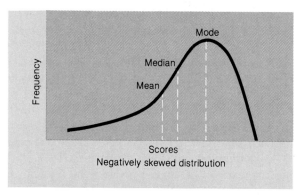

Mode

Median

Mean

Frequency

Scores
Negatively skewed distribution

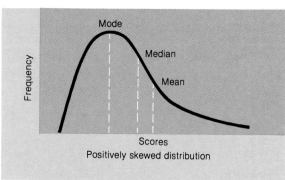

Mode

Median

Mean

Frequency

Scores
Positively skewed distribution

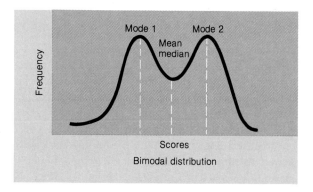

Mode 1   Mode 2
Mean
median

Frequency

Scores
Bimodal distribution

FIGURE A.2 *Common types of frequency distributions.*

In the curve representing such a distribution, the "tail," or portion which contains few scores, is to the left of the mean. In such a distribution the mean is smaller than the median, since it is more affected by the few extremely low scores. The mode is, in turn, larger than the median. One might expect a negatively skewed distribution for a very easy classroom test on which the majority of students obtain high scores. In a **positively skewed distribution,** the mean is larger than the median, which is, in turn, larger than the mode. A very difficult test might produce such a distribution of scores.

Our final distribution in Figure A.2 is called a *bimodal distribution* because there are two modes rather than one. We might obtain a bimodal distribution on a classroom examination for which some class members had studied diligently and others had not.

Measures of variability

Measures of central tendency provide us with a single score which typifies the distribution. But in order to describe a distribution adequately, we need to know more. One critical question concerns the amount of variability there is among scores. Do they tend to cluster about the mean, or do they vary widely? **Measures of variability** provide us with answers to this question.

The quickest, but least informative, measure of variability is the **range.** The range is simply the difference between the highest and the lowest score in a distribution. If, in a distribution of 20 IQ scores, the highest IQ is 160 and the lowest is 70, then the range is 90 ($160 - 70 = 90$). But supposing the other 18 people all have IQs of 110? If we knew only the range of scores, we might be led to believe that the scores in this distribution vary far more than they actually do. Far more useful and accurate than the range would be a measure of how much each score varies from the mean *on the average.*

Such a measure is provided by the **variance** and its

close relative, the **standard deviation.** The variance is the mean of the squared differences between each individual score and the mean of the distribution. The standard deviation is the square root of the variance. These definitions are probably quite intimidating, so let's analyze them more closely by showing how the variance and standard deviation are computed for the distributions of scores in Table A.3.

First we take each score (X) and subtract the mean of the distribution $(\overline{X})$ from it. In this manner we obtain the *deviation*, or distance, of each score from the group mean. The symbol for the deviation of $X - \overline{X}$ is the lower-case x. Having obtained the deviation for each score, our next step is to square these deviations and add them up. We then divide by the total number of scores (in this case, 10) to obtain the mean of the squared deviation scores. This is the variance (S^2). The reason we square the deviation scores is to eliminate

their positive and negative signs. If we simply summed the x's, the positive and negative values would always cancel each other out, resulting in $\Sigma x = 0$. We are interested in the *average* deviation of the scores from the mean without regard to direction (above or below the mean).

Once we have obtained the variance, we can easily obtain the *standard deviation* (SD) by taking the square root of the variance. Since we squared the deviation scores to compute the variance, we can now get back to the original scale of measurement by taking the square root of the variance. Psychologists tend to prefer the

TABLE A.3 COMPUTATION OF THE VARIANCE AND STANDARD DEVIATION FOR TWO DISTRIBUTIONS OF SCORES WITH IDENTICAL MEANS

DISTRIBUTION A			DISTRIBUTION B		
X	$X - \overline{X} = x$	x^2	X	$X - \overline{X} = x$	x^2
12	+2	4	18	+8	64
12	+2	4	18	+8	64
11	+1	1	15	+5	25
11	+1	1	15	+5	25
10	0	0	10	0	0
10	0	0	10	0	0
9	−1	1	5	−5	25
9	−1	1	5	−5	25
8	−2	4	2	−8	64
8	−2	4	2	−8	64
$\Sigma X = 100$	$\Sigma x = 0$	$\Sigma x^2 = 20$	$\Sigma X = 100$	$\Sigma x = 0$	$\Sigma x^2 = 356$
$N = 10$			$N = 10$		
$\overline{X} = 10$			$\overline{X} = 10$		

x (deviation) $= X - \overline{X}$

S^2 (variance) $= \dfrac{\Sigma x^2}{N} = \dfrac{20}{10} = 2.00$ $S^2 = \dfrac{\Sigma x^2}{N} = \dfrac{356}{10} = 35.6$

SD (standard deviation) $= \sqrt{2.00} = 1.414$ $SD = \sqrt{35.6} = 5.967$

standard deviation over the variance as a measure of variability because the SD is expressed in the same unit of measurement as the original (raw) data.

Besides showing how the variance and standard deviation are calculated, Table A.3 illustrates how these measures of variability provide us with important descriptive information. Note that distribution A and distribution B have an identical mean of 10. However, it is clear that there is more variability in B than in A. In fact, calculation of the standard deviations for the two sets of scores shows that the average deviation from the mean of distribution B is more than four times greater than the average deviation from the mean of distribution A.

Standard scores

The standard deviation provides us with important descriptive information about distributions. It is also the basis for computing **standard scores,** which have many important uses in psychology. Standard scores allow us to compare scores from different distributions, even those using very different units of measurement. In a sense, we can indeed compare apples and oranges!

In order to compare scores directly, we need to be able to place scores from different distributions on a common scale of measurement. The way this can be done is to express the original scores in terms of how far they deviate from the mean of their distribution. The original scores are now expressed in terms of standard scores, known as **z scores.** To calculate a z score, we simply subtract the distribution mean from the subject's score $(X - \overline{X} = x)$ and divide x by the standard deviation of the distribution—that is,

$$z = \frac{x}{\text{SD}}$$

The z score tells us how many standard deviations the score is from the group mean. The larger the z score, either positive (above the mean) or negative (below the mean), the farther the raw (original) score deviates from the average. A z score of -0.50 tells us that the raw score falls half a standard deviation below the mean of its distribution; a z score of $+1.00$ indicates a score exactly one standard deviation above its mean.

To illustrate the comparison of raw scores from different distributions, let us return to Table A.3. Assume that distribution A consists of scores on a math test and distribution B contains scores on a biology test. Each test contained 20 items. You obtained a score of 12 on the math test and a score of 15 on the biology exam. On which test did you perform better?

The answer depends on how we choose to define "better." Certainly you obtained a higher raw score on the biology test, so you did better in biology in that sense. But suppose we ask which test you did better on in relation to other students who took the tests? Converting your raw scores to standard z scores provides an answer to this question. Recall that both distributions had a mean of 10. Your z score on the math test is thus

$$z = \frac{x}{\text{SD}} = \frac{12 - 10}{1.414} = \frac{2}{1.414} = 1.41$$

We can similarly compute your z score on the biology test:

$$z = \frac{x}{\text{SD}} = \frac{15 - 10}{5.967} = \frac{5}{5.967} = 0.84$$

Examining your scores in terms of standard deviation units thus provides us with a different perspective on your performance on the tests. While you obtained above average scores on both tests, your higher z score on the math test shows that, relative to other students, you did far better on that test than on the biology test.

Standard scores have many applications in psychology. Many scores on psychological tests are expressed as standard scores. Your college entrance examination scores were expressed as standard scores, which allowed you and college officials not only to compare your performance with that of students across the nation, but also to compare your subtest scores (mathematics, social studies, verbal skills) with one another.

THE NORMAL CURVE

Earlier we described several types of frequency distributions, including symmetrical, skewed, and bimodal. One type of distribution which is of particular importance in statistics is the **normal curve.** In this bell-shaped symmetrical curve, 50 percent of the cases fall on each side of the mean. The median and the mode have exactly the same value as the mean. As we move away from the mean, the number of scores steadily decreases. As we noted previously, the normal curve is important because so many phenomena—weight, height, IQ, anxiety, to name a few—are distributed in the population in this fashion.

The normal curve is a statistician's delight because it has certain specific and very important properties. Of greatest importance is the fact that in a normal distribution, the standard deviation can be used to divide the distribution into areas containing known percentages of the total sample.

Figure A.3 shows a normal curve and illustrates its statistical properties. In a normal curve, nearly all of the cases fall between 3 standard deviations above and 3 standard deviations below the mean. Note that the standard *(z)* scores described in the last section correspond to the standard deviations of the normal curve. For example, a *z* score of +1.0 is exactly 1 standard deviation above the mean. A *z* score of −2.0 is 2 standard deviations below the mean.

If we know that a characteristic is normally distributed (as many are), then we can use the statistical prop-

erties of the normal curve to deduce more information about the characteristic. For example, IQ scores as measured by the Wechsler tests (see Chapter 12) are normally distributed with a mean of 100 and a standard deviation of 15. Knowing this, we can use our knowledge of the normal curve to answer questions like these:

1. What percentage of people have IQs below 115? (Approximately 84 percent—the 50 percent having IQs below 100 plus the 34 percent having IQs between 100 and 115, which is one standard deviation above the mean.)

2. What percentage of people have IQs between 70 and 130? (Approximately 95 percent. These scores are −2 and +2 SD from the mean. This area of the curve includes 13.59 + 34.13 + 34.13 + 13.59 percent of the cases, or 95.44 percent.)

3. What is the probability that a person selected at

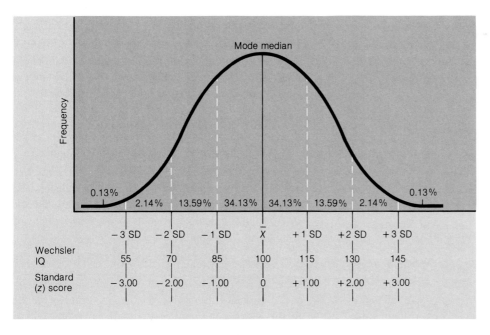

FIGURE A.3 *The figure shows the normal curve and the Wechsler IQ scores corresponding to standard deviation (SD) units. Also shown is the percentage of cases falling within each area of the curve.*

random from the population will have an IQ of 145 or more?

(Approximately one-tenth of 1 percent. The probability corresponds to the area under the curve beyond +3 SD, or 0.13 percent.)

The last example points to an important use of the normal curve. We can use it to make probability statements, that is, to estimate the likelihood that a given event will occur. Indeed, the statistical tests we describe next are methods for arriving at probability statements based on the assumption that the phenomena being investigated are normally distributed. Thus, the normal curve not only mirrors reality in many cases, but it helps us to arrive at probability statements, which are as close as we can come to "truth" in science. We shall have more to say about this point when we discuss the concept of statistical significance.

STATISTICAL METHODS FOR DATA ANALYSIS

As we have seen, we use descriptive statistics to summarize the characteristics of sets of data. But psychologists want to do more than simply describe behavior. They want to be able to *understand* behavior and its causes. From a scientific point of view the only way in which we can understand behavior is to determine how it *is related* to other things. In psychology, then, scientific understanding involves establishing exactly how a behavioral phenomenon is related to other behaviors, to the characteristics of individuals, and to environmental events. Thus, all of the statistical methods we now describe are methods for assessing relationships among variables and for drawing inferences about the meaning of those relationships.

A key concept: Variance accounted for

Behavior varies. It varies between individuals and it varies for the same individual at different times. Why?

This question is the reason we have a science of psychology. The psychologist's goal is to explain varia-

tions in behavior, or **behavioral variance.** Specifically, we want to know how much of the variation we observe in a given behavior, the dependent variable, can be accounted for by differences in some other variable or set of variables, the independent variable(s). Note that we are now using the term variance in a general sense to refer to total variation, rather than in reference to the specific statistical measure of variation described earlier.

Because the concept of **variance accounted for** is a key one in understanding the rationale for statistical tests, let us approach it from a somewhat more direct perspective. In any research study, the total amount of variation in a behavior or characteristic may be divided into two components: the amount of variance that is due to differences in the independent variable(s) that we have measured or manipulated, and the amount of variance that is left over or cannot be accounted for in terms of the factors we have manipulated. Thus

$$\text{Total variance} = \begin{array}{l} \textit{Variance accounted for} \\ \textit{(due to independent variables)} \\ + \\ \textit{Variance not accounted for} \\ \textit{(due to random, unmeasured,} \\ \textit{or uncontrolled factors)} \end{array}$$

As an example, let us assume that an experiment is conducted to study how the number of other bystanders present (none, one other, or three others) influences the speed with which subjects go to the aid of a person in distress. In this instance the number of bystanders present is the experimental (independent) variable and speed of helping (in seconds) is the dependent variable. The results of this experiment show that 20 percent of the variance in the speed with which subjects helped another person in distress could be accounted for in terms of the number of other bystanders who were present. This means that the experimental or independent variable (number of other bystanders) accounted for one-fifth of the total variance in speed of helping by all subjects in the experiment. This is shown schematically in Figure A.4. The other 80 percent of the helping variance (the unshaded portion of the circle) is due to other factors which were not controlled in the experiment. Some of these other factors are simply random factors beyond the control of the experimenter which

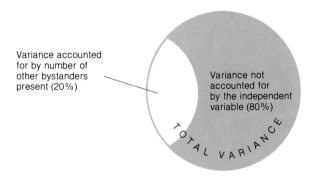

Variance accounted for by number of other bystanders present (20%)

Variance not accounted for by the independent variable (80%)

TOTAL VARIANCE

FIGURE A.4 *The total variance or variation in speed of helping another person in distress is represented within the circle. The total variance may be divided into that portion accounted for by the experimental (independent) variable (number of other bystanders) and that portion not accounted for by the independent variable.*

produce **error variance.** For example, some subjects may have been tired or preoccupied with personal problems and thus responded more slowly than they would have otherwise. The rest of the unexplained variance is the result of factors which do systematically affect speed of helping, but which the experimenter either does not know about or which were not controlled for in the experimental design. Such variables may include personality characteristics, sex of subject, victim, and other bystanders, nature of the emergency, and so forth. As other independent variables are studied in future experiments, we should be able to increase the size of the shaded area in Figure A.4 by increasing the amount of variance accounted for.

Viewed from this perspective, understanding behavior involves isolating factors which account for behavioral variance. The more important a particular variable is, the more highly it is related to the behavior of interest and the more variance it helps us account for. As scientific research proceeds, the goal is to discover new variables that account for additional portions of the total variance. To be sure, we can never completely eliminate the random factors that produce error variance. But the more variance we are able to account for, the more understanding we have of the behavior in question.

Correlational methods

As we noted earlier, the way in which understanding is achieved in science is by identifying relationships among events. When variables are related to one another, they are said to *covary*, or vary together in some systematic fashion, such that changes in one variable are associated with changes in the other. The varying together of two sets of measures is known as **correlation.** In other words, the measures are *co*-related to one another in some fashion.

In this section we describe three statistical techniques that assess relationships among variables. The *correlation coefficient* provides the psychologist with a numerical index of the strength and direction (positive or negative) of the relationship between two variables. Another technique that is a more complex application of correlational analysis, *factor analysis*, allows us to reduce a large number of measures to a smaller number of factors, or clusters of variables that are highly correlated with one another, and thereby to identify "underlying" dimensions or variables. We will discuss this approach in a later section.

THE CORRELATION COEFFICIENT

Relationships among variables can differ in terms of the *direction* of the relationship and the *magnitude* of the relationship. To illustrate, examine the relationships between the five sets of X and Y scores in Table A.4. In each instance, we have a score on variable X and a score on variable Y for each of six individuals. Of interest is the manner in which X and Y scores are related to one another. In set A the relationship is *positive* in direction. That is, high scores on variable X are associated with high scores on Y, and low scores on X are associated with low scores on Y. The opposite direction of relationship is seen in set E. Here there is a perfect inverse ordering of scores on X and Y; low scores on X are associated with high Y scores, and vice versa. Thus,

TABLE A.4 FIVE SETS OF DATA INDICATING VARIOUS RELATIONSHIPS THAT MAY EXIST BETWEEN TWO VARIABLES

SUBJECT	SET A X	SET A Y	SET B X	SET B Y	SET C X	SET C Y	SET D X	SET D Y	SET E X	SET E Y
1	1	2	1	4	1	4	1	6	1	8
2	2	4	2	5	2	8	2	8	2	6
3	3	5	3	2	3	5	3	10	3	5
4	4	6	4	10	4	2	4	4	4	4
5	5	8	5	6	5	6	5	2	5	2
6	6	10	6	8	6	6	6	1	6	1
$N = 6$	$r = +1.00$		$r = +.58$		$r = +.02$		$r = -.75$		$r = -1.00$	

Each set consists of the scores of six subjects on two variables, X and Y. The product-moment correlation coefficient (r) has been computed for each set. The computational formula for the product-moment correlation coefficient is presented at the bottom of the table.

$$r = \frac{N\,(\Sigma X_i Y_i) - (\Sigma X_i)\,(\Sigma Y_i)}{\sqrt{[N\,(\Sigma X_i^2) - (\Sigma X_i)^2][N\,(\Sigma Y_i^2) - (\Sigma Y_i)^2]}}$$

Where X_i = each subject's score on variable X; ΣX_i = sum of Xs.
$\quad\quad Y_i$ = each subject's score on variable Y; ΣY_i = sum of Ys.
$\quad\quad N$ = total number of subjects.

in set E we have a *negative* relationship between X and Y. In set C the pairs of X and Y scores bear no clear relationship to one another; they show no tendency to covary in either a positive or negative direction. They show a *zero relationship*; they are not correlated. Thus, in sets A, C, and E we see three different types of relationships—positive, none (zero), and negative.

The second way in which relationships vary is in the *magnitude* of the relationship. To illustrate differences in magnitude, let us compare set A with set B and set D with set E. In set A the pairs of scores have the same rank order; there is a perfect positive relationship. In set B individuals having high X scores tend to also have high Y scores, but the ordering is not as perfect as in set A. In other words, the positive relationship is not as strong in magnitude. Likewise, in set D there is an overall negative relationship between X and Y scores, but the magnitude of the relationship is less than the perfect negative relationship which exists in set E.

Is it possible to be more precise about the magnitude of relationships in the sets of measures in Table A.4? There is a statistic, the **product-moment correlation coefficient,** that provides us with a precise numerical index of the direction and magnitude of the relationship between two variables.

The correlation coefficient (designated r) can range in magnitude from -1.00 to $+1.00$. If $r = -1.00$, there is a perfect negative relationship between X and Y scores, as in set E of Table A.4. A correlation coefficient of $+1.00$ signifies a perfect positive relationship, as in set A. Correlations close to .00 indicate no systematic relationship between the variables, as in set C.

In actual research a correlation of -1.00 or $+1.00$ is very rare, since psychological variables tend to be imperfectly correlated with one another. More typically, correlation coefficients resemble those in sets B $(r = +.58)$ and D $(r = -.75)$. An important point to remember is that it is the *magnitude* of the correlation coefficient and not its sign (direction) that indicates the degree to which two variables are related to one another. Thus, X and Y are more strongly related in set D ($r = -.75$) than in set B ($r = +.58$), even though the correlation is a negative one in set D.

The correlation coefficient has one very important and useful property which is pertinent to the researcher's goal of accounting for variance. If the product-moment correlation coefficient (the type of coefficient most frequently used) is squared, the squared coefficient (r^2) indicates the amount of variance which the two variables share or have in common. Stated another way, r^2 tells us how much of the variance in one measure can be accounted for by differences in the other measure. For example, suppose that a correlation of $+.50$ is obtained between scores on a mechanical aptitude test and grades in an engineering course. Squaring the correlation coefficient—$(.50)^2 = .25$—tells us that 25 percent of the total variance in course grades can be accounted for by differences in mechanical aptitude scores. The reverse is also true, because we are indicating the amount of variance shared by the two measures, as illustrated in Figure A.5. Obviously, the more highly two variables are correlated (either positively or negatively), the more common variance they share. If the two variables in Figure A.5 correlated $\pm.70$, the area of overlap would include about half of each circle, since $(.70)^2 = .49$.

At this point it is well to emphasize an important point discussed in Chapter 2, namely, that a correlation between two variables does *not* allow us to conclude that one caused the other. We know only that they are related to one another. If variables A and B are correlated, it is possible that A causes B, B causes A, or that both A and B are caused by some other variable, C. We cannot infer causality from correlation. If this point is not entirely clear, you may wish to refer to Chapter 2 for a fuller discussion of the issue.

CORRELATION AND PREDICTION

In addition to providing us with information concerning the strength and direction of the relationship between two variables and giving us the basis for determining how much of the variance in each variable can be accounted for by the other variable, correlation coefficients have another function. They can help us to make predictions. If two variables are highly correlated with one another and we know an individual's score on one variable, then we can predict his or her score on the other variable. The more highly the variables are correlated, the more accurate our predictions will be. In statistical prediction based on correlation, we are thus taking advantage of lawful relationships among variables to predict to the individual case.

There are many practical applications for predictions based on correlational analysis. In industry, for example, on-the-job performance is often found to be correlated with scores on various aptitude tests. Personnel managers can therefore use these test scores to predict which of their applicants are most likely to perform well. The more highly the test scores, or **predictor variables,** are correlated with job performance, the more correct decisions will be made.

FACTOR ANALYSIS

Another important correlational technique is **factor analysis.** The technique provides us with a tool for reducing a large number of measures to a smaller number of clusters or factors on the basis of correlations

FIGURE A.5 *The correlation coefficient may be used to estimate the amount of variance shared by two variables. In this instance, r = .50, indicating that 25 percent of the variance on each measure can be accounted for by differences on the other measure.*

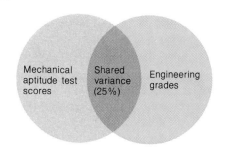

among the original measures. Just as complex chemical compounds can be analyzed to discover the basic elements they consist of, factor analysis can help us identify the basic dimensions or "factors" that underlie a large number of measures and account for the relationships among them.

Factor analysis is a highly complex statistical procedure, and we need not be concerned with its mathematical basis. Our interest is in how psychologists use it as a research tool. As an example, psychologists have long been interested in determining the basic mental abilities which people possess. How many are there? Are there hundreds, or are there perhaps only a few basic abilities involved in the performance of many different tasks? What is the nature of these abilities? To answer questions like these, let us assume that a psychologist administers 40 different and varied tests to a large number of subjects and correlates all of the test scores with one another. She reasons that tests that correlate highly with one another are probably measuring the same "underlying" ability because the underlying ability that enables people to do well on one test also enables them to do well on the others. Further, if there are clusters of tests that correlate highly with one another, but are not correlated with tests in other clusters, then these test clusters probably reflect different and distinct mental abilities. Thus, from her table of correlations, the psychologist hopes to determine the number of test clusters and to use this information to infer the nature of the underlying abilities.

When each of the 40 test scores is correlated with the other 39 scores, our psychologist will have 1560 (40 × 39) separate correlation coefficients. She will need to work with only half of the total because each correlation repeats (the correlation between variable 1 and 2 is the same as that between 2 and 1). That still leaves 780 correlations. Now, obviously, trying to determine by visual examination which tests cluster together by virtue of their correlation with one another (and lack of correlation with other tests) is a hopelessly complex task with this large number of correlations. It is in instances like this that factor analysis comes to the rescue, for it is one of the most powerful methods for reducing variable complexity to greater simplicity. In less than a minute a modern computer can analyze the table of correlations and perform a factor analysis which will tell the psychologist which tests or measures

TABLE A.5 CORRELATIONS AMONG SIX ABILITY TESTS

TEST	1	2	3	4	5	6
1	1.00	.84	.71	.04	.11	−.07
2		1.00	.79	.12	.01	.00
3			1.00	−.05	.12	.08
4				1.00	.69	.74
5					1.00	.92
6						1.00

Note: There are two sets, or clusters, of tests which correlate highly with one another but do not correlate with tests in the other cluster.

belong together, that is, which ones measure virtually the same thing and how much they do so. The "underlying" or unobserved variables (or abilities in this case) which presumably explain these obtained relationships are called **factors.**

To illustrate with a highly simplified example the kind of clustering of tests that we are interested in, let us assume that Table A.5 shows the correlations among only 6 of the 40 measures. Such a table is called a *correlation matrix.* Since the bottom of the matrix would contain the same correlations as the top, we need concern ourselves only with the upper half. The correlation coefficients of 1.00 along the diagonal of the matrix reflect the fact that, of course, each variable correlates perfectly with itself.

Examination of Table A.5 indicates the presence of two clear clusters of tests which correlate highly with one another. Test 1 correlates .84 with test 2 and .71 with test 3, while test 2 correlates .79 with test 3. Likewise, test 4 correlates .69 with test 5 and .74 with test 6, while tests 5 and 6 correlate .92. Also of great importance is the fact that tests 1, 2, and 3 have very low correlations with tests 4, 5, and 6. This indicates that the two sets of tests are measuring different things. We have determined that there are two different factors.

But what are these two groups of tests measuring? This question cannot be answered by the factor analysis; it can only identify the clusters for us. It is up to the psychologist to decide what the underlying factors might be by examining the nature of the tests within each cluster. Suppose, for example, that test 1 is a measure of vocabulary, test 2 measures the ability to construct words out of groups of random letters, and test 3 requires subjects to complete sentences having missing words. Since all of these tasks involve the use of words, the psychologist might decide to call the underlying factor "verbal ability." What she calls the factor is up to her; some other psychologist might decide that a better name for the factor would be "word fluency." What matters is that we have reduced six variables to two variables, based on the correlations among them and have arrived at some idea of what the underlying factors might be. In psychology, where we frequently wish to identify basic dimensions of behavior, factor analysis has become a valuable tool.

Inferential statistics and hypothesis testing

Correlational research is one way in which we try to understand behaviors by determining what they are related to. Another way of assessing relationships is by studying behavioral differences between groups that are known to differ in some way. In some instances, the groups differ in terms of a subject variable such as sex, high versus low anxiety, or schizophrenic versus nonschizophrenic. These groups are then compared on some behavior which is assumed to be affected by the subject variable. In other cases, the experimenter "creates" different groups by manipulating some experimental variable which is assumed to affect the behavior of interest. For example, in a study on aggression, subjects may be randomly assigned to one of two groups. One group (the experimental group) is frustrated in some way, while the other group (the control group) is not. Differences in subsequent aggression by the two groups are then measured to determine whether frustration is related to aggression.

In experiments like these, we are typically interested in overall differences between the groups. The question we usually ask is whether the means of the two groups differ enough for us to conclude that the independent and dependent variables are truly related to one another. Methods known as **inferential statistics** allow us to draw conclusions and test hypotheses by

telling us how likely it is that observed differences between groups occurred by chance alone and do not reflect a "real" difference between the groups.

But if we have observed a difference, why do we need to ask whether the difference is "real" or not? The reason is that our observations are based on only a **sample** of people drawn from a larger **population.** How do we know that the same difference would occur if we tested every member of the population? Perhaps for one reason or another, the groups we tested were not truly *representative* of the populations from which they were drawn and the differences we observed were the result of chance alone.

In most instances, researchers do not have access to the entire population of interest (for example, to all schizophrenics and all nonschizophrenic people). They must be satisfied with studying a relatively small sample of subjects. On the basis of results obtained from their samples, they want to generalize to the population as a whole. Inferential statistics provide a means of determining how much confidence we can have in results obtained from samples by telling us exactly how likely it is that the results occurred by chance alone. In actual practice, we (or our trusty computer) need only perform a series of statistical computations and then consult some special tables which tell us the precise likelihood that our sample differences do not reflect a corresponding difference in the populations from which the sample is drawn. This probability is called the **level of statistical significance.** Psychologists typically consider results to be statistically significant only if they could have occurred by chance alone less than 5 times in 100.

The logic underlying tests of statistical significance is related to our previous discussion of the normal curve and its statistical properties. Determining the level of statistical significance is in many ways similar to the problem which we presented earlier in the appendix: If IQ is normally distributed with a mean of 100 and a standard deviation of 15, what is the likelihood of randomly selecting a person with an IQ of 145?

To answer that question, all we had to do was to determine what proportion of cases are 3 standard deviations above the mean in a normal distribution. We found that proportion to be about one tenth of 1 percent. Thus, we would expect to randomly select a person with an IQ that high about once in 1000 times—pretty small odds. With this example in mind, let us consider the logic of statistical inference in greater detail.

Suppose we are interested in the effects of a stress management program on the academic performance of freshman college students who are high in test anxiety. We hypothesize that learning to control anxiety during tests will result in better performance. We randomly assign 40 students who have received high scores on a self-report measure of test anxiety to either an experimental group of 20 subjects who participate in a stress management program for test anxiety, or to a control group which receives no guidance or treatment. All of the students take the same required courses, and at the end of the academic year we compare the mean grade point averages of the two groups. We find that the experimental group, which went through the training program, obtains a mean grade point of 3.17 (A = 4.0), whereas the control group has a mean grade point of 2.61. How can we now decide whether the grade point difference in the two samples reflects a difference in the respective populations (that is, all high test-anxious students who might participate in a stress management program and all who do not)?

Suppose that we repeated our experiment a large number of times with different samples of high-anxiety subjects. If we did, we would surely find that the means for the two samples would vary in each experiment. The next time we performed the study the means might be 2.94 (experimental) and 2.77 (control), the next time 3.34 and 2.31, the next time 2.89 and 2.83, and so on. Since each of the means would vary with each study, the *differences* between the means of the experimental and control groups would vary, too. By repeating the experiment a great many times, we could actually create a distribution of experimental versus control difference scores, and mathematical theory tells us that this distribution would be a *normal* distribution. This, then, gives us the key. Because we have a normal distribution, we can assess the likelihood of randomly obtaining any particular difference between our sample

means, just as we could arrive at the exact likelihood of randomly selecting a person with an IQ of 145, 92, or 71. But in order to do this, we must know what the mean and standard deviation of our distribution of differences are. One way to determine these values would be to perform our experiment a large number of times. But, fortunately, we can estimate these values on the basis of a single experiment. Here's how it works.

If there is no real difference in grade point between the populations of trained and untrained test-anxious students, and if we repeated our experiment a great

---

FIGURE A.6 *A theoretical frequency distribution of differences in grade point average between means of test-anxious samples who do or do not receive stress management training. Assuming no difference between the populations from which the samples were drawn (the null hypothesis), the difference scores would be normally distributed with a mean of zero. The values of the standard deviation of difference scores estimated from the hypothetical experiment in the text are presented here.*

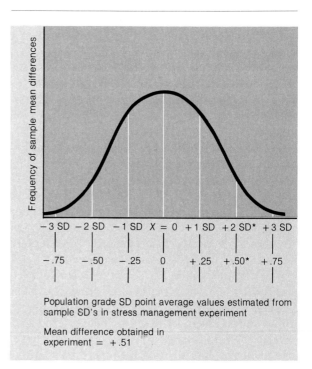

Population grade SD point average values estimated from sample SD's in stress management experiment

Mean difference obtained in experiment = +.51

many times, then we would expect the mean of our distribution of difference scores to be around zero. The normal distribution of difference scores would cluster around this mean in the manner shown in Figure A.6. The standard deviation of this normal distribution can be estimated from the standard deviations of the two samples, although the mathematics need not concern us here.

Statistical analysis involves testing the **null hypothesis**, which assumes that the difference between the two population means is zero, and that any observed differences between the samples are due to chance. In our hypothetical experiment, we obtained grade point means of 3.17 for the experimental group and 2.61 for the controls, a difference of +0.51. Let us now suppose that the standard deviation of our distribution of differences between means was estimated on the basis of our samples to be .25. Thus, our obtained difference is slightly more than 2 SD above the mean (0) of the null hypothesis distribution. From the properties of the normal curve, we know that more than 95 percent of the cases fall in the area of the curve between −2 SD and +2 SD. Thus, if the null hypothesis were true, we would expect a difference in means as large as .51 (in either direction from the mean) less than 5 percent of the time on the basis of chance factors. This is another way of saying that our level of statistical significance is less than .05. In view of this fact, we would probably reject the null hypothesis and conclude that there is a real difference in grade point in the two populations. Thus, our experimental hypothesis that the stress management program resulted in a higher level of academic performance would be supported. Note that we used the term *supported*, not proven, because we are making an inference based on a probability statement. There is, after all, a 5 percent chance that the null hypothesis is true. This is one reason why repeating or replicating research studies is so valuable. If another study also yields statistically significant results, we can have more confidence that the difference we obtained reflects a real relationship between the independent variable (stress management training) and the dependent variable (academic performance). But no matter how many times we repeat the experiment, we shall never escape from the world of probability into the world of absolute truth.

STUDY OUTLINE

DESCRIPTIVE STATISTICS (p. 657)

1. Descriptive statistics allow us to summarize and describe the characteristics of whole sets, or distributions, of data. A frequency distribution shows how many subjects received each score and indicates the pattern of scores. Histograms are pictorial representations of frequency distributions.

2. Measures of central tendency—the mode, the mean, and the median—describe a distribution in terms of a single score that is typical of the sample as a whole. The mode is the most frequently occurring score in a distribution. The mean is the arithmetic average, while the median is the point that divides the distribution in half. The median is less affected by extreme scores than the mean is.

3. In symmetrical distributions, scores are distributed in essentially the same manner above and below the mean. In skewed distributions, scores tend to cluster at the high (negatively skewed) or low (positively skewed) ends of the distribution. A bimodal distribution has two modes rather than one; it resembles a camel's back.

4. Measures of variability tell us how much variation there is among scores. The difference between the highest and the lowest scores in the distribution is the range. The variance and the standard deviation are the most useful measures of variability. The variance is the mean of the squared differences between each score and the mean of the distribution. The standard deviation is the square root of the variance.

5. The standard deviation is used to compute standard scores, which allow direct comparisons of scores from different distributions in standard deviation units. The z score tells us how many standard deviations a score is from the mean.

THE NORMAL CURVE (p. 662)

A normal curve is a symmetrical bell-shaped curve. Fifty percent of the cases fall on each side of the mean. The mean, median, and mode all have the same value. The standard deviation can be used to divide the distribution into areas containing known percentages of the total sample. Probability statements are based on the assumption that the phenomena being studied are distributed normally in the population.

VARIANCE ACCOUNTED FOR (p. 664)

A major goal of psychological research is to determine how much behavioral variance can be accounted for by relationships between variables, including experimental manipulations, and how much is due to random, unmeasured, or uncontrolled factors. Random factors that are beyond the experimenter's control produce error variance.

CORRELATIONAL METHODS (p. 665)

1. In science, understanding is achieved by identifying relationships among events. Variables that are related covary in some systematic fashion; covariation in two groups of measures is called correlation.

2. The correlation coefficient is a numerical index of the direction and magnitude of the relationship between two variables. Correlations may be positive, negative, or zero, as well as weak or strong.

3. Squaring the correlation coefficient tells us how much of the variance in one measure can be accounted for by differences in the other measure. Although correlation does not allow us to assume causality, correlations are often the basis for predictions.

4. Factor analysis allows us to use correlations to reduce a large number of measures to a smaller number of clusters in which the measures are highly correlated with one another and presumably measuring the same psychological dimension. Factor analysis only identifies the clusters; the researcher must infer the nature of the underlying factors.

INFERENTIAL STATISTICS AND HYPOTHESIS TESTING (p. 669)

1. Inferential statistics allow us to draw conclusions and test hypotheses because they tell us how likely it is that differences between groups or correlations among

variables are the result of chance alone. Inferential statistics are needed because most research is done with samples, and conclusions must be generalized to the population from which the sample was drawn.

2. The probability that relationships shown among variables do not reflect a corresponding relationship in the population is called the level of statistical significance. Statistical analysis involves testing the null hypothesis, which assumes that any observed relationship is due to chance, or that the difference between the two population means is zero. Inferential statistics yield probability statements, not proof.

KEY TERMS AND CONCEPTS

descriptive statistics

frequency distribution

histogram

measure of central tendency

mode

mean

median

symmetrical distribution

positively/negatively skewed distribution

measure of variability

range

variance

standard deviation

standard score

z score

normal curve

behavioral variance

variance accounted for

error variance

correlation

product-moment correlation coefficient

predictor variable

factor analysis

factor

inferential statistics

sample

population

level of statistical significance

null hypothesis

SUGGESTED READINGS

KERLINGER, F. N. (1979). *Behavioral research: A conceptual approach.* New York: Holt, Rinehart and Winston. An excellent introduction to research design and methods with clear, nonmathematical explanations of statistical techniques.

KIMBLE, G. (1978). *How to use (and mis-use) statistics.* Englewood Cliffs, N.J.: Prentice-Hall. A brief text on statistical methods written especially for people with a limited background in mathematics; it includes many practical examples of the use of statistics in psychology.

PAGANO, R. R. (1986). *Understanding statistics in the behavioral sciences* (2d ed.). St. Paul, Minn.: West. An extremely readable text that covers statistical concepts and methods of computation of commonly used statistical techniques, along with many practice problems; more mathematical than the Kerlinger and Kimble books.

GLOSSARY

a = a   as in *back*

ah = a   as in *ha*

aw = aw   as in *shawl* or a as in *tall*

ay = a   as in *play*

e = e   as in *set*

ee = e   as in *see*

ew = eu   as in *blue* or ew as in *few*

i or ih = i   as in *sit*

igh = i   as in *high*

oh = o   as in *pole*

u = u   as in *yule* or ou as in *you*

uh = u   as in *tub*

Exceptions are sometimes made when syllables are clearly pronounceable.
Examples: shun = *tion*   hy = *hy*   type = *type*

ablation (ab-LAY-shun)   Surgical removal; more specifically, surgical removal of parts of the brain in the study of the function of particular structures.

absolute threshold   The amount of energy a stimulus must exert before we can detect its presence. When the level is below absolute threshold, there is no sensation; when it is above the threshold, a stimulus can be sensed and experienced. For research purposes the absolute threshold is defined as the stimulus intensity at which a stimulus can be detected 50 percent of the time.

abstract code   The storage of memory by a symbolic rather than visual representation of the stimulus. Examples include language, musical notation, computer languages.

accommodation   The process by which the lens of the eye changes shape in accordance with the distance of the object being viewed.

acetylcholine (ACh) (uh-seet-l-KOH-leen)   A chemical transmitter substance secreted into the synapse that combines with a receptor chemical in the membrane of the dendrite or soma of the receiving cell. The chemical reaction that results makes possible firing of the receiving neuron.

achievement motivation   The desire to compete successfully with standards of excellence.

achievement test   A measure of an individual's degree of accomplishment in a particular subject or task based on a relatively standardized set of experiences—for example, a particular mathematics course—rather than on broad knowledge gained over a long period of time from many sources.

acquired immune deficiency syndrome (AIDS)   A contagious disorder that involves a failure of the body's immune system, thus making a person susceptible to death from normally nonfatal infections.

action potential   The change in cell polarity that takes place during the passage of a nerve impulse. The membrane becomes permeable to sodium, and sodium ions flow into the interior of the cell.

acupuncture (AK-yu-punk-cher)   Ancient Chinese medical procedure involving the insertion of long, fine needles into precise points on the skin to relieve various illnesses.

additive (AD-uh-tiv) **model**   A theory of information integration that says that one person's impression of another is based simply on the sum of reactions to all the information about that person.

adrenal (uh-DREE-nuhl) **gland**   One of a pair of endocrine glands, one situated over each kidney. Its two main parts are the adrenal cortex and the adrenal medulla.

afferent neurons (AF-uh-runt NU-rahnz)   Those nerves that carry messages from the periphery of the body and the internal organs to the spinal cord and brain; also called sensory neurons.

affiliation (uh-FIL-ee-ay-shun)   The association or connection of oneself with other people.

age-related process   An aspect of development that occurs naturally as an individual becomes older. Motor and cognitive skills are examples. Age-related processes are differentiated from history-related events and unique life events.

aggregate (AG-ri-guht)   A collection of people who have no real relationship—for example, people waiting at a bus stop or members of a crowd.

aggression   Any behavior intended to harm another. The term does not include the emotions that may underly the behavior.

agoraphobia (AG-or-ah-FOH-bee-ah)   Pathological fear of open spaces.

alarm reaction   The first stage of the *general adaptation syndrome* to stress described by Selye. The other stages are resistance and exhaustion.

algorithm (AL-guh-rith-uhm)   A method of problem solving that will, if properly used, automatically generate a correct solution. Examples of algorithms are rules for multiplication or addition or such formulas as time = distance ÷ speed.

alpha rhythm The brain wave pattern of 8 to 12 cycles per second characteristic of humans in a relaxed waking state.

altruism (ALL-true-is-um) Voluntary helping acts that are carried out regardless of the possibility of a reward.

Alzheimer's (ALTS-hi-merz) **disease** A chronic brain disorder, occurring as early as 40 years of age, that involves progressive destruction of nervous tissue that results in slurring of speech and gradual intellectual deterioration with growing lapses of memory.

ambiguity (AM-bi-gue-i-tee) A condition whose meaning is uncertain. In ambiguous situations, help is less likely to be offered because the potential helper is not certain of the meaning of all aspects of the event.

amine (AH-meen) **hypothesis of depression and mania** A theory stating that depression may be associated with too little activity of the amine neurotransmitters and mania with their overactivity.

amine neurotransmitter systems The body's source of a group of short-lived chemical compounds that are important in transferring a nerve impulse from one neuron to another.

amphetamine (am-FET-uh-meen) A type of stimulant sold under such trade names as Benzedrine, Dexadrine, and Methadrine and popularly known as speed, uppers, and bennies. Use of large quantities of the drugs can cause heart failure, cerebral hemorrhage, brain damage, or paranoid delusions.

anal (AY-nuhl) **stage** The second stage of psychosexual development as described by Freud. It begins at about age 2. In this stage the anal area becomes more strongly associated with sexual gratification than the oral area.

analytical psychology The system of psychodynamic psychology originated by Carl Jung. The focus is the study of the unconscious, with a particular emphasis on the use of dreams as reflections of inherited wisdom and as guides to living.

androgen (AN-druh-juhn) The male sex hormone. Genetically programmed release during pregnancy determines the development of male characteristics.

anorexia nervosa (ah-noh-REX-ia ner-VOH-sa) An eating disorder characterized by a phobia toward eating, resulting in a severe weight loss.

antecedents (an-ti-SEE-dents) Specific aspects of a situation that trigger particular behaviors.

antianxiety drugs (minor tranquilizers) Substances prescribed to reduce anxiety but not to reduce mental capabilities of patients.

antidepressant drugs A group of medications used to reduce symptoms of depression.

antipsychotic (an-tigh-sigh-KAHT-ik) **drugs** (major tranquilizers) Substances such as chlorpromazine, often prescribed for patients who are hallucinating, having delusions, or are extremely withdrawn or highly excited. They are frequently used in the treatment of schizophrenia. Many patients relapse if they stop taking such medication.

antisocial personality disorder A condition characterized by chronic antisocial behavior, beginning before the age of 15 and continuing into adult life. Before the age of 18, such behavior is called a conduct disorder. The behavior tends to impair the rights of others and to be marked by an impaired capacity for close relationships.

anxiety An unpleasant emotional state accompanied both by physiological arousal and by cognitive elements, such as a sense of impending disaster. It differs from fear in that it is a general response rather than a reaction to a specific object or situation.

anxiety disorder Formerly called neurosis of neurotic disorder. Characterized by some form of anxiety as the most prominent symptom. Includes panic disorder, phobic disorder, obsessive compulsive disorder and generalized anxiety disorder.

aphasia (uh-FAY-zhi-uh) An inability to understand language or to express it.

applied behavior analysis The use of monitoring to determine under what specific conditions of reinforcement certain precisely identified behaviors occur.

approach-approach conflict Conflict produced by the necessity of choosing between two desirable objects or consequences.

approach-avoidance conflict Conflict produced when a single object or activity is simultaneously attractive and unattractive.

aptitude test A measure of a person's ability to profit from further training or experience in an occupation or skill. It is usually based on a measure of skills gained over a period of time rather than during a specific course of study.

archetype (AHR-kuh-type) A mythological image or a predisposition to characteristic thoughts that is represented in such universal concepts as God; the wisdom of the old; the young and potent hero; resurrection; and evil spirits. It is a term used by Jung for the contents of the collective unconscious.

arousal A state of heightened stimulation or excitement.

artificial intelligence The use of computer program models to reproduce as closely as possible some aspects of intellectual functioning.

assertiveness training A combined cognitive and behavioral approach designed to increase the frequency of behavior that defends or maintains the person's rights and enables him or her to state positions with appropriate emphasis.

association areas Those regions of the cerebral cortex that do not have sensory or motor functions. These areas, which include the majority of the cortex, are involved in perception, language, and thought.

associative strategies Pain-control techniques that involve focusing in an unemotional way on the painful bodily sensations.

attachment The tendency of an infant during the first two years of life to be most receptive to being cared for and approached by a certain person or persons. In the company of this person or persons the infant is also less afraid of a strange environment.

attitude A relatively long-lasting set of beliefs, feelings, or behaviors directed at a person, object, or situation.

attribution The process of pinpointing the cause of behavior or answering the question "Why?" in relation to behavior.

autokinetic (aw-toh-ki-NET-ik) **effect** An illusion of apparent movement of a small stationary light in a totally dark room; used by Sherif to study conformity.

autonomic (aw-toh-NAHM-ik) **nervous system** A division of the peripheral nervous system that directs the activity of the glands and internal organs of the body. It is especially important in emotional behavior.

autoradiography (aw-toh-ray-dee-AH-graf-ee) A method for photographing the amount of radioactive substance absorbed by neurons to determine how active they were. See deoxyglucose technique.

avoidance-avoidance conflict Conflict produced by the necessity of choosing between two undesirable objects or consequences.

avoidance conditioning A procedure in which the subject learns to make a response when a warning signal occurs and thereby avoids an aversive stimulus.

axon (AK-sahn) An extension from one side of the cell body that conducts electrical impulses away from the cell body to other neurons, muscles, or glands.

baseline measure Assessment of a phenomenon that is made before an intervention is begun.

basilar (BAH-si-ler) **membrane** A membrane in the cochlea whose movement stimulates the auditory receptors in the organ of Corti.

Beck's cognitive theory of depression The idea proposed by A. T. Beck that depressed individuals have a distorted view of their environment that maintains their depressed state by misinterpretation of events and an imperviousness to feedback.

behavioral assessment A technique of systematically observing certain classes of responses and the situations in which they occur.

behavioral constraint A term used in environmental psychology to describe the idea that crowding makes people feel that their freedom of behavior is threatened or eliminated.

behavioral medicine An area of study emphasizing the importance of psychological factors in patient evaluation and treatment—for example, the study of how to increase the likelihood that a person will follow the prescribed course of treatment including medication, diet, exercise, and other life style changes that may be necessary.

behavioral perspective A view that behavior results from an organism's interaction with its environment; the belief that human beings are basically reactors and that the factors controlling human behavior reside in the external environment rather than within the individual. Behavior is determined by how the individual has been conditioned previously and the stimuli within his or her immediate environment.

behavior genetics The study of the inheritance of behavioral characteristics or predispositions.

behaviorism A school of psychology that holds that scientific psychology should focus only on observable stimuli and responses.

Binet (bih-NAY) **tests** Adaptations of intelligence tests developed by Alfred Binet. The tests reflect a global view of intelligence. Among the most famous of the Binet tests is the Stanford-Binet.

binocular (bigh-NAH-kyu-lahr) **disparity** The slightly different view of an object experienced by each eye which results in depth perception.

biological perspective The view of human behavior that emphasizes organic factors, such as brain processes and genetic determinants.

bipedalism (bigh-PED-al-is-uhm) The ability to walk upright on the hind limbs.

bipolar (bigh-POH-ler) **cells** In the visual system, the second-order cells that synapse with the rods and cones.

bipolar disorder An affective disorder including periods of depression and periods of mania.

blind spot The point in the retina of the eye where the optic nerve exits from the eye and in which there is no vision.

blobs Recently discovered patches of feature detectors in the visual cortex that are sensitive to color.

blocking An experimental procedure in which classical conditioning of a response to a new conditioned stimulus is blocked by a previously established conditioned stimulus.

bodily assessment The use of sophisticated physiological techniques to monitor blood pressure, heart rate, electrical skin conductance, and so on.

bonding period A developmental period occurring in some animals and thought by some researchers to occur in human infants. Physical closeness during this period has specific long-term effects on later relationships as well as on the infant's behavior.

borderline personality disorder A condition characterized by impulsive and unpredictable behavior and marked shifts in mood. Instability may affect personal relationships, behavior, mood, and image of self.

bottom-up processing A cognitive approach in which all the parts of the stimulus are surveyed separately and then combined to give them meaning.

brain slice A microscopically thin sheet of living nerve tissue that can be studied biochemically.

brain stem The portion of the brain between the spinal cord and the cerebellum made of the pons and the medulla. It contains many ascending and descending fibers that connect the higher and lower levels of the central nervous system.

bulimia (bu-LEE-mee-a) An eating disorder characterized by uncontrolled binges followed by purging through the use of laxatives and/or vomiting.

burnout A type of stress reaction often seen in people who have extremely demanding and frustrating jobs.

calpain An enzyme in the membrane of neurons that, when released by stimulation, breaks down a portion of the membrane to expose more neurotransmitter receptors so as to increase the neuron's sensitivity to further stimulation.

Cannon-Bard theory of emotion The idea that the thalamus responds to emotion-arousing stimuli by sending messages simultaneously to the cerebral cortex and to the visceral and skeletal muscles. Messages to the cortex are responsible for the "feelings" of emotion and the messages to the visceral and skeletal muscles for the physiological and overt behavior responses.

catecholamine (kat-uh-KOHL-uh-meen) A neurotransmitter; a chemical compound in the body that aids in the transmission of impulses across the synaptic gap.

central nervous system One of the major divisions of the nervous system; includes all the neurons in the brain and spinal cord and is the integrating center for all behavior and bodily functions.

cerebellum (ser-uh-BEL-uhm) An area of the hindbrain that controls the coordination of motor activity.

cerebral (se-REE-bruhl) **hemispheres** The largest part of the human brain, consisting of outer gray cortex composed primarily of neuron cell bodies and unmyelinated fibers and an internal white core composed primarily of myelinated fibers.

cerebral ventricles Cavities in the brain that are connected to the central canal of the spinal cord and that contain cerebrospinal fluid.

cerebrum (se-REE-bruhm) The portion of the brain consisting of the two cerebral hemispheres. These constitute the bulk of the brain in humans and other higher animals.

chromosome (KROH-muh-zohm) A rodlike unit carrying specific hereditary factors, or genes.

chunk In the study of memory, sensory stimulation that can be recognized as one unit. Multistore theorists think that about seven chunks can be retained in short-term memory at one time.

ciliary (SIL-ee-er-ee) **muscle** The muscle that acts on the lens of the eye to adjust its shape for viewing at various distances.

circadian (ser-KAH-dee-ahn) **rhythm** Cyclical changes in body temperature, blood pressure, blood plasma volume, hormonal secretions into the bloodstream, and other body processes that occur in humans and other mammals during periods of about 24 hours.

classical conditioning A technique originated by Pavlov that produces learning by pairing a neutral stimulus with a stimulus that already evokes a response. The neutral stimulus will eventually evoke the same response when presented alone.

client-centered therapy A type of psychotherapy developed by Carl Rogers, in which the therapist neither provides interpretations nor gives advice, but tries to create an environment in which clients can reorganize their subjective world.

clinical psychology The field of psychology concerned with diagnosis and treatment of psychological disturbances and with research on personality, psychological tests, and deviant behavior.

clitoris (KLIT-uh-ris) An extremely sensitive part of the female external genitalia.

closure Gestalt perceptual law that states that when there are open edges or gaps in a figure, the individual tends to fill them in to make the stimulus complete.

cocaine (koh-KAYN) A stimulant, derived from the coca plant that is either inhaled or injected and may induce euphoria, excitation, anxiety, a sense of increased muscular strength, talkativeness, and liveliness. Overdoses can depress breathing and heart functions and therefore cause death. Users may develop a strong psychological dependence, although there is no evidence that they become physically dependent.

cochlea (COKE-lee-uh) Coiled tubes filled with fluid in the inner ear that contain the organs of Corti, the tiny hair cells that transform sound vibrations into nerve impulses.

cocktail party effect The phenomenon in which a person's attention suddenly shifts from one stimulus to another because of the personal relevance of the second stimulus.

coding The process by which information is condensed into meaningful units as an aid to memory.

cognitive (KAGH-ni-tiv) **appraisal** The process of evaluating, interpreting, and giving meaning to external stimuli and one's own behavior.

cognitive assessment Behavioral methods for studying individuals' thoughts. These include questionnaires and time signals that alert an individual to report what thoughts were occurring at a particular time.

cognitive behavior modification A procedure in which subjects learn to control and change self-instructional statements that affect their feelings and behavior.

cognitive complexity The idea that attitudes, though usually simple likes or dislikes, have as their basis a complex set of facts, some of which may be opposed to the final attitude.

cognitive dissonance The state of tension resulting from the experience by the individual of two cognitions that are psychologically inconsistent. In order to reduce the tension, the individual will either change one of the cognitions or add more cognitions to explain the inconsistency. The term was first used by Leon Festinger.

cognitive perspective A view of behavior as the result of the individual's thoughts, understandings, interpretations, and ideas about the environment. This point of view emphasizes the ways in which individuals process, evaluate, and respond to stimuli.

cohesion A group characteristic that involves high attraction, commitment, and involvement among group members and a tendency to stick together under adversity.

cohort The general group of which an individual is a part—for example, because of similar birth data or attendance at the same institution at the same time.

collective unconscious A term used by Carl Jung for the part of the human unconscious that consists of memories accumulated throughout the history of the human race. It contains archetypes, or mythological images or predispositions to certain thoughts that are reflected in universal concepts, such as God, resurrection, and evil spirits.

community approach   The viewpoint that much maladaptive behavior results from poor living conditions, discrimination, and so on. Emphasis is on preventive activities.

companionate love   A deep, close, caring friendship that may exist together with, or separate from, sexual love.

comparative outcome research   Research to determine the relative effects of different types of therapy, their results with different types of clients, and their effectiveness compared to no treatment.

concordance (kuhn-KOR-duhns) **rate**   A measure used by researchers studying hereditary characteristics; the probability or risk that one of a pair of individuals in a population will show a particular characteristic if the other individual has the characteristic.

concrete operations period   A term used by Piaget for the third of the four major stages in the continuous process of growth and change in cognitive development during childhood. It runs from about age 7 to age 12. In this period children acquire a whole new set of skills called operations, which involve the ability to understand that certain mental processes are reversible.

concussion (kuhn-KUH-shun)   A violent shock or jarring of the brain against the skull that often results in a temporary loss of consciousness.

conditioned response (CR)   In classical conditioning, the response that is eventually evoked by the conditioned stimulus. Although based on the unconditioned response, the CR is generally not identical with it in all respects.

conditioned stimulus (CS)   In classical conditioning, the neutral stimulus that, as a result of being paired with the unconditioned stimulus, becomes capable of evoking a conditioned response.

cone   Structure within the retina of the eye that constitutes the color receptors. It functions only at relatively high levels of illumination.

confounding   The mixing of two or more variables in an experiment so that it is impossible to know for certain which variable produced the effect.

conjugate (KAHN-ju-gat) **reinforcement**   A reinforcement technique in which the rate or size of the response has a similar effect on the rate or amount of reinforcement delivered. It results in rapid learning and enhanced learning transfer from task to task.

consanguinity (kahn-sang-GWIN-uh-tee) **study**   A method of examining inheritance that contrasts the statistical probability of occurrence of a trait in close relatives, distant relatives, and the general population.

conscious   The psychoanalytic term describing the mental events of which we are presently aware.

consequences   A term used in behavior therapy to focus on the results from a particular behavior.

constituent   The basic unit into which a spoken sentence is

organized. After each of the units is understood, they are combined so that the whole sentence can be understood.

construct (KAHN-strukt)   A word or concept that represents a nonmaterial idea rather than an object. Examples are aggression, stress, learning.

contingency (kuhn-TIN-juhn-see) **model**   A theory of leadership advanced by Fred Fiedler, in which leadership performance is a joint function of the goals of the leader and of the amount of situational control he or she has.

continuity   Gestalt perceptual law that states that the individual tends to see shapes, lines, and angles following the same direction established by previous elements.

continuous reinforcement   A procedure used in operant conditioning in which there is reinforcement after every response.

contraprepared behaviors   Behaviors that an organism has great difficulty learning because they are contrary to evolutionary survival requirements of the species.

control group   A group of subjects in an experiment that experiences all the same conditions as those of the experimental group except for the condition under investigation.

contusion (kuhn-TU-shun)   A bruising of the brain; more severe injury than a concussion, usually with longer-lasting and more severe effects.

copulin (KAHP-yu-lin)   Vaginal secretion whose odors sexually arouse males.

corpus callosum (KOR-pus Kal-OH-suhm)   A large band of fibers that connects the two hemispheres of the brain and allows them to function as a single unit.

correlational studies   A way of determining the degree of correspondence between two sets of paired measurements. Correlational studies cannot establish a cause-and-effect relationship.

correlation coefficient   A statistical measure that expresses the degree of relationship between two variables. It can range from $+1.00$ to -1.00. A positive correlation indicates that high scorers on one of the variables also have high scores on the other. A negative correlation indicates that high scorers on one variable have low scores on the other. A correlation of .00 means that there is no statistical relationship between two sets of scores.

cortex (KOR-tex)   The outer layer of an organ. When used alone, the term refers to the furrowed or convoluted part of the brain that lies above the brain stem and covers the cerebrum and cerebellum.

cortical (KOR-ti-kuhl) **columns**   Vertical arrangements of cells in the cerebral cortex that are maximally sensitive to specific stimulus features.

cortical projection areas   The specific regions of the cerebral cortex to which input from the various senses is directed.

corticotropin (KORT-i-koh-TROH-pin) **releasing factor**

(CRF) A chemical produced by the hypothalamus that travels to the pituitary gland and brain stem and triggers them to produce a response to stress.

cost-reward analysis A way of predicting whether or not helping behavior will occur by considering the rewards and costs of helping.

countertransference The irrational reactions of the therapist to the client based on the therapist's own past associations.

couples therapy A therapeutic program in which both members of a couple work with the therapist to understand and alter the factors that are producing a troubled relationship.

covert behavior Internal, objectively unobservable processes, such as thoughts and images.

critical period A point in development during which certain experiences are most likely to elicit particular responses and the growth of particular skills. If the eliciting experiences do not occur at that point, the failure to establish the response or skill cannot be compensated for later in development. See also *sensitive period*.

cross-sectional method A technique of studying development by comparing the characteristics of groups of individuals of different ages.

crystallized abilities Intellectual abilities that depend on a store of information and the acquisition of particular skills. See also *fluid abilities*.

CT SCAN (computerized axial tomography) A method of examining the brain with narrow X rays. The data are analyzed by a computer that generates a picture of the brain's anatomical features.

cunnilingus (kuhn-ih-LING-gus) Oral stimulation of the female genitals.

dark adaptation The process though which visual pigments regenerate so that the visual system becomes more sensitive to low levels of illumination.

decibel (DEH-si-buhl) Logarithmic unit used to measure noise. For example, a change in level from 10 decibels to 20 decibels represents an increase of 10 times in sound intensity. Sound of 90 decibels can cause permanent loss of hearing.

declarative representation scheme A way of accessing stored information by the use of explicit relationship—for instance, in a computer program.

deep structure A linguistic term that refers to the underlying meaning of a spoken or written sentence. The meanings that make up deep structure are stored as concepts and rules in long-term memory.

defense mechanism A psychoanalytic term for various kinds of psychic operations that are used by the ego to prevent awareness of anxiety-evoking or unpleasant stimuli. These stimuli may come form the id, the superego, or the external world.

dehumanization The tendency to perceive others as objects rather than as people having feelings similar to one's own.

deindividuation The feelings of loss of behavioral restraint that may accompany the anonymity people feel as part of a group.

delayed sleep syndrome A form of insomnia characterized by an inability to fall asleep.

delusion An incorrect belief about an object or event that an individual maintains even in the face of clear evidence to the contrary.

demand characteristics Stimuli that exist in many research situations that give subjects information about how they are expected to behave. Subjects may not all be affected in the same way by these stimuli.

dementia praecox (dih-MEN-chee-ya Pree-kox) The original term for schizophrenia used by Emil Kraepelin.

dendrite (DEN-drite) One of many small fibers that extend from the soma or cell body and receive electrical messages from adjacent cells that are then conducted to the cell body.

deoxyglucose (dee-AK-see-GLU-kohs) **technique** A method for studying the activity of the brain by measuring the amount of radioactive deoxyglucose absorbed by specific groups of neurons.

deoxyribonucleic (dee-AK-cee-RIGH-boh-nu-klee-ik) **acid (DNA)** A chemical compound that occurs in the cell nucleus and is important in the transmission of heredity. The DNA molecule can unzip up the center and reproduce the missing halves so that each new molecule contains the complete genetic code contained in the original.

dependent personality disorder A disorder characterized by an inability to make major decisions and a belittling of a person's own abilities and assets. Intense discomfort is experienced if the person remains alone for more than a brief period.

dependent variable In an experiment, the behavior that is measured to determine any changes caused by manipulation of the independent variable.

depression An affective disorder characterized by intense, inappropriate, and lasting sadness. If it occurs in combination with mania, it is called a bipolar disorder.

descriptive statistics Procedures used to summarize groups of individual observations, the most common being measures of central tendency and measures of variability.

developmental psychology The branch of psychology concerned with growth and development of the organism from before birth through old age.

dichromat (DIGH-kroh-mat) A person who is color-blind due to a defect in either the yellow-blue or red-green color systems.

difference threshold The smallest difference between two stimuli that can be consistently detected.

diffusion of responsibility The feeling of reduced responsibility for one's own actions when in a group; it allows the individual to behave in ways he or she ordinarily would not if alone.

discriminative stimuli Stimuli that signal to the organism the consequences that are likely to follow certain responses.

dissociation The splitting off or coexistence without awareness of mental processes.

dissociative strategies Pain-control strategies that involve ignoring or deflecting attention away from painful sensations.

dominance hierarchy A characteristic form of social organization that includes a definite power structure in which every individual is in either a dominant or a submissive position in relationship to the others.

dominant characteristic A genetic effect that will be produced whether either one or both members of a gene pair are present.

dopamine (DOH-puh-meen) One of the groups of neurotransmitters called catecholamines.

dopamine hypothesis of schizophrenia The idea that schizophrenic behavior is related to an excess of the neurotransmitter dopamine at certain synapses within the brain.

Down syndrome A rather common type of retardation caused by a chromosomal abnormality. It was formerly known as mongolism; also called trisomy 21.

dream work The process by which the latent dream content is transformed for defensive purposes into the manifest dream content.

DSM III *Diagnostic and Statistical Manual of the American Psychiatric Association*, 3rd ed.; the classification system for abnormal behavior used in the United States for diagnosis, record keeping, and insurance reimbursement.

dualism The philosophical position that there are separate physical and mental or spiritual realities.

duplex theory (of memory) One of a number of theories of memory that divide it into two parts, one for long-term and one for short-term storage.

Durham Test A legal procedure based in the *Durham* decision of 1954. It differs from the *M'Naghten Rule* in holding that an individual is not criminally responsible for an unlawful act if the act was "the product of mental disease or mental defect." In this case the person should be treated and rehabilitated instead of being sent to prison.

dysphoric (dis-FOHR-ik) **mood** A mood characterized by symptoms of depression and feelings of hopelessness; the opposite of eurphoric mood.

eardrum A movable membrane that vibrates in response to sound waves.

echoic (e-KOH-ik) **store** The sensory store for auditory information.

E. coli A bacterium used as the host organism in recombinant DNA research.

ectomorphy (EK-toh-mor-fee) A body build that is delicate, with long, thin bones and small muscles.

educational psychology The branch of psychology concerned with all aspects of the educational process, including learning, classroom instruction, vocational counseling, and testing of abilities and attitudes.

efferent neurons (EF-uh-runt NU-rahnz) Those nerves that transmit impulses from the brain and spinal cord to the muscles and organs of the body; also called motor neurons.

ego The psychoanalytic term for the part of the psyche that is conscious and is most closely in touch with reality. It functions as an integrating mechanism for the impulses from the id and the directives from the superego to make them conform to the demands of external reality.

elaborative (ee-LAB-uh-ruh-tiv) **rehearsal** The process of repeating material with the intent to remember it permanently and to fit it into the memory system.

electrical stimulation of the brain (ESB) The process of implanting tiny electrodes in various areas of the brain to which mild electrical stimulation is delivered. This can bring about marked changes in behavior.

electroconvulsive therapy (ECT) A form of treatment of mental disorders, particularly depression, in which electrodes are placed on one or both sides of the patient's head and a controlled current is applied for a fraction of a second. This produces a convulsion followed by a brief period of coma.

electroencephalograph (ee-LEK-troh-en-SE-fo-lo-graf) **(EEG)** A device to record the electrical activity of the brain by attaching electrodes to the scalp. The EEG records the simultaneous activity of millions of neurons.

elicited (ee-LIS-uh-tud) **behavior** A term used to refer to behavior that naturally occurs in the presence of a particular stimulus.

emitted behavior A term used in operant conditioning to describe the choice made by the organism of when to respond in a situation that contains many stimuli, rather than responding at a particular time to a particular stimulus, as in classical conditioning.

emotion A subjective feeling state involving cognitive appraisal, physiological arousal, and possible expressive or instrumental behaviors.

empathic (em-PATH-ik) **inference** Piaget's term for the process of carefully observing how children approach problems and then attempting to infer how they must have experienced the situation in order to respond as they did.

empirical Referring to information obtained through observation and experimentation.

encounter group A group therapy in which a therapist and group members attempt to reexamine their behavior through training exercises that increase psychological intimacy among group members.

endocrine (EN-doh-krin) **system** The system of the body composed of the glands that secrete hormones. These chemicals act to regulate metabolism and coordinate various body processes and are associated with emotion.

endomorphy (EN-doh-mor-fee) A body build that is flabby and weak in muscular development.

endorphins (en-DOR-finz) A class of neuropeptides in the body that have pain-reducing qualities similar to morphine; literally, "morphine within."

epilepsy (EP-uh-lep-see) A disorder characterized by sudden electrical changes in the brain that produce seizures or changes in consciousness.

epinephrine (ep-uh-NEF-rin) A hormone secreted by the adrenal glands. Secretion is associated with fear and anger; also called adrenaline.

episodic memory   A person's mental record of personal life experiences.

equity theory   A theory of interpersonal attraction that predicts that the costs and rewards of the relationship for each individual involved must be balanced if the relationship is to form or continue.

Erikson's theory of psychosocial development   A stage theory using the psychodynamic perspective that emphasizes cognitive and social changes occurring over the entire life span.

erogenous (eh-RAH-juhn-uhs) **zone**   Any part of the body sensitive to sexual stimulation.

erotic (er-AH-tik)   Tending to arouse sexual interest.

escape conditioning   A process whereby a subject learns to escape from an aversive stimulus. The escape response is strengthened by negative reinforcement.

estimated learning potential (ELP)   The measure of ability obtained from the SOMPA battery of tests.

ethologist (eth-AHL-uh-jist)   A scientist who studies the behavior of animals in their natural habitat.

evaluation apprehension   The fear of being thought to be foolish or inadequate. In helping situations, it is a deterrent to action by the helper.

evaluative simplicity   The social psychological idea that even though an attitude may be based on a complex group of facts, these facts are combined to produce a simple like or dislike.

event schemata   Cognitive structures that organize expectations of what is to be encountered in particular situations.

excitement phase   The initial phase of the human sexual response characterized by increased physiological arousal.

exhaustion   The third stage in the *general adaptation syndrome* of stress described by Selye. The first two stages are alarm and resistance.

expanding   The process by which an adult restates a child's simple speech by converting it into a grammatically correct adult sentence.

expectancy   A predictive statement or belief that involves relationships between events—either between two or more stimuli or between behaviors and their consequences.

expectancy X value theory   A cognitive approach to motivation that says that the direction and intensity of goal-directed behavior are jointly determined by the strength of the person's expectation that certain actions will lead to the desired goal and by the value of the goal for the individual.

experiment   A scientific procedure in which one or more conditions (independent variables) are manipulated in a systematic manner to determine their effects on other conditions (dependent variables).

experimental group   The group of subjects in an experiment who are exposed to the experimental manipulation of the condition under investigation. Their responses are compared to those of the control group, who are not exposed to the experimental manipulation.

experimental psychology   That branch of psychology that studies basic psychological processes such as learning, per-

ception, and cognition, usually under controlled laboratory conditions.

experimenter expectancy effect   A modification of experimental results caused in part by the experimenter's unintentional cues to the subject to respond in the manner anticipated by the experimenter.

expressed emotion   A term used to describe the family environment of some individuals diagnosed as schizophrenic. The family members are often harsh, overcritical, and highly involved in each others' lives.

expressive behaviors   Overt behaviors that reflect one's emotional state.

external locus of control   A concept introduced by Rotter that describes individuals who feel at the mercy of the environment.

extinction   The weakening and eventual disappearance of a learned behavior as a result of nonreinforcement.

extraversion-introversion   One of three dimensions of personality used in the theory of Hans Eysenck. It is thought to reflect differing levels of excitation and inhibition in the brain. Other dimensions are neuroticism and psychoticism.

extrinsic motivation   The tendency to perform a behavior because of some external reinforcer rather than simply because the behavior is rewarding in and of itself.

factor analysis   A sophisticated statistical technique that permits a researcher to reduce a large number of measures to a small number of clusters or factors. It identifies the clusters of behavior that are highly correlated with one another.

family therapy   A specialized type of group therapy employed when the problems of one or more family members seem interrelated. The therapist encourages family members to deal as a group with their attitudes and feelings toward one another.

father attachment   A bond, initially thought to occur only with an infant's mother, that has been found to occur with fathers as well, even when the father spends a relatively small amount of time with the infant.

fear-avoidance theory of pain   A theory that links the development of chronic pain behavior to an avoidance of further pain following an injury.

fear of success   A tendency to avoid being successful because of fears of negative consequences such as rejection or disapproval from others.

feature detectors   Sensory neurons that show maximum activity in response to stimuli which have specific properties, such as corners or certain angles.

fellatio (feh-LAH-shee-oh)   Oral stimulation of the male genitals.

field experiment   An investigation performed in a natural setting with the variables of interest manipulated by the experimenter.

field study   An investigative technique that involves observing and recording behavior in its natural setting with no attempt to manipulate variables or to influence individuals being studied.

fixed ratio schedule   A reinforcement schedule in which reinforcement follows the first response after a fixed number of responses—for example, after every tenth response.

flooding Clinical treatment used for phobic disorders. Extinction is forced by preventing avoidance responses and exposing individuals to the feared conditioned stimulus in the absence of the unconditioned stimulus with which it was originally paired.

fluid abilities The aspect of intelligence that involves working out an answer on the basis of some stimulus clues. See also *crystallized abilities.*

forebrain The foremost of the three major divisions of the brain, including the cerebrum, thalamus, and hypothalamus.

forensic (for-REN-sik) **psychology** An area of specialization that deals with psychological aspects of the legal system.

formal operational period A term used by Piaget for the fourth major stage in the continual process of growth and change in cognitive development. It usually begins around age 11. In this period children become capable of deductive logic (if-then reasoning).

fovea (FO-vee-uh) Small central region in the retina of the eye that contains only cones.

fraternal twins Two infants developing from the fertilization at the same time of two eggs by two different sperm; also called dizygotic twins. The genetic relationship of the twins is no closer than that among any brothers or sisters. See also *identical,* or monozygotic, *twins.*

free-association In psychoanalysis, the technique of having the patient report every thought as it occurs.

frequency distribution A table showing the number of subjects who obtained each score on a specific variable.

frequency theory A theory of pitch perception which states that at low frequencies the number of nerve impulses sent to the auditory cortex corresponds with the frequency of the sound wave.

Freud's theory of psychosexual development Sigmund Freud's ideas of the development of personality in the changing focus of the libido through a series of pleasure-giving zones. Freud believed that this process, occurring in the first 5 years of life, is crucial for adjustment in later life.

frontal lobe One of the four divisions of each cerebral hemisphere. It controls speech and skeletal-motor functions.

fully functioning person Carl Rogers's concept of individuals who have reached a high level of adjustment in which they can be natural and no longer feel forced to adopt artificial roles.

functional distance The likelihood of contact based on customary travel patterns rather than on amounts of physical separation.

functional fixedness A phenomenon, often found in problem-solving tasks, in which the customary use of an object interferes with its application in a novel situation.

fundamental attribution error The tendency to place blame for others' actions on their personal characteristics while fixing blame on the situation for one's own negative behavior.

galvanic (gal-VAN-ik) **skin response (GSR)** A measure of the drop in electrical resistance of the skin caused by the activity of the sweat glands when an individual becomes emotionally aroused.

Garcia (gar-SEE-yah) **effect** A classical conditioning phenomenon in which animals acquire an aversion to a food which has been treated with a nausea-producing substance.

gender identity The individual's sensation of being either male or female. It is a part of the self-concept expressed through a broad range of behaviors, attitudes, and fantasies.

gene The unit of hereditary transmission contained within the chromosome. Each chromosome contains many genes. These occur in pairs, and the offspring receives one of each parent's pair of each type of gene.

general (g) factor The component of intelligence that determines ability in all areas. Defined by C. Spearman as the purely intellective element of "mind," as distinct from acquired understanding, emotion, and temperament.

general adaptation syndrome (GAS) Three-stage cycle of bodily stress reactions described by Hans Selye. The first stage, an alarm reaction, involves physiological changes generally associated with emotion; the second stage, resistance, is the time when the body recovers from the stress reaction and begins to cope with the situation. If the stress continues, the final stage, exhaustion, is reached, during which the adrenal gland can no longer function and the body begins to break down.

generalized anxiety disorder A type of anxiety disorder characterized by nonspecific or free-floating anxiety and physical symptoms such as rapid heart rate and profuse sweating.

General Problem Solver A computer simulation developed by Newell and Simon that uses means-ends analyses or heuristics in a manner similar to that used by human beings.

generational factors in development Those historical events such as wars or depressions that may affect the development of people who experience them.

genital (JEN-uh-tuhl) **stage** The last of the series of psychosexual stages described by Freud. It begins in adolescence.

genotype (JEN-oh-type) A term that refers to the total genetic material that people inherit. See also *phenotype.*

Gestalt (gesh-TAHLT) **laws of perception** Principles of perceptual organization, including the laws of similarity, proximity, closure, and continuity.

Gestalt psychology A view that emphasizes the form, pattern, or configuration of the stimulus as a whole. Gestalt psychologists believe that principles of perceptual organization are built into the nervous system.

Gestalt therapy A treatment procedure originated by Fritz Perls, in which the client experiences strong emotions through techniques such as role playing.

gonadotropic (go-nad-oh-TRAWP-ik) **hormones**   Hormones that stimulate the testes or ovary.

Grant study   A longitudinal investigation with a psychodynamic perspective, involving men who were Harvard undergraduates in the late 1930s.

gray matter   Nervous tissue consisting primarily of neuron cell bodies.

group   A collection of people who feel some relationship or connection with each other.

group polarization   The tendency of groups of people who hold similar attitudes to become more extreme in their attitudes as a result of group discussion.

group therapy   Psychotherapy carried out with several clients interacting both among themselves and with the therapist.

groupthink   Unanimity of commitment to a course of action, which tends to occur under stressful conditions in highly cohesive groups. Group members who express reservations about the group's policy are faced with immediate and direct pressure to conform.

habituation   The lessened magnitude of a response because the stimulus has become familiar.

halfway house   Transitional living facility that accommodates, usually for a short period of time, newly discharged mental patients or others who have been institutionalized and are in the process of returning to life in the community.

hallucination (hal-lu-sin-AY-shun)   A sensory perception that takes place in the absence of an external stimulus.

hallucinogenic (hal-lu-sin-oh-JEN-ik) drug   A substance that distorts or intensifies sense perception and blurs the boundaries between fact and fantasy. Such a drug is apparently not physically addictive, but psychological dependence may develop.

health psychology   A new field of study concerned with the acquisition of healthful behavior patterns. Emphasis is on the role of individual responsibility in the prevention of illness.

heritability   A mathematical index of the amount of variation in a specific characteristic that can be attributed to genetic factors.

heuristic (hyu-RIS-tik)   A method of problem solving characterized by quick and easy search procedures similar to rules of thumb. Heuristics can be used to make approximations of the answers. In complex problems heuristics may be more useful than algorithms.

hierarchical (high-RARK-i-kal) **network**   A theoretical view of memory structure in which concepts are organized and assessed in subordinate-superordinate relationships.

high-risk children   Children who, because of heredity or because of a less than desirable environment, tend to have a greater than average chance of developing some physical or psychological problem.

higher-order conditioning   A classical conditioning procedure in which a previously established conditioned stimulus serves as the unconditioned stimulus that is paired with a new conditioned stimulus.

history-related events   Events that affect large numbers of people, such as war, economic depression, famine, or other disasters. They influence development together with age-related events and unique life events, such as a death in the family.

homeostasis (hoh-mee-oh-STAY-sis)   The processes by which an organism maintains a stable internal state.

hormone (HOR-mohn)   A chemical secreted by the glands of the endocrine system. The chemical messengers convey information from one area of the body to another through the bloodstream.

humanistic perspective   The view that emphasizes the individual's creative potential and ability for personal growth. Abraham Maslow and Carl Rogers are examples of humanistic theorists.

hypercolumn   Group of cell columns in the cerebral cortex that are believed to be the basic integrating units in the sensory cortex.

hypnosis (hip-NO-sis)   An artificially induced state characterized by exaggerated suggestibility.

hypothalamus (high-po-THAL-uh-mus)   A part of the forebrain consisting of a group of small nuclei lying at the base of the brain above the roof of the mouth. Known to be involved in sexual behavior, temperature regulation, sleeping, eating, aggression, and emotional behavior.

hypothesis (high-PAH-thuh-sis)   A predicted relationship between two or more events. A hypothesis must be checked by comparing its predictions with already known facts or by testing them with new research. The results may reject or support the hypothesis, but cannot conclusively prove it.

iconic (igh-KAHN-ik) **store**   The sensory store for visual information.

id   The psychoanalytic term for that part of the psyche in which all instinctual impulses and repressed mental contents are stored; the true unconscious.

identical twins   Two infants developing from the fertilization of a single egg that splits at an early stage of growth; also called monozygotic twins. They are genetically identical. See also *fraternal*, or dizygotic, *twins*.

identification   A process described by Freud in which the child unconsciously seeks to become as similar as possible to its perception of the same-sex parent. The term is also used to describe the normal process of acquiring appropriate social behavior through imitation.

illusion   A false perception of a stimulus that is actually present.

impotence (IM-poh-tuhns)   A form of male sexual dysfunction in which the man consistently has difficulty in achieving or maintaining an erection.

imprinting   A species-specific form of learning that occurs within a limited period of time early in life and is virtually unmodifiable thereafter. For example, ducklings will learn to follow any object (including the mother) that is consistently present within 11 to 18 hours after birth.

independent variable   The variable, or factor, in the experiment that is manipulated by the experimenter.

indiscriminate attachment   The first phase of the developmental process of attachment. During this phase, which lasts until age 6 or 7 months, the child responds similarly to anyone who interacts with it.

individual psychology A personality theory originated by Alfred Adler that stresses the importance of social rather than sexual needs in the motivation of behavior.

industrial psychology A branch of psychology concerned with applying psychological principles to work situations and problems arising in the industrial field. These include selection and training of workers, conditions of work, and other personnel problems.

inferential statistics Procedures used to draw conclusions about data based on the laws of probability.

information processing An approach to the study of cognitive behavior that analyzes the steps in acquiring and using information. Computer programs are often used as models of information processing.

ingroup The group with which an individual identifies and that he or she sees as positive, as opposed to others who form the negative outgroup.

inner ear The internal portion of the ear that contains the vestibular apparatus and the cochlea. The receptors of the cochlea transform sound vibrations to nerve impulses. The inner ear also contains semicircular canals that, together with the vestibular sacs, control the sense of equilibrium.

input The first step in the information processing view of memory. The others are coding and storage, and retrieval.

insecure attachment A term used to describe the behavior of a child who is anxious before separation and is ambivalent toward its mother after separation.

insight The sudden perception of the solution to a problem. In psychotherapy, the discovery of therapeutically important material by the client.

insomnia (in-SOM-nee-ah) A sleep disorder characterized by difficulties in going to sleep or early awakening.

instrumental behavior Behavior that is directed toward goal attainment.

instrumental conditioning The strengthening of behavior by the presentation of a reinforcing stimulus when the response occurs but not otherwise; also called operant conditioning.

intelligence The capacity to acquire and apply knowledge.

intelligence quotient (IQ) Originally defined for the Binet test as mental age (MA) divided by chronological age (CA) multiplied by 100: $IQ = (MA/CA) \times 100$. An IQ of 100 indicates that an individual is average for his or her age group. IQ scores are now available from many intelligence tests, usually by consulting conversion tables.

interferon (in-ter-FEER-ohn) An antivirus and antitumor substance produced naturally in the body's cells and artificially through recombinant DNA techniques.

internal locus of control A concept introduced by Rotter that describes individuals who view what happens to them as something that they can influence.

interneuron A neuron that is neither sensory nor motor in its functioning but, rather, has an associative function.

interview A face-to-face meeting often used for diagnostic purposes. The clinician may follow a prescribed series of questions or may vary the topics. Observations of behavior are usually combined with verbal content in analyzing the information gained from the interview.

intrinsic (in-TRIN-sik) **motivation** Motivation to engage in certain activities because they are enjoyable or rewarding in and of themselves.

involuntary commitment The legal decision to hold someone in a mental institution against his or her will.

invulnerable A term describing someone whose development appears excellent in spite of poor environmental conditions and possible hereditary difficulties.

IQ See *intelligence quotient*.

James-Lange (LAHNG-uh) **theory of emotion** The idea that one's experience of emotion is really the perception of bodily changes that follow the emotional stimulus. For example, we are afraid because we ran away, rather than running away because we are afraid.

jigsaw program An educational approach developed by Elliot Aronson in which mutual interdependence is used to foster students' academic achievement and liking for one another.

just noticeable difference (jnd) The smallest difference people can perceive between two stimuli; also called differential threshold.

Kaufman Assessment Battery for Children (K-ABC) A test incorporating ideas from cognitive psychology and neuropsychology that attempts to reduce social and cultural bias in test scores.

labeling A cognitive device for classifying one's emotions or one's reactions to other people. The classification then serves as an explanation for future behavior.

latency stage The fourth in a series of psychosexual stages described by Freud. It begins at about age 6 and is characterized by dormancy of the sexual instinct.

latent dream content Psychoanalytic term for the true psychological meaning of the dream.

lateral hypothalamus (high-po-THAL-uh-mus) A portion of the hypothalamus that was once viewed as an "eating center." When stimulated, it increased food intake; when destroyed, eating is markedly reduced.

law of effect The principle that an individual tends to repeat behaviors that have produced positive outcomes and does not repeat those that produce neutral or negative outcomes. This principle is a cornerstone of operant conditioning.

learned helplessness A concept originated by Martin Seligman to refer to a learned belief that one has no control over aversive stimuli in the environment.

learned mastery A learned belief that one has the ability to cope with aversive situations that then facilitates coping with new aversive situations.

learning A change in potential behavior that occurs as the result of experience. There are three major types of learning: classical conditioning, instrumental or operant conditioning, and observational learning.

lens The elastic structure within the eye that changes shape in accordance with the distance of the object being viewed. It becomes thinner when distant objects are viewed and thicker when nearby objects are seen.

lesioning (LEE-zhuhn-ing) A technique for studying the function of particular parts of the brain by destroying tissue.

level of significance In inferential statistics, the probability that the results obtained with a sample occurred by chance alone and do not reflect a similar relationship in the population.

libido (luh-BEE-do) In psychoanalytic theory, the psychic energy that is generated by instinctual drives and that constantly presses for discharge.

life changes Events that occur in an individual's life that may singly or together produce stress. They are sometimes referred to as life events and used as a measure of stress that has been experienced.

Life Experiences Survey (LES) A measure of the changes that have occurred in a person's recent life and of their perceived positive or negative impact.

life span development The product of the interaction of biology and environment in an individual from conception to death.

limbic (LIM-bik) **system** A portion of the forebrain that consists of a number of structures lying deep inside the cerebral hemispheres around the central core of the brain. It has many neural interconnections with the hypothalamus. It seems to be involved in organizing the activities needed to satisfy the basic motivational and emotional needs regulated by the hypothalamus.

linguistic relativism The idea that people's language determines the ways in which they perceive and think about their world; also called linguistic relativity or Whorfian hypothesis (named for Benjamin Whorf, a noted linguist).

lithium (lithium carbonate) A chemical salt used in the treatment of bipolar disorder.

locus of control In Julian Rotter's theory, generalized expectancies or beliefs that one has control over one's outcomes (internal locus) or that one's outcomes are caused by factors outside of oneself, such as luck or powerful others (external locus).

longitudinal approach A technique of studying development by periodically measuring changes in the same individual or group as time passes.

long-term memory The relatively permanent part of the memory system that has a very large capacity. It holds all memories that are retained for more than a few brief moments and that are not in active use at any particular time. See also *short-term memory*.

long-term potentiation An increased sensitivity of neurons to further stimulation that may be the neural basis of learning.

lysergic (luh-SER-jik) **acid diethylamide** (digh-eth-uhl-AM-ide) **(LSD-25)** One of the most potent of the hallucinogenic drugs. A small dose can produce an 8- to 16-hour "trip," during which many perceptual distortions occur.

maintenance rehearsal The process of keeping material available in memory for immediate use by constantly repeating it without intending to remember it.

mania (MAY-nee-a) One of the affective disorders, sometimes of psychotic proportions, that is characterized by a high level of uncontrolled excitement.

manifest dream content A psychoanalytic term that describes the story or symbol the dreamer reports.

MAO inhibitor A drug used to prevent the monoamine oxidase enzyme from chemically breaking down the neurotransmitter. It is used in the treatment of depression.

marijuana (mer-i-WA-nuh) A hallucinogenic drug derived from the hemp plant that affects the user's mood and thought patterns. It is usually either smoked in a cigarette or eaten when mixed with food. While under the influence of marijuana, an individual's ability to make decisions may be affected.

maturation The process of physical and cognitive growth over time culminating in the fullest possible development the person is able to achieve.

mean The statistical term for the arithmetic average, computed by summing all the scores and dividing by the total number of scores.

means-end analysis A kind of heuristic problem-solving device in which subjects first define a subgoal that they hope to achieve (an "end"). They then compare that subgoal with their present state of knowledge, and if there is a discrepancy between them, try to find the means to reduce the difference.

measure of central tendency A single score that characterizes the level of performance of a group. The most commonly used measures of central tendency are the mean, median, and mode.

measures of variability Statistics that indicate the amount of scatter or dispersion among scores, the most common being the range, the variance, and the standard deviation.

median The statistical term for the point that cuts a distribution in half if all scores are arranged in order from lowest to highest. Half the scores lie above and half below it.

medulla (muh-DUHL-uh) A portion of the brain stem that plays a vital role in bodily functions, such as heart rate and respiration. It also contains all the sensory and motor nerve tracts coming up from the spinal cord and descending from the brain.

menopause (MEN-oh-paws) The cessation of menstruation, or the period of time during which ovarian function gradually diminishes and the menstrual cycle eventually ceases.

mental age A measure of childhood intellectual functioning derived by matching an individual's score with the average age at which that score is generally attained. That age then becomes the individual's mental age and may be higher or lower than his or her chronological or calendar age.

mental set A habitual approach to problems that focuses on what has worked before rather than on an analysis of the current situation; a readiness to think about a problem in a particular way.

mesmerism (MEZ-mer-ism) A hypnotic technique developed by Anton Mesmer that attempted to cure patients through magnetic forces radiated from the planets.

mesomorphy (MEZ-oh-mor-fee) A body build that has well-developed muscle structure and is large and squarish in overall shape.

meta-analysis A technique for statistical analysis combining a large number of data sets from different studies.

metacognition A person's knowledge of his or her own cognitive processes and the products of these processes.

metalinguistic awareness A person's awareness of the language processes. See also *metacognition*.

midbrain The portion of the brain lying just above the hindbrain and containing a number of important sensory and motor nuclei and also many sensory and motor pathways.

middle ear A portion of the ear that includes three small bones called hammer, anvil, and stirrup. These bones pass the vibration of the eardrum along to the oval window, the boundary between the middle and inner ear.

mindguards The individuals within groups undergoing groupthink who suppress the discussion of information inconsistent with the group's decision.

Minnesota Multiphasic Personality Inventory (MMPI) A test used to assess broad personality traits and to help diagnose psychopathology. The items are varied in content and were obtained by finding items that patients with different psychiatric diagnoses responded to in different ways.

M'Naghten (M-NAW-ten) **Rule** Legal precedent in English law, originating in 1843, that provides for acquittal if an accused person is found to be not responsible for the crime—that is, if he or she could not distinguish between "right and wrong."

mnemonic (ni-MAHN-ik) **technique** A way of organizing material to be remembered so that easily remembered cues are available when the material is later accessed. Examples are the peg word technique or a rhyme that contains the needed information.

monism (MOHN-isem) The philosophical view that body and mind are reducible to common physiological processes.

monoamine oxidase (mohn-oh-AM-een AHX-i-dayz) **(MAO)** An enzyme that renders neurotransmitters chemically inactive.

monocular (mah-NAHK-yuh-ler) **depth cue** A cue used in depth perception that requires only one eye, such as perspective, decreasing size, height of the horizontal plane, texture, clarity, and interposition of other objects.

monozygotic (mohn-oh-zigh-GAHT-ik) **twins** Two individu-

als produced from a single fertilized egg. They are genetically identical.

morpheme (MOR-feem) The smallest unit of meaning in a given language. English morphemes include whole words, prefixes, and suffixes. There are over 100,000 English morphemes.

motivation A general term referring to internal forces regulating the direction, vigor, and persistence of goal-directed behavior.

multiple personality A rare, dramatic type of dissociative reaction in which two or more separate and markedly different personalities coexist within the same individual.

myelin (MIGH-uh-luhn) The sheath of fatty tissue that covers the axons of many neurons. The sheath serves to increase speed of neural transmission.

nalaxone (nuh-LAHK-sohn) A drug that counteracts the pain-reducing effects of the endorphins.

narcolepsy (NAR-koh-lep-see) A sleep disorder characterized by sudden and unpredictable sleep attacks during waking hours.

narcotics Substances that act on the central and autonomic nervous system and are used therapeutically to ease pain. Examples are opium, morphine, and heroin. Tolerance for and physiological and psychological dependence on narcotic analgesics develop quickly.

natural experiment A field study carried out to coincide with the occurrence of a natural event, in which the investigator can observe the effects of a variable but cannot (or does not) manipulate it.

natural selection Darwin's proposal that over time any inheritable characteristic that increases the likelihood of survival of the species will be maintained in the species. Those characteristics that do not improve chances for survival will be eliminated over time.

need for power (n Power) A technique devised by David McClelland to measure an individual's need to exert control over the lives of others. McClelland divided power motivation into two kinds: (1) oriented toward winning over adversaries and (2) socially acceptable helping or inspiring.

negative reinforcement In operant conditioning, anything that will serve to increase the behavior that results in its removal; not to be confused with *punishment*.

negative symptom A symptom characteristic of Type II schizophrenia, in which a lack of affect and response is prominent.

negative transference See *transference*.

neural plasticity The capacity of the nervous system to recover its function following injury.

neuron A nerve cell. It consists of three main parts: the soma, dendrites, and an axon.

neurosis (new-roh-suhs)   See *anxiety disorder.*

neuroticism (new-RAHT-uh-sis-uhm)   A personality dimension in tests developed by Hans Eysenck. It refers to the tendency to be emotionally overreactive and socially dependent. Other dimensions are psychoticism and introversion-extraversion.

neurotic paradox (new-RAHT-ik PAR-uh-dox)   The tendency of neurotics to engage in behaviors that are, in the long run, self-defeating, but that have immediate positive consequences such as anxiety reduction.

neurotransmitter (new-roh-trans-MIT-er)   Chemical produced in the body that provides transmission of the nerve impulse across the synapse.

New York Longitudinal Study   A longitudinal investigation of the effects of temperament on psychological development, carried out by Thomas and Chess.

norepinephrine (nor-ep-uh-NEF-rin)   A hormone produced by the adrenal medulla that functions as a synaptic transmitter and thus allows nerve impulses to pass from one neuron to the next. Norepinephrine is found in high concentrations in brain structures, and many drugs that influence mood and emotions have an effect on brain levels of norepinephrine. Norepinephrine also produces physiological arousal.

normal distribution   A frequency distribution in the shape of a symmetrical, or bell-shaped, curve that satisfies certain mathematical conditions deduced from the theory of probability.

nuclear magnetic resonance (NMR)   A method developed for producing a computer-generated picture of an internal organ by measuring the reactions of atoms to a magnetic field.

object constancy   The concept that objects remain the same even if they appear to change. For example, water poured from a tall, thin glass to a short, fat glass is still the same amount of water; an object viewed at different distances appears different in size, but is actually the same. According to Piaget, this concept is acquired during the sensorimotor period.

observational learning   The process by which behavior is changed through observations of others' behavior and its consequences.

occipital (ahk-SIP-uh-tuhl) **lobe**   One of the four lobes into which each cerebral hemisphere of the brain is divided. It lies at the rear of the brain and contains the visual reception area.

operant (AH-puh-runt) **conditioning**   The strengthening or weakening of behavior through systematic manipulation of its consequences.

operational definition   The description or specification of a concept in terms of some observable event that can be measured.

opponent-process theory (motivation)   A theory that states that because of the body's tendency toward homeostasis, any emotional response is followed shortly by its opposite, and that the latter becomes stronger over time.

opponent-process theory (vision)   A theory of color vision based on Hering's theory that there are three types of cones, one for red/green, one for blue/yellow, and one for black/white reception. Each type of receptor can respond in one of two ways, and its specific response determines which of the two colors is sensed.

optic chiasma (AHP-tik kigh-AZ-muh)   The point at which the optic nerves cross after leaving the eye.

oral stage   The first in a series of psychosexual stages as described by Freud. It occurs in earliest infancy. The sucking response first associated with feeding becomes involved in obtaining pleasure that is not completely nutritional in nature. Indiscriminate sucking by infants is typical oral stage behavior.

organ of Corti (KOR-ti)   The thousands of tiny hair cells in the inner ear that are the actual sound receptors of the body. Their movement sets off the electrical potential that results in nerve impulses being sent to the brain through the auditory nerve.

orgasm (OR-gaz-uhm)   The sexual climax, characterized by muscle contractions and a surging release of accumulated tension.

orgasmic (OR-gaz-mik) **dysfunction**   Disturbances in sexual functioning among women that may involve pain and negative emotions as well as apathy and inability to respond.

outgroup   Those who are not included in the group with whom a person identifies (the ingroup). The outgroup is usually regarded in a negative light.

overjustification hypothesis   The hypothesis that if extrinsic reinforcement is given for an act that is intrinsically rewarding, individuals will come to see themselves as performing the act because of the external reinforcer and will be less likely to perform it if that reinforcer is withdrawn.

overload model   A concept used in environmental psychology to explain the effects of overcrowding. It presumes that if individuals receive more stimulation from the environment than they can tolerate, they respond by withdrawing, becoming aloof, or giving less attention to low-priority items.

overt behavior   Behavior that can be externally observed.

parasympathetic (PAR-uh-sim-puh-THET-ik) **nervous system**   That portion of the autonomic nervous system that slows down bodily processes and reduces physiological arousal.

parietal (puh-RIGH-uh-tuhl) **lobe**   One of the four divisions of each cerebral hemisphere. It lies behind the frontal lobe and contains the body sense area.

partial reinforcement   A procedure used in operant conditioning in which not all responses are followed by reinforcement.

passionate love   Sexual love and arousal.

pedigree analysis   The study of the past and present family of a person who has a specific characteristic, in an attempt to identify a pattern of genetic inheritance.

peg word system   A mnemonic technique based on a rhyme. Each word in the rhyme is combined in a visual image with a word in the list to be learned. The words in the rhyme then aid in later access to the material by serving as a series of cues.

peptides Chemical substances (including endorphins) released in various parts of the body, including the liver and the brain, that regulate many bodily functions as well as the experiencing of pain.

perception The interpretation of sensation by the individual into subjective experience.

perceptual constancy The phenomenon that although the particular sensory stimuli for objects may change, our recognition and perception of the objects do not change.

perceptual defense A proposed attentional filtering process that serves a defensive function and protects the individual from perceiving threatening stimuli.

peripheral (per-IF-uh-ruhl) **nervous system** One of the two major divisions of the nervous system; it is made up of all neurons connecting the central nervous system with the muscles, glands, and sensory receptors. This system may be further subdivided into the somatic nervous system and the autonomic nervous system.

personal attribution The pinpointing of the cause of a person's behavior on that individual's personality characteristics rather than on the environment.

personal constructs (KAHN-strukts) Categories used by George Kelly to describe the manner in which individuals construct reality by sorting out persons and events in their lives. They are the rules an individual uses to assign events to categories, and his or her ideas about how the categories relate to each other.

personal factor in stress Individual characteristic such as self-confidence and general anxiety that influences response to a stressor. See also *situational factor in stress*.

personality The collection of attributes, dispositions, and tendencies that make up a single individual.

personality disorder A deeply ingrained, inflexible, maladaptive pattern of thought and behavior that persists throughout a person's life.

personal unconscious Carl Jung's term for information unique to the individual, of which he or she is not aware. It corresponds to Freud's categories of the unconscious and the preconscious.

person schemata The generalized set of characteristics that are used to simplify understanding of the behavior of persons in a specific category—for instance, "teachers pet."

person × situation interaction The idea that behavior is influenced by the characteristics of the person, the elements of the situation, and the way in which these two sets of factors influence each other.

PET scan A method of examining the living brain to determine the amount of radioactive deoxyglucose absorbed by active neurons.

phallic (FAL-ik) **stage** The third in the stages of psychosexual development described by Freud. It begins at about age 4 and peaks at 5 or 6. In this stage the genitals gradually replace the anal zone as a major location of sexual pleasure. The Oedipal crisis occurs during the phallic stage.

phenomenological Relating to the study of human experience without concern for objective reality. Emphasis is placed on what is perceived rather than on why it is perceived.

phenotype (FEE-noh-tighp) The observable appearance of an organism that is determined by both environmental and genetic factors.

phobia (FOH-bee-uh) A type of generalized anxiety disorder characterized by highly specific and irrational fears.

phoneme (FO-neem) The smallest unit of sound in a language; the vowel and consonant sounds that are recognized in any given language. English has 45 phonemes.

physiological psychology The branch of psychology that studies neurological, genetic, and hormonal bases of behavior.

placebo (pluh-SEE-boh) A substance, such as a sugar pill, that has no curative power. It is sometimes prescribed for patients whose complaints seem to have no physical cause.

plasticity (plas-TIS-uh-tee) **of development** The idea that later experiences can make up for negative early experiences that have produced maladjusted behavior.

plateau phase A phase of the sexual response cycle characterized by a high state of tension and arousal preceding orgasm.

pleasure principle The Freudian idea that the organism is impelled toward immediate impulsive action and gratification of need independently of all other considerations. Freud thought that this was the principle motivating the individual in early life and that it continued as a guiding concept of the unconscious.

polygraph (PAHL-ee-graf) An instrument that measures emotional responses through various physiological reactions, such as heart rate, blood pressure, breathing, and galvanic skin response.

pons (PAHNZ) The portion of the brain stem that lies just above the medulla. Contains many ascending and descending fibers that connect the higher and lower levels of the central nervous system, and also nuclei that carry sensory information to the brain from the sense organs in the head and that are involved in respiration.

population All of the subjects who comprise a definable group; all possible or potential subjects who might be observed.

pornography (por-NAH-grah-fee) Material that aims to arouse the viewer or reader sexually and that is characterized by obscenity.

positive reinforcement Any stimulus or event that increases the likelihood of behavior on which it is made contingent.

positive transference See *transference*.

positive symptom Term used to describe the hallucinations, delusions, and disordered thinking of Type I schizophrenia, in which the individual still shows some emotional response.

posttraumatic (post-trow-MAT-ik) **stress reaction** A psychological response to a stressful situation that develops after the event is over. It usually consists of a repetitive reliving of the experience.

preferential looking procedure A method of studying attention, vision, and learning in very young infants by providing them with visual choices and noting the direction and duration of their gaze; also called Fantz visual preference technique.

prejudice A set of beliefs based on inaccurate or incomplete information. These beliefs and the feelings and behavioral tendencies that accompany them are directed toward members of particular groups.

Premack (PREE-mak) **principle** The notion that the opportunity to engage in a high-frequency behavior may be used to reinforce a lower-probability behavior.

premature ejaculation (ee-jak-yu-LAY-shun) A form of male sexual dysfunction that involves a consistent inability to delay ejaculation long enough for mutually satisfying sexual intercourse.

preoperation period The term used by Piaget for the second of the four major stages in the continuous process of growth and change in cognitive development during childhood. It lasts about age 2 to 7. A major accomplishment of the period is the understanding that objects can be classified and grouped.

preparedness Martin Seligman's notion that as a result of the evolutionary history of each species, members of the species are prepared to learn certain behaviors but not others.

primacy effect A situation in which information received first has the greatest effect on an individual's behavior. See also *recency effect*.

primary appraisal The first cognitive review of an event, in which an individual assesses the possible outcome as harmful or harmless. See also *secondary appraisal*.

primary mental abilities A series of cognitive skills including spatial ability, perceptual speed, numerical ability, verbal comprehension, memory, verbal fluency, and inductive reasoning. These were defined by L. L. Thurstone on the basis of his factor analysis of intelligence test items.

primary reinforcement A situation in which an object or condition does not require prior association with other reinforcers in order to have reinforcement properties. Primary reinforcement satisfies biological needs.

priming effect The notion that the stimulation of any single component in an associative network tends to evoke the network's other components as well.

proactive (proh-AK-tiv) **interference** The process by which earlier learning can interfere with the ability to recall newly learned material.

projective test A type of test that involves stimuli that are relatively unclear and ambiguous and that give subjects a wide range of possible responses. Such tests have been used to study unconscious processes and are often used by psychodynamically oriented psychologists. Examples of projective assessments are the Rorschach inkblots and Thematic Apperception Test.

proposition In the propositional model of organization of information, a piece of information simple enough to be expressed as a statement that can be converted into a question answerable with yes or no. For example, "Mary is a girl" can be changed to "Is Mary a girl?"

prosocial behavior Helping activity that may or may not be motivated by the idea of reward.

proximity (prahk-SIM-uh-tee) Gestalt perceptual law that states that elements near each other are perceived as part of the same configuration.

psychodynamic (sigh-koh-digh-NAM-ik) **perspective** A view of behavior that focuses on inner causes, especially motivations, feelings, conflicts, and other unconscious factors in behavior. Freud's ideas formed the basis for this view.

psycholinguistics The study of the manner in which symbols and sounds are translated into language as well as the psychological processes involved in that translation.

psychological maturation The cognitive, perceptual, and social changes that occur naturally if development takes place in an environment that provides for basic needs.

psychology The scientific study of behavior and consciousness.

psychophysics (sigh-koh-FIZ-iks) The scientific study of the relationship between physical properties of stimuli and the perceptual experience to which they give rise.

psychosexual (sigh-koh-SEKS-yu-uhl) **stages** A series of specific levels of development believed by Freud to make up a universal pattern of sexual development.

psychosocial (sigh-koh-SOH-shuhl) **stage theory** The developmental theory of Erik Erikson that extended the age range of Freud's psychosexual theory and changed the emphasis to the important effects of social problems encountered at different developmental stages.

psychoticism (sigh-KOT-i-sis-uhm) A dimension used by Hans Eysenck in his personality theory, along with neuroticism and introversion-extraversion. It is associated with distractibility and generally disordered thought.

punishment A negative consequence that follows an undesirable response and that decreases the future occurrence of that response.

random sampling A procedure in which the probability that each person in the population will be included in the sample is independent of whether or not any other member is selected. Chance plays a greater role in random sampling than in *representative sampling*.

range A simple measure of variability that gives the difference between the highest and the lowest score.

rape trauma syndrome A response pattern, seen in many rape victims, that involves initial upset or hysteria followed by fear of being assaulted again and, in some cases, a decrease in the capacity to enjoy sexual intercourse.

rapid eye movement (REM) Physiological manifestation that occurs about 20 times per second during a fifth sleep stage that begins about an hour after the person falls asleep and occurs approximately every 90 minutes thereafter. REM periods seem to coincide with periods of dreaming.

rational-emotive therapy A type of psychotherapy developed by Albert Ellis, aimed at changing irrational beliefs that cause maladaptive feelings and behaviors.

reaction range The genetically influenced limit within which environmental factors can exert their effects on an organism.

reactivity Changes in behavior that occur because subjects know they are being observed or studied.

reality principle In psychoanalytic theory, a guide by which the ego functions at the conscious level. It takes into account reality demands and restrictions in obtaining gratification.

recall The technique by which persons retrieve and reproduce material that they have previously learned.

recency effect A situation in which the most recent information has the strongest effects on behavior. See also *primacy effect*.

recessive characteristic A hereditary trait that is not apparent unless both genes in the gene pair are recessive. If the individual has only one recessive gene in the pair, its effect is masked by its dominant partner gene.

reciprocity (re-ci-PROS-i-tee) A mutual or cooperative interchange of favors or privileges.

recognition A technique used in verbal learning, in which the subject is asked to pick out from a list of old and new items those that he or she has previously learned.

recombinant (ree-KOHM-buh-nuhnt) **DNA techniques** Procedures that permit scientists to splice genetic material to create new genetic forms.

reconstructive memory The filling in of omissions in memory with material that seems logical or appears to fit.

reference group A term describing that social group with whose standards and beliefs an individual identifies.

refractory (ri-FRAHK-tuh-ree) **period** The period of time following orgasm in males in which they are unresponsive to sexual stimulation. Also, the brief period following an action potential during which a neuron cannot be stimulated.

reinforcement In classical conditioning, each pairing of the conditioned stimulus with the unconditioned stimulus; in operant conditioning, the following of the operant response by the reinforcing stimulus. In general, it refers to any stimulation that serves to strengthen a response.

reinforcement/affect theory A theory of interpersonal attraction based on the idea that people like others who are kind or helpful to them. Because of these reinforcements, liking may also develop for other individuals associated with the one initially liked.

reinforcement contingency In operant conditioning, the relationship between a behavior and its consequences.

releaser A term used by ethologists to refer to a specific stimulus that triggers innate behavior patterns in animals.

reliability The consistency of a test as a measuring instru-

ment, or its lack of measurement error. Reliability is measured by the coefficient of correlation between scores on two halves of a test, on alternate forms of a test, or on retests with the same test.

REM rebound effect The tendency of subjects deprived of REM sleep to exhibit more REM sleep on subsequent nights.

representative sampling A technique in which the numbers of individuals sampled from various groups are proportional to the size of these groups in the population. This type of sampling is used by most public opinion polling organizations. See also *random sampling*.

resistance The therapeutic client's maneuvers to avoid the anxiety associated with understanding why he or she behaves in a particular manner. Also the second stage of the general adaptation syndrome described by Hans Selye.

resolution phase The phase of the sexual response cycle following orgasm in which the body returns to a nonaroused state.

resting potential The voltage generated by unequal distribution of ions inside and outside the cell membrane when the neuron is in its resting state.

retarded ejaculation A form of sexual dysfunction in which the male finds it difficult or impossible to ejaculate within a reasonable period of sexual stimulation.

reticular (ri-TIK-yuh-luhr) **formation** A large bundle of neurons in the midbrain that controls the activation level of the cortex. It seems to be involved with control of certain aspects of motor behavior and to have a central role in consciousness, attention, and sleep.

retina (RET-in-uh) The portion of the eye that contains the visual receptors.

retroactive interference The process by which new learning can interfere with the ability to recall previously learned material.

reversal condition In a behavior therapy study, the reestablishment of the conditions that existed prior to the specific intervention.

rod A structure within the retina of the eye that is sensitive to light and movement but not to color.

role schemata An organized set of ideas that are used by an individual in understanding and reacting to the behavior of people considered to constitute a homogeneous group.

Rorschach (ROR-shak) **test** A projective assessment in which subjects are shown a series of inkblots one at a time and asked what the blot looks like and what it might be. Many scoring systems have been developed for the Rorschach test.

sadomasochism (say-doh-MAS-uh-kiz-uhm) The achievement of sexual pleasure by inflicting pain on one's partner (sadism) or by suffering pain (masochism).

sample The limited number of subjects from a large group or population, selected for testing and statistical treatment. The assumption is made that the sample may be representative of the whole group.

schemata (ski-MAH-ta) Organized representations of experience from the past that are used to interpret present experience.

schizoid personality disorder Classification used for withdrawn individuals who are not disturbed by their lack of social relationships. These people have flat emotional responses and often seem cold and detached.

schizophrenia (skit-suh-FREE-nee-uh) A type of psychosis characterized by a loss of contact with reality, blunting of emotions, and disturbance of thinking. Behavior is often so bizarre that individuals must be hospitalized.

schizotypal (skit-suh-TIGH-pal) **personality disorder** Diagnosis for a person who shows some of the symptoms of schizophrenia, but not in as extreme a form. People with this disorder include those formerly classified with the label "simple schizophrenic." It differs from schizoid personality disorder in that it includes eccentricities of communication and behavior not seen in introverted personality.

Scholastic Aptitude Test (SAT) A screening examination for college admission, required of applicants by many colleges in the United States.

secondary appraisal The second cognitive review of a situation, after it has been assessed as possibly harmful or stressful; it is a consideration of one's ability to deal with the situation and the appropriate action called for. See also *primary appraisal.*

secondary drive A motive that develops as a result of learning, presumably by virtue of being associated with satisfaction of biologically based (primary) drives.

secondary reinforcement The situation in which reinforcing properties are acquired by one object or event beause it is associated with other reinforcers.

securely attached A term used by Ainsworth to describe infants who use their mothers as a secure base but who also engage in away-from-mother exploratory behavior.

selective breeding A procedure that involves mating animals that have selected characteristics with other animals having the same or different selected characteristics in order to produce offspring with certain specific traits.

selective processing The procedure by which some but not all of the material from the sensory store is chosen for transfer into memory.

self-actualization In humanistic theory, the inborn tendency of human beings to develop and work toward their ultimate potential.

self-concept An individual's organized perceptions of the "I" or "me" and perceptions of the relationship of the "I" or "me" to others and to various aspects of life.

self-control The idea that a person has choices and by monitoring and being aware of behavior can alter his or her responses.

self-disclosure The willingness to tell someone else one's thoughts and feelings as well as less personal information about oneself.

self-efficacy According to Albert Bandura, an expectancy concept relating to confidence in one's ability to perform the behaviors necessary to obtain reinforcement.

self-instructional training (SIT) A method of teaching children to develop control over their own behavior in a series of graded steps. The child is first told what to do, then gives self-instructions aloud, and finally thinks, but does not speak, the self-instructions.

self-perception theory A theory suggested by Bem to explain cognitive dissonance phenomena; the idea that people infer their own attitudes by observing their own behavior in particular situations.

self-regulation Changes in behavior that occur because of internal reinforcement rather than external reinforcement.

self schemata The cognitive structures that a person uses to describe his or her own behavior and personal characteristics.

self-selection A threat to representative sampling resulting from the fact that people who volunteer to participate in research may be atypical of the population as a whole.

self-theory Carl Rogers's theory of personality, based on the way a person perceives the environment rather than on the characteristics of the environment itself.

semantic memory The organized knowledge we have about words and other verbal symbols, including their meaning and the things to which they refer, relationships among them, and rules for manipulating them.

sensation The physical process of detecting environmental stimuli and of transmitting information about them through the nervous system.

sensation-seeking motive The tendency to seek novelty and high levels of stimulation.

sensitive-period A period of development during which a behavior is most easily established. It is distinct from a *critical period*, which is assumed to be the only time during development when a behavior can be established.

sensorimotor period A term used by Piaget for the first of four major stages in the continuous process of growth and change in cognitive development during childhood. The period begins at birth and lasts until about 18 months of age. Children's functioning in this period is at the action level involving sensing and motor movement. They have not fully developed internal representations of objects or mental images.

sequential design A combination of longitudinal, cross-sectional, and time lag techniques for the study of development. It is impractical to execute fully because of time and cost factors.

serial position curve A function showing that material presented at the beginning and end of a list is remembered better than material in the middle of the list.

serotonin (ser-oh-TOHN-in) One of a group of chemical neurotransmitters, thought to be involved in some types of depression.

sexism A form of prejudice and stereotyping based on whether a person is male or female.

sex role The appropriate behavior assigned by a culture to a person of a particular sex.

sexual dysfunction Sexual difficulties experienced by a man or a woman that have detrimental effects on sexual performance and satisfaction.

sexual identity The image that an individual has about the sex to which he or she belongs.

shadowing A technique for studying shifts of attention. Subjects are asked to listen to two messages simultaneously and to repeat, or shadow, one of them word for word.

shaping A method used to train animals and humans to perform novel and complex behaviors. The process involves finding a behavior that the subject can already perform and reinforcing gradual changes in the direction of the desired behavior; also called the method of successive approximations.

short-term memory The component of the memory that holds information only briefly until it is either processed and retained or is lost when it is displaced by new material. See also *long-term memory*.

signal detection theory The idea that there is no fixed probability that a subject will detect a signal of a particular intensity and that the concept of "fixed absolute threshold" is largely meaningless. The subject's decision criterion or standard is far more influential than the actual physical intensity of the stimulus.

similarity Gestalt perceptual law that states that when parts of the stimulus configuration are perceived as similar, they will also be perceived as belonging together.

single-subject research Behaviorally oriented research in which each subject's behavior is studied under a variety of conditions. These conditions usually include a baseline measure and periods of treatment separated by a period of no treatment.

situational adjustment Necessary responses to deal with changes in environmental circumstances that are stress-producing.

situational attribution The tendency to pinpoint the cause of a person's behavior on the environment at the time rather than on his or her personality characteristics.

situational factor in stress A person's assessment of the impact of a stressor, based on its duration, severity, predictability, controllability, and suddenness of onset. Compare to *personal factors in stress*.

Skinner box A piece of scientific apparatus designed by B. F. Skinner for use in operant conditioning studies. The typical box contains a lever that the animal may press and a method of delivering some kind of reinforcement, usually a food pellet.

sleep apnea (AP-nee-ah) A serious sleep disorder characterized by a cessation of breathing due to a collapse of the pharynx.

sleep factor A hypothesized sleep-inducing chemical compound in the blood.

slow-wave sleep The deep sleep of stages 3 and 4, characterized by a slow, irregular EEG pattern.

social cognition The study of the general processes that people use to make sense out of the behavior of other people and of their own behavior.

social exchange theory A theory concerned with the effects of rewards and costs that are exchanged within relationships.

social facilitation The ability of the presence of observers to enhance or impair performance by increasing arousal that energizes dominant correct or incorrect responses.

social learning A cognitive-behavioral theory of social behavior that focuses on how such behavior develops and changes.

social phobia A type of irrational fear of situations in which a person will be exposed to the scrutiny of others. The most common types of fears are of blushing, public speaking, eating in public, writing in public, and using public toilets.

social psychology The area of psychology that studies the behavior of the individual in relation to his or her social environment. The study includes such topics as psychological conditions that lead to the development of social groups, attitude formation and change, affiliation, interpersonal attraction, conformity, and group processes.

social support Factors, such as the presence of close interpersonal ties or knowledge of the availability of helpers, that serve to moderate the impact of stress.

Social Support Questionnaire A paper and pencil test designed to measure an individual's perception of the number of people available to provide help and psychological comfort if they are needed.

socialization The developmental process by which the individual (especially the child) comes to recognize and identify with basic values and attitudes of the dominant institutions and representatives of the society in which he or she lives and to practice them as a part of ordinary behavior.

sociobiology A biologically based evolutionary approach to understanding behavior which holds that much social behavior is aimed at preserving one's genes in the gene pool.

soma (SOH-muh) The cell body of a neuron that contains its nucleus.

somatic (soh-MAT-ik) **nervous system** A division of the peripheral nervous system that provides input from the sensory system and output to the skeletal muscles that are responsible for voluntary movement.

somatotype (so-MAHT-uh-type) The three-digit number that represents William Sheldon's description of a particular body type in his system of constitutional psychology.

SOMPA (System of Multicultural Pluralistic Assessment) A testing procedure developed by Jane Mercer to measure the level of intellectual functioning of minority and culturally deprived children.

spatial frequency model A theory of visual perception which hold that differences in patterns of light and darkness (spatial frequency curves) are the basic stimulus feature to which the visual system responds.

specific attachment A selectivity in response to care-giving figures. It usually occurs among human infants 6 to 7 months of age.

split-brain patient A patient whose corpus callosum has been severed surgically to prevent the spread of a type of epileptic seizure from one side of the brain to the other hemisphere. Examination of such patients has indicated that the two halves of the brain have somewhat different functions.

spontaneous recovery The reappearance of a classically conditioned response after a period of time during which it seemed to be extinguished.

stable attribution Assignment of the cause of behavior to personal or situational factors that might be expected to be the same on most occasions.

stages of cognitive development The idea that thinking and logic progress in a series of clearly definable steps that alternate with longer periods during which little change occurs.

stage of development The particular grouping of behaviors, in a predetermined series of groupings, that describes an individual at a particular point in time.

stages of dying A series of responses in anticipation of one's own death or that of a loved one. According to Kübler-Ross, these include denial, anger, bargaining, depression, and acceptance.

stages of moral reasoning A series of cognitive stages, derived from the work of Kohlberg, that are based on developmental differences in the solution of moral dilemmas.

standard deviation A measure of variation computed by finding the difference, or deviation, between each score and the mean, squaring and summing the deviations, dividing them by the total number of scores minus 1, and then calculating the square root of this value.

standard error The statistical expression of the difference between the actual score an individual makes on a test and his or her "true score," or the average score he or she would make if the test were taken an infinite number of times.

standard score A statistical formula used to convert a variety of measures to the same scale of measurement so that they can be compared. It is calculated by subtracting each score from the mean and then dividing this by the standard deviation of the entire set of scores.

Stanford-Binet (bih-NAY) The revision of the original Binet intelligence test by Lewis Terman of Stanford University. Later revisions of the Binet test have continued to use this name.

state-dependent memory A phenomenon in which improved recall occurs if the mood at the time of recall is the same as it was when learning occurred.

state-specific experience An experience that occurs in a specific state of consciousness and that cannot be recalled or expressed in other states.

stereopsis (STER-ee-AHP-sis) Depth perception based on the different view of an object from each eye.

stereotype (STER-ee-oh-type) An idea about members of a group based not on experience but on selective observation of behavior that fits in with earlier expectations.

stimulus control procedure A behavior modification technique that involves arranging the environment so that specific stimuli will come to elicit desired behaviors.

storage One of four stages in information processing. After the input of information, it is coded and stored, ready for later retrieval.

stress A concept that refers to a person's perception of a situation as demanding, challenging, and requiring some sort of response.

stress-coping skills Techniques used by an individual to deal effectively with problem situations.

stress-induced analgesia A decreased sensitivity to pain under severe stress; it is apparently caused by the release of endorphins.

stressor Some element of a situation that makes demands on the individual.

stroke A rupturing of one or more blood vessels in the brain; also known as a cerebral vascular accident (CVA).

structuralism An early school of psychology that sought to analyze the mind in terms of sensations, thought to be its basic components.

sublimation (sub-li-MAY-shun) The process by which an individual channels unacceptable impulses into socially acceptable behavior.

subliminal (sub-LIM-uhn-uhl) **perception** Perception of stimuli that are so weak or brief that they cannot be consciously perceived.

sudden infant death syndrome (SIDS) A fatal disorder in which infants cease respiration and die from lack of oxygen.

superego In psychoanalytic theory, that part of the psyche that is developed by internalized parental standards and identification. There are two parts to the superego: the ego ideal, which represents identification with parents and desired standards of conduct, and the conscience, which includes moralistic attitudes and values.

suppression A defense mechanism that consciously excludes anxiety-producing material from awareness.

surface structure A linguistic term for the words and organization of a spoken or written sentence. Two sentences may have quite different surface structure but still mean the same thing.

survey study A technique used to obtain information about opinions and attitudes by questioning individuals directly.

sympathetic nervous system That portion of the autonomic nervous system that speeds up bodily processes and increases physiological arousal.

synapse (SIN-aps) The junction between nerve cells across which the nerve impulse must pass.

systematic desensitization A therapeutic process for reducing specific fears by pairing a series of increasingly intense fear-producing stimuli with a relaxed state.

tardive dyskinesia (TAHR-dihv dis-ki-NEE-see-uh) A disorder involving uncontrolled body movement, particularly of the lips and tongue, that may result from treatment with antipsychotic drugs.

target behavior In behavior therapy, the specific activity identified by an individual on which efforts for change are to be focused.

Terman study A longitudinal study of the development of highly intelligent children, begun at Stanford University by Lewis Terman in 1922.

test anxiety A set of stress responses that may be both cognitive and physiological and that occur when an individual is evaluated.

testis (TES-tis), **testes** (TES-teez) The male gland that produces the sperm cells needed for reproduction and also androgens, or male hormones.

testosterone (tes-TAH-stuh-rohn) Male sex hormone produced by the testes. It is important in puberty for the growth of the male sex organs and the development of secondary sex characteristics.

test standardization A term that can refer both to test procedures and to the development of norms. The way a test is given, the materials used, and the method of scoring must be fixed, so that the test can be administered the same way each time. Then tables of norms representing the range of scores earned by representative subjects can also be compiled.

T group The name for human relations training groups that are designed to enhance the interpersonal reactions of already well functioning individuals.

thalamus (THAL-uh-muhs) A large group of nuclei, located above the midbrain, that are an important sensory relay system.

Thematic Apperception Test (TAT) A projective assessment developed by Henry Murray that consists of 30 pictures, including one blank card. The subjects are asked to tell a story for each somewhat ambiguous picture. A number of scoring systems have been developed for the TAT.

theory A system of generalizations that specify the relationships between specific behaviors and their causes.

theory of reasoned action A model developed by Fishbein and Ajzen to predict whether behavior will be consistent with a given attitude.

theory of social impact The theory, advanced by Latané and others, which states that any social pressure directed toward a group is diffused among its members, decreasing feelings of personal accountability as group size increases.

time lag study An approach to the study of development that attempts to control for historical factors. A longitudinal study of new groups of similar subjects is begun at several time periods, and the results are compared.

tip of the tongue phenomenon A situation in which a person is unable to remember a particular item, but at the same time is able to produce clues to the correct answer. It implies that the item has not been forgotten, but that the retrieval mechanism is temporarily faulty.

token economy A programmed therapeutic environment based on learning theory principles, in which patients, by performing certain behaviors, earn tokens that can be exchanged for various privileges.

trait A distinguishing feature of an individual, usually thought to be consistent over time.

Transactional Analysis (TA) A group therapy method that focuses on increased understanding of the way people use their interpersonal needs and conflicts as a basis for interacting with others.

transfer of excitation The notion that the arousal component of one emotion may be channeled into and become part of another emotional response.

transcendental meditation A quasi-religious technique founded by Maharishi Mahesh Yogi that involves dwelling on a thought, sensation, word, or object in an attempt to achieve inner peace.

transduction The process whereby sensory systems convert various forms of physical energy into nerve impulses.

transference Psychoanalytic term that refers to the displacement of affect from one person to another. Patterns of feelings and behavior originally experienced with significant figures in childhood are displaced or attached to individuals in one's current relationships (e.g., a psychotherapist). In positive transference, the client reacts to the therapist as a helping, caring, emotionally supportive figure. In negative transference, the client responds to the therapist with negative feelings derived from past relationships.

transitional adjustment The need to accommodate to a new situation caused by movement to a new developmental stage.

transsexual One who feels an intense desire to change his or her body to that of the opposite sex.

transvestite (trans-VES-tight) One who obtains sexual satisfaction by dressing in the clothing of the opposite sex (crossdressing).

treatment contingency In behavior therapy, the specific environmental manipulation that is implemented in an attempt to modify a behavior.

tricyclic (trigh-SIGH-klik) **antidepressants** A group of drugs used to treat depression. They are thought to block the reuptake of neurotransmitters into the cell bodies so that more of the chemical remains active in the neural synapse. Common trade names are Tofranel and Elavil.

two-factor theory of avoidance learning A theory that incorporates both classical and operant conditioning factors. The warning stimulus evokes a classically conditioned fear response. The fear response motivates the operant avoidance behavior. The resulting anxiety reduction is a powerful reinforcer.

Type I schizophrenia A pathological condition involving

delusions, hallucinations, and disordered symptoms but without a flattened affect and poverty of speech.

Type II schizophrenia A disorder in which flattened affect and changes in speech are prominent.

unconditioned stimulus (UCS) A stimulus that evokes an unconditioned response. A neutral stimulus that is paired with a UCS may become capable of evoking a conditioned response.

unconscious In psychoanalytic theory, a dynamic body of wishes, feelings, and impulses of which the individual is unaware.

unipolar disorder Term for an affective disorder in which only depression occurs. There are no episodes of mania.

unique life events Occurrences, not related to either historical events or the general maturational process, that may have an effect on the course of development. Examples are a death in the family, a serious accident or illness, or the move to a new and very different environment.

unobtrusive measures Naturally occurring behaviors or environmental effects of behavior that can be used as measures without the subjects being aware that they are being studied.

unstable attribution Assignment of the cause of an individual's behavior to personal or environmental factors that may differ from time to time.

vaginismus (vaj-in-IZ-mus) A form of female sexual dysfunction involving involuntary contraction and tightening of the vagina when intercourse is attempted.

validity The degree to which a test measures what it is supposed to measure or accomplishes the purpose for which it is intended. Validity is measured by the coefficient of correlation between a test and some other criterion.

variability, measures of Measures of the dispersion of values in a distribution of scores. The range and standard deviation are two measures of variability.

variable Any characteristic of a person or situation that can vary in some way.

variable-interval schedule A reinforcement schedule in which reinforcement follows the first response after a varying but average amount of time.

variable-ratio schedule A reinforcement schedule in which reinforcement follows the first response after a varying but average number of responses.

vicarious (vigh-KAYR-ee-uhs) **learning** See *observational learning.*

visual code The storage in memory of an object or event by a picturelike representation of its important features.

visually evoked potential (VEP) A measure of electrical activity of a large group of neurons in the visual cortex through electrodes attached to the scalp.

vulnerability Greater than average susceptibility to the effects of either general or specific stressors.

vulnerability hypothesis of schizophrenia The idea that schizophrenia is not a permanent disorder but rather that an individual may have a permanent risk of developing schizophrenic behavior when he or she is under stress.

WAIS-R The Wechsler Adult Intelligence Scale, revised version. An improved version of the Wechsler scales, it is made up of six verbal subtests and five performance subtests.

Weber's (VAY-ber) **law** A hypothesis that states that there is a constant ratio between the intensity of the stimulus and the amount that a second stimulus must differ from it before the perceiver can detect the difference.

Wechsler (WEKS-ler) **tests** A group of intelligence tests, for different age levels, that follow the pattern of the original tests designed by David Wechsler. The tests include the Wechsler Intelligence Scale for Children (WISC-R), the Wechsler Preschool and Primary Scale of Intelligence (WPPSI), and the Wechsler Adult Intelligence Scale (WAIS-R).

white matter Nervous tissue consisting of myelinated nerve fibers.

WISC-R The Wechsler Intelligence Scale for Children, revised edition. It is part of the Wechsler test series, with 5 verbal and 5 performance tests intended for children ages 7–16.

WPPSI Wechsler Preschool and Primary Scale of Intelligence. The version of the Wechsler scales for children 4 to 6.5 years of age, it yields verbal, performance, and overall scores.

Yerkes-Dodson law A hypothesis that states that there is an optimal level of arousal for the performance of any given task. For difficult tasks the optimal level of arousal for performance is lower than for easy tasks.

Young-Helmholtz theory The theory of color vision that assumes that there are three types of color receptors in the retina, one sensitive to blue, one to green, and one to red.

BIBLIOGRAPHY

ABBOTT, B., SCHOEN, L., and BADIA, P. (1984). Choosing between predictable shock schedules: Long vs. short-duration signals. *Journal of the Experimental Analysis of Behavior, 41 (3),* 319–327.

ABRAMSON, L., SELIGMAN, M. E. P., and TEASDALE, J. D. (1978). Learned helplessness in humans: Critique and reformulation. *Journal of Abnormal Psychology, 87,* 49–74.

ACREDOLO, L. P., and HAKE, J. L. (1982). Infant perception. In B. B. Wolman (Ed.), *Handbook of developmental psychology.* Englewood Cliffs, N.J.: Prentice-Hall.

ADKINSON, C. D., and BERG, W. K. (1976). Cardiac deceleration in newborns: Habituation, dishabituation, and offset response. *Journal of Experimental Child Psychology, 21,* 46–60.

AHLES, T. A., BLANCHARD, E. B., and LEVENTHAL, H. (1983). Cognitive control of pain: Attention to the sensory aspects of the cold pressor stimulus. *Cognitive Therapy and Research, 1,* 159–178.

AINSWORTH, M. D. S. (1963). The development of infant-mother interaction among the Ganda. In B. M. Foss (Ed.), *Determinants of infant behavior,* Vol. 2. New York: Wiley.

AINSWORTH, M. D. S., BELL, S. M., and SLAYTON, D. J. (1972). Individual differences in the development of some attachment behaviors. *Merrill-Palmer Quarterly, 18,* 123–143.

AJZEN, I., and FISHBEIN, M. (1980). *Understanding attitudes and predicting social behavior.* Englewood Cliffs, N.J.: Prentice-Hall.

AKISKAL, H. S. (1981). Concepts of depression. In E. Friedman, J. Mann, and S. Gershon (Eds.), *Depression and antidepressants: Implications for cause and treatment.* New York: Raven Press.

ALLEN, V. L., and GREENBERGER, D. B. (1980). Destruction and perceived control. In A. Baum and J. E. Singer (Eds.), *Advances in environmental psychology,* Vol. 2. Hillsdale, N.J.: Erlbaum.

ALLGEIER, E. R., and McCORMICK, N. B. (Eds.) (1983). *Changing boundaries: Gender roles and sexual behavior.* Palo Alto, Calif.: Mayfield.

AMABILE, T. M. (1985). Motivation and creativity: Effects of motivational orientation on creative writers. *Journal of Personality and Social Psychology, 48,* 393–399.

AMES, L. B., GILLESPIE, C., HAINES, J., and ILG, G. L. (1979). *The Gesell Institute's child from one to six: Evaluating the behavior of the preschool child.* New York: Harper & Row.

AMOORE, J. E. (1969). A plan to identify most of the primary odors. In C. Pfaffman (Ed.), *Olfaction and taste,* Vol. 3. New York: Rockefeller University Press.

ANASTASI, A. (1982). *Psychological testing* (5th ed.). New York: Macmillan.

ANDERSEN, S. M. (1984). Self-knowledge and social inference: II. The diagnosticity of cognitive/affective and behavioral data. *Journal of Personality and Social Psychology*, 46, 294–307.

ANDERSEN, S. M., and BEM, S. L. (1981). Sex typing and androgyny in dyadic interaction: Individual differences in responsiveness to physical attractiveness. *Journal of Personality and Social Psychology*, 41, 74–86.

ANDERSON, J. R. (1980). *Cognitive psychology and its implications.* San Francisco: Freeman.

ANDERSON, U. E. (1972). *Discussion.* In L. Ehrman, G. S. Omenn, and E. Caspari (Eds.), *Genetics, environment and behavior.* New York: Academic Press.

ANDREASEN, N. C. (1979). Thought, language and communication disorders: II. Diagnostic significance. *Archives of General Psychiatry*, 36, 1325–1330.

ANGST, J., FREY, R., LOHMEYER, B., ZERKIN-RIIDIN, E. (1980). Bipolar manic-depressive psychoses. *Human Genetics*, 55, 237–254.

ANONYMOUS (1977). Letter to the editor. *Schizophrenia Bulletin*, 3, 4.

ARCHER, D., and GARTNER, R. (1984). *Violence and crime in cross-national perspective.* New Haven: Yale University Press.

ARENBERG, D., and ROBERTSON-TCHABO, E. A. (1977). Learning and aging. In J. E. Birren and K. W. Schaie (Eds.), *Handbook of the psychology of aging.* New York: Van Nostrand Reinhold.

ARKIN, R. M., APPELMAN, A. J., and BURGER, J. M. (1980). Social anxiety, self-presentation, and self-serving bias in causal attributions. *Journal of Personality and Social Psychology*, 38, 23–35.

ARONSON, E. (1984). *The social animal.* (4th ed.). San Francisco: Freeman.

ARONSON, E., STEPHAN, C., SIKES, J., BLANEY, N., and SNAPP, M. (1978). *The jigsaw classroom.* Beverly Hills, Calif.: Sage.

ASCH, S. E. (1951). Effects of group pressure upon the modification and distortion of judgment. In H. Guetzkow (Ed.), *Groups, leadership, and men.* Pittsburgh: Carnegie Press.

ASCH, S. E. (1952). *Social psychology.* Englewood Cliffs, N.J.: Prentice-Hall.

ASCH, S. E. (1956). Studies of independence and conformity: I. A minority of one against a unanimous majority. *Psychological Monographs*, 70, 9 (Whole No. 416).

ATKINSON, J., BRADDICK, O., and FRENCH, J. (1979). Contrast sensibility of the human neonate measured by the visual evoked potential. *Investigations of Ophthalmological and Visual Science*, 18, 210–213.

ATKINSON, J. W., and BIRCH, D. (1978). *An introduction to motivation.* New York: Van Nostrand.

AUDEN, W. H. (1940). In memory of Sigmund Freud. *Another time.* London: Faber.

AVERILL, J. A. (1980). A constructivist view of emotion. In R. Plutchik and H. Kellerman (Eds.), *Emotion: Theory, research, and experience.* Vol. 1, *Theories of emotion.* New York: Academic Press.

AXELROD, S., and APSCHE, J. (Eds.) (1983). *The effects of punishment on human behavior.* New York: Academic Press.

AYLLON, T., and AZRIN, N. H. (1965). The measurement and reinforcement of behavior of psychotics. *Journal of the Experimental Analysis of Behavior*, 8, 357–383.

AYLLON, T., GARBER, S. W., and ALLISON, M. G. (1977). Behavioral treatment of childhood neurosis. *Psychiatry*, 40, 315–322.

BADDELEY, A. (1982a). *Your memory, a user's guide.* Harmondsworth, England: Penguin Books.

BADDELEY, A. D. (1982b). Domains of recollection. *Psychological Review*, 89, 708–729.

BAKER, L., and SANTA, J. L. (1977). Context, integration, and retrieval. *Memory and Cognition*, 5, 308–314.

BALES, R. F., and SLATER, P. E. (1955). Role differentiation in small decision-making groups. In T. Parsons and R. F. Bales (Eds.), *Family, socialization, and interaction process.* New York: Free Press.

BALSAM, R. M., and BALSAM, A. (1984). *Becoming a psychotherapist.* (2nd ed.). Chicago: University of Chicago Press.

BALTES, P. B., REESE, H. W., and LIPSITT, L. P. (1980). Life span developmental psychology. In M. R. Rosenzweig and L. W. Porter (Eds.), *Annual review of psychology.* Palo Alto, Calif.: Annual Reviews.

BANCROFT, J. (1984). Hormones and human sexual behavior. *Journal of Sex and Marital Therapy*, 10, 3–21.

BANDURA, A. (1965). Influence of models' reinforcement contingencies on the acquisition of imitated responses. *Journal of Personality and Social Psychology*, 1, 589–595.

BANDURA, A. (1969). *Principles of behavior modification.* New York: Holt, Rinehart and Winston.

BANDURA, A. (1973). *Aggression: A social learning analysis.* Englewood Cliffs, N.J.: Prentice-Hall.

BANDURA, A. (1978). The self-system in reciprocal determinism. *American Psychologist, 33,* 344–358.

BANDURA, A. (1981). In search of pure unidirectional determinants. *Behavior Therapy, 12,* 30–40.

BANDURA, A. (1982). Self-efficacy mechanism in human agency. *American Psychologist, 37,* 122–147.

BARASH, D. P. (1982). *Sociobiology and behavior.* (2nd ed.). New York: Elsevier.

BARBER, J. (1977). Rapid induction analgesia. *American Journal of Clinical Hypnosis, 19,* 138–143.

BARBER, T. X., and CALVERLEY, D. S. (1964). Experimental studies in "hypnotic" behavior: Suggested deafness evaluated by delayed auditory feedback. *British Journal of Psychology, 55,* 439–446.

BARBER, T. X., SPANOS, N. P., and CHAVES, J. F. (1974). *Hypnosis, imagination, and human potentialities.* Elmsford, N.Y.: Pergamon Press.

BARGH, J. A., and COHEN, J. L. (1978). Mediating factors in the arousal-performance relationship. *Motivation and Emotion, 2,* 243–256.

BARKER, R. (1972). The effects of REM sleep on the retention of a visual task. *Psychophysiology, 9,* 107.

BARKER, R. G., and SCHOGGEN, P. (1973). *Qualities of community life.* San Francisco: Jossey-Bass.

BARLOW, D. H., ABEL, G. G., and BLANCHARD, E. B. (1979). Gender identity change in transsexuals. *Archives of General Psychiatry, 36,* 1001–1007.

BARLOW, D. H., and WOLFE, B. E. (1981). Behavioral approaches in anxiety disorders: A report on the NIMH-SUNY, Albany Research Conference. *Journal of Consulting and Clinical Psychology, 49,* 448–454.

BARNETT, M. A., KING, L. M., and HOWARD, J. A. (1979). Inducing affect about self or other: Effects on generosity in children. *Developmental Psychology, 15,* 164–167.

BARON, R. A. (1977). *Human aggression.* New York: Plenum.

BARON, R. A., and BYRNE, D. (1984). *Social psychology: Understanding human interaction.* (4th ed.). Boston: Allyn and Bacon.

BARR, A., and FEIGENBAUM, E. A. (Eds.) (1981). *The handbook of artificial intelligence.* Stanford, Calif.: Heiris Tech Press.

BARTLETT, F. C. (1932). *Remembering: A study in experimental and social psychology.* New York: Cambridge University Press.

BATES, J. E. (1982). *Temperament as a part of social relationships: Implications of perceived infant difficultness.* Paper presented at International Conference on Infant Studies, Austin, Texas, March 1982.

BATSON, C. D., COCHRAN, P. J., BIEDENMAN, M. F., BLOSSER, J. L., RYAN, M. J., and VOOT, B. (1978). Failure to help when in a hurry: Callousness or conflict? *Personality and Social Psychology Bulletin, 4,* 97–101.

BAUER, K. E., and MCCANNE, T. R. (1980). Autonomic and central nervous system responding during hypnosis and simulation of hypnosis. *International Journal of Clinical and Experimental Hypnosis, 28,* 148–163.

BAUMRIND, D. (1964). Some thoughts on ethics in research: After reading Milgram's "Behavioral study of obedience." *American Psychologist, 19,* 421–423.

BEACH, F. A. (1969). It's all in your mind. *Psychology Today, 3,* 33–35.

BECK, A. T. (1967). *Depression: Clinical, experimental, and theoretical aspects.* New York: Hoeber.

BECK, A. T. (1976). *Cognitive therapy and the emotional disorders.* New York: International Universities Press.

BECK, A. T., RUSH, J. A., SHAW, B. R., and EMERY, G. (1978). *Cognitive therapy of depression: A treatment manual.* Copyright A. T. Beck, M.D.

BECKER, J., and SCHUCKIT, M. A. (1978). The comparative efficacy of cognitive therapy and pharmacotherapy in the treatment of depressions. *Cognitive Therapy and Research, 2,* 193–197.

BEECHER, H. K. (1959). Generalization from pain of various types and diverse origins. *Science, 130,* 267–268.

BEKERIAN, D. A., and BOWERS, J. M. (1983). Eyewitness testimony: Were we misled? *Journal of Experimental Psychology: Learning, Memory, and Cognition, 9,* 39–145.

BELL, A. P., and WEINBERG, S. (1978). *Homosexualities: A study of diversity among men and women.* New York: Simon & Schuster.

BELSKY, J. (1981). Early human experience: A family perspective. *Developmental Psychology, 17,* 3–23.

BELT, J., and HOLDEN, P. (1978). Polygraphic usage among major U.S. corporations. *Personnel Journal, 57,* 80.

BEM, D. J. (1972). Self-perception theory. In L. Berkowitz (Ed.), *Advances in experimental social psychology*, Vol. 1. New York: Academic Press.

BEM, D. J., and ALLEN, A. (1974). On predicting some of the people some of the time: The search for cross-situational consistencies in behavior. *Psychological Review, 81,* 506–520.

BENNETT, H. L. (1983). Remembering drink orders: The memory skills of cocktail waitresses. *Human Learning, 2,* 157–169.

BENSON, H. (1975). *The relaxation response.* New York: Morrow.

BEN-VENISTE, R. (1971). Pornography and sex crime: The Danish experience. In *Technical report of the Commission on Obscenity and Pornography*, Vol. 7. Washington, D.C.: Government Printing Office.

BERGER, S. M. (1962). Conditioning through vicarious instigation. *Psychological Review, 69,* 450–466.

BERGER, T. W. (1984). Long-term potentiation of hippocampal synaptic transmission affects rate of behavioral learning. *Science, 224,* 627–629.

BERKOWITZ, L. (1984). Some effects of thoughts on anti- and prosocial influences of media events: A cognitive-neoassociation analysis. *Psychological Bulletin, 95,* 410–427.

BERLYNE, D. E. (1978). Curiosity and learning. *Learning and Motivation, 2,* 99–175.

BERSCHEID, E. (1983). Emotion. In H. H. Kelley and others (Eds.), *Close relationships.* San Francisco: Freeman.

BERSCHEID, E. (1984). *The problem of emotion in close relationships.* New York: Plenum.

BINET, A. (1890). Perceptions d'enfants. *Revue Philosophique, 30,* 582–611.

BINET, A., and FERE, C. (1901). *Animal magnetism.* New York: Appleton.

BINET, A., and SIMON, T. (1909). L'Intelligence des imbeciles. *L'Année Psychologique, 15,* 1–147.

BIRCH, E. B., and HEIDT, R. (1983). The development of binocular summation in human infants. *Investigative ophthalmology and visual science, 24,* 1103–1107.

BLACK, I. B. (Ed.). (1984). *Cellular and molecular biology of neuronal development.* New York: Plenum.

BLAKEMORE, C., and COOPER, G. F. (1970). Development of the brain depends on visual environment. *Nature, 228,* 477–478.

BLATT, S. J., D'AFFLITI, J. P., and QUINLAN, D. M. (1976). Experiences of depression in normal young adults. *Journal of Abnormal Psychology, 85,* 383–389.

BLEULER, M. (1972). *The schizophrenic psychosis in light of long-term case and family histories.* Stuttgart: George Thieme Verlag.

BLEULER, M. (1973). Today's concept of schizophrenia. *Transactions and Studies of the College of Physicians of Philadelphia, 41,* 69–80.

BLOOD, R. O., JR., and BLOOD, M. (1978). *Marriage.* (3rd ed.). New York: Free Press.

BLOOM, B. L., ASHER, S. S., and WHITE, S. W. (1978). Marital disruption as a stressor: A review and analysis. *Psychological Bulletin, 85,* 867–894.

BLOOM, F. E. (1983). Ultimate chemistry. *Psychology Today, 17,* (9), 49–55.

BLOOM, F. E., LAZERSON, A., and HOFSTADTER, L. (1984). *Brain, mind, and behavior.* New York: Freeman.

BLUMBERG, S. R., and HOKANSON, J. E. (1983). The effects of another person's response style on interpersonal behavior in depression. *Journal of Abnormal Psychology, 92,* 196–209.

BOFFEY, P. M. (1984, September 13). Failure is found in the discharge of the mentally ill. *New York Times,* p. 1.

BOLLES, R. C. (1979). *Learning theory* (2nd ed.). New York: Holt, Rinehart and Winston.

BOLLES, R. C. (1980). Ethological learning theory. In G. M. Gazda and R. J. Corsini (Eds.), *Theories of learning: A comparative approach.* Itaska, Ill.: Peacock.

BOTTOMLEY, P. A., HACK, H. R., EDELSTEIN, W. A., SCHENCK, J. F., SMITH, L. S., LEUE, W. M., MUELLER, O. M., and REDINGTON, R. W. (1984). Anatomy and metabolism of the normal human brain studied by magnetic resonance at 1.5 Tesla. *Radiology, 150,* 441–446.

BOUCHARD, T. (in press). Traits and the concepts of convergence and divergence in the development of human personality. *Acta Geneticae Medicae et Gemellologiae.*

BOUCHER, J. D., and EKMAN, P. (1975). Facial areas and emotional information. *Journal of Communication, 25,* 21–29.

BOWER, G. H. (1981). Mood and memory. *American Psychologist. 36,* 129–148.

BOWER, G. H., and HILGARD, E. R. (1981). *Theories of learning.* (5th ed.). Englewood Cliffs, N.J.: Prentice Hall.

BOWER, G. H., MONTEIRO, K. P., and GILLIGAN, S. C. (1978). Emotional mood as a context for learning and recall. *Journal of Verbal Learning and Verbal Behavior, 17,* 573–585.

BOWERS, K. S. (1976). *Hypnosis for the seriously curious.* Monterey, Calif.: Brooks/Cole.

BOWLBY, J. (1969). *Attachment and loss.* Vol. 1, *Attachment.* New York: Basic Books.

BOWLBY, J. (1973). *Attachment and loss.* Vol. 2, *Separation—Anxiety and anger.* New York: Basic Books.

BOWLBY, J. (1980). *Attachment and loss.* Vol. 3, *Loss: Sadness and depression.* New York: Basic Books.

BRADY, J. V. (1958). Ulcers in "executive monkeys." *Scientific American, 199,* 95–103.

BRAINERD, C. J. (1983). Modifiability of cognitive development. In S. Meadows (Ed.), *Developing thinking.* London: Methuen.

BRANSFORD, J. D. (1979). *Human cognition.* Belmont, Calif.: Wadsworth.

BRAVEMAN, N. S., and BRONSTEIN, P. (1985). Conference on experimental assessments and clinical applications of conditioned food aversions. New York: Annals of the New York Academy of Sciences.

BREGMAN, E. O. (1934). An attempt to modify the emotional attitudes of infants by the conditioned response technique. *Journal of Genetic Psychology, 45,* 169–198.

BREHM, S. S. (1985). *Intimate relationships.* New York: Random House.

BRENNER, C. (1974). On the nature and development of affects: A unified theory. *Psychoanalytic Quarterly, 43,* 532–556.

BRIGHAM, J. C. (1980). Limiting conditions of the physical attractiveness stereotype: Attributions about divorce. *Journal of Research in Personality, 14,* 365–375.

BRODY, N. (1980). Social motivation. *Annual Review of Psychology, 31,* 143–168.

BROWN, G. W., and HARRIS, T. (1978). Social origins of depression: A reply. *Psychological Medicine, 8,* 577–588.

BROWN, J. S., and BURTON, R. R. (1978). Diagnostic models for procedural bugs in basic mathematical skills. *Cognitive Science, 2,* 155–192.

BROWN, R. (1973). Schizophrenia, language, and reality. *American Psychologist, 28,* 395–403.

BROWN, R., CAZDEN, C., and BELLUGI, U. (1969). The child's grammar from I to III. In J. P. Hill (Ed.). *Minnesota symposium on child psychology,* Vol. 2. Minneapolis: University of Minnesota Press.

BROWN, T. S., and WALLACE, P. (1980). *Physiological psychology.* New York: Academic Press.

BROWNMILLER, S. (1975). *Against our will: Men, women and rape.* New York: Simon & Schuster.

BROWNELL, K. D. (1982). Obesity: Behavioral treatments for a serious, prevalent, and refractory disorder. In R. K. Goodstein (Ed.), *Eating and weight disorders: Current developments.* New York: Springer.

BRUNER, J. B. (1983). *In Search of mind.* New York: Harper & Row.

BRUNER, J. S. (1975). The ontogenesis of speech acts. *Journal of Child Language, 2,* 1–19.

BRUNER, J. S. (1978a). Acquiring the uses of language. *Canadian Journal of Psychology, 32,* 204–218.

BRUNER, J. S. (1978b). Learning the mother tongue. *Human Nature, 1,* 42–48.

BUCHSBAUM, M. S., and HAIER, R. J. (1978). Biological homogeneity, symptom heterogeneity and the diagnosis of schizophrenia. *Schizophrenia Bulletin, 4,* 473–475.

BUCHSBAUM, M. S., and HAIER, R. J. (1983). Psychopathology: Biological approaches. *Annual Review of Psychology, 34,* 401–430.

BUCK, R., MILLER, R. E., and CAUL, W. F. (1974). Sex, personality, and physiological variables in the communication of affect via facial expression. *Journal of Personality and Social Psychology, 30,* 587–596.

BULLOUGH, J. L. (1981). Age at menarche: A misunderstanding. *Science, 213 (17),* 365–366.

BURGESS, A. W., and HOLMSTROM, L. L. (1974). Rape trauma syndrome. *American Journal of Psychiatry, 131,* 981–986.

BURKS, B. (1938). On the relative contributions of nature and nurture to average group differences in intelligence. *Proceedings of the National Academy of Sciences, 24,* 276–282.

BURKS, B. S. (1928). The relative influence of nature and nurture upon mental development: A comparative study of foster parent–foster child resemblance and true parents–true child resemblance. *27th yearbook of the National Society for the Study of Education, 27 (1),* 219–316.

BURNSTEIN, E. (1983). Persuasion as argument processing. In M. Brandstatter, J. H. Davis, and G. Stocker-Kreichgauer (Eds.), *Group decision processes.* London: Academic Press.

BUSS, A. H., and PLOMIN, R. (1984). *Temperament.* Hillsdale, N.J.: Erlbaum.

BUTLER, R. A. (1954). Curiosity in monkeys. *Scientific American, 190,* 70–75.

BUTLER, S., (1978). *Conspiracy of silence.* San Francisco: New Glide Publications.

BYRNE, D. (1971). *The attraction paradigm.* New York: Academic Press.

BYRNE, D., and CLORE, G. L. (1970). A reinforcement model of evaluative responses. *Personality: An International Journal, 1,* 103–128.

CACIOPPO, J. T., and PETTY, R. E. (Eds.) (1983). *Social psychophysiology: A sourcebook.* New York: Guilford Press.

CADORET, R. J., and CAIN, C. (1981). Environmental and genetic factors in predicting adolescent antisocial behavior in adoptees. *The Psychiatric Journal of University of Ottawa, 6* (4), 220–225.

CADORET, R. J., and WINOKUR, G. (1975). X-linkage in manic-depressive illness. *Annual Review of Medicine, 26,* 21–25.

CAIRNS, H. (1952). Disturbances of consciousness in lesions of the mid-brain and diencephalon. *Brain, 75,* 107–114.

CALHOUN, J. B. (1962). Population density and social pathology. *Scientific American, 206,* 139–148.

CAMPBELL, E. A., COPE, S. J., and TEASDALE, J. D. (1983). Social factors and affective disorder: An investigation of Brown and Harris' model. *British Journal of Psychiatry, 143,* 548–553.

CAMPIONE, J. C., BROWN, A. L., and FERRARA, R. A. (1982). Mental retardation and intelligence. In R. J. Sternberg (Ed.), *Handbook of Human Intelligence.* Cambridge: Cambridge University Press.

CAMPOS, J. J., LANGER, A., and KROWITZ, A. (1970). Cardiac responses on the visual cliff in prelocomotor human infants. *Science, 170,* 195–196.

CANTOR, G. N., DUNLAP, L. L., and RETTIE, C. S. (1982). Effects of reception and discovery instruction on kindergartners' performance on probability tasks. *American Educational Research Journal. 19,* 453–463.

CARLSON, R. F., KINCORD, J. P., LANCE, S., and HODGEON, T. (1976). Spontaneous use of mnemonics and grade point average. *Journal of Psychology, 92,* 117–122.

CARMICHAEL, L., HOGAN, H. P., and WALTER, A. A. (1932). An experimental study of the effect of language on the reproduction of visually perceived form. *Journal of Experimental Psychology, 15,* 73–86.

CARPENTER, W. T., JR., and HEINRICHS, D. W. (1983). Early intervention, time-limited, targeted pharmacotherapy of schizophrenia. *Schizophrenia Bulletin, 9,* 533–542.

CARR, E. G., and LOVAAS, O. I. (1983). Contingent electric shock as a treatment for severe behavioral problems. In S. Axelrod and J. Apsche (Eds.), *The effects of punishment on human behavior.* New York: Academic Press.

CARROLL, J. B. (1982). The measurement of intelligence. In R. T. Sternberg (Ed.), *Handbook of Human Intelligence.* Cambridge, England: Cambridge University Press.

CARRON, A. V. (1984). Cohesion in sport teams. In J. M. Silva and R. S. Weinberg (Eds.), *Psychological foundations of sport.* Champaign, Ill.: Human Kinetics.

CARRON, A. V., and CHELLADURAI, P. (1982). Cohesiveness, coach-athlete compatibility, participation, orientation, and their relationship to relative performance and satisfaction. Paper presented at North American Society for the Psychology of Sport and Physical Activity Conference, College Park, Maryland.

CARTWRIGHT, R. C. (1977). *Night life: Explorations in dreaming.* Englewood Cliffs, N.J.: Prentice-Hall.

CAVANAUGH, J. C., and PERLMUTTER, M. (1982). Metamory: A critical examination. *Child Development, 53,* 11–28.

CENTERS FOR DISEASE CONTROL (1984). Update: Acquired immune deficiency syndrome (AIDS), United States. *Morbidity and Mortality Weekly Report, 32,* (52), 688–691.

CHANDLER, M. J. (1973). Egocentrism and antisocial behavior: The assessment and training of social perspective taking skills. *Developmental Psychology, 9,* 326–332.

CHAPMAN, J. (1966). The early symptoms of schizophrenia. *British Journal of Psychiatry, 112,* 225–251.

CHARGOFF, E. (1976). On the dangers of genetic meddling. *Science, 192,* 938.

CHASE, W. G., and SIMON, H. A. (1973). The mind's eye in chess. In W. G. Chase (Ed.), *Visual information processing.* New York: Academic Press.

CHASE, M. H., and WEITZMAN, E. D., (Eds.) (1983). *Sleep disorders: Basic and clinical research.* New York: Spectrum.

CHELLADURAI, P. (1984). Leadership in sports. In J. M. Silva and R. S. Weinberg (Eds.), *Psychological foundations of sports.* Champaign, Ill.: Human Kinetics.

CHELLADURAI, P., and SALEH, S. D. (1978). Preferred

leadership in sports. *Canadian Journal of Applied Sport Science*, 3, 85–92.

CHELLADURAI, P., and SALEH, S. D. (1980). Dimensions of leader behavior in sports: Development of a leadership scale. *Journal of Sport Psychology*, 2, 34–45.

CHEN, A., DWORKIN, S., and BLOOMQUIST, D. S. (1981). Cortical power spectrum analysis of hypnotic pain control in surgery. *International Journal of Neuroscience*, 13, 127–134.

CHESS, S. (1979). Developmental theory revisited. *Canadian Journal of Psychiatry*, 24, 101–112.

CHESS, S., and THOMAS, A. (1983). Infant bonding: Mystique and reality. *American Journal of Orthopsychiatry*, 52, (2), 213–222.

CHI, M. T. H., FELTOVICH, P. S., and GLASER, R. (1981). Categorization and representation of physics problems by experts and novices. *Cognitive Science*, 5, 121–152.

CHOMSKY, N. (1968). *Language and mind*. New York: Harcourt Brace Jovanovich.

CHOMSKY, N. (1975). *Reflections on language*. New York: Pantheon Books.

CHRISTMAN, R. J. (1979). *Sensory experience*. (2nd ed.). New York: Harper & Row.

CIALDINI, R. B., BAUMANN, D. J., and KENRICK, D. T. (1981). Insights from sadness: A three-step model of the development of altruism as hedonism. *Developmental Review*, 1, 207–223.

CLARK, E. V. (1983). Meanings and concepts. In P. H. Mussen (Ed.), *Handbook of Child Psychology*. New York: Wiley.

CLARK, H. H., and CARLSON, T. B. (1981). Context for comprehension. In J. Long and A. Baddeley (Eds.), *Attention and performance IX*. Hillsdale, N.J.: Erlbaum.

CLARK, H. H., and CLARK, E. V. (1977). *Psychology and language*. New York: Harcourt Brace Jovanovich.

CLARK, K., and CLARK, M. (1947). Racial identification and preference in Negro children. In T. Newcomb and E. Hartley (Eds.), *Readings in social psychology*. New York: Holt, Rinehart and Winston.

CLARKE, A. M., and CLARKE, A. D. B. (1976). *Early experience: Myth and evidence*. New York: Free Press.

COE, W. C. (1980). Expectations, hypnosis, and suggestion in change. In F. H. Kanfer and A. P. Goldstein (Eds.), *Helping people change: A textbook of methods*. (2nd ed.). New York: Pergamon Press.

COHEN, G. (1983). *The psychology of cognition*. New York: Academic Press.

COHEN, L. B. (1979). Our developing knowledge of infant perception. *American Psychologist*, 34, 894–899.

COHEN, S. (1980). Coca paste and freebase: New fashions in cocaine use. *Drug Abuse and Alcoholism Newsletter*, 9, (3).

COHEN, S., EVANS, G. W., KRANTZ, D. S., and STOKOLS, D. (1980). Physiological, motivational, and cognitive effects of aircraft noise on children: Moving from the laboratory to the field. *American Psychologist*, 35, 231–243.

COHEN, S., EVANS, G. W., KRANTZ, D. S., STOKOLS, D., and KELLY, S. (1981). Aircraft noise and children: Longitudinal and cross-sectional evidence on adaptation to noise and the effectiveness of noise abatement. *Journal of Personality and Social Psychology*, 40, 331–345.

COLBY, A., KOHLBERG, L., GIEBS, J., CANDEE, D., SPEICHER-DUBIN, B., KAUFFMAN, K., HEWER, A., and POWER, C. (1983). *Measurement of moral judgments: A manual and its results*. New York: Cambridge University Press.

COLBY, K. M. (1977). On the way people and models do it. *Perspectives in Biology and Medicine*, 21, 99–104.

COLLIGAN, M. J., FROCKT, W., and TASTO, D. L. (1978). Frequency of sickness, absence, and worksite clinic visits and function of shift. *Journal of Environmental Pathology*, 2, 125–148.

COLLINS, A. M., and QUILLIAN, M. R. (1969). Retrieval time from semantic memory. *Journal of Verbal Learning and Verbal Behavior*, 2, 240–247.

COMMONS, M. L., RACHLIN, H., and NEVIN, J. A. (Eds.) (1984). *Quantitative analyses of behavior*. Vol. 5, *Reinforcement value: The effect of delay and intervening events*. Cambridge, Mass.: Ballinger.

COOK, T. D., and CAMPBELL, D. T. (1979). *Quasiexperimentation*. Chicago: Rand McNally.

COOPER, J. E., KENDALL, R. E., GURLAND, B. J., SHARPE, L., COPELAND, J. R. M., and SIMON, R. J. (1972). *Psychiatric diagnoses in New York and London: A comparative study of mental hospital admissions* (Maudsley Monograph No. 20). London: Oxford University Press.

Costantini, E., and Craik, K. H. (1980). Personality and politicians: California party leaders, 1960–1976. *Journal of Personality and Social Psychology, 38,* 641–661.

Cowen, E. L. (1982). Help is where you find it: Four informational helping groups. *American Psychologist, 37,* 385–395.

Coyne, J. C., Kahn, J., and Gotlib, I. H. (in press). Depression. In T. Jacobs (Ed.), *Family interaction and psychopathology.* New York: Plenum Press.

Craik, F. I. M. (1977). Age differences in human memory. In J. E. Birrer and K. W. Schaie (Eds.) *Handbook of the psychology of aging.* New York: Van Nostrand and Reinhold.

Craik, F. I. M. (1981). Encoding and retrieval effects in human memory: A partial review. In J. Long and A. Baddeley (Eds.). *Attention and performance IX.* Hillsdale, N.J.: Erlbaum.

Craik, F. I. M., and Lockhart, R. S. (1972). Levels of processing: A framework for memory research. *Journal of Verbal Learning and Verbal Behavior, 11,* 671–684.

Cronbach, L. J. (1984). *Essentials of psychological testing.* (4th ed.). New York: Harper & Row.

Crow, T. J. (1980). Molecular pathology of schizophrenia: More than one disease process? *British Medical Journal, 280,* 66–68.

Crowe, R. (1974). An adoption study of antisocial personality. *Archives of General Psychiatry, 31,* 785–791.

Crowe, R. R. (1984). Electroconvulsive therapy—a current perspective. *New England Journal of Medicine, 311,* 163–167.

Curtiss, S. (1977). *Genie: A psycholinguistic study of a modern-day "wild child."* New York: Academic Press.

Damon, W. (1977). *The social world of the child.* San Francisco: Jossey-Bass.

Darwin, C. (1955) (originally published 1872). *The expression of emotions in man and animals.* New York: Philosophical Library.

Davidson, R. J. (1978). Specificity and patterning in biobehavioral systems: Implications for behavior change. *American Psychologist, 33,* 430–436.

Davitz, J. R. (1970). A dictionary and grammar of emotion. In M. Arnold (Ed.), *Feelings and emotions.* New York: Academic Press.

de Araujo, G., van Arsdel, P. P., Jr., Holmes, T. H., and Dudley, D. L. (1973). Life change, coping ability, and chronic intrinsic asthma. *Journal of Psychosomatic Research, 17,* 359–363.

Deaux, K., and Wrightsman, L. S. (1984). *Social psychology in the 80s.* (4th ed.). Monterey, Calif.: Brooks/Cole.

deCharms, R., and Moeller, G. H. (1962). Values expressed in American children's readers: 1800 to 1950. *Journal of Abnormal and Social Psychology, 64,* 135–142.

Dekker, E., and Groen, J. (1956). Reproducible psychogenic attacks of asthma. *Journal of Psychosomatic Research, 1,* 56–67.

Delgado, J. M. R. (1967). Social rank and radio-stimulated aggressiveness in monkeys. *Journal of Nervous and Mental Disease, 144,* 383–390.

DeMaris, A., and Leslie, G. R. (1984). Cohabitation with the future spouse: Its influence upon marital satisfaction and communication. *Journal of Marriage and the Family, 46,* 77–84.

Dement, W. C. (1974). *Some must watch while some must sleep.* San Francisco: Freeman.

Dement, W. C. (1983). A life in sleep research. In M. H. Chase and E. D. Weitzman (Eds.), *Sleep disorders: Basic and clinical research.* New York: Spectrum.

Derliga, V. J., and Chaikin, A. L. (1975). *Sharing intimacy: What we reveal to others and why.* Englewood Cliffs, N.J.: Prentice-Hall.

De Valois, R. L., and De Valois, K. K. (1980). Spatial vision. *Annual Review of Psychology, 31,* 309–341.

Dewald, P. A. (1972). *The psychoanalytic process: A case illustration.* New York: Basic Books.

Diamond, M., and Karlen, A. (1980). *Sexual decisions.* Boston: Little, Brown.

Diener, E. (1980). Deindividuation: The absence of self-awareness and self-regulation in group members. In P. B. Paulus (Ed.), *The psychology of group influence.* Hillsdale, N.J.: Erlbaum.

Diener, E. (1984). Subjective well-being. *Psychological Bulletin, 95,* 542–575.

Dienstbier, R. A. (1979). Attraction increases and decreases as a function of emotion-attribution and appropriate social cues. *Motivation and Emotion, 3,* 201–213.

Dingledine, R. (Ed.) (1984). *Brain slices.* New York: Plenum.

Dinner, D. S., Luders, H., Morris, H. H., and Lesser, R. P. (1984). Polysomnograms before and after uvulo-palato-pharyngoplasty for obstructive sleep apnea. *Sleep Research, 13,* 139.

Dion, K. (1972). Physical attractiveness and the evaluation of children's transgressions. *Journal of Personality and Social Psychology, 24,* 207–213.

DION, K. K. (1981). Physical attractiveness, sex roles and heterosexual attraction. In M. Cook (Ed.), *The bases of human sexual attraction*. London: Academic Press.

DION, K. K., BERSCHEID, E., and WALSTER, E. (1972). What is beautiful is good. *Journal of Personality and Social Psychology, 24*, 285–290.

DIXON, N. F. (1971). *Subliminal perception: The nature of a controversy*. London: McGraw-Hill.

DIXON, N. F. (1981). *Preconscious processing*. New York: Wiley.

DOANE, J. A., WEST, K. L., GOLDSTEIN, M. J., RODNICK, E. H., and JONES, J. E. (1981). Parental affective style and communication deviance as predictors of subsequent schizophrenia spectrum disorders in vulnerable adolescents. *Archives of General Psychiatry, 38*, 679–685.

DOBSON, V., TELLER, D. Y., LEE, C. P., and WADE, B. (1978). A behavioral method for efficient screening of visual acuity in young infants. *Investigative Ophthalmology and Visual Science, 17*, 1142–1150.

DOLLARD, J., and MILLER, N. (1950). *Personality and psychotherapy*. New York: McGraw-Hill.

DONCHIN, E. (Ed.) (1984). *Cognitive psychophysiology: Event-related potentials and the study of cognition*. Hillsdale, N.J.: Erlbaum.

DONNERSTEIN, E., and BERKOWITZ, L. (1981). Victim reactions in aggressive erotic films as a factor in violence against women. *Journal of Personality and Social Psychology, 41*, 710–724.

DOOLING, D. J., and CHRISTIAANSEN, R. E. (1977). Episodic and semantic aspects of memory for prose. *Journal of Experimental Psychology: Human Learning and Memory, 3*, 428–436.

DOWNEY, L. (1980). Intergenerational change in sex behavior: A belated look at Kinsey's males. *Archives of Sexual Behavior, 4*, 267–317.

DRACHMAN, D., DE CARUFEL, A., and INSKO, C. A. (1978). The extra credit effect in interpersonal attraction. *Journal of Experimental Social Psychology, 14*, 458–465.

DUDA, R. O., and SHORTLIFFE, E. H. (1983). Expert systems research. *Science, 220*, 261–268.

DUEHRSSEN, A., and JORSWIEK, E. (1965). An empirical and statistical inquiry into the therapeutic potential of psychoanalytic treatment. *Der Nervenarzt, 36*, 166–169.

DUGUAY, M., GAGNON, I., DEMERS, L., and MONTPLAISIR, J. (1984). Effect of autogenic training and psychomotor relaxation therapy on insomnia. *Sleep Research, 13*, 140.

DUNCKER, K. (1945). On problem solving. *Psychological Monographs, 58*, 270.

DURKIN, K. (1983). Language development—past, present, and later. *Bulletin of the British Psychological Society, 36*, 193–196.

EAGLY, A. H., and STEFFEN, V. J. (1984). Gender stereotypes stem from the distribution of women and men into social roles. *Journal of Personality and Social Psychology, 46*, 735–754.

EDWARDS, A. E. (1962). A demonstration of the long-term retention of a conditioned galvanic skin response. *Psychosomatic Medicine, 24*, 459–463.

EGELAND, J. A. (1983). Bipolarity: The iceberg of affective disorders. *Comprehensive Psychiatry, 24*, 337–343.

EIBL-EIBESFELDT, I. (1973). The expressive behavior of the deaf-and-blind-born. In M. von Cranach and I. Vine (Eds.), *Social communication and movement*. New York: Academic Press, 1973.

EICH, J. E. (1980). The cue-dependent nature of state-dependent retrieval. *Memory and Cognitions, 8*, 157–173.

EIMAS, P. (1976). Speech perception in infancy. Paper presented at the International Congress of Psychology, Paris.

EIMAS, P., SIQUELAND, E. R., JUSCZYK, P., and VIGORITO, J. (1971). Speech perception in infants. *Science, 171*, 303–306.

EINOLANDER, J. C. (1976). Vandalism at Red Rock. In S. Alfano and A. Magill (Eds.), *Vandalism and outdoor recreation: Symposium proceedings*. USDA Forest Service Technical Report, PSW-17.

EISELEY, L. (1946). *The immense journey*. New York: Random House.

EKMAN, P. (Ed.) (1982). *Emotion in the human face.* (2nd ed.). New York: Cambridge University Press.

EKMAN, P., FRIESEN, W. V., and ELLSWORTH, P. (1982). What are the relative contributions of facial behavior and contextual information to the judgment of emotion? In P. Ekman (Ed.), *Emotion in the human face* (2nd ed.). New York: Cambridge University Press.

ELIOT, R. S., and BUELL, J. C. (1983). The role of the CNS in cardiovascular disorder. *Hospital Practice, 18* (5), 189–193, 197–199.

ELLIS, A. (1962). *Reason and emotion in psychotherapy.* Secausus, N.J.: Stuart.

ELLIS, A. (1970). Rational-emotive therapy. In L. Hersher (Ed.), *Four psychotherapies.* New York: Appleton-Century-Crofts.

ELLIS, A. (1973). *Humanistic psychotherapy.* New York: McGraw-Hill.

ELLIS, A., and GRIEGER, R. (Eds.) (1977). *Handbook of rational-emotive therapy.* New York: Springer.

ELTON, D., STANLEY, G., and BURROWS, G. (1983). *Psychological control of pain.* New York: Grune & Stratton.

ENDLER, N. S. (1982). *Holiday of darkness.* New York: Wiley-Interscience.

EPSTEIN, A. N. (1982). The physiology of thirst. In D. W. Pfaff (Ed.), *The physiological mechanisms of motivation.* New York: Springer-Verlag.

EPSTEIN, M. L. (1980). The relationship of mental imagery and mental rehearsal to performance of a motor task. *Journal of Sport Psychology, 2,* 211–220.

EPSTEIN, R., LANZA, R. P., and SKINNER, B. F. (1980). Symbolic communication between two pigeons. *[Columbia livia domestica]. Science, 2,* 220–221.

ERIKSON, E. (1963). *Childhood and society.* New York: Norton.

ERIKSON, E. (1974). *Dimensions of a new identity: The 1973 Jefferson lectures in the humanities.* New York: Norton.

ERLE, F. J. (1981). *Leadership in competitive and recreational sport.* Master's thesis, University of Western Ontario.

ESTES, W. K. (1982). Learning, memory and intelligence. In R. J. Sternberg (Ed.), *Handbook of human intelligence.* Cambridge, England: Cambridge University Press.

EVANS, G. W. (1979). Behavioral and physiological consequences of crowding in humans. *Journal of Applied Social Psychology, 9,* 27–46.

EVANS, M. B., and PAUL, G. L. (1970). Effects of hypnotically suggested analgesia on physiological and subjective responses to cold stress. *Journal of Consulting and Clinical Psychology, 35,* 362–371.

EVANS, R. I., ROZELLE, R. M., LASATER, T. M., DEMBROWSKI, T. M., and ALLEN, B. P. (1970). Fear arousal, persuasion, and actual vs. implied behavioral change: New perspectives utilizing a real-life dental hygiene program. *Journal of Personality and Social Psychology, 16,* 220–227.

EVERETT, P. B. (1977). *A behavior science approach to transportation systems management.* Unpublished manuscript, Pennsylvania State University.

EWIN, D. M. (1984). Hypnosis in surgery and anesthesia. In W. C. Wester and A. H. Smith (Eds.), *Clinical hypnosis: A multidisciplinary approach.* Philadelphia: Lippincott.

EYER, J., and STERLING, P. (1973). *Work in America.* Cambridge, Mass.: MIT Press.

EYSENCK, H. J. (1952). The effects of psychotherapy: An evaluation. *Journal of Consulting Psychology, 16,* 319–324.

FAGAN, J. F., and McGRATH, S. K. (1981). Infant recognition memory and later intelligence. *Intelligence, 5,* 121–130.

FALLOON, I. R. H., and LIBERMAN, R. P. (1983). Interactions between drug and psychosocial therapy in schizophrenia. *Schizophrenia Bulletin, 9(4),* 543–554.

FANSELOW, M. S. (1984). Shock-induced analgesia on the formalin test: Effects of shock severity, naloxone, hypophysectomy, and associative variables. *Behavioral Neuroscience, 98,* 79–95.

FARRELL, M. P., and ROSENBERG, S. D. (1981). *Men at midlife.* Boston: Auburn House.

FARRELL, P. A. (1985). Exercise and endorphins—male responses. *Medicine and Science in Sports and Exercise, 17,* 89–93.

FERBER, P. (Ed.) (1974). *Mountaineering: The freedom of the hills.* (3rd ed.). Seattle: The Mountaineers.

FERNALD, A. (1979). Four month olds prefer to listen to "motherese." Paper presented at the Society for Research in Child Development, San Francisco.

FERNALD, A., and KUHL, P. (1981). Fundamental frequency as an acoustic determinant of infant preference for "motherese." Paper presented at the Society for Research in Child Development, Boston.

FERSTER, C. B., and SKINNER, B. F. (1957). *Schedules of reinforcement.* Englewood Cliffs, N.J.: Prentice-Hall.

FESHBACH, N. D. (1978). Studies of empathetic behavior in children. In B. A. Maher (Ed.), *Progress in experimental personality research,* Vol. 8. New York: Academic Press.

FESHBACH, N. D., and FESHBACH, S. (1982). Empathy training and the regulation of aggression: Potentialities and limitations. *Academic Psychology Bulletin, 4,* 399–413.

FESTINGER, L., and CARLSMITH, L. M. (1959). Cognitive consequences of forced compliance. *Journal of Abnormal and Social Psychology, 58,* 203–210.

FESTINGER, L., PEPITONE, A., and NEWCOMB, T. (1952). Some consequences of deindividuation in a group. *Journal of Abnormal and Social Psychology*, 47, 382–389.

FESTINGER, L., SCHACHTER, S., and BACK, K. (1950). *Social pressures in informal groups: A study of a housing community*. New York: Harper & Row.

FIEDLER, F. E. (1967). *A theory of leadership effectiveness*. New York: McGraw-Hill.

FIEDLER, F. E. (1978). The contingency model and the dynamics of the leadership process. In L. Berkowitz (Ed.), *Advances in experimental and social psychology*, Vol. 2. New York: Academic Press.

FIELDS, H. L. (1978). Secrets of the placebo. *Psychology Today*, 12, 172.

FINK, M. K. (1977). Myths of "shock therapy." *American Journal of Psychiatry*, 134, 991–996.

FISHBEIN, M., and AJZEN, I. (1975). *Belief, attitude, and behavior: An introduction to theory and research*. Reading, Mass.: Addison-Wesley.

FISHER, D., and BYRNE, D. (1978). Sex differences in response to erotica? Love versus lust. *Journal of Personality and Social Psychology*, 36, 117–125.

FISHER, J. D., and BARON, R. M. (1982). An equity-based model of vandalism. *Population and Environment*, 5, 182–200.

FISHER, J. D., BELL, P. A., and BAUM, A. (1984). *Environmental psychology*. (2nd ed.). New York: Holt, Rinehart, and Winston.

FISHER, S. (1984). *Stress and the perception of control*. Hillsdale, N.J.: Erlbaum.

FISKE, S. T., and TAYLOR, S. E. (1984). *Social cognition*. Reading, Mass.: Addison-Wesley.

FLAVELL, J. H. (1976). Metacognitive aspects of problem solving. In L. G. Resnick (Ed.), *The nature of intelligence*. Hillsdale, N.J.: Erlbaum.

FLEMING, J. F. (1974). Field report: The state of the apes. *Psychology Today*, 7, 31–38.

FLOOD, J. F., LANDRY, D. W., and JARVIK, M. I. (1981). Cholinergic receptor interactions and their effects on long-term memory processing. *Brain Research*, 215, 177–185.

FLYNN, J. P. (1975). Experimental analysis of aggression and its neural basis. In J. P. Flynn (Ed.), *Advances in behavioral biology, the neurophysiology of aggression*. New York: Academic Press.

FLYNN, J. R. (1984). The mean IQ of Americans: Massive gains 1932 to 1978. *Psychological Bulletin*, 95, 29–51.

FOWLER, J. W., and PETERSON, P. L. (1981). Increasing reading persistence and altering attributional style of learned helplessness in children. *Journal of Educational Psychology*, 73, 251–260.

FOX, J. L. (1983). Memories are made of this. *Science*, 222, 1318.

FRANK, E., ANDERSON, C., and RUBINSTEIN, D. (1978). Frequency of sexual dysfunction in "normal" couples. *New England Journal of Medicine*, 299, 111–115.

FRANKENBURG, W. K., and DODDS, J. B. (1967). The Denver Developmental Screening Test. *Journal of Pediatrics*, 71, 181–191 (Fig. 12.5).

FREAN, J. F. (1982). Infant memory. In T. M. Field, A. Huston, H. C. Quay, L. Troll, and G. E. Finley, *Review of human development*. New York: Wiley.

FREDERIKSEN, N. (1984). Implications of cognitive theory for instruction in problem solving. *Review of Educational Research*, 54, 313–407.

FRERICHS, R. R., ANESHENSEL, C. S., and CLARK, V. A. (1981). Prevalence of depression in Los Angeles County. *American Journal of Epidemiology*, 113, 691–699.

FREUD, S. (1917/1957). Mourning and melancholia. In J. Stachey (Ed.), *The standard edition of the complete psychological works of Sigmund Freud*, 14. London: Hogarth.

FREUD, S. (1957) (originally published 1914). On the history of the psychoanalytic movement—papers on metapsychology and other works. In J. Strachey (Ed.), *The standard edition of the complete psychological works of Sigmund Freud*, Vol. 14. London: Hogarth Press.

FREUD, S. (1950a) (originally published 1924). *Collected papers, Vol. 2*. London: Hogarth Press.

FREUD, S. (1950b). (originally published 1909). *Selected papers*. In J. Strachey (Ed.), *The standard edition of the complete psychological works of Sigmund Freud*, Vol. 3. London: Hogarth Press.

FRIED, R., and BERKOWITZ, L. (1979). Music hath charms . . . and can influence helpfulness. *Journal of Applied Social Psychology*, 9, 199–208.

FRIEDHOFF, A. S. (1983). A diology for developing novel drugs for the treatment of schizophrenia. *Schizophrenia Bulletin*, 9(4), 555–562.

FRIEDMAN, M., and ROSENMAN, R. H. (1974). *Type A behavior and your heart.* New York: Knopf.

FRIEZE, I. H., PARSONS, J. E., JOHNSON, B. P., RUBLE, D. N., and ZELLMAN, G. L. (1979). *Women and sex roles: A social psychological perspective.* New York: Norton.

FRISBY, J. P. (1980). *Seeing: Illusion, brain, and mind.* Oxford, England: Oxford University Press.

FRODI, A. N., LAMB, M. E., LEAVITT, L. A., DONOVAN, W. L., NEFF, C., and SHERRY, D. (1978). Fathers' and mothers' responses to the faces and cries of normal and premature infants. *Developmental Psychology, 14,* 190–198.

FROMM, E. (1960). Psychoanalysis and Zen Buddhism. In D. T. Suzuki, E. Fromm, and R. DeMartino (Eds.), *Zen Buddhism and psychoanalysis.* New York: Grove Press.

FULLER, B. (1967). Man with a chronofile. *Saturday Review,* April, pp. 14–18.

GAENSBAUER, T. J. (1982). Regulation of emotional expression in infants from two contrasting caretaking environments. *Journal of the American Academy of Child Psychiatry, 21,* 163–170.

GAGNON, J. (1965). Female child victims of sex offenses. *Social Problems, 13,* 176–192.

GALANTER, E. (1962). Contemporary psychophysics. In R. Brown and others (Eds.), *New directions in psychology.* New York: Holt, Rinehart and Winston.

GALLE, O. R., and GOVE, W. R. (1979). Crowding and behavior in Chicago, 1940–1970. In J. R. Aiello and A. Baum (Eds.), *Residential crowding and design.* New York: Plenum.

GALLUP, G. G., JR. (1979). Self-awareness in primates. *American Scientist, 67,* 417–421.

GARCIA, J., McGOWAN, B. K., and GREEN, K. F. (1972). Biological constraints on conditioning. In A. H. Block and W. F. Prokasy (Eds.), *Classical conditioning: II. Current theory and research.* New York: Appleton-Century-Crofts.

GARDNER, H. (1983). *Frames of mind.* New York: Basic Books.

GAREY, R. E.(1979). PCP (Phencyclidine): An update. *Journal of Psychedelic Drugs, 11,* 265–275.

GARFINKEL, P. E., and GARNER, D. M. (1982). *Anorexia nervosa: A multidimensional perspective.* New York: Brunner/Mazel.

GARMEZY, N. (1974). Children at risk: The search for the antecedents of schizophrenia: I. Conceptual models and research methods. *Schizophrenia Bulletin, 9,* 55–125.

GARMEZY, N. (1976). Vulnerable and invulnerable children: Theory, research and intervention. Master lecture on developmental psychology, Washington, D.C. American Psychology Association (No. 1337).

GARNER, D. M., and GARFINKEL, P. E. (1984). *Handbook of psychotherapy for anorexia nervosa and bulimia.* New York: Guilford Press.

GATCHEL, R. J., and BAUM, A. (1983). *An introduction to health psychology.* Reading, Mass.: Addison-Wesley.

GAZZANIGA, M. S. (1967). The split brain in man. *Scientific American, 217,* 24–29.

GAZZANIGA, M. S. (1983). Right hemisphere language following brain bisection: A 20-year perspective. *American Psychologist, 38,* 525–537.

GAZZANIGA, M. S., and SMYLIE, C. S. (1983). Facial recognition and brain asymmetries: Clues to underlying mechanisms. *Annals of Neurology, 13,* 536–540.

GAZZANIGA, M. S., STEEN, D., and VOLPE, B. T. (1979). *Functional neuroscience.* New York: Harper & Row.

GEBHARD, P. H., GAGNON, J. H., POMEROY, W. B., and CHRISTENSON, C. V. (1965). *Sex offenders: An analysis of types.* New York: Harper & Row.

GEEN, R. G., BEATTY, W. W., and ARKIN, R. M. (1984). *Human motivation: Physiological, behavioral, and social approaches.* Boston: Allyn and Bacon.

GEER, J., HERMAN, J., and LEITENBERG, H. (1984). *Human sexuality.* Englewood Cliffs, N.J.: Prentice-Hall.

GEISELMAN, R. E., and BJORK, R. A. (1980). Primary versus secondary rehearsal in imagined voices: Differential effects on recognition. *Cognitive Psychology, 12,* 188–205.

GELLER, E. S., WINNETT, R. A., and EVERETT, P. B. (1982). *Preserving the environment: New strategies for behavior change.* Elmsford, N.Y.: Pergamon.

GEORGE, C., and MAIN, M. (1979). Social interactions of young abused children: Approach, avoidance, and aggression. *Child Development, 50,* 306–318.

GEORGESON, M. (1979). Spatial fourier analysis and human vision. In N. S. Sutherland (Ed.), *Tutorial essays in psychology: A guide to recent advances,* Vol. 2. Hillsdale, N.J.: Erlbaum.

GERGEN, K. L., GERGEN, M., and METER, K. (1972). Individual orientations to prosocial behavior. *Journal of Social Issues, 8,* 105–130.

GERON, M. E., and CADORET, R. J. (1977). Genetic aspects of manic-depressive disease in family practice. *Journal of Family Practice, 4,* 453–456.

GIBSON, E. J., and WALK, R. D. (1960). The "visual cliff." *Scientific American, 202,* 64–71.

GILHOOLY, K. J. (1982). *Thinking: Directed, undirected, and creative.* New York: Academic Press.

GILL, D. L. (1984). Individual and group performance in sport. In J. M. Silva and R. S. Weinberg (Eds.), *Psychological foundations of sport.* Champaign, Ill.: Human Kinetics.

GILLUND, G., and SHIFFRIN, R. M. (1984). A retrieval model for both recognition and recall. *Psychological Review, 91,* 1–67.

GLASS, D., and SINGER, J. (1972). *Urban stress: Experiments on noise and social stressors.* New York: Academic Press.

GLASS, G. V., and ELLETT, F. S. (1980). Evaluation research. *Annual Review of Psychology, 31,* 211–228.

GLUCKSBERG, S., and WEISBERG, R. W. (1966). Verbal behavior and problem solving: Some effects of labeling in a functional fixedness problem. *Journal of Experimental Psychology, 71,* 659–664.

GODDEN, D. R., and BADDELEY, A. D. (1975). Context-dependent memory in two natural environments: On land and under water. *British Journal of Psychology, 66,* 325–332.

GODDEN, D. R., and BADDELEY, A. D. (1980). When does context influence recognition? *British Jounral of Psychology, 71,* 99–104.

GOLDBERG, S. (1983). Parent-Infant Bonding: Another look. *Child Development, 54,* 1355–1382.

GOLDBERGER, L., and BREZNITZ, S. (Eds.) (1982). *Handbook of stress.* New York: Free Press.

GOLDSTEIN, E. B. (1984). *Sensation and perception.* Belmont, Calif.: Wadsworth.

GOLDSTEIN, G., and HERSEN, M. (Eds.) (1984). *Handbook of psychological assessment.* Elmsford, N.Y.: Pergamon Press.

GOLEMAN, D. J. (1977). *Varieties of the meditative experience.* New York: Dutton.

GOODHART, D. E. (1985). Some psychological effects associated with positive and negative thinking about stressful event outcomes: Was Pollyanna right? *Journal of Personality and Social Psychology, 48,* 216–232.

GORMAN, J. M., FYER, A. F., GLICKLICH, J., KING, D. L., and KLEIN, D. F. (1981). Mitral valve prolapse and panic disorders: Effect of imipramine. In Klein, D. F., and Rabkin, J. (Eds.), *Anxiety: New research and changing concepts.* New York: Raven Press.

GOTTESMAN, I. I. (1963). Heritability of personality: A demonstration. *Psychological Monographs, 77* (Whole No. 572).

GOTTESMAN, I. I. (1974). *Developmental genetics and ontogenetic psychology.* Minneapolis: University of Minnesota Press.

GREEN, R. (1974). *Sexual identity conflicts in children and adults.* New York: Basic Books.

GREENBERG, J., PYSZEZYNSKI, T., and SOLOMON, S. (1982). The self-serving attributional bias: Beyond self-presentation. *Journal of Experimental Social Psychology, 18,* 56–67.

GREENO, J. G. (1976). Indefinite goals in well-structured problems. *Psychological Review, 83,* 479–491.

GREENWALD, A. G. (1975). On the inconclusiveness of "crucial" cognitive tests of dissonance vs. self-perception theories. *Journal of Experimental Social Psychology, 11,* 490–499.

GREENWALD, A. G. (1980). The totalitarian ego: Fabrication and revision of personal history. *American Psychologist, 35,* 603–618.

GREGORY, R. L. (1966). *Eye and brain.* New York: McGraw-Hill.

GRIFFITT, W., and HATFIELD, E. (1985). *Human sexual behavior.* Glenview, Ill.: Scott, Foresman.

GRIMM, L. G. (1983). The relation between self-evaluation and self-reward: A test of Kanfer's self-regulation model. *Cognitive Therapy and Research, 7,* 245–250.

GRINKER, J. A. (1982). Physiological and behavioral basis of human obesity. In D. W. Pfaff (Ed.), *The physiological mechanisms of motivation.* New York: Springer-Verlag.

GROFFMAN, K. H. (1970). Life-span developmental psychology in Europe. In L. R. Goulet and P. B. Baltes (Eds.), *Life-span developmental psychology: Research and theory.* New York: Academic Press.

GROSS, A. E. (1978). The male role and heterosexual behavior. *Journal of Social Issues, 34,* 87–107.

GROSSBERG, J. M., and GRANT, B. (1978). Clinical psychophysics: Applications of ratio scaling and signal detection methods to research on pain, fear, drugs, and medical decision making. *Psychological Bulletin, 85,* 1154–1176.

GROTH, A. N. (1979). *Men who rape: The psychology of the offender.* New York: Plenum.

GUILLEMINAULT, C., ELDRIDGE, F. L., and DEMENT, W. C. (1973). Insomnia with sleep apnea: A new syndrome. *Science, 181,* 856–858.

GUNDERSON, J. G., SIEVER, L. J., and SPAULDING, E. (1983). The search for a schizotype. *Archives of General Psychiatry, 40,* 15–22.

GUNTER, B., BERRY, C., and CLIFFORD, B. (1982). Remembering broadcast news: The implications of experimental research for production technique. *Human Learning, 1,* 13–29.

HAAS, H., FINK, H., and HARTFELDER, G., (1959). Das placeboproblem (translation). *Psychopharmacology Service Center Bulletin, 2,* 1–65. (U.S. Public Health Service).

HACKER, H. M. (1981). Blabbermouths and clams: Sex differences in self-disclosure in same-sex and cross-sex friendship dyads. *Psychology of Women Quarterly, 5,* 385–401.

HAILMAN, J. P. (1982). Evolution and behavior: An iconoclastic view. In H. C. Plotkin (Ed.), *Learning development and culture: Essays in evolutionary epistemology.* London: Wiley.

HAMBLIN, R. L., BUCKHOLDT, D., FERRITOR, D., KOZLOFF, M., and BLACKWELL, L. (1971). *The humanization process: A social, behavioral analysis of children's problems.* New York: Wiley.

HAN, J. S., KAUFMAN, B. ALFIDI, R. J., YEUNG, H. N., BENSON, J. E., HAAGA, J. R., EL YOUSEF, S. J., CLAMPITT, M. E., BONSTELLE, C. T., and HUSS, R. (1984). Head trauma evaluated by magnetic resonance and computed tomography: A comparison. *Radiology, 150,* 71–77.

HANDSFIELD, H. H. (1984). Causes of acquired immune deficiency syndrome. *Journal of the American Medical Association, 251,* 341.

HANIN, I. (Ed.) (1984). *Dynamics of neurotransmitter function.* New York: Raven Press.

HARACZ, J. L. (1982). The dopamine hypotheses: An overview of studies with schizophrenic patients. *Schizophrenia Bulletin, 8,* 438–468.

HARKINS, S. G., and PETTY, R. E. (1982). Effects of task difficulty and task uniqueness on social loafing. *Journal of Personality and Social Psychology, 43,* 1214–1229.

HARLOW, H. F. (1950). Learning and satiation of response in intrinsically motivated complex puzzle performance by monkeys. *Journal of Comparative and Physiological Psychology, 43,* 289–294.

HARPER, R. M. (1983). Cardiorespiratory and state control in infants at risk for the sudden death syndrome. In

M. H. Chase and E. D. Weitzman (Eds.). *Sleep disorders: Basic and clinical research.* New York: Spectrum.

HARRIS, R. J. (1977). Comprehension of pragmatic implications in advertising. *Journal of Applied Psychology, 62,* 603–608.

HARROW, M., GRINKER, R. R. SILVERSTEIN, M. L., and HOLZMAN, P. (1978). Is modern-day schizophrenic outcome still negative? *American Journal of Psychiatry, 135,* 1156–1162.

HARTL, E. M., MONNELLY, E. P., and ELDERKIN, R. D. (1982). *Physique and delinquent behavior.* New York: Academic Press.

HARVEY, J. H., and WEARY, G. (1984). Current issues in attribution theory and research. *Annual review of psychology, 35,* 427–459.

HASSETT, J. (1978). Sex and smell. *Psychology Today, 12,* 40–45.

HASTORF, A., and CANTRIL, H. (1954). They saw a game: A case study. *Journal of Abnormal and Social Psychology, 49,* 129–134.

HATFIELD, E. (1983). What do women and men want from love and sex? In E. R. Allgeier and N. B. McCormick (Eds.), *Changing boundaries: Gender roles and sexual behavior.* Palo Alto, Calif.: Mayfield.

HEBB, D. O. (1949). *The organization of behavior.* New York: Wiley.

HECKHAUSEN, H. (1977). Achievement motivation and its constructs: A cognitive model. *Motivation and Emotion, 1,* 283–330.

HEIBY, E. M. (1983). Depression as a function of the interaction of self and environmentally controlled reinforcement. *Behavior Therapy, 14,* 430–433.

HEIDER, E. R., and OLIVIER, D. (1972). The structure of the color space in naming and memory for two languages. *Cognitive Psychology, 3,* 337–354.

HEIMAN, J. R., LoPICCOLO, I., and LoPICCOLO, J. (1976). *Becoming orgasmic.* Englewood Cliffs, N.J.: Prentice-Hall.

HEIMBERG, R. G., and BECKER, R. E. (1984). Comparative outcome research. In M. Hersen, L. Michelson, and A. S. Bellack, *Issues in psychotherapy research.* New York: Plenum.

HELLER, J., GROFF, B., and SOLOMON, S. (1977). Toward an understanding of crowding: The role of physical interaction. *Journal of Personality and Social Psychology, 35,* 183–190.

HENDERSON, N. D. (1982). Human behavior genetics. *Annual Review of Psychology, 33,* 403–440.

HERBERT, W. (1982). Sleeping pills and apnea linked in elderly. *Science, 121,* 421.

HERMAN, J. H., ELLMAN, S. J., and ROFFWARG, H P. (1978). The problem of NREM dream recall re-examined. In A. M. Arkin, J. S. Antrobus, and S. J. Ellman (Eds.), *The mind in sleep: Psychology and psychophysiology.* Hillsdale, N. J.: Erlbaum.

HEROLD, E. S., and WAY, L. (1983). Oral-genital sexual behavior in a sample of university females. *Journal of Sex Research, 19,* 327–338.

HERON, W. (1961). Cognitive and physiological effects of perceptual isolation. In P. Solomon and others (Eds.), *Sensory deprivation.* Cambridge, Mass.: Harvard University Press.

HETHERINGTON, E. M., COX, M., and COX, R. (1979). Play and social interaction in children following divorce. *Journal of Social Issues, 35 (4),* 26–49.

HIBLER, N. S. (1984). Investigative aspects of forensic hypnosis. In W. C. Webster and A. H. Smith (Eds.), *Clinical hypnosis: A multidisciplinary approach.* Philadelphia: Lippincott.

HIGGINS, E. T., and MCCANN, C. D. (1984). Social encoding and subsequent attitudes, impressions and memory: "Context-driven" and motivational aspects of processing. *Journal of Personality and Social Psychology, 47,* 26–39.

HILGARD, E. R. (1977). *Divided consciousness: Multiple controls in human thought and action.* New York: Wiley.

HILGARD, J. R. (1970). *Personality and hypnosis.* Chicago: University of Chicago Press.

HILL, C. T., RUBIN, Z., and PEPLAU, L. A. (1976). Breakups before marriage: The end of 103 affairs. *Journal of Social Issues, 32,* 147–168.

HILL, C. T., and STULL, D.E. (1981). Sex differences in effects of social and value similarity in same-sex friendship. *Journal of Personality and Social Psychology, 41,* 488–502.

HILLYARD, S. A., and KUTAS, M. (1983). Electrophysiology of cognitive processing. *Annual Review of Psychology, 34,* 33–61.

HINKEL, L. E., JR., WHITNEY, L. H., LEHMAN, E. W., DUNN, J., BENJAMIN, B., KING, R., PLAKUN, A., and FLEAHINGER, B. (1968). Occupation, education, and coronary heart disease. *Science, 161,* 238–246.

HINSLEY, D., HAYES, J. R., and SIMON, H. A. (1977). From words to equations: Meaning and representation in algebra word problems. In P. Carpenter and M. Just (Eds.), *Cognitive processes in comprehension.* Hillsdale, N.J.: Erlbaum.

HITE, S. (1976). *The Hite Report.* New York: Macmillan.

HITE, S. (1981). *The Hite Report on Male Sexuality.* New York: Knopf.

HOFMANN, A. (1980). *LSD, my problem child.* New York: McGraw-Hill.

HOLAHAN, C. K. (1984). Marital attitudes over 40 years: A longitudinal and cohort analysis. *Journal of Gerontology, 39,* 49–57.

HOLMES, D. S. (1984). Meditation and somatic arousal reduction: A review of the experimental evidence. *American Psychologist, 39,* 1–10.

HOLMES, M.R., and ST. LAWRENCE, J. S. (1983). Treatment of rape-induced trauma: Proposed behavioral conceptualization and review of the literature. *Clinical Psychology Review, 3,* 417–433.

HOLMES, T. H., and RAHE, R. H. (1967). The social readjustment rating scale. *Journal of Psychosomatic Research, 11,* 213–218.

HOLZMAN, P. S. (1978). Cognitive impairment and cognitive stability: Toward a theory of thought disorder. In G. Serban (Ed.), *Cognitive defects in the development of mental illness.* New York: Brunner/Mazel.

HONIG, B., DINUR, U., NAKANISHI, K., BALOUGH-NAIR, V., GAWINOWICZ, M. A., ARNABOLDI, M., and MOTTO, M. G. (1979). An external point-charge model for wavelength regulation in visual pigments. *Journal of the American Chemical Society, 101,* 7084–7086.

HORN, J. L., and CATTELL, R. B. (1966). Refinement and test of the theory of fluid and crystallized intelligence. *Journal of Educational Psychology, 57,* 253–276.

HORN, J. M., LOEHLIN, J. C., and WILLERMAN, L. (1979). Intellectual resemblance among adoptive and biological relatives: The Texas Adoption Project. *Behavior Genetics, 9,* 177–207.

HORNE, J. A. (1978). A review of the biological effects of total sleep deprivation in man. *Biological Psychology, 7,* 55–102.

HOUCK, J. C., KIMBALL, C., CHANG, C., PEDIGO, N. W., and YAMAMURA, H. I. (1980). Placental B-endorphin-like peptides. *Science, 207,* 78–79.

HOVLAND, C. I., JANIS, I. L., and KELLEY, H. H. (1953). *Communication and persuasion*. New Haven: Yale University Press, 1953.

HOWES, E. R. (1977, September 11). Twin speech: A language of their own. *New York Times*, p. 54.

HOYENGA, K. B., and HOYENGA, K. T. (1984). *Motivational explanations of behavior: Evolutionary, physiological and cognitive ideas*. Monterey, Calif.: Brooks/Cole.

HUBEL, D. H. (1979). The visual cortex of normal and deprived monkeys. *American Scientist, 67*, 532–543.

HUBEL, D. H. (1982). Explorations of the primary visual cortex. *Nature, 299*, 515–524.

HUBEL, D. H., and LIVINGSTONE, M. (1983). Blobs and color vision. *Canadian Journal of Physiology and Pharmacology, 61*, 1433–1441.

HUBEL, D. H., and WIESEL, T. N. (1959). Receptive fields of single neurons in the cat's striate cortex. *Journal of Physiology, 147*, 226–238.

HUBEL, D. H., and WIESEL, T. N. (1979). Brain mechanisms of vision. *Scientific American, 241*, 150–162.

HUGHES, M. (1984). Learning about numbers. *Economic and Social Research Council Newsletter*, June, pp. 9–11.

HUNT, D. D., and HAMPSON, J. L. (1980). Follow-up of 17 biological male transsexuals after sex-reassignment surgery. *American Journal of Psychiatry, 137*, 432–438.

HUNT, E., and PELLEGRINO, J. (1985). Using interactive computing to expand intelligence testing: A critique and prospectus. *Intelligence, 9*, 207–236.

HUNT, M. (1974). *Sexual behavior in the 1970's*. Chicago: Playboy Press.

HUNTER, I. M. L. (1957). *Memory: Facts and fallacies*. Baltimore: Penguin.

HURSCH, C. (1977). *The trouble with rape*. Chicago: Nelson-Hall.

HURVICH, L. M. (1978). Two decades of opponent processes. In F. W. Billmeyer and G. Wyszecki (Eds.), *Color 77*. Bristol, England: Adam-Hilger.

HUTTENLOCHER, P. R. (1979). Synaptic density in human frontal cortex: Developmental changes and effects of aging. *Brain Research, 163*, 195–205.

HYGGE, S., and OHMAN, A. (1978). Modeling processes in the acquisition of fears: Vicarious electrodermal conditioning to fear-relevant stimuli. *Journal of Personality and Social Psychology, 36*, 271–279.

IKEMI, Y., and NAKAGAWA, A. (1962). A psychosomatic study of contagious dermatitis. *Kyushu Journal of Medical Science, 13*, 335–350.

INGVAR, D. H., and LASSEN, N. A. (Eds.) (1977). Cerebral function, metabolism and circulation. *Acta Neurologica Scandanavica, 56* (Suppl. 64), 1–560.

INHELDER, B., and PIAGET, J. (1980). Procedures and structures. In D. R. Olson (Ed.), *The social foundations of language and thought*. Essays in honor of Jerome S. Brunner. New York: Norton.

IVERSEN, L. L. (1979). The chemistry of the brain. *Scientific American, 241*, 134–149.

IZARD, C. T. (1984). Emotion-cognition relationships and human development. In C. E. Izard, J. Kagan, and R. B. Zajonc (Eds.), *Emotion, cognitions, and behavior*. New York: Cambridge University Press.

JACKSON, R. (1980). The Scholastic Aptitude Test: A response to Slack and Porter's critical appraisal. *Harvard Educational Review, 50*, 382–391.

JACOBSON, N. S., WALDRON, H., and MOORE, D. (1980). Toward a behavioral profile of marital distress. *Journal of Consulting and Clinical Psychology, 48*, 696–703.

JAMES, W. (1890). *The principles of psychology*. New York: Holt.

JAMES, W. (1902). *The varieties of religious experience: A study in human nature*. New York: Longmans, Green.

JAMISON, K. R., GERNER, R. H., HAMMEN, C., and PADESKY, C. (1980). Clouds and silver linings: Positive experiences associated with primary affective disorders. *American Journal of Psychology, 137*, 198–202.

JANIS, I. L. (1958). *Psychological stress*. New York: Wiley.

JANIS, I. L. (1982). *Groupthink*. Boston: Houghton Mifflin.

JANIS, I. L. (1983). *Groupthink: Psychological studies of policy decisions and fiascos*. (2nd ed.). Boston: Houghton Mifflin.

JOHANSSON, G. (1977). *Case report on female catecholamine excretion in response to examination stress* (Department of Psychology Report No. 515). Stockholm: University of Stockholm.

JOHNSON, D. L. (1981). Naturally acquired learned helplessness: The relationship of school failure to achievement behavior, attributions and self-concept. *Journal of Educational Psychology, 73*, 174–180.

JOHNSON, K. S. (1979). The leading question: Isn't there an effect? Doctoral dissertation, University of Washington, Seattle.

JOHNSON, R. D. (1977). *Space settlements: A design*

study. Washington, D.C.: National Aeronautics and Space Administration, Scientific and Technical Information Office.

JOHNSON, V. S. (1985). Electrophysiological changes induced by androstenol: A potential human pheromone. Unpublished manuscript, New Mexico State University.

JOHNSTON, D., and BROWN, T. H. (1984). Biophysics and microphysiology of synaptic transmission in the hippocampus. In R. Dingledine (Ed.), *Brain slices*. New York: Plenum.

JONES, K. L., SHAINBERG, L. W., and BYER, C. O. (1977). *Sex and people*. New York: Harper & Row.

JONES, K. R., and FISCHI, T. R. (1979). The impact of alcohol, drug abuse and mental health treatment on medical core utilization: A review of the research literature. *Medical Care*, 17, 1–82.

JONES, M. (1979). "Law tied everyone's hands," says suicide victim's mother. *Seattle Times*, Feb. 4, A21.

JONES, M. B. (1974). Regressing group on individual effectiveness. *Organizational Behavior and Human Performance*, 11, 426–451.

JONES, M. C. (1965). Psychological correlates of somatic development. *Child Development*, 36, 899–911.

JONES, M. C., and MUSSEN, P. H. (1958). Self-conceptions, motivations, and interpersonal attitudes of early-and-late maturing girls. *Child Development*, 29, 491–501.

JOURARD, S. M., and LANDSMAN, T. (1980). *Healthy personality: An approach from the viewpoint of humanistic psychology*. New York: Macmillan.

JULIEN, R. M. (1985). *A primer of drug action*. (4th ed.). New York: Freeman.

JUNG, J. (1978). *Understanding human motivation: A cognitive approach*. New York: Macmillan.

KAGAN, J. (1984). *Emotions, cognition and behavior*. Cambridge, England: Cambridge University Press.

KAHNEMAN, D., and TREISMAN, A. (1984). Changing views of attention and automaticity. In R. Parasuraman and D. R. Davies (Eds.), *Varieties of attention*. New York: Academic Press.

KALLMANN, F. J., and JARVIK, L. F. (1959). Individual differences in constitution and genetic background. In J. E. Birren (Ed.), *Handbook of aging and the individual*. Chicago: University of Chicago Press.

KALTER, N. (1977). Children of divorce in an outpatient psychiatric population. *American Journal of Orthopsychiatry*, 47, 40–51.

KANFER, F. H. (1980). Self-management methods. In

F. H. Kanfer and A. P. Goldstein (Eds.), *Helping people change*. (2nd ed.). Elmsford, N.Y.: Pergamon Press.

KANIN, E. J., and PARCELL, S. R. (1977). Sexual aggression: A second look at the offended female. *Archives of Sexual Behavior*, 6, 67–76.

KAPLAN, H. S. (1974). *The new sex therapy*. New York: Brunner/Mazel.

KAPLAN, R. M. (1982). Nader's raid on the testing industry. *American Psychologist*, 37, 15–23.

KAROLY, P., and KANFER, F. H. (Eds.) (1982). *Self-management and behavior change*. Elmsford, N.Y.: Pergamon Press.

KASTENBAUM, R. (1975). Is death a life crisis? On the confrontation with death in theory and practice. In N. Datan and L. H. Ginsberg (Eds.), *Life span developmental psychology: Normative life crises*. New York: Academic Press.

KATCHADOURIAN, H. A., and LUNDE, D. T. (1979). *Fundamentals of human sexuality*. (3rd ed.). New York: Holt, Rinehart and Winston.

KATKIN, E. S., and GOLDBAND, S. (1980). Biofeedback. In F. H. Kanfer and A. P. Goldstein (Eds.), *Helping people change*. (2nd ed.). Elmsford, N.Y.: Pergamon Press.

KATKIN, E. S., and HASTRUP, J. L. (1982). Psychophysiological methods in clinical research. In P. C. Kendall and J. N. Butcher (Eds.), *Handbook of research methods in clinical psychology*. New York: Wiley.

KAUFMAN, A. S. (1979). *Intelligence testing with the WISC-R*. New York: Wiley.

KAY, P. (1975). Synchronic variability and diachronic changes in basic color terms. *Language in Society*, 4, 257–270.

KEEN, E. (1970). *Three faces of being: Toward an existential clinical psychology*. Englewood Cliffs, N.J.: Prentice-Hall.

KELLER, H. (1955). *The story of my life*. New York: Doubleday.

KELLEY, H. H. (1973). The process of causal attribution. *American Psychologist*, 28, 107–128.

KELLEY, H. H. (1983). Love and commitment. In H. H. Kelley, E. Berschied, A. Christensen, J. H. Harvey, T. L. Huston, G. Levinger, E. McClintock, L. Peplau, and D. R. Peterson, *Close relationships*. San Francisco: Freeman.

KELLEY, H. H., and THIBAUT, J. W. (1978). *Interpersonal relations: A theory of interdependence*. New York: Wiley-Interscience.

KELLY, G. A. (1955). *The psychology of personal constructs*, Vols. 1 & 2. New York: Norton.

KENDALL, P. C., and KOGESKI, G. P. (1979). Assessment and cognitive-behavioral interventions. *Cognitive Therapy and Research*, 3, 1–21.

KENDLER, K. S., and ROBINETTE, C. D. (1983). Schizophrenia in the National Academy of Sciences–National Research Council Twin Regency: A 16-year update. *American Journal of Psychology*, 140, 1551–1563.

KERR, N. L., and BRUUN, S. E. (1983). The dispensability of member effort and group motivation losses: Free-rider effects. *Journal of Personality and Social Psychology*, 44, 78–94.

KEVERNE, E. B. (1977). Pheromones and sexual behavior. In J. Money and M. Musaph (Eds.), *Handbook of sexology*. Amsterdam: Excerpta Medica.

KEY, W. B. (1972). *Subliminal seduction*. New York: New American Library (Signet).

KIESLER, C. A. (1982). Mental hospitals and alternative care. *American Psychologist*, 37, 349–360.

KIHLSTROM, J. F., and SHOR, R. E. (1978). Recall and recognition during posthypnotic amnesia. *International Journal of Clinical and Experimental Hypnosis*, 26, 330–349.

KINDER, D. R., and SEARS, D. O. (1985). Public opinion and political action. In G. Lindzey and E. Aronson (Eds.), *Handbook of social psychology*. (3rd ed.). Reading, Mass.: Addison-Wesley.

KINSBOURNE, M., and SMITH, W. L. (Eds.) (1974). *Hemispheric disconnection and cerebral function*. Springfield, Ill.: Thomas.

KINSEY, A. C., POMEROY, W. B., and MARTIN, C. E. (1948). *Sexual behavior in the human male*. Philadelphia: Saunders.

KINSEY, A. C., POMEROY, W. B., MARTIN, C. E., and GEBHARD, P. H. (1953). *Sexual behavior in the human female*. Philadelphia: Saunders.

KLAUS, M. H., and KENNELL, J. H. (1976). *Maternal infant bonding*. St. Louis: Mosby.

KLEIN, M., and CHRISTIANSEN, G. (1969). Group composition, group structure, and group effectiveness of bas-ketball teams. In J. W. Loy and G. S. Kenyon (Eds.), *Sport, culture, and society*. New York: Macmillan.

KLEINMUNTZ, B. (1980). *Essentials of abnormal psychology*. (2nd ed.). New York: Harper & Row.

KLEINMUNTZ, B., and SZUCKO, J. J. (1984a). Lie detection in ancient and modern times: A call for contemporary scientific study. *American Psychologist*, 39, 766–776.

KLEINMUNTZ, B., and SZUCKO, J. J. (1984b). A field study of the fallibility of polygraphic lie detection. *Nature*, 38, 449–450.

KLERMAN, G. L. (1975). Overview of depression. In A. M. Friedman, H. L. Kaplan, and B. Sadock (Eds.), *Comprehensive textbook of psychiatry*. Baltimore: Williams and Wilkins.

KLERMAN, G. L., DIMASCIO, A., WEISSMAN, M., PRUSOFF, B., and PAYKEL, E. S. (1974). Treatment of depression by drugs and psychotherapy. *American Journal of Psychiatry*, 131, 186–191.

KLINGER, E., BARTA, S. G., and MAXEINER, M. E. (1981). Current concerns: Assessing therapeutically relevant motivation. In P. C. Kendall and S. D. Hollon (Eds.), *Assessment strategies for cognitive-behavioral interventions*. New York: Academic Press.

KLONOFF, H. (1974). Marijuana and driving in real-life situations. *Science*, 186, 317–324.

KLUCKHOHN, C., and MURRAY, H. A. (1953). Personality formation: The determinants. In C. Kluckhorn, H. A. Murray, and D. M. Schneider (Eds.), *Personality in nature, society, and culture*. (2nd ed.). New York: Knopf.

KNIGHT, R. A., ROFF, J. D., BARNETT, J., and MOSS, J. L. (1979). Concurrent and predictive validity of thought disorder and affectivity: A 22-year follow-up of acute schizophrenics. *Journal of Abnormal Psychology*, 88, 1–12.

KOBASA, S. C. (1979). Stressful life events, personality, and health: An inquiry into hardiness. *Journal of Personality and Social Psychology*, 37, 1–11.

KOBASA, S. C., MADDI, S. R., and KAHNS, S. (1982). Hardiness and health: A prospective study. *Journal of Personality and Social Psychology*, 42, 168–177.

KOHLBERG, L. (1964). Development of moral character and moral ideology. In M. L. Hoffman and L. W. Hoffman (Eds.), *Review of child development research*, Vol 1. New York: Russell Sage Foundation.

KOHLER, W. (1925). *The mentality of apes*. London: Routledge and Kegan Paul.

KOHN, P. M., and COULAS, J. T. (1985). Sensation-seeking, augmenting-reducing, and the perceived and preferred effects of drugs. *Journal of Personality and Social Psychology, 48,* 99–106.

KOLATA, G. (1984a). Puberty mystery solved. *Science, 223,* 272.

KOLATA, G. (1984b). Studying learning in the womb. *Science, 225* (4659), 302–303.

KOLB, B., and WHISHAW, I. Q. (1985). *Fundamentals of human neuropsychology.* (2nd ed.). New York: Freeman.

KOLLAR, E. J., and FISHER, C. (1980). Tooth induction in chick epithelium: Expression of quiescent genes for enamel synthesis. *Science, 207,* 993–995.

KOOB, G., LEMOAL, M., and BLOOM, F. E. (1984). The role of endorphins in neurobiology, behavior, and psychiatric disorders. In C. B. Nemeroff and A. J. Dunn (Eds.), *Peptides, hormones, and behavior.* New York: Spectrum.

KOSAMBI, D. D. (1967). Living prehistory in India. *Scientific American, 216,* 105.

KOSSLYN, S. M. (1975). Information representation in visual images. *Cognitive Psychology, 7,* 341–370.

KOSSLYN, S. M., and SHWARTZ, S. P. (1981). Empirical constraints on theories of visual mental imagery. In J. Long and A. Baddeley (Eds.), *Attention and performance IX.* Hillsdale, N.J.: Erlbaum.

KOVACS, M., RUSH, A. J., BECK, A. T., and HOLLON, S. C. (1981). Depressed outpatients treated with cognitive therapy or pharmacotherapy: A one-year follow-up. *Archives of General Psychiatry, 38,* 33–39.

KRAEPELIN, E. (1914). *Clinical psychology.* New York: Wood.

KRAFT, C. L. (1978). A psychophysical contribution to air safety: Simulator studies of visual illusions in night visual approaches. In H. L. Pick, Jr., H. W. Leibowitz, J. E. Singer, A. Steinschneider, and H. W. Stevenson (Eds.), *Psychology: From research to practice.* New York: Plenum.

KRANTZ, D.S., and SCHULZ, R. (1980). A model of life crisis, control, and health outcomes: Cardiac rehabilitation and relocation of the elderly. In A. Baum and J. E. Singer (Eds.), *Advances in environmental psychology,* Vol. 2. Hillsdale, N.J.: Erlbaum.

KROEBER, A. L. (1948). *Anthropology.* New York: Harcourt Brace Jovanovich.

KROMER, L. F., BJORKLUND, A., and STENEVI, U. (1981). Innervation of embryonic hippocampal implants by regenerating axons of cholinergic septal neurons in the adult rat. *Brain Research, 210,* 153–171.

KÜBLER-ROSS, E. (1969) *On death and dying.* New York: Macmillan.

KÜBLER-ROSS, E. (1974). *Questions and answers on death and dying.* New York: Macmillan.

KUHL, J., and BLANKENSHIP, V. (1979). The dynamic theory of achievement motivation: From episodic to dynamic thinking. *Psychological Review, 86,* 141–151.

KUKLA, A. (1975). Preferences among impossibly difficult and trivially easy tasks: A revision of Atkinson's theory of choice. *Journal of Personality and Social Psychology, 32,* 338–345.

KURIANSKY, S. B., GURLAND, B. J., SPITZER, R. L., and ENDICOTT, S. (1977). Trends in the frequency of schizophrenia by different diagnostic criteria. *American Journal of Psychiatry, 134,* 631–636.

LACHAPELLE, E. R. (1978). The ABC of avalanche safety. Seattle: The Mountaineers.

LADER, M. H., and WING, L. (1966). Physiological measures, sedative, and morbid anxiety. *Maudsley Monograph.* London: Oxford University Press.

LAING, R. D. (1967). *The politics of experience.* New York: Pantheon Books.

LAING, R. D. (1969). *The divided self.* New York: Pantheon Books.

LAMB, M. E. (1979). Paternal influences and the father's role. *American Psychologist, 34,* 938–943.

LAMBERT, N. (1978). Exhibit C: IQ trail. *APA Monitor,* April, p. 9.

LAMM, H. G., and MYERS, D. G. (1978). Group-induced polarization of attitudes and behavior. In L. Berkowitz (Ed.), *Advances in experimental social psychology,* Vol. 10. New York: Academic Press.

LANDIS, J. (1956). Experiences of 500 children with adult sexual deviation. *Psychiatric Quarterly Supplement, 30,* 91–109.

LANG, A. R., GOECKNER, D. J., ADESSO, V. J., and MARLATT, G. A. (1975). Effects of alcohol and aggression in male social drinkers. *Journal of Abnormal Psychology, 84,* 508–518.

LANGER, E. J., RODIN, J., BECK, P., WEINMAN, C., and SPITZER, L. (1979). Environmental determinants of memory improvement in late adulthood. *Journal of Personality and Social Psychology, 37,* 2003–2013.

LANGLEY, P. (1983). Exploring the space of cognitive architectures. *Behavior Research Methods and Instrumentation, 15,* 289–299.

LANGLOIS, J. H., and STEPHAN, C. (1981). Beauty and the beast: The role of physical attractiveness in the development of peer relations and social behavior. In S. S. Brehm, S. M. Kassin, and F. X. Gibbons (Eds.), *Developmental social psychology.* New York: Oxford University Press.

LATANÉ, B., and DARLEY, B. (1970). *The unresponsive bystander: Why doesn't he help?* Englewood Cliffs, N.J.: Prentice-Hall.

LATANÉ, B., HARKINS, S. G., and WILLIAMS, K. D. (1980). *Many hands make light the work: Social loafing as a social disease.* Unpublished manuscript, Ohio State University.

LATANÉ, B., and NIDA, S. (1981). Ten years of research on group size and helping. *Psychological Bulletin, 89,* 308–334.

LATANÉ, B., WILLIAMS, K. D., and HARKINS, S. G. (1979). Many hands make light the work: The causes and consequences of social loafing. *Journal of Personality and Social Psychology, 37,* 822–832.

LAU, R. R. (1984). Dynamics of the attribution process. *Journal of Personality and Social Psychology, 46,* 1017–1028.

LAU, R. R., and RUSSELL, D. (1980). Attribution in the sports pages. *Journal of Personality and Social Psychology, 39,* 29–38.

LAURENCE, J. R., and PERRY, C. (1983). Hypnotically created memory among highly hypnotizable subjects. *Science, 222,* 523–524.

LAZARUS, R. S. (1984). On the primacy of cognition. *American Psychologist, 39,* 124–129.

LEAHY, A. M. (1935). Nature-nurture and intelligence. *Genetic Psychology Monographs, 17,* 237–308.

LEBON, G. (1903). *The crowd.* London: Allen and Unwin.

LECKMAN, J. F., WEISSMAN, M. M., MERIKANGAS, K. R., PAULS, D. L., and PRUSOFF, B. A. (1983). Panic disorder and major depression: Increased risk of depression, alcoholism, panic, and phobic disorders in families of depressed probands with panic disorder. *Archives of General Psychiatry, 40,* 1055–1060.

LEFF, J., KUIPERS, L., BERKOWITZ, R., EBERKEUB-VRIES,

R., and STURGEON, D. (1982). A controlled trial of social intervention in the families of schizophrenic patients. *British Journal of Psychology, 141,* 121–134.

LEFF, J., and VAUGHN, C. (1981). The role of maintenance therapy and relatives' expressed emotion in relapse of schizophrenia: A two-year follow-up. *British Journal of Psychiatry, 139,* 102–104.

LEITENBERG, H., GROSS, J., PETERSON, J., and ROSEN, J. C. (1984). Analysis of an anxiety model and the process of change during exposure plus response prevention treatment of bulimia nervosa. *Behavior Therapy, 15,* 3–20.

LENNEBERG, E. H. (1967). *Biological foundations of language.* New York: Wiley.

LENNEBERG, E. H., REBELSKY, F. G., and NICHOLS, I. A. (1965). The vocalizations of infants born to deaf and hearing parents. *Human Development, 8,* 23–37.

LEPPER, M. R., and GREENE, D. (1978). *The hidden costs of reward: New perspectives on the psychology of motivation.* Hillsdale, N.J.: Erlbaum.

LERNER, P. (1984). Projective techniques and personality assessment: The current perspective. In N. S. Endler and J. M. Hunt (Eds.), *Personality and the behavioral disorders.* New York: Ronald.

LERNER, R. M., and LERNER, J. (1977). Effects of age, sex, and physical attractiveness on child-peer relations, academic performance and elementary school adjustment. *Developmental Psychology, 13,* 585–590.

LERNER, S. E., and BURNS, R. S. (1978). PCP use among youth: History, epidemiology, and acute and chronic intoxication. In R. C. Petersen and R. C. Stillman (Eds.), *PCP phencyclidine abuse: An appraisal (NIDA Research Monograph No. 21).* Washington, D.C.: Department of Health, Education, and Welfare.

LETHEM, J., SLADE, P. O., TROUP, J. D. G., and BENTLEY, G. (1983). Outline of a fear-avoidance model of exaggerated pain perception: I. *Behaviour Research and Therapy, 21,* 401–408.

LEVINE, L. E., and HOFFMAN, M. L. (1975). Empathy and cooperation in four-year-olds. *Developmental Psychology, 11,* 533–534.

LEVINE, S. B., and LOTHSTEIN, L. M. (1981). Transsexualism or the gender dysphoria syndromes. *Journal of Sex and Marital Therapy, 7,* 85–113.

LEVINSON, D. J., with DARROW, C. N., KLEIN, E. B., LEVINSON, M. H., and McKEE, B. (1978). *The seasons of a man's life.* New York: Knopf.

LEVY, C. M. (1983). Microcomputer-based tutorials for

teaching statistics. *Behavior Research Methods and Instrumentation*, 15, 127–130.

Levy, J. (1983). Language, cognition, and the right hemisphere: A response to Gazzaniga. *American Psychologist*, 38, 538–541.

Levy, J. (1985). Right brain, left brain: Fact and fiction. *Psychology Today*, 19, 38–44.

Levy, R. I., and Moskowitz, J. (1982). Cardiovascular research: Decades of progress, a decade of promise. *Science*, 217, 121–129.

Lewis, J. F., and Mercer, J. R. (1978). The system of multicultural pluralistic assessment: SOMPA. In W. A. Coulter and H. W. Morrow (Eds.), *Adaptive behavior: Concepts and measurements*. New York: Grune & Stratton.

Lewinsohn, P. M., Mischel, W., Chaplin, W., and Barton, R. (1980). Social competence and depression: The role of illusory self-perceptions. *Journal of Abnormal Psychology*, 89, 203–212.

Lightman, E. S. (1982). Technique bias in measuring acts of altruism. *Social Science and Medicine*, 16, 1627–1633.

Lindsay, P. H., and Norman, D. A. (1977). *Human information processing: An introduction to psychology.* (2nd ed.). New York: Academic Press.

Lion, J. R., Bach-y-Rita, G., and Ervin, F. R. (1969). Enigmas of violence. *Science*, 164, 1465.

Lipowski, J. (1977). Psychosomatic medicine in the seventies: An overview. *American Journal of Psychiatry*, 134, 233–244.

Lipsitt, L. (1982). Infant learning. In T. M. Field, A. Huston, H. C. Quay, L. Troll, and G. E. Finley (Eds.), *Review of human development*. New York: Wiley.

Lobnitz, W. C., and Post, R. D. (1979). Parameters of self-reinforcement and depression. *Journal of Abnormal Psychology*, 88, 33–41.

Loehlin, J. C., and Nichols, R. C. (1976). *Heredity, environment, and personality: A study of 850 sets of twins*. Austin: University of Texas Press.

Loftus, E. F. (1981). Mentalmorphosis: Alterations in memory produced by the mental bonding of new information to old. In J. Long and A. Baddeley (Eds.), *Attention and performance IX*. Hillsdale, N.J.: Erlbaum.

Loftus, E. F., and Loftus, G. R. (1980). On the permanence of stored information in the human brain. *American Psychologist*, 35, 409–420.

London, P. (1970). The rescuers: Motivational hypotheses about Christians who saved Jews from the Nazis. In J. Maecaulay and L. Berkowitz (Eds.), *Altruism and helping behavior*. New York: Academic Press.

Long, J., and Vaillant, G. (1984). Natural history of male psychological health: XI. Escape from the underclass. *American Journal of Psychiatry*, 141, 341–346.

Longfellow, C. (1979). Divorce in context: Its impact on children. In G. Levinger and O. C. Moles (Eds.), *Divorce and separation*. New York: Basic Books.

Lorenz, K. (1966). *On aggression*. New York: Harcourt Brace Jovanovich.

Lovaas, O. I. (1973). *Behavioral treatment of autistic children*. Morristown, N.J.: General Learning Press.

Lovaas, O. I. (1977). *The autistic child*. New York: Irvington.

Lumry, A., Gottesman, I. I., and Tuason, V. B. (1982). MMPI state dependency during the course of bipolar psychosis. *Psychiatry Research*, 7 (1), 59–67.

Luria, A. (1961). The role of speech in the regulation of normal and abnormal behavior. New York: Liveright.

Lykken, D. T. (1984). Polygraphic interrogation. *Nature*, 307, 681–684.

Lynch, G., and Baudry, M. (1984). The biochemistry of memory: A new and specific hypothesis. *Science*, 224, 1057–1063.

Lynch, G., Kessler, M., and Baudry, M. (1984). Correlated electrophysiological and biochemical studies of hippocampal slices. In R. Dingledine (Ed.), *Brain slices*. New York: Plenum.

Maass, A., and Clark, R. D., III (1984). Hidden impact of minorities: Fifteen years of minority influence research. *Psychological Bulletin*, 95, 428–450.

Maccoby, E. E., and Maccoby, N. (1954). The interview: A tool of social science. In G. Lindzey (Ed.), *Handbook of social psychology*. Cambridge, Mass.: Addison-Wesley.

MacCulloch, M. J., Snowden, P. R., Wood, P. J. W., and Mills, H. E. (1983). Sadistic fantasy, sadistic behaviour and offending. *British Journal of Psychiatry*, 143, 20–29.

MacDonald, N. (1960). Living with schizophrenia. *Canadian Medical Association Journal*, 82, 218–221.

MACKIE, D., and COOPER, J. (1984). Attitude polarization: Effects of group membership. *Journal of Personality and Social Psychology, 46*, 575–585.

MACKLIN, E. D. (1978). Review of research on nonmarital cohabitation in the United States. In B. I. Murstein (Ed.), *Exploring intimate lifestyles*. New York: Springer.

MAHONEY, M. J. (1980). *Abnormal psychology: Perspectives on human variance*. New York: Harper & Row.

MALAMUTH, N. M., and CHECK, J. V. P. (1981). The effects of mass media exposure on acceptance of violence against women: A field experiment. *Journal of Research in Personality, 15*, 436–446.

MALAMUTH, N. M., and DONNERSTEIN, E. (1983). The effects of aggressive-erotic stimuli. In L. Berkowitz (Ed.), *Advances in experimental social psychology*, Vol. 15. New York: Academic Press.

MALLICK, S. K., and McCANDLESS, B. R. (1966). A study of catharsis of aggression. *Journal of Personality and Social Psychology, 4*, 591–596.

MANDELL, A. (1978). The Sunday syndrome. *Proceedings of the National Amphetamine Conference*, San Francisco, September.

MANDLER, G. (1984). *Mind and body: Psychology of emotion and stress*. New York: Norton.

MANN, L. (1981). The baiting crowd in episodes of threatened suicide. *Journal of Personality and Social Psychology, 41*, 703–709.

MANSTEAD, A. S. R., PROFFITT, C. T., and SMART, S. L. (1983). Predicting and understanding mothers' infant-feeding intentions and behavior: Testing the theory of reasoned action. *Journal of Personality and Social Psychology, 44*, 657–671.

MARCUS, R. F., TELLEEN, S., and ROKE, E. J. (1979). Relations between cooperation and empathy in young children. *Developmental Psychology, 15*, 346–347.

MARKMAN, E. M. (1977). Realizing that you don't understand: A preliminary investigation. *Child Development, 48*, 986–992.

MARKS, I. M., and LADER, M. (1973). Anxiety states (anxiety neurosis): A review. *Journal of Nervous and Mental Disease, 156*, 3–18.

MARKUS, H., and SENTIS, K. (1982). The self in social information processing. In J. Suls (Ed.), *Social psychological perspectives on the self*. Hillsdale, N.J.: Erlbaum.

MARLATT, G. A., and GORDON, J. R. (1985). *Relapse prevention: Maintenance strategies in the treatment of addictive behaviors*. New York: Guilford.

MARLATT, G. A., and ROHSENOW, D. J. (1980). Cognitive processes in alcohol use: Expectancy and the balanced placebo design. In N. K. Mello (Ed.), *Advances in substance abuse: Behavioral and biological research*. Greenwich, Conn.: JAI Press.

MARLER, P. (1967). Animal communication signals. *Science, 157*, 769–774.

MARMOT, M. G., and SYME, S. L. (1976). Acculturation and coronary heart disease in Japanese-Americans. *American Journal of Epidemiology, 104*, 225–247.

MARSHALL, J. F. (1984). Brain function: Neural adaptations and recovery from injury. *Annual Review of Psychology, 35*, 277–308.

MARSLEN-WILSON, W. D., and WELSH, A. (1978). Processing interactions and lexical access during word recognition in continuous speech. *Cognitive Psychology, 10*, 29–63.

MARTENS, R., LANDERS, D. M., and LOY, J. (1972). *Sport cohesiveness questionnaire*. Washington: American Alliance on Health, Physical Education, and Recreation.

MARTIN, E. (1970). Toward an analysis of subjective phrase structure. *Psychological Bulletin, 74*, 153–166.

MARZILLIER, J. S., and BIRCHWOOD, M. S. (1981). Behavioral treatment of cognitive disorders. In L. Michelson, M. Hersen, and S. M. Turner (Eds.), *Future perspectives on behavior therapy*. New York: Plenum.

MASER, J. D., and KEITH, S. J. (1983). CT scans and schizophrenia: Report on a workshop. *Schizophrenia Bulletin, 9*, 265–283.

MASLOW, A. H. (1968). Toward the study of violence. In L. Ng (Ed.), *Alternatives to violence*. New York: Time-Life.

MASLOW, A. H. (1970). *Motivation and personality*. (2nd ed.). New York: Harper & Row.

MASLOW, A. H. (1971). *The farther reaches of human nature*. New York: Viking Press.

MASTERS, W. H., and JOHNSON, V. E. (1966). *Human sexual response*. Boston: Little, Brown.

MASTERS, W. H., and JOHNSON, V. E. (1970). *Human sexual inadequacy*. Boston: Little, Brown.

MASTERS, W. H., and JOHNSON, V. E. (1979). *Homosexuality in perspective*. Boston: Little, Brown.

MATSUMOTO, Y. S. (1970). Social stress and coronary heart disease in Japan: A hypothesis. *Millbank Memorial Fund Quarterly, 68*, 9–36.

MAUGH, T. H., II (1982). Sleep-promoting factor isolated. *Science, 216*, 1400.

MAVLIGIT, G. M. (1984). Chronic immune stimulation by sperm alloantigens: Support for the hypothesis that spermatazoa induce immune deregulation in homosexual males. *Journal of the American Medical Association, 251,* 237–241.

MAY, R. (1961). The emergence of existential psychology. In R. May (Ed.), *Existential psychology.* New York: Random House.

MAYNARD, J. (1972). The embarrassment of virginity. *Mademoiselle, 411,* 258–259.

MAYNARD, J. F. (1979). Infant perception of auditory-visual synchrony. Master's thesis, University of Illinois.

MAZUR, A. (1983). Hormones, aggression, and dominance in humans. In B. B. Svare (Ed.), *Hormones and aggressive behavior.* New York: Plenum.

MCARTHUR, J. W. (1985). Endorphins and exercise in females: Possible connection with reproductive function. *Medicine and Science in Sports and Exercise, 17,* 82–88.

MCCARLEY, R. W. (1983). REM dreams, REM sleep, and their isomorphisms. In M. H. Chase and E. D. Weitzman (Eds.), *Sleep disorders: Basic and clinical research,* Vol. 8. New York: Spectrum.

MCCAUL, K. D., and MALOTT, J. J. (1984). Distraction and coping with pain. *Psychological Bulletin, 95,* 516–533.

MCCAULEY, C., STITT, C. L., and SEGAL, M. (1980). Stereotyping: From prejudice to prediction. *Psychological Bulletin, 87,* 195–208.

MCCLELLAND, D. C. (1975). *Power: The inner experience.* New York: Irvington.

MCCLELLAND, D. C. (1985). *Human motivation.* Glenview, Ill.: Scott, Foresman.

MCCLELLAND, D. C., ATKINSON, J. W., CLARK, R. A., and LOWELL, E. L. (1953). *The achievement motive.* Englewood Cliffs, N.J.: Prentice-Hall.

MCCLELLAND, D. C., DAVIS, W. N., KALIN, R., and WANNER, E. (1972). *The drinking man.* New York: Free Press.

MCCLINTOCK, M. K. (1971). Menstrual synchrony and suppression. *Nature, 229,* 244–245.

MCCORMICK, D. A., and THOMPSON, R. (1984). Cerebellum: Essential involvement in the classically conditioned eyelid response. *Science, 223,* 296–299.

MCGARRIGLE, J., and DONALDSON, M. (1974–1975). Conservation accidents. *Cognition, 3,* 341–350.

MCGAUGH, J. L. (1983). Hormonal influences on memory. *Annual Review of Psychology, 34,* 297–324.

MCGLASHAN, T. H. (1983). The borderline syndrome. *Archives of General Psychiatry, 40,* 1319–1323.

MCGUIRE, W. J., and PAPAGEORGIS, D. (1961). The relative efficacy of various types of prior belief-defense in producing immunity against persuasion. *Journal of Abnormal and Social Psychology, 62,* 327–337.

MEDNICK, S. A., POLLOCK, V., VOLAVKA, J., and GABRIELLI, W. F. (1982). Biology and violence. In M. E. Wolfgang and N. A Weiner (Eds.) *Criminal violence.* Beverly Hills, Calif.: Sage.

MEGARGEE, E. I. (1966). Undercontrolled and overcontrolled personality types in extreme anti-social aggression. *Psychological Monographs, 80* (Whole No. 611).

MEICHENBAUM, D. (1977). *Cognitive-behavior modification: An integrative approach.* New York: Plenum.

MEISELMAN, K. C. (1980). Personality characteristics of incest history psychotherapy patients: A research note. *Archives of Sexual Behavior, 9,* 195–197.

MELAMED, B. G. (1979). Behavioral approaches to fear in dental settings. In M. Hersen, R. M. Eisler, and P. M. Miller (Eds.), *Progress in behavior modification, 7.* New York: Academic Press.

MELTZOFF, A. N., and MOORE, M. K. (1983). Newborn infants imitate adult facial gestures. *Child Development, 54,* 702–709.

MELZACK, R. (1973). *The puzzle of pain.* New York: Basic Books.

MENDLEWICZ, J., and RAINIER, J. D. (1974). Morbidity risk and genetic transmission in manic-depressive illness. *American Journal of Human Genetics, 26,* 692–701.

MERCER, J. R., and LEWIS, J. F. (1978). *System of multicultural pluralistic assessment* (SOMPA). New York: Psychological Corporation.

MESSENGER, J. C. (1971). Sex and repression in an Irish folk community. In D. S. Marshall and R. C. Suggs (Eds.), *Human sexual behavior,* Englewood Cliffs, N.J.: Prentice-Hall.

MESSICK, S. (1980). Test validity and the ethics of assessment. *American Psychologist, 35,* 1012–1027.

METROPOLITAN LIFE STATISTICAL BULLETIN (1975). *55* (2), 3–5.

MEYER, J. K., and RETER, D. J. (1979). Sex reassignment: Follow-up. *Archives of General Psychiatry, 36,* 1010–1015.

MEYERS, A. W., ARTZ, L. M., and CRAIGHEAD, W. E. (1976). The effects of instructions, incentives and feedback on a community problem: Dormitory noise. *Journal of Applied Behavior Analysis, 9,* 445–457.

MICHAELS, J. W., BLOMMEL, J. M., BROCATO, R. M., LINKOUS, R. A., and ROWE, J. S. (1982). Social facilitation and inhibition in a natural setting. *Replications in Social Psychology, 2,* 21–24.

MICHELS, R. (1984). First rebuttal. *American Journal of Psychiatry. 141 (4),* 548–551.

MIDLARSKY, E., and MIDLARSKY, M. (1973). Some determinants of aiding under experimentally induced stress. *Journal of Personality, 41,* 305–327.

MILES, L. E., and SIMMONS, F. B. (1984). Evaluation of 190 patients with loud and disruptive snoring. *Sleep Research, 13,* 154.

MILGRAM, S. (1964). Issues in the study of obedience: A reply to Baumrind. *American Psychologist, 19,* 848–852.

MILGRAM, S. (1974). *Obedience to authority: An experimental view.* New York: Harper & Row.

MILLAR, D. G. (1983). Hostile emotion and obsessional neuroses. *Psychological Medicine, 13,* 813–819.

MILLER, D. R. (1985). Some electrophysiological correlates of affect and memory. Doctoral dissertation, New Mexico State University.

MILLER, G. A. (1981). *Language and speech.* San Francisco: Freeman.

MILLER, N. E. (1959). Liberalization of basic S-R concepts: Extensions to conflict behavior, motivation, and social learning. In S. Koch (Ed.), *Psychology: A study of a science,* Vol. 2. New York: McGraw-Hill.

MILLER, N. E. (1983). Behavioral medicine: Symbiosis between laboratory and clinic. *Annual Review of Psychology, 34,* 1–32.

MILLER, S., ROSSBACH, J., and MUNSON, R. (1981). Social density and affiliative tendency as determinants of dormitory residential outcomes. *Journal of Applied Social Psychology, 11,* 356–365.

MILNER, B. (1966). Amnesia following operations on the temporal lobes. In C. W. M. Whitty and O. L. Zangwill (Eds.), *Amnesia.* London: Butterworths.

MILNER, B., BRANCH, C., and RASMUSSEN, T. (1966). Evidence for bilateral representation in non-right-handers. *Transactions of the American Neurological Association, 91,* 306–308.

MINEKA, S. (1979). The role of fear in theories of avoidance learning, flooding, and extinction. *Psychological Bulletin, 86,* 985–1010.

MINER, G. D. (1973). The evidence for genetic components in the neuroses. *Archives of General Psychiatry, 29,* 111–118.

MINTUN, M. A., RAICHLE, M. E., KILBOURN, M. R., WOOTEN, G. F., and WELCH, M. J. (1984). A quantitative model for the *in vitro* assessment of drug binding sites with positron emission tomography. *Annals of Neurology, 15,* 217–227.

MISCHEL, W. (1973). Toward a cognitive social learning reconceptualization of personality. *Psychological Review, 75,* 252–283.

MISCHEL, W. (1979). On the interface of cognition and personality: Beyond the person–situation debate. *American Psychologist, 34,* 740–754.

MISCHEL, W. (1981). *Introduction to personality* (3rd ed.). Englewood Cliffs, N.J.: Prentice-Hall.

MISHKIN, M., and PETRI, H. L. (in press). Memories and habits: Some implications for the analysis of learning and retention. In N. Butters and L. Squire (Eds.), *Neuropsychology of memory.* New York: Guilford Press.

MISSEL, P., and SOMMER, G. (1983). Depression and self-verbalization. *Cognitive Therapy and Research, 7,* 141–148.

MITA, T. H., DERMER, M., and KNIGHT, J. (1977). Reversed facial images and the mere exposure hypotheses. *Journal of Personality and Social Psychology, 35,* 597–601.

MOLFESE, D. L., NUNEZ, V., SEIBERT, S. M., and RAMANAIATT, N. V. (1976). Cerebral asymmetry: Changes in factors affecting its development. In S. H. R. Harnad, H. D. Sterlis, and J. Lancaster (Eds.), *Origins and evaluation of language and speech.* New York: New York Academy of Sciences.

MONEY, J., and EHRHARDT, A. A. (1972). *Man and woman, boy and girl.* Baltimore: Johns Hopkins University Press.

MOORE-EDE, M. C., and CZEISLER, C. A. (Eds.) (1984). *Mathematical models of the circadian sleep-wake cycle.* New York: Raven Press.

MOORE-EDE, M. C., SULZMAN, F. M., and FULLER, C. A. (1982). *The clocks that time us.* Cambridge, Mass.: Harvard University Press.

MORELAND, R. L., and ZAJONC, R. B. (1982). Exposure effects in person perception: Familiarity, similarity and attraction. *Journal of experimental social psychology, 18,* 395–415.

MORGAN, J. J. B. (1941). *Psychology*. New York: Farrar and Rinehart.

MORGAN, W. P. (1984). Mind over matter. In W. F. Straub and J. M. Williams (Eds.), *Cognitive sport psychology*. Lansing, N.Y.: Sport Science Associates.

MORGAN, W. P. (1985). Affective beneficence of vigorous physical activity. *Medicine and Science in Sports and Exercise, 17,* 94–100.

MORGAN, W. P., HORSTMAN, D. H., CYMERMAN, A., and STOKES, J. (1983). Facilitation of physical performance by means of a cognitive strategy. *Cognitive Therapy and Research, 7,* 251–264.

MORIN, S. F., and BATCHELOR, W. F. (1984). Responding to the psychological crisis of AIDS. *Public Health Reports, 99,* 4–9.

MORRIS, D., COLLETT, P., MARSH, P., and O'SHAUGHNESSY, M. (1979). *Gestures*. New York: Stein & Day.

MORRIS, L. W. (1979). *Extraversion and introversion: An interactional perspective*. Washington, D.C.: Hemisphere.

MORRIS, N. M., and UDRY, J. R. (1978). Pheromonal influences on human sexual behavior: An experimental search. *Journal of Biosocial Science, 10,* 147–157.

MORRIS, R. J. (1980). Fear reduction methods. In F. H. Kanfer and A. P. Goldstein (Eds.), *Helping people change* (2nd ed.). Elmsford, N.Y.: Pergamon Press.

MORRISON, A. R. (1983). A window on the sleeping brain. *Scientific American, 248,* 94–102.

MOSKOWITZ, B. A. (1978). The acquisition of language. *Scientific American, 239,* 92–108.

MOSS, C. S. (1972). *Recovery with aphasia*. Urbana: University of Illinois Press.

MOSS, M. K., and PAGE, R. A. (1972). Reinforcement and helping behavior. *Journal of Applied Social Psychology, 2,* 360–371.

MOWRER, O. H. (1950). *Learning theory and personality dynamics*. New York: Ronald Press.

MUMFORD, E., SCHLESINGER, H. J., and GLASS, G. V. (1978). A critical review and indexed bibliography of the literature up to 1978 on the effects of psychotherapy on medical utilization. Report to NIMHI, Rockville, Md.

MUMFORD, E., SCHLESINGER, H. J., GLASS, G. V., PATRICK, C., and CUERDON, T. (1984). A new look at evidence about reduced cost of medical utilization following mental health treatment. *The American Journal of Psychiatry, 141,* 1145–1158.

MURDOCK, B. B., JR. (1974). *Human memory: Theory and data*. Potomac, Md.: Erlbaum.

MURPHY, G. E. (1983). The problems in studying suicide. *Psychiatric Developments, 4,* 339–350.

NAIRN, A., & ASSOCIATES. (1980). *The reign of ETS: The corporation that makes up minds*. Washington, D.C.: Ralph Nader.

NAKANISHI, K., BALOUGH-NAIR, V., GAWINOWICZ, M. A., Arnaboldi, M., Motto, M., and HONIG, B. (1979). Hydroretinals and hydrorhodopsins. *Photochemical Photobiology, 29,* 657.

NATIONAL ACADEMY OF SCIENCES (1982). *Marijuana and health*. Washington, D.C.: National Academy Press.

NEISWORTH, J. T., and MOORE, F. (1972). Operant treatment of asthmatic responding with the parent as therapist. *Behavior Therapy, 3,* 95–99.

NELSON, K. (1973). Structure and strategy in learning to talk. *Monographs of the Society for Research in Child Development, 38,* 1–2, (Whole No. 149).

NELSON, T. O. (1977). Repetition and depth of processing. *Journal of Verbal Learning and Verbal Behavior, 16,* 161–171.

NESSELROADE, J. R., SCHAIE, K. W., and BALTES, P. B. (1972). Ontogenetic and generational components of structural and quantitative change in adult cognitive behavior. *Journal of Gerontology, 27,* 222–228.

NEUGARTEN, B. L. (1976). Adaptation and the life cycle. *The Counseling Psychologist, 6,* 16–20.

NEUMAN, W. R. (1976). Patterns of recall among television news viewers. *Public Opinion Quarterly, 40,* 115–123.

NEWCOMB, M. D., and BENTLER, P. M. (1981). Marital breakdown. In S. Duck and R. Gilmour (Eds.), *Personal relationships: Personal relationships in disorder*. New York: Academic Press.

NEWCOMB, T. M. (1961). *The acquaintance process*. New York: Holt, Rinehart and Winston.

NEWCOMB, T. M. (1963). Persistence and regression of changed attitudes: Long-range studies. *Journal of Social Issues, 19,* 3–14.

NEWELL, A., and SIMON, H. (1972). *Human problem solving*. Englewood Cliffs, N.J.: Prentice-Hall.

NIELSEN, A. C., III, and WILLIAMS, T. A. (1981). Depression in ambulatory medical patients: Prevalence by self-report questionnaire and recognition by non-phychiatric physicians. *Archives of General Psychiatry*, 38, 133–137.

NOSSITER, B. D. (1980). World population explosion is slowing, U.N. finds. *New York Times*, June 15, p. 10.

NOVACO, R. (1975). *Anger control: The development and evaluation of an experimental treatment.* Lexington, Mass.: Heath.

NOVAK, M. A., and HARLOW, H. F. (1975). Social recovery of monkeys isolated for the first year of life: I. Rehabilitation and therapy. *Developmental Psychology*, 11, 453–465.

NUCKOLLS, K. B., CASSEL, J., and KAPLAN, B. H. (1972). Psychosocial assets, life crisis and the prognosis of pregnancy. *American Journal of Epidemiology*, 95, 431–441.

O'BRIEN, M., HUSTON, A. C., and RISLEY, T. (in press). Sex-typed play of toddlers in a daycare center. *Journal of Applied Developmental Psychology*.

OHMAN, A., FREDRICKSON, M., and OLOFSSON, C. (1975). One-trial learning and superior resistance to extinction of autonomic responses conditioned to potentially phobic stimuli. *Journal of Comparative and Physiological Psychology*, 88, 619–627.

OLDS, J., and OLDS, M. E. (1965). Drives, rewards, and the brain. In F. Barron, W. C. Dement, W. Edwards, H. Lindman, and L. D. Phillips (Eds.), *New directions in psychology*, Vol. 2. New York: Holt, Rinehart and Winston.

OLWEUS, D. (1980). Familial and temperamental determinants of aggressive behavior in adolescent boys: A causal analysis. *Developmental Psychology*, 16, 644–666.

OLWEUS, D., MATTSSON, A., SCHALLING, D., and Low, H. (1980). Testosterone, aggression, physical and personality dimensions in normal adolescent males. *Psychosomatic Medicine*, 42, 253–269.

ORNE, M. T. (1962). On the social psychology of the psychological experiment: With particular reference to demand characteristics and their implications. *American Psychologist*, 17, 776–783.

ORNE, M. T. (1959). The nature of hypnosis: Artifact and essence. *Journal of Abnormal and Social Psychology*, 58, 277–299.

ORNSTEIN, R. E. (1977). *The psychology of consciousness.* (2nd ed.). New York: Harcourt Brace Jovanovich.

ORTON, I. K., BEIMAN, I., LaPOINTE, K., and LANKSFORD, A. (1983). Induced states of anxiety and depression: Effects on self-reported affect and tonic psycho-

physiological response. *Cognitive Therapy and Research*, 1, 233–244.

OVERMEIER, J. B., and WIELKIEWICZ, R. M. (1983). On unpredictability as a causal factor in "learned helplessness." *Learning and Motivation*, 14, 324–337.

PAGANO, R. R., AKOTS, N. J., and WALL, T. W. (1985). *Hypnosis, cerebral laterality, and relaxation.* Unpublished manuscript, University of Washington.

PAGANO, R. R., and WARRENBURG, S. (1983). Meditation: In search of a unique effect. In R. J. Davidson, G. E. Schwartz, and D. Shapiro (Eds.), *Consciousness and self-regulation*, Vol. 3. New York: Plenum.

PAIVIO, A. (1978). Comparisons of mental clocks. *Journal of Experimental Psychology: Human Perception and Performance*, 4, 61–71.

PAIVIO, A., and DE LINDE, J. (1982). Imagery, memory and the brain. *Canadian Journal of Psychology*, 36, 243–272.

PALERMO, D. S. (1978). *Psychology of language.* Glenview, Ill.: Scott, Foresman.

PARIS, S. G., and LINDAUER, B. K. (1982). The development of cognitive skills during childhood (pp. 333–349). In B. B. Wolman (Ed.). *Handbook of developmental psychology.* Englewood Cliffs, N.J.: Prentice-Hall.

PARK, B., and ROTHBART, M. (1982). Perception of outgroup homogeneity and levels of social categorization: Memory for subordinate attributes of in-group and outgroup members. *Journal of Personality and Social Psychology*, 42, 1051–1068.

PARKE, R. D., BERKOWITZ, L., LEYENS, J. P., WEST, S. G., and SEBASTIAN, R. J. (1977). Some effects of violent and nonviolent movies on the behavior of juvenile delinquents. In L. Berkowitz (Ed.), *Advances in experimental social psychology*, Vol. 10. New York: Academic Press.

PARKE, R. D., and SLABY, R. G. (1983). The development of aggression. In P. H. Mussen (Ed.), *Handbook of child psychology*, Vol. 4. (4th ed.). New York: Wiley.

PARKER, G., TUPLING, H., and BROWN, L. B. (1979). A parental bonding instrument. *British Journal of Medical Psychology*, 52, 1–10.

PARLOFF, M. B. (1979). Can psychotherapy research guide the policymaker? A little knowledge may be a dangerous thing. *American Psychology*, 34, 296–306.

PATTERSON, G. R. (1982). *Coercive family processes.* Eugene, Oreg.: Castilia Press.

PATTERSON, G. R., LITTMAN, R. A., and BRICKER, W.

(1967). Assertive behavior in children: A step toward a theory of aggression. *Monographs of the Society for Research in Child Development*, 32 (Whole No. 5).

PAULUS, P. B. (1980). Crowding. In P. B. Paulus (Ed.), *Psychology of group influence*. Hillsdale, N.J.: Erlbaum.

PAZULINEC, R., MEYERROSE, M., and SAJWAJ, T. (1983). Punishment via response cost. In S. Avelrod and J. Apsche (Eds.), *The effects of punishment on human behavior*. New York: Academic Press.

PEET, M., and COPPEN A. (1980). Lithium treatment and prophylaxis in unipolar depression. *Psychosomatics*, 21, 303–313.

PERLMUTER, L. C., and MONTY, R. A. (Eds.) (1979). *Choice and perceived control*. Hillsdale, N.J.: Erlbaum.

PERLS, F. S. (1969). *Gestalt therapy verbatim*. Lafayette, Calif.: Real People Press.

PEROUTKA, S. J., and SNYDER, S. H. (1980). Relationship of neuroleptic drug effects at brain dopamine, serotonin, αadrenergic, and histamine receptors to clinical potency. *American Journal of Psychiatry*, 137, 1518–1522.

PESKIN, H. (1973). Influence of the developmental schedule of puberty on learning and ego functioning. *Journal of Youth and Adolescence*, 2, 273–290.

PETERSON, A. C. (1979). Female pubertal development. In M. Sugar (Ed.), *Female adolescent development*. New York: Brunner/Mazel.

PETERSON, L., SCHULTHEIS, K., RIDLEY-JOHNSON, R., MILLER, D. J., and TRACY, K. (1984). Comparison of three modeling procedures on the presurgical and postsurgical reactions of children. *Behavior Therapy*, 15, 197–203.

PETERSON, L. R., and PETERSON, M. J. (1959). Short-term retention of individual verbal items. *Journal of Experimental Psychology*, 58, 193–198.

PETTY, R. E., HARKINS, S. G., and WILLIAMS, K. D. (1980). The effects of group diffusion of cognitive effort on attitudes: An information-processing view. *Journal of Personality and Social Psychology*. 38, 81–92.

PETTY, R. E., WILLIAMS, K. D., HARKINS, S. G., and LATANÉ, B. (1977). Social inhibition of helping yourself: Bystander response to a cheeseburger. *Personality and Social Psychology Bulletin*, 3, 571–574.

PFAFF, D. W. (Ed.) (1982). *The physiological mechanisms of motivation*. New York: Springer-Verlag.

PHARES, E. J. (1984). *Introduction to personality*. Columbus, Ohio: Merrill.

PHARES, E. J., and LAMIELL, J. T. (1975). Internal-external control, interpersonal judgments of others in need, and attribution of responsibility. *Journal of Personality*, 43, 23–38.

PHILLIPP, S. F., and CICCIARELLA, C. F. (1983). An Apple II package for computer-assisted telephone interviewing. *Behavior Research Methods and Instrumentation*, 15, 456–458.

PHILLIPS, D. P. (in press). The impact of mass media on homicide and suicide. In L. Berkowitz (Ed.), *Advances in Experimental Social Psychology*. New York: Academic Press.

PHILLIPS, D. P. (1983). The impact of mass media violence on U.S. homicides. *American Sociological Review*, 48, 560–568.

PHILLIPS, D. P., and BRUGGE, J. F. (1985). Progress in neurophysiology of sound localization. *Annual Review of Psychology*, 36, 245–274.

PIAGET, J. (1970). Piaget's theory. In P. H. Mussen (Ed.), *Carmichael's manual of child psychology*. New York: Wiley.

PILBEAM, D. (1984). The descent of hominoids and hominids. *Scientific American*, 250, 84–97.

PILIAVIN, J., and PILIAVIN, I. (1972). Effects of blood on reactions to a victim. *Journal of Personality and Social Psychology*, 23, 353–361.

PILISUK, M. (1982). Delivery of social support—the social inoculation. *American Journal of Orthopsychiatry*, 52, 20–31.

PI-SUNYEN, X., KISSILEFF, H. R., THORNTON, J., and SMITH, G. P. (1982). C-terminal octapeptide of cholecystokinin decreases food intake in obese men. *Physiology of Behavior*, 29, 627–630.

PITZ, G. F., and SACHS, N. J. (1984). Judgment and decision: Theory and application. *Annual Review of Psychology*, 35, 139–163.

PLOMIN, R., DEFRIES, J. C., and McCLEARN, G. E. (1980). *Behavior genetics: A Primer*. San Francisco: Freeman.

PLUTCHIK, R. (1980). *Emotion: A psychoevolutionary synthesis*. New York: Harper & Row.

POGGIO, G. F., and FISCHER, B. (1977). Binocular interaction and depth sensitivity of striate and prestriate cortical neurons of behaving rhesus monkeys. *Journal of Neurophysiology, 40,* 1392–1405.

POLIVY, J., and HERMAN, C. P. (1985). Dieting and binging: A causal analysis. *American Psychologist, 40,* 193–201.

POMEROY, W. B. (1969). Homosexuality. In R. W. Weltage (Ed.), *The same sex.* Philadelphia: Pilgrim Press.

PORRINO, L. J., ESPOSITO, R. U., SEEGER, T. F., CRANE, A. M., PERT, A., and SOKOLOFF, L. (1984). Metabolic mapping of the brain during rewarding self-stimulation. *Science, 224,* 306–308.

POSTMAN, L., and PHILLIPS, L. W. (1965). Short-term temporal changes in free recall. *Quarterly Journal of Experimental Psychology, 17* (2), 132–138.

PREMACK, D. (1965). Reinforcement theory. In D. Levine (Ed.), *Nebraska symposium on motivation.* Lincoln: University of Nebraska Press.

PRENTICE-DUNN, S., and ROGERS, R. W. (1982). Effects of public and private self-awareness on deindividuation and aggression. *Journal of Personality and Social Psychology, 43,* 503–513.

PRENTICE-DUNN, S., and ROGERS, R. W. (1983). Deindividuation in aggression. In R. Geen and E. Donnerstein (Eds.), *Aggression: Theoretical and empirical reviews.* New York: Academic Press.

PRIBRAM, K. H. (1980). The biology of emotions and other feelings. In R. Plutchik and H. Kellerman (Eds.), *Emotion: Theory, research, and experience.* Vol. 1, *Theories of emotion.* New York: Academic Press.

QANTRY, M. B. (1976). Aggression catharsis: Experimental investigations and implications. In R. G. Geen and E. C. O'Neal (Eds.), *Perspectives on aggression.* New York: Academic Press.

QUINSEY, V. L., MAGUIRE, A., and VARNEY, G. W. (1983). Assertion and overcontrolled hostility among mentally disordered murderers. *Journal of Consulting and Clinical Psychology, 51,* 550–566.

QUINTON, D., and RUTTER, M. (1976). Early hospital admissions and later disturbances of behavior: An attempted replication of Douglas' findings. *Developmental Medicine and Child Neurology, 18,* 447–459.

RAAHEIM, K. (1974). *Problem solving and intelligence.* Oslo: Universitetforlaget.

RABKIN, J. (1979). Criminal behavior of discharged mental patients: A critical appraisal of the research. *Psychological Bulletin, 86,* 1–27.

RACHMAN, S. J., and HODGSON, R. J. (1980). *Obsessions and compulsions.* Englewood Cliffs, N.J.: Prentice-Hall.

RADA, R. T. (1978). *Clinical aspects of the rapist.* New York: Grune & Stratton.

RAICHLE, M. E., and TER-POGOSSIAN, M. M. (1984). PET scan controversy. *Science, 224,* 934.

RAINES, M. P. (1982). A conceptual framework for life transitions. Paper presented at the National Conference of the National Association for Student Personnel Administration, Boston.

RAMSAY, R. W. (1976). *Grief.* Film presented to the meeting of the European Association of Behavior Therapy, Spetsae, Greece (Columbia Broadcasting Company).

RANDICH, A., and ROSS, R. T. (1984). Mechanisms of blocking by contextual stimuli. *Learning and Motivation, 15,* 106–117.

RAVEN, B. H., and RUBIN, J. Z. (1983). *Social psychology.* (2nd ed.). New York: Wiley.

RAY, O. S. (1978). *Drugs, society, and human behavior* (2nd ed.). St. Louis: Mosby.

RAY, O. S. (1983). *Drugs, society, and human behavior.* (3rd ed.). St. Louis: Mosby.

RAYNOR, J. O. (1970). Relationships between achievement-related motives, future orientation, and academic performance. *Journal of Personality and Social Psychology, 15,* 28–33.

REDSON, J. T., and MYCHIELSKA, K. (1982). *Absent-minded: The psychology of mental lapses and everyday errors.* Englewood Cliffs, N.J.: Prentice-Hall.

REIS, H. T., and NEZLEK, J. (1980). Physical attractiveness in social interaction. *Journal of Personality and Social Psychology, 38,* 604–617.

REMMERS, J. E. (1983). Obstructive sleep apnea: Reflections on breathing and the sleeping brain. In M. H. Chase and E. D. Weitzman (Eds.), *Sleep disorders: Basic and clinical research.* New York: Spectrum.

RESCHLY, D. J. (1981). Evaluation of the effects of SOMPA measures on classification of students as mildly retarded. *American Journal of Mental Deficiency, 86,* 16–20.

RESCORLA, R. A., DURLACH, P. J., and GRAU, J. W. (1985). Context learning in Pavlovian conditioning. In P. D. Balsam and A. Tomie (Eds.), *Context and learning.* Hillsdale, N.J.: Erlbaum.

RESCORLA, R. A., and HOLLAND, P. C. (1982). Behavioral studies of associative learning in animals. In M. R. Rosenzweig and L. W. Porter (Eds.), *Annual Review of Psychology, 33,* 265–308.

RESCORLA, R. A., and SOLOMON, R. L. (1967). Two-process learning theory: Relationships between Pavlovian conditioning and instrumental learning. *Psychological Review, 74,* 151–182.

REST, J. R. (1983). Morality. In P. H. Mussen (Ed.), *Handbook of child psychology,* Vol. 3. (4th ed.). New York: Wiley.

RICHMOND, R. S. (1975). Donating blood. *Journal of the American Medical Association, 232* (7), 753–754.

RIDGWAY, J. (1981). Toward a symbiosis of cognitive psychology and psychometrics. In M. P. Friedman, J. P. Das, and N. O'Connor (Eds.), *Intelligence and learning.* New York: Plenum.

RIESEN, A. H. (1965). Effects of early deprivation of photic stimulation. In S. Oster and R. Cooke (Eds.), *The biosocial basis of mental retardation.* Baltimore: Johns Hopkins University Press.

RIESS, M., and SCHLENKER, B. R. (1977). Attitude change and responsibility avoidance as modes of dilemma resolution in forced-compliance situations. *Journal of Personality and Social Psychology, 35,* 21–30.

RIMM, D. C., and MASTERS, J. C. (1979). *Behavior therapy: Techniques and empirical findings.* (2nd ed.). New York: Academic Press.

RIORDAN, C. A., QUIGLEY-FERNANDEZ, B. T., and TEDESCHI, J. T. (1982). Some variables affecting changes in interpersonal attraction. *Journal of Experimental Social Psychology, 18,* 358–374.

ROBBINS, M., and JENSEN, G. (1977). Multiple orgasm in males. In R. Gemme and C. Wheeler (Eds.), *Progress in sexology.* New York: Plenum.

ROBERTS, E. J., KLINE, D., and GAGNON, J. (1978). *Family life and sexual learning,* Vol. 1. Cambridge, Mass.: Population Education.

ROBINS, L. N., HELZER, J. E., CROUGHAN, J., and RATCLIFF, K. (1981). National Institute of Mental Health Diagnostic Interview Schedule: Its history, characteristics, and validity. *Archives of General Psychiatry, 38,* 381–389.

ROCKWELL, R. C., and ELDER, G. H., JR. (1982). Economic deprivation and problem behavior: Childhood and adolescence in the Great Depression. In J. A. Meacham and H. Thomae (Eds.), *Human development.* Basel: S. Karger.

RODIN, J. (1981). Current status of the internal-external hypothesis for obesity: What went wrong? *American Psychologist, 36,* 361–372.

ROGERS, C. R. (1951). *Client-centered therapy.* Boston: Houghton Mifflin.

ROGERS, C. R. (1959). A theory of therapy, personality and interpersonal relationships, as developed in the client-centered framework. In S. Koch (Ed.), *Psychology: A study of a science,* Vol. 3. New York: McGraw-Hill.

ROGERS, C. R. (1970). *Carl Rogers on encounter groups.* New York: Harper & Row.

ROGERS, C. R. (1977). *Carl Rogers on personal power.* New York: Delacorte.

ROGERS, C. R. (1981). *A way of being.* Boston: Houghton Mifflin.

ROGERS, R. F. (1984). Theories of adult development: Research status and counseling implications. In S. D. Brown and R. W. Lent (Eds.), *Handbook of counseling psychology.* New York: Wiley-Interscience.

ROGERS, R. W., and MEWBORN, R. (1976). Fear appeals and attitude change: Effects of a threat's noxiousness, probability of occurrence, and the efficiency of coping responses. *Journal of Personality and Social Psychology, 34,* 54–61.

ROMANCZYK, R. G. (1985). *Clinical utilization of microcomputer technology.* Elmsford, N.Y.: Pergamon Press.

ROOT, M. P. P. (1983). Bulimia: A descriptive and treatment outcome study. Doctoral dissertation, University of Washington.

ROSCH, E. (1973). On the internal structure of perceptual and semantic categories. In T. E. Moore (Ed.), *Cognitive development and the acquisition of language.* New York: Academic Press.

ROSEKIND, M. R., COATES, T. J., and THORESEN, C. E. (1978). Telephone transmission of all-night polysomnographic data from subjects' homes. *Journal of Nervous and Mental Disease, 166,* 438–441.

ROSEN, J. C., and LEITENBERG, H. (1982). Bulimia nervosa: Treatment with exposure and response prevention. *Behavior Therapy, 13,* 117–124.

ROSEN, R., and HALL, E. (1984). *Sexuality.* New York: Random House.

ROSENBAUM, M., and BEN-ARI, K. (1985). Learned helplessness and learned resourcefulness: Effects of noncontingent success and failure on individuals differing in self-control skills. *Journal of Personality and Social Psychology, 48,* 198–215.

ROSENHAN, D. L. (1973). On being sane in insane places. *Science, 179,* 250–258.

ROSENMAN, R. H., BRAND, R. J., JENKINS, C. D., FRIEDMAN, M., STRAUS, R., and WURM, M. (1975). Coronary heart disease in the Western Collaborative Group Study. *Journal of the American Medical Association, 233,* 872–877.

ROSENTHAL, D. (Ed.) (1963). *The Genain quadruplets: A case study and theoretical analysis of heredity and environment in schizophrenia.* New York: Basic Books.

ROSENTHAL, R. (1966). *Experimenter effects in behavioral research.* (Enlarged ed.). New York: Halsted Press.

ROSENTHAL, R., ARCHER, D., DiMATTEO, M. R., KOIVUMAKI, J. H., and ROGERS, P. L. (1974). Body talk and tone of voice: The language without words. *Psychology Today, 2,* 64–71.

ROSENZWEIG, M. R. (1984). Experiences, memory and the brain. *American Psychologist, 39,* 365–376.

ROSS, L. (1977). The intuitive psychologist and his shortcomings: Distortions in the attribution process. In L. Berkowitz (Ed.), *Advances in experimental social psychology, Vol. 10.* New York: Academic Press.

ROTH, T., and ZORICK, F. (1983). The use of hypnotics in specific disorders of initiating and maintaining sleep. In M. H. Chase and E. D. Weitzman (Eds.), *Sleep disorders: Basic and clinical research.* New York: Spectrum.

ROTTER, J. B. (1980). Interpersonal trust, trustworthiness, and gullibility. *American Psychologist, 35,* 1–7.

ROUTH, D. K. (1982). *Learning, speech, and the complex effects of punishment.* New York: Plenum.

ROVEE-COLLIER, C. (1984). The ontogeny of learning and memory in human infancy. In R. Kail and N. E. Spear (Eds.), *Comparative perspectives on the development of memory.* Hillsdale, N.J.: Erlbaum.

ROY, A. (1983). Family history of suicide. *Archives of General Psychiatry, 40,* 971–974.

RUBIN, J. Z., PROVENZANO, F. J., and LURIA, Z. (1974). The eye of the beholder: Parents' view on sex of newborns. *American Journal of Orthopsychiatry, 44,* 512–519.

RUBIN, Z. (1970). Measurement of romantic love. *Journal of Personality and Social Psychology, 116,* 265–273.

RUBIN, Z. (1973). *Liking and loving: An invitation to social psychology.* New York: Holt, Rinehart and Winston.

RUCH, L. O., and CHANDLER, S. M. (1983). Sexual assault trauma during the acute phase: An exploratory model and univariate analysis. *Journal of Health & Social Behavior, 24,* 174–185.

RUMBAUGH, D. M. (Ed.) (1977). *Language learning by a chimpanzee: The Lana Project.* New York: Academic Press.

RUMELHART, D. E., LINDSAY, P., and NORMAN, D. A. (1972). A process model for long-term memory. In E. Tulving and W. Donaldson (Eds.), *Organization of memory.* New York: Academic Press.

RUNNION, A., WATSON, J. D., and McWHORTER, J. (1978). Energy savings in interstate transportation through feedback and reinforcement. *Journal of Organizational Behavior Management, 1,* 180–191.

RUNYAN, W. McK. (1979). Perceived determinants of highs and lows in life satisfaction. *Developmental Psychology, 15,* 331–333.

RUSBULT, C. E., ZEMBRODT, I. M., and GUNN, L. K. (1982). Exit, voice, loyalty, and neglect: Responses to dissatisfaction in romantic involvements. *Journal of Personality and Social Psychology, 19,* 274–293.

RUSH, A. J., BECK, A. T., KOVACS, M., and HOLLON, S. (1977). Comparative efficacy of cognitive therapy and pharmacotherapy in the treatment of depressed outpatients. *Cognitive Therapy and Research, 1,* 17–37.

RUSHTON, J. P., and CAMPBELL, A. C. (1977). Modeling, vicarious reinforcement and extraversion on blood donating in adults: Immediate and long-term effects. *European Journal of Social Psychology, 7,* 297–306.

RUSHTON, J. P., CHRISJOHN, R. D., and FERREN, G. C. (1981). The altruistic personality and the self-report altruism scale. *Personality and Individual Differences, 2,* 293–302.

RUTTER, M. (1978). Family, area, and school influences in the genesis of conduct disorders. In L. Hersov, M. Berger, and D. Shaffer (Eds.), *Aggression and antisocial behavior in childhood and adolescence* (Journal of Child Psychology and Psychiatry Book Series, No. 1). Oxford, England: Pergamon.

RUTTER, M. (1979). Protective factors in children's responses to stress and disadvantage. In M. W. Kent and J. E. Rolf (Eds.), *Primary prevention of psychopathology.* Vol. 3, *Promoting social competence and coping in children.* Hanover, N.H.: University Press of New England.

RUTTER, M. (1983). Continuities and discontinuities in socio-emotional development: Empirical and conceptual perspectives. In R. Emde and R. Harmon (Eds.), *Continuities and discontinuities in development.* New York: Plenum.

RUTTER, M., and GARMEZY, N. (1983). Developmental psychopathology. In P. H. Mussen (Ed.), *Handbook of child psychology.* (4th ed.). New York: Wiley.

RUTTER, M., QUINTON, D., and LIDDLE, C. (1983). Parenting in two generations: Looking backwards and looking forwards. In N. Madge (Ed.), *Families at risk*. London: Heinemann.

RUTTER, M., and SHAFFER, D. (1980). DSM III: A step forward or back in terms of the classification of child psychiatric disorders? *Journal of the American Academy of Child Psychiatry, 19,* 371–394.

SAGAR, H. A., and SCHOFIELD, J. W. (1980). Racial and behavioral cues in black and white children's perceptions of ambiguously aggressive acts. *Journal of Personality and Social Psychology, 39,* 590–598.

SAGHIR, M. T., and ROBINS, E. (1973). *Male and female homosexuality: A comprehensive investigation*. Baltimore: Williams & Wilkins.

SALANS, L. B., KNITTLE, J. L., and HIRSCH, J. (1968). The role of adipose cell size and adipose tissue sensitivity in the carbohydrate intolerance of human obesity. *Journal of Clinical Investigation, 47,* 153–165.

SALES, E., BAUM, M., and SHORE, B. (1984). Victim readjustment following assault. *Journal of Social Issues, 40,* 117–136.

SAMEROFF, A. J. (1972). Learning and adoption in infancy: A comparison of models. In H. W. Reese (Ed.), *Advances in child development and behavior*, Vol. 7. New York: Academic Press.

SAMEROFF, A. J., CASHMORE, T. F., and DYKES, A. C. (1973). Heart rate deceleration during visual fixation in human newborns. *Developmental Psychology, 8,* 117–119.

SANDERS, G. S. (1981). Driven by distraction: An integrative review of social facilitation theory and research. *Journal of Experimental Social Psychology, 17,* 227–251.

SANTA, J. L., and RANKEN, H. B. (1972). Effects of verbal coding on recognition memory. *Journal of Experimental Psychology, 93,* 268–278.

SANTA, J. L., RUSKIN, A. B., SNUTTJER, D., and BAKER, L. (1975). Retrieval and cued recall. *Memory and Cognition, 3,* 341–348.

SARASON, I. G. (1980). *Test anxiety: Theory, research, and applications*. Hillsdale, N.J.: Erlbaum.

SARASON, I. G. (1981). The revised Life Experiences Survey. Unpublished manuscript, University of Washington.

SARASON, I. G., JOHNSON, J. H., and SIEGEL, J. M. (1978). Assessing the impact of life stress: Development of the Life Experiences Survey. *Journal of Consulting and Clinical Psychology, 46,* 932–946.

SARASON, I. G., LEVINE, H. M., BASHAM, R. B., and SARASON, B. R. (1983). Assessing social support: The Social Support Questionnaire. *Journal of Personality and Social Psychology, 39,* 472–480.

SARASON, I. G., and SARASON, B. R. (1984). *Abnormal psychology*. (4th ed.). Englewood Cliffs, N.J.: Prentice-Hall.

SARBIN, T. R., and COE, W. C. (1972). *Hypnosis: A social psychological analysis of influence communication*. New York: Holt, Rinehart and Winston.

SARGENT, M. (1980). "Photos" of living human brain reveal functions of specific areas. *ADAMHA News, 6,* 1, 2.

SARREL, P., and SARREL, L. (1980). The Redbook report on sexual relationships. *Redbook, 155,* 73–80.

SARTRE, J-P. (1956). *Being and nothingness*. New York: Philosophical Library.

SAVAGE-RUMBAUGH, E. S., PATE, J. L., LAWSON, J., SMITH, S. T., and ROSENBAUM, S. (1983). Can a chimpanzee make a statement? *Journal of Experimental Psychology: General, 112,* 457–492.

SAXE, L., DOUGHERTY, D., and CROSS, T. (1985). The validity of polygraph testing: Scientific analysis and public controversy. *American Psychologist, 40,* 355–366.

SCARR, S. T., and CARTER-SALTZMAN, L. (1982). Genetics and intelligence. In R. J. Sternberg (Ed.), *Handbook of human intelligence*. Cambridge, England: Cambridge University Press.

SCARR, S., and WEINBERG, R. A. (1977). Intellectual similarities within families of both adopted and biological children. *Intelligence, 1 (2),* 170–191.

SCARR, S., and WEINBERG, R. A. (1978). The influence of "family background" on intellectual attainment. *American Social Review, 43,* 674–692.

SCHACHTER, D. L. (1983). Amnesia observed: Remembering and forgetting in a natural environment. *Journal of Abnormal Psychology, 92,* 236–242.

SCHACHTER, S. (1966). The interaction of cognitive and physiological determinants of emotional state. In C. D. Spielberger (Ed.), *Anxiety and behavior*. New York: Academic Press.

SCHACHTER, S. (1971). Some extraordinary facts about obese humans and rats. *American Psychologist, 26*, 129–144.

SCHACHTER, S., and WHEELER, L. (1962). Epinephrine, chlorpromazine, and amusement. *Journal of Abnormal and Social Psychology, 65*, 121–128.

SCHÄFER, S. (1976). Sexual and social problems of lesbians. *Journal of Sex Research, 12*, 50–69.

SCHAFFER, H. R., and EMERSON, P. (1964). The development of social attachments in infancy. *Monographs of the Society for Research in Child Development, 20*, (whole No. 94).

SCHAIE, K. W. (1965). A general model for the study of developmental problems. *Psychological Bulletin, 64*, 92–107.

SCHAIE, K. W. (1979). The primary mental abilities in adulthood: An exploration in the development of psychometric intelligence. In P. B. Baltes and O. G. Brim, Jr. (Eds.), *Life span development and behavior*, Vol. 2. New York: Academic Press.

SCHAIE, K. W. (1983). The Seattle longitudinal study: A 21-year exploration of psychometric intelligence in adulthood. In K. W. Schaie (Ed.), *Longitudinal Studies of Adult Psychology Development*. New York: Guilford Press.

SCHANK, R. C. (1982). *Dynamic memory*. New York: Cambridge University Press.

SCHLESIER-STROPP, B. (1984). Bulimia: A review of the literature. *Psychological Bulletin, 95*, 247–257.

SCHLESINGER, H. J., MUMFORD, E., and GLASS, G. V., and others. (1983). Mental health treatment and medical care utilization in a fee-for-service system: Outpatient mental health treatment following the onset of a chronic disease. *American Journal of Public Health, 73*, 422–429.

SCHMALING, K. B., SARASON, I. G., SARASON, B. R., and BASHAM, R. B. (1984). Parental attachment, social support and current life situation. Paper presented at the meeting of the Western Psychological Association, Los Angeles.

SCHMIDT, G. (1975). Male-female differences in sexual arousal during and after exposure to sexually erotic stimuli. *Archives of Sexual Behavior, 4*, 353–364.

SCHNEIDMAN, N. N. (1979). Soviet sport psychology in the 1970s and the superior athlete. In P. Klavora and J. V. Daniel (Eds.), *Coach, athlete, and the sport psychologist*. Champaign, Ill.: Human Kinetics.

SCHOEN, L., KRAMER, M., ANAND, V. K., and WEISENBERGER, S. (1984). Efficacy of UPPP in patients with obstructive sleep apnea. *Sleep Research, 13*, 164.

SCHREURS, B. G., GORMEZANO, I., and HARVEY, J. A. (1983). Apple II/First system control of electrical brain stimulation in the rabbit. *Behavior Research Methods and Instrumentation, 15*, 167–170.

SCHWARTZ, L. L., and KASLOW, F. W. (1981). The cult phenomenon: Historical, sociological, and familial factors contributing to their development and appeal. *Marriage and Family Review, 4*, 3–30.

SCHWARTZ, R. (1984). Body weight regulation. *University of Washington Medicine, 10*, 16–20.

SEARS, D. O., FREEDMAN, J. L., and PEPLAU, L. A. (1985). *Social psychology*. Englewood Cliffs, N.J.: Prentice-Hall.

SEBEOK, T. A., and UMIKER-SEBEOK, D. J. (Eds.) (1980). *Speaking of apes: A critical anthology of two-way communication with man*. New York: Plenum.

SEEMAN, M. V. (1983). Schizophrenia and family studies. *The Psychiatric Journal of the University of Ottowa*, June, pp. 38–43.

SEIDMAN, J. (1983). Schizophrenia and brain dysfunction: An integration of recent neurodiagnostic findings. *Psychological Bulletin, 94* (2), 195–238.

SELIGMAN, M. E. P. (1970). On the generality of the laws of learning. *Psychological Review, 77*, 406–418.

SELIGMAN, M. E. P. (1975). *Helplessness: On depression, development, and death*. San Francisco: Freeman.

SELYE, H. (1976). *The stress of life*. (Rev. ed.). New York: McGraw-Hill.

SENDEN, M. VON (1960). *Space and sight: The perception of space and shape in the congenitally blind before and after operation* (trans. by P. Heath). New York: Free Press.

SHAPIRO, A. K. (1963). Psychological aspects of medication. In H. I. Lief, V. F. Lief, and N. R. Lief (Eds.), *The psychological basis of medical practice*. New York: Harper & Row.

SHAPIRO, D. H., and WALSH, R. N. (Eds.) (1984). *Meditation: Classical and contemporary perspectives*. Hawthorne, N.Y.: Aldine.

SHAPIRO, K. J. (1984). Ethical treatment of animals. In R. Corsini (Ed.), *Encyclopedia of psychology*. New York: Wiley.

SHARAN, S., KUSSELL, P., BROSH, T., and PELEG, R. (1984). *Cooperative learning in the classroom: Research in desegregated schools*. Hillsdale, N.J.: Erlbaum.

SHAVER, P., and FREEDMAN, J. (1976). Your pursuit of happiness. *Psychology Today, 10*, 26–32.

SHAVIT, Y., LEWIS, J. W., TERMAN, G. W., GALE, R. P., and LIEBESKIND, J. C. (1984). Opioid peptides mediate the suppressive effect of stress on natural killer cell cytotoxicity. *Science*, 223, 188–190.

SHEEHAN, D. V. (1982). Panic attacks and phobias. *New England Journal of Medicine*, 307, 156–158.

SHELDON, W. H. (with the collaboration of S. S. Stevens) (1942). *The varieties of temperament: A psychology of constitutional differences.* New York: Harper & Row.

SHELDON, W. H. (with the collaboration of C. W. Dupertuis and E. McDermott). (1954). *Atlas of men: A guide for somatotyping the adult male at all ages.* New York: Harper & Row.

SHERIF, M. (1935). A study of some social factors in perception. *Archives of Psychology* (No. 187).

SHERIF, M., HARVEY, O., WHITE, B., HOOD, W., and SHERIF, C. (1961). *Intergroup conflict and cooperation: The Robbers Cave experiment.* Norman: Institute of Group Relations, University of Oklahoma.

SHERRINGTON, C. S. (1950). The physical basis of mind. In P. Laslett (Ed.), *The physical basis of mind.* New York: Macmillan.

SHERROD, D. R., HAGE, J. N., HALPERN, P. L., and MOORE, B. S. (1977). Effects of personal causation and perceived control on responses to an aversive environment: The more control, the better. *Journal of Experimental Social Psychology*, 13, 14–27.

SHIPLEY, R. H., BUTT, J. H., and HORWITZ, E. A. (1979). Preparation to reexperience a stressful medical examination: Effect of repetitious videotape exposure and coping style. *Journal of Consulting and Clinical Psychology*, 47, 485–492.

SHNEIDMAN, E. S. (1973). *Deaths of man.* New York: Quadrangle.

SHOCK, N. W. (1962). The physiology of aging. *Scientific American*, 206, (1), 101.

SHOTLAND, R. L., and STRAW, M. K. (1976). Bystander response to an assault: When a man attacks a woman. *Journal of Personality and Social Psychology*, 34, 990–999.

SIEGEL, O. (1982). Personality development in adolescence. In B. B. Wolman (Ed.), *Handbook of developmental psychology.* Englewood Cliffs, N.J.: Prentice-Hall.

SIEGEL, R. K. (1978). Phencyclidine, criminal behavior, and the defense of diminished capacity. In R. C. Petersen and R. C. Stillman (Eds.), *Phencyclidine (PCP) abuse: An appraisal* (NIDA Research Monograph No. 21). Washington, D.C.: National Institute of Drug Abuse, Department of Health, Education, and Welfare.

SIEGEL, S. (1978). Tolerance to the hyperthermic effect of morphine in the rat is a learned response. *Journal of Comparative and Physiological Psychology*, 92, 1137–1149.

SIEGEL, S., HINSON, R. E., KRANK, M. D., and MCCULLY, J. (1982). Heroin overdose death: Contribution of drug-associated environmental cues. *Science*, 216, 436–437.

SILVA, J. M., and WEINBERG, R. S. (Eds.) (1984). *Psychological foundations of sport.* Champaign, Ill.: Human Kinetics.

SILVERMAN, L. H., LOCHMAN, I. M., and MILICH, R. H. (1984). *The search for oneness.* New York: International Universities Press.

SILVERMAN, L. H., ROSS, D. C., ADLER, J. M., and LUSTIG, D. A. (1978). Simple research paradigm for demonstrating subliminal psychodynamic activation: Effects of Oedipal stimuli on dart-throwing accuracy in college males. *Journal of Abnormal Psychology*, 87, 341–357.

SINGER, M. T. (1979). Coming out of the cults. *Psychology Today*, 12, 72–82.

SINSHEIMER, R. (1975). Troubled dawn for genetic engineering. *New Scientist*, 68 (971), 148–151.

SKEELS, H. M. (1938). Mental development in children in foster homes. *Journal of Consulting Psychology*, 2, 33–43.

SKINNER, B. F. (1957). *Verbal behavior.* Englewood Cliffs, N.J.: Prentice-Hall.

SKINNER, B. F. (1959). A case history in scientific method. In S. Koch (Ed.), *Psychology: A study of a science*, Vol. 2. New York: McGraw-Hill.

SKINNER, B. F. (1983). *A matter of consequences.* New York: Knopf.

SKODAK, M. (1938). Children in foster homes. *University of Iowa Child Welfare*, 15 (4), 191.

SKODAK, M., and SKEELS, H. (1949). A final follow-up study of one hundred adopted children. *Journal of Genetic Psychology*, 75, 85–125.

SLADE, P. D., TROUP, J. D. G., LETHEM, J., and BENTLEY, G. (1983). The fear-avoidance model of exaggerated pain perception: II. Preliminary studies of coping strategies for pain. *Behaviour Research and Therapy*, 21, 409–416.

SLOANE, R. B., STAPLES, F. R., CRISTOL, A. H., YORKSTON, N. G., and WHIPPLE, K. (1975). *Short-term analytically oriented psychotherapy versus behavior therapy.* Cambridge, Mass.: Harvard University Press.

SMITH, C., and LAPP, L. (1984). Prolonged increases in PS and number of REMS following shuttle box training. In M. H. Chase, W. B. Webb, and R. Wilder-Jones (Eds.), *Sleep research*, Vol. 13. Los Angeles: Brain Information Service.

SMITH, C. A. (1951). *The physiology of the newborn infant.* (2nd ed.). Springfield, Ill.: Thomas.

SMITH, E. R., and MANARD, B. B. (1980). Causal attributions and medical school admissions. *Personality and Social Psychology Bulletin, 6,* 644–650.

SMITH, G. P., GIBBS, J., KULKOSKY, P. J., and BOURNE, E. W. (1982). Relationships between brain-gut peptides and neurons in the control of food intake. In B. G. Hoebel and D. Novin (Eds.), *The neural basis of feeding and reward.* Brunswick, Maine: Hoer Institute.

SMITH, M. C. (1983). Hypnotic memory enhancement of witnesses: Does it work? *Psychological Bulletin, 94,* 387–407.

SMITH, M. L., and GLASS, G. V. (1977). Meta-analyses of psychotherapy outcome studies. *American Psychologist, 32,* 752–760.

SMITH, M. L., GLASS, G. V., and MILLER, T. I. (1980). *The benefits of psychotherapy.* Baltimore: Johns Hopkins University Press.

SMITH, O. A., and DEVITO, J. (1984). Central neural integration of autonomic responses associated with emotion. *Annual Review of Neuroscience, 7,* 43–65.

SMITH, R. E., SMOLL, F. L., and CURTIS, B. (1978). Coaching behaviors in Little League baseball. In F. L. Smoll and R. E. Smith (Eds.), *Psychological perspectives in youth sports.* Washington, D.C.: Hemisphere.

SMITH, R. E., SMOLL, F. L., and CURTIS, B. (1979). Coach Effectiveness Training: A cognitive-behavioral approach to enhancing relationship skills in youth sport coaches. *Journal of Sport Psychology, 1,* 59–75.

SMITH, S. E. (1979). Remembering in and out of context. *Journal of Experimental Psychology, Human Learning and Memory, 5,* 460–471.

SMOLL, F. L., and SMITH, R. E. (1984). Leadership research in youth sports. In J. M. Silva and R. S. Weinberg (Eds.), *Psychological foundations of sport.* Champaign, Ill.: Human Kinetics.

SNOW, C. E., ARLMAN-RUPP, A., HASSING, Y., JOBS, J., JOOSTEN, J., and VORSTER, J. (1976). Mother's speech in three social classes. *Journal of Psycholinguistic Research, 5,* 1–20.

SNOWDON, C. T. (1983). Ethology, comparative psychology, and animal behavior. *Annual Review of Psychology, 34,* 63–94.

SOKOL, S. (1978). Measurement of infant visual acuity from pattern reversal cvoked potentials. *Vision Research, 18,* 33–39.

SOKOL, S. (1984). The use of event-related potentials in the study of human pattern vision. In R. Hilfer and J. B. Sheffield (Eds.), *Molecular and cellular basis of visual acuity.* New York: Springer-Verlag.

SOKOLOFF, L., REIVICH, M., KENNEDY, C., DESROSIERS, M. H., PATLACK, C. S., PETTIGREW, K. D., SAKURADA, O., and SHINOHARA, M. (1977). The [14C] deoxyglucose method for the measurement of local cerebral glucose utilization: Theory, procedure, and normal values in the conscious and anesthetized albino rat. *Journal of Neurochemistry, 28,* 897–916.

SOLOFF, P. H., and MILLWARD, J. W. (1983). Psychiatric disorders in the families of borderline patients. *Archives of General Psychiatry, 40,* 37–44.

SOLOMON, R. L. (1982). The opponent process in acquired motivation. In D. W. Pfaff (Ed.), *The physiological mechanisms of motivation.* New York: Springer-Verlag.

SORENSEN, R. C. (1973). *Adolescent sexuality in contemporary America.* New York: World Publishing.

SOSA, R., KENNELL, J., KLAUS, M., ROBERTSON, S., and URRUTIA, J. (1980). The effect of a supportive companion on perinatal problems, length of labor, and mother-infant interaction. *New England Journal of Medicine, 303,* 597–600.

SPACAPAN, S., and COHEN, S. (1983). Effects and after-effects of stressor expectations. *Journal of Personality and Social Psychology, 45,* 1243–1254.

SPAULDING, W., CRINEAN, W. J., and MARTIN, T. (1983). Microcomputerized clinical and research laboratories in in-patient settings. *Behavior Research Methods and Instrumentation, 15,* 171–176.

SPEISMAN, J. C., LAZARUS, R. S., MORDKOFF, A. M., and DAVIDSON, L. A. (1964). The experimental reduction of stress based on ego-defense theory. *Journal of Abnormal and Social Psychology, 68,* 367–380.

SPERLING, G. (1960). The information available in brief visual presentations. *Psychological Monographs, 74,* 11 (Whole No. 498).

SPERLING, G. (1984). A unified theory of attention and signal detection. In R. Parasuraman and D. R. Davies (Eds.), *Varieties of attention.* New York: Academic Press.

SPERRY, R. W. (1970). Perception in the absence of neocortical commissures. In *Perception and its disorders.* Association for Research in Nervous and Mental Disease. New York: Williams and Wilkins.

SPIELBERGER, C. D., and DE NIKE, L. D. (1966). Descriptive behaviorism versus cognitive theory in verbal operant conditioning. *Psychological Review*, 73, 306–326.

SPITZ, R. A. (1946). Anaclitic depression. *Psychoanalytic Study of the Child*, 2, 313–342.

SPRAFKIN, J. N., LIEBERT, R.M., and POULOS, R. W. (1975). Effects of a prosocial televised example on children's helping. *Journal of Experimental Child Psychology*, 20, 119–126.

SPRINGER, S. P., and DEUTSCH, G. (1985). *Left brain, right brain*. (Rev. ed.). New York: Freeman.

SROUFE, L. A. (1983). Infant-caregiver attachment and patterns of adaptation in preschool: The roles of maladaptation and competence. In M. Perlmutter (Ed.), *The Minnesota Symposia on Child Psychology*, Vol. 16. Hillsdale, N.J.: Erlbaum.

SROUFE, L. A., FOX, N. E., and PANCAKE, V. R. (1983). Attachment and dependency in developmental perspective. *Child Development*, 54, 1615–1627.

STAATS, A. W. (1971). Linguistic-mentalistic theory versus explanatory S-R learning theory of language development. In D. I. Slobin (Ed.), *The ontogenesis of grammar: Some facts and several theories*. New York: Academic Press.

STAATS, A. W. (1975). *Social behaviorism*. Homewood, Ill.: Dorsey Press.

STAGNER, R. (1984). Trait psychology. In N. S. Endler and J. McV. Hunt (Eds.), *Personality and the behavioral disorders*, Vol. 1. (2nd ed.). New York: Wiley.

STAIB, A. R., and LOGAN, D. R. (1977). Hypnotic stimulation of breast growth. *American Journal of Clinical Hypnosis*, 19, 201–207.

STARKEY, D. (1981). The origins of concept formation: Object sorting and object preference in early infancy. *Child Development*, 52, 489–497.

STAUB, E. (1978). Predicting prosocial behavior: A model for specifying the nature of personality-situation interaction. In L. A. Pervin and M. Lewis (Eds.), *Perspectives in interactional psychology*. New York: Plenum.

STEINBERG, R., and SHAPIRO, S. (1982). Sex differences in personality traits of female and male master of business administration students. *Journal of Applied Psychology*, 67, 306–310.

STEPHAN, W. (1978). School desegregation: An evaluation of predictions made in Brown v. Board of Education. *Psychological Bulletin*, 85, 217–238.

STEPHENS, J. H. (1978). Long-term prognosis and follow-up in schizophrenia. *Schizophrenia Bulletin*, 4, 25–47.

STERN, R. S., and COBB, J. P. (1978). Phenomenology of obsessive-compulsive neuroses. *British Journal of Psychiatry*, 182, 233–239.

STERN, R. M., RAY, J. W., and DAVIS, C. M. (1980). *Psychophysiological recording*. New York: Oxford University Press.

STERNBERG, R. J., and GRAJEK, S. (1984). The nature of loving. *Journal of Personality and Social Psychology*, 47, 312–329.

STERNBERG, R. J., KETRON, J. L., and POWELL, J. S. (1982). Componential approaches to the training of intelligent performance. In D. K. Detterman and R. J. Sternberg (Eds.), *How and how much can intelligence be increased?* Norwood, N.J.: Ablex.

STERNBERG, R. J., and SALTER, W. (1982). Conceptions of intelligence. In R. J. Sternberg (Ed.), *Handbook of human intelligence*. Cambridge, England: Cambridge University Press.

STERNBERG, R. S., and POWELL, J. S. (1983). Comprehending verbal comprehension. *American Psychologist*, 38, 878–893.

STEVENS, C. F. (1979). The neuron. *Scientific American*, 241, 54–65.

STEVENSON, H. (1983). How children learn—the quest for a theory. In P. Mussen (Ed.), *Handbook of child psychology*. (4th ed.). New York: Wiley.

STINE, E. L., and BOHANNON, J. N., III (1983). Imitations, interactions, and language acquisition. *Journal of Child Language*, 10, 589–603.

STOKOLS, D. (1976). The experience of crowding in primary and secondary environments. *Environment and Behavior*, 8, 49–86.

STOKOLS, D. (1978). A typology of crowding experiences. In A. Baum and Y. Epstein (Eds.), *Human response to crowding*. Hillsdale, N.J.: Erlbaum.

STONE, M. H. (1980). *The borderline syndromes*. New York: Methuen.

STONE, M. H. (1981). Borderline syndrome: Consideration of subtypes and an overview, direction for research. *Psychiatric Clinics of North America*, 4, 3–24.

STORR, A. (1980). *The art of psychotherapy*. New York: Methuen.

Stouffer, S. A., Lumsdaine, A. A., Lumsdaine, M. H., Williams, R. M., Smith, M. B., Janis, I. L., Star, S. A., and Cottrell, L. S. (1949). *The American soldier.* Vol. 2, *Combat and its aftermath.* Princeton, N.J.: Princeton University Press.

Straus, M. A., Gelles, R. J., and Steinmetz, S. K. (1980). *Behind closed doors: Violence in the American family.* Garden City, N.Y.: Doubleday (Anchor).

Stuart, R. B. (1981). *Violent behavior: Social learning approaches to prediction, management, and treatment.* New York: Brunner/Mazel.

Stunkard, A. J. (1982). Obesity. In A. S. Bellak, M. Hersen, and A. E. Kazdin (Eds.), *International handbook of behavior modification and therapy.* New York: Plenum.

Stuss, D. T., and Benson, D. F. (1984). Neuropsychological studies of the frontal lobes. *Psychological Bulletin,* 95, 3–28.

Sugarman, S. (1983). Why talk? Comment on Savage-Rumbaugh, et al. *Journal of Experimental Psychology: General, 112,* 493–497.

Suggs, R. (1962). *The hidden worlds of Polynesia.* New York: Harcourt Brace Jovanovich.

Sulin, R. A., and Dooling, D. J. (1974). Intrusions of a thematic idea in retention of prose. *Journal of Experimental Psychology, 103,* 255–262.

Suomi, S. J., and Harlow, H. F. (1978). Early experience and social development in Rhesus monkeys. In M. E. Lamb (Ed.), *Social and personality development.* New York: Holt, Rinehart and Winston.

Tageson, C. W. (1982). *Humanistic psychology: A synthesis.* Homewood, Ill.: Dorsey Press.

Tajfel, H., and Turner, J. (1979). An integrative theory of intergroup conflict. In W. G. Autin and S. Worchel (Eds.), *The social psychology of intergroup relations.* Monterey, Calif.: Brooks/Cole.

Tallman, J. F., Paul, S. M., Skolnick, P., and Gallager, D. W. (1980). Receptors for the age of anxiety: Pharmacology of the benzodiazepines. *Science, 207,* 274–281.

Taylor, S. E. (1983). Adjustment to threatening events: A theory of cognitive adaptation. *American Psychologist,* 38, 1161–1173.

Tearnan, B. H., Telch, M. J., and Keefe, P. (1984). Etiology and onset of agoraphobia: A critical review. *Comprehensive Psychiatry, 25 (1),* 51–61.

Television and Behavior: Ten Years of Scientific Progress and Implications for the Eighties. (1982). Rockville, Md.: U.S. Department of Health and Human Services.

Tellegen, A. (1979). On measures and conceptions of hypnosis. *American Journal of Clinical Hypnosis, 21,* 219–237.

Teplin, L. A. (1977). Preference versus prejudice: A multimethod analysis of children's discrepant racial choices. *Social Science Quarterly, 58,* 390–406.

Terrace, H. S., Petito, L. A., Sanders, R. J., and Bever, T. G. (1979). Can an ape create a sentence? *Science, 206,* 891–902.

Tesser, A., and Paulhus, D. L. (1976). Toward a causal model of love. *Journal of Personality and Social Psychology, 34,* 1095–1105.

Tharp, R. G., and Gallimore, R. (1976). What a coach can teach a teacher. *Psychology Today,* Jan., 75–78.

Thelmar, E. (1932). *The maniac: A realistic study of madness from a maniac's point of view.* (2nd ed.). London: Watts.

Thomas, A., and Chess, S. (1984). Genesis and evolution of behavioral disorders: From infancy to early adult life. *American Journal of Psychiatry, 141,* 1–9.

Thomas, C. B. (1982). Stamina—the thread of human life. *Psychotherapy and Psychosomatics, 38,* 74–80.

Thomas, J. (Ed.) (1984). *Motor development during childhood and adolescence.* Minneapolis: Burgess.

Thompson, R. F., Berger, T. W., and Madden, J., IV (1983). Cellular processes of learning and memory in the mammalean CNS. *Annual Review of Neurosciences, 6,* 447–491.

Thompson, R. F., and Robinson, D. N. (1979). Physiological psychology. In E. Hearsh (Ed.), *The first century of experimental psychology.* Hillsdale, N.J.: Erlbaum.

Thompson, W. C., Cowan, C. L., and Rosenhan, D. L. (1980). Focus of attention mediates the impact of negative affect on altruism. *Journal of Personality and Social Psychology, 38,* 291–300.

Thornton, B. (1984). Defensive attribution of responsibility: Evidence for an arousal-based motivational bias. *Journal of Personality and Social Psychology, 46,* 721–734.

Thurstone, L. L. (1938). Primary mental abilities. *Psychometric Monographs,* No. 1.

Tilker, H. A. (1970). Socially responsible behavior as a function of observer responsibility and victim feedback. *Journal of Personality and Social Psychology, 14,* 95–100.

Tilson, H. A., and Mitchell, C. L. (1984). Neurobehavioral techniques to assess the effects of chemicals on

Harper & Row
STUDY-AID

School is tough enough.
Get an edge on studying this semester with STUDY-AID.

STUDY-AID is a new computer program for the Apple, the Macintosh, and the IBM PC (and most IBM PC compatible) computers keyed directly to your text.

After reading each chapter in the text, you can use STUDY-AID to review how much you have learned with various types of exercises and self-tests. Automatic scoring enables you to check your progress as you learn.

If you do not own a computer, ask your instructor where you can use one on campus.

As a special offer, you can have the STUDY-AID disk and the printed Study Guide as a package for only $19.95.

To purchase a copy, check with your local college bookstore. To order by mail or telephone, complete the card or call Soft Productions, Inc. at (219) 255-3911. Be sure to indicate the type of computer disk you want and to include your method of payment. If the order card has been removed, mail your order to Soft Productions, Inc., P.O. Box 1003, Notre Dame, IN 46556. Be sure to indicate the title and author of the text and the type of computer disk you want (Apple, Macintosh, or IBM) and to include your method of payment.

(Cut along dotted lines and mail card below.)

Offer available in the
U.S. and Canada only.

NO POSTAGE
NECESSARY
IF MAILED
IN THE
UNITED STATES

BUSINESS REPLY MAIL
FIRST CLASS   PERMIT NO. 4501   NOTRE DAME, IN

POSTAGE WILL BE PAID BY ADDRESSEE

Soft Productions, Inc.
P.O. Box 1003
Notre Dame, IN 46556

the nervous system. *Annual Review of Pharmacology and Toxicology, 24*, 425–450.

TIMEROS, P. S. (1972). *Developmental psychology and aging.* New York: Macmillan.

TIZARD, B., and HODGES, J. (1978). The effect of early institutional rearing on the development of eight-year-old children. *Journal of Child Psychology and Psychiatry, 19*, 99–118.

TOCH, H. (1969). *Violent men.* Chicago: Aldine.

TOLMAN, E. C., and HONZIK, C. H. (1930). Introduction and removal of reward, and maze performance in rats. *University of California Publications in Psychology, 4*, 257–275.

TOMKINS, S. S. (1982). Affect theory. In P. Ekman (Ed.), *Emotion in the human face.* (2nd ed.). New York: Cambridge University Press.

TORTORA, G. J., and ANAGNOSTAKOS, N. P. (1984). *Principles of anatomy and physiology.* (4th ed.). New York: Harper & Row.

TRIPLETT, N. (1898). The dynamogenic factors in pace-making and competition. *American Journal of Psychology, 9*, 507–533.

TSAI, M., FELDMAN-SUMMERS, S., and EDGAR, M. (1979). Childhood molestation: Variables related to differential impacts on psychosexual functioning in adult women. *Journal of Abnormal Psychology, 88*, 407–417.

TULVING, E. (1972). Episodic and semantic memory. In E. Tulving and W. Donaldson (Eds.), *Organization of memory.* New York: Academic Press.

TULVING, E. (1984). Précis of elements of episodic memory. *The Behavioral and Brain Sciences, I*, 223–268.

TULVING, E., and THOMSON, D. M. (1973). Encoding specificity and retrieval processes in episodic memory. *Journal of Experimental Psychology, 80*, 352–373.

TURNER, J. (1984). Social identification and psychological group formation. In H. Tajfel (Ed.), *The social dimension.* Cambridge, England: Cambridge University Press.

TURNBULL, C. M. (1961). Some observations regarding the experiences and behavior of the Ba Mbuti pygmies. *American Journal of Psychology, 74*, 304–308.

UNDHEIM, J. (1981). On intelligence: IV. Toward a restoration of general intelligence. *Scandinavian Journal of Psychology, 22*, 251–266.

U.S. BUREAU OF THE CENSUS (1979). Marital status and living arrangements: March 1978. *Current Population Reports* (Series P-20, No. 303). Washington, D.C.: Government Printing Office.

UTTAL, W. R. (1973). *The psychobiology of sensory coding.* New York: Harper & Row.

VAILLANT, G. E. (1977). *Adaptation to life.* Boston: Little, Brown.

VAILLANT, G. E. (1984). The disadvantages of DSM-III outweigh the advantages. *American Journal of Psychiatry, 141* (4), 542–545.

VALENTI, A., and DOWNING, L. (1975). Differential effects of jury size on verdicts following deliberation as a function of the apparent guilt of the defendant. *Journal of Personality and Social Psychology, 32*, 655–663.

VAN HOUTEN, R. (1983). Punishment: From the animal laboratory to the applied setting. In S. Axelrod and J. Apsche (Eds.), *The effects of punishment on human behavior.* New York: Academic Press.

VASTA, R., and BROCKNER, J. (1979). Self-esteem and self-evaluative covert statements. *Journal of Consulting and Clinical Psychology, 47*, 776–777.

VAUGHN, E. D. (1977). Misconceptions about psychology among introductory psychology students. *Teaching of Psychology*, October, pp. 138–141.

VISCHI, T. R., JONES, K. R., SHANK, E. L., and LIMA, L. H. (1980). *The alcohol, drug abuse, and mental health national data book.* Rockville, Md.: Alcohol, Drug Abuse, and Mental Health Administration.

VOLPICELLI, J. R., ULM, R. R., ALTENOR, A., and SELIGMAN, M. E. P. (1983). Learned mastery in the rat. *Learning and Motivation, 14*, 204–222.

VON DER HEYDT, R., ADORJANI, C., HANNEY, P., and BAUMGARTNER, G. (1978). Disparity, sensitivity, and receptive field incongruity of units in the cat striate cortex. *Experimental Brain Research, 31*, 523–545.

VON FRISCH, F. (1967). *The dance language and orientation of bees* (trans. by C. E. Chadwick). Cambridge, Mass.: Harvard University Press (Belknap Press).

VONNEGUT, M. (1975). *The Eden express.* New York: Bantam Books.

WALEN, S. (1980). Cognitive factors in sexual behavior. *Journal of Sex and Marital Therapy, 6*, 87–101.

WALKER, T. G., and MAIN, E. C. (1973). Choice-shifts in political decision making: Federal judges and civil liberties cases. *Journal of Applied Social Psychology, 2*, 39–48.

WALL, T. W. (1984). Hypnotic phenomena. In W. C. Wester and A. H. Smith (Eds.), *Clinical hypnosis: A multidisciplinary approach*. Philadelphia: Lippincott.

WALLERSTEIN, J. S., and KELLY, J. B. (1980). *Surviving the breakup: How children and parents cope with divorce*. New York: Basic Books.

WALSH, R. (1980). The consciousness disciplines and the behavioral sciences: Questions of comparison and assessment. *American Journal of Psychiatry, 137*, 663–673.

WALSTER, E., and PILIAVIN, J. A. (1972). Equity and the innocent bystander. *Journal of Social Issues, 28*, 165–189.

WALSTER, E., and WALSTER, G. W. (1978). *A new look at love*. Reading, Mass.: Addison-Wesley.

WALSTER, E., WALSTER, G. W., and BERSCHEID, E. (1978). Equity: Theory and research. *Journal of Personality and Social Psychology, 36*, 82–92.

WANNER, E., and GLEITMAN, L. R. (Eds.) (1982). *Language acquisition: The state of the art*. New York: Cambridge University Press.

WARSHAK, R. A., and SANTROCK, J. W. (1983). Children of divorce: Impact of custody disposition on social development. In E. Callahan and K. McCluskey (Eds.), *Life span developmental psychology: Non-normative life events*. New York: Academic Press.

WATERS, E., VAUGHN, B. E., and EGELAND, B. R. (1980). Individual differences in infant-mother attachment relationships at age one: Antecedents in neonatal behavior in an urban economically disadvantaged sample. *Child Development, 51*, 208–216.

WATSON, D. L., and THARP, R. G. (1981). *Self-directed behavior: Self-modification for personal adjustment*. (3rd ed.). Monterey, Calif.: Brooks/Cole.

WATSON, J. B., and RAYNER, R. (1920). Conditioned emotional reactions. *Journal of Experimental Psychology, 3*, 1–14.

WEBB, E. J., CAMPBELL, D. T., SCHWARTZ, R. D., and SECHREST, L. (1966). *Unobtrusive measures: Nonreactive research in the social sciences*. Chicago: Rand McNally.

WEHR, T. A., TILLIN, J. C., and WOODWIN, F. K. (1983). Sleep and circadian rhythms in depression. In M. H. Chase and E. D. Weitzman (Eds.), *Sleep disorders: Basic and clinical research*. New York: Spectrum.

WEINBERG, M. S., and WILLIAMS, C. J. (1974). *Male homosexuals: Their problems and adaptations*. New York: Oxford University Press.

WEINBERG, R. S., and GENUCHI, M. (1980). Relationship between competitive trait anxiety, state anxiety, and performance: A field study. *Journal of Sport Psychology, 2*, 148–154.

WEINBERGER, D. R., WAGNER, R. L., and WYATT, R. J. (1983). Neuropathological studies of schizophrenia: A selective review. *Schizophrenia Bulletin, 9*, 193–212.

WEINER, B. (1980). *Human motivation*. New York: Holt, Rinehart and Winston.

WEISBERG, L., NICE, C., and KATZ, M. (1984). *Cerebral computed tomography*. Philadelphia: Saunders.

WEISS, J. M. (1971). Effects of coping behavior in different warning signal conditions in stress pathology in rats. *Journal of Comparative and Physiological Psychology, 77*, 1–13.

WEISSBERG, R. P., COWEN, E. L., and LATYCZEWSKI, B. S. (1982). The primary mental health project: Seven consecutive years of program outcome research. *Journal of Counseling and Clinical Psychology, 51*, 100–107.

WEISSMAN, M. M., GESHON, E. S., KIDD, K. K., PRUSOFF, B. A., LECKMAN, J. F., DIBBLE, E., HAMOVIT, J., THOMPSON, W. D., PAULS, D. L., and GUROFF, J. J. (1984). Psychiatric disorder in the relatives of probands with affective disorders. *Archives of General Psychiatry, 41*, 13–21.

WEISSMAN, M. M., KLERMAN, G. L., PAYKEL, E. S., PRUSOFF, B., and HANSON, B. (1974). Treatment effects on the social adjustment of depressed patients. *Archives of General Psychiatry, 30*, 771–778.

WEISSMAN, M., MYERS, J. K., and THOMPSON, W. D. (1981). Depression and its treatment in a U.S. urban community, 1975–1976. *Archives of General Psychiatry, 38*, 417–421.

WEITZMAN, E. D., CZEISLER, C. A., ZIMMERMAN, J. C., MOORE-EDE, M. C., and RONDA, J. M. (1983). Biological rhythms in man: Internal organization of the physiology during non-entrained (free-running) conditions and applied to delayed sleep phase syndrome. In M. H. Chase and E. D. Weitzman (Eds.), *Sleep disorders: Basic and clinical research*. New York: Spectrum.

WELLS, K. C., CONNERS, C. K., IMBER, L., and DELAMATER, A. (1981). Use of single subject methodology in clinical decision making with a hyperactive child on the psychiatric inpatient unit. *Behavioral Assessment, 3*, 359–369.

WERNER, E. E., BIERMAN, J. M., and FRENCH, F. E. (1971). *The children of Kauai*. Honolulu: University of Hawaii Press.

WERNER, E. E., and SMITH, R. S. (1977). *Kauai's children come of age*. Honolulu: University of Hawaii Press.

WERNER, E. E., and SMITH, R. S. (1982). *Vulnerable but invincible.* New York: McGraw-Hill.

WERNER, P. D., ROSE, T. L., and YESAVAGE, J. A. (1983). Reliability, accuracy, and decision-making strategy in clinical predictions. *Journal of Consulting and Clinical Psychology, 51,* 815–825.

WEST, J. B. (1984). Human physiology at extreme altitudes on Mt. Everest. *Science, 223,* 784–788.

WESTHEIMER, G. (1984). Spatial vision. *Annual Review of Psychology, 35,* 201–226.

WHALEN, R. E., and SIMON, N. G. (1984). Biological motivation. *Annual Review of Psychology, 35,* 257–276.

WHITE, G. L., and KIGHT, T. D. (1984). Misattribution of arousal and attraction: Effects of salience of explanations for arousal. *Journal of Experimental Social Psychology, 20,* 55–64.

WHITE, R. K. (1968). *Nobody wanted war.* Garden City, N.Y.: Doubleday.

WHITEHURST, G. J., and VASTA, R. (1975). Is language acquired through imitation? *Journal of Psycholinguistic Research, 4,* 37–60.

WHITMONT, E. C., and KAUFMANN, Y. (1973). Analytical psychotherapy. In R. Corsini (Ed.), *Current psychotherapies.* Itasca, Ill.: Peacock.

WICKELGREN, W. A. (1981). Human learning and memory. *Annual Review of Psychology, 32,* 21–52.

WIDOM, C. S. (1983). A methodology for studying noninstitutionalized psychopaths. In R. D. Hare and D. A. Schaling (Eds.), *Psychopathic behavior: Approaches to research.* Chichester, England: Wiley.

WILCOXON, H. C., DRAGOIN, W. B., and KRAL, P. A. (1971). Illness-induced aversions in rat and quail: Relative salience of visual and gustatory cues. *Science, 171,* 826–828.

WILLARD, R. D. (1977). Breast enlargement through visual imagery and hypnosis. *American Journal of Clinical Hypnosis, 19,* 195–199.

WILLIAMS, J. E. (1974). Stimulation of breast growth by hypnosis. *Journal of Sex Research, 10,* 316–325.

WILLIAMS, M. D. (1976). Retrieval from very long-term memory. Doctoral dissertation, University of California, San Diego.

WILSON, E. O. (1975). *Sociobiology: The new synthesis.* Cambridge, Mass.: Harvard University Press.

WILSON, I. C., GARBUTT, U.C., LANIER, C. F., MOYLAN, J., NELSON, W. T., and PRANGE, A. J., JR. (1983). Is there a tardive dysmentia? *Schizophrenia Bulletin, 9,* 187–192.

WILSON, R. S. (1983). The Louisville twin study: Developmental synchronies in behavior. *Child Development, 54,* 298–316.

WIMER, R. E., and WIMER, C. C. (1985). Animal behavior genetics: A search for the biological foundation of behavior. *Annual Review of Psychology, 36,* 171–218.

WINTER, D. G. (1973). *The power motive.* New York: Free Press.

WINTER, D. G., and STEWART, A. J. (1978). The power motive. In H. London and J. Exner (Eds.), *Dimensions of personality.* Hillsdale, N.J.: Erlbaum.

WINTER, D. G., STEWART, A. J., and McCLELLAND, D. C. (1977). Husband's motives and wife's career level. *Journal of Personality and Social Psychology, 35,* 159–166.

WINTER, L., and ULEMAN, S. (1984). When are social judgments made? Evidence for the spontaneousness of trait interference. *Journal of Personality and Social Psychology, 47* (2), 237–252.

WOLFE, L. (1980). The sexual profile of that Cosmopolitan girl. *Cosmopolitan, 189,* 254–257, 263–265.

WOLPE, J., and RACHMAN, S. (1960). Psychoanalytic "evidence": A critique based on Freud's case of Little Hans. *Journal of Nervous and Mental Disease, 131,* 135–147.

WOODS, S. C. (1978). Conditioned insulin secretion. In Y. Katsuki, M. Sato, S. F. Takagi, and Y. Oomura (Eds.), *Food intake and the chemical senses.* Tokyo: University of Tokyo Press.

WOODS, S. C., and KULKOSKY, P. J. (1976). Classically conditioned changes in blood glucose level. *Psychosomatic Medicine, 38,* 201–219.

WOOLEY, S. C., WOOLEY, O. W., and DYRENFORTH, S. R. (1979). Theoretical, practical, and social issues in behavioral treatments of obesity. *Journal of Applied Behavior Analysis, 12,* 3–25.

WULACH, J. S. (1983). Diagnosing the DSM-III antisocial personality disorder. *Professional Psychology: Research and Practice, 14,* 330–340.

WYLIE, R. C. (1978). *The self concept* (Vol. 2). *Theory and research on selected topics.* Lincoln: University of Nebraska Press.

YABLONSKY, L. (1962). *The violent gang.* New York: Macmillan.

YALOM, I. D. (1975). *The theory and practice of group psychotherapy.* (2nd ed.). New York: Basic Books.

YALOM, I. D. (1980). *Existential psychotherapy.* New York: Basic Books.

YARROW, M. R., CAMPBELL, J. D., and BURTON, R. V. (1970). Recollections of childhood: A study of the retrospective method. *Monographs of the Society for Research in Child Development,* Serial No. 138, 35 (5), 83.

YERKES, R. M., and DODSON, J. D. (1908). The relation of strength of stimulus to rapidity of habit-formation. *Journal of Comparative Neurological Psychology, 18,* 459–482.

YIN, T. C. T., and KUWADA, S. (1984). Neuronal mechanisms of binaural interaction. In G. M. Edelman, W. M. Cowan, and W. E. Gall (Eds.), *Dynamic aspects of neocortical function.* New York: Wiley.

ZAIDEL, E. (1983). A response to Gazzaniga: Language in the right hemisphere, convergent perspectives. *American Psychologist, 38,* 542–546.

ZAJONC, R. B. (1965). Social facilitation. *Science, 149,* 269–274.

ZAJONC, R. B. (1980). Feeling and thinking: Preferences need no inferences. *American Psychologist, 35,* 151–175.

ZAJONC, R. B. (1980). Compresence. In P. Paulus (Ed.), *The psychology of group influence.* Hillsdale, N.J.: Erlbaum.

ZAJONC, R. B. (1984). On the primacy of affect. *American Psychologist, 39,* 117–123.

ZELNICK, M., KANTNER, J. F., and FORD, K. (1981). *Sex and pregnancy in adolescence.* Beverly Hills, Calif.: Sage.

ZILBERGELD, B. (1978). *Male sexuality.* New York: Bantam.

ZILBERGELD, B., and EVANS, M. (1980). The inadequacy of Masters and Johnson. *Psychology Today, 14,* 29–43.

ZILLMANN, D. (1979). *Hostility and aggression.* New York: Halsted Press.

ZILLMANN, D. (1983). Transfer of excitation in emotional behavior. In J. T. Capioppo and R. E. Petty (Eds.), *Social psychophysiology: A sourcebook.* New York: Guilford Press.

ZILLMANN, D. (1984). *Connections between sex and aggression.* Hillsdale, N.J.: Erlbaum.

ZIMBARDO, P. G. (1972). Pathology of imprisonment. *Society, 9 (6),* 4–8.

ZIMBARDO, P. G., HANEY, C., BANKS, W. C., and JAFFE, D. (1973). The mind is a formidable jailer: A Pirandellian prison. *New York Times Magazine,* April 8.

ZUBIN, J., MAGAZINER, J., and STEINHAUER, S. R. (1982). *The metamorphosis of schizophrenia: From chronicity to vulnerability.* Unpublished paper.

ZUBIN, J., and SPRING, B. (1977). Vulnerability—a new view of schizophrenia. *Journal of Abnormal Psychology, 86,* 103–126.

ZUBIN, J., and STEINHAUER, S. (1982). How to break the logjam in schizophrenia. *Journal of Nervous and Mental Disease, 169,* 477–492.

ZUCKERMAN, M. (1979). *Sensation seeking: Beyond the optimal level of arousal.* Hillsdale, N.J.: Erlbaum.

ZUCKERMAN, M., BUCHSBAUM, M. S., and MURPHY, D. L. (1980). Sensation seeking and its biological correlates. *Psychological Bulletin, 88,* 187–214.

ZUCKERMAN, M., HALL, J. A., DeFRANK, R. S., and ROSENTHAL, R. (1976). Encoding and decoding of spontaneous and posed facial expressions. *Journal of Personality and Social Psychology, 34,* 966–977.

PHOTOGRAPH AND ILLUSTRATION ACKNOWLEDGMENTS

Collins and M. R. Quillian, "Retrieval time from semantic memory." *Journal of Verbal Learning and Verbal Behavior*, 2, 240–247/ p. 256, Used with permission of the authors and the publishers, from G. R. Loftus and E. F. Loftus, *Human Memory: The Processing of Information*. Hillsdale, N.J.: Erlbaum, 1976/ p. 261, Adapted from W. K. Estes, "Learning, memory and intelligence." In R. J. Sternberg, Ed., *Handbook of Human Intelligence*. Cambridge, Eng.: Cambridge University Press/ p. 262, Adapted from L. Postman and L. Phillips, "Short-term temporal changes in free recall." *Quarterly Journal of Experimental Psychology*, 17(2), 132–138. Reprinted by permission of the Experimental Psychological Society.

Chapter Eight: Page 271, Burroughs/NYT Pictures/ p. 272, Schaefer, The Picture Cube/ p. 275, Friends of Washoe, Roger S. Fouts/ p. 276, From A. J. Premack and D. Premack, "Teaching language to an ape." Copyright © 1972 by Scientific American, Inc. All rights reserved/ p. 277 (top), Yerkes Regional Primate Research Center of Emory University; (bottom), N. A. Baxley (Producer), 1982. *Cognition, Creativity, and Behavior: The Columban Simulations*. (film). Champaign, Ill.: Research Press/ p. 283, General Electric Company/ p. 286 (top), © Brilliant, The Picture Cube; (middle), Pacheco, EKM-Nepenthe/ p. 289, John B. West, M.D., Ph.D./ p. 292 (bottom), The Psychological Corporation, Cleveland, Ohio/ p. 294, Reproduced by permission of Harcourt Brace Jovanovich from the Otis-Lennon Mental Ability Test, Copyright 1967/ p. 295, Courtesy of Harcourt Brace Jovanovich, Inc./ p. 300, Reproduced by permission of American Guidance Service, Inc., Publishers' Bldg., Circle Pines, MN 55014. *Kaufman Assessment Battery for Children* by Alan S. Kaufman and Nadeen L. Kaufman © 1983.

Chapter Nine: Page 311, From *How To Make Yourself Miserable: A Vital Training Manual* by Dan Greenburg, with Marcia Jacobs. Illustrations by Marvin Rubin. © 1966 by Dan Greenburg. Reprinted by permission of Random House, Inc., p. 9/ p. 312, Arthur Leipzig © 1960/ p. 313, Conklin, Monkmeyer/ p. 314 (bottom), *U.S. News & World Report*/ p. 317, A. N. Meltzoff and M. K. Moore, "Imitation of facial and manual gestures by human neonates." *Science*, 1977, 198:75. Copyright 1977 by the American Association for the Advancement of Science/ p. 319 (bottom, left), Forsyth, Monkmeyer; (right), AP/Wide World/ p. 325 (top, left), © Ylla, Rapho/Photo Researchers; (right), © Canty, Stock, Boston; (middle), AP/Wide World; (bottom), © Gatewood, Image Works/ p. 327, Hankin, Stock, Boston/ p. 331, Devendra Singh/ p. 334, Eckert, EKM-Nepenthe/ p. 337, University of Wisconsin Primate Laboratory.

Chapter Ten: Page 349, © Kroll, Taurus/ p. 352, Wallace Kirkland, LIFE Magazine © 1948 Time, Inc./ p. 355, Halstead, Gamma/Liaison/ p. 356, Raymond C Rosen, Ph.D., Dept. of Psychiatry, Rutgers/ p. 358, Sobol, Stock, Boston/ p. 362, © Arms, 1982, Jeroboam/ p. 365, Schrut, Taurus/ p. 367 (left), Berndt, Stock, Boston; (right), © 1978, Lawrence Frank/ p. 368 (left), UPI/Bettmann Newsphotos; (right), © Henry Grossman/ p. 369, Berndt, Stock, Boston/ p. 376, Webb, Magnum/ p. 377, *The Seattle Post-Intelligencer*/ p. 379, Ron Smith.

Chapter Eleven: Page 391, © Crews, Stock, Boston/ p. 396, Adapted from R. C. Rockwell, and G. H. Elder, Jr., "Economic deprivation and problem behavior: Childhood and adolescence in the great depression." In J. A. Meacham and H. Thomas, Eds., *Human Development*. Basel: S. Karger, 1982/ p. 403, © Holland, Stock, Boston/ p. 406, © George W. Gardner, 1972/ p. 407, Adapted from D. J. Levinson, with C. N. Darrow, E. B. Klein, M. H. Levinson, and B. McKee, *The Seasons of a Man's Life*. New York: Knopf, 1978/ p. 408, © 1976, Hamlin, Stock, Boston/ p. 409 (left, top and bottom), Zimbel, Monkmeyer Press Photo Service; (right), © Shelton, Monkmeyer Press Photo Service/ p. 415, From *To Live Until We Say Good-bye* by Elisabeth Kübler-Ross. Photographs by Mal Warshaw. © 1978 by Ross Medical Associates, S.C. and Mal Warshaw. Published by Prentice-Hall, Inc., Englewood, Cliffs, N.J.

Chapter Twelve: Page 419, Sarason, 1972a, frontispiece, p. 40/ p. 423, Reprinted from *Handbook of Aging and the Individual*, edited by James E. Birren, by permission of the University of Chicago Press. Copyright 1959 by the University of Chicago Press/ p. 426, V. Dobson, D. Y. Teller, C. P. Lee, and B. Wade, "A behavioral method for efficient screening of visual acuity in young infants." *Investigative Ophthamology and Visual Science*, 1978, 17, p. 1143/ p. 427, V. Dobson, D. Y. Teller, C. P. Lee, and B. Wade, "A behavioral method for efficient screening of visual acuity in young infants." *Investigative Ophthamology and Visual Science*, 1978, 17, p. 1144/ p. 428, William Vandivert and *Scientific American*/ p. 429, E. R. Siqueland and L. P. Lipsitt, *Journal of Experimental Child Psychology*, 1966, 3, 356–376/ p. 430, E. R. Siqueland and L. P. Lipsitt, *Journal of Experimental Child Psychology*, 1966, 3, 356–376/ p. 431, © Arms, Jeroboam/ p. 433, Adapted from K. W. Schaie, "The Seattle longitudinal study: A 21-year exploration of psychometric intelligence in adulthood." In K. W. Schaie, Ed., *Longitudinal Studies in Adult Psychology Development*. New York: Guilford, 1983/ p. 435, Thomas McAvoy, LIFE Magazine © 1955 Time, Inc./ p. 436, H. F. Harlow, University of Wisconsin Primate Laboratory/ p. 438, Ballard, EKM-Nepenthe/ p. 439, Holland, Stock, Boston/ p. 440, Adapted from M. O'Brien, A. C. Anston, and T. Risley, "Sex-typed play of toddlers in a daycare center." *Journal of Applied Developmental Psychology* (in press)/ p. 441, University of Wisconsin Primate Laboratory/ p. 444, Dullea, 1980, p. 34. © 1980 by The New York Times Company. Reprinted by permission.

Chapter Thirteen: Page 453, Eckert, EKM-Nepenthe/ p. 455, Clark University/ p. 460, Courtesy of the Adler family/ p. 462, Carl Rogers/ p. 464, Ohio State University/ p. 466 (top), Albert Bandura/ p. 468 (left), Carrey, The Picture Cube; (middle), © Beckley, Southern Light; (right), Syndication International, Photo Trends/ p. 469, Pictorial Parade/ p. 470 (top), Vandermark, Stock, Boston; (bottom), © Myers, Stock, Boston/ p. 477, THE GRANGER COLLECTION, New York/ p. 478, Reprinted by permission of the publishers from Henry A. Murray, Thematic Apperception Test. Cambridge, Mass.: Harvard University Press. Copyright circa 1943 by the President and Fellows of Harvard College. Renewed 1971 by Henry A. Murray/ p. 479, AP/ Wide World/ p. 480, Courtesy, Spacelabs, Inc., Redmond, WA.

Chapter Fourteen: Page 485, Courtesy, International Institute of Stress/ p. 486, Reproduced with permission from *The Story of the Adaptation Syndrome* by Hans Selye. Montreal: Acta Inc., Medical Publishers, 1952, p. 169/ p. 493, AP/ Wide World/ p. 494, Hayman, Stock, Boston/ p. 502, Reprinted with permission from *Journal of Psychosomatic Research,* 17. G. de Araujo, P. P. van Arsdel, Jr., T. H. Holmes, and D. L. Dudley, "Life changes, coping ability, and chronic intrinsic asthma." Copyright 1973, Pergamon Press, Ltd./ p. 504, Maher, EKM-Nepenthe.

Chapter Fifteen: Page 518, Karlin, Leo de Wys, Inc./ p. 520, Forsyth, Monkmeyer/ p. 522, Friedman, Black Star/ p. 528, Joyce Dopkeen/NYT Pictures/ p. 533, Adapted from I. G. Sarason and B. R. Sarason, *Abnormal Psychology,* 4th ed. Englewood Cliffs, N.J.: Prentice-Hall, 1984/ p. 583, UPI/Bettmann Newsphotos/ p. 541, National Institute of Mental Health/ p. 542, Dr. Monte S. Buchsbaum/ p. 544, Dr. Monte S. Buchsbaum/ p. 547, Adapted from J. S. Marzillier and M. J. Birchwood, "Behavioral treatment of cognitive disorders." In L. Michelson, M. Hersen, and S. M. Turner, Eds., *Future Perspectives on Behavior Therapy.* New York: Plenum Press, 1981.

Chapter Sixteen: Page 552, Mary Evans/Sigmund Freud Copyrights/ p. 558, Adapted from K. C. Wells, C. K. Conners, L. Imber, and A. Delamater, "Use of single subject methodology in clinical decision making with a hyperactive child on the psychiatric inpatient unit." *Behavioral Assessment,* 1981, 3, 359–369/ p. 560, Sedwick, The Picture Cube/ p. 565, Ballard, EKM-Nepenthe/ p. 569, © Paul Fusco, Magnum/ p. 570, Adapted from M. L. Smith, G. V. Glass, and T. I. Miller, *The Benefits of Psychotherapy.* Baltimore: The John Hopkins University Press, 1980/ p. 577 (top), Beckley, Southern Light.

Chapter Seventeen: page 589, Adapted from H. A. Sagar and J. W. Schofield, "Racial and behavioral cues in black and white children's perceptions of ambiguously aggressive acts." *Journal of Personality and Social Psychology,* 1980, 39, 590–598/ p. 591 (top), Zeiberg, Taurus; (middle, left), Antman, Image Works; (middle, right), Carlson, Stock, Boston; (bottom), © Heyman, Archive Pictures/ p. 592 (top), Karfo, The Picture Cube; (bottom), Adapted from L. Festinger, S. Schachter, and K. Back, *Social Pressures in Informal Groups: A Study of a Housing Community.* New York: Harper & Row, 1950/ p. 593, Adapted from L. Festinger, S. Schachter, and K. Back, *Social Pressures in Informal Groups: A Study of a Housing Community.* New York: Harper & Row, 1950/ p. 594 (left), Franken, Stock, Boston; (middle), Fullman, The Picture Cube; (right), Carlson, Stock, Boston/ p. 595, Adapted from C. A. Riordan, B. T. Quigley-Fernandez, and J. T. Tedeschi, "Some variables affecting changes in interpersonal attraction." *Journal of Experimental Social Psychology,* 1982, 18, 358–374/ p. 597, Herwig, Stock, Boston/ p. 599, Adapted from D. O. Sears, J. L. Freedman, and L. A. Peplau, *Social Psychology.* Englewood Cliffs, N.J.: Prentice-Hall, 1985/ p. 601, AP/Wide World/ p. 602 (bottom), Adapted from B. Park and M. Rothbart, "Perceptions of out-group homogeneity and levels of social categorization: Memory for subordinate attributes of in-group and out-group members." *Journal of Personality and Social Psychology,* 1982, 42, 1051–1068/ p. 603, Adapted from R. Steinberg and S. Shapiro, "Sex differences in personality traits of female and male master of business administration students." *Journal of Applied Psychology,* 1982, 67, 306–310/ p. 604 (*a*), From *Shrew Bettina's Birthday* by John S. Goodall. Harcourt Brace Jovanovich, Inc., 1970, first American edition, 1971; (*b*), From *Sylvester and the Magic Pebble* by William Steig. Copyright © 1969 by William Steig. Reprinted by permission of Simon & Schuster, a Division of Gulf & Western Corporation; (*c*), From *Pop Corn and Ma Goodness* by Edna Mitchell Preston. Illustrated by Robert Andrew Parker. Reprinted by permission of Viking Penguin Inc.; (*d*), From *The Quitting Deal* by Tobi Tobias. Illustrated by Trina Schart Hyman. Reprinted by permission of Viking Penguin Inc./ p. 608, American Cancer Society/ p. 609, Adapted from R. W. Rogers and R. Mewborn, "Fear appeals and attitude change: Effects of a threat's noxiousness, probability of occurrence, and the efficiency of coping response." *Journal of Personality and Social Psychology*, 1976, 34, 54–61/ p. 611, Adapted from M. A. Barnett, L. M. King, and J. A. Howard, "Inducing affect about self or others: Effects on generosity in children." *Developmental Psychology*, 1979, 15, 164–167/ p. 614 (left), Cheney, EKM-Nepenthe; (right), Strickler, The

Picture Cube/ p. 615 (left), Maynard, Stock, Boston; (right), Used with permission of the Health Sciences Center for Educational Resources, University of Washington.

Chapter Eighteen: Page 620, Courtesy, Philip G. Zimbardo, Inc./ p. 622 (top, left), Reuters/Bettmann Newsphotos; (top, right), Herwig, Stock, Boston; (bottom), Bross, Stock, Boston/ p. 624, William Vandivert, Courtesy of Scientific American/ p. 626, AP/Wide World/ p. 627, AP/Wide World/ p. 630, Focus on Sports/ p. 633 (right), Strickler, Monkmeyer/ p. 638 (all photos), AP/Wide World/ p. 641 (top), Muzafer Sherif and Carolyn W. Sherif, *Groups in Harmony and Tension*. New York: Harper & Row, 1953; (bottom), © Hamlin, 1976, Stock, Boston/ p. 645, Ronald Smith/ p. 647, National Institute of Mental Health/ p. 649, © Eckert, 1982, The Picture Cube/ p. 651, Beckwith Studios.

NAME INDEX

Abbott, B., 502
Abel, G. G., 367
Abramson, L., 532
Acredolo, L. P., 426
Adesso, V. J., 49, 50
Adkinson, C. D., 426
Adler, J. M., 474
Agnew, N. M., 63
Ahles, T. A., 189
Ainsworth, M. D. S., 434, 437
Ajzen, I., 604
Akiskal, H. S., 527
Akots, N., 128
Allen, A., 471
Allen, V. L., 650
Allgeier, E. R., 360
Allison, M. G., 557
Altenor, A., 228
Amabile, T., 327
Amoore, J. E., 161
Anagnostakos, N. P., 69, 79, 333
Anastasi, A., 294
Anderson, C., 371
Anderson, J. R., 251, 256
Anderson, S. M., 596
Anderson, V. E., 285
Andreasen, N. C., 545
Aneshensel, C. S., 527
Appelman, A. J., 588
Archer, D., 21
Arenberg, D., 433
Arkin, R. M., 318, 347, 588
Arlman-Rupp, A., 272
Aronson, E., 640, 641
Artz, L. M., 651
Asch, S. E., 624, 625
Aserinsky, E., 114
Asher, S. S., 443
Atkinson, J., 427
Atkinson, J. W., 338, 339
Averill, J. A., 308

Auden, W. H., 402
Ayllon, T., 557, 546
Azrin, N. H., 546

Bach-y-Rita, G., 23
Back, K., 593
Baddeley, A. D., 253, 264
Badia, P., 502
Baker, L., 249
Bales, R. F., 639
Balsam, A., 555
Balsam, R. M., 555
Baltes, P. B., 394
Bancroft, J., 366
Bandura, A., 20, 28, 216, 230, 466, 525
Banks, W. C., 621
Barash, D., 14
Barber, J., 126
Barber, T. X., 124, 125, 126
Bard, L. L., 320
Bargh, J. A., 318
Barker, R. G., 585
Barlow, D. H., 367
Barnett, J., 539
Barnett, M. A., 610
Baron, R. A., 28, 364, 650
Barta, S. G., 480
Bartlett, F. C., 254
Barton, R., 530, 533
Basham, R. B., 492
Bates, J. E., 24
Batson, C. D., 613
Baudry, M., 82, 102, 235
Bauer, K., 383
Bauer, K. E., 127
Baum, A., 496, 655
Baum, M., 379
Baumann, D. J., 613
Baumrind, D., 54
Beatty, W. W., 318, 347

Beck, A. T., 229, 531, 562, 574
Beck, P., 434
Becker, J., 574
Becker, R. E., 574
Beecher, H. K., 186
Beiman, I., 310
Bekerian, D. A., 260
Bekesy, G., 159
Bell, A., 375
Bell, P. A., 655
Bell, S. M., 437
Belsky, J., 437
Belt, J., 314
Bellugi, U., 271
Bem, D. J., 471, 606
Benjamin, B., 499
Bennett, H. L., 248
Benson, D. F., 92
Bentler, P. M., 597
Bentley, G., 186
Ben-Veniste, R., 358
Berg, W. K., 426
Berger, S. M., 231
Berger, T. W., 88, 235
Berkowitz, L., 27, 310, 323, 613
Berkowitz, R., 546
Berlyne, D. E., 336
Berry, C., 258
Berscheid, E., 362, 364, 593, 597
Bever, T. G., 278
Biedenman, M. F., 613
Bierman, J. M., 442
Binet, A., 122, 268
Birch, D., 339
Birch, E. B., 427
Bjork, R. A., 253
Bjorklund, A., 98
Black, I. B., 80
Blackwell, L., 207
Blakemore, C., 181, 182
Blanchard, E. B., 189, 367

Blaney, N., 641
Blankenship, V., 339
Blatt, S. J., 527
Bleuler, M., 539
Blommel, J. M., 632
Blood, M., 364
Blood, R. O., 364
Bloom, B. L., 443
Bloom, F. E., 82, 108
Bloomquist, D. S., 128
Blosser, J. L., 613
Blumberg, S. R., 530
Boffey, P. M., 579
Bohannon, J. N., 271
Bolles, R. C., 224, 232, 238
Bottomley, P. A., 103
Bouchard, T., 22, 75
Boucher, J. D., 316
Bower, G. H., 253, 259, 323, 324
Bowers, J. M., 260
Bowers, K., 111
Bowlby, J., 434
Braddick, O., 427
Brady, J. V., 33, 34
Braid, J., 122
Brainerd, C. J., 411
Brand, R. J., 499
Braveman, N. S., 232
Bregman, M., 233
Breland, K., 231
Breland, M., 231
Brehm, S., 361
Brenner, C., 328
Breznitz, S., 486
Brigham, J. C., 593
Brocato, R. M., 632
Brockner, J., 229
Brody, N., 339
Bronstein, P., 232
Brown, A. L., 289
Brown, G. W., 534
Brown, J. S., 282
Brown, R., 271, 276, 545
Brown, T. S., 331
Brownmiller, S., 358
Brownell, K. D., 503
Brugge, J. F., 179
Bruner, J. B., 270
Bruner, J. S., 272
Bruun, S. E., 633
Buchsbaum, M. S., 536

Buckholdt, D., 207
Buell, J., 500
Burger, J. M., 588
Burks, B. S., 287
Burnstein, E., 636
Burrows, G., 187
Burton, R. R., 282
Burton, R. V., 393
Buss, A. H., 467
Butt, J. H., 501
Byer, C. O., 370
Byrne, D., 356, 364, 596, 597

Cacioppo, J. T., 480
Cadoret, R. J., 519, 536
Cain, C., 519
Cairns, H., 88
Calhoun, J. B., 647
Calverley, D. S., 124
Campbell, D. T., 53
Campbell, E. A., 534
Campbell, J. D., 393
Campione, J. C., 289
Campos, J. J., 428
Candee, D., 412
Cannon, W., 320
Cantor, G. N., 411
Cantril, H., 166
Carlsmith, L. M., 605
Carlson, R. F., 249
Carmichael, L., 280
Carpenter, W. T., Jr., 568
Carr, E. G., 217
Carron, A. V., 643
Carter-Saltzman, L., 287
Cartwright, R. D., 117, 119, 144
Cashmore, T. F., 426
Cassel, J., 502
Cattell, R. B., 299
Cavanaugh, J. C., 252
Cazden, C., 271
Chandler, S. M., 379
Chaplin, W., 530, 533
Chapman, J., 545
Chargoff, E., 72
Chase, M. H., 118
Chase, W. G., 247
Chaves, J. F., 125, 126
Check, J. V. P., 358
Chelladurai, P., 643
Chen, A., 128

Chess, S., 399, 400, 436, 445
Chi, M. T. H., 283
Chomsky, N., 270, 271
Chrisjohn, R. D., 613
Christiaansen, R. E., 255
Christiansen, G., 643
Christman, R. J., 147
Cialdini, R. B., 613
Cicciarella, C. F., 61
Clark, E. V., 269, 273, 432
Clark, H. H., 269, 273
Clark, K., 600
Clark, M., 600
Clark, R. D., III, 338, 625
Clark, V. A., 527
Clarke, A. D. B., 278, 440
Clarke, A. M., 278, 440
Clifford, B., 258
Clore, G. L., 596
Coates, T. J., 114
Cochran, P. J., 613
Coe, W. C., 126, 127
Cohen, J. L., 318
Cohen, L. B., 270
Cohen, S., 138, 493, 650
Colby, A., 412
Colby, K. M., 513
Collett, P., 317
Colligan, M. J., 114
Collins, A. M., 250
Commons, M. L., 218
Cooper, G., 181, 182
Cooper, J. E., 515, 635
Cope, S. J., 534
Copeland, J. R. M., 515
Coppen, A., 536
Costantini, E., 639
Cottrell, L. S., 36
Coulas, J. T., 337
Cowan, C. L., 613
Cowen, E. L., 492, 577
Cox, M., 443
Cox, R., 443
Coyne, J. C., 533
Craighead, W. E., 651
Craik, F. I. M., 263, 264, 433
Craik, K. H., 639
Crinean, W. J., 61
Cristol, A. H., 574
Cronbach, L. J., 293, 294, 296
Crooks, R., 383

Cross, T., 314
Croughan, J., 522
Crow, T. J., 536, 538
Crowder, R. G., 242
Crowe, R., 570
Crowe, R. R., 519
Cuerdon, T., 573
Curtis, B., 644
Curtiss, S., 441
Czeisler, C. A., 113

D'Affliti, J. P., 527
Damon, W., 439
Darley, B., 611
Darrow, C. N., 406, 407
Darwin, C., 12, 316
Darwin, C. T., 242
Davidson, L. A., 321
Davidson, R. J., 121
Davis, C. M., 313
Davitz, J. R., 308
de Araujo, G., 502
Deaux, K., 634
deCarufel, A., 595
deCharms, R., 339
Defries, J. C., 75, 108
Dekker, E., 202
Delgado, J., 23, 27
deLinde, J., 256
DeMaris, A., 361
Dement, W., 115, 117, 119
DeNike, L. D., 226
Dermer, M., 592
Des Rosiers, M. H., 102
Deutsch, G., 92, 95, 108
DeVito, J., 103
Dewald, P. A., 554
Diamond, M., 367, 371
Dibble, E., 536
Diener, E., 310, 628
Dienstbier, R., 363
Dimascio, A., 574
Dingledine, R., 102
Dinner, D. S., 119
Dion, K. K., 593, 594
Dixon, N., 164, 165, 167
Doane, J. A., 545
Dobson, V., 427
Dodson, J. D., 318
Dollard, J., 465
Donaldson, M., 411

Donchin, E., 100, 111
Donnerstein, E. I., 31, 358, 361
Donovan, W. L., 316
Dooling, D. J., 255
Dougherty, D., 314
Downey, L., 354
Downing, L., 634
Drachman, D., 595
Dragoin, W. B., 232
Dudley, D. L., 502
Duehrssen, A., 572
Duguay, M., 118
Duncker, K., 284
Dunlap, L. L., 411
Dunn, J., 499
Durkin, K., 273
Dworkin, S., 128
Dykes, A. C., 426
Dyrenforth, S. R., 333

Eagly, A. H., 604
Eberkeub-Vries, R., 546
Edgar, M., 381
Edwards, A. E., 199
Egeland, B. R., 437
Egeland, J. A., 535
Ehrhardt, A. A., 366
Eibl-Eibesfeldt, I., 316
Eimas, P., 272
Einolander, J. C., 650
Ekman, P., 316, 318
Elder, G. H., Jr., 395
Elderkin, R. D., 469
Eldridge, F. L., 119
Eliot, R., 500
Ellett, F. S., 255
Ellis, A., 310, 561, 562
Ellman, S. J., 115
Elton, D., 187
Emerson, P., 434
Emery, G., 562
Endler, N. S., 527
Epstein, M. L., 330
Epstein, R., 277
Erikson, E., 404
Erle, F. J., 644
Ervin, F. R., 23
Estes, W. K., 285
Evans, G. W., 648, 650
Evans, M. B., 126
Everett, P. B., 651

Eyer, J., 34
Eysenck, H. J., 571

Fagan, J. F., 431
Falloon, I. R. H., 569
Fanselow, M., 185, 202
Farrell, M. P., 392
Farrell, P. A., 185
Feldman-Summers, S., 381
Feltovich, P. S., 283
Ferber, P., 279
Fere, C., 122
Fernald, A., 272
Ferrara, R. A., 289
Ferren, G. C., 613
Ferritor, D., 207
Ferster, C. B., 213
Feschbach, N. D., 610
Festinger, L., 593, 605, 628
Fiedler, F. E., 639
Fischer, B., 179
Fischi, T. R., 133, 572
Fishbein, M., 604
Fisher, C., 69
Fisher, J., 650
Fisher, S., 490, 502
Fisher, W., 356
Fiske, S. T., 588, 589
Fleahinger, B., 499
Fleming, J. F., 275
Flood, J. F., 258
Flynn, J. P., 23
Ford, K., 353
Fowler, J. W., 228
Fox, J. L., 259
Frank, E., 371
Frank, M. D., 343
Fredrickson, M., 233
Freedman, J., 361
French, F. E., 442
French, J., 427
Frerichs, R. R., 527
Freud, S., 14, 15, 116, 328, 361, 393, 525, 533

NAME INDEX

Fried, R., 613
Friedhoff, A. S., 568
Friedman, M., 498, 499
Frieze, I. H., 603
Frisby, J. P., 168, 175, 191
Frockt, W., 114
Frodi, A. N., 316
Fromm, E., 140
Fuller, C. A., 112, 144
Fuller, R. B., 652
Fyer, A. F., 523

Gabrielli, W. F., 519
Gaensbauer, T. J., 425
Gagnon, J., 380
Gallager, D. W., 132
Galle, O. R., 648
Gallimore, R., 479
Gallup, G. G., 111
Garber, S. W., 557
Garbutt, U. C., 539
Garcia, J., 232
Gardner, H., 288
Garey, R. E., 137
Garfinkel, P. E., 334
Garmezy, N., 441, 442
Garner, D. M., 334
Gartner, R., 21
Gatchel, R. J., 496
Gazzaniga, M. S., 68, 87, 96, 97, 98, 108, 331
Gebhard, P., 351, 380
Geen, R. G., 31, 318, 347
Geer, J., 366, 373
Geiselman, R. E., 253
Geller, E. S., 651
Gelles, R. J., 28
Genuchi, M., 318
George, C., 216
Gergen, K. L., 615
Gergen, M., 615
Gerner, R. H., 569
Geron, M. E., 536
Geshon, E. S., 527
Gibbs, J., 332
Gibson, E., 427
Giebs, J., 412
Gill, D., 642
Gilligan, S. C., 253
Gillund, G., 251
Glaser, R., 283

Glass, D., 649
Glass, G. V., 255, 571, 572, 573
Glicklich, J., 523
Glucksberg, S., 284
Godden, D. R., 253
Goeckner, D. J., 49, 50
Goldband, S., 127
Goldberg, S., 436
Goldberger, L., 486
Goldstein, A., 184
Goldstein, E. B., 169, 175, 185, 191
Goldstein, G., 475
Goldstein, M. J., 545
Goleman, D., 120
Gordon, J., 132
Gorman, J. M., 523
Gormezano, I., 61
Gotlib, I. H., 533
Gottesman, I. I., 22, 73, 536
Gove, W. R., 648
Grajek, S., 590, 596
Grant, B., 164
Green, R., 367
Greenberg, J., 588
Greenberger, D. B., 650
Greene, D., 327
Greenwald, A. G., 588, 606
Gregory, R. L., 171
Grieger, R., 310, 561
Griffitt, W., 368
Grinker, J. A., 333
Grinker, R. R., 539
Groen, J., 202
Groff, B., 648
Groffman, K. H., 388
Gross, A. E., 380
Grossberg, J., 164
Groth, N., 380
Guilleminault, C., 119
Gunderson, J. G., 518
Gunn, L. K., 598
Gunter, B., 258
Gurland, B. J., 515
Guroff, J. J., 536

Haas, H., 187
Hage, J. N., 650
Haier, R. J., 536
Hake, J. L., 426
Hall, E., 361
Halpern, P. L., 650

Hamblin, R. L., 207
Hammen, C., 569
Hamovit, J., 536
Hampson, J. L., 368
Han, J. S., 103
Handsfield, H. H., 376
Haney, C., 621
Hanin, I., 81
Hanson, B., 535, 574
Harkins, S. G., 612, 633
Harlow, H. F., 336, 441
Harper, R. M., 119
Harris, R. J., 256
Harris, T., 534
Harrow, M., 539
Hartl, E. M., 469
Harvey, J. A., 61
Harvey, J. H., 588
Hassett, J., 162
Hassing, Y., 272
Hastorf, A., 166
Hatfield, E., 368
Hayes, J. R., 281
Heatherington, E. M., 443
Hebb, D. O., 235
Heckhausen, H., 326
Heiby, E., 229
Heider, E. R., 280
Heidt, R., 427
Heiman, J., 366, 373
Heimberg, R. G., 574
Heinrichs, D. W., 568
Heller, J., 648
Helmholtz, H., 152
Helzer, J. E., 522
Henderson, N. D., 73, 74
Herbart, J. F., 16
Herbert, W., 119
Hering, E., 152
Herman, J. H., 115
Herman, P., 335
Herold, E. S., 354
Heron, W., 336
Hersen, M., 475
Hewer, A., 412
Hibler, N., 124
Higgins, E. T., 607
Hilgard, E. R., 128
Hilgard, J. R., 128
Hill, C. T., 364, 590
Hillyard, S. A., 101

Hinkle, L. E., Jr., 499
Hinsley, D., 281
Hinson, R. E., 343
Hite, S., 352, 353
Hitler, A., 26
Hodgeon, T., 249
Hodges, J., 440
Hodgson, R. J., 524
Hoff, J. D., 539
Hoffman, M. L., 613
Hofmann, A., 137
Hofstadter, L., 82, 108
Hogan, H. P., 280
Hokanson, J. E., 530
Holahan, C. K., 397
Holden, P., 314
Holland, P. C., 198, 225
Hollon, S. C., 229, 576
Holmes, D. S., 121
Holmes, M. R., 379
Holmes, T. H., 443, 495, 502
Holzman, P. S., 539, 545
Honig, B., 154
Honzik, C. H., 224
Horn, J. L., 299
Horn, J. M., 285
Horne, J. A., 112
Horwitz, E. A., 501
Houck, J. C., 185
Hovland, C. I., 607
Howard, J. A., 610
Hoyenga, K. B., 344, 366
Hoyenga, K. T., 344, 366
Hubel, D., 91, 168, 169, 180, 181
Huck, S. W., 63
Hughes, M., 409
Hunt, D. D., 368
Hunt, E., 61
Hunt, M., 352, 354
Hursch, C., 378
Hurvich, L. M., 154
Huttenlocher, P., 98
Huxley, A., 4
Hygge, S., 233, 309

Ikemi, Y., 125
Ingvar, D. H., 96
Inhelder, B., 408
Insko, C. A., 595
Iversen, L. L., 85
Izard, C., 310, 316

Jackson, R., 297
Jacobson, N. S., 566
Jaffe, D., 621
James, W., 9, 17, 141, 179, 320
Jamison, K. R., 569
Janis, I. L., 36, 501, 607, 636
Jarvik, L. F., 422
Jarvik, M. I., 258
Jenkins, C. D., 499
Jobs, J., 272
Johansson, G., 487
Johnson, B. P., 603
Johnson, D. L., 228
Johnson, J. H., 495
Johnson, K. S., 256
Johnson, R. D., 652
Johnson, V. E., 349, 351, 354, 369
Johnson, V. S., 162
Jones, J. E., 545
Jones, K. L., 370
Jones, K. R., 572
Jones, M., 576
Jones, M. B., 642
Jones, M. C., 421, 422
Joosten, J., 272
Jorswick, E., 572
Jourard, S., 29
Julien, R. M., 130
Jung, J., 326
Jusczyk, P., 272

Kagan, J., 425, 445
Kahn, J., 533
Kahneman, D., 164
Kahns, S., 505
Kallmann, F. J., 422
Kalter, N., 443
Kanfer, F. H., 220, 223, 490
Kanin, E. J., 380
Kantner, J. F., 353
Kaplan, B. H., 502
Kaplan, H., 373
Kaplan, R. M., 297
Karlen, A., 367, 371
Karoly, P., 490
Kaslow, F. W., 627
Kastenbaum, R., 415
Katchadourian, H., 103, 349
Katkin, E. S., 39, 127
Kauffman, K., 412
Kaufman, A. S., 294

Kaufmann, Y., 117
Kawada, S., 179
Kay, P., 280
Keefe, P., 522
Keen, E., 556
Keith, S. J., 539
Kelley, H. H., 361, 464, 587, 597, 607
Kelly, J. B., 443
Kelly, S., 650
Kendall, P. C., 480
Kendall, R. E., 515
Kendler, K. S., 540
Kennedy, C., 102
Kennell, J. H., 435, 503
Kenrick, D. T., 613
Kerlinger, F. N., 672
Kerr, N. L., 633
Kessler, M., 102
Ketron, J. L., 289
Keverne, E. B., 163
Key, W. B., 165
Kidd, K. K., 536
Kiesler, C. A., 576
Kight, T. D., 363
Kihlstrom, J., 124
Kimble, G., 674
Kincord, J. P., 249
Kinder, D. R., 600
King, D. L., 523
King, L. M., 610
King, R., 499
Kinsey, A., 349
Klaus, M. H., 435, 503
Klein, D. F., 523
Klein, E. B., 406, 407
Klein, M., 643
Kleinmuntz, B., 313, 314, 535
Kleitman, N., 114
Klerman, G. L., 535, 574
Klinger, E., 480
Kluckhohn, C., 454
Knight, J., 592
Knight, R. A., 539

Kobasa, S. C., 505
Kohlberg, L., 411, 412
Kohler, W., 17, 224
Kohn, P. M., 337
Kolata, G., 421, 430
Kolb, B., 312
Kollar, E. J., 69
Korgeski, G. P., 480
Kosambi, D. D., 186
Kosslyn, S. M., 245
Kovacs, M., 229, 574
Kozloff, M., 207
Kraepelin, E., 539
Kraft, C. L., 173
Kral, P. A., 232
Krantz, D. S., 502, 650
Kroeber, A. L., 186
Kromer, L. F., 98
Krowitz, A., 428
Kübler-Ross, E., 414, 415
Kuhl, J., 339
Kuhl, P., 272
Kuipers, L., 546
Kukla, A., 338
Kulkosky, P. J., 202, 332
Kutas, M., 101

Lachappelle, E. R., 279
Lader, M. H., 521, 522
Laing, R. D., 21, 546
Lam, H. G., 635
Lamb, M. E., 316, 437
Lambert, N., 297
Lamiell, J. T., 613
Lance, S., 249
Landers, D. M., 643
Landis, J., 380
Landry, D. W., 258
Landsman, T., 29
Lang, A. R., 49, 50
Lange, C., 320
Langer, A., 428
Langer, E. J., 434
Langlois, J. H., 24
Lanier, C. F., 539
Lanksford, A., 310
Lanza, R. P., 277
LaPointe, K., 310
Lashley, K., 12
Lassen, N. A., 96
Latane, B., 611, 612, 633, 642

Latyczewski, B. S., 577
Lau, R. R., 586, 587, 588
Laurence, J. R., 124
Lawson, J., 276
Lazarus, R. S., 310, 315, 321
Lazerson, A., 82, 108
Leavitt, L. A., 316
Le Bon, G., 628
Leckman, J. F., 521, 536
Lee, C. P., 427
Leff, J., 545, 546
Lehman, E. R., 499
Leitenberg, H., 335, 366, 373
Lenneberg, E. H., 273
Lepper, M., 327
Lerine, H. M., 492
Lerner, J., 24
Lerner, P., 478
Lerner, R. M., 24
Leslie, G. R., 361
Lethem, J., 186
Leventhal, H., 189
Levine, L. E., 613
Levine, S. B., 366
Levinson, D. J., 406, 407
Levinson, M. H., 406, 407
Levy, C. M., 61
Levy, J., 96, 274
Levy, R. I., 498
Lewin, K., 341
Lewinsohn, P. M., 530, 533
Lewis, J. F., 298
Liberman, R. P., 569
Libert, R. M., 610
Lightman, E. S., 615
Lindauer, B. K., 432
Lindsay, P. H., 171, 251
Linkous, R. A., 632
Lion, J. R., 23
Lipowski, J., 497
Lipsitt, L., 430
Livingstone, M., 169
Lobnitz, W. C., 532
Lochman, I. M., 423
Locke, J., 18
Lockhart, R. S., 263–264
Loehlin, J. C., 22, 285
Loftus, E. F., 255, 259, 260
Loftus, G. R., 259
Logan, D. R., 125
London, P., 610

Long, J., 445
Longfellow, C., 442
Lo Piccolo, J., 373
Lorenz, K., 22
Lothstein, L. M., 366
Lovaas, O. I., 217, 271
Low, H., 24
Lowell, E. L., 338
Loy, J., 643
Lumry, A., 536
Lumsdaine, A. A., 36
Lunde, D. T., 103, 349
Luria, A., 562
Luria, Z., 437
Lustig, D. A., 474
Lykken, D., 314
Lynch, G., 82, 102, 235

Maass, A., 625
McCann, C. D., 607
McCanne, T. R., 127
McCarley, R., 115
McCaul, K. D., 188, 189
McCauley, C., 600
McClearn, G. E., 75, 108
McClelland, D. C., 324, 326, 338, 340, 341, 347
McClintock, M., 162
Maccoby, E. E., 476
Maccoby, N., 476
McCormick, N. B., 360
MacCulloch, M. J., 358
McCully, J., 343
MacDonald, N., 545
McGarrigle, J., 411
McGlashan, T. H., 519
McGrath, S. K., 431
McGuire, W. J., 608
McKee, B., 406, 407
Mackie, D., 635
Macklin, E. D., 361
McWhorter, J., 651
Madden, J., IV, 88
Maddi, S. R., 505
Maguire, A., 25
Mahoney, M., 227
Main, E. C., 635
Main, M., 216
Malamuth, N., 358, 361
Malott, J. J., 188, 189
Manard, B. B., 588

Mandell, A., 134
Mandler, G., 312, 315, 320, 362
Mann, L., 628
Manstead, A. S. R., 605
Marcus, R. F., 613
Markman, E. M., 252
Marks, I. M., 521
Markus, H., 589
Marlatt, G. A., 49, 50, 132
Marmot, M. G., 500
Marsh, P., 317
Marshall, J. F., 98
Marslen-Wilson, W. D., 244
Martens, R., 643
Martin, C. E., 351
Martin, E., 269
Martin, T., 61
Maser, J. D., 539
Maslow, A., 20, 328–329
Masters, J. C., 559, 560
Masters, W. H., 349, 351, 354, 369
Matsumoto, Y. S., 501
Mattsson, A., 24
Maugh, T. H., 112
Mavligit, G., 376
Maxeiner, M. E., 480
May, R., 21
Maynard, J., 427, 625
Mednick, S. A., 519
Megargee, E. I., 25
Meiselman, K. C., 380
Melamed, B. G., 501
Meltzoff, A. W., 317
Melzack, R., 184, 191
Mendel, G., 69
Mendlewicz, J., 536
Mercer, J. R., 298
Merikangas, K. R., 521
Mesmer, A., 121
Messenger, J. C., 360
Messick, S., 297
Meter, K., 615
Mewborn, R., 608
Meyer, J. K., 368, 527
Meyers, A. W., 651
Michaels, J. W., 632
Michels, R., 517
Midlarsky, E., 613
Midlarsky, M., 613
Miles, L. E., 119
Milgram, S., 42, 47, 48, 54, 56

Milich, R. H., 473
Miller, D. J., 501
Miller, D. R., 162
Miller, I. W., III, 228
Miller, N. E., 34, 342, 465
Miller, S., 649
Miller, T. I., 571
Milligan, B., 110
Mills, H. E., 358
Millward, J. W., 519
Milner, B., 91
Mineka, S., 215
Miner, G. D., 526
Mintun, M. A., 103
Mischel, W., 229, 267, 467, 530, 533
Mishkin, M., 259
Missel, P., 229
Mita, T. H., 592
Mitchell, C. L., 82, 86
Moeller, G. H., 339
Money, J., 366
Monnelly, E. P., 469
Monteiro, K. P., 253
Monty, R. A., 502
Moore, B. S., 650
Moore, D., 566
Moore, F., 50
Moore, M. K., 317
Moore-Ede, M. C., 112, 113
Mordkoff, A. M., 321
Moreland, R. L., 592
Morgan, J. J. B., 281
Morgan, W. P., 185, 189
Morris, D., 317
Morris, L. W., 469
Morris, N. M., 163
Morris, R. J., 215
Morrison, A. R., 116
Moskowitz, B. A., 272
Moskowitz, J., 498
Moss, C. S., 93
Moss, J. L., 539
Moss, M. K., 610
Mowrer, O. H., 218, 413
Moylan, J., 539
Mumford, E., 572, 573
Munson, R., 649
Murdock, 257
Murphy, G. E., 529
Murray, H. A., 454

Mussen, P. H., 422
Mychielska, K., 475
Myers, D. G., 635

Nairn, A., 297
Nakagawa, A., 125
Nakanishi, K., 154
Navarick, D. J., 238
Neff, C., 316
Neisworth, J. T., 50
Nelson, K., 271
Nelson, T. O., 264
Nelson, W. T., 539
Nesselroade, J. R., 394
Neugarten, B. L., 392
Nevin, J. A., 218
Neuman, W. R., 258
Newcomb, M. D., 597
Newcomb, T., 623
Newell, A., 282
Nezlek, J., 594
Nichols, I. A., 272
Nichols, R. C., 22
Norman, D. A., 171
Nida, S., 611
Nielsen, A. C., 527
Norman, D. A., 251
Norman, W. H., 228
Nossiter, B. D., 646
Novaco, R., 490
Novak, M. A., 441
Nuckolls, K. B., 502

Ohman, A., 233, 309
Olivier, D., 280
Olofsson, C., 233
Olweus, D., 24
Orne, M. T., 53, 127
Ornstein, R., 96
Orton, I. K., 310
O'Shaughnessy, M., 317
Overmier, J. B., 227

Padesky, C., 569

Pagano, R. R., 63, 120, 121, 673
Page, R. A., 610
Paivio, A., 245, 256
Papageorgis, D., 608
Parcell, S. R., 380
Paris, S. G., 432
Park, B., 602
Parke, R. D., 28, 29
Parloff, M. B., 574
Parsons, J. E., 603
Pate, J. L., 276
Patlack, C. S., 102
Patrick, C., 573
Patterson, G. R., 209
Paul, G., 126
Paul, S. M., 132
Paulhus, D. L., 362
Pauls, D. L., 521, 536
Paulus, P. B., 648
Pavlov, I., 197
Paykel, E. S., 535, 574
Peet, M., 536
Pellegrino, J., 61
Peplau, L. A., 364, 590
Pepitone, A., 628
Perls, F. S., 564
Perlmuter, L. C., 502
Perlmutter, M., 252
Peroutka, S. J., 541
Perry, C., 124
Peskin, H., 421, 422
Peterson, L., 501
Peterson, L. R., 242
Peterson, M. J., 242
Peterson, P. L., 228
Petito, L. A., 278
Pettigrew, K. D., 102
Petty, R. E., 480, 612, 633
Pfaff, D. W., 326
Phares, E. J., 471, 613
Phillipp, S. F., 61
Phillips, D. P., 28, 44, 179
Piaget, J., 18, 408, 411
Pilbeam, D., 13
Piliavin, I., 613
Piliavin, J. A., 612, 613
Pilisuk, M., 492
Pi-Sunyen, X., 334
Pitz, G. F., 164
Plakun, A., 499
Plomin, R., 75, 108, 467

Plutchik, R., 316
Poggio, G. F., 179
Polivy, J., 335
Pollock, V., 519
Pomeroy, W., 351, 374
Poppen, P., 31
Post, R. D., 532
Poulos, R. W., 610
Powell, J. S., 289
Power, C., 412
Prange, A. J., 539
Premack, D., 222
Prentice-Dunn, S., 628, 629
Pribram, K., 312
Proffitt, C. T., 605
Prusoff, B. A., 521, 536, 574
Pyke, S. W., 63
Pyszezynski, T., 588

Quigley-Fernandez, B. T., 595
Quillian, M. R., 250
Quinlan, D. M., 527
Quinsey, V. L., 25
Quinton, D., 442

Raaheim, K., 281
Rachlin, H., 218
Rachman, S. J., 524, 525
Rahe, R. H., 443, 495
Raichle, M. E., 103
Raines, M. P., 392
Rainier, J. D., 536
Ramsay, R. W., 559
Ranken, H. B., 280
Ratcliff, K., 522
Raven, B., 634, 637
Ray, J. W., 313
Ray, O., 131, 144
Rayner, R., 200
Raynor, J. O., 338
Reason, J. T., 475
Rebelsky, F. G., 273
Reis, H. T., 594
Reivich, M., 102
Remmers, J. E., 119
Reschly, D. J., 298
Rescorla, R. A., 198, 214, 225
Rest, J. R., 413
Reter, D. J., 368
Rettie, C. S., 411
Richmond, R. S., 615

Ricks, D., 31
Ridley-Johnson, R., 501
Riesen, A., 180
Riess, M., 606
Rimm, D. C., 559, 560
Ringelmann, E., 632
Riordan, C. A., 595
Robbins, M., 355
Robertson, S., 503
Robertson-Tchabo, E. A., 433
Robinette, C. D., 540
Robins, E., 374
Robins, L., 522
Robinson, D. N., 11
Rockwell, R. C., 395
Rodin, J., 333, 434
Rodnick, E. H., 545
Roffwarg, H. P., 115
Rogers, C. R., 20, 29, 462, 463, 555, 556, 565
Rogers, R. F., 392
Rogers, R. W., 608, 628, 629
Rohsenow, D. J., 50
Roisenberg, S. D., 392
Roke, E. J., 613
Romanczyk, R. G., 61
Root, M. P. P., 335
Rosch, E., 280
Rosekind, M. R., 114
Roseman, R. H., 498, 499
Rosen, J. C., 335
Rosen, R., 361
Rosenbaum, S., 276
Rosenhan, D. L., 40, 613
Rosenthal, D., 542, 543
Rosenthal, R., 54, 318
Rosenzweig, M. R., 235, 258
Ross, D. G., 474
Ross, L., 585
Rossbach, J., 649
Roth, T., 118
Rothbart, M., 602
Rotter, J. B., 467
Routh, D., 216
Rovee-Collier, C., 431
Rowe, J. S., 632
Roy, A., 529
Rubin, J. Z., 437, 634, 637
Rubin, Z., 364, 590, 596
Rubinstein, D., 371
Ruble, D. N., 603

Ruch, L. O., 379
Rumbaugh, D. M., 276
Rumelhart, D. E., 251
Runnion, A., 651
Runyan, W. McK., 397
Rusbult, C. E., 598
Rush, A. J., 229, 562, 574
Rushton, J. P., 613
Russell, D., 587, 588
Russell, M., 162
Rutter, M., 440, 442, 517
Ryan, M. J., 613

Sachs, N. J., 164
Sagar, H. A., 589
Saghir, M. T., 375
St. Lawrence, J. S., 379
Sakurado, O., 102
Salans, L. B., 333
Saleh, S. D., 644
Sales, E., 379
Salter, W., 289
Sameroff, A. J., 426, 430
Sanders, G. S., 631
Sanders, R. J., 278
Sandler, H. M., 63
Santa, J. L., 249, 280
Santrock, J. W., 444
Sarason, B. R., 492
Sarason, I. G., 319, 492, 495
Sarbin, T., 127
Sargent, M., 102
Sarrel, L., 352
Sarrel, P., 352
Sartre, J. P., 20
Savage-Rumbaugh, E. S., 276
Saxe, L., 314
Scarr, S. T., 285, 287
Schachter, D. L., 263
Schachter, S., 320, 322, 595
Schafer, S., 375
Schaffer, H. R., 434
Schaie, K. W., 394, 395, 432
Schalling, D., 24
Schlenker, B. R., 606
Schlesier-Stropp, B., 335
Schlesinger, H. J., 572, 573
Schmidt, G., 356, 357
Schneidman, N. N., 8, 415
Schoen, L., 119, 502

Schofield, J. W., 589
Schoggen, P., 585
Schreurs, B. G., 61
Schuckit, M. A., 574
Schulz, R., 502
Schultheis, K., 501
Schwartz, L. L., 627
Schwartz, R., 331, 332
Schwartz, R. D., 53
Sears, D. O., 600
Sebeok, T. A., 278
Sechrest, L., 53
Seeman, M. V., 540
Segal, M., 600
Seidman, J., 541
Seligman, M. E. P., 34, 228, 232, 532
Selye, H., 486
Senden, M. von, 182
Sentis, K., 589
Shaffer, D., 517
Shainberg, L. W., 370
Shapiro, A. K., 40
Shapiro, K. J., 55, 120
Shapiro, S., 603
Sharan, S., 641
Sharpe, L., 515
Shaver, K., 361
Shavit, Y., 185
Shaw, B. R., 562
Shaw, M. K., 612
Sheehan, D. R., 522, 523
Sheldon, W. H., 467
Sherif, C., 640
Sherif, M., 623, 640
Sherrington, C., 146
Sherrod, D. R., 650
Sherry, D., 316
Shiffrin, R. M., 251
Shinohara, M., 102
Shipley, R. H., 501
Shor, R. E., 124
Shore, B., 379
Shotland, R. L., 612
Shwartz, S. P., 245
Siegel, J. M., 495
Siegel, R. K., 137
Siegel, S., 343–344, 421
Siever, L. J., 518
Sikes, J., 641
Silva, J. M., 642

Silverman, L. H., 473, 474
Silverstein, M. L., 539
Simmons, F. B., 119
Simon, H., 282
Simon, H. A., 247, 281
Simon, N. G., 332
Simon, R. J., 515
Singer, J. L., 649
Singer, M. T., 627
Singer, P., 55
Sinsheimer, R., 72
Siqueland, E. R., 272
Skeels, H. M., 287
Skinner, B. F., 19, 35, 204, 222, 271, 277
Skodak, M., 287
Skolnick, P., 132
Slaby, R. G., 28, 29
Slade, P. O., 186
Slater, P. E., 639
Slayton, D. J., 437
Sloane, R. B., 574
Smart, S. L., 605
Smith, A. H., 144
Smith, C. A., 420
Smith, E. R., 588
Smith, G. P., 332
Smith, M. B., 36
Smith, M. C., 124
Smith, M. L., 571
Smith, O. A., 103
Smith, R. E., 644, 645, 646
Smith, R. S., 442, 445
Smith, S. E., 253
Smith, S. T., 276
Smoll, F. L., 644, 645, 646
Smylie, C. S., 95
Snapp, M., 641
Snow, C. E., 272
Snowden, P. R., 358
Snowdon, C., 14, 163
Snyder, S. H., 541
Sokol, S., 101, 427

Sokoloff, L., 102, 235
Soloff, P. H., 519
Solomon, R. L., 214, 343–344
Solomon, S., 588, 648
Sommer, G., 229
Sosa, R., 503
Spacapan, S., 493
Spanos, N. P., 125, 126
Spaulding, E., 518
Spaulding, W., 61
Speicher-Dubin, B., 412
Speisman, J. C., 321
Sperling, G., 167, 241
Sperry, R. W., 93
Spielberger, C. D., 226
Spitz, R. A., 434
Spitzer, L., 434
Sprafkin, J. N., 610
Spring, B., 546
Springer, S. P., 92, 95, 108
Sroufe, L. A., 437
Staats, A. W., 20, 202, 271
Stagner, R., 471
Staib, A. R., 125
Stanley, G., 187
Staples, F. R., 574
Star, S. A., 36
Starkey, D., 432
Staub, E., 615
Steen, D., 68, 87, 97, 331
Steffen, V. J., 604
Steinberg, R., 603
Steinhauer, S., 546
Steinmetz, S. K., 28
Stephan, C., 24, 641
Stephan, W., 640, 641
Stephens, J. H., 539
Stenevi, U., 98
Sterling, P., 34
Stern, R. M., 313
Sternberg, R. J., 289, 290, 596
Stevens, C. F., 77, 79
Stevenson, H., 430
Stewart, A. J., 340, 341
Stine, E. L., 271
Stitt, C. L., 600
Stokols, D., 648
Stone, M. H., 519
Storr, A., 575
Stouffer, S. A., 36
Straus, R., 28, 499

Stull, D. E., 590
Stunkard, A., 332
Sturgeon, D., 546
Stuss, D. T., 92
Sugarman, S., 278
Suggs, R., 360
Sulin, R. A., 255
Sulzman, F. M., 112, 144
Suomi, S. J., 441
Syme, S. L., 500
Szucko, J. J., 313, 314

Tageson, C. W., 21
Tajfel, H., 601
Tallman, J. F., 132
Tasto, D., 114
Taylor, S. E., 489, 588, 589
Tearnan, B. H., 522
Teasdale, J. D., 532
Tedeschi, J. T., 595
Telch, M. J., 522
Telleen, S., 613
Tellegen, A., 123
Teller, D. Y., 427
Teplin, L. A., 600
Ter-Poggosian, M. M., 103
Terrace, H., 278
Tesser, A., 362
Tharp, R. G., 220, 223, 238, 479
Thelmar, E., 538
Thibaut, J. W., 597
Thomas, A., 399, 400, 436, 445
Thomas, C. B., 504
Thomas, J., 642
Thompson, D. M., 253
Thompson, R. F., 11, 88, 235
Thompson, W. C., 613
Thompson, W. D., 527, 536
Thoresen, C., 114
Thorndike, E. L., 203
Thornton, B., 588
Thurstone, L. L., 288
Tilker, H., 48
Tilson, H. A., 82, 86
Tizard, B., 440
Toch, H., 25
Tolman, E. C., 224
Tomkins, S., 316
Tortora, G. J., 69, 79, 333
Tracy, K., 501
Treisman, A., 164

Triplett, N., 631
Tripp, P., 112
Troup, J. D. G., 186
Tsai, M., 381
Tuason, V. B., 536
Tulving, E., 253, 256
Turnbull, C. M., 180
Turner, J., 601
Turvey, M. T., 242

Udry, J. R., 163
Uleman, S., 587
Ulm, R. R., 228
Umiker-Sebeok, D. J., 278
Undheim, J., 300
Urrutia, J., 503
Uttal, W., 147

Vaillant, G. E., 401, 402, 445, 515
Valenti, A., 634
van Arsdel, P. P., Jr., 502
Van Houten, R., 216
Varney, G. W., 25
Vasta, R., 229, 271
Vaughn, B. E., 437
Vaughn, C., 545
Vaughn, E. D., 584
Verbeek, G., 172
Vigorito, J., 272
Volavka, J., 519
Volpe, B. T., 68, 87, 97, 108, 331
Volpicelli, J. R., 228
Von Frisch, F., 275
Vonnegut, M., 538
Voot, B., 613
Vorster, J., 272

Wade, B., 427
Wagner, R. L., 541
Waldron, H., 566
Walen, S., 373
Walk, R., 427
Walker, T. G., 635
Wall, T., 128, 129
Wallace, P., 331
Wallerstein, J. S., 443
Walsh, R. N., 120, 138
Walster, E., 362, 593, 596, 597, 612
Walster, G. W., 362, 596, 597
Walter, A. A., 280
Wandersman, A., 31

Warrenburg, S., 120, 121
Warshak, R. A., 444
Waters, E., 437
Watson, D. L., 220, 223, 238
Watson, J. B., 18, 200
Watson, J. D., 651
Way, L., 354
Weary, G., 588
Webb, E. J., 53
Weber, E., 165
Weinberg, M. S., 375
Weinberg, R. A., 285, 287, 318, 642
Weinberger, D. R., 541
Weiner, B., 339
Weinman, C., 434
Weisberg, L., 284
Weiss, J., 34, 35
Weissberg, R. P., 577
Weissman, M. M., 521, 527, 536, 574
Weitzman, E. D., 118
Welsh, A., 244
Werner, E. E., 442, 445
West, J. B., 288
West, K. L., 545
Wertheimer, M. A., 31
Wester, W. C., 144
Westheimer, G., 169
Whalen, R. E., 332
Wheeler, L., 322
Whipple, K., 574
Whishaw, I. Q., 312

White, G. L., 363
White, S. W., 443
Whitehurst, G. J., 271
Whitmont, E. C., 117
Whitney, L. H., 499
Wickelgren, W. A., 264
Widom, C. S., 519
Wielkiewicz, R. M., 227
Wiesel, T., 91, 168
Wilcoxon, H. C., 232
Willard, R. D., 125
Willerman, L., 285
Williams, J. E., 125
Williams, K. D., 612, 633
Williams, M. D., 240
Williams, R. M., 36
Williams, T. A., 527
Wilson, E. O., 609
Wilson, I. C., 539
Wilson, R. S., 14
Wimer, C. C., 75
Wimer, R. E., 75
Wing, L., 522
Winnett, R. A., 651
Winokur, R. J., 536
Winter, D. G., 340, 341
Winter, L., 587
Wolpe, J., 525
Wood, P. J. W., 358
Woods, S. C., 202
Wooley, O. W., 333
Wooley, S. C., 333

Wrightsman, L., 634
Wulach, J. S., 519
Wundt, W., 16
Wurm, M., 499
Wyatt, R. J., 541
Wylie, R. C., 29, 167, 218

Yablonsky, L., 27
Yalom, I., 29
Yarrow, M. R., 393
Yerkes, R. M., 318
Yin, T. C. T., 179
Yorkston, N. J., 574
Young, T., 152

Zaidel, E., 96
Zajonc, R. B., 592, 631
Zellman, G. L., 603
Zelnick, M., 353
Zilbergeld, B., 373
Zillmann, D., 27, 362
Zimbardo, P. G., 620, 621
Zubin, J., 546
Zuckerman, M., 309, 318, 337

SUBJECT INDEX

A-B-A-B experimental design, 557–558
Abnormal behavior, 512
Abstract codes, 245, 246–247
Achievement motivation, 338–340
Achievement tests, 290, 294, 302
Acquisition, of language, 272
Activation-synthesis model, 115–116
Addictions, 130, 343–344
Ajustment, over time, 401
Adjustment disorder, 516
Adler, A., personality theory of, 460
Adolescence, 405
  growth in, 421
  and suicide, 528
Adulthood, 405–406
Affective disorder, 516, 527–536, 548
  and borderline personality disorder, 519
Affiliation, 590
Age-related development, 389, 391–392
Aging, 391–392
  and intellectual performance, 432
  physical changes in, 422
Aggregate, 629
Agoraphobia, 522
Alarm reaction, 486
Alcohol, 131–132
Alcoholism
  and panic disorder, 521
  therapeutic approach to, 561
Algorithm, 281, 302
Altruism, 609–617
  and personality, 613
Alzheimer's disease, 263
Ambiguity, and helping, 611
Amine neurotransmitter systems, 529
Amphetamines, 133–134
Analogy, 302
Anal stage, 404

Analytic psychology, 460, 481
Anger, 414
  control of, 490
Angina pectoris, 498
Animals, language in, 275–279
Anisomycin, 258
Anorexia nervosa, 334
Antecedents, of behavior, 490
Antianxiety drugs, 567–568
Antidepressant drugs, 530, 567, 569
Antimanic drugs, 567, 569
Antipsychotic drugs, 569–570
Antisocial behavior, and personality disorder, 520
Antisocial personality disorders, 519, 548
Anxiety, 457, 485, 520
  therapy for, 559
Anxiety disorders, 516, 520–521, 548
Aphasia, 92–93
Applied behavior analysis, 557, 578
Appraisal, of stressor, 484
Aptitude tests, 290, 293–294, 297, 302
Archetypes, 460
Arguments, effectiveness of, 608
Arousal, in stressful situations, 486–487
Artificial intelligence, 241, 283
Assertiveness training, 560, 578
Assessment
  of intelligence, 290–301
  of personality, 475–481
Associative pain-control strategies, 187–188
Atherosclerosis, 498
Attachment, 434–437, 446
Attention, 166–167
Attitude
  and attraction, 590
  components of, 598

  toward victims, 588
Attitude change, 607
Attitudes, 598
  and behavior, 617
  over time, 397
Attraction, 590, 616–617
  and helping, 595
Attractiveness
  and attraction, 593–594
  and the impressions of personality, 593–594
Attribution, 585, 616
  in depression, 532
  rules of, 587
Audition, 156–159
Auditory input, 242
Auditory localization, 179
Autokinetic effect, 623–624
Autonomic nervous system, 98–104
Aversive punishment, 215–217
Avoidance conditioning, 213–215
Awareness and learning, 225–227

Babbling, 272–273, 301
Barbiturates, 132–133
Basilar membrane, 158–159
Battered wives, 520
Beck's theory of depression, 531–532
Behavior, and attitude, 604
Behavioral assessment, 478–479, 557
  of athletic coaches, 479, 646–647
Behavioral medicine, 496, 506
Behavioral perspective
  of abnormal behavior, 512
  on anxiety disorders, 524–525
  on attitude formation, 599
  on depression, 530–531
  and intelligence, 287
  and language, 277
  in memory, 260
  of morality, 413

on motivation, 326
in schizophrenia, 546
on sex roles, 438–439
Behavioral prediction, 604
Behavior genetics, 14, 22, 73–76
Behaviorism, 18–20
Behavior therapy, 556–557, 578
Berkeley Guidance Study, 397
Binet test, 268, 291
Biological development, 420, 446
Biological factors in personality, 481–482
Biological perspective, 11–14
    of abnormal behavior, 512
    on aggression, 22–24
    on anxiety disorders, 526
    on bipolar disorders, 536
    on helping, 609
    and intelligence, 285
    and language, 270
    in language development, 273
    on learning, 231–235
    in memory, 259
    on motivation, 326
    and personality, 467
    in schizophrenia, 542
Biological state, and memory, 258
Biological therapy, 564, 578–579
Bipolar disorder, 526, 535, 548
    drug treatment for, 568
Blobs, 169
Blood donations, 614
Bodily assessment, 480
Body type, and personality, 467–468, 482
Bonding, 435
Borderline personality, 519, 548
Bottom-up processing, 244, 265
Brain, 84–98, 100–103
    and aggression, 23
Brain damage, 96–98
Brain slices, 102
Brainwashing, 626
Brief psychotherapy, 554
Bulimia, 334–335
Burnout, 495, 506

California Children of Divorce Project, 443
Calpain, 235

Caticholamines, and heart disease, 498
Central tendency, measures of, 56, 658–659
Cerebellum, 87
Cerebral ventricles, 541–542
Cerebrum, 88–96
    and oxygen deprivation, 288
Chemical factors, in memory, 265
Chemical senses (taste and smell), 159–161
Childhood disorders, 516–517
Child molestation, 380–381
Child rearing practices, and psychological perspective, 424
Chronic disease, and psychotherapy, 573
Chunking, 246–247, 265
Circadian rhythms, 113–114
Classical conditioning, 197–203, 557, 559
    and attitudes, 202–203
    of fear, 214–215
    in infancy, 429–431
    and psychosomatic disorders, 202
    therapies based on, 559
Classification, of abnormal behavior, 515–517, 547–548
Classification system, principles of, 515–517
Class inclusion, 410
Clever Hans, 278
Client-centered therapy, 463–464, 555–559, 578
Cocaine, 134
Cochlea, 158
Cocktail party phenomenon, 243
Coding of information, 265
Cognition
    and language, 279–280, 302
    social, 588–590
Cognitions, and attitude, 599–600
Cognitive appraisal, 310, 320–323, 371–373
Cognitive assessment, 480
Cognitive-behavioral modification, 557, 561–562, 578
Cognitive-behavioral perspective, and personality, 464–467
Cognitive complexity, 599–600
Cognitive development, 407–411, 446

lifespan changes in, 429–434
measures in infancy, 431–432
stages of, 408–411
Cognitive dissonance, 605–606, 617
Cognitive elements, in emotion, 425–426
Cognitive functioning, and age, 432
Cognitive mechanisms, in prejudice, 607
Cognitive perspective, 16–18, 407–408
    of abnormal behavior, 512
    on aggression, 26–27
    on anxiety disorder, 525–526
    on depression, 531–533
    on helping, 610–611
    in intelligence, 288
    on learning, 221, 224–231
    on motivation, 326–327
    and personality, 464–465
    in schizophrenia, 545
    on sex roles, 439–440
Cognitive psychology, and intelligence, 289–290
Cognitive skills, sex differences, 421
Cognitive stages, in intelligence, 288
Cognitive therapy, 561, 578
Cognitive training, for anger, 491
Collective unconscious, 460–461
Color, perception of, 280
Color blindness, 155–156
Color vision, 151–154
Community approach, 552
Community psychology, 577–578
Comparative outcome research, in therapy, 574–575
Complementarity, and attraction, 590
Complex stimuli, 264
Compulsion, 523
Computer axial tomography. *See* CT scan
Computer programs, problem solving, 282–283
Computers, 60–61
    in primate language, 276

Computer simulation, 513
Concrete operational period, 409–410
Conditioned response, 197–199
Conditioned stimulus, 197–199
Cones, 148–154
  and color vision, 151–154
Conflict, 341–342
  intergroup, 640
  motivational, 341–342
  resolution of intergroup, 640–641
Conformity, 624–625
Confounding, 52–53
Conjugate reinforcement, 430
Consequences, of behavior, 490–491
Conservation, 410
  and sex roles, 439–440
Consistency, in behavior, 471
Constituents, in language, 269
Construct, 37
Context, 253
  in memory, 264
Control, and attribution, 589
Control group, 47
"Cool reactors," 500
Coping, 502
  rigidity in, 517–518
  with stress, 488–500
Coping strategies, 506
Coronary heart disease, 498–501
Correlation, 44–46, 665–667
  and prediction, 45–46, 667
Cortical columns, 168
Cortical hypercolumns, 168
Corticotropin releasing factor (CRF),
  486
Cost reward analysis, and helping,
  612–613
Costs, in relationship, 597
Countertransference, 553–554
Couples therapy, 565–566, 578
Credibility, in communicator, 607
Criminal responsibility, 575–576
Criterion, test, 290
Critical period, 278–279, 440–441,
  446
Cross-cultural data, and heart disease,
  499–500
Cross-sectional study, 393
Crowding, 646–648
  versus density, 648
  effects on behavior, 647–649
Crystallized abilities, 299–301

CT scan, 102, 541–542, 548, 549
Cults, 626–627
Culture fair tests, 293
Custody, and developmental out-
  come, 444–446

Dark adaption, 150–151
Deafness, and language, 272–273
Death, preparation for, 414–415
Decibel, 157–158
Decision making, 635–637
  group polarization and, 635
  groupthink, 636
Declarative representation schemes,
  250
Deep structure, 269, 301
Defense mechanisms, 457–459, 481
Deindividuation, 628–629
Delusions, 536–539
Demand characteristics, 53
Dementia praecox, 539–542
Denial, 414, 458
Density, 648–649
  versus crowding, 648
Deoxyglucose technique, 102
Dependent personality disorder, 520,
  548
Dependent variable, 46
Depressant drugs, 130–133
Depression, 415, 526–528
  aggression in, 473–475
  cognitive therapy for, 562
  drug treatment for, 569
  and panic disorder, 521–522
  treatment effectiveness in, 574–575
Deprivation, and development, 396,
  440–441
Depth perception, 176–179
  binocular cues, for, 178–179
  in infancy, 427–428
  monocular cues, for, 176–178
Development
  Freud's theory of, 402–404
  of language, 270–273
  perspectives on, 402–414
Developmental research techniques,
  416
Developmental theory, practical applications, 391–392
Discrimination, 200–201, 619
  in infants, 426–427
  and language, 280

Displacement, 458
  of memories, 260
Dissociation, 110, 128–129
Dissociative disorders, 516–517
Dissociative pain-control strategies,
  187–188
Divorce, 392
  and development, 443–446
Dopamine, 529
Dopamine hypothesis, 540–541
Dramatic behavior, 518–520
Dreams, 115–119
  and memory consolidation, 117
Drugs, 130–138
  and memory, 258
Drug therapy, 566–569, 578
DSM-111, 515–517
Duplex theory, of memory, 261–263,
  265–266
Durham test, 575
Dysphoric mood, 527

Eccentric behavior, 518
Echoic store, 242, 261
ECT. See Electroconvulsive therapy
Ectomorphy, 468–469
Effectiveness, of psychotherapy, 571–
  573
Ego, 456–457
Egocentrism, 440
Elaboration, in memory, 263–264
Electroconvulsive therapy (ECT),
  569–570, 579
Emotion, 308–324, 424–425
  and attitude, 598–599
  behavior and, 314–319
  cognitive component, 310–311
  development of, 424–425
  interactions among components,
  320–324
  physiological process, 310–312
  theories of, 320–321
Empathy, 610
Encounter groups, 564–565, 578
Endocrine system, 104–105
Endomorphy, 468–469
Endorphins, 134, 184–185
Environment, and intelligence, 285–
  287
Environmental psychology, 646
Epinephrine, 487
Episodic memory, 256–257, 265

Equity, 361, 597
  norm of, 652
Erikson, E., developmental theory of,
  404–407, 416
Erogenous zone, 403
Erratic behavior, 518–520
Escape conditioning, 213
Estimated learning potential, 298
Evaluation apprehension, and help-
  ing, 614–615
Evaluative simplicity, 599–600
Event-related potentials, 100–101
Evolution, 12–14
Exhibitionism, 377–378
Existential therapy, 556
Expanding, 271–272
Expectancies, 227–228
Experiential groups, 564–565
Experiment, 46–54
  confounding of variables, 52–53
  single-subject, 50–51
Experimental group, 46–47
Experimentor expectancies, 53–54
Expressed emotions, 545–546
Extinction, 199, 208–210
Extraversion, 461, 469–470
Eysenck, H., theory of personality,
  469–472

Factitious disorders, 516
Factor analysis, 278–288, 302, 667–
  669
Factor analytic theories, of intelli-
  gence, 287–288
Familiarity, and attraction, 592–594
Family therapy, 565–566, 578
Farsightedness, 155
Father, role in attachment, 437
Fear, and persuasion, 608–609
Fear-avoidance theory of chronic
  pain, 185–186
Feature detectors, 168–170
Feedback, in language, 272, 301–302
Fels study, 397
Field experiment, 585
Field study, 587
Fixation, 403
Flooding, 559
Fluid abilities, 299–300
Forensic psychology, 7
Forgetting, 257–259, 265
Formal operation period, 409

Free association, 553–554
Freud's developmental theories, 402–
  404, 416
Freud's personality theories, 454–459
Freud's theory, 14–15, 24
Fully functioning person, 463
Functional fixedness, 283–284
Fundamental attribution error, 585–
  589, 616

Gate control theory of pain, 184
Genain sisters, 542–544
Gender, cognitive understanding,
  438–440
Gender identity, 365–368
General adaptation syndrome (GAS),
  486, 505
General factor, in intelligence, 288
Generalization, 200–201
Generalized anxiety disorder, 521,
  526, 548
General Problem Solver, 282–283
Generational factors, in development,
  394–396
Generativity, 275–278
Genetic counseling, 286–287
Genetic damage, and intelligence,
  285–287
Genetic engineering, 72–73
Genetic factors in schizophrenia,
  540–542, 548
Genetics, 68–76
Genic, case of, 441
Genital stage, 404
Gestalt organizing principles, 170–
  171
Gestalt psychology, 17
Gestalt therapy, 563–565, 566
Glaucoma, 155
Grant study, 400–402, 416
Group, 629
Group competition, 601
Group tests, of intelligence, 291, 293–
  301
Group therapy, 563, 578
Gustation, 160

Habituation, 431
Halfway houses, 576–577
Hallucinations, 536–538
Hallucinogens, 135–137

Health
  and coping, 503
  and exercise, 503–504
Health care costs, and psychotherapy,
  571–573
Health psychology, 7, 496–497, 506
Heart attack, Type A and, 500
Hemispheric localization, 92–96
Heredity, and intelligence, 285–287
Hering theory of color vision, 152–
  154
Heritability index, 74
Hertz (Hz), 157
Heuristics, 282–284, 302
Hierarchical network, 250–251
High altitude, and intellectual skills,
  288
High-risk children, 441–446
History-related events, in develop-
  ment, 389–390
Homosexuality, 374–377
"Hot reactors," 500
Humanistic-existential perspective,
  20–21, 414–415
  of abnormal behavior, 514
  on aggression, 29
  on anxiety disorder, 526
  on depression, 534
  on motivation, 328–329
  in schizophrenia, 546
  of personality, 461–462
Humanistic-existential therapies, 555–
  556, 578
Hunger, 330–332
Hypnosis, 121–129
  and pain tolerance, 125–126
Hypothalamus, 88
Hypothesis, 35
  perception as, 171–174

Iconic store, 242
Id, 456–457
Identification, 440, 609–610
Illness
  psychological factors in recovery,
  501–503

Illness (*Continued*)
  stress-related, 493
Illusions, 172–175
Imitation, and language, 271–272
Impairment, of memory, 263
Imprinting, 278–279, 434–437
Impulse control, disorders of, 516
Independent variable, 46
Individual difference variable, 390
Individual psychology, 460, 481
Infancy
  cognitive development in, 431–432
  growth in, 420
  measurement techniques for, 426–427
Inferiority, 460
Information, and stress, 501–502
Information processing, 240–251, 264–266
Ingroup, 601–602
Inoculation, in attitude, 608
Input, of information, 241–242
Insanity, 579
Insight, 525
Insomnia, 118
Institutionalization, 576–578
Intellectual development, age related changes and, 432–434
Intellectualization, 458
Intellectual performance, and aging, 432–434
Intelligence, 285–290, 302
Intelligence quotient (IQ), 294–296, 302
Intelligence tests, 290–301, 302
Interference, 258, 265
Interpersonal attraction, theories of, 596–597
Introversion, 461, 469–471, 482
Introversion-extraversion, 461, 469–471, 482
Interviews, as assessment, 476
Invulnerability, 441–446
IQ. *See* Intelligence quotient
Irrational beliefs, 561

Jung, personality theory of, 460–461

Kaufman Assessment Battery (K-ABC), 298–301
Kelly, personality theory of, 464–465

Kinesthesis, 161–162
Kohlberg, theory of development, 416
Kohlberg's theory of moral development, 411–414
Kübler-Ross, developmental theories of, 416
Kübler-Ross's theory, 414–415

Labeling, 465–466, 481
Language, 268–281, 301–302
  biological basis, 302
  private, 271–272
  in schizophrenia, 545
Larry P. V. Wilson Riles, 297
Latency, 404–405
Lateralization, 273–274
Leadership, 637–640
  contingency model of, 639
  styles of, 639
  traits and, 628–638
Learned helplessness, 227–228, 532–533
Learned mastery, 228
Learning, 197
  biological constraints on, 231–234
  cooperative, 640
  in infancy, 429–431
Learning perspective
  on helping, 610
  and intelligence, 288–289
  and language, 272
Learning techniques, in aging, 432–434
Level of significance, 59, 669
Levels of processing, 263–264
Libido, 454–456
Lie detection, 313–314
Life events, 495–496
  unique, 390
Life Experiences Survey (LES), 495
Life satisfaction, 398
Life span approach, 388–396, 415
Liking, 616–617
  and familiarity, 592–593
  and helping, 594–596
Liking Scale, 596–598
Limbic system, 88
Linguistic determinism, 279–280
Linguistic relativism, 279–280, 302
Lithium, 530, 569
Little Hans, case of, 525

Locomotor-genital stage, 405
Locus of control, 467
  and helping, 613
Longevity, and behavior, 505
Longitudinal approach, in development, 393–402
Longitudinal studies, of development, 416
Longitudinal study, 395–402
  of divorce, 443–445
  high-risk children, 442–443, 445–446
  intellectual development, 432
  moral reasoning, 412–414
Long-term memory, 261–264
Long-term potentiation, 235
Loss
  and depression, 534
  of memory, 259–260
Loudness perception, 159
Love, 590, 596, 616–617
  cognitive arousal theory of, 362–364
  and sexuality, 360
Love Scale, 596, 598
LSD, 136–137

Maintenance rehearsal, 264
Mania, 526–527, 534–536, 548
MAO inhibitors, 530
Marijuana (*cannabis*), 137–138
Maslow's need hierarchy, 328–329
Maslow's personality theory, 461–462
Maturation, 390, 416
Maturity, 406
  in development, 406
Mean, 56, 658
Means-ends analysis, 282, 302
Measurement, of sensory skills, 426–427
Median, 659
Meditation, 120–121
  and stress reduction, 120–121
Medulla, 85
Memory, 268
  complex stimuli, 254–255
  distortion of, 392–393
  and language, 280
Memory aids, and age, 432–434
Memory trace circuits, 259
Mental representation, principle of, 410

Mental set, 284
Mesmerism, 121–122
Mesomorphy, 468–469
Meta-analysis, 571, 572–573
Metacognition, 251, 252–253, 265, 289–290
Metalinguistic awareness, 273
Middle age, 391–392
Minnesota Multiphasic Personality Inventory (MMPI), 476–477
M'Naghten rule, 575
Mnemonics, 248–249, 264, 265
Mode, 56, 658
Modeling, 28, 229–230
    and aggressive behavior, 28
    as therapy, 559–561
Monoamine oxidase, 530, 569
Mood
    and helping, 613
    and memory, 253, 258–259
Moral reasoning, stages of, 412–414
Morphemes, 268–269
Motivation, 324–344
    attribution, 588
    extrinsic, 326–327
    for helping, 614–616
    intrinsic, 326–327
Motor skills
    in infancy, 423–424
    sex difference in, 420–424
Multiaxial classification, 517
Muscular-anal stage, 405
Myocardial infarction, 498–500

Narcolepsy, 118
Narcotics, 134–135
Natural experiment, 587
Nearsightedness, 154–155
Need for power, 340–341
Negative reinforcement, 213, 218
Negative symptoms, 539
Neoanalytic theories, of personality, 459
Nerve conduction, 78–82
Neural plasticity, 97–98
Neuron, 77–82
Neuropsychologists, 288
Neuroses. See Anxiety disorders
Neuroticism, 469–470
Neurotransmitters, 81–82, 529
    in schizophrenia, 540–542

News, memory for, 258
New York Longitudinal Study, 399–400, 416
Noise, 649–650
Nonverbal ability, 288
Norepinephrine, 529
Normal curve, 662–664
Norms, for tests, 291
Nuclear magnetic resonance, 103

Oakland Growth Study, 397
Obesity, 333–334
Object classification, 410
Object-consistency, 410
Object permanence, 410
Object representation, 410
Observational learning, 466–467
Observational research, 40–44
    on sexual behavior, 354–355
Obsession, 523
Obsessive-compulsive disorder, 523–524, 548
Olfaction, 160–161
    and sexual behavior, 162–163
Operant conditioning, 203–219, 557–559
    in infancy, 430–431
    therapies based on, 557–559
Operational definition, 38
Operations, 410
Opponent process theory
    of color vision, 152–154
    of emotion, 343–344, 364
Oral-sensory stage, 405
Oral stage, 403
Organic mental disorders, 516
Organization, of memory, 249–251
Organ of Corti, 159
Outcome measures, for therapy, 575
Outgroup, 601–602
Overgeneralization, in depression, 562
Overjustification hypothesis, 326–327

Pain control, 187–188
Pain perception, 161, 183–188
Panic attacks, 526
Panic disorder, 521–522, 548
Paranoid disorders, 516
Paranoid thinking, 513
Parasympathetic nervous system, 103

Pase v. Hannon, 297
PCP, 137
Peg words, 265
Perceived control, and health, 502
Perception, 146, 165–189
    in infancy, 426–428
    and language, 279–280, 302
Perceptual constancies, 174–175
Perceptual defense, 167
Perceptual development, 179–182
Personal constructs, 465, 481
Personal factors, in stress, 485
Personality, continuity in, 401–402
Personality assessment, 482
Personality characteristics, and helping, 613–614, 617
Personality development, 434–446
Personality disorders, 516, 517–520, 548
Personal unconscious, 460–461
Person × situation interaction, 399–400
    in helping, 611–616, 617
    and personality, 472–478, 482
    and psychoanalytic theory, 459
    in schizophrenia, 546–547
    in stress, 484–485
Persuasion, 607–610, 617
PET scan, 541–544, 549
Phallic stage, 404
Phobia, 521–523, 548
Phonemes, 268–269
Physical change, in development, 420–422
Physical condition, psychological factors affecting, 516
Piaget's theories, 407–411
    of development, 416
    and helping, 610–611
Pitch perception, 159
Plasticity of development, 440
Pleasure principle, 456–457
Polygraph, 313–314
Pons, 85–86
Pornography, 357–359

Positive reinforcement, 206–208
Positive symptoms, 538–539
Position emission tomography. *See*
    PET scan
Posttraumatic stress disorder, 548
Posttraumatic stress reactions, 494
Preconscious, 456
Predictability, and health, 502
Preferential looking procedure, 426–
    427
Prejudice, 589–590, 600–604, 617
Preoperational period, 409–411
Preparedness, 232–234
Prevention
    of mental disorder, 577–578
    programs for, 391–392
Primacy effect, in memory, 262
Primary mental abilities, 288
Primate language, 273–276
Privacy, and tests, 481
Proactive interference, 258
Problem solving, 281–285
Processes, in development, 389–390
Prognosis, in schizophrenia, 538–539
Programming, for language, 270–273
Projection, 458
Projective techniques, 477–478
Prosocial behavior, 609–616, 617
Proximity, and attraction, 592–593
Psychoanalysis, 553–555, 578
Psychoanalytic concepts, research on,
    473–475
Psychoanalytic theory, of personality,
    481
Psychodynamic perspective, 14–15
    of abnormal behavior, 512
    on aggression, 24–25
    on anxiety disorders, 524
    on depression, 533–534
    on development, 402–407
    on helping, 609–610
    on motivation, 327–328
    on personality development, 459
    in schizophrenia, 545–546
    and sex roles, 440
    in memory, 259–260
Psychodynamic therapies, 552–555,
    578
Psycholinguistics, 268, 301
Psychological factors, in illness and
    recovery, 501–505

Psychological hardiness, 504–505
Psychology, 4
Psychophysiological disorders, 497–
    498
Psychosexual development, 402–404
Psychosexual disorders, 516–517
Psychosocial development, 404–407
Psychotherapy, 552–555
Psychotic disorders, 516
Psychoticism, 470
Public Law, 94–142, 297
Public policy, and disordered behav-
    ior, 575–578, 579
Punishment, 215–218

Questionnaires, as personality meas-
    ures, 476–478
Questions, in language development,
    273

Rape, 378–380
Rapists, 380
Rational-emotive therapy, 561–562
Rationalization, in memory, 255
Reaction formation, 458
Reaction range, 73–74
Reactivity, 53
Recall, 253, 262–263, 265
Reciprocity, in relationship, 594–595
Recognition, 251, 253, 265
Recombinant DNA techniques, 72–
    73
Reconstructive memory, 255–256,
    259, 265
Reference group, 622–623
Regression, 403, 458
Rehearsal, in memory, 242–243
Reinforcement
    in depression, 530–531
    and helping, 610–611
Reinforcement/affect theory, 596–597
Relationship development, in mon-
    keys, 436–437
Relationships
    factors in, 594–598
    termination of, 597–598
    theories of, 617
Reliability
    in classification, 515
    of tests, 290
Repetition, in memory, 264

Replacement, in memory, 265
Repression, 457
Research ethics, 54–55
Research methods, in social psychol-
    ogy, 584–588, 616
Research techniques, developmental,
    392–396
Resistance, 554
Response cost, 217–218
Responsibility, diffusion of, 611–616
Reticular formation, 86
Retirement, 392
Retrieval, from memory, 251–260,
    264, 265
Retrieval cue, 258–259
Retrieval failure, 257–259, 265
Retroactive interference, 258
Retrospective data, 392–396
Rh factor, 286–287
Rods, 148–154
Rogers' personality theory, 462–464
Role theory of hypnosis, 127
Rorschach inkblots, 477–478
Rubella, 287

Schedules of reinforcement, 209–212
    effects on learning, extinction, 212–
    213
Schemata, 591–592, 618
    in depression, 532–533
Schizoid personality disorder, 518,
    548
Schizophrenia, drugs for, 570–571.
    See also Schizophrenic disorders
Schizophrenic disorders, 516, 536–
    540, 548–549
Schizotypal personality disorder, 518,
    548
Scholastic Aptitude Test (SAT), 294,
    297, 302
Seattle Longitudinal Study, 432
Selective processing, 243–244
Selection, and tests, 296–301
Self, 462–464, 481
Self-actualization, 461–464, 481
Self-control of behavior, 490–491
    and health, 503–505
Self-control strategies, 220–223
Self-disclosure, 595–596
Self-discovery, in learning, 408–411
Self-efficient, 560–561

Self-esteem, 588
Self-instructional training, 562–563
Self-instructions, 491
Self-monitoring, 489
  in therapy, 566
Self-perception theory, 606–607
Self-presentation, 588
Self-regulation, 466–467
Self-reinforcement, 228–229, 466–467
Self-Report Altruism Scale, 613
Self-schemata, 589
Self-theory, 462–464
Semantic memory, 249, 256–257, 265
Sensation, 146–165
Sensation Seeking Scale, 336–337
Sensitive period, 279
Sensorimotor period, 409–411
Sensory needs, 335–338
Sensory skills, 426–428
Sensory stores, 242, 261
Separation
  and depression, 534
  and development, 441
Sequential design, 395–396
Sequential processing, 298–301
Serial position curve, 262–263
Serotonin, 529
Set-point theory, 332
Sex differences
  in childhood skills, 420
  in development, 446
Sexism, 603–604
Sex-role development, 437–440, 446
Sexual abuse, 380–381
Sexual dysfunction, 370–373
  treatment of, 373–375
Sexual identity, 437–440, 446
Sexuality
  and aging, 369–370
  childhood, 361–365, 402–415
Shaping, 207–208, 223
Sheldon's theory of personality, 467–468
Short-term memory, 261, 263, 264
Signal detection theory, 163–164
Sign language, 275–276
Similarity, and attraction, 590–591
Simplification, in language, 273
Simultaneous processing, 299–301

Situational factors, in stress, 484–485
Sleep, 112–119
Sleep apnea, 119
Sleep disorders, 118–119
Slip of the tongue, 456
Slow learners, 296–297
Social anxiety, 487–488, 590
Social cognition, 588–616
Social competition, 601–604
Social development, 434–440, 446
Social-exchange theory, 597, 598
Social facilitation, 631–632
  and performance, 631
  distraction-conflict model of, 631
  drive theory of, 631
Social impact theory, 633
Social issues, and testing, 296, 302
Socialization, 437–440, 446
Social learning, 557
  and prejudice, 600–601
Social learning theory, 481
  and helping, 610
  and personality, 465–467
  therapies based on, 559–561
Social learning therapy, 578
Social loafing, 632–634
Social norms, 621–624
Social perception, 585–588, 616
Social phobia, 522
Social power, 637
Social roles, 621–622
Social support, 491–492, 502–503, 506
Social Support Questionnaire (SSQ), 492
Sociobiology, 14
Somatoform disorders, 516
Somatotype, 468–469
Spatial frequency receptors, 169–170
Specific brain functioning, in intelligence, 288–290
Speech discrimination, in infancy, 272–273
Speech sounds, 272–273
Spinal cord, 84
Spontaneous recovery, 198
Sport psychology, 7–8, 642–646
Sports, 642–646
  arousal and performance in, 319
  group dynamics in, 642–646
  leadership in, 646–648

Stages of development, 390
Stage theories, 390–396
Stamina, 504–505
Standard deviation, 57, 661
Standardization, of tests, 290–291
Standard score, 296, 662
Stanford Binet, 291
State-specific experiences, 142
Statistics, 555–557, Appendix
  descriptive, 56–57, 657–662
  inferential, 58–59, 669–671
Stereopsis, 178
Stereotypes, 600–601
Stimulus control, 27, 205–206, 222, 472
"Strange situation," the, 436–437
Strategies, in problem solving, 282–285
Stress, 505
  in schizophrenia, 546–547
Stress-coping skills, 489
Stress-induced analgesia, 185
Stress reactions, 506
Stress-related disorders, 497–498
Sublimation, 458
Subliminal perception, 164–165
Sudden infant death syndrome (SIDS), 119
Suicide, 528–529
Superego, 456–457, 609–610
Suppression, 457–459
Surface structure, 269
Surgery, and memory, 259
Survey studies, of sexuality, 351–353
Survey study, 584–585
Sympathetic nervous system, 103
Synapse, 80–82
Syntax, 270–272
Systematic desensitization, 561
  and flooding, 578
Study of Multicultural Pluralistic Assessment (SOMPA), 298

Tardive dyskinesia, 568–569
Target behavior, 490–491

Task orientation, 506
Task-oriented response, 488–490
Television, influence on behavior of, 610
Terman study, 397–399, 416
Test-anxiety, 476–477, 487–488
Test-retest reliability, 290–291
Tests
  of intelligence, 290–301
  of personality, 475–481
T groups, 564–565, 578
Thalamus, 87
Thematic Apperception Test, 478
Theory, 35–36
Theory of reasoned action, 604–605, 617
Therapeutic effectiveness, 570–575
Therapeutic improvement, criteria for, 571–573
Therapies, evaluation, 579
Thinking, 268
Thirst, 330
Thresholds, 163–165
  absolute, 163–165
  differential, 165
Time-lag study, 393–396
Time pressure, and helping, 613
Tip of the tongue phenomenon, 260, 265
Token economy, 546

Top-down processing, 244, 265
TOT. *See* Tip of the tongue phenomenon
Trait theories, of personality, 471–472, 482
Tranquilizer drugs, 132–133, 526, 567
Transactional analysis, 563, 578
Transference, 553–554
Transformation, in memory, 255
Transition, adjustment to, 487–488
Transitions
  developmental, 406–407
  life, 392
Transsexualism, 366–368
Tricyclics, 569, 574–575
Type A behavior, 499–501, 506
Type 1 schizophrenia, 538–539
Type 2 schizophrenia, 538–539

Unconditioned response, 197–199
Unconditioned stimulus, 197–199
Unconscious, 456
Understanding, 36–37
  after-the-fact, 36
  through prediction and control, 37
Unipolar disorder, 526

Validity, of tests, 290, 481
Variability, measures of, 57, 660–662

Variance
  behavioral, 664
  measures of, 661
Verbal ability, 287–288
Vestibular sense, 161–162
Vicarious learning, 466
Victim, attitude toward, 588
Vision, in infancy, 426–428
Visual cliff, 427–428
Visual codes, 244–246
Visual defects, 154–156
Visual inputs, 241–242
Visually evoked potentials (VEP), 427
Vocabulary, 273
Vulnerability, 506
  in children, 399–400
  to depression, 534
  in schizophrenia, 546–547
  and social support, 491–492
  to stress, 488

WAIS-R, 291–293
Wechsler tests, 291–293, 295–296, 302
WISC, 292, 298
WPPSI, 292

X-linked inheritance, 536

Young adulthood, 405
Young-Helmholtz theory of color vision, 152–154